The Writer's Presence

A Pool of Readings
Sixth Edition

EDITED BY

DONALD MCQUADE
University of California, Berkeley

ROBERT ATWAN
Series Editor, The Best American Essays
Director, The Blue Hills Writing Institute at Curry College

Bedford / St. Martin's   Boston ◆ New York

For Bedford/St. Martin's

Developmental Editor: Nathan Odell
Editorial Assistant: Nina Gantcheva
Production Supervisor: Sarah Ulicny
Marketing Manager: Molly Parke
Project Management: Books By Design, Inc.
Cover Design: Donna L. Dennison
Cover Photo: Dougal Waters, *Open Book by Window Overlooking Sea*.
   Getty Images.
Composition: Books By Design, Inc.
Printing and Binding: RR Donnelley & Sons Company

President: Joan E. Feinberg
Editorial Director: Denise B. Wydra
Editor in Chief: Karen S. Henry
Director of Development: Erica Appel
Director of Marketing: Karen R. Soeltz
Director of Editing, Design, and Production: Marcia Cohen
Assistant Director of Editing, Design, and Production: Elise S. Kaiser
Manager, Publishing Services: Emily Berleth

Library of Congress Control Number: 2008933817

Manufactured in the United States of America.

3 2 1
f

For information, write: Bedford/St. Martin's, 75 Arlington Street, Boston, MA 02116   (617-399-4000)

ISBN-10: 0-312-48686-3
ISBN-13: 978-0-312-48686-0

Acknowledgments

Preface for Instructors _____

At the center of our work on this new edition of *The Writer's Presence* is our commitment to creating an effective tool for teaching critical reading and writing. This commitment is reflected in our efforts to design *The Writer's Presence* to achieve three fundamental objectives: to introduce students to a wide range of prose genres emphasizing a strong authorial presence and voice; to allow writing instructors maximum flexibility in assigning reading materials and writing models; and to support composition teachers and students as effectively as possible with helpful, though unobtrusive, editorial and pedagogical features. We are confident that the readings we have selected, the ways we have chosen to arrange that material, and the instructional resources we have provided both in the book and in the comprehensive instructor's manual and on-line support will make this a uniquely useful collection that will satisfy the requirements of most first-year writing programs.

The Writer's Presence combines eminently readable—and teachable— writing with a simple organization and minimal editorial apparatus. Each selection showcases a writer's unique voice and provides students with accessible models they can use to develop their own voices in the writing they produce. Engaging readings arranged alphabetically by author and by four types of writing—personal, expository, and argumentative essays, as well as short fiction—offer instructors the freedom to explore a wide range of pedagogical options, readily adaptable to the specific abilities and needs of particular students.

ESTABLISHED FEATURES OF *THE WRITER'S PRESENCE*

We continue to work diligently to ensure that the book's enduring features are as useful to instructors and as helpful to students as possible. (For information on features new to this edition, see page vi.)

Diverse Selections with a Strong Writer's Presence

Each of the selections in *The Writer's Presence* displays the distinctive signature that characterizes memorable prose: the presence of a lively individual imagination attempting to explore the self, shape information into meaning, or contend with issues. The 119 essays, 3 graphic selections, 6 short stories, and 28 writer's commentaries offer an array of voices, genres, and styles from different times and cultures. Women and writers of color are strongly represented. Ranging widely across subjects, methods of development, and stylistic patterns, the selections also illustrate both the expectations and the uncertainties that surface when a writer attempts to create a memorable presence in prose.

We have built this book—like previous editions—out of first-rate teaching material proven to work in the writing classroom. We continue to feature a large number of authors whose works instructors have repeatedly enjoyed teaching over the years. These classroom favorites include such respected writers as Maya Angelou, James Baldwin, Joan Didion, Annie Dillard, Edward Hoagland, Langston Hughes, Jamaica Kincaid, George Orwell, Scott Russell Sanders, Jonathan Swift, Mark Twain, Alice Walker, E. B. White, and Virginia Woolf. In fact, as this list of writers clearly indicates, *The Writer's Presence* could be used as an introduction to the essay or to literary nonfiction in general. For instructors with even more literary ambitions, we have included paired selections so that certain writers can be shown working in two different genres. These writers are Raymond Carver, Sherman Alexie, and George Orwell.

Flexible Organization

The organization of *The Writer's Presence* displays a broad range of private, personal, expository, argumentative, and creative writing without imposing an order or specifying an instructional context in which to work with individual selections. In that sense, the contents of *The Writer's Presence* can truly be called "a pool of readings." The nonfiction selections that constitute the first three parts are divided into the three most commonly taught types of nonfiction—personal essays, exposition, and argumentation. That is the extent of the book's overarching structure. Within each part, we present the writers in alphabetical order to make the selections easy to retrieve, assign, analyze, and interpret, regardless of instructional emphasis. To make it even easier to explore different approaches, *The Writer's Presence* includes alternate tables of contents that allow the book to be used as a thematic reader, a rhetorical reader, or a contemporary argument reader, with each selection carefully chosen to play multiple roles.

Helpful and Unobtrusive Apparatus

As in previous editions, we continue to keep instructional apparatus to a minimum, striving for a middle ground between too much and too little. The headnotes in *The Writer's Presence* provide important biographical data and publication lists, along with intriguing quotations, and are as attentive as possible to a selection's original source. Many selections provide provocative glimpses of lives and places, and readers naturally want to know when a selection was written and how and where it originally appeared. We don't want readers to infer mistakenly that an excerpt is actually an essay as this would distort their approach to the selection and may also be unfair to the author. For example, we want readers to know at the outset that Maya Angelou's "'What's Your Name, Girl?'" is taken from her award-winning autobiography, *I Know Why the Caged Bird Sings*, and was not originally intended to stand alone as an essay.

It is our experience that many students can be guided in their assessment or rereading of a selection by carefully constructed follow-up questions. In this edition we have retained "The Reader's Presence," the small collection of questions after each selection. These questions can be used by student readers and writers to enhance their understanding of the selection, or the questions can stimulate productive analysis and group discussion in the classroom.

We have designed "The Reader's Presence" to cover some of the dominant features of the selection and to refer to matters of content, style, and structure. As the title indicates, the questions will often draw attention to the specific ways in which readers are present in a piece of writing — either as an implied reader (the reader imagined by the writer) or as an actual reader. The concept of presence — both the writer's and the reader's — is discussed more fully in the "Introduction for Students."

"Writer at Work" Selections

These twenty-four supplemental readings include excerpts from interviews and essays in which authors discuss their writing processes and their identities as writers or in which a writer's work or development process is usefully analyzed. We chose each to show students that effective writing is thoughtful work done by real people.

Uniquely Extensive Instructor's Manual

Although the amount of instructional apparatus in *The Writer's Presence* is carefully managed, a wealth of specific instructional activities appears in *Resources for Teaching THE WRITER'S PRESENCE*, the most comprehensive instructor's manual available for any composition reader. The resources in this guide to *The Writer's Presence* include the following four parts in each entry:

- "Approaching the Essay" provides a thorough overview of pedagogically effective ways to work with the essay in the classroom.

- The "Additional Activity" offers imaginative classroom activities, connections to other essays in the book, and collaborative projects.

- "Generating Writing" includes a range of writing exercises— from suggestions for informal writing to essay assignments and ideas for research papers.

- "The Reader's Presence" addresses the questions that follow each selection in the text, pointing to illuminating passages in the selection and anticipating possible responses from students.

FEATURES NEW TO THIS EDITION

For the sixth edition of *The Writer's Presence*, we have strengthened the book's key features: its flexible format and its emphasis on authorial presence. We have also introduced new features that we believe will enhance the book's appeal to teachers and students in and beyond the classroom.

Forty-Three New Selections

The compelling new essays include works by such well-known contemporary authors as Kwame Anthony Appiah, Rick Bass, Rita Dove, Brian Doyle, Richard Ford, Henry Louis Gates Jr., Adam Gopnik, Louis Menand, Camille Paglia, Steven Pinker, William Safire, and Andrew Sullivan.

Authors Relatively New to Anthologies

To present the freshest and most compelling nonfiction available, *The Writer's Presence* complements the work of established and frequently anthologized authors with that of writers who are now finding their way into major collections: Meghan Daum, Debra Dickerson, Mark Edmundson, Daniel Harris, Charles McGrath, Errol Morris, Virginia Postrel, Marjane Satrapi, and Ellen Ullman. Included here are Marie Arana reflecting on her Peruvian childhood, James McBride exploring the global significance of hip-hop, and Michael Pollan arguing against the American farm system and the junk food it produces.

We have also made an effort to include contemporary writers and thinkers who, though professionally established, are not often included in composition readers; in this edition, we are pleased to include essays by such well-known authors and public figures as Yale legal scholar Akhil Reed Amar, video game designer Will Wright, economist Steven D. Levitt and journalist Stephen J. Dubner of *Freakonomics* fame, literary scholar Walter Benn Michaels, and psychologist Barry Schwartz. Featured, too, is the candid opening section of Barack Obama's now famous memoir, *Dreams from My Father.*

More Emphasis on Academic Writing

It is likely that the Internet, instant messaging, and text messaging have had more of an influence on the writing lives of today's students than has formal academic composition. For this reason, there is a need for material that helps students transition from the conventions of their daily correspondence to the conventions of academic writing. For the sixth edition of *The Writer's Presence*, we have removed the "Informal Writing" section to make room for more expository and argumentative essays. (You will find the most popular pieces—journal entries from Joan Didion, Anne Frank, Michihiko Hachiya, and Adam Mayblum—in the "Personal Writing" section.) *The Writer's Presence* now features four documented essays, and many selections that are more academic in voice and subject than what one would typically find in a college composition reader. To name a few, we have added Akhil Reed Amar's "Second Thoughts: What the Right to Bear Arms Really Means," a legal scholar's look at the nuances of the second amendment; Daniel Akst's "What Meets the Eye" and Daniel Harris's "Celebrity Bodies," contrapuntal cultural critique on obesity and celebrity in America; and Kwame Anthony Appiah's "The Case for Contamination," a thoughtful exploration of the cultural impact of globalization.

Unique Academic Voice Pairings

The new academic voice pairings in the sixth edition of *The Writer's Presence* demonstrate how professional writers adjust their voice to suit their audience by pairing essays written for a lay audience with excerpts from the authors' academic articles on the same subject. These unique tools for teaching academic writing will help students analyze the shifts in tone, structure, and appeals that make writing more formal. This edition features pairings by public intellectuals such as Jared Diamond, Peter Singer, and Martha Nussbaum.

New "Writer at Work" Selections

For the sixth edition of *The Writer's Presence* we have expanded the acclaimed "Writer at Work" commentaries in which authors discuss their writing habits and identities as writers. This edition features commentaries from Barack Obama on the hazards of autobiography, graphic memoirist Marjane Satrapi on the language of words and images, and Jerald Walker's suggestions on how to tell a compelling story. This edition also introduces a new feature, "The Critic at Work," showing why one writer considers Flannery O'Connor's "A Good Man Is Hard to Find" the best southern short story ever written.

New Attention to Visual Texts

The Writer's Presence includes selections from some of the best contemporary graphic writing — a newly appreciated literary genre with cross-generational appeal. New selections include Marjane Satrapi's short graphic essay describing her complicated visit to West Point and several selections that feature writing that analyzes accompanying visuals, such as Errol Morris's examination of what photographs can and cannot tell us.

More Ways to Explore the Connections among Readings

At the request of instructors, we have strengthened the questions connecting two or more readings — questions aimed at helping students see the many thematic and stylistic links between and among selections. In addition to these questions and to the connections identified in the alternate tables of contents, *The Writer's Presence* now offers a "Connections Explorer" feature on the companion Web site to enable students and instructors to find selections in the book linked by theme, rhetorical mode, or any combination of these attributes. Each fiction selection is also connected to at least one nonfiction piece on a related theme, usually by the same writer.

ACKNOWLEDGMENTS

Each revision of *The Writer's Presence* has been developed through frequent correspondence and conversations — on the phone, in person, in letters, and on the Internet — with the many teachers and an appreciable number of students who have worked with *The Writer's Presence* in their writing classes. We continue to learn a great deal from these discussions, and we are grateful to the colleagues and friends who graciously have allowed us into their already crowded lives to seek advice and encouragement. Since its inception, *The Writer's Presence* has been and continues to be a truly collaborative enterprise.

In the same way we originally developed *The Writer's Presence*, this revision has emerged from spirited discussions with instructors. We are grateful to these colleagues across the country who took the time to tell us about what did—and did not—work well when they used the fifth edition: Natalie Bakopoulos, University of Michigan; Anne Balay, University of Illinois at Chicago; Greg Bryant, Highland Community College; Jan Carpenter, College of Southern Idaho; Louis Cicciarelli, University of Michigan; Lisa Del Torto, University of Michigan; Gayatri Devi, Lock Haven University of Pennsylvania; Emily Dial-Driver, Rogers State University; Clark Draney, College of Southern Idaho; Nina Dulin-Mallory, LaGrange College; Adria Fulkerson, Clackamas Community College; Deborah Garfinkle, College of San Mateo/De Anza College; Michael Gorman, University of Nebraska–Lincoln; Russell Green, North Shore Community College; Brenda S. Hines, Highland Community College; Dianne Layden, Central New Mexico Community College; Jennifer Liddell, California State University, Fullerton; Diana Lurz, Rogers State University; Laura McBride, College of Southern Nevada; Elizabeth McConnell, New England Institute of Art; Michele F. McGinn, Lake Highland Preparatory School; Paul Mendonca, North Shore Community College; Kathy O'Shaughnessy, Portland Community College; Sally Parr, Ithaca College; Kimberly Skeen, College of Southern Idaho; Karen Stewart, Norwich University; Damon Tutunjian, University of Michigan; and Anthony Wilson, LaGrange College.

We would also like to acknowledge those instructors who offered thoughtful responses and imaginative suggestions for improving previous editions: James Adams, Boston College; Susan J. Allspaw, Boston College; Lisa Altomari, Vermont Technical College; Linda Baker, Portland Community College; Helen Barnes, Boise State University; Maurice H. Barr, Spokane Community College; Bette Bauer, College of Saint Mary; Todd W. Bersley, California State University, Northridge; Gerri Black, Stockton State College; Scott Brookman, Virginia Commonwealth University; Ann Lightcap Bruno, Boston College; Larry Brunt, Highline Community College; Jennifer Buckley, John Carroll University; Irene Burgess, State University of New York, Cortland; Ruth Elizabeth Burks, Tufts University; Deborah Burnham, University of Pennsylvania; Dolores M. Burton, Boston University; Susan Cannata, University of North Carolina–Pembroke; Diane Challis, Virginia Commonwealth University; Jimmy Cheshire, Wright State University; Chet Childress, Virginia Commonwealth University; Alice Cleveland, College of Mareu; Rosanne Colosi, Boston College; Michel S. Connell, University of Iowa; Kimberly Connor, University of San Francisco; Chase Crossingham, University of South Carolina; Ruth Y. Davidson, Pennsylvania State University Schuylkill; Ellen Davis, Boston University; Michael G. Davros, University of Illinois at Chicago; Peggy C. de Broux, Peninsula College; Jessica Deforest, Michigan State University; Mary Devaney,

Rutgers University–Newark; Debra DiPiazza, Bernard M. Baruch College, City University of New York; Trevor Dodge, Boise State University; Jamye Doerfler, Virginia Commonwealth University; Maria Rowena P. Dolorico, Bristol Community College; Eileen Donovan-Kranz, Boston College; Susan M. Eisenthal, University of Massachusetts–Boston; Alex Fagan, Virginia Commonwealth University; Grace Farrell, Butler University; Todd Fox, California State University, Long Beach; Joan Gabriele, University of Colorado; Christie Anderson Garcia, Spokane Falls Community College; Jane Gatewood, Mary Washington College; Sharon Gerring, Buffalo State College; Rae Greiner, Radford University; Brian Hale, University of South Carolina; Sarah Hanselman, Tufts University; Lee Harrison, Houston Community College; Lori Harrison-Kahan, Boston College; Dave Hendrickson, Virginia Commonwealth University; Curtis W. Herr, Kutztown University; Benjamin Hoffman, Boston College; Tim Hohmann, Arizona State University; Susanna Horng, New York University; Jack Jacobs, Auburn University; Goldie Johnson, Winona State University; Nancy B. Johnson, Pace University; Matthew Kelley, University of Michigan; Kate Kessler, James Madison University; Ronald L. King, Virginia Commonwealth University; Laura Kjosen, Arapahoe Community College; Elizabeth Klem, Atlantic Cape Community College; Mary Ann Lee, Longview Community College; Donna Levy, University of Richmond and J. Sargeant Reynolds Community College; Anthony W. Lilly II, Tufts University; Genoveva Llosa, Boston College; Terri Long, Boston College; Harriet Malinowitz, Hunter College, City University of New York; Barbara Mallonee, Loyola College; Denice Martone, New York University; Debra Matier, College of Southern Idaho; Robert Mayer, College of Southern Idaho; Ilene Miele, Moorpark College; Andrew Mossin, Temple University; Cathryn A. Myers, Virginia Commonwealth University; Lolly Ockerstrom, Virginia Commonwealth University; Barbara Ohrstrom, University of Michigan; Jean Pace, Emerson College; Cheryl Pallant, Virginia Commonwealth University; Marty Patton, University of Missouri–Columbia; Jesse Peters, University of North Carolina–Pembroke; Gary D. Pratt, Brandeis University; Catherine S. Quick, University of Missouri–Columbia; Colleen Richmond, George Fox College; Larry Rodgers, Kansas State University; Robert Rogan, University of North Carolina Wilmington; Jan Zlotnick Schmidt, State University of New York, New Paltz; Lissa Schneider, University of Miami; Erin Scott, Illinois College; Marilyn S. Scott, California State University Hayward; Larry Severeid, College of Eastern Utah; Joanne Sibicky, Virginia Commonwealth University; Andrew Sidle, Northern Illinois University; Robert Singleton, State University of New York, New Paltz; Constance Fletcher Smith, Mary Washington College; Nancy Sorenson, California State University; Roger Sorkin, University of Massachusetts–Dartmouth; Robert L. Stapleton, Long Beach City College; J. F. Stenerson, Pace University; Chad R. Stockton, Emerson College; Steven Strang, Massachusetts Institute of Technology; Pamela Topping, Long Island University–Southampton College; Mary Turnbull, University of Puget Sound; Donna M. Turner, University of North Dakota; Sandra Urban, Loyola University of Chicago; Jennifer Lynne Von Ammon, Florida State University; Michael M. Walker, Palomar College; Kathleen G. White, Bellevue Community College; Mary Robin Whitney, John Jay College, City University of New York; Ed Wiltse, Tufts University; and Sallie Wolf, Arapahoe Community College.

We would especially like to acknowledge our colleagues from the Expository Writing Program at New York University who talked with us and shared their ideas as we planned the first edition of this book — Lisa Altomari, Karen Boiko, Darlene Forrest, Alfred Guy, Mary Helen Kolisnyk, Jim Marcall, Denice Martone, and Will McCormack.

We also extend our thanks to the professional staff at Bedford/ St. Martin's for their innumerable contributions to this revision. We are grateful for the unfailing support and imaginative and convincing recommendations we received from our previous editors, especially Carolyn Lengel. We are most grateful to Nathan Odell, who has managed every aspect of this sixth edition with great insight, excellent judgment, and unfailing dedication. We are also grateful to Nina Gantcheva for her fine work bringing together the inevitable and the innumerable loose ends throughout the project's development. Many thanks to Herb Nolan of Books By Design, Inc., for his outstanding work moving this large manuscript through production with such good cheer and exemplary professionalism. Special thanks to Emily Berleth for managing the entire process — again — with impeccable and quiet attentiveness and intelligence.

As ever, Joan Feinberg, the president of Bedford/St. Martin's, offered us spirited encouragement and first-rate and rigorous advice, as well as engaging suggestions for improving the project. When our conversations veered occasionally toward uncertainty, we relied on her steady editorial presence to help us convert pedagogical principle into sound instructional practice.

Mary Jo Thomas, Ph.D., prepared the comprehensive instructor's manual that accompanies this collection, *Resources for Teaching THE WRITER'S PRESENCE*. Dr. Thomas, formerly a professor of English and composition at Berea College, is now an independent writer and scholar. We are very grateful to Dr. Thomas for the intelligence, imagination, energy, and wealth of teaching experience she brings to the project. Her work is an invaluable pedagogical tool to help instructors teach their students to read and write more effectively. We continue to be grateful to Cassandra Cleghorn of Williams College; Alfred Guy of Yale University; Joanna Imm of the University of Arizona; Jon Roberts of St. Thomas Aquinas College; Shelley Salamensky of the University of California, Los Angeles; Alix Schwartz of the University of California, Berkeley; Kate Silverstein; their very helpful suggestions are still amply evident in the instructor's manual. Darryl Stephens once again offered invaluable assistance in strengthening the pedagogy of this project. Jan Weber continued to handle the headnote research and writing for this edition; we are enormously grateful to her yet again for all of her fine efforts. We extend our thanks as well to Sandy Schechter and Diane Kraut, who managed the challenging process of securing reprint permissions with great skill and attentiveness. Helane Prottas made the work of art research and permissions process seem effortless; she far exceeded our expectations, and we'd like to acknowledge her work with special thanks. Finally, we hope that Hélène, Gregory, and Emily Atwan, along with Susanne, Christine, and Marc McQuade, will once again share our satisfaction in seeing this project in print and our pleasure in continuing our productive collaboration.

Donald McQuade
Robert Atwan
August 2008

Contents

I. PERSONAL WRITING: Exploring Our Own Lives   11

"A smart Indian is a dangerous person, widely feared and ridiculed by Indians and non-Indians alike. I fought with my classmates on a daily basis. They wanted me to stay quiet when the non-Indian teacher asked for answers, for volunteers, for help. We were Indian children who were expected to be stupid."

"Every person I knew had a hellish horror of being 'called out of his name.' It was a dangerous practice to call a Negro anything that could be loosely construed as insulting because of the centuries of their having been called niggers, jigs, dinges, blackbirds, crows, boots, and spooks."

"I knew, with a certainty I could feel in my bones, that I was deeply Peruvian. That I was rooted to the Andean dust. That I believed in ghosts.

"Dolls are the ultimate symbol of childhood; they are toy children. Though I realize that playing with dolls is supposed to mimic the adult act of caring for children, playing with dolls always struck me as nothing more but childhood squared, a child doing a childish thing with a simulacrum of a child. It was like some hideous vortex."

"My first notebook was a Big Five tablet, given to me by my mother with the sensible suggestion that I stop whining and learn to amuse myself by writing down my thoughts."

"The more I read, the more I was led to abhor and detest my enslavers. I could regard them in no other light than a band of successful robbers, who had left their homes, and gone to Africa, and stolen us from our homes, and in a strange land reduced us to slavery. I loathed them as being the meanest as well as the most wicked of men."

"'You can always get warm, but it's hard to stay cool.' My mother's words, muttered every summer since I can remember, rang like a mantra in my head as I stood in the uncut grass of a football field (the 20-yard line, to be precise), knees locked and eyes forward, arms akimbo, to balance a 28-inch-long metal stick at a 45-degree angle, just so."

"A friend has two jobs in our town: policeman and soldier. In both, he is the guy who knocks on doors to tell mothers and fathers, wives and husbands that their son or daughter, husband or wife is dead. He has to knock on a door five or six times a year. He had become a student of doors and how people open them."

"Who can write about New Orleans now? Tell us what it's like there. Bring us near to what people are experiencing, to their loss, to what will survive. People who are close should write that. Only they're in the city, or they're on a bus, or they're seeking shelter. We don't know where they are."

"The communities I grew up in were dangerous and poor, and it was the common opinion of nearly everyone I knew that, when all was said and done, whites were to blame. Whites discriminated against us. Whites denied us decent housing. Whites caused us to have high unemployment and failed schools. Crack had come from whites, and so too had AIDS. Whites, in some vague and yet indisputable way, made the winos drink and gangbangers kill."

   "The paranoia created by racism, it seems to me, is often worse than racism itself, in the way that not knowing something is often worse than knowing. The phrase, '*Please*, Doc, just give it to me straight!' comes to mind."

"Summertime, oh, summertime, pattern of life indelible, the fade-proof lake, the woods unshatterable, the pasture with the sweetfern and the juniper forever and ever, summer without end."

   "There is one thing the essayist cannot do . . . he cannot indulge himself in deceit or in concealment, for he will be found out in no time."

II. EXPOSITORY WRITING: Shaping Information 279

"Attractive people are paid more on the job, marry more desirable spouses, and are likelier to get help from others when in evident need. Nor is this all sheer, baseless prejudice. Human beings appear to be hard-wired to respond to how people and objects look, an adaptation without which the species might not have made it this far."

"So what *does* the Second Amendment mean? A lot, says the National Rifle Association. Not much, say gun-control groups. Until recently, it didn't much matter who was right—on all but the mildest of measures, the NRA had the votes (and the cash), and that was that. Then came Littleton. Now proposals for serious federal gun controls are in the air."

"The first time a student asked me about my 'grading system,' I was nonplused—and a bit intimidated. It was an innocent question, but I heard it as a challenge: I was a 25-year-old graduate student teaching my first section in an English-literature class at the University of Virginia, and I really didn't know *what* my grading system was. Nor did I feel comfortable saying, 'Well, it's like Justice Stewart's definition of pornography, really—I simply know an A paper when I see one.'"

"It is appalling that Americans know so little about one another. It is appalling that many of us are so narrow-minded that we can't tolerate a few people with ideas significantly different from our own. It's appalling that evangelical Christians are practically absent from entire professions, such as academia, the media, and filmmaking. It's appalling that people should be content to cut themselves off from everyone unlike themselves."

"Bertrand Russell once observed that animal behaviorists studying the problem-solving abilities of chimpanzees consistently seemed to detect in their experimental subjects the 'national characteristics' of the scientists themselves. A divergence in the findings of the practical-minded Americans and the theoretically inclined Germans was particularly apparent."

"The first point to understand about the difference between honesty and integrity is that a person may be entirely honest without ever engaging in the hard work of discernment that integrity requires; she may tell us quite truthfully what she believes without ever taking the time to figure out whether what she believes is good and right and true."

"Smiles are associated with joy, relief, and amusement. But smiles are by no means limited to the expression of positive emotions: People of many different cultures smile when they are frightened, embarrassed, angry, or miserable."

"We like to think America invented the future. We are comfortable with the future, intimate with it. But there are disturbances now, in large and small ways, a chain of reconsiderations. Where we live, how we travel, what we think about when we look at our children."

"A Romantic, says Nietzsche, is someone who always wants to be elsewhere. If that's so, then the children of the Internet are Romantics, for they perpetually wish to be someplace else, and the laptop reliably helps take them there—if only in imagination. The e-mailer, the instant messenger, the Web browser are all dispersing their energies and interests outward, away from the present, the here and now. The Internet user is constantly connecting with people and institutions far away, creating surrogate communities that displace the potential community at hand."

to add or detract. The world will little note, nor long remember, what we say here, but can never forget what they did here. It is

"This defiant culture of song, graffiti, and dance, collectively known as hip-hop, has ripped popular music from its moorings in every society it has permeated. In Brazil, rap rivals samba in popularity. In China, teens spray-paint graffiti on the Great Wall. In France it has been blamed, unfairly, for the worst civil unrest that country has seen in decades."

"If u cn rd these days, and, just as important, if your thumbs are nimble enough so that u cn als snd, you can conduct your entire emotional life just by transmitting and receiving messages on the screen of your cellphone."

"Try getting a teen-ager to appreciate a grilled ramp. Try getting a teen-ager to appreciate another person, for that matter."

"Almost every American food—from Egg Foo Yung to empanadas—is covered in the phone book under the generic heading 'Restaurants.' Only pizza stands alone. Pizza, a Johnny-come-lately, compared with such long-standing national favorites as the hamburger and hot dog, has secured a special place on the American table."

·LOMBARDI'S · 1905·

"Loneliness is an aspect of the land. All things in the plain are isolate; there is no confusion of objects in the eye, but *one* hill or *one* tree or *one* man. To look upon that landscape in the early morning, with the sun at your back, is to lose the sense of proportion. Your imagination comes to life, and this, you think, is where Creation was begun."

"Teaching in the Islamic Republic, like any other vocation, was subservient to politics and subject to arbitrary rules. Always, the joy of teaching was marred by diversions and considerations forced on us by the regime—how well could one teach when the main concern of university officials was not the quality of one's work but the color of one's lips, the subversive potential of a single strand of hair?"

"If this were a movie, he'd score a perfect 1600 and be off to Princeton on full scholarship. But Harlem isn't Hollywood, and the challenges in real life are infinitely more complex."

"Political language—and with variations this is true of all political parties, from Conservatives to Anarchists—is designed to make lies sound truthful and murder respectable, and to give an appearance of solidity to pure wind."

"Putting aside the need to earn a living, I think there are four great motives for writing, at any rate for writing prose."

"Instead of looking at kids to 'prove' that differences in behavior by sex are innate, we can look at the ways we raise kids as an index to how unfinished the feminist revolution really is, and how tentatively it is embraced even by adults who fully expect their daughters to enter previously male-dominated professions and their sons to change diapers."

"In the nomenclature struggle, who names an issue usually carries the day."

"Wonderful smells drifted through the hallways, men and women in neat white lab coats cheerfully went about their work, and hundreds of little glass bottles sat on laboratory tables and shelves. . . . The long chemical names on the little white labels were as mystifying to me as medieval Latin. These odd-sounding things would be mixed and poured and turned into new substances, like magic potions."

"Can one experience nostalgia for a time and place one did not know? I believe so. You could put me in solitary with Abbott's photograph of 'Blossom Restaurant' and I wouldn't notice the months pass away as I studied the menu chalked on the blackboard at its entrance."

"I just found out that our family is no longer what the Census Bureau calls a traditional American family, and I want everyone to know that this is not our fault."

"Ignorance of the cause augmented the sense of horror. Of the real carriers, rats and fleas, the fourteenth century had no suspicion, perhaps because they were so familiar."

"We live in a culture of simulation. Our games, our economic and political systems, and the ways architects design buildings, chemists envisage molecules, and surgeons perform operations all use simulation technology. In ten years the degree to which simulations are embedded in every area of life will have increased exponentially. We need to develop a new form of media literacy: readership skills for the culture of simulation."

"As I picked out six limes, not a bruise or blemish on them, it occurred to me that I was not really worried about robots becoming sentient, human, indistinguishable from us. That long-standing fear—robots who fool us into taking them for humans—suddenly seemed a comic-book peril, born of another age, as obsolete as a twenty-five-year-old computer."

"According to the National Science Board's 2002 study *Science and Engineering Indicators*, only one-third of Americans can 'adequately explain what it means to study something scientifically.' Which presumably leaves those who would exploit scientific claims with two suckers born every three minutes."

"People often refer to being 'hooked on TV.' Does this, too, fall into the lighthearted category of cookie eating and other pleasures that people pursue with unusual intensity? Or is there a kind of television viewing that falls into the more serious category of destructive addiction?"

"'Hooking up' was a term known in the year 2000 to almost every American child over the age of nine, but to only a relatively small percentage of their parents, who, even if they heard it, thought it was being used in the old sense of 'meeting' someone. Among the children, hooking up was always a sexual experience, but the nature and extent of what they did could vary widely."

"In the eyes of American law today, most of the community of life on Earth remains mere property. . . . This means that environmentalists are seldom seen as activists fighting to uphold fundamental rights, but rather as criminals who infringe upon the property rights of others."

"Asteroids hurtling at us beyond our control don't figure high on our list of imminent dangers. To save ourselves, we don't need new technology: we just need the political will to face up to our problems of population and the environment."

▶ THE ACADEMIC VOICE
"Surprisingly, many educated people who should know better deny the seriousness of the risks ahead of us. History has important lessons to teach such people. Collapse has already befallen many societies that were at less risk than our societies are today."

"We rarely wonder about or discuss the brother who shot him because we already know everything about him. When the call came, my first thought was the same one I'd had when I'd heard about Rosa Parks's beating: a brother did it."

"We can live any way we want. People take vows of poverty, chastity, and obedience—even of silence—by choice. The thing is to stalk your calling in a certain skilled and supple way, to locate the most tender and live spot and plug into that pulse. This is yielding, not fighting."

▶ THE WRITER AT WORK
"One of the few things I know about writing is this: spend it all, shoot it, play it, lose it, all, right away, every time. Do not hoard what seems good for a later place in the book, or for another book; give it, give it all, give it now."

"In the fairly near future, a standard item in the trunks of American police cruisers—perhaps even on each officer's belt—may be a DNA analyzer. As a suspect is arrested, police will quickly swipe the inside of his cheek with a cotton swab and pop the results into the scanner."

"I could have lived with 'flag' and 'faith' as neotraditional values—not happily, but I could have managed—until 'family' was press-ganged into joining them."

have been the veterans of creative suffering. Continue to work with the faith that unearned suffering is redemptive."

"Abused and scorned though we may be, our destiny is tied up with the destiny of America. Before the pilgrims landed at Plymouth, we were here. Before the pen of Jefferson etched across the pages of history the majestic words of the Declaration of Independence, we were here."

"As love has increasingly become the center of all emotional expression in the popular imagination, anxiety about obtaining it in sufficient quantities—and for sufficient duration—suffuses the population. Everyone knows that as the demands and expectations on couples escalated, so did divorce rates. And given the current divorce statistics (roughly 50 percent of all marriages end in divorce), all indications are that whomever you love today—your beacon of hope, the center of all your optimism—has a good chance of becoming your worst nightmare tomorrow."

"Most families don't shop for baby names in Hollywood. They look to the family just a few blocks over, the one with the bigger house and newer car. The kind of families that were the first to call their daughters Amber or Heather, and are now calling them Alexandra or Katherine."

"[P]eople think about 'global warming' in the way they think about 'violence on television' or 'growing trade deficits,' as a marginal concern to them, if a concern at all. Enlightened governments make smallish noises and negotiate smallish treaties; enlightened people look down on America for its blind piggishness. Hardly anyone, however, has fear in their guts."

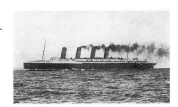

"Inside the door of Kelley's Bar and Lounge I was flagged by a guy collecting a cover charge and told I couldn't enter wearing my Malcolm X hat. I asked why; the guy hesitated, conferred for a moment with his partner, then declared that Malcolm X hats were against the dress code."

"Most statistics tell us that breast cancer is genetic, hereditary, with rising percentages attached to fatty diets, childlessness, or becoming pregnant after thirty. What they don't say is that living in Utah may be the greatest hazard of all."

"When I began reading and studying history, I kept coming across incidents and events that led me to think, *Wow, what a movie this would make.* I would look to see if a movie had been made about it, but I'd never find one. It took me a while to realize that Hollywood isn't going to make movies like the ones I imagined. Hollywood isn't going to make movies that are class-conscious, or antiwar, or conscious of the need for racial equality or gender equality."

IV. VOICES OF MODERN FICTION:
Six Short Stories

"Victor didn't have any money. Who does have money on a reservation, except the cigarette and fireworks salespeople? His father had a savings account waiting to be claimed, but Victor needed to find a way to get to Phoenix. Victor's mother was just as poor as he was, and the rest of his family didn't have any use at all for him."

"Of course, the birthday party never happened. The birthday boy was in the hospital instead. The mother sat by the bed. She was waiting for the boy to wake up. The father hurried over from his office. He sat next to the mother. So now the both of them waited for the boy to wake up. They waited for hours, and then the father went home to take a bath."

"Wash the white clothes on Monday and put them on the stone heap; wash the color clothes on Tuesday and put them on the clothesline to dry; don't walk barehead in the hot sun."

Alternate Tables of Contents _____

Selections Arranged by Theme

BUSINESS, ECONOMICS, AND CONSUMERISM

CHILDHOOD AND FAMILY

EDUCATION

ETHICS AND MORALITY

LANGUAGE AND LITERATURE

LAW, POLITICS, AND SOCIETY

THE NATURAL ENVIRONMENT

PHILOSOPHY, SPIRITUALITY, AND RELIGION

POPULAR CULTURE AND MASS MEDIA

PSYCHOLOGY AND HUMAN BEHAVIOR

RACIAL AND ETHNIC IDENTITY

SCIENCE AND TECHNOLOGY

A SENSE OF PLACE

Selections Arranged by Common Rhetorical Modes and Patterns of Development

CONSTRUCTING NARRATIVES

Narratives That Lead to a Sudden Insight or a Decision

Narratives That Report Facts and Historical Events

Narratives That Illustrate a Position or a Philosophical Perspective

USING COMPARISONS

DEFINING WORDS AND CONCEPTS

SUPPLYING INSTANCES AND EXAMPLES

CLASSIFYING IDEAS

ANALYZING AND DESCRIBING PROCESSES

ANALYZING AND DESCRIBING IMAGES

ESTABLISHING CAUSES AND EFFECTS

FORMING ANALOGIES

Countering Other Arguments

Arguing from Personal Authority and Expertise

Introduction for Students:
The Writer's Presence

Presence is a word—like *charisma*—that we reserve for people who create powerful and memorable impressions. Many public figures and political leaders are said to "have presence"—Martin Luther King Jr. and Eleanor Roosevelt are two superb examples—as well as many athletes, dancers, and musicians. In fact, the quality of presence is found abundantly in the performing arts, where top entertainers and actors self-consciously fashion—through style, costume, and gesture—an instantly recognizable public presence. Clearly, people with presence are able to command our attention. How do they do it?

Presence is far easier to identify than it is to define. We recognize it when we see it, but how do we capture it in words? Virtually everyone would agree, for example, that when LeBron James steps onto a basketball court, he displays an exceptional degree of presence; we acknowledge this regardless of whether we are basketball fans. But what is it about such individuals that commands our attention? How can we begin to understand this elusive characteristic known as presence?

On one level, *presence* simply means "being present." But the word is more complex than that; it suggests much more than the mere fact of being physically present. Most dictionaries define *presence* as an ability to project a sense of self-assurance, poise, ease, or dignity. We thus speak of someone's "stage presence" or "presence of mind." But the word is also used today to suggest an impressive personality, an individual who can make his or her presence felt. As every college student knows, to be present in a classroom is not the same thing as *having a presence* there. We may be present in body but not in spirit. In that sense, presence is also a matter of individual energy and exertion, of putting something of ourselves into whatever we do.

Presence is especially important in writing, which is what this book is about. Just as we notice individual presence in sports, or music, or conversation, so too we discover it in good writing. If what we read seems dreary, dull, or dead, it's usually because the writer forgot to include an important ingredient: *personal presence*. That doesn't mean that your essays should be written *in* the first-person singular (this book contains many exceptional essays that aren't) but that your essays should be written *by* the first-person singular. Interesting essays are produced by a real and distinct person, not an automaton following a set of mechanical rules and abstract principles.

PRESENCE IN WRITING

How can someone be present in writing? How can you project yourself into an essay so that it seems that you're personally there, even though all your reader sees are words on a piece of paper?

The Writer's Presence shows you how this is done. It shows how a wide variety of talented writers establish a distinct presence in many different kinds of writing and for many different purposes and audiences. Although the book offers numerous examples of methods for establishing presence, several are worth pointing out at the start. Let's examine four of the chief ways an experienced writer can be present in an essay.

1. *Through Personal Experience*. One of the most straightforward ways for the writer to make his or her presence felt in an essay is to include appropriate personal experiences. Of course, many assignments may call for a personal essay and, in those cases, you will naturally be putting episodes from your own life at the center of your writing. But writers also find ways to build their personal experiences into essays that are informative or argumentative, essays on topics other than themselves. They do this to show their close connection with a subject, to offer testimony, or to establish their personal authority on a subject. Many of the essays in this collection offer clear illustrations of how writers incorporate personal experience into an essay on a specific topic or issue.

Look, for example, at the essay by Amy Cunningham, "Why Women Smile" (page 324). This essay is primarily an explanation of a cultural phenomenon—the way women are socially conditioned to maintain a smiling attitude. However, Cunningham begins the essay not with a general observation but with a personal anecdote: "After smiling brilliantly for nearly four decades, I now find myself trying to quit." Although her essay is not "personal," her opening sentence, besides establishing her own connection with the topic, provides readers with a personal motive for her writing.

One of the first places to look for the writer's presence is in the motive, the purpose, for putting words down on paper or on the computer screen. The extent of your success in making clear your motive for writing will largely depend on your interest both in the subject and in your ideas about the subject. It is extremely difficult for any writer to establish a presence when he or she is either bored with—or simply uninterested in—the subject at hand. But a writer who demonstrates what Virginia

Woolf calls a "fierce attachment to an idea" can create a presence that attracts and holds a reader's attention.

2. *Through Voice*. Another way a writer makes his or her presence felt is through creating a distinctive and identifiable *voice*. All words are composed of sounds, and language itself is something nearly all of us originally learned through *hearing*. Any piece of writing can be read aloud, though many readers have developed such ingrained habits of silent reading that they no longer *hear* the writing. Good writers, however, want their words to be heard. They want their sentences to have rhythm, cadence, and balance. Experienced authors revise a great deal of their writing just to make sure the sentences *sound* right. They're writing for the reader's ear as well as the reader's mind.

In many respects, voice is the writer's "signature," what finally distinguishes the work of one writer from another. Consider how quickly we recognize voice. We've *heard* only the opening lines of a comedy routine on television, yet we instantly recognize the speaker. So, too, whenever we read a piece of writing, we ought to think of it as an experience similar to listening to someone speak aloud. Doing so adds drama to writing and reading. Here is what the poet Robert Frost has to say on the subject:

> Everything written is as good as it is dramatic. . . . A dramatic necessity goes deep into the nature of the sentence. Sentences are not different enough to hold the attention unless they are dramatic. No ingenuity of varying structure will do. All that can save them is the speaking tone of voice somehow entangled in the words and fastened to the page for the ear of the imagination. That is all that can save poetry from singing, all that can save prose from itself. (Preface to *A Way Out*, in *Selected Prose of Robert Frost*)

Frost spent a good portion of his celebrated public life encouraging people to cultivate what he called "the hearing imagination."

A more specific dimension of voice is *tone*, which refers not only to the implied relationship of the writer to the reader but also to the manner the writer adopts in addressing the reader. Tone suggests not the writer's attitudes themselves but the way those attitudes are revealed. In either projecting or analyzing tone, writers and readers ought to consider its intensity, the force with which the writer's attitudes are expressed. The strength of the writer's tone depends on such factors as the seriousness of the situation, the nature and extent of the writer's involvement in the situation, and the control the writer exercises over expression. In practical terms, tone is usually a matter of diction and individual word choice.

A writer's voice is usually fairly consistent from essay to essay and can be detected quickly by an experienced reader who pays attention to "the hearing imagination." To be distinctive and effective, a writer's voice need not be strange, artificial, or self-consciously literary. Many essayists develop a casual, familiar, flexible tone of voice that allows them to range easily from the intimate to the intellectual. Sentence rhythm and word choice play a large part in determining a writer's tone of voice. Observe how Raymond Carver begins an essay about his father (page 57):

> My dad's name was Clevie Raymond Carver. His family called him Raymond and friends called him C.R. I was named Raymond Clevie Carver, Jr. I hated the "Junior" part. When I was little my dad called me Frog, which was okay. . . .

Carver's voice here is casual and almost childlike, a quality he is striving for in an essay intended to be candid, intimate, and low-key. Throughout the essay, for example, he rarely uses the word *father* but always the more colloquial *dad*. If you read this passage aloud, you will get the feeling that someone is speaking directly to you.

3. *Through Point of View.* Another sure way for writers to establish presence is through the point of view they adopt toward a subject. In this sense, point of view comprises the "where" of the writer's presence. Sometimes a point of view can be a literal reality, an actual place or situation in which writers physically locate themselves. This occurs most frequently in autobiographical essays in which the writer is present both as the narrator and as a character. For example, in "A Clack of Tiny Sparks: Remembrances of a Gay Boyhood" (page 75), Bernard Cooper is always meticulous about telling us his actual location at any given moment in his writing. The essay begins, "Theresa Sanchez sat behind me in ninth-grade algebra."

Or consider the tremendous importance of point of view — this time in terms of perspective — to another essayist in the volume, Brent Staples, in "Just Walk on By: A Black Man Ponders His Power to Alter Public Space" (page 240). This is how Staples opens his essay:

> My first victim was a woman — white, well dressed, probably in her early twenties. I came upon her late one evening on a deserted street in Hyde Park, a relatively affluent neighborhood in an otherwise mean, impoverished section of Chicago. As I swung onto the avenue behind her, there seemed to be a discreet, uninflammatory distance between us. Not so. She cast back a worried glance. To her, the youngish black man — a broad six feet two inches with a beard and billowing hair, both hands shoved into the pockets of a bulky military jacket — seemed menacingly close. After a few more quick glimpses, she picked up her pace and was soon running in earnest. Within seconds she disappeared into a cross street.

To see why he frightens people, Staples needs to see himself in the stereotypical ways that others see him. Thus, by the middle of this opening paragraph (in the sentence beginning "To her"), he literally switches the point of view from his own perspective to that of the young and terrified white woman, describing his appearance as she would perceive it.

Point of view is not always a matter of a specific location or position. Writers are not always present in their essays as dramatic characters. In many reflective, informative, or argumentative essays, the point of view is determined more by a writer's intellectual attitude or opinions — an angle of vision — than by a precise physical perspective. As an example of how a writer establishes a personal perspective without a dominant first-person narrator, consider the following passage from John Taylor Gatto's "Against School" (page 682), an argumentative essay against America's traditional school system. Although Gatto from time to time introduces his own personal background, he makes his point of view—opposition to modern education—clear to the reader without ever referring directly to himself. Note his comparison between how schools train children and how concerned parents might better handle the job:

> Now for the good news. Once you understand the logic behind modern schooling, its tricks and traps are fairly easy to avoid. School trains children to be employees and consumers; teach your own to be leaders and adventurers. School trains children to obey reflexively; teach your own to think critically and independently. Well-schooled kids have a low threshold for boredom; help your own to develop an inner life so that they'll never be bored. Urge them to take on the serious material, the *grown-up* material, in history, literature, philosophy, music, art, economics, theology—all the stuff schoolteachers know well enough to avoid. Challenge your kids with plenty of solitude so that they can learn to enjoy their own company, to conduct inner dialogues.

There is no first-person singular here, nor a dramatically rendered self. Yet this passage conveys a distinct point of view.

4. *Through Verbal Patterns.* A writer can also be present in an essay as a *writer*—that is, as a person consciously crafting and shaping his or her work. This artistic presence is not always obvious. Yet when we begin to detect in our reading certain kinds of repeated elements—a metaphor or an image, a twist on an earlier episode, a conclusion that echoes the opening—we become aware that someone is deliberately shaping experience or ideas in a special manner. We often find this type of presence in imaginative literature—especially in novels and poems—as well as in essays that possess a distinct literary flavor.

To see an example of creating a presence through verbal patterns, look at the opening paragraph of E. B. White's now-classic essay, "Once More to the Lake" (page 270).

> One summer, along about 1904, my father rented a camp on a lake in Maine and took us all there for the month of August. We all got ringworm from some kittens and had to rub Pond's Extract on our arms and legs night and morning, and my father rolled over in a canoe with all his clothes on; but outside of that the vacation was a success and from then on none of us ever thought there was any place in the world like that lake in Maine. We returned summer after summer—always on August 1st for one month. I have since become a salt-water man, but sometimes in summer there are days when the restlessness of the tides and the fearful cold of the sea water and the incessant wind that blows across the afternoon and into the evening make me wish for the placidity of a lake in the woods. A few weeks ago this feeling got so strong I bought myself a couple of bass hooks and a spinner and returned to the lake where we used to go, for a week's fishing and to revisit old haunts.

If, in rereading this opening, you circle every use of the word *and*, you will clearly see a pattern of repetition. *And*, of course, is a very unobtrusive word, and you may not notice right away how White keeps it present throughout the passage. This repetition alone may strike you at first as of no special importance, but as you read through the essay and see how much of White's central theme depends on the idea of return and repetition, you will get a better sense of why the little word *and*—a word that subtly reinforces the idea of repetition itself—is so significant.

E. B. White is present in his essay in more obvious ways—he is both telling the story and appearing in it as a character. But he is also present to us as a writer, someone consciously shaping the language and form of his essay. We are dealing here with three levels of presence (which might also be described as three levels of "I"). If this sounds confusing, just think of a movie in which a single person directs, stars, and perhaps plays one or more other roles in the making of the film. It's not that uncommon. If you watch the 2004 film *Million Dollar Baby*, for example, you can observe the multiple presences of Clint Eastwood. Not only is Eastwood visibly present in the film as one of the main characters, but we also can detect his creative and shaping presence as the director and as a producer (roles for which he won two Oscars), and as the composer of the film's score. The audience can directly see him on the screen as an actor; the audience can also infer his presence as a composer, a producer, and especially as a director—presences that, though less directly observable, are still original and powerful.

THE SELECTIONS IN THIS BOOK

Many of the selections in this book feature the first-person point of view directly. These selections appear mostly in the first part, "Personal Writing: Exploring Our Own Lives." In most of these selections, the writer will appear as both narrator and main character, and the writer's presence will be quite observable.

But private and personal writing provide only a fraction of the different types of nonfiction that appear regularly in books, newspapers, and magazines. Many essays are written on specific topics and deal with specific issues. Most of the essays appearing in America's dominant periodicals, for example, are intended to be either informative or persuasive; the author wants to convey information about a particular subject (a Civil War battle, for example) or wants to express an opinion about a particular issue (such as how to deal with terrorism). The book's second and third parts, "Expository Writing: Shaping Information" and "Argumentative Writing: Contending with Issues," contain a large number of selections that illustrate writing intended to inform, argue, and persuade.

You'll notice, however, a strong writer's presence in many of the informative and persuasive essays. This is deliberate. To write informatively or persuasively about subjects other than yourself doesn't mean that you have to disappear as a writer. Sometimes you will want to insert your own experiences and testimony into an argumentative essay; at other times you will want to assume a distinct viewpoint concerning a piece of information; and at still other times—though you may not introduce the first-person singular—you will make your presence strongly felt in your tone of voice or simply in the way you arrange your facts and juxtapose details (see the Gatto passage on page 5). At the heart of the word *information* is *form.* Writers don't passively receive facts and information in a totally finished format; they need to shape their information, to give it form. This shaping or patterning is something the writer *contributes.* A large part of the instructional purpose of this collection is to encourage you to pay more attention to the different ways writers are present in their work.

Presence in Fiction

An individual writer's presence and voice are perhaps more easily discerned in nonfiction than in fiction. The reason for this is that a novelist or short story writer invents and gives voices to numerous characters who should not be confused with the author. Sometimes a story is told by an invented character who also should not be closely identified with his or her author. A good example of this technique can be found in John Updike's "A & P" (page 967), in which a story is narrated in the distinctive voice of its main character, Sammy, a teenager who is working at a small suburban supermarket. Although the story is written in the first-person singular—exactly like most personal essays—the character and voice are fictional and do not correspond to any real person. Sammy is not John Updike, nor does he necessarily speak like John Updike would if we met him.

To further complicate matters, this biographical gap between narrator and author remains even when a story that is told in the third person appears to be written in the voice of the author. The third-person narrator is also invented, and the narrative voice and presence may have little to do with the life of the author who created it. So in what ways can the writer's presence be observed in a story if we cannot attach to its teller any biographical connection with its author? In fiction, we often find a writer's presence in a distinctive style of writing; in certain repeated patterns; in the dynamics of structure and plot; and, of course, in the ethical, spiritual, or intellectual values a story may be intended to illustrate. In certain stories, to be sure, a particular character may clearly represent the author's own values, and in those cases we might argue that the writer becomes "present" in that character. As we can see in the fourth part, "Voices of Modern Fiction: Six Short Stories," an author may refuse to locate his or her moral and psychological values within a particular character but will expect instead that the reader will derive these values from the overall perspective of the story itself. Unlike essayists, short story writers rarely state their ethical or aesthetic values directly and explicitly. As the novelist D. H. Lawrence aptly put it, in fiction we must trust the tale and not the teller.

THE READER'S PRESENCE

Because almost all writing (and *all* published writing) is intended to be read, we can't dismiss the importance of the reader. Just as we find different levels of a writer's presence in a given piece of writing, so too can we detect different ways in which a reader can be present.

An author writes a short essay offering an opinion about gun control. The author herself has been the victim of a shooting, and her piece, though it includes her personal experiences, is largely made up of a concrete plan to eliminate all guns—even hunting rifles—from American life. She would like lawmakers to adopt her plan. Yet, in writing her essay, she imagines that there will be a great deal of resistance to her argument. In other words, she imagines a reader who will most likely disagree with her and who needs to be won over. Let's imagine she gets her essay published in *Newsweek*.

Now imagine three people in a dentist's office who within the same afternoon pick up this issue of *Newsweek* and read the essay. One of them has also been victimized by guns (her son was accidentally wounded by a hunter), and she reads the essay with great sympathy and conviction. She understands perfectly what this woman has gone through and believes in her plan completely. The next reader, a man who has never once in his life committed a crime and has no tolerance for criminals, is outraged by the essay. He was practically brought up in the woods and loves to hunt. He could never adopt a gun control plan that would in effect criminalize hunting. He's ready to fire off a letter attacking this woman's plan. The third reader also enjoys hunting and has always felt that hunting rifles should be exempt from any government regulation of firearms. But he finds the writer's plan convincing and feasible. He spends the rest of the day trying to think of counterarguments.

Obviously, these are only three of many possibilities. But you can see from this example the differences between the reader imagined by the writer and some actual readers. The one person who completely agreed with the writer was not the kind of reader the author had originally imagined or was trying to persuade; she was already persuaded. And though the other two readers were part of her intended audience, one of them could never be persuaded to her point of view, whereas the other one might.

The differences briefly outlined here are distinctions between what can be called *implied readers* and *actual readers*. The implied reader is the reader imagined by the writer for a particular piece of writing. In constructing arguments, for example, it is usually effective to imagine readers we are *trying* to win over to our views. Otherwise, we are simply asking people who already agree with us to agree with us—what's commonly known as "preaching to the converted" or "preaching to the choir."

In informative or critical essays, a writer also needs to be careful about the implied reader. For example, it's always important to ask how much your intended audience may already know about your subject.

Here's a practical illustration. If you were asked to write a review of a recent film for your college newspaper, you would assume your readers had not yet seen it (or else you might annoy them by giving away some surprises). However, if you were asked to write a critical essay about the same movie for a film course, you could assume your readers had seen it. It's the same movie, and you have the same opinions about it, but your two essays have two different purposes, and in the process of writing them you imagine readers with two different levels of knowledge about the film.

Actual readers, of course, differ from implied readers in that they are real people who read the writing—not readers intended or imagined by the writer. As you read the essays in this collection, you should be aware of at least two readers—(1) the reader you think the writer imagines for the essay and (2) the reader you are in actuality. Sometimes you will seem very close to the kind of reader the writer is imagining. In those cases, you might say that you "identify" with a particular writer, essay, or point of view. At other times, however, you will notice a great distance between the reader the author imagines and you as an actual reader. For example, you may feel excluded by the author on the basis of race, gender, class, or expected knowledge and educational level. Or you may feel you know more than the author does about a particular topic.

To help you get accustomed to your role as a reader, each selection in the book is followed by a set of questions, "The Reader's Presence." These questions are designed to orient you to the various levels of reading suggested by the selection. Some of the questions will ask you to identify the kind of reader you think the author imagines; other questions will prompt you to think about specific ways you may differ from the author's intended reader; still others will help you to make connections between and among the selections and authors. In general, the questions are intended to make you more deeply aware of your *presence* as a reader.

In this brief introduction, we covered only two levels of readers (imagined and actual), but some literary essays, such as Jonathan Swift's "A Modest Proposal" (page 866), demand more complex consideration. Whenever we think more than these two types of readers need to be identified in an essay, we will introduce this information in the questions.

We hope you will find *The Writer's Presence* a stimulating book to read and think about. To make our presence felt as writers is as much a matter of self-empowerment as it is of faith. It requires the confidence that we can affect others, or determine a course of action, or even surprise ourselves by new ideas or by acquiring new powers of articulation.

Part of the enduring pleasure of writing is precisely that element of surprise, of originality—that lifelong pleasure of discovering new resources of language, finding new means of knowing ourselves, and inventing new ways to be present in the world.

Part I

Personal Writing: Exploring Our Own Lives

Sherman Alexie

The Joy of Reading and Writing: Superman and Me

Sherman Alexie (b. 1966) is a Spokane/Coeur d'Alene Indian who grew up on the Spokane Indian Reservation in Wellpinit, Washington. He was born hydrocephalic and underwent a brain operation at the age of six months, which he was not expected to survive. As a youth, Alexie left the reservation for a public high school where he excelled in academics and became a star player on the basketball team. He attended Gonzaga University in Spokane on a scholarship and then transferred to Washington State University, where his experience in a poetry workshop encouraged him to become a writer. Soon after graduation he received the Washington State Arts Commission Poetry Fellowship and a National Endowment for the Arts Poetry Fellowship. His first collection of short stories, The Lone Ranger and Tonto Fistfight in Heaven *(1993), received a PEN/Hemingway Award for Best First Book of Fiction. He was subsequently named one of* Granta's Best of Young American Novelists *and published a novel titled* Reservation Blues *(1995), followed the next year by* Indian Killer *(1996). Since 1997 Alexie has written for the screen; his screenplay for the movie* Smoke Signals, *based on his short story "This Is What It Means to Say Phoenix, Arizona" (page 909), received the Christopher Award in 1999. He has published eighteen books of fiction and poetry, including* Ten Little Indians *(2003), short stories;* Dangerous Astronomy *(2005), poetry;* Flight *(2007), a novel; and* The Absolutely True Diary of a Part-Time Indian *(2007), his first book aimed at young adults, which won the 2007 National Book Award for Young People's Literature.*

Alexie has commented on his own work, "I'm a good writer who may be a great writer one day. I'm harder on myself than anybody."

I learned to read with a Superman comic book. Simple enough, I suppose. I cannot recall which particular Superman comic book I read, nor can I remember which villain he fought in that issue. I cannot remember the plot, nor the means by which I obtained the comic book. What I can remember is this: I was 3 years old, a Spokane Indian boy living with his family on the Spokane Indian Reservation in eastern Washington state.

13

We were poor by most standards, but one of my parents usually managed to find some minimum-wage job or another, which made us middle-class by reservation standards. I had a brother and three sisters. We lived on a combination of irregular paychecks, hope, fear, and government surplus food.

My father, who is one of the few Indians who went to Catholic school on purpose, was an avid reader of westerns, spy thrillers, murder mysteries, gangster epics, basketball player biographies, and anything else he could find. He bought his books by the pound at Dutch's Pawn Shop, Goodwill, Salvation Army, and Value Village. When he had extra money, he bought new novels at supermarkets, convenience stores, and hospital gift shops. Our house was filled with books. They were stacked in crazy piles in the bathroom, bedrooms, and living room. In a fit of unemployment-inspired creative energy, my father built a set of bookshelves and soon filled them with a random assortment of books about the Kennedy assassination, Watergate, the Vietnam War, and the entire 23-book series of the Apache westerns. My father loved books, and since I loved my father with an aching devotion, I decided to love books as well.

I can remember picking up my father's books before I could read. The words themselves were mostly foreign, but I still remember the exact moment when I first understood, with a sudden clarity, the purpose of a paragraph. I didn't have the vocabulary to say "paragraph," but I realized that a paragraph was a fence that held words. The words inside a paragraph worked together for a common purpose. They had some specific reason for being inside the same fence. This knowledge delighted me. I began to think of everything in terms of paragraphs. Our reservation was a small paragraph within the United States. My family's house was a paragraph, distinct from the other paragraphs of the LeBrets to the north, the Fords to our south, and the Tribal School to the west. Inside our house, each family member existed as a separate paragraph but still had genetics and common experiences to link us. Now, using this logic, I can see my changed family as an essay of seven paragraphs: mother, father, older brother, the deceased sister, my younger twin sisters, and our adopted little brother.

At the same time I was seeing the world in paragraphs, I also picked up that Superman comic book. Each panel, complete with picture, dialogue, and narrative was a three-dimensional paragraph. In one panel, Superman breaks through a door. His suit is red, blue, and yellow. The brown door shatters into many pieces. I look at the narrative above the picture. I cannot read the words, but I assume it tells me that "Superman is breaking down the door." Aloud, I pretend to read the words and say, "Superman is breaking down the door." Words, dialogue, also float out of Superman's mouth. Because he is breaking down the door, I assume he says, "I am breaking down the door." Once again, I pretend to read the words and say aloud, "I am breaking down the door." In this way, I learned to read.

This might be an interesting story all by itself. A little Indian boy teaches   5
himself to read at an early age and advances quickly. He reads "Grapes of
Wrath" in kindergarten when other children are struggling through "Dick
and Jane." If he'd been anything but an Indian boy living on the reservation, he might have been called a prodigy. But he is an Indian boy living on
the reservation and is simply an oddity. He grows into a man who often
speaks of his childhood in the third person, as if it will somehow dull the
pain and make him sound more modest about his talents.

A smart Indian is a dangerous person, widely feared and ridiculed by
Indians and non-Indians alike. I fought with my classmates on a daily
basis. They wanted me to stay quiet when the non-Indian teacher asked
for answers, for volunteers, for help. We were Indian children who were
expected to be stupid. Most lived up to those expectations inside the
classroom but subverted them on the outside. They struggled with basic
reading in school but could remember how to sing a few dozen powwow
songs. They were monosyllabic in front of their non-Indian teachers but
could tell complicated stories and jokes at the dinner table. They submis-
sively ducked their heads when confronted by a non-Indian adult but
would slug it out with the Indian bully who was 10 years older. As Indian
children, we were expected to fail in the non-Indian world. Those who
failed were ceremonially accepted by other Indians and appropriately
pitied by non-Indians.

I refused to fail. I was smart. I was arrogant. I was lucky. I read books
late into the night, until I could barely keep my eyes open. I read books at
recess, then during lunch, and in the few minutes left after I had finished
my classroom assignments. I read books in the car when my family traveled to powwows or basketball games. In shopping malls, I ran to the
bookstores and read bits and pieces of as many books as I could. I read
the books my father brought home from the pawnshops and secondhand.
I read the books I borrowed from the library. I read the backs of cereal
boxes. I read the newspaper. I read the bulletins posted on the walls of
the school, the clinic, the tribal offices, the post office. I read junk mail. I
read auto-repair manuals. I read magazines. I read anything that had
words and paragraphs. I read with equal parts joy and desperation. I
loved those books, but I also knew that love had only one purpose. I was
trying to save my life.

Despite all the books I read, I am still surprised I became a writer. I
was going to be a pediatrician. These days, I write novels, short stories,
and poems. I visit schools and teach creative writing to Indian kids. In all
my years in the reservation school system, I was never taught how to
write poetry, short stories, or novels. I was certainly never taught that Indians wrote poetry, short stories, and novels. Writing was something beyond Indians. I cannot recall a single time that a guest teacher visited the
reservation. There must have been visiting teachers. Who were they?
Where are they now? Do they exist? I visit the schools as often as possible.

The Indian kids crowd the classroom. Many are writing their own poems, short stories, and novels. They have read my books. They have read many other books. They look at me with bright eyes and arrogant wonder. They are trying to save their lives. Then there are the sullen and already defeated Indian kids who sit in the back rows and ignore me with theatrical precision. The pages of their notebooks are empty. They carry neither pencil nor pen. They stare out the window. They refuse and resist. "Books," I say to them. "Books," I say. I throw my weight against their locked doors. The door holds. I am smart. I am arrogant. I am lucky. I am trying to save our lives.

The Reader's Presence

1. What does literacy mean to Alexie? What are his associations with reading? with writing? How does he use his reading and his writing to establish his ties to the community? What aspects of his identity are bound up with reading and writing?

2. How did the young Alexie use popular culture to educate himself? What did comic books teach him? How does Alexie use the figure of Superman, and aspects of action-hero stories more generally, to give structure and coherence to his essay?

3. Alexie uses the metaphor of "breaking down the door" to describe the act of learning to read. What are the connotations of this metaphor? How does it compare with Frederick Douglass's account of his acquisition of literacy in "Learning to Read and Write" (page 94) in which he says that he sometimes felt as though "learning to read had been a curse rather than a blessing"? As he encountered arguments for and against slavery in the books he read, Douglass felt that reading deepened his already vivid experience of slavery: "It had given me a view of my wretched condition, without the remedy" (paragraph 6). Is literacy a means to freedom for Alexie as it was, ultimately, for Douglass? If so, freedom from what or freedom to do what?

Maya Angelou

"What's Your Name, Girl?"

Maya Angelou (b. 1928) grew up in St. Louis, Missouri, and in Stamps, Arkansas, a victim of poverty, discrimination, and abuse. Angelou confronts the pain and injustice of her childhood in I Know Why the Caged Bird Sings *(1969), from which the selection "'What's Your Name, Girl?'" is taken. James Baldwin, who suggested she write about her childhood, praised this book as the mark of the "beginning of a new era in the minds and hearts of all black men and women." Angelou, who has received more than a hundred honorary degrees, is currently Reynolds Professor of American Studies at Wake Forest University. In addition to the several volumes of her autobiography, Angelou is the author of articles, short stories, and poetry. Her most recent publications are* Hallelujah! The Welcome Table *(2004), a collection of essays, and several books of poetry, including* Amazing Peace: A Christmas Poem *(2005),* Mother: A Cradle to Hold Me *(2006), and* Poetry for Young People: Maya Angelou *(2007). Her recording of her autobiographical work* A Song Flung Up to Heaven *won a Grammy in 2002.*

Angelou describes a typical day in her life as a writer in this way: "When I'm writing, everything shuts down. I get up about five. . . . I get in my car and drive off to a hotel room: I can't write in my house, I take a hotel room and ask them to take everything off the walls so there's me, the Bible, Roget's Thesaurus, and some good, dry sherry and I'm at work by 6:30. I write on the bed lying down—one elbow is darker than the other, really black from leaning on it—and I write in longhand on yellow pads. Once into it, all disbelief is suspended, it's beautiful. I hate to go, but I've set for myself 12:30 as the time to leave, because after that it's an indulgence, it becomes stuff I am going to edit out anyway. . . . After dinner I re-read what I have written . . . if April is the cruellest month, then 8:00 at night is the cruellest hour because that's when I start to edit and all that pretty stuff I've written gets axed out. So if I've written ten or twelve pages in six hours, it'll end up as three or four if I'm lucky."

Recently a white woman from Texas, who would quickly describe herself as a liberal, asked me about my hometown. When I told her that in Stamps[1] my grandmother had owned the only Negro general merchandise store since the turn of the century, she exclaimed, "Why, you were a debutante." Ridiculous and even ludicrous. But Negro girls in small Southern towns, whether poverty-stricken or just munching along on a few of life's necessities, were given as extensive and irrelevant preparations for adulthood as rich white girls shown in magazines. Admittedly the training was not the same. While white girls learned to waltz and sit gracefully with a teacup balanced on their knees, we were lagging behind, learning

---

[1]*Stamps:* A town in southwestern Arkansas. —EDS.

the mid-Victorian values with very little money to indulge them. (Come
and see Edna Lomax spending the money she made picking cotton on five
balls of ecru tatting thread. Her fingers are bound to snag the work and
she'll have to repeat the stitches time and time again. But she knows that
when she buys the thread.)

We were required to embroider and I had trunkfuls of colorful dish-
towels, pillowcases, runners, and handkerchiefs to my credit. I mastered
the art of crocheting and tatting, and there was a lifetime's supply of
dainty doilies that would never be used in sacheted dresser drawers. It
went without saying that all girls could iron and wash, but the finer
touches around the home, like setting a table with real silver, baking roasts,
and cooking vegetables without meat, had to be learned elsewhere. Usually
at the source of those habits. During my tenth year, a white woman's
kitchen became my finishing school.

Mrs. Viola Cullinan was a plump woman who lived in a three-
bedroom house somewhere behind the post office. She was singularly unattractive until she smiled, and then the lines around her eyes and mouth
which made her look perpetually dirty disappeared, and her face looked
like the mask of an impish elf. She usually rested her smile until late afternoon when her women friends dropped in and Miss Glory, the cook,
served them cold drinks on the closed-in porch.

The exactness of her house was inhuman. This glass went here and
only here. That cup had its place and it was an act of impudent rebellion
to place it anywhere else. At twelve o'clock the table was set. At 12:15
Mrs. Cullinan sat down to dinner (whether her husband had arrived or
not). At 12:16 Miss Glory brought out the food.

It took me a week to learn the difference between a salad plate, a   5
bread plate, and a dessert plate.

Mrs. Cullinan kept up the tradition of her wealthy parents. She was
from Virginia. Miss Glory, who was a descendant of slaves that had
worked for the Cullinans, told me her history. She had married beneath
her (according to Miss Glory). Her husband's family hadn't had their
money very long and what they had "didn't 'mount to much."

As ugly as she was, I thought privately, she was lucky to get a husband
above or beneath her station. But Miss Glory wouldn't let me say a thing
against her mistress. She was very patient with me, however, over the
housework. She explained the dishware, silverware, and servants' bells.

The large round bowl in which soup was served wasn't a soup bowl,
it was a tureen. There were goblets, sherbet glasses, ice-cream glasses,
wine glasses, green glass coffee cups with matching saucers, and water
glasses. I had a glass to drink from, and it sat with Miss Glory's on a separate shelf from the others. Soup spoons, gravy boat, butter knives, salad
forks, and carving platter were additions to my vocabulary and in fact almost represented a new language. I was fascinated with the novelty, with
the fluttering Mrs. Cullinan and her Alice-in-Wonderland house.

Her husband remains, in my memory, undefined. I lumped him with all the other white men that I had ever seen and tried not to see.

On our way home one evening, Miss Glory told me that Mrs. Cullinan   10
couldn't have children. She said that she was too delicate-boned. It was hard to imagine bones at all under those layers of fat. Miss Glory went on to say that the doctor had taken out all her lady organs. I reasoned that a pig's organs included the lungs, heart, and liver, so if Mrs. Cullinan was walking around without these essentials, it explained why she drank alcohol out of unmarked bottles. She was keeping herself embalmed.

When I spoke to Bailey[2] about it, he agreed that I was right, but he also informed me that Mr. Cullinan had two daughters by a colored lady and that I knew them very well. He added that the girls were the spitting image of their father. I was unable to remember what he looked like, although I had just left him a few hours before, but I thought of the Coleman girls. They were very light-skinned and certainly didn't look very much like their mother (no one ever mentioned Mr. Coleman).

My pity for Mrs. Cullinan preceded me the next morning like the Cheshire cat's smile. Those girls, who could have been her daughters, were beautiful. They didn't have to straighten their hair. Even when they were caught in the rain, their braids still hung down straight like tamed snakes. Their mouths were pouty little cupid's bows. Mrs. Cullinan didn't know what she missed. Or maybe she did. Poor Mrs. Cullinan.

For weeks after, I arrived early, left late, and tried very hard to make up for her barrenness. If she had had her own children, she wouldn't have had to ask me to run a thousand errands from her back door to the back door of her friends. Poor old Mrs. Cullinan.

Then one evening Miss Glory told me to serve the ladies on the porch. After I set the tray down and turned toward the kitchen, one of the women asked, "What's your name, girl?" It was the speckled-face one. Mrs. Cullinan said, "She doesn't talk much. Her name's Margaret."

"Is she dumb?"   15

"No. As I understand it, she can talk when she wants to but she's usually quiet as a little mouse. Aren't you, Margaret?"

I smiled at her. Poor thing. No organs and couldn't even pronounce my name correctly.[3]

"She's a sweet little thing, though."

"Well, that may be, but the name's too long. I'd never bother myself. I'd call her Mary if I was you."

I fumed into the kitchen. That horrible woman would never have the   20
chance to call me Mary because if I was starving I'd never work for her. I decided I wouldn't pee on her if her heart was on fire. Giggles drifted in

---

[2]*Bailey:* Angelou's brother. —EDS.
[3]*couldn't even pronounce my name correctly:* Angelou's first name is actually Marguerite. —EDS.

off the porch and into Miss Glory's pots. I wondered what they could be laughing about.

Whitefolks were so strange. Could they be talking about me? Everybody knew that they stuck together better than the Negroes did. It was possible that Mrs. Cullinan had friends in St. Louis who heard about a girl from Stamps being in court and wrote to tell her. Maybe she knew about Mr. Freeman.[4]

My lunch was in my mouth a second time and I went outside and relieved myself on the bed of four-o'clocks. Miss Glory thought I might be coming down with something and told me to go on home, that Momma would give me some herb tea, and she'd explain to her mistress.

I realized how foolish I was being before I reached the pond. Of course Mrs. Cullinan didn't know. Otherwise she wouldn't have given me the two nice dresses that Momma cut down, and she certainly wouldn't have called me a "sweet little thing." My stomach felt fine, and I didn't mention anything to Momma.

That evening I decided to write a poem on being white, fat, old, and without children. It was going to be a tragic ballad. I would have to watch her carefully to capture the essence of her loneliness and pain.

The very next day, she called me by the wrong name. Miss Glory and   25
I were washing up the lunch dishes when Mrs. Cullinan came to the doorway. "Mary?"

Miss Glory asked, "Who?"

Mrs. Cullinan, sagging a little, knew and I knew. "I want Mary to go down to Mrs. Randall's and take her some soup. She's not been feeling well for a few days."

Miss Glory's face was a wonder to see. "You mean Margaret, ma'am. Her name's Margaret."

"That's too long. She's Mary from now on. Heat that soup from last night and put it in the china tureen and, Mary, I want you to carry it carefully."

Every person I knew had a hellish horror of being "called out of   30
his name." It was a dangerous practice to call a Negro anything that could be loosely construed as insulting because of the centuries of their having been called niggers, jigs, dinges, blackbirds, crows, boots, and spooks.

Miss Glory had a fleeting second of feeling sorry for me. Then as she handed me the hot tureen she said, "Don't mind, don't pay that no mind. Sticks and stones may break your bones, but words . . . You know, I been working for her for twenty years."

She held the back door open for me. "Twenty years; I wasn't much older than you. My name used to be Hallelujah. That's what Ma named me, but my mistress give me 'Glory,' and it stuck. I likes it better too."

---

[4]**Mr. Freeman:** A friend of Angelou's mother; he was convicted of raping Angelou when she was a child. —EDS.

I was in the little path that ran behind the houses when Miss Glory shouted, "It's shorter too."

For a few seconds it was a toss-up over whether I would laugh (imagine being named Hallelujah) or cry (imagine letting some white woman rename you for her convenience). My anger saved me from either outburst. I had to quit the job, but the problem was going to be how to do it. Momma wouldn't allow me to quit for just any reason.

"She's a peach. That woman is a real peach." Mrs. Randall's maid   35
was talking as she took the soup from me, and I wondered what her name used to be and what she answered to now.

For a week I looked into Mrs. Cullinan's face as she called me Mary. She ignored my coming late and leaving early. Miss Glory was a little annoyed because I had begun to leave egg yolk on the dishes and wasn't putting much heart in polishing the silver. I hoped that she would complain to our boss, but she didn't.

Then Bailey solved my dilemma. He had me describe the contents of the cupboard and the particular plates she liked best. Her favorite piece was a casserole shaped like a fish and the green glass coffee cups. I kept his instructions in mind, so on the next day when Miss Glory was hanging out clothes and I had again been told to serve the old biddies on the porch, I dropped the empty serving tray. When I heard Mrs. Cullinan scream, "Mary!" I picked up the casserole and two of the green glass cups in readiness. As she rounded the kitchen door I let them fall on the tiled floor.

I could never absolutely describe to Bailey what happened next, because each time I got to the part where she fell on the floor and screwed up her ugly face to cry, we burst out laughing. She actually wobbled around on the floor and picked up shards of the cups and cried, "Oh, Momma. Oh, dear Gawd. It's Momma's china from Virginia. Oh, Momma, I sorry."

Miss Glory came running in from the yard and the women from the porch crowded around. Miss Glory was almost as broken up as her mistress. "You mean to say she broke our Virginia dishes? What we gone do?"

Mrs. Cullinan cried louder. "That clumsy nigger. Clumsy little black   40
nigger."

Old speckled-face leaned down and asked, "Who did it, Viola? Was it Mary? Who did it?"

Everything was happening so fast I can't remember whether her action preceded her words, but I know that Mrs. Cullinan said, "Her name's Margaret, goddamn it, her name's Margaret!" And she threw a wedge of the broken plate at me. It could have been the hysteria which put her aim off, but the flying crockery caught Miss Glory right over her ear and she started screaming.

I left the front door wide open so all the neighbors could hear.

Mrs. Cullinan was right about one thing. My name wasn't Mary.

The Reader's Presence

1. At the center of this autobiographical episode is the importance of people's names in African American culture. Where does Angelou make this point clear? If she hadn't explained the problem of names directly, how might your interpretation of the episode be different? To what extent do the names of things also play an important role in the essay? What does it mean to be "called out of [one's] name" (paragraph 30)?

2. Consider Marguerite's final act carefully. What turns her sympathetic feelings for Mrs. Cullinan to anger? Why does she respond by deliberately destroying Mrs. Cullinan's china? What else could she have done? Why was that act especially appropriate? What does the china represent? How does Angelou establish our sympathy, or lack thereof, for Marguerite in the final paragraphs?

3. Many coming-of-age stories involve an account not only of the child's acquisition of language but also, and perhaps more important, of the importance of social context to communication. Miss Glory's training of Marguerite as a maid involves "additions to [her] vocabulary and in fact almost represented a new language" (paragraph 8). How does her education compare to that of Malcolm X in "Homeboy" (page 168) when he arrives in the Roxbury ghetto (paragraph 15 and following)? What is the relation between language and power in each essay?

Marie Arana

Ghosts/Pishtacos

Journalist, editor, author, and literary critic Marie Arana was born in Lima, Peru, in 1949 of an American mother and a Peruvian father. In 1959, the family moved to the United States and settled in suburban Summit, New Jersey, where Arana grew up as "Latina and gringa." She received a BA in Russian language and literature from Northwestern University in 1971; she then spent time in Hong Kong where she received a certificate of scholarship in Mandarin through Yale University in China and an MA in linguistics from British University. Returning

*to the United States, she began her career as an editor, first at Harcourt, Brace,
Jovanovich and then at Simon & Schuster. In 1992, Arana joined the* Washington
Post *as a writer and an editor and, in 1999, became editor-in-chief of the* Post's
book review section, Book World. *Her memoir,* American Chica: Two Worlds,
One Childhood *(2001) was her first departure from being "the critic" to being
"the writer," and she was nominated as a finalist for the National Book Award.
This selection, "Ghosts/Pishtacos," is taken from that book. Arana edited the
essay collection,* The Writing Life: Writers on How They Think and Work *(2003);
she published her first novel,* Cellophane, *in 2006.*

In a 2007 interview for the Washington Post's *"Off the Page," Arana responded to the ultimate question posed to writers: Why do you write? "There is
no why. I just do. When I was very young, I used to write poetry, and I found
that enormously satisfying: whittling language down to its purest element....
Now, it's as if I have no choice. I don't ever set out with a program of what I
want to write. I simply love to weave the words and then the words become a
story and then the story has a life of its own. I write because I have to. The way a
shark needs to swim in order to breathe."*

The corridors of my skull are haunted. I carry the smell of sugar
there. The odors of a factory—wet cane, dripping iron, molasses pits—
are up behind my forehead, deep inside my throat. I'm reminded of those
scents when children offer me candy from a damp palm, when the man
I love sighs with wine upon his tongue, when I inhale the heartbreaking sweetness of rotting fruit and human waste that rises from garbage
dwellers' camps along the road to Lima.

I am always surprised to learn that people do not live with memories
of fragrance as I do. The smell of sugar is so strong in my head. That they
could have spent the first years of their lives in places like Pittsburgh or
Hong Kong and not gone for the rest of their days with the stench of a
steel furnace or the aromas of fungus and salt shrimp tucked into some
netherworld of cortex—how is that possible?

I had a friend once, from Bombay, who told how baffling it was to
travel this world smelling turmeric, coriander, and cardamom in the most
improbable corners of Nantucket or Palo Alto, only to find they were
Lorelei[1] of the olfactory, whiffs of his imagination, sirens of his mother's
curry, wafting in like she-cats, flicking seductive tails.

He chased after those smells, cooking up curries in rented houses in
New Jersey, in tidy chalets in Switzerland, in motel rooms along the
Shenandoah, mixing pastes from powders out of bottles with Scottish
surnames, searing ghees[2] in Sara Lee aluminum, washing out lunch boxes
in Maryland rest stops, trying to bring it back. Bring it back. Up into the
sinus, trailing down the throat. He was never quite able to recapture that

---

[1]*Lorelei:* A siren (sea nymph) of German legend whose singing lures sailors to ship-
wrecks.—EDS.
[2]*ghees:* Ghee is a semifluid, clarified butter used in Indian cooking.—EDS.

childhood blend: mashed on stone, dried in a Mahabharatan[3] sun, stuffed into earthenware, sold in an old man's shop, carried home in string-tied packages, measured onto his mother's mortar, locked into the chambers of his heart.

So it has been with me and sugar. I look back and see piles of it, glit-   5
tering crystals of it—burned, powdered, superfine. I smell sugar every-where. On whispers, in books, in the loam of a garden. In every cranny of life. And always—always—it is my father's sugar I am longing for: raw, rough, Cartavio brown.

Cartavio was the name of our hacienda[4]: a company town as single of purpose as Akron or Erie or Turin or anyplace where pistons and steel drive residents' lives. It was the mid-1950s, boom days for sugar in Peru, and the American industrial giant W. R. Grace was making the most of it in this remote coastal hamlet, five hundred miles north of Lima. Cartavio was surrounded by fields of sugarcane, fringed by a raging Pacific, and life in it was an eerie mirror or Peru's conquistador past. On one side of the hacienda were the cinnamon-skinned indigenous in a warren[5] of cinder block. On the other, in houses whose size and loveliness depended on the rank of their inhabitants, lived Peruvians of Spanish ancestry, Europeans, North Americans, the elite. There was a church on the square, a mansion for the manager, a Swiss-style guest house, a country club, and a clinic. But in the middle, with smokestacks thrusting so high there could be no doubt as to why the unlikely multitude was there: my father's factories.

Cartavio was nestled in the heart of the nation, just under the left breast of the female torso that Peru's landmass defines. But it was, in many ways, a foreign place, a twentieth-century invention, a colony of the world. Its driving force was industry, and the people who had gathered there were, one way or another, single-minded industrialists. The Americans had come with dollars; the Limeños with political power; the villagers with hands. Although their objectives were shared—a humming produc-tion of sugar and paper—Cartavio citizens lived in uncertain harmony. The laborers were willing to surrender themselves to the practicalities of an iron city by day, but under their own roofs by night they returned to ancient superstitions. The Lima engineers were willing to obey the gringo directives, but they suspected they knew a great deal more about those factories than any mahogany-desk boss in New York. The Americans soon learned that if the indigenous believed in ghosts and the *criollo*[6] overlords resented gringo power, then Grace's fortunes turned on such chimera as phantoms and pride. They understood the social dynamic, used it, and with old-fashioned American pragmatism, made it work for them.

---

[3]*Mahabharatan:* Mahabharata is an ancient religious epic of India.—EDS.
[4]*hacienda:* Spanish for property, estate.—EDS.
[5]*warren:* An elaborate system of burrows where rabbits live, a mazelike place in which it's easy to lose oneself.—EDS.
[6]*criollo:* Spanish for *Creole.* In Latin America, *criollos* are people of Spanish descent who were not born in Spain.—EDS.

I knew, with a certainty I could feel in my bones, that I was deeply Peruvian. That I was rooted to the Andean dust. That I believed in ghosts. That they lived in the trees, in my hair, under the *aparador*[7], lurking behind the silver, slipping in and out of the whites of my ancestors' portraits' eyes. I also knew that, for all his nods and smiles at the gringos, my father believed in ghosts, too. How could he not? He faced them every day.

To the hacienda of Cartavio, Papi was *Doctor Ingeniero*, the young Peruvian engineer in charge of the people and the maintenance of this whirring, spewing, U.S.-owned mill town. He was a sunny man with an open face. Although his hands were small, they were clever. Although he was not tall, his shoulders filled a room. There were photographs my mother would point to when she wanted us to know she thought him handsome, but they were of a man I didn't recognize—gaunt and angular, black wavy hair, eyes as wide as a calf's, mouth in a curl. The Papi I knew was barrel-chested, full-lipped. His hair had receded to a V. His cheeks were cherubic and round. His eyes bulged. In the subequatorial heat, he wore his shirt out, and it flapped in the breeze, revealing skin that was brown, smooth, and hairless. He was not fat but taut as a sausage—*bien papeado*, as Peruvians like to say. Potato-tight. When he laughed, he made no sound. He would lean forward as if something had leapt on his back and held him in an irresistible tickle. His eyes would squint, the tip of his tongue would push out, and his shoulders would bound vigorously. He'd laugh long and hard like that—silent, save for the hiss that issued from between his teeth—until he was short of breath, red-faced, and weeping. When he wasn't laughing, he was barking orders. When he wasn't doing that, his mouth was ringing a cigarette, sucking hard, his eyelids fluttering in thought.

Papi would not so much walk as strut. Not so much drink as guzzle. Not so much chat with a woman as flirt, wink, and ogle. He was clearly not the slender, soulful man in Mother's photographs. Not anymore. From the moment he registered on my brain, he was straining buttons, *bien papeado*—threatening to burst. 10

He was a machine virtuoso, improvising ways to go from desert to sugar, from burned plants to Herculean rolls of paper. He could take a field of sugarcane into his steel colossus, shove it through squealing threshers, wet it down with processed seawater, suck it dry of crystals, and feed it onto the rollers to emerge warm and dry from the other end as flying sheets of paper. He could take a faulty German turbine whose only hope for survival was a spare part eight thousand miles away in Stuttgart and, with a knickknack here, a length of wire there, make it hum again. He could pacify the gringos when they came from New York, matching them eye for eye on the intricacies of marcomechanics or spherical trigonometry or particle physics. He inspired fervent loyalty from his

---

[7] *aparador:* Spanish for china cabinet, dresser, or cupboard. —Eds.

laborers, striding through his iron city in an impeccably white suit, teaching them the way to an industrial future. The American way.

Every morning he would head for the belching beast long before the whistle sounded. In late afternoons, he returned to survey his pretty wife over lunch and take a brief siesta in his chair. But there seemed to be no end to his work. Even as he walked back through the gate for a late lunch or dinner and the servants fluttered into the kitchen to announce the *señor* was home, he was on call. Ready to pull away.

That he had to work with ghosts was a fact of life and everybody knew it. A worker's hand might be drawn into the iron jaws of the *trapiche*[8] as it gathered cane into its mandibles and pulled the mass into its threshers. A finger, a foot, a dog, a whole man might be lost to that ravenous maw as it creaked and shook and thrashed and sifted everything down to liquid sugar and a fine bagasse.

Los pishtacos, the workers would say to one another whenever such tragedies occurred. *Pishtacos*, their wives and mothers would whisper the next day as they combed the market or polished the silver services on the richly carved *aparadores* of the engineers. Ghosts. Machine ghosts. *Pishtacos norteamericanos*. And as anyone who knew Peruvian *historias* understood: They needed the fat of *indios* to grease their machines.

Our house stood on the corner of prime real estate, behind the offices of head engineers but far enough from the factory to allow us to ignore the less pleasant aspects of a churning industry. Finished in white stucco and shielded by manicured rows of tropical botanica, the house loomed above its compound walls like a castle behind a barricade. Flowers cascaded from its ramparts. In the garden, trees pushed forth pineapples, lucuma, bananas, and mango. An iron gate shut out the world. Behind the gate and the wall and the garden, the house itself was impervious to vendors, to factory workers, to ordinary Peruvians, to the sprawl of humanity that struggled a few hundred feet from its door.   15

The house was skirted by a capacious veranda. Inside, it was filled with high-ceilinged white rooms, heavy doors, yawning keyholes, arched passageways, Spanish tile. The living room—the *sala*—was dominated by my mother's ornate ebony piano. The master bedroom lay behind it, on the other side of a carved double door, so that when those doors were thrown open, the entire *sala* was surveyable from my parents' bed—a bizarre feature, but houses in outlying haciendas were often capricious and irregular. Through an open arch, you could go from our *sala* to the dining room, which held two massive pieces of furniture—a table and an *aparador*, carved with undulating scallops and garlands. The kitchen was stark, a workroom for servants, stripped down and graceless. A cavernous enamel sink—pocked and yellow—jutted from the wall. There was a simple blue table where we three children and our servants took meals. The

---

[8]*trapiche:* Spanish for a machine used in the sugar-refining process.—EDS.

kitchen door led to a back atrium garden. On the other side of that, behind a wall, were the servants' quarters, a shabby little building that could sleep six in two spare rooms. There was a stall with a spigot where our *mayordomo*[9] and *amas*[10] could wash, a storage area, and a concrete staircase that led to their rooms. To the left of those stairs, under a shed of bare wood and chicken wire, were the animal cages. At four I was told very clearly—as my older brother and sister, George and Vicki, had been—that I was not allowed in the servants' quarters. The cages were my demarcation line; they were the point beyond which I could not go.

Our own rooms were upstairs, well away from our parents' bedroom and out of the circuit of revelers when a party was afoot. After dinner, which we regularly took in the kitchen, the *amas* would trot us upstairs and bathe us, struggling with their small arms to balance us in the tubs. We would loll about in our pajamas thereafter. There never seemed any urgency to get us to bed, which was just as well because all three of us were terrified of the dark, afraid to look out the windows at tree branches, so well had our *amas* taught us that *pishtacos* were perched there, slavering and squinting in.

Had we overcome our fears and looked out those windows onto Cartavio's main residential street beyond our own house, we would have seen five other houses of the first rank, equally grand, equally walled. Behind them, a row of modest ones for the lesser company families. Our immediate neighbors were the Lattos, freckle-faced Scots whose brogue-filtered Spanish made George and me horselaugh into our hands. Their eight-year-old son, Billy, was the undisputed object of Vicki's affection. He was a straight, good-looking boy with an easy smile. He would direct his grins freely to Vicki, but George and I—who thought ourselves far more appealing than our prickly sister—had to work hard to draw his charms: We'd stand on our heads, swing from trees, make fools of ourselves if we had to, for the incomparable joy of gazing on his teeth.

As a young child, my days unfolded in the garden. It was, as every garden in that coastal desert is, an artificial paradise: invented, deceptive, precarious. Without human hands to tend it, the lush vegetation would have dried to a husk and sifted down into an arid dune. For years, I did not know how tentative that childhood environment was. Walled in, with green crowding our senses and the deep sweetness of fruit and sugar in the air, I felt a sense of entitlement, as if my world would ever be so richly hung. But it was an illusion, and many had labored to create it: to make us feel as if we were emperors of a verdant oasis on the banks of the Amazon just north of the Andes, where the green was unrestrained.

Fooled, happy, ignorant, George and I would splash in the duck pond our father had built for us. Or we would play with the animals we kept in the cages out back where the servants lived. We'd pet the rabbits, feed them

[9]*mayordomo:* Spanish for steward, butler.—EDS.
[10]*amas:* Spanish for homemakers.—EDS.

fragrant verbena. We'd put chickens on the backs of goats and shriek with laughter as the bewildered creatures scrambled around in circles, the goats wild-eyed under their unruly riders, the chickens pounding the air.

George was my hero, my general, my god. He was as bright and beautiful as I was fat and slow. He could prance and swagger as well as any cowboy in Mother's storybook litany of Wild West valiants. He would hector;[11] I would follow. He'd do mischief; I'd do cover-up. He'd get caught; I'd confess to everything. He'd be spanked; I'd yank down my pants. He'd yawp; I'd bawl louder. And so we spent our days, crawling under the house, devising schemes to scandalize the *mayordomo*, scare Claudia the cook out of her wits, or pester Vicki, whose prissy ways cried out for redress and revenge. If only to force her to look at us over an eternal rim of books.

After lunch, after my father had come home, gazed at his wife's Hollywood face, dozed off, and gone back to work, Mother came to the kitchen looking for us. First she'd put George in bed for his nap, then she'd lead me to her room for a musical siesta.

My mother did not tell us much about herself beyond the fact that she had been a violinist when she and Papi had met in Boston. She was different, odd, that much I knew: porcelain-fair, near translucent, throwing off a kind of shimmer wherever she went. She spoke a halting Spanish, every bit as strange as that of our Scots neighbors; I recall peering into other people's faces to see if it would make them laugh. Often, it would. But she did not mix much with Peruvians if my father was not about. She was not a social person. She seemed more inclined to spend time with her children than with women her age. Then again, she was so unlike any other woman in Cartavio. What distinguished her most from them was the way she moved, like no Peruvian I'd ever seen—straight ahead, gliding—a motion that led from the rib cage, not the hips. It was the kind of walk that tells you little about a body. Her clothes told less: They were loose and silky, more likely to drape from her shoulders than reveal her essential lineaments. She did not own a tightly belted, bust-hoisting, hip-flaunting dress, like those the Peruvian *señoras* wore.

Very early somehow—I don't recall exactly why—in the same way that I dared not imagine what was beneath her frocks, I learned not to ask about her life before she married Papi. The sweet mildness of her demeanor, like the silk of her clothes, masked some indeterminate thing beneath. There was a hardness behind her glow. An ice. I felt I could quiz her to my heart's content about music, which came to be the langauge between us. But beyond that—like the point beyond the animal cages—lay a zone I was not supposed to know.

Her past was the only thing Mother was stingy about. Attentive to her children to the point of obsession, she doted on us, worried about us.

25

---

[11]*hector:* To intimidate, to behave like a bully, to swagger. —EDS.

Every headache was the start of some dread calenture[12] of the brain. Every bellyache, the possibility that we were teeming with tropical parasites. I could make her ooze with love by telling her that I had eaten a wild strawberry from the roadside: She would be anxious for days that I had contracted some rare, Andean disease, taking my temperature at every opportunity, padding into my bedroom at night to lay a cool hand on my brow. Nowhere was her love more evident, however, than in the way she imparted her music to her children. It was, for her, a constant vocation. Any drama, any spectacle, any mathematical conundrum had a corresponding phrase of music, a melody that might frame it more effectively than words. It was as if she needed to impart English. She would teach all three of us the language of music to some degree, but with time it became clear that I was the one she had chosen to be the beneficiary of this particular gift, and it was through music that she ultimately spoke to me most directly.

At siesta time, she'd recite long strings of poetry from memory for me. Or she'd try singing me to sleep—hopeless enterprises, since I found her poetry and songs more seductive than any prospect of slumber. Outside her room, I spoke Spanish. But inside, we were range-roving Americans, heirs of the king's English, and Mother unfolded that world in verse: Whitman's "Leaves of Grass," Coleridge's "Rime of the Ancient Mariner," Gilbert and Sullivan's pirates and maidens, Stephen Foster's dreamers and chariots, Robert Burns's banks and brae, George M. Cohan's flag and salute, Irving Berlin's moon and champagne.

I would lie big-eyed, starstruck, as she spun visions of a faraway country where cowboys reigned, valleys were green, wildflowers sprang from the feet of great oaks, water was sipped—unboiled—from streams, opera houses were lined with red velvet, and sidewalks winked with radiant flecks of mica. "You'll see it all someday, Mareezie," she'd say of her melody-filled *historias*. "You'll see it for yourself."

She would sing, then peek to see if I had drifted off. Into the fifth or sixth song, I knew to pretend. I'd burrow my ear into the place between her shoulder and her large, firm breast, reach an arm across her white throat to feel her corn-silk hair, and feign a deep, heavy breathing. When she stopped singing, I'd open one eye and see that she was asleep.

She was a beautiful woman. Big-boned yet slender. Her forehead was deep, unlined, nearly browless, which gave her the look of a perpetually startled doll. She painted her lips to a fullness they did not have, and, when they were in repose, you could see their thinness beneath the color. It was a beguiling mouth, sloped slightly to one side, so that if you positioned yourself to her left you saw someone pensive, to her right, someone playful. "My slop-pail mug," she called it, leaving me to wonder, in my narrow Peruvianness, what any one of those inexplicable American words—*slop*,

---

[12]*calenture:* A tropical disease once believed to be caused by heat; from the Spanish "to heat." —EDS.

pail, or *mug*—could possibly have to do with that lovely face. When she smiled and showed the little space between her two front teeth, it was enough to break my heart.

I loved to watch her sleep, for there was a vulnerability in her face then that was not there when her eyes were fixed on me. Ordinarily, her stare was as hard as a statue's, unreadable, until something brought her to the verge of anger, at which point her blue eyes would turn a harrowing shade of green. It was a color I did not like to see. But her most disturbing features, by far, were her violinist's hands, which were large and square, with meaty, muscled fingers that seemed to belong to another body, not to the delicate queen who lay on the wide carved bed.

When I had had my fill of studying her, I'd slip carefully out of her arms. I'd tiptoe off to wake up George, and in no time we were out in the garden with pockets full of bread—free of parents, free of the snoring *mayordomo* and the *amas*. Alone. Ready for our daily ritual with *El Gringo*.

More vivid than any other sound in memory—the crow of the cock at dawn, the cooing of mourning doves—was the rhythm of his advance. A tap, thump, drag—ominous and regular—as he made his way down the street. We would stand under the lucuma tree and listen for his step, cock our ears toward it, feel the hairs rise against our collars as it approached.

El loco, we'd whisper—the madman—and watch the black grow large in each other's eyes. By the time we'd made it under the verbena, he was rapping the white stucco with his knuckles, bone-hard and sharp as weapons. When he reached the gate, we'd see the whole man. Eyeless. Rags like leathery wings. A purple stump where a foot should have been. Dried sugarcane for a crutch. When he threw back his head and let the sun fill his eye sockets, a wail would rise from his chest like the keen of a wounded animal. And then a stream of words, sliding at us in a high whinny so that we'd have to strain to catch it. *Out, you little bastards!* And he'd wham the fence with his makeshift staff. *Out! Or I'll call on the* pishtacos! *They'll pluck you from that bush and eat your pygmy hearts!*

El Gringo, people called him. The American. Somehow, we believed he was one, although all evidence was to the contrary. He was small. Almost as small as we were. Dark. Like us.

Weren't all Americans as big, blond, and clear-eyed as our mother? We had serious reservations about her—she was so otherworldly, so ill-at-ease, so unwilling to conform, so *mad* in her own way—but it was terrifying to think she'd end up crazed and blind, staggering through some remote Andean backwater looking for her luminous land. Holding our breath against his stench, we crept out with our bread, dropped the offerings one by one into El Gringo's grimy sack—buying our mother's future, keeping the *pishtacos* at bay. Then we raced away, gasping and squealing, to our crawl space under the house. From there we would watch as he hobbled off to the neighbors. And we would worry.

But there were afternoons when my mother would sing and I'd actually fall asleep. Then it would be her turn to slip away.

One day, I woke to see the double doors wide open and her sitting in the *sala*, cameolike, her profile outlined against the wood of her piano.

She was not alone.

She was poised on one side of the sofa—its back toward me—her armed stretched out along its spine. Across, in the other corner of the same sofa, was a man. I did not know his name. His arm, like hers, was stretched along the back, and its was long and ruddy, with a halo of down against the skin. Their fingers were close. But did not touch.

The *casa de solteros*, the bachelors' quarters, was across from us.   40
There, a rotating corps of young Americans and Northern Europeans came for Third World adventure and a shot at the boom. They were rough-hewn, long-legged. Almost as golden as my mother. More often than not they were war veterans—ex-army engineers—rail-hanging habitués of the bottle, with tales of hard-won battle.

"Over here, let me tell you how I nearly got greased at Midway!" one would shout over a brimming glass of rum at one of my parents' garden parties. Off they'd go, weaving legends, each one braver than the last.

I liked these *solteros*. I liked them because they seemed to be at the white-hot core of a kid-hearted craziness that overtook the grown-ups from time to time. I liked them because of their laughter. I liked them for their sweet smell of Cartavio rum. I liked them most of all because, when their long limbs ambled through our gates, the sky would open and my mother's eyes would dance.

The man sitting with my mother was a *soltero*. Of that I was sure. Whether or not they'd been talking, I could not tell. I rubbed my eyes and focused closer. My mother had a sweet, peaceful expression on her face. The man looked at her, perfectly calm, and said something I could not hear.

Suddenly, her outstretched hand flew to her forehead, and her long, thick fingers rested there for what seemed a great while, her eyes cast down. Then he stood, bowed awkwardly, and walked away.

It was a fleeting gesture, that manual flutter from chair to brow, but I   45
can see it still, engraved in memory like some irrevocable omen. Up, press. *Presto, fermata.*[13] A passage that sounds again and again, as if its notes should lead to something else, some other movement. But that something else bows and spins and floats away. Off. Up. Out of sight, never to be explained.

My mother's hand floated down. She turned her face to the open doors of the bedroom and looked deep into my eyes. A pause, and then a radiant smile. "You slept this time!" she said. Her voice was so full of joy that my heart slipped a bit. There was no cause for joy in my napping. It had been a terrible lapse on my part: I had not awakened George. I had slept through our rendezvous with El Gringo. I had not given the beggar his sacramental scraps of bread. I had not kept the ghouls away. I had not protected my mother from a stone-blind fate.

[13]*fermata:* A musical term for an indefinite prolongation of a note or chord. —EDS.

Her blue eyes were looking at me now with such love, though, I had to grin back. I flung myself off the bed, slipped into George's old boots, and marched into the afternoon.

I asked about the stranger on the sofa many times in decades to come—even caused a harrowing scene with my questions—but she only shook her head and said she had no recollection of him. "I can't imagine who you saw there, Mareezie. I just can't imagine." Until I thought perhaps the whole thing had been a dream, and the man another ghost in my head.

The Reader's Presence

1. "I wanted to capture the sense of all things that exist beyond the parameters of what we can control, that make one's life what it is," said Marie Arana in commenting on her book *American Chica: Two Worlds, One Childhood*, from which "*Ghosts*/Pishtacos" is drawn. What worlds has Arana captured in this essay? What specific "sense" of these worlds does she convey? And what aspects of these worlds would you characterize as "beyond" Arana's control?

2. What expectations of this essay did its title generate for you? To what extent—and in what specific ways—did your understanding of the title change after you read the essay? As you reread Arana's essay, you might pay particular attention to the ways in which Arana invokes ghosts, or the idea of ghosts. How does she thread the notion of ghosts throughout the piece? What, from Arana's childhood and adult perspectives, are the meanings of ghosts?

3. Outline—and then characterize the effectiveness of—the structure of Arana's piece. You might find it helpful to create a list of brief summaries of each paragraph to identify the major moves Arana makes in the essay, or to create a map of the locations she describes, or to do both. Based on this outline and the inferences you draw from it, how would you describe the essay's structure? How does this structure help Arana capture a rich sense of her childhood worlds?

4. Both Arana and Richard Rodriguez (see "Aria: A Memoir of a Bilingual Childhood" page 210) write about their childhoods from an adult perspective. Reread each essay with an eye to the compositional strategies each writer uses to establish an adult perspective on that experience, then compare and contrast the effectiveness of the presence each writer creates for the child and for the adult in both essays.

James Baldwin

Notes of a Native Son

James Baldwin (1924–1987) grew up in New York City but moved to France in 1948 because he felt personally and artistically stifled as a gay African American man in the United States. His first novels, Go Tell It on the Mountain *(1956) and* Giovanni's Room *(1956), and his first collection of essays,* Notes of a Native Son *(1955), were published during Baldwin's first stay abroad, where he was able to write critically about race, sexual identity, and social injustice in America. "Once I found myself on the other side of the ocean," he told an interviewer, "I could see where I came from very clearly, and I could see that I carried myself, which is my home, with me. You can never escape that. I am the grandson of a slave, and I am a writer. I must deal with both."*

After nearly a decade in France, he returned to New York and became a national figure in the civil rights movement. After Baldwin's death, Henry Louis Gates Jr. eulogized him as the conscience of the nation, for he "educated an entire generation of Americans about the civil-rights struggle and the sensibility of Afro-Americans as we faced and conquered the final barriers in our long quest for civil rights." Baldwin continues to educate through his essays, collected in The Price of the Ticket: Collected Nonfiction *(1985).*

When asked if he approached the writing of fiction and nonfiction in different ways, Baldwin responded, "Every form is different, no one is easier than another. . . . An essay is not simpler, though it may seem so. An essay is clearly an argument. The writer's point of view in an essay is always absolutely clear. The writer is trying to make the readers see something, trying to convince them of something. In a novel or a play you're trying to show them something. The risks, in any case, are exactly the same."

The title essay of the book Notes of a Native Son *first appeared in* Harper's *magazine in 1955. In it, Baldwin recounts the death of his father, whose funeral took place on Baldwin's nineteenth birthday—the same day a bloody race riot broke out in Harlem.*

ONE

On the twenty-ninth of July, in 1943, my father died. On the same day, a few hours later, his last child was born. Over a month before this, while all our energies were concentrated in waiting for these events, there had been, in Detroit, one of the bloodiest race riots of the century. A few hours after my father's funeral, while he lay in state in the undertaker's chapel, a race riot broke out in Harlem. On the morning of the third of August, we drove my father to the graveyard through a wilderness of smashed plate glass.

The day of my father's funeral had also been my nineteenth birthday. As we drove him to the graveyard, the spoils of injustice, anarchy, discontent, and hatred were all around us. It seemed to me that God himself had devised, to mark my father's end, the most sustained and brutally dissonant of codas. And it seemed to me, too, that the violence which rose all about us as my father left the world had been devised as a corrective for the pride of his eldest son. I had declined to believe in that apocalypse which had been central to my father's vision; very well, life seemed to be saying, here is something that will certainly pass for an apocalypse until the real thing comes along. I had inclined to be contemptuous of my father for the conditions of his life, for the conditions of our lives. When his life had ended I began to wonder about that life and also, in a new way, to be apprehensive about my own.

I had not known my father very well. We had got on badly, partly because we shared, in our different fashions, the vice of stubborn pride. When he was dead I realized that I had hardly ever spoken to him. When he had been dead a long time I began to wish I had. It seems to be typical of life in America, where opportunities, real and fancied, are thicker than anywhere else on the globe, that the second generation has no time to talk to the first. No one, including my father, seems to have known exactly how old he was, but his mother had been born during slavery. He was of the first generation of free men. He, along with thousands of other Negroes, came North after 1919 and I was part of that generation which had never seen the landscape of what Negroes sometimes call the Old Country.

He had been born in New Orleans and had been quite a young man there during the time that Louis Armstrong, a boy, was running errands for the dives and honky-tonks of what was always presented to me as one of the most wicked of cities—to this day, whenever I think of New Orleans, I also helplessly think of Sodom and Gomorrah. My father never mentioned Louis Armstrong, except to forbid us to play his records; but there was a picture of him on our wall for a long time. One of my father's strong-willed female relatives had placed it there and forbade my father to take it down. He never did, but he eventually maneuvered her out of the house and when, some years later, she was in trouble and near death, he refused to do anything to help her.

He was, I think, very handsome. I gather this from photographs and from my own memories of him, dressed in his Sunday best and on his way to preach a sermon somewhere, when I was little. Handsome, proud, and ingrown, "like a toenail," somebody said. But he looked to me, as I grew older, like pictures I had seen of African tribal chieftains: he really should have been naked, with warpaint on and barbaric mementos, standing among spears. He could be chilling in the pulpit and indescribably cruel in his personal life and he was certainly the most bitter man I have ever met; yet it must be said that there was something else in him, buried in him, which lent him his tremendous power and, even, a rather crushing

5

charm. It had something to do with his blackness, I think—he was very black—with his blackness and his beauty, and with the fact that he knew that he was black but did not know that he was beautiful. He claimed to be proud of his blackness but it had also been the cause of much humiliation and it had fixed bleak boundaries to his life. He was not a young man when we were growing up and he had already suffered many kinds of ruin; in his outrageously demanding and protective way he loved his children, who were black like him and menaced, like him; and all these things sometimes showed in his face when he tried, never to my knowledge with any success, to establish contact with any of us. When he took one of his children on his knee to play, the child always became fretful and began to cry; when he tried to help one of us with our homework the absolutely unabating tension which emanated from him caused our minds and our tongues to become paralyzed, so that he, scarcely knowing why, flew into a rage and the child, not knowing why, was punished. If it ever entered his head to bring a surprise home for his children, it was, almost unfailingly, the wrong surprise and even the big watermelons he often brought home on his back in the summertime led to the most appalling scenes. I do not remember, in all those years, that one of his children was ever glad to see him come home. From what I was able to gather of his early life, it seemed that this inability to establish contact with other people had always marked him and had been one of the things which had driven him out of New Orleans. There was something in him, therefore, groping and tentative, which was never expressed and which was buried with him. One saw it most clearly when he was facing new people and hoping to impress them. But he never did, not for long. We went from church to smaller and more improbable church, he found himself in less and less demand as a minister, and by the time he died none of his friends had come to see him for a long time. He had lived and died in an intolerable bitterness of spirit and it frightened me, as we drove him to the graveyard through those unquiet, ruined streets, to see how powerful and overflowing this bitterness could be and to realize that this bitterness now was mine.

When he died I had been away from home for a little over a year. In that year I had had time to become aware of the meaning of all my father's bitter warnings, had discovered the secret of his proudly pursed lips and rigid carriage: I had discovered the weight of white people in the world. I saw that this had been for my ancestors and now would be for me an awful thing to live with and that the bitterness which had helped to kill my father could also kill me.

He had been ill a long time—in the mind, as we now realized, reliving instances of his fantastic intransigence in the new light of his affliction and endeavoring to feel a sorrow for him which never, quite, came true. We had not known that he was being eaten up by paranoia, and the discovery that his cruelty, to our bodies and our minds, had been one of the symptoms of his illness was not, then, enough to enable us to forgive him. The younger children felt, quite simply, relief that he would not be coming home anymore. My mother's observation that it was he, after all, who had kept them alive all these years meant nothing because the problems of keeping children alive are not real for children. The older children felt, with my father gone, that they could invite their friends to the house without fear that their friends would be insulted or, as had sometimes happened with me, being told that their friends were in league with the devil and intended to rob our family of everything we owned. (I didn't fail to wonder, and it made me hate him, what on earth we owned that anybody else would want.)

His illness was beyond all hope of healing before anyone realized that he was ill. He had always been so strange and had lived, like a prophet, in such unimaginably close communion with the Lord that his long silences which were punctuated by moans and hallelujahs and snatches of old songs while he sat at the living-room window never seemed odd to us. It was not until he refused to eat because, he said, his family was trying to poison him that my mother was forced to accept as a fact what had, until then, been only an unwilling suspicion. When he was committed, it was discovered that he had tuberculosis and, as it turned out, the disease of his mind allowed the disease of his body to destroy him. For the doctors could not force him to eat, either, and, though he was fed intravenously, it was clear from the beginning that there was no hope for him.

In my mind's eye I could see him, sitting at the window, locked up in his terrors; hating and fearing every living soul including his children who had betrayed him, too, by reaching toward the world which had despised him. There were nine of us. I began to wonder what it could have felt like for such a man to have had nine children whom he could barely feed. He used to make little jokes about our poverty, which never, of course, seemed very funny to us; they could not have seemed very funny to him, either, or else our all too feeble response to them would never have caused such rages. He spent great energy and achieved, to our chagrin, no small amount of success in keeping us away from the people who surrounded us, people who had all-night rent parties[1] to which we listened when we should have been sleeping, people who cursed and drank and flashed razor blades on Lenox Avenue. He could not understand why, if they had so much energy to spare, they could not use it to make their lives better. He treated almost everybody on our block with a most uncharitable asperity and neither they, nor, of course, their children were slow to reciprocate.

The only white people who came to our house were welfare workers   10
and bill collectors. It was almost always my mother who dealt with them, for my father's temper, which was at the mercy of his pride, was never to be trusted. It was clear that he felt their very presence in his home to be a

---

[1]*rent parties:* Part of a Harlem tradition; musicians were often hired and contributions taken to help pay the rent for needy tenants. —EDS.

violation: this was conveyed by his carriage, almost ludicrously stiff, and by his voice, harsh and vindictively polite. When I was around nine or ten I wrote a play which was directed by a young, white schoolteacher, a woman, who then took an interest in me, and gave me books to read and, in order to corroborate my theatrical bent, decided to take me to see what she somewhat tactlessly referred to as "real" plays. Theater-going was forbidden in our house, but, with the really cruel intuitiveness of a child, I suspected that the color of this woman's skin would carry the day for me. When, at school, she suggested taking me to the theater, I did not, as I might have done if she had been a Negro, find a way of discouraging her, but agreed that she should pick me up at my house one evening. I then, very cleverly, left all the rest to my mother, who suggested to my father, as I knew she would, that it would not be very nice to let such a kind woman make the trip for nothing. Also, since it was a schoolteacher, I imagine that my mother countered the idea of sin with the idea of "education," which word, even with my father, carried a kind of bitter weight.

Before the teacher came my father took me aside to ask *why* she was coming, what *interest* she could possibly have in our house, in a boy like me. I said I didn't know but I, too, suggested that it had something to do with education. And I understood that my father was waiting for me to say something—I didn't quite know what; perhaps that I wanted his protection against this teacher and her "education." I said none of these things and the teacher came and we went out. It was clear, during the brief interview in our living room, that my father was agreeing very much against his will and that he would have refused permission if he had dared. The fact that he did not dare caused me to despise him: I had no way of knowing that he was facing in that living room a wholly unprecedented and frightening situation.

Later, when my father had been laid off from his job, this woman became very important to us. She was really a very sweet and generous woman and went to a great deal of trouble to be of help to us, particularly during one awful winter. My mother called her by the highest name she knew: she said she was a "Christian." My father could scarcely disagree but during the four or five years of our relatively close association he never trusted her and was always trying to surprise in her open, Midwestern face the genuine, cunningly hidden, and hideous motivation. In later years, particularly when it began to be clear that this "education" of mine was going to lead me to perdition, he became more explicit and warned me that my white friends in high school were not really my friends and that I would see, when I was older, how white people would do anything to keep a Negro down. Some of them could be nice, he admitted, but none of them were to be trusted and most of them were not even nice. The best thing was to have as little to do with them as possible. I did not feel this way and I was certain, in my innocence, that I never would.

But the year which preceded my father's death had made a great change in my life. I had been living in New Jersey, working in defense plants, working and living among southerners, white and black. I knew about the south, of course, and about how southerners treated Negroes and how they expected them to behave, but it had never entered my mind that anyone would look at me and expect *me* to behave that way. I learned in New Jersey that to be a Negro meant, precisely, that one was never looked at but was simply at the mercy of the reflexes the color of one's skin caused in other people. I acted in New Jersey as I had always acted, that is as though I thought a great deal of myself—I had to *act* that way—with results that were, simply, unbelievable. I had scarcely arrived before I had earned the enmity, which was extraordinarily ingenious, of all my superiors and nearly all my co-workers. In the beginning, to make matters worse, I simply did not know what was happening. I did not know what I had done, and I shortly began to wonder what *anyone* could possibly do, to bring about such unanimous, active, and unbearably vocal hostility. I knew about Jim Crow but I had never experienced it. I went to the same self-service restaurant three times and stood with all the Princeton boys before the counter, waiting for a hamburger and coffee; it was always an extraordinarily long time before anything was set before me; but it was not until the fourth visit that I learned that, in fact, nothing had ever been set before me: I had simply picked something up. Negroes were not served there, I was told, and they had been waiting for me to realize that I was always the only Negro present. Once I was told this, I determined to go there all the time. But now they were ready for me and, though some dreadful scenes were subsequently enacted in that restaurant, I never ate there again.

It was the same story all over New Jersey, in bars, bowling alleys, diners, places to live. I was always being forced to leave, silently, or with mutual imprecations. I very shortly became notorious and children giggled behind me when I passed and their elders whispered or shouted— they really believed that I was mad. And it did begin to work on my mind, of course; I began to be afraid to go anywhere and to compensate for this I went places to which I really should not have gone and where, God knows, I had no desire to be. My reputation in town naturally enhanced my reputation at work and my working day became one long series of acrobatics designed to keep me out of trouble. I cannot say that these acrobatics succeeded. It began to seem that the machinery of the organization I worked for was turning over, day and night, with but one aim: to eject me. I was fired once, and contrived, with the aid of a friend from New York, to get back on the payroll; was fired again, and bounced back again. It took a while to fire me for the third time, but the third time took. There were no loopholes anywhere. There was not even any way of getting back inside the gates.

That year in New Jersey lives in my mind as though it were the year during which, having an unsuspected predilection for it, I first contracted some dread, chronic disease, the unfailing symptom of which is a kind of   15 blind fever, a pounding in the skull and fire in the bowels. Once this disease is contracted, one can never be really carefree again, for the fever, without an instant's warning, can recur at any moment. It can wreck more important things than race relations. There is not a Negro alive who does not have this rage in his blood—one has the choice, merely, of living with it consciously or surrendering to it. As for me, this fever has recurred in me, and does, and will until the day I die.

My last night in New Jersey, a white friend from New York took me to the nearest big town, Trenton, to go to the movies and have a few drinks. As it turned out, he also saved me from, at the very least, a violent whipping. Almost every detail of that night stands out very clearly in my memory. I even remember the name of the movie we saw because its title impressed me as being so patly ironical. It was a movie about the German occupation of France, starring Maureen O'Hara and Charles Laughton and called *This Land Is Mine*. I remember the name of the diner we walked into when the movie ended: it was the "American Diner." When we walked in the counterman asked what we wanted and I remember answering with the casual sharpness which had become my habit: "We want a hamburger and a cup of coffee, what do you think we want?" I do not know why, after a year of such rebuffs, I so completely failed to anticipate his answer, which was, of course, "We don't serve Negroes here." This reply failed to discompose me, at least for the moment. I made some sardonic comment about the name of the diner and we walked out into the streets.

This was the time of what was called the "brownout," when the lights in all American cities were very dim. When we reentered the streets something happened to me which had the force of an optical illusion, or a nightmare. The streets were very crowded and I was facing north. People were moving in every direction but it seemed to me, in that instant, that all of the people I could see, and many more than that, were moving toward me, against me, and that everyone was white. I remember how their faces gleamed. And I felt, like a physical sensation, a *click* at the nape of my neck as though some interior string connecting my head to my body had been cut. I began to walk. I heard my friend call after me, but I ignored him. Heaven only knows what was going on in his mind, but he had the good sense not to touch me—I don't know what would have happened if he had—and to keep me in sight. I don't know what was going on in my mind, either; I certainly had no conscious plan. I wanted to do something to crush these white faces, which were crushing me. I walked for perhaps a block or two until I came to an enormous, glittering, and fashionable restaurant in which I knew not even the intercession of the Virgin would cause me to be served. I pushed through the doors and took the first vacant seat I saw, at a table for two, and waited.

I do not know how long I waited and I rather wonder, until today, what I could possibly have looked like. Whatever I looked like, I frightened the waitress who shortly appeared, and the moment she appeared all of my fury flowed toward her. I hated her for her white face, and for her great, astounded, frightened eyes. I felt that if she found a black man so frightening I would make her fright worthwhile.

She did not ask me what I wanted, but repeated, as though she had learned it somewhere, "We don't serve Negroes here." She did not say it with the blunt, derisive hostility to which I had grown so accustomed, but, rather, with a note of apology in her voice, and fear. This made me colder and more murderous than ever. I felt I had to do something with my hands. I wanted her to come close enough for me to get her neck between my hands.

So I pretended not to have understood her, hoping to draw her closer.   20
And she did step a very short step closer, with her pencil poised incongruously over her pad, and repeated the formula: ". . . don't serve Negroes here."

Somehow, with the repetition of that phrase, which was already ringing in my head like a thousand bells of a nightmare, I realized that she would never come any closer and that I would have to strike from a distance. There was nothing on the table but an ordinary watermug half full of water, and I picked this up and hurled it with all my strength at her. She ducked and it missed her and shattered against the mirror behind the bar. And, with that sound, my frozen blood abruptly thawed, I returned from wherever I had been, I *saw*, for the first time, the restaurant, the people with their mouths open, already, as it seemed to me, rising as one man, and I realized what I had done, and where I was, and I was frightened. I rose and began running for the door. A round, potbellied man grabbed me by the nape of the neck just as I reached the doors and began to beat me about the face. I kicked him and got loose and ran into the streets. My friend whispered, *"Run!"* and I ran.

My friend stayed outside the restaurant long enough to misdirect my pursuers and the police, who arrived, he told me, at once. I do not know what I said to him when he came to my room that night. I could not have said much. I felt, in the oddest, most awful way, that I had somehow betrayed him. I lived it over and over and over again, the way one relives an automobile accident after it has happened and one finds oneself alone and safe. I could not get over two facts, both equally difficult for the imagination to grasp, and one was that I could have been murdered. But the other was that I had been ready to commit murder. I saw nothing very clearly but I did see this: that my life, my *real* life, was in danger, and not from anything other people might do but from the hatred I carried in my own heart.

TWO

I had returned home around the second week in June — in great haste because it seemed that my father's death and my mother's confinement were both but a matter of hours. In the case of my mother, it soon became clear that she had simply made a miscalculation. This had always been her tendency and I don't believe that a single one of us arrived in the world, or has since arrived anywhere else, on time. But none of us dawdled so intolerably about the business of being born as did my baby sister. We sometimes amused ourselves, during those endless, stifling weeks, by picturing the baby sitting within in the safe, warm dark, bitterly regretting the necessity of becoming a part of our chaos and stubbornly putting it off as long as possible. I understood her perfectly and congratulated her on showing such good sense so soon. Death, however, sat as purposefully at my father's bedside as life stirred within my mother's womb and it was harder to understand why he so lingered in that long shadow. It seemed that he had bent, and for a long time, too, all of his energies toward dying. Now death was ready for him but my father held back.

All of Harlem, indeed, seemed to be infected by waiting. I had never before known it to be so violently still. Racial tensions throughout this country were exacerbated during the early years of the war, partly because the labor market brought together hundreds of thousands of ill-prepared people and partly because Negro soldiers, regardless of where they were born, received their military training in the south. What happened in defense plants and army camps had repercussions, naturally, in every Negro ghetto. The situation in Harlem had grown bad enough for clergymen, policemen, educators, politicians, and social workers to assert in one breath that there was no "crime wave" and to offer, in the very next breath, suggestions as to how to combat it. These suggestions always seemed to involve playgrounds, despite the fact that racial skirmishes were occurring in the playgrounds, too. Playground or not, crime wave or not, the Harlem police force had been augmented in March, and the unrest grew — perhaps, in fact, partly as a result of the ghetto's instinctive hatred of policemen. Perhaps the most revealing news item, out of the steady parade of reports of muggings, stabbings, shootings, assaults, gang wars, and accusations of police brutality, is the item concerning six Negro girls who set upon a white girl in the subway because, as they all too accurately put it, she was stepping on their toes. Indeed she was, all over the nation.

I had never before been so aware of policemen, on foot, on horse-   25 back, on corners, everywhere, always two by two. Nor had I ever been so aware of small knots of people. They were on stoops and on corners and in doorways, and what was striking about them, I think, was that they did not seem to be talking. Never, when I passed these groups, did the usual sound of a curse or a laugh ring out and neither did there seem to be any hum of gossip. There was certainly, on the other hand, occurring between them communication extraordinarily intense. Another thing that was striking was the unexpected diversity of the people who made up these groups. Usually, for example, one would see a group of sharpies standing on the street corner, jiving the passing chicks; or a group of older men, usually, for some reason, in the vicinity of a barber shop, discussing baseball scores, or the numbers, or making rather chilling observations about women they had known. Women, in a general way, tended to be seen less often together — unless they were church women, or very young girls, or prostitutes met together for an unprofessional instant. But that summer I saw the strangest combinations: large, respectable, churchly matrons standing on the stoops or the corners with their hair tied up, together with a girl in sleazy satin whose face bore the marks of gin and the razor, or heavy-set, abrupt, no-nonsense older men, in company with the most disreputable and fanatical "race" men,[2] or these same "race" men with the sharpies, or these sharpies with the churchly women. Seventh Day Adventists and Methodists and Spiritualists seemed to be hobnobbing with Holyrollers and they were all, alike, entangled with the most flagrant disbelievers; something heavy in their stance seemed to indicate that they had all, incredibly, seen a common vision, and on each face there seemed to be the same strange, bitter shadow.

The churchly women and the matter-of-fact, no-nonsense men had children in the Army. The sleazy girls they talked to had lovers there, the sharpies and the "race" men had friends and brothers there. It would have demanded an unquestioning patriotism, happily as uncommon in this country as it is undesirable, for these people not to have been disturbed by the bitter letters they received, by the newspaper stories they read, not to have been enraged by the posters, then to be found all over New York, which described the Japanese as "yellow-bellied Japs." It was only the "race" men, to be sure, who spoke ceaselessly of being revenged — how this vengeance was to be exacted was not clear — for the indignities and dangers suffered by Negro boys in uniform; but everybody felt a directionless, hopeless bitterness, as well as that panic which can scarcely be suppressed when one knows that a human being one loves is beyond one's reach, and in danger. This helplessness and this gnawing uneasiness does something, at length, to even the toughest mind. Perhaps the best way to sum all this up is to say that the people I knew felt, mainly, a peculiar kind of relief when they knew that their boys were being shipped out of the south, to do battle overseas. It was, perhaps, like feeling that the most dangerous part of a dangerous journey had been passed and that now, even if death should come, it would come with honor and without the complicity of their countrymen. Such a death would be, in short, a fact with which one could hope to live.

It was on the twenty-eighth of July, which I believe was a Wednesday, that I visited my father for the first time during his illness and for the last time in his life. The moment I saw him I knew why I had put off this visit so long. I had told my mother that I did not want to see him because I hated him. But this was not true. It was only that I *had* hated him and I wanted to hold on to this hatred. I did not want to look on him as a ruin: it was not a ruin I had hated. I imagine that one of the reasons people

---

[2]*"race" men:* Baldwin seems to be thinking of self-appointed spokesmen for racial consciousness and not serious black leaders. — EDS.

cling to their hates so stubbornly is because they sense, once hate is gone, that they will be forced to deal with pain.

We traveled out to him, his older sister and myself, to what seemed to be the very end of a very Long Island. It was hot and dusty and we wrangled, my aunt and I, all the way out, over the fact that I had recently begun to smoke and, as she said, to give myself airs. But I knew that she wrangled with me because she could not bear to face the fact of her brother's dying. Neither could I endure the reality of her despair, her unstated bafflement as to what had happened to her brother's life, and her own. So we wrangled and I smoked and from time to time she fell into a heavy reverie. Covertly, I watched her face, which was the face of an old woman; it had fallen in, the eyes were sunken and lightless; soon she would be dying, too.

In my childhood—it had not been so long ago—I had thought her beautiful. She had been quick-witted and quick-moving and very generous with all the children and each of her visits had been an event. At one time one of my brothers and myself had thought of running away to live with her. Now she could no longer produce out of her handbag some unexpected and yet familiar delight. She made me feel pity and revulsion and fear. It was awful to realize that she no longer caused me to feel affection. The closer we came to the hospital the more querulous she became and at the same time, naturally, grew more dependent on me. Between pity and guilt and fear I began to feel that there was another me trapped in my skull like a jack-in-the-box who might escape my control at any moment and fill the air with screaming.

She began to cry the moment we entered the room and she saw him 30 lying there, all shriveled and still, like a little black monkey. The great, gleaming apparatus which fed him and would have compelled him to be still even if he had been able to move brought to mind, not beneficence, but torture; the tubes entering his arm made me think of pictures I had seen when a child, of Gulliver, tied down by the pygmies on that island. My aunt wept and wept, there was a whistling sound in my father's throat; nothing was said; he could not speak. I wanted to take his hand, to say something. But I do not know what I could have said, even if he could have heard me. He was not really in that room with us, he had at last really embarked on his journey; and though my aunt told me that he said he was going to meet Jesus, I did not hear anything except that whistling in his throat. The doctor came back and we left, into that unbearable train again, and home. In the morning came the telegram saying that he was dead. Then the house was suddenly full of relatives, friends, hysteria, and confusion and I quickly left my mother and the children to the care of those impressive women, who, in Negro communities at least, automatically appear at times of bereavement armed with lotions, proverbs, and patience, and an ability to cook. I went downtown. By the time I returned, later the same day, my mother had been carried to the hospital and the baby had been born.

THREE

For my father's funeral I had nothing black to wear and this posed a nagging problem all day long. It was one of those problems, simple, or impossible of solution, to which the mind insanely clings in order to avoid the mind's real trouble. I spent most of that day at the downtown apartment of a girl I knew, celebrating my birthday with whisky and wondering what to wear that night. When planning a birthday celebration one naturally does not expect that it will be up against competition from a funeral and this girl had anticipated taking me out that night, for a big dinner and a night club afterwards. Sometime during the course of that long day we decided that we would go out anyway, when my father's funeral service was over. I imagine I decided it, since, as the funeral hour approached, it became clearer and clearer to me that I would not know what to do with myself when it was over. The girl, stifling her very lively concern as to the possible effects of the whisky on one of my father's chief mourners, concentrated on being conciliatory and practically helpful. She found a black shirt for me somewhere and ironed it and, dressed in the darkest pants and jacket I owned, and slightly drunk, I made my way to my father's funeral.

The chapel was full, but not packed, and very quiet. There were, mainly, my father's relatives, and his children, and here and there I saw faces I had not seen since childhood, the faces of my father's one-time friends. They were very dark and solemn now, seeming somehow to suggest that they had known all along that something like this would happen. Chief among the mourners was my aunt, who had quarreled with my father all his life; by which I do not mean to suggest that her mourning was insincere or that she had not loved him. I suppose that she was one of the few people in the world who had, and their incessant quarreling proved precisely the strength of the tie that bound them. The only other person in the world, as far as I knew, whose relationship to my father rivaled my aunt's in depth was my mother, who was not there.

It seemed to me, of course, that it was a very long funeral. But it was, if anything, a rather shorter funeral than most, nor, since there were no overwhelming, uncontrollable expressions of grief, could it be called — if I dare to use the word — successful. The minister who preached my father's funeral sermon was one of the few my father had still been seeing as he neared his end. He presented to us in his sermon a man whom none of us had ever seen — a man thoughtful, patient, and forbearing, a Christian inspiration to all who knew him, and a model for his children. And no doubt the children, in their disturbed and guilty state, were almost ready to believe this; he had been remote enough to be anything and, anyway, the shock of the incontrovertible, that it was really our father lying up there in that casket, prepared the mind for anything. His sister moaned and this grief-stricken moaning was taken as corroboration. The other faces held a dark, noncommittal thoughtfulness. This was not the man they had known, but they had scarcely expected to be confronted with *him*; this was, in a sense deeper than questions of fact, the man they had not known, and the man they had not known may have been the real one. The real man, whoever he had been, had suffered and now he was dead: this was all that was sure and all that mattered now. Every man in the chapel hoped that when his hour came he, too, would be eulogized, which is to say forgiven, and that all of his lapses, greeds, errors, and strayings from the truth would be invested with coherence and looked upon with charity. This was perhaps the last thing human beings could give each other and it was what they demanded, after all, of the Lord. Only the Lord saw the midnight tears, only He was present when one of His children, moaning and wringing hands, paced up and down the room. When one slapped one's child in anger the recoil in the heart reverberated through heaven and became part of the pain of the universe. And when the children were hungry and sullen and distrustful and one watched them, daily, growing wilder, and further away, and running headlong into danger, it was the Lord who knew what the charged heart endured as the strap was laid to the backside; the Lord alone who knew what one *would* have said if one had had, like the Lord, the gift of the living word. It was the Lord who knew of the impossibility every parent in that room faced: how to prepare the child for the day when the child would be despised and how to *create* in the child—by what means?—a stronger antidote to this poison than one had found for oneself. The avenues, side streets, bars, billiard halls, hospitals, police stations, and even the playgrounds of Harlem—not to mention the houses of correction, the jails, and the morgue—testified to the potency of the poison while remaining silent as to the efficacy of whatever antidote, irresistibly raising the question of whether or not such an antidote existed; raising, which was worse, the question of whether or not an antidote was desirable; perhaps poison should be fought with poison. With these several schisms in the mind and with more terrors in the heart than could be named, it was better not to judge the man who had gone down under an impossible burden. It was better to remember: *Thou knowest this man's fall; but thou knowest not his wrassling.*

While the preacher talked and I watched the children—years of changing their diapers, scrubbing them, slapping them, taking them to school, and scolding them had had the perhaps inevitable result of making me love them, though I am not sure I knew this then—my mind was busily breaking out with a rash of disconnected impressions. Snatches of popular songs, indecent jokes, bits of books I had read, movie sequences, faces, voices, political issues—I thought I was going mad; all these impressions suspended, as it were, in the solution of the faint nausea produced in me by the heat and liquor. For a moment I had the impression that my alcoholic breath, inefficiently disguised with chewing gum, filled the entire chapel. Then someone began singing one of my father's favorite songs and, abruptly, I was with him, sitting on his knee, in the hot, enormous, crowded church which was the first church we attended. It was the

Abyssinian Baptist Church on 138th Street. We had not gone there long. With this image, a host of others came. I had forgotten, in the rage of my growing up, how proud my father had been of me when I was little. Apparently, I had had a voice and my father had liked to show me off before the members of the church. I had forgotten what he had looked like when he was pleased but now I remembered that he had always been grinning with pleasure when my solos ended. I even remembered certain expressions on his face when he teased my mother—had he loved her? I would never know. And when had it all begun to change? For now it seemed that he had not always been cruel. I remembered being taken for a haircut and scraping my knee on the footrest of the barber's chair and I remembered my father's face as he soothed my crying and applied the stinging iodine. Then I remembered our fights, fights which had been of the worst possible kind because my technique had been silence.

I remembered the one time in all our life together when we had really spoken to each other.

It was on a Sunday and it must have been shortly before I left home. We were walking, just the two of us, in our usual silence, to or from church. I was in high school and had been doing a lot of writing and I was, at about this time, the editor of the high school magazine. But I had also been a Young Minister and had been preaching from the pulpit. Lately, I had been taking fewer engagements and preached as rarely as possible. It was said in the church, quite truthfully, that I was "cooling off."

My father asked me abruptly, "You'd rather write than preach, wouldn't you?"

I was astonished at his question—because it was a real question. I answered, "Yes."

That was all we said. It was awful to remember that that was all we had *ever* said.

The casket now was opened and the mourners were being led up the aisle to look for the last time on the deceased. The assumption was that the family was too overcome with grief to be allowed to make this journey alone and I watched while my aunt was led to the casket and, muffled in black, and shaking, led back to her seat. I disapproved of forcing the children to look on their dead father, considering that the shock of his death, or, more truthfully, the shock of death as a reality, was already a little more than a child could bear, but my judgment in this matter had been overruled and there they were, bewildered and frightened and very small, being led, one by one, to the casket. But there is also something very gallant about children at such moments. It has something to do with their silence and gravity and with the fact that one cannot help them. Their legs, somehow, seem *exposed*, so that it is at once incredible and terribly clear that their legs are all they have to hold them up.

I had not wanted to go to the casket myself and I certainly had not wished to be led there, but there was no way of avoiding either of these forms. One of the deacons led me up and I looked on my father's face. I

cannot say that it looked like him at all. His blackness had been equivo-
cated by powder and there was no suggestion in that casket of what his
power had or could have been. He was simply an old man dead, and it
was hard to believe that he had ever given anyone either joy or pain. Yet,
his life filled that room. Further up the avenue his wife was holding his
newborn child. Life and death so close together, and love and hatred, and
right and wrong, said something to me which I did not want to hear concerning man, concerning the life of man.

After the funeral, while I was downtown desperately celebrating my
birthday, a Negro soldier, in the lobby of the Hotel Braddock, got into a
fight with a white policeman over a Negro girl. Negro girls, white policemen, in or out of uniform, and Negro males—in or out of uniform—were
part of the furniture of the lobby of the Hotel Braddock and this was certainly not the first time such an incident had occurred. It was destined,
however, to receive an unprecedented publicity, for the fight between the policeman and the soldier ended with the shooting of the soldier. Rumor, flowing immediately to the streets outside, stated that the soldier had been shot
in the back, an instantaneous and revealing invention, and that the soldier
had died protecting a Negro woman. The facts were somewhat different—
for example, the soldier had not been shot in the back, and was not dead,
and the girl seems to have been as dubious a symbol of womanhood as her
white counterpart in Georgia usually is, but no one was interested in the
facts. They preferred the invention because this invention expressed and
corroborated their hates and fears so perfectly. It is just as well to remember that people are always doing this. Perhaps many of those legends, including Christianity, to which the world clings began their conquest of the
world with just some such concerted surrender to distortion. The effect, in
Harlem, of this particular legend was like the effect of a lit match in a tin of
gasoline. The mob gathered before the doors of the Hotel Braddock simply
began to swell and to spread in every direction, and Harlem exploded.

The mob did not cross the ghetto lines. It would have been easy, for
example, to have gone over Morningside Park on the west side or to have
crossed the Grand Central railroad tracks at 125th Street on the east side,
to wreak havoc in white neighborhoods. The mob seems to have been
mainly interested in something more potent and real than the white face,
that is, in white power, and the principal damage done during the riot of
the summer of 1943 was to white business establishments in Harlem. It
might have been a far bloodier story, of course, if, at the hour the riot
began, these establishments had still been open. From the Hotel Braddock
the mob fanned out, east and west along 125th Street, and for the entire
length of Lenox, Seventh, and Eighth avenues. Along each of these avenues,
and along each major side street—116th, 125th, 135th, and so on—bars,
stores, pawnshops, restaurants, even little luncheonettes had been smashed
open and entered and looted—looted, it might be added, with more haste
than efficiency. The shelves really looked as though a bomb had struck
them. Cans of beans and soup and dog food, along with toilet paper, corn

flakes, sardines and milk tumbled every which way, and abandoned cash registers and cases of beer leaned crazily out of the splintered windows and were strewn along the avenues. Sheets, blankets, and clothing of every description formed a kind of path, as though people had dropped them while running. I truly had not realized that Harlem *had* so many stores until I saw them all smashed open; the first time the word *wealth* ever entered my mind in relation to Harlem was when I saw it scattered in the streets. But one's first, incongruous impression of plenty was countered immediately by an impression of waste. None of this was doing anybody any good. It would have been better to have left the plate glass as it had been and the goods lying in the stores.

It would have been better, but it would also have been intolerable, for Harlem had needed something to smash. To smash something is the ghetto's chronic need. Most of the time it is the members of the ghetto who smash each other, and themselves. But as long as the ghetto walls are standing there will always come a moment when these outlets do not work. That summer, for example, it was not enough to get into a fight on Lenox Avenue, or curse out one's cronies in the barber shops. If ever, indeed, the violence which fills Harlem's churches, pool halls, and bars erupts outward in a more direct fashion, Harlem and its citizens are likely to vanish in an apocalyptic flood. That this is not likely to happen is due to a great many reasons, most hidden and powerful among them the Negro's real relation to the white American. This relation prohibits, simply, anything as uncomplicated and satisfactory as pure hatred. In order really to hate white people, one has to blot so much out of the mind—and the heart—that this hatred itself becomes an exhausting and self-destructive pose. But this does not mean, on the other hand, that love comes easily: the white world is too powerful, too complacent, too ready with gratuitous humiliation, and, above all, too ignorant and too innocent for that. One is absolutely forced to make perpetual qualifications and one's own reactions are always canceling each other out. It is this, really, which has driven so many people mad, both white and black. One is always in the position of having to decide between amputation and gangrene. Amputation is swift but time may prove that the amputation was not necessary—or one may delay the amputation too long. Gangrene is slow, but it is impossible to be sure that one is reading one's symptoms right. The idea of going through life as a cripple is more than one can bear, and equally unbearable is the risk of swelling up slowly, in agony, with poison. And the trouble, finally, is that the risks are real even if the choices do not exist.

"But as for me and my house," my father had said, "we will serve the   45
Lord." I wondered, as we drove him to his resting place, what this line had meant for him. I had heard him preach it many times. I had preached it once myself, proudly giving it an interpretation different from my father's. Now the whole thing came back to me, as though my father and I were on our way to Sunday school and I were memorizing the golden text: *And if it seem evil unto you to serve the Lord, choose you this day whom you*

will serve; whether the gods which your fathers served that were on the other side of the flood, or the gods of the Amorites, in whose land ye dwell: but as for me and my house, we will serve the Lord. I suspected in these familiar lines a meaning which had never been there for me before. All of my father's texts and songs, which I had decided were meaningless, were arranged before me at his death like empty bottles, waiting to hold the meaning which life would give them for me. This was his legacy: nothing is ever escaped. That bleakly memorable morning I hated the unbelievable streets and the Negroes and whites who had, equally, made them that way. But I knew that it was folly, as my father would have said, this bitterness was folly. It was necessary to hold on to the things that mattered. The dead man mattered, the new life mattered; blackness and whiteness did not matter; to believe that they did was to acquiesce in one's own destruction. Hatred, which could destroy so much, never failed to destroy the man who hated and this was an immutable law.

It began to seem that one would have to hold in the mind forever two ideas which seemed to be in opposition. The first idea was acceptance, the acceptance, totally without rancor, of life as it is, and men as they are: in the light of this idea, it goes without saying that injustice is a commonplace. But this did not mean that one could be complacent, for the second idea was of equal power: that one must never, in one's own life, accept these injustices as commonplace but must fight them with all one's strength. This fight begins, however, in the heart and it now had been laid to my charge to keep my own heart free of hatred and despair. This intimation made my heart heavy and, now that my father was irrecoverable, I wished that he had been beside me so that I could have searched his face for the answers which only the future would give me now.

The Reader's Presence

1. Why does Baldwin open with three events: his father's death, his youngest sibling's birth, and the race riots in Detroit and Harlem? How did the death of his father serve to change Baldwin's thinking about how he would deal with racism in his life? How does Baldwin make peace with his father's memory?

2. At the end of the essay, Baldwin remembers a biblical passage his father used to quote. How does Baldwin reinterpret the passage after his father's death? What does it mean in the context of being his father's son? How does it help him make sense of the race riots in Harlem?

3. Examine Baldwin's description of the Harlem race riots in the third section of his essay. How does Baldwin approach the riots as a native of Harlem and as an African American? What explanations does he give for the violence? How does he use the riots to

explain the relations between white and black America? Compare Baldwin's discussion of the Harlem race riots to Martin Luther King Jr.'s consideration of nonviolence in "Letter from Birmingham Jail" (page 730) written eight years later. Which author takes a more personal view of race relations at the time? In your opinion, would King concur with Baldwin's assessment of the riots? Do you think after reading Baldwin's essay that Baldwin would agree with King's philosophy? These are long essays and among the most important documents of African American literary history. How would you compare and contrast the racial attitudes of both Baldwin and King as reflected in these two outstanding works?

THE WRITER AT WORK

James Baldwin on Black English

> *In the following piece, Baldwin takes up a subject that is periodically scrutinized by the American mass media: Is black English a language and, if so, what kind of language is it? Whatever its current status in the eyes of the dominant society, black English is an indisputable fact of everyday life for many Americans. When Baldwin writes that blacks have "endured and transcended" American racism by means of language, he echoes William Faulkner's belief that our compulsion to talk is what will save the human race.*
>
> *Since Baldwin wrote this piece in 1979, the language he so ardently defends as necessary to African American strength in the face of "brutal necessity" (that is, in defense against racism) has entered the mainstream through the spread of hip-hop culture. What might Baldwin say about white speakers of black English? Are they simply another example of the appropriation of subcultural forms by the dominant culture, a means of containing or defusing resistance? The "rules of the language are dictated by what the language must convey," Baldwin writes. Who is using black English today? For what purposes?*

The argument concerning the use, or the status, or the reality, of black English is rooted in American history and has absolutely nothing to do with the question the argument supposes itself to be posing. The argument has nothing to do with language itself but with the *role* of language. Language, incontestably, reveals the speaker. Language, also, far more dubiously, is meant to define the other—and, in this case, the other is refusing to be defined by a language that has never been able to recognize him.

People evolve a language in order to describe and thus control their circumstances, or in order not to be submerged by a reality that they cannot articulate. (And, if they cannot articulate it, they *are* submerged.) A Frenchman living in Paris speaks a subtly and crucially different language from that of the man living in Marseilles; neither sounds very much like a man living in Quebec; and they would all have great difficulty in apprehending what the man from Guadeloupe, or Martinique, is saying, to say nothing of the man from Senegal—although the "common" language of all these areas is French. But each has paid, and is paying, a different price for this "common" language, in which, as it turns out, they are not saying, and cannot be saying, the same things: They each have very different realities to articulate, or control.

What joins all languages, and all men, is the necessity to confront life, in order, not inconceivably, to outwit death: The price for this is the acceptance, and achievement, of one's temporal identity. So that, for example, though it is not taught in the schools (and this has the potential of becoming a political issue) the south of France still clings to its ancient and musical Provençal, which resists being described as a "dialect." And much of the tension in the Basque countries, and in Wales, is due to the Basque and Welsh determination not to allow their languages to be destroyed. This determination also feeds the flames in Ireland, for among the many indignities the Irish have been forced to undergo at English hands is the English contempt for their language.

It goes without saying, then, that language is also a political instrument, means, and proof of power. It is the most vivid and crucial key to identity: It reveals the private identity, and connects one with, or divorces one from, the larger, public, or communal identity. There have been, and are, times, and places, when to speak a certain language could be dangerous, even fatal. Or, one may speak the same language, but in such a way that one's antecedents are revealed, or (one hopes) hidden. This is true in France, and is absolutely true in England: The range (and reign) of accents on that damp little island make England coherent for the English and totally incomprehensible for everyone else. To open your mouth in England is (if I may use black English) to "put your business in the street": You have confessed your parents, your youth, your school, your salary, your self-esteem, and, alas, your future.

Now, I do not know what white Americans would sound like if there had never been any black people in the United States, but they would not sound the way they sound. *Jazz*, for example, is a very specific sexual term, as in *jazz me, baby*, but white people purified it into the Jazz Age. *Sock it to me*, which means, roughly, the same thing, has been adopted by Nathaniel Hawthorne's descendants with no qualms or hesitations at all, along with *let it all hang out* and *right on! Beat to his socks*, which was once the black's most total and despairing image of poverty, was transformed into a thing called the Beat Generation, which phenomenon was, largely, composed of *uptight*, middle-class white people, imitating poverty, trying to *get down*, to get *with it*, doing their *thing*, doing their despairing best to be *funky*, which we, the blacks, never dreamed of doing—we *were* funky, baby, like *funky* was going out of style.

Now, no one can eat his cake and have it, too, and it is late in the day to attempt to penalize black people for having created a language that

5

permits the nation its only glimpse of reality, a language without which the nation would be even more *whipped* than it is.

I say that the present skirmish is rooted in American history, and it is. Black English is the creation of the black diaspora. Blacks came to the United States chained to each other, but from different tribes: Neither could speak the other's language. If two black people, at that bitter hour of the world's history, had been able to speak to each other, the institution of chattel slavery could never have lasted as long as it did. Subsequently, the slave was given, under the eye, and the gun, of his master, Congo Square, and the Bible—or in other words, and under these conditions, the slave began the formation of the black church, and it is within this unprecedented tabernacle that black English began to be formed. This was not, merely, as in the European example, the adoption of a foreign tongue, but an alchemy that transformed ancient elements into a new language: *A language comes into existence by means of brutal necessity, and the rules of the language are dictated by what the language must convey.*

There was a moment, in time, and in this place, when my brother, or my mother, or my father, or my sister, had to convey to me, for example, the danger in which I was standing from the white man standing just behind me, and to convey this with a speed, and in a language, that the white man could not possibly understand, and that, indeed, he cannot understand, until today. He cannot afford to understand it. This understanding would reveal to him too much about himself, and smash that mirror before which he has been frozen for so long.

Now, if this passion, this skill, this (to quote Toni Morrison) "sheer intelligence," this incredible music, the mighty achievement of having brought a people utterly unknown to, or despised by "history"—to have brought this people to their present, troubled, troubling, and unassailable and unanswerable place—if this absolutely unprecedented journey does not indicate that black English is a language, I am curious to know what definition of language is to be trusted.

A people at the center of the Western world, and in the midst of so   10
hostile a population, has not endured and transcended by means of what is patronizingly called a "dialect." We, the blacks, are in trouble, certainly, but we are not doomed, and we are not inarticulate because we are not compelled to defend a morality that we know to be a lie.

The brutal truth is that the bulk of white people in America never had any interest in educating black people, except as this could serve white purposes. It is not the black child's language that is in question, it is not his language that is despised: It is his experience. A child cannot be taught by anyone who despises him, and a child cannot afford to be fooled. A child cannot be taught by anyone whose demand, essentially, is that the child repudiate his experience, and all that gives him sustenance, and enter a limbo in which he will no longer be black, and in which he knows that he can never become white. Black people have lost too many black children that way.

And, after all, finally, in a country with standards so untrustworthy, a country that makes heroes of so many criminal mediocrities, a country unable to face why so many of the nonwhite are in prison, or on the needle, or standing, futureless, in the streets—it may very well be that both the child, and his elder, have concluded that they have nothing whatever to learn from the people of a country that has managed to learn so little.

Thomas Beller

The Problem with T-Shirts

A born and bred New Yorker, Thomas Beller (b. 1965) has used his hometown as a location for much of his writing. Beller received his BA from Vassar College and his MFA from Columbia University. He and his family live in New York City and in Roanoke, Virginia, where he is visiting assistant professor of English at Hollins University. His short stories, essays, and reportage have appeared in numerous magazines, newspapers, and anthologies, including the New Yorker, Spin, Harper's Bazaar, Vogue, Slate, *the* New York Times, *the* Village Voice, Ploughshares, *and the* Southwest Review. *He is a contributing editor to* Travel and Leisure *magazine, and the* Cambodia Daily *in Phnom Penh, whose mission is "to establish a foundation for a free press in Cambodia and to train its journalists." Beller is the co-founder and editor of the literary magazine,* Open City, *and the Web-zine,* Mr. Beller's Neighborhood. *The site has published over 1,000 pieces of original writing and was nominated for a Webby Award in 2002. Beller's anthology* Before and After: Stories from New York *(2002) is a collection of pieces from that site. His books include* Seduction Theory *(1995), a story collection;* The Sleep-Over Artist *(2000), a novel; and* How to Be a Man: Scenes from a Protracted Boyhood *(2005), a collection of personal essays, from which this essay is taken.*

In a 2006 interview with Robert Birnbaum on identitytheory.com, Beller spoke about the relationship between his fiction and non-fiction writing: "Well, these things that I call essays I am prepared to stand up and say this is me writing about something that happened to me, and the fiction, I am not prepared to do that. The fiction is often informed by autobiography a lot, but it's twisted enough so that I want to take that feeling of responsibility out of it. It's true that sometimes my fiction swerves into this essayistic discussing mode and some of these pieces function like short stories, I think."

The other day I went to a party wearing an old T-shirt to which I had grown attached. You should never wear a beloved item of clothing out in public, if that item of clothing happens to be a T-shirt. This shirt had existed in a state of semiretirement for a while on account of its age, but I was wearing it to amuse a friend, who had once edited a magazine whose name was now on my chest. The magazine had lasted a year. The T-shirt had outlasted it by more than a decade.

Halfway through the party someone said, "What's up with all the holes?" She flicked her hand at one of them, somewhere below the chest. Was this a hostile gesture? Flirtatious? Was she thinking about another friend of mine, who had strung her along for such a long time and then announced that he was engaged to someone else?

I don't know. I don't think she intended to rip the shirt off my back, but that was what happened. The whole shirt rolled itself up like a window shade and more or less vanished, leaving the collar around my neck and some material hanging on my back. I changed into another shirt and brought the T-shirt home. It was beyond repair, more of a shroud than a shirt, but it took a few weeks of moving it around the house from one place to another before I realized I finally had to throw it out. I had this realization, and then put the shroud back in a drawer, where it hung around for another year or so before I came to my senses and got rid of it.

There are those for whom a T-shirt is just another name for an undershirt, the sort of thing that never sees the light of day. But for a lot of others, myself included, T-shirts often are a staple.

Like most people, my T-shirt collection has developed in a haphazard manner—a free one here, an impulse buy there. Even at the time of their acquisition, they are negligible possessions, and get treated as such. No other item of clothing is valued less than T-shirts, in spite of the fact that a T-shirt single-handedly turns its wearer into a walking billboard (even the plain white ones carry a kind of James Dean circa *Rebel Without a Cause* message). They are often drenched in sweat during some strenuous physical exercise, or spattered with bits of food, since the state of hyperawareness that exists while eating in a nice dress shirt is absent while eating in a T-shirt, which of course is part of its appeal. Then they get crumpled up and thrown in a corner or rudely stuffed in a hamper.

Socks admittedly give it competition in the No Respect category, but sock enthusiasts will point out that socks are capable of levels of style and elegance that a T-shirt could never attain. The other logical competition for lowest spot on the wardrobe totem pole would be underwear, but we live in the age of underwear—Victoria's Secret has built an Empire of Underwear. Entire museum exhibitions are dedicated to it, and walking around New York these days, one is surrounded by a kaleidoscope of underwear imagery: on buses, on billboards, and on people.

Now and then a T-shirt fad will pop up, but they're never very convincing. Once there was "Frankie Says Relax,"[1] then the Phillies Blunt[2] logo, then old concert T-shirts from dinosaur rock bands, and the innocent high school sports T-shirts from small-town America.

I've always preferred more eclectic T-shirts, such as the one that promotes a publication called *Pain Digest*. It got sent to me by a friend who works in the pharmaceutical industry. The logo sprawls across the chest, big white letters against dark blue, and the phrase "Advanced Literature for Pain" runs across the back. This item always draws out a few curious stares.

T-shirts get worn all year, but warm weather is their prime time. Recently, with the arrival of T-shirt weather, I found myself in a contemplative mood, staring into a drawer devoted exclusively to T-shirts. I had just done the wash, and they lay in two neat square piles, like a multicolored layer cake. Some were fairly new, while others were nearly twenty years old. Each of the older ones had been acquired during a long-departed era. They were like souvenirs from a trip I'd once taken. I reached into the pile and felt fabrics as soft as cashmere and as cool and smooth as silk.

And here is the real problem with T-shirts. They improve with age, getting better and better, until one day they disappear. Their finest moment is their grand finale. This is true of shoes and jeans, too, but shoes can always be resoled and jeans can be patched, and both, when all is finally lost, still have a physical presence, a weight you can feel on your hands. But T-shirts will just keep getting thinner and finer until they're gone. One moment it is perfect, and then a tiny hole appears, and then another; a tear along the seam might develop, and one day you reach into your drawer and pull out what to the untrained eye would look like a handkerchief. Or someone touches your shirt at a party and it disappears off your back. What then?

Of course you just throw it out. But there's a catch. One doesn't have to be wildly sentimental to get attached to a T-shirt that used to belong to an old flame, or the one advertising a high school or college in faded letters, or even that ridiculous thing that one swore would never see the light of day but has taken on some importance because you were a whole other person when you first slipped it on. These objects are as evocative as snapshots. They're documents, but they can't be reproduced.

My own solution, I discovered that day, is an informal T-shirt Hall of Fame. Way down at the bottom of the drawer several T-shirts are lying in state, like antiquities. Sometimes, when I'm fumbling around for a newer model, I'll reach down into the cool darkness and brush against their fragile surfaces, waiting there like understudies for one last day in the sun.

10

---

[1]*"Frankie Say[s] Relax":* One of the political T-shirts by Katharine E. Hamnett (b. 1947), an English fashion designer. In the early 1980s, Hamnett produced oversized T-shirts with large block-letter slogans that were worn by pop music groups, including Frankie Goes to Hollywood. The popularity of their song "Relax" led to other T-shirts with such slogans as "FRANKIE SAY WAR! HIDE YOURSELF" and "FRANKIE SAY ARM THE UNEMPLOYED." Counterfeit shirts featured the word "SAYS" instead of "SAY." —EDS.

[2]*Phillies Blunt:* A brand name for a cigar. —EDS.

The Reader's Presence

1. Beller's essay "The Problem with T-Shirts" consists of a series of assertions about the functions and value of one of the "most negligible possessions" in anyone's wardrobe. As you reread Beller's essay, develop a list of these functions and then comment on the accuracy of each of Beller's claims about the utility and fashionableness of the T-shirt. Which of his claims do you find most convincing? most surprising? most debatable? Which seem counter to your own experience of wearing T-shirts? Explain why in each instance.

2. Beller's essay is part of a book titled *How to Be a Man: Scenes from a Protracted Boyhood* (2005). To what extent is wearing a T-shirt restricted by gender? What "rules" or suggestions, adapted from those Beller provides, would you articulate for women who choose to wear T-shirts?

3. Near the end of his essay, Beller observes that T-shirts don't die, they "just keep getting thinner and finer until they're gone" (paragraph 10). He reminds his readers that the wearer "doesn't have to be wildly sentimental to get attached to a T-shirt. . . . These objects," he declares, "are as evocative as snapshots" (paragraph 11). In "Toy Children" (page 83), Meghan Daum talks about being a child who hated dolls: "By 'hate,' I'm not talking about a cool indifference. I'm talking about a palpable loathing" (paragraph 1). She declares, "Dolls are the ultimate symbol of childhood; they are toy children" (paragraph 4). Compare and contrast the specific ways in which Beller and Daum invoke T-shirts and dolls as "snapshots," and as "symbols" of different gender roles and ages.

Raymond Carver

My Father's Life

Son of a laborer and a homemaker in Clatskanie, Oregon, Raymond Carver (1938–1988) resembled the characters in the short stories for which he is widely acclaimed. Once a manual laborer, a gas station attendant, and a janitor himself, Carver acquired his vision of the working class and the desperate lives of ordinary folk through direct experience. The Pacific Northwest of Carver's writing is peopled with types such as "the waitress, the bus driver, the mechanic, the hotel keeper"—people Carver feels are "good people." First published in Esquire *in 1984, "My Father's Life," Carver's account of his father's hardships during the Great Depression, puts a biographical spin on these "good people." Carver's short story collections,* Will You Please Be Quiet, Please? *(1976),* Cathedral *(1984), and* Where I'm Calling From *(1988), were all nominated for the National Book Critics Circle Award. Both* Cathedral *and* Where I'm Calling From *were also nominated for the Pulitzer Prize for fiction in 1985 and 1989, respectively. Carver's poetry is collected in* Where Water Comes Together with Other Water *(1985), recipient of the 1986 Los Angeles* Times Book Prize; Ultramarine *(1986); and* A New Path to the Waterfall *(1989).*

In his essay "On Writing," Carver states, "Writers don't need tricks or gimmicks or even necessarily to be the smartest fellows on the block. At the risk of appearing foolish, a writer sometimes needs to be able to just stand and gape at this or that thing—a sunset or an old shoe—in absolute and simple amazement."

For an example of Carver's fiction, see "The Bath" (page 919).

My dad's name was Clevie Raymond Carver. His family called him Raymond and friends called him C. R. I was named Raymond Clevie Carver, Jr. I hated the "Junior" part. When I was little my dad called me Frog, which was okay. But later, like everybody else in the family, he began calling me Junior. He went on calling me this until I was thirteen or fourteen and announced that I wouldn't answer to that name any longer. So he began calling me Doc. From then until his death, on June 17, 1967, he called me Doc, or else Son.

When he died, my mother telephoned my wife with the news. I was away from my family at the time, between lives, trying to enroll in the School of Library Science at the University of Iowa. When my wife answered the phone, my mother blurted out, "Raymond's dead!" For a moment, my wife thought my mother was telling her that I was dead. Then my mother made it clear *which* Raymond she was talking about and my wife said, "Thank God. I thought you meant *my* Raymond."

My dad walked, hitched rides, and rode in empty boxcars when he went from Arkansas to Washington State in 1934, looking for work. I don't know whether he was pursuing a dream when he went out to

Washington. I doubt it. I don't think he dreamed much. I believe he was
simply looking for steady work at decent pay. Steady work was meaningful work. He picked apples for a time and then landed a construction laborer's job on the Grand Coulee Dam. After he'd put aside a little money,
he bought a car and drove back to Arkansas to help his folks, my grandparents, pack up for the move west. He said later that they were about to
starve down there, and this wasn't meant as a figure of speech. It was
during that short while in Arkansas, in a town called Leola, that my
mother met my dad on the sidewalk as he came out of a tavern.

"He was drunk," she said. "I don't know why I let him talk to me. His
eyes were glittery. I wish I'd had a crystal ball." They'd met once, a year or
so before, at a dance. He'd had girlfriends before her, my mother told me.
"Your dad always had a girlfriend, even after we married. He was my first
and last. I never had another man. But I didn't miss anything."

They were married by a justice of the peace on the day they left for   5
Washington, this big, tall country girl and a farmhand-turned-construction
worker. My mother spent her wedding night with my dad and his folks, all
of them camped beside the road in Arkansas.

In Omak, Washington, my dad and mother lived in a little place not
much bigger than a cabin. My grandparents lived next door. My dad was
still working on the dam, and later, with the huge turbines producing
electricity and the water backed up for a hundred miles into Canada, he
stood in the crowd and heard Franklin D. Roosevelt when he spoke at the
construction site. "He never mentioned those guys who died building that
dam," my dad said. Some of his friends had died there, men from Arkansas,
Oklahoma, and Missouri.

He then took a job in a sawmill in Clatskanie, Oregon, a little town
alongside the Columbia River. I was born there, and my mother has a picture of my dad standing in front of the gate to the mill, proudly holding
me up to face the camera. My bonnet is on crooked and about to come
untied. His hat is pushed back on his forehead, and he's wearing a big grin.
Was he going in to work or just finishing his shift? It doesn't matter. In either case, he had a job and a family. These were his salad days.

In 1941 we moved to Yakima, Washington, where my dad went to
work as a saw filer, a skilled trade he'd learned in Clatskanie. When war
broke out, he was given a deferment because his work was considered necessary to the war effort. Finished lumber was in demand by the armed services, and he kept his saws so sharp they could shave the hair off your arm.

After my dad had moved us to Yakima, he moved his folks into the
same neighborhood. By the mid-1940s the rest of my dad's family—his
brother, his sister, and her husband, as well as uncles, cousins, nephews,
and most of their extended family and friends—had come out from
Arkansas. All because my dad came out first. The men went to work at
Boise Cascade, where my dad worked, and the women packed apples in
the canneries. And in just a little while, it seemed—according to my

mother—everybody was better off than my dad. "Your dad couldn't keep money," my mother said. "Money burned a hole in his pocket. He was always doing for others."

The first house I clearly remember living in, at 1515 South Fifteenth Street, in Yakima, had an outdoor toilet. On Halloween night, or just any night, for the hell of it, neighbor kids, kids in their early teens, would carry our toilet away and leave it next to the road. My dad would have to get somebody to help him bring it home. Or these kids would take the toilet and stand it in somebody else's backyard. Once they actually set it on fire. But ours wasn't the only house that had an outdoor toilet. When I was old enough to know what I was doing, I threw rocks at the other toilets when I'd see someone go inside. This was called bombing the toilets. After a while, though, everyone went to indoor plumbing until, suddenly, our toilet was the last outdoor one in the neighborhood. I remember the shame I felt when my third-grade teacher, Mr. Wise, drove me home from school one day. I asked him to stop at the house just before ours, claiming I lived there.

I can recall what happened one night when my dad came home late to find that my mother had locked all the doors on him from the inside. He was drunk, and we could feel the house shudder as he rattled the door. When he'd managed to force open a window, she hit him between the eyes with a colander and knocked him out. We could see him down there on the grass. For years afterward, I used to pick up this colander— it was as heavy as a rolling pin—and imagine what it would feel like to be hit in the head with something like that.

It was during this period that I remember my dad taking me into the bedroom, sitting me down on the bed, and telling me that I might have to go live with my Aunt LaVon for a while. I couldn't understand what I'd done that meant I'd have to go away from home to live. But this, too—whatever prompted it—must have blown over, more or less, anyway, because we stayed together, and I didn't have to go live with her or anyone else.

I remember my mother pouring his whiskey down the sink. Sometimes she'd pour it all out and sometimes, if she was afraid of getting caught, she'd only pour half of it out and then add water to the rest. I tasted some of his whiskey once myself. It was terrible stuff, and I don't see how anybody could drink it.

After a long time without one, we finally got a car, in 1949 or 1950, a 1938 Ford. But it threw a rod the first week we had it, and my dad had to have the motor rebuilt.

"We drove the oldest car in town," my mother said. "We could have had a Cadillac for all he spent on car repairs." One time she found someone else's tube of lipstick on the floorboard, along with a lacy handkerchief. "See this?" she said to me. "Some floozy left this in the car."

Once I saw her take a pan of warm water into the bedroom where my dad was sleeping. She took his hand from under the covers and held it in the water. I stood in the doorway and watched. I wanted to know what was going on. This would make him talk in his sleep, she told me. There were things she needed to know, things she was sure he was keeping from her.

Every year or so, when I was little, we would take the North Coast Limited across the Cascade Range from Yakima to Seattle and stay in the Vance Hotel and eat, I remember, at a place called the Dinner Bell Cafe. Once we went to Ivar's Acres of Clams and drank glasses of warm clam broth.

In 1956, the year I was to graduate from high school, my dad quit his job at the mill in Yakima and took a job in Chester, a little sawmill town in northern California. The reasons given at the time for his taking the job had to do with a higher hourly wage and the vague promise that he might, in a few years' time, succeed to the job of head filer in this new mill. But I think, in the main, that my dad had grown restless and simply wanted to try his luck elsewhere. Things had gotten a little too predictable for him in Yakima. Also, the year before, there had been the deaths, within six months of each other, of both his parents.

But just a few days after graduation, when my mother and I were packed to move to Chester, my dad penciled a letter to say he'd been sick for a while. He didn't want us to worry, he said, but he'd cut himself on a saw. Maybe he'd got a tiny sliver of steel in his blood. Anyway, something had happened and he'd had to miss work, he said. In the same mail was an unsigned postcard from somebody down there telling my mother that my dad was about to die and that he was drinking "raw whiskey."

When we arrived in Chester, my dad was living in a trailer that belonged to the company. I didn't recognize him immediately. I guess for a moment I didn't want to recognize him. He was skinny and pale and looked bewildered. His pants wouldn't stay up. He didn't look like my dad. My mother began to cry. My dad put his arm around her and patted her shoulder vaguely, like he didn't know what this was all about, either. The three of us took up life together in the trailer, and we looked after him as best we could. But my dad was sick, and he couldn't get any better. I worked with him in the mill that summer and part of the fall. We'd get up in the mornings and eat eggs and toast while we listened to the radio, and then go out the door with our lunch pails. We'd pass through the gate together at eight in the morning, and I wouldn't see him again until quitting time. In November I went back to Yakima to be closer to my girlfriend, the girl I'd made up my mind I was going to marry.

He worked at the mill in Chester until the following February, when he collapsed on the job and was taken to the hospital. My mother asked if I would come down there and help. I caught a bus from Yakima to Chester, intending to drive them back to Yakima. But now, in addition to being physically sick, my dad was in the midst of a nervous breakdown, though none of us knew to call it that at the time. During the entire trip back to Yakima, he didn't speak, not even when asked a direct question.

20

("How do you feel, Raymond?" "You okay, Dad?") He'd communicate, if he communicated at all, by moving his head or by turning his palms up as if to say he didn't know or care. The only time he said anything on the trip, and for nearly a month afterward, was when I was speeding down a gravel road in Oregon and the car muffler came loose. "You were going too fast," he said.

Back in Yakima a doctor saw to it that my dad went to a psychiatrist. My mother and dad had to go on relief, as it was called, and the county paid for the psychiatrist. The psychiatrist asked my dad, "Who is the President?" He'd had a question put to him that he could answer. "Ike," my dad said. Nevertheless, they put him on the fifth floor of Valley Memorial Hospital and began giving him electroshock treatment. I was married by then and about to start my own family. My dad was still locked up when my wife went into this same hospital, just one floor down, to have our first baby. After she had delivered, I went upstairs to give my dad the news. They let me in through a steel door and showed me where I could find him. He was sitting on a couch with a blanket over his lap. *Hey*, I thought. *What in hell is happening to my dad?* I sat down next to him and told him he was a grandfather. He waited a minute and then he said, "I feel like a grandfather." That's all he said. He didn't smile or move. He was in a big room with a lot of other people. Then I hugged him, and he began to cry.

Somehow he got out of there. But now came the years when he couldn't work and just sat around the house trying to figure what next and what he'd done wrong in his life that he'd wound up like this. My mother went from job to crummy job. Much later she referred to that time he was in the hospital, and those years just afterward, as "when Raymond was sick." The word *sick* was never the same for me again.

In 1964, through the help of a friend, he was lucky enough to be hired on at a mill in Klamath, California. He moved down there by himself to see if he could hack it. He lived not far from the mill, in a one-room cabin not much different from the place he and my mother had started out living in when they went west. He scrawled letters to my mother, and if I called she'd read them aloud to me over the phone. In the letters, he said it was touch and go. Every day that he went to work, he felt like it was the most important day of his life. But every day, he told her, made the next day that much easier. He said for her to tell me he said hello. If he couldn't sleep at night, he said, he thought about me and the good times we used to have. Finally, after a couple of months, he regained some of his confidence. He could do the work and didn't think he had to worry that he'd let anybody down ever again. When he was sure, he sent for my mother.

He'd been off from work for six years and had lost everything in that time—home, car, furniture, and appliances, including the big freezer that had been my mother's pride and joy. He'd lost his good name too—Raymond Carver was someone who couldn't pay his bills—and his self-respect

25

was gone. He'd even lost his virility. My mother told my wife, "All during that time Raymond was sick we slept together in the same bed, but we didn't have relations. He wanted to a few times, but nothing happened. I didn't miss it, but I think he wanted to, you know."

During those years I was trying to raise my own family and earn a living. But, from one thing and another, we found ourselves having to move a lot. I couldn't keep track of what was going down in my dad's life. But I did have a chance one Christmas to tell him I wanted to be a writer. I might as well have told him I wanted to become a plastic surgeon. "What are you going to write about?" he wanted to know. Then, as if to help me out, he said, "Write about stuff you know about. Write about some of those fishing trips we took." I said I would, but I knew I wouldn't. "Send me what you write," he said. I said I'd do that, but then I didn't. I wasn't writing anything about fishing, and I didn't think he'd particularly care about, or even necessarily understand, what I was writing in those days. Besides, he wasn't a reader. Not the sort, anyway, I imagined I was writing for.

Then he died. I was a long way off, in Iowa City, with things still to say to him. I didn't have the chance to tell him goodbye, or that I thought he was doing great at his new job. That I was proud of him for making a comeback.

My mother said he came in from work that night and ate a big supper. Then he sat at the table by himself and finished what was left of a bottle of whiskey, a bottle she found hidden in the bottom of the garbage under some coffee grounds a day or so later. Then he got up and went to bed, where my mother joined him a little later. But in the night she had to get up and make a bed for herself on the couch. "He was snoring so loud I couldn't sleep," she said. The next morning when she looked in on him, he was on his back with his mouth open, his cheeks caved in. *Graylooking*, she said. She knew he was dead—she didn't need a doctor to tell her that. But she called one anyway, and then she called my wife.

Among the pictures my mother kept of my dad and herself during those early days in Washington was a photograph of him standing in front of a car, holding a beer and a stringer of fish. In the photograph he is wearing his hat back on his forehead and has this awkward grin on his face. I asked her for it and she gave it to me, along with some others. I put it up on my wall, and each time we moved, I took the picture along and put it up on another wall. I looked at it carefully from time to time, trying to figure out some things about my dad, and maybe myself in the process. But I couldn't. My dad just kept moving further and further away from me and back into time. Finally, in the course of another move, I lost the photograph. It was then that I tried to recall it, and at the same time make an attempt to say something about my dad, and how I thought that in some important ways we might be alike. I wrote the poem when I was living in an apartment house in an urban area south of San Fran-

cisco, at a time when I found myself, like my dad, having trouble with alcohol. The poem was a way of trying to connect up with him.

PHOTOGRAPH OF MY FATHER IN HIS TWENTY-SECOND YEAR

October. Here in this dank, unfamiliar kitchen
I study my father's embarrassed young man's face.
Sheepish grin, he holds in one hand a string
of spiny yellow perch, in the other
a bottle of Carlsberg beer.

In jeans and flannel shirt, he leans
against the front fender of a 1934 Ford.
He would like to pose brave and hearty for his posterity,
wear his old hat cocked over his ear.
All his life my father wanted to be bold.

But the eyes give him away, and the hands
that limply offer the string of dead perch
and the bottle of beer. Father, I love you,
yet how can I say thank you, I who can't hold my liquor either
and don't even know the places to fish.

The poem is true in its particulars, except that my dad died in June   30
and not October, as the first word of the poem says. I wanted a word
with more than one syllable to it to make it linger a little. But more than
that, I wanted a month appropriate to what I felt at the time I wrote the
poem—a month of short days and failing light, smoke in the air, things
perishing. June was summer nights and days, graduations, my wedding
anniversary, the birthday of one of my children. June wasn't a month
your father died in.

After the service at the funeral home, after we had moved outside, a
woman I didn't know came over to me and said, "He's happier where he
is now." I stared at this woman until she moved away. I still remember
the little knob of a hat she was wearing. Then one of my dad's cousins—
I didn't know the man's name—reached out and took my hand. "We all
miss him," he said, and I knew he wasn't saying it just to be polite.

I began to weep for the first time since receiving the news. I hadn't
been able to before. I hadn't had the time, for one thing. Now, suddenly,
I couldn't stop. I held my wife and wept while she said and did what she
could do to comfort me there in the middle of that summer afternoon.

I listened to people say consoling things to my mother, and I was glad
that my dad's family had turned up, had come to where he was. I thought
I'd remember everything that was said and done that day and maybe find a
way to tell it sometime. But I didn't. I forgot it all, or nearly. What I do remember is that I heard our name used a lot that afternoon, my dad's name
and mine. But I knew they were talking about my dad. *Raymond,* these
people kept saying in their beautiful voices out of my childhood. *Raymond.*

The Reader's Presence

1. You may have noticed that Carver begins and ends his essay with a reference to his and his father's name. Of what importance is this information at the opening? What do we learn about his relationship with his father through their names? How do names matter in the final paragraph?

2. Reread the essay with particular attention to the conversations between father and son. How many reported conversations can you find? What do the conversations sound like? Can you find any pattern to them? If so, describe that pattern. To what extent do these conversations help you understand Carver's relationship with his father?

3. Carver includes one of his own poems in his essay, as does Alice Walker in "Beauty: When the Other Dancer Is the Self" (page 258). How do these writers explore the margins between poetry and prose? What do you think a poem communicates that a passage of prose may not?

Judith Ortiz Cofer

Silent Dancing

Born in Puerto Rico in 1952, Judith Ortiz Cofer moved to New Jersey in 1955. Her poetry has appeared in numerous literary magazines, and several collections of her poems have been published. Her first novel, The Line of the Sun *(1989), was nominated for the Pulitzer Prize. "Silent Dancing" is from Cofer's 1990 essay collection,* Silent Dancing: A Partial Remembrance of a Puerto Rican Childhood, *which won a PEN/Martha Albrand special citation for nonfiction. Among her notable books are* The Latin Deli: Prose and Poetry *(1993),* An Island Like You: Stories of the Barrio *(1995),* Woman in Front of the Sun *(2000),* The Meaning of Consuelo *(2003), and* Call Me Maria *(2004). Her third volume of poetry,* A Love Story Beginning in Spanish, *was published in 2005.*

Reflecting on her life as a writer, Cofer has said, "The 'infinite variety' and power of language interest me. I never cease to experiment with it. As a native Puerto Rican, my first language was Spanish. It was a challenge, not only to learn English, but to master it enough to teach it and — the ultimate goal — to write poetry in it." Cofer is professor of English and creative writing at the University of Georgia.

We have a home movie of this party. Several times my mother and I have watched it together, and I have asked questions about the silent revelers coming in and out of focus. It is grainy and of short duration, but it's a great visual aid to my memory of life at that time. And it is in color—the only complete scene in color I can recall from those years.

We lived in Puerto Rico until my brother was born in 1954. Soon after, because of economic pressures on our growing family, my father joined the United States Navy. He was assigned to duty on a ship in Brooklyn Yard—a place of cement and steel that was to be his home base in the States until his retirement more than twenty years later. He left the Island first, alone, going to New York City and tracking down his uncle who lived with his family across the Hudson River in Paterson, New Jersey. There my father found a tiny apartment in a huge tenement that had once housed Jewish families but was just being taken over and transformed by Puerto Ricans, overflowing from New York City. In 1955 he sent for us. My mother was only twenty years old, I was not quite three, and my brother was a toddler when we arrived at *El Building*, as the place had been christened by its newest residents.

My memories of life in Paterson during those first few years are all in shades of gray. Maybe I was too young to absorb vivid colors and details, or to discriminate between the slate blue of the winter sky and the darker hues of the snow-bearing clouds, but that single color washes over the whole period. The building we lived in was gray, as were the streets, filled with slush the first few months of my life there. The coat my father had bought for me was similar in color and too big; it sat heavily on my thin frame.

I do remember the way the heater pipes banged and rattled, startling all of us out of sleep until we got so used to the sound that we automatically shut it out or raised our voices above the racket. The hiss from the valve punctuated my sleep (which has always been fitful) like a nonhuman presence in the room—a dragon sleeping at the entrance of my childhood. But the pipes were also a connection to all the other lives being lived around us. Having come from a house designed for a single family back in Puerto Rico—my mother's extended-family home—it was curious to know that strangers lived under our floor and above our heads, and that the heater pipe went through everyone's apartments. (My first spanking in Paterson came as a result of playing tunes on the pipes in my room to see if there would be an answer.) My mother was as new to this concept of beehive life as I was, but she had been given strict orders by my father to keep the doors locked, the noise down, ourselves to ourselves.

It seems that Father had learned some painful lessons about prejudice while searching for an apartment in Paterson. Not until years later did I hear how much resistance he had encountered with landlords who were panicking at the influx of Latinos into a neighborhood that had been Jewish for a couple of generations. It made no difference that it was the

American phenomenon of ethnic turnover which was changing the urban core of Paterson, and that the human flood could not be held back with an accusing finger.

"You Cuban?" one man had asked my father, pointing at his name   5
tag on the Navy uniform—even though my father had the fair skin and light-brown hair of his northern Spanish background, and the name Ortiz is as common in Puerto Rico as Johnson is in the United States.

"No," my father had answered, looking past the finger into his adversary's angry eyes. "I'm Puerto Rican."

"Same shit." And the door closed.

My father could have passed as European, but we couldn't. My brother and I both have our mother's black hair and olive skin, and so we lived in El Building and visited our great-uncle and his fair children on the next block. It was their private joke that they were the German branch of the family. Not many years later that area too would be mainly Puerto Rican. It was as if the heart of the city map were being gradually colored brown—*café con leche*[1] brown. Our color.

The movie opens with a sweep of the living room. It is "typical" immigrant Puerto Rican decor for the time: The sofa and chairs are square and hard-looking, upholstered in bright colors (blue and yellow in this instance), and covered with the transparent plastic that furniture salesmen then were so adept at convincing women to buy. The linoleum on the floor is light blue; if it had been subjected to spike heels (as it was in most places), there were dime-sized indentations all over it that cannot be seen in this movie. The room is full of people dressed up: dark suits for the men, red dresses for the women. When I have asked my mother why most of the women are in red that night, she has shrugged, "I don't remember. Just a coincidence." She doesn't have my obsession for assigning symbolism to everything.

The three women in red sitting on the couch are my mother, my   10
eighteen-year-old cousin, and her brother's girlfriend. The novia *is just up from the Island, which is apparent in her body language. She sits up formally, her dress pulled over her knees. She is a pretty girl, but her posture makes her look insecure, lost in her full-skirted dress, which she has carefully tucked around her to make room for my gorgeous cousin, her future sister-in-law. My cousin has grown up in Paterson and is in her last year of high school. She doesn't have a trace of what Puerto Ricans call* la mancha *(literally, the stain: the mark of the new immigrant—something about the posture, the voice, or the humble demeanor that makes it obvious to everyone the person has just arrived on the mainland). My cousin is wearing a tight, sequined, cocktail dress. Her brown hair has been lightened with peroxide around the bangs, and she is holding a cigarette*

[1]*café con leche:* Coffee with cream. In Puerto Rico it is sometimes prepared with boiled milk. — COFER'S NOTE.

*expertly between her fingers, bringing it up to her mouth in a sensuous
arc of her arm as she talks animatedly. My mother, who has come up to
sit between the two women, both only a few years younger than herself,
is somewhere between the poles they represent in our culture.*

It became my father's obsession to get out of the barrio, and thus we
were never permitted to form bonds with the place or with the people who
lived there. Yet El Building was a comfort to my mother, who never got
over yearning for *la isla*. She felt surrounded by her language: The walls
were thin, and voices speaking and arguing in Spanish could be heard all
day. *Salsas* blasted out of radios, turned on early in the morning and left
on for company. Women seemed to cook rice and beans perpetually—the
strong aroma of boiling red kidney beans permeated the hallways.

Though Father preferred that we do our grocery shopping at the supermarket when he came home on weekend leaves, my mother insisted that she
could cook only with products whose labels she could read. Consequently,
during the week I accompanied her and my little brother to *La Bodega*—a
hole-in-the-wall grocery store across the street from El Building. There we
squeezed down three narrow aisles jammed with various products. Goya's
and Libby's—those were the trademarks that were trusted by her *mamá*, so
my mother bought many cans of Goya beans, soups, and condiments, as
well as little cans of Libby's fruit juices for us. And she also bought Colgate
toothpaste and Palmolive soap. (The final *e* is pronounced in both these
products in Spanish, so for many years I believed that they were manufactured on the Island. I remember my surprise at first hearing a commercial
on television in which Colgate rhymed with "ate.") We always lingered at
La Bodega, for it was there that Mother breathed best, taking in the familiar aromas of the foods she knew from Mamá's kitchen. It was also there
that she got to speak to the other women of El Building without violating
outright Father's dictates against fraternizing with our neighbors.

Yet Father did his best to make our "assimilation" painless. I can still
see him carrying a real Christmas tree up several flights of stairs to our
apartment, leaving a trail of aromatic pine. He carried it formally, as if it
were a flag in a parade. We were the only ones in El Building that I knew
of who got presents on both Christmas day and *dia de Reyes*, the day
when the Three Kings brought gifts to Christ and to Hispanic children.

Our supreme luxury in El Building was having our own television set.
It must have been a result of Father's guilty feelings over the isolation he
had imposed on us, but we were among the first in the barrio to have one.
My brother quickly became an avid watcher of Captain Kangaroo and
Jungle Jim, while I loved all the series showing families. By the time I
started first grade, I could have drawn a map of Middle America as exemplified by the lives of characters in "Father Knows Best," "The Donna Reed
Show," "Leave It to Beaver," "My Three Sons," and (my favorite) "Bachelor Father," where John Forsythe treated his adopted teenage daughter like

a princess because he was rich and had a Chinese houseboy to do everything for him. In truth, compared to our neighbors in El Building, *we* were rich. My father's Navy check provided us with financial security and a standard of life that the factory workers envied. The only thing his money could not buy us was a place to live away from the barrio—his greatest wish, Mother's greatest fear.

In the home movie the men are shown next, sitting around a card table   15
set up in one corner of the living room, playing dominoes. The clack of the
ivory pieces was a familiar sound. I heard it in many houses on the Island
and in many apartments in Paterson. In Leave It to Beaver, *the Cleavers*
played bridge in every other episode; in my childhood, the men started
every social occasion with a hotly debated round of dominoes. The women
would sit around and watch, but they never participated in the games.
   Here and there you can see a small child. Children were always
brought to parties and, whenever they got sleepy, were put to bed in the
host's bedroom. Babysitting was a concept unrecognized by the Puerto
Rican women I knew: A responsible mother did not leave her children
with any stranger. And in a culture where children are not considered in-
trusive, there was no need to leave the children at home. We went where
our mother went.

Of my preschool years I have only impressions: the sharp bite of the wind in December as we walked with our parents toward the brightly lit stores downtown; how I felt like a stuffed doll in my heavy coat, boots, and mittens; how good it was to walk into the five-and-dime and sit at the counter drinking hot chocolate. On Saturdays our whole family would walk downtown to shop at the big department stores on Broadway. Mother bought all our clothes at Penney's and Sears, and she liked to buy her dresses at the women's specialty shops like Lerner's and Diana's. At some point we'd go into Woolworth's and sit at the soda fountain to eat.

We never ran into other Latinos at these stores or when eating out, and it became clear to me only years later that the women from El Building shopped mainly in other places—stores owned by other Puerto Ricans or by Jewish merchants who had philosophically accepted our presence in the city and decided to make us their good customers, if not real neighbors and friends. These establishments were located not downtown but in the blocks around our street, and they were referred to generically as *La Tienda, El Bazar, La Bodega, La Botánica.* Everyone knew what was meant. These were the stores where your face did not turn a clerk to stone, where your money was as green as anyone else's.

One New Year's Eve we were dressed up like child models in the Sears catalogue: my brother in a miniature man's suit and bow tie, and I in black patent-leather shoes and a frilly dress with several layers of crinoline underneath. My mother wore a bright red dress that night, I remember, and spike heels; her long black hair hung to her waist. Father, who usually wore his Navy uniform during his short visits home, had put on a dark civilian suit for the occasion: We had been invited to his uncle's house for a big celebration. Everyone was excited because my mother's brother Hernan — a bachelor who could indulge himself with luxuries — had bought a home movie camera, which he would be trying out that night.

Even the home movie cannot fill in the sensory details such a gathering left imprinted in a child's brain. The thick sweetness of women's perfumes mixing with the ever-present smells of food cooking in the kitchen: meat and plantain *pasteles,* as well as the ubiquitous rice dish made special with pigeon peas — *gandules* — and seasoned with precious *sofrito*[2] sent up from the Island by somebody's mother or smuggled in by a recent traveler. *Sofrito* was one of the items that women hoarded, since it was hardly ever in stock at La Bodega. It was the flavor of Puerto Rico.   20

The men drank Palo Viejo rum, and some of the younger ones got weepy. The first time I saw a grown man cry was at a New Year's Eve party: He had been reminded of his mother by the smells in the kitchen. But what I remember most were the boiled *pasteles* — plantain or yucca rectangles stuffed with corned beef or other meats, olives, and many other savory ingredients, all wrapped in banana leaves. Everybody had to fish one out with a fork. There was always a "trick" pastel — one without stuffing — and whoever got that one was the "New Year's Fool."

There was also the music. Long-playing albums were treated like precious china in these homes. Mexican recordings were popular, but the songs that brought tears to my mother's eyes were sung by the melancholy Daniel Santos, whose life as a drug addict was the stuff of legend. Felipe Rodríguez was a particular favorite of couples, since he sang about faithless women and brokenhearted men. There is a snatch of one lyric that has stuck in my mind like a needle on a worn groove: *De piedra ha de ser mi cama, de piedra la cabezera . . . la mujer que a mi me quiera . . . ha de quererme de veras. Ay, Ay, Ay, corazón, porque no amas.*[3] . . . I must have heard it a thousand times since the idea of a bed made of stone, and its connection to love, first troubled me with its disturbing images.

The five-minute home movie ends with people dancing in a circle — the creative filmmaker must have set it up so that all of them could file past him. It is both comical and sad to watch silent dancing. Since there is no justification for the absurd movements that music provides for some

---

[2]*sofrito:* A cooked condiment. A sauce composed of a mixture of fatback, ham, tomatoes, and many island spices and herbs. It is added to many Puerto Rican dishes for a distinctive flavor. — COFER'S NOTE.

[3]*De piedra ha de ser . . . amas:* Lyrics from a popular romantic balled (called a *bolero* in Puerto Rico). Freely translated: "My bed will be made of stone, of stone also my headrest (or pillow), the woman who (dares to) love me, will have to love me for real. Ay, Ay, Ay, my heart, why can't you (let me) love. . . ." — COFER'S NOTE.

of us, people appear frantic, their faces embarrassingly intense. It's as if you were watching sex. Yet for years I've had dreams in the form of this home movie. In a recurring scene, familiar faces push themselves forward into my mind's eyes, plastering their features into distorted close-ups. And I'm asking them: "Who is *she*? Who is the old woman I don't recognize? Is she an aunt? Somebody's wife? Tell me who she is."

"See the beauty mark on her cheek as big as a hill on the lunar landscape of her face—well, that runs in the family. The women on your father's side of the family wrinkle early; it's the price they pay for that fair skin. The young girl with the green stain on her wedding dress is *La Novia*—just up from the Island. See, she lowers her eyes when she approaches the camera, as she's supposed to. Decent girls never look at you directly in the face. *Humilde*, humble, a girl should express humility in all her actions. She will make a good wife for your cousin. He should consider himself lucky to have met her only weeks after she arrived here. If he marries her quickly, she will make him a good Puerto Rican–style wife; but if he waits too long, she will be corrupted by the city—just like your cousin there."

"She means me. I do what I want. This is not some primitive island I live on. Do they expect me to wear a black mantilla on my head and go to mass every day? Not me. I'm an American woman, and I will do as I please. I can type faster than anyone in my senior class at Central High, and I'm going to be a secretary to a lawyer when I graduate. I can pass for an American girl anywhere—I've tried it. At least for Italian, anyway—I never speak Spanish in public. I hate these parties, but I wanted the dress. I look better than any of these *humildes* here. My life is going to be different. I have an American boyfriend. He is older and has a car. My parents don't know it, but I sneak out of the house late at night sometimes to be with him. If I marry him, even my name will be American. I hate rice and beans—that's what makes these women fat."

"Your *prima*[4] is pregnant by that man she's been sneaking around with. Would I lie to you? I'm your *Tía Política*,[5] your great-uncle's common-law wife—the one he abandoned on the Island to go marry your cousin's mother. *I* was not invited to this party, of course, but I came anyway. I came to tell you that story about your cousin that you've always wanted to hear. Do you remember the comment your mother made to a neighbor that has always haunted you? The only thing you heard was your cousin's name, and then you saw your mother pick up your doll from the couch and say: 'It was as big as this doll when they flushed it down the toilet.' This image has bothered you for years, hasn't it? You had nightmares about babies being flushed down the toilet, and you wondered why anyone would do such a horrible thing. You didn't dare ask your mother about it. She would only tell you that you had not heard her right, and yell

[4]*prima:* Female cousin. —Cofer's Note.
[5]*Tía Política:* Aunt by marriage. —Cofer's Note.

at you for listening to adult conversations. But later, when you were old enough to know about abortions, you suspected.

"I am here to tell you that you were right. Your cousin was growing an *Americanito* in her belly when this movie was made. Soon after she put something long and pointy into her pretty self, thinking maybe she could get rid of the problem before breakfast and still make it to her first class at the high school. Well, *Niña*,[6] her screams could be heard downtown. Your aunt, her mamá, who had been a midwife on the Island, managed to pull the little thing out. Yes, they probably flushed it down the toilet. What else could they do with it—give it a Christian burial in a little white casket with blue bows and ribbons? Nobody wanted that baby—least of all the father, a teacher at her school with a house in West Paterson that he was filling with real children, and a wife who was a natural blonde.

"Girl, the scandal sent your uncle back to the bottle. And guess where your cousin ended up? Irony of ironies. She was sent to a village in Puerto Rico to live with a relative on her mother's side: a place so far away from civilization that you have to ride a mule to reach it. A real change in scenery. She found a man there—women like that cannot live without male company—but believe me, the men in Puerto Rico know how to put a saddle on a woman like her. *La Gringa*,[7] they call her. Ha, ha, ha. *La Gringa* is what she always wanted to be. . . ."

The old woman's mouth becomes a cavernous black hole I fall into. And as I fall, I can feel the reverberations of her laughter. I hear the echoes of her last mocking words: *La Gringa, La Gringa!* And the conga line keeps moving silently past me. There is no music in my dream for the dancers.

When Odysseus visits Hades to see the spirit of his mother, he makes an offering of sacrificial blood, but since all the souls crave an audience with the living, he has to listen to many of them before he can ask questions. I, too, have to hear the dead and the forgotten speak in my dream. Those who are still part of my life remain silent, going around and around in their dance. The others keep pressing their faces forward to say things about the past.

My father's uncle is last in line. He is dying of alcoholism, shrunken   25 and shriveled like a monkey, his face a mass of wrinkles and broken arteries. As he comes closer I realize that in his features I can see my whole family. If you were to stretch that rubbery flesh, you could find my father's face, and deep within *that* face—my own. I don't want to look into those eyes ringed in purple. In a few years he will retreat into silence, and take a long, long time to die. *Move back, Tío,* I tell him. *I don't want to hear what you have to say. Give the dancers room to move. Soon it will be midnight. Who is the New Year's Fool this time?*

---

[6]*Niña:* Girl.—COFER'S NOTE.
[7]*La Gringa:* Derogatory epithet used here to ridicule a Puerto Rican girl who wants to look like a blonde North American.—COFER'S NOTE.

The Reader's Presence

1. In "Silent Dancing," Cofer explores the personal, familial, and communal transformations that resulted from moving in the 1950s to Paterson, New Jersey—to "a huge tenement that had once housed Jewish families" and to a new community that emerged from the sprawling barrio that Puerto Ricans "overflowing from New York City" called home. Reread the essay carefully, and summarize the transformations that occurred in the life of the narrator, her family, and their larger Puerto Rican community.

2. Cofer uses an account of a home movie to create a structure for her essay. What are the specific advantages and disadvantages of this strategy? How, for example, does the home movie serve as "a great visual aid" to recounting life in the barrio of Paterson, New Jersey? What effect does the fact that the home movie is in color have on what Cofer notices? on how she writes?

3. Because Cofer's essay is built around the occasion of watching a home movie, the narrator assumes the position of an observer of the scenes and people Cofer describes. What specific strategies as a writer does Cofer use to establish a presence for herself in this narrative and descriptive account of growing up?

4. In his attempt to aid the family's "assimilation" into American culture, Cofer's father forbids his wife and children from making friends in "El Building." Cofer and her mother were expected "to keep the doors locked, the noise down, ourselves to ourselves" (paragraph 3). As a result, Cofer at times feels alienated from her own relatives. How does her situation compare to that of the narrator of Maxine Hong Kingston's "No Name Woman" (page 447)?

THE WRITER AT WORK

Judith Ortiz Cofer on Memory and Personal Essays

In setting out to write essays recounting her family history, Judith Ortiz Cofer found in Virginia Woolf a brilliant mentor and guide who taught her how to release the creative power of memory. In the following preface to Silent Dancing: A Partial Remembrance of a Puerto Rican Childhood, *Cofer pays tribute to Woolf, who "understood that the very act of reclaiming her memories could provide a writer with confidence in the power of art to discover meaning and truth in ordinary events." How do Cofer's remarks in the preface (which she called "Journey to a Summer's Afternoon"), along with Woolf's "The Death of the Moth" (page 601), help illuminate the artistry of Cofer's own essay, "Silent Dancing"?*

As one gets older, childhood years are often conveniently consolidated into one perfect summer's afternoon. The events can be projected on a light blue screen; the hurtful parts can be edited out, and the moments of joy brought in sharp focus to the foreground. It is our show. But with all that on the cutting room floor, what remains to tell?

Virginia Woolf, whose vision guided my efforts as I tried to recall the faces and words of the people who are a part of my "summer's afternoon," wrote of the problem of writing truth from memory. In "A Sketch of the Past" she says, "But if I turn to my mother, how difficult it is to single her out as she really was; to imagine what she was thinking, to put a single sentence into her mouth." She accepts the fact that in writing about one's life, one often has to rely on that combination of memory, imagination, and strong emotion that may result in "poetic truth." In preparing to write her memoirs Woolf said, "I dream, I make up pictures of a summer's afternoon."

In one of her essays from her memoir *Moments of Being*, Woolf recalls the figure of her beautiful and beloved mother who died while the author was still a child, leaving her a few precious "moments of being" from which the mature woman must piece together a childhood. And she does so not to showcase her life, extraordinary as it was, but rather out of a need most of us feel at some point to study ourselves and our lives in retrospect; to understand what people and events formed us (and, yes, what and who hurt us, too).

From "A Sketch of the Past": "Many bright colors; many distinct sounds; some human beings, caricatures; several violent moments of being, always including a circle of the scene they cut out: and all surrounded by a vast space — that is a rough visual description of childhood. This is how I shape it; and how I see myself as a child. . . ."

This passage illustrates the approach that I was seeking in writing   5
about my family. I wanted the essays to be, not just family history, but also creative explorations of known territory. I wanted to trace back through scenes based on my "moments of being" the origins of my creative imagination. As a writer, I am, like most artists, interested in the genesis of ideas: How does a poem begin? Can the process be triggered at will? What compels some of us to examine and re-examine our lives in poems, stories, novels, memoirs?

Much of my writing begins as a meditation on past events. But memory for me is the "jumping off" point; I am not, in my poetry and my fiction writing, a slave to memory. I like to believe that the poem or story contains the "truth" of art rather than the factual, historical truth that the journalist, sociologist, scientist — most of the rest of the world — must adhere to. Art gives me that freedom. But in writing these "essays" (the Spanish word for essay, *ensayo*, suits my meaning here better — it can mean "a rehearsal," an exercise or practice), I faced the possibility that the past is mainly a creation of the imagination also, although there are facts one can research and confirm. The biographer's time-honored task can be employed on one's own life too. There are birth, marriage, and death certificates on file, there are letters and family photographs in someone's desk or attic; and there are the relatives who have assigned themselves the role of genealogist or family bard, recounting at the least instigation the entire history of your clan. One can go to these sources and come up with a *Life* in several volumes that will make your mother proud and give you the satisfaction of having "preserved" something. I am not interested in merely "canning" memories, however, and Woolf gave me the focus that I needed to justify this work. Its intention is not to chronicle my life—which in my case is still very much "in-progress," nor are there any extraordinary accomplishments to showcase; neither is it meant to be a record of public events and personal histories (in fact, since most of the characters in these essays are based on actual, living persons and real places, whenever I felt that it was necessary to protect their identities, I changed names, locations, etc.). Then, what is the purpose of calling this collection nonfiction or a memoir? Why not just call it fiction? Once again I must turn to my literary mentor for this project, Virginia Woolf, for an answer: like her, I wanted to try to connect myself to the threads of lives that have touched mine and at some point converged into the tapestry that is my memory of childhood. Virginia Woolf understood that the very act of reclaiming her memories could provide a writer with confidence in the power of art to discover meaning and truth in ordinary events. She was a time-traveler who saw the past as a real place one could return to by following the tracks left by strong emotions: "I feel that strong emotion must leave its trace; and it is only a question of discovering how we can get ourselves attached to it, so that we shall be able to live our lives through from the start."[1]

It was this winding path of memory, marked by strong emotions, that I followed in my *ensayos* of a life.

---

[1]All quotes by Virginia Woolf are from *Moments of Being* (Harcourt Brace Jovanovich, Inc.).—AUTHOR'S NOTE.

Bernard Cooper

A Clack of Tiny Sparks: Remembrances of a Gay Boyhood

Born (1951), raised, and still residing in Los Angeles, Bernard Cooper received his BFA and MFA from the California Institute of the Arts. He has taught at the Otis/Parsons Institute of Art and Design and Southern California Institute of Architecture, Los Angeles, and at the UCLA writing program; he is now an art critic for Los Angeles Magazine. *His two collections of personal essays,* Maps to Anywhere *(1990) and* Truth Serum *(1996), cover a wide range of topics from the aging of his father, to his gay awakening, to the future of American life and culture. A collection of short stories,* Guess Again, *was published in 2000 and his latest memoir,* The Bill from My Father, *in 2006. Cooper contributes to various periodicals such as* Harper's, *where "A Clack of Tiny Sparks: Remembrances of a Gay Boyhood" first appeared in January 1991.*

Commenting on his 1993 novel, A Year of Rhymes, *Cooper notes, "One of the reasons why there is so much detail in my work is that I'm a person that essentially shies away from abstractions, from Large Issues and Big Ideas. The world only seems real and vivid and meaningful to me in the smaller details, what's heard and felt and smelled and tasted."*

Theresa Sanchez sat behind me in ninth-grade algebra. When Mr. Hubbley faced the blackboard, I'd turn around to see what she was reading; each week a new book was wedged inside her copy of *Today's Equations*. The deception worked; from Mr. Hubbley's point of view, Theresa was engrossed in the value of *X*, but I knew otherwise. One week she perused *The Wisdom of the Orient*, and I could tell from Theresa's contemplative expression that the book contained exotic thoughts, guidelines handed down from high. Another week it was a paperback novel whose title, *Let Me Live My Life*, appeared in bold print atop every page, and whose cover, a gauzy photograph of a woman biting a strand of pearls, head thrown back in an attitude of ecstasy, confirmed my suspicion that Theresa Sanchez was mature beyond her years. She was the tallest girl in school. Her bouffant hairdo, streaked with blond, was higher than the flaccid bouffants of other girls. Her smooth skin, plucked eyebrows, and painted fingernails suggested hours of pampering, a worldly and sensual vanity that placed her within the domain of adults. Smiling dimly, steeped in daydreams, Theresa moved through the crowded halls with a languid, self-satisfied indifference to those around her. "You are merely children," her posture seemed to say. "I can't be bothered." The week Theresa hid *101 Ways to Cook Hamburger* behind her algebra book, I could stand it no longer and, after the bell rang, ventured a question.

"Because I'm having a dinner party," said Theresa. "Just a couple of intimate friends."

No fourteen-year-old I knew had ever given a dinner party, let alone used the word "intimate" in conversation. "Don't you have a mother?" I asked.

Theresa sighed a weary sigh, suffered my strange inquiry. "Don't be so naïve," she said. "Everyone has a mother." She waved her hand to indicate the brick school buildings outside the window. "A higher education should have taught you that." Theresa draped an angora sweater over her shoulders, scooped her books from the graffiti-covered desk, and just as she was about to walk away, she turned and asked me, "Are you a fag?"

There wasn't the slightest hint of rancor or condescension in her   5
voice. The tone was direct, casual. Still I was stunned, giving a sidelong glance to make sure no one had heard. "No," I said. Blurted really, with too much defensiveness, too much transparent fear in my response. Octaves lower than usual, I tried a "Why?"

Theresa shrugged. "Oh, I don't know. I have lots of friends who are fags. You remind me of them." Seeing me bristle, Theresa added, "It was just a guess." I watched her erect, angora back as she sauntered out the classroom door.

She had made an incisive and timely guess. Only days before, I'd invited Grady Rogers to my house after school to go swimming. The instant Grady shot from the pool, shaking water from his orange hair, freckled shoulders shining, my attraction to members of my own sex became a matter I could no longer suppress or rationalize. Sturdy and boisterous and gap-toothed, Grady was an inveterate backslapper, a formidable arm wrestler, a wizard at basketball. Grady was a boy at home in his body.

My body was a marvel I hadn't gotten used to; my arms and legs would sometimes act of their own accord, knocking over a glass at dinner or flinching at an oncoming pitch. I was never singled out as a sissy, but I could have been just as easily as Bobby Keagan, a gentle, intelligent, and introverted boy reviled by my classmates. And although I had always been aware of a tacit rapport with Bobby, a suspicion that I might find with him a rich friendship, I stayed away. Instead, I emulated Grady in the belief that being seen with him, being like him, would somehow vanquish my self-doubt, would make me normal by association.

Apart from his athletic prowess, Grady had been gifted with all the trappings of what I imagined to be a charmed life: a fastidious, aproned mother who radiated calm, maternal concern; a ruddy, stoic father with a knack for home repairs. Even the Rogerses' small suburban house in Hollywood, with its spindly Colonial furniture and chintz curtains, was a testament to normalcy.

Grady and his family bore little resemblance to my clan of Eastern European Jews, a dark and vociferous people who ate with abandon—matzo   10 and halvah and gefilte fish; foods the goyim couldn't pronounce—who cajoled one another during endless games of canasta, making the simplest remark about the weather into a lengthy philosophical discourse on the sun and the seasons and the passage of time. My mother was a chain-smoker, a dervish in a frowsy housedress. She showed her love in the most peculiar and obsessive ways, like spending hours extracting every seed from a watermelon before she served it in perfectly bite-sized, geometric pieces. Preoccupied and perpetually frantic, my mother succumbed to bouts of absentmindedness so profound she'd forget what she was saying midsentence, smile and blush and walk away. A divorce attorney, my father wore roomy, iridescent suits, and the intricacies, the deceits inherent in his profession, had the effect of making him forever tense and vigilant. He was "all wound up," as my mother put it. But when he relaxed, his laughter was explosive, his disposition prankish: "Walk this way," a waitress would say, leading us to our table, and my father would mimic the way she walked, arms akimbo, hips liquid, while my mother and I were wracked with laughter. Buoyant or brooding, my parents' moods were unpredictable, and in a household fraught with extravagant emotion it was odd and awful to keep my longing secret.

One day I made the mistake of asking my mother what a "fag" was. I knew exactly what Theresa had meant but hoped against hope it was not what I thought; maybe "fag" was some French word, a harmless term like "naïve." My mother turned from the stove, flew at me, and grabbed me by the shoulders. "Did someone call you that?" she cried.

"Not me," I said. "Bobby Keagan."

"Oh," she said, loosening her grip. She was visibly relieved. And didn't answer. The answer was unthinkable.

For weeks after, I shook with the reverberations from that afternoon in the kitchen with my mother, pained by the memory of her shocked expression and, most of all, her silence. My longing was wrong in the eyes of my mother, whose hazel eyes were the eyes of the world, and if that longing continued unchecked, the unwieldy shape of my fate would be cast, and I'd be subjected to a lifetime of scorn.

During the remainder of the semester, I became the scientist of my own desire, plotting ways to change my yearning for boys into a yearning for girls. I had enough evidence to believe that any habit, regardless of how compulsive, how deeply ingrained, could be broken once and for all: The plastic cigarette my mother purchased at the Thrifty pharmacy—one end was red to approximate an ember, the other tan like a filtered tip—was designed to wean her from the real thing. To change a behavior required self-analysis, cold resolve, and the substitution of one thing for another: plastic, say, for tobacco. Could I also find a substitute for Grady? What I needed to do, I figured, was kiss a girl and learn to like it.

This conclusion was affirmed one Sunday morning when my father, seeing me wrinkle my nose at the pink slabs of lox he layered on a bagel, tried to convince me of its salty appeal. "You should try some," he said. "You don't know what you're missing."

"It's loaded with protein," added my mother, slapping a platter of sliced onions onto the dinette table. She hovered above us, cinching her housedress, eyes wet from onion fumes, the mock cigarette dangling from her lips.

My father sat there chomping with gusto, emitting a couple of hearty grunts to dramatize his satisfaction. And still I was not convinced. After a loud and labored swallow, he told me I may not be fond of lox today, but sooner or later I'd learn to like it. One's tastes, he assured me, are destined to change.

"Live," shouted my mother over the rumble of the Mixmaster. "Expand your horizons. Try new things." And the room grew fragrant with the batter of a spice cake.

The opportunity to put their advice into practice, and try out my plan to adapt to girls, came the following week when Debbie Coburn, a member of Mr. Hubbley's algebra class, invited me to a party. She cornered me in the hall, furtive as a spy, telling me her parents would be gone for the evening and slipping into my palm a wrinkled sheet of notebook paper. On it were her address and telephone number, the lavender ink in a tidy cursive. "Wear cologne," she advised, wary eyes darting back and forth. "It's a make-out party. Anything can happen."

The Santa Ana wind blew relentlessly the night of Debbie's party, careening down the slopes of the Hollywood hills, shaking the road signs and stoplights in its path. As I walked down Beachwood Avenue, trees thrashed, surrendered their leaves, and carob pods bombarded the pavement. The sky was a deep but luminous blue, the air hot, abrasive, electric. I had to squint in order to check the number of the Coburns' apartment, a three-story building with glitter embedded in its stucco walls. Above the honeycombed balconies was a sign that read BEACHWOOD TERRACE in lavender script resembling Debbie's.

From down the hall, I could hear the plaintive strains of Little Anthony's "I Think I'm Going Out of My Head." Debbie answered the door bedecked in an Empire dress, the bodice blue and orange polka dots, the rest a sheath of black and white stripes. "Op art," proclaimed Debbie. She turned in a circle, then proudly announced that she'd rolled her hair in orange juice cans. She patted the huge unmoving curls and dragged me inside. Reflections from the swimming pool in the courtyard, its surface ruffled by wind, shuddered over the ceiling and walls. A dozen of my classmates were seated on the sofa or huddled together in corners, their whispers full of excited imminence, their bodies barely discernible in the dim light. Drapes flanking the sliding glass doors bowed out with every gust of wind, and it seemed that the room might lurch from its foundations and sail with its cargo of silhouettes into the hot October night.

Grady was the last to arrive. He tossed a six-pack of beer into Debbie's arms, barreled toward me, and slapped my back. His hair was slicked back with Vitalis, lacquered furrows left by the comb. The wind hadn't shifted a single hair. "Ya ready?" he asked, flashing the gap between his front teeth and leering into the darkened room. "You bet," I lied.

Once the beers had been passed around, Debbie provoked everyone's attention by flicking on the overhead light. "Okay," she called. "Find a partner." This was the blunt command of a hostess determined to have her guests aroused in an orderly fashion. Everyone blinked, shuffled about, and grabbed a member of the opposite sex. Sheila Garabedian landed beside me—entirely at random, though I wanted to believe she was driven by passion—her timid smile giving way to plain fear as the light went out. Nothing for a moment but the heave of the wind and the distant banter of dogs. I caught a whiff of Sheila's perfume, tangy and sweet as Hawaiian Punch. I probed her face with my own, grazing the small scallop of an ear, a velvety temple, and though Sheila's trembling made me want to stop, I persisted with my mission until I found her lips, tightly sealed as a private letter. I held my mouth over hers and gathered her shoulders closer, resigned to the possibility that, no matter how long we stood there, Sheila would be too scared to kiss me back. Still, she exhaled through her nose, and I listened to the squeak of every breath as though it were a sigh of inordinate pleasure. Diving within myself, I monitored my heartbeat and respiration, trying to will stimulation into being, and all the while an image intruded, an image of Grady erupting from our pool, rivulets of water sliding down his chest. "Change," shouted Debbie, switching on the light. Sheila thanked me, pulled away, and continued her routine of gracious terror with every boy throughout the evening. It didn't matter whom I held— Margaret Sims, Betty Vernon, Elizabeth Lee—my experiment was a failure; I continued to picture Grady's wet chest, and Debbie would bellow "change" with such fervor, it could have been my own voice, my own incessant reprimand.

Our hostess commandeered the light switch for nearly half an hour. 25 Whenever the light came on, I watched Grady pivot his head toward the newest prospect, his eyebrows arched in expectation, his neck blooming with hickeys, his hair, at last, in disarray. All that shuffling across the carpet charged everyone's arms and lips with static, and eventually, between low moans and soft osculations, I could hear the clack of tiny sparks and see them flare here and there in the dark like meager, short-lived stars.

I saw Theresa, sultry and aloof as ever, read three more books—*North American Reptiles*, *Bonjour Tristesse*, and *MGM: A Pictorial History*—before she vanished early in December. Rumors of her fate abounded. Debbie Coburn swore that Theresa had been "knocked up" by an older man, a traffic cop, she thought, or a grocer. Nearly quivering with relish, Debbie told me and Grady about the home for unwed mothers in the San Fernando Valley, a compound teeming with pregnant girls who had nothing to do but touch their stomachs and contemplate their mistake. Even Bobby Keagan, who took Theresa's place behind me in algebra, had a theory regarding her disappearance colored by his own wish for escape; he imagined that Theresa, disillusioned with society, booked passage to a tropical island, there to live out the rest of her days without restrictions or ridicule. "No wonder she flunked out of school," I overheard Mr. Hubbley tell a fellow teacher one afternoon. "Her head was always in a book."

Along with Theresa went my secret, or at least the dread that she might divulge it, and I felt, for a while, exempt from suspicion. I was, however, to run across Theresa one last time. It happened during a period of torrential rain that, according to reports on the six o'clock news, washed houses from the hillsides and flooded the downtown streets. The halls of Joseph Le Conte Junior High were festooned with Christmas decorations: crepe-paper garlands, wreaths studded with plastic berries, and one requisite Star of David twirling above the attendance desk. In Arts and Crafts, our teacher, Gerald (he was the only teacher who allowed us— *required* us—to call him by his first name), handed out blocks of balsa wood and instructed us to carve them into bugs. We would paint eyes and antennae with tempera and hang them on a Christmas tree he'd made the previous night. "Voilà," he crooned, unveiling his creation from a burlap sack. Before us sat a tortured scrub, a wardrobe-worth of wire hangers that were bent like branches and soldered together. Gerald credited his inspiration to a Charles Addams cartoon he's seen in which Morticia, grimly preparing for the holidays, hangs vampire bats on a withered pine. "All that red and green," said Gerald. "So predictable. *So boring.*"

As I chiseled a beetle and listened to rain pummel the earth, Gerald handed me an envelope and asked me to take it to Mr. Kendrick, the drama teacher. I would have thought nothing of his request if I hadn't seen Theresa on my way down the hall. She was cleaning out her locker, blithely dropping the sum of its contents—pens and textbooks and mimeographs—into a trash can. "Have a nice life," she sang as I passed. I mustered the courage to ask her what had happened. We stood alone in the silent hall, the reflections of wreaths and garlands submerged in brown linoleum.

"I transferred to another school. They don't have grades or bells, and you get to study whatever you want." Theresa was quick to sense my incredulity. "Honest," she said. "The school is progressive." She gazed into a glass cabinet that held the trophies of track meets and intramural spelling bees. "God," she sighed, "this place is so . . . barbaric." I was still trying to decide whether or not to believe her story when she asked me where I was headed. "Dear," she said, her exclamation pooling in the silence, "that's no ordinary note, if you catch my drift." The envelope was blank and white; I looked up at Theresa, baffled. "Don't be so naïve," she muttered, tossing an empty bottle of nail polish into the trash can. It struck bottom with a resolute thud. "Well," she said, closing her locker and breathing deeply, "bon voyage." Theresa swept through the double doors and in seconds her figure was obscured by rain.

As I walked toward Mr. Kendrick's room, I could feel Theresa's insinuation burrow in. I stood for a moment and watched Mr. Kendrick through the pane in the door. He paced intently in front of the class, handsome in his shirt and tie, reading from a thick book. Chalked on the blackboard behind him was THE ODYSSEY BY HOMER. I have no recollection of how Mr. Kendrick reacted to the note, whether he accepted it with pleasure or embarrassment, slipped it into his desk drawer or the pocket of his shirt. I have scavenged that day in retrospect, trying to see Mr. Kendrick's expression, wondering if he acknowledged me in any way as his liaison. All I recall is the sight of his mime through a pane of glass, a lone man mouthing an epic, his gestures ardent in empty air.

Had I delivered a declaration of love? I was haunted by the need to know. In fantasy, a kettle shot steam, the glue released its grip, and I read the letter with impunity. But how would such a letter begin? Did the common endearments apply? This was a message between two men, a message for which I had no precedent, and when I tried to envision the contents, apart from a hasty, impassioned scrawl, my imagination faltered.

Once or twice I witnessed Gerald and Mr. Kendrick walk together into the faculty lounge or say hello at the water fountain, but there was nothing especially clandestine or flirtatious in their manner. Besides, no matter how acute my scrutiny, I wasn't sure, short of a kiss, exactly what to look for—what semaphore of gesture, what encoded word. I suspected there were signs, covert signs that would give them away, just as I'd unwittingly given myself away to Theresa.

In the school library, a *Webster's* unabridged dictionary lay on a wooden podium, and I padded toward it with apprehension; along with clues to the bond between my teachers, I risked discovering information that might incriminate me as well. I had decided to consult the dictionary during lunch period, when most of the students would be on the playground. I clutched my notebook, moving in such a way as to appear both studious and nonchalant, actually believing that, unless I took precautions, someone would see me and guess what I was up to. The closer I came to the podium, the more obvious, I thought, was my endeavor; I felt like the model of The Visible Man in our science class, my heart's undulations, my overwrought nerves legible through transparent skin. A couple of kids riffled through the card catalogue. The librarian, a skinny woman whose perpetual whisper and rubber-soled shoes caused her to drift through the room like a phantom, didn't seem to register my presence. Though I'd looked up dozens of words before, the pages felt strange beneath my fingers. *Homer* was the first word I saw. *Hominid. Homogenize.* I feigned interest and skirted other words before I found the word I was after. Under the heading HO·MO·SEX·U·AL was the terse definition: *adj. Pertaining to, characteristic of, or exhibiting homosexuality.* —*n. A homosexual person.* I read the definition again and again, hoping the words would yield more than they could. I shut the dictionary, swallowed hard, and, none the wiser, hurried away.

As for Gerald and Mr. Kendrick, I never discovered evidence to prove or dispute Theresa's claim. By the following summer, however, I had overheard from my peers a confounding amount about homosexuals: They wore green on Thursday, couldn't whistle, hypnotized boys with a piercing glance. To this lore, Grady added a surefire test to ferret them out.

"A test?" I said.

35

"You ask a guy to look at his fingernails, and if he looks at them like this" — Grady closed his fingers into a fist and examined his nails with manly detachment — "then he's okay. But if he does this" — he held out his hands at arm's length, splayed his fingers, and coyly cocked his head — "you'd better watch out." Once he'd completed his demonstration, Grady peeled off his shirt and plunged into our pool. I dove in after. It was early June, the sky immense, glassy, placid. My father was cooking spareribs on the barbecue, an artist with a basting brush. His apron bore the caricature of a frazzled French chef. Mother curled on a chaise lounge, plumes of smoke wafting from her nostrils. In a stupor of contentment she took another drag, closed her eyes, and arched her face toward the sun.

Grady dog-paddled through the deep end, spouting a fountain of chlorinated water. Despite shame and confusion, my longing for him hadn't diminished; it continued to thrive without air and light, like a luminous fish in the dregs of the sea. In the name of play, I swam up behind him, encircled his shoulders, astonished by his taut flesh. The two of us flailed, pretended to drown. Beneath the heavy press of water, Grady's orange hair wavered, a flame that couldn't be doused.

I've lived with a man for seven years. Some nights, when I'm half-asleep and the room is suffused with blue light, I reach out to touch the expanse of his back, and it seems as if my fingers sink into his skin, and I feel the pleasure a diver feels the instant he enters a body of water.

I have few regrets. But one is that I hadn't said to Theresa, "Of course I'm a fag." Maybe I'd have met her friends. Or become friends with her. Imagine the meals we might have concocted: hamburger Stroganoff, Swedish meatballs in a sweet translucent sauce, steaming slabs of Salisbury steak.

The Reader's Presence

1. Cooper's first stirrings of attraction for his friend Grady occur in a swimming pool. What importance does swimming play in Cooper's essay? How does it provide him with a cluster of images for sexual experience?

2. Why does Cooper attend the "make-out party"? What does he hope will happen? Why do you think he ends his description of the party with the observation of the "clack of tiny sparks"? Why do you think he used that image for his title?

3. In paragraph 15, Cooper writes that he became "the scientist of
   [his] own desire," as he tried to understand—and to resist—his
   "yearning for boys." In what ways does Cooper's experience resemble Andrew Sullivan's in "The M-Word: Why It Matters to
   Me" (page 246). What differences do you find in the author's
   process of self-discovery? Children often turn to dictionaries to
   solve mysteries they are too shy to ask people about. How does
   Cooper's discovery of the definition of "homosexual" compare to
   Frederick Douglass's attempt to discover the meaning of "abolition" in "Learning to Read and Write" (page 94)?

Meghan Daum

Toy Children

*Author and journalist, Meghan Daum (b. 1970), was born in California,
grew up in Ridgewood, New Jersey, and spent several years living in New York
City after receiving her MFA from Columbia University's School of the Arts. In
1999, Daum decided to quit New York and move to Nebraska, out of which
came her 2003 novel,* The Quality of Life Report, *a* New York Times *Notable
Book in 2003. Her essay "Toy Children" comes from her 2001 essay collection,*
My Misspent Youth. *Daum is a frequent contributor to such publications as the*
New Yorker, GQ, Self, Harper's, *the* Village Voice, *and the* New York Times
Book Review. *Her commentaries and audio essays have been heard on National
Public Radio's* Morning Edition, Marketplace, Talk of the Nation, *and* This
American Life. *Daum lives in Los Angeles, where she writes a weekly op-ed col-
umn about current social and cultural issues for the* Los Angeles Times.*

In a conversation between Meghan Daum and Joan Didion that appeared in
BlackBook *in 2004, they talked about the differences between essays and memoir.*

***Daum:** I also think that many people don't make any distinction between an
essay and a memoir or confession, and I always want to be really clear with people that for me an essay is an outward inquiry, it's trying to figure out a problem,
and I would never ever sit down to write an essay unless it was going to transcend
my own experience.*

***Didion:** Right, but it is built on personal reference points because an essay
has an "I" in it.*

***Daum:** Yeah, but it's not memoir. Memoir is allowed to stop at the end of
the specific experience, and I think the essay demands transcendence and a thesis.
I don't see it as confessional, because I think you should know everything about*

the narrator but nothing about the author, which I always felt you pulled off
beautifully. As readers, we're very much at arm's length the whole time.

Though I had a stuffed-animal collection that rivaled the inventory of
a Toys "R" Us, I was a child who hated dolls. By "hate," I'm not talking
about a cool indifference. I'm talking about a palpable loathing, a dislike
so intense that my salient memory of doll ownership concerns a plastic
baby whose duty among my playthings consisted solely of being thrown
against the wall repeatedly and then smudged with a combination of red
lipstick, purple Crayola, and, when available, spaghetti sauce. This was
done in an effort to simulate severe injury, possibly even internal bleeding, and this doll, who, if I recall correctly, had eyes that opened and shut
and therefore had come preassigned with the name Baby Drowsy, spent
most of her time in a shoe box in my closet. This was the intensive care
unit, the place where, when I could no longer stand the sight of Baby
Drowsy's fat, contusion-ridden face, I would Scotch-tape a folded Kleenex
to her forehead and announce to my mother that Baby Drowsy had been
in yet another massive car wreck. I would then proceed to tend with
painstaking care to my thirty-plus animals, all of whom I had personally
christened with names like Excellent Eagle, Mr. Nice, and Soft Koala, and
who, I was entirely certain, could communicate with both myself and
each other through a complex telepathy. I say complex because, even at
five, I had the ability to convey my thoughts to individual animals and
then conference-in others should the discussion be relevant. They could
do the same when they talked amongst themselves. Eeyore could discuss
the events of the day with Squiffy. Peter Panda could alert Bunny Rabbit
that he had fallen behind the bed. Everyone knew about Baby Drowsy's
frequent mishaps. And none of us really cared. In the social hierarchy of
my bedroom, animals ranked highest. Dolls were somewhere between dust
balls and cockroaches. They were uninvited guests that gathered in the
corners, something to be stomped on.

But since I was a girl, I had dolls. People gave them to me, though
Baby Drowsy was unquestionably subject to the most abuse. Something
about the word "drowsy" struck me as flaccid, even masochistic;[1] it was
as if drowsy was baby talk for "drown me," and the beatings seemed to
emerge out of a sense that she was asking for it. The handful of other
dolls had the luck of being simply ignored. I had a Raggedy Ann, whose
stuffed-animal-like properties redeemed her enough so that she would occasionally be placed next to—though never in the pile with—the dogs
and bears. My mother, perhaps worried about whatever maternal instincts were failing to develop in me, spent several years trying to find a
doll I might actually like. With chubby baby dolls clearly out of the question, she tried to introduce me to more sophisticated dolls, older girls in

---

[1]***masochistic:*** Adjective describing someone who derives pleasure from being abused,
punished, or dominated. — EDS.

higher quality plastic, dolls with hair to be brushed and tasteful clothes to be changed. Nothing amused me. I loved my animals, furry, long-tongued creatures who were safe from the hair-braiding, cradle-rocking proclivities of playmates, some of whom had the hubris, not to mention the bad sense, to bring their own dolls with them when visiting my house. By the time I was old enough to enter into the world of Barbies, my mother's quest to make a nurturer of me was subsumed by her feminist impulses. I was given no Barbies and received stuffed animals every Christmas until I was approximately twenty-seven.

While it might seem that my intense dislike for dolls is simply a dramatic manifestation of my intense affection for animals, I suspect that the whole doll issue is part of a larger semiotic[2] equation, an entire genre of girlhood—and childhood in general—that I could just never get with. While I can't say that I had an unhappy childhood, I was unhappy being a child. Just as there has not been a morning of my adult life when I don't wake up and thank the gods that I am no longer a kid, there was hardly a day between the ages of three and eighteen that I didn't yearn for the time when I would be a grown-up. Aside from the usual headaches of being a kid—the restricted freedoms, the semi-citizenship—what really ailed me were the trappings of kid-dom: the mandatory hopscotch, the inane cartoons, the cutesy names ascribed to daycare centers and recreation programs, like Little Rascals Preschool and Tiny Tot Tumbling. Why was a simple burger and fries called The Lone Ranger? Why did something as basic as food have to be repackaged to resemble a toy? Even as a child I resented this lowbrow aesthetic—the alphabet-block designs on everything, the music-box soundtrack, the relentless kitsch of it all.

Dolls are the ultimate symbol of childhood; they are toy children. Though I realize that playing with dolls is supposed to mimic the adult act of caring for children, playing with dolls always struck me as nothing more but childhood squared, a child doing a childish thing with a simulacrum[3] of a child. It was like some hideous vortex. Adults think it's cute when girls burp their dolls. We buy them dolls that cry, and dolls that pee. I think there's even a doll that spits up. Most people see this as endearing, even healthy in a biological imperative sense. I see it as an exercise in narcissism. But I suppose that says more about me than about the doll-buying public or the doll-diapering girls who are supposedly doing the thing that comes naturally to them but just didn't to me.

I read somewhere that women who choose not to have children are more likely to have grown up preferring stuffed animals to dolls. Though I'm probably still too young to make pronouncements about my wish to forgo motherhood, I must say that, at thirty, my desire for children is all but nil. Though it's not impossible for me to enjoy other people's kids, my biological clock seems to reside permanently in a time zone to my

5

---

[2]*semiotic:* Relating to the study of meaning in language forms, the relationship between signs and symbols, also called semantics.—EDS.

[3]*simulacrum:* An image or a representation.—EDS.

west. Babies amuse me only mildly, toddlers not at all, and children of the talking, television-watching, Happy-Meal–eating variety fill me with a kind of queasy empathy. When I see a mother with her child, I identify not with the adult but with the small person who, in my mind, seems trapped in a world governed by romanticized, consumer-driven notions of childhood. I see a kid and I think to myself, "I'm sorry you have to be a kid right now. I'm sorry you have to play with Legos. I'm sorry you have to ride in the back seat."

A psychiatrist would see this as regressive. A lot of other people would argue that childhood is about as pure as anything gets, that the preadolescent mind enjoys some kind of blissful exemption from adult concerns, and that little girls and, when given the opportunity, little boys, gravitate naturally towards dolls. Dolls, say the experts, are merely objects on which to practice the care-giving skills we need to survive as a species.

Though I can understand that, I still can't relate to it. To me, a child with a doll is a child who has been railroaded by the trappings of childhood. She has already acquired her first accessory, an inanimate version of herself, one that possibly even requires batteries. She has already tied up one hand, already spent more time looking down than looking around. You might ask how I make a distinction between the dreaded doll and the adored stuffed animal. Why is it that I can smile at the child with a bear but always end up pitying the child with a doll? Perhaps it's because animals are more closely connected with the imaginative world than dolls are. They are ageless, genderless, and come in colors that defy nature. To play with a stuffed panda, or, in my case, to telepathically communicate with one, is a creative act. To play with a doll is to stare yourself in the face, to gaze at an object that is forever trapped in infancy. Maybe that's why dolls frighten me so much. Forever trapped in babyhood, they threaten the very essence of life's possibilities. They're my greatest nightmare come true. They never, ever grow up.

The Reader's Presence

1. What do dolls represent to Daum? What explanation does she offer to account for the fact that she "hated dolls" when she was a child? Why did she prefer playing with stuffed animals to dolls? What did playing with stuffed animals provide that playing with dolls did not? Identify the specific anecdotes and examples Daum invokes to support her assertions, and comment on the effectiveness of each.

2. In paragraph 7, Daum declares: "To me, a child with a doll is a child who has been railroaded by the trappings of childhood." What does she mean by "the trappings of childhood"? What specific examples does she offer to substantiate her assertion? How

reasonable, accurate, and convincing do you find her claims? Apply this same standard to judge Daum's claim that "dolls are the ultimate symbol of childhood; they are toy children. Though I realize that playing with dolls is supposed to mimic the adult act of caring for children, playing with dolls always struck me as nothing more but childhood squared, a child doing a childish thing with a simulacrum of a child" (paragraph 4).

3. When and how does Daum anticipate the reader's response to her essay? To what extent did she anticipate *your* responses to each of the points she makes? Please support each point you make with detailed references to—and an analysis of—specific words and phrases.

4. In paragraph 5, Daum declares: "When I see a mother with her child, I identify not with the adult but with the small person who, in my mind, seems trapped in a world governed by romanticized, consumer-driven notions of childhood." Compare and contrast the pressures imposed on Daum's conception of self-identity in "Toy Children" with the expectations imposed on Judith Ortiz Cofer by members of her family in "Silent Dancing" (page 64). Which writer handles these pressures more effectively? Explain why.

Joan Didion

On Keeping a Notebook

The author of novels, short stories, screenplays, and essays, Joan Didion (b. 1934) began her career in 1956 as a staff writer at Vogue *magazine in New York. In 1963, she published her first novel,* Run River, *and the following year returned to her native California. Didion's essays have appeared in periodicals ranging from* Mademoiselle *to the* National Review. *Her essay "On Keeping a Notebook" can be found in her collection of essays,* Slouching Towards Bethlehem *(1968). Didion's other nonfiction publications include* The White Album *(1979),* Salvador *(1983),* Miami *(1987),* After Henry *(1992),* Political Fictions *(2001),* Fixed Ideas: America since 9.11 *(2003), and* Where I Was From *(2003). Her essays, written between 1968 and 2003, are collected in* We Tell Ourselves Stories in Order to Live *(2006).* The Year of Magical Thinking *(2005), Didion's account of grief and survival after the loss of her husband of forty years, John Gregory Dunne, and the near-fatal illness of their only child, won the 2005*

National Book Award for Nonfiction; Didion adapted her tragic memoir into a play, which opened on Broadway in 2007, starring Vanessa Redgrave and directed by David Hare.

Didion has defined a writer as "a person whose most absorbed and passionate hours are spent arranging words on pieces of paper. I write entirely to find out what's on my mind, what I'm thinking, what I'm looking at, what I'm seeing and what it means, what I want and what I'm afraid of." She has also said that "all writing is an attempt to find out what matters, to find the pattern in disorder, to find the grammar in the shimmer. Actually I don't know whether you find the grammar in the shimmer or you impose a grammar on the shimmer, but I am quite specific about the grammar — I mean it literally. The scene that you see in your mind finds its own structure; the structure dictates the arrangement of the words. . . . All the writer has to do really is to find the words." However, she warns, "You have to be alone to do this."

"'That woman Estelle,'" the note reads, "'is partly the reason why George Sharp and I are separated today.' *Dirty crepe-de-Chine wrapper, hotel bar, Wilmington RR, 9:45 a.m. August Monday morning.*"

Since the note is in my notebook, it presumably has some meaning to me. I study it for a long while. At first I have only the most general notion of what I was doing on an August Monday morning in the bar of the hotel across from the Pennsylvania Railroad station in Wilmington, Delaware (waiting for a train? missing one? 1960? 1961? why Wilmington?), but I do remember being there. The woman in the dirty crepe-de-Chine wrapper had come down from her room for a beer, and the bartender had heard before the reason why George Sharp and she were separated today. "Sure," he said, and went on mopping the floor. "You told me." At the other end of the bar is a girl. She is talking, pointedly, not to the man beside her but to a cat lying in the triangle of sunlight cast through the open door. She is wearing a plaid silk dress from Peck & Peck, and the hem is coming down.

Here is what it is: The girl has been on the Eastern Shore, and now she is going back to the city, leaving the man beside her, and all she can see ahead are the viscous summer sidewalks and the 3 a.m. long-distance calls that will make her lie awake and then sleep drugged through all the steaming mornings left in August (1960? 1961?). Because she must go directly from the train to lunch in New York, she wishes that she had a safety pin for the hem of the plaid silk dress, and she also wishes that she could forget about the hem and the lunch and stay in the cool bar that smells of disinfectant and malt and make friends with the woman in the crepe-de-Chine wrapper. She is afflicted by a little self-pity, and she wants to compare Estelles. That is what that was all about.

Why did I write it down? In order to remember, of course, but exactly what was it I wanted to remember? How much of it actually happened? Did any of it? Why do I keep a notebook at all? It is easy to deceive oneself on all those scores. The impulse to write things down is a peculiarly compulsive one, inexplicable to those who do not share it, useful only accidentally, only secondarily, in the way that any compulsion tries to justify itself. I suppose that it begins or does not begin in the cradle. Although I have felt compelled to write things down since I was five years old, I doubt that my daughter ever will, for she is a singularly blessed and accepting child, delighted with life exactly as life presents itself to her, unafraid to go to sleep and unafraid to wake up. Keepers of private notebooks are a different breed altogether, lonely and resistant rearrangers of things, anxious malcontents, children afflicted apparently at birth with some presentiment of loss.

My first notebook was a Big Five tablet, given to me by my mother   5
with the sensible suggestion that I stop whining and learn to amuse myself by writing down my thoughts. She returned the tablet to me a few years ago; the first entry is an account of a woman who believed herself to be freezing to death in the Arctic night, only to find, when day broke, that she had stumbled onto the Sahara Desert, where she would die of the heat before lunch. I have no idea what turn of a five-year-old's mind could have prompted so insistently "ironic" and exotic a story, but it does reveal a certain predilection for the extreme which has dogged me into adult life; perhaps if I were analytically inclined I would find it a truer story than any I might have told about Donald Johnson's birthday party or the day my cousin Brenda put Kitty Litter in the aquarium.

So the point of my keeping a notebook has never been, nor is it now, to have an accurate factual record of what I have been doing or thinking. That would be a different impulse entirely, an instinct for reality which I sometimes envy but do not possess. At no point have I ever been able successfully to keep a diary; my approach to daily life ranges from the grossly negligent to the merely absent, and on those few occasions when I have tried dutifully to record a day's events, boredom has so overcome me that the results are mysterious at best. What is this business about "shopping, typing piece, dinner with E, depressed"? Shopping for what? Typing what piece? Who is E? Was this "E" depressed, or was I depressed? Who cares?

In fact I have abandoned altogether that kind of pointless entry; instead I tell what some would call lies. "That's simply not true," the members of my family frequently tell me when they come up against my memory of a shared event. "The party was *not* for you, the spider was *not* a black widow, *it wasn't that way at all*." Very likely they are right, for not only have I always had trouble distinguishing between what happened and what merely might have happened, but I remain unconvinced that the distinction, for my purposes, matters. The cracked crab that I recall having for lunch the day my father came home from Detroit in 1945 must certainly be embroidery, worked into the day's pattern to lend verisimilitude; I was ten years old and would not now remember the cracked crab. The day's events did not turn on cracked crab. And yet it is precisely that fictitious crab that makes me see the afternoon all over again, a home movie run all too often, the father bearing gifts, the child weeping, an exercise in family love and guilt. Or that is what it was to me. Similarly, perhaps it never did snow that August in Vermont; perhaps there never were flurries in the night wind, and maybe no one else felt the ground hardening and summer already dead even as we pretended to bask in it, but that was how it felt to me, and it might as well have snowed, could have snowed, did snow.

How it felt to me: that is getting closer to the truth about a notebook. I sometimes delude myself about why I keep a notebook, imagine that some thrifty virtue derives from preserving everything observed. See enough and write it down, I tell myself, and then some morning when the world seems drained of wonder, some day when I am only going through the motions of doing what I am supposed to do, which is write — on that bankrupt morning I will simply open my notebook and there it will all be, a forgotten account with accumulated interest, paid passage back to the world out there: dialogue overheard in hotels and elevators and at the hatcheck counter in Pavillon (one middle-aged man shows his hat check to another and says, "That's my old football number"); impressions of Bettina Aptheker and Benjamin Sonnenberg and Teddy ("Mr. Acapulco") Stauffer; careful *aperçus*[1] about tennis bums and failed fashion models and Greek shipping heiresses, one of whom taught me a significant lesson (a lesson I could have learned from F. Scott Fitzgerald, but perhaps we all must meet the very rich for ourselves) by asking, when I arrived to interview her in her orchid-filled sitting room on the second day of a paralyzing New York blizzard, whether it was snowing outside.

I imagine, in other words, that the notebook is about other people. But of course it is not. I have no real business with what one stranger said to another at the hatcheck counter in Pavillon; in fact I suspect that the line "That's my old football number" touched not my own imagination at all, but merely some memory of something once read, probably "The Eighty-Yard Run."[2] Nor is my concern with a woman in a dirty crepe-de-Chine wrapper in a Wilmington bar. My stake is always, of course, in the unmentioned girl in the plaid silk dress. *Remember what it was to be me*: that is always the point.

It is a difficult point to admit. We are brought up in the ethic that   10
others, any others, all others, are by definition more interesting than ourselves; taught to be diffident, just this side of self-effacing. ("You're the least important person in the room and don't forget it," Jessica Mitford's[3] governess would hiss in her ear on the advent of any social occasion; I copied that into my notebook because it is only recently that I have been

---

[1] *aperçus*: Summarizing glimpse or insight (French).—Eds.
[2] *"The Eighty-Yard Run"*: Popular short story by Irwin Shaw.—Eds.
[3] *Jessica Mitford* (1917–1996): British satirical writer.—Eds.

able to enter a room without hearing some such phrase in my inner ear.) Only the very young and the very old may recount their dreams at breakfast, dwell upon self, interrupt with memories of beach picnics and favorite Liberty lawn dresses and the rainbow trout in a creek near Colorado Springs. The rest of us are expected, rightly, to affect absorption in other people's favorite dresses, other people's trout.

And so we do. But our notebooks give us away, for however dutifully we record what we see around us, the common denominator of all we see is always, transparently, shamelessly, the implacable "I." We are not talking here about the kind of notebook that is patently for public consumption, a structural conceit for binding together a series of graceful *pensées*;[4] we are talking about something private, about bits of the mind's string too short to use, an indiscriminate and erratic assemblage with meaning only for its maker.

And sometimes even the maker has difficulty with the meaning. There does not seem to be, for example, any point in my knowing for the rest of my life that, during 1964, 720 tons of soot fell on every square mile of New York City, yet there it is in my notebook, labeled "FACT." Nor do I really need to remember that Ambrose Bierce liked to spell Leland Stanford's[5] name "£eland $tanford" or that "smart women almost always wear black in Cuba," a fashion hint without much potential for practical application. And does not the relevance of these notes seem marginal at best?:

> In the basement museum of the Inyo County Courthouse in Independence, California, sign pinned to a mandarin coat: "This MANDARIN COAT was often worn by Mrs. Minnie S. Brooks when giving lectures on her TEAPOT COLLECTION."

> Redhead getting out of car in front of Beverly Wilshire Hotel, chinchilla stole, Vuitton bags with tags reading:

> > MRS. LOU FOX
> > HOTEL SAHARA
> > VEGAS

Well, perhaps not entirely marginal. As a matter of fact, Mrs. Minnie S. Brooks and her MANDARIN COAT pull me back into my own childhood, for although I never knew Mrs. Brooks and did not visit Inyo County until I was thirty, I grew up in just such a world, in houses cluttered with Indian relics and bits of gold ore and ambergris and the souvenirs my Aunt Mercy Farnsworth brought back from the Orient. It is a long way from that world to Mrs. Lou Fox's world, where we all live now, and is it not just as well to remember that? Might not Mrs. Minnie S. Brooks help me to remember what I am? Might not Mrs. Lou Fox help me to remember what I am not?

---

[4]*pensées:* Thoughts or reflections (French).—EDS.
[5]*Bierce . . . Stanford's:* Ambrose Bierce (1842–1914?), American journalist and short story writer known for his savage wit; Leland Stanford (1824–1893), wealthy railroad builder who was a governor of California and the founder of Stanford University.—EDS.

But sometimes the point is harder to discern. What exactly did I have in mind when I noted down that it cost the father of someone I know $650 a month to light the place on the Hudson in which he lived before the Crash? What use was I planning to make of this line by Jimmy Hoffa:[6] "I may have my faults, but being wrong ain't one of them"? And although I think it interesting to know where the girls who travel with the Syndicate have their hair done when they find themselves on the West Coast, will I ever make suitable use of it? Might I not be better off just passing it on to John O'Hara?[7] What is a recipe for sauerkraut doing in my notebook? What kind of magpie keeps this notebook? "*He was born the night the* Titanic *went down.*" That seems a nice enough line, and I even recall who said it, but is it not really a better line in life than it could ever be in fiction?

But of course that is exactly it: not that I should ever use the line, but that I should remember the woman who said it and the afternoon I heard it. We were on her terrace by the sea, and we were finishing the wine left from lunch, trying to get what sun there was, a California winter sun. The woman whose husband was born the night the *Titanic* went down wanted to rent her house, wanted to go back to her children in Paris. I remember wishing that I could afford the house, which cost $1,000 a month. "Someday you will," she said lazily. "Someday it all comes." There in the sun on her terrace it seemed easy to believe in someday, but later I had a low-grade afternoon hangover and ran over a black snake on the way to the supermarket and was flooded with inexplicable fear when I heard the checkout clerk explaining to the man ahead of me why she was finally divorcing her husband. "He left me no choice," she said over and over as she punched the register. "He has a little seven-month-old baby by her, he left me no choice." I would like to believe that my dread then was for the human condition, but of course it was for me, because I wanted a baby and did not then have one and because I wanted to own the house that cost $1,000 a month to rent and because I had a hangover.

It all comes back. Perhaps it is difficult to see the value in having one's self back in that kind of mood, but I do see it; I think we are well advised to keep on nodding terms with the people we used to be whether we find them attractive company or not. Otherwise they turn up unannounced and surprise us, come hammering on the mind's door at 4 a.m. of a bad night and demand to know who deserted them, who betrayed them, who is going to make amends. We forget all too soon the things we thought we could never forget. We forget the loves and the betrayals alike, forget what we whispered and what we screamed, forget who we were. I have already

[margin: 15]

[6]*Jimmy Hoffa* (1913–1975?): Controversial leader of the Teamsters Union who disappeared in the mid-seventies.—EDS.
[7]*John O'Hara* (1905–1970): American novelist who wrote several books about gangsters.—EDS.

lost touch with a couple of people I used to be; one of them, a seventeen-year-old, presents little threat, although it would be of some interest to me to know again what it feels like to sit on a river levee drinking vodka-and-orange-juice and listening to Les Paul and Mary Ford[8] and their echoes sing "How High the Moon" on the car radio. (You see I still have the scenes, but I no longer perceive myself among those present, no longer could even improvise the dialogue.) The other one, a twenty-three-year-old, bothers me more. She was always a good deal of trouble, and I suspect she will reappear when I least want to see her, skirts too long, shy to the point of aggravation, always the injured party, full of recriminations and little hurts and stories I do not want to hear again, at once saddening me and angering me with her vulnerability and ignorance, an apparition all the more insistent for being so long banished.

It is a good idea, then, to keep in touch, and I suppose that keeping in touch is what notebooks are all about. And we are all on our own when it comes to keeping those lines open to ourselves: your notebook will never help me, nor mine you. "*So what's new in the whiskey business?*" What could that possibly mean to you? To me it means a blonde in a Pucci bathing suit sitting with a couple of fat men by the pool at the Beverly Hills Hotel. Another man approaches, and they all regard one another in silence for a while. "So what's new in the whiskey business?" one of the fat men finally says by way of welcome, and the blonde stands up, arches one foot and dips it in the pool, looking all the while at the cabaña where Baby Pignatari is talking on the telephone. That is all there is to that, except that several years later I saw the blonde coming out of Saks Fifth Avenue in New York with her California complexion and a voluminous mink coat. In the harsh wind that day she looked old and irrevocably tired to me, and even the skins in the mink coat were not worked the way they were doing them that year, not the way she would have wanted them done, and there is the point of the story. For a while after that I did not like to look in the mirror, and my eyes would skim the newspapers and pick out only the deaths, the cancer victims, the premature coronaries, the suicides, and I stopped riding the Lexington Avenue IRT because I noticed for the first time that all the strangers I had seen for years—the man with the seeing-eye dog, the spinster who read the classified pages every day, the fat girl who always got off with me at Grand Central—looked older than they once had.

It all comes back. Even that recipe for sauerkraut: even that brings it back. I was on Fire Island when I first made that sauerkraut, and it was raining, and we drank a lot of bourbon and ate the sauerkraut and went to bed at ten, and I listened to the rain and the Atlantic and felt safe. I made the sauerkraut again last night and it did not make me feel any safer, but that is, as they say, another story.

---

[8]***Les Paul and Mary Ford:*** Husband-and-wife musical team of the forties and fifties who had many hit records.—EDS.

The Reader's Presence

1. Notice that Didion begins her essay not with a general comment about notebooks but with an actual notebook entry. What does the entry sound like at first? What effect do you think Didion wants it to have on you as a reader?

2. Consider the comparison Didion makes in paragraph 6 between a notebook and a diary. How do they differ? Why is she fond of one and not the other? How does her example of a diary entry support her distinction?

3. Didion's notebook entries were never intended to have an audience. How is that apparent from the entries themselves? Compare Didion's ideas about keeping a notebook to Anne Frank's ideas about keeping a diary (page 115). In what ways do Frank's reasons for keeping a diary resemble Didion's? In what ways do their motivations differ? Where do you fit in as a reader of Didion's work? of Frank's work? Do you think the two writers would agree about the uses of private writing? Explain your answer.

Frederick Douglass

Learning to Read and Write

Born into slavery, Frederick Douglass (1817?–1895) was taken from his mother as an infant and denied any knowledge of his father's identity. He escaped to the north at the age of twenty-one and created a new identity for himself as a free man. He educated himself and went on to become one of the most eloquent orators and persuasive writers of the nineteenth century. He was a national leader in the abolition movement and, among other activities, founded and edited the North Star *and* Douglass' Monthly. *His public service included appointments as U.S. marshal and consul general to the Republic of Haiti. His most lasting literary accomplishment was his memoirs, which he revised several times before they were published as* The Life and Times of Frederick Douglass *(1881 and 1892). "Learning to Read and Write" is taken from these memoirs.*

Douglass overcame his initial reluctance to write his memoirs because, as he put it, "not only is slavery on trial, but unfortunately, the enslaved people are also on trial. It is alleged that they are, naturally, inferior; that they are so low in the scale of humanity, and so utterly stupid, that they are unconscious of their wrongs, and do not apprehend their rights." Therefore, wishing to put his talents to work "to the benefit of my afflicted people," Douglass agreed to write the story of his life.

I lived in Master Hugh's family about seven years. During this time, I succeeded in learning to read and write. In accomplishing this, I was compelled to resort to various stratagems. I had no regular teacher. My mistress, who had kindly commenced to instruct me, had, in compliance with the advice and direction of her husband, not only ceased to instruct, but had set her face against my being instructed by anyone else. It is due, however, to my mistress to say of her, that she did not adopt this course of treatment immediately. She at first lacked the depravity indispensable to shutting me up in mental darkness. It was at least necessary for her to have some training in the exercise of irresponsible power, to make her equal to the task of treating me as though I were a brute.

My mistress was, as I have said, a kind and tender-hearted woman; and in the simplicity of her soul she commenced, when I first went to live with her, to treat me as she supposed one human being ought to treat another. In entering upon the duties of a slaveholder, she did not seem to perceive that I sustained to her the relation of a mere chattel, and that for her to treat me as a human being was not only wrong, but dangerously so. Slavery proved as injurious to her as it did to me. When I went there, she was a pious, warm, and tender-hearted woman. There was no sorrow or suffering for which she had not a tear. She had bread for the hungry, clothes for the naked, and comfort for every mourner that came within her reach. Slavery soon proved its ability to divest her of these heavenly qualities. Under its influence, the tender heart became stone, and the lamb-like disposition gave way to one of tiger-like fierceness. The first step in her downward course was in her ceasing to instruct me. She now commenced to practice her husband's precepts. She finally became even more violent in her opposition than her husband himself. She was not satisfied with simply doing as well as he had commanded; she seemed anxious to do better. Nothing seemed to make her more angry than to see me with a newspaper. She seemed to think that here lay the danger. I have had her rush at me with a face made all up of fury, and snatch from me a newspaper, in a manner that fully revealed her apprehension. She was an apt woman; and a little experience soon demonstrated, to her satisfaction, that education and slavery were incompatible with each other.

From this time I was most narrowly watched. If I was in a separate room any considerable length of time, I was sure to be suspected of having a book, and was at once called to give an account of myself. All this, however, was too late. The first step had been taken. Mistress, in teaching me the alphabet, had given me the *inch*, and no precaution could prevent me from taking the *ell*.

The plan which I adopted, and the one by which I was most successful, was that of making friends of all the little white boys whom I met in

the street. As many of these as I could, I converted into teachers. With
their kindly aid, obtained at different times and in different places, I finally succeeded in learning to read. When I was sent to errands, I always
took my book with me, and by doing one part of my errand quickly, I
found time to get a lesson before my return. I used also to carry bread
with me, enough of which was always in the house, and to which I was
always welcome; for I was much better off in this regard than many of the
poor white children in our neighborhood. This bread I used to bestow
upon the hungry little urchins, who, in return, would give me that more
valuable bread of knowledge. I am strongly tempted to give the names of
two or three of those little boys, as a testimonial of the gratitude and affection I bear them; but prudence forbids—not that it would injure me,
but it might embarrass them; for it is almost an unpardonable offense to
teach slaves to read in this Christian country. It is enough to say of the
dear little fellows, that they lived on Philpot Street, very near Durgin and
Bailey's ship-yard. I used to talk this matter of slavery over with them. I
would sometimes say to them, I wished I could be as free as they would
be when they got to be men. "You will be free as soon as you are twenty-
one, *but I am a slave for life*! Have not I as good a right to be free as you
have?" These words used to trouble them; they would express for me the
liveliest sympathy, and console me with the hope that something would
occur by which I might be free.

I was now about twelve years old, and the thought of being *a slave*   5
for life began to bear heavily upon my heart. Just about this time, I got
hold of a book entitled *The Columbian Orator*. Every opportunity I got, I
used to read this book. Among much of other interesting matter, I found
in it a dialogue between a master and his slave. The slave was represented
as having run away from his master three times. The dialogue represented
the conversation which took place between them, when the slave was re-
taken the third time. In this dialogue, the whole argument in behalf of
slavery was brought forward by the master, all of which was disposed of
by the slave. The slave was made to say some very smart as well as impressive things in reply to his master—things which had the desired
though unexpected effect; for the conversation resulted in the voluntary
emancipation of the slave on the part of the master.

In the same book, I met with one of Sheridan's[1] mighty speeches on
and in behalf of Catholic emancipation. These were choice documents to
me. I read them over and over again with unabated interest. They gave
tongue to interesting thoughts of my own soul, which had frequently
flashed through my mind, and died away for want of utterance. The
moral which I gained from the dialogue was the power of truth over the
conscience of even a slaveholder. What I got from Sheridan was a bold
denunciation of slavery, and a powerful vindication of human rights. The

---

[1]*Sheridan's:* Richard Brinsley Butler Sheridan (1751–1816), Irish dramatist and orator.
—EDS.

reading of these documents enabled me to utter my thoughts, and to meet the arguments brought forward to sustain slavery; but while they relieved me of one difficulty, they brought on another even more painful than the one of which I was relieved. The more I read, the more I was led to abhor and detest my enslavers. I could regard them in no other light than a band of successful robbers, who had left their homes, and gone to Africa, and stolen us from our homes, and in a strange land reduced us to slavery. I loathed them as being the meanest as well as the most wicked of men. As I read and contemplated the subject, behold! that very discontentment which Master Hugh had predicted would follow my learning to read had already come, to torment and sting my soul to unutterable anguish. As I writhed under it, I would at times feel that learning to read had been a curse rather than a blessing. It had given me a view of my wretched condition, without the remedy. It opened my eyes to the horrible pit, but to no ladder upon which to get out. In moments of agony, I envied my fellow-slaves for their stupidity. I have often wished myself a beast. I preferred the condition of the meanest reptile to my own. Anything, no matter what, to get rid of thinking! It was this everlasting thinking of my condition that tormented me. There was no getting rid of it. It was pressed upon me by every object within sight or hearing, animate or inanimate. The silver trump of freedom had roused my soul to eternal wakefulness. Freedom now appeared, to disappear no more forever. It was heard in every sound, and seen in every thing. It was ever present to torment me with a sense of my wretched condition. I saw nothing without seeing it, I heard nothing without hearing it, and felt nothing without feeling it. It looked from every star, it smiled in every calm, breathed in every wind, and moved in every storm.

I often found myself regretting my own existence, and wishing myself dead; and but for the hope of being free, I have no doubt but that I should have killed myself, or done something for which I should have been killed. While in this state of mind, I was eager to hear anyone speak of slavery. I was a ready listener. Every little while, I could hear something about the abolitionists. It was some time before I found what the word meant. It was always used in such connections as to make it an interesting word to me. If a slave ran away and succeeded in getting clear, or if a slave killed his master, set fire to a barn, or did anything very wrong in the mind of a slaveholder, it was spoken of as the fruit of *abolition*. Hearing the word in this connection very often, I set about learning what it meant. The dictionary afforded me little or no help. I found it was "the act of abolishing"; but then I did not know what was to be abolished. Here I was perplexed. I did not dare to ask anyone about its meaning, for I was satisfied that it was something they wanted me to know very little about. After a patient waiting, I got one of our city papers, containing an account of the number of petitions from the North, praying for the abolition of slavery in the District of Columbia, and of the slave trade between the States. From this time I understood the words *abolition* and *abolitionist*, and always drew near when that word was spoken, expecting to hear something of importance to myself and fellow-slaves. The light broke in upon me by degrees. I went one day down on the wharf of Mr. Waters; and seeing two Irishmen unloading a scow of stone, I went, unasked, and helped them. When we had finished, one of them came to me and asked me if I were a slave. I told him I was. He asked, "Are ye a slave for life?" I told him that I was. The good Irishman seemed to be deeply affected by the statement. He said to the other that it was a pity so fine a little fellow as myself should be a slave for life. He said it was a shame to hold me. They both advised me to run away to the North; that I should find friends there, and that I should be free. I pretended not to be interested in what they said, and treated them as if I did not understand them; for I feared they might be treacherous. White men have been known to encourage slaves to escape, and then, to get the reward, catch them and return them to their masters. I was afraid that these seemingly good men might use me so; but I nevertheless remembered their advice, and from that time I resolved to run away. I looked forward to a time at which it would be safe for me to escape. I was too young to think of doing so immediately; besides, I wished to learn how to write, as I might have occasion to write my own pass. I consoled myself with the hope that I should one day find a good chance. Meanwhile, I would learn to write.

The idea as to how I might learn to write was suggested to me by being in Durgin and Bailey's ship-yard, and frequently seeing the ship carpenters, after hewing, and getting a piece of timber ready for use, write on the timber the name of that part of the ship for which it was intended. When a piece of timber was intended for the larboard side, it would be marked thus—"L." When a piece was for the starboard side, it would be marked thus—"S." A piece for the larboard side forward, would be marked thus—"L.F." When a piece was for starboard side forward, it would be marked thus—"S.F." For larboard aft, it would be marked thus—"L.A." For starboard aft, it would be marked thus—"S.A." I soon learned the names of these letters, and for what they were intended when placed upon a piece of timber in the shipyard. I immediately commenced copying them, and in a short time was able to make the four letters named. After that, when I met with any boy who I knew could write, I would tell him I could write as well as he. The next word would be, "I don't believe you. Let me see you try it." I would then make the letters which I had been so fortunate as to learn, and ask him to beat that. In this way I got a good many lessons in writing, which it is quite possible I should never have gotten in any other way. During this time, my copy-book was the board fence, brick wall, and pavement; my pen and ink was a lump of chalk. With these, I learned mainly how to write. I then commenced and continued copying the Italics in *Webster's Spelling Book*, until I could make them all without looking in the book. By this time, my little Master Thomas had gone to school, and learned how to write, and had written over a number of copy-books. These had been brought home, and shown to some of our near neighbors, and then laid aside. My mistress used to go to class meeting at the Wilk Street meeting-house every Monday afternoon, and leave me to take care of the house. When left thus, I used to spend the time in writing in the spaces left in Master Thomas's copy-book, copying what he had written. I continued to do this until I could write a hand very similar to that of Master Thomas. Thus, after a long, tedious effort for years, I finally succeeded in learning how to write.

The Reader's Presence

1. What sort of audience does Douglass anticipate for his reminiscence? How much does he assume his readers know about the conditions of slavery?

2. What books seem to matter most to Douglass? Why? What are his motives for wanting to read and write? For Douglass, what is the relationship between literacy and freedom? How does he move from curiosity to anguish to "eternal wakefulness" in paragraph 6? What is the relationship between learning to read and learning to write?

3. Read Azar Nafisi's excerpt from "Reading *Lolita* in Tehran" (page 493) and consider Nafisi's students' challenges in obtaining an education. What obstacles do the girls overcome to join Nafisi's class? How do the difficulties Douglass faced in getting an education compare with those of Nafisi's students?

Rita Dove

Major Steps

Rita Dove (b. 1952) has received numerous literary and academic awards during her career as a poet, writer, and scholar. Born and raised in Akron, Ohio, Dove graduated from Miami University of Ohio, became a Fulbright scholar at the Universität Tübingen in Germany, and earned her MFA from the University of Iowa. Dove's first book of poetry, The Yellow House on the Corner, *was published in 1980, followed by seven more collections, including* Thomas and Beulah, *which was published in 1986 and won the Pulitzer Prize for poetry. Her latest book of poetry is* American Smooth *(2004). Dove's broad array of work includes her 1992 novel,* Through the Ivory Gate; *a collection of short stories; a collection of essays; and a play,* The Darker Face of the Earth, *produced at the Kennedy Center in Washington, D.C., and the Royal National Theatre in London. Dove was chosen as Poet Laureate of the United States and consultant to the Library of Congress from 1993 to 1995, and Poet Laureate of the commonwealth of Virginia from 2004 to 2006. She continues to teach creative writing at the University of Virginia, Charlottesville. Dove's essay, "Major Steps," appeared in the July 10, 2005, issue of the* Washington Post Magazine.

In an interview with the American Poetry Review, *Dove spoke about the process of writing the poems about her grandparents in* Thomas and Beulah, *a process that bears a strong resemblance to the process of writing a memoir. "I know that when I was writing the poems that went into* Thomas and Beulah, *I felt that I was, at least for myself, doing something very new. I felt I was moving into a territory that I wasn't quite sure of, but it was immensely exciting, and the more that I wrote the more I realized that what I was trying to tell, let's say, was not a narrative as we know narratives but actually the moments that matter most in our lives. I began to think, how do we remember our lives? How do we think of our lives or shape our lives in our own consciousnesses, and I realize that we don't actually think of our lives in very cohesive strands but we remember as beads on a necklace, moments that matter to us, come to us in flashes, and the connections are submerged."*

"You can always get warm, but it's hard to stay cool." My mother's words, muttered every summer since I can remember, rang like a mantra in my head as I stood in the uncut grass of a football field (the 20-yard line, to be precise), knees locked and eyes forward, arms akimbo, to balance a 28-inch-long metal stick at a 45-degree angle, just so. Perspiration trickled down my temples and collected under my jaw, but I held still. Since reaching my teens, I'd come to dread the wasteland of summer vacation—heat and more heat, the sodden press of humidity that could force my painfully coifed pageboy to retract its hooks, sun that turned my caramel complexion to burnt umber if I forgot to wear a hat.

It was the 19th of August, 1968, four days until the Soap Box Derby Parade and nine days before my 16th birthday, and I still hadn't figured out how to keep my minimalist emergency 'do (French twist with bangs pinned to the side) from shrinking to that fine corona of frizz usually found in the *National Geographic* photographs of ostrich heads. Why, oh why was I standing here at attention like a tin soldier, ankle-deep in crabgrass in the middle of a sweltering Midwestern summer, sweating out all the good sense Mom had pressed into the curls on my head?

Four months earlier, in April, a week or so after Martin Luther King Jr.'s murder, I was packing up my cello one afternoon after orchestra practice when Rhonda bounced up, flute propped on her shoulder like a baseball bat, and clapped me on the back. Rhonda was always doing things like that; copper-skinned and confident (even in glasses!) to the point of being uncomfortably gung-ho, she was what my grandmother would call, wrinkling her nose, *sturdy.* I started to straighten up, but she couldn't wait. "Rita," she whispered, "I've got a terrific idea. Let's try out for the majorette squad!"

Funny thing is, even though I gulped and felt my heart pound into my throat, I thought it was a great idea, too. In the Byzantine hierarchy of high school, majorettes and cheerleaders were the Cream. Cheerleaders enjoyed a noisy devotion from the masses, but majorettes were the serene wizards, the silvery circumferences of their batons humming before them like horizontal pirouettes. If I said yes, if I tried out and actually made the squad, maybe I could finally be . . . I closed my eyes to savor the possibility—*popular.*

Just thinking the word sent a shiver of longing through me. What was it like? Ever since junior high, I'd been called "brainiac." I thought I was used to it, but sometimes, on pale green spring mornings or glimpsing the tentative expression on my face reflected in a store window, I'd wonder. Although I'd never been exactly reviled, had never borne the brunt of schoolyard taunts or classroom pranks, I'd also never been pursued by a boy, at least not ardently. I could not imagine attaining the courtly cool of Carla, every hair in perfect alignment against her cocoa profile. Nor could I ever hope for the effervescent cuteness of Quinita, barely 5 feet tall, with wide-spaced, tilted almond eyes large enough to bring any basketball player down to her size. I just wanted . . . well, not to be regarded with dread or, worse, utter indifference. But how to accomplish that, skinny-Minnie me with my Cat-woman glasses and hair that frizzled in the rain because I was not allowed to put a relaxer in it? How could someone who attended all AP classes and played cello in the school orchestra become popular?

I picked up my bow from the music stand and loosened it, slowly. "Why not?" I replied, utterly *cool.*

We figured the only way to break the barrier of the all-white majorette squad was to make it impossibly hard for them to refuse us. Rhonda had taken twirling lessons before and volunteered to coach me during the open training session offered by the senior majorettes during the last weeks of the school year.

We joined the other supplicants after school in the incandescent gloom of the band room for a crash course in twirls—verticals and frontals, figure eights, around the worlds—which Rhonda supplemented later in her basement, enthusiastically breaking down each sleight of hand into its elemental actions: wrist down then wrist up, clockwise then counter.

For the second week, we broke into groups to learn a routine of our choice, which we were expected to perform for auditions that Friday. Rhonda made for Donna's corner. I followed, reluctantly; Donna was a senior and the best twirler on the team, and I found the gleaming blond waves capping her stocky frame rather frightening. But when she announced, "This routine is hard, you'll have to work," looking each of us in the eye without much hope or even sympathy, I began to like her: Fair

was fair. By audition time, I knew the routine as well as Rhonda; we
had even invented a few moves of our own. We were careful not to show
our cards, though; we never stood next to each other during practice or
laughed at each other's jokes. An old survival trick: Don't give them a
chance to cry disrespect; if they're going to dismiss you, at least make
them scramble for their excuses.

And so it happened that in Akron, Ohio, for the 1968–69 school
year, two Negroes joined the Buchtel High School majorettes: a Historic
First. The neighborhood buzzed, my mother beamed, the president of the
local NAACP chapter came up after church to shake my hand; even my
father, usually dismissive of nonintellectual pursuits, pulled out his camera as I struck a few poses in the driveway.

The first item on the outgoing majorettes' agenda was to form a new
Line. We were ranked by height, then shuffled among the returning twirlers
with adjustments for body build, hair color and style—and complexion.
No one mentioned race, but it was on everyone's mind that year, and it
hung in the meeting room until Rhonda blurted out: "What are we, a handful of M&M's?" We all laughed, and that was that. There were too many
other things demanding our attention: marching techniques and stand-
alone routines, halftime formations and pep rally drills. We practiced
every afternoon after school in the deserted hallways. The seniors stood
apart, arms crossed, forbearing and aloof. Beth, Cindy, Toni: veterans on
the Line, proprietors of all Knowledge, purveyors of Secret Remedies
(Vaseline on bare legs in winter, Band-Aids on heels to prevent blisters),

our shepherds through the Valley of the Shadow of Football Seasons Past. It was heady but confusing: Flash a smile but maintain synchronicity, switch your hips while lifting your knees, high step and sashay. The amount of paraphernalia was staggering—two uniforms (cotton for summer parades, corduroy for the fall), regulation boots with pompoms, kid gloves for November games. When Donna offered to sell me her gear, I hesitated, sniffing condescension. (*All Blacks are poor, live in the ghetto,* etc.), until she pointed out that we were about the same height and it was silly to waste money on a vaguely militaristic outfit I'd wear for four months out of the year. So I walked with her to the white neighborhood two blocks the other way from school and sat on a chenille bedspread eerily similar to my own as she rummaged through her closet. Two grocery bags full: She even threw in the corduroy underwear.

"Hey, you finally got one!" I ducked my head to hide my irritation, but the pigtailed little girl squatting in the grass could not be deterred. "That's good!" she said. "Aren't you glad?" I stole a glance at Rhonda throwing aerials at the far end of the yard to the oohs and aahs of a pack of neighborhood kids. Big deal. After snatching at air for a half-hour, it was about time I caught the thing.

My champion twitched her fat braids—now she was irritated, too—and called out, "Hey, she caught it!"

Rhonda trotted over. "I told you it'd work itself out! You just have to plug away until your arm remembers by itself!"

Rhonda was the technique guru, while I thrived on artistic expression; we pushed each other. Every weekend that spring found us in my side yard, polishing the routines and trying out new tricks. The secret to retrieving a baton tossed into the air—as I was to learn that afternoon of miss upon near-miss, the kids squealing in delight as they rippled to a safe orbit—is not to try too hard to catch it. Once you send the baton spinning skyward, calmly released from the upturned palm, all you have to do is wait, gauging the instant when it will return to waist level, then reach and pluck it out of the air, like a flower. Easy enough, once you know.

15

The school year ended in the usual flurry of exams and social events; band and majorette practice would resume three weeks before Derby Day in August, when kids from all over the world descended upon Akron to race their motorless wooden cars in the All American Soap Box Derby. I took a vacation from twirling and spent a few weeks curled on the couch reading before growing restless—in the wake of Bobby Kennedy's assassination, with the accelerating madness of Vietnam in plain television view, it seemed the entire country was growing more and more restless. But while the streets seethed with angry, disheartened protesters, I checked out library books on Eastern philosophies and sat cross-legged on the floor of my room, shades drawn and incense burning, hip sockets screeching in agony as I intoned "Om" to a recording of Buddhist monks. Nirvana escaped me, but it didn't matter: August neared, with the promise of being allowed onto our Half-Time Stage: the Gridiron.

Beth's whistle pumped out the beat: 1, 2, 3, 4. Hard to stay cool, indeed: I was delirious with heat, my temples throbbing in march tempo while we advanced on burning feet up the ragged field, my fingers thick and slick as sausages—which meant slippage, a slower baton, more wrist action, more effort, more sweat. Wait till winter, the freshly risen seniors warned with a chuckle, it'll freeze to your fingers. *Then* try catching an aerial! They loved scaring us, it was part of the ritual. Rhonda and I vowed we would show them.

Right now, though, this slithery silver was not behaving. I cast a surreptitious look down the Line: Ruthie, shortest and terminally cute, was the veteran among us juniors, having already marched in her sophomore year. Elaine's brown hair curled gently around her roses-and-cream complexion; she constantly had to be told not to slump. Jackie was tall, too, and dark in a Mediterranean way, with a nose that jutted out like Cher's—Rhonda and I agreed it looked sexy.

Caught up in my own deficiencies, I couldn't understand that each girl had her secret shortcomings—Jackie wanted Ruthie's pert nose, Ruthie covertly envied Beth's narrow one; Cindy deplored her skinny legs, which Elaine coveted. Christine despaired over her hair, fine and blond, which she claimed was unmanageable. How could I ever fit into this group that laughed so easily and seemed not to mind the heat? But it was more than that: They possessed the power of assumption; they'd grown up assuming the world was theirs to grow up into. Every little detail of their daily lives—flesh-toned Band-Aids and nude-colored brassieres, the shades of face powder available at Woolworth's cosmetic counter and, yes, the hair products lining the shelves—was buoyed by the mainstream they floated in.

As we ran through the roster for Derby Day (which would be our first gig, replete with real celebrities—Trini Lopez!—in the grandstand and tens of thousands of spectators), the seniors doled out anecdotes and advice in equally sadistic measures. Take salt tablets to counteract the fluids you lose, so you don't faint. Sweat? You haven't seen sweat yet . . . it'll blind you, pool in your boots. Apropos boots—wear at least two pairs of bobby socks. Better your feet burn up than getting blisters! You'll forget your feet, anyway—too much noise and bright lights. Then, after you've marched past Polsky's department store, after you can't hear the horns anymore because those guys' lips are blown and all you can do is try to find the bass drum beat in that racket (refrain from licking your sweat, let it drip gracefully) . . . after you've given up trying to smile at the crowds lining the curb and you just want to sit down and pull off those ridiculous pom-pommed boots that weigh a ton by now and make you feel like a Clydesdale while looking like a Lipizzaner—then comes Derby Hill.

Oh, it's a mean hill, they exclaimed, steep and single-minded! You march your weary thighs to the starting line, wait for the trumpet fanfare, then step over the precipice. Pure perpendicular, braking with your heels, your calf muscles screaming as they contract. You don't know pain until you do the Hill.

"C'mon, Rita, it's easy!" Jackie pushed her way through the gaggle of girls, her smooth, locket-shaped face thrust forward, laughing. Now the world would know. Come one, come all: Behold the asphalt flower in her reinforced tennis shoes!

I scanned the circle: barefoot, every one of them. How could these white girls have this over me, too? Every summer I tried, but my tender soles kept me from going any farther than our gravel driveway. Wasn't I supposed to have come from the jungle to these shores, in chains and certainly barefoot? What had happened to my gene pool?

"It's all grass. Padded—just like your carpet at home!"

Who said that? Had to be a senior. I peered over Jackie's shoulder   25
and caught sight of Rhonda, hanging back at the fringe, grinning.

"You'll be much cooler. And you won't run a blister," said Christine, whose nose was beginning to peel despite the floppy cotton hat she's screwed on over her limp hair.

It was the perspiration sheen across Christine's cheeks that convinced me. If she could suffer, so could I. I wriggled out of my sneakers, wavered on damp, puckery feet. Hoots and whistles. Rhonda's clomping applause. We fell in at the 50-yard line and waited for the whistle's count before peeling into the "Colonel Bogey March," with its easy reverse vertical twirls low to one side, then the swooping back-bending strut that looked so hard but was breezingly simple—perfect for the end of a long parade and the approach to Derby Hill, where leaning backward would counterbalance the pitch of the racetrack slope.

The grass was cool, the ground deliciously warm underneath. After a few measures I got used to the feathery pokes between my toes, an occasional flicker tickling my ankle. My knees snapped to my chest as I high-stepped, switching my hips. How tantalizing it was after all these years, to feel the earth under the soft skin of my feet!

Then I stopped mid-step, howling: A pain suffused me, immediate and pure, almost sweet in its ferocity. It seemed to shoot out of the earth, straight up from Hell's flame pits. I dropped and rolled, clutching my right foot. Instinct, it seemed, knew right away where it hurt, while my overactive brain went nova. Jackie was the first one over, but Elaine made the pronouncement: "You've been stung!" She gently unfolded my clenched toes to expose the dull red stinger, still lodged in the crevice of my little toe. Stung? By what? I was incredulous. A bee sting hurts this much? Somewhere behind the throbbing and a sympathetic headache, I was ashamed of my ignorance. Ruthie ran for the first-aid kit and pulled the stinger out.

I insisted on walking the few blocks home. When I stumbled into the   30
kitchen, Mom lit into action, popping ice cubes into a pail of water. My
brother, dangerously allergic to bee stings, took one look, panicked, and
began pacing, so Mom sent him upstairs for iodine just as 10-year-old
Robin, sensing family drama, rushed in from play. "Ooh, that's nasty!"
she shrieked, plainly delighted. "How ya gonna march now?"

Although Mom applied crushed aspirin directly to the puncture, by
dinnertime not even a sandal fit over my swollen foot. Yet I remained
calm. One thing was certain: I would march on Derby Day, even if I had
to hop on one boot.

I spent the next day on the couch, foot propped up, but demanded to
attend practice the last afternoon before the parade. Mom dropped me
off at the edge of the field and I limped to the bleachers to watch. That
night, a dry run with gauze and one sock instead of two: Tears shot into
my eyes when we maneuvered the boot on. By the time we'd jimmied it
off and I had taken my clump foot and ice pack to bed, I was too wrung
out to despair.

Derby Day dawned clear and hot. By rush hour, downtown was thick
with enflamed smog from the tire factories. Stir in the kind of mugginess
the Midwest does best, and by 7 in the evening we'd be slogging through
warm pudding.

A funny thing: Pain endured in service of desire, even one as trivial as
marching in a parade, doesn't stay still. It may hide a bit at first so you
think you've got the upper hand, but then it crescendos—threatening,
testing. And if you don't panic, if you accept and even invite that pain to
become a part of yourself (I thought of the Buddhist monks and chanted
silently with them), then you can turn the corner and go on forever. I remember every minute of that parade—the grit flying in our faces when we
turned off Main Street, the weird way buildings amplified or swallowed
the music, how I quenched my thirst with my own sweat and how the
taste changed from salty to bitter, the wink Rhonda threw me in the middle of our high school's fight song, just before the right turn. And there it
was: the Hill.

We paused on the crest, hands on our hips in identical chevrons, our   35
black-and-white uniforms looking crisp despite the heat. A faint wind
teased, a cool sigh sweeping up the torched asphalt; at the bottom of the
incline autumn waited with the promise of football sweaters, frosty nights
and hot chocolate. Suddenly Beth's whistle blew, more a shriek than a
call to arms; the band lurched into the perky opening measures of the
"Colonel Bogey March," and we stepped off.

Why did marching down the Hill feel so good that August evening? It
was the last hurdle, of course, in a transition I had hoped to negotiate
with some measure of grace. But it was more physical and metaphysical
than that. As the ground under my feet *gave way*, I trusted the laws of
gravity and physics, and they did not let me down; instead, I lay back,
and they held me on a cushion of air plumped by the throbbing of the

band behind me, pulsing in time with my swollen toe way down there nestled in gauze and one cotton sock, safe in my spanking-white boot. The Hill was beneath me and we were all going down at the same time, the I gloriously aware that as long as she was part of the We there would be no slipping—just lay back and let the ground tug you along.

And in that instant of buoyant locomotion I knew, suddenly and very clearly, that being a majorette wasn't going to make me popular. Maybe even the opposite—boys would be scared of Little Miss Overachiever more than ever. I no longer cared. I'd be sunburnt red as a brick, windchapped and rusty-shinned, and oh, what a mess my hair would be; but it all would be over too soon, like the summer I'd left at the top of the hill.

The Reader's Presence

1. One feature of Dove's prose is her use of adjectives and figurative language to reinforce her anxiety as she set out to march in a new direction in terms of her identity. As you reread Dove's essay, identify as many examples as possible of her use of adjectives, similes, and metaphors. Choose three examples, and explain—as specifically as possible—why these compositional choices are so effective.

2. In paragraph 4, Dove talks about the "Byzantine hierarchy of high school," and cites the distinctions between majorettes and cheerleaders to illustrate her point: "Cheerleaders enjoyed a noisy devotion from the masses, but majorettes were the serene wizards, the silvery circumferences of their batons humming before them like horizontal pirouettes." Take a few moments to reflect on the specific ways in which you came to experience hierarchy in high school. After you summarize these distinctions, identify the ways in which students expressed this hierarchy. What specific metaphors did they use to differentiate one peer group from another? How did this hierarchy change, if at all, as you progressed from one year to the next?

3. Dove opens her essay with a surprising statement: "You can always get warm, but it's hard to stay cool." After reading "Major Steps," what would you identify as the nature of the surprise in this sentence? How does Dove's essay illustrate the paradox embedded in this statement? What are the specific—and various—ways the word "cool" is defined and exemplified in the essay? In "*Ghosts*/Pishtacos" (page 22), Marie Arana begins her essay about growing up in "two different worlds" with a similarly remarkable line: "The corridors of my skull are haunted." Compare and contrast the effectiveness of these opening sentences and how each anticipates larger thematic issues in each essay. Which do you think is more effective? Explain why.

Brian Doyle

The Knock

Journalist, essayist, and editor, Brian Doyle (b. 1956) was born in New York, educated "fitfully" at the University of Notre Dame, and now lives and works in Portland, Oregon, where he is the editor of Portland Magazine *at the University of Portland. Doyle is noted for writing books with spiritual and religious themes, including* Two Voices: A Father and Son Discuss Family and Faith *(1998), co-written with his father, Jim Doyle;* Credo *(1999);* Saints Passionate and Peculiar: Brief Exuberant Essays for Teens *(2002);* Leaping: Revelations and Epiphanies *(2003);* Spirited Men: Story, Soul, and Substance *(2004); and* The Wet Engine: Exploring the Mad Wild Miracle of the Heart *(2005). His latest book is* The Grail: A Year Ambling and Shambling through an Oregon Vineyard in Pursuit of the Best Pinot Noir Wine in the Whole Wild World *(2006). He edited the anthology* God Is Love: Essays from *Portland Magazine (2003). Doyle's own essays and poems have appeared in numerous magazines, journals, and newspapers, including the* Atlantic Monthly, Harper's, Orion, *the* American Scholar, *the* Georgia Review, *the* Times of London, *the* Sydney Morning Herald, *the* Kansas City Star, *the* San Francisco Chronicle, Newsday, *and* Commonweal, *in which his essay, "The Knock," appeared in 2007.*

In a 2006 essay, "What If?" in Portland Magazine, *Doyle wrote about those deep spiritual realizations that not only inspire him as a person but are at the very heart of his writing: "I still have faith in faith, despite all the evidence that religions are merely nutty hobbies, like being a Cubs fan. I keep thinking that under the rituals of religion there is a crucial wriggling possibility for what we might someday be. It's the same possibility you see sometimes under patriotism or sport or families; a humor and mercy, a grace and mercy, a warmth beyond all sense. Sometimes, for an instant, at a game, a wedding, a park, you get a flash of connective energy with your fellow beings—just a hint, a shiver of inexplicable peace and joy."*

A friend has two jobs in our town: policeman and soldier. In both, he is the guy who knocks on doors to tell mothers and fathers, wives and husbands that their son or daughter, husband or wife is dead. He has to knock on a door five or six times a year. He has become a student of doors and how people open them.

First, you never bang on the door, even if you are knocking for the fifth time and have been freezing on the porch for ten minutes. "I always start with my knuckles, then go to the knocker or the bell if I have to. Most doors have a good loud hollow sound. Usually people answer right away. You would think that with houses bigger than they used to be, people wouldn't hear a knock. But this isn't so. Women who answer the door look first to see who you are. Men just open it. I don't think I have ever had a child open the door.

"When I wear my Army uniform, people know immediately why I am there, whereas if I am a policeman, it could be for anything. I have had people cry in my arms. Some invite me in and give me tea, even after I have delivered the news. It's like their automatic-pilot function is to show courtesy. I've had some people refuse to believe me, and some who got angry and asked me to leave. I've never had someone swing at me, but I have heard stories like that.

"The thing I look for is shock. I've had people faint, men as well as women. People can go into serious shock and you have to be prepared for that. I carry a medical kit in the car. I try to visit in the late morning. I stay as long as necessary. I have been in some houses for hours. Sometimes I have waited with a person all afternoon until his or her spouse comes home from work. You mostly just listen.

"People tell stories. Often their first reaction, after the initial shock   5
and grief, is to tell stories. They have to get their feelings out. I have heard thousands of these stories. Friends tell me I should write them down, but I say they are a private matter, that it wouldn't be right. I also convey information about counseling, funeral arrangements, and legal matters. Most people aren't ready to discuss the details. They are too stunned. But they do want to discuss the facts of the death.

"It is a difficult job and it wears you down. I try to do it with as much dignity and courtesy as possible. There are more visits now with the wars, but I still make more calls as a policeman. The message I deliver most is that a loved one has been killed in an automobile accident. Often teenagers. The hardest messages to deliver are about the deaths of children. There is nothing I can say—other than the facts—to a mother or a father in that situation. So I don't try. I have often thought that what I am doing is a communal act, that it represents the town itself, standing there on the porch. I stand straight, speak clearly, and wear the full uniform. I ask permission to enter the domicile but never sit down. It's easier to speak directly if you stand. I remove my hat, make sure the person is sitting down if possible, and deliver the message. I take as much time as is needed. When I am absolutely sure the initial shock has lessened and the person is safe to be alone in the house, I express my condolences and prepare to leave. At the door, before I put on my hat, I usually add that I will keep the deceased in my prayers. I make it clear that I am saying this as a private citizen, not as a soldier or a policeman. In my experience, saying that and meaning it matters a lot. Generally, I stop at the church on the way back and say the rosary. It's become a form of closure for me, a way to hand over the pain.

"That's about it. I'll check in on the person or family if necessary, and I keep abreast of funeral details but rarely go to the services. I don't want to be a disruptive presence. I keep the deceased in my prayers for at least a month, longer if the person was a child. Generally, I direct my prayers to the Madonna. At one point, I wrote down all the names of the deceased, but I don't do that anymore. The list was getting too long, and I realized Mary knows all their names, especially the children's."

The Reader's Presence

1. Why do you think Doyle put almost the entire essay in the words of his friend? What effect does that have on you as a reader? Can you think of other ways he might have composed the essay? Try, for example, rewriting the second paragraph in the same way the first is written, without direct quotations from Doyle's friend. How does that alter the tone of the essay?

2. How does Doyle's friend manage to sound both official and personal? Identify expressions in the essay that sound as though they come from a police officer or soldier. Identify a few that seem to come from "a private citizen." How would you characterize Doyle's friend as a private citizen? What do you think Doyle's friend means when he says he often thinks that what he's doing is "a communal act"?

3. Compare "The Knock" with another short selection that deals with the way we respond to the deaths of others, Abraham Lincoln's "Gettysburg Address" (page 460). What kind of consolation does each selection offer? In which selection does religion play a larger role? Explain your answer. How can each selection be considered in terms of "a communal act"?

Richard Ford

A City Beyond the Reach of Empathy

Richard Ford is a writer of many hometowns. He was born in 1944 in Jackson, Mississippi and raised there and in Little Rock, Arkansas, and educated in the Midwest and on the West Coast. After graduating from Michigan State University, Ford first chose law school but left after one year to pursue a career as a writer. He received his MFA in 1970 from the University of California, Irvine (where he studied with E. L. Doctorow), and has taught at both Princeton and Harvard universities. His first novel, A Piece of My Heart, was published in 1976, followed by The Ultimate Good Luck (1981), The Sportswriter (1986), and Wildlife (1990). Independence Day (1995) was the first novel ever to win both the Pulitzer Prize and the PEN/Faulkner Award. His latest novel is The Lay of the Land (2006), one of the New York Times 10 Best Books of 2006. Ford's short fiction collections include Rock Springs (1987), Women with Men: Three Stories

(1997), A Multitude of Sins *(2002), and* Vintage Ford *(2003), his collected sto-ries. Among the anthologies he has edited are* The Granta Book of the American Short Story *(1992) and* The Best American Sports Writing *(1999).*

On August 28, 2005, Hurricane Katrina slammed into the southern coast of the United States and inflicted devastating damage: more than 1,800 people lost their lives and more than $81 billion dollars in property was destroyed. As the center of Katrina passed east of New Orleans on August 29, winds and tidal surges caused more than fifty levee breaches, precipitating the worst engineering disaster in U.S. history. By August 31, 80 percent of New Orleans was flooded, with some parts under fifteen feet of water. This essay was published in the New York Times *within a week of this national catastrophe.*

Who can write about New Orleans now? Tell us what it's like there. Bring us near to what people are experiencing, to their loss, to what will survive. People who are close should write that. Only they're in the city, or they're on a bus, or they're seeking shelter. We don't know where they are.

It's just a keyhole, and a small one, onto this great civic tragedy. The people who should be writing of it can't be found. An attempt to set out a vocabulary for empathy and for reckoning is frustrated in a moment of sorest need by the plain terms of the tragedy that wants telling. There are many such keyholes.

In America, even with our incommensurable memories of 9/11, we still do not have an exact human vocabulary for the loss of a city—our great iconic city, so graceful, livable, insular, self-delighted, eccentric, the one New Orleanians always said, with a wink, that care forgot and that sometimes, it might seem, forgot to care. Other peoples have experienced their cities' losses. Some bombed away (sometimes by us). Others gone in the flood. Here now is one more tragedy that we thought, by some divin-ity's grace that didn't arrive, we'd miss. But not. And our inept attempts at words run only to lists, costs, to assessing blame. It's like Hiroshima, a public official said. But not. It's not like anything. It's what it is. That's the hard part. He, with all of us, lacked the words.

For those away from New Orleans—most all of us—in this week of tears and wrenching, words fail. Somehow our hearts' reach comes short and we've been left with an aching, pointless inwardness. "All memory resolves itself in gaze," the poet Richard Hugo wrote once about another town that died.

Empathy is what we long for—not sadness for a house we own, or owned once—now swept away. Not even for the felt miracle of two wide-eyed children whirled upward into a helicopter as if into clouds. And we want more than that, even at this painful long distance: we want to project our sympathies straight into the life of a woman standing waist-deep in a glistening toxic current with a whole city's possessions all floating about, her own belongings in a white plastic bag, and who has no particular reason for hope, and so is just staring up. We would all give   5

Remains of a home, Ninth Ward neighborhood. Photo by Chris Jordan.

her hope. Comfort. A part of ourselves. Perform an act of renewal. It's hard to make sense of this, we say. But it makes sense. Making sense just doesn't help.

Tell me what you feel, a woman in Los Angeles said to me today by telephone. (I have a telephone, of course.) Tell me what you think of when you think of New Orleans. There must be special things you feel the loss of. Memories. And I realized, by her voice, that she had made a firm decision already about this loss.

Oh, yes, I said, though not always the memories you'd think. I have a picture of my parents on V-J Day, in City Park, holding a baby, staring at the camera and the sun. They are all dressed up and happy. The baby is me. So, I wonder, how is that park faring tonight.

I have a memory of my father and my mother drunk as loons on New Year's Eve, in front of Antoine's. It was nearly midnight, 1951. There was no place to leave me, so they had their fight (only an argument, really) in front of me. My father held my mother against a wall on St. Louis Street and shouted at her. About what I don't know. Later, when we were in bed in the Hotel Monteleone, with me between them and the ceiling fan turning, they both cried. So. What of Antoine's now? What of the waiters who a week ago stood out on the street in tuxedo aprons and smoked? What of St. Louis Street?

I have a memory of a hot and breathless summer. It is many summers joined into one. My mother took me onto the Algiers Ferry, an open boat with cars driven onto the deck. Out on the great sliding brown river there was the only hint of breeze you could find anywhere. Back and across to the foot of Canal Street. Back and across, we went. She bought me pralines. I held her hand during it all, until the sun finally fell and the hot night rose. So, now, what of that river? And the Algiers Ferry? And Algiers? All memory resolves itself in gaze.

And a last one, more up to date. My wife and I are walking home   10 from a friend's house down tree-shrouded Coliseum Street. It is 2003, and 11 o'clock on a warm January night. We are only steps from our door, just in a cone of street light, when a boy hops out of a car and says he will definitely kill us if we don't hand it over right away. He has a little silver pistol to persuade us. Let's say he's 16. And he is serious. But he laughs when we tell him we don't have a penny. And it's true. I pull my pockets out like a bum. "You people," he says, almost happily, his gun become an afterthought. "You shouldn't be out here this way." He shakes his head, looks at the pavement, then gets in his car and drives away. He, that boy—he'd be 19—I hope he's safe somewhere.

It is—New Orleans is—a city foremost for special projections, for the things you can't do, see, think, consume, feel, forget up in Jackson or Little Rock or home in Topeka. "We're at the jumping-off place," Eudora Welty wrote. This was about Plaquemines, just across the river. It is— New Orleans—the place where the firm ground ceases and the unsound footing begins. A certain kind of person likes such a place. A certain kind of person wants to go there and never leave.

And there are the streetcars (or there were). And there are the oak trees and the lovely French boulevards and the stately rich men's houses. And Buddy Bolden[1] was born there and Satchmo[2] grew up in Storyville. Huey Long[3] lived in the Roosevelt Hotel, where he really had a "de-duct box." His brother, Uncle Earl,[4] was crazy as a betsy-bug.[5] If you knew a waiter you could get a table anywhere. You couldn't get divorced or married or sell your house on Fat Tuesday.[6] And while they didn't let Jews and blacks in the Boston Club, the races still mingled and often people danced in the streets. They subscribed to the Napoleonic Code.[7]

---

[1]***Buddy Bolden:*** Buddy Bolden (1877–1931) was a celebrated African American musician whose cornet playing helped popularize New Orleans–style "rag-time" music that later became known as jazz.—Eds.

[2]***Satchmo:*** The nickname of Louis Armstrong (1901–1971), one of the most celebrated trumpeters and singers in the history of American jazz.—Eds.

[3]***Huey Long:*** Huey Pierce Long Jr. (1893–1935), nicknamed The Kingfish, served as governor (1928–1932) and as senator of Louisiana (1932–1935).—Eds.

[4]***Uncle Earl:*** Earl Kemp Long (1895–1960) was the flamboyant three-time Democratic governor of Louisiana, serving from 1939 to 1940, 1948 to 1952, and 1956 to 1960.—Eds.

[5]***betsy-bug:*** Another term for bedbug.—Eds.

[6]***Fat Tuesday:*** *Mardi Gras* is the French expression for "Fat Tuesday," the day before Ash Wednesday. Mardi Gras is the final day of Carnival, the three-day period preceding the beginning of Lent, which in most Christian denominations is the forty-day liturgical season of fasting and prayer before Easter.—Eds.

[7]***Napoleonic Code:*** The French civil code, established under Napoleon I and implemented in 1804, emphasized clearly written and accessible law.—Eds.

But so much for memory now. It charms, but it confuses and possibly holds us back. It's hard enough to take things in. When I think of my friends in the city this morning, I think of them as high and dry, as being where they belong, being themselves in their normal life that was. I turn off the TV, as I did four years ago next week, just to think my own sorrowing and prospective thoughts of them.

From the ruins it's not easy to know what's best to think. Even the president may have felt that way in his low pass over that wide sheet of onyx water, the bobbing roofs peeking above the surfaces, the vast collapse, the wind-riddled buildings, that little figure (could he see who she was?) staring skyward. Something will be there when the flood recedes. We know that. It will be those people now standing in the water, and on those rooftops—many black, many poor. Homeless. Overlooked. And it will be New Orleans—though its memory may be shortened, its self-gaze and eccentricity scoured out so that what's left is a city more like other cities, less insular, less self-regarding, but possibly more self-knowing after today. A city on firmer ground.

I write in the place of others, today, for the ones who can't be found.   15 And there is a blunt ending now, one we always feared, never wished for, and do not deserve. Don't get me wrong. We would all turn the days back if we could, have those old problems, those old eccentricities again. But today is a beginning. There's no better way to think of it now. Those others surely will be writing soon.

The Reader's Presence

1. Ford's essay is "an attempt to set out a vocabulary for empathy and for reckoning," but these efforts, he discovers, are "frustrated in a moment of sorest need by the plain terms of the tragedy that wants telling" (paragraph 2). If, as Ford says, "People who are close should write that" (paragraph 1), then to what extent—and how—does Ford succeed in developing terms for his readers to understand and appreciate "this great civic tragedy"?

2. In paragraph 2, Ford uses the metaphor of a "keyhole" to describe his efforts at finding adequate language to describe the personal—and civic—devastation inflicted on New Orleans. What specific compositional strategies does Ford use to develop this metaphor and to create a structure for his essay? How does Ford try to "make sense" of what happened in—and to—New Orleans? What role(s) do memory and photographs play in Ford's essay? What are the effects of his saying "But so much for memory now" (paragraph 13)? What prompts him to "turn off the TV"? How do these decisions anticipate—and reflect—the final paragraph of his essay? Please be as specific as possible in your response.

3. In paragraph 3, Ford rejects the efforts of "a public official" to compare the devastation in New Orleans to that in Hiroshima after the dropping of the atomic bomb at the end of World War II. Ford counters this effort by noting simply: "It's not like anything." In an excerpt from *Hiroshima Diary* (page 131), Michihiko Hachiya offers one of the most vivid accounts of the bombing and of the immediate aftermath of the destruction caused by it. What similarities—and differences—do you notice between Hachiya's and Ford's accounts of these scenes of devastation, and to what extent—and how—does each writer use similar compositional strategies to recount the aftermath of events that defy adequate language?

Anne Frank

From *The Diary of a Young Girl*

On her thirteenth birthday (June 12, 1942), and as World War II raged on, Anne Frank began a diary that she called "Kitty." Less than a month later, she and her family went into hiding in a cramped attic in Amsterdam, Holland, in hopes of escaping the Nazis. She continued to keep her diary, addressing it in the form of letters that candidly and freely expressed her most personal thoughts and feelings. Living in conditions that allowed for little privacy, she cherished the secrecy her diary provided: "Who besides me will ever read these letters?" she writes, never dreaming that after her death her intimate diary would be found, published, and read by millions throughout the world.

In August 1944 the Frank family's hiding place was discovered by the Nazis and in March 1945, three months before her sixteenth birthday, Anne died in the concentration camp at Bergen-Belsen. As they searched the attic for valuables and important documents, the Nazis left behind on the floor an insignificant-looking little red-checkered cloth book. Anne Frank: The Diary of a Young Girl *was first published in 1952.*

THINGS THAT LIE BURIED DEEP IN MY HEART

Saturday, June 20, 1942

I haven't written for a few days, because I wanted first of all to think about my diary. It's an odd idea for someone like me to keep a diary; not only because I have never done so before, but because it seems to me that neither I—nor for that matter anyone else—will be interested in the un-bosomings of a thirteen-year-old schoolgirl. Still, what does that matter? I want to write, but more than that, I want to bring out all kinds of things that lie buried deep in my heart.

There is a saying that "paper is more patient than man"; it came back to me on one of my slightly melancholy days, while I sat chin in hand, feeling too bored and limp even to make up my mind whether to go out or stay at home. Yes, there is no doubt that paper is patient and as I don't intend to show this cardboard-covered notebook, bearing the proud name of "diary," to anyone, unless I find a real friend, boy or girl, proba-bly nobody cares. And now I come to the root of the matter, the reason for my starting a diary: it is that I have no such real friend.

Let me put it more clearly, since no one will believe that a girl of thirteen feels herself quite alone in the world, nor is it so. I have darling parents and a sister of sixteen. I know about thirty people whom one might call friends—I have strings of boy friends, anxious to catch a glimpse of me and who, failing that, peep at me through mirrors in class. I have relations, aunts and uncles, who are darlings too, a good home, no—I don't seem to lack anything. But it's the same with all my friends, just fun and joking, nothing more. I can never bring myself to talk of anything outside the common round. We don't seem to be able to get any closer, that is the root of the trouble. Perhaps I lack confidence, but anyway, there it is, a stubborn fact and I don't seem to be able to do anything about it.

Hence, this diary. In order to enhance in my mind's eye the picture of the friend for whom I have waited so long, I don't want to set down a series of bald facts in a diary like most people do, but I want this diary itself to be my friend, and I shall call my friend Kitty. No one will grasp what I'm talking about if I begin my letters to Kitty just out of the blue, so albeit unwillingly, I will start by sketching in brief the story of my life.

My father was thirty-six when he married my mother, who was then   5 twenty-five. My sister Margot was born in 1926 in Frankfurt-on-Main, I followed on June 12, 1929, and, as we are Jewish, we emigrated to Hol-land in 1933, where my father was appointed Managing Director of Travies N.V. This firm is in close relationship with the firm of Kolen & Co. in the same building, of which my father is a partner.

The rest of our family, however, felt the full impact of Hitler's anti-Jewish laws, so life was filled with anxiety. In 1938 after the pogroms, my two uncles (my mother's brothers) escaped to the U.S.A. My old grand-mother came to us, she was then seventy-three. After May 1940 good times rapidly fled: first the war, then the capitulation, followed by the ar-rival of the Germans, which is when the sufferings of us Jews really began. Anti-Jewish decrees followed each other in quick succession. Jews must wear a yellow star, Jews must hand in their bicycles, Jews are banned from trains and are forbidden to drive. Jews are only allowed to do their shopping between three and five o'clock and then only in shops which bear the placard "Jewish shop." Jews must be indoors by eight o'clock and cannot even sit in their own gardens after that hour. Jews are forbidden to visit theaters, cinemas, and other places of entertainment. Jews may not take part in public sports. Swimming baths, tennis courts, hockey fields, and other sports grounds are all prohibited to them. Jews may not visit Christians. Jews must go to Jewish schools, and many more restrictions of a similar kind.

So we could not do this and were forbidden to do that. But life went on in spite of it all. Jopie[1] used to say to me, "You're scared to do anything, because it may be forbidden." Our freedom was strictly limited. Yet things were still bearable.

Granny died in January 1942; no one will ever know how much she is present in my thoughts and how much I love her still.

In 1934 I went to school at the Montessori Kindergarten and continued there. It was at the end of the school year, I was in form 6B, when I had to say good-by to Mrs. K. We both wept, it was very sad. In 1941 I went, with my sister Margot, to the Jewish Secondary School, she into the fourth form and I into the first.

So far everything is all right with the four of us and here I come to the   10
present day.

I ALWAYS COME BACK TO MY DIARY

Saturday, November 7, 1942

Dear Kitty,

Mummy is frightfully irritable and that always seems to herald unpleasantness for me. Is it just chance that Daddy and Mummy never rebuke Margot and that they always drop on me for everything? Yesterday evening, for instance: Margot was reading a book with lovely drawings in it; she got up and went upstairs, put the book down ready to go on with it later. I wasn't doing anything, so picked up the book and started looking at the pictures. Margot came back, saw "her" book in my hands, wrinkled her forehead and asked for the book back. Just because I wanted to look a little further on, Margot got more and more angry. Then Mummy joined in: "Give the book to Margot; she was reading it," she said. Daddy came into the room. He didn't even know what it was all about, but saw the injured look on Margot's face and promptly dropped on me: "I'd like to see what you'd say if Margot ever started looking at one of your books!" I gave way at once, laid the book down, and left the room — offended, as they thought. It so happened I was neither offended

---

[1]*Jopie:* A girlfriend. — EDS.

nor cross, just miserable. It wasn't right of Daddy to judge without knowing what the squabble was about. I would have given Margot the book
myself, and much more quickly, if Mummy and Daddy hadn't interfered.
They took Margot's part at once, as though she were the victim of some
great injustice.

It's obvious that Mummy would stick up for Margot; she and Margot always do back each other up. I'm so used to that that I'm utterly
indifferent to both Mummy's jawing and Margot's moods.

I love them; but only because they are Mummy and Margot. With
Daddy it's different. If he holds Margot up as an example, approves of
what she does, praises and caresses her, then something gnaws at me inside,
because I adore Daddy. He is the one I look up to. I don't love anyone in
the world but him. He doesn't notice that he treats Margot differently
from me. Now Margot is just the prettiest, sweetest, most beautiful girl in
the world. But all the same I feel I have some right to be taken seriously
too. I have always been the dunce, the ne'er-do-well of the family, I've always had to pay double for my deeds, first with the scolding and then
again because of the way my feelings are hurt. Now I'm not satisfied with
this apparent favoritism any more. I want something from Daddy that he
is not able to give me.

I'm not jealous of Margot, never have been. I don't envy her good
looks or her beauty. It is only that I long for Daddy's real love: not only
as his child, but for me—Anne, myself.

I cling to Daddy because it is only through him that I am able to retain   15
the remnant of family feeling. Daddy doesn't understand that I need to give
vent to my feelings over Mummy sometimes. He doesn't want to talk about
it; he simply avoids anything which might lead to remarks about Mummy's
failings. Just the same, Mummy and her failings are something I find harder
to bear than anything else. I don't know how to keep it all to myself. I can't
always be drawing attention to her untidiness, her sarcasm, and her lack of
sweetness, neither can I believe that I'm always in the wrong.

We are exact opposites in everything; so naturally we are bound to
run up against each other. I don't pronounce judgment on Mummy's
character, for that is something I can't judge. I only look at her as a
mother, and she just doesn't succeed in being that to me; I have to be my
own mother. I've drawn myself apart from them all; I am my own skipper
and later on I shall see where I come to land. All this comes about particularly because I have in my mind's eye an image of what a perfect mother
and wife should be; and in her whom I must call "Mother" I find no trace
of that image.

I am always making resolutions not to notice Mummy's bad example. I want to see only the good side of her and to seek in myself what I
cannot find in her. But it doesn't work; and the worst of it is that neither
Daddy nor Mummy understands this gap in my life, and I blame them for
it. I wonder if anyone can ever succeed in making their children absolutely content.

Sometimes I believe that God wants to try me, both now and later on; I must become good through my own efforts, without examples and without good advice. Then later on I shall be all the stronger. Who besides me will ever read these letters? From whom but myself shall I get comfort? As I need comforting often, I frequently feel weak, and dissatisfied with myself; my shortcomings are too great. I know this, and every day I try to improve myself, again and again.

My treatment varies so much. One day Anne is so sensible and is allowed to know everything; and the next day I hear that Anne is just a silly little goat who doesn't know anything at all and imagines that she's learned a wonderful lot from books. I'm not a baby or a spoiled darling any more, to be laughed at, whatever she does. I have my own views, plans, and ideas, though I can't put them into words yet. Oh, so many things bubble up inside me as I lie in bed, having to put up with people I'm fed up with, who always misinterpret my intentions. That's why in the end I always come back to my diary. That is where I start and finish, because Kitty is always patient. I'll promise her that I shall persevere, in spite of everything, and find my own way through it all, and swallow my tears. I only wish I could see the results already or occasionally receive encouragement from someone who loves me.

Don't condemn me; remember rather that sometimes I too can reach   20
the bursting point.

Yours, Anne

A SWEET SECRET

Wednesday, January 5, 1944

Dear Kitty,

I have two things to confess to you today, which will take a long time. But I must tell someone and you are the best one to tell, as I know that, come what may, you always keep a secret.

The first is about Mummy. You know that I've grumbled a lot about Mummy, yet still tried to be nice to her again. Now it is suddenly clear to me what she lacks. Mummy herself has told us that she looked upon us more as her friends than her daughters. Now that is all very fine, but still, a friend can't take a mother's place. I need my mother as an example which I can follow, I want to be able to respect her. I have the feeling that Margot thinks differently about these things and would never be able to understand what I've just told you. And Daddy avoids all arguments about Mummy.

I imagine a mother as a woman who, in the first place, shows great tact, especially towards her children when they reach our age, and who does not laugh at me if I cry about something—not pain, but other things—like "Mums" does.

One thing, which perhaps may seem rather fatuous, I have never forgiven her. It was on a day that I had to go to the dentist. Mummy and Margot were going to come with me, and agreed that I should take my bicycle. When we had finished at the dentist, and were outside again, Margot and Mummy told me that they were going into the town to look at something or buy something—I don't remember exactly what. I wanted to go, too, but was not allowed to, as I had my bicycle with me. Tears of rage sprang into my eyes, and Mummy and Margot began laughing at me. Then I became so furious that I stuck my tongue out at them in the street just as an old woman happened to pass by, who looked very shocked! I rode home on my bicycle, and I know I cried for a long time.

It is queer that the wound that Mummy made then still burns, when I think of how angry I was that afternoon.   25

The second is something that is very difficult to tell you, because it is about myself.

Yesterday I read an article about blushing by Sis Heyster. This article might have been addressed to me personally. Although I don't blush very easily, the other things in it certainly all fit me. She writes roughly something like this—that a girl in the years of puberty becomes quiet within and begins to think about the wonders that are happening to her body.

I experience that, too, and that is why I get the feeling lately of being embarrassed about Margot, Mummy, and Daddy. Funnily enough, Margot, who is much more shy than I am, isn't at all embarrassed.

I think what is happening to me is so wonderful, and not only what can be seen on my body, but all that is taking place inside. I never discuss myself or any of these things with anybody; that is why I have to talk to myself about them.

Each time I have a period—and that has only been three times—I   30
have the feeling that in spite of all the pain, unpleasantness, and nastiness, I have a sweet secret, and that is why, although it is nothing but a nuisance to me in a way, I always long for the time that I shall feel that secret within me again.

Sis Heyster also writes that girls of this age don't feel quite certain of themselves, and discover that they themselves are individuals with ideas, thoughts, and habits. After I came here, when I was just fourteen, I began to think about myself sooner than most girls, and to know that I am a "person." Sometimes, when I lie in bed at night, I have a terrible desire to feel my breasts and to listen to the quiet rhythmic beat of my heart.

I already had these kinds of feelings subconsciously before I came here, because I remember that once when I slept with a girl friend I had a strong desire to kiss her, and that I did do so. I could not help being terribly inquisitive over her body, for she had always kept it hidden from me. I asked her whether, as proof of our friendship, we should feel one another's breasts, but she refused. I go into ecstasies every time I see the naked figure of a woman, such as Venus, for example. It strikes me as so wonderful and exquisite that I have difficulty in stopping the tears rolling down my cheeks.

If only I had a girl friend!

Yours, Anne

The Reader's Presence

1. Why do you think the thirteen-year-old Frank feels compelled to write? Does she have a purpose for keeping a diary?

2. Speculate why her diary is addressed to "Kitty." What is the effect of personalizing her diary in this way? What does that personalization allow her to do as a person and as a writer?

3. Frank wrote during wartime, but the bulk of her diary is devoted to her relationships with family and friends, and to her experiences as a teenager whose mind and body are changing. Michihiko Hachiya (page 131) also kept a diary during wartime. How do these two very different writers deal with the terrible events going on around them? How do they deal with their feelings? Why do you think their diaries have become major contributions to twentieth-century history? What experiences do they offer readers about events that we might otherwise not know?

Henry Louis Gates Jr.

In the Kitchen

The critic, educator, writer, and activist Henry Louis Gates Jr. (b. 1950) is perhaps the most recent in a long line of African American intellectuals who are also public figures. In 1979 he became the first African American to earn a PhD from Cambridge University in its eight-hundred-year history. He has been the recipient of countless honors, including a Carnegie Foundation Fellowship, a Mellon Fellowship, a MacArthur "genius" grant for his work in literary theory, and the 1998 National Medal for the Humanities. Gates is the Alphonse Fletcher University Professor and the director of the W. E. B. Du Bois Institute for African and African American Research at Harvard University. He has been at the forefront of the movement to expand the literary canon that is studied in American schools to include the works of non-European authors. He is also known for his

*work as a "literary archaeologist," uncovering literally thousands of previously
unknown stories, poems, and reviews written by African American authors between 1829 and 1940 and making those texts available to modern readers. He
is co-editor with Kwame Anthony Appiah of* Encarta Africana, *an encyclopedia
of the African diaspora published on CD-ROM, and in print as* Africana: The Encyclopedia of the African and African American Experience *(1999); the expanded
five-volume edition was published in 2005. Gates has written and produced a
number of documentaries aired on public television, including* African American
Lives *in 2006, and* Oprah's Roots: An African American Lives Special *in 2007,
which further examined the genealogical and genetic heritage of African Americans. His latest documentary work is the four-hour sequel to* African American
Lives, *which aired on PBS in February 2008.*

    Among Gates's most recent books are America Behind the Color Line: Dia-
logues with African Americans *(2004),* The Annotated Uncle Tom's Cabin *(2006),
and* Finding Oprah's Roots, Finding Your Own *(2007), a companion book to the
PBS documentary.*

    "In the Kitchen" is taken from Gates's 1995 book Colored People, *a memoir
of his early life as part of the middle-class "colored" community of Piedmont,
West Virginia. About* Colored People, *Gates says, "I'm trying to recollect a lost
era, what I can call a* sepia time, *a whole world that simply no longer exists."*

    We always had a gas stove in the kitchen, though electric cooking be-
came fashionable in Piedmont, like using Crest toothpaste rather than
Colgate, or watching Huntley and Brinkley rather than Walter Cronkite.
But for us it was gas, Colgate, and good ole Walter Cronkite, come what
may. We used gas partly out of loyalty to Big Mom, Mama's mama, because she was mostly blind and still loved to cook, and she could feel her
way better with gas than with electric.

    But the most important thing about our gas-equipped kitchen was
that Mama used to do hair there. She had a "hot comb"—a fine-tooth
iron instrument with a long wooden handle—and a pair of iron curlers
that opened and closed like scissors: Mama would put them into the gas
fire until they glowed. You could smell those prongs heating up.

    I liked what that smell meant for the shape of my day. There was an
intimate warmth in the women's tones as they talked with my mama
while she did their hair. I knew what the women had been through to get
their hair ready to be "done," because I would watch Mama do it herself.
How that scorched kink could be transformed through grease and fire
into a magnificent head of wavy hair was a miracle to me. Still is.

    Mama would wash her hair over the sink, a towel wrapped round
her shoulders, wearing just her half-slip and her white bra. (We had no
shower until we moved down Rat Tail Road into Doc Wolverton's house,
in 1954.) After she had dried it, she would grease her scalp thoroughly
with blue Bergamot hair grease, which came in a short, fat jar with a picture of a beautiful colored lady on it. It's important to grease your scalp
real good, my mama would explain, to keep from burning yourself.

    Of course, her hair would return to its natural kink almost as soon
as the hot water and shampoo hit it. To me, it was another miracle how

hair so "straight" would so quickly become kinky again once it even ap-   5
proached some water.

My mama had only a "few" clients whose heads she "did"—and did,
I think, because she enjoyed it, rather than for the few dollars it brought
in. They would sit on one of our red plastic kitchen chairs, the kind with
the shiny metal legs, and brace themselves for the process. Mama would
stroke that red-hot iron, which by this time had been in the gas fire for a
half hour or more, slowly but firmly through their hair, from scalp to
strand's end. It made a scorching, crinkly sound, the hot iron did, as it
burned its way through the damp kink, leaving in its wake the straightest
of hair strands, each of them standing up long and tall but drooping at the
end, like the top of a heavy willow tree. Slowly, steadily, with deftness and
grace, Mama's hands would transform a round mound of Odetta kink[1]
into a darkened swamp of everglades. The Bergamot made the hair shiny;
the heat of the hot iron gave it a brownish-red cast. Once all the hair was
as straight as God allows kink to get, Mama would take the well-heated
curling iron and twirl the straightened strands into more or less loosely
wrapped curls. She claimed that she owed her strength and skill as a hair-
dresser to her wrists, and her little finger would poke out the way it did
when she sipped tea. Mama was a southpaw, who wrote upside down and
backwards to produce the cleanest, roundest letters you've ever seen.

The "kitchen" she would all but remove from sight with a pair of
shears bought for this purpose. Now, the *kitchen* was the room in which
we were sitting, the room where Mama did hair and washed clothes, and

Odetta Holmes Felious Gorden

[1]*Odetta kink:* A reference to Odetta Holmes Felious Gorden, a popular African American folk singer of the 1960s who helped popularize the hairstyle known as the "afro."
—EDS.

where each of us bathed in a galvanized tub. But the word has another meaning, and the "kitchen" I'm speaking of now is the very kinky bit of hair at the back of the head, where our neck meets the shirt collar. If there ever was one part of our African past that resisted assimilation, it was the kitchen. No matter how hot the iron, no matter how powerful the chemical, no matter how stringent the mashed-potatoes-and-lye formula of a man's "process," neither God nor woman nor Sammy Davis, Jr., could straighten the kitchen. The kitchen was permanent, irredeemable, invincible kink. Unassimilably African. No matter what you did, no matter how hard you tried, nothing could dekink a person's kitchen. So you trimmed it off as best you could.

When hair had begun to "turn," as they'd say, or return to its natural kinky glory, it was the kitchen that turned first. When the kitchen started creeping up the back of the neck, it was time to get your hair done again. The kitchen around the back, and nappy edges at the temples.

Sometimes, after dark, Mr. Charlie Carroll would come to have his hair done. Mr. Charlie Carroll was very light-complected and had a ruddy nose, the kind of nose that made me think of Edmund Gwenn playing Kris Kringle in *Miracle on 34th Street*. At the beginning, they did it after Rocky and I had gone to sleep. It was only later that we found out he had come to our house so Mama could iron his hair—not with a comb and curling iron but with our very own Proctor-Silex steam iron. For some reason, Mr. Charlie would conceal his Frederick Douglass mane[2] under a big white Stetson hat, which I never saw him take off. Except when he came to our house, late at night, to have his hair pressed.

Frederick Douglass

---

[2]***Frederick Douglass mane:*** Frederick Douglass (1817?–1895), an escaped slave who became a prominent African American writer, abolitionist, and orator (see page 125). —EDS.

(Later, Daddy would tell us about Mr. Charlie's most prized piece of   10
knowledge, which the man would confide only after his hair had been
pressed, as a token of intimacy. "Not many people know this," he'd say
in a tone of circumspection, "but George Washington was Abraham Lincoln's daddy." Nodding solemnly, he'd add the clincher: "A white man
told me." Though he was in dead earnest, this became a humorous refrain around the house — "a white man told me" — used to punctuate especially preposterous assertions.)

My mother furtively examined my daughters' kitchens whenever we
went home for a visit in the early eighties. It became a game between us. I
had told her not to do it, because I didn't like the politics it suggested of
"good" and "bad" hair. "Good" hair was straight. "Bad" hair was kinky.
Even in the late sixties, at the height of Black Power, most people could
not bring themselves to say "bad" for "good" and "good" for "bad."
They still said that hair like white hair was "good," even if they encapsu-
lated it in a disclaimer like "what we used to call 'good.'"

Maggie would be seated in her high chair, throwing food this way
and that, and Mama would be cooing about how cute it all was, remembering how I used to do the same thing, and wondering whether Maggie's
flinging her food with her left hand meant that she was going to be a
southpaw too. When my daughter was just about covered with Franco-
American SpaghettiOs, Mama would seize the opportunity and wipe her
clean, dipping her head, tilted to one side, down under the back of Maggie's neck. Sometimes, if she could get away with it, she'd even rub a curl
between her fingers, just to make sure that her bifocals had not deceived
her. Then she'd sigh with satisfaction and relief, thankful that her prayers
had been answered. No kink . . . yet. "Mama!" I'd shout, pretending to
be angry. (Every once in a while, if no one was looking, I'd peek too.)

I say "yet" because most black babies are born with soft, silken hair.
Then, sooner or later, it begins to "turn," as inevitably as do the seasons
or the leaves turn on a tree. And if it's meant to turn, it *turns*, no matter
how hard you try to stop it. People once thought baby oil would stop it.
They were wrong.

Everybody I knew as a child wanted to have good hair. You could be
as ugly as homemade sin dipped in misery and still be thought attractive
if you had good hair. Jesus Moss was what the girls at Camp Lee, Virginia, had called Daddy's hair during World War II. I know he played
that thick head of hair for all it was worth, too. Still would, if he could.

My own hair was "not a bad grade," as barbers would tell me when   15
they cut my head for the first time. It's like a doctor reporting the overall
results of the first full physical that he had given you. "You're in good
shape" or "Blood pressure's kind of high; better cut down on salt."

I spent much of my childhood and adolescence messing with my hair.
I definitely wanted straight hair. Like Pop's.

When I was about three, I tried to stick a wad of Bazooka bubble
gum to that straight hair of his. I suppose what fixed that memory for me

is the spanking I got for doing so: he turned me upside down, holding me by the feet, the better to paddle my behind. Little *nigger*, he shouted, walloping away. I started to laugh about it two days later, when my behind stopped hurting.

When black people say "straight," of course, they don't usually mean "straight" literally, like, say, the hair of Peggy Lipton (the white girl on *The Mod Squad*) or Mary of Peter, Paul and Mary fame; black people call that "stringy" hair. No, "straight" just means not kinky, no matter what contours the curl might take. Because Daddy had straight hair, I would have done *anything* to have straight hair—and I used to try everything to make it straight, short of getting a process, which only riffraff were dumb enough to do.

Of the wide variety of techniques and methods I came to master in the great and challenging follicle prestidigitation, almost all had two things in common: a heavy, oil-based grease and evenly applied pressure. It's no accident that many of the biggest black companies in the fifties and sixties made hair products. Indeed, we do have a vast array of hair grease. And I have tried it all, in search of that certain silky touch, one that leaves neither the hand nor the pillow sullied by grease.

I always wondered what Frederick Douglass put on *his* hair, or Phillis Wheatley.[3] Or why Wheatley has that rag on her head in the little engraving in the frontispiece of her book. One thing is for sure: you can bet that when Wheatley went to England to see the Countess of Huntington, she did not stop by the Queen's Coiffeur on the way. So many black people still get their hair straightened that it's a wonder we don't have a national holiday for Madame C. J. Walker, who invented the process for straightening kinky hair, rather than for Dr. King. Jheri-curled or "relaxed"— it's still fried hair.

I used all the greases, from sea-blue Bergamot, to creamy vanilla Duke (in its orange-and-white jar), to the godfather of grease, the formidable Murray's. Now, Murray's was some *serious* grease. Whereas Bergamot was like oily Jell-O and Duke was viscous and sickly sweet, Murray's was light brown and *hard*. Hard as lard and twice as greasy, Daddy used to say whenever the subject of Murray's came up. Murray's came in an orange can with a screw-on top. It was so hard that some people would put a match to the can, just to soften it and make it more manageable. In the late sixties, when Afros came into style, I'd use Afro-Sheen. From Murray's to Duke to Afro-Sheen: that was my progression in black consciousness.

We started putting hot towels or washrags over our greased-down Murray's-coated heads, in order to melt the wax into the scalp and follicles. Unfortunately, the wax had a curious habit of running down your neck, ears, and forehead. Not to mention your pillowcase.

20

---

[3]*Phillis Wheatley* (1753?–1784): An African-born slave who became America's first major black poet.—EDS.

Another problem was that if you put two palmfuls of Murray's on your head, your hair turned white. Duke did the same thing. It was a challenge: if you got rid of the white stuff, you had a magnificent head of wavy hair. Murray's turned kink into waves. Lots of waves. Frozen waves. A hurricane couldn't have blown those waves around.

That was the beauty of it. Murray's was so hard that it froze your hair into the wavy style you brushed it into. It looked really good if you wore a part. A lot of guys had parts *cut* into their hair by a barber, with clippers or a straight-edge razor. Especially if you had kinky hair—in which case you'd generally wear a short razor cut, or what we called a Quo Vadis.

Being obsessed with our hair, we tried to be as innovative as possible.   25
Everyone knew about using a stocking cap, because your father or your uncle or the older guys wore them whenever something really big was about to happen, secular or sacred, a funeral or a dance, a wedding or a trip in which you confronted official white people, or when you were trying to look really sharp. When it was time to be clean, you wore a stocking cap. If the event was really a big one, you made a new cap for the occasion.

A stocking cap was made by asking your mother for one of her hose, cutting it with a pair of scissors about six inches or so from the open end, where the elastic goes to the top of the thigh. Then you'd knot the cut end, and behold—a conical-shaped hat or cap, with an elastic band that you pulled down low on your forehead and down around your neck in the back. A good stocking cap, to work well, had to fit tight and snug, like a press. And it had to fit that tightly because it *was* a press: it pressed your hair with the force of the hose's elastic. If you greased your hair down real good and left the stocking cap on long enough—*voilà*: you got a head of pressed-against-the-scalp waves. If you used Murray's, and if you wore a stocking cap to sleep, you got a *whole lot* of waves. (You also got a ring around your forehead when you woke up, but eventually that disappeared.)

And then you could enjoy your concrete 'do. Swore we were bad, too, with all that grease and those flat heads. My brother and I would brush it out a bit in the morning so it would look—ahem—"natural."

Grown men still wear stocking caps, especially older men, who generally keep their caps in their top drawer, along with their cuff links and their see-through silk socks, their Maverick tie, their silk handkerchief, and whatever else they prize most.

A Murrayed-down stocking cap was the respectable version of the process, which, by contrast, was most definitely not a cool thing to have, at least if you weren't an entertainer by trade.

Zeke and Keith and Poochie and a few other stars of the basketball team all used to get a process once or twice a year. It was expensive, and to get one you had to go to Pittsburgh or D.C. or Uniontown, someplace where there were enough colored people to support a business. They'd disappear, then reappear a day or two later, strutting like peacocks, their hair burned slightly red from the chemical lye base. They'd also wear "rags" or cloths or handkerchiefs around it when they slept or played

basketball. Do-rags, they were called. But the result was *straight* hair with   30
a hint of wave. No curl. Do-it-yourselfers took their chances at home
with a concoction of mashed potatoes and lye.

The most famous process, outside of what Malcolm X describes in
his *Autobiography* and maybe that of Sammy Davis, Jr., was Nat King
Cole's. Nat King Cole had patent-leather hair.

"That man's got the finest process money can buy." That's what
Daddy said the night Cole's TV show aired on NBC, November 5, 1956.
I remember the date because everyone came to our house to watch it and
to celebrate one of Daddy's buddies' birthdays. Yeah, Uncle Joe chimed
in, they can do shit to his hair that the average Negro can't even *think*
about—secret shit.

Nat King Cole was *clean*. I've had an ongoing argument with a
Nigerian friend about Nat King Cole for twenty years now. Not whether
or not he could sing; any fool knows that he could sing. But whether or
not he was a handkerchief-head for wearing that patent-leather process.

Sammy Davis's process I detested. It didn't look good on him. Worse
still, he liked to have a fried strand dangling down the middle of his forehead, shaking it out from the crown when he sang. But Nat King Cole's
hair was a thing unto itself, a beautifully sculpted work of art that he and
he alone should have had the right to wear.

The only difference between a process and a stocking cap, really, was   35
taste; yet Nat King Cole—unlike, say, Michael Jackson—looked *good* in
his process. His head looked like Rudolph Valentine's in the twenties, and

Nat King Cole

some say it was Valentine that the process imitated. But Nat King Cole wore a process because it suited his face, his demeanor, his name, his style. He was as clean as he wanted to be.

I had forgotten all about Nat King Cole and that patent-leather look until the day in 1971 when I was sitting in an Arab restaurant on the island of Zanzibar, surrounded by men in fezzes and white caftans, trying to learn how to eat curried goat and rice with the fingers of my right hand, feeling two million miles from home, when all of a sudden the old transistor radio sitting on top of a china cupboard stopped blaring out its Swahili music to play "Fly Me to the Moon" by Nat King Cole. The restaurant's din was not affected at all, not even by half a decibel. But in my mind's eye, I saw it: the King's sleek black magnificent tiara. I managed, barely, to blink back the tears.

The Reader's Presence

1. At what point in the essay do you, as a reader, begin to become aware of the social or political significance of the hair-straightening process? At what point in his own development does Gates begin to ascribe a political significance to hair? How would you describe his attitude toward the "kitchen"? toward the "process"? toward the prominent black Americans whom he names in the essay?

2. How would you characterize the author's voice in this essay? Which words and phrases hark back to the language of his home and family? How does Gates integrate these words and phrases into the text? What difference, if any, does it make to you as a reader when he puts certain words, such as *kitchen* or *good*, in quotation marks, as opposed to the passages in which phrases (such as "ugly as homemade sin dipped in misery" [paragraph 14]) are not set off in the text in this way?

3. Gates makes explicit reference to Malcolm X's description of his own first home hair-straightening process (paragraph 31). Reread that description in "Homeboy" (page 168, paragraph 69 to end). How do the two descriptions compare in terms of detail and tone? Are both essays staging an argument? If so, what are their main assertions, and what do they use as evidence? Might Gates's essay be read as a response to Malcolm X's admission of shame? If so, what sort of response is it?

THE WRITER AT WORK

Henry Louis Gates Jr. on the Writer's Voice

Skilled at critical and academic writing, Henry Louis Gates Jr. hoped to find ways to tell stories about his growing up in a small West Virginia community. In writing his memoir, Colored People, *Gates found the voice he wanted. The following comments appeared in a 1995 collection,* Swing Low: Black Men Writing, *edited by Rebecca Carroll.*

My father told stories all the time when I was growing up. My mother used to call them "lies." I didn't know that "lies" was the name for stories in the black vernacular, I just thought it was her own word that she had made up. I was inspired by those "lies," though, and knew that I wanted to tell some too one day.

When I was ten or twelve, I had a baseball column in the local newspaper. I was the scorekeeper for the minor-league games in my town—I would compile all of the facts, and then the editor and I would put together a narrative. I did that every week during the summer. The best part was seeing my name in print. After that, I was hooked—hooked to seeing my name in black and white on paper.

At fourteen or fifteen, I read James Baldwin's work and became fascinated with the idea of writing. When I started reading about black people through the writings of black people, suddenly I was seized by the desire to write. I was in awe of how writers were able to take words and create an illusion of the world that people could step into—a world where people opened doors and shut doors, fell in love and out of love, where people lived and died. I wanted to be able to create those worlds too. I knew I had a voice even before I knew what a "writer's voice" meant. I didn't know what it was, but I could hear it, and I knew when my rhythm was on—it was almost as if I could hear myself write. I thought I had a unique take on the world and trusted my sensibility. It struck me that perhaps it would be a good thing to share it with other people. . . .

I don't think that the prime reason for writing is to save the world, or to save black people. I do it because it makes me feel good. I want to record my vision and to entertain people. When I was writing reviews, although it was an intriguing way to discuss literature, I would have a lot of black people say to me, "I'm having a hard time understanding you, brother." I've always had two conflicting voices within me, one that wants to be outrageous and on the edge, always breaking new ground, and another that wants to be loved by the community for that outrageousness. It is very difficult to expect that people will let you have it both ways like that. Those who really care about a community are the ones who push the boundaries and create new definitions, but generally they get killed for doing that, which is what I mean when I refer to myself as a griot in the black community—the one who makes the wake-up call, who loves his people enough to truly examine the status quo.

The wonderful thing about *Colored People* is that everybody gets it   5
and can appreciate it because it is a universal story. It is my segue from
nonfiction to fiction. I wrote it to preserve a world that has passed away,
and to reveal some secrets — not for the shock value, but because I want
to re-create a voice that black people use when there are no white people
around. Oftentimes in black literature, black authors get all lockjawed in
their writing because they are doing it for a white audience, and not for
themselves. You don't hear the voice of black people when it's just us in
the kitchen, talking out the door and down the road, and that is the voice
that I am trying to capture in *Colored People*. Integration may have cost
us that voice. We cannot take it for granted and must preserve it whenever possible. I don't know what kind of positive language and linguistic
rituals are being passed down in the fragmented, dispossessed black un-
derclass. I think it's very different from when and where I was raised,
when there was a stronger sense of community, and that language was
everywhere I turned.

Michihiko Hachiya
From *Hiroshima Diary*

*On August 6, 1945, the United States dropped an atomic bomb on the
Japanese city of Hiroshima and introduced a new, devastating weapon into modern war. Two days later, the military dropped another bomb on Nagasaki, forcing the Japanese government into an unconditional surrender. For years, the
Japanese survivors of the blasts suffered from unhealing burns, radiation poisoning, cancers, and a score of other illnesses. At first, the Japanese had no idea what
had hit them, though rumors of a new secret weapon circulated rapidly. Most
Americans today know of the bombing mainly through repeated images of the
mushroom cloud itself; rarely do they see photographs or footage of the destruction and casualties. One of the most vivid accounts of the bombing and its immediate aftermath can be found in a diary kept by a Hiroshima physician, Michihiko
Hachiya, who, though severely injured himself, miraculously found the time to
record both his professional observations of a medical nightmare and his human
impressions of an utterly destroyed community. Published on the tenth anniversary of the bombing of Hiroshima,* Hiroshima Diary *(1955) gained widespread
attention. The diary runs only for some two months, from the moment of the
blast on the sunny morning of August 6 to the end of September, when the American occupation was well under way.*

WHAT HAD HAPPENED?
August 6, 1945

Badly injured from the blast, Dr. Hachiya managed to make his way to the hospital where he served as director and which, fortunately, was quite near his house. He spent several days in bed and did not begin writing his diary until August 8. As we can see from the following passage, however, the events were still fresh in his mind.

The hour was early; the morning still, warm, and beautiful. Shimmering leaves, reflecting sunlight from a cloudless sky, made a pleasant contrast with shadows in my garden as I gazed absently through wide-flung doors opening to the south.

Clad in drawers and undershirt, I was sprawled on the living room floor exhausted because I had just spent a sleepless night on duty as an air warden in my hospital.

Suddenly, a strong flash of light startled me — and then another. So well does one recall little things that I remember vividly how a stone lantern in the garden became brilliantly lit and I debated whether this light was caused by a magnesium flare or sparks from a passing trolley.

Garden shadows disappeared. The view where a moment before all had been so bright and sunny was now dark and hazy. Through swirling dust I could barely discern a wooden column that had supported one corner of my house. It was leaning crazily and the roof sagged dangerously.

Moving instinctively, I tried to escape, but rubble and fallen timbers   5
barred the way. By picking my way cautiously I managed to reach the *rōka*[1] and stepped down into my garden. A profound weakness overcame me, so I stopped to regain my strength. To my surprise I discovered that I was completely naked. How odd! Where were my drawers and undershirt?

What had happened?

All over the right side of my body I was cut and bleeding. A large splinter was protruding from a mangled wound in my thigh, and something warm trickled into my mouth. My cheek was torn, I discovered as I felt it gingerly, with the lower lip laid wide open. Embedded in my neck was a sizable fragment of glass which I matter-of-factly dislodged, and with the detachment of one stunned and shocked I studied it and my blood-stained hand.

Where was my wife?

Suddenly thoroughly alarmed, I began to yell for her: "Yaeko-san! Yaeko-san! Where are you?"

Blood began to spurt. Had my carotid artery been cut? Would I bleed   10
to death? Frightened and irrational, I called out again: "It's a five-hundred-ton bomb! Yaeko-san, where are you? A five-hundred-ton bomb has fallen!"

---

[1]*rōka:* A narrow outside hall. — EDS.

Yaeko-san, pale and frightened, her clothes torn and blood-stained, emerged from the ruins of our house holding her elbow. Seeing her, I was reassured. My own panic assuaged, I tried to reassure her.

"We'll be all right," I exclaimed. "Only let's get out of here as fast as we can."

She nodded, and I motioned for her to follow me.

The shortest path to the street lay through the house next door so through the house we went—running, stumbling, falling, and then running again until in headlong flight we tripped over something and fell sprawling into the street. Getting to my feet, I discovered that I had tripped over a man's head.

"Excuse me! Excuse me, please!" I cried hysterically.   15

There was no answer. The man was dead. The head had belonged to a young officer whose body was crushed beneath a massive gate.

We stood in the street, uncertain and afraid, until a house across from us began to sway and then with a rending motion fell almost at our feet. Our own house began to sway, and in a minute it, too, collapsed in a cloud of dust. Other buildings caved in or toppled. Fires sprang up and whipped by a vicious wind began to spread.

It finally dawned on us that we could not stay there in the street, so we turned our steps towards the hospital. Our home was gone; we were wounded and needed treatment; and after all, it was my duty to be with my staff. This latter was an irrational thought—what good could I be to anyone, hurt as I was.

We started out, but after twenty or thirty steps I had to stop. My breath became short, my heart pounded, and my legs gave way under me. An overpowering thirst seized me and I begged Yaeko-san to find me some water. But there was no water to be found. After a little my strength somewhat returned and we were able to go on.

I was still naked, and although I did not feel the least bit of shame, I   20
was disturbed to realize that modesty had deserted me. On rounding a corner we came upon a soldier standing idly in the street. He had a towel draped across his shoulder, and I asked if he would give it to me to cover my nakedness. The soldier surrendered the towel quite willingly but said not a word. A little later I lost the towel, and Yaeko-san took off her apron and tied it around my loins.

Our progress towards the hospital was interminably slow, until finally, my legs, stiff from drying blood, refused to carry me farther. The strength, even the will, to go on deserted me, so I told my wife, who was almost as badly hurt as I, to go on alone. This she objected to, but there was no choice. She had to go ahead and try to find someone to come back for me.

Yaeko-san looked into my face for a moment, and then, without saying a word, turned away and began running towards the hospital. Once, she looked back and waved and in a moment she was swallowed up in the gloom. It was quite dark now, and with my wife gone, a feeling of dreadful loneliness overcame me.

I must have gone out of my head lying there in the road because the next thing I recall was discovering that the clot on my thigh had been dislodged and blood was again spurting from the wound. I pressed my hand to the bleeding area and after a while the bleeding stopped and I felt better.

Could I go on?

I tried. It was all a nightmare — my wounds, the darkness, the road 25 ahead. My movements were ever so slow; only my mind was running at top speed.

In time I came to an open space where the houses had been removed to make a fire lane. Through the dim light I could make out ahead of me the hazy outlines of the Communications Bureau's big concrete building, and beyond it the hospital. My spirits rose because I knew that now someone would find me; and if I should die, at least my body would be found.

I paused to rest. Gradually things around me came into focus. There were the shadowy forms of people, some of whom looked like walking ghosts. Others moved as though in pain, like scarecrows, their arms held out from their bodies with forearms and hands dangling. These people puzzled me until I suddenly realized that they had been burned and were holding their arms out to prevent the painful friction of raw surfaces rubbing together. A naked woman carrying a naked baby came into view. I averted my gaze. Perhaps they had been in the bath. But then I saw a naked man, and it occurred to me that, like myself, some strange thing had deprived them of their clothes. An old woman lay near me with an expression of suffering on her face; but she made no sound. Indeed, one thing was common to everyone I saw — complete silence. . . .

PIKADON
August 9, 1945

As the wounded poured into Dr. Hachiya's hospital, the physicians tried to make sense of the symptoms and injuries, which did not resemble those of ordinary bombings. Because many of the patients with horrible symptoms showed no obvious signs of injuries, Dr. Hachiya could only speculate about what might have occurred. He had no idea as yet what type of weapon had been used against them.

Today, Dr. Hanaoka's[2] report on the patients was more detailed. One observation particularly impressed me. Regardless of the type of injury, nearly everybody had the same symptoms. All had a poor appetite, the majority had nausea and gaseous indigestion, and over half had vomiting.

Not a few had shown improvement since yesterday. Diarrhea, though, continued to be a problem and actually appeared to be increasing. Distinctly alarming was the appearance of blood in the stools of patients who

---

[2]*Dr. Hanaoka:* Head of internal medicine. — EDS.

People walking through the ruins of Hiroshima in the weeks following the atomic bomb blast. Photo by Bernard Hoffman.

earlier had only diarrhea. The isolation of these people was becoming increasingly difficult.

One seriously ill man complained of a sore mouth yesterday, and today, numerous small hemorrhages began to appear in his mouth and under his skin. His case was the more puzzling because he came to the hospital complaining of weakness and nausea and did not appear to have been injured at all.   30

This morning, other patients were beginning to show small subcutaneous hemorrhages, and not a few were coughing and vomiting blood in addition to passing it in their stools. One poor woman was bleeding from her privates. Among these patients there was not one with symptoms typical of anything we knew, unless you could excuse those who developed signs of severe brain disease before they died.

Dr. Hanaoka believed the patients could be divided into three groups:

1. Those with nausea, vomiting, and diarrhea who were improving.
2. Those with nausea, vomiting, and diarrhea who were remaining stationary.
3. Those with nausea, vomiting, and diarrhea who were developing hemorrhage under the skin or elsewhere.

Had these patients been burned or otherwise injured, we might have tried to stretch the logic of cause and effect and assume that their bizarre symptoms were related to injury, but so many patients appeared to have received no injury whatsoever that we were obliged to postulate an insult heretofore unknown.

The only other possible cause for the weird symptoms observed was a sudden change in atmospheric pressure. I had read somewhere about bleeding that follows ascent to high altitudes and about bleeding in deep sea divers who ascend too rapidly from the depths. Having never seen such injury I could not give much credence to my thoughts.

Still, it was impossible to dismiss the thought that atmospheric pressure   35
had had something to do with the symptoms of our patients. During my student days at Okayama University, I had seen experiments conducted in a pressure chamber. Sudden, temporary deafness was one symptom everyone complained of if pressure in the chamber was abruptly altered.

Now, I could state positively that I heard nothing like an explosion when we were bombed the other morning, nor did I remember any sound during my walk to the hospital as houses collapsed around me. It was as though I walked through a gloomy, silent motion picture. Others whom I questioned had had the same experience.

Those who experienced the bombing from the outskirts of the city characterized it by the word: *pikadon*.[3]

How then could one account for my failure and the failure of others to hear an explosion except on the premise that a sudden change in atmospheric pressure had rendered those nearby temporarily deaf: Could the bleeding we were beginning to observe be explained on the same basis?

Since all books and journals had been destroyed, there was no way to corroborate my theories except by further appeal to the patients. To that end Dr. Katsube[4] was asked to discover what else he could when he made ward rounds.

It was pleasing to note my scientific curiosity was reviving, and I lost   40
no opportunity to question everyone who visited me about the bombing of Hiroshima. Their answers were vague and ambiguous, and on one point only were they in agreement: a new weapon had been used. *What* the new weapon was became a burning question. Not only had our books been destroyed, but our newspapers, telephones, and radios as well. . . .

---

[3]*pikadon:* *Pika* means a glitter, sparkle, or bright flash of light, like a flash of lightning. *Don* means a boom! or loud sound. Together, the words came to mean to the people of Hiroshima an explosion characterized by a flash and a boom. Hence: "flash-boom!" Those who remember the flash only speak of the "*pika*"; those who were far enough from the hypocenter to experience both speak of the "*pikadon*." —EDS.
[4]**Dr. Katsube:** Chief of surgery. —EDS.

The Reader's Presence

1. In many ways it is fortunate that one of the diaries kept immediately after the atomic blast was written by a medical doctor. Why? How does it contribute to the diary's historical value? Could this be a disadvantage? Would you have preferred to read a patient's diary instead? If so, why?

2. Hachiya's first entry on August 6 was written a few days after the events it depicts. What indications do you receive from the writing that the entry was predated? Can you detect any differences from the second entry (August 9), which was apparently composed on the stated day?

3. Hachiya's confusion reveals itself in his writing in many ways: short paragraphs, multiple questions, and unconfirmed guesses. Throughout, his matter-of-fact language belies his panic. How does Hachiya's characterization of the bombing of Hiroshima compare with Don DeLillo's account of the attack on the World Trade Center (page 332)? Is a survivor's account of a disaster necessarily more vivid than that of someone who witnesses it from a distance?

Edward Hoagland

On Stuttering

Edward Hoagland (b. 1932) is an essayist, nature writer, and novelist. Before his graduation from Harvard University, his first novel, Cat Man *(1956), was accepted for publication and won the Houghton Mifflin Literary Fellowship Award. He has received several other honors, including a Guggenheim Fellowship, an O. Henry Award, an award from the American Academy of Arts and Letters, and a Lannan Foundation Award. Having taught at Bennington College in Vermont for almost twenty years, Hoagland retired in 2005. Hoagland's essays cover a wide range of topics, such as personal experiences, wild animals, travels to other countries, and ecological crises. Among his many highly regarded books are* Walking the Dead Diamond River *(1973),* African Calliope *(1979),* Balancing Acts *(1992), and* Tigers and Ice *(1999). His latest book of essays,* Hoagland on Nature, *was published in 2004.*

In his memoir, Compass Points *(2001), Hoagland writes: "Most of us live like stand-up comedians on a vaudeville stage—the way an essayist does—by our humble wits, messing up, swallowing an aspirin, knowing Hollywood won't call, thinking no one we love will die today, just another day of sunshine and rain."*

Stuttering is like trying to run with loops of rope around your feet. And yet you feel that you do want to run because you may get more words out that way before you trip: an impulse you resist so other people won't tell you to "calm down" and "relax." Because they themselves may stammer a little bit when jittery or embarrassed, it's hard for a real stutterer like me to convince a new acquaintance that we aren't perpetually in such a nervous state and that it's quite normal for us to be at the mercy of strangers. Strangers are usually civilized, once the rough and sometimes inadvertently hurtful process of recognizing what is wrong with us is over (that we're not laughing, hiccuping, coughing, or whatever) and in a way we plumb them for traces of schadenfreude. A stutterer knows who the good guys are in any crowded room, as well as the location of each mocking gleam, and even the St. Francis type, who will wait until he thinks nobody is looking to wipe a fleck of spittle off his face.

I've stuttered for more than sixty years, and the mysteries of the encumbrance still catch me up: being reminded every morning that it's engrained in my fiber, although I had forgotten in my dreams. Life can become a matter of measuring the importance of anything you have to say. Is it better to remain a pleasant cipher who ventures nothing in particular but chuckles immoderately at everyone else's conversation, or instead to subject your several companions to the ordeal of watching you struggle to expel opinions that are either blurred and vitiated, or made to sound too emphatic, by all the huffing and puffing, the facial contortions, tongue biting, blushing, and suffering? "Write it down," people often said to me in school; indeed I sold my first novel before I left college.

Self-confidence can reduce a stutter's dimensions (in that sense you do "outgrow" it), as will affection (received or felt), anger, sexual arousal, and various other hormonal or pheromonal states you may dip into in the shorter term. Yet it still lurks underfoot, like a trapdoor. I was determined not to be impeded and managed to serve a regular stint in the Army by telling the draft-board psychiatrist that I wanted to and was only stammering from "nervousness" with him. Later I also contrived to become a college professor, thanks to the patience of my early students. Nevertheless, through childhood and adolescence, when I was almost mute in public, I could talk without much difficulty to one or two close friends, and then to the particular girl I was necking with. In that case, an overlapping trust was then the lubricant, but if it began to evaporate as our hopes for permanence didn't pan out, I'd start regretfully, apologetically but willy-nilly, to stutter with her again. Adrenaline, when I got mad, operated in a similar fashion, though only momentarily. That is, if somebody made fun of me or treated me cavalierly and a certain threshold was crossed, a spurt of chemistry would suddenly free my mouth and—like Popeye grabbing a can of spinach—I could answer

him. Poor Billy Budd[1] didn't learn this technique (and his example frightened me because of its larger implications). Yet many stutterers develop
a snappish temperament, and from not just sheer frustration but the fact
that being more than ready to "lose one's temper" (as Billy wasn't) actually helps. As in jujitsu, you can trap an opponent by employing his
strength and cruelty against him; and bad guys aren't generally smart
enough to know that if they wait me out, I'll bog down helplessly all
over again.

Overall, however, stuttering is not so predictable. Whether rested or
exhausted, fibbing or speaking the Simon-pure truth, and when in the
company of chums or people whom I don't respect, I can be fluent or tied
in knots. I learned young to be an attentive listener, both because my empathy for others' worries was honed by my handicap and because it was in
my best interest that they talk a lot. And yet a core in you will hemorrhage
if you become a mere assenter. How many opinions can you keep to
yourself before you choke on them (and turn into a stick of furniture for
everybody else)? So, instead, you measure what's worth specifying. If you
agree with two-thirds of what's being suggested, is it worth the labor of
breathlessly elaborating upon the one-third where you differ? There were
plenty of times when a subject might come up that I knew more about
than the rest of the group, and it used to gall me if I had held my peace till
maybe closeted afterward with a close friend. A stymieing bashfulness can
also slide a stutterer into slack language because accurate words are so
much harder to say than bland ones. You're tempted to be content with
an approximation of what you mean in order to escape the scourge of
being exact. A sort of football game is going on in your head—the tacklers live there too—and the very effort of pausing to figure out the right
way to describe something will alert them to how to pull you down.
Being glib and sloppy generates less blockage.

But it's important not to err in the opposite direction, on the side of   5
tendentiousness, and insist on equal time only because you are a pain in
the neck with a problem. You can stutter till your tongue bleeds and
your chest is sore from heaving, but so what, if you haven't anything to
say that's worth the humiliation? Better to function as a kind of tuning
fork, vibrating to other people's anguish or apprehensiveness, as well as
your own. A handicap can be cleansing. My scariest moments as a stutterer have been (1) when my daughter was learning to talk and briefly
got the impression that she was supposed to do the same; (2) once when
I was in the woods and a man shot in my direction and I had to make
myself heard loud and fast; and (3) when anticipating weddings where I
would need either to propose a toast or say "I do." Otherwise my impediment ceased to be a serious blight about the time I lost my virginity:

---

[1]*Poor Billy Budd:* a reference to the main character in Herman Melville's novella, *Billy
Budd* (published 1924). Billy Budd's speech impediment plays a pivotal role in the plot,
leading to his hanging.—EDS.

just a sort of cleft to step around—a squint and gasp of hesitation that indicated to people I might want to be friends with or interview that I wasn't perfect either and perhaps they could trust me.

At worst, during my teens, when I was stuttering on vowels as well as consonants and spitting a few words out could seem interminable, I tried some therapies. But "Slow Speech" was as slow as the trouble itself; and repeatedly writing the first letter of the word that I was stuttering on with my finger in my pocket looked peculiar enough to attract almost as much attention. It did gradually lighten with my maturity and fatherhood, professional recognition, and the other milestones that traditionally help. Nothing "slew" it, though, until at nearly 60 I went semiblind for a couple of years, and this emergency eclipsed—completely trumped—the lesser difficulty. I felt I simply had to talk or die, and so I talked. Couldn't do it gratuitously or lots, but I talked enough to survive. The stutter somehow didn't hold water and ebbed away, until surgery restored my vision and then it returned, like other normalcies.

Such variations can make a stutter seem like a sort of ancillary eccentricity, or a personal Godzilla. But the ball carrier in your head is going to have his good days too—when he can swivel past the tacklers, improvising a broken-field dash so that they are out of position—or even capture their attention with an idea so intriguing that they stop and listen. Not for long, however: The message underlying a stutter is rather like mortality, after all. Real reprieves and fluency are not for you and me. We blunder along, stammering—then not so much—through minor scrapes and scares, but not unscathed. We're not Demosthenes, of course. And poor Demosthenes, if you look him up, ended about as sadly as Billy Budd. People tend to.

The Reader's Presence

1. Why does Hoagland compare his stutter to a football game (paragraph 4)? Explore the metaphor fully. For example, what position does Hoagland play? Who are the tacklers who are trying to pull him down? How many touchdowns does he score in his life, according to his essay? What strategies does he develop to avoid anticipated blockers? Would you say he's winning or losing? Why?

2. In what specific ways do Hoagland's sentences and paragraphs begin and end as you might have anticipated? Can you detect written signs of his stutter? What kinds of verbal hesitations and restatements happen when someone stutters? Where—and with what effects—are there similar hesitations and restatements in Hoagland's essay? Imagine Hoagland speaking this essay. At which points do you think that he would hesitate? Rewrite a paragraph to include the imagined stuttering and compare it to the original paragraph. What changes in meaning occur in the rewritten version?

3. Read David Sedaris's "Me Talk Pretty One Day" (page 235) and compare the two authors' approaches to handling difficulties with speech. What strategies do they use to deal with being less than fluent? To what extent do their limitations affect their feelings about themselves? about the world around them? Who deals more effectively with not being able to communicate easily? Why?

THE WRITER AT WORK

Edward Hoagland on What an Essay Is

Known as one of America's finest essayists, Edward Hoagland began his career writing fiction. In this passage from his Introduction to The Best American Essays 1999, *Hoagland describes how he thinks essays work and the idiosyncratic ways essayists—like himself—approach the act of writing them. Essays, he reminds us, are different from articles and documents: They don't necessarily offer objective information and they don't require their writers to be authorities about anything other than their own experiences. All good essays, he suggests, encapsulate their writer's presence. In these literary beliefs he is a direct descendent of Montaigne (1533–1592), whom many consider the inventor of the modern essay. Montaigne, too, was skeptical of authority and wrote essays that appear to follow the drifts of an interior dialogue carried on with himself. After reading Hoagland's brief but thoughtful passage, consider how it comments on his essay on stuttering.*

Essays are how we speak to one another in print—caroming thoughts not merely in order to convey a certain packet of information, but with a special edge or bounce of personal character in a kind of public letter. You multiply yourself as a writer, gaining height as though jumping on a trampoline, if you can catch the gist of what other people have also been feeling and clarify it for them. Classic essay subjects, like the flux of friendship, "On Greed," "On Religion," "On Vanity," or solitude, lying, self-sacrifice, can be major-league yet not require Bertrand Russell to handle them. A layman who has diligently looked into something, walking in the mosses of regret after the death of a parent, for instance, may acquire an intangible authority, even without being memorably angry or funny or possessing a beguiling equanimity. *He* cares; therefore, if he has tinkered enough with his words, we do too.

An essay is not a scientific document. It can be serendipitous or domestic, satire or testimony, tongue-in-cheek or a wail of grief. Mulched perhaps in its own contradictions, it promises no sure objectivity, just the condiment of opinion on a base of observation, and sometimes such leaps of illogic or superlogic that they may work a bit like magic realism in a novel: namely, to simulate the mind's own processes in a murky and incongruous world. More than being instructive, as a magazine article is, an essay has a slant, a seasoned personality behind it that ought to weather well. Even if we think the author is telling us the earth is flat, we might want to listen to him elaborate upon the fringes of his premise because the bristle of his narrative and what he's seen intrigues us. He has a cutting edge, yet balance too. A given body of information is going to be eclipsed, but what lives in art is spirit, not factuality, and we respond to Montaigne's human touch despite four centuries of technological and social change.

Langston Hughes

Salvation

One of the leading figures of the Harlem Renaissance, Langston Hughes (1902–1967) was a prolific writer. He started his career as a poet, but he also wrote fiction, autobiography, biography, history, and plays, and he worked at various times as a journalist. One of his most famous poems, "The Negro Speaks of Rivers," was written while he was in high school. Although Langston Hughes traveled widely, most of his writings are concerned with the lives of urban working-class African Americans.

Hughes used the rhythms of blues and jazz to bring to his writing a distinctive expression of black culture and experience. His work continues to be popular today, especially collections of short stories such as The Ways of White Folks *(1934), volumes of poetry such as* Montage of a Dream Deferred *(1951), and his series of vignettes on the character Jesse B. Simple, collected and published from 1950 to 1965. Hughes published two volumes of autobiography; "Salvation" is taken from the first of these,* The Big Sea *(1940).*

Throughout his work, Hughes refused to idealize his subject. "Certainly," he said, "I personally knew very few people anywhere who were wholly beautiful and wholly good. Besides I felt that the masses of our people had as much in their lives to put into books as did those more fortunate ones who had been born with some means and the ability to work up to a master's degree at a Northern college." Expressing the writer's truism on writing about what one knows best, he continued, "Anyway, I didn't know the upper-class Negroes well enough to write much about them. I only knew the people I had grown up with, and they weren't the people whose shoes were always shined, who had been to Harvard, or who had heard of Bach. But they seemed to me good people too."

I was saved from sin when I was going on thirteen. But not really saved. It happened like this. There was a big revival at my Auntie Reed's church. Every night for weeks there had been much preaching, singing, praying, and shouting, and some very hardened sinners had been brought to Christ, and the membership of the church had grown by leaps and bounds. Then just before the revival ended, they held a special meeting for children, "to bring the young lambs to the fold." My aunt spoke of it for days ahead. That night I was escorted to the front row and placed on the mourners' bench with all the other young sinners, who had not yet been brought to Jesus.

My aunt told me that when you were saved you saw a light, and something happened to you inside! And Jesus came into your life! And God was with you from then on! She said you could see and hear and feel Jesus in your soul. I believed her. I had heard a great many old people say the same thing and it seemed to me they ought to know. So I sat there calmly in the hot, crowded church, waiting for Jesus to come to me.

The preacher preached a wonderful rhythmical sermon, all moans and shouts and lonely cries and dire pictures of hell, and then he sang a song about the ninety and nine safe in the fold, but one little lamb was left out in the cold. Then he said: "Won't you come? Won't you come to Jesus? Young lambs, won't you come?" And he held out his arms to all us young sinners there on the mourners' bench. And the little girls cried. And some of them jumped up and went to Jesus right away. But most of us just sat there.

A great many old people came and knelt around us and prayed, old women with jet-black faces and braided hair, old men with work-gnarled hands. And the church sang a song about the lower lights are burning, some poor sinners to be saved. And the whole building rocked with prayer and song.

Still I kept waiting to *see* Jesus.   5

Finally all the young people had gone to the altar and were saved, but one boy and me. He was a rounder's son named Westley. Westley and I were surrounded by sisters and deacons praying. It was very hot in the church, and getting late now. Finally Westley said to me in a whisper: "God damn! I'm tired o' sitting here. Let's get up and be saved." So he got up and was saved.

Then I was left all alone on the mourners' bench. My aunt came and knelt at my knees and cried, while prayers and song swirled all around me in the little church. The whole congregation prayed for me alone, in a mighty wail of moans and voices. And I kept waiting serenely for Jesus, waiting, waiting—but he didn't come. I wanted to see him, but nothing happened to me. Nothing! I wanted something to happen to me, but nothing happened.

I heard the songs and the minister saying: "Why don't you come? My dear child, why don't you come to Jesus? Jesus is waiting for you. He wants you. Why don't you come? Sister Reed, what is this child's name?"

"Langston," my aunt sobbed.

"Langston, why don't you come? Why don't you come and be saved?   10
Oh, Lamb of God! Why don't you come?"

Eight Studies for the Book of Genesis, #3: And God said "Let the earth bring forth the grass, trees, fruit, and herbs." By Jacob Lawrence, 1989.

© 2008 The Jacob and Gwendolyn Lawrence Foundation, Seattle/Artists Rights Society (ARS), New York. Photo credit: The Jacob and Gwendolyn Lawrence Foundation/ Art Resource, NY.

Now it was really getting late. I began to be ashamed of myself, holding everything up so long. I began to wonder what God thought about Westley, who certainly hadn't seen Jesus either, but who was now sitting proudly on the platform, swinging his knickerbockered legs and grinning down at me, surrounded by deacons and old women on their knees praying. God had not struck Westley dead for taking his name in vain or for lying in the temple. So I decided that maybe to save further trouble, I'd better lie, too, and say that Jesus had come, and get up and be saved.

So I got up.

Suddenly the whole room broke into a sea of shouting, as they saw me rise. Waves of rejoicing swept the place. Women leaped in the air. My aunt threw her arms around me. The minister took me by the hand and led me to the platform.

When things quieted down, in a hushed silence, punctuated by a few ecstatic "Amens," all the new young lambs were blessed in the name of God. Then joyous singing filled the room.

That night, for the first time in my life but one — for I was a big boy   15
twelve years old — I cried. I cried, in bed alone, and couldn't stop. I
buried my head under the quilts, but my aunt heard me. She woke up and
told my uncle I was crying because the Holy Ghost had come into my life,
and because I had seen Jesus. But I was really crying because I couldn't
bear to tell her that I had lied, that I had deceived everybody in the
church, that I hadn't seen Jesus, and that now I didn't believe there was a
Jesus anymore, since he didn't come to help me.

The Reader's Presence

1. Pay close attention to Hughes's two opening sentences. How would
   you describe their tone? How do they suggest the underlying pattern of the essay? How do they introduce the idea of deception
   right from the start? Who is being deceived in the essay? Is it the
   congregation? God? Hughes's aunt? the reader?

2. Hughes's essay is full of hyperbole, much of it expressing the
   heightened emotion of religious conversion. What is the purpose of
   the exclamation points Hughes uses in paragraph 2? Who is speaking these sentences? Where are other examples of overstatement?
   How does Hughes incorporate lyrics from songs into his prose (see
   especially paragraph 3)? Why not simply quote from the songs directly? How do these stylistic decisions affect your sense of the
   scene? Do you feel aligned with Hughes? Why or why not?

3. How does Hughes use the character of Westley? Is he essential
   to the narrative? If so, why? How does his role compare to secondary characters in other essays — for example, Theresa in
   Bernard Cooper's "A Clack of Tiny Sparks" (page 75) or Shorty
   in Malcolm X's "Homeboy" (page 168)?

THE WRITER AT WORK

Langston Hughes on *How to Be a Bad Writer* *(in Ten Easy Lessons)*

*Established authors are frequently asked for tips on writing. Here Langston
Hughes reverses the practice and offers young writers some memorable advice on
how to write poorly. "How to Be a Bad Writer" first appeared in the* Harlem
Quarterly *(Spring 1950). Some of his suggestions no longer seem applicable
today, thanks in part to his own literary efforts. But which lessons do you think
are still worth paying attention to?*

1. Use all the clichés possible, such as "He had a gleam in his eye," or "Her teeth were white as pearls."

2. If you are a Negro, try very hard to write with an eye dead on the white market—use modern stereotypes of older stereotypes—big burly Negroes, criminals, low-lifers, and prostitutes.

3. Put in a lot of profanity and as many pages as possible of near-pornography and you will be so modern you pre-date Pompei in your lonely crusade toward the best-seller lists. By all means be misunderstood, unappreciated, and ahead of your time in print and out, then you can be felt-sorry-for by your own self, if not the public.

4. Never characterize characters. Just name them and then let them go for themselves. Let all of them talk the same way. If the reader hasn't imagination enough to make something out of cardboard cut-outs, shame on him!

5. Write about China, Greece, Tibet, or the Argentine pampas—   5
anyplace you've never seen and know nothing about. Never write about anything you know, your home town, or your home folks, or yourself.

6. Have nothing to say, but use a great many words, particularly high-sounding words, to say it.

7. If a playwright, put into your script a lot of hand-waving and spirituals, preferably the ones everybody has heard a thousand times from Marion Anderson to the Golden Gates.

8. If a poet, rhyme June with moon as often and in as many ways as possible. Also use *thee*'s and *thou*'s and *'tis* and *o'er*, and invert your sentences all the time. Never say, "The sun rose, bright and shining." But, rather, "Bright and shining rose the sun."

9. Pay no attention to spelling or grammar or the neatness of the manuscript. And in writing letters, never sign your name so anyone can read it. A rapid scrawl will better indicate how important and how busy you are.

10. Drink as much liquor as possible and always write under the influ-   10
ence of alcohol. When you can't afford alcohol yourself, or even if you can, drink on your friends, fans, and the general public.

If you are white, there are many more things I can advise in order to be a bad writer, but since this piece is for colored writers, there are some things I know a Negro just will not do, not even for writing's sake, so there is no use mentioning them.

Geeta Kothari

If You Are What You Eat, Then What Am I?

Writer and educator Geeta Kothari (b. 1928) was born in New York City of Indian parents whose "back home" was New Delhi, India. Kothari is the editor of the literary journal the Kenyon Review *and teaches at the University of Pittsburgh. She is a two-time recipient of the fellowship in literature from the Pennsylvania Council on the Arts and the editor of an anthology,* Did My Mama Like to Dance? and Other Stories about Mothers and Daughters *(1994). Her fiction and nonfiction work has appeared in a number of journals, including the* Massachusetts Review *and* Fourth Genre. *Her essay "If You Are What You Eat, Then What Am I?" was first published in the* Kenyon Review *in 1999 and was selected for the* Best American Essays 2000.

Kothari clearly understands the relationship among culture, family, and food and "the tacit codes of the people you live with," as the Michael Ignatieff quotation that opens the essay underscores.

To belong is to understand the tacit codes of the people you live with.

—Michael Ignatieff, *Blood and Belonging*

I

The first time my mother and I open a can of tuna, I am nine years old. We stand in the doorway of the kitchen, in semi-darkness, the can tilted toward daylight. I want to eat what the kids at school eat: bologna, hot dogs, salami—foods my parents find repugnant because they contain pork and meat by-products, crushed bone and hair glued together by chemicals and fat. Although she has never been able to tolerate the smell of fish, my mother buys the tuna, hoping to satisfy my longing for American food.

Indians, of course, do not eat such things.

The tuna smells fishy, which surprises me because I can't remember anyone's tuna sandwich actually smelling like fish. And the tuna in those sandwiches doesn't look like this, pink and shiny, like an internal organ. In fact, this looks similar to the bad foods my mother doesn't want me to eat. She is silent, holding her face away from the can while peering into it like a half-blind bird.

"What's wrong with it?" I ask.

She has no idea. My mother does not know that the tuna everyone else's mothers made for them was tuna *salad*.

5

"Do you think it's botulism?"

I have never seen botulism, but I have read about it, just as I have read about but never eaten steak and kidney pie.

There is so much my parents don't know. They are not like other parents, and they disappoint me and my sister. They are supposed to help us negotiate the world outside, teach us the signs, the clues to proper behavior: what to eat and how to eat it.

We have expectations, and my parents fail to meet them, especially my mother, who works full time. I don't understand what it means, to have a mother who works outside and inside the home; I notice only the ways in which she disappoints me. She doesn't show up for school plays. She doesn't make chocolate-frosted cupcakes for my class. At night, if I want her attention, I have to sit in the kitchen and talk to her while she cooks the evening meal, attentive to every third or fourth word I say.

We throw the tuna away. This time my mother is disappointed. I   10
go to school with tuna eaters. I see their sandwiches, yet cannot explain the discrepancy between them and the stinking, oily fish in my mother's hand. We do not understand so many things, my mother and I.

II

On weekends, we eat fried chicken from Woolworth's on the back steps of my father's first-floor office in Murray Hill. The back steps face a small patch of garden—hedges, a couple of skinny trees, and gravel instead of grass. We can see the back windows of the apartment my parents and I lived in until my sister was born. There, the doorman watched my mother, several months pregnant and wearing a sari, slip on the ice in front of the building.

My sister and I pretend we are in the country, where our American friends all have houses. We eat glazed doughnuts, also from Woolworth's, and french fries with catsup.

III

My mother takes a catering class and learns that Miracle Whip and mustard are healthier than mayonnaise. She learns to make egg salad with chopped celery, deviled eggs with paprika, a cream cheese spread with bits of fresh ginger and watercress, chicken liver pâté, and little brown and white checkerboard sandwiches that we have only once. She makes chicken *à la king* in puff pastry shells and eggplant parmesan. She acquires smooth wooden paddles, whose purpose is never clear, two different egg slicers, several wooden spoons, icing tubes, cookie cutters, and an electric mixer.

IV

I learn to make tuna salad by watching a friend. My sister never acquires a taste for it. Instead, she craves:

bologna
hot dogs
bacon
sausages

and a range of unidentifiable meat products forbidden by my parents. Their restrictions are not about sacred cows, as everyone around us assumes; in a pinch, we are allowed hamburgers, though lamb burgers are preferable. A "pinch" means choosing not to draw attention to ourselves as outsiders, impolite visitors who won't eat what the host serves. But bologna is still taboo.

V

Things my sister refuses to eat: butter, veal, anything with *jeera*.[1] The babysitter tries to feed her butter sandwiches, threatens her with them, makes her cry in fear and disgust. My mother does not disappoint her; she does not believe in forcing us to eat, in using food as a weapon. In addition to pbj, my sister likes pasta and marinara sauce, bologna and Wonder bread (when she can get it), and fried egg sandwiches with turkey, cheese, and horseradish. Her tastes, once established, are predictable.

VI

When we visit our relatives in India, food prepared outside the house is carefully monitored. In the hot, sticky monsoons in New Delhi and Bombay, we cannot eat ice cream, salad, cold food, or any fruit that can't be peeled. Definitely no meat. People die from amoebic dysentery, unexplained fevers, strange boils on their bodies. We drink boiled water only, no ice. No sweets except for jalebi, thin fried twists of dough in dripping hot sugar syrup. If we're caught ouside with nothing to drink, Fanta, Limca, Thums Up (after Coca-Cola is thrown out by Mr. Gandhi) will do. Hot tea sweetened with sugar, served with thick creamy buffalo milk, is preferable. It should be boiled, to kill the germs on the cup.

My mother talks about "back home" as a safe place, a silk cocoon frozen in time where we are sheltered by family and friends. Back home, my sister and I do not argue about food with my parents. Home is where

---

[1]*jeera:* Cumin. — EDS.

they know all the rules. We trust them to guide us safely through the maze of city streets for which they have no map, and we trust them to feed and take care of us, the way parents should.

Finally, though, one of us will get sick, hungry for the food we see our cousins and friends eating, too thirsty to ask for a straw, too polite to insist on properly boiled water.

At my uncle's diner in New Delhi, someone hands me a plate of aloo tikki, fried potato patties filled with mashed channa dal[2] and served with a sweet and sour chutney. The channa, mixed with hot chilies and spices, burned my tongue and throat. I reach for my Fanta, discard the paper straw, and gulp the sweet orange soda down, huge draughts that sting rather than soothe.

When I throw up later that day (or is it the next morning, when a   20
stomachache wakes me up from deep sleep?), I cry over the frustration of being singled out, not from the pain my mother assumes I'm feeling as she holds my hair back from my face. The taste of orange lingers in my mouth, and I remember my lips touching the cold glass of the Fanta bottle.

At that moment, more than anything, I want to be like my cousins.

VII

In New York, at the first Indian restaurant in our neighborhood, my father orders with confidence, and my sister and I play with the silverware until the steaming plates of lamb biryani[3] arrive.

What is Indian food? my friends ask, their noses crinkling up.

Later, this restaurant is run out of business by the new Indo-Pak-Bangladeshi combinations up and down the street, which serve similar food. They use plastic cutlery and Styrofoam cups. They do not distinguish between North and South Indian cooking, or between Indian, Pakistani, and Bangladeshi cooking, and their customers do not care. The food is fast, cheap, and tasty. Dosa, a rice flour crepe stuffed with masala[4] potato, appears on the same trays as chicken makhani.[5]

Now my friends want to know, Do you eat curry at home?   25

One time, my mother makes lamb vindaloo[6] for guests. Like dosa, this is a South Indian dish, one that my Punjabi mother has to learn from a cookbook. For us, she cooks everyday food—yellow dal, rice, chapati, bhaji. Lentils, rice, bread, and vegetables. She has never referred to anything on our table as "curry" or "curried," but I know she has made

---

[2]*channa dal:* A dish made of the split kernel of beans in the chickpea family.—EDS.
[3]*lamb biryani:* A dish made of lamb, spices, basmati rice, and yogurt.—EDS.
[4]*masala:* A blend of spices common to Indian food, often includes cinnamon, cardamom, cumin, caraway, and many others.—EDS.
[5]*chicken makhani:* A dish combining chicken with a butter-based tomato sauce.—EDS.
[6]*lamb vindaloo:* A spicy marinated lamb dish.—EDS.

chicken curry for guests. Vindaloo, she explains, is a curry too. I understand, then, that curry is a dish created for guests, outsiders, a food for people who eat in restaurants.

VIII

I have inherited brown eyes, black hair, a long nose with a crooked bridge, and soft teeth with thin enamel. I am in my twenties, moving to a city far from my parents, before it occurs to me that jeera, the spice my sister avoids, must have an English name. I have to learn that haldi = turmeric, methi = fenugreek. What to make with fenugreek, I do not know. My grandmother used to make methi roti[7] for our breakfast, corn bread with fresh fenugreek leaves served with a lump of homemade butter. No one makes it now that she's gone, though once in a while my mother will get a craving for it and produce a facsimile ("The corn meal here is wrong") that only highlights what she's really missing: the smells and tastes of her mother's house.

I will never make my grandmother's methi roti or even my mother's unsatisfactory imitation of it. I attempt chapati:[8] it takes six hours, three phone calls home, and leaves me with an aching back. I have to write translations down: jeera = cumin. My memory is unreliable. But I have always known garam = hot.

IX

My mother learns how to make brownies and apple pie. My father makes only Indian food, except for loaves of heavy, sweet, brown bread that I eat with thin slices of American cheese and lettuce. The recipe is a secret, passed on to him by a woman at work. Years later, when he finally gives it to me, when I ask for it, I end up with three bricks of gluten that even the birds and my husband won't eat.

X

My parents send me to boarding school, outside of London. They imagine that I will overcome my shyness and find a place for myself in this all-girls' school. They have never lived in England, but as former subjects of the British Empire, they find London familiar, comfortable in a way New York—my mother's home for over twenty years by now—is not. Americans still don't know what to call us; their Indians live on

30

[7] *roti:* A round puffy flatbread. —EDS.
[8] *chapati:* A type of roti, or flatbread. —EDS.

reservations, not in Manhattan. Because they understand the English, my parents believe the English understand us.

I poke at my first school lunch—thin, overworked pastry in a puddle of lumpy gravy. The lumps are chewy mushrooms, maybe, or overcooked shrimp.

"What is this?" I don't want to ask, but I can't go on eating without knowing.

"Steak and kidney pie."

The girl next to me, red-haired, freckled, watches me take a bite from my plate. She has been put in charge of me, the new girl, and I follow her around all day, a foreigner at the mercy of a reluctant and angry tour guide. She is not used to explaining what is perfectly and utterly natural.

"What, you've never had steak and kidney pie? Bloody hell."   35

My classmates scoff, then marvel, then laugh at my ignorance. After a year, I understand what is on my plate: sausage rolls, blood pudding, Spam, roast beef in a thin, greasy gravy, all the bacon and sausage I could possibly want. My parents do not expect me to starve.

The girls at school expect conformity; it has been bred into them, through years of uniforms and strict rules about proper behavior. I am thirteen and contrary, even as I yearn for acceptance. I declare myself a vegetarian and doom myself to a diet of cauliflower cheese and baked beans on toast. The administration does not question my decision; they assume it's for vague, undefined religious reasons, although my father, the doctor, tells them it's for my health. My reasons, from this distance of many years, remain murky to me.

Perhaps I am my parents' daughter after all.

XI

When she is three, sitting on my cousin's lap in Bombay, my sister reaches for his plate and puts a chili in her mouth. She wants to be like the grown-ups who dip green chilies in coarse salt and eat them like any other vegetable. She howls inconsolable animal pain for what must be hours. She doesn't have the vocabulary for the oily heat that stings her mouth and tongue, burns a trail through her small tender body. Only hot, sticky tears on my father's shoulder.

As an adult, she eats red chili paste, mango pickle, kimchee,[9] foods   40
that make my eyes water and my stomach gurgle. My tastes are milder. I order raita[10] at Indian restaurants and ask for food that won't sear the roof of my mouth and scar the insides of my cheeks. The waiters nod,

[9]*kimchee:* A spicy Korean dish made of fermented cabbage and other vegetables. —EDS.

[10]*raita:* A yogurt-based condiment, often including cilantro, mint, and cucumber. —EDS.

and their eyes shift—a slight once-over that indicates they don't believe me. I am Indian, aren't I? My father seems to agree with them. He tells me I'm asking for the impossible, as if he believes the recipes are immutable, written in stone during the passage from India to America.

XII

I look around my boyfriend's freezer one day and find meat: pork chops, ground beef, chicken pieces, Italian sausage. Ham in the refrigerator, next to the homemade Bolognese sauce. Tupperware filled with chili made from ground beef and pork.

He smells different from me. Foreign. Strange.

I marry him anyway.

He has inherited blue eyes that turn gray in bad weather, light brown hair, a sharp pointy nose, and excellent teeth. He learns to make chili with ground turkey and tofu, tomato sauce with red wine and portobello mushrooms, roast chicken with rosemary and slivers of garlic under the skin.

He eats steak when we are in separate cities, roast beef at his mother's house, hamburgers at work. Sometimes I smell them on his skin. I hope he doesn't notice me turning my face, a cheek instead of my lips, my nose wrinkled at the unfamiliar, musky smell.

45

XIII

And then I realize I don't want to be a person who can find Indian food only in restaurants. One day, my parents will be gone, and I will long for the foods of my childhood, the way they long for theirs. I prepare for this day the way people on TV prepare for the end of the world. They gather canned goods they will never eat while I stockpile recipes I cannot replicate. I am frantic, disorganized, grabbing what I can, filing scribbled notes haphazardly. I regret the tastes I've forgotten, the meals I have inhaled without a thought. I worry that I've come to this realization too late.

XIV

Who told my mother about Brie? One day we were eating Velveeta, the next day Brie, Gouda, Camembert, Port Salut, Havarti with caraway, Danish fontina, string cheese made with sheep's milk. Who opened the door to these foreigners that sit on the refrigerator shelf next to last night's dal?

Back home, there is one cheese only, which comes in a tin, looks like Bakelite, and tastes best when melted.

And how do we go from Chef Boyardee to fresh pasta and home-made sauce, made with Redpack tomatoes, crushed garlic, and dried oregano? Macaroni and cheese, made with fresh cheddar and whole milk, sprinkled with bread crumbs and paprika. Fresh eggplant and ricotta ravioli, packed with marinara sauce and fresh mozzarella.

My mother will never cook beef or pork in her kitchen, and the foods   50
she knew in her childhood are unavailable. Because the only alternative to the supermarket, with its TV dinners and canned foods, is the gourmet Italian deli across the street, by default our meals become socially acceptable.

XV

If I really want to make myself sick, I worry that my husband will one day leave me for a meat-eater, for someone familiar who doesn't sniff him suspiciously for signs of alimentary infidelity.

XVI

Indians eat lentils. I understand this as absolute, a decree from an unidentifiable authority that watches and judges me.

So what does it mean that I cannot replicate my mother's dal? She and my father show me repeatedly, in their kitchen, in my kitchen. They coach me over the phone, buy me the best cookbooks, and finally write down their secrets. Things I'm supposed to know but don't. Recipes that should be, by now, engraved on my heart.

Living far from the comfort of people who require no explanation for what I do and who I am, I crave the foods we have shared. My mother convinces me that moong is the easiest dal to prepare, and yet it fails me every time: bland, watery, a sickly greenish-yellow mush. These imperfect imitations remind me only of what I'm missing.

But I have never been fond of moong dal.[11] At my mother's table it is   55
the last thing I reach for. Now I worry that this antipathy toward dal signals something deeper, that somehow I am not my parents' daughter, not Indian, and because I cannot bear the touch and smell of raw meat, though I can eat it cooked (charred, dry, and overdone), I am not American either.

I worry about a lifetime purgatory in Indian restaurants where I will complain that all the food looks and tastes the same because they've used the same masala.

---

[11]*moong dal:* A dish made of split green lentils. —EDS.

XVII

About the tuna and her attempts to feed us, my mother laughs. She says, "You were never fussy. You ate everything I made and never complained."

My mother is at the stove, wearing only her blouse and petticoat, her sari carefully folded and hung in the closet. She does not believe a girl's place is in the kitchen, but she expects me to know that too much hing can ruin a meal, to know without being told, without having to ask or write it down. Hing = asafoetida.

She remembers the catering class. "Oh, that class. You know, I had to give it up when we got to lobster. I just couldn't stand the way it looked."

She says this apologetically, as if she has deprived us, as if she suspects that having a mother who could feed us lobster would have changed the course of our lives.   60

Intellectually, she understands that only certain people regularly eat lobster, people with money or those who live in Maine, or both. In her catering class there were people without jobs for whom preparing lobster was a part of their professional training as caterers. Like us, they wouldn't be eating lobster at home. For my mother, however, lobster was just another American food, like tuna—different, strange, not natural yet somehow essential to belonging.

I learned how to prepare and eat lobster from the same girl who taught me tuna salad. I ate bacon at her house, too. And one day this girl, with her houses in the country and Martha's Vineyard, asked me how my uncle was going to pick me up from the airport in Bombay. In 1973, she was surprised to hear that he used a car, not an elephant. At home, my parents and I laughed, and though I never knew for sure if she was making fun of me, I still wanted her friendship.

My parents were afraid my sister and I would learn to despise the foods they loved, replace them with bologna and bacon and lose our taste for masala. For my mother, giving up her disgust of lobster, with its hard exterior and foreign smell, would mean renouncing some essential difference. It would mean becoming, decidedly, definitely, American—unafraid of meat in all its forms, able to consume large quantities of protein at any given meal. My willingness to toss a living being into boiling water and then get past its ugly appearance to the rich meat inside must mean to my mother that I am, somehow, someone she is not.

But I haven't eaten lobster in years. In my kitchen cupboards, there is a thirteen-pound bag of basmati rice, jars of lime pickle, mango pickle, and ghee,[12] cans of tuna and anchovies, canned soups, coconut milk, and tomatoes, rice noodles, several kinds of pasta, dried mushrooms, and unlabeled bottles of spices: haldi, jeera, hing. When my husband tries to help me cook, he cannot identify all the spices. He gets confused when I

---

[12]*ghee:* Clarified butter. —EDS.

forget their English names and remarks that my expectations of him are unreasonable.

I am my parents' daughter. Like them, I expect knowledge to pass   65
from me to my husband without one word of explanation or translation. I want him to know what I know, see what I see, without having to tell him exactly what it is. I want to believe the recipes never change.

The Reader's Presence

1. Kothari worries in the essay whether she is "her parents' daughter." Why is this of concern? How is that concern related to the title of her essay? At the end of the essay, she says definitively: "I am my parents' daughter." How has she reached that conclusion in the process of writing the essay?

2. Consider the ways food relates to cultural identity. How does Kothari characterize American foods? In what ways does she enjoy them? In what ways does she find them distasteful? For example, how is her husband—who is never named—described in terms of his favorite foods? In what ways do husband and wife differ from each other? How does Kothari suggest that their culinary differences could affect their relationship?

3. Read Kothari's essay in conjunction with Amy Tan's "Mother Tongue" (page 249). Though one writes about food and the other about language, discuss how each writer deals with the conflict between a family's ethnic values and its assimilation into American culture. You also might consider ethnic cuisine in contrast to American fast food as described by Eric Schlosser in "Why McDonald's Fries Taste So Good" (page 528). Do you think fast-food chains help undermine cultural heritage as it is expressed in various ethnic cuisines, such as Kothari's Indian recipes? Why or why not?

Nancy Mairs

On Being a Cripple

Nancy Mairs (b. 1943) has contributed poetry, short stories, articles, and essays to numerous journals. "On Being a Cripple" comes from Plaintext, *a collection of essays published in 1986. Her books include* Remembering the Bone House: An Erotics of Time and Space *(1989);* Carnal Acts *(1990);* Ordinary Time: Cycles in Marriage, Faith, and Renewal *(1993);* Waist-High in the World *(1997);* A Troubled Guest: Life and Death Stories *(2001); and her most recent,* A Dynamic God: Living an Unconventional Catholic Faith *(2007). From 1983 to 1985 Mairs served as assistant director of the Southwest Institute for Research on Women, and she has also taught at the University of Arizona and at UCLA.*

In Voice Lessons: On Becoming a (Woman) Writer *(1994), she writes, "I want a prose that is allusive and translucent, that eases you into me and embraces you, not one that baffles you or bounces you around so that you can't even tell where I am. And so I have chosen to work, very, very carefully, with the language we share, faults and all, choosing each word for its capacity, its ambiguity, the space it provides for me to live my life within it, relating rather than opposing each word to the next, each sentence to the next, 'starting on all sides at once . . . twenty times, thirty times, over': the stuttering adventure of the essay."*

To escape is nothing. Not to escape is nothing.

—Louise Bogan

The other day I was thinking of writing an essay on being a cripple. I was thinking hard in one of the stalls of the women's room in my office building, as I was shoving my shirt into my jeans and tugging up my zipper. Preoccupied, I flushed, picked up my book bag, took my cane down from the hook, and unlatched the door. So many movements unbalanced me, and as I pulled the door open I fell over backward, landing fully clothed on the toilet seat with my legs splayed in front of me: the old beetle-on-its-back routine. Saturday afternoon, the building deserted, I was free to laugh aloud as I wriggled back to my feet, my voice bouncing off the yellowish tiles from all directions. Had anyone been there with me, I'd have been still and faint and hot with chagrin. I decided that it was high time to write the essay.

First, the matter of semantics. I am a cripple. I choose this word to name me. I choose from among several possibilities, the most common of which are "handicapped" and "disabled." I made the choice a number of years ago, without thinking, unaware of my motives for doing so. Even now, I'm not sure what those motives are, but I recognize that they are complex and not entirely flattering. People—crippled or not—wince at the word "cripple," as they do not at "handicapped" or "disabled." Perhaps I want them to wince. I want them to see me as a tough customer, one to whom the fates/gods/viruses have not been kind, but who can face the brutal truth of her existence squarely. As a cripple, I swagger.

But, to be fair to myself, a certain amount of honesty underlies my choice. "Cripple" seems to me a clean word, straightforward and precise. It has an honorable history, having made its first appearance in the Lindisfarne Gospel in the tenth century. As a lover of words, I like the accuracy with which it describes my condition: I have lost the full use of my limbs. "Disabled," by contrast, suggests any incapacity, physical or mental. And I certainly don't like "handicapped," which implies that I have deliberately been put at a disadvantage, by whom I can't imagine (my God is not a Handicapper General), in order to equalize chances in the great race of life. These words seem to me to be moving away from my condition, to be widening the gap between word and reality. Most remote is the recently coined euphemism "differently abled," which partakes of the same semantic hopefulness that transformed countries from "undeveloped" to "underdeveloped," then to "less developed," and finally to "developing" nations. People have continued to starve in those countries during the shift. Some realities do not obey the dictates of language.

Mine is one of them. Whatever you call me, I remain crippled. But I don't care what you call me, so long as it isn't "differently abled," which strikes me as pure verbal garbage designed, by its ability to describe anyone, to describe no one. I subscribe to George Orwell's thesis that "the slovenliness of our language makes it easier for us to have foolish thoughts."[1] And I refuse to participate in the degeneration of the language to the extent that I deny that I have lost anything in the course of this calamitous disease; I refuse to pretend that the only differences between you and me are the various ordinary ones that distinguish any one person from another. But call me "disabled" or "handicapped" if you like. I have long since grown accustomed to them; and if they are vague, at least they hint at the truth. Moreover, I use them myself. Society is no readier to accept crippledness than to accept death, war, sex, sweat, or wrinkles. I would never refer to another person as a cripple. It is the word I use to name only myself.

I haven't always been crippled, a fact for which I am soundly grate-   5
ful. To be whole of limb is, I know from experience, infinitely more pleasant and useful than to be crippled: and if that knowledge leaves me open to bitterness at my loss, the physical soundness I once enjoyed (though I did not enjoy it half enough) is well worth the occasional stab of regret. Though never any good at sports, I was a normally active child and young adult. I climbed trees, played hopscotch, jumped rope, skated,

---

[1] *Orwell:* From his essay "Politics and the English Language" (page 533).—Eds.

swam, rode my bicycle, sailed. I despised team sports, spending some of the wretchedest afternoons of my life, sweaty and humiliated, behind a field-hockey stick and under a basketball hoop. I tramped alone for miles along the bridle paths that webbed the woods behind the house I grew up in. I swayed through countless dim hours in the arms of one man or another under the scattered shot of light from mirrored balls, and gyrated through countless more as Tab Hunter and Johnny Mathis gave way to the Rolling Stones, Creedence Clearwater Revival, Cream. I walked down the aisle. I pushed baby carriages, changed tires in the rain, marched for peace.

When I was twenty-eight I started to trip and drop things. What at first seemed my natural clumsiness soon became too pronounced to shrug off. I consulted a neurologist, who told me that I had a brain tumor. A battery of tests, increasingly disagreeable, revealed no tumor. About a year and a half later I developed a blurred spot in one eye. I had, at last, the episodes "disseminated in space and time" requisite for a diagnosis: multiple sclerosis. I have never been sorry for the doctor's initial misdiagnosis, however. For almost a week, until the negative results of the tests were in, I thought that I was going to die right away. Every day for the past nearly ten years, then, has been a kind of gift. I accept all gifts.

Multiple sclerosis is a chronic degenerative disease of the central nervous system, in which the myelin that sheathes the nerves is somehow eaten away and scar tissue forms in its place, interrupting the nerves' signals. During its course, which is unpredictable and uncontrollable, one may lose vision, hearing, speech, the ability to walk, control of bladder and/or bowels, strength in any or all extremities, sensitivity to touch, vibration, and/or pain, potency, coordination of movements—the list of possibilities is lengthy and, yes, horrifying. One may also lose one's sense of humor. That's the easiest to lose and the hardest to survive without.

In the past ten years, I have sustained some of these losses. Characteristic of MS are sudden attacks, called exacerbations, followed by remissions, and these I have not had. Instead, my disease has been slowly progressive. My left leg is now so weak that I walk with the aid of a brace and a cane; and for distances I use an Amigo, a variation on the electric wheelchair that looks rather like an electrified kiddie car. I no longer have much use of my left hand. Now my right side is weakening as well. I still have the blurred spot in my right eye. Overall, though, I've been lucky so far. My world has, of necessity, been circumscribed by my losses, but the terrain left me has been ample enough for me to continue many of the activities that absorb me: writing, teaching, raising children and cats and plants and snakes, reading, speaking publicly about MS and depression, even playing bridge with people patient and honorable enough to let me scatter cards every which way without sneaking a peek.

Lest I begin to sound like Pollyanna, however, let me say that I don't like having MS. I hate it. My life holds realities—harsh ones, some of them—that no right-minded human being ought to accept without grumbling. One of them is fatigue. I know of no one with MS who does not complain of bone-weariness; in a disease that presents an astonishing variety of symptoms, fatigue seems to be a common factor. I wake up in the morning feeling the way most people do at the end of a bad day, and I take it from there. As a result, I spend a lot of time *in extremis* and, impatient with limitation, I tend to ignore my fatigue until my body breaks down in some way and forces rest. Then I miss picnics, dinner parties, poetry readings, the brief visits of old friends from out of town. The offspring of a puritanical tradition of exceptional venerability, I cannot view these lapses without shame. My life often seems a series of small failures to do as I ought.

I lead, on the whole, an ordinary life, probably rather like the one I   10
would have led had I not had MS. I am lucky that my predilections were already solitary, sedentary, and bookish—unlike the world-famous French cellist I have read about, or the young woman I talked with one long afternoon who wanted only to be a jockey. I had just begun graduate school when I found out something was wrong with me, and I have remained, interminably, a graduate student. Perhaps I would not have if I'd thought I had the stamina to return to a full-time job as a technical editor; but I've enjoyed my studies.

In addition to studying, I teach writing courses. I also teach medical students how to give neurological examinations. I pick up freelance editing jobs here and there. I have raised a foster son and sent him into the world, where he has made me two grandbabies, and I am still escorting my daughter and son through adolescence. I go to Mass every Saturday. I am a superb, if messy, cook. I am also an enthusiastic laundress, capable of sorting a hamper full of clothes into five subtly differentiated piles, but a terrible housekeeper. I can do italic writing and, in an emergency, bathe an oil-soaked cat. I play a fiendish game of Scrabble. When I have the time and the money, I'd like to sit on my front steps with my husband, drinking Amaretto and smoking a cigar, as we imagine our counterparts in Leningrad and make sure that the sun gets down once more behind the sharp childish scrawl of the Tucson Mountains.

This lively plenty has its bleak complement, of course, in all the things I can no longer do. I will never run again, except in dreams, and one day I may have to write that I will never walk again. I like to go camping, but I can't follow George and the children along the trails that wander out of a campsite through the desert or into the mountains. In fact, even on the level I've learned never to check the weather or try to hold a coherent conversation: I need all my attention for my wayward feet. Of late, I have begun to catch myself wondering how people can propel themselves without canes. With only one usable hand, I have to select my clothing with care not so much for style as for ease of ingress and egress, and even so, dressing can be laborious. I can no longer do fine stitchery, pick up babies, play the piano, braid my hair. I am immobilized by acute attacks of depression, which may or may not be physiologically related to MS but are certainly its logical concomitant.

These two elements, the plenty and the privation, are never pure, nor are the delight and wretchedness that accompany them. Almost every pickle that I get into as a result of my weakness and clumsiness—and I get into plenty—is funny as well as maddening and sometimes painful. I recall one May afternoon when a friend and I were going out for a drink after finishing up at school. As we were climbing into opposite sides of my car, chatting, I tripped and fell, flat and hard, onto the asphalt parking lot, my abrupt departure interrupting him in mid-sentence. "Where'd you go?" he called as he came around the back of the car to find me hauling myself up by the door frame. "Are you all right?" Yes, I told him, I was fine, just a bit rattly, and we drove off to find a shady patio and some beer. When I got home an hour or so later, my daughter greeted me with "What have you done to yourself?" I looked down. One elbow of my white turtleneck with the green froggies, one knee of my white trousers, one white kneesock were blood-soaked. We peeled off the clothes and inspected the damage, which was nasty enough but not alarming. That part wasn't funny: The abrasions took a long time to heal, and one got a little infected. Even so, when I think of my friend talking earnestly, suddenly, to the hot thin air while I dropped from his view as though through a trap door, I find the image as silly as something from a Marx Brothers movie.

I may find it easier than other cripples to amuse myself because I live propped by the acceptance and the assistance and, sometimes, the amusement of those around me. Grocery clerks tear my checks out of my checkbook for me, and sales clerks find chairs to put into dressing rooms when I want to try on clothes. The people I work with make sure I teach at times when I am least likely to be fatigued, in places I can get to, with the materials I need. My students, with one anonymous exception (in an end-of-the-semester evaluation), have been unperturbed by my disability. Some even like it. One was immensely cheered by the information that I paint my own fingernails; she decided, she told me, that if I could go to such trouble over fine details, she could keep on writing essays. I suppose I became some sort of bright-fingered muse. She wrote good essays, too.

The most important struts in the framework of my existence, of course, are my husband and children. Dismayingly few marriages survive the MS test, and why should they? Most twenty-two- and nineteen-year-olds, like George and me, can vow in clear conscience, after a childhood of chicken pox and summer colds, to keep one another in sickness and in health so long as they both shall live. Not many are equipped for catastrophe: the dismay, the depression, the extra work, the boredom that a degenerative disease can insinuate into a relationship. And our society, with its emphasis

15

on fun and its association of fun with physical performance, offers little encouragement for a whole spouse to stay with a crippled partner. Children experience similar stresses when faced with a crippled parent, and they are more helpless, since parents and children can't usually get divorced. They hate, of course, to be different from their peers, and the child whose mother is tacking down the aisle of a school auditorium packed with proud parents like a Cape Cod dinghy in a stiff breeze jolly well stands out in a crowd. Deprived of legal divorce, the child can at least deny the mother's disability, even her existence, forgetting to tell her about recitals and PTA meetings, refusing to accompany her to stores or church or the movies, never inviting friends to the house. Many do.

But I've been limping along for ten years now, and so far George and the children are still at my left elbow, holding tight. Anne and Matthew vacuum floors and dust furniture and haul trash and rake up dog droppings and button my cuffs and bake lasagna and Toll House cookies with just enough grumbling so I know that they don't have brain fever. And far from hiding me, they're forever dragging me by racks of fancy clothes or through teeming school corridors, or welcoming gaggles of friends while I'm wandering through the house in Anne's filmy pink babydoll pajamas. George generally calls before he brings someone home, but he does just as many dumb thankless chores as the children. And they all yell at me, laugh at some of my jokes, write me funny letters when we're apart—in short, treat me as an ordinary human being for whom they have some use. I think they like me. Unless they're faking. . . .

Faking. There's the rub. Tugging at the fringes of my consciousness always is the terror that people are kind to me only because I'm a cripple. My mother almost shattered me once, with that instinct mothers have— blind, I think, in this case, but unerring nonetheless—for striking blows along the fault-lines of their children's hearts, by telling me, in an attack on my selfishness, "We all have to make allowances for you, of course, because of the way you are." From the distance of a couple of years, I have to admit that I haven't any idea just what she meant, and I'm not sure that she knew either. She was awfully angry. But at the time, as the words thudded home, I felt my worst fear, suddenly realized. I could bear being called selfish: I am. But I couldn't bear the corroboration that those around me were doing in fact what I'd always suspected them of doing, professing fondness while silently putting up with me because of the way I am. A cripple. I've been a little cracked ever since.

Along with this fear that people are secretly accepting shoddy goods comes a relentless pressure to please—to prove myself worth the burdens I impose, I guess, or to build a substantial account of good will against which I may write drafts in times of need. Part of the pressure arises from social expectations. In our society, anyone who deviates from the norm had better find some way to compensate. Like fat people, who are expected to be jolly, cripples must bear their lot meekly and cheerfully. A grumpy cripple isn't playing by the rules. And much of the pressure is self-generated. Early on I vowed that, if I had to have MS, by God I was going to do it well. This is a class act, ladies and gentlemen. No tears, no recriminations, no faint-heartedness.

One way and another, then, I wind up feeling like Tiny Tim,[2] peering over the edge of the table at the Christmas goose, waving my crutch, piping down God's blessing on us all. Only sometimes I don't want to play Tiny Tim; I'd rather be Caliban,[3] a most scurvy monster. Fortunately, at home no one much cares whether I'm a good cripple or a bad cripple as long as I make vichyssoise with fair regularity. One evening several years ago, Anne was reading at the dining-room table while I cooked dinner. As I opened a can of tomatoes, the can slipped in my left hand and juice spattered me and the counter with bloody spots. Fatigued and infuriated, I bellowed, "I'm so sick of being crippled!" Anne glanced at me over the top of her book. "There now," she said, "do you feel better?" "Yes," I said, "yes, I do." She went back to her reading. I felt better. That's about all the attention my scurviness ever gets.

Because I hate being crippled, I sometimes hate myself for being a crip-   20
ple. Over the years I have come to expect—even accept—attacks of violent self-loathing. Luckily, in general our society no longer connects deformity and disease directly with evil (though a charismatic once told me that I have MS because a devil is in me) and so I'm allowed to move largely at will, even among small children. But I'm not sure that this revision of attitude has been particularly helpful. Physical imperfection, even freed of moral disapprobation, still defies and violates the ideal, especially for women, whose confinement in their bodies as objects of desire is far from over. Each age, of course, has its ideal, and I doubt that ours is any better or worse than any other. Today's ideal woman, who lives on the glossy pages of dozens of magazines, seems to be between the ages of eighteen and twenty-five; her hair has body, her teeth flash white, her breath smells minty, her underarms are dry; she has a career but is still a fabulous cook, especially of meals that take less than twenty minutes to prepare; she does not ordinarily appear to have a husband or children; she is trim and deeply tanned; she jogs, swims, plays tennis, rides a bicycle, sails, but does not bowl; she travels widely, even to out-of-the-way places like Finland and Samoa, always in the company of the ideal man, who possesses a nearly identical set of characteristics. There are a few exceptions. Though usually white and often blonde, she may be black, Hispanic, Asian, or Native American, so long as she is unusually sleek. She may be old, provided she is selling a laxative or is Lauren Bacall. If she is selling a detergent, she may be married and have a flock of strikingly messy children. But she is never a cripple.

Like many women I know, I have always had an uneasy relationship with my body. I was not a popular child, largely, I think now, because I was peculiar: intelligent, intense, moody, shy, given to unexpected actions

[2]*Tiny Tim:* Crippled boy in Charles Dickens's *A Christmas Carol.*—Eds.
[3]*Caliban:* A character in William Shakespeare's play *The Tempest.*—Eds.

and inexplicable notions and emotions. But as I entered adolescence, I believed myself unpopular because I was homely; my breasts too flat, my mouth too wide, my hips too narrow, my clothing never quite right in fit or style. I was not, in fact, particularly ugly, old photographs inform me, though I was well off the ideal; but I carried this sense of self-alienation with me into adulthood, where it regenerated in response to the depredations of MS. Even with my brace I walk with a limp so pronounced that, seeing myself on the videotape of a television program on the disabled, I couldn't believe that anything but an inchworm could make progress humping along like that. My shoulders droop and my pelvis thrusts forward as I try to balance myself upright, throwing my frame into a bony S. As a result of contractures, one shoulder is higher than the other and I carry one arm bent in front of me, the fingers curled into a claw. My left arm and leg have wasted into pipe-stems, and I try always to keep them covered. When I think about how my body must look to others, especially to men, to whom I have been trained to display myself, I feel ludicrous, even loathsome.

At my age, however, I don't spend much time thinking about my appearance. The burning egocentricity of adolescence, which assures one that all the world is looking all the time, has passed, thank God, and I'm generally too caught up in what I'm doing to step back, as I used to, and watch myself as though upon a stage. I'm also too old to believe in the accuracy of self-image. I know that I'm not a hideous crone, that in fact, when I'm rested, well dressed, and well made up, I look fine. The self-loathing I feel is neither physically nor intellectually substantial. What I hate is not me but a disease.

I am not a disease.

And a disease is not — at least not singlehandedly — going to determine who I am, though at first it seemed to be going to. Adjusting to a chronic incurable illness, I have moved through a process similar to that outlined by Elisabeth Kübler-Ross in *On Death and Dying*. The major difference — and it is far more significant than most people recognize — is that I can't be sure of the outcome, as the terminally ill cancer patient can. Research studies indicate that, with proper medical care, I may achieve a "normal" life span. And in our society, with its vision of death as the ultimate evil, worse even than decrepitude, the response to such news is, "Oh well, at least you're not going to *die*." Are there worse things than dying? I think that there may be.

I think of two women I know, both with MS, both enough older than 25
I to have served me as models. One took to her bed several years ago and has been there ever since. Although she can sit in a high-backed wheelchair, because she is incontinent she refuses to go out at all, even though incontinence pants, which are readily available at any pharmacy, could protect her from embarrassment. Instead, she stays at home and insists that her husband, a small quiet man, a retired civil servant, stay there with her except for a quick weekly foray to the supermarket. The other

woman, whose illness was diagnosed when she was eighteen, a nursing student engaged to a young doctor, finished her training, married her doctor, accompanied him to Germany when he was in the service, bore three sons and a daughter, now grown and gone. When she can, she travels with her husband; she plays bridge, embroiders, swims regularly; she works, like me, as a symptomatic-patient instructor of medical students in neurology. Guess which woman I hope to be.

At the beginning, I thought about having MS almost incessantly. And because of the unpredictable course of the disease, my thoughts were always terrified. Each night I'd get into bed wondering whether I'd get out again the next morning, whether I'd be able to see, to speak, to hold a pen between my fingers. Knowing that the day might come when I'd be physically incapable of killing myself, I thought perhaps I ought to do so right away, while I still had the strength. Gradually I came to understand that the Nancy who might one day lie inert under a bedsheet, arms and legs paralyzed, unable to feed or bathe herself, unable to reach out for a gun, a bottle of pills, was not the Nancy I was at present, and that I could not presume to make decisions for that future Nancy, who might well not want in the least to die. Now the only provision I've made for the future Nancy is that when the time comes—and it is likely to come in the form of pneumonia, friend to the weak and the old—I am not to be treated with machines and medications. If she is unable to communicate by then, I hope she will be satisfied with these terms.

Thinking all the time about having MS grew tiresome and intrusive, especially in the large and tragic mode in which I was accustomed to considering my plight. Months and even years went by without catastrophe (at least without one related to MS), and really I was awfully busy, what with George and children and snakes and students and poems, and I hadn't the time, let alone the inclination, to devote myself to being a disease. Too, the richer my life became, the funnier it seemed, as though there were some connection between largesse and laughter, and so my tragic stance began to waver until, even with the aid of a brace and a cane, I couldn't hold it for very long at a time.

After several years I was satisfied with my adjustment. I had suffered my grief and fury and terror, I thought, but now I was at ease with my lot. Then one summer day I set out with George and the children across the desert for a vacation in California. Part way to Yuma I became aware that my right leg felt funny. "I think I've had an exacerbation," I told George. "What shall we do?" he asked. "I think we'd better get the hell to California," I said, "because I don't know whether I'll ever make it again." So we went on to San Diego and then to Orange, up the Pacific Coast Highway to Santa Cruz, across to Yosemite, down to Sequoia and Joshua Tree, and so back over the desert to home. It was a fine two-week trip, filled with friends and fair weather, and I wouldn't have missed it for the world, though I did in fact make it back to California two years later. Nor would there have been any point in missing it, since in MS, once the symptoms have appeared, the neurological damage has been done, and there's no way to predict or prevent that damage.

The incident spoiled my self-satisfaction, however. It renewed my grief and fury and terror, and I learned that one never finishes adjusting to MS. I don't know now why I thought one would. One does not, after all, finish adjusting to life, and MS is simply a fact of my life—not my favorite fact, of course—but as ordinary as my nose and my tropical fish and my yellow Mazda station wagon. It may at any time get worse, but no amount of worry or anticipation can prepare me for a new loss. My life is a lesson in losses. I learn one at a time.

And I had best be patient in the learning, since I'll have to do it like it   30
or not. As any rock fan knows, you can't always get what you want. Particularly when you have MS. You can't, for example, get cured. In recent years researchers and the organizations that fund research have started to pay MS some attention even though it isn't fatal; perhaps they have begun to see that life is something other than a quantitative phenomenon, that one may be very much alive for a very long time in a life that isn't worth living. The researchers have made some progress toward understanding the mechanism of the disease: It may well be an autoimmune reaction triggered by a slow-acting virus. But they are nowhere near its prevention, control, or cure. And most of us want to be cured. Some, unable to accept incurability, grasp at one treatment after another, no matter how bizarre: megavitamin therapy, gluten-free diet, injections of cobra venom, hypothermal suits, lymphocytopharesis, hyperbaric chambers. Many treatments are probably harmless enough, but none are curative.

The absence of a cure often makes MS patients bitter toward their doctors. Doctors are, after all, the priests of modern society, the new shamans, whose business is to heal, and many an MS patient roves from one to another, searching for the "good" doctor who will make him well. Doctors too think of themselves as healers, and for this reason many have trouble dealing with MS patients, whose disease in its intransigence defeats their aims and mocks their skills. Too few doctors, it is true, treat their patients as whole human beings, but the reverse is also true. I have always tried to be gentle with my doctors, who often have more at stake in terms of ego than I do. I may be frustrated, maddened, depressed by the incurability of my disease, but I am not diminished by it, and they are. When I push myself up from my seat in the waiting room and stumble toward them, I incarnate the limitation of their powers. The least I can do is refuse to press on their tenderest spots.

This gentleness is part of the reason that I'm not sorry to be a cripple. I didn't have it before. Perhaps I'd have developed it anyway—how could I know such a thing?—and I wish I had more of it, but I'm glad of what I have. It has opened and enriched my life enormously, this sense that my frailty and need must be mirrored in others, that in searching for and shaping a stable core in a life wrenched by change and loss, change and loss, I must recognize the same process, under individual conditions, in the lives around me. I do not deprecate such knowledge, however I've come by it.

All the same, if a cure were found, would I take it? In a minute. I may be a cripple, but I'm only occasionally a loony and never a saint. Anyway, in my brand of theology God doesn't give bonus points for a limp. I'd take a cure; I just don't need one. A friend who also has MS startled me once by asking, "Do you ever say to yourself, 'Why me, Lord?'" "No, Michael, I don't," I told him, "because whenever I try, the only response I can think of is 'Why not?'" If I could make a cosmic deal, who would I put in my place? What in my life would I give up in exchange for sound limbs and a thrilling rush of energy? No one. Nothing. I might as well do the job myself. Now that I'm getting the hang of it.

The Reader's Presence

1. Mairs's approach to her multiple sclerosis may come across as ironic, jaunty, or tough. Near the beginning of the essay she assumes that her reader is fundamentally alienated from her: "I refuse to pretend that the only differences between you and me are the various ordinary ones that distinguish any one person from another" (paragraph 4). What are those differences? How does the essay attempt to move the reader away from awkwardness or suspicion or hostility? Does it succeed? Why or why not?

2. What does the epigraph from Louise Bogan mean to you? What might it signify in relation to Mairs's essay? What is "escape," in Mairs's context? What meanings might the word *nothing* have?

3. "Lest I begin to sound like Pollyanna, however, let me say that I don't like having MS. I hate it" (paragraph 9). Discuss Mairs's admission of hatred for the disease—and for herself (paragraph 20)—in relation to Alice Walker's "abuse" of her injured eye (paragraph 30) in "Beauty: When the Other Dancer Is the Self" (page 258). What is the role of self-loathing in personal growth?

THE WRITER AT WORK

Nancy Mairs on Finding a Voice

In writing workshops and lectures, the essayist Nancy Mairs is often asked what appears to be a simple question: How did you find your voice as a writer? Yet is the question truly a simple one? In the following passage from her book "on becoming a (woman) writer," Voice Lessons, Mairs closely examines the question and suggests a way it might be answered. You might want to compare her concern about finding a voice to that of Henry Louis Gates Jr. in The Writer at Work *on page 130.*

The question I am most often asked when I speak to students and others interested in writing is, How did you find your voice? I have some trouble with this locution because "find" always suggests to me the discovery, generally fortuitous, of some lack or loss. I have found an occasional four-leaf clover. I have found a mate. I have, more than once, found my way home. But is a voice susceptible of the same sort of revelation or retrieval? Hasn't mine simply always been there, from my earliest lallation to the "I love you" I called after my husband on his way to school several hours ago?

But of course, I remind myself, the question doesn't concern *my* voice at all but the voice of another woman (also named Nancy Mairs, confusingly enough) whose "utterances" are, except for the occasional public reading, literally inaudible: not, strictly speaking, a voice at all, but a fabrication, a device. And when I look again at the dictionary, I see that "find" can indeed also mean "devise." The voice in question, like the woman called into being to explain its existence, is an invention.

But of whom? For simplicity's sake, we assume that the voice in a work is that of the writer (in the case of nonfiction) or one invented by her (in the case of fiction). This assumption describes the relationship between writer (the woman in front of a luminous screen) and persona (whoever you hear speaking to you right now) adequately for most readers. And maybe for most writers, too. Until that earnest student in the second row waves a gnawed pencil over her head and asks, timidly as a rule because hers is the first question, "How did you find your voice?"

As though "you" were a coherent entity already existing at some original point, who had only to open her mouth and agitate her vocal chords— or, to be precise, pick up her fingers and diddle the keys—to call the world she had in mind into being. Not just a writer, an Author. But I've examined this process over and over in myself, and the direction of this authorial plot simply doesn't ring true. In the beginning, remember, was the *Word*. Not me. And the question, properly phrased, should probably be asked of my voice: How did you find (devise, invent, contrive) your Nancy?

Malcolm X

Homeboy

Malcolm X (1925–1965) is regarded as one of the most influential figures in the struggle for racial equality. Born Malcolm Little in Omaha, Nebraska, his family was frequently the target of racist violence: white supremacists burned their home, and his father, a Baptist minister, was horribly murdered. After his father's death, Malcolm's mother was hospitalized for mental illness, and Malcolm and his seven brothers and sisters were placed in foster homes. Although a gifted student, Malcolm was discouraged by a racist teacher and quit high school. He lived for a while in Lansing, Michigan, and later moved to Boston, where he engaged in various illegal activities, became addicted to narcotics, and was imprisoned for robbery. While in jail Malcolm made extensive use of the prison library and studied philosophy, politics, and the teachings of the Black Muslims' Nation of Islam. After his release from prison, Malcolm worked with Elijah Muhammad, founder and leader of the Nation of Islam, and changed his name to Malcolm X. He became known as an outspoken and articulate minister, championing racial separatism, faith in Allah, and rejection of white society, and he quickly rose to a position of prominence within the organization. While on a pilgrimage to Mecca in 1964, Malcolm X became an orthodox Muslim, adopted the name El-Hajj Malik El-Shabazz, and formed his own religious organization. Hostilities grew between his followers and the Black Muslims, and in 1965 Malcolm X was assassinated in a Harlem ballroom. The Autobiography of Malcolm X (1965), from which "Homeboy" is taken, was written with Alex Haley and was published posthumously.

I looked like Li'l Abner. Mason, Michigan, was written all over me. My kinky, reddish hair was cut hick style, and I didn't even use grease in it. My green suit's coat sleeves stopped above my wrists, the pants legs showed three inches of socks. Just a shade lighter green than the suit was my narrow-collared, three-quarter length Lansing department store topcoat. My appearance was too much for even Ella.[1] But she told me later she had seen countrified members of the Little family come up from Georgia in even worse shape than I was.

Ella had fixed up a nice little upstairs room for me. And she was truly a Georgia Negro woman when she got into the kitchen with her pots and pans. She was the kind of cook who would heap up your plate with such as ham hock, greens, black-eyed peas, fried fish, cabbage, sweet potatoes, grits and gravy, and cornbread. And the more you put away, the better she felt. I worked out at Ella's kitchen table like there was no tomorrow.

Ella still seemed to be as big, black, outspoken, and impressive a woman as she had been in Mason and Lansing. Only about two weeks before I arrived, she had split up with her second husband—the soldier, Frank, whom I had met there the previous summer; but she was taking it right in stride. I could see, though I didn't say, how any average man would find it almost impossible to live for very long with a woman whose every instinct was to run everything and everybody she had anything to do with—including me. About my second day there in Roxbury, Ella told me that she didn't want me to start hunting for a job right away, like most newcomer Negroes did. She said that she had told all those she'd brought North to take their time, to walk around, to travel the buses and the subway, and get the feel of Boston, before they tied themselves down

---

[1]*Ella:* Malcolm's older sister. He left Lansing, Michigan, and moved to her house in the Roxbury section of Boston in 1948.—EDS.

working somewhere, because they would never again have the time to really see and get to know anything about the city they were living in. Ella said she'd help me find a job when it was time for me to go to work.

So I went gawking around the neighborhood—the Waumbeck and Humboldt Avenue Hill section of Roxbury, which is something like Harlem's Sugar Hill, where I'd later live. I saw those Roxbury Negroes acting and living differently from any black people I'd ever dreamed of in my life. This was the snooty-black neighborhood; they called themselves the "Four Hundred," and looked down their noses at the Negroes of the black ghetto, or so-called "town" section where Mary, my other half-sister, lived.

What I thought I was seeing there in Roxbury were high-class, educated, important Negroes, living well, working in big jobs and positions. Their quiet homes sat back in their mowed yards. These Negroes walked along the sidewalks looking haughty and dignified, on their way to work, to shop, to visit, to church. I know now, of course, that what I was really seeing was only a big-city version of those "successful" Negro bootblacks and janitors back in Lansing. The only difference was that the ones in Boston had been brainwashed even more thoroughly. They prided themselves on being incomparably more "cultured," "cultivated," "dignified," and better off than their black brethren down in the ghetto, which was no further away than you could throw a rock. Under the pitiful misapprehension that it would make them "better," these Hill Negroes were breaking their backs trying to imitate white people.

Any black family that had been around Boston long enough to own the home they lived in was considered among the Hill elite. It didn't make any difference that they had to rent out rooms to make ends meet. Then the native-born New Englanders among them looked down upon recently migrated Southern home-owners who lived next door, like Ella. And a big percentage of the Hill dwellers were in Ella's category—Southern strivers and scramblers, and West Indian Negroes, whom both the New Englanders and the Southerners called "Black Jews." Usually it was the Southerners and the West Indians who not only managed to own the places where they lived, but also at least one other house which they rented as income property. The snooty New Englanders usually owned less than they.

In those days on the Hill, any who could claim "professional" status—teachers, preachers, practical nurses—also considered themselves superior. Foreign diplomats could have modeled their conduct on the way the Negro postmen, Pullman porters, and dining car waiters of Roxbury acted, striding around as if they were wearing top hats and cutaways.

I'd guess that eight out of ten of the Hill Negroes of Roxbury, despite the impressive-sounding job titles they affected, actually worked as menials and servants. "He's in banking," or "He's in securities." It sounded as though they were discussing a Rockefeller or a Mellon—and not some grayheaded, dignity-posturing bank janitor, or bond-house messenger.

"I'm with an old family" was the euphemism used to dignify the professions of white folks' cooks and maids who talked so affectedly among their own kind in Roxbury that you couldn't even understand them. I don't know how many forty- and fifty-year-old errand boys went down the Hill dressed like ambassadors in black suits and white collars, to downtown jobs "in government," "in finance," or "in law." It has never ceased to amaze me how so many Negroes, then and now, could stand the indignity of that kind of self-delusion.

Soon I ranged out of Roxbury and began to explore Boston proper. Historic buildings everywhere I turned, and plaques and markers and statues for famous events and men. One statue in the Boston Commons astonished me: a Negro named Crispus Attucks, who had been the first man to fall in the Boston Massacre. I had never known anything like that.

I roamed everywhere. In one direction, I walked as far as Boston University. Another day, I took my first subway ride. When most of the people got off, I followed. It was Cambridge, and I circled all around in the Harvard University campus. Somewhere, I had already heard of Harvard—though I didn't know much more about it. Nobody that day could have told me I would give an address before the Harvard Law School Forum some twenty years later.

I also did a lot of exploring downtown. Why a city would have *two* big railroad stations—North Station and South Station—I couldn't understand. At both of the stations, I stood around and watched people arrive and leave. And I did the same thing at the bus station where Ella had met me. My wanderings even led me down along the piers and docks where I read plaques telling about the old sailing ships that used to put into port there.

In a letter to Wilfred, Hilda, Philbert, and Reginald back in Lansing, I told them about all this, and about the winding, narrow, cobblestoned streets, and the houses that jammed up against each other. Downtown Boston, I wrote them, had the biggest stores I'd ever seen, and white people's restaurants and hotels. I made up my mind that I was going to see every movie that came to the fine, air-conditioned theaters.

On Massachusetts Avenue, next door to one of them, the Loew's State Theater, was the huge, exciting Roseland State Ballroom. Big posters out in front advertised the nationally famous bands, white and Negro, that had played there. "COMING NEXT WEEK," when I went by that first time, was Glenn Miller.[2] I remember thinking how nearly the whole evening's music at Mason High School dances had been Glenn Miller's records. What wouldn't that crowd have given, I wondered, to be standing where Glenn Miller's band was actually going to play? I didn't know how familiar with Roseland I was going to become.

10

[2]***Miller:*** One of America's most popular band leaders of the 1940s.—EDS.

Ella began to grow concerned, because even when I had finally had enough sight-seeing, I didn't stick around very much on the Hill. She kept dropping hints that I ought to mingle with the "nice young people my age" who were to be seen in the Townsend Drugstore two blocks from her house, and a couple of other places. But even before I came to Boston, I had always felt and acted toward anyone my age as if they were in the "kid" class, like my younger brother Reginald. They had always looked up to me as if I were considerably older. On weekends back in Lansing where I'd go to get away from the white people in Mason, I'd hung around in the Negro part of town with Wilfred's and Philbert's set. Though all of them were several years older than me, I was bigger, and I actually looked older than most of them.

I didn't want to disappoint or upset Ella, but despite her advice, I began   15
going down into the town ghetto section. That world of grocery stores, walk-up flats, cheap restaurants, poolrooms, bars, storefront churches, and pawnshops seemed to hold a natural lure for me.

Not only was this part of Roxbury much more exciting, but I felt more relaxed among Negroes who were being their natural selves and not putting on airs. Even though I did live on the Hill, my instincts were never—and still aren't—to feel myself any better than any other Negro.

I spent my first month in town with my mouth hanging open. The sharp-dressed young "cats" who hung on the corners and in the poolrooms, bars and restaurants, and who obviously didn't work anywhere, completely entranced me. I couldn't get over marveling at how their hair was straight and shiny like white men's hair; Ella told me this was called a "conk." I had never tasted a sip of liquor, never even smoked a cigarette, and here I saw little black children, ten and twelve years old, shooting craps, playing cards, fighting, getting grown-ups to put a penny or a nickel on their number for them, things like that. And these children threw around swear words I'd never heard before, even, and slang expressions that were just as new to me, such as "stud" and "cat" and "chick" and "cool" and "hip." Every night as I lay in bed I turned these new words over in my mind. It was shocking to me that in town, especially after dark, you'd occasionally see a white girl and a Negro man strolling arm in arm along the sidewalk, and mixed couples drinking in the neon-lighted bars— not slipping off to some dark corner, as in Lansing. I wrote Wilfred and Philbert about that, too.

I wanted to find a job myself, to surprise Ella. One afternoon, something told me to go inside a poolroom whose window I was looking through. I had looked through that window many times. I wasn't yearning to play pool; in fact, I had never held a cue stick. But I was drawn by the sight of the cool-looking "cats" standing around inside, bending over the big, green, felt-topped tables, making bets and shooting the bright-colored balls into the holes. As I stared through the window this particular afternoon, something made me decide to venture inside and talk to a dark, stubby, conk-headed fellow who racked up balls for the pool-players, whom I'd heard called "Shorty." One day he had come outside and seen me standing there and said "Hi, Red," so that made me figure he was friendly.

As inconspicuously as I could, I slipped inside the door and around the side of the poolroom, avoiding people, and on to the back, where Shorty was filling an aluminum can with the powder that pool players dust on their hands. He looked up at me. Later on, Shorty would enjoy teasing me about how with that first glance he knew my whole story. "Man, that cat still *smelled* country!" he'd say, laughing. "Cat's legs was so long and his pants so short his knees showed—an' his head looked like a briar patch!"

But that afternoon Shorty didn't let it show in his face how "country" I appeared when I told him I'd appreciate it if he'd tell me how could somebody go about getting a job like his.

"If you mean racking up balls," said Shorty, "I don't know of no pool joints around here needing anybody. You mean you just want any slave you can find?" A "slave" meant work, a job.

He asked what kind of work I had done. I told him that I'd washed restaurant dishes in Mason, Michigan. He nearly dropped the powder can. "My homeboy! Man, gimme some skin! I'm from Lansing!"

I never told Shorty—and he never suspected—that he was about ten years older than I. He took us to be about the same age. At first I would have been embarrassed to tell him, later I just never bothered. Shorty had dropped out of first-year high school in Lansing, lived a while with an uncle and aunt in Detroit, and had spent the last six years living with his cousin in Roxbury. But when I mentioned the names of Lansing people and places, he remembered many, and pretty soon we sounded as if we had been raised in the same block. I could sense Shorty's genuine gladness, and I don't have to say how lucky I felt to find a friend as hip as he obviously was.

"Man, this is a swinging town if you dig it," Shorty said. "You're my homeboy—I'm going to school you to the happenings." I stood there and grinned like a fool. "You got to go anywhere now? Well, stick around until I get off."

One thing I liked immediately about Shorty was his frankness. When I told him where I lived, he said what I already knew—that nobody in town could stand the Hill Negroes. But he thought a sister who gave me a "pad," not charging me rent, not even running me out to find "some slave," couldn't be all bad. Shorty's slave in the poolroom, he said, was just to keep ends together while he learned his horn. A couple of years before, he'd hit the numbers and bought a saxophone. "Got it right in there in the closet now, for my lesson tonight." Shorty was taking lessons "with some other studs," and he intended one day to organize his own small band. "There's a lot of bread to be made gigging right around here

20

25

in Roxbury," Shorty explained to me. "I don't dig joining some big band, one-nighting all over just to say I played with Count or Duke or somebody." I thought that was smart. I wished I had studied a horn; but I never had been exposed to one.

All afternoon, between trips up front to rack balls, Shorty talked to me out of the corner of his mouth: which hustlers—standing around, or playing at this or that table—sold "reefers," or had just come out of prison, or were "second-story men." Shorty told me that he played at least a dollar a day on the numbers. He said as soon as he hit a number, he would use the winnings to organize his band.

I was ashamed to have to admit that I had never played the numbers. "Well, you ain't never had nothing to play with," he said, excusing me, "but you start when you get a slave, and if you hit, you got a stake for something."

He pointed out some gamblers and some pimps. Some of them had white whores, he whispered. "I ain't going to lie—I dig them two-dollar white chicks," Shorty said. "There's a lot of that action around here, nights: you'll see it." I said I already had seen some. "You ever had one?" he asked.

My embarrassment at my inexperience showed. "Hell, man," he said, "don't be ashamed. I had a few before I left Lansing—them Polack chicks that used to come over the bridge. Here, they're mostly Italians and Irish. But it don't matter what kind, they're something else! Ain't no different nowhere—there's nothing they love better than a black stud."

Through the afternoon, Shorty introduced me to players and loungers. "My homeboy," he'd say, "he's looking for a slave if you hear anything." They all said they'd look out.

At seven o'clock, when the night ball-racker came on, Shorty told me he had to hurry to his saxophone lesson. But before he left, he held out to me the six or seven dollars he had collected that day in nickel and dime tips. "You got enough bread, homeboy?"

I was okay, I told him—I had two dollars. But Shorty made me take three more. "Little fattening for your pocket," he said. Before we went out, he opened his saxophone case and showed me the horn. It was gleaming brass against the green velvet, an alto sax. He said, "Keep cool, homeboy, and come back tomorrow. Some of the cats will turn you up a slave."

When I got home, Ella said there had been a telephone call from somebody named Shorty. He had left a message that over at the Roseland State Ballroom, the shoeshine boy was quitting that night, and Shorty had told him to hold the job for me.

"Malcolm, you haven't had any experience shining shoes," Ella said. Her expression and tone of voice told me she wasn't happy about my taking that job. I didn't particularly care, because I was already speechless thinking about being somewhere close to the greatest bands in the world. I didn't even wait to eat any dinner.

The ballroom was all lighted when I got there. A man at the front 35
door was letting in members of Benny Goodman's band. I told him I
wanted to see the shoeshine boy, Freddie.

"You're going to be the new one?" he asked. I said I thought I was,
and he laughed, "Well, maybe you'll hit the numbers and get a Cadillac,
too." He told me that I'd find Freddie upstairs in the men's room on the
second floor.

But downstairs before I went up, I stepped over and snatched a
glimpse inside the ballroom. I just couldn't believe the size of that waxed
floor! At the far end, under the soft, rose-colored lights, was the band-
stand with the Benny Goodman musicians moving around, laughing and
talking, arranging their horns and stands.

A wiry, brown-skinned, conked fellow upstairs in the men's room
greeted me. "You Shorty's homeboy?" I said I was, and he said he was
Freddie. "Good old boy," he said. "He called me, he just heard I hit the
big number, and he figured right I'd be quitting." I told Freddie what the
man at the front door had said about a Cadillac. He laughed and said,
"Burns them white cats up when you get yourself something. Yeah, I told
them I was going to get me one—just to bug them."

Freddie then said for me to pay close attention, that he was going to
be busy and for me to watch but not get in the way, and he'd try to get
me ready to take over at the next dance, a couple of nights later.

As Freddie busied himself setting up the shoeshine stand, he told me, 40
"Get here early . . . your shoeshine rags and brushes by this footstand . . .
your polish bottles, paste wax, suede brushes over here . . . everything in
place, you get rushed, you never need to waste motion. . . ."

While you shined shoes, I learned, you also kept watch on customers
inside, leaving the urinals. You darted over and offered a small white
hand towel. "A lot of cats who ain't planning to wash their hands, sometimes you can run up with a towel and shame them. Your towels are really
your best hustle in here. Cost you a penny apiece to launder—you always
get at least a nickel tip."

The shoeshine customers, and any from the inside rest room who
took a towel, you whiskbroomed a couple of licks. "A nickel or a dime
tip, just give 'em that," Freddie said. "But for two bits, Uncle Tom a little
—white cats especially like that. I've had them to come back two, three
times a dance."

From down below, the sound of the music had begun floating up. I
guess I stood transfixed. "You never seen a big dance?" asked Freddie.
"Run on awhile, and watch."

There were a few couples already dancing under the rose-colored
lights. But even more exciting to me was the crowd thronging in. The most
glamorous-looking white women I'd ever seen—young ones, old ones,
white cats buying tickets at the window, sticking big wads of green bills
back into their pockets, checking the women's coats, and taking their arms
and squiring them inside.

Freddie had some early customers when I got back upstairs. Between   45
the shoeshine stand and thrusting towels to me just as they approached
the wash basin, Freddie seemed to be doing four things at once. "Here,
you can take over the whiskbroom," he said, "just two or three licks—
but let 'em feel it."

When things slowed a little, he said, "You ain't seen nothing tonight.
You wait until you see a spooks' dance! Man, our own people carry *on*!"
Whenever he had a moment, he kept schooling me. "Shoelaces, this
drawer here. You just starting out, I'm going to make these to you as a
present. Buy them for a nickel a pair, tell cats they need laces if they do,
and charge two bits."

Every Benny Goodman record I'd ever heard in my life, it seemed,
was filtering faintly into where we were. During another customer lull,
Freddie let me slip back outside again to listen. Peggy Lee was at the mike
singing. Beautiful! She had just joined the band and she was from North
Dakota and had been singing with a group in Chicago when Mrs. Benny
Goodman discovered her, we had heard some customers say. She finished
the song and the crowd burst into applause. She was a big hit.

"It knocked me out, too, when I first broke in here," Freddie said,
grinning, when I went back in there. "But, look, you ever shined any
shoes?" He laughed when I said I hadn't excepting my own. "Well, let's
go to work. I never had neither." Freddie got on the stand and went to
work on his own shoes. Brush, liquid polish, brush, paste wax, shine rag,
lacquer sole dressing . . . step by step, Freddie showed me what to do.

"But you got to get a whole lot faster. You can't waste time!" Freddie
showed me how fast on my own shoes. Then, because business was taper-
ing off, he had time to give me a demonstration of how to make the shine
rag pop like a firecracker. "Dig the action?" he asked. He did it in slow
motion. I got down and tried it on his shoes. I had the principle of it.
"Just got to do it faster," Freddie said. "It's a jive noise, that's all. Cats
tip better, they figure you're knocking yourself out!"

By the end of the dance, Freddie had let me shine the shoes of three   50
or four stray drunks he talked into having shines, and I had practiced
picking up my speed on Freddie's shoes until they looked like mirrors.
After we had helped the janitors to clean up the ballroom after the dance,
throwing out all the paper and cigarette butts and empty liquor bottles,
Freddie was nice enough to drive me all the way home to Ella's on the
Hill in the second-hand maroon Buick he said he was going to trade in on
his Cadillac. He talked to me all the way. "I guess it's all right if I tell
you, pick up a couple of dozen packs of rubbers, two-bits apiece. You notice some of those cats that came up to me around the end of the dance?
Well, when some have new chicks going right, they'll come asking you for
rubbers. Charge a dollar, generally you'll get an extra tip."

He looked across at me. "Some hustles you're too new for. Cats will
ask you for liquor, some will want reefers. But you don't need to have
nothing except rubbers—until you can dig who's a cop.

"You can make ten, twelve dollars a dance for yourself if you work everything right," Freddie said, before I got out of the car in front of Ella's. "The main thing you got to remember is that everything in the world is a hustle. So long, Red."

The next time I ran into Freddie I was downtown one night a few weeks later. He was parked in his pearl gray Cadillac, sharp as a tack, "cooling it."

"Man, you sure schooled me!" I said, and he laughed; he knew what I meant. It hadn't taken me long on the job to find out that Freddie had done less shoeshining and towel-hustling than selling liquor and reefers, and putting white "Johns" in touch with Negro whores. I also learned that white girls always flocked to the Negro dances—some of them whores whose pimps brought them to mix business and pleasure, others who came with their black boy friends, and some who came in alone, for a little freelance lusting among a plentiful availability of enthusiastic Negro men.

At the white dances, of course, nothing black was allowed, and that's where the black whores' pimps soon showed a new shoeshine boy what he could pick up on the side by slipping a phone number or address to the white Johns who came around the end of the dance looking for "black chicks."

55

Most of Roseland's dances were for whites only, and they had white bands only. But the only white band ever to play there at a Negro dance to my recollection, was Charlie Barnet's. The fact is that very few white bands could have satisfied the Negro dancers. But I know that Charlie Barnet's "Cherokee" and his "Redskin Rhumba" drove those Negroes wild. They'd jampack that ballroom, the black girls in way-out silk and satin dresses and shoes, their hair done in all kinds of styles, the men sharp in their zoot suits and crazy conks, and everybody grinning and greased and gassed.

Some of the bandsmen would come up to the men's room at about eight o'clock and get shoeshines before they went to work. Duke Ellington, Count Basie, Lionel Hampton, Cootie Williams, Jimmie Lunceford were just a few of those who sat in my chair. I would really make my shine rag sound like someone had set off Chinese firecrackers. Duke's great alto sax-man, Johnny Hodges—he was Shorty's idol—still owes me for a shoeshine I gave him. He was in the chair one night, having a friendly argument with the drummer, Sonny Greer, who was standing there, when I tapped the bottom of his shoes to signal that I was finished. Hodges stepped down, reaching his hand in his pocket to pay me, but then snatched his hand out to gesture, and just forgot me, and walked away. I wouldn't have dared to bother the man who could do what he did with "Day-dream" by asking him for fifteen cents.

I remember that I struck up a little shoeshine-stand conversation with Count Basie's great blues singer, Jimmie Rushing. (He's the one famous for

"Sent For You Yesterday, Here You Come Today" and things like that.) Rushing's feet, I remember, were big and funny-shaped—not long like most big feet, but they were round and roly-poly like Rushing. Anyhow, he even introduced me to some of the other Basie cats, like Lester Young, Harry Edison, Buddy Tate, Don Byas, Dickie Wells, and Buck Clayton. They'd walk in the rest room later, by themselves. "Hi, Red." They'd be up there in my chair, and my shine rag was popping to the beat of all of their records, spinning in my head. Musicians never have had, anywhere, a greater shoeshine-boy fan than I was. I would write to Wilfred and Hilda and Philbert and Reginald back in Lansing, trying to describe it.

I never got any decent tips until the middle of the Negro dances, which is when the dancers started feeling good and getting generous. After the white dances, when I helped to clean out the ballroom, we would throw out perhaps a dozen empty liquor bottles. But after the Negro dances, we would have to throw out cartons full of empty fifth bottles—not rotgut, either, but the best brands, and especially Scotch.

During lulls up there in the men's room, sometimes I'd get in five minutes of watching the dancing. The white people danced as though somebody had trained them—left, one, two; right, three, four—the same steps and patterns over and over, as though somebody had wound them up. But those Negroes—nobody in the world could have choreographed the way they did whatever they felt—just grabbing partners, even the white chicks who came to the Negro dances. And my black brethren today may hate me for saying it, but a lot of black girls nearly got run over by some of those Negro males scrambling to get at those white women; you would have thought God had lowered some of his angels. Times have sure changed; if it happened today, those same black girls would go after those Negro men—and the white women, too.

Anyway, some couples were so abandoned—flinging high and wide, improvising steps and movements—that you couldn't believe it. I could feel the beat in my bones, even though I had never danced.

"*Showtime!*" people would start hollering about the last hour of the dance. Then a couple of dozen really wild couples would stay on the floor, the girls changing to low white sneakers. The band now would really be blasting, and all the other dancers would form a clapping, shouting circle to watch that wild competition as it began, covering only a quarter or so of the ballroom floor. The band, the spectators and the dancers, would be making the Roseland Ballroom feel like a big rocking ship. The spotlight would be turning, pink, yellow, green, and blue, picking up the couples lindy-hopping as if they had gone mad. "*Wail, man, wail!*" people would be shouting at the band; and it *would* be wailing, until first one and then another couple just ran out of strength and stumbled off toward the crowd, exhausted and soaked with sweat. Sometimes I would be down there standing inside the door jumping up and down in

60

my gray jacket with the whiskbroom in the pocket, and the manager would have to come and shout at me that I had customers upstairs.

The first liquor I drank, my first cigarettes, even my first reefers, I can't specifically remember. But I know they were all mixed together with my first shooting craps, playing cards, and betting my dollar a day on the numbers, as I started hanging out at night with Shorty and his friends. Shorty's jokes about how country I had been made us all laugh. I still was country, I know now, but it all felt so great because I was accepted. All of us would be in somebody's place, usually one of the girls', and we'd be turning on, the reefers making everybody's head light, or the whiskey aglow in our middles. Everybody understood that my head had to stay kinky a while longer, to grow long enough for Shorty to conk it for me. One of these nights, I remarked that I had saved about half enough to get a zoot.

"*Save?*" Shorty couldn't believe it. "Homeboy, you never heard of credit?" He told me he'd call a neighborhood clothing store the first thing in the morning, and that I should be there early.

A salesman, a young Jew, met me when I came in. "You're Shorty's friend?" I said I was; it amazed me—all of Shorty's contacts. The salesman wrote my name on a form, and the Roseland as where I worked, and Ella's address as where I lived. Shorty's name was put down as recommending me. The salesman said, "Shorty's one of our best customers."

65

I was measured, and the young salesman picked off a rack a zoot suit that was just wild: sky-blue pants thirty inches in the knee and angle-narrowed down to twelve inches at the bottom, and a long coat that pinched my waist and flared out below my knees.

As a gift, the salesman said, the store would give me a narrow leather belt with my initial "L" on it. Then he said I ought to also buy a hat, and I did—blue, with a feather in the four-inch brim. Then the store gave me another present: a long, thick-lined, gold-plated chain that swung down lower than my coat hem. I was sold forever on credit.

When I modeled the zoot for Ella, she took a long look and said, "Well, I guess it had to happen." I took three of those twenty-five-cent sepia-toned, while-you-wait pictures of myself, posed the way "hipsters" wearing their zoots would "cool it"—hat dangled, knees drawn close together, feet wide apart, both index fingers jabbed toward the floor. The long coat and swinging chain and the Punjab pants were much more dramatic if you stood that way. One picture, I autographed and airmailed to my brothers and sisters in Lansing, to let them see how well I was doing. I gave another one to Ella, and the third to Shorty, who was really moved: I could tell by the way he said, "Thanks, homeboy." It was part of our "hip" code not to show that kind of affection.

Shorty soon decided that my hair was finally long enough to be conked. He had promised to school me in how to beat the barbershops' three- and four-dollar price by making up congolene, and then conking ourselves.

I took the little list of ingredients he had printed out for me, and went   70
to a grocery store, where I got a can of Red Devil lye, two eggs, and two
medium-sized white potatoes. Then at a drugstore near the poolroom, I
asked for a large jar of vaseline, a large bar of soap, a large-toothed comb
and a fine-toothed comb, one of those rubber hoses with a metal spray-
head, a rubber apron, and a pair of gloves.

"Going to lay on that first conk?" the drugstore man asked me. I
proudly told him, grinning, "Right!"

Shorty paid six dollars a week for a room in his cousin's shabby apartment. His cousin wasn't at home. "It's like the pad's mine, he spends so
much time with his woman," Shorty said. "Now, you watch me—"

He peeled the potatoes and thin-sliced them into a quart-sized Mason
fruit jar, then started stirring them with a wooden spoon as he gradually
poured in a little over half the can of lye. "Never use a metal spoon; the
lye will turn it black," he told me.

A jelly-like, starchy-looking glop resulted from the lye and potatoes,
and Shorty broke in the two eggs, stirring real fast—his own conk and
dark face bent down close. The congolene turned pale-yellowish. "Feel
the jar," Shorty said. I cupped my hand against the outside, and snatched
it away. "Damn right, it's hot, that's the lye," he said. "So you know it's
going to burn when I comb it in—it burns *bad*. But the longer you can
stand it, the straighter the hair."

He made me sit down, and he tied the string of a new rubber apron   75
tightly around my neck, and combed up my bush of hair. Then, from the
big vaseline jar, he took a handful and massaged it hard all through my hair
and into the scalp. He also thickly vaselined my neck, ears and forehead.
"When I get to washing out your head, be sure to tell me anywhere you feel
any little stinging," Shorty warned me, washing his hands, then pulling on
the rubber gloves, and tying on his own rubber apron. "You always got to
remember that any congolene left in burns a sore into your head."

The congolene just felt warm when Shorty started combing it in. But
then my head caught fire.

I gritted my teeth and tried to pull the sides of the kitchen table together. The comb felt as if it was raking my skin off.

My eyes watered, my nose was running. I couldn't stand it any longer;
I bolted to the washbasin. I was cursing Shorty with every name I could
think of when he got the spray going and started soap-lathering my head.

He lathered and spray-rinsed, lathered and spray-rinsed, maybe ten
or twelve times, each time gradually closing the hot-water faucet, until
the rinse was cold, and that helped some.

"You feel any stinging spots?"   80

"No," I managed to say. My knees were trembling.

"Sit back down, then. I think we got it all out okay."

The flame came back as Shorty, with a thick towel, started drying my
head, rubbing hard. "*Easy, man, easy!*" I kept shouting.

"The first time's always worst. You get used to it better before long. You took it real good, homeboy. You got a good conk."

When Shorty let me stand up and see in the mirror, my hair hung   85
down in limp, damp strings. My scalp still flamed, but not as badly; I could bear it. He draped the towel around my shoulders, over my rubber apron, and began again vaselining my hair.

I could feel him combing, straight back, first the big comb, then the fine-tooth one.

Then, he was using a razor, very delicately, on the back of my neck. Then, finally, shaping the sideburns.

My first view in the mirror blotted out the hurting. I'd seen some pretty conks, but when it's the first time, on your *own* head, the transformation, after the lifetime of kinks, is staggering.

The mirror reflected Shorty behind me. We both were grinning and sweating. And on top of my head was this thick, smooth sheen of shining red hair — real red — as straight as any white man's.

How ridiculous I was! Stupid enough to stand there simply lost in ad-   90
miration of my hair now looking "white," reflected in the mirror in Shorty's room. I vowed that I'd never again be without a conk, and I never was for many years.

This was my first really big step toward self-degradation: when I endured all of that pain, literally burning my flesh to have it look like a white man's hair. I had joined that multitude of Negro men and women in America who are brainwashed into believing that the black people are "inferior" — and white people "superior" — that they will even violate and mutilate their God-created bodies to try to look "pretty" by white standards.

Look around today, in every small town and big city, from two-bit catfish and soda-pop joints into the "integrated" lobby of the Waldorf-Astoria, and you'll see conks on black men. And you'll see black women wearing these green and pink and purple and red and platinum-blond wigs. They're all more ridiculous than a slapstick comedy. It makes you wonder if the Negro has completely lost his sense of identity, lost touch with himself.

You'll see the conk worn by many, many so-called "upper class" Negroes, and, as much as I hate to say it about them, on all too many Negro entertainers. One of the reasons that I've especially admired some of them, like Lionel Hampton and Sidney Poitier, among others, is that they have kept their natural hair and fought to the top. I admire any Negro man who has never had himself conked, or who has had the sense to get rid of it — as I finally did.

I don't know which kind of self-defacing conk is the greater shame — the one you'll see on the heads of the black so-called "middle class" and "upper class," who ought to know better, or the one you'll see on the heads of the poorest, most downtrodden, ignorant black men. I mean the legal-minimum-wage ghetto-dwelling kind of Negro, as I was when I got my first one. It's generally among these poor fools that you'll see a black kerchief over the man's head, like Aunt Jemima; he's trying to make his conk last longer, between trips to the barbershop. Only for special occasions is this kerchief-protected conk exposed—to show off how "sharp" and "hip" its owner is. The ironic thing is that I have never heard any woman, white or black, express any admiration for a conk. Of course, any white woman with a black man isn't thinking about his hair. But I don't see how on earth a black woman with any race pride could walk down the street with any black man wearing a conk—the emblem of his shame that he is black.

To my own shame, when I say all of this I'm talking first of all about myself—because you can't show me any Negro who ever conked more faithfully than I did. I'm speaking from personal experience when I say of any black man who conks today, or any white-wigged black woman, that if they gave the brains in their heads just half as much attention as they do their hair, they would be a thousand times better off.

95

The Reader's Presence

1. The young Malcolm resists Ella's pressure to imitate white lifestyles to get ahead. Instead, he seeks the company of his brethren in the black ghetto (paragraph 15) from whom he learns that "everything in the world is a hustle" (paragraph 52). What might this resistance signify politically? What relation might it bear to his later name changes, from Malcolm Little to Malcolm X and, finally, to El-Hajj Malik El-Shabazz? What elements of African American identity appeal to the young Malcolm Little?

2. The writer, of course, was a courageous African American leader who was assassinated in 1965, when he was only forty years old. How does this knowledge affect your reading of this account of his early years? How does Malcolm himself indicate the difference in time between the events he is relating and the time at which he is writing?

3. In "People Like Us" (page 306) David Brooks notes, "Human beings are capable of drawing amazingly subtle social distinctions and then shaping their lives around them." What kinds of social distinctions does Malcolm X draw about the neighborhoods he describes in Boston? How does he seek to fit in where he most wants to belong?

David Mamet

The Rake: A Few Scenes from My Childhood

David Mamet (b. 1947) is a playwright, screenwriter, and director whose work is appreciated for the attention he pays to language as it is spoken by ordinary people in the contemporary world. His 1984 Pulitzer Prize–winning play, Glengarry Glen Ross, *explores the psychology of ambition, competition, failure, and despair among a group of Chicago real estate agents who are driven to sell worthless property to unsuspecting customers.*

Mamet has said that "playwriting is simply showing how words influence actions and vice versa. All my plays attempt to bring out the poetry in the plain, everyday language people use. That's the only way to put art back in the theater." Mamet's sensitivity to working-class language and experience is due in part to his own work experience in factories, at a real estate agency, and as a window washer, office cleaner, and taxi driver. Mamet has taught theater at several leading universities and published a number of books about theater and film, including True and False: Heresy and Common Sense for the Actor *(1997),* Three Uses of the Knife: On the Nature and Purpose of Drama *(1998), and* Bambi vs. Godzilla: On the Nature, Purpose, and Practice of the Movie Business. *Mamet's plays include the often revived* American Buffalo *(1977) and* Speed the Plow *(1988), and, more recently,* Ricky Jay: On the Stem *(2002),* Dr. Faustus *(2004),* Romance *(2005), and* November, *his take on politics that opened in New York City in 2008. He has written and directed several films, including Oscar-nominated movies,* The Verdict *(1982) and* Wag the Dog *(1997),* State and Main *(2000), and* Heist *(2001). He was also the producer and writer of the television series,* The Unit *(2006–2007). "The Rake: A Few Scenes from My Childhood" appeared in* Harper's *in 1992.*

There was the incident of the rake and there was the incident of the school play, and it seems to me that they both took place at the round kitchen table.

The table was not in the kitchen proper but in an area called "the nook," which held its claim to that small measure of charm by dint of a waist-high wall separating it from an adjacent area known as the living room.

All family meals were eaten in the nook. There was a dining room to the right, but, as in most rooms of that name at the time and in those surroundings, it was never used.

The round table was of wrought iron and topped with glass; it was noteworthy for that glass, for it was more than once and rather more than several times, I am inclined to think, that my stepfather would grow so angry as to bring some object down on the glass top, shattering it, thus giving us to know how we had forced him out of control.

And it seems that most times when he would shatter the table, as   5
often as that might have been, he would cut some portion of himself on the glass, or that he or his wife, our mother, would cut their hands on picking up the glass afterward, and that we children were to understand, and did understand, that these wounds were our fault.

So the table was associated in our minds with the notion of blood.

The house was in a brand-new housing development in the southern suburbs. The new community was built upon, and now bordered, the remains of what had once been a cornfield. When our new family moved in, there were but a few homes in the development completed, and a few more under construction. Most streets were mud, and boasted a house here or there, and many empty lots marked out by white stakes.

The house we lived in was the development's Model Home. The first time we had seen it, it had signs plastered on the front and throughout the interior telling of the various conveniences it contained. And it had a lawn, and was one of the only homes in the new community that did.

My stepfather was fond of the lawn, and he detailed me and my sister to care for it, and one fall afternoon we found ourselves assigned to rake the leaves.

Why this chore should have been so hated I cannot say, except that   10
we children, and I especially, felt ourselves less than full members of this new, cobbled-together family, and disliked being assigned to the beautification of a home that we found unbeautiful in all respects, and for which we had neither natural affection nor a sense of proprietary interest.

We went to the new high school. We walked the mile down the open two-lane road on one side of which was the just-begun suburban community and on the other side of which was the cornfield.

The school was as new as the community, and still under construction for the first three years of its occupancy. One of its innovations was the notion that honesty would be engendered by the absence of security, and so the lockers were designed and built both without locks and without the possibility of attaching locks. And there was the corresponding rash of thievery and many lectures about the same from the school administration, but it was difficult to point with pride to any scholastic or community tradition supporting the suggestion that we, the students, pull together in this new, utopian way. We were, in school, in an uncompleted building in the midst of a mud field in the midst of a cornfield. Our various sports teams were called The Spartans; and I played on those teams, which were of a wretchedness consistent with their novelty.

Meanwhile my sister interested herself in the drama society. The year after I had left the school she obtained the lead in the school play. It called for acting and singing, both of which she had talent for, and it looked to be a signal triumph for her in her otherwise unremarkable and unenjoyed school career.

On the night of the play's opening, she sat down to dinner with our mother and our stepfather. It may be that they ate a trifle early to allow her to get to the school to enjoy the excitement of opening night. But however it was, my sister had no appetite, and she nibbled a bit at her food, and then she got up from the table to carry her plate back to scrape it in the sink, when my mother suggested that she sit down, as she had not finished her food. My sister said she really had no appetite, but my mother insisted that, as the meal had been prepared, it would be good form to sit and eat it.

My sister sat down with the plate and pecked at her food and she   15
tried to eat a bit, and told my mother that, no, really, she possessed no appetite whatever, and that was due, no doubt, not to the food, but to her nervousness and excitement at the prospect of opening night.

My mother, again, said that, as the food had been cooked, it had to be eaten, and my sister tried and said that she could not; at which my mother nodded. She then got up from the table and went to the telephone and looked the number up and called the school and got the drama teacher and identified herself and told him that her daughter wouldn't be coming to school that night, that, no, she was not ill, but that she would not be coming in. Yes, yes, she said, she knew her daughter had the lead in the play, and, yes, she was aware that many children and teachers had worked hard for it, et cetera, and so my sister did not play the lead in her school play. But I was long gone, out of the house by that time, and well out of it. I heard that story, and others like it, at the distance of twenty-five years.

In the model house our rooms were separated from their room, the master bedroom, by a bathroom and a study. On some weekends I would go alone to visit my father in the city and my sister would stay and sometimes grow frightened or lonely in her part of the house. And once, in the period when my grandfather, then in his sixties, was living with us, she became alarmed at a noise she had heard in the night; or perhaps she just became lonely, and she went out of her room and down the hall, calling for my mother, or my stepfather, or my grandfather, but the house was dark, and no one answered.

And, as she went farther down the hall, toward the living room, she heard voices, and she turned the corner, and saw a light coming from under the closed door in the master bedroom, and heard my stepfather crying, and the sound of my mother weeping. So my sister went up to the door, and she heard my stepfather talking to my grandfather and saying, "Jack. Say the words. Just say the words . . ." And my grandfather in his Eastern European accent, saying with obvious pain and difficulty, "No.

No. I can't. Why are you making me do this? Why?" And the sound of my mother crying convulsively.

My sister opened the door, and she saw my grandfather sitting on the bed, and my stepfather standing by the closet and gesturing. On the floor of the closet she saw my mother, curled in a fetal position, moaning and crying and hugging herself. My stepfather was saying, "Say the words. Just say the words." And my grandfather was breathing fast and repeating, "I can't. She knows how I feel about her. I can't." And my stepfather said, "Say the words, Jack. Please. Just say you love her." At which my mother would moan louder. And my grandfather said, "I can't."

My sister pushed the door open farther and said—I don't know what she said, but she asked, I'm sure, for some reassurance, or some explanation, and my stepfather turned around and saw her and picked up a hairbrush from a dresser that he passed as he walked toward her, and he hit her in the face and slammed the door on her. And she continued to hear "Jack, say the words."   20

She told me that on weekends when I was gone my stepfather ended every Sunday evening by hitting or beating her for some reason or other. He would come home from depositing his own kids back at their mother's house after their weekend visitation, and would settle down tired and angry, and, as a regular matter on those evenings, would find out some intolerable behavior on my sister's part and slap or hit or beat her.

Years later, at my mother's funeral, my sister spoke to our aunt, my mother's sister, who gave a footnote to this behavior. She said when they were young, my mother and my aunt, they and their parents lived in a small flat on the West Side. My grandfather was a salesman on the road from dawn on Monday until Friday night. Their family had a fiction, and that fiction, that article of faith, was that my mother was a naughty child. And each Friday, when he came home, his first question as he climbed the stairs was, "What has she done this week . . . ?" At which my grandmother would tell him the terrible things that my mother had done, after which she, my mother, was beaten.

This was general knowledge in my family. The footnote concerned my grandfather's behavior later in the night. My aunt had a room of her own, and it adjoined her parents' room. And she related that each Friday, when the house had gone to bed, she, through the thin wall, heard my grandfather pleading for sex. "Cookie, please." And my grandmother responding, "No, Jack." "Cookie, please." "No, Jack." "Cookie, please."

And once, my grandfather came home and asked, "What has she done this week?" and I do not know, but I imagine that the response was not completed, and perhaps hardly begun; in any case, he reached and grabbed my mother by the back of the neck and hurled her down the stairs.

And once, in our house in the suburbs there had been an outburst by   25
my stepfather directed at my sister. And she had, somehow, prevailed. It was, I think, that he had the facts of the case wrong, and had accused her

of the commission of something for which she had demonstrably had no opportunity, and she pointed this out to him with what I can imagine, given the circumstances, was an understandable, and, given my prejudice, a commendable degree of freedom. Thinking the incident closed she went back to her room to study, and, a few moments later, saw him throw open her door, bat the book out of her hands, and pick her up and throw her against the far wall, where she struck the back of her neck on the shelf.

She was told, the next morning, that her pain, real or pretended, held no weight, and that she would have to go to school. She protested that she could not walk, or, if at all, only with the greatest of difficulty and in great pain; but she was dressed and did walk to school, where she fainted, and was brought home. For years she suffered various headaches; an X-ray taken twenty years later for an unrelated problem revealed that when he threw her against the shelf he had cracked her vertebrae.

When we left the house we left in good spirits. When we went out to dinner, it was an adventure, which was strange to me, looking back, because many of these dinners ended with my sister or myself being banished, sullen or in tears, from the restaurant, and told to wait in the car, as we were in disgrace.

These were the excursions that had ended, due to her or my intolerable arrogance, as it was explained to us.

The happy trips were celebrated and capped with a joke. Here is the joke: My stepfather, my mother, my sister, and I would exit the restaurant, my stepfather and mother would walk to the car, telling us that they would pick us up. We children would stand by the restaurant entrance. They would drive up in the car, open the passenger door, and wait until my sister and I had started to get in. They would then drive away.

They would drive ten or fifteen feet, and open the door again, and we would walk up again, and they would drive away again. They sometimes would drive around the block. But they would always come back, and by that time the four of us would be laughing in camaraderie and appreciation of what, I believe, was our only family joke.

We were raking the lawn, my sister and I. I was raking, and she was stuffing the leaves into a bag. I loathed the job, and my muscles and my mind rebelled, and I was viciously angry, and my sister said something, and I turned and threw the rake at her and hit her in the face.

The rake was split bamboo and metal, and a piece of metal caught her lip and cut her badly.

We were both terrified, and I was sick with guilt, and we ran into the house, my sister holding her hand to her mouth, and her mouth and her hand and the front of her dress covered in blood.

We ran into the kitchen where my mother was cooking dinner, and my mother asked what happened.

Neither of us, myself out of guilt, of course, and my sister out of a de-   35
sire to avert the terrible punishment she knew I would receive, neither of
us would say what occurred.

My mother pressed us, and neither of us would answer. She said that
until one or the other answered, we would not go to the hospital; and so
the family sat down to dinner where my sister clutched a napkin to her
face and the blood soaked the napkin and ran down onto her food, which
she had to eat; and I also ate my food and we cleared the table and went
to the hospital.

I remember the walks home from school in the frigid winter, along the
cornfield that was, for all its proximity to the city, part of the prairie. The
winters were viciously cold. From the remove of years, I can see how
the area might and may have been beautiful. One could have walked in the
stubble of the cornfields, or hunted birds, or enjoyed any of a number of
pleasures naturally occurring.

The Reader's Presence

1. Interwoven through Mamet's essay are descriptions of suburban
   developments and model homes; he even uses the word "utopian"
   (paragraph 12). What is Mamet's attitude toward these ideals?
   What is his tone in discussing them? Mamet says that he and his
   sister hate doing yardwork, in part because they "had neither natural affection nor a sense of proprietary interest" (paragraph 10)
   toward their house. What does this mean?

2. Near the end of the essay, Mamet recalls a "joke" that his family
   shared. How does he present the joke to the reader? Do you think
   Mamet wants the reader to think the joke is funny? Why or why
   not? Would the joke seem different if Mamet had told it at the beginning of the essay? How does he connect this joke back to the
   story about the rake?

3. Mamet says that "the table was associated in our minds with the
   notion of blood" (paragraph 6). Do you think the rake also has
   symbolic value? If so, what does it represent? How does Mamet's
   use of symbolic objects compare to George Orwell's treatment of
   the gun and the elephant in "Shooting an Elephant" (page 203)?
   How does Mamet's account of his relationship with his sister
   compare to Alice Walker's account of her brothers' role in the
   "accident" in which she lost the sight in her eye in "Beauty: When
   the Other Dancer Is the Self" (page 258)?

Adam Mayblum

The Price We Pay

Adam Mayblum, the 35-year-old managing director of the May Davis Group private investment firm, was in his office on the eighty-seventh floor of the North Tower of the World Trade Center when one of the hijacked planes struck on September 11, 2001. He escaped just before the tower's collapse. The following day, at his home in New Rochelle, New York, Mayblum composed a terse, harrowing e-mail describing his experience and sent the 2,100-word piece out to friends and family. This e-mail quickly circulated throughout the world, bringing Mayblum more than 1,000 responses from strangers offering thanks, sympathy, and prayers. One woman wrote, "The fact that you survived . . . helped to lift the terrible weight from my heart." Mayblum, who disclaims the label of "hero" by pointing out that firefighters and police officers were the ones who rushed in to save lives, attributes the enormous outpouring of support to the fact that his e-mail "helped a lot of people understand what was going on inside the building at the same time they had seen what was going on outside." Mayblum's e-mail was first published as an essay in DoubleTake Magazine, *and was selected for* The Best American Essays 2002.

My name is Adam Mayblum. I am alive today. I am committing this to "paper" so I never forget. SO WE NEVER FORGET. I am sure that this is one of thousands of stories that will emerge over the next several days and weeks.

I arrived as usual a little before 8 a.m. My office was on the eighty-seventh floor of 1 World Trade Center, aka: Tower 1, aka: the North Tower. Most of my associates were in by 8:30 a.m. We were standing around, joking around, eating breakfast, checking e-mails, and getting set for the day when the first plane hit just a few stories above us. I must stress that we did not know that it was a plane. The building lurched violently and shook as if it were an earthquake. People screamed. I watched out my window as the building seemed to move ten to twenty feet in each direction. It rumbled and shook long enough for me to get my wits about myself and grab a coworker and seek shelter under a doorway. Light fixtures and parts of the ceiling collapsed. The kitchen was destroyed. We were certain that it was a bomb. We looked out the windows. Reams of paper were flying everywhere, like a ticker tape parade. I looked down at the street. I could see people in Battery Park City looking up. Smoke started billowing in through the holes in the ceiling. I believe that there were thirteen of us.

We did not panic. I can only assume that we thought that the worst was over. The building was standing and we were shaken but alive. We checked the halls. The smoke was thick and white and did not smell like I imagined smoke should smell. Not like your BBQ or your fireplace or even a bonfire. The phones were working. My wife had taken our nine-month-old for his checkup. I called my nanny at home and told her to page my wife, tell her that a bomb went off, I was O.K., and on my way out, I grabbed my laptop. Took off my T-shirt and ripped it into three pieces. Soaked it in water. Gave two pieces to my friends. Tied my piece around my face to act as an air filter. And we all started moving to the staircase. One of my dearest friends said that he was staying until the police or firemen came to get him. In the halls there were tiny fires and sparks. The ceiling had collapsed in the men's bathroom. It was gone along with anyone who may have been in there. We did not go in to look. We missed the staircase on the first run and had to double back. Once in the staircase we picked up fire extinguishers just in case. On the eighty-fifth floor a brave associate of mine and I headed back up to our office to drag out my partner who stayed behind. There was no air, just white smoke. We made the rounds through the office calling his name. No response. He must have succumbed to the smoke. We left defeated in our efforts and made our way back to the stairwell. We proceeded to the seventy-eighth floor where we had to change over to a different stairwell. Seventy-eight is the main junction to switch to the upper floors. I expected to see more people. There were some fifty to sixty more. Not enough. Wires and fires all over the place. Smoke too. A brave man was fighting a fire with the emergency hose. I stopped with friends to make sure that everyone from our office was accounted for. We ushered them and confused people into the stairwell. In retrospect, I recall seeing Harry, my head trader, doing the same several yards behind me. I am only thirty-five. I have known him for over fourteen years. I headed into the stairwell with two friends.

We were moving down very orderly in Stairwell A. Very slowly. No panic. At least not overt panic. My legs could not stop shaking. My heart was pounding. Some nervous jokes and laughter. I made a crack about ruining a brand new pair of Merrells. Even still, they were right, my feet felt great. We all laughed. We checked our cell phones. Surprisingly, there was a very good signal, but the Sprint network was jammed. I heard that the BlackBerry two-way e-mail devices worked perfectly. On the phones, one out of twenty dial attempts got through. I knew I could not reach my wife so I called my parents. I told them what happened and that we were all O.K. and on the way down. Soon, my sister-in-law reached me. I told her we were fine and moving down. I believe that was about the sixty-fifth floor. We were bored and nervous. I called my friend Angel in San Francisco. I knew he would be watching. He was amazed I was on the phone. He told me to get out, that there was another plane on its way. I did not know what he was talking about. By now the second plane had struck Tower 2. We were so deep into the middle of our building that we did not hear or feel anything. We had no idea what was really going on. We kept making way for wounded to go down ahead of us. Not many of them, just a few. No one seemed seriously wounded. Just some cuts and scrapes. Everyone cooperated. Everyone was a hero yesterday. No questions asked. I had coworkers in another office on the seventy-seventh floor. I tried dozens of times to get them on their cell phones or office lines. It was futile. Later I found that they were alive. One of the many miracles on a day of tragedy.

On the fifty-third floor we came across a very heavyset man sitting on the stairs. I asked if he needed help or was he just resting. He needed help. I knew I would have trouble carrying him because I have a very bad back. But my friend and I offered anyway. We told him he could lean on us. He hesitated, I don't know why. I said do you want to come or do you want us to send help for you. He chose for help. I told him he was on the fifty-third floor in Stairwell A and that's what I would tell the rescue workers. He said O.K. and we left.

On the forty-fourth floor my phone rang again. It was my parents. They were hysterical. I said relax, I'm fine. My father said get out, there is a third plane coming. I still did not understand. I was kind of angry. What did my parents think? Like I needed some other reason to get going? I couldn't move the thousand people in front of me any faster. I know they love me, but no one inside understood what the situation really was. My parents did. Starting around this floor the firemen, policemen, WTC K-9 units without the dogs, anyone with a badge, started coming up as we were heading down. I stopped a lot of them and told them about the man on Fifty-three and my friend on Eighty-seven. I later felt terrible about this. They headed up to find those people and met death instead.

On the thirty-third floor I spoke with a man who somehow knew most of the details. He said two small planes hit the building. Now we all started talking about which terrorist group it was. Was it an internal organization or an external one? The overwhelming but uninformed opinion was Islamic fanatics. Regardless, we now knew that it was not a bomb and there were potentially more planes coming. We understood.

On the third floor the lights went out and we heard and felt this rumbling coming towards us from above. I thought the staircase was collapsing upon itself. It was 10 a.m. now and that was Tower 2 collapsing next door. We did not know that. Someone had a flashlight. We passed it forward and left the stairwell and headed down a dark and cramped corridor to an exit. We could not see at all. I recommended that everyone place a hand on the shoulder of the person in front of them and call out if they hit an obstacle so others would know to avoid it. They did. It worked perfectly. We reached another stairwell and saw a female officer emerge soaking wet and covered in soot. She said we could not go that way, it was blocked. Go up to Four and use the other exit. Just as we started up she said it was O.K. to go down instead. There was water everywhere. I called out for hands on shoulders again and she said that was a great idea. She stayed behind instructing people to do that. I do not know what happened to her.

We emerged into an enormous room. It was light but filled with smoke. I commented to a friend that it must be under construction. Then we realized where we were. It was the second floor. The one that overlooks the lobby. We were ushered out into the courtyard, the one where the fountain used to be. My first thought was of a TV movie I saw once about nuclear winter and fallout. I could not understand where all of the debris came from. There was at least five inches of this gray pasty dusty drywall soot on the ground as well as a thickness of it in the air. Twisted steel and wires. I heard there were bodies and body parts as well, but I did not look. It was bad enough. We hid under the remaining overhangs and moved out to the street. We were told to keep walking towards Houston Street. The odd thing is that there were very few rescue workers around. Less than five. They all must have been trapped under the debris when Tower 2 fell. We did not know that and could not understand where all of that debris came from. It was just my friend Kern and I now. We were hugging but sad. We felt certain that most of our friends ahead of us died and we knew no one behind us.

We came upon a post office several blocks away. We stopped and   10 looked up. Our building, exactly where our office is (was), was engulfed in flame and smoke. A postal worker said that Tower 2 had fallen down. I looked again and sure enough it was gone. My heart was racing. We kept trying to call our families. I could not get in touch with my wife. Finally I got through to my parents. Relieved is not the word to explain their feelings. They got through to my wife, thank G–d, and let her know I was alive. We sat down. A girl on a bike offered us some water. Just as she took the cap off her bottle we heard a rumble. We looked up and our building, Tower 1, collapsed. I did not note the time, but I am told it was 10:30 a.m. We had been out less than fifteen minutes.

We were mourning our lost friends, particularly the one who stayed in the office, as we were now sure that he had perished. We started walking towards Union Square. I was going to Beth Israel Medical Center to be looked at. We stopped to hear the president speaking on the radio. My phone rang. It was my wife. I think I fell to my knees crying when I heard her voice. Then she told me the most incredible thing. My partner who had stayed behind called her. He was alive and well. I guess we just lost him in the commotion. We started jumping and hugging and shouting. I told my wife that my brother had arranged for a hotel in midtown. He can be very resourceful in that way. I told her I would call her from there. My brother and I managed to get a gypsy cab to take us home to Westchester instead. I cried on my son and held my wife until I fell asleep. As it turns out, my partner, the one who I thought had stayed behind, was behind us with Harry Ramos, our head trader. This is now secondhand information. They came upon Victor, the heavyset man on the fifty-third floor. They helped him. He could barely move. My partner bravely/stupidly tested the elevator on the fifty-second floor. He rode it down to the sky lobby on Forty-four. The doors opened, it was fine. He rode it back up and got Harry and Victor. I don't yet know if anyone else joined them. Once on Forty-four they made their way back into the stairwell. Someplace around the thirty-ninth to thirty-sixth floors they felt the same rumble I felt on the third floor. It was 10 a.m. and Tower 2 was coming down. They had about thirty minutes to get out. Victor said he could no longer move. They offered to have him lean on them. He said he couldn't do it. My partner hollered at him to sit on his butt and scooch down the steps. He said he was not capable of doing it. Harry told my partner to go ahead of them. Harry once had a heart attack and was worried about this man's heart. It was his nature to be this way. He was/is one of the kindest people I know. He would not leave a man behind. My partner went ahead and made it out. He said he was out maybe ten minutes before the building came down. This means that Harry had maybe twenty-five minutes to move Victor thirty-six floors. I guess they moved one floor every 1.5 minutes. Just a guess. This means Harry was around the twentieth floor when the building collapsed. As of now twelve of thirteen people are accounted for. As of 6 p.m. yesterday his wife had not heard from him. I fear that Harry is lost. However, a short while ago I heard that he may be alive. Apparently there is a Web site with survivor names on it and his appears there. Unfortunately, Ramos is not an uncommon name in New York. Pray for him and all those like him.

With regards to the firemen heading upstairs, I realize that they were going up anyway. But it hurts to know that I may have made them move quicker to find my friend. Rationally, I know this is not true and that I am not the responsible one. The responsible ones are in hiding some-where on this planet and damn them for making me feel like this. But they should know that they failed in terrorizing us. We were calm. Those men and women that went up were heroes in the face of it all. They must have known what was going on and they did their jobs. Ordinary people were heroes, too. Today the images that people around the world equate with power and democracy are gone, but "America" is not an image, it is a concept. That concept is only strengthened by our pulling together as a team. If you want to kill us, leave us alone because we will try to do it by ourselves. If you want to make us stronger, attack and we unite. This is the ultimate failure of terrorism against the United States and the ultimate price we pay to be free, to decide where we want to work, what we want to eat, and when and where we want to go on vacation. The very moment the first plane was hijacked, democracy won.

The Reader's Presence

1. Whom does Mayblum talk to as he moves down the stairs? What subject(s) do they discuss? Whom did you talk to following the attacks on the World Trade Center? To what extent do these conversations confirm Mayblum's claim that "If you want to make us stronger, attack and we unite" (paragraph 12)?

2. As Mayblum mentions the floors he passes in his descent, how does the countdown affect his overall story? Point to specific parts of his story that are more hurried than other parts. What about the moments in which he pauses? How do these moments affect your reading?

3. Compare Mayblum's account with Don DeLillo's essay on the terrorist attack on the World Trade Center ("In the Ruins of the Future," page 332) and with Richard Ford's essay on the aftermath of the impact of Hurricane Katrina ("A City Beyond Empathy," page 110). How does each writer position himself in relation to the catastrophic experience related in each essay? Which account do you find most moving? most effective? Why?

Barack Obama

Origins

America's forty-fourth president, Barack Obama (b. 1961) was born in Honolulu, Hawaii, to a Kansas-born American mother and a Kenyan father, who met and married when they were students at the University of Hawaii. The effects of his parent's interracial marriage, his father's return to Kenya, and his parents' subsequent divorce when he was very young are central to his memoir, Dreams from My Father: A Story of Race and Inheritance *(1995; reprinted in 2004), from which the piece that follows is excerpted. A 1995 review in the* New York Times Book Review *said that Obama's memoir "persuasively describes the phenomenon of belonging to two different worlds, and thus belonging to neither." After graduating from Columbia University in 1983, Obama worked as a community organizer in Chicago, then went on to Harvard University, where he became the first African American president of the* Harvard Law Review; *he received his law degree in*

1991. Turning down a prestigious judicial clerkship, he chose instead to practice civil rights law in Chicago and to teach constitutional law at the University of Chicago. He served in the Illinois State Senate from 1997 to 2003 and was elected to the U.S. Senate in 2004. In addition to his memoir, Obama *wrote* The Audacity of Hope: Thoughts on Reclaiming the American Dream, *published in 2006.*

A few months after my twenty-first birthday, a stranger called me to give me the news. I was living in New York at the time, on Ninety-fourth between Second and First, part of the unnamed, shifting border between East Harlem and the rest of Manhattan. It was an uninviting block, treeless and barren, lined with soot-colored walk-ups that cast heavy shadows for most of the day. The apartment was small, with slanting floors and irregular heat and a buzzer downstairs that didn't work, so that visitors had to call ahead from a pay phone at the corner gas station, where a black Doberman the size of a wolf paced through the night in vigilant patrol, its jaws clamped around an empty beer bottle.

None of this concerned me much, for I didn't get many visitors. I was impatient in those days, busy with work and unrealized plans, and prone to see other people as unnecessary distractions. It wasn't that I didn't appreciate company exactly. I enjoyed exchanging Spanish pleasantries with my mostly Puerto Rican neighbors, and on my way back from classes I'd usually stop to talk to the boys who hung out on the stoop all summer long about the Knicks or the gunshots they'd heard the night before. When the weather was good, my roommate and I might sit out on the fire escape to smoke cigarettes and study the dusk washing blue over the city, or watch white people from the better neighborhoods nearby walk their dogs down our block to let the animals shit on our curbs—"Scoop the poop, you bastards!" my roommate would shout with impressive rage, and we'd laugh at the faces of both master and beast, grim and unapologetic as they hunkered down to do the deed.

I enjoyed such moments—but only in brief. If the talk began to wander, or cross the border into familiarity, I would soon find reason to excuse myself. I had grown too comfortable in my solitude, the safest place I knew.

I remember there was an old man living next door who seemed to share my disposition. He lived alone, a gaunt, stooped figure who wore a heavy black overcoat and a misshapen fedora on those rare occasions when he left his apartment. Once in a while I'd run into him on his way back from the store, and I would offer to carry his groceries up the long flight of stairs. He would look at me and shrug, and we would begin our ascent, stopping at each landing so that he could catch his breath. When we finally arrived at his apartment, I'd carefully set the bags on the floor and he would offer a courtly nod of acknowledgment before shuffling inside and closing the latch. Not a single word would pass between us, and not once did he ever thank me for my efforts.

The old man's silence impressed me; I thought him a kindred spirit. Later, my roommate would find him crumpled up on the third-floor landing, his eyes wide open, his limbs stiff and curled up like a baby's. A crowd gathered; a few of the women crossed themselves, and the smaller children whispered with excitement. Eventually the paramedics arrived to take away the body and the police let themselves into the old man's apartment. It was neat, almost empty—a chair, a desk, a faded portrait of a woman with heavy eyebrows and a gentle smile atop the mantelpiece. Somebody opened the refrigerator and found close to a thousand dollars in small bills rolled up inside wads of old newspaper and carefully arranged behind mayonnaise and pickle jars.

The loneliness of the scene affected me, and for the briefest moment I wished that I had learned the old man's name. Then, almost immediately, I regretted my desire, along with its companion grief. I felt as if an understanding had been broken between us—as if, in that barren room, the old man was whispering an untold history, telling me things I preferred not to hear.

It must have been a month or so later, on a cold, dreary November morning, the sun faint behind a gauze of clouds, that the other call came. I was in the middle of making myself breakfast, with coffee on the stove and two eyes in the skillet, when my roommate handed me the phone. The line was thick with static.

"Barry? Barry, is this you?"

"Yes. . . . Who is this?"

"Yes, Barry . . . this is your Aunt Jane. In Nairobi. Can you hear me?"   10

"I'm sorry—who did you say you were?"

"Aunt Jane. Listen, Barry, your father is dead. He is killed in a car accident. Hello? Can you hear me? I say, your father is dead. Barry, please call your uncle in Boston and tell him. I can't talk now, okay, Barry. I will try to call you again. . . ."

That was all. The line cut off, and I sat down on the couch, smelling eggs burn in the kitchen, staring at cracks in the plaster, trying to measure my loss.

At the time of his death, my father remained a myth to me, both more and less than a man. He had left Hawaii back in 1963, when I was only two years old, so that as a child I knew him only through the stories that my mother and grandparents told. They all had their favorites, each one seamless, burnished smooth from repeated use. I can still picture Gramps leaning back in his old stuffed chair after dinner, sipping whiskey and cleaning his teeth with the cellophane from his cigarette pack, recounting the time that my father almost threw a man off the Pali Lookout because of a pipe. . . .

"See, your mom and dad decided to take this friend of his sightseeing   15 around the island. So they drove up to the Lookout, and Barack was probably on the wrong side of the road the whole way over there—"

"Your father was a terrible driver," my mother explains to me. "He'd end up on the left-hand side, the way the British drive, and if you said something he'd just huff about silly American rules—"

"Well, this particular time they arrived in one piece, and they got out and stood at the railing to admire the view. And Barack, he was puffing away on his pipe that I'd given him for his birthday, pointing out all the sights with the stem, like a sea captain—"

"Your father was really proud of this pipe," my mother interrupts again. "He'd smoke it all night while he studied, and sometimes—"

"Look, Ann, do you want to tell the story or are you going to let me finish?"

"Sorry, Dad. Go ahead."

20

"Anyway, this poor fella—he was another African student, wasn't he? Fresh off the boat. This poor kid must've been impressed with the way Barack was holding forth with this pipe, 'cause he asked if he could give it a try. Your dad thought about it for a minute, and finally agreed, and as soon as the fella took his first puff, he started coughing up a fit. Coughed so hard that the pipe slipped out of his hand and dropped over the railing, a hundred feet down the face of the cliff."

Gramps stops to take another nip from his flask before continuing. "Well, now, your dad was gracious enough to wait until his friend stopped coughing before he told him to climb over the railing and bring the pipe back. The man took one peek down this ninety-degree incline and told Barack that he'd buy him a replacement—"

"Quite sensibly," Toot says from the kitchen. (We call my grandmother Tutu, Toot for short; it means "grandparent" in Hawaiian, for she decided on the day I was born that she was still too young to be called Granny.) Gramps scowls but decides to ignore her.

"—but Barack was adamant about getting *his* pipe back, because it was a gift and couldn't be replaced. So the fella took another look, and shook his head again, and that's when your dad picked him clear off the ground and started dangling him over the railing!"

Gramps lets out a hoot and gives his knee a jovial slap. As he laughs, 25 I imagine myself looking up at my father, dark against the brilliant sun, the transgressor's arms flailing about as he's held aloft. A fearsome vision of justice.

"He wasn't really holding him over the railing, Dad," my mother says, looking to me with concern, but Gramps takes another sip of whiskey and plows forward.

"At this point, other people were starting to stare, and your mother was begging Barack to stop. I guess Barack's friend was just holding his breath and saying his prayers. Anyway, after a couple of minutes, your dad set the man back down on his feet, patted him on the back, and suggested, calm as you please, that they all go find themselves a beer. And don't you know, that's how your dad acted for the rest of the tour—like nothing happened. Of course, your mother was still pretty upset when they got home. In fact, she was barely talking to your dad. Barack wasn't helping matters any, either, 'cause when your mother tried to tell us what had happened he just shook his head and started to laugh. 'Relax, Anna,' he said to her—your dad had this deep baritone, see, and this British accent." My grandfather tucks his chin into his neck at this point, to capture the full effect. "'Relax, Anna,' he said. 'I only wanted to teach the chap a lesson about the proper care of other people's property!'"

Gramps would start to laugh again until he started to cough, and Toot would mutter under her breath that she supposed it was a good thing that my father had realized that dropping the pipe had just been an accident because who knows what might have happened otherwise, and my mother would roll her eyes at me and say they were exaggerating.

"Your father can be a bit domineering," my mother would admit with a hint of a smile. "But it's just that he is basically a very honest person. That makes him uncompromising sometimes."

She preferred a gentler portrait of my father. She would tell the story of when he arrived to accept his Phi Beta Kappa key in his favorite outfit —jeans and an old knit shirt with a leopard-print pattern. "Nobody told him it was this big honor, so he walked in and found everyone standing around this elegant room dressed in tuxedos. The only time I ever saw him embarrassed."

And Gramps, suddenly thoughtful, would start nodding to himself. "It's a fact, Bar," he would say. "Your dad could handle just about any situation, and that made everybody like him. Remember the time he had to sing at the International Music Festival? He'd agreed to sing some African songs, but when he arrived it turned out to be this big to-do, and the woman who performed just before him was a semiprofessional singer, a Hawaiian gal with a full band to back her up. Anyone else would have stopped right there, you know, and explained that there had been a mistake. But not Barack. He got up and started singing in front of this big crowd—which is no easy feat, let me tell you—and he wasn't great, but he was so sure of himself that before you knew it he was getting as much applause as anybody."

My grandfather would shake his head and get out of his chair to flip on the TV set. "Now there's something you can learn from your dad," he would tell me. "*Confidence*. The secret to a man's success."

That's how all the stories went—compact, apocryphal, told in rapid succession in the course of one evening, then packed away for months, sometimes years, in my family's memory. Like the few photographs of my father that remained in the house, old black-and-white studio prints that I might run across while rummaging through the closets in search of Christmas ornaments or an old snorkle set. At the point where my own memories begin, my mother had already begun a courtship with a man who would become her second husband, and I sensed without explanation why the photographs had to be stored away. But once in a while, sitting on the floor with my mother, the smell of dust and mothballs rising from the crumbling album, I would stare at my father's likeness—the dark laughing face, the prominent forehead and thick glasses that made him appear older than his years—and listen as the events of his life tumbled into a single narrative.

He was an African, I would learn, a Kenyan of the Luo tribe, born on the shores of Lake Victoria in a place called Alego. The village was poor, but his father—my other grandfather, Hussein Onyango Obama—had been a prominent farmer, an elder of the tribe, a medicine man with healing powers. My father grew up herding his father's goats and attending the local school, set up by the British colonial administration, where he had shown great promise. He eventually won a scholarship to study in Nairobi; and then, on the eve of Kenyan independence, he had been selected by Kenyan leaders and American sponsors to attend a university in the United States, joining the first large wave of Africans to be sent forth to master Western technology and bring it back to forge a new, modern Africa.

In 1959, at the age of twenty-three, he arrived at the University of Hawaii as that institution's first African student. He studied econometrics, worked with unsurpassed concentration, and graduated in three years at the top of his class. His friends were legion, and he helped organize the International Students Association, of which he became the first president. In a Russian language course, he met an awkward, shy American girl, only eighteen, and they fell in love. The girl's parents, wary at first, were won over by his charm and intellect; the young couple married, and she bore them a son, to whom he bequeathed his name. He won another scholarship—this time to pursue his Ph.D. at Harvard—but not the money to take his new family with him. A separation occurred, and he returned to Africa to fulfill his promise to the continent. The mother and child stayed behind, but the bond of love survived the distances. . . .

There the album would close, and I would wander off content, swaddled in a tale that placed me in the center of a vast and orderly universe. Even in the abridged version that my mother and grandparents offered, there were many things I didn't understand. But I rarely asked for the details that might resolve the meaning of "Ph.D." or "colonialism," or locate Alego on a map. Instead, the path of my father's life occupied the same terrain as a book my mother once bought for me, a book called *Origins*, a collection of creation tales from around the world, stories of Genesis and the tree where man was born, Prometheus and the gift of fire, the tortoise of Hindu legend that floated in space, supporting the weight of the world on its back. Later, when I became more familiar with the narrower path to happiness to be found in television and the movies, I'd become troubled by questions. What supported the tortoise? Why did an omnipotent God let a snake cause such grief? Why didn't my father return? But at the age of five or six I was satisfied to leave these distant

35

mysteries intact, each story self-contained and as true as the next, to be carried off into peaceful dreams.

That my father looked nothing like the people around me—that he was black as pitch, my mother white as milk—barely registered in my mind.

In fact, I can recall only one story that dealt explicitly with the subject of race; as I got older, it would be repeated more often, as if it captured the essence of the morality tale that my father's life had become. According to the story, after long hours of study, my father had joined my grandfather and several other friends at a local Waikiki bar. Everyone was in a festive mood, eating and drinking to the sounds of a slack-key guitar, when a white man abruptly announced to the bartender, loudly enough for everyone to hear, that he shouldn't have to drink good liquor "next to a nigger." The room fell quiet and people turned to my father, expecting a fight. Instead, my father stood up, walked over to the man, smiled, and proceeded to lecture him about the folly of bigotry, the promise of the American dream, and the universal rights of man. "This fella felt so bad when Barack was finished," Gramps would say, "that he reached into his pocket and gave Barack a hundred dollars on the spot. Paid for all our drinks and puu-puus for the rest of the night—and your dad's rent for the rest of the month."

By the time I was a teenager, I'd grown skeptical of this story's veracity and had set it aside with the rest. Until I received a phone call, many years later, from a Japanese-American man who said he had been my father's classmate in Hawaii and now taught at a midwestern university. He was very gracious, a bit embarrassed by his own impulsiveness; he explained that he had seen an interview of me in his local paper and that the sight of my father's name had brought back a rush of memories. Then, during the course of our conversation, he repeated the same story that my grandfather had told, about the white man who had tried to purchase my father's forgiveness. "I'll never forget that," the man said to me over the phone; and in his voice I heard the same note that I'd heard from Gramps so many years before, that note of disbelief—and hope.

The Reader's Presence

1. When Obama wrote his memoir *Dreams from My Father*, he enjoyed a small reputation as the first African American to be president of the *Harvard Law Review*, but he was hardly the national public figure he is today. So those who first read the memoir in 1995 would have considered it a literary account by a young writer intent on telling his life story. Though the words have not changed, how might the current context of his political career affect your reading?

2. Note the many times Obama mentions the mysteries surrounding his father and his skepticism toward many of the stories he hears. How does this affect your response to both his childhood and his father? How does it relate to the opening portion of the selection when Obama talks about an old man who lived next door to him?

3. Father-and-son relationships figure prominently in literature. You might compare Obama's account of his father with James Baldwin's description of his father in "Notes of a Native Son" (page 33), Henry Louis Gates Jr's in "In the Kitchen" (page 121), or Raymond Carver's in "My Father's Life" (see page 57). Do you think Obama's account was more challenging for him to write than the other accounts were for their respective authors? Explain what problems Obama might have encountered. What advantages might his situation have offered him?

THE WRITER AT WORK

Barack Obama on the Hazards of Autobiography

While a student at Harvard Law School, Barack Obama began an autobiography that would describe his somewhat unusual background and life experiences. Dreams from My Father: A Story of Race and Inheritance *was published in 1995 to excellent reviews, but it quickly disappeared in a sudden avalanche of memoirs. It was not until 2004, when the author became a major political figure in Illinois politics, that his publishers decided to reissue the autobiography with a new preface by Obama. The new edition quickly climbed to the top of the* New York Times *best-seller list. The following thoughts on the dangers of writing autobiography are from the book's original 1995 introduction.*

I learned long ago to distrust my childhood and the stories that shaped it. It was only many years later, after I had sat at my father's grave and spoken to him through Africa's red soil, that I could circle back and evaluate these early stories for myself. Or, more accurately, it was only then that I understood that I had spent much of my life trying to rewrite these stories, plugging up holes in the narrative, accommodating unwelcome details, projecting individual choices against the blind sweep of history, all in the hope of extracting some granite slab of truth upon which my unborn children can firmly stand.

At some point, in spite of a stubborn desire to protect myself from scrutiny, in spite of the periodic impulse to abandon the entire project, what has found its way onto these pages is a record of a personal, interior

journey—a boy's search for his father, and through that search a work-
able meaning for his life as a black American. The result is autobiographical, although whenever someone's asked me over the course of these last
three years just what the book is about, I've usually avoided such a description. An autobiography promises feats worthy of record, conversations with famous people, a central role in important events. There is
none of that here. At the very least, an autobiography implies a summing
up, a certain closure, that hardly suits someone of my years, still busy
charting his way through the world. I can't even hold up my experience
as being somehow representative of the black American experience
("After all, you don't come from an underprivileged background," a
Manhattan publisher helpfully points out to me); indeed, learning to accept that particular truth—that I can embrace my black brothers and sisters, whether in this country or in Africa, and affirm a common destiny
without pretending to speak to, or for, all our various struggles—is part
of what this book's about.

Finally, there are the dangers inherent in any autobiographical work:
the temptation to color events in ways favorable to the writer, the tendency to overestimate the interest one's experiences hold for others, selective lapses of memory. Such hazards are only magnified when the writer
lacks the wisdom of age; the distance that can cure one of certain vanities.
I can't say that I've avoided all, or any, of these hazards successfully. Although much of this book is based on contemporaneous journals or the
oral histories of my family, the dialogue is necessarily an approximation
of what was actually said or relayed to me. For the sake of compression,
some of the characters that appear are composites of people I've known,
and some events appear out of precise chronology. With the exception of
my family and a handful of public figures, the names of most characters
have been changed for the sake of their privacy.

George Orwell
Shooting an Elephant

George Orwell (1903–1950) was born Eric Arthur Blair in Bengal, India, the son of a colonial administrator. He was sent to England for his education and attended Eton on a scholarship, but rather than go on to university in 1922 he returned to the East and served with the Indian Imperial Police in Burma. Orwell hated his work and the colonial system; published posthumously, the essay "Shooting an Elephant" was based on his experience in Burma and is found in Shooting an Elephant and Other Essays *(1950). In 1927, Orwell returned to England and began a career as a professional writer. He served briefly in the Spanish Civil War until he was wounded and then settled in Hertfordshire. Best remembered for his novels* Animal Farm *(1945) and* Nineteen Eighty-Four *(1949), Orwell also wrote articles, essays, and reviews, usually with a political point in mind. In 1969, Irving Howe honored Orwell as "the best English essayist since Hazlitt, perhaps since Dr. Johnson. He was the greatest moral force in English letters during the last several decades: craggy, fiercely polemical, sometimes mistaken, but an utterly free man."*

In his 1946 essay "Why I Write," Orwell said that from a very early age "I knew that when I grew up I should be a writer." At first he saw writing as a remedy for loneliness, but as he grew up his reasons for writing expanded: "Looking back through my work, I see it is invariably when I lacked a political purpose that I wrote lifeless books." In his mature work, he relied on simple, clear prose to express his political and social convictions: "Good prose," he once wrote, "is like a windowpane."

In Moulmein, in Lower Burma, I was hated by large numbers of people — the only time in my life that I have been important enough for this to happen to me. I was subdivisional police officer of the town, and in an aimless, petty kind of way anti-European feeling was very bitter. No one had the guts to raise a riot, but if a European woman went through the bazaars alone somebody would probably spit betel juice over her dress. As a police officer I was an obvious target and was baited whenever it seemed safe to do so. When a nimble Burman tripped me up on the football field and the referee (another Burman) looked the other way, the crowd yelled with hideous laughter. This happened more than once. In the end the sneering yellow faces of young men that met me everywhere, the insults hooted after me when I was at a safe distance, got badly on my nerves. The young Buddhist priests were the worst of all. There were several thousands of them in the town and none of them seemed to have anything to do except stand on street corners and jeer at Europeans.

All this was perplexing and upsetting. For at that time I had already made up my mind that imperialism was an evil thing and the sooner I chucked up my job and got out of it the better. Theoretically—and secretly, of course—I was all for the Burmese and all against the oppressors, the British. As for the job I was doing, I hated it more bitterly than I can perhaps make clear. In a job like that you see the dirty work of Empire at close quarters. The wretched prisoners huddling in the stinking cages of the lockups, the grey, cowed faces of the long-term convicts, the scarred buttocks of the men who had been flogged with bamboos—all these oppressed me with an intolerable sense of guilt. But I could get nothing into perspective. I was young and ill-educated and I had had to think out my problems in the utter silence that is imposed on every Englishman in the East. I did not even know that the British Empire is dying, still less did I know that it is a great deal better than the younger empires that are going to supplant it. All I knew was that I was stuck between my hatred of the empire I served and my rage against the evil-spirited little beasts who tried to make my job impossible. With one part of my mind I thought of the British Raj[1] as an unbreakable tyranny, as something clamped down, *in saecula saeculorum,*[2] upon the will of prostrate peoples; with another part I thought that the greatest joy in the world would be to drive a bayonet into a Buddhist priest's guts. Feelings like these are the normal by-products of imperialism; ask any Anglo-Indian official, if you can catch him off duty.

One day something happened which in a roundabout way was enlightening. It was a tiny incident in itself, but it gave me a better glimpse than I had had before of the real nature of imperialism—the real motives for which despotic governments act. Early one morning the subinspector at a police station the other end of town rang me up on the phone and said that an elephant was ravaging the bazaar. Would I please come and do something about it? I did not know what I could do, but I wanted to see what was happening and I got on to a pony and started out. I took my rifle, an old .44 Winchester and much too small to kill an elephant, but I thought the noise might be useful *in terrorem.*[3] Various Burmans stopped me on the way and told me about the elephant's doings. It was not, of course, a wild elephant, but a tame one which had gone "must."[4] It had been chained up, as tame elephants always are when their attack of "must" is due, but on the previous night it had broken its chain and escaped. Its mahout,[5] the only person who could manage it when it was in that state, had set out in pursuit, but had taken the wrong direction and was now twelve hours' journey away, and in the morning the elephant had suddenly reappeared in the town. The Burmese population had no weapons and were quite helpless against it. It had already destroyed somebody's bamboo hut, killed a cow, and raided some fruit stalls and

[1]*Raj:* The British administration.—EDS.
[2]*in saecula saeculorum:* Forever and ever (Latin).—EDS.
[3]*in terrorem:* As a warning (Latin).—EDS.
[4]*"must":* Sexual arousal.—EDS.
[5]*mahout:* Keeper (Hindi).—EDS.

devoured the stock; also it had met the municipal rubbish van and, when the driver jumped out and took to his heels, had turned the van over and inflicted violence upon it.

The Burmese subinspector and some Indian constables were waiting for me in the quarter where the elephant had been seen. It was a very poor quarter, a labyrinth of squalid bamboo huts, thatched with palmleaf, winding all over a steep hillside. I remember that it was a cloudy, stuffy morning at the beginning of the rains. We began questioning the people as to where the elephant had gone and, as usual, failed to get any definite information. That is invariably the case in the East; a story always sounds clear enough at a distance, but the nearer you get to the scene of events the vaguer it becomes. Some of the people said that the elephant had gone in one direction, some said that he had gone in another, some professed not even to have heard of any elephant. I had almost made up my mind that the whole story was a pack of lies, when we heard yells a little distance away. There was a loud, scandalized cry of "Go away, child! Go away this instant!" and an old woman with a switch in her hand came round the corner of a hut, violently shooing away a crowd of naked children. Some more women followed, clicking their tongues and exclaiming; evidently there was something that the children ought not to have seen. I rounded the hut and saw a man's dead body sprawling in the mud. He was an Indian, a black Dravidian[6] coolie, almost naked, and he could not have been dead many minutes. The people said that the elephant had come suddenly upon him round the corner of the hut, caught him with its trunk, put its foot on his back, and ground him into the earth. This was the rainy season and the ground was soft, and his face had scored a trench a foot deep and a couple of yards long. He was lying on his belly with arms crucified and head sharply twisted to one side. His face was coated with mud, the eyes wide open, the teeth bared and grinning with an expression of unendurable agony. (Never tell me, by the way, that the dead look peaceful. Most of the corpses I have seen looked devilish.) The friction of the great beast's foot had stripped the skin from his back as neatly as one skins a rabbit. As soon as I saw the dead man I sent an orderly to a friend's house nearby to borrow an elephant rifle. I had already sent back the pony, not wanting it to go mad with fright and throw me if it smelled the elephant.

The orderly came back in a few minutes with a rifle and five cartridges, and meanwhile some Burmans had arrived and told us that the elephant was in the paddy fields below, only a few hundred yards away. As I started forward practically the whole population of the quarter flocked out of the houses and followed me. They had seen the rifle and were all shouting excitedly that I was going to shoot the elephant. They had not shown much interest in the elephant when he was merely ravaging their homes, but it was different now that he was going to be shot. It was a bit of fun to them, as it would be to an English crowd; besides, they wanted

[6]**Dravidian:** A populous Indian group. —EDS.

the meat. It made me vaguely uneasy. I had no intention of shooting the elephant—I had merely sent for the rifle to defend myself if necessary—and it is always unnerving to have a crowd following you. I marched down the hill, looking and feeling a fool, with the rifle over my shoulder and an ever-growing army of people jostling at my heels. At the bottom, when you got away from the huts, there was a metalled road and beyond that a miry waste of paddy fields a thousand yards across, not yet ploughed but soggy from the first rains and dotted with coarse grass. The elephant was standing eight yards from the road, his left side towards us. He took not the slightest notice of the crowd's approach. He was tearing up bunches of grass, beating them against his knees to clean them and stuffing them into his mouth.

I had halted on the road. As soon as I saw the elephant I knew with perfect certainty that I ought not to shoot him. It is a serious matter to shoot a working elephant—it is comparable to destroying a huge and costly piece of machinery—and obviously one ought not to do it if it can possibly be avoided. And at that distance, peacefully eating, the elephant looked no more dangerous than a cow. I thought then and I think now that his attack of "must" was already passing off; in which case he would merely wander harmlessly about until the mahout came back and caught him. Moreover, I did not in the least want to shoot him. I decided that I would watch him for a little while to make sure that he did not turn savage again, and then go home.

But at that moment, I glanced round at the crowd that had followed me. It was an immense crowd, two thousand at the least and growing every minute. It blocked the road for a long distance on either side. I looked at the sea of yellow faces above the garish clothes—faces all happy and excited over this bit of fun, all certain that the elephant was going to be shot. They were watching me as they would watch a conjuror about to perform a trick. They did not like me, but with the magical rifle in my hands I was momentarily worth watching. And suddenly I realized that I should have to shoot the elephant after all: The people expected it of me and I had got to do it; I could feel their two thousand wills pressing me forward, irresistibly. And it was at this moment, as I stood there with the rifle in my hands, that I first grasped the hollowness, the futility of the white man's dominion in the East. Here was I, the white man with his gun, standing in front of the unarmed native crowd—seemingly the leading actor of the piece; but in reality I was only an absurd puppet pushed to and fro by the will of those yellow faces behind. I perceived in this moment that when the white man turns tyrant it is his own freedom that he destroys. He becomes a sort of hollow, posing dummy, the conventionalized figure of a sahib. For it is the condition of his rule that he shall spend his life in trying to impress the "natives," and so in every crisis he has got to do what the "natives" expect of him. He wears a mask, and his face grows to fit it. I had got to shoot the elephant. I had committed myself to doing it when I sent for the rifle. A sahib has got to act like a sahib; he has got to appear resolute, to know his own mind and do definite things. To come all that way, rifle in hand, with two thousand people marching at my heels, and then to trail feebly away, having done nothing—no, that was impossible. The crowd would laugh at me. And my whole life, every white man's life in the East, was one long struggle not to be laughed at.

But I did not want to shoot the elephant. I watched him beating his bunch of grass against his knees, with that preoccupied grandmotherly air that elephants have. It seemed to me that it would be murder to shoot him. At that age I was not squeamish about killing animals, but I had never shot an elephant and never wanted to. (Somehow it always seems worse to kill a *large* animal.) Besides, there was the beast's owner to be considered. Alive, the elephant was worth at least a hundred pounds; dead, he would only be worth the value of his tusks, five pounds, possibly. But I had got to act quickly. I turned to some experienced-looking Burmans who had been there when we arrived, and asked them how the elephant had been behaving. They all said the same thing: He took no notice of you if you left him alone, but he might charge if you went too close to him.

It was perfectly clear to me what I ought to do. I ought to walk up to within, say, twenty-five yards of the elephant and test his behavior. If he charged, I could shoot; if he took no notice of me, it would be safe to leave him until the mahout came back. But also I knew that I was going to do no such thing. I was a poor shot with a rifle and the ground was soft mud into which one would sink at every step. If the elephant charged and I missed him, I should have about as much chance as a toad under a steamroller. But even then I was not thinking particularly of my own skin, only of the watchful yellow faces behind. For at that moment, with the crowd watching me, I was not afraid in the ordinary sense, as I would have been if I had been alone. A white man mustn't be frightened in front of "natives"; and so, in general, he isn't frightened. The sole thought in my mind was that if anything went wrong those two thousand Burmans would see me pursued, caught, trampled on, and reduced to a grinning corpse like that Indian up the hill. And if that happened it was quite probable that some of them would laugh. That would never do. There was only one alternative. I shoved the cartridges into the magazine and lay down on the road to get a better aim.

The crowd grew very still, and a deep, low, happy sigh, as of people who see the theatre curtain go up at last, breathed from innumerable throats. They were going to have their bit of fun after all. The rifle was a beautiful German thing with cross-hair sights. I did not then know that in shooting an elephant one would shoot to cut an imaginary bar running from ear-hole to ear-hole. I ought, therefore, as the elephant was sideways on, to have aimed straight at his ear-hole; actually I aimed several inches in front of this, thinking the brain would be further forward.

When I pulled the trigger I did not hear the bang or feel the kick—one never does when a shot goes home—but I heard the devilish roar of glee

10

that went up from the crowd. In that instant, in too short a time, one would have thought, even for the bullet to get there, a mysterious, terrible change had come over the elephant. He neither stirred nor fell, but every line of his body had altered. He looked suddenly stricken, shrunken, immensely old, as though the frightful impact of the bullet had paralyzed him without knocking him down. At last, after what seemed a long time — it might have been five seconds, I dare say — he sagged flabbily to his knees. His mouth slobbered. An enormous senility seemed to have settled upon him. One could have imagined him thousands of years old. I fired again into the same spot. At the second shot he did not collapse but climbed with desperate slowness to his feet and stood weakly upright, with legs sagging and head drooping. I fired a third time. That was the shot that did it for him. You could see the agony of it jolt his whole body and knock the last remnant of strength from his legs. But in falling he seemed for a moment to rise, for as his hind legs collapsed beneath him he seemed to tower upward like a huge rock toppling, his trunk reaching skywards like a tree. He trumpeted, for the first and only time. And then down he came, his belly towards me, with a crash that seemed to shake the ground even where I lay.

I got up. The Burmans were already racing past me across the mud. It was obvious that the elephant would never rise again, but he was not dead. He was breathing very rhythmically with long rattling gasps, his great mound of a side painfully rising and falling. His mouth was wide open. I could see far down into caverns of pale pink throat. I waited a long time for him to die, but his breathing did not weaken. Finally, I fired my two remaining shots into the spot where I thought his heart must be. The thick blood welled out of him like red velvet, but still he did not die. His body did not even jerk when the shots hit him, the tortured breathing continued without a pause. He was dying, very slowly and in great agony, but in some world remote from me where not even a bullet could damage him further. I felt I had got to put an end to that dreadful noise. It seemed dreadful to see the great beast lying there, powerless to move and yet powerless to die, and not even to be able to finish him. I sent back for my small rifle and poured shot after shot into his heart, and down his throat. They seemed to make no impression. The tortured gasps continued as steadily as the ticking of a clock.

In the end I could not stand it any longer and went away. I heard later that it took him half an hour to die. Burmans were bringing dahs[7] and baskets even before I left, and I was told they had stripped his body almost to the bones by the afternoon.

Afterwards, of course, there were endless discussions about the shooting of the elephant. The owner was furious, but he was only an Indian and could do nothing. Besides, legally I had done the right thing, for a mad elephant has to be killed, like a mad dog, if its owner fails to control it. Among the Europeans opinion was divided. The older men said I was right, the younger men said it was a damn shame to shoot an elephant for

---

[7]*dahs:* Large knives. — EDS.

killing a coolie, because the elephant was worth more than any damn Coringhee coolie. And afterwards I was very glad that the coolie had been killed; it put me legally in the right and it gave me sufficient pretext for shooting the elephant. I often wondered whether any of the others grasped that I had done it solely to avoid looking a fool.

The Reader's Presence

1. At the end of paragraph 2, Orwell gives the perfect expression of ambivalence, the simultaneous holding of two opposed feelings or opinions: "With one part of my mind . . . with another part . . ." How would you describe Orwell's dilemma? How would you react in such a situation? Is Orwell recommending that readers see his behavior as a model of what to do in such a conflict? To what extent is Orwell responsible for the situation in which he finds himself? What does he mean when he says that his conflicted feelings "are the normal by-products of imperialism"?

2. Some literary critics doubt that Orwell really did shoot an elephant in Burma. No external historical documentation has ever been found to corroborate Orwell's account. Yet what *internal* elements in the essay—what details or features—suggest that the episode is fact and not fiction? In other words, what makes this piece seem to be an essay and not a short story?

3. Orwell's essay describes a state of extreme personal self-consciousness, even vigilance, in a situation in which one's behavior feels somehow "scripted" by society. Orwell writes, "in reality I was only an absurd puppet pushed to and fro by the will of those yellow faces behind" (paragraph 7). How does Orwell's essay compare with Brent Staples's essay "Just Walk on By: A Black Man Ponders His Power to Alter Public Space" (page 240)? Compare especially Orwell's use of the word *fool* in his last paragraph and Staples's use of the same word in the second paragraph of the alternate version of his essay. Do you believe both authors?

Richard Rodriguez

Aria: A Memoir of a Bilingual Childhood

Richard Rodriguez (b. 1944) has contributed articles to many magazines and newspapers, including Harper's, American Scholar, *the* Los Angeles Times, *and the* New York Times. *He is an editor at* Pacific News Services *and a regular essayist on the* News Hour with Jim Lehrer, *for which he received the 1997 George Foster Peabody Award. His most sensational literary accomplishment, however, is his intellectual autobiography,* Hunger of Memory: The Education of Richard Rodriguez *(1982). In it, Rodriguez outlines his positions on issues such as bilingualism, affirmative action, and assimilation, and he concludes that current policies in these areas are misguided and serve only to reinforce current social inequalities. Other books include* Days of Obligations: An Argument with My Mexican Father *(1992) and* Brown: The Last Discovery of America *(2002).*

About the experience of writing his autobiography, Rodriguez comments, "By finding public words to describe one's feelings, one can describe oneself to oneself. . . . I have come to think of myself as engaged in writing graffiti."

The following essay originally appeared in the American Scholar *(winter 1980/81) and later served as the opening chapter in his autobiography* Hunger of Memory *(1982).*

I remember, to start with, that day in Sacramento, in a California now nearly thirty years past, when I first entered a classroom — able to understand about fifty stray English words. The third of four children, I had been preceded by my older brother and sister to a neighborhood Roman Catholic school. But neither of them had revealed very much about their classroom experiences. They left each morning and returned each afternoon, always together, speaking Spanish as they climbed the five steps to the porch. And their mysterious books, wrapped in brown shopping-bag paper, remained on the table next to the door, closed firmly behind them.

An accident of geography sent me to a school where all my classmates were white and many were the children of doctors and lawyers and business executives. On that first day of school, my classmates must certainly have been uneasy to find themselves apart from their families, in the first institution of their lives. But I was astonished. I was fated to be the "problem student" in class.

The nun said, in a friendly but oddly impersonal voice: "Boys and girls, this is Richard Rodriguez." (I heard her sound it out: *Rich-heard Road-ree-guess.*) It was the first time I had heard anyone say my name in

English. "Richard," the nun repeated more slowly, writing my name down in her book. Quickly I turned to see my mother's face dissolve in a watery blur behind the pebbled-glass door.

Now, many years later, I hear of something called "bilingual educa-tion"—a scheme proposed in the late 1960s by Hispanic-American so-cial activists, later endorsed by a congressional vote. It is a program that seeks to permit non-English-speaking children (many from lower class homes) to use their "family language" as the language of school. Such, at least, is the aim its supporters announce. I hear them, and am forced to say no: It is not possible for a child, any child, ever to use his family's language in school. Not to understand this is to misunder-stand the public uses of schooling and to trivialize the nature of inti-mate life.

Memory teaches me what I know of these matters. The boy reminds the adult. I was a bilingual child, but of a certain kind: "socially dis-advantaged," the son of working-class parents, both Mexican immigrants.

In the early years of my boyhood, my parents coped very well in America. My father had steady work. My mother managed at home. They were nobody's victims. When we moved to a house many blocks from the Mexican-American section of town, they were not intimidated by those two or three neighbors who initially tried to make us unwel-come. ("Keep your brats away from my sidewalk!") But despite all they achieved, or perhaps because they had so much to achieve, they lacked any deep feeling of ease, of belonging in public. They regarded the people at work or in crowds as being very distant from us. Those were the oth-ers, *los gringos*. That term was interchangeable in their speech with an-other, even more telling: *los americanos*.

I grew up in a house where the only regular guests were my relations. On a certain day, enormous families of relatives would visit us, and there would be so many people that the noise and the bodies would spill out to the backyard and onto the front porch. Then for weeks no one would come. (If the doorbell rang, it was usually a salesman.) Our house stood apart—gaudy yellow in a row of white bungalows. We were the people with the noisy dog, the people who raised chickens. We were the foreign-ers on the block. A few neighbors would smile and wave at us. We waved back. But until I was seven years old, I did not know the name of the old couple living next door or the names of the kids living across the street.

In public, my father and mother spoke a hesitant, accented, and not always grammatical English. And then they would have to strain, their bodies tense, to catch the sense of what was rapidly said by *los gringos*. At home, they returned to Spanish. The language of their Mexican past sounded in counterpoint to the English spoken in public. The words would come quickly, with ease. Conveyed through those sounds was the pleasing, soothing, consoling reminder that one was at home.

During those years when I was first learning to speak, my mother and father addressed me only in Spanish; in Spanish I learned to reply. By contrast, English (*inglés*) was the language I came to associate with gringos, rarely heard in the house. I learned my first words of English overhearing my parents speaking to strangers. At six years of age, I knew just enough words for my mother to trust me on errands to stores one block away—but no more.

I was then a listening child, careful to hear the very different sounds   10
of Spanish and English. Wide-eyed with hearing, I'd listen to sounds more than to words. First, there were English (gringo) sounds. So many words still were unknown to me that when the butcher or the lady at the drugstore said something, exotic polysyllabic sounds would bloom in the midst of their sentences. Often the speech of people in public seemed to me very loud, booming with confidence. The man behind the counter would literally ask, "What can I do for you?" But by being so firm and clear, the sound of his voice said that he was a gringo; he belonged in public society. There were also the high, nasal notes of middle-class American speech—which I rarely am conscious of hearing today because I hear them so often, but could not stop hearing when I was a boy. Crowds at Safeway or at bus stops were noisy with the birdlike sounds of *los gringos*. I'd move away from them all—all the chirping chatter above me.

My own sounds I was unable to hear, but I knew that I spoke English poorly. My words could not extend to form complete thoughts. And the words I did speak I didn't know well enough to make distinct sounds. (Listeners would usually lower their heads to hear better what I was trying to say.) But it was one thing for *me* to speak English with difficulty; it was more troubling to hear my parents speaking in public: their high-whining vowels and guttural consonants; their sentences that got stuck with "eh" and "ah" sounds; the confused syntax; the hesitant rhythm of sounds so different from the way gringos spoke. I'd notice, moreover, that my parents' voices were softer than those of gringos we would meet.

I am tempted to say now that none of this mattered. (In adulthood I am embarrassed by childhood fears.) And, in a way, it didn't matter very much that my parents could not speak English with ease. Their linguistic difficulties had no serious consequences. My mother and father made themselves understood at the county hospital clinic and at government offices. And yet, in another way, it mattered very much. It was unsettling to hear my parents struggle with English. Hearing them, I'd grow nervous, and my clutching trust in their protection and power would be weakened.

There were many times like the night at a brightly lit gasoline station (a blaring white memory) when I stood uneasily hearing my father talk to a teenage attendant. I do not recall what they were saying, but I cannot forget the sounds my father made as he spoke. At one point his words slid together to form one long word—sounds as confused as the threads of blue and green oil in the puddle next to my shoes. His voice rushed through what he had left to say. Toward the end, he reached falsetto notes, appealing to his listener's understanding. I looked away at the lights of passing automobiles. I tried not to hear any more. But I heard only too well the attendant's reply, his calm, easy tones. Shortly afterward, headed for home, I shivered when my father put his hand on my shoulder. The very first chance that I got, I evaded his grasp and ran on ahead into the dark, skipping with feigned boyish exuberance.

But then there was Spanish: *español*, the language rarely heard away from the house; *español*, the language which seemed to me therefore a private language, my family's language. To hear its sounds was to feel myself specially recognized as one of the family, apart from *los otros*. A simple remark, an inconsequential comment could convey that assurance. My parents would say something to me and I would feel embraced by the sounds of their words. Those sounds said: *I am speaking with ease in Spanish. I am addressing you in words I never use with los gringos. I recognize you as someone special, close, like no one outside. You belong with us. In the family. Ricardo.*

At the age of six, well past the time when most middle-class children   15
no longer notice the difference between sounds uttered at home and words spoken in public, I had a different experience. I lived in a world compounded of sounds. I was a child longer than most. I lived in a magical world, surrounded by sounds both pleasing and fearful. I shared with my family a language enchantingly private—different from that used in the city around us.

Just opening or closing the screen door behind me was an important experience. I'd rarely leave home all alone or without feeling reluctance. Walking down the sidewalk, under the canopy of tall trees, I'd warily notice the (suddenly) silent neighborhood kids who stood warily watching me. Nervously, I'd arrive at the grocery store to hear there the sounds of the gringo, reminding me that in this so-big world I was a foreigner. But if leaving home was never routine, neither was coming back. Walking toward our house, climbing the steps from the sidewalk, in summer when the front door was open, I'd hear voices beyond the screen door talking in Spanish. For a second or two I'd stay, linger there listening. Smiling, I'd hear my mother call out, saying in Spanish, "Is that you, Richard?" Those were her words, but all the while her sounds would assure me: *You are home now. Come closer inside. With us.* "*Sí,*" I'd reply.

Once more inside the house, I would resume my place in the family. The sounds would grow harder to hear. Once more at home, I would grow less conscious of them. It required, however, no more than the blurt of the doorbell to alert me all over again to listen to sounds. The house would turn instantly quiet while my mother went to the door. I'd hear her hard English sounds. I'd wait to hear her voice turn to soft-sounding Spanish, which assured me, as surely as did the clicking tongue of the lock on the door, that the stranger was gone.

Plainly it is not healthy to hear such sounds so often. It is not healthy to distinguish public from private sounds so easily. I remained cloistered by sounds, timid and shy in public, too dependent on the voices at home. And yet I was a very happy child when I was at home. I remember many nights when my father would come back from work, and I'd hear him call out to my mother in Spanish, sounding relieved. In Spanish, his voice would sound the light and free notes that he never could manage in English. Some nights I'd jump up just hearing his voice. My brother and I would come running into the room where he was with our mother. Our laughing (so deep was the pleasure!) became screaming. Like others who feel the pain of public alienation, we transformed the knowledge of our public separateness into a consoling reminder of our intimacy. Excited, our voices joined in a celebration of sounds. *We are speaking now the way we never speak out in public—we are together*, the sounds told me. Some nights no one seemed willing to loosen the hold that sounds had on us. At dinner we invented new words that sounded Spanish, but made sense only to us. We pieced together new words by taking, say, an English verb and giving it Spanish endings. My mother's instructions at bedtime would be lacquered with mock-urgent tones. Or a word like *sí*, sounded in several notes, would convey added measures of feeling. Tongues lingered around the edges of words, especially fat vowels. And we happily sounded that military drum roll, the twirling roar of the Spanish *r*. Family language, my family's sounds: the voices of my parents and sisters and brother. Their voices insisting: *You belong here. We are family members. Related. Special to one another. Listen!* Voices singing and sighing, rising and straining, then surging, teeming with pleasure which burst syllables into fragments of laughter. At times it seemed there was steady quiet only when, from another room, the rustling whispers of my parents faded and I edged closer to sleep.

Supporters of bilingual education imply today that students like me miss a great deal by not being taught in their family's language. What they seem not to recognize is that, as a socially disadvantaged child, I regarded Spanish as a private language. It was a ghetto language that deepened and strengthened my feeling of public separateness. What I needed to learn in school was that I had the right, and the obligation, to speak the public language. The odd truth is that my first-grade classmates could have become bilingual, in the conventional sense of the word, more easily than I. Had they been taught early (as upper middle-class children often are taught) a "second language" like Spanish or French, they could have regarded it simply as another public language. In my case, such bilingualism could not have been so quickly achieved. What I did not believe was that I could speak a single public language.

Without question, it would have pleased me to have heard my teachers address me in Spanish when I entered the classroom. I would have felt much less afraid. I would have imagined that my instructors   20 were somehow "related" to me; I would indeed have heard their Spanish as my family's language. I would have trusted them and responded with ease. But I would have delayed—postponed for how long?—having to learn the language of public society. I would have evaded—and for how long?—learning the great lesson of school: that I had a public identity.

Fortunately, my teachers were unsentimental about their responsibility. What they understood was that I needed to speak public English. So their voices would search me out, asking me questions. Each time I heard them I'd look up in surprise to see a nun's face frowning at me. I'd mumble, not really meaning to answer. The nun would persist. "Richard, stand up. Don't look at the floor. Speak up. Speak to the entire class, not just to me!" But I couldn't believe English could be my language to use. (In part, I did not want to believe it.) I continued to mumble. I resisted the teacher's demands. (Did I somehow suspect that once I learned this public language my family life would be changed?) Silent, waiting for the bell to sound, I remained dazed, diffident, afraid.

Because I wrongly imagined that English was intrinsically a public language and Spanish was intrinsically private, I easily noted the difference between classroom language and the language of home. At school, words were directed to a general audience of listeners. ("Boys and girls . . .") Words were meaningfully ordered. And the point was not self-expression alone, but to make oneself understood by many others. The teacher quizzed: "Boys and girls, why do we use that word in this sentence? Could we think of a better word to use there? Would the sentence change its meaning if the words were differently arranged? Isn't there a better way of saying much the same thing?" (I couldn't say. I wouldn't try to say.)

Three months passed. Five. A half year. Unsmiling, ever watchful, my teachers noted my silence. They began to connect my behavior with the slow progress my brother and sisters were making. Until, one Saturday morning, three nuns arrived at the house to talk to our parents. Stiffly they sat on the blue living-room sofa. From the doorway of another room, spying on the visitors, I noted the incongruity, the clash of two worlds, the faces and voices of school intruding upon the familiar setting of home. I overheard one voice gently wondering, "Do your children speak only Spanish at home, Mrs. Rodriguez?" While another voice added, "That Richard especially seems so timid and shy."

That Rich-heard!

With great tact, the visitors continued, "Is it possible for you and your husband to encourage your children to practice their English when they are home?" Of course my parents complied. What would they not do for their children's well-being? And how could they question the Church's authority which those women represented? In an instant they agreed to give up the language (the sounds) which had revealed and accentuated our family's closeness. The moment after the visitors left, the change was observed. "*Ahora,* speak to us only *en inglés,*" my father and mother told us.

25

At first, it seemed a kind of game. After dinner each night, the family gathered together to practice "our" English. It was still then *inglés*, a language foreign to us, so we felt drawn to it as strangers. Laughing, we would try to define words we could not pronounce. We played with strange English sounds, often over-anglicizing our pronunciations. And we filled the smiling gaps of our sentences with familiar Spanish sounds. But that was cheating, somebody shouted, and everyone laughed.

In school, meanwhile, like my brother and sisters, I was required to attend a daily tutoring session. I needed a full year of this special work. I also needed my teachers to keep my attention from straying in class by calling out, "*Rich-heard!*"—their English voices slowly loosening the ties to my other name, with its three notes, *Ri-car-do*. Most of all, I needed to hear my mother and father speak to me in a moment of seriousness in "broken"—suddenly heartbreaking—English. This scene was inevitable. One Saturday morning I entered the kitchen where my parents were talking, but I did not realize that they were talking in Spanish until, the moment they saw me, their voices changed and they began speaking English. The gringo sounds they uttered startled me. Pushed me away. In that moment of trivial misunderstanding and profound insight, I felt my throat twisted by unsounded grief. I simply turned and left the room. But I had no place to escape to where I could grieve in Spanish. My brother and sisters were speaking English in another part of the house.

Again and again in the days following, as I grew increasingly angry, I was obliged to hear my mother and father encouraging me: "Speak to us *en inglés*." Only then did I determine to learn classroom English. Thus, sometime afterward it happened: one day in school, I raised my hand to volunteer an answer to a question. I spoke out in a loud voice and I did not think it remarkable when the entire class understood. That day I moved very far from being the disadvantaged child I had been only days earlier. Taken hold at last was the belief, the calming assurance, that I *belonged* in public.

Shortly after, I stopped hearing the high, troubling sounds of *los gringos*. A more and more confident speaker of English, I didn't listen to how strangers sounded when they talked to me. With so many English-speaking people around me, I no longer heard American accents. Conversations quickened. Listening to persons whose voices sounded eccentrically pitched, I might note their sounds for a few seconds, but then I'd concentrate on what they were saying. Now when I heard someone's tone of voice—angry or questioning or sarcastic or happy or sad—I didn't distinguish it from the words it expressed. Sound and word were thus tightly wedded. At the end of each day I was often bemused, and always relieved, to realize how "soundless," though crowded with words, my day in public had been. An eight-year-old boy, I finally came to accept what had been technically true since my birth: I was an American citizen.

But diminished by then was the special feeling of closeness at home. 30 Gone was the desperate, urgent, intense feeling of being at home among those with whom I felt intimate. Our family remained a loving family, but one greatly changed. We were no longer so close, no longer bound tightly together by the knowledge of our separateness from *los gringos*. Neither my older brother nor my sisters rushed home after school any more. Nor did I. When I arrived home, often there would be neighborhood kids in the house. Or the house would be empty of sounds.

Following the dramatic Americanization of their children, even my parents grew more publicly confident—especially my mother. First she learned the names of all the people on the block. Then she decided we needed to have a telephone in our house. My father, for his part, continued to use the word *gringo*, but it was no longer charged with bitterness or distrust. Stripped of any emotional content, the word simply became a name for those Americans not of Hispanic descent. Hearing him, sometimes, I wasn't sure if he was pronouncing the Spanish word *gringo*, or saying gringo in English.

There was a new silence at home. As we children learned more and more English, we shared fewer and fewer words with our parents. Sentences needed to be spoken slowly when one of us addressed our mother or father. Often the parent wouldn't understand. The child would need to repeat himself. Still the parent misunderstood. The young voice, frustrated, would end up saying, "Never mind"—the subject was closed. Dinners would be noisy with the clinking of knives and forks against dishes. My mother would smile softly between her remarks; my father, at the other end of the table, would chew and chew his food while he stared over the heads of his children.

My mother! My father! After English became my primary language, I no longer knew what words to use in addressing my parents. The old Spanish words (those tender accents of sound) I had earlier used—*mamá* and *papá*—I couldn't use any more. They would have been all-too-painful reminders of how much had changed in my life. On the other hand, the words I heard neighborhood kids call their parents seemed equally unsatisfactory. "Mother" and "father," "ma," "papa," "pa," "dad," "pop" (how I hated the all-American sound of that last word)—all these I felt were unsuitable terms of address for *my* parents. As a result, I never used them at home. Whenever I'd speak to my parents, I would try to get their attention by looking at them. In public conversations, I'd refer to them as my "parents" or my "mother" and "father."

My mother and father, for their part, responded differently, as their children spoke to them less. My mother grew restless, seemed troubled and anxious at the scarceness of words exchanged in the house. She would question me about my day when I came home from school. She smiled at my small talk. She pried at the edges of my sentences to get me to say something more. ("What . . . ?") She'd join conversations she overheard, but her intrusions often stopped her children's talking. By contrast, my father seemed to grow reconciled to the new quiet. Though his English somewhat improved, he tended more and more to retire into silence. At dinner he spoke very little. One night his children and even his wife helplessly giggled at his garbled English pronunciation of the Catholic "Grace Before Meals." Thereafter he made his wife recite the prayer at the start of each meal, even on formal occasions when there were guests in the house.

Hers became the public voice of the family. On official business it was she, not my father, who would usually talk to strangers on the phone or in stores. We children grew so accustomed to his silence that years later we would routinely refer to his "shyness." (My mother often tried to explain: Both of his parents died when he was eight. He was raised by an uncle who treated him as little more than a menial servant. He was never encouraged to speak. He grew up alone—a man of few words.) But I realized my father was not shy whenever I'd watch him speaking Spanish with relatives. Using Spanish, he was quickly effusive. Especially when talking with other men, his voice would spark, flicker, flare alive with varied sounds. In Spanish he expressed ideas and feelings he rarely revealed when speaking English. With firm Spanish sounds he conveyed a confidence and authority that English would never allow him.   35

The silence at home, however, was not simply the result of fewer words passing between parents and children. More profound for me was the silence created by my inattention to sounds. At about the time I no longer bothered to listen with care to the sounds of English in public, I grew careless about listening to the sounds made by the family when they spoke. Most of the time I would hear someone speaking at home and didn't distinguish his sounds from the words people uttered in public. I didn't even pay much attention to my parents' accented and ungrammatical speech—at least not at home. Only when I was with them in public would I become alert to their accents. But even then their sounds caused me less and less concern. For I was growing increasingly confident of my own public identity.

I would have been happier about my public success had I not recalled, sometimes, what it had been like earlier, when my family conveyed its intimacy through a set of conveniently private sounds. Sometimes in public, hearing a stranger, I'd hark back to my lost past. A Mexican farm worker approached me one day downtown. He wanted directions to some place. "*Hijito* . . . ," he said. And his voice stirred old longings. Another time I was standing beside my mother in the visiting room of a Carmelite convent, before the dense screen which rendered the nuns shadowy figures. I heard several of them speaking Spanish in their busy, singsong, overlapping voices, assuring my mother that, yes, yes, we were remembered, all our family was remembered, in their prayers. Those voices echoed faraway family sounds. Another day a dark-faced old woman touched my shoulder lightly to steady herself as she boarded a bus. She murmured something to me I couldn't quite comprehend. Her Spanish voice came near, like the face of a never-before-seen relative in the instant before I was kissed. That voice, like so many of the Spanish voices I'd hear in public, recalled the golden age of my childhood.

Bilingual educators say today that children lose a degree of "individuality" by becoming assimilated into public society. (Bilingual schooling is a program popularized in the seventies, that decade when middle-class "ethnics" began to resist the process of assimilation—the "American melting pot.") But the bilingualists oversimplify when they scorn the value and necessity of assimilation. They do not seem to realize that a person is individualized in two ways. So they do not realize that, while one suffers a diminished sense of *private* individuality by being assimilated into public society, such assimilation makes possible the achievement of *public* individuality.

Simplistically again, the bilingualists insist that a student should be reminded of his difference from others in mass society, of his "heritage." But they equate mere separateness with individuality. The fact is that only in private—with intimates—is separateness from the crowd a prerequisite for individuality; an intimate "tells" me that I am unique, unlike all others, apart from the crowd. In public, by contrast, full individuality is achieved, paradoxically, by those who are able to consider themselves members of the crowd. Thus it happened for me. Only when I was able to think of myself as an American, no longer an alien in gringo society, could I seek the rights and opportunities necessary for full public individuality. The social and political advantages I enjoy as a man began on the day I came to believe that my name is indeed *Rich-heard Road-ree-guess*. It is true that my public society today is often impersonal; in fact, my public society is usually mass society. But despite the anonymity of the crowd, and despite the fact that the individuality I achieve in public is often tenuous—because it depends on my being one in a crowd—I celebrate the day I acquired my new name. Those middle-class ethnics who scorn assimilation seem to me filled with decadent self-pity, obsessed by the burden of public life. Dangerously, they romanticize public separateness and trivialize the dilemma of those who are truly socially disadvantaged.

If I rehearse here the changes in my private life after my Americanization, it is finally to emphasize a public gain. The loss implies the gain. The house I returned to each afternoon was quiet. Intimate sounds no longer greeted me at the door. Inside there were other noises. The telephone rang. Neighborhood kids ran past the door of the bedroom where I was reading my schoolbooks—covered with brown shopping-bag paper. Once I learned the public language, it would never again be easy for me to hear intimate family voices. More and more of my day was spent hearing words, not sounds. But that may only be a way of saying that on the day I raised my hand in class and spoke loudly to an entire roomful of faces, my childhood started to end.

I grew up the victim of a disconcerting confusion. As I became fluent in English, I could no longer speak Spanish with confidence. I continued to understand spoken Spanish, and in high school I learned how to read and write Spanish. But for many years I could not pronounce it. A powerful guilt blocked my spoken words; an essential glue was missing whenever I would try to connect words to form sentences. I would be unable to break a barrier of sound, to speak freely. I would speak, or try to speak, Spanish, and I would manage to utter halting, hiccuping sounds which betrayed my unease. (Even today I speak Spanish very slowly, at best.)

When relatives and Spanish-speaking friends of my parents came to the house, my brother and sisters would usually manage to say a few words before being excused. I never managed so gracefully. Each time I'd hear myself addressed in Spanish, I couldn't respond with any success. I'd know the words I wanted to say, but I couldn't say them. I would try to speak, but everything I said seemed to me horribly anglicized. My mouth wouldn't form the sounds right. My jaw would tremble. After a phrase or two, I'd stutter, cough up a warm, silvery sound, and stop.

My listeners were surprised to hear me. They'd lower their heads to grasp better what I was trying to say. They would repeat their questions in gentle, affectionate voices. But then I would answer in English. No, no, they would say, we want you to speak to us in Spanish ("*en español*"). But I couldn't do it. Then they would call me *Pocho*. Sometimes playfully, teasing, using the tender diminutive—*mi pochito*. Sometimes not so playfully but mockingly, *pocho*. (A Spanish dictionary defines that word as an adjective meaning "colorless" or "bland." But I heard it as a noun, naming the Mexican-American who, in becoming an American, forgets his native society.) "*¡Pocho!*" my mother's best friend muttered, shaking her head. And my mother laughed, somewhere behind me. She said that her children didn't want to practice "our Spanish" after they started going to school. My mother's smiling voice made me suspect that the lady who faced me was not really angry at me. But searching her face, I couldn't find the hint of a smile.

Embarrassed, my parents would often need to explain their children's inability to speak fluent Spanish during those years. My mother encountered the wrath of her brother, her only brother, when he came up from Mexico one summer with his family and saw his nieces and nephews for the very first time. After listening to me, he looked away and said what a disgrace it was that my siblings and I couldn't speak Spanish, "*su propria idioma.*" He made that remark to my mother, but I noticed that he stared at my father.

One other visitor from those years I clearly remember: a long-time   45
friend of my father from San Francisco who came to stay with us for several days in late August. He took great interest in me after he realized that I couldn't answer his questions in Spanish. He would grab me, as I started to leave the kitchen. He would ask me something. Usually he wouldn't

bother to wait for my mumbled response. Knowingly, he'd murmur, "*¿Ay pocho, pocho, donde vas?*" And he would press his thumbs into the upper part of my arms, making me squirm with pain. Dumbly I'd stand there, waiting for his wife to notice us and call him off with a benign smile. I'd giggle, hoping to deflate the tension between us, pretending that I hadn't seen the glittering scorn in his glance.

I recount such incidents only because they suggest the fierce power that Spanish had over many people I met at home, how strongly Spanish was associated with closeness. Most of those people who called me a *pocho* could have spoken English to me, but many wouldn't. They seemed to think that Spanish was the only language we could use among ourselves, that Spanish alone permitted our association. (Such persons are always vulnerable to the ghetto merchant and the politician who have learned the value of speaking their clients' "family language" so as to gain immediate trust.) For my part, I felt that by learning English I had somehow committed a sin of betrayal. But betrayal against whom? Not exactly against the visitors to the house. Rather, I felt I had betrayed my immediate family. I knew that my parents had encouraged me to learn English. I knew that I had turned to English with angry reluctance. But once I spoke English with ease, I came to feel guilty. I sensed that I had broken the spell of intimacy which had once held the family so close together. It was this original sin against my family that I recalled whenever anyone addressed me in Spanish and I responded, confounded.

Yet even during those years of guilt, I was coming to grasp certain consoling truths about language and intimacy—truths that I learned gradually. Once, I remember playing with a friend in the backyard when my grandmother appeared at the window. Her face was stern with suspicion when she saw the boy (the *gringo* boy) I was with. She called out to me in Spanish, sounding the whistle of her ancient breath. My companion looked up and watched her intently as she lowered the window and moved (still visible) behind the light curtain, watching us both. He wanted to know what she had said. I started to tell him, to translate her Spanish words into English. The problem was, however, that though I knew how to translate exactly what she had told me, I realized that any translation would distort the deepest meaning of her message: it had been directed only to me. This message of intimacy could never be translated because it did not lie in the actual words she had used but passed through them. So any translation would have seemed wrong; the words would have been stripped of an essential meaning. Finally I decided not to tell my friend anything—just that I didn't hear all she had said.

This insight was unfolded in time. As I made more and more friends outside my house, I began to recognize intimate messages spoken in English in a close friend's confidential tone or secretive whisper. Even more remarkable were those instances when, apparently for no special reason, I'd become conscious of the fact that my companion was speaking *only to me.* I'd marvel then, just hearing his voice. It was a stunning event to be able to break through the barrier of public silence, to be able to hear the voice of the other, to realize that it was directed just to me. After such moments of intimacy outside the house, I began to trust what I heard intimately conveyed through my family's English. Voices at home at last punctured sad confusion. I'd hear myself addressed as an intimate — in English. Such moments were never as raucous with sound as in past times, when we had used our "private" Spanish. (Our English-sounding house was never to be as noisy as our Spanish-sounding house had been.) Intimate moments were usually moments of soft sound. My mother would be ironing in the dining room while I did my homework nearby. She would look over at me, smile, and her voice sounded to tell me that I was her son. *Richard.*

Intimacy thus continued at home; intimacy was not stilled by English. Though there were fewer occasions for it — a change in my life that I would never forget — there were also times when I sensed the deep truth about language and intimacy: *Intimacy is not created by a particular language; it is created by intimates.* Thus the great change in my life was not linguistic but social. If, after becoming a successful student, I no longer heard intimate voices as often as I had earlier, it was not because I spoke English instead of Spanish. It was because I spoke public language for most of my day. I moved easily at last, a citizen in a crowded city of words.

As a man I spend most of my day in public, in a world largely devoid   50
of speech sounds. So I am quickly attracted by the glamorous quality of certain alien voices. I still am gripped with excitement when someone passes me on the street, speaking in Spanish. I have not moved beyond the range of the nostalgic pull of those sounds. And there is something very compelling about the sounds of lower-class blacks. Of all the accented versions of English that I hear in public, I hear theirs most intently. The Japanese tourist stops me downtown to ask me a question and I inch my way past his accent to concentrate on what he is saying. The eastern European immigrant in the neighborhood delicatessen speaks to me and, again, I do not pay much attention to his sounds, nor to the Texas accent of one of my neighbors or the Chicago accent of the woman who lives in the apartment below me. But when the ghetto black teenagers get on the city bus, I hear them. Their sounds in my society are the sounds of the outsider. Their voices annoy me for being so loud — so self-sufficient and unconcerned by my presence, but for the same reason they are glamorous: a romantic gesture against public acceptance. And as I listen to their shouted laughter, I realize my own quietness. I feel envious of them — envious of their brazen intimacy.

I warn myself away from such envy, however. Overhearing those teenagers, I think of the black political activists who lately have argued in favor of using black English in public schools — an argument that varies only slightly from that of foreign-language bilingualists. I have heard "radical" linguists make the point that black English is a complex and intricate version of English. And I do not doubt it. But neither do I think that black English should be a language of public instruction. What makes it inappropriate in classrooms is not something in the language itself but, rather, what lower-class speakers make of it. Just as Spanish would have been a dangerous language for me to have used at the start of my education, so black English would be a dangerous language to use in the schooling of teenagers for whom it reinforces feelings of public separateness.

This seems to me an obvious point to make, and yet it must be said. In recent years there have been many attempts to make the language of the alien a public language. "Bilingual education, two ways to understand . . ." television and radio commercials glibly announce. Proponents of bilingual education are careful to say that above all they want every student to acquire a good education. Their argument goes something like this: Children permitted to use their family language will not be so alienated and will be better able to match the progress of English-speaking students in the crucial first months of schooling. Increasingly confident of their ability, such children will be more inclined to apply themselves to their studies in the future. But then the bilingualists also claim another very different goal. They say that children who use their family language in school will retain a sense of their ethnic heritage and their family ties. Thus the supporters of bilingual education want it both ways. They propose bilingual schooling as a way of helping students acquire the classroom skills crucial for public success. But they likewise insist that bilingual instruction will give students a sense of their identity apart from the English-speaking public.

Behind this scheme gleams a bright promise for the alien child: One can become a public person while still remaining a private person. Who would not want to believe such an appealing idea? Who can be surprised that the scheme has the support of so many middle-class ethnic Americans? If the barrio or ghetto child can retain his separateness even while being publicly educated, then it is almost possible to believe that no private cost need be paid for public success. This is the consolation offered by any of the number of current bilingual programs. Consider, for example, the bilingual voter's ballot. In some American cities one can cast a ballot printed in several languages. Such a document implies that it is possible for one to exercise that most public of rights — the right to vote — while still keeping oneself apart, unassimilated in public life.

It is not enough to say that such schemes are foolish and certainly doomed. Middle-class supporters of public bilingualism toy with the confusion of those Americans who cannot speak standard English as well as they do. Moreover, bilingual enthusiasts sin against intimacy. A Hispanic-American tells me, "I will never give up my family language," and he clutches a group of words as though they were the source of his family ties. He credits to language what he should credit to family members. This is a convenient mistake, for as long as he holds on to certain familiar words, he can ignore how much else has actually changed in his life.

It has happened before. In earlier decades, persons ambitious for so- 55 cial mobility, and newly successful, similarly seized upon certain "family words." Workingmen attempting to gain political power, for example, took to calling one another "brother." The word as they used it, however, could never resemble the word (the sound) "brother" exchanged by two people in intimate greeting. The context of its public delivery made it at best a metaphor; with repetition it was only a vague echo of the intimate sound. Context forced the change. Context could not be overruled. Context will always protect the realm of the intimate from public misuse. Today middle-class white Americans continue to prove the importance of context as they try to ignore it. They seize upon idioms of the black ghetto, but their attempt to appropriate such expressions invariably changes the meaning. As it becomes a public expression, the ghetto idiom loses its sound, its message of public separateness and strident intimacy. With public repetition it becomes a series of words, increasingly lifeless.

The mystery of intimate utterance remains. The communication of intimacy passes through the word and enlivens its sound, but it cannot be held by the word. It cannot be retained or ever quoted because it is too fluid. It depends not on words but on persons.

My grandmother! She stood among my other relations mocking me when I no longer spoke Spanish. *Pocho*, she said. But then it made no difference. She'd laugh, and our relationship continued because language was never its source. She was a woman in her eighties during the first decade of my life—a mysterious woman to me, my only living grandparent, a woman of Mexico in a long black dress that reached down to her shoes. She was the one relative of mine who spoke no word of English. She had no interest in gringo society and remained completely aloof from the public. She was protected by her daughters, protected even by me when we went to Safeway together and I needed to act as her translator. An eccentric woman. Hard. Soft.

When my family visited my aunt's house in San Francisco, my grandmother would search for me among my many cousins. When she found me, she'd chase them away. Pinching her granddaughters, she would warn them away from me. Then she'd take me to her room, where she had prepared for my coming. There would be a chair next to the bed, a dusty jellied candy nearby, and a copy of *Life en Español* for me to examine. "There," she'd say. And I'd sit content, a boy of eight. *Pocho*, her favorite. I'd sift through the pictures of earthquake-destroyed Latin-American cities and blonde-wigged Mexican movie stars. And all the while I'd listen to the sound of my grandmother's voice. She'd pace around the room, telling me stories of her life. Her past. They were stories so familiar that I couldn't remember when I'd heard them for the first time. I'd look up sometimes to listen. Other times she'd look over at me, but she never expected a response. Sometimes I'd smile or nod. (I understood exactly what she was saying.) But it never seemed to matter to her one way or the other. It was enough that I was there. The words she spoke were almost irrelevant to that fact. We were content. And the great mystery remained: intimate utterance.

I learn nothing about language and intimacy listening to those social activists who propose using one's family language in public life. I learn much more simply by listening to songs on a radio, or hearing a great voice at the opera, or overhearing the woman downstairs at an open window singing to herself. Singers celebrate the human voice. Their lyrics are words, but, animated by voice, those words are subsumed into sounds. (This suggests a central truth about language: All words are capable of becoming sounds as we fill them with the "music" of our life.) With excitement I hear the words yielding their enormous power to sound, even though their meaning is never totally obliterated. In most songs, the drama or tension results from the way that the singer moves between words (sense) and notes (song). At one moment the song simply "says" something; at another moment the voice stretches out the words and moves to the realm of pure sound. Most songs are about love: lost love, celebrations of loving, pleas. By simply being occasions when sounds soar through words, however, songs put me in mind of the most intimate moments of life.

Finally, among all types of music, I find songs created by lyric poets most compelling. On no other public occasion is sound so important for me. Written poems on a page seem at first glance a mere collection of words. And yet, without musical accompaniment, the poet leads me to hear the sounds of the words that I read. As song, a poem moves between the levels of sound and sense, never limited to one realm or the other. As a public artifact, the poem can never offer truly intimate sound, but it helps me to recall the intimate times of my life. As I read in my room, I grow deeply conscious of being alone, sounding my voice in search of another. The poem serves, then, as a memory device; it forces remembrance. And it refreshes; it reminds me of the possibility of escaping public words, the possibility that awaits me in intimate meetings. 60

The child reminds the adult: To seek intimate sounds is to seek the company of intimates. I do not expect to hear those sounds in public. I would dishonor those I have loved, and those I love now, to claim anything else. I would dishonor our intimacy by holding on to a particular language and calling it my family language. Intimacy cannot be trapped within words; it passes through words. It passes. Intimates leave the room. Doors close. Faces move away from the window. Time passes, and voices recede into the dark. Death finally quiets the voice. There is no way to deny it, no way to stand in the crowd claiming to utter one's family language.

The last time I saw my grandmother I was nine years old. I can tell you some of the things she said to me as I stood by her bed, but I cannot quote the message of intimacy she conveyed with her voice. She laughed, holding my hand. Her voice illumined disjointed memories as it passed them again. She remembered her husband—his green eyes, his magic name of Narcissio, his early death. She remembered the farm in Mexico, the eucalyptus trees nearby (their scent, she remembered, like incense). She remembered the family cow, the bell around its neck heard miles away. A dog. She remembered working as a seamstress, how she'd leave her daughters and son for long hours to go into Guadalajara to work. And how my mother would come running toward her in the sun—in her bright yellow dress—on her return. "MMMAAAAMMMMÁÁÁÁÁ," the old lady mimicked her daughter (my mother) to her daughter's son. She laughed. There was the snap of a cough. An aunt came into the room and told me it was time I should leave. "You can see her tomorrow," she promised. So I kissed my grandmother's cracked face. And the last thing I saw was her thin, oddly youthful thigh, as my aunt rearranged the sheet on the bed.

At the funeral parlor a few days after, I remember kneeling with my relatives during the rosary. Among their voices I traced, then lost, the sounds of individual aunts in the surge of the common prayer. And I heard at that moment what since I have heard very often—the sound the women in my family make when they are praying in sadness. When I went up to look at my grandmother, I saw her through the haze of a veil draped over the open lid of the casket. Her face looked calm—but distant and unyielding to love. It was not the face I remembered seeing most often. It was the face she made in public when the clerk at Safeway asked her some question and I would need to respond. It was her public face that the mortician had designed with his dubious art.

The Reader's Presence

1. The writer blames the intrusion of English into his family's private language, Spanish, for a breakdown of communication, and even of caring. How does the Spanish language appear in the essay? What associations does it have for the author? Why does Rodriguez end the essay with the scene of his dying grandmother followed by a glimpse of her corpse?

2. Rodriguez's rhetorical style alternates between persuasive argument and personal drama. Find examples of each. Do these divergent tactics undercut or reinforce each other? Why? What is the purpose of the exclamation points at the beginning of paragraph 33?

3. Rodriguez opposes proposals to teach bilingual children in their native languages, wishing to keep native language "private" and fearing that teaching bilingual children in their native languages

will further contribute to the marginalization of minorities. Read Walter Benn Michaels's essay, "The Trouble with Diversity" (page 766). Based on your analysis and understanding of Michaels's argument, how do you think Michaels would react to Rodriguez's proposition about bilingual education? Which writer do you find more persuasive, and why?

THE WRITER AT WORK

Richard Rodriguez on a Writer's Identity

How important is cultural or ethnic identity to a writer? Some writers clearly draw creative strength from their allegiances and affiliations, whereas others prefer to remain independent of groups, even those they are undeniably part of. In the following passage from a 1997 interview published in The Sun *magazine, Scott London asks Richard Rodriguez some tough questions about Rodriguez's various "identities." Could you have anticipated his responses based on his essay, "Aria: A Memoir of a Bilingual Childhood"?*

London: Many people feel that the call for diversity and multiculturalism is one reason the American educational system is collapsing.

Rodriguez: It's no surprise that at the same time that American universities have engaged in a serious commitment to diversity, they have been thought-prisons. We are not talking about diversity in any real way. We are talking about brown, black, and white versions of the same political ideology. It is very curious that the United States and Canada both assume that diversity means only race and ethnicity. They never assume it might mean more Nazis, or more Southern Baptists. That's diversity, too, you know.

London: What do *you* mean by diversity?

Rodriguez: For me, diversity is not a value. Diversity is what you find in Northern Ireland. Diversity is Beirut. Diversity is brother killing brother. Where diversity is *shared*—where I share with you my difference—that can be valuable. But the simple fact that we are unlike each other is a terrifying notion. I have often found myself in foreign settings where I became suddenly aware that I was not like the people around me. That, to me, is not a pleasant discovery.

London: You've said that it's tough in America to lead an intellectual life outside the universities. Yet you made a very conscious decision to leave academia.   5

Rodriguez: My decision was sparked by affirmative action. There was a point in my life when affirmative action would have meant something to me—when my family was working-class, and we were struggling. But very early in life I became part of the majority culture and now don't think of myself as a minority. Yet the university said I was one.

Anybody who has met a real minority—in the economic sense, not the numerical sense—would understand how ridiculous it is to describe a young man who is already at the university, already well into his studies in Italian and English Renaissance literature, as a minority. Affirmative action ignores our society's real minorities—members of the disadvantaged classes, no matter what their race. We have this ludicrous, bureaucratic sense that certain racial groups, regardless of class, are minorities. So what happens is those "minorities" at the very top of the ladder get chosen for everything.

London: Is that what happened to you?

Rodriguez: Well, when it came time for me to look for jobs, the jobs came looking for me. I had teaching offers from the best universities in the country. I was about to accept one from Yale when the whole thing collapsed on me.

London: What do you mean?

Rodriguez: I had all this anxiety about what it meant to be a minority. My professors—these same men who taught me the intricacies of language—just shied away from the issue. They didn't want to talk about it, other than to suggest I could be a "role model" to other Hispanics—when I went back to my barrio, I suppose. I came from a white, middle-class neighborhood. Was I expected to go back there and teach the woman next door about Renaissance sonnets? The embarrassing truth of the matter was that I was being chosen because Yale University had some peculiar idea about what my skin color or ethnicity signified. Who knows what Yale thought it was getting when it hired Richard Rodriguez? The people who offered me the job thought there was nothing wrong with that. I thought there was something very wrong. I still do. I think race-based affirmative action is crude and absolutely mistaken.

London: I noticed that some university students put up a poster outside the lecture hall where you spoke the other night. It said, "Richard Rodriguez is a disgrace to the Chicano community."

Rodriguez: I sort of like that. I don't think writers should be convenient examples. I don't think we should make people feel settled. I don't try to be a gadfly, but I do think that real ideas are troublesome. There should be something about my work that leaves the reader unsettled. I intend that. The notion of the writer as a kind of sociological sample of a community is ludicrous. Even worse is the notion that writers should provide an example of how to live. Virginia Woolf ended her life by putting a rock in her sweater one day and walking into a lake. She is not a model for how I want to live my life. On the other hand, the bravery of her syntax, of her sentences, written during her deepest depression, is a kind of example for me. But I do not want to become Virginia Woolf. That is not why I read her.

London: What's wrong with being a role model?

Rodriguez: The popular idea of a role model implies that an adult's influence on a child is primarily occupational, that all a black child needs is to see a black doctor, and then this child will think, "Oh, I can become a doctor, too." I have a good black friend who is a doctor, but he didn't become a doctor because he saw other black men who were doctors. He became a doctor because his mother cleaned office buildings at night, and because she loved her children. She grew bowlegged from cleaning office buildings at night, and in the process she taught him something about courage and bravery and dedication to others. I became a writer not because my father was one — my father made false teeth for a living. I became a writer because the Irish nuns who educated me taught me something about bravery with their willingness to give so much to me.

London: There used to be a category for writers and thinkers and   15
intellectuals — "the intelligentsia." But not anymore.

Rodriguez: No, I think the universities have co-opted the intellectual, by and large. But there is an emerging intellectual set coming out of Washington think tanks now. There are people who are leaving the universities and working for the government or in think tanks, simply looking for freedom. The university has become so stultified since the sixties. There is so much you can't do at the university. You can't say this, you can't do that, you can't think this, and so forth. In many ways, I'm free to range as widely as I do intellectually precisely because I'm not at a university. The tiresome Chicanos would be after me all the time. You know: "We saw your piece yesterday, and we didn't like what you said," or, "You didn't sound happy enough," or, "You didn't sound proud enough."

London: You've drawn similar responses from the gay community, I understand.

Rodriguez: Yes, I've recently gotten in trouble with certain gay activists because I'm not gay enough! I am a morose homosexual. I'm melancholy. *Gay* is the last adjective I would use to describe myself. The idea of being gay, like a little sparkler, never occurs to me. So if you ask me if I'm gay, I say no.

After the second chapter of *Days of Obligation*, which is about the death of a friend of mine from AIDS, was published in *Harper's*, I got this rather angry letter from a gay-and-lesbian group that was organizing a protest against the magazine. It was the same old problem: political groups have almost no sense of irony. For them, language has to say exactly what it means. "Why aren't you proud of being gay?" they wanted to know. "Why are you so dark? Why are you so morbid? Why are you so sad? Don't you realize, we're all OK? Let's celebrate that fact." But that is not what writers do. We don't celebrate being "OK." If you want to be OK, take an aspirin.

London: Do you consider yourself more Mexican, or more American?   20

Rodriguez: In some ways I consider myself more Chinese, because I live in San Francisco, which is becoming a predominantly Asian city. I avoid falling into the black-and-white dialectic in which most of America still seems trapped. I have always recognized that, as an American, I am in relationships with other parts of the world; that I have to measure myself against the Pacific, against Asia. Having to think of myself in relationship to that horizon has liberated me from the black-and-white checkerboard.

Marjane Satrapi

My Speech at West Point

Writer-illustrator and graphic novelist Marjane Satrapi (b. 1969) was born in Iran and, after a sojourn in Europe and a return to Tehran, now lives and works in France. Her graphic memoir, Persepolis: The Story of a Childhood *(2003), recounts in comic-book form growing up in Iran from ages six to fourteen, years that saw the overthrow of the Shah, the triumph of the Islamic Revolution, and the devastating effects of war with Iraq. The book was an immediate hit in France, selling more than 150,000 copies, and has been translated into numerous languages. In the United States,* Persepolis *was named a* New York Times *Notable Book and one of* Time *magazine's "Best Comix of the Year." Satrapi co-directed the feature film,* Persepolis, *which won numerous awards including an Oscar nomination for Best Animated Feature Film of 2007.* Persepolis 2: The Story of a Return *(2004) picks up her story with Satrapi's departure for Austria when she was fourteen and continues through her college years back in Tehran. Satrapi's most recent graphic memoirs are* Embroideries *(2005) and* Chicken with Plums *(2006). She has also written several children's books, and her commentary and comics appear in newspapers and magazines around the world, including the* New York Times *and the* New Yorker.*

Satrapi was invited to West Point to speak in 2005. After her visit, her book Persepolis *was put on the required reading list at the academy. "My Speech at West Point" appeared on the Op-Ed page of the* New York Times *on May 29, 2005.*

In an interview with Believer *magazine, Satrapi talked about what she learned not only at West Point but also through traveling and listening to people from so many disparate cultures: "I figured out a long time ago that, whatever I think I know, I don't know anything. Once I realized that, I really started learning. That's a great strength: I know that I don't know. There are some people in Iran who are fundamentalist and others who are not. I have very good Israeli friends. And I have very good American friends. We come from different cultures but share points of view. It's humanism, which we're steadily losing. That's what the comics are about in a way, trying to stop that loss."*

When I was invited to speak at West Point, this is how I thought it would be: I'll go to West Point...

The major will show me around without saying a word...

Then, he will shout at me...

YOU DON'T SMOKE HERE

Then, I'll eat with 4,000 cadets in the mess hall...

The meal won't be tasty... pizza... half pepperoni

half cheese

After lunch, I will speak in front of 600 people...

I AM AGAINST THE WAR IN IRAQ.

They will all shout at me again...

I will have to continue my speech...

Democracy is not a present you give to people by bombing them.

Their general will order them to hang me...

I will die...

BUT...

Here we are!

The major shows me around...

Here they play football. You should come and watch a game sometime!

great...

Can I smoke?

Of course!

I eat with 4,000 cadets in the mess hall...

The half-pepperoni, half-cheese pizza is worse than what I thought

After my speech, the cadets come to talk to me...

What you said was so inspiring!

It's great to discover another point of view!

They are lovely and intelligent and much more open-minded than I am!

I go back to Manhattan...

I know that I don't know anything

That makes my life even more complicated...

Later, in my hotel room...

Seven American soldiers and 10 Iraqis died today in Baghdad!

There's still things I know that I know: I'm against the war and democracy is not a present you give to people by bombing them

The Reader's Presence

1. How would you describe Satrapi's expectations of West Point as opposed to what she actually experienced on her visit? What do her expectations imply about her view of the military academy? Where may she have received these views? In what ways do they complicate her experience? What elements of Satrapi's narrative do you find humorous? Why?

2. Satrapi's personal narrative is not just told but drawn in black and white. How would you describe her artistic style? What sort of imagery does it resemble? Do you think that the way she depicts herself in the art reinforces the way she describes herself in words? Why or why not? Explain how you see the interrelation of words and images in this graphic essay.

3. Consider Satrapi's graphic essay in connection with other short personal narratives that dramatize a complicated personal experience, such as Jerald Walker's "Scattered Inconveniences" (page 205) or Brent Staples's "Just Walk on By: A Black Man Ponders His Power to Alter Public Space" (page 240). How do these narratives convey complicated moments and emotions and introduce competing perspectives? Of the three selections, choose the one you believe achieves the most satisfying resolution and explain your reasons.

THE GRAPHIC MEMOIRIST AT WORK

Marjane Satrapi on the Language of Words and Images

In an interview with the literary journal Fourth Genre, *Marjane Satrapi spoke about the unique interaction of words and images in her graphic memoirs and comics in general. The interview was conducted in November 2006 by the journal's interview editor, Robert Root, and it was published in Fall 2007.*

Root: I'm interested in the use of illustration in the service of autobiography or memoir or other kinds of nonfiction and how that affects the "nonfictionness" of it, the truth of it. People keep referring to your books and to Art Spiegelman's *Maus* and to Alison Bechdel's *Fun Home* as "graphic novels," but it seems to me that a more accurate term would be "graphic memoirs," since they are all autobiographical on some level.

Satrapi: Yes, they *are* autobiographical, but at the same time they search for truth . . . If you're looking for truth you have to ask it from the Fox News and the *New York Times*. As soon as you write your story, it is a story; this is not a documentary. Of course you have to make fiction, you have to cheat, you have to make some angle around there, because the story has to turn, so that is the reconstruction of what we do. For instance, I don't know, when I write something about people and I'm mean to them, of course I would not use the real names and the real figures, even not the real story. I will create this new personage around myself. Of course, they will always be related to my experiences—what I have seen and what I have heard, or whatever—but any writer will do that, even in science fiction you do that. So the use of the drawing for me is that first of all, I am a very lousy writer. I have tried actually, you know, at one time to write. If I had to write this short article or something, here I am good. But for a novel, just forget about it. I lose all my sense of humor, I lose completely all my decency, and I become completely lousy and pathetic. If I say to myself, "Now you are a serious girl and now you are going to make some serious work," there's nothing worse than wanting to make a serious work for me. So drawing gives me the possibility of this sense of saying what I want to say.

Also, there are many things that you can say through images that you cannot say with the writing. The comics is the only media in the whole world that you can use the image plus the writing plus the imagination and plus be active while reading it. When you watch a picture, a movie, you are passive. Everything is coming to you. When you are reading comics, between one frame to the other what is happening, you have to imagine it yourself. So you are active; you have to take part actually when you read the story. It is the only medium that uses the images in this way. So, for me, comics has only convenience. . . .

Root: You've mentioned before the two languages that you work with, the language of words and the language of image, and how they come together. I wish you would elaborate a little more on that. You've said that you don't write the story and then find images to illustrate the text, that they go together and bounce off of one another. How does that work?

Satrapi: I have a small page on which I know more or less what I want to write in my story. When I start, I have these small little sketches with small drawings of people, and I have short, short dialogues going together, and once in a while I write the dialogue, and once in a while I go the other way. It's like a baby growing up. You don't have first the nose come up and then one eye and then one hand or one leg—all of it grows at the same time. Another thing also: when I work, you know, I am completely in a trance. I'm so concentrated on the work that I don't look at myself working. And I work alone on my books. So since I don't watch myself, it's very difficult for me to know what I'm doing, since I don't see what I'm doing.

David Sedaris

Me Talk Pretty One Day

David Sedaris (b. 1956) was born in Johnson City, New York, and raised in Raleigh, North Carolina. He is a dramatist whose plays, written in collaboration with his sister, Amy (one of which won an Obie Award), have been produced at La Mama and Lincoln Center. Sedaris launched his career as a wry, neurotically self-disparaging humorist on National Public Radio's Morning Edition, *when he read aloud from "The Santaland Diaries," an autobiographical piece about working as a Christmas elf at Macy's. He has since published a number of best-selling collections, including* Barrel Fever *(1994),* Naked *(1997),* Holiday on Ice *(1997),* Me Talk Pretty One Day *(2000),* Dress Your Family in Corduroy and Denim *(2004), and his latest,* When You Are Engulfed in Flames *(2008). His essays appear regularly in the* New Yorker *and* Esquire. *In 2001, Sedaris was named Humorist of the Year by* Time *magazine and received the Thurber Prize for American Humor.* New York Magazine *had dubbed Sedaris "the most brilliantly witty New Yorker since Dorothy Parker." He currently divides his time between France and New York City.*

Sedaris, who for two years taught writing at the Art Institute of Chicago, laments that the students in his writing classes "were ashamed of their middle-class background . . . they felt like unless they grew up in poverty, they had nothing to write about." Sedaris feels that "it doesn't really matter what your life was like, you can write about anything. It's just the writing of it that is the challenge."

At the age of forty-one, I am returning to school and have to think of myself as what my French textbook calls "a true debutant." After paying my tuition, I was issued a student ID, which allows me a discounted entry fee at movie theaters, puppet shows, and Festyland, a far-flung amusement park that advertises with billboards picturing a cartoon stegosaurus sitting in a canoe and eating what appears to be a ham sandwich.

I've moved to Paris with hopes of learning the language. My school is an easy ten-minute walk from my apartment, and on the first day of class I arrived early, watching as the returning students greeted one another in the school lobby. Vacations were recounted, and questions were raised concerning mutual friends with names like Kang and Vlatnya. Regardless of their nationalities, everyone spoke in what sounded to me like excellent French. Some accents were better than others, but the students exhibited an ease and confidence I found intimidating. As an added discomfort, they were all young, attractive, and well dressed, causing me to feel not unlike Pa Kettle trapped backstage after a fashion show.

The first day of class was nerve-racking because I knew I'd be expected to perform. That's the way they do it here—it's everybody into the language pool, sink or swim. The teacher marched in, deeply tanned from a recent vacation, and proceeded to rattle off a series of administrative announcements. I've spent quite a few summers in Normandy, and I took a monthlong French class before leaving New York. I'm not completely in the dark, yet I understood only half of what this woman was saying.

"If you have not *meimslsxp* or *lgpdmurct* by this time, then you should not be in this room. Has everyone *apzkiubjxow*? Everyone? Good, we shall begin." She spread out her lesson plan and sighed, saying, "All right, then, who knows the alphabet?"

It was startling because (a) I hadn't been asked that question in a   5 while and (b) I realized, while laughing, that I myself did *not* know the alphabet. They're the same letters, but in France they're pronounced differently. I knew the shape of the alphabet but had no idea what it actually sounded like.

"Ahh." The teacher went to the board and sketched the letter *a*. "Do we have anyone in the room whose first name commences with an *ahh*?"

Two Polish Annas raised their hands, and the teacher instructed them to present themselves by stating their names, nationalities, occupations, and a brief list of things they liked and disliked in this world. The first Anna hailed from an industrial town outside of Warsaw and had front teeth the size of tombstones. She worked as a seamstress, enjoyed quiet times with friends, and hated the mosquito.

"Oh, really," the teacher said. "How very interesting. I thought that everyone loved the mosquito, but here, in front of all the world, you claim to detest him. How is it that we've been blessed with someone as unique and original as you? Tell us, please."

The seamstress did not understand what was being said but knew that this was an occasion for shame. Her rabbity mouth huffed for breath, and she stared down at her lap as though the appropriate comeback were stitched somewhere alongside the zipper of her slacks.

The second Anna learned from the first and claimed to love sunshine   10 and detest lies. It sounded like a translation of one of those Playmate of the Month data sheets, the answers always written in the same loopy handwriting: "Turn-ons: Mom's famous five-alarm chili! Turnoffs: insecurity and guys who come on too strong!!!!"

The two Polish Annas surely had clear notions of what they loved and hated, but like the rest of us, they were limited in terms of vocabulary, and this made them appear less than sophisticated. The teacher forged on, and we learned that Carlos, the Argentine bandonion player, loved wine, music, and, in his words, "making sex with the womens of the world." Next came a beautiful young Yugoslav who identified herself as an optimist, saying that she loved everything that life had to offer.

The teacher licked her lips, revealing a hint of the saucebox we would later come to know. She crouched low for her attack, placed her hands on the young woman's desk, and leaned close, saying, "Oh yeah? And do you love your little war?"

While the optimist struggled to defend herself, I scrambled to think of an answer to what had obviously become a trick question. How often is one asked what he loves in this world? More to the point, how often is one asked and then publicly ridiculed for his answer? I recalled my mother, flushed with wine, pounding the tabletop late one night, saying, "Love? I love a good steak cooked rare. I love my cat, and I love . . ." My sisters and I leaned forward, waiting to hear our names. "Tums," our mother said. "I love Tums."

The teacher killed some time accusing the Yugoslavian girl of masterminding a program of genocide, and I jotted frantic notes in the margins of my pad. While I can honestly say that I love leafing through medical textbooks devoted to severe dermatological conditions, the hobby is beyond the reach of my French vocabulary, and acting it out would only have invited controversy.

When called upon, I delivered an effortless list of things that I detest: 15
blood sausage, intestinal pâtés, brain pudding. I'd learned these words the hard way. Having given it some thought, I then declared my love for IBM typewriters, the French word for *bruise*, and my electric floor waxer. It was a short list, but still I managed to mispronounce *IBM* and assign the wrong gender to both the floor waxer and the typewriter. The teacher's reaction led me to believe that these mistakes were capital crimes in the country of France.

"Were you always this *palicmkrexis*?" she asked. "Even a *fiuscrzsa ticiwelmun* knows that a typewriter is feminine."

I absorbed as much of her abuse as I could understand, thinking—but not saying—that I find it ridiculous to assign a gender to an inanimate object incapable of disrobing and making an occasional fool of itself. Why refer to Lady Crack Pipe or Good Sir Dishrag when these things could never live up to all that their sex implied?

The teacher proceeded to belittle everyone from German Eva, who hated laziness, to Japanese Yukari, who loved paintbrushes and soap. Italian, Thai, Dutch, Korean, and Chinese—we all left class foolishly believing that the worst was over. She'd shaken us up a little, but surely that was just an act designed to weed out the deadweight. We didn't know it then, but the coming months would teach us what it was like to spend time in the presence of a wild animal, something completely unpredictable. Her temperament was not based on a series of good and bad days but, rather, good and bad moments. We soon learned to dodge chalk and protect our heads and stomachs whenever she approached us with a question. She hadn't yet punched anyone, but it seemed wise to protect ourselves against the inevitable.

Though we were forbidden to speak anything but French, the teacher would occasionally use us to practice any of her five fluent languages.

"I hate you," she said to me one afternoon. Her English was flawless.   20
"I really, really hate you." Call me sensitive, but I couldn't help but take it personally.

After being singled out as a lazy *kfdtinvfm*, I took to spending four hours a night on my homework, putting in even more time whenever we were assigned an essay. I suppose I could have gotten by with less, but I was determined to create some sort of identity for myself: David the hard worker, David the cut-up. We'd have one of those "complete this sentence" exercises, and I'd fool with the thing for hours, invariably settling on something like "A quick run around the lake? I'd love to! Just give me a moment while I strap on my wooden leg." The teacher, through word and action, conveyed the message that if this was my idea of an identity, she wanted nothing to do with it.

My fear and discomfort crept beyond the borders of the classroom and accompanied me out onto the wide boulevards. Stopping for a coffee, asking directions, depositing money in my bank account: these things were out of the question, as they involved having to speak. Before beginning school, there'd been no shutting me up, but now I was convinced that everything I said was wrong. When the phone rang, I ignored it. If someone asked me a question, I pretended to be deaf. I knew my fear was getting the best of me when I started wondering why they don't sell cuts of meat in vending machines.

My only comfort was the knowledge that I was not alone. Huddled in the hallways and making the most of our pathetic French, my fellow students and I engaged in the sort of conversation commonly overheard in refugee camps.

"Sometime me cry alone at night."

"That be common for I, also, but be more strong, you. Much work and someday you talk pretty. People start love you soon. Maybe tomorrow, okay."

Unlike the French class I had taken in New York, here there was no sense of competition. When the teacher poked a shy Korean in the eyelid with a freshly sharpened pencil, we took no comfort in the fact that, unlike Hyeyoon Cho, we all knew the irregular past tense of the verb *to defeat*. In all fairness, the teacher hadn't meant to stab the girl, but neither did she spend much time apologizing, saying only, "Well, you should have been *vkkdyo* more *kdeynfulh*."

Over time it became impossible to believe that any of us would ever improve. Fall arrived and it rained every day, meaning we would now be scolded for the water dripping from our coats and umbrellas. It was mid-October when the teacher singled me out, saying, "Every day spent with you is like having a cesarean section." And it struck me that, for the first time since arriving in France, I could understand every word that someone was saying.

Understanding doesn't mean that you can suddenly speak the language. Far from it. It's a small step, nothing more, yet its rewards are intoxicating and deceptive. The teacher continued her diatribe and I settled back, bathing in the subtle beauty of each new curse and insult.

"You exhaust me with your foolishness and reward my efforts with nothing but pain, do you understand me?"

The world opened up, and it was with great joy that I responded,   30
"I know the thing that you speak exact now. Talk me more, you, plus,
please, plus."

The Reader's Presence

1. How did Sedaris take his experience—auditing a beginner's lan-
   guage class—and turn it into a humorous essay? What were the
   funniest parts of the essay? An interviewer once wrote that
   Sedaris's signature is "deadpan" humor. What is deadpan humor?
   Identify—and characterize the effectiveness of—examples of it in
   "Me Talk Pretty One Day."

2. Which English words would you substitute for the nonsense words
   that represent Sedaris's difficulties understanding his teacher's
   French? Have a classmate tell you what he or she thinks such
   words as *meimslsxp* (paragraph 4), *palicmkrexis* (paragraph 16),
   or *kdeynfulh* (paragraph 26) might mean. Did he or she pick the
   same or similar words to the ones you picked? Point to the clues
   Sedaris includes in the essay to hint at what such words mean.
   How would you rewrite the passage with different clues to indicate a different possible meaning for the nonsense words?

3. How surprised were you by the last line in the essay? To what extent did you expect that Sedaris would speak fluently because he
   understood his teacher's French perfectly? Look at some other unexpected last lines in essays that you've read in this collection.
   Choose two surprising last lines and identify how each author
   goes about setting up the surprise. When you look back, at what
   point in each essay might you have expected the unexpected? Be
   as specific as possible in your response.

Brent Staples

Just Walk on By: A Black Man Ponders His Power to Alter Public Space

As he describes in Parallel Time: Growing Up in Black and White *(1994), Brent Staples (b. 1951) escaped a childhood of urban poverty through success in school and his determination to be a writer. Although Staples earned a PhD in psychology from the University of Chicago in 1982, his love of journalism led him to leave the field of psychology and start a career that has taken him to the* New York Times, *where he has served on the editorial board since 1990. Staples contributes to several national magazines, including* Harper's, *the* New York Times Magazine, *and* Ms., *in which "Just Walk on By" appeared in 1986.*

Staples's 1994 memoir, Parallel Time, *received the Anisfield Wolff Book Award, previously won by such writers as James Baldwin, Ralph Ellison, and Zora Neale Hurston. In it he remembers how in Chicago he prepared for his writing career by keeping a journal. "I wrote on buses, on the Jackson Park el — though only at the stops to keep the writing legible. I traveled to distant neighborhoods, sat on their curbs, and sketched what I saw in words. Thursdays meant free admission at the Art Institute. All day I attributed motives to people in paintings, especially people in Rembrandts. At closing time I went to a nightclub in The Loop and spied on patrons, copied their conversations and speculated about their lives. The journal was more than 'a record of my inner transactions.' It was a collection of stolen souls from which I would one day construct a book."*

My first victim was a woman — white, well dressed, probably in her early twenties. I came upon her late one evening on a deserted street in Hyde Park, a relatively affluent neighborhood in an otherwise mean, impoverished section of Chicago. As I swung onto the avenue behind her, there seemed to be a discreet, uninflammatory distance between us. Not so. She cast back a worried glance. To her, the youngish black man — a broad six feet two inches with a beard and billowing hair, both hands shoved into the pockets of a bulky military jacket — seemed menacingly close. After a few more quick glimpses, she picked up her pace and was soon running in earnest. Within seconds she disappeared into a cross street.

That was more than a decade ago. I was twenty-two years old, a graduate student newly arrived at the University of Chicago. It was in the echo of that terrified woman's footfalls that I first began to know the unwieldy inheritance I'd come into — the ability to alter public space in ugly ways. It was clear that she thought herself the quarry of a mugger, a rapist, or worse. Suffering a bout of insomnia, however, I was stalking sleep, not defenseless wayfarers. As a softy who is scarcely able to take a knife to a raw chicken — let alone hold it to a person's throat — I was surprised, embarrassed, and dismayed all at once. Her flight made me feel

like an accomplice in tyranny. It also made it clear that I was indistinguishable from the muggers who occasionally seeped into the area from
the surrounding ghetto. That first encounter, and those that followed, signified that a vast, unnerving gulf lay between nighttime pedestrians—
particularly women—and me. And I soon gathered that being perceived
as dangerous is a hazard in itself. I only needed to turn a corner into a
dicey situation, or crowd some frightened, armed person in a foyer somewhere, or make an errant move after being pulled over by a policeman.
Where fear and weapons meet—and they often do in urban America—
there is always the possibility of death.

In that first year, my first away from my hometown, I was to become
thoroughly familiar with the language of fear. At dark, shadowy intersections in Chicago, I could cross in front of a car stopped at a traffic light
and elicit the *thunk, thunk, thunk, thunk* of the driver—black, white,
male, or female—hammering down the door locks. On less traveled
streets after dark, I grew accustomed to but never comfortable with people who crossed to the other side of the street rather than pass me. Then
there were the standard unpleasantries with police, doormen, bouncers,
cabdrivers, and others whose business is to screen out troublesome individuals *before* there is any nastiness.

I moved to New York nearly two years ago and I have remained an
avid night walker. In central Manhattan, the near-constant crowd cover
minimizes tense one-on-one street encounters. Elsewhere—visiting friends
in Soho,[1] where sidewalks are narrow and tightly spaced buildings shut
out the sky—things can get very taut indeed.

Black men have a firm place in New York mugging literature. Norman   5
Podhoretz[2] in his famed (or infamous) 1963 essay, "My Negro Problem—
And Ours," recalls growing up in terror of black males; they "were tougher
than we were, more ruthless," he writes—and as an adult on the Upper
West Side of Manhattan, he continues, he cannot constrain his nervousness
when he meets black men on certain streets. Similarly, a decade later, the
essayist and novelist Edward Hoagland extols a New York where once
"Negro bitterness bore down mainly on other Negroes." Where some see
mere panhandlers, Hoagland sees "a mugger who is clearly screwing up his
nerve to do more than just *ask* for money." But Hoagland has "the New
Yorker's quick-hunch posture for broken-field maneuvering," and the bad
guy swerves away.

I often witness that "hunch posture," from women after dark on the
warrenlike streets of Brooklyn where I live. They seem to set their faces
on neutral and, with their purse straps strung across their chests bandolier
style, they forge ahead as though bracing themselves against being tackled. I understand, of course, that the danger they perceive is not a halluci-
nation. Women are particularly vulnerable to street violence, and young

---

[1]*Soho:* A district of lower Manhattan known for its art galleries.—EDS.
[2]*Podhoretz:* A well-known literary critic and editor of *Commentary* magazine.—EDS.

black males are drastically overrepresented among the perpetrators of that violence. Yet these truths are no solace against the kind of alienation that comes of being ever the suspect, against being set apart, a fearsome entity with whom pedestrians avoid making eye contact.

It is not altogether clear to me how I reached the ripe old age of twenty-two without being conscious of the lethality nighttime pedestrians attributed to me. Perhaps it was because in Chester, Pennsylvania, the small, angry industrial town where I came of age in the 1960s, I was scarcely noticeable against a backdrop of gang warfare, street knifings, and murders. I grew up one of the good boys, had perhaps a half-dozen fistfights. In retrospect, my shyness of combat has clear sources.

Many things go into the making of a young thug. One of those things is the consummation of the male romance with the power to intimidate. An infant discovers that random flailings send the baby bottle flying out of the crib and crashing to the floor. Delighted, the joyful babe repeats those motions again and again, seeking to duplicate the feat. Just so, I recall the points at which some of my boyhood friends were finally seduced by the perception of themselves as tough guys. When a mark cowered and surrendered his money without resistance, myth and reality merged— and paid off. It is, after all, only manly to embrace the power to frighten and intimidate. We, as men, are not supposed to give an inch of our lane on the highway; we are to seize the fighter's edge in work and in play and even in love; we are to be valiant in the face of hostile forces.

Unfortunately, poor and powerless young men seem to take all this nonsense literally. As a boy, I saw countless tough guys locked away; I have since buried several, too. They were babies, really—a teenage cousin, a brother of twenty-two, a childhood friend in his midtwenties—all gone down in episodes of bravado played out in the streets. I came to doubt the virtues of intimidation early on. I chose, perhaps even unconsciously, to remain a shadow—timid, but a survivor.

The fearsomeness mistakenly attributed to me in public places often has a perilous flavor. The most frightening of these confusions occurred in the late 1970s and early 1980s when I worked as a journalist in Chicago. One day, rushing into the office of a magazine I was writing for with a deadline story in hand, I was mistaken for a burglar. The office manager called security and, with an ad hoc posse, pursued me through the labyrinthine halls, nearly to my editor's door. I had no way of proving who I was. I could only move briskly toward the company of someone who knew me.

Another time I was on assignment for a local paper and killing time before an interview. I entered a jewelry store on the city's affluent Near North Side. The proprietor excused herself and returned with an enormous red Doberman pinscher straining at the end of a leash. She stood, the dog extended toward me, silent to my questions, her eyes bulging nearly out of her head. I took a cursory look around, nodded, and bade her good night. Relatively speaking, however, I never fared as badly as another black male journalist. He went to nearby Waukegan, Illinois, a couple of summers ago to work on a story about a murderer who was born there. Mistaking the reporter for the killer, police hauled him from his car at gunpoint and but for his press credentials would probably have tried to book him. Such episodes are not uncommon. Black men trade tales like this all the time.

In "My Negro Problem—And Ours," Podhoretz writes that the hatred he feels for blacks makes itself known to him through a variety of avenues—one being his discomfort with that "special brand of paranoid touchiness" to which he says blacks are prone. No doubt he is speaking here of black men. In time, I learned to smother the rage I felt at so often being taken for a criminal. Not to do so would surely have led to madness—via that special "paranoid touchiness" that so annoyed Podhoretz at the time he wrote the essay.

I began to take precautions to make myself less threatening. I move about with care, particularly late in the evening. I give a wide berth to nervous people on subway platforms during the wee hours, particularly when I have exchanged business clothes for jeans. If I happen to be entering a building behind some people who appear skittish, I may walk by, letting them clear the lobby before I return, so as not to seem to be following them. I have been calm and extremely congenial on those rare occasions when I've been pulled over by the police.

And on late-evening constitutionals along streets less traveled by, I employ what has proved to be an excellent tension-reducing measure: I whistle melodies from Beethoven and Vivaldi and the more popular classical composers. Even steely New Yorkers hunching toward nighttime destinations seem to relax, and occasionally they even join in the tune. Virtually everybody seems to sense that a mugger wouldn't be warbling bright, sunny selections from Vivaldi's *Four Seasons*. It is my equivalent of the cowbell that hikers wear when they know they are in bear country.

The Reader's Presence

1. Why does Staples use the word *victim* in his opening sentence? In what sense is the white woman a "victim"? How is Staples using the term? As readers, how might we interpret the opening sentence upon first reading? How does the meaning of the term change in rereading?

2. In rereading the essay, pay close attention to the way Staples handles points of view. When does he shift viewpoints or perspectives? What is his purpose in doing so? What are some of the connections Staples makes in this essay between the point of view one chooses and one's identity?

3. How does Staples behave on the street? How does he deal with the
   woman's anxiety? How has he "altered" his own public behavior?
   In what ways is his behavior on the street similar to his "behavior" as a writer? Compare this version of the essay to the alternate
   version that follows. What are the changes and how do those
   changes influence the essay's effect on the reader? How do you
   compare Staples's strategies—in both versions—to those of Malcolm X in "Homeboy" (page 168)?

THE WRITER AT WORK

Another Version of *Just Walk on By*

When he published his memoir, Parallel Time, *in 1994, Brent Staples decided
to incorporate his earlier essay into the book. He also decided to revise it substantially. As you compare the two versions, note the passages Staples retained and
those he chose not to carry forward into book form. Do you agree with his
changes? Why in general do you think he made them? If you had been his editor,
what revision strategy would you have suggested?*

At night, I walked to the lakefront whenever the weather permitted. I
was headed home from the lake when I took my first victim. It was late
fall, and the wind was cutting. I was wearing my navy pea jacket, the collar turned up, my hands snug in the pockets. Dead leaves scuttled in
shoals along the streets. I turned out of Blackstone Avenue and headed
west on 57th Street, and there she was, a few yards ahead of me, dressed
in business clothes and carrying a briefcase. She looked back at me once,
then again, and picked up her pace. She looked back again and started to
run. I stopped where I was and looked up at the surrounding windows.
What did this look like to people peeking out through their blinds? I was
out walking. But what if someone had thought they'd seen something
they hadn't and called the police. I held back the urge to run. Instead, I
walked south to The Midway, plunged into its darkness, and remained on
The Midway until I reached the foot of my street.

I'd been a fool. I'd been walking the streets grinning good evening at
people who were frightened to death of me. I did violence to them by just
being. How had I missed this? I kept walking at night, but from then on I
paid attention.

I became expert in the language of fear. Couples locked arms or
reached for each other's hand when they saw me. Some crossed to the
other side of the street. People who were carrying on conversations went
mute and stared straight ahead, as though avoiding my eyes would save
them. This reminded me of an old wives' tale: that rabid dogs didn't bite
if you avoided their eyes. The determination to avoid my eyes made me
invisible to classmates and professors whom I passed on the street.

It occurred to me for the first time that I was big. I was 6 feet 1½ inches tall, and my long hair made me look bigger. I weighed only 170 pounds. But the navy pea jacket that Brian had given me was broad at the shoulders, high at the collar, making me look bigger and more fearsome than I was.

I tried to be innocuous but didn't know how. The more I thought   5
about how I moved, the less my body belonged to me; I became a false character riding along inside it. I began to avoid people. I turned out of my way into side streets to spare them the sense that they were being stalked. I let them clear the lobbies of buildings before I entered, so they wouldn't feel trapped. Out of nervousness I began to whistle and discovered I was good at it. My whistle was pure and sweet—and also in tune. On the street at night I whistled popular tunes from the Beatles and Vivaldi's *Four Seasons*. The tension drained from people's bodies when they heard me. A few even smiled as they passed me in the dark.

Then I changed. I don't know why, but I remember when. I was walking west on 57th Street, after dark, coming home from the lake. The man and the woman walking toward me were laughing and talking but clammed up when they saw me. The man touched the woman's elbow, guiding her toward the curb. Normally I'd have given way and begun to whistle, but not this time. This time I veered toward them and aimed myself so that they'd have to part to avoid walking into me. The man stiffened, threw back his head and assumed the stare: eyes dead ahead, mouth open. His face took on a bluish hue under the sodium vapor streetlamps. I suppressed the urge to scream into his face. Instead I glided between them, my shoulder nearly brushing his. A few steps beyond them I stopped and howled with laughter. I called this game Scatter the Pigeons.

Fifty-seventh Street was too well lit for the game to be much fun; people didn't feel quite vulnerable enough. Along The Midway were heart-stopping strips of dark sidewalk, but these were so frightening that few people traveled them. The stretch of Blackstone between 57th and 55th provided better hunting. The block was long and lined with young trees that blocked out the streetlight and obscured the heads of people coming toward you.

One night I stooped beneath the branches and came up on the other side, just as a couple was stepping from their car into their town house. The woman pulled her purse close with one hand and reached for her husband with the other. The two of them stood frozen as I bore down on them. I felt a surge of power: these people were mine; I could do with them as I wished. If I'd been younger, with less to lose, I'd have robbed them, and it would have been easy. All I'd have to do was stand silently before them until they surrendered their money. I thundered, "Good evening!" into their bleached-out faces and cruised away laughing.

I held a special contempt for people who cowered in their cars as they waited for the light to change at 57th and Woodlawn. The intersection was always deserted at night, except for a car or two stuck at the red. *Thunk! Thunk! Thunk!* they hammered down the door locks when I came into view. Once I had hustled across the street, head down, trying to seem harmless. Now I turned brazenly into the headlights and laughed. Once across, I paced the sidewalk, glaring until the light changed. They'd made me terrifying. Now I'd show them how terrifying I could be.

Andrew Sullivan

The M-Word: Why It Matters to Me

Andrew Sullivan (b. 1963) was born in southern England, and grew up near his birthplace. He attended Oxford University, where he studied modern history and modern languages. In 1984, he won a Harkness Fellowship to the John F. Kennedy School of Government at Harvard University, and graduated with a master's degree in Public Administration in 1986. Upon graduation, he began PhD work at Harvard in political science, and from 1991 to 1996 he was acting editor of the New Republic.

Openly gay, Sullivan has been an outspoken advocate of gay issues. His 1993 New Republic *essay, "The Politics of Homosexuality," remains one of the most influential articles of the decade on the subject of gay rights; his controversial essay, "Why Men Are Different," put him on the cover of* Time *magazine. Sullivan has worked as a contributing writer and columnist for the* New York Times Magazine, *a regular contributor to the* New York Times Book Review, *and a weekly columnist for the* Sunday Times of London. *He writes a regular column for* Time *magazine, in which his essay, "The M-Word: Why It Matters to Me," appeared in 2004. Sullivan's books include* Virtually Normal: An Argument About Homosexuality *(1995),* Love Undetectable: Notes on Friendship, Sex, and Survival *(1998), and, most recently,* The Conservative Soul *(2006). Sullivan took up blogging in 2000 and writes daily on his blog,* The Daily Dish *on the* Atlantic Online.

What's in a name?

Perhaps the best answer is a memory.

As a child, I had no idea what homosexuality was. I grew up in a traditional home — Catholic, conservative, middle class. Life was relatively simple: education, work, family. I was brought up to aim high in life, even though my parents hadn't gone to college. But one thing was instilled in me. What matters is not how far you go in life, how much money you make, how big a name you make for yourself. What really matters is family, and the love you have for one another. The most important day of your life was not graduation from college or your first day at work or a raise or even your first house. The most important day of your life was when you got married. It was on that day that all your friends and all your family got together to celebrate the most important thing in life: your happiness, your ability to make a new home, to form a new but connected family, to find love that puts everything else into perspective.

But as I grew older, I found that this was somehow not available to me. I didn't feel the things for girls that my peers did. All the emotions and social rituals and bonding of teenage heterosexual life eluded me. I didn't know why. No one explained it. My emotional bonds to other boys were one-sided; each time I felt myself falling in love, they sensed it, pushed it away. I didn't and couldn't blame them. I got along fine with my buds in a nonemotional context; but something was awry, something not right. I came to know almost instinctively that I would never be a part of my family the way my siblings one day might be. The love I had inside me was unmentionable, anathema — even, in the words of the Church I attended every Sunday, evil. I remember writing in my teenage journal one day: "I'm a professional human being. But what do I do in my private life?"

So, like many gay men of my generation, I retreated. I never discussed my real life. I couldn't date girls and so immersed myself in schoolwork, in the debate team, school plays, anything to give me an excuse not to confront reality. When I looked toward the years ahead, I couldn't see a future. There was just a void. Was I going to be alone my whole life? Would I ever have a "most important day" in my life? It seemed impossible, a negation, an undoing. To be a full part of my family I had to somehow not be me. So like many gay teens, I withdrew, became neurotic, depressed, at times close to suicidal. I shut myself in my room with my books, night after night, while my peers developed the skills needed to form real relationships, and loves. In wounded pride, I even voiced a rejection of family and marriage. It was the only way I could explain my isolation.

It took years for me to realize that I was gay, years later to tell others, and more time yet to form any kind of stable emotional bond with another man. Because my sexuality had emerged in solitude — and without any link to the idea of an actual relationship — it was hard later to reconnect sex to love and self-esteem. It still is. But I persevered, each relationship slowly growing longer than the last, learning in my twenties and thirties what my straight friends found out in their teens. But even then, my parents and friends never asked the question they would have asked automatically if I were straight: So when are you going to get married? When is your relationship going to be public? When will we be able to celebrate it and affirm it and support it? In fact, no one — no one — has yet asked me that question.

When people talk about "gay marriage," they miss the point. This isn't about gay marriage. It's about marriage. It's about family. It's about love. It isn't about religion. It's about civil marriage licenses — available

to atheists as well as believers. These family values are not options for a
happy and stable life. They are necessities. Putting gay relationships in
some other category—civil unions, domestic partnerships, civil partnerships, whatever—may alleviate real human needs, but, by their very euphemism, by their very separateness, they actually build a wall between
gay people and their own families. They put back the barrier many of us
have spent a lifetime trying to erase.

It's too late for me to undo my own past. But I want above everything
else to remember a young kid out there who may even be reading this
now. I want to let him know that he doesn't have to choose between himself and his family any more. I want him to know that his love has dignity,
that he does indeed have a future as a full and equal part of the human
race. Only marriage will do that. Only marriage can bring him home.

The Reader's Presence

1. Why do you think Sullivan uses the term *M-Word* in his title?
   Would you know before reading the essay what it stands for? Why
   not simply use the full word? In what way does using only the letter to stand for the word affect the way you consider that word?

2. In paragraph 7, Sullivan refers to a "euphemism"? What is a euphemism and what examples does he give? In what way do euphemisms "build a wall between gay people and their own families?" Given his argument, do you think Sullivan would consider
   the term *same-sex marriage* (which he doesn't use) a euphemism?
   Why or why not?

3. Compare Sullivan's essay to Calvin Trillin's "A Traditional Family" (page 545) and Barbara Ehrenreich's "Family Values" (page
   669). Which essayist in your opinion is most committed to traditional family values? What evidence can you supply to support
   your opinion?

Amy Tan

Mother Tongue

Amy Tan (b. 1952) was born in California several years after her parents im-migrated to the United States from China. She started writing as a child and won a writing contest at age eight. As an adult, Tan made her living as a freelance business writer for many years. In 1989 she published a best-selling novel, The Joy Luck Club, *followed by the novel* The Kitchen God's Wife *(1991); the chil-dren's books* The Moon Lady *(1992) and* The Chinese Siamese Cat *(1994); and the novels* The Hundred Secret Senses *(1995) and* The Bonesetter's Daughter *(2001). Her latest books are* The Opposite of Fate *(2003), a collection of autobio-graphical essays, and* Saving Fish from Drowning *(2005), a novel. "Mother Tongue" originally appeared in the* Threepenny Review *in 1990.*

Commenting on the art of writing, Tan has said, "I had a very unliterary background, but I had a determination to write for myself." She believes that the goal of every serious writer of literature is "to try to find your voice and your art, because it comes from your own experiences, your own pain."

I am not a scholar of English or literature. I cannot give you much more than personal opinions on the English language and its variations in this country or others.

I am a writer. And by that definition, I am someone who has always loved language. I am fascinated by language in daily life. I spend a great deal of my time thinking about the power of language—the way it can evoke an emotion, a visual image, a complex idea, or a simple truth. Lan-guage is the tool of my trade. And I use them all—all the Englishes I grew up with.

Recently, I was made keenly aware of the different Englishes I do use. I was giving a talk to a large group of people, the same talk I had already given to half a dozen other groups. The nature of the talk was about my writing, my life, and my book, *The Joy Luck Club*. The talk was going along well enough, until I remembered one major difference that made the whole talk sound wrong. My mother was in the room. And it was perhaps the first time she had heard me give a lengthy speech, using the kind of English I have never used with her. I was say-ing things like "The intersection of memory upon imagination" and "There is an aspect of my fiction that relates to thus-and-thus"—a speech filled with carefully wrought grammatical phrases, burdened, it suddenly seemed to me, with nominalized forms, past perfect tenses, conditional phrases, all the forms of standard English that I had learned in school and through books, the forms of English I did not use at home with my mother.

Just last week, I was walking down the street with my mother, and I again found myself conscious of the English I was using, the English I do use with her. We were talking about the price of new and used furniture and I heard myself saying this: "Not waste money that way." My husband was with us as well, and he didn't notice any switch in my English. And then I realized why. It's because over the twenty years we've been together I've often used that same kind of English with him, and sometimes he even uses it with me. It has become our language of intimacy, a different sort of English that relates to family talk, the language I grew up with.

So you'll have some idea of what this family talk I heard sounds like,   5
I'll quote what my mother said during a recent conversation which I videotaped and then transcribed. During this conversation, my mother was talking about a political gangster in Shanghai who had the same last name as her family's, Du, and how the gangster in his early years wanted to be adopted by her family, which was rich by comparison. Later, the gangster became more powerful, far richer than my mother's family, and one day showed up at my mother's wedding to pay his respects. Here's what she said in part:

"Du Yusong having business like fruit stand. Like off the street kind. He is Du like Du Zong — but not Tsung-ming Island people. The local people call putong, the river east side, he belong to that side local people. That man want to ask Du Zong father take him in like become own family. Du Zong father wasn't look down on him, but didn't take seriously, until that man big like become a mafia. Now important person, very hard to inviting him. Chinese way, came only to show respect, don't stay for dinner. Respect for making big celebration, he shows up. Mean gives lots of respect. Chinese custom. Chinese social life that way. If too important won't have to stay too long. He come to my wedding. I didn't see, I heard it. I gone to boy's side, they have YMCA dinner. Chinese age I was nineteen."

You should know that my mother's expressive command of English belies how much she actually understands. She reads the *Forbes* report, listens to *Wall Street Week*, converses daily with her stockbroker, reads all of Shirley MacLaine's books with ease — all kinds of things I can't begin to understand. Yet some of my friends tell me they understand 50 percent of what my mother says. Some say they understand 80 to 90 percent. Some say they understand none of it, as if she were speaking pure Chinese. But to me, my mother's English is perfectly clear, perfectly natural. It's my mother tongue. Her language, as I hear it, is vivid, direct, full of observation and imagery. That was the language that helped shape the way I saw things, expressed things, made sense of the world.

Lately, I've been giving more thought to the kind of English my mother speaks. Like others, I have described it to people as "broken" or "fractured" English. But I wince when I say that. It has always bothered me that I can think of no way to describe it other than "broken," as if it were damaged and needed to be fixed, as if it lacked a certain wholeness and soundness. I've heard other terms used, "limited English," for example. But they seem just as bad, as if everything is limited, including people's perceptions of the limited English speaker.

I know this for a fact, because when I was growing up, my mother's "limited" English limited *my* perception of her. I was ashamed of her English. I believed that her English reflected the quality of what she had to say. That is, because she expressed them imperfectly her thoughts were imperfect. And I had plenty of empirical evidence to support me: the fact that people in department stores, at banks, and at restaurants did not take her seriously, did not give her good service, pretended not to understand her, or even acted as if they did not hear her.

My mother has long realized the limitations of her English as well.   10
When I was fifteen, she used to have me call people on the phone to pretend I was she. In this guise, I was forced to ask for information or even to complain and yell at people who had been rude to her. One time it was a call to her stockbroker in New York. She had cashed out her small portfolio and it just so happened we were going to go to New York the next week, our very first trip outside California. I had to get on the phone and say in an adolescent voice that was not very convincing, "This is Mrs. Tan."

And my mother was standing in the back whispering loudly, "Why he don't send me check, already two weeks late. So mad he lie to me, losing me money."

And then I said in perfect English, "Yes, I'm getting rather concerned. You had agreed to send the check two weeks ago, but it hasn't arrived."

Then she began to talk more loudly. "What he want, I come to New York tell him front of his boss, you cheating me?" And I was trying to calm her down, make her be quiet, while telling the stockbroker, "I can't tolerate any more excuses. If I don't receive the check immediately, I am going to have to speak to your manager when I'm in New York next week." And sure enough, the following week there we were in front of this astonished stockbroker, and I was sitting there red-faced and quiet, and my mother, the real Mrs. Tan, was shouting at his boss in her impeccable broken English.

We used a similar routine just five days ago, for a situation that was far less humorous. My mother had gone to the hospital for an appointment, to find out about a benign brain tumor a CAT scan had revealed a month ago. She said she had spoken very good English, her best English, no mistakes. Still, she said, the hospital did not apologize when they said they had lost the CAT scan and she had come for nothing. She said they did not seem to have any sympathy when she told them she was anxious to know the exact diagnosis, since her husband and son had both died of brain tumors. She said they would not give her any more information until the next time and she would have to make another appointment for that. So she said she would not leave until the doctor called her daughter.

She wouldn't budge. And when the doctor finally called her daughter, me, who spoke in perfect English—lo and behold—we had assurances the CAT scan would be found, promises that a conference call on Monday would be held, and apologies for any suffering my mother had gone through for a most regrettable mistake.

I think my mother's English almost had an effect on limiting my possibilities in life as well. Sociologists and linguists probably will tell you that a person's developing language skills are more influenced by peers. But I do think that the language spoken in the family, especially in immigrant families which are more insular, plays a large role in shaping the language of the child. And I believe that it affected my results on achievement tests, IQ tests, and the SAT. While my English skills were never judged as poor, compared to math, English could not be considered my strong suit. In grade school I did moderately well, getting perhaps B's, sometimes B-pluses, in English and scoring perhaps in the sixtieth or seventieth percentile on achievement tests. But those scores were not good enough to override the opinion that my true abilities lay in math and science, because in those areas I achieved A's and scored in the ninetieth percentile or higher. 15

This was understandable. Math is precise; there is only one correct answer. Whereas, for me at least, the answers on English tests were always a judgment call, a matter of opinion and personal experience. Those tests were constructed around items like fill-in-the-blank sentence completion, such as "Even though Tom was _____, Mary thought he was _____." And the correct answer always seemed to be the most bland combinations of thoughts, for example, "Even though Tom was shy, Mary thought he was charming," with the grammatical structure "even though" limiting the correct answer to some sort of semantic opposites, so you wouldn't get answers like, "Even though Tom was foolish, Mary thought he was ridiculous." Well, according to my mother, there were very few limitations as to what Tom could have been and what Mary might have thought of him. So I never did well on tests like that.

The same was true with word analogies, pairs of words in which you were supposed to find some sort of logical, semantic relationship—for example, "*Sunset* is to *nightfall* as _____ is to _____." And here you would be presented with a list of four possible pairs, one of which showed the same kind of relationship: *red* is to *stoplight, bus* is to *arrival, chills* is to *fever, yawn* is to *boring.* Well, I could never think that way. I knew what the tests were asking, but I could not block out of my mind the images already created by the first pair, "*sunset* is to *nightfall*"—and I would see a burst of colors against a darkening sky, the moon rising, the lowering of a curtain of stars. And all the other pairs of words—red, bus, stoplight, boring—just threw up a mass of confusing images, making it impossible for me to sort out something as logical as saying: "A sunset precedes nightfall" is the same as "a chill precedes a fever." The only way I would have gotten that answer right would have been to imagine an associative situation, for example, my being disobedient and staying out past sunset, catching a chill at night, which turns into feverish pneumonia as punishment, which indeed did happen to me.

I have been thinking about all this lately, about my mother's English, about achievement tests. Because lately I've been asked, as a writer, why there are not more Asian Americans represented in American literature. Why are there few Asian Americans enrolled in creative writing programs? Why do so many Chinese students go into engineering? Well, these are broad sociological questions I can't begin to answer. But I have noticed in surveys — in fact, just last week — that Asian students, as a whole, always do significantly better on math achievement tests than in English. And this makes me think that there are other Asian-American students whose English spoken in the home might also be described as "broken" or "limited." And perhaps they also have teachers who are steering them away from writing and into math and science, which is what happened to me.

Fortunately, I happen to be rebellious in nature and enjoy the challenge of disproving assumptions made about me. I became an English major my first year in college, after being enrolled as pre-med. I started writing nonfiction as a freelancer the week after I was told by my former boss that writing was my worst skill and I should hone my talents toward account management.

But it wasn't until 1985 that I finally began to write fiction. And at   20 first I wrote using what I thought to be wittily crafted sentences, sentences that would finally prove I had mastery over the English language. Here's an example from the first draft of a story that later made its way into *The Joy Luck Club*, but without this line: "That was my mental quandary in its nascent state." A terrible line, which I can barely pronounce.

Fortunately, for reasons I won't get into today, I later decided I should envision a reader for the stories I would write. And the reader I decided upon was my mother, because these were stories about mothers. So with this reader in mind — and in fact she did read my early drafts — I began to write stories using all the Englishes I grew up with: the English I spoke to my mother, which for lack of a better term might be described as "simple"; the English she used with me, which for lack of a better term might be described as "broken"; my translation of her Chinese, which could certainly be described as "watered down"; and what I imagined to be her translation of her Chinese if she could speak in perfect English, her internal language, and for that I sought to preserve the essence, but neither an English nor a Chinese structure. I wanted to capture what language ability tests can never reveal: her intent, her passion, her imagery, the rhythms of her speech, and the nature of her thoughts.

Apart from what any critic had to say about my writing, I knew I had succeeded where it counted when my mother finished reading my book and gave me her verdict: "So easy to read."

The Reader's Presence

1. In paragraph 2, Tan mentions "all the Englishes" she grew up with. What were those "Englishes"? What is odd about the term? How does the oddity of the word reinforce the point of her essay?

2. In paragraph 20, Tan gives an example of a sentence that she once thought showed her "mastery" of English. What does she now find wrong with that sentence? What do you think of it? What would her mother have thought of it? What sort of reader does that sentence anticipate?

3. What exactly is Tan's "mother tongue"? What does the phrase usually mean? Would you call her mother's English "broken English"? What does that phrase imply? Why does Tan write with her mother in mind as her ideal reader? How does Tan's determination to keep her mother linked to her writing compare with Richard Rodriguez's profound sense of having irrecoverably lost a connection with his parents in "Aria: A Memoir of a Bilingual Childhood" (page 210)? Does Rodriguez's distinction between private and public languages hold true for Tan?

Garry Trudeau

My Inner Shrimp

Garry Trudeau (b. 1948), creator of the popular comic strip "Doonesbury," has contributed articles to such publications as Harper's, Rolling Stone, *the* New Republic, *the* New Yorker, New York Magazine, *and the* Washington Post. *He received bachelor's and master's degrees from Yale University. Trudeau won a Pulitzer Prize in 1975 and in 1994 received the award for best comic strip from the National Cartoonists Society. For five years he was an occasional columnist for the* New York Times *opinion and editorial page. Currently, he is a contributing essayist for* Time *magazine. He lives in New York City with his wife, Jane Pauley, and their three children. This essay originally appeared in the* New York Times Magazine *on March 31, 1996.*

For the rest of my days, I shall be a recovering short person. Even from my lofty perch of something over six feet (as if I don't know within a micron), I have the soul of a shrimp. I feel the pain of the diminutive, irrespective of whether they feel it themselves, because my visit to the planet of the teenage midgets was harrowing, humiliating, and extended. I even perceive my last-minute escape to have been flukish, somehow un-earned—as if the Commissioner of Growth Spurts had been an old class-mate of my father.

My most recent reminder of all this came the afternoon I went hunt-ing for a new office. I had noticed a building under construction in my neighborhood—a brick warren of duplexes, with wide, westerly facing windows, promising ideal light for a working studio. When I was ushered into the model unit, my pulse quickened: The soaring, twenty-two-foot living room walls were gloriously aglow with the remains of the day. I bonded immediately.

Almost as an afterthought, I ascended the staircase to inspect the loft, ducking as I entered the bedroom. To my great surprise, I stayed ducked: The room was a little more than six feet in height. While my head techni-cally cleared the ceiling, the effect was excruciatingly oppressive. This cer-tainly wasn't a space I wanted to spend any time in, much less take out a mortgage on.

Puzzled, I wandered down to the sales office and asked if there were any other units to look at. No, replied a resolutely unpleasant reception-ist, it was the last one. Besides, they were all exactly alike.

"Are you aware of how low the bedroom ceilings are?" I asked.   5

She shot me an evil look. "Of course we are," she snapped. "There were some problems with the building codes. The architect knows all about the ceilings.

"He's not an idiot, you know," she added, perfectly anticipating my next question.

She abruptly turned away, but it was too late. She'd just confirmed that a major New York developer, working with a fully licensed architect, had knowingly created an entire twelve-story apartment building virtually uninhabitable by anyone of even average height. It was an exclusive high-rise for shorties.

Once I knew that, of course, I couldn't stay away. For days thereafter, as I walked to work, some perverse, unreasoning force would draw me back to the building. But it wasn't just the absurdity, the stone silliness of its design that had me in its grip; it was something far more compelling. Like some haunted veteran come again to an ancient battlefield, I was re-visiting my perilous past.

When I was fourteen, I was the third-smallest in a high school class of   10 one hundred boys, routinely mistaken for a sixth grader. My first week of school, I was drafted into a contingent of students ignominiously dubbed the "Midgets," so grouped by taller boys presumably so they could taunt us with more perfect efficiency. Inexplicably, some of my fellow Midgets refused to be diminished by the experience, but I retreated into self-pity.

"Doonesbury" by Garry Trudeau. February 9, 2003.

I sent away for a book on how to grow tall, and committed to memory its tips on overcoming one's genetic destiny — or at least making the most of a regrettable situation. The book cited historical figures who had gone the latter route — Alexander the Great, Caesar, Napoleon (the mind involuntarily added Hitler). Strategies for stretching the limbs were suggested — hanging from door frames, sleeping on your back, doing assorted floor exercises — all of which I incorporated into my daily routine (get up, brush teeth, hang from door frame). I also learned the importance of meeting girls early in the day, when, the book assured me, my rested spine rendered me perceptibly taller.

For six years, my condition persisted; I grew, but at nowhere near the rate of my peers. I perceived other problems as ancillary, and loaded up the stature issue with freight shipped in daily from every corner of my life. Lack of athletic success, all absence of a social life, the inevitable run-ins with bullies — all could be attributed to the missing inches. The night I found myself sobbing in my father's arms was the low point; we both knew it was one problem he couldn't fix.

Of course what we couldn't have known was that he and my mother already had. They had given me a delayed developmental timetable. In my seventeenth year, I miraculously shot up six inches, just in time for graduation and a fresh start. I was, in the space of a few months, reborn — and I made the most of it. Which is to say that thereafter, all of life's disappointments, reversals, and calamities still arrived on schedule — but blissfully free of subtext.

Once you stop being the butt, of course, any problem recedes, if only to give way to a new one. And yet the impact of being literally looked down on, of being *made* to feel small, is forever. It teaches you how to stretch, how to survive the scorn of others for things that are beyond your control. Not growing forces you to grow up fast.

Sometimes I think I'd like to return to a high-school reunion to surprise my classmates. Not that they didn't know me when I finally started catching up. They did, but I doubt they'd remember. Adolescent hierarchies have a way of enduring; I'm sure I am still recalled as the Midget I myself have never really left behind.

Of course, if I'm going to show up, it'll have to be soon. I'm starting 15 to shrink.

The Reader's Presence

1. It is said that "beauty is in the eye of the beholder"; Trudeau's testimony challenges this old saw. Does Trudeau's piece convince you that imagined shortcomings are nearly as ruinous as those apparent to others? Why or why not?

2. Locate examples of exaggeration or hyperbole in the essay. Does this descriptive technique support or weaken Trudeau's case, and why? What phrase does Trudeau's title intentionally echo? Why?

3. "Not growing forces you to grow up fast" (paragraph 13), Trudeau writes near the end of the essay—a general truth that can apply to any reader, tall or short. Compare this essay to Nancy Mairs's "On Being a Cripple" (page 157). Their respective subjects differ, of course, but both writers strive to make their essays speak to a wide audience. How do they do this?

Alice Walker

Beauty: When the Other Dancer Is the Self

Alice Walker (b. 1944) was awarded the Pulitzer Prize and the American Book Award for her second novel, The Color Purple *(1982), which was made into a popular film. This novel helped establish Walker's reputation as one of America's most important contemporary writers. In both her fiction and nonfiction, she shares her compassion for the black women of America whose lives have long been largely excluded from or distorted in literary representation. Walker is also the author of other novels, short stories, several volumes of poetry, a children's biography of Langston Hughes, essays, and criticism. Her books of poetry and prose include* By the Light of My Father's Smile *(1998),* The Way Forward Is with a Broken Heart *(2000),* Absolute Trust in the Goodness of the Earth *(2003), and* Now Is the Time to Open Your Heart *(2004). Her most recent work includes a collection of essays and ruminations,* We Are the Ones We Have Been Waiting For *(2006), and an illustrated poem for children,* Why War Is Never a Good Idea *(2007). "Beauty: When the Other Dancer Is the Self" comes from her 1983 collection,* In Search of Our Mothers' Gardens.

When asked by an interviewer about her writing habits, Walker replied, "I think it was Hemingway who said that each day that you write, you don't try to write to the absolute end of what you feel and think. You leave a little, you know, so that the next day you have something else to go on. And I would take it a little further—the thing is being able to create out of fullness, and that in order to create out of fullness, you have to let it well up. . . . In creation you must always leave something. You have to go to the bottom of the well with creativity. You have to give it everything you've got, but at the same time you have to leave that last drop for the creative spirit or for the earth itself."

It is a bright summer day in 1947. My father, a fat, funny man with beautiful eyes and a subversive wit, is trying to decide which of his eight children he will take with him to the county fair. My mother, of course, will not go. She is knocked out from getting most of us ready: I hold my neck stiff against the pressure of her knuckles as she hastily completes the braiding and the beribboning of my hair.

My father is the driver for the rich old white lady up the road. Her name is Miss Mey. She owns all the land for miles around, as well as the house in which we live. All I remember about her is that she once offered to pay my mother thirty-five cents for cleaning her house, raking up piles of her magnolia leaves, and washing her family's clothes, and that my mother—she of no money, eight children, and a chronic earache—refused it. But I do not think of this in 1947. I am two-and-a-half years old. I want to go everywhere my daddy goes. I am excited at the prospect of riding in a car. Someone has told me fairs are fun. That there is room in the car for only three of us doesn't faze me at all. Whirling happily in my starchy frock, showing off my biscuit-polished patent-leather shoes and lavender socks, tossing my head in a way that makes my ribbons bounce, I stand, hands on hips, before my father. "Take me, Daddy," I say with assurance; "I'm the prettiest!"

Later, it does not surprise me to find myself in Miss Mey's shiny black car, sharing the back seat with the other lucky ones. Does not surprise me that I thoroughly enjoy the fair. At home that night I tell the unlucky ones all I can remember about the merry-go-round, the man who eats live chickens, and the teddy bears, until they say: that's enough, baby Alice. Shut up now, and go to sleep.

It is Easter Sunday, 1950. I am dressed in a green, flocked, scalloped-hem dress (handmade by my adoring sister, Ruth) that has its own smooth satin petticoat and tiny hot-pink roses tucked into each scallop. My shoes, new T-strap patent leather, again highly biscuit-polished. I am six years old and have learned one of the longest Easter speeches to be heard that day, totally unlike the speech I said when I was two: "Easter lilies / pure and white / blossom in / the morning light." When I rise to give my speech I do so on a great wave of love and pride and expectation. People in the church stop rustling their new crinolines. They seem to hold their breath. I can tell they admire my dress, but it is my spirit, bordering on sassiness (womanishness), they secretly applaud.

"That girl's a little *mess*," they whisper to each other, pleased.   5

Naturally I say my speech without stammer or pause, unlike those who stutter, stammer, or, worst of all, forget. This is before the word "beautiful" exists in people's vocabulary, but "Oh, isn't she the *cutest* thing!" frequently floats my way. "And got so much sense!" they gratefully add . . . for which thoughtful addition I thank them to this day.

It was great fun being cute. But then, one day, it ended.

I am eight years old and a tomboy. I have a cowboy hat, cowboy boots, checkered shirt and pants, all red. My playmates are my brothers, two and four years older than I. Their colors are black and green, the only difference in the way we are dressed. On Saturday nights we all go to the picture show, even my mother; Westerns are her favorite kind of movie. Back home, "on the ranch," we pretend we are Tom Mix, Hopa-long Cassidy, Lash LaRue (we've even named one of our dogs Lash LaRue); we chase each other for hours rustling cattle, being outlaws, delivering damsels from distress. Then my parents decide to buy my brothers guns. These are not "real" guns. They shoot BBs, copper pellets my brothers say will kill birds. Because I am a girl, I do not get a gun. Instantly I am relegated to the position of Indian. Now there appears a great distance between us. They shoot and shoot at everything with their new guns. I try to keep up with my bow and arrows.

One day while I am standing on top of our makeshift "garage"—pieces of tin nailed across some poles—holding my bow and arrow and looking out toward the fields, I feel an incredible blow in my right eye. I look down just in time to see my brother lower his gun.

Both brothers rush to my side. My eye stings, and I cover it with my hand. "If you tell," they say, "we will get a whipping. You don't want that to happen, do you?" I do not. "Here is a piece of wire," says the older brother, picking it up from the roof; "say you stepped on one end of it and the other flew up and hit you." The pain is beginning to start. "Yes," I say. "Yes, I will say that is what happened." If I do not say this is what happened, I know my brothers will find ways to make me wish I had. But now I will say anything that gets me to my mother.

Confronted by our parents we stick to the lie agreed upon. They place me on a bench on the porch and I close my left eye while they examine the right. There is a tree growing from underneath the porch that climbs past the railing to the roof. It is the last thing my right eye sees. I watch as its trunk, its branches, and then its leaves are blotted out by the rising blood.

I am in shock. First there is intense fever, which my father tries to break using lily leaves bound around my head. Then there are chills: my mother tries to get me to eat soup. Eventually, I do not know how, my parents learn what has happened. A week after the "accident" they take me to see a doctor. "Why did you wait so long to come?" he asks, looking into my eye and shaking his head. "Eyes are sympathetic," he says. "If one is blind, the other will likely become blind too."

This comment of the doctor's terrifies me. But it is really how I look that bothers me most. Where the BB pellet struck there is a glob of whitish scar tissue, a hideous cataract, on my eye. Now when I stare at people—a favorite pastime, up to now—they will stare back. Not at the "cute" little girl, but at her scar. For six years I do not stare at anyone, because I do not raise my head.

10

Years later, in the throes of a mid-life crisis, I ask my mother and sister whether I changed after the "accident." "No," they say, puzzled. "What do you mean?"

What do I mean?   15

I am eight, and, for the first time, doing poorly in school, where I have been something of a whiz since I was four. We have just moved to the place where the "accident" occurred. We do not know any of the people around us because this is a different county. The only time I see the friends I knew is when we go back to our old church. The new school is the former state penitentiary. It is a large stone building, cold and drafty, crammed to overflowing with boisterous, ill-disciplined children. On the third floor there is a huge circular imprint of some partition that has been torn out.

"What used to be here?" I ask a sullen girl next to me on our way past it to lunch.

"The electric chair," says she.

At night I have nightmares about the electric chair, and about all the people reputedly "fried" in it. I am afraid of the school, where all the students seem to be budding criminals.

"What's the matter with your eye?" they ask, critically.   20

When I don't answer (I cannot decide whether it was an "accident" or not), they shove me, insist on a fight.

My brother, the one who created the story about the wire, comes to my rescue. But then brags so much about "protecting" me, I become sick.

After months of torture at the school, my parents decide to send me back to our old community, to my old school. I live with my grandparents and the teacher they board. But there is no room for Phoebe, my cat. By the time my grandparents decide there *is* room, and I ask for my cat, she cannot be found. Miss Yarborough, the boarding teacher, takes me under her wing, and begins to teach me to play the piano. But soon she marries an African—a "prince," she says—and is whisked away to his continent.

At my old school there is at least one teacher who loves me. She is the teacher who "knew me before I was born" and bought my first baby clothes. It is she who makes life bearable. It is her presence that finally helps me turn on the one child at the school who continually calls me "one-eyed bitch." One day I simply grab him by his coat and beat him until I am satisfied. It is my teacher who tells me my mother is ill.

My mother is lying in bed in the middle of the day, something I have   25
never seen. She is in too much pain to speak. She has an abscess in her ear. I stand looking down on her, knowing that if she dies, I cannot live. She is being treated with warm oils and hot bricks held against her cheek. Finally a doctor comes. But I must go back to my grandparents' house. The weeks pass but I am hardly aware of it. All I know is that my mother might die, my father is not so jolly, my brothers still have their guns, and I am the one sent away from home.

"You did not change," they say.

Did I imagine the anguish of never looking up?

I am twelve. When relatives come to visit I hide in my room. My cousin Brenda, just my age, whose father works in the post office and whose mother is a nurse, comes to find me. "Hello," she says. And then she asks, looking at my recent school picture, which I did not want taken, and on which the "glob," as I think of it, is clearly visible, "You still can't see out of that eye?"

"No," I say, and flop back on the bed over my book.

That night, as I do almost every night, I abuse my eye. I rant and rave   30 at it, in front of the mirror. I plead with it to clear up before morning. I tell it I hate and despise it. I do not pray for sight. I pray for beauty.

"You did not change," they say.

I am fourteen and baby-sitting for my brother Bill, who lives in Boston. He is my favorite brother and there is a strong bond between us. Understanding my feelings of shame and ugliness he and his wife take me to a local hospital, where the "glob" is removed by a doctor named O. Henry. There is still a small bluish crater where the scar tissue was, but the ugly white stuff is gone. Almost immediately I become a different person from the girl who does not raise her head. Or so I think. Now that I've raised my head I win the boyfriend of my dreams. Now that I've raised my head I have plenty of friends. Now that I've raised my head classwork comes from my lips as faultlessly as Easter speeches did, and I leave high school as valedictorian, most popular student, and *queen*, hardly believing my luck. Ironically, the girl who was voted most beautiful in our class (and was) was later shot twice through the chest by a male companion, using a "real" gun, while she was pregnant. But that's another story in itself. Or is it?

"You did not change," they say.

It is now thirty years since the "accident." A beautiful journalist comes to visit and to interview me. She is going to write a cover story for her magazine that focuses on my latest book. "Decide how you want to look on the cover," she says. "Glamorous, or whatever."

Never mind "glamorous," it is the "whatever" that I hear. Suddenly   35 all I can think of is whether I will get enough sleep the night before the photography session: If I don't, my eye will be tired and wander, as blind eyes will.

At night in bed with my lover I think up reasons why I should not appear on the cover of a magazine. "My meanest critics will say I've sold out," I say. "My family will now realize I write scandalous books."

"But what's the real reason you don't want to do this?" he asks.

"Because in all probability," I say in a rush, "my eye won't be straight."

"It will be straight enough," he says. Then, "Besides, I thought you'd made your peace with that."

And I suddenly remember that I have.   40

I remember:

I am talking to my brother Jimmy, asking if he remembers anything unusual about the day I was shot. He does not know I consider that day the last time my father, with his sweet home remedy of cool lily leaves, chose me, and that I suffered and raged inside because of this. "Well," he says, "all I remember is standing by the side of the highway with Daddy, trying to flag down a car. A white man stopped, but when Daddy said he needed somebody to take his little girl to the doctor, he drove off."

I remember:

I am in the desert for the first time. I fall totally in love with it. I am so overwhelmed by its beauty, I confront for the first time, consciously, the meaning of the doctor's words years ago: "Eyes are sympathetic. If one is blind, the other will likely become blind too." I realize I have dashed about the world madly, looking at this, looking at that, storing up images against the fading of the light. *But I might have missed seeing the desert!* The shock of that possibility—and gratitude for over twenty-five years of sight—sends me literally to my knees. Poem after poem comes—which is perhaps how poets pray.

ON SIGHT

I am so thankful I have seen
The Desert
And the creatures in the desert
And the desert Itself.

The desert has its own moon
Which I have seen
With my own eye.
There is no flag on it.

Trees of the desert have arms
All of which are always up
That is because the moon is up
The sun is up
Also the sky
The Stars
Clouds
None with flags.

If there were flags, I doubt
the trees would point.
Would you?

But mostly, I remember this: 45

I am twenty-seven, and my baby daughter is almost three. Since her birth I have worried about her discovery that her mother's eyes are different from other people's. Will she be embarrassed? I think. What will she say? Every day she watches a television program called *Big Blue Marble*. It begins with a picture of the earth as it appears from the moon. It is bluish, a little battered-looking, but full of light, with whitish clouds swirling around it. Every time I see it I weep with love, as if it is a picture of Grandma's house. One day when I am putting Rebecca down for her nap, she suddenly focuses on my eye. Something inside me cringes, gets ready to try to protect myself. All children are cruel about physical differences, I know from experience, and that they don't always mean to be is another matter. I assume Rebecca will be the same.

But no-o-o-o. She studies my face intently as we stand, her inside and me outside her crib. She even holds my face maternally between her dimpled little hands. Then, looking every bit as serious and lawyerlike as her father, she says, as if it may just possibly have slipped my attention: "Mommy, there's a *world* in your eye." (As in, "Don't be alarmed, or do anything crazy.") And then, gently, but with great interest: "Mommy, where did you *get* that world in your eye?"

For the most part, the pain left then. (So what, if my brothers grew up to buy even more powerful pellet guns for their sons and to carry real guns themselves. So what, if a young "Morehouse[1] man" once nearly fell off the steps of Trevor Arnett Library because he thought my eyes were blue.) Crying and laughing I ran to the bathroom, while Rebecca mumbled and sang herself to sleep. Yes indeed, I realized, looking into the mirror. There *was* a world in my eye. And I saw that it was possible to love it: that in fact, for all it had taught me of shame and anger and inner vision, I *did* love it. Even to see it drifting out of orbit in boredom, or rolling up out of fatigue, not to mention floating back at attention in excitement (bearing witness, a friend has called it), deeply suitable to my personality, and even characteristic of me.

That night I dream I am dancing to Stevie Wonder's song "Always" (the name of the song is really "As," but I hear it as "Always"). As I dance, whirling and joyous, happier than I've ever been in my life, another bright-faced dancer joins me. We dance and kiss each other and hold each other through the night. The other dancer has obviously come through all right, as I have done. She is beautiful, whole, and free. And she is also me.

---

[1]*Morehouse:* Morehouse College, a black men's college in Atlanta, Georgia. —Eds.

The Reader's Presence

1. In her opening paragraph, Walker refers to her father's "beautiful eyes." How does that phrase take on more significance in rereading? Can you find other words, phrases, or images that do the same? For example, why might Walker have mentioned the pain of having her hair combed?

2. Note that Walker uses the present tense throughout the essay. Why might this be unusual, given her subject? What effect does it have for both writer and reader? Try rewriting the opening paragraph in the past tense. What difference do you think it makes?

3. What is the meaning of Walker's occasional italicized comments? What do they have in common? Whose comments are they? To whom do they seem addressed? What time frame do they seem to be in? What purpose do you think they serve? How do they compare to those of Judith Ortiz Cofer in "Silent Dancing" (page 64)?

Jerald Walker

Scattered Inconveniences

Jerald Walker (b. 1964) was born and raised on Chicago's South Side. He attended the Iowa Writers' Workshop and later earned a PhD in interdisciplinary studies from the University of Iowa. Currently, he is an assistant professor of English at Bridgewater State College. A recipient of a James A. Michener Fellowship, his works have appeared in publications such as the Missouri Review, *the* Iowa Review, *the* Chronicle of Higher Education, Outsmart, *the* Barcelona Review, *and the* New Delta Review. *One of his essays, "Dragon Slayers," first published in the* Iowa Review, *was selected for* The Best American Essays 2007. *"Scattered Inconveniences" appeared in the* North American Review *in 2006.*

He barreled up on our left, momentarily matched our speed, then surged forward and waved a cowboy hat out the window, a bull rider in a brown Chevy. Somehow I knew he would swerve into our lane and slow down, and as he did the sound of his horn came to us over the rumble of our truck's engine. We were in a seventeen-foot Ryder that held everything we owned, junk, pretty much, with ten feet to spare. Those were, we believed, the final days of poverty. After not being able to find a teaching job for three years since completing her doctorate in art history, my wife had landed a rare tenure-track position at a state college in New England, twelve hundred miles east of Iowa City where we'd spent ten years living with tornadoes, academics, and hippies. I was going to be a stay-at-home dad, watching our fifteen-month-old during the day and writing at night. It was the perfect scenario, one we'd dreamt of for so long. All I had to do now was prevent the man in the Chevy from killing us.

I gripped the steering wheel tighter, checked the rearview mirrors in case a sudden maneuver was necessary. There were no vehicles within twenty yards, besides our reckless escort, just ten feet away.

"This guy's drunk or something," Brenda said.

I shook my head. "I *told you* we shouldn't drive in the middle of the night."

"It's only eight." 5

I checked the clock on the dashboard. "8:10."

"Well, you could just *slow down*," she said, "and let him go."

"Or," I responded, "I could crush him."

"And injure your son in the process?"

I glanced to my right. Adrian slept between us in his child seat, oblivious that we were being menaced by a fool, and that his daddy, in certain situations, particularly those that involved motor vehicles and testosterone, was a fool, too. I tugged at his harness, and confirmed that it was secure, then gunned the engine and lurched the truck forward. Brenda punched my arm. I lifted my foot off the accelerator and watched the speedometer topple from 70 to 55, where I leveled off. For a few seconds there was a gentlemanly distance between us and the Chevy, and then it slowed, too, until it was again ten feet from our bumper. This time I held my ground. I could feel Brenda tensing. I lowered my window and gave him the finger, Adrian stirring as wind tore into the cab. Brenda called me an ass, though not audibly. We'd been together long enough that the actual use of words, at times like those, was unnecessary. 10

The Chevy suddenly braked and I had to as well to avoid a collision. My heart was racing now. I tried hard to believe that we weren't dealing with something more ominous than a souse. We were in Indiana, a state I vaguely remembered hearing was a breeding ground for racists; perhaps the random sight of a black family had proved too irresistible, a cat straying into an angry dog's view.

But I had heard similar things about Iowa, only later to experience no problems. "No problems" is not to say "nothing," though, for there were what a black intellectual referred to as "scattered inconveniences"—women crossing the street or removing their purses from grocery carts at my approach, security guards following me in department stores. Once, while I was working out in the university's gym, two young men, looking my way and laughing, began mimicking the walk of a gorilla. Silly, all of it, confirmation that the bigotry my parents faced no longer exists, that its sledgehammer impact has been reduced, for the most part, to pebbles pitched from a naughty child's hand. I tell myself to find victory in encounters such as these. And I usually do. But sometimes I can't because of one simple truth: I am a racist.

Like a recovering alcoholic, I recognize that to define myself by my disease is in some way to help guard against relapse, that there is daily salvation in this constant reminder of who and what I am. My quest to be rid of all traces of this scourge has not been easy, though I have made good progress, considering I was born during the sixties in a segregated Chicago. The communities I grew up in were dangerous and poor, and it was the common opinion of nearly everyone I knew that, when all was said and done, whites were to blame. Whites discriminated against us. Whites denied us decent housing. Whites caused us to have high unemployment and failed schools. Crack had come from whites, and so too had AIDS. Whites, in some vague and yet indisputable way, made the winos drink and gangbangers kill. I came to believe, at a very early age, that in order to succeed I would have to beat the system through the mastery of some criminal enterprise, or join it in the form of a Sambo, a sell-out, an Oreo, an Uncle Tom. In other words, I'd have to be my brother Clyde.

Clyde, who said things like, "Whites aren't an obstacle to success," and "Only *you* can stop *you*."

We didn't like Clyde. 15

We watched him with disgust as he became a teenager and continued to speak without slang or profanity. He wore straight-legs and loafers instead of bellbottoms and four-inch stacks, his only concession to soulful style an afro, which *could* have been bigger. He held a job during high school and still earned straight A's. After graduation he studied computers when his friends aspired to be postal clerks or pimps.

Our father threw him out. He was twenty-one. My twin brother and I, at fourteen, just on the threshold of a decade of lawlessness, had come home one night drunk. Clyde beat us sober with a pool stick. Outside of a few times at church, it was many years before we saw him socially again. I didn't know where he spent his exile. I was not surprised, though, when he resurfaced in the eighties in a Ford AeroStar with a Ronald Reagan sticker on his bumper. He'd rejected liberal black ideology his whole life, and so his emergence as a staunch conservative made perfect sense, as much sense as me, twenty years later, being tempted to crush a white man on I-80.

The Chevy switched lanes again, this time to the right. The driver was shouting at us through his opened window. I ignored him. He blew his horn.

Brenda asked, "What do you think he wants?"

"Our lives," I said.   20

He blew his horn again.

"I'm going to open my window and see what he wants."

"Do *not* do that!"

She opened her window. I couldn't make out what he was saying, and Brenda was practically hanging out the window to hear him. I leaned towards them while trying to keep the truck steady. Brenda suddenly whirled to face me. Her eyes were wide. "Stop the truck!" she demanded.

"*Why?*"   25

"The back door is open! The washer's about to fall out!"

We were towing our car behind us; the perilousness of the situation was instantly clear.

I put on my right signal and began to work my way to the shoulder. The man tooted his horn and gave me a thumbs-up, then rode off into the night. Adrian was crying and I wondered for how long. His pacifier had fallen. Brenda rooted it from his seat and slipped it between his lips. He puffed on it fiendishly, like it was long-denied nicotine.

We'd come to a stop. Our hazards were flashing. Cars and trucks rocked us gently as they hurled themselves east, towards the Promised Land. Before I opened my door, Brenda and I exchanged a quick glance. I did not have to actually say I was sorry. She did not have to actually say she forgave me.

The Reader's Presence

1. Why does Walker title his essay "Scattered Inconveniences?" Where in the essay do we find the phrase used? Who said it and in what context does it appear? What meaning does it take on with respect to racism? Do you think the incident Walker describes is an example of a scattered inconvenience in the same sense that the phrase appears in the essay? Explain why or why not?

2. In paragraph 12, Walker admits to being "a racist." In what sense is he one? Is his racism shown in the essay? If so, how? If not, why does he introduce the subject? Consider Walker's brother Clyde, who plays a fairly large part in this brief essay. What does Clyde's presence have to do with Walker's main point in the essay?

3. Consider Walker's essay along with another essay on a similar topic, John Edgar Wideman's "The Night I Was Nobody" (page 886). How similar are the incidents each author encounters? Given the two personal accounts of racist incidents, how would you describe the essential differences between each writer?

THE WRITER AT WORK

Jerald Walker on Telling a Good Story

As a creative writing instructor, Jerald Walker wants his students to concentrate more on story telling *and less on the lesson or point they want to make. Nevertheless, invited by the editors to discuss his own essay and what it means to him as a reader (and not as a writer), Walker discovers that it contains a moral or point he did not set out to make. His brief explanation makes us aware that writing to a large extent is an act of discovery. But that discovery could only happen in the process of constructing the story.*

One thing I constantly urge my creative writing students to do is to lay off the metaphors. Go easy on morals, lessons, and "points"—it's the reader's job to worry about those. Your job is simply to try to tell a good story. That was what I tried to do in "Scattered Inconveniences." However, much to my delight (I was tempted to say "surprise," but I've come to expect surprises in the act of writing, so now I'm merely delighted when they occur), I later discovered it to be highly metaphorical. As a *reader* of this essay, I could make a case that the man in the Chevy represents the sin of American racism—slavery, discrimination, and other forms of bigotry that may at any moment barrel forth to make terribly disruptive appearances in our lives. When it cannot appear itself, which these days is more often the case than not, for an exceedingly long and reckless life has left it frail and feeble, it sends an able representative, known as paranoia. I have experienced a great deal of paranoia in the black community. On Chicago's South Side, where I was raised, there always seemed to be the suspicion, if not the outright prediction, that the blatant racism practiced in previous generations would make a triumphant comeback—indeed, in the minds of some people it never left. The paranoia created by racism, it seems to me, is often worse than racism itself, in the way that not knowing something is often worse than knowing. The phrase, *"Please,* Doc, just give it to me straight!" comes to mind.

But as my wife, son, and I traveled in our truck through Indiana, I could not have it given to me straight. I did not know the intentions of the man in the Chevy. And so, regrettably, I assumed the worst. Here my actions were metaphorical, too, for what better way to express how so many racial conflicts could be averted if we simply learned to give each other the benefit of the doubt. For me, that is sometimes easier said than done, but it is what I—what we all—must constantly aspire to if complete racial reconciliation will ever be achieved. Which leads me to another metaphor, as embodied in Adrian, my toddler, sleeping so peacefully until I lost my cool; he is, of course, the future. As a result of fear and mistrust, the future is placed in jeopardy. Perhaps that is ultimately the lesson of "Scattered Inconveniences"; maybe that is its moral or "point." I will leave that for each reader to decide, because, as the *writer,* I did not set out with any of these in mind. I was simply trying to tell a good story.

E. B. White

Once More to the Lake

Elwyn Brooks White (1899–1985) started contributing to the New Yorker *soon after the magazine began publication in 1925, and in the "Talk of the Town" and other columns helped establish the magazine's reputation for precise and brilliant prose. Collections of his contributions can be found in* Every Day Is Saturday *(1934),* Quo Vadimus? *(1939), and* The Wild Flag *(1946). He also wrote essays for* Harper's *on a regular basis; these essays include "Once More to the Lake" and are collected in* One Man's Meat *(1941). In his comments on this work, the critic Jonathan Yardley observed that White is "one of the few writers of this or any century who has succeeded in transforming the ephemera of journalism into something that demands to be called literature."*

Capable of brilliant satire, White could also be sad and serious, as in his compilation of forty years of writing, Essays *(1977). Among his numerous awards and honors, White received the American Academy of Arts and Letters Gold Medal (1960), a Presidential Medal of Freedom (1963), and a National Medal for Literature (1971). He made a lasting contribution to children's literature with* Stuart Little *(1945),* Charlotte's Web *(1952), and* The Trumpet of the Swan *(1970).*

White has written, "I have always felt that the first duty of a writer was to ascend—to make flights, carrying others along if he could manage it." According to White, the writer needs not only courage, but also hope and faith to accomplish this goal: "Writing itself is an act of faith, nothing else. And it must be the writer, above all others, who keeps it alive—choked with laughter, or with pain."

One summer, along about 1904, my father rented a camp on a lake in Maine and took us all there for the month of August. We all got ringworm from some kittens and had to rub Pond's Extract on our arms and legs night and morning, and my father rolled over in a canoe with all his clothes on; but outside of that the vacation was a success and from then on none of us ever thought there was any place in the world like that lake in Maine. We returned summer after summer—always on August 1st for one month. I have since become a salt-water man, but sometimes in summer there are days when the restlessness of the tides and the fearful cold of the sea water and the incessant wind that blows across the afternoon and into the evening make me wish for the placidity of a lake in the woods. A few weeks ago this feeling got so strong I bought myself a couple of bass hooks and a spinner and returned to the lake where we used to go, for a week's fishing and to revisit old haunts.

I took along my son, who had never had any fresh water up his nose and who had seen lily pads only from train windows. On the journey over to the lake I began to wonder what it would be like. I wondered how time would have marred this unique, this holy spot—the coves and streams, the hills that the sun set behind, the camps and the paths behind the camps. I was sure that the tarred road would have found it out and I wondered in what other ways it would be desolated. It is strange how much you can remember about places like that once you allow your mind to return into the grooves that lead back. You remember one thing, and that suddenly reminds you of another thing. I guess I remembered clearest of all the early mornings, when the lake was cool and motionless, remembered how the bedroom smelled of the lumber it was made of and the wet woods whose scent entered through the screen. The partitions in the camp were thin and did not extend clear to the top of the rooms, and as I was always the first up I would dress softly so as not to wake the others, and sneak out into the sweet outdoors and start out in the canoe, keeping close along the shore in the long shadows of the pines. I remembered being very careful never to rub my paddle against the gunwale for fear of disturbing the stillness of the cathedral.

The lake had never been what you would call a wild lake. There were cottages sprinkled about the shores, and it was in farming country although the shores of the lake were quite heavily wooded. Some of the cottages were owned by nearby farmers, and you would live at the shore and eat your meals at the farmhouse. That's what our family did. But although it wasn't wild, it was a fairly large and undisturbed lake and there were places in it which, to a child at least, seemed infinitely remote and primeval.

I was right about the tar: It led to within half a mile of the shore. But when I got back there, with my boy, and we settled into a camp near a farmhouse and into the kind of summertime I had known, I could tell that it was going to be pretty much the same as it had been before— I knew it, lying in bed the first morning, smelling the bedroom, and hearing the boy sneak quietly out and go off along the shore in a boat. I began to sustain the illusion that he was I, and therefore, by simple transposition, that I was my father. This sensation persisted, kept cropping up all the time we were there. It was not an entirely new feeling, but in this setting it grew much stronger. I seemed to be living a dual existence. I would be in the middle of some simple act, I would be picking up a bait box or laying down a table fork, or I would be saying something, and suddenly it would be not I but my father who was saying the words or making the gesture. It gave me a creepy sensation.

We went fishing the first morning. I felt the same damp moss covering the worms in the bait can, and saw the dragonfly alight on the tip of my rod as it hovered a few inches from the surface of the water. It was the arrival of this fly that convinced me beyond any doubt that everything was as it always had been, that the years were a mirage and there had been no years. The small waves were the same, chucking the rowboat under the chin as we fished at anchor, and the boat was the same boat, the same color green and the ribs broken in the same places, and under the floor-boards the same fresh-water leavings and debris—the dead hellgrammite, the wisps of moss, the rusty discarded fishhook, the dried

5

blood from yesterday's catch. We stared silently at the tips of our rods, at the dragonflies that came and went. I lowered the tip of mine into the water, tentatively, pensively dislodging the fly, which darted two feet away, poised, darted two feet back, and came to rest again a little farther up the rod. There had been no years between the ducking of this dragon-fly and the other one—the one that was part of memory. I looked at the boy, who was silently watching his fly, and it was my hands that held his rod, my eyes watching. I felt dizzy and didn't know which rod I was at the end of.

We caught two bass, hauling them in briskly as though they were mackerel, pulling them over the side of the boat in a businesslike manner without any landing net, and stunning them with a blow on the back of the head. When we got back for a swim before lunch, the lake was ex-actly where we had left it, the same number of inches from the dock, and there was only the merest suggestion of a breeze. This seemed an utterly enchanted sea, this lake you could leave to its own devices for a few hours and come back to, and find that it had not stirred, this constant and trustworthy body of water. In the shallows, the dark, watersoaked sticks and twigs, smooth and old, were undulating in clusters on the bot-tom against the clean ribbed sand, and the track of the mussel was plain. A school of minnows swam by, each minnow with its small individual shadow, doubling the attendance, so clear and sharp in the sunlight. Some of the other campers were in swimming, along the shore, one of them with a cake of soap, and the water felt thin and clear and unsubstantial. Over the years there had been this person with the cake of soap, this cultist, and here he was. There had been no years.

Up to the farmhouse to dinner through the teeming, dusty field, the road under our sneakers was only a two-track road. The middle track was missing, the one with the marks of the hooves and splotches of dried, flaky manure. There had always been three tracks to choose from in choosing which track to walk in; now the choice was narrowed down to two. For a moment I missed terribly the middle alternative. But the way led past the tennis court, and something about the way it lay there in the sun reassured me; the tape had loosened along the backline, the alleys were green with plantains and other weeds, and the net (installed in June and removed in September) sagged in the dry noon, and the whole place steamed with midday heat and hunger and emptiness. There was a choice of pie for dessert, and one was blueberry and one was apple, and the waitresses were the same country girls, there having been no passage of time, only the illusion of it as in a dropped curtain—the waitresses were still fifteen; their hair had been washed, that was the only difference—they had been to the movies and seen the pretty girls with the clean hair.

Summertime, oh summertime, pattern of life indelible, the fade-proof lake, the woods unshatterable, the pasture with the sweetfern and the ju-niper forever and ever, summer without end; this was the background, and the life along the shore was the design, the cottages with their innocent and tranquil design, their tiny docks with the flagpole and the American flag floating against the white clouds in the blue sky, the little paths over the roots of the trees leading from camp to camp and the paths leading back to the outhouses and the can of lime for sprinkling, and at the souvenir counters at the store the miniature birch-bark canoes and the post cards that showed things looking a little better than they looked. This was the American family at play, escaping the city heat, wondering whether the newcomers in the camp at the head of the cove were "common" or "nice," wondering whether it was true that the people who drove up for Sunday dinner at the farmhouse were turned away because there wasn't enough chicken.

It seemed to me, as I kept remembering all this, that those times and those summers had been infinitely precious and worth saving. There had been jollity and peace and goodness. The arriving (at the beginning of August) had been so big a business in itself, at the railway station the farm wagon drawn up, the first smell of the pine-laden air, the first glimpse of the smiling farmer, and the great importance of the trunks and your father's enormous authority in such matters, and the feel of the wagon under you for the long ten-mile haul, and at the top of the last long hill catching the first view of the lake after eleven months of not seeing this cherished body of water. The shouts and cries of the other campers when they saw you, and the trunks to be unpacked, to give up their rich burden. (Arriving was less exciting nowadays, when you sneaked up in your car and parked it under a tree near the camp and took out the bags and in five minutes it was all over, no fuss, no loud wonderful fuss about trunks).

Peace and goodness and jollity. The only thing that was wrong now,   10
really, was the sound of the place, an unfamiliar nervous sound of the outboard motors. This was the note that jarred, the one thing that would sometimes break the illusion and set the years moving. In those other summertimes all motors were inboard; and when they were at a little distance, the noise they made was a sedative, an ingredient of summer sleep. They were one-cylinder and two-cylinder engines, and some were make-and-break and some were jump-spark, but they all made a sleepy sound across the lake. The one-lungers throbbed and fluttered, and the twin-cylinder ones purred and purred, and that was a quiet sound too. But now the campers all had outboards. In the daytime, in the hot mornings, these motors made a petulant, irritable sound; at night, in the still evening when the afterglow lit the water, they whined about one's ears like mosquitoes. My boy loved our rented outboard, and his great desire was to achieve singlehanded mastery over it, and authority, and he soon learned the trick of choking it a little (but not too much), and the adjustment of the needle valve. Watching him I would remember the things you could do with the old one-cylinder engines with the heavy flywheel, how you could have it eating out of your hand if you got really close to it spiritually. Motor boats in those days didn't have clutches, and you would make a landing by shutting off the motor at the proper time and coasting in

with a dead rudder. But there was a way of reversing them, if you learned the trick, by cutting the switch and putting it on again exactly on the final dying revolution of the flywheel, so that it would kick back against compression and begin reversing. Approaching a dock in a strong following breeze, it was difficult to slow up sufficiently by the ordinary coasting method, and if a boy felt he had complete mastery over his motor, he was tempted to keep it running beyond its time and then reverse it a few feet from the dock. It took a cool nerve, because if you threw the switch a twentieth of a second too soon you could catch the flywheel when it still had speed enough to go up past center, and the boat would leap ahead, charging bull-fashion at the dock.

We had a good week at the camp. The bass were biting well and the sun shone endlessly, day after day. We would be tired at night and lie down in the accumulated heat of the little bedrooms after the long hot day and the breeze would stir almost imperceptibly outside and the smell of the swamp drift in through the rusty screens. Sleep would come easily and in the morning the red squirrel would be on the roof, tapping out his gay routine. I kept remembering everything, lying in bed in the mornings — the small steamboat that had a long rounded stern like the lip of a Ubangi, and how quietly she ran on the moonlight sails, when the older boys played their mandolins and the girls sang and we ate doughnuts dipped in sugar, and how sweet the music was on the water in the shining night, and what it had felt like to think about girls then. After breakfast we would go up to the store and the things were in the same place — the minnows in a bottle, the plugs and spinners disarranged and pawed over by the youngsters from the boys' camp, the Fig Newtons and the Beeman's gum. Outside, the road was tarred and cars stood in front of the store. Inside, all was just as it had always been, except there was more Coca-Cola and not so much Moxie and root beer and birch beer and sarsaparilla. We would walk out with a bottle of pop apiece and sometimes the pop would backfire up our noses and hurt. We explored the streams, quietly, where the turtles slid off the sunny logs and dug their way into the soft bottom; and we lay on the town wharf and fed worms to the tame bass. Everywhere we went I had trouble making out which was I, the one walking at my side, the one walking in my pants.

One afternoon while we were there at that lake a thunderstorm came up. It was like the revival of an old melodrama that I had seen long ago with childish awe. The second-act climax of the drama of the electrical disturbance over a lake in America had not changed in any important respect. This was the big scene, still the big scene. The whole thing was so familiar, the first feeling of oppression and heat and a general air around camp of not wanting to go very far away. In midafternoon (it was all the same) a curious darkening of the sky, and a lull in everything that had made life tick; and then the way the boats suddenly swung the other way at their moorings with the coming of a breeze out of the new quarter, and the premonitory rumble. Then the kettle drum, then the snare, then the bass drum and cymbals, then crackling light against the dark, and the gods grinning and licking their chops in the hills. Afterward the calm, the rain steadily rustling in the calm lake, the return of light and hope and spirits, and the campers running out in joy and relief to go swimming in the rain, their bright cries perpetuating the deathless joke about how they were getting simply drenched, and the children screaming with delight at the new sensation of bathing in the rain, and the joke about getting drenched linking the generations in a strong indestructible chain. And the comedian who waded in carrying an umbrella.

When the others went swimming my son said he was going in too. He pulled his dripping trunks from the line where they had hung all through the shower, and wrung them out. Languidly, and with no thought of going in, I watched him, his hard little body, skinny and bare, saw him wince slightly as he pulled up around his vitals the small, soggy, icy garment. As he buckled the swollen belt suddenly my groin felt the chill of death.

The Reader's Presence

1. In paragraph 2, White begins to reflect on the way his memory works. How does he follow the process of remembering throughout the essay? Are his memories of the lake safely stored in the past? If not, why not?

2. Go through the essay and identify words and images having to do with the sensory details of seeing, hearing, touching, and so on. How do these details contribute to the overall effect of the essay? How do they anticipate White's final paragraph?

3. In paragraph 4, White refers to a "creepy sensation." What is the basis of that sensation? Why is it "creepy"? What is the "dual existence" White feels he is living? How does the essay build the story of White's relationships with both his father and his son? Compare this account of intergenerational intimacy to Raymond Carver's essay "My Father's Life" (page 57).

THE WRITER AT WORK

E. B. White on the Essayist

For several generations, E. B. White has remained America's best known essayist, his works widely available and widely anthologized. Yet in the foreword to his 1977 collected essays, when he addresses the role of the essayist, he sounds wholly modest not only about his career but about his chosen genre: In the world of literature, he writes, the essayist is a "second-class citizen." Why do you think

*White thinks of himself that way, and how might that self-deprecation be recon-
ciled with the claims of his final two paragraphs? Do you think White's description of himself as an essayist matches the actual essayist we encounter in "Once
More to the Lake"? Also, do you think his persistent use of the male pronoun is
merely for grammatical convenience (the essay was written in 1977) or reflects a
gender bias on his part?*

The essayist is a self-liberated man, sustained by the childish belief
that everything he thinks about, everything that happens to him, is of
general interest. He is a fellow who thoroughly enjoys his work, just as
people who take bird walks enjoy theirs. Each new excursion of the essayist, each new "attempt," differs from the last and takes him into new
country. This delights him. Only a person who is congenitally self-centered
has the effrontery and the stamina to write essays.

There are as many kinds of essays as there are human attitudes or
poses, as many essay flavors as there are Howard Johnson ice creams.
The essayist arises in the morning and, if he has work to do, selects his
garb from an unusually extensive wardrobe: he can pull on any sort of
shirt, be any sort of person, according to his mood or his subject matter—
philosopher, scold, jester, raconteur, confidant, pundit, devil's advocate,
enthusiast. I like the essay, have always liked it, and even as a child was
at work, attempting to inflict my young thoughts and experiences on others by putting them on paper. I early broke into print in the pages of
St. Nicholas. I tend still to fall back on the essay form (or lack of form)
when an idea strikes me, but I am not fooled about the place of the essay in
twentieth century American letters—it stands a short distance down the
line. The essayist, unlike the novelist, the poet, and the playwright, must be
content in his self-imposed role of second-class citizen. A writer who has his
sights trained on the Nobel Prize or other earthly triumphs had best write a
novel, a poem, or a play, and leave the essayist to ramble about, content
with living a free life and enjoying the satisfactions of a somewhat undisci-
plined existence. (Dr. Johnson called the essay "an irregular, undigested
piece"; this happy practitioner has no wish to quarrel with the good doctor's characterization.)

There is one thing the essayist cannot do, though—he cannot indulge
himself in deceit or in concealment, for he will be found out in no time.
Desmond MacCarthy, in his introductory remarks to the 1928 E. P. Dutton
& Company edition of Montaigne, observes that Montaigne "had the gift
of natural candor. . . ." It is the basic ingredient. And even the essayist's escape from discipline is only a partial escape: the essay, although a relaxed
form, imposes its own disciplines, raises its own problems, and these disciplines and problems soon become apparent and (we all hope) act as a de-
terrent to anyone wielding a pen merely because he entertains random
thoughts or is in a happy or wandering mood.

I think some people find the essay the last resort of the egoist, a much
too self-conscious and self-serving form for their tastes; they feel that it is

presumptuous of a writer to assume that his little excursions or his small observations will interest the reader. There is some justice in their complaint. I have always been aware that I am by nature self-absorbed and egoistical; to write of myself to the extent I have done indicates a too great attention to my own life, not enough to the lives of others. I have worn many shirts, and not all of them have been a good fit. But when I am discouraged or downcast I need only fling open the door of my closet, and there, hidden behind everything else, hangs the mantle of Michel de Montaigne, smelling slightly of camphor.

Part II

Expository Writing: Shaping Information

Daniel Akst

What Meets the Eye

New York–born writer Daniel Akst (b. 1956) divides his time between fiction and nonfiction, journalism and commentary. He has written two novels, St. Burl's Obituary *(1996), a PEN/Faulkner Award finalist, and* The Webster Chronicle *(2001). His nonfiction account of financial fraud in southern California,* Wonder Boy, *was listed in* Business Week's *best books of 1990. Akst began his career in journalism while still attending college at the University of Pennsylvania, and continued as a reporter while at New York University, where he took graduate courses in economics and finance. Akst has been a regular columnist for the* Los Angeles Times *and the Sunday business section of the* New York Times, *writing, as he describes it, "about the intersection of money and culture." He is a regular contributor to the* Wall Street Journal *and his articles have appeared in numerous publications, including* Salon, *the* Christian Science Monitor, Forbes, Fortune, Money, Newsday, Slate, *and* Smithsonian. *His commentaries have been aired on NPR's* Marketplace, *and* Nightly Business Report *for PBS. He is a contributing editor at the* Wilson Quarterly, *in which this essay, "What Meets the Eye" first appeared in 2005.*

Everyone knows looks shouldn't matter. Beauty, after all, is only skin deep, and no right-thinking person would admit to taking much account of how someone looks outside the realm of courtship, that romantic free-trade zone traditionally exempted from the usual tariffs of rationality. Even in that tender kingdom, where love at first sight is still readily indulged, it would be impolitic, if not immature, to admit giving too much weight to a factor as shallow as looks. Yet perhaps it's time to say what we all secretly know, which is that looks do matter, maybe even more than most of us think.

We infer a great deal from people's looks — not just when it comes to mating (where looks matter profoundly), but in almost every other aspect of life as well, including careers and social status. It may not be true that blondes have more fun, but it's highly likely that attractive people do, and they start early. Mothers pay more attention to good-looking babies, for example, but, by the same token, babies pay more attention to prettier adults who wander into their fields of vision. Attractive people are paid more on the job, marry more desirable spouses, and are likelier to get help from others when in evident need. Nor is this all sheer, baseless prejudice. Human beings appear to be hard-wired to respond to how people and objects look, an adaptation without which the species might not have made it this far. The unpleasant truth is that, far from being only skin deep, our looks reflect all kinds of truths about difference and desire — truths we are, in all likelihood, biologically programmed to detect.

Sensitivity to the signals of human appearances would naturally lead to successful reproductive decisions, and several factors suggest that this sensitivity may be bred in the bone. Beauty may even be addictive. Researchers at London's University College have found that human beauty stimulates a section of the brain called the ventral striatum, the same region activated in drug and gambling addicts when they're about to indulge their habit. Photos of faces rated unattractive had no effect on the volunteers to whom they were shown, but the ventral striatum did show activity if the picture was of an attractive person, especially one looking straight at the viewer. And the responses occurred even when the viewer and the subject of the photo were of the same sex. Good-looking people just do something to us, whether we like it or not.

People's looks speak to us, sometimes in a whisper and sometimes in a shout, of health, reproductive fitness, agreeableness, social standing, and intelligence. Although looks in mating still matter much more to men than to women, the importance of appearance appears to be rising on both sides of the gender divide. In a fascinating cross-generational study of mating preferences, every 10 years different groups of men and women were asked to rank 18 characteristics they might want enhanced in a mate. The importance of good looks rose "dramatically" for both men and women from 1939 to 1989, the period of the study, according to David M. Buss, an evolutionary psychologist at the University of Texas. On a scale of 1 to 3, the importance men gave to good looks rose from 1.50 to 2.11. But for women, the importance of good looks in men rose from 0.94 to 1.67. In other words, women in 1989 considered a man's looks even more important than men considered women's looks 50 years earlier. Since the 1930s, Buss writes, "physical appearance has gone up in importance for men and women about equally, corresponding with the rise in television, fashion magazines, advertising, and other media depictions of attractive models."

In all likelihood this trend will continue, driven by social and techno- 5 logical changes that are unlikely to be reversed anytime soon—changes such as the new ubiquity of media images, the growing financial independence of women, and the worldwide weakening of the institution of marriage. For better or worse, we live now in an age of appearances. It looks like looks are here to stay.

The paradox, in such an age, is that the more important appearances become, the worse most of us seem to look — and not just by comparison with the godlike images alternately taunting and bewitching us from every billboard and TV screen. While popular culture is obsessed with fashion and style, and our prevailing psychological infirmity is said to be narcissism, fully two-thirds of American adults have abandoned conventional ideas of attractiveness by becoming overweight. Nearly half of this group is downright obese. Given their obsession with dieting—a $40 billion-plus industry in the United States—it's not news to these people that they're sending an unhelpful message with their inflated bodies, but it's worth noting here nonetheless.

Social scientists have established what most of us already know in this regard, which is that heavy people are perceived less favorably in a variety of ways. Across cultures—even in places such as Fiji, where fat is the norm—people express a preference for others who are neither too slim nor too heavy. In studies by University of Texas psychologist Devendra Singh, people guessed that the heaviest figures in photos were eight to 10 years older than the slimmer ones, even though the faces were identical. (As the nation's bill for hair dye and facelifts attests, looking older is rarely desirable, unless you happen to be an underage drinker.)

America's weight problem is one dimension of what seems to be a broader-based national flight from presentability, a flight that manifests itself unmistakably in the relentless casualness of our attire. Contrary to the desperate contentions of some men's clothiers, for example, the suit is really dying. Walk around midtown Manhattan, and these garments are striking by their absence. Consumer spending reflects this. In 2004, according to NPD Group, a marketing information firm, sales of "active sportswear," a category that includes such apparel as warm-up suits, were $39 billion, nearly double what was spent on business suits and other tailored clothing. The irony is that the more athletic gear we wear, from plum-colored velour track suits to high-tech sneakers, the less athletic we become.

The overall change in our attire did not happen overnight. America's clothes, like America itself, have been getting more casual for decades, in a trend that predates even Nehru jackets and the "full Cleveland" look of a pastel leisure suit with white shoes and belt, but the phenomenon reaches something like an apotheosis in the vogue for low-riding pajama bottoms and flip-flops outside the home. Visit any shopping mall in summer—or many deep-Sunbelt malls year round—and you'll find people of all sizes, ages, and weights clomping through the climate-controlled spaces in tank tops, T-shirts, and running shorts. Tops—and nowadays often bottoms—emblazoned with the names of companies, schools, and places make many of these shoppers look like walking billboards. Bulbous athletic shoes, typically immaculate on adults who go everywhere by car, are the functional equivalent of SUVs for the feet. Anne Hollander, an observant student of clothing whose books include *Sex and Suits* (1994), has complained that we've settled on "a sandbox aesthetic" of sloppy comfort, the new classics—sweats, sneakers, and jeans—persist year after year, transcending fashion altogether.

We've come to this pass despite our seeming obsession with how we   10
look. Consider these 2004 numbers from the American Society of Plastic
Surgeons: 9.2 million cosmetic surgeries (up 24 percent from 2000) at a
cost of $8.4 billion, and that doesn't count 7.5 million "minimally inva-
sive" procedures, such as skin peels and Botox injections (collectively up
36 percent). Cosmetic dentistry is also booming, as is weight-loss surgery.
Although most of this spending is by women, men are focusing more and
more on their appearance as well, which is obvious if you look at the evolution of men's magazines over the years. Further reflecting our concern
with both looks and rapid self-transformation is a somewhat grisly new
genre of reality TV: the extreme makeover show, which plays on the audience's presumed desire to somehow look a whole lot better fast.

But appearances in this case *are* deceiving. The evidence suggests that
a great many of us do not care nearly enough about how we look, and
that even those who care very much indeed still end up looking terrible.
In understanding why, it's worth remembering that people look the way
they do for two basic reasons—on purpose and by accident—and both
can be as revealing as a neon tube top.

Let's start with the purposeful. Extremes in casual clothing have several important functions. A big one nowadays is camouflage. Tent-like
T-shirts and sweatsuits cover a lot of sins, and the change in our bodies
over time is borne out by the sizes stores find themselves selling. In 1985,
for example, the top-selling women's size was eight. Today, when, as a
result of size inflation, an eight (and every other size) is larger than it used
to be, NPD Group reports that the top-selling women's size is 14. Camouflage may also account for the popularity of black, which is widely perceived as slimming as well as cool.

That brings us to another motive for dressing down—way down—
which is status. Dressing to manifest disregard for society—think of
the loose, baggy hipsters in American high schools—broadcasts self-
determination by flaunting the needlessness of having to impress anybody
else. We all like to pretend we're immune to "what people think," but
reaching for status on this basis is itself a particularly perverse—and egregious—form of status seeking. For grownups, it's also a way of pretending to be young, or at least youthful, since people know instinctively that
looking young often means looking good. Among the truly young, dressing down is a way to avoid any embarrassing lapses in self-defining rebelliousness. And for the young and fit, sexy casual clothing can honestly
signal a desire for short-term rather than long-term relationships. Indeed,
researchers have shown that men respond more readily to sexy clothing
when seeking a short-term relationship, perhaps because more modest attire is a more effective signal of sexual fidelity, a top priority for men in
the marriage market, regardless of nation or tribe.

Purposeful slovenliness can have its reasons, then, but what about
carelessness? One possible justification is that, for many people, paying
attention to their own looks is just too expensive. Clothes are cheap,

thanks to imports, but looking good can be costly for humans, just as it is for other species. A signal such as beauty, after all, is valuable in reproductive terms only if it has credibility, and it's been suggested that such signals are credible indicators of fitness precisely because in evolutionary terms they're so expensive. The peacock's gaudy tail, for example, attracts mates in part because it signals that the strutting bird is robust enough not only to sustain his fancy plumage but to fend off predators it also attracts. Modern humans who want to strut their evolutionary stuff have to worry about their tails too. They have to work them off. Since most of us are no longer paid to perform physical labor, getting exercise requires valuable time and energy, to say nothing of a costly gym membership. And then there is the opportunity cost—the pleasure lost by forgoing fried chicken and Devil Dogs. Eating junk food, especially fast food, is probably also cheaper, in terms of time, than preparing a low-calorie vegetarian feast at home.

These costs apparently strike many Americans as too high, which may   15
be why we as a culture have engaged in a kind of aesthetic outsourcing, transferring the job of looking good—of providing the desired supply of physical beauty—to the specialists known as "celebrities," who can afford to devote much more time and energy to the task. Offloading the chore of looking great into a small, gifted corps of professionals saves the rest of us a lot of trouble and expense, even if it has opened a yawning aesthetic gulf between the average person (who is fat) and the average model or movie star (who is lean and toned within an inch of his or her life).

Although the popularity of Botox and other such innovations suggests that many people do want to look better, it seems fair to conclude that they are not willing to pay any significant price to do so, since the great majority do not in fact have cosmetic surgery, exercise regularly, or maintain anything like their ideal body weight. Like so much in our society, physical attractiveness is produced by those with the greatest comparative advantage, and consumed vicariously by the rest of us—purchased, in a sense, ready made.

Whether our appearance is purposeful or accidental, the outcome is the same, which is that a great many of us look awful most of the time, and as a consequence of actions or inactions that are at least substantially the result of free will.

Men dressed like boys? Flip-flops at the office? Health care workers who never get near an operating room but nevertheless dress in shapeless green scrubs? These sartorial statements are not just casual. They're also of a piece with the general disrepute into which looking good seems to have fallen. On its face, so to speak, beauty presents some serious ideological problems in the modern world. If beauty were a brand, any focus group that we convened would describe it as shallow and fleeting or perhaps as a kind of eye candy that is at once delicious and bad for you. As a society, we consume an awful lot of it, and we feel darn guilty about it.

Why should this be so? For one thing, beauty strikes most of us as a natural endowment, and as a people we dislike endowments. We tax inheritances, after all, on the premise that they are unearned by their recipients and might produce something like a hereditary aristocracy, not unlike the one produced by the competition to mate with beauty. Money plays a role in that competition; there's no denying that looks and income are traditionally awfully comfortable with each other, and today affluent Americans are the ones least likely to be overweight. By almost any standard, then, looks are a seemingly unfair way of distinguishing oneself, discriminating as they do on the basis of age and generally running afoul of what the late political scientist Alan Wildavsky called "the rise of radical egalitarianism," which was at the very least suspicious of distinction and advantage, especially a distinction as capricious and as powerful as appearance.

Appearance can be a source of inequality, and achieving some kind   20
of egalitarianism in this arena is a longstanding and probably laudable American concern. The Puritans eschewed fancy garb, after all, and Thoreau warned us to beware of enterprises that require new clothes. Nowadays, at a time of increased income inequality, our clothes paradoxically confer less distinction than ever. Gender distinctions in clothing, for instance, have been blurred in favor of much greater sartorial androgyny, to the extent that nobody would any longer ask who wears the pants in any particular household (because the correct answer would be, "everybody"). The same goes for age distinctions (short pants long ago lost their role as uniform of the young), class distinctions (the rich wear jeans too), and even distinctions between occasions such as school and play, work and leisure, or public and private. Who among us hasn't noticed sneakers, for example, at a wedding, in a courtroom, or at a concert, where you spot them sometimes even on the stage?

The problem is that, if anything, looks matter even more than we think, not just because we're all hopelessly superficial, but because looks have always told us a great deal of what we want to know. Looks matter for good reason, in other words, and delegating favorable appearances to an affluent elite for reasons of cost or convenience is a mistake, both for the individuals who make it and for the rest of us as well. The slovenliness of our attire is one of the things that impoverish the public sphere, and the stunning rise in our weight (in just 25 years) is one of the things that impoverish our health. Besides, it's not as if we're evolving anytime soon into a species that's immune to appearances. Looks seem to matter to all cultures, not just our image-besotted one, suggesting that efforts to stamp out looksism (which have yet to result in hiring quotas on behalf of the homely) are bucking millions of years of evolutionary development.

The degree of cross-cultural consistency in this whole area is surprising. Contrary to the notion that beauty is in the eye of the beholder, or at the very least in the eye of the culture, studies across nations and tribal societies have found that people almost everywhere have similar ideas about what's attractive, especially as regards the face (tastes in bodies seem to vary a bit more, perhaps allowing for differing local evolutionary ecologies). Men everywhere, even those few still beyond the reach of Hollywood and Madison Avenue, are more concerned about women's looks than women are about men's, and their general preference for women who look young and healthy is probably the result of evolutionary adaptation.

The evidence for this comes from the field of evolutionary psychology. Whatever one's view of this burgeoning branch of science, one thing it has produced (besides controversy) is an avalanche of disconcerting research about how we look. Psychologists Michael R. Cunningham, of the University of Louisville, and Stephen R. Shamblen cite evidence that babies as young as two or three months old look longer at more attractive faces. New mothers of less attractive offspring, meanwhile, have been found to pay more attention to other people (say, hospital room visitors) than do new mothers of better-looking babies. This may have some basis in biological necessity, if you bear in mind that the evolutionary environment, free as it was of antibiotics and pediatricians, might have made it worthwhile indeed for mothers to invest themselves most in the offspring likeliest to survive and thrive.

The environment today, of course, is very different, but it may only amplify the seeming ruthlessness of the feelings and judgments we make. "In one study," reports David M. Buss, the evolutionary psychologist who reported on the multi-generational study of mating preferences, "after groups of men looked at photographs of either highly attractive women or women of average attractiveness, they were asked to evaluate their commitment to their current romantic partner. Disturbingly, the men who had viewed pictures of attractive women thereafter judged their actual partners to be less attractive than the men who had viewed analogous pictures of women who were average in attractiveness. Perhaps more important, the men who had viewed attractive women thereafter rated themselves as less committed, less satisfied, less serious, and less close to their actual partners." In another study, men who viewed attractive nude centerfolds promptly rated themselves as less attracted to their own partners.

Even if a man doesn't personally care much what a woman looks like, he knows that others do. Research suggests that being with an attractive woman raises a man's status significantly, while dating a physically unattractive woman moderately lowers a man's status. (The effect for women is quite different; dating an attractive man raises a woman's status only somewhat, while dating an unattractive man lowers her status only nominally.) And status matters. In the well-known "Whitehall studies" of British civil servants after World War II, for example, occupational grade was strongly correlated with longevity. The higher the bureaucrat's ranking, the longer the life. And it turns out that Academy Award–winning actors and actresses outlive other movie performers by about four years at least according to a study published in the *Annals of*

Internal Medicine in 2001. "The results," write authors Donald A. Redelmeier and Sheldon M. Singh, "suggest that success confers a survival advantage." So if an attractive mate raises a man's status, is it really such a wonder that men covet trophy wives?

In fact, people's idea of what's attractive, influenced by the body types that are associated with status in a given time and place (which suggests that culture plays at least some role in ideas of attractiveness). As any museumgoer can tell you, the big variation in male preferences across time and place is in plumpness, and Buss contends that this is a status issue: In places where food is plentiful, such as the United States, high-status people distinguish themselves by being thin.

There are reasons besides sex and status to worry about how we look. For example, economists David S. Hamermesh, of the University of Texas, and Jeff E. Biddle, of Michigan State University, have produced a study suggesting that better-looking people make more money. "Holding constant demographic and labor-market characteristics," they wrote in a well-known 1993 paper, "plain people earn less than people of average looks, who earn less than the good-looking. The penalty for plainness is five to 10 percent, slightly larger than the premium for beauty." A 1998 study of attorneys (by the same duo) found that some lawyers also benefit by looking better. Yet another study found that better-looking college instructors—especially men—receive higher ratings from their students.

Hamermesh and some Chinese researchers also looked into whether primping pays, based on a survey of Shanghai residents. They found that beauty raises women's earnings (and, to a lesser extent, men's), but that spending on clothing and cosmetics helps only a little. Several studies have even found associations between appearance preferences and economic cycles. Psychologists Terry F. Pettijohn II, of Ohio State University, and Abraham Tesser, of the University of Georgia, for example, obtained a list of the Hollywood actresses with top box-office appeal in each year from 1932 to 1995. The researchers scanned the actresses' photos into a computer, did various measurements, and determined that, lo and behold, the ones who were most popular during social and economic good times had more "neoteny"—more childlike features, including bigger eyes, smaller chins, and rounder cheeks. During economic downturns, stronger and more rectangular female faces—in other words, faces that were more mature—were preferred.

It's not clear whether this is the case for political candidates as well, but looks matter in this arena too. In a study that appeared recently [2005] in *Science*, psychologist Alexander Todorov and colleagues at Princeton University showed photographs of political candidates to more than 800 students, who were asked to say who had won and why based solely on looks. The students chose correctly an amazing 69 percent of the time, consistently picking candidates they judged to look the most competent, meaning those who looked more mature. The losers were more likely to have babyfaces, meaning some combination of a round face, big eyes, small nose, high forehead, and small chin. Those candidates apparently have a hard time winning elections.

To scientists, a convenient marker for physical attractiveness in people is symmetry, as measured by taking calipers to body parts [such] as wrists, elbows, and feet to see how closely the pairs match. The findings of this research can be startling. As summarized by biologist Randy Thornhill and psychologist Steven W. Gangestad, both of the University of New Mexico, "In both sexes, relatively low asymmetry seems to be associated with increased genetic, physical, and mental health, including cognitive skill and IQ. Also, symmetric men appear to be more muscular and vigorous, have a lower basal metabolic rate, and may be larger in body size than asymmetric men. . . . Symmetry is a major component of developmental health and overall condition and appears to be heritable." The researchers add that more symmetrical men have handsomer faces, more sex partners, and their first sexual experience at an earlier age, and they get to sex more quickly with a new romantic partner. "Moreover," they tell us, "men's symmetry predicts a relatively high frequency of their sexual partners' copulatory orgasms."

Those orgasms are sperm retaining, suggesting that symmetric men may have a greater chance of getting a woman pregnant. It doesn't hurt that the handsomest men may have the best sperm, at least according to a study at Spain's University of Valencia, which found that men with the healthiest, fastest sperm were those whose faces were rated most attractive by women. There's evidence that women care more about men's looks for short-term relationships than for marriage, and that as women get closer to the most fertile point of the menstrual cycle, their preference for "symmetrical" men grows stronger, according to Thornhill and Gangestad. Ovulating woman prefer more rugged, masculinized faces, whereas the rest of the time they prefer less masculinized or even slightly feminized faces. Perhaps predictably, more-symmetrical men are likelier to be unfaithful and tend to invest less in a relationship.

Asymmetric people may have some idea that they're behind the eight ball here. William Brown and his then-colleague at Dalhousie University in Halifax, Nova Scotia, looked at 50 people in heterosexual relationships, measuring such features as hands, ears, and feet, and then asked about jealousy. The researchers found a strong correlation between asymmetry and romantic jealousy, suggesting that asymmetrical lovers may suspect they're somehow less desirable. Brown's explanation: "If jealousy is a strategy to retain your mate, then the individual more likely to be philandered on is more likely to be jealous."

In general, how we look communicates something about how healthy we are, how fertile, and probably how useful in the evolutionary environment. This may be why, across a range of cultures, women prefer tall, broad-shouldered men who seem like good reproductive specimens, in addition to offering the possibility of physical protection. Men, meanwhile, like pretty women who appear young. Women's looks seem to vary depending on where they happen to be in the monthly fertility cycle. The University of Liverpool biologist John Manning measured women's ears and fingers and had the timing of their ovulation confirmed by pelvic exams. He found a 30 percent decline in asymmetries in the 24 hours before ovulation — perhaps more perceptible to our sexual antennae than to the conscious mind. In general, symmetrical women have more sex partners, suggesting that greater symmetry makes women more attractive to men.

To evolutionary biologists, it makes sense that men should care more about the way women look than vice versa, because youth and fitness matter so much more in female fertility. And while male preferences do vary with time and place there's also some remarkable underlying consistency. Devendra Singh, for instance, found that the waist-to-hip ratio was the most important factor in women's attractiveness to men in 18 cultures he studied. Regardless of whether lean or voluptuous women happen to be in fashion, the favored shape involves a waist/hip ratio of about 0.7. "Audrey Hepburn and Marilyn Monroe represented two very different images of beauty to filmgoers in the 1950s," writes Nancy Etcoff, who is a psychologist at Massachusetts General Hospital. "Yet the 36-24-34 Marilyn and the 31.5-22-31 Audrey both had versions of the hourglass shape and waist-to-hip ratios of 0.7." Even Twiggy, in her 92-pound heyday, had a waist/hip ratio of 0.73.

Is it cause for despair that looks are so important? The bloom of youth   35
is fleeting, after all, and the bad news that our appearance will inevitably broadcast about us cannot be kept under wraps forever. Besides, who could live up to the impossible standards propagated by our powerful aesthetic-industrial complex? It's possible that the images of models and actresses and even TV newscasters, most of them preternaturally youthful and all selected for physical fitness, have driven most Americans to quit the game, insisting that they still care about how they look even as they retire from the playing field to console themselves with knife and fork.

If the pressure of all these images has caused us to opt out of caring about how we look, that's a shame, because we're slaves of neither genes nor fashion in this matter. By losing weight and exercising, simply by making ourselves healthier, we can change the underlying data our looks report. The advantages are almost too obvious to mention, including lower medical costs, greater confidence, and a better quality of life in virtually every way.

There's no need to look like Brad Pitt or Jennifer Lopez, and no reason for women to pursue Olive Oyl[1] thinness (a body type men do not especially prefer). Researchers, in fact, have found that people of both sexes

---

[1]*Olive Oyl:* a cartoon character created in 1919 by Elzie Crisler Segar for his comic strip "Thimble Theater," which later was renamed "Popeye," to recognize the popularity of the sailor character featured in the comic strip. — EDS.

Despite wildly divergent public images, actresses Audrey Hepburn, in black, and Marilyn Monroe shared one thing: A waist/hip ration of 0.7.

tend to prefer averageness in members of the opposite sex: The greater the number of faces poured (by computer) into a composite, the higher it's scored in attractiveness by viewers. That's in part because "bad" features tend to be averaged out. But the implication is clear: You don't need to look like a movie star to benefit from a favorable appearance, unless, of course, you're planning a career in movies.

To a bizarre extent, looking good in America has become the province of an appearance aristocracy — an elect we revere for their seemingly unattainable endowment of good looks. Physical attractiveness has become too much associated with affluence and privilege for a country as democratically inclined as ours. We can be proud at least that these lucky lookers no longer have to be white or even young. Etcoff notes that, in tracking cosmetic surgery since the 1950s, the American Academy of Facial

Plastic and Reconstructive Surgery reports a change in styles toward wider, fuller-tipped noses and narrower eyelids, while makeup styles have tended toward fuller lips and less pale skin shades. She attributes these changes to the recalibration of beauty norms as the result of the presence of more Asian, African, and Hispanic features in society.

But what's needed is a much more radical democratization of physical beauty, a democratization we can achieve not by changing the definition of beauty but by changing ourselves. Looking nice is something we need to take back from the elites and make once again a broadly shared, everyday attribute, as it once was when people were much less likely to be fat and much more likely to dress decently in public. Good looks are not just an endowment, and the un-American attitude that looks are immune to self-improvement only breeds the kind of fatalism that is blessedly out of character in America.

As a first step, maybe we can stop pretending that our appearance   40
doesn't—or shouldn't—matter. A little more looksism, if it gets people to shape up, would probably save some lives, to say nothing of some marriages. Let's face it. To a greater extent than most of us are comfortable with, looks tell us something, and right now what they say about our health, our discipline, and our mutual regard isn't pretty.

The Reader's Presence

1. If, as Daniel Akst notes, humans are "hard-wired to respond to how people and objects look," why has society developed attitudes that consider beauty as "only skin deep"? How does the author explain this apparent inconsistency? Discuss why you agree or disagree with his explanation.

2. Note that Akst's essay on a common subject—the significance of good looks—relies on a number of scientific and professional studies. Make a list of the various disciplines that help provide Akst with evidence and support. For example, how does research in evolutionary biology contribute? How does economics contribute? What reports, if any, did you find either surprising or obvious, and why?

3. Read Akst's essay in conjunction with Daniel Harris's "Celebrity Bodies" (page 425) and Camille Paglia's "The Pitfalls of Plastic Surgery" (page 791). Explain how Harris and Paglia's responses to the subject of looks and beauty conform to Akst's. How do Harris and Paglia offer alternative insights into the topic? For example, how are Paglia's norms about beauty different from those Akst cites in his research? Which author do you agree with most on the significance of good looks, and why?

Akhil Reed Amar

Second Thoughts: What the Right to Bear Arms Really Means

Constitutional law scholar Akhil Reed Amar (b. 1958) is the Southmayd Professor of Law and Political Science at Yale University. He teaches constitutional law at both Yale College, from which he graduated in 1980, and Yale Law School, where he received his law degree in 1984. Before joining the Yale faculty in 1985, Amar served as law clerk to Stephen Breyer, who is now a Supreme Court Justice. He co-edited, with other noted experts, a leading constitutional law casebook, Process of Constitutional Decisionmaking: Cases and Materials *(2002), and has authored many law review articles and scholarly books, including* The Constitution and Criminal Procedure: First Principles *(1997);* For the People: What the Constitution Really Says About Your Rights *(1998), co-written with Alan Hirsch;* The Bill of Rights: Creation and Reconstruction *(1998); and his most recent book,* America's Constitution: A Biography *(2005). Amar's articles on constitutional issues have been published in the* New York Times, *the* Washington Post, *the* Los Angeles Times, *the* American Lawyer, Slate, *and the* New Republic, *where his essay "Second Thoughts: What the Right to Bear Arms Really Means" appeared in 1999. In another essay, titled "Rethinking Originalism" (2005), Amar jokes about the importance of context in analyzing the Second Amendment: "As I see it, text without context is empty. Constitutional interpretation heedless of enactment history becomes a pun-game: The right to 'bear arms' could mean no more than an entitlement to possess the stuffed forelimbs of grizzlies and Kodiaks."*

So what *does* the Second Amendment mean? A lot, says the National Rifle Association. Not much, say gun-control groups. Until recently, it didn't much matter who was right—on all but the mildest of measures, the NRA had the votes (and the cash), and that was that. Then came Littleton. Now proposals for serious federal gun controls are in the air. Thus far, the House and Senate have failed to agree on any specific gun measures, and whatever Congress ultimately decides in conference promises to be modest at best, targeting only gun shows and youngsters. But prominent politicians and civic leaders are now arguing for far more sweeping restrictions on guns, including mandatory licensing schemes and strict limits on the number of weapons that may be purchased in a single transaction. Would such measures violate the Constitution? Is the NRA right after all? No, but neither are its leading critics. Properly construed, the Second Amendment means quite a lot, but not what the NRA thinks.

Begin with the words of the amendment itself: "A well regulated militia being necessary to the security of a free state, the right of the people to keep and bear arms shall not be infringed." This curious syntax has perplexed most modern readers. How do the two main clauses with different subject-nouns fit together? Do these words guarantee a right of militias, as the second clause seems to say? In one corner, gun controllers embrace a narrow, statist reading, insisting that the amendment merely confers a right on state governments to establish professional state militias like the National Guard or local SWAT teams. No ordinary citizen is covered by the amendment in this view. In the other corner, gun owners and their supporters read the amendment in a broad, libertarian way, arguing that it protects a right of every individual to have guns for self-protection, for hunting, and even for sport. Virtually nothing having to do with personal weaponry is outside the amendment in this view. Both readings are wrong.

The statist reading sidesteps the obvious fact that the amendment's actual command language — "shall not be infringed" — appears in its second clause, which speaks of "the people" and not "the states." A quick look at the Tenth Amendment — which draws a sharp distinction between "the states" and "the people" — makes clear that these two phrases are not identical and that the Founders knew how to say "states" when they meant states. What's more, the eighteenth-century "militia" referred to by the first clause was not remotely like today's National Guard. It encompassed virtually all voters — somewhat like today's Swiss militia — rather than a small group of paid, semiprofessional volunteers.

But the libertarian reading must contend with textual embarrassments of its own. The amendment speaks of a right of "the people" collectively rather than a right of "persons" individually. And it uses a distinctly military phrase: "bear arms." A deer hunter or target shooter carries a gun but does not, strictly speaking, bear arms. The military connotation was even more obvious in an earlier draft of the amendment, which contained additional language that "no one religiously scrupulous of bearing arms shall be compelled to render military service in person." Even in the final version, note how the military phrase "bear arms" is sandwiched between a clause that talks about the "militia" and a clause (the Third Amendment) that regulates the quartering of "soldiers" in times of "war" and "peace." Likewise, state constitutions in place in 1789 consistently used the phrase "bear arms" in military contexts and no other.

By now it should be evident that we need to understand how all the words of the amendment fit together, and how they, in turn, mesh with other words in the Constitution. The amendment's syntax seems odd only because modern readers persistently misread the words "militia" and "people," imposing twentieth-century assumptions on an eighteenth-century text. The key subject-nouns were simply different ways of saying the same thing: at the Founding, the militia was the people and the people were the militia. Indeed, the earlier draft of the amendment linked the two clauses with linchpin language speaking of "a well regulated militia, composed of the body of the people." The linchpin was later pulled out as clumsy and redundant. A modern translation of the amendment might thus be: "An armed and militarily trained citizenry being conducive to freedom, the right of the electorate to organize itself militarily shall not be infringed."

Call this the communitarian reading as opposed to the statist and libertarian readings that dominate modern discourse. Statists anachronistically read the "militia" to mean the government (the paid professional officialdom) rather than the people (the ordinary citizenry). Equally anachronistically, libertarians read "the people" to mean atomized private persons, each hunting in his own private Idaho, rather than the citizenry acting collectively. But, when the Constitution speaks of "the people" rather than "persons," the collective connotation is primary. "We the People" in the preamble do ordain and establish the Constitution as public citizens meeting together in conventions and acting in concert, not as private individuals pursuing our respective hobbies. The only other reference to "the people" in the Philadelphia Constitution of 1787 appears a sentence away from the preamble, and here, too, the meaning is public and political, not private and individualistic. Every two years, "the people"—that is, the voters—elect the House. To see the key distinction another way, recall that women in 1787 had the rights of "persons" (such as freedom to worship and protections of privacy in their homes) but did not directly participate in the acts of "the people"—they did not vote in constitutional conventions or for Congress, nor were they part of the militia/people at the heart of the Second Amendment.

The rest of the Bill of Rights confirms this communitarian reading. The core of the First Amendment's assembly clause, which textually abuts the Second Amendment, is the right of "the people"—in essence, voters—to "assemble" in constitutional conventions and other political conclaves. So, too, the core rights retained and reserved to "the people" in the Ninth and Tenth Amendments were rights of the people collectively to govern themselves democratically. The Fourth Amendment is trickier: "The right of the people to be secure in their persons, houses, papers, and effects against unreasonable searches and seizures, shall not be violated." Here, the collective "people" wording is paired with more individualistic language of "persons." And these words obviously focus on the private domain, protecting individuals in their private homes more than in the public square. Why, then, did the Fourth Amendment use the words "the people" at all? Probably to highlight the role that jurors—acting collectively and representing the electorate—would play in deciding which searches were reasonable and how much to punish government officials who searched and seized improperly. An early draft of James Madison's amendment protecting jury rights helps make this linkage obvious and also resonates with the language of the Second Amendment: "[T]he trial by jury, as one of the best securities to the rights of the people, ought to remain inviolate." Note the obvious echoes here—"security" (Second Amendment), "secure" (Fourth Amendment), and "securities" (draft amendment); "shall not be infringed," "shall not be violated," and "ought to remain inviolate"; and, of course, "the right of the people" in all three places.

If we want an image of the people's militia at the Founding, we should think first of the militia's cousin, the jury. Like the militia, the jury was a local body countering imperial power—summoned by the government but standing outside it, representing the people, collectively. Like jury service, militia participation was both a right and a duty of qualified voters who were regularly summoned to discharge their public obligations. Like the jury, the militia was composed of amateurs arrayed against, and designed to check, permanent and professional government officials (judges and prosecutors, in the case of the jury; a standing army in the case of the militia). Like the jury, the militia embodied collective political action rather than private pursuits.

Founding history confirms this. The Framers envisioned Minutemen bearing guns, not Daniel Boone gunning bears. When we turn to state constitutions, we consistently find arms-bearing and militia clauses intertwined with rules governing standing armies, troop-quartering, martial law, and civilian supremacy. Libertarians cannot explain this clear pattern that has everything to do with the military and nothing to do with hunting. Conversely, statists make a hash of all these state constitutional provisions using language very similar to the Second Amendment to affirm rights *against* state governments.

Keeping the jury-militia analogy in mind, we can see the kernel of   10
truth in these competing accounts and also what's missing from each. Statists are right to see the amendment as localist and to note that law and government help bring the militia together. So, too, with the jury. Twelve private citizens who simply get together on their own to announce the guilt of a fellow citizen are not a lawful jury but a lynch mob. Similarly, private citizens who choose to own guns today are not a well-regulated militia of the people; they are gun clubs. But what the statist reading misses is that, when the law summons the citizenry together, these citizens act as the people *outside* of government, rather than as a professional and permanent government bureaucracy. A lynch mob is not a jury, but neither is the Occupational Safety and Health Administration. Likewise, the NRA and other gun clubs are not the militia, but neither is the National Guard. Libertarians rightly recoil at the authoritarianism of their opponents in the debate but wrongly privatize what is an inherently collective and political right. It is as if Ross Perot[1] insisted that the First Amendment guaranteed him the right to conduct his own poll and, on the basis of this private poll, to proclaim himself president.

But to see all this is to see what makes the Second Amendment so slippery today: the legal and social structure on which the amendment is built no longer exists. The Founders' juries—grand, petit, and civil—are still

---

[1]*Ross Perot:* (b. 1930) an American businessman from Texas, who founded Electronic Data Systems (EDS) in 1962. He sold EDS to General Motors in 1984, and founded Perot Systems in 1988. One of the wealthiest Americans, Perot is most widely known as a candidate for president of the United States in 1992 and 1996.—EDS.

around today, but the Founders' militia is not. America is not Switzerland. Voters no longer muster for militia practice in the town square.

Of course, we are free today to read the Second Amendment more broadly if we choose. Thoughtful legal scholars of all stripes—from Sanford Levinson on the left to Eugene Volokh on the right—have reminded us that other amendments have been read generously; why not the Second? But, given that a broad reading is a policy choice rather than a clear constitutional command, it must be functionally justified. And the mere fact that, say, the First Amendment has been read expansively is not an automatic argument for equal treatment for the Second. For example, violent felons, even while in prison and especially after their release, obviously have a First Amendment right to print their opinions in newspapers. Yet such felons have never had a Second Amendment right to own guns. Even the NRA accepts this double standard. But what underlies it? The obvious functional idea that sticks and stones and guns in the hands of dangerous felons can indeed hurt others in ways that their words cannot. Especially today's guns. At the Founding, single-fire muskets had certain attractive and democratic properties. A person had to get close to you to kill you, and, in getting close, he typically rendered himself vulnerable to counterattack. It took time to reload, and so one person could not kill dozens in a few seconds. One person, one gun, one shot was not as perfect a system of majority rule as one person, one vote, but the side with the most men often won; and, as lawyer Brent McIntosh emphasizes in a forthcoming [1999][2] essay in the *Alabama Law Review*, there was a rough proportionality of capacity to kill and be killed. Virtually all male citizens were trained in the use of weapons and had them handy. What's more, madmen were constrained by the strong social network of the well-regulated militia. Today, technological and social limits have been loosened, perhaps rendering madmen more dangerous.

So, if we seek broad readings of the amendment faithful to the core values of the Founding, here are a few that the NRA hasn't proposed but that are at least as plausible as their preferred broad readings:

Take the "mil" out of the militia. In highly sophisticated scholarship transcending the typical statist-versus-libertarian debate, Indiana law professor David Williams has emphasized how the militia bound citizens together in a common venture. It played an important social function in the community and embodied a democratic culture in which rich and poor citizens from all walks of life came together as equals—as with the jury. Without some forms of democratic glue, our culture risks flying apart, especially in today's world of increasing demographic diversity and specialization of labor. Thus, a broad modern reading of the amendment would

15

[2]Brent J. MacIntosh, "The Revolutionary Second Amendment," 51 (2000): 673. http://www.saf.org/LawReviews/McIntosh1.htm.—EDS.

call for compulsory or quasi-compulsory national service, with both military and nonmilitary alternatives, like Volunteers in Service to America or the Civilian Conservation Corps. (Recall that an early version of the amendment provided for compulsory military service with an opt-out for conscientious objectors.) Instead of bowling alone, Americans would band together, building a more solid base of social capital and civic virtue.

Create an Army that truly looks like America. At the Founding, a standing army in peacetime was viewed with dread and seen as the Other—mercenaries, convicts, vagrants, aliens—rather than ordinary citizens. Today, we view our professional Armed Forces with pride. These forces represent Us, not Them. As lawyer-journalist Alan Hirsch has noted, the Founders' militia has begun to morph into today's Army. If so, women and gays should play as equal a role as possible in today's institutions of collective self-defense. The militia celebrated by the Second Amendment should reflect the people, just as the jury should. To put the point another way, the Second Amendment says that voters should bear arms and that arms-bearers should vote. Since the Nineteenth Amendment has made women equal voters, the Second Amendment demands that they be given equal status in arms. (Allowing women to buy guns at the local Wal-Mart might make them equal in communitarian arms-bearing—it fails to include them on equal terms in modern America's militia-substitute.)

And what's true for women may also be true for gay men: the Armed Forces' discrimination on grounds of sexual orientation is, formally at least, discrimination on grounds of sex, in tension with this Nineteenth Amendment ideal. (If Leslie has sex with John, it is a form of sex discrimination to treat Leslie one way if she is a woman and a different way if he is a man.) Formal sex discriminations can be justified in some cases, but they should be closely interrogated. For example, separate bathrooms for men and women are, formally, a kind of sex discrimination, but this arrangement is widely seen as justified by legitimate privacy concerns. So, too, certain sex-based exclusions in military policy might be justifiable, where these exclusions reflect real physical differences relevant to modern warfare. But, where exclusions of women and gays are justified merely by the need to maintain "morale" and "unit cohesion," we should be wary: similar arguments were once used to maintain racial discrimination in our Armed Forces.

Rethink presidential power to use military force unilaterally. At the Founding, standing armies were feared as engines of executive despotism and military adventurism. If the president could simply command hired guns who would mindlessly obey, he would have less need to persuade his fellow citizens before pursuing risky policies. Thus, the Founders' reliance on a militia effectively decentralized and democratized decisions about whether and how to go to war. In a brilliant article in the May 1991 *University of Pennsylvania Law Review*, Harvard's Elaine Scarry argues that our modern military system has betrayed the values and vision of the Second Amendment. Today's Minuteman missiles, she suggests, are far less democratic than the Founders' Minuteman muskets.

These, then, are a few broad readings that in various ways try to stay true to the vision of the Founders' Second Amendment while also making modern sense. None of these readings is compelled, and all of them would require much more elaboration before they should be accepted.

But is there nothing to be said for the strong libertarian view? In fact,   20
there is a great deal to be said on behalf of an individual right to keep a gun in one's home for self-defense, as even Harvard Law School's Laurence Tribe—no pawn of the NRA—has publicly acknowledged of late. But the best constitutional arguments for this view come not from the Founding but from the Reconstruction some fourscore years later.

Even with regard to the Founding, it's simplistic to deny any link between collective self-protection and individual self-defense. Lawyer and legal scholar Don Kates reminds us that, somewhat like standing armies, roving bands of thugs and pirates posed a threat to law-abiding citizens, and a trusty musket in every home was indeed part of a system of community policing against predators. (Note that the amendment encompasses the right to "keep" as well as "bear" arms.) But this was not the main image of the Second Amendment at the Founding. Rather, the amendment was about Lexington and Concord and Bunker Hill. When arms were outlawed, only the king's men would have arms.

The amendments forged in the afterglow of the Revolution reflected obvious anxiety about a standing army controlled by the new imperial government and affection for the good old militia. But things looked different to Americans after a bloody Civil War. Massachusetts militiamen had once died for liberty at Bunker Hill, but more recently Mississippi militiamen had killed for slavery at Vicksburg. The imperial Redcoats at the Founding were villains, but the boys in blue who had won under Grant and Sherman were heroes—at least in the eyes of Reconstruction Republicans. And, when this generation took its turn rewriting the Constitution, it significantly recast the right to weapons. Textually, the Fourteenth Amendment proclaimed the need to protect fundamental "privileges" and "immunities" of citizens. The amendment explicitly limited state governments, but its authors made clear that no government, state or federal, had the right to violate fundamental rights of citizens. Although the Supreme Court ignored this language for almost a century, there are recent signs that suggest the justices may be willing to give this clause a second look.

And, if they do, gun groups would have reason to cheer. As scholars such as Stephen Halbrook, Michael Kent Curtis, Robert Cottrol, and Ray Diamond have documented in great detail, the framers of the Fourteenth

Amendment strongly believed in an individual right to own and keep guns in one's home for self-protection. Most obviously, blacks and Unionists down South could not always count on the local police to keep white night-riders at bay. When guns were outlawed, only Klansmen would have guns. Thus, the Reconstruction Congress made quite clear that a right to keep a gun at home for self-protection was indeed a constitutional right—a true "privilege" or "immunity" of citizens.

That's the good news for the NRA—with the even better news that, if the Court took this Reconstruction vision seriously, state and local governments would be limited along with federal officials. But the bad news, at least for the most ardent gun lovers, is that whatever Fourteenth Amendment right exists is a limited one. Virtually no one today is seriously arguing to take away all guns from homes. (And actually trying to do so would be a nightmare for anyone who cares about liberty and privacy, given that guns are stashed everywhere and may well outnumber people in America.) Instead, most proposals seek to regulate rather than prohibit—limiting the amount and type of ammunition, restricting the number of guns one can buy in a given week, and so on. Requiring registration of guns and even licenses with practical and book tests, on the model of licensing drivers, sends some gun lovers up the wall—the first step toward confiscation, they predict in dire tones. But this is hard to take seriously. The authors of the Second Amendment, after all, were perfectly comfortable knowing that the government would know who had guns—every voter—and also were perfectly comfortable requiring those who owned guns to be properly trained and monitored in their use. Realistic gun control today may not be exactly what the Framers had in mind when they said that the armed citizenry should be "well regulated." But— at least in a world that is so distant from the Founders—it's close enough.

The Reader's Presence

1. In paragraph 2, Akhil Reed Amar summarizes the "statist" and the "libertarian" readings of the Second Amendment to the U.S. Constitution. Summarize the particular points of reasoning that inform each interpretation." What specific terms does Amar use to characterize each? Amar ends the second paragraph by asserting: "Both readings are wrong. Summarize the main points he offers for his alternative reading of the Second Amendment, and then discuss the extent to which you find his analysis reasonable and convincing. How does Amar's own interpretation take into account "the kernel of truth [he sees] in these competing accounts and also what's missing from each" (paragraph 10)? Summarize— and then characterize—the relevance of his jury-militia analogy to his interpretation of the Second Amendment.

2. What do you notice about the syntax and tone in the opening paragraph of Amar's essay? What would you identify as the pivotal sentence in this paragraph? What changes in syntax and tone do you notice after this point? With what effect(s)? In the second sentence of his first paragraph Amar sets up a contrast between those who think that the second amendment means "A lot," and those who think that it means "Not much." What moves does Amar make in this paragraph in order to stake out a position between these two extremes? With what effect(s)? How might the structure of this opening paragraph be said to represent the structure for the rest of Amar's analysis of the different interpretations of the Second Amendment? Please be as specific as possible.

3. After you have settled into an understanding of Amar's interpretation of the Second Amendment—and especially his analysis of its phrasing—read Stephen Jay Gould's essay "Sex, Drugs, Disasters, and the Extinction of Dinosaurs" (page 417). Which essay do you think is more successful in making observations—and drawing reasonable inferences—about what Gould calls the failure "to separate fascinating claims" from the methods used to establish facts? Point to specific examples to support your responses. Explain why you think one writer is more successful in unpacking the distinctions others use to construct their analyses and arguments, what Gould calls "testable proposals," "intriguing ideas," and "useless speculation." Do you find Amar's or Gould's analysis more engaging and reasonable? Explain why.

Michael Bérubé

Analyze, Don't Summarize

Michael Bérubé, born in New York City in 1961, is the Paterno Family Professor in Literature at Pennsylvania State University, where he teaches literature and cultural studies or, as he calls it, "dangeral studies" for the controversy such studies engender. "I would be selling students short if my classes did not reflect some of my beliefs about literary theory, or feminism, or postmodernism, or multiculturalism, since I have spent my entire adult life studying such things," he told a reporter in 2006. Known for sparring with conservative critics of academia, Bérubé has become a noted advocate of "liberal" liberal education, a defender of the humanities, and "the professor the right loves to hate." His books include Marginal Forces/Cultural Centers: Tolson, Pynchon, and the Politics of the Canon *(1992);* Public Access: Literary Theory and American Cultural Politics *(1994); and* The Employment of English: Theory, Jobs, and the Future of Literary Studies *(1998). His 1996 book dealing with his son born with Down syndrome,* Life as We Know It: A Father, a Family, and an Exceptional Child *(1996), was a* New York Times Notable Book of the Year. *His most recent works are* What's Liberal About the Liberal Arts? Classroom Politics and "Bias" in Higher Education *(2006) and* Rhetorical Occasions: Essays on Humans and the Humanities *(2006). He has written articles for many publications, including* Harper's, *the* New Yorker, Dissent, *the* New York Times Magazine, *the* Village Voice, *the* Washington Post, *and the* Nation, *as well as numerous scholarly journals such as the* Chronicle of Higher Education, *where his essay, "Analyze, Don't Summarize," appeared in 2004.*

The first time a student asked me about my "grading system," I was nonplused—and a bit intimidated. It was an innocent question, but I heard it as a challenge: I was a 25-year-old graduate student teaching my first section in an English-literature class at the University of Virginia, and I really didn't know *what* my grading system was. Nor did I feel comfortable saying, "Well, it's like Justice Stewart's definition of pornography, really—I simply know an A paper when I see one."

I fumbled my way through a reply, but I was unsettled enough by the exchange to seek the advice of the professor in charge of the course (and roughly a dozen teaching assistants). He went on a sublime rant that I've never forgotten, though I'm sure I've embellished it over the years. "These students come in here," he fumed, "with the idea that *you* have to explain yourself. 'You gave me a B-plus,' they say. 'What did you take points off for?' I tell them, 'Your paper was not born with an A. Your paper was born with a "nothing," and I made up my mind about it as I read it. That's what the marginalia are—they're the record of my responses to your arguments.'"

Today I've incorporated versions of that rant into my own teaching handouts: I try to explain the differences among superior, mediocre, and failing papers, and I tell students that my skills as a reader have been honed by my many experiences with professional editors, who attend carefully to paragraph transitions, dangling modifiers, and inaccurate citations. But I've never been able to give my students a visceral idea of what goes through my head as I read their work—until now.

Like many sports fans, I've grown a bit tired of ESPN's 25th-anniversary hyper-self-awareness of itself as a sports medium. While it's great to see the network poke fun at its early years, when its anchors wore dorky sport coats and weren't always sure when they were on the air, it's really quite tedious to be reminded of how sports-television hype helped hype TV sports.

The show *Around the Horn* has come to epitomize the general decline to me. Another half-hour program with which it's paired, *Pardon*   5 *the Interruption*, gives us two volatile, opinionated sportscasters disagreeing with each other in rapid-fire fashion, with but a handful of seconds devoted to each topic. *Around the Horn* takes that format and makes a game show of it, offering us sportswriters competing for whose commentary will "win" by the end of the show.

I still play an organized sport — ice hockey — and as an amateur (and aged) player, I have to say that sports talk shows like this make me wonder whether some people don't see sports as simply an opportunity for endless metacommentary . . . and, of course, as gainful employment for an entire entourage of chattering parasites. In all that noise, I think, where are the games themselves?

Imagine my surprise, then, when I watched *Around the Horn* one afternoon and realized that here, at last, was my grading system in practice.

The idea behind *Around the Horn* is simple. There are a host and four contestants, each of whom speaks briefly on a series of up-to-the-moment sports topics. Points are awarded for smart — or merely plausible — remarks, and points are deducted for obviously foolish or factually inaccurate ones. There's a mute button involved, too, and players get eliminated as the show progresses (but those aspects of the game, so far as I can tell, have no counterpart in the world of paper-grading). And — of course, for this is the point of all such sports metacommentary — the viewers at home get to disagree with and complain about the commentary, as well as the officiating.

My standard undergraduate survey-course guides for paper-writing tells students things like this: "Assume a hypothetical readership composed of people who have already read the book. That means you shouldn't say, 'In class, we discussed the importance of the clam chowder in Chapter Five.' But more important, it means *you don't have to summarize the novel.* We're your readers, and we've read the book. However, we haven't read it in quite the way *you're* reading it. We haven't focused on the same scenes and passages you're bringing to our attention, and we haven't yet seen how your argument might make sense of the book for us."

But not all of my students see the point. Every semester I'm approached   10
by some who don't quite understand why they're being asked to make an *argument* out of literary criticism. Why shouldn't they simply record their impressions of the works before them? When I tell them that an observation is not a thesis, and that their thesis isn't sufficiently specific or useful if they can't imagine anyone plausibly disagreeing with it, they ask me why they can't simply explain *what happens in the novel.*

But in what world, exactly, would such an enterprise count as analysis? Not in any world I know — not even in the ephemeral pop-culture world of sports metacommentary. Can you imagine someone showing up on *Around the Horn* and saying to host Tony Reali, "Well, Tony, let me point out that last night, the Red Sox swept the Tigers and crept to within three games of the Yankees."

"And?"

"And nothing. I'm just pointing out that the Sox won, 3–1, on a four-hitter by Schilling, while the Yanks blew another late-inning lead."

No one does that, because no one in the sports world confuses summaries with analyses.

I also tell students that an essay of 2,000 words doesn't give them all   15
that much space to get going.

"You've only got a few pages to make that argument of yours. You don't need a grand introductory paragraph that begins, 'Mark Twain is one of Earth's greatest writers.' It's far better to start by giving us some idea of what you'll be arguing and why. If you like, you can even begin by pointing us to a particularly important passage that will serve as the springboard for your larger discussion: 'Not long after the second scaffold scene in *The Scarlet Letter*, when Arthur Dimmesdale joins hands with Hester Prynne and her daughter Pearl, Nathaniel Hawthorne asks us to reconsider the meaning of the scarlet A on Hester's breast.'"

On *Around the Horn*, commentators have to make their points in 15 seconds, which, as people who know me can testify, just happens to be roughly the amount of time it takes me to utter 2,000 words. So here, too, the analogy holds up.

Seriously, the sports-talk analogy is useful simply as a handy way of distinguishing between summary and analysis—and, more important, as an illustration of what happens in my grading process when a student paper cites textual evidence so compelling and unusual that it makes me go back and reread the passage in question (good!), suggests that a novel's conclusion fails to resolve the questions and tensions raised by the rest of the narrative (interesting!—possibly good, depending on the novel we're talking about), or makes claims that are directly contradicted by the literary text itself (bad! the mute button for you!).

So in a sense, I do "take off" points as I go—but then I add them back on as well, sentence by sentence, paragraph by paragraph, as I weigh the claims my students advance and the means by which they advance them.

The rules for literary analysis are the same rules in play for any kind   20
of analysis: mastery of the material. Cogency of supporting evidence. Ability to imagine and rebut salient counterarguments. Extra points for wit and style, points off for mind-numbing clichés, and permanent suspension for borrowing someone else's argument without proper attribution.

And yet, every year, I'm left with a handful of students who tell me that if *that's* what I want, I should simply assign topics to each student. "Not a chance," I reply. "Most of the mental labor of your paper takes place when you try to figure out just what you want to argue and why." As books like Thomas McLaughlin's *Street Smarts and Critical Theory* and Gerald Graff's *Clueless in Academe* have argued (with wit and style), students seem to understand this principle perfectly well when it comes to music, sports, and popular culture. It's our job to show them how it might apply to the study of literature.

My students, too, are often suspicious of what they regard as an idiosyncratic and a subjective enterprise that varies from English professor to English professor. But I can tell them there's really nothing mysterious about its mechanics. In fact, if they want to watch it in action, they can tune in to ESPN any weekday afternoon, 5 p.m. Eastern.

The Reader's Presence

1. Michael Bérubé creates an analogy between grading student essays and watching sports commentary on ESPN. Outline the points of similarity between an instructor's responding to student writing and a television commentator's comments about sports. Which aspects of this analogy do you find most—and least—convincing? What aspects of this analogy, if any, has Bérubé omitted? Summarize the distinctions Bérubé draws between "analysis" and "summary." What is the significance of Bérubé's point that "an observation is not a thesis" (paragraph 10)?

2. In paragraph 21, Bérubé notes, "As books like Thomas McLaughlin's *Street Smarts and Critical Theory* and Gerald Graff's *Clueless in Academe* have argued (with wit and style), students seem to understand this principle perfectly well when it comes to music, sports, and popular culture." Explain the extent to which you agree—or disagree—with Bérubé's assertion here. What evidence can you point to in support of—or to argue against—the spirit and substance of Bérubé's claim?

3. As you reread Bérubé's essay, what are the specific words and phrases that you think most accurately and effectively characterize his tone toward grading student essays? Toward television commentators on sports? What do you notice about Bérubé's choice of adjectives and verbs? What are his attitudes toward what he calls "marginalia" (paragraph 2)? What do you understand him to mean when he talks about "sports as simply an opportunity for metacommentary" (paragraph 6)? Comment on the effectiveness of his use of "entourage" in the phrase "an entire entourage of chattering parasites" (paragraph 6). Examine carefully Bérubé's "rules for literary analysis" in paragraph 20. Apply these criteria to the strengths and weaknesses of his essay. Which of these rules does his essay most—and least—effectively illustrate? Please be as specific as possible in your response.

4. In his essay "Politics and the English Language," George Orwell observes: "Modern English, especially written English, is full of bad habits which spread by imitation and which can be avoided if one is willing to take the necessary trouble" (paragraph 2, page 510). Orwell proceeds to list—and then illustrate and analyze—six rules

for writing good prose. Compare and contrast Orwell's and
Bérubé's rules of writing. Based on these rules, which writer practices his craft more effectively? Explain why, and support your response with detailed analyses of each writer's prose.

David Brooks

People Like Us

*David Brooks (b. 1961) was born in Toronto and grew up in New York City
and in a suburb of Philadelphia. A journalist, columnist, and self-described "comic
sociologist," Brooks has authored two books of cultural commentary,* Bobos in
Paradise *(2001) and* On Paradise Drive: How We Live Now (and Always Have)
in the Future Tense *(2004), and he edited the anthology* Backward and Upward:
The New Conservative Writing *(1995). After graduating from the University of
Chicago, Brooks worked as a reporter for the* Wall Street Journal. *Since that time,
he has served as a senior editor at the* Weekly Standard *and as a contributing
editor at the* Atlantic *and* Newsweek, *where the managing editor praised his
"dead-on eye for the foibles of the Beltway—and his strong sense of how what
happens in the capital's conservative circles affects the rest of the country."
Brooks presents commentary on* National Public Radio *and on* The Newshour
with Jim Lehrer. *In 2003 he joined the* New York Times *as an op-ed columnist.*

*In a PBS interview in 2000, Brooks argued that people tend to gravitate to
like-minded, like-cultured people—a "congealing pot" of people just like themselves: "Now if you look at the* New York Times *wedding page, it's this great
clash of résumés. . . . Harvard marries Yale. Princeton marries Stanford. Magna
cum laude marries magna cum laude. You never get a magna cum laude marrying
a summa cum laude because the tensions would be too great in that wedding."
"People Like Us" first appeared in the* Atlantic *in 2003.*

Maybe it's time to admit the obvious. We don't really care about diversity all that much in America, even though we talk about it a great
deal. Maybe somewhere in this country there is a truly diverse neighborhood in which a black Pentecostal minister lives next to a white anti-
globalization activist, who lives next to an Asian short-order cook, who
lives next to a professional golfer, who lives next to a postmodern-literature
professor and a cardiovascular surgeon. But I have never been to or heard
of that neighborhood. Instead, what I have seen all around the country is

people making strenuous efforts to group themselves with people who are basically like themselves.

Human beings are capable of drawing amazingly subtle social distinctions and then shaping their lives around them. In the Washington, D.C., area Democratic lawyers tend to live in suburban Maryland, and Republican lawyers tend to live in suburban Virginia. If you asked a Democratic lawyer to move from her $750,000 house in Bethesda, Maryland, to a $750,000 house in Great Falls, Virginia, she'd look at you as if you had just asked her to buy a pickup truck with a gun rack and to shove chewing tobacco in her kid's mouth. In Manhattan the owner of a $3 million SoHo loft would feel out of place moving into a $3 million Fifth Avenue apartment. A West Hollywood interior decorator would feel dislocated if you asked him to move to Orange County. In Georgia a barista from Athens would probably not fit in serving coffee in Americus.

It is a common complaint that every place is starting to look the same. But in the information age, the late writer James Chapin once told me, every place becomes more like itself. People are less often tied down to factories and mills, and they can search for places to live on the basis of cultural affinity. Once they find a town in which people share their values, they flock there, and reinforce whatever was distinctive about the town in the first place. Once Boulder, Colorado, became known as congenial to politically progressive mountain bikers, half the politically progressive mountain bikers in the country (it seems) moved there; they made the place so culturally pure that it has become practically a parody of itself.

But people love it. Make no mistake—we are increasing our happiness by segmenting off so rigorously. We are finding places where we are comfortable and where we feel we can flourish. But the choices we make toward that end lead to the very opposite of diversity. The United States might be a diverse nation when considered as a whole, but block by block and institution by institution it is a relatively homogeneous nation.

When we use the word "diversity" today we usually mean racial integration. But even here our good intentions seem to have run into the brick wall of human nature. Over the past generation reformers have tried heroically, and in many cases successfully, to end housing discrimination. But recent patterns aren't encouraging: according to an analysis of the 2000 census data, the 1990s saw only a slight increase in the racial integration of neighborhoods in the United States. The number of middle-class and upper-middle-class African-American families is rising, but for whatever reasons—racism, psychological comfort—these families tend to congregate in predominantly black neighborhoods.

In fact, evidence suggests that some neighborhoods become more segregated over time. New suburbs in Arizona and Nevada, for example, start out reasonably well integrated. These neighborhoods don't yet have reputations, so people choose their houses for other, mostly economic reasons. But as neighborhoods age, they develop personalities (that's where the Asians live, and that's where the Hispanics live), and segmentation occurs. It could be that in a few years the new suburbs in the Southwest will be nearly as segregated as the established ones in the Northeast and the Midwest.

Even though race and ethnicity run deep in American society, we should in theory be able to find areas that are at least culturally diverse. But here, too, people show few signs of being truly interested in building diverse communities. If you run a retail company and you're thinking of opening new stores, you can choose among dozens of consulting firms that are quite effective at locating your potential customers. They can do this because people with similar tastes and preferences tend to congregate by ZIP code.

The most famous of these precision marketing firms is Claritas, which breaks down the U.S. population into sixty-two psycho-demographic clusters, based on such factors as how much money people make, what they like to read and watch, and what products they have bought in the past. For example, the "suburban sprawl" cluster is composed of young families making about $41,000 a year and living in fast-growing places such as Burnsville, Minnesota, and Bensalem, Pennsylvania. These people are almost twice as likely as other Americans to have three-way calling. They are two and a half times as likely to buy Light n' Lively Kid Yogurt. Members of the "towns & gowns" cluster are recent college graduates in places such as Berkeley, California, and Gainesville, Florida. They are big consumers of DoveBars and *Saturday Night Live*. They tend to drive small foreign cars and to read *Rolling Stone* and *Scientific American*.

Looking through the market research, one can sometimes be amazed by how efficiently people cluster—and by how predictable we all are. If you wanted to sell imported wine, obviously you would have to find places where rich people live. But did you know that the sixteen counties with the greatest proportion of imported-wine drinkers are all in the same three metropolitan areas (New York, San Francisco, and Washington, D.C.)? If you tried to open a motor-home dealership in Montgomery County, Pennsylvania, you'd probably go broke, because people in this ring of the Philadelphia suburbs think RVs are kind of uncool. But if you traveled just a short way north, to Monroe County, Pennsylvania, you would find yourself in the fifth motor-home-friendliest county in America.

Geography is not the only way we find ourselves divided from people   10
unlike us. Some of us watch Fox News, while others listen to NPR. Some like David Letterman, and others—typically in less urban neighborhoods— like Jay Leno. Some go to charismatic churches; some go to mainstream churches. Americans tend more and more often to marry people with education levels similar to their own, and to befriend people with backgrounds similar to their own.

My favorite illustration of this latter pattern comes from the first, noncontroversial chapter of *The Bell Curve*. Think of your twelve closest friends, Richard J. Herrnstein and Charles Murray write. If you had chosen them randomly from the American population, the odds that half of your twelve closest friends would be college graduates would be six in a thousand. The odds that half of the twelve would have advanced degrees would be less than one in a million. Have any of your twelve closest friends graduated from Harvard, Stanford, Yale, Princeton, Caltech, MIT, Duke, Dartmouth, Cornell, Columbia, Chicago, or Brown? If you chose your friends randomly from the American population, the odds against your having four or more friends from those schools would be more than a billion to one.

Many of us live in absurdly unlikely groupings, because we have organized our lives that way.

It's striking that the institutions that talk the most about diversity often practice it the least. For example, no group of people sings the diversity anthem more frequently and fervently than administrators at just such elite universities. But elite universities are amazingly undiverse in their values, politics, and mores. Professors in particular are drawn from a rather narrow segment of the population. If faculties reflected the general population, 32 percent of professors would be registered Democrats and 31 percent would be registered Republicans. Forty percent would be evangelical Christians. But a recent study of several universities by the conservative Center for the Study of Popular Culture and the American Enterprise Institute found that roughly 90 percent of those professors in the arts and sciences who had registered with a political party had registered Democratic. Fifty-seven professors at Brown were found on the voter-registration rolls. Of those, fifty-four were Democrats. Of the forty-two professors in the English, history, sociology, and political-science departments, all were Democrats. The results at Harvard, Penn State, Maryland, and the University of California at Santa Barbara were similar to the results at Brown.

What we are looking at here is human nature. People want to be around others who are roughly like themselves. That's called community. It probably would be psychologically difficult for most Brown professors to share an office with someone who was pro-life, a member of the National Rifle Association, or an evangelical Christian. It's likely that hiring committees would subtly—even unconsciously—screen out any such people they encountered. Republicans and evangelical Christians have sensed that they are not welcome at places like Brown, so they don't even consider working there. In fact, any registered Republican who contemplates a career in academia these days is both a hero and a fool. So, in a semi–self-selective pattern, brainy people with generally liberal social mores flow to academia, and brainy people with generally conservative mores flow elsewhere.

The dream of diversity is like the dream of equality. Both are based   15
on ideals we celebrate even as we undermine them daily. (How many times have you seen someone renounce a high-paying job or pull his child from an elite college on the grounds that these things are bad for equality?) On

the one hand, the situation is appalling. It is appalling that Americans know so little about one another. It is appalling that many of us are so narrow-minded that we can't tolerate a few people with ideas significantly different from our own. It's appalling that evangelical Christians are practically absent from entire professions, such as academia, the media, and filmmaking. It's appalling that people should be content to cut themselves off from everyone unlike themselves.

The segmentation of society means that often we don't even have arguments across the political divide. Within their little validating communities, liberals and conservatives circulate half-truths about the supposed awfulness of the other side. These distortions are believed because it feels good to believe them.

On the other hand, there are limits to how diverse any community can or should be. I've come to think that it is not useful to try to hammer diversity into every neighborhood and institution in the United States. Sure, Augusta National should probably admit women, and university sociology departments should probably hire a conservative or two. It would be nice if all neighborhoods had a good mixture of ethnicities. But human nature being what it is, most places and institutions are going to remain culturally homogeneous.

It's probably better to think about diverse lives, not diverse institutions. Human beings, if they are to live well, will have to move through a series of institutions and environments, which may be individually homogeneous but, taken together, will offer diverse experiences. It might also be a good idea to make national service a rite of passage for young people in this country: it would take them out of their narrow neighborhood segment and thrust them in with people unlike themselves. Finally, it's probably important for adults to get out of their own familiar circles. If you live in a coastal, socially liberal neighborhood, maybe you should take out a subscription to *The Door*, the evangelical humor magazine; or maybe you should visit Branson, Missouri. Maybe you should stop in at a megachurch. Sure, it would be superficial familiarity, but it beats the iron curtains that now separate the nation's various cultural zones.

Look around at your daily life. Are you really in touch with the broad diversity of American life? Do you care?

The Reader's Presence

1. Brooks begins his argument by "admit[ting] the obvious": Americans don't care about diversity, they just like to talk as if they do. What was your initial reaction to Brooks's so-called admission? What is the effect of admitting something that many of his readers will instinctually reject? How is your opinion affected by his evidence? How well has he supported this assertion by the end of the essay?

2. Brooks claims that it is human nature for people to group together with those who have similar ideals and backgrounds. What might be the advantages of such grouping? What might be lost if Americans were truly integrated? What is lost by segregating by religion, politics, race, class, profession, and sexuality?

3. Compare Brooks's observations about how we prefer to be around "people who are basically like themselves" to E. B. White's classic essay "Once More to the Lake" (page 270). In what ways can Brooks's point play a factor in an evaluation of White's essay, which was written decades earlier? In what ways does White's lake community support Brooks's perspective on diversity? For a more direct comparison of ideas, compare Brooks's essay with Walter Benn Michaels's "The Trouble with Diversity" (page 766). After reading each selection closely, list the points both writers agree on and those they don't. What major differences do you see between the conclusions each writer reaches?

Stephen Budiansky

The Physics of Gridlock

Author, historian, and journalist Stephen Budiansky (b. 1957) has written extensively on science and the natural world, and on military history and foreign affairs. Budiansky studied chemistry at Yale University and applied mathematics at Harvard University, where he received his masters in applied mathematics in 1979. As a journalist, he was national security correspondent, deputy editor, and foreign editor of U.S. News & World Report *and Washington editor of the international scientific journal* Nature. *Budiansky is currently a correspondent for the* Atlantic Monthly *and has written on a broad range of topics for the* New York Times, *the* Washington Post, *and the* Wall Street Journal. *Early in his career, Budiansky was a congressional fellow at the U.S. Congress Office of Technology Assessment, where he co-authored a classified study on the future role of "smart" weapons technology in warfare. Today, Budiansky is a noted military historian, specializing in cryptology (the study of ciphers and codes), he is a member of the editorial board of* Cryptologia, *and he serves on the usage panel of the* American Heritage Dictionary. *His books include* Battle of Wits: The Complete Story of Codebreaking in World War II *(2000),* Air Power: The Men, Machines, and Ideas that Revolutionized War, from Kitty Hawk to Gulf War II *(2004),* Her Majesty's Spymaster: Elizabeth I, Sir Francis Walsingham, and the Birth of Modern Espionage *(2005), and* The Bloody Shirt: Terror After Appomattox *(2008). Though he says he wasn't even allowed to have a pet frog as a child, his interest in animal behavior and the bond between humans and animals are the source for several books, including,* The Covenant of the Wild *(2002),* The Nature of Horses *(1997),* If a Lion Could Talk *(1998),* The Truth about Dogs *(2000), and* The Character of Cats *(2002). His essay, "The Physics of Gridlock," appeared in the* Atlantic *in 2000.*

Bertrand Russell[1] once observed that animal behaviorists studying the problem-solving abilities of chimpanzees consistently seemed to detect in their experimental subjects the "national characteristics" of the scientists themselves. A divergence in the findings of the practical-minded Americans and the theoretically inclined Germans was particularly apparent.

> Animals studied by Americans rush about frantically, with an incredible display of hustle and pep, and at last achieve the desired result by chance. Animals observed by Germans sit still and think, and at last evolve the solution out of their inner consciousness.

In science, Germans tend to come up with things like the uncertainty principle. Americans tend to come up with things like the atomic bomb.

The latest field to host this conflict of national styles is one that seems at first glance to offer little prospect of a sporting contest. Bigger and better highways are as American as fast-food restaurants and sport utility vehicles, and when it comes to making the crooked straight and the rough places plain, the practicality of American traffic engineers is hard to argue with. As an American academic discipline, traffic engineering is centered in civil-engineering departments, and civil engineers tend to believe in solving problems by going at them head on. A recent study funded by nine state departments of transportation to examine the doubling in congestion on urban highways and primary roads that has occurred over the past two decades listed in its final report various ways that traffic engineers have tried to alleviate the problem. These included "add road space" and "lower the number of vehicles." This would not, as the saying goes, appear to be rocket science.

Even when American traffic engineers have ventured closer to rocket science, with computer simulations of traffic flow on multi-lane highways, the results have tended to reinforce the American reputation for practicality and level-headedness. The mathematical and computer models indicate that when traffic jams occur, they are the result of bottlenecks (merging lanes, bad curves, accidents), which constrict flow. Find a way to eliminate the bottlenecks and flow will be restored.

Such was the happy, practical, and deterministic state of affairs up until a few years ago, when several German theoretical physicists began

---

[1]*Russell:* (1872–1970) A British philosopher, historian, logician, mathematician, advocate for social reform, and pacifist. — EDS.

publishing papers on traffic flow in *Physical Review Letters*, *Journal of Physics*, *Nature*, and other publications not normally read by civil engineers. The Germans had noticed that if one simulated the movement of cars and trucks on a highway using the well-established equations that describe how the molecules of gas move, some distinctly eerie results emerged. Cars do not behave exactly like gas molecules, to be sure: for example, drivers try to avoid collisions by slowing down when they get too near another car, whereas gas molecules have no such aversion. But the physicists added some terms to the equations to take the differences into account, and the overall description of traffic as a flowing gas has proved to be a very good one. The moving-gas model of traffic reproduces many phenomena seen in real-world traffic. When a flowing gas encounters a bottleneck, for example, it becomes compressed as the molecules suddenly crowd together—and that compression travels back through the stream of oncoming gas as a shock wave. That is precisely analogous to the well-known slowing and queuing of cars behind a traffic bottleneck: as cars slow at the obstruction, cars behind them slow too, which causes a wave of stop-and-go movement to be transmitted "upstream" along the highway.

The eeriest thing that came out of these equations, however, was the implication that traffic congestion can arise completely spontaneously under certain circumstances. No bottlenecks or other external causes are necessary. Traffic can be flowing freely along, at a density still well below what the road can handle, and then suddenly gel into a slow-moving ooze. Under the right conditions a small, brief, and local fluctuation in the speed or spacing of cars—the sort of fluctuation that happens all the time just by chance on a busy highway—is all it takes to trigger a system-wide breakdown that persists for hours after the blip that triggered it is gone. In fact, the Germans' analysis suggested, such spontaneous breakdowns in traffic flow probably occur quite frequently on highways.

Though a decidedly unnerving discovery, this was very much of a piece with the results of mathematical models of many physical and biological systems that exhibit the phenomena popularized under the heading "chaos theory." In any complex interacting system with many parts, each of which affects the others, tiny fluctuations can grow in huge but unpredictable ways. Scientists refer to those as nonlinear phenomena—phenomena in which seemingly negligible changes in one variable can have disproportionately great consequences. Nonlinear properties have been discovered in the mathematical equations that describe weather, chemical reactions, and populations of biological organisms. Some combinations of variables for these equations give rise to sudden "phase shifts," in which the solution to the equation jumps abruptly from one value to another; others set off truly chaotic situations in which for a time the solution to the equation fluctuates wildly and without any seeming pattern, and then suddenly calms down.

Such mathematical discoveries do seem to be borne out in the real world. Biological populations often exhibit erratic booms and busts that cannot be explained by any external cause. Long-term weather patterns defy prediction by the most powerful supercomputers. And a whole class of chemical reactions has been discovered in which the chemicals do not merely react and create a product, as they did in high school chemistry class, but oscillate back and forth between reactants and products. (Some especially nice ones cause color changes in the solution, so you can sit there and watch the stuff in the beaker go back and forth every few seconds.) The consistent story in all these discoveries is that the components of the system and their interactions *themselves* — rather than any external cause — give rise to the nonlinear behavior of the system as a whole. A rough analogy is a dozen dogs standing on a water bed. If one dog moves, he starts the bed sloshing around, which causes another dog to lose his balance and shift his weight, which sets up another wave of disturbance, until true chaos is reached.

In the case of traffic, the German physicists — principally Dirk Helbing and Boris Kerner, of Stuttgart — found that given a certain combination of vehicle density and vehicle flow rate along a highway, the solution to their equations undergoes a sudden phase shift from freely moving traffic to what they call "synchronized traffic." Cars in all lanes abruptly slow down and start moving at the same speed as the cars in adjacent lanes, which makes passing impossible and can cause the whole system to jam up for hours.

In the traditional picture of traffic flow and congestion, the number of cars per minute that pass a given point on the highway at first steadily increases as the density of cars on the highway increases. (As long as everything keeps moving freely, the more cars there are on a mile of highway, the more flow by per minute.) Eventually, however, further increases in density will cause a decrease in flow, as drivers begin braking to maintain a safe distance from the cars in front of them. A graph of flow versus density thus forms an inverted *V* shape. The uphill side corresponds to free flow, the downhill to congested flow. The Germans found, in effect, that under the right (or, rather, wrong) circumstances the solution to the equations can tunnel right through this hill without ever reaching the top, jumping from a state of (submaximal) free flow straight to congestion.

Such a leap from one state to another is like what happens when a chemical substance changes phase from vapor to liquid. It often happens that water in a cloud remains in the gas phase even after temperature and density have reached the point where it could condense into water droplets. Only when a speck of dust happens along, providing a surface on which condensation can take place (a "condensation nucleus"), does the transition finally occur. Helbing and Kerner basically found that free flow

10

and synchronized flow can occur under the same conditions, and that under such "metastable" conditions a small fluctuation in traffic density can act as the speck of dust causing the shift from one to the other.

Worse, they found that it is easier to start a traffic jam than to stop one. The phase shifts they discovered exhibit what is known in the terminology of nonlinear phenomena as *hysteresis*. That is, a small and transient increase in, say, the number of cars entering a highway from a ramp can trigger a breakdown in flow, but even after the on-ramp traffic drops to its original level (in fact, even after it drops well below its original level), the traffic jam persists. Looking at actual data recorded by sensors on Dutch and German highways, the physicists found apparent examples of this phenomenon in action, in which a sluggish synchronized flow came on suddenly and persisted for hours, even after the density of traffic had dropped.

If breakdowns in flow can result from such small and random fluctuations, then the world is a very different place from the one that most traffic engineers are accustomed to. The very notion of maximum capacity for a highway is called into question, because even at traffic densities well below what a highway is designed to handle, jams can spontaneously arise. "If this flow breakdown can take place just anywhere," says James Banks, a professor of civil and environmental engineering at San Diego State University, "then we're in trouble, because there's a lot more potential for congested traffic than we thought was the case. And it makes a control strategy much more difficult."

For example, it may not be enough simply to limit the rate at which cars are allowed to enter a highway, as is now done on some congested freeways; rather, it may be necessary to time each car's entry precisely to coincide with a transient drop in density along the main road, thus aiming to smooth out the fluctuations that can trigger a phase shift. There may even be situations in which widening roads or "metering" on-ramp flow could backfire, making flow breakdowns more likely. Preventing flow breakdowns in a nonlinear, chaotic world could ultimately require realizing an Orwellian idea that has been suggested from time to time: directly controlling the speed and spacing of individual cars along a highway with central computers and sensors that communicate with each car's engine and brake controls.

To say that not all American traffic engineers like these discoveries in chaos theory and their implications for traffic is an understatement. Banks acknowledges that there has been a strong, almost visceral, reaction against the Germans' conclusion, because of its assault on rational determinism and common sense, and also on what might be termed culture-of-science grounds. "Scientists and engineers are human beings," he says, "and the first reaction is, These guys are not only physicists — they also have a knack for getting themselves in the press. So right away there's an envy factor: Who do these guys think they are?" It doesn't help that the German theoreticians' papers are very difficult to understand. "They're written in such a way that those of us who aren't physicists never know if it's their English, or whether they're using physics jargon, or whether they just don't make sense," Banks says.

The Americans also question how well the Germans' theoretical results   15
relate to traffic in the real world. All mathematical models involve assumptions, and just because a model re-creates certain real-world phenomena doesn't mean it accurately reflects reality in toto; there is always the possibility that the weird properties of the equations are artifacts of the model itself and its assumptions. The Germans' theory "is one plausible description," says Carroll Messer, a research engineer at Texas A&M University, using words that are obviously chosen carefully, "but that's not saying it's been verified." Indeed, some American researchers have questioned whether elaborate chaos-theory interpretations are needed at all, since at least some of the traffic phenomena the Germans' theories predict seem to be much like things that have been appearing in the traffic-engineering literature under other names for years, and these have straightforward cause-and-effect explanations. Banks published a paper in 1999 pointing out that data from monitors that record how many cars pass a fixed point—the sort of data the Germans obtained from Dutch and German highways, which they say verify their predictions—often fail to capture the complete picture of what is happening on the road. He suggests that the behavior of drivers may in fact offer a simpler explanation for the phase shifts and other nonlinear features of the Germans' theoretical models. A sudden slowdown in traffic may have less to do with chaos theory and self-organizing phenomena of systems than with driver psychology. Synchronized flow, for example, has appeared in American traffic literature for decades, under the name "speed sympathy," and Banks says it often happens as traffic gets heavier simply because of the way individual drivers react to changing conditions. As the passing lane gets more crowded, aggressive drivers move to other lanes to try to pass, which also tends to homogenize the speed between lanes. Another leveling force is that when a driver in a fast lane brakes a bit to maintain a safe distance, the shock wave travels back much more rapidly than it would in other lanes, because each following driver has to react more quickly. So as a road becomes congested, the faster-moving traffic is the first to slow down.

Thus many American traffic engineers insist that when breakdowns in flow occur for no apparent reason, it is only because no one has looked hard enough to find the reason, which could be anything from a bad stretch of pavement to a deer running across the road. Much work is now under way on both sides of the Atlantic on a "theory of bottlenecks" that may help to settle the matter.

Even if traffic engineers manage to slay the mathematical bogeyman that theoretical physics and chaos theory have unleashed, another bogeyman may be lurking nearby. It turns out that the properties collectively exhibited by large numbers of cars moving over a network of roadways have many mathematical features in common with the behavior of other things that flow over networks, such as data carried by telephone lines and the Internet. The mathematics of networks is a well-studied topic in communications research, and a recent paper draws on this body of theory to establish an interesting paradox about the flow of vehicular traffic: adding a new road segment to an existing network of roadways can under certain circumstances reduce the car-carrying capacity of the network as a whole. The safest advice for budding engineers may be, If you want determinacy, stick to something simple—like rockets or atomic bombs.

The Reader's Presence

1. In Stephen Budiansky's insightful analysis of what causes traffic jams, he establishes polar differences between the research of "practical-minded Americans" and the "theoretically inclined Germans" (paragraph 1), between American civil engineering and German physics. What are the specific strategies Budiansky uses as a writer to develop this fundamental competition between ways of solving theoretical and real-world problems? Which approach to science does Budiansky seem to favor, or is he able to remain neutral? In effect, would you characterize Budiansky as being more interested in science as theory or as practicality? Explain. In supporting your response, comment on the tone of Budiansky's essay and his use of irony.

2. Budiansky uses analogy to make the complexities of science accessible to readers of the *Atlantic*. Choose one of these analogies and discuss what is particularly effective about the ways Budiansky unfolds it. Budiansky also relies on metaphor to help explain such theoretical concepts as chaos theory and the "moving-gas model of traffic" (paragraph 4). What does he mean when he talks about "metastable conditions" (paragraph 10) or when he talks about how a solution to a problem is able to "tunnel right through this hill without ever reaching the top" (paragraph 9)? How effectively does he define and illustrate what German physicists call "synchronized traffic" (paragraph 8)? Discuss the specific ways in which you have experienced this phenomenon and your reactions to it.

3. What are the practical consequences of the findings of German physicists on traffic jams? In what specific ways would their findings "require realizing an Orwellian idea" (paragraph 13)? Summarize the reactions of other scientists to the analysis of traffic jams proposed by German physicists. On what evidentiary grounds

are other scientists advocating—or resisting—their claims? Do you find these objections convincing? Why or why not?

4. Budiansky's essay focuses on a common question in everyday life—what causes traffic jams? This seemingly simple question serves as an opportunity to examine the substantial differences in the ways science is conducted in the United States and in Germany as well as the competitive nature of international science. Eric Schlosser tackles another equally simple question in his essay "Why McDonald's Fries Taste So Good" (page 528). Compare and contrast the specific ways in which Schlosser and Budiansky establish the basis for their questions and the extent to which each writer succeeds at unfolding and answering his question. Which essay do you find more engaging? more successful? Explain why.

Stephen L. Carter

The Insufficiency of Honesty

Law professor and writer Stephen L. Carter (b. 1954) is an insightful and incisive critic of contemporary cultural politics. His first book, Reflections of an Affirmative Action Baby *(1992), criticizes affirmative action policies that reinforce racial stereotypes rather than break down structures of discrimination. Carter's critique emerges from his own experience as an African American student at Stanford University and at Yale University Law School. After graduating from Yale, Carter served as a law clerk for Supreme Court justice Thurgood Marshall and eventually joined the faculty at Yale as professor of law, where he has served since 1991 as the William Cromwell Professor of Law. Carter has published widely on legal and social topics, including his books* The Culture of Disbelief: How American Law and Politics Trivialize Religious Devotion *(1993),* The Confirmation Mess *(1994),* Civility: Manners, Morals, and the Etiquette of Democracy *(1998),* The Dissent of the Governed: A Meditation on Law, Religion, and Loyalty *(1998), and* God's Name in Vain *(2000). Carter's most recent work is the novel* New England White *(2007).*

Carter's best-selling novel The Emperor of Ocean Park *(2002) took him four years to complete. Carter says, "One of the best pieces of advice about writing I ever received was from a professor at law school who said to me, 'Stephen, there's no piece of writing that can't be improved by spending more time on it. The discipline is to make yourself stop.'"*

"The Insufficiency of Honesty" first appeared in Integrity *in 1996.*

A couple of years ago I began a university commencement address by telling the audience that I was going to talk about integrity. The crowd broke into applause. Applause! Just because they had heard the word "integrity": that's how starved for it they were. They had no idea how I was using the word, or what I was going to say about integrity, or, indeed, whether I was for it or against it. But they knew they liked the idea of talking about it.

Very well, let us consider this word "integrity." Integrity is like the weather: everybody talks about it but nobody knows what to do about it. Integrity is that stuff that we always want more of. Some say that we need to return to the good old days when we had a lot more of it. Others say that we as a nation have never really had enough of it. Hardly anybody stops to explain exactly what we mean by it, or how we know it is a good thing, or why everybody needs to have the same amount of it. Indeed, the only trouble with integrity is that everybody who uses the word seems to mean something slightly different.

For instance, when I refer to integrity, do I mean simply "honesty"? The answer is no; although honesty is a virtue of importance, it is a different virtue from integrity. Let us, for simplicity, think of honesty as not lying; and let us further accept Sissela Bok's[1] definition of a lie: "any intentionally deceptive message which is *stated*." Plainly, one cannot have integrity without being honest (although, as we shall see, the matter gets complicated), but one can certainly be honest and yet have little integrity.

When I refer to integrity, I have something very specific in mind. Integrity, as I will use the term, requires three steps: discerning what is right and what is wrong; acting on what you have discerned, even at personal cost; and saying openly that you are acting on your understanding of right and wrong. The first criterion captures the idea that integrity requires a degree of moral reflectiveness. The second brings in the ideal of a person of integrity as steadfast, a quality that includes keeping one's commitments. The third reminds us that a person of integrity can be trusted.

The first point to understand about the difference between honesty and integrity is that a person may be entirely honest without ever engaging in the hard work of discernment that integrity requires; she may tell us quite truthfully what she believes without ever taking the time to figure out whether what she believes is good and right and true. The problem may be as simple as someone's foolishly saying something that hurts a friend's feelings; a few moments of thought would have revealed the likelihood of the hurt and the lack of necessity for the comment. Or the problem may be more complex, as when a man who was raised from birth in a society that preaches racism states his belief in one race's inferiority as a fact, without ever really considering that perhaps this deeply

5

---

[1] *Bok:* (b. 1934) a Swedish-born scholar, philosopher, ethicist, and the author of many books, including *Lying: Moral Choice in Public and Private Life* (1978). She is the wife of Derek Bok, an interim president (2006–2007) of Harvard. —EDS.

held view is wrong. Certainly the racist is being honest—he is telling us what he actually thinks—but his honesty does not add up to integrity.

TELLING EVERYTHING YOU KNOW

A wonderful epigram sometimes attributed to the filmmaker Sam Goldwyn goes like this: "The most important thing in acting is honesty; once you learn to fake that, you're in." The point is that honesty can be something one *seems* to have. Without integrity, what passes for honesty often is nothing of the kind; it is fake honesty—or it is honest but irrelevant and perhaps even immoral.

Consider an example. A man who has been married for fifty years confesses to his wife on his deathbed that he was unfaithful thirty-five years earlier. The dishonesty was killing his spirit, he says. Now he has cleared his conscience and is able to die in peace.

The husband has been honest—sort of. He has certainly unburdened himself. And he has probably made his wife (soon to be his widow) quite miserable in the process, because even if she forgives him, she will not be able to remember him with quite the vivid image of love and loyalty that she had hoped for. Arranging his own emotional affairs to ease his transition to death, he has shifted to his wife the burden of confusion and pain, perhaps for the rest of her life. Moreover, he has attempted his honesty at the one time in his life when it carries no risk; acting in accordance with what you think is right and risking no loss in the process is a rather thin and unadmirable form of honesty.

Besides, even though the husband has been honest in a sense, he has now twice been unfaithful to his wife: once thirty-five years ago, when he had his affair, and again when, nearing death, he decided that his own peace of mind was more important than hers. In trying to be honest he has violated his marriage vow by acting toward his wife not with love but with naked and perhaps even cruel self-interest.

As my mother used to say, you don't have to tell people everything you know. Lying and nondisclosure, as the law often recognizes, are not the same thing. Sometimes it is actually illegal to tell what you know, as, for example, in the disclosure of certain financial information by market insiders. Or it may be unethical, as when a lawyer reveals a confidence entrusted to her by a client. It may be simple bad manners, as in the case of a gratuitous comment to a colleague on his or her attire. And it may be subject to religious punishment, as when a Roman Catholic priest breaks the seal of the confessional—an offense that carries automatic excommunication.

In all the cases just mentioned, the problem with telling everything you know is that somebody else is harmed. Harm may not be the intention, but it is certainly the effect. Honesty is most laudable when we risk harm to ourselves; it becomes a good deal less so if we instead risk harm

10

to others when there is no gain to anyone other than ourselves. Integrity may counsel keeping our secrets in order to spare the feelings of others. Sometimes, as in the example of the wayward husband, the reason we want to tell what we know is precisely to shift our pain onto somebody else—a course of action dictated less by integrity than by self-interest. Fortunately, integrity and self-interest often coincide, as when a politician of integrity is rewarded with our votes. But often they do not, and it is at those moments that our integrity is truly tested.

ERROR

Another reason that honesty alone is no substitute for integrity is that if forthrightness is not preceded by discernment, it may result in the expression of an incorrect moral judgment. In other words, I may be honest about what I believe, but if I have never tested my beliefs, I may be wrong. And here I mean "wrong" in a particular sense: the proposition in question is wrong if I would change my mind about it after hard moral reflection.

Consider this example. Having been taught all his life that women are not as smart as men, a manager gives the women on his staff less-challenging assignments than he gives the men. He does this, he believes, for their own benefit: he does not want them to fail, and he believes that they will if he gives them tougher assignments. Moreover, when one of the women on his staff does poor work, he does not berate her as harshly as he would a man, because he expects nothing more. And he claims to be acting with integrity because he is acting according to his own deepest beliefs.

The manager fails the most basic test of integrity. The question is not whether his actions are consistent with what he most deeply believes but whether he has done the hard work of discerning whether what he most deeply believes is right. The manager has not taken this harder step.

Moreover, even within the universe that the manager has constructed for himself, he is not acting with integrity. Although he is obviously wrong to think that the women on his staff are not as good as the men, even were he right, that would not justify applying different standards to their work. By so doing he betrays both his obligation to the institution that employs him and his duty as a manager to evaluate his employees.

The problem that the manager faces is an enormous one in our practical politics, where having the dialogue that makes democracy work can seem impossible because of our tendency to cling to our views even when we have not examined them. As Jean Bethke Elshtain[2] has said, borrowing

[2]**Elshtain** (b. 1941) a feminist political philosopher and Professor of Social and Political Ethics at the University of Chicago Divinity School. She serves on the Board of Advisors of the Bible Literacy Project, publishers of the curriculum "The Bible and Its Influence" for public high school literature courses.—EDS.

from John Courtney Murray,[3] our politics are so fractured and contentious that we often cannot reach *disagreement*. Our refusal to look closely at our own most cherished principles is surely a large part of the reason. Socrates thought the unexamined life not worth living. But the unhappy truth is that few of us actually have the time for constant reflection on our views—on public or private morality. Examine them we must, however, or we will never know whether we might be wrong.

None of this should be taken to mean that integrity as I have described it presupposes a single correct truth. If, for example, your integrity-guided search tells you that affirmative action is wrong, and my integrity-guided search tells me that affirmative action is right, we need not conclude that one of us lacks integrity. As it happens, I believe—both as a Christian and as a secular citizen who struggles toward moral understanding—that we *can* find true and sound answers to our moral questions. But I do not pretend to have found very many of them, nor is an exposition of them my purpose here.

It is the case not that there aren't any right answers but that, given human fallibility, we need to be careful in assuming that we have found them. However, today's political talk about how it is wrong for the government to impose one person's morality on somebody else is just mindless chatter. *Every* law imposes one person's morality on somebody else, because law has only two functions: to tell people to do what they would rather not or to forbid them to do what they would.

And if the surveys can be believed, there is far more moral agreement in America than we sometimes allow ourselves to think. One of the reasons that character education for young people makes so much sense to so many people is precisely that there seems to be a core set of moral understandings—we might call them the American Core—that most of us accept. Some of the virtues in this American Core are, one hopes, relatively noncontroversial. About 500 American communities have signed on to Michael Josephson's[4] program to emphasize the "six pillars" of good character: trustworthiness, respect, responsibility, caring, fairness, and citizenship. These virtues might lead to a similarly noncontroversial set of political values: having an honest regard for ourselves and others, protecting freedom of thought and religious belief, and refusing to steal or murder.

HONESTY AND COMPETING RESPONSIBILITIES

A further problem with too great an exaltation of honesty is that it   20
may allow us to escape responsibilities that morality bids us bear. If hon-

---

[3]*John Courtney Murray, SJ:* (1904–1967), a Jesuit priest, theologian, and widely respected intellectual who was especially known for his efforts to reconcile Catholicism and religious pluralism, religious freedom, and American politics.—EDS.

[4]*Josephson:* (b. 1942) a prominent ethicist as well as founder and president of Josephson Institute and its CHARACTER COUNTS! Project.—EDS.

esty is substituted for integrity, one might think that if I say I am not planning to fulfill a duty, I need not fulfill it. But it would be a peculiar morality indeed that granted us the right to avoid our moral responsibilities simply by stating our intention to ignore them. Integrity does not permit such an easy escape.

Consider an example. Before engaging in sex with a woman, her lover tells her that if she gets pregnant, it is her problem, not his. She says that she understands. In due course she does wind up pregnant. If we believe, as I hope we do, that the man would ordinarily have a moral responsibility toward both the child he will have helped to bring into the world and the child's mother, then his honest statement of what he intends does not spare him that responsibility.

This vision of responsibility assumes that not all moral obligations stem from consent or from a stated intention. The linking of obligations to promises is a rather modern and perhaps uniquely Western way of looking at life, and perhaps a luxury that the well-to-do can afford. As Fred and Shulamit Korn (a philosopher and an anthropologist) have pointed out, "If one looks at ethnographic accounts of other societies, one finds that, while obligations everywhere play a crucial role in social life, promising is not preeminent among the sources of obligation and is not even mentioned by most anthropologists." The Korns have made a study of Tonga, where promises are virtually unknown but the social order is remarkably stable. If life without any promises seems extreme, we Americans sometimes go too far the other way, parsing not only our contracts but even our marriage vows in order to discover the absolute minimum obligation that we have to others as a result of our promises.

That some societies in the world have worked out evidently functional structures of obligation without the need for promise or consent does not tell us what *we* should do. But it serves as a reminder of the basic proposition that our existence in civil society creates a set of mutual responsibilities that philosophers used to capture in the fiction of the social contract. Nowadays, here in America, people seem to spend their time thinking of even cleverer ways to avoid their obligations, instead of doing what integrity commands and fulfilling them. And all too often honesty is their excuse.

The Reader's Presence

1. If Carter intends his essay to be a discussion of honesty, why does he begin with a consideration of the concept of integrity? How are the terms related? In what important ways are they different? What does integrity involve that honesty doesn't?

2. Notice that in this essay Carter never once offers a dictionary definition of the words *honesty* and *integrity*. Look up each term in a

standard dictionary. As a reader, do you think such definitions would have made Carter's distinctions clearer? Why or why not? Why do you think he chose not to define the words according to their common dictionary meanings? How does he define them? How are his considerations of honesty and integrity related to his conclusion?

3. In the following selection "Why Women Smile," Amy Cunningham argues that women often "smile in lieu of showing what's really on [their] minds." Would Carter classify this kind of smiling as insufficiently honest? Why or why not? Cunningham notes that she is "trying to quit" smiling; would not smiling show greater integrity, as Carter explains it?

Amy Cunningham
Why Women Smile

Amy Cunningham (b. 1955) has been writing on psychological issues and modern life for magazines such as Redbook, Glamour, *and the* Washington Post Magazine *since she graduated from the University of Virginia in 1977 with a BA in English. Cunningham says that the essay reprinted here grew out of her own experience as an "easy to get along with person" who was raised by southerners in the suburbs of Chicago. She also recalls that when writing it, "I was unhappy with myself for taking too long, for not being efficient the way I thought a professional writer should be—but the work paid off and now I think it is one of the best essays I've written." "Why Women Smile" originally appeared in* Lear's *in 1993.*

Looking back on her writing career, Cunningham notes, "When I was younger I thought if you had talent you would make it as a writer. I'm surprised to realize now that good writing has less to do with talent and more to do with the discipline of staying seated in the chair, by yourself, in front of the computer and getting the work done."

After smiling brilliantly for nearly four decades, I now find myself trying to quit. Or, at the very least, seeking to lower the wattage a bit.

Not everyone I know is keen on this. My smile has gleamed like a cheap plastic night-light so long and so reliably that certain friends and relatives worry that my mood will darken the moment my smile dims.

"Gee," one says, "I associate you with your smile. It's the essence of you. I should think you'd want to smile more!" But the people who love me best agree that my smile — which springs forth no matter where I am or how I feel — hasn't been serving me well. Said my husband recently, "Your smiling face and unthreatening demeanor make people like you in a fuzzy way, but that doesn't seem to be what you're after these days."

Smiles are not the small and innocuous things they appear to be: Too many of us smile in lieu of showing what's really on our minds. Indeed, the success of the women's movement might be measured by the sincerity — and lack of it — in our smiles. Despite all the work we American women have done to get and maintain full legal control of our bodies, not to mention our destinies, we still don't seem to be fully in charge of a couple of small muscle groups in our faces.

We smile so often and so promiscuously — when we're angry, when we're tense, when we're with children, when we're being photographed, when we're interviewing for a job, when we're meeting candidates to employ — that the Smiling Woman has become a peculiarly American archetype. This isn't entirely a bad thing, of course. A smile lightens the load, diffuses unpleasantness, redistributes nervous tension. Women doctors smile more than their male counterparts, studies show, and are better liked by their patients.

Oscar Wilde's old saw that "a woman's face is her work of fiction" is   5
often quoted to remind us that what's on the surface may have little connection to what we're feeling. What is it in our culture that keeps our smiles on automatic pilot? The behavior seems to be an equal blend of nature and nurture. Research has demonstrated that since females often mature earlier than males and are less irritable, girls smile more than boys from the very beginning. But by adolescence, the differences in the smiling rates of boys and girls are so robust that it's clear the culture has done more than its share of the dirty work. Just think of the mothers who painstakingly embroidered the words ENTER SMILING on little samplers, and then hung their handiwork on doors by golden chains. Translation: "Your real emotions aren't welcome here."

Clearly, our instincts are another factor. Our smiles have their roots in the greetings of monkeys, who pull their lips up and back to show their fear of attack, as well as their reluctance to vie for a position of dominance. And like the opossum caught in the light by the clattering garbage cans, we, too, flash toothy grimaces when we make major mistakes. By declaring ourselves nonthreatening, our smiles provide an extremely versatile means of protection.

Our earliest baby smiles are involuntary reflexes having only the vaguest connection to contentment or comfort. In short, we're genetically wired to pull on our parents' heartstrings. As Desmond Morris explains in *Babywatching*, this is our way of attaching ourselves to our caretakers, as truly as baby chimps clench their mothers' fur. Even as babies we're capable of projecting onto others (in this case, our parents) the feelings we know we need to get back in return.

Bona fide social smiles occur at two-and-a-half to three months of age, usually a few weeks after we first start gazing with intense interest into the faces of our parents. By the time we are six months old, we are smiling and laughing regularly in reaction to tickling, feedings, blown raspberries, hugs, and peekaboo games. Even babies who are born blind intuitively know how to react to pleasurable changes with a smile, though their first smiles start later than those of sighted children.

Psychologists and psychiatrists have noted that babies also smile and laugh with relief when they realize that something they thought might be dangerous is not dangerous after all. Kids begin to invite their parents to indulge them with "scary" approach-avoidance games; they love to be chased or tossed up into the air. (It's interesting to note that as adults, we go through the same gosh-that's-shocking-and-dangerous-but-it's-okay-to-laugh-and-smile cycles when we listen to raunchy stand-up comics.)

From the wilds of New Guinea to the sidewalks of New York, smiles are associated with joy, relief, and amusement. But smiles are by no means limited to the expression of positive emotions: People of many different cultures smile when they are frightened, embarrassed, angry, or miserable. In Japan, for instance, a smile is often used to hide pain or sorrow.

Psychologist Paul Ekman, the head of the University of California's Human Interaction Lab in San Francisco, has identified 18 distinct types of smiles, including those that show misery, compliance, fear, and contempt. The smile of true merriment, which Dr. Ekman calls the Duchenne

10

These photos from Paul Ekman's study show the difference between the social smile (left) and the true enjoyment smile (right).

Smile, after the nineteenth-century French doctor who first studied it, is characterized by heightened circulation, a feeling of exhilaration, and the employment of two major facial muscles: the zygomaticus major of the lower face, and the orbicularis oculi, which crinkles the skin around the eyes. But since the average American woman's smile often has less to do with her actual state of happiness than it does with the social pressure to smile no matter what, her baseline social smile isn't apt to be a felt expression that engages the eyes like this. Ekman insists that if people learned to read smiles, they could see the sadness, misery, or pain lurking there, plain as day.

Evidently, a woman's happy, willing deference is something the world wants visibly demonstrated. Woe to the waitress, the personal assistant or receptionist, the flight attendant, or any other woman in the line of public service whose smile is not offered up to the boss or client as proof that there are no storm clouds—no kids to support, no sleep that's been missed—rolling into the sunny workplace landscape. Women are expected to smile no matter where they line up on the social, cultural, or economic ladder: College professors are criticized for not smiling, political spouses are pilloried for being too serious, and women's roles in films have historically been smiling ones. It's little wonder that men on the street still call out, "Hey, baby, smile! Life's not *that* bad, is it?" to women passing by, lost in thought.

A friend remembers being pulled aside by a teacher after class and asked, "What is wrong, dear? You sat there for the whole hour looking so sad!" "All I could figure," my friend says now, "is that I wasn't smiling. And the fact that *she* felt sorry for me for looking normal made me feel horrible."

Ironically, the social laws that govern our smiles have completely reversed themselves over the last two thousand years. Women weren't always expected to seem animated and responsive; in fact, immoderate laughter was once considered one of the more conspicuous vices a woman could have, and mirth was downright sinful. Women were kept apart, in some cultures even veiled, so that they couldn't perpetuate Eve's seductive, evil work. The only smile deemed appropriate on a privileged woman's face was the serene, inward smile of the Virgin Mary at Christ's birth, and even that expression was best directed exclusively at young children. Cackling laughter and wicked glee were the kinds of sounds heard only in hell.

What we know of women's facial expressions in other centuries comes 15 mostly from religious writings, codes of etiquette, and portrait paintings. In fifteenth century Italy, it was customary for artists to paint lovely, blank-faced women in profile. A viewer could stare endlessly at such a woman, but she could not gaze back. By the Renaissance, male artists were taking some pleasure in depicting women with a semblance of complexity, Leonardo da Vinci's *Mona Lisa*, with her veiled enigmatic smile, being the most famous example.

The Golden Age of the Dutch Republic marks a fascinating period for studying women's facial expressions. While we might expect the drunken young whores of Amsterdam to smile devilishly (unbridled sexuality and lasciviousness were *supposed* to addle the brain), it's the faces of the Dutch women from fine families that surprise us. Considered socially more free, these women demonstrate a fuller range of facial expressions than their European sisters. Frans Hals's 1622 portrait of Stephanus Geraerdt and Isabella Coymans, a married couple, is remarkable not just for the full, friendly smiles on each face but for the frank and mutual pleasure the couple take in each other.

In the 1800s, sprightly, pretty women began appearing in advertisements for everything from beverages to those newfangled Kodak Land cameras. Women's faces were no longer impassive, and their willingness to bestow status, to offer, proffer, and yield, was most definitely promoted by their smiling images. The culture appeared to have turned the smile, originally a bond shared between intimates, into a socially required display that sold capitalist ideology as well as kitchen appliances. And female viewers soon began to emulate these highly idealized pictures. Many longed to be more like her, that perpetually smiling female. She seemed so beautiful. So content. So whole.

By the middle of the nineteenth century, the bulk of America's smile burden was falling primarily to women and African-American slaves, providing a very portable means of protection, a way of saying, "I'm harmless. I won't assert myself here." It reassured those in power to see signs of gratitude and contentment in the faces of subordinates. As long ago as 1963, adman David Ogilvy declared the image of a woman smiling approvingly at a product clichéd, but we've yet to get the message. Cheerful Americans still appear in ads today, smiling somewhat less disingenuously than they smiled during the middle of the century, but smiling broadly nonetheless.

Other countries have been somewhat reluctant to import our "Don't worry, be happy" American smiles. When McDonald's opened in Moscow not long ago and when EuroDisney debuted in France last year [1992], the Americans involved in both business ventures complained that they couldn't get the natives they'd employed to smile worth a damn.

Europeans visiting the United States for the first time are often surprised at just how often Americans smile. But when you look at our history, the relentless good humor (or, at any rate, the pretense of it) falls into perspective. The American wilderness was developed on the assumption that this country had a shortage of people in relation to its possibilities. In countries with a more rigid class structure or caste system, fewer people are as captivated by the idea of quickly winning friends and influencing people. Here in the States, however, every stranger is a potential associate. Our smiles bring new people on board. The American smile is a democratic version of a curtsy or doffed hat, since, in this land of free equals, we're not especially formal about the ways we greet social superiors.

The civil rights movement never addressed the smile burden by name, but activists worked on their own to set new facial norms. African-American males stopped smiling on the streets in the 1960s, happily aware of the unsettling effect this action had on the white population. The image of the simpleminded, smiling, white-toothed black was rejected as blatantly racist, and it gradually retreated into the distance. However, like the women of Sparta and the wives of samurai, who were expected to look happy upon learning their sons or husbands had died in battle, contemporary American women have yet to unilaterally declare their faces their own property.

For instance, imagine a woman at a morning business meeting being asked if she could make a spontaneous and concise summation of a complicated project she's been struggling to get under control for months. She might draw the end of her mouth back and clench her teeth — Eek! — in a protective response, a polite, restrained expression of her surprise, not

20

unlike the expression of a conscientious young schoolgirl being told to get out paper and pencil for a pop quiz. At the same time, the woman might be feeling resentful of the supervisor who sprang the request, but she fears taking that person on. So she holds back a comment. The whole performance resolves in a weird grin collapsing into a nervous smile that conveys discomfort and unpreparedness. A pointed remark by way of explanation or self-defense might've worked better for her—but her mouth was otherwise engaged.

We'd do well to realize just how much our smiles misrepresent us, and swear off for good the self-deprecating grins and ritual displays of deference. Real smiles have beneficial physiological effects, according to Paul Ekman. False ones do nothing for us at all.

"Smiles are as important as sound bites on television," insists producer and media coach Heidi Berenson, who has worked with many of Washington's most famous faces. "And women have always been better at understanding this than men. But the smile I'm talking about is not a cutesy smile. It's an authoritative smile. A genuine smile. Properly timed, it's tremendously powerful."

To limit a woman to one expression is like editing down an orchestra   25
to one instrument. And the search for more authentic means of expression isn't easy in a culture in which women are still expected to be magnanimous smilers, helpmates in crisis, and curators of everybody else's morale. But change is already floating in the high winds. We see a boon in assertive female comedians who are proving that women can *dish out* smiles, not just wear them. Actress Demi Moore has stated that she doesn't like to take smiling roles. Nike is running ads that show unsmiling women athletes sweating, reaching, pushing themselves. These women aren't overly concerned with issues of rapport; they're not being "nice" girls—they're working out.

If a woman's smile were truly her own, to be smiled or not, according to how the *woman* felt, rather than according to what someone else needed, she would smile more spontaneously, without ulterior, hidden motives. As Rainer Maria Rilke wrote in *The Journal of My Other Self*, "Her smile was not meant to be seen by anyone and served its whole purpose in being smiled."

That smile is my long-term aim. In the meantime, I hope to stabilize on the smile continuum somewhere between the eliciting grin of Farrah Fawcett and the haughty smirk of Jeane Kirkpatrick.

The Reader's Presence

1. Cunningham presents an informative précis of the causes and effects of smiling in Western culture. Consider the points of view

from which she addresses this subject. Summarize and evaluate her treatment of smiling from psychological, physiological, sociological, and historical points of view. Which do you find most incisive? Why? What other points of view does she introduce into her discussion of smiling? What effects do they create? What does she identify as the benefits (and the disadvantages) of smiling?

2. At what point in this essay does Cunningham address the issue of gender? Characterize the language she uses to introduce this issue. She distinguishes between the different patterns—and the consequences—experienced by men and women who smile. Summarize these differences and assess the nature and the extent of the evidence she provides for each of her points. What more general distinctions does she make about various kinds of smiles? What are their different purposes and degrees of intensity? What information does she provide about smiling as an issue of nationality and race? What is the overall purpose of this essay? Where—and how—does Cunningham create and sustain a sense of her own presence in this essay? What does she set as her personal goal in relation to smiling?

3. Cunningham presents an explanation of the causes of an activity that few of her readers think of in both scientific and historical terms. Compare her use of science and history to that of Stephen Jay Gould in "Sex, Drugs, Disasters, and the Extinction of Dinosaurs" (page 417). How does each writer establish her or his authority in these fields? What is each writer's argument? To what extent does each argument depend on factual evidence?

Don DeLillo

In the Ruins of the Future: Reflections on Terror, Loss, and Time in the Shadow of September

Don DeLillo was born in the Bronx, New York, in 1936, the son of Italian immigrants, and grew up in an Italian American neighborhood. He attended Cardinal Hayes High School and then majored in communication arts at Fordham University, graduating with a BA in 1958. During the 1960s, he worked as a copywriter for the renowned ad agency Ogilvy and Mather. He did not start writing his first novel, Americana, until about 1967. But after it appeared in print in 1971, he continued to write prolifically, publishing five novels in only seven years: End Zone *(1972),* Great Jones Street *(1973),* Ratner's Star *(1976),* Players *(1977), and* Running Dog *(1978). Although popular with reviewers and a small but fanatical readership, DeLillo had difficulty reaching a wide audience until the publication of* White Noise *(1985), which won the National Book Award, and* Mao II *(1991), which won the PEN/Faulkner Award. DeLillo's work surveys recent history and portrays American culture since the 1950s, dealing with such themes as paranoia, terrorist violence, and consumerism. His novels include* Libra *(1988),* Underworld *(1997),* The Body Artist *(2001),* Cosmopolis *(2003), and* Falling Man *(2007), which traces the changes in people's perception of the world and themselves after 9/11. His essay "In the Ruins of the Future," which first appeared in* Harper's *in December 2001, was written just weeks after the September 11 attack and appears to be the seed from which his later novel emerged.*

DeLillo's work reflects a fascination with language — its power to free the writer and to shape narrative and history. "Language lives in everything it touches and can be an agent of redemption, the thing that delivers us, paradoxically, from history's flat, thin, tight, and relentless designs, its arrangement of stark pages, and that allows us to find an unconstraining otherness, a free veer from time and place and fate."

I

In the past decade the surge of capital markets has dominated discourse and shaped global consciousness. Multinational corporations have come to seem more vital and influential than governments. The dramatic climb of the Dow and the speed of the Internet summoned us all to live permanently in the future, in the utopian glow of cyber-capital, because there is no memory there and this is where markets are uncontrolled and investment potential has no limit.

All this changed on September 11. Today, again, the world narrative belongs to terrorists. But the primary target of the men who attacked the Pentagon and the World Trade Center was not the global economy. It is America that drew their fury. It is the high gloss of our modernity. It is the thrust of our technology. It is our perceived godlessness. It is the blunt force of our foreign policy. It is the power of American culture to penetrate every wall, home, life, and mind.

Terror's response is a narrative that has been developing over years, only now becoming inescapable. It is *our* lives and minds that are occupied now. This catastrophic event changes the way we think and act, moment to moment, week to week, for unknown weeks and months to come, and steely years. Our world, parts of our world, have crumbled into theirs, which means we are living in a place of danger and rage.

The protesters in Genoa, Prague, Seattle, and other cities want to decelerate the global momentum that seemed to be driving unmindfully toward a landscape of consumer-robots and social instability, with the chance of self-determination probably diminishing for most people in most countries. Whatever acts of violence marked the protests, most of the men and women involved tend to be a moderating influence, trying to slow things down, even things out, hold off the white-hot future.

The terrorists of September 11 want to bring back the past.   5

II

Our tradition of free expression and our justice system's provisions for the rights of the accused can only seem an offense to men bent on suicidal terror.

We are rich, privileged, and strong, but they are willing to die. This is the edge they have, the fire of aggrieved belief. We live in a wide world, routinely filled with exchange of every sort, an open circuit of work, talk, family, and expressible feeling. The terrorist, planted in a Florida town, pushing his supermarket cart, nodding to his neighbor, lives in a far narrower format. This is his edge, his strength. Plots reduce the world. He builds a plot around his anger and our indifference. He lives a certain kind of apartness, hard and tight. This is not the self-watcher, the soft white dangling boy who shoots someone to keep from disappearing into himself. The terrorist shares a secret and a self. At a certain point he and his brothers may begin to feel less motivated by politics and personal hatred than by brotherhood itself. They share the codes and protocols of their mission here and something deeper as well, a vision of judgment and devastation.

Does the sight of a woman pushing a stroller soften the man to her humanity and vulnerability, and her child's as well, and all the people he is here to kill?

This is his edge, that he does not see her. Years here, waiting, taking flying lessons, making the routine gestures of community and home, the credit card, the bank account, the post-office box. All tactical, linked, layered. He knows who we are and what we mean in the world—an idea, a righteous fever in the brain. But there is no defenseless human at the end of his gaze.

The sense of disarticulation we hear in the term "Us and Them" has   10
never been so striking, at either end.

We can tell ourselves that whatever we've done to inspire bitterness, distrust, and rancor, it was not so damnable as to bring this day down on our heads. But there is no logic in apocalypse. They have gone beyond the bounds of passionate payback. This is heaven and hell, a sense of armed martyrdom as the surpassing drama of human experience.

He pledges his submission to God and meditates on the blood to come.

III

The Bush Administration was feeling a nostalgia for the Cold War. This is over now. Many things are over. The narrative ends in the rubble, and it is left to us to create the counter-narrative.

There are a hundred thousand stories crisscrossing New York, Washington, and the world. Where we were, whom we know, what we've seen or heard. There are the doctors' appointments that saved lives, the cell phones that were used to report the hijackings. Stories generating others and people running north out of the rumbling smoke and ash. Men running in suits and ties, women who'd lost their shoes, cops running from the skydive of all that towering steel.

People running for their lives are part of the story that is left to us.   15

There are stories of heroism and encounters with dread. There are stories that carry around their edges the luminous ring of coincidence, fate, or premonition. They take us beyond the hard numbers of dead and missing and give us a glimpse of elevated being. For a hundred who are arbitrarily dead, we need to find one person saved by a flash of forewarning. There are configurations that chill and awe us both. Two women on two planes, best of friends, who die together and apart, Tower 1 and Tower 2. What desolate epic tragedy might bear the weight of such juxtaposition? But we can also ask what symmetry, bleak and touching both, takes one friend, spares the other's grief?

The brother of one of the women worked in one of the towers. He managed to escape.

In Union Square Park, about two miles north of the attack site, the improvised memorials are another part of our response. The flags, flower beds, and votive candles, the lamppost hung with paper airplanes, the passages from the Koran and the Bible, the letters and poems, the cardboard John Wayne, the children's drawings of the Twin Towers, the hand-painted signs for Free Hugs, Free Back Rubs, the graffiti of love and peace on the tall equestrian statue.

There are many photographs of missing persons, some accompanied by hopeful lists of identifying features. (Man with panther tattoo, upper right arm.) There is the saxophonist, playing softly. There is the sculptured flag of rippling copper and aluminum, six feet long, with two young people still attending to the finer details of the piece.

Then there are the visitors to the park. The artifacts on display represent the confluence of a number of cultural tides, patriotic and multidevotional and retro hippie. The visitors move quietly in the floating aromas of candlewax, roses, and bus fumes. There are many people this mild evening, and in their voices, manner, clothing, and in the color of their skin they recapitulate the mix we see in the photocopied faces of the lost.

For the next fifty years, people who were not in the area when the attacks occurred will claim to have been there. In time, some of them will believe it. Others will claim to have lost friends or relatives, although they did not.

This is also the counter-narrative, a shadow history of false memories and imagined loss.

The Internet is a counter-narrative, shaped in part by rumor, fantasy, and mystical reverberation.

The cell phones, the lost shoes, the handkerchiefs mashed in the faces of running men and women. The box cutters and credit cards. The paper that came streaming out of the towers and drifted across the river to Brooklyn back yards: status reports, résumés, insurance forms. Sheets of paper driven into concrete, according to witnesses. Paper slicing into truck tires, fixed there.

These are among the small objects and more marginal stories in the sifted ruins of the day. We need them, even the common tools of the terrorists, to set against the massive spectacle that continues to seem unmanageable, too powerful a thing to set into our frame of practiced response.

IV

Ash was spattering the windows. Karen was half dressed, grabbing the kids and trying to put on some clothes and talking with her husband and scooping things to take out to the corridor, and they looked at her, twin girls, as if she had fourteen heads.

They stayed in the corridor for a while, thinking there might be secondary explosions. They waited, and began to feel safer, and went back to the apartment.

At the next impact, Marc knew in the sheerest second before the shock wave broadsided their building that it was a second plane, impossible, striking the second tower. Their building was two blocks away, and he'd thought the first crash was an accident.

They went back to the hallway, where others began to gather, fifteen or twenty people.

Karen ran back for a cell phone, a cordless phone, a charger, water,   30
sweaters, snacks for the kids, and then made a quick dash to the bedroom for her wedding ring.

From the window she saw people running in the street, others locked shoulder to shoulder, immobilized, with debris coming down on them. People were trampled, struck by falling objects, and there was ash and paper everywhere, paper whipping through the air, no sign of light or sky.

Cell phones were down. They talked on the cordless, receiving information measured out in eyedrops. They were convinced that the situation outside was far more grave than it was here.

Smoke began to enter the corridor.

Then the first tower fell. She thought it was a bomb. When she talked to someone on the phone and found out what had happened, she felt a surreal relief. Bombs and missiles were not falling everywhere in the city. It was not all-out war, at least not yet.

Marc was in the apartment getting chairs for the older people, for the   35
woman who'd had hip surgery. When he heard the first low drumming rumble, he stood in a strange dead calm and said, "Something is happening." It sounded exactly like what it was, a tall tower collapsing.

The windows were surfaced with ash now. Blacked out completely, and he wondered what was out there. What remained to be seen and did he want to see it?

They all moved into the stairwell, behind a fire door, but smoke kept coming in. It was gritty ash, and they were eating it.

He ran back inside, grabbing towels off the racks and washcloths out of drawers and drenching them in the sink, and filling his bicycle water bottles, and grabbing the kids' underwear.

He thought the crush of buildings was the thing to fear most. This is what would kill them.

Karen was on the phone, talking to a friend in the district attorney's   40
office, about half a mile to the north. She was pleading for help. She begged, pleaded, and hung up. For the next hour a detective kept calling with advice and encouragement.

Marc came back out to the corridor. I think we *might* die, he told himself, hedging his sense of what would happen next.

The detective told Karen to stay where they were.

When the second tower fell, my heart fell with it. I called Marc, who is my nephew, on his cordless. I couldn't stop thinking of the size of the towers and the meager distance between those buildings and his. He answered, we talked. I have no memory of the conversation except for his final remark, slightly urgent, concerning someone on the other line, who might be sending help.

Smoke was seeping out of the elevator shaft now. Karen was saying goodbye to her father in Oregon. Not hello-goodbye. But goodbye-I-think-we-are-going-to-die. She thought smoke would be the thing that did it.

People sat on chairs along the walls. They chatted about practical 45
matters. They sang songs with the kids. The kids in the group were coop-
erative because the adults were damn scared.

There was an improvised rescue in progress. Karen's friend and a colleague made their way down from Centre Street, turning up with two policemen they'd enlisted en route. They had dust masks and a destination,
and they searched every floor for others who might be stranded in the
building.

They came out into a world of ash and near night. There was no one
else to be seen now on the street. Gray ash covering the cars and pavement, ash falling in large flakes, paper still drifting down, discarded shoes,
strollers, briefcases. The members of the group were masked and toweled,
children in adults' arms, moving east and then north on Nassau Street, trying not to look around, only what's immediate, one step and then another,
all closely focused, a pregnant woman, a newborn, a dog.

They were covered in ash when they reached shelter at Pace University, where there was food and water, and kind and able staff members,
and a gas-leak scare, and more running people.

Workers began pouring water on the group. *Stay wet, stay wet.* This
was the theme of the first half hour.

Later a line began to form along the food counter. 50

Someone said, "I don't want cheese on that."

Someone said, "I like it better not so cooked."

Not so incongruous really, just people alive and hungry, beginning to
be themselves again.

V

Technology is our fate, our truth. It is what we mean when we call
ourselves the only superpower on the planet. The materials and methods
we devise make it possible for us to claim our future. We don't have to
depend on God or the prophets or other astonishments. We are the astonishment. The miracle is what we ourselves produce, the systems and networks that change the way we live and think.

But whatever great skeins of technology lie ahead, ever more complex, 55
connective, precise, micro-fractional, the future has yielded, for now, to
medieval expedience, to the old slow furies of cutthroat religion.

Kill the enemy and pluck out his heart.

If others in less scientifically advanced cultures were able to share,
wanted to share, some of the blessings of our technology, without a threat
to their faith or traditions, would they need to rely on a God in whose
name they kill the innocent? Would they need to invent a God who rewards
violence against the innocent with a promise of "infinite paradise," in the
words of a handwritten letter found in the luggage of one of the hijackers?

For all those who may want what we've got, there are all those who
do not. These are the men who have fashioned a morality of destruction.

They want what they used to have before the waves of Western influence. They surely see themselves as the elect of God whether or not they follow the central precepts of Islam. It is the presumptive right of those who choose violence and death to speak directly to God. They will kill and then die. Or they will die first, in the cockpit, in clean shoes, according to instructions in the letter.

Six days after the attacks, the territory below Canal Street is hedged with barricades. There are few civilians in the street. Police at some check-points, troops in camouflage gear at others, wearing gas masks, and a pair of state troopers in conversation, and ten burly men striding east in hard hats, work pants, and NYPD jackets. A shop owner tries to talk a cop into letting him enter his place of business. He is a small elderly man with a Jewish accent, but there is no relief today. Garbage bags are everywhere in high broad stacks. The area is bedraggled and third-worldish, with an air of permanent emergency, everything surfaced in ash.

It is possible to pass through some checkpoints, detour around others.   60
At Chambers Street I look south through the links of the National Rent-A-Fence barrier. There stands the smoky remnant of filigree that marks the last tall thing, the last sign in the mire of wreckage that there were towers here that dominated the skyline for over a quarter of a century.

Ten days later and a lot closer, I stand at another barrier with a group of people, looking directly into the strands of openwork facade. It is al-most too close. It is almost Roman, I-beams for stonework, but not nearly so salvageable. Many here describe the scene to others on cell phones.

"Oh my god I'm standing here," says the man next to me.

The World Trade towers were not only an emblem of advanced tech-nology but a justification, in a sense, for technology's irresistible will to realize in solid form whatever becomes theoretically allowable. Once de-fined, every limit must be reached. The tactful sheathing of the towers was intended to reduce the direct threat of such straight-edge enormity, a giantism that eased over the years into something a little more familiar and comfortable, even dependable in a way.

Now a small group of men have literally altered our skyline. We have fallen back in time and space. It is their technology that marks our mo-ments, the small lethal devices, the remote-control detonators they fashion out of radios, or the larger technology they borrow from us, passenger jets that become manned missiles.

Maybe this is a grim subtext of their enterprise. They see something   65
innately destructive in the nature of technology. It brings death to their customs and beliefs. Use it as what it is, a thing that kills.

VI

Nearly eleven years ago, during the engagement in the Persian Gulf, people had trouble separating the war from coverage of the war. After the first euphoric days, coverage became limited. The rush of watching all that eerie green night-vision footage, shot from fighter jets in combat, had been so intense that it became hard to honor the fact that the war was still going on, untelevised. A layer of consciousness had been stripped away. People shuffled around, muttering. They were lonely for their war.

The events of September 11 were covered unstintingly. There was no confusion of roles on TV. The raw event was one thing, the coverage another. The event dominated the medium. It was bright and totalizing, and some of us said it was unreal. When we say a thing is unreal, we mean it is too real, a phenomenon so unaccountable and yet so bound to the power of objective fact that we can't tilt it to the slant of our perceptions. First the planes struck the towers. After a time it became possible for us to absorb this, barely. But when the towers fell. When the rolling smoke began moving downward, floor to floor. This was so vast and terrible that it was outside imagining even as it happened. We could not catch up to it. But it was real, punishingly so, an expression of the physics of structural limits and a void in one's soul, and there was the huge antenna falling out of the sky, straight down, blunt end first, like an arrow moving backward in time.

The event itself has no purchase on the mercies of analogy or simile. We have to take the shock and horror as it is. But living language is not diminished. The writer wants to understand what this day has done to us. Is it too soon? We seem pressed for time, all of us. Time is scarcer now. There is a sense of compression, plans made hurriedly, time forced and distorted. But language is inseparable from the world that provokes it. The writer begins in the towers, trying to imagine the moment, desperately. Before politics, before history and religion, there is the primal terror. People falling from the towers hand in hand. This is part of the counter-narrative, hands and spirits joining, human beauty in the crush of meshed steel.

In its desertion of every basis for comparison, the event asserts its singularity. There is something empty in the sky. The writer tries to give memory, tenderness, and meaning to all that howling space.

VII

We like to think America invented the future. We are comfortable with the future, intimate with it. But there are disturbances now, in large and small ways, a chain of reconsiderations. Where we live, how we travel, what we think about when we look at our children. For many people, the event has changed the grain of the most routine moment.

We may find that the ruin of the towers is implicit in other things. The new PalmPilot at fingertip's reach, the stretch limousine parked outside the hotel, the midtown skyscraper under construction, carrying the name of a major investment bank—all haunted in a way by what has happened, less assured in their authority, in the prerogatives they offer.

There is fear of other kinds of terrorism, the prospect that biological and chemical weapons will contaminate the air we breathe and the water we drink. There wasn't much concern about this after earlier terrorist acts. This time we are trying to name the future, not in our normally hopeful way but guided by dread.

What has already happened is sufficient to affect the air around us, psychologically. We are all breathing the fumes of lower Manhattan, where traces of the dead are everywhere, in the soft breeze off the river, on rooftops and windows, in our hair and on our clothes.

Think of a future in which the components of a microchip are the size of atoms. The devices that pace our lives will operate from the smart quantum spaces of pure information. Now think of people in countless thousands massing in anger and vowing revenge. Enlarged photos of martyrs and holy men dangle from balconies, and the largest images are those of a terrorist leader.

Two forces in the world, past and future. With the end of Communism, the ideas and principles of modern democracy were seen clearly to prevail, whatever the inequalities of the system itself. This is still the case. But now there is a global theocratic state, unboundaried and floating and so obsolete it must depend on suicidal fervor to gain its aims.

Ideas evolve and de-evolve, and history is turned on end.

75

VIII

On Friday of the first week a long series of vehicles moves slowly west on Canal Street. Dump trucks, flatbeds, sanitation sweepers. There are giant earthmovers making a tremendous revving sound. A scant number of pedestrians, some in dust masks, others just standing, watching, the indigenous people, clinging to walls and doorways, unaccustomed to traffic that doesn't bring buyers and sellers, goods and cash. The fire rescue car and state police cruiser, the staccato sirens of a line of police vans. Cops stand at the sawhorse barriers, trying to clear the way. Ambulances, cherry pickers, a fleet of Con Ed trucks, all this clamor moving south a few blocks ahead, into the cloud of sand and ash.

One month earlier I'd taken the same walk, early evening, among crowds of people, the panethnic swarm of shoppers, merchants, residents and passersby, with a few tourists as well, and the man at the curbstone doing acupoint massage, and the dreadlocked kid riding his bike on the sidewalk. This was the spirit of Canal Street, the old jostle and stir unchanged for many decades and bearing no sign of SoHo just above, with its restaurants and artists' lofts, or TriBeCa below, rich in architectural textures. Here were hardware bargains, car stereos, foam rubber and industrial plastics, the tattoo parlor and the pizza parlor.

Then I saw the woman on the prayer rug. I'd just turned the corner, heading south to meet some friends, and there she was, young and slender, in a silk headscarf. It was time for sunset prayer, and she was kneeling, upper body pitched toward the edge of the rug. She was partly concealed by a couple of vendors' carts, and no one seemed much to notice her. I think there was another woman seated on a folding chair near the curbstone. The figure on the rug faced east, which meant most immediately a storefront just a foot and a half from her tipped head but more distantly and pertinently toward Mecca, of course, the holiest city of Islam.

Some prayer rugs include a *mihrab* in their design, an arched element representing the prayer niche in a mosque that indicates the direction of Mecca. The only locational guide the young women needed was the Manhattan grid. 80

I looked at her in prayer and it was clearer to me than ever, the daily sweeping taken-for-granted greatness of New York. The city will accommodate every language, ritual, belief, and opinion. In the rolls of the dead of September 11, all these vital differences were surrendered to the impact and flash. The bodies themselves are missing in large numbers. For the survivors, more grief. But the dead are their own nation and race, one identity, young or old, devout or unbelieving—a union of souls. During the *hadj*, the annual pilgrimage to Mecca, the faithful must eliminate every sign of status, income, and nationality, the men wearing identical strips of seamless white cloth, the women with covered heads, all recalling in prayer their fellowship with the dead.

Allahu akbar. God is great.

The Reader's Presence

1. From the title's linking of the past and the future to statements such as "history is turned on end" (paragraph 76), DeLillo's essay is absorbed with time. Trace the way time is used in the piece. How does the writer make schematic use of past and future to evoke the warring forces of the world? How does he vary tenses and points of view to report the events of September 11 and their aftermath? Why is time central to DeLillo's understanding of these events?

2. For the most part, DeLillo's discussion of the terrorists themselves is unspecific with respect to nationality, religion, or political affiliation. He first mentions Islam several pages into the essay, in section V. How does DeLillo build the reader's sense of "the enemy"? How is Islam woven through the essay? Why might DeLillo resist giving too narrow an articulation of "us" and "them"?

3. Compare DeLillo's account of the very recent past to Barbara Tuchman's history of the distant past in " 'This Is the End of the World': The Black Death" (page 548). Which sections of DeLillo's essay read like a historian's account and which read more like the primary accounts of the plague's disastrous effects? Compare section IV to

Michihiko Hachiya's journal of the days immediately following the bombing of Hiroshima in "From *Hiroshima Diary*" (page 131). Why do you think DeLillo varies his style so dramatically from section to section? What are the advantages and disadvantages of writing about an event whose meaning is still being discovered?

Mark Edmundson
Dwelling in Possibilities

Author and scholar Mark Edmundson (b. 1952) is an award-winning professor of English at the University of Virginia, where he teaches Romantic poetry and literary theory. A self-described "pedagogical pragmatist," Edmundson is well known, in and out of academic circles, for his belief in the value of liberal arts and the humanities for the students he teaches and for the larger culture. On being honored as a National Endowment for the Humanities Distinguished Professor, he said, "Pursuing meaning is a splendid and useful thing, but we must go beyond meaning to ask questions about what value literature and history and philosophy might have for conduct in life." Edmundson has published numerous books of literary and cultural criticism, including Literature Against Philosophy, Plato to Derrida: A Defense of Poetry *(1995);* Nightmare on Main Street: Angels, Sado-Masochism, and the Culture of Gothic *(1997); and his latest work,* The Death of Sigmund Freud: Fascism, Psychoanalysis and the Rise of Fundamentalism *(2007). Edmundson's 2004 book* Why Read? *is about the transformative effects of reading;* Teach: The One Who Made the Difference *(2002) is a memoir about the high school teacher who transformed his life and set him on the path to teaching. Widely read, Edmundson is a contributing editor to* Harper's *and to the journal* Raritan. *His articles appear frequently in the* New York Times, *the* New York Times Magazine *and* Book Review, *the* Nation, *the* American Scholar, *and the* Chronicle of Higher Education, *where his essay "Dwelling in Possibilities" appeared in March 2008.*

At the beginning of school last fall, I ran into a student on the University of Virginia Lawn, not far from the famous statue of Homer instructing an admiring pupil. Homer's student is in a toga. Mine was wearing wraparound sunglasses like Bono's, black jeans, and a red T-shirt emblazoned with Chinese characters in white. Over his shoulder he carried his laptop.

We asked each other the usual question: What did you do over the summer? What he did, as I recall, was a brief internship at a well-regarded

Internet publication, a six-country swing through Europe, then back to enjoy his family and home, reconnect with high-school friends, and work on recording a rock CD. What had I done? I had written five drafts of a chapter for a book on the last two years of Sigmund Freud's life. I had traveled to Crozet, a few miles away, to get pizza. I'd sojourned overnight in Virginia Beach, the day after I woke up distressed because I couldn't figure out how to begin my chapter. I'd driven to the beach, figured it out (I thought), and then I'd come home. My young friend looked at me with a mixture of awe and compassion. I felt a little like one of those aged men of the Earth who populate Wordsworth's[1] poetry. One of them, the Old Cumberland Beggar, goes so slowly that you never actually see him move, but if you return to the spot where you first encountered him two hours past, lo, he has gone a little way down the road. The footprints are there to prove it.

I headed back to my office for draft No. 6, or something comparably glamorous. Where was my student going? He was no doubt heading into a more turbocharged version of his summer, a life of supreme intensity created in collaboration with the laptop slung over his shoulder. For his student generation is a singular one, at least in my experience of 30 or so years teaching: Its members have a spectacular hunger for life and more life. They want to study, travel, make friends, make more friends, read everything (superfast), take in all the movies, listen to every hot band, keep up with everyone they've ever known. And there's something else, too, that distinguishes them: They live to multiply possibilities. They're enemies of closure. For as much as they want to do and actually manage to do, they always strive to keep their options open, never to shut possibilities down before they have to.

This hunger for life has a number of consequences, for now and for the future. It's part of what makes this student generation appealing, highly promising—and also radically vulnerable. These students may go on to do great and good things, but they also present dangers to themselves and to the common future. They seem almost to have been created, as the poet says, "half to rise and half to fall."[2] As a teacher of theirs (and fellow citizen), I'm more than a little concerned about which it's going to be.

Internet technology was on hand for my current students from about   5
the time they were eight years old; it was in 1995 that the Netscape browser made the Internet accessible to everyone. And the Internet seems to me to have shaped their generation as much as the multichannel TV, with that critical device, the remote control, shaped the students who registered for my classes a decade ago. What is the Internet to current students?

---

[1]**Wordsworth:** William Wordsworth (1770–1850) was a major English poet associated with the Romantic movement along with his friend Samuel Taylor Coleridge (1772–1834), who is mentioned later in the essay.—EDS.

[2]*"half to rise and half to fall":* The phrase is from the poem "An Essay on Man" by the English poet, Alexander Pope (1688–1744).—EDS.

Consider first what it is not. A friend of mine, who has assiduously kept a journal for 40 years, calls the journal, which now runs to about 40 volumes, a "life thickener." His quotations and pictures and clips and drawings and paintings give density and meaning to the blind onrush that life can be. He looks back through the volumes and sees that there was a life and that to him it meant something. To my students, I suspect, my friend would look like a medieval monk, laboring over his manuscripts, someone with a radically pre-postmodern feel for time, someone who did not, in fact, understand what time actually is.

An Internet-linked laptop, one may safely say, is not a life thickener. At the fingertips of my students, the laptop is a multiplier of the possible. "I dwell in possibility," says Emily Dickinson, "a fairer house than prose." Well, my students want to dwell there with her and, it seems, to leave me in the weed-grown bungalow, prose.

My university recently passed an edict: No one, damn it (insofar as edicts can say damn it), is going to triple major. Everyone now who is worth his tuition money double majors: The students in my classes are engineering/English; politics/English; chemistry/English. An urban legend in my leaf-fringed 'hood is that someone got around this inane dictum about triple majors by majoring in four subjects—there was, it seems, no rule against that. The top students at my university, the ones who set the standard for the rest, even if they drive the rest a little crazy, connect with every likely person who has a page on Facebook, have 30 pages on Facebook, be checked in with and check in at every moment.

One day I tried an experiment in a class I was teaching on English and American Romanticism. We had been studying Thoreau and talking about his reflections (sour) on the uses of technology or communication. ("We are in great haste," he famously said, "to construct a magnetic telegraph from Maine to Texas; but Maine and Texas, it may be, have nothing important to communicate.") I asked the group, "How many places were you simultaneously yesterday—at the most?" Suppose you were chatting on your cell phone, partially watching a movie in one corner of the computer screen, instant messaging with three people (a modest number), and glancing occasionally at the text for some other course than ours—grazing, maybe, in Samuelson's *Economics* rather than diving deep into Thoreau's "Economy"—and then, also, tossing the occasional word to your roommate? Well, that would be seven, seven places at once. Some students—with a little high-spirited hyperbole thrown in, no doubt—got into double digits. Of course it wouldn't take the Dalai Lama or Thoreau to assure them that anyone who is in seven places at once is not anywhere in particular—not present, not here now. Be everywhere now—that's what the current technology invites, and that's what my students aspire to do.

Internet-linked computers are of course desiring machines—machines for the stimulation of desire. But so is a TV, so in a certain sense is a movie screen. What makes the Internet singular is its power to expand desire, expand possibility beyond the confines of prior media. (My students   10 are possibility junkies.) You can multiply the number of possible clothing purchases to near infinity and do it with stunning speed. You can make all the pleated skirts in the world appear almost all at once, for you to choose from. As we talked about this in class—with Thoreau's disapproving specter looking on (sometimes it appears that Thoreau disapproves of everything, except the drinking of cold water)—something surprising came out. The moment of maximum Internet pleasure was not the moment of closure, where you sealed the deal; it was the moment when the choices had been multiplied to the highest sum. It was the moment of maximum promise, when you touched the lip of the possible: of four majors and eight courses per term and a gazillion hits on your Facebook page, and being everyplace (almost) at once, and gazing upon all the pleated skirts that the world doth hold.

This is what Immanuel Kant, were he around to see it, might have called the computer sublime (he called something like it mathematical sublimity). The moment when you make the purchase, close the deal, pick a girlfriend, set a date: All those things, the students around the Thoreau table concurred, were a letdown, consummations not really to be wished for. The students were a little surprised by the conclusions they came to about themselves. "It's when I can see it all in front of me," one young woman said, "that's when I'm the happiest."

Ask an American college student what he's doing on Friday night. Ask him at 5:30 Friday afternoon. "I don't know" will likely be the first response. But then will come a list of possibilities to make the average Chinese menu look sullenly costive: the concert, the play, the movie, the party, the stay-at-home, chilling (or chillaxing), the monitoring of *Sports-Center*, the reading (fast, fast) of an assignment or two. University students now are virtual Hamlets of the virtual world, pondering possibility, faces pressed up against the sweet-shop window of their all-purpose desiring machines. To ticket or not to ticket, buy or not to, party or no: or perhaps to simply stay in and to multiply options in numberless numbers, never to be closed down.

And once you do get somewhere, wherever it might be, you'll find that, as Gertrude Stein has it, there's "no there there." At a student party, about a fourth of the people have their cell phones locked to their ears. What are they doing? "They're talking to their friends." About? "About another party they might conceivably go to." And naturally the simulation party is better than the one that they're now at (and not at), though of course there will be people at that party on their cell phones, talking about other simulacrum gatherings, spiraling on into M. C. Escher[3] infinity.

It's possible that recent events in the world have added intensity to students' quest for more possibilities, more and more life. The events of

---

[3]*Escher:* The Dutch artist M(aritus) C(ornelius) Escher (1898–1972) is famous for his intriguing drawings of objects in repeated loops that appear to approach infinity—for example, a picture of two hands in which each hand is drawing the other.—EDS.

September 11, which current college students experienced in their early teens, were an undoubted horror. But they had the effect, I think, of waking America's young people up from a pseudo-nihilistic doze. Before New York, Pennsylvania, and Virginia, the middle-class American teenager's world had been a pleasure dome, full of rare delights. It was the reign of television: the oracle that knows everything and can take you anywhere. Television brought images of bliss, and its ads showed you the products that you needed to buy in order to achieve it. The well-known Jeep ad that depicted hip kids tossing Frisbees and laughing like rock stars had nothing to do with the properties of a Jeep. It was a persona ad that advertised the sort of person you'd be when you acquired the product. The ad was an emblem of the consumer moment: Buy in order to be.

Students wanted to be cool. They wanted to be beyond reproach. There was a sense abroad that if you simply did what you were supposed to do, kept low to the ground and stayed on the conveyor belt, the future that TV promised would be yours. Everything was a mode of entertainment, or could be transformed into one, after it had been submitted to Letterman-like or Leno-like ridicule. The president was a genial boy from Arkansas who awoke one day and found himself in office. But that had not slaked his boyishness at all. He still wanted a version of what everyone did: all-nighters, pizza, and his pals. The president was a dog who couldn't stay on the porch. My students—the guys in particular—often found him the perfect image of success: You need never grow up; need never abandon college-boy mode. The couch where you sat, hours a day, in lordly condescension, monitoring the box, would in time morph into an airship to swoosh you into your dreams.

But then there came the day of near apocalypse in America, September 11, 2001. The prospect of hanging, Doctor Johnson[4] observed, does wonders to concentrate the mind. Well, the mind of America has been concentrated. No one believes that the whole edifice is likely to come down around us soon. But everyone now lives charged with the knowledge that today, tomorrow, next week, we can suffer an event that will change everything drastically. A dirty bomb in the middle of a great city, poison wafting in soft clouds through a subway system, a water supply subtly tainted: Such things would not only derange the lives of those they touch directly, they'd discompose and remake America in ways that would be, to say the least, none too sweet. Tomorrow the deck may be shuffled and recut by the devil's hand. So what shall we do now?

The answer that comes from current students would seem to be this: Live, live. Before the bombs go off in San Francisco or the water goes vile in New York, and the new Mahdi appears on a billion screens at once to pronounce another turn in the holy war that, for him, has been going on since the first crusader scraped an armored foot on the soil of the Holy Land. On that bad day there will be, at the very least, the start of a com-

15

---

[4]***Doctor Johnson:*** The English essayist, critic, and lexicographer Samuel Johnson (1709–1784).—EDS.

prehensive closing down. There will be no more free travel, no more easy money, and much less loose talk. Life will become a confinement, a prison, a pound. So now, as James's Strether instructs Little Bilham,[5] you must "live all you can; it's a mistake not to." There's a humane hunger to my students' hustle for more life — but I think it's possible that down below bubbles a fear. Do it now, for later may be too late.

It's clearly a new university world that I'm living in, though it took me some time to see it. My revelation occurred a few months ago. Up to that point, I was always happy to see students bringing their laptops to class. The sight of them conjured up visions of upbeat newsmagazine covers: Kids in ordered rows behind their computers, tapping in the new millennium. And the students who brought their laptops seemed to be the most engaged: They'd be skittering fast across the keys, alert and alive, and glancing up from time to time to toss a few sentences into the conversation. These were the plugged-in kids, the committed ones. But then one day I made a rare trip to the blackboard and on the way glanced over a laptopper's shoulder. There was what appeared to be YouTube in one corner (Shakira? The *Hips Don't Lie* video?) and e-mail front and center — but nothing much to do with the ostensible subject of the class. How could I have missed it? This sort of thing is now the way of the classroom world.

Three thousand first-year students entered my university last year, and 2,906 of them brought laptops with them; 90 brought desktops. Four students — the incoming James Deans and Marlon Brandos? — showed up computerless. (Ten years ago, half of our first-year students came to school without computers.) At Virginia, as at just about every other university, almost all buildings are now equipped with wireless routers. This began to happen about four years ago, and many of us professors barely noticed it, in part because we generally travel only from office to classroom. But our students are nomads, on the move all day. Wherever they sit, they set up Internet Command Central. Now students in almost any classroom can get directly onto the Internet and, given the shieldlike screens on their laptops, they can call up what they like. Especially in the big lecture classes now, everyone's flitting from Web site to Web site, checking e-mail, and instant messaging. Do they pay any attention to the class? My students tell me that they're experts in paying attention to many things at once: It's no problem at all.

A Romantic, says Nietzsche, is someone who always wants to be else-   20
where. If that's so, then the children of the Internet are Romantics, for they perpetually wish to be someplace else, and the laptop reliably helps take them there — if only in imagination. The e-mailer, the instant messenger, the Web browser are all dispersing their energies and interests outward, away from the present, the here and now. The Internet user is constantly connecting with people and institutions far away, creating surrogate communities that displace the potential community at hand.

---

[5]*James Strether . . . Little Bilham:* Characters in *The Ambassadors*, the 1903 novel by the American writer, Henry James (1843–1916). — EDS.

Then too, booking by computer has made travel easier and, by eliminating a certain number of middlemen, kept it reasonably cheap. So there's an inducement to take off physically as well. The Internet is perhaps the most centrifugal technology ever devised. The classroom, where you sit down in one space at one time and ponder a text or an issue in slow motion, is coming to feel ever more antiquated. What's at a premium now is movement, making connections, getting all the circuitry fizzing and popping.

For students now, life is elsewhere. Classes matter to them, but classes are just part of an ever-enlarging web of activities and diversions. Students now seek to master their work—not to be taken over by it and consumed. They want to dispatch it, do it well and quickly, then get on to the many other things that interest them. For my students live in the future and not in the present; they live with their prospects for success and pleasure. They dwell in possibility.

"By their drugs shall ye know them," it says somewhere in the Scriptures, no doubt. The answer to the question, "What drugs are college students taking now?" is, as it has been for some time, "All of the above." But the drugs that have most recently entered the scene and had an impact are the ones designed to combat attention-deficit disorder (ADD): Adderall, Ritalin, Concerta, and Daytrana, which delivers the meds through a patch. These are all pharmaceuticals, obtained by prescription, though often the people taking them have never gotten diagnosed. The ADD drugs seem to be omnipresent; they're on sale in every dorm at prices that rise exponentially as the week of final exams approaches. "Twenty dollars for a hit," one student told me, "on the night before an exam in the intro econ class." Their effect is, pretty subtly, but pretty surely, to speed the taker up. They kick him forward, give him fresh juice to keep exploring possibilities, buying and doing and buying and doing.

The idea is to keep moving, never to stop. It's now become so commonplace as to be beneath notice, but there was a time that every city block contiguous to a university did not contain a shop dispensing a speed-you-up drug and inviting people to sit down and enjoy it along with wireless computer access. Laptops seem to go with coffee and other stimulants, in much the way that blood-and-gold sunsets went with LSD and Oreo cookies with weed. (It's possible, I sometimes think, that fully half of the urban Starbucks in America are located in rental properties that, in an earlier incarnation, were head shops.) Nor were there always energy drinks: vile-tasting concoctions coming in cans costumed like superheroes, designed to make you run as fast and steady as your computer, your car, and—this is Darwinian capitalism after all—your colleagues. You've got to keep going. Almost all of my students have one book—an old book—that they've read and treasured, and read again. It's the American epic of free movement, *On the Road*,[6] a half-century old last year, but to them one of the few things in the culture of my generation that's still youthful.

---

[6]**On the Road:** The now-classic American novel published in 1957 by Jack Kerouac (1922–1969), known as "king of the beats."—EDS.

The sports that this generation has put its stamp on—X-games sorts   25
of things, like snowboarding, surfing, and skateboarding—are all about
velocity, motion, skimming. They're about speeding flawlessly through
space, without being diverted, shut down, or captured by mere gravity.
(Gravity, in all senses, is what my students are out to avoid.) Like the
drugs, the sports help to keep the kids moving elsewhere.

How about their music? It's a little hard to say. Students no longer turn
their speakers out the dorm window and blast the quad with Poco's "Deliv-
erin'." Music now comes personal, a whisper in the ear, through the iPod,
so that everyone can walk around with the soundtrack to his own movie
purring. This constant music plug-in is another mode of being elsewhere,
about right for the current dispensation. As to the sort of music, well, the
kind of stuff that runs through iPods is varied. Many of my students delight in listening to bands that absolutely no one but themselves seems to
have heard of. When I ask them in class to tell me their favorite tunes, I'm
reminded of the days when my friends and I would show each other our
baseball cards. As you flipped yours over, the other guy responded with
"Got it. Got it. Don't got it. Got it." "Don't got it" came with a wince.
The coolest kid in the room now is clearly the one whose favorite bands
are the ones the others wince most over—the ones they don't got.

But the students have a collective musical taste, too. When they're together at a party, when they've unplugged their iPods and put their cell
phones, temporarily, on vibrate, what they generally want is rap. Whatever the content of rap, its form is propulsive forward motion—the beat,
the energy pulse, is what it's about. It drives you forward, runs gas through
the motor. Rap is part of the constant stimulation that students seem unable to live without.

When a seminar is over now, the students reach their hands into their
pockets and draw—it looks a little like *Gunfight at the O.K. Corral.* But
what they're reaching for, after discussing Thoreau, say, on the pleasures
of solitude, are their cell phones. They've been unwired, off the drug, for
more than an hour, and they need a fix. The cell phoning comes as a relief: The students have been (give or take) in one place, at one time, pondering a few passages from *Walden.* Now they need to disperse themselves again, get away from the immediate, dissolve the present away.

But I teach at a university known for high-powered students who
are also sometimes high-octane partiers. Is what I'm saying true of all
universities? Well, I do some traveling and talking to colleagues at other
places, and from what I can tell, the more high-prestige the institution,
the more frenetic and centrifugal the pace. At Harvard and Yale, I'd now
expect to find kids who've hit a white incandescence or maybe who've
fused completely with the Internet, living within it, like characters out of
Neuromancer,[7] finding in their merger with the machine a kind of high
that can take the place of happiness.

---

[7]**Neuromancer:** The 1984 novel by William Gibson that coined the word "cyberspace." For more on Gibson, see page 691.—EDS.

Skate fast over the surfaces of life and cover all the extended space you   30
can, says the new ethos. Perhaps the greatest of all surface skimmers, the
poet laureate of the way we live now at college, was William Wordsworth's
arch-antagonist, George Gordon, Lord Byron. The poetry of Wordsworth, the explorer of inner space, is deliberate, slow, ponderous, like
those old men of the woods he loves to depict, and that I perhaps resemble to my fast-skimming students. The complaint against Wordsworth is
that he is tiresome—he has no time for sex or violence, just muted natural
beauty and a mystical sublime. Byron—rich, beautiful, glamorous, with
startlingly white skin, black hair, and swanlike neck—doesn't celebrate
violence. Sex is his game. In *Don Juan*, the hero skims and skips from one
encounter to the next. His desires are mobile: He can play the woman's
part as well as the man's. Desire doesn't provoke complex ambivalence in
Byron, just the need to move from one beckoning satisfaction to the next.
Byron's poetry has all the velocity of this ever-moving, ever-changing desire: His rhymes are shrewd, arch, unexpected, and seem to be turned
with a flick of his wrist. Thus Byron or Wordsworth's good friend Samuel
Taylor Coleridge, who has just published his *Biographia Literaria*, a
book Byron dislikes because it is dense and difficult, something you must
read at least twice: "And Coleridge, too, has lately taken wing. / But like
a hawk encumbered with his hood,—/ Explaining metaphysics to the nation—/ I wish he would explain his Explanation."

Byron claimed to compose best on horseback and to be able to concoct dozens of lines in an outing. Wordsworth shouted his lines aloud as
he trudged through the Lake District, his dog browsing ahead of him to
bark if strangers, who might hear his bellowing and think him mad, appeared on the trail. Byron disliked Wordsworth for one reason above all
the rest: boring. The poet of "rocks and stones and trees" was boring.
Byron wished never to be bored. So he kept moving, kept accelerating
from one point to the next, not in hopes of being satisfied—that he took
to be an illusion—but so as not to be overcome by the noontide demon,
ennui. In 1825, the year after Byron died, the first passenger locomotive
appeared, and maybe, says Camille Paglia,[8] Byron's aristocratic spirit
flew by metempsychosis into the machine. Well, perhaps Byron's restless
demon has migrated again, this time from locomotive to laptop.

Students now are Romantics—of a Byronic sort. He would have
adored their world of fast travel, fast communication—and fast relationships. There is no more Byronic form of erotic life than the hookup.
When after the publication of *Childe Harold* Byron became a celebrity—
"I awoke and found myself famous," he said—he was beset with erotic
opportunities. Women sent him notes begging for liaisons; they followed
his carriage through the streets; they smuggled themselves into his rooms.
And frequently Byron, who was probably more often seduced than seduc-

---

[8]***Paglia:*** American cultural critic known for her strong and controversial opinions. For
more on Paglia, see page 791.—EDS.

ing, was pleased to comply. In his superspeed erotic life, Byron is said to have hooked up hundreds of times.

What exactly does it mean to hook up? It means managing to have good sex without activating all the strong feelings that sex usually brings. Hooking up is a fantasy of frictionless sex—sex free of deep emotion. It's sex that lets you keep on sliding over surfaces, moving from partner to partner as smoothly as you move from site to site on a laptop. In fact, the Internet-linked computer is an erotic bazaar, a hookup machine. All of those personal pages on MySpace and Facebook are, among other things, personal ads. (Byron would love shopping there—and, more, being shopped for.) Here students can find objects more alluring and numerous than pleated skirts. They can find sexual possibilities without end.

Hooking up, of course, is a kind of myth. Sex usually does provoke strong feelings, even when people swear to each other that—this time, this time—it won't. Not everyone is wired like Lord Byron. Students often find that they need continuity and comfort in what can be a harsh college world. Many of them hold faithfully to boyfriends and girlfriends through all four years of school (albeit sometimes with special spring-break dispensations). And a few of those students busting out of my class, grabbing for their cell phones, are calling not the alluring near stranger who just IM-ed them, but their parents. In every class I teach, there are at least two or three students who call home every day.

For the way that my students live now is dangerous—some of them 35 know it, some learn in time. "In skating over thin ice," Emerson says, "our safety is in our speed." But sometimes, like it or not, we're slowed down or stopped, and then trouble begins. Last term a young woman, an art-history and commerce major in one of my classes, stopped by my office. She's a marvelous student; I've never taught anyone who could read poetry with much more subtlety and feeling. She was pale, sleepless; her teeth were chattering softly. I invited her to sit down and then asked some questions. "How many courses are you taking?" Five, no six, seven. "Audits?" Yes, one. "A thesis?" Almost done: She planned to knock out 40 pages over the weekend, but now her father, whom she clearly adored, was sick, and she'd have to go home and then how could she. . . .

"It's too much," I said. "What?" She hadn't heard me exactly. "What you're doing? It's too much." And then came—as it almost always does when I say these words, or something like them—a feeling of great relief. Someone with a claim to authority has said that it's OK to be tired, OK to ease up. OK to rest. When my students crash on their own, they crash like helicopters dropping straight out of the sky. They're often unaware that they're on the verge of trouble. They're doing what they are supposed to do, what their parents want, with all those courses and the multiple majors, and they haven't got much of any resources to look inside and see that matters are out of joint—no one has thought to help them acquire those. Did Byron ever fall apart, victim of his own hunger for speed and space? If so, he told us little about it.

I wonder, thinking back to that fall day on the Lawn, was it something like an encounter I had had — to take the reincarnation trope a step further — with Lord Byron? He was all for glamour and motion. I was all for — well, what was I for? Was it the magic of the fifth draft on a project about a thinker, Freud, about whom — let us be generous — not everyone seems to care a great deal? I admit that I love that line of Yeats's about how writing is ceaseless stitching and unstitching, but "if it does not seem a moment's thought / Our stitching and unstitching has been naught." The stitching-unstitching business fascinates me. Yet my student had been to six countries, six! — and that was only part of his summer's story. If you asked returning students now for that old composition standard, What I Did This Summer, they'd have to hit you with three-decker novels.

And what do I have to offer the speedsters, I, a slow person from the generation of one kind of Coke, three TV stations, one mom and one dad? How exactly do we professors teach this kind of student? What does she need to know?

Many of my colleagues have a ready answer, and its essence is this: If you can't lick 'em, join 'em. In effect, they've made the courses an extension of the Internet. Their classes are laser-and-light shows, fast-moving productions that mime the colors and sound and above all the velocity of the laptop. There are movie screens, sound systems, Internet tie-ins. And, these colleagues say, it works. One professor I know of equips his students with handheld wireless input devices that have 12 buttons and look a lot like TV remotes. Every five minutes or so, he stops teaching and polls the kids to see how well they're doing. I admire the resourcefulness that's on display here — and I admire the skill and energy that many of my fellow teachers have deployed to meet students halfway. And yet. . . .

Not long ago, a younger colleague came by my office to chat and at   40
a certain point informed me that her son, who was 4 years old, had a favorite dinosaur and that it was called the Edmontosaurus. ("Edmundosaurus" is what I could have sworn she said.) She remarked, with what seemed untainted good will, that this may be the very oldest of dinosaurs. A few weeks later she came by again — was she wheeling a TV in front of her, taking it to class? — and ended up telling me about this "Edmundosaurus" one more time. Well, the kind of schooling I endorse goes back at least as far as Socrates or maybe further, though not quite full-throttle to the thunder lizards.

If Socrates looked out on the current dispensation, what would he see? He'd see the velocity and the hunger for more life, faster, faster — sure. But given his interests, he'd notice something else, too. He'd see that by the time students get to college, they have been told who they are and what the world is many times over. Parents and friends, teachers, counselors, priests and rabbis, ministers and imams have had their say. They've let each student know how they size him up, and they've let him know what they think he should value. Every student has been submitted to what Socrates liked to called *doxa*, common sense, general belief.

And a student may be all the things the people who raised her say she is; she may want the things they have shown her are worth wanting. She may genuinely be her father and mother's daughter. But then again, she may not.

The primary reason to study Blake and Dickinson and Freud and Dickens is not to become more cultivated, or more articulate, or to be someone who at a cocktail party is never embarrassed (but can embarrass others). The ultimate reason to read them is to see if they may know you better than you know yourself. They may help you to cut through established opinion—*doxa*—about who you are and what the world is. They may give you new ways of seeing and saying things, and those ways may be truer for you than the ones that you grew up with. Genuine education is a process that gives students a second chance. They've been socialized once by their parents and teachers; now it's time for a second, maybe a better, shot. It's time—to be a little idealizing about it—for Socrates to have a turn.

For a student to be educated, she has to face brilliant antagonists. She has to encounter thinkers who see the world in different terms than she does. Does she come to college as a fundamentalist guardian of crude faith? Then two necessary books for her are Freud's *Future of an Illusion* and Nietzsche's *The Anti-Christ*. Once she's weathered the surface insults, she may find herself in an intellectual version of paradise, where she can defend her beliefs or change them, and where what's on hand is not a chance conversation, as Socrates liked to say, but a dialogue about how to live. Is the student a scion of high-minded liberals who think that religion is the OxyContin—the redneck heroin—of Redneck Nation? Then on might come William James and *The Varieties of Religious Experience* or Schopenhauer's essays on faith. It's this kind of dialogue, deliberate, gradual, thoughtful, that immersion in the manic culture of the Internet and Adderall conditions students not to have. The first step for the professor now is to slow his classroom down. The common phrase for what he wants to do is telling: We "stop and think." Stop. Our students rarely get a chance to stop. They're always in motion, always spitting out what comes first to mind, never challenging, checking, revising.

Not long ago a young man came to my office, plopped down, and looked at me with tired urgency. "Give me 10 minutes on Freud," he said. "Convince me that he really has something important to tell me." Despite appearances, this was a good moment. It was a chance to try to persuade him to slow it down. Get one of Freud's books—*Civilization and Its Discontents* is usually the best place to start—read it once and again, then let's talk.

When you have that kind of conversation, one on one, you begin, however modestly, to create a university. Why does the encounter need to take place face to face? The student and teacher need to create a bond of good feeling, where they are free to speak openly with each other. They need to connect not just through cold print, but through gestures, intonations, jokes. The student needs to discover what the teacher knows, and what she exemplifies about how to live. The teacher needs contact with the student's energy and hopes. That kind of connection happens best in person; perhaps it can happen only that way.

It's not a luxury, this Socratic education whose goal is self-knowledge. Constantly I see my students leaving the university, determined to do not what they want and need to do, but what their parents and their friends believe they ought to do. And in this they can in some measure succeed. Society has a great span of resources to assist someone in doing what he's not cut out for yet still must be done. Alcohol, drugs, divorce, and buying, buying, buying what you don't need will all help you jam your round peg of a self into this or that square-holed profession.

But those students who, through whatever form of struggle, really have come to have an independent sense of who they are and what they want genuinely seem to thrive in the world. Thoreau says that if you advance in the direction of your dreams, you'll find uncommon success, and teaching a few generations of students has persuaded me that he is right. The ones who do what they love without a lot of regard for conventional success tend to turn out happy and strong. As to those willing to advance in the direction of other people's dreams—well, prime the credit cards, crank the porn channel!

We teachers need to remind ourselves from time to time that our primary job is not to help our students to acquire skills, marketable skills, bankables. And we don't preeminently teach communication and computation and instill habits of punctuality and thoroughness. We're not here to help our students make their minds resemble their laptops, fast and feverish. We didn't get into teaching to make trains of thought run on time.

As to our students, all honor to them: They may have much to teach   50
the five-drafter. By their hunger for more life they convey hope that the world is still in some measure a splendid place, worth seeing and appreciating. Into spontaneity they can liberate us. But life is more than spontaneity and whim. To live well, we must sometimes stop and think, and then try to remake the work in progress that we currently are. There's no better place for that than a college classroom where, together, we can slow it down and live deliberately, if only for a while.

And to that end—Edmundosaurus, take the mike!—starting this year, no more laptops in my classroom. You can leave them at home. You can check 'em at the door.

The Reader's Presence

1. Why do you think Edmundson opens his essay by describing a brief encounter with a student? What does the encounter allow him to establish? How does Edmundson's description provide you with a contrast between himself and the younger generation that the student represents? As a student, do you consider Edmundson's

characterization of the younger generation fair and accurate? Do you take any issue with it? Explain your answers.

2. Edmundson's essay contains many literary and philosophical references. The author clearly expects his readers to recognize them. How many did you not recognize? Did you find the references distracting? How do these references help you identify the audience Edmundson targets for his essay? How would you describe that audience? To what extent did you or did you not feel included as a reader? Explain how Edmundson's numerous references help reinforce the main point of the essay.

3. Read Edmundson's essay in conjunction with John Taylor Gatto's "Against School" (page 682). One essay addresses college-level educational issues; the other examines our public schools. What similarities can you find between the two essays? How does Edmundson deal with the issue of conformity? Do you think Gatto's observations about the ineffectiveness of our public school systems can be applied to America's universities? Explain why or why not.

Lars Eighner

On Dumpster Diving

Lars Eighner (b. 1948) was born in Texas and attended the University of Texas at Austin. An essayist and fiction writer, he contributes regularly to the Threepenny Review, Advocate Men, the Guide, *and* Inches. *He has published several collections of short stories, essays, and gay erotica. His most recent publications include a camp novel,* Pawn to Queen Four *(1995); a collection of essays,* Gay Cosmos *(1995); an erotic short story collection,* Whispered in the Dark *(1995); and* WANK: The Tapes *(1998). Eighner writes a blog on his Web site,* larseighner.com.

Eighner became homeless in 1988, after he lost his job as a mental-hospital attendant. "On Dumpster Diving" is Eighner's prize-winning essay based on this experience, later reprinted as part of his full-length book about homelessness, Travels with Lizbeth: Three Years on the Road and on the Streets *(1993). Eighner and Lizbeth, Eighner's dog, became homeless again in 1996. Friends organized a fund under the auspices of the* Texas Observer *and obtained an apartment for Eighner and Lizbeth in Austin. Lizbeth has since passed away.*

On what is required to find success as a writer, Eighner has said, "I was not making enough money to support myself as a housed person, but I was writing well before I became homeless. . . . A writer needs talent, luck, and persistence. You can make do with two out of three, and the more you have of one, the less you need of the others."

Long before I began Dumpster diving I was impressed with Dumpsters, enough so that I wrote the Merriam-Webster research service to discover what I could about the word "Dumpster." I learned from them that "Dumpster" is a proprietary word belonging to the Dempster Dumpster company.

Since then I have dutifully capitalized the word although it was lowercased in almost all of the citations Merriam-Webster photocopied for me. Dempster's word is too apt. I have never heard these things called anything but Dumpsters. I do not know anyone who knows the generic name for these objects. From time to time, however, I hear a wino or hobo give some corrupted credit to the original and call them Dipsy Dumpsters.

I began Dumpster diving about a year before I became homeless.

I prefer the term "scavenging" and use the word "scrounging" when I mean to be obscure. I have heard people, evidently meaning to be polite, using the word "foraging," but I prefer to reserve that word for gathering nuts and berries and such which I do also according to the season and the opportunity. "Dumpster diving" seems to me to be a little too cute and, in my case, inaccurate because I lack the athletic ability to lower myself into the Dumpsters as the true divers do, much to their increased profit.

I like the frankness of the word "scavenging," which I can hardly think of without picturing a big black snail on an aquarium wall. I live from the refuse of others. I am a scavenger. I think it a sound and honorable niche, although if I could I would naturally prefer to live the comfortable consumer life, perhaps—and only perhaps—as a slightly less wasteful consumer owing to what I have learned as a scavenger.

While my dog Lizbeth and I were still living in the house on Avenue B in Austin, as my savings ran out, I put almost all my sporadic income into rent. The necessities of daily life I began to extract from Dumpsters. Yes, we ate from Dumpsters. Except for jeans, all my clothes came from Dumpsters. Boom boxes, candles, bedding, toilet paper, medicine, books, a typewriter, a virgin male love doll, change sometimes amounting to many dollars: I acquired many things from the Dumpsters.

I have learned much as a scavenger. I mean to put some of what I have learned down here, beginning with the practical art of Dumpster diving and proceeding to the abstract.

What is safe to eat?

After all, the finding of objects is becoming something of an urban art. Even respectable employed people will sometimes find something tempting sticking out of a Dumpster or standing beside one. Quite a number of people, not all of them of the bohemian type, are willing to brag that they found this or that piece in the trash. But eating from Dumpsters is the thing that separates the dilettanti from the professionals.

Eating safely from the Dumpsters involves three principles: using the senses and common sense to evaluate the condition of the found materials, knowing the Dumpsters of a given area and checking them regularly, and seeking always to answer the question "Why was this discarded?" 10

Perhaps everyone who has a kitchen and a regular supply of groceries has, at one time or another, made a sandwich and eaten half of it before discovering mold on the bread or got a mouthful of milk before realizing the milk had turned. Nothing of the sort is likely to happen to a Dumpster diver because he is constantly reminded that most food is discarded for a reason. Yet a lot of perfectly good food can be found in Dumpsters.

Canned goods, for example, turn up fairly often in the Dumpsters I frequent. All except the most phobic people would be willing to eat from a can even if it came from a Dumpster. Canned goods are among the safest of foods to be found in Dumpsters, but are not utterly foolproof.

Although very rare with modern canning methods, botulism is a possibility. Most other forms of food poisoning seldom do lasting harm to a healthy person. But botulism is almost certainly fatal and often the first symptom is death. Except for carbonated beverages, all canned goods should contain a slight vacuum and suck air when first punctured. Bulging, rusty, dented cans and cans that spew when punctured should be avoided, especially when the contents are not very acidic or syrupy.

Heat can break down the botulin, but this requires much more cooking than most people do to canned goods. To the extent that botulism occurs at all, of course, it can occur in cans on pantry shelves as well as in cans from Dumpsters. Need I say that home-canned goods found in Dumpsters are simply too risky to be recommended.

From time to time one of my companions, aware of the source of my provisions, will ask, "Do you think these crackers are really safe to eat?" For some reason it is most often the crackers they ask about. 15

This question always makes me angry. Of course I would not offer my companion anything I had doubts about. But more than that I wonder why he cannot evaluate the condition of the crackers for himself. I have no special knowledge and I have been wrong before. Since he knows where the food comes from, it seems to me he ought to assume some of the responsibility for deciding what he will put in his mouth.

For myself I have few qualms about dry foods such as crackers, cookies, cereal, chips, and pasta if they are free of visible contaminants and still dry and crisp. Most often such things are found in the original packaging, which is not so much a positive sign as it is the absence of a negative one.

Raw fruits and vegetables with intact skins seem perfectly safe to me, excluding of course the obviously rotten. Many are discarded for minor imperfections which can be pared away. Leafy vegetables, grapes, cauliflower, broccoli, and similar things may be contaminated by liquids and may be impractical to wash.

Candy, especially hard candy, is usually safe if it has not drawn ants. Chocolate is often discarded only because it has become discolored as the cocoa butter de-emulsified. Candying after all is one method of food preservation because pathogens do not like very sugary substances.

All of these foods might be found in any Dumpster and can be evalu-   20
ated with some confidence largely on the basis of appearance. Beyond these are foods which cannot be correctly evaluated without additional information.

I began scavenging by pulling pizzas out of the Dumpster behind a pizza delivery shop. In general prepared food requires caution, but in this case I knew when the shop closed and went to the Dumpster as soon as the last of the help left.

Such shops often get prank orders, called "bogus." Because help seldom stays long at these places pizzas are often made with the wrong topping, refused on delivery for being cold, or baked incorrectly. The products to be discarded are boxed up because inventory is kept by counting boxes: A boxed pizza can be written off; an unboxed pizza does not exist.

I never placed a bogus order to increase the supply of pizzas and I believe no one else was scavenging in this Dumpster. But the people in the shop became suspicious and began to retain their garbage in the shop overnight.

While it lasted I had a steady supply of fresh, sometimes warm pizza. Because I knew the Dumpster I knew the source of the pizza, and because I visited the Dumpster regularly I knew what was fresh and what was yesterday's.

The area I frequent is inhabited by many affluent college students. I   25
am not here by chance; the Dumpsters in this area are very rich. Students throw out many good things, including food. In particular they tend to throw everything out when they move at the end of a semester, before and after breaks, and around midterm when many of them despair of college. So I find it advantageous to keep an eye on the academic calendar.

The students throw food away around the breaks because they do not know whether it has spoiled or will spoil before they return. A typical discard is a half jar of peanut butter. In fact nonorganic peanut butter does not require refrigeration and is unlikely to spoil in any reasonable time. The student does not know that, and since it is Daddy's money, the student decides not to take a chance.

Opened containers require caution and some attention to the question "Why was this discarded?" But in the case of discards from student apartments, the answer may be that the item was discarded through carelessness, ignorance, or wastefulness. This can sometimes be deduced when the item is found with many others, including some that are obviously perfectly good.

Some students, and others, approach defrosting a freezer by chucking out the whole lot. Not only do the circumstances of such a find tell the story, but also the mass of frozen goods stays cold for a long time and items may be found still frozen or freshly thawed.

Yogurt, cheese, and sour cream are items that are often thrown out while they are still good. Occasionally I find a cheese with a spot of mold, which of course I just pare off, and because it is obvious why such a cheese was discarded, I treat it with less suspicion than an apparently perfect cheese found in similar circumstances. Yogurt is often discarded, still sealed, only because the expiration date on the carton had passed. This is one of my favorite finds because yogurt will keep for several days, even in warm weather.

Students throw out canned goods and staples at the end of semesters and when they give up college at midterm. Drugs, pornography, spirits, and the like are often discarded when parents are expected—Dad's day, for example. And spirits also turn up after big party weekends, presumably discarded by the newly reformed. Wine and spirits, of course, keep perfectly well even once opened.

My test for carbonated soft drinks is whether they still fizz vigorously. Many juices or other beverages are too acid or too syrupy to cause much concern provided they are not visibly contaminated. Liquids, however, require some care.

One hot day I found a large jug of Pat O'Brien's Hurricane mix. The jug had been opened, but it was still ice cold. I drank three large glasses before it became apparent to me that someone had added the rum to the mix, and not a little rum. I never tasted the rum and by the time I began to feel the effects I had already ingested a very large quantity of the beverage. Some divers would have considered this a boon, but being suddenly and thoroughly intoxicated in a public place in the early afternoon is not my idea of a good time.

I have heard of people maliciously contaminating discarded food and even handouts, but mostly I have heard of this from people with vivid imaginations who have had no experience with the Dumpsters themselves. Just before the pizza shop stopped discarding its garbage at night, jalapeños began showing up on most of the discarded pizzas. If indeed this was meant to discourage me it was a wasted effort because I am a native Texan.

For myself, I avoid game, poultry, pork, and egg-based foods whether I find them raw or cooked. I seldom have the means to cook what I find, but when I do I avail myself of plentiful supplies of beef which is often in very good condition. I suppose fish becomes disagreeable before it becomes dangerous. The dog is happy to have any such thing that is past its prime and, in fact, does not recognize fish as food until it is quite strong.

Home leftovers, as opposed to surpluses from restaurants, are very often bad. Evidently, especially among students, there is a common type of personality that carefully wraps up even the smallest leftover and shoves it into the back of the refrigerator for six months or so before discarding it. Characteristic of this type are the reused jars and margarine tubs which house the remains.

30

35

I avoid ethnic foods I am unfamiliar with. If I do not know what it is supposed to look like when it is good, I cannot be certain I will be able to tell if it is bad.

No matter how careful I am I still get dysentery at least once a month, oftener in warm weather. I do not want to paint too romantic a picture. Dumpster diving has serious drawbacks as a way of life.

I learned to scavenge gradually, on my own. Since then I have initiated several companions into the trade. I have learned that there is a predictable series of stages a person goes through in learning to scavenge.

At first the new scavenger is filled with disgust and self-loathing. He is ashamed of being seen and may lurk around, trying to duck behind things, or he may try to dive at night.

(In fact, most people instinctively look away from a scavenger. By skulking around, the novice calls attention to himself and arouses suspicion. Diving at night is ineffective and needlessly messy.)

Every grain of rice seems to be a maggot. Everything seems to stink. He can wipe the egg yolk off the found can, but he cannot erase the stigma of eating garbage out of his mind.

That stage passes with experience. The scavenger finds a pair of running shoes that fit and look and smell brand new. He finds a pocket calculator in perfect working order. He finds pristine ice cream, still frozen, more than he can eat or keep. He begins to understand: People do throw away perfectly good stuff, a lot of perfectly good stuff.

At this stage, Dumpster shyness begins to dissipate. The diver, after all, has the last laugh. He is finding all manner of good things which are his for the taking. Those who disparage his profession are the fools, not he.

He may begin to hang onto some perfectly good things for which he has neither a use nor a market. Then he begins to take note of the things which are not perfectly good but are nearly so. He mates a Walkman with broken earphones and one that is missing a battery cover. He picks up things which he can repair.

At this stage he may become lost and never recover. Dumpsters are full of things of some potential value to someone and also of things which never have much intrinsic value but are interesting. All the Dumpster divers I have known come to the point of trying to acquire everything they touch. Why not take it, they reason, since it is all free.

This is, of course, hopeless. Most divers come to realize that they must restrict themselves to items of relatively immediate utility. But in some cases the diver simply cannot control himself. I have met several of these pack-rat types. Their ideas of the values of various pieces of junk verge on the psychotic. Every bit of glass may be a diamond, they think, and all that glistens, gold.

I tend to gain weight when I am scavenging. Partly this is because I always find far more pizza and doughnuts than water-packed tuna, non-fat yogurt, and fresh vegetables. Also I have not developed much faith in the reliability of Dumpsters as a food source, although it has been proven to me many times. I tend to eat as if I have no idea where my next meal is coming from. But mostly I just hate to see food go to waste and so I eat much more than I should. Something like this drives the obsession to collect junk.

As for collecting objects, I usually restrict myself to collecting one kind of small object at a time, such as pocket calculators, sunglasses, or campaign buttons. To live on the street I must anticipate my needs to a certain extent: I must pick up and save warm bedding I find in August because it will not be found in Dumpsters in November. But even if I had a home with extensive storage space I could not save everything that might be valuable in some contingency.

I have proprietary feelings about my Dumpsters. As I have suggested, it is no accident that I scavenge from Dumpsters where good finds are common. But my limited experience with Dumpsters in other areas suggests to me that it is the population of competitors rather than the affluence of the dumpers that most affects the feasibility of survival by scavenging. The large number of competitors is what puts me off the idea of trying to scavenge in places like Los Angeles.

Curiously, I do not mind my direct competition, other scavengers, so   50
much as I hate the can scroungers.

People scrounge cans because they have to have a little cash. I have tried scrounging cans with an able-bodied companion. Afoot a can scrounger simply cannot make more than a few dollars a day. One can extract the necessities of life from the Dumpsters directly with far less effort than would be required to accumulate the equivalent value in cans.

Can scroungers, then, are people who *must* have small amounts of cash. These are drug addicts and winos, mostly the latter because the amounts of cash are so small.

Spirits and drugs do, like all other commodities, turn up in Dumpsters and the scavenger will from time to time have a half bottle of a rather good wine with his dinner. But the wino cannot survive on these occasional finds; he must have his daily dose to stave off the DTs. All the cans he can carry will buy about three bottles of Wild Irish Rose.

I do not begrudge them the cans, but can scroungers tend to tear up the Dumpsters, mixing the contents and littering the area. They become so specialized that they can see only cans. They earn my contempt by passing up change, canned goods, and readily hockable items.

There are precious few courtesies among scavengers. But it is a com-   55
mon practice to set aside surplus items: pairs of shoes, clothing, canned goods, and such. A true scavenger hates to see good stuff go to waste and what he cannot use he leaves in good condition in plain sight.

Can scroungers lay waste to everything in their path and will stir one of a pair of good shoes to the bottom of a Dumpster, to be lost or ruined in the muck. Can scroungers will even go through individual garbage cans, something I have never seen a scavenger do.

Individual garbage cans are set out on the public easement only on garbage days. On other days going through them requires trespassing close to a dwelling. Going through individual garbage cans without scattering litter is almost impossible. Litter is likely to reduce the public's tolerance of scavenging. Individual garbage cans are simply not as productive as Dumpsters; people in houses and duplexes do not move as often and for some reason do not tend to discard as much useful material. Moreover, the time required to go through one garbage can that serves one household is not much less than the time required to go through a Dumpster that contains the refuse of twenty apartments.

But my strongest reservation about going through individual garbage cans is that this seems to me a very personal kind of invasion to which I would object if I were a householder. Although many things in Dumpsters are obviously meant never to come to light, a Dumpster is somehow less personal.

I avoid trying to draw conclusions about the people who dump in the Dumpsters I frequent. I think it would be unethical to do so, although I know many people will find the idea of scavenger ethics too funny for words.

Dumpsters contain bank statements, bills, correspondence, and other documents, just as anyone might expect. But there are also less obvious sources of information. Pill bottles, for example. The labels on pill bottles contain the name of the patient, the name of the doctor, and the name of the drug. AIDS drugs and antipsychotic medicines, to name but two groups, are specific and are seldom prescribed for any other disorders. The plastic compacts for birth control pills usually have complete label information.

Despite all of this sensitive information, I have had only one apartment resident object to my going through the Dumpster. In that case it turned out the resident was a university athlete who was taking bets and who was afraid I would turn up his wager slips.

Occasionally a find tells a story. I once found a small paper bag containing some unused condoms, several partial tubes of flavored sexual lubricant, a partially used compact of birth control pills, and the torn pieces of a picture of a young man. Clearly she was through with him and planning to give up sex altogether.

Dumpster things are often sad—abandoned teddy bears, shredded wedding books, despaired-of sales kits. I find many pets lying in state in Dumpsters. Although I hope to get off the streets so that Lizbeth can have a long and comfortable old age, I know this hope is not very realistic. So I suppose when her time comes she too will go into a Dumpster. I will have no better place for her. And after all, for most of her life her livelihood has come from the Dumpster. When she finds something I think is safe that has been spilled from the Dumpster I let her have it. She already knows the route around the best Dumpsters. I like to think that if she sur-

60

vives me she will have a chance of evading the dog catcher and of finding her sustenance on the route.

Silly vanities also come to rest in the Dumpsters. I am a rather accomplished needleworker. I get a lot of materials from the Dumpsters. Evidently sorority girls, hoping to impress someone, perhaps themselves, with their mastery of a womanly art, buy a lot of embroider-by-number kits, work a few stitches horribly, and eventually discard the whole mess. I pull out their stitches, turn the canvas over, and work an original design. Do not think I refrain from chuckling as I make original gifts from these kits.

I find diaries and journals. I have often thought of compiling a book   65
of literary found objects. And perhaps I will one day. But what I find is hopelessly commonplace and bad without being, even unconsciously, camp. College students also discard their papers. I am horrified to discover the kind of paper which now merits an A in an undergraduate course. I am grateful, however, for the number of good books and magazines the students throw out.

In the area I know best I have never discovered vermin in the Dumpsters, but there are two kinds of kitty surprise. One is alley cats which I meet as they leap, claws first, out of Dumpsters. This is especially thrilling when I have Lizbeth in tow. The other kind of kitty surprise is a plastic garbage bag filled with some ponderous, amorphous mass. This always proves to be used cat litter.

City bees harvest doughnut glaze and this makes the Dumpster at the doughnut shop more interesting. My faith in the instinctive wisdom of animals is always shaken whenever I see Lizbeth attempt to catch a bee in her mouth, which she does whenever bees are present. Evidently some birds find Dumpsters profitable, for birdie surprise is almost as common as kitty surprise of the first kind. In hunting season all kinds of small game turn up in Dumpsters, some of it, sadly, not entirely dead. Curiously, summer and winter, maggots are uncommon.

The worst of the living and near-living hazards of the Dumpsters are the fire ants. The food that they claim is not much of a loss, but they are vicious and aggressive. It is very easy to brush against some surface of the Dumpster and pick up half a dozen or more fire ants, usually in some sensitive area such as the underarm. One advantage of bringing Lizbeth along as I make Dumpster rounds is that, for obvious reasons, she is very alert to ground-based fire ants. When Lizbeth recognizes the signs of fire ant infestation around our feet she does the Dance of the Zillion Fire Ants. I have learned not to ignore this warning from Lizbeth, whether I perceive the tiny ants or not, but to remove ourselves at Lizbeth's first pas de bourrée.[1] All the more so because the ants are the worst in the months I wear flip-flops, if I have them.

---

[1]*pas de bourrée:* A transitional ballet step. — EDS.

(Perhaps someone will misunderstand the above. Lizbeth does the Dance of the Zillion Fire Ants when she recognizes more fire ants than she cares to eat, not when she is being bitten. Since I have learned to react promptly, she does not get bitten at all. It is the isolated patrol of fire ants that falls in Lizbeth's range that deserves pity. Lizbeth finds them quite tasty.)

By far the best way to go through a Dumpster is to lower yourself   70
into it. Most of the good stuff tends to settle at the bottom because it is usually weightier than the rubbish. My more athletic companions have often demonstrated to me that they can extract much good material from a Dumpster I have already been over.

To those psychologically or physically unprepared to enter a Dumpster, I recommend a stout stick, preferably with some barb or hook at one end. The hook can be used to grab plastic garbage bags. When I find canned goods or other objects loose at the bottom of a Dumpster I usually can roll them into a small bag that I can then hoist up. Much Dumpster diving is a matter of experience for which nothing will do except practice.

Dumpster diving is outdoor work, often surprisingly pleasant. It is not entirely predictable; things of interest turn up every day and some days there are finds of great value. I am always very pleased when I can turn up exactly the thing I most wanted to find. Yet in spite of the element of change, scavenging more than most other pursuits tends to yield returns in some proportion to the effort and intelligence brought to bear. It is very sweet to turn up a few dollars in change from a Dumpster that has just been gone over by a wino.

The land is now covered with cities. The cities are full of Dumpsters. I think of scavenging as a modern form of self-reliance. In any event, after ten years of government service, where everything is geared to the lowest common denominator, I find work that rewards initiative and effort refreshing. Certainly I would be happy to have a sinecure again, but I am not heartbroken not to have one anymore.

I find from the experience of scavenging two rather deep lessons. The first is to take what I can use and let the rest go by. I have come to think that there is no value in the abstract. A thing I cannot use or make useful, perhaps by trading, has no value however fine or rare it may be. I mean useful in a broad sense — so, for example, some art I would think useful and valuable, but other art might be otherwise for me.

I was shocked to realize that some things are not worth acquiring,   75
but now I think it is so. Some material things are white elephants that eat up the possessor's substance.

The second lesson is of the transience of material being. This has not quite converted me to a dualist, but it has made some headway in that direction. I do not suppose that ideas are immortal, but certainly mental things are longer-lived than other material things.

Once I was the sort of person who invests material objects with sentimental value. Now I no longer have those things, but I have the sentiments yet.

Many times in my travels I have lost everything but the clothes I was wearing and Lizbeth. The things I find in Dumpsters, the love letters and ragdolls of so many lives, remind me of this lesson. Now I hardly pick up a thing without envisioning the time I will cast it away. This I think is a healthy state of mind. Almost everything I have now has already been cast out at least once, proving that what I own is valueless to someone.

Anyway, I find my desire to grab for the gaudy bauble has been largely sated. I think this is an attitude I share with the very wealthy—we both know there is plenty more where what we have came from. Between us are the rat-race millions who have confounded their selves with the objects they grasp and who nightly scavenge the cable channels looking for they know not what.

I am sorry for them.   80

The Reader's Presence

1. At the center of "On Dumpster Diving" is Eighner's effort to bring out from the shadows of contemporary American life the lore and practices of scavenging, what he calls "a modern form of self-reliance." His essay also provides a compelling account of his self-education as he took to the streets for "the necessities of life." Outline the stages in this process, and summarize the ethical and moral issues and the questions of decorum that Eighner confronted along the way. Show how this process reflects the structure of his essay, "beginning with the practical art of Dumpster diving and proceeding to the abstract."

2. One of the most remarkable aspects of Eighner's essay is the tone (the attitude) he expresses toward his subject. Select a paragraph from the essay. Read it aloud. How would you characterize the sound of his voice? Does he sound, for example, tough-minded? polite? strident? experienced? cynical? something else? Consider, for example, paragraph 34, where he notes: "For myself, I avoid game, poultry, pork, and egg-based foods whether I find them raw or cooked." Where have you heard talk like this before? Do you notice any changes as the essay develops, or does Eighner maintain the same tone in discussing his subject? What responses does he elicit from his readers when he speaks of scavenging as a "profession" and a "trade"?

3. Consider Eighner's relationship with his readers. Does he consider himself fundamentally different from or similar to his audience? In

what specific ways? Consider, for example, the nature of the information Eighner provides in the essay. Does he expect his readers to be familiar with the information? How does he characterize his own knowledgeability about this often-noticed but rarely discussed activity in urban America? Comment on his use of irony in presenting information about Dumpster diving and in anticipating his readers' responses to the circumstances within which he does the work of his trade.

4. Compare Eighner's description of Dumpster diving to one of the most famous essays in the English language, Jonathan Swift's "A Modest Proposal" (page 866). Both essays deal with economics and the effects of poverty. In what ways does each author use humor and satire? How does each author introduce us to the grim realities of poverty? What role does food play in each essay? You might also compare Eighner's essay to Peter Singer's "The Singer Solution to World Poverty" (page 849). Discuss how applicable you find Singer's "solution" to Eighner's problems.

Joseph Epstein

The Perpetual Adolescent

A self-described "stickler for language," Joseph Epstein (b. 1937) has authored eighteen books of literary criticism, social commentary, personal essays, and fiction. His essays and articles are found in numerous publications, including Commentary, *the* New Yorker, Harper's, *the* New Republic, *and the* New York Review of Books. *He was a lecturer in English and writing at Northwestern University from 1974 to 2002 and an editor of the Phi Beta Kappa magazine* American Scholar *for more than two decades. In his "Life and Letters" column in that magazine, Epstein declared his principles regarding the use and abuse of language: "Take out all language that is pretentious and imprecise, undereducated and over-intellectualized. Question all language that says more than it means, that leaves the ground but doesn't really fly. Question authority only after you have first seriously consulted it; it isn't always as stupid as it looks. Never forget that today's hot new phrase becomes tomorrow's cold dead cliché." Now retired from teaching, Epstein has continued to write prodigiously; his books of essays and stories include* Narcissus Leaves the Pool *(1999),* Snobbery *(2002),* Envy *(2003),* Fabulous Small Jews *(2003),* Friendship: An Exposé *(2006), and* In a Cardboard Belt! Essays Personal, Literary, and Savage *(2007).*

In a 2003 interview, Epstein described writing about people who are "caught in a cultural switch. That is to say they grew up with one set of values and now there is another. . . . I like to think of myself as a kind of chronicler of people caught in the switch." In his essay "The Perpetual Adolescent," Epstein comments on such a "cultural switch" in the United States since World War II. The essay is taken from the March 15, 2003, issue of the Weekly Standard, *to which Epstein is a regular contributor.*

Whenever anyone under the age of 50 sees old newsreel film of Joe DiMaggio's 56-game hitting streak of 1941, he is almost certain to be brought up by the fact that nearly everyone in the male-dominated crowds—in New York, Boston, Chicago, Detroit, Cleveland—seems to be wearing a suit and a fedora or other serious adult hat. The people in those earlier baseball crowds, though watching a boyish game, nonetheless had a radically different conception of themselves than most Americans do now. A major depression was ending, a world war was on. Even though they were watching an entertainment that took most of them back to their boyhoods, they thought of themselves as adults, no longer kids, but grown-ups, adults, men.

How different from today, when a good part of the crowd at any ballgame, no matter what the age, is wearing jeans and team caps and T-shirts; and let us not neglect those (one hopes) benign maniacs who paint their faces in home-team colors or spell out, on their bare chests, the letters of the names of star players: S-O-S-A.

Part of the explanation for the suits at the ballpark in DiMaggio's day is that in the 1940s and even '50s there weren't a lot of sport, or leisure, or casual clothes around. Unless one lived at what H. L. Mencken[1] called "the country-club stage of culture"—unless, that is, one golfed, played tennis, or sailed—one was likely to own only the clothes one worked in or better. Far from casual Fridays, in those years there weren't even casual Sundays. Wearing one's "Sunday best," a cliché of the time, meant wearing the good clothes one reserved for church.

Dressing down may first have set in on the West Coast, where a certain informality was thought to be a new way of life. In the 1960s, in universities casual dress became absolutely *de rigueur* among younger faculty, who, in their ardor to destroy any evidence of their being implicated in evil hierarchy, wished not merely to seem in no wise different from their students but, more important, to seem always young; and the quickest path to youthfulness was teaching in jeans, T-shirts, and the rest of it.

This informality has now been institutionalized. Few are the restaurants that could any longer hope to stay in business if they required men to wear a jacket and tie. Today one sees men wearing baseball caps—some worn backwards—while eating indoors in quite good restaurants. In

5

[1]H(enry) L(ouis) "H. L." *Mencken:* (1880–1956), an influential journalist, essayist, magazine editor, satirist, and critic of American life and culture.—EDS.

an episode of *The Sopranos*, Tony Soprano, the mafia don, representing life of a different day, finds this so outrages his sense of decorum that, in a restaurant he frequents, he asks a man, in a quiet but entirely menacing way, to remove his goddamn hat.

Life in that different day was felt to observe the human equivalent of the Aristotelian unities: to have, like a good drama, a beginning, middle, and end. Each part, it was understood, had its own advantages and detractions, but the middle—adulthood—was the lengthiest and most earnest part, where everything serious happened and much was at stake. To violate the boundaries of any of the three divisions of life was to go against what was natural and thereby to appear unseemly, to put one's world somehow out of joint, to be, let us face it, a touch, and perhaps more than a touch, grotesque.

Today, of course, all this has been shattered. The ideal almost everywhere is to seem young for as long as possible. The health clubs and endemic workout clothes, the enormous increase in cosmetic surgery (for women and men), the special youth-oriented television programming and moviemaking, all these are merely the more obvious signs of the triumph of youth culture. When I say youth culture, I do not mean merely that the young today are transcendent, the group most admired among the various age groups in American society, but that youth is no longer viewed as a transitory state, through which one passes on the way from childhood to adulthood, but an aspiration, a vaunted condition in which, if one can only arrange it, to settle in perpetuity.

This phenomenon is not something that happened just last night; it has been underway for decades. Nor is it something that can be changed even by an event as cataclysmic as that of September 11, which at first was thought to be so sobering as to tear away all shreds of American innocence. As a generalization, it allows for a wide variety of exceptions. There still are adults in America; if names are wanted, I would set out those of Alan Greenspan, Jeane Kirkpatrick, Robert Rubin, Warren Buffett, Sol Linowitz,[2] and many more. But such men and women, actual grown-ups, now begin to appear a bit anomalous; they no longer seem representative of the larger culture.

The shift into youth culture began in earnest, I suspect, during the 10 or so years following 1951, the year of the publication of *Catcher in the Rye*. Salinger's novel exalts the purity of youth and locates the enemy—a clear case of Us versus Them—in those who committed the sin of having grown older, which includes Holden Caulfield's pain-in-the-neck parents, his brother (the sellout screenwriter), and just about everyone else who has passed beyond adolescence and had the rather poor taste to remain alive.

---

[2]*Alan Greenspan . . . Sol Linowitz:* Greenspan: Five-term chairman of the Federal Reserve System; Kirkpatrick: former Reagan cabinet member and United Nations representative; Rubin: Secretary of the Treasury under President Clinton; Buffett: world-famous multibillionaire; Linowitz (d. 2005): cofounder and chairman of Xerox, who also served in the Johnson and Carter administrations.—EDS.

The case for the exaltation of the young is made in Wordsworth's   10
"Intimation of Immortality," with its idea that human beings are born
with great wisdom from which life in society weans them slowly but inexorably. Plato promulgated this same idea long before: For him we all had
wisdom in the womb, but it was torn from us at the exact point that we
came into the world. Rousseau gave it a French twist, arguing that human
beings are splendid all-around specimens—noble savages, really—with
life out in society turning us mean and loutish, which is another way of
saying that the older we are, the worse we get. We are talking about Romanticism here, friend, which never favors the mature, let alone the aged.

The triumph of youth culture has conquered perhaps nowhere more
completely than in the United States. The John F. Kennedy administration,
with its emphasis on youthfulness, beginning with its young president—the
first president routinely not to wear a serious hat—gave it its first public
prominence. Soon after the assassination of Kennedy, the Free Speech
Movement, which spearheaded the student revolution, positively enshrined
the young. Like Yeats's Byzantium, the sixties utopia posited by the student
radicals was "no country for old men"[3] or women. One of the many tenets
in its credo—soon to become a cliché, but no less significant for that—was
that no one over 30 was to be trusted. (If you were part of that movement
and 21 years old in 1965, you are 60 today. Good morning, Sunshine.)

Music was a key element in the advance of youth culture. The dividing moment here is the advent of Elvis. On one side were those who
thought Elvis an amusing and largely freakish phenomenon—a bit of
a joke—and on the other, those who took him dead seriously as a figure
of youthful rebellion, the musical equivalent of James Dean in the
movie *Rebel Without a Cause* [1955], another early winning entry in the
glorification-of-youth sweepstakes then forming. Rock 'n' roll presented a
vinyl curtain, with those committed to retaining their youth on one side,
those wanting to claim adulthood on the other. The Beatles, despite the
very real charms of their non-druggie music, solidified things. So much of
hard rock 'n' roll came down to nothing more than a way of saying bug-
ger off to adult culture.

Reinforcement for these notions—they were not yet so coherent as to
qualify as ideas—was to be found in the movies. Movies for some years
now have been made not only increasingly for the young but by the
young. I once worked on a movie script with a producer who one day announced to me that it was his birthday. When I wished him happy returns
of the day, he replied that it wasn't so happy for him; he was turning 41,
an uncomfortably old age in Hollywood for someone who hadn't many
big success-scalps on his belt.

Robert Redford, though now in his mid-sixties, remains essentially a
guy in jeans, a handsome graduate student with wrinkles. Paul Newman,

---

[3]*"no country for old men":* One of the most famous poems by Irish poet William Butler Yeats, "Sailing to Byzantium," begins: "That is no country for old men."—EDS.

now in his late seventies, seems uncomfortable in a suit. Hugh Grant, the English actor, may be said to be professionally boyish, and in a recent role, in the movie *About a Boy*, is described in the *New York Times* as a character who "surrounds himself with gadgets, videos, CDs, and other toys" and who "is doing everything in his power to avoid growing up." The actor Jim Carrey, who is 42, not long ago said of the movie *The Majestic*, in which he stars, "It's about manhood. It's about adulthood," as if italicizing the rarity of such movies. He then went on to speak about himself in standard self-absorbed adolescent fashion: "You've got that hole you're left with by whatever your parents couldn't give you." Poor baby.

Jim Carrey's roles in movies resemble nothing so much as comic-book characters come to life. And why, just now, does so much of contemporary entertainment come in the form of animation or comic-book cartooning? Such television shows as *The Simpsons* and *King of the Hill*, the occasional back page in the *New York Times Book Review* or the *New Yorker* and the comic-book novel, all seem to feel that the animated cartoon and comic-book formats are very much of the moment. They are of course right, at least if you think of your audience as adolescent, or, more precisely, as being unwilling quite to detach themselves from their adolescence.

15

Recent history has seemed to be on the side of keeping people from growing up by supplying only a paucity of stern tests of the kind out of which adulthood is usually formed. We shall never have another presidential candidate tested by the Depression or by his experience in World War II. These were events that proved crucibles for the formation of adult character, not to say manliness. Henceforth all future presidential—and congressional—candidates will come with a shortage of what used to pass for significant experience. Crises for future politicians will doubtless be about having to rethink their lives when they didn't get into Brown or found themselves unequipped emotionally for Stanford Business School.

Corporate talent these days feels no weightier. Pictures of heads of corporations in polo shirts with designer logos in the business section of the *New York Times*, fresh from yet another ephemeral merger, or acquiring an enormous raise after their company has recorded another losing year, do not inspire confidence. "The trouble with Enron," said an employee of the company in the aftermath of that corporation's appalling debacle, "is that there weren't any grown-ups."

The increasing affluence the United States enjoyed after World War II, extending into the current day, also contributed heavily to forming the character I've come to think of as the perpetual American adolescent. Earlier, with less money around, people were forced to get serious, to grow up—and fast. How quickly the Depression generation was required to mature! How many stories one used to hear about older brothers going to work at 18 or earlier, so that a younger brother might be allowed to go to college, or simply to help keep the family afloat! With lots of money around, certain kinds of pressure were removed. More and more people nowadays are working, as earlier generations were not, with a strong safety net of money under them. All options opened, they now swim in what Kierkegaard[4] called "a sea of possibilities," and one of these possibilities in America is to refuse to grow up for a longer period than has been permitted any other people in history.

All this is reinforced by the play of market forces, which strongly encourage the mythical dream of perpetual youthfulness. The promise behind 95 percent of all advertising is that of recaptured youth, whose deeper promise is lots more sex yet to go. The ads for the $5,000 wristwatch, the $80,000 car, the khakis, the vodka, the pharmaceuticals to regrow hair and recapture ardor, all whisper display me, drive me, wear me, drink me, swallow me, and you stop the clock—youth, Baby, is yours.

The whole sweep of advertising, which is to say of market, culture since soon after World War II has been continuously to lower the criteria of youthfulness while extending the possibility for seeming youthful to older and older people. To make the very young seem older—all those 10- and 12-year-old Britney Spears and Jennifer Lopez imitators, who already know more about brand-name logos than I do about English literature—is another part of the job. It's not a conspiracy, mind you, not six or eight international ad agencies meeting in secret to call the shots, but the dynamics of marketing itself, finding a way to make it more profitable all around by convincing the young that they can seem older and the old that they can seem a lot younger. Never before has it been more difficult to obey the injunction to act one's age.   20

Two of the great television sitcom successes of recent years, *Seinfeld* and *Friends*, though each is different in its comic tone, are united by the theme of the permanent adolescent loose in the big city. One takes the characters in *Seinfeld* to be in their middle to late thirties, those in *Friends* in their late twenties to early thirties. Charming though they may be, both sets of characters are oddly stunted. They aren't quite anywhere and don't seem to be headed anywhere, either. Time is suspended for them. Aimless and shameless, they are in the grip of the everyday *Sturm und Drang*[5] of adolescent self-absorption. Outside their rather temporary-looking apartments, they scarcely exist. Personal relations provide the full drama of their lives. Growth and development aren't part of the deal. They are still, somehow, in spirit, locked in a high school of the mind, eating dry cereal, watching a vast quantity of television, hoping to make ecstatic sexual scores. Apart from the high sheen of the writing and the comic skill of the casts, I wonder if what really attracts people to these shows—*Friends* still, *Seinfeld* in its reruns—isn't the underlying identification with the characters because of the audience's own longing for a

---

[4]***Kierkegaard:*** Soren Kierkegaard (1813–1855), Danish philosopher.—Eds.

[5]**Sturm und Drang:** German for "storm and stress." The phrase refers to a literary movement in the late eighteenth century that emphasized the emotional conflicts of unconventional youth.—Eds.

perpetual adolescence, cut loose, free of responsibility, without the real pressures that life, that messy business, always exerts.

Time for the perpetual adolescents is curiously static. They are in no great hurry: to succeed, to get work, to lay down achievements. Perhaps this is partly because longevity has increased in recent decades—if one doesn't make it to 90 nowadays, one feels slightly cheated—but more likely it is that time doesn't seem to the perpetual adolescent the excruciatingly finite matter, the precious commodity, it indubitably is. For the perpetual adolescent, time is almost endlessly expandable. Why not go to law school in one's late thirties, or take the premed requirements in one's early forties, or wait even later than that to have children? Time enough to toss away one's twenties, maybe even one's thirties; 40 is soon enough to get serious about life; maybe 50, when you think about it, is the best time really to get going in earnest.

The old hunger for life, the eagerness to get into the fray, has been replaced by an odd patience that often looks more like passivity. In the 1950s, people commonly married in their twenties, which may or may not have been a good thing, but marriage did prove a forcing house into adulthood, for men and women, especially where children issued from the marriage, which they usually did fairly quickly. I had two sons by the time I was 26, which, among other things, made it impossible, either physically or spiritually, for me to join the general youth movement of the 1960s, even though I still qualified by age. It also required me to find a vocation. By 30, one was supposed to be settled in life: wife, children, house, job—"the full catastrophe," as Zorba the Greek[6] liked to say. But it was also a useful catastrophe. Today most people feel that they can wait to get serious about life. Until then one is feeling one's way, still deciding, shopping around, contributing to the formation of a new psychological type: the passive-nonaggressive.

Not everywhere is nonaggression the psychological mode of choice. One hears about the young men and women working the 14-hour days at low six-figure jobs in front-line law firms; others sacrificing to get into MBA programs, for the single purpose of an early financial score. But even here one senses an adolescent spirit to the proceedings. The old model for ambition was solid hard work that paid off over time. One began at a low wage, worked one's way up through genuine accomplishment, grew wealthier as one grew older, and, with luck, retired with a sense of financial security and pleasure in one's achievement. But the new American ambition model features the kid multimillionaire—the young man or woman who breaks the bank not long out of college. An element of adolescent impatience enters in here—I want it, *now!*—and also an element of continued youthfulness.

The model of the type may be the professional athlete. "The growth of professional basketball over the past twenty-odd years, from a rela-   25

---

[6]***Zorba the Greek:*** Nikos Kazantzakis's *Zorba the Greek* was published in the United States in 1953 and became a major film in 1964.—Eds.

tively minor spectator sport to a mass-cultural phenomenon," notes Rebecca Mead, in the *New Yorker*, "is an example of the way in which all of American culture is increasingly geared to the tastes of teenage boys." Mead writes this in an article about Shaquille O'Neal, the 32-year-old center for the Los Angeles Lakers, who earns, with endorsements, 30-odd million dollars a year and lives the life of the most privileged possible junior high school boy: enjoying food fights, go-carts, motorcycles, the run of high rides at amusement parks. It may be a wonderful, but it's also a strange life.

And yet what is so wrong about any of this? If one wants to dress like a kid, spin around the office on a scooter, not make up one's mind about what work one wants to do until one is 40, be noncommittal in one's relationships—what, really, are the consequences? I happen to think that the consequences are genuine, and fairly serious.

"Obviously it is normal to think of oneself as younger than one is," W. H. Auden, a younger son, told Robert Craft,[7] "but fatal to want to be younger." I'm not sure about fatal, but it is at a minimum degrading for a culture at large to want to be younger. The tone of national life is lowered, made less rich. The first thing lowered is expectations, intellectual and otherwise. To begin with education, one wonders if the dumbing down of culture one used to hear so much about and which continues isn't connected to the rise of the perpetual adolescent.

Consider contemporary journalism, which tends to play everything to lower and lower common denominators. Why does the *New York Times*, with its pretensions to being our national newspaper, choose to put on its front pages stories about Gennifer Flowers's career as a chanteuse in New Orleans, the firing of NFL coaches, the retirement of Yves Saint Laurent, the canceling of the singer Mariah Carey's recording contract? Slow-news days is a charitable guess; a lowered standard of the significant is a more realistic one. Since the advent of its new publisher, a man of the baby boomer generation, an aura of juvenilia clings to the paper. Frank Rich and Maureen Dowd, two of the paper's most-read columnists, seem not so much the type of the bright college student but of the sassy high-school student—the clever, provocative editor of the school paper out to shock the principal—even though both are in their early fifties.

Television comes closer and closer to being a wholly adolescent form of communication. Clicking the remote from major network news shows, one slides smoothly from superficiality to triviality. When Tom Brokaw announces that some subject will be covered "In Depth," what he really means is that roughly 90 seconds, perhaps two minutes, will be devoted to it. It's scarcely original to note that much of contemporary journalism,

---

[7]***Robert Lawson Craft:*** (b. 1923) an American conductor and writer.—EDS.

print and electronic, is pitched to the short attention span, the soundbite, photo-op, quickie take, the deep distaste for complexity—in short, so much is pitched to the adolescent temperament.

Political correctness and so many of the political fashions of our day— 30 from academic feminism to cultural studies to queer theory—could only be perpetrated on adolescent minds: minds, that is, that are trained to search out one thing and one thing only: Is my teacher, or this politician, or that public spokesman, saying something that is likely to be offensive to me or members of any other victim group? Only an adolescent would find it worthwhile to devote his or her attention chiefly to the hunting of offenses, the possibility of slights, real and imagined.

Self-esteem, of which one currently hears so much, is at bottom another essentially adolescent notion. The great psychological sin of our day is to violate the self-esteem of adolescents of all ages. One might have thought that such self-esteem as any of us is likely to command would be in place by the age of 18. (And what is the point of having all that much self-esteem anyhow, since its logical culminating point can only be smug complacence?) Even in nursing homes, apparently, patients must be guarded against a feeling of their lowered consequence in the world. Self-esteem has become a womb to tomb matter, so that, in contemporary America, the inner and the outer child can finally be made one in the form of the perpetual adolescent.

The coarsening of American culture seems part of the adolescent phenomenon. Television commercials have gotten grosser and grosser. The level of profanity on prime-time television shows has risen greatly over the years. Flicks known to their audiences as "gross-out movies," featuring the slimy and hideous, are part of the regular film menu. Florence King, writing about this phenomenon in her column in the *National Review*, noted: "Since arrested development is as American as apple pie, it is easy to identify the subconscious motivation of the adult male Ughs who produce all these revolting movies and commercials." What makes these things possible is what is known as "niche programming," or the aiming of entertainment at quite specific segments of the audience—African Americans, or teenagers, or the educated classes, or the beer brutes. But increasingly, apparently, we are all being forced into that largest of niches, the American adolescent mentality.

Consider now what must be taken as the most consequential adolescent act in American history during the past half century: the Bill Clinton–Monica Lewinsky relationship. I hesitate to call it an affair, because an affair implies a certain adult style: the good hotel room, the bottle of excellent wine, the peignoir, the Sulka pajamas. With Bill and Monica, you had instead the pizza, the canoodling under the desk, the cigar business, even the whole thing going without consummation. No matter what one's politics, one has to admit that our great national scandal was pure high school.

In a 1959 review of Iona and Peter Opie's *The Lore and Language of School Children*, the poet Philip Larkin[8] revealed first sensing a sharp waning of his interest in Christianity when he read the Bible verse that promises one will return to one's childish state upon entry into Heaven. Larkin wanted nothing more to do with being a child or with the company of children. He looked forward to "money, keys, wallets, letters, books, long-playing records, drinks, the opposite sex, and other solaces of adulthood."

I wanted these things, too, and as soon as possible. From roughly the age of 14, I wanted to stay out all night, to dress like Fred Astaire, to drink and smoke cigarettes with the elegance of William Powell, to have the company of serious women like Susan Hayward and Ingrid Bergman.[9] As I grew older, I sadly began to realize it wasn't going to happen, at least not in the way I had hoped. What happened instead was the triumph of youth culture, with its adoration of youth, in and for itself, and as a time in one's life of purity and goodness always in danger of being despoiled by the corruption of growing older, which is also to say, of "growing up." 35

At a certain point in American life, the young ceased to be viewed as a transient class and youth as a phase of life through which everyone soon passed. Instead, youthfulness was vaunted and carried a special moral status. Adolescence triumphed, becoming a permanent condition. As one grew older, one was presented with two choices, to seem an old fogey for attempting to live according to one's own standard of adulthood, or to go with the flow and adapt some variant of pulling one's long gray hair back into a ponytail, struggling into the spandex shorts, working on those abs, and ending one's days among the Rip Van With-Its. Not, I think, a handsome set of alternatives.

The greatest sins, Santayana[10] thought, are those that set out to strangle human nature. This is of course what is being done in cultivating perpetual adolescence, while putting off maturity for as long as possible. Maturity provides a more articulated sense of the ebb and flow, the ups and downs, of life, a more subtly reticulated graph of human possibility. Above all, it values a clear and fit conception of reality. Maturity is ever cognizant that the clock is running, life is finite, and among the greatest mistakes is to believe otherwise. Maturity doesn't exclude playfulness or high humor. Far from it. The mature understand that the bitterest joke of all is that the quickest way to grow old lies in the hopeless attempt to stay forever young.

---

[8]*Larkin:* A British poet (1922–1985) who was known for his witty formal verse. — EDS.
[9]*Susan Hayward . . . Bergman:* Glamorous film stars of the 1940s and 1950s. — EDS.
[10]*Santayana:* Spanish-born George Santayana (1863–1952) was an influential American philosopher. — EDS.

The Reader's Presence

1. What does Epstein believe caused the shift toward adolescent culture? When did it happen? What are some of the earliest examples he cites of youth culture triumphing over maturity? Do you agree that most Americans behave in an "adolescent" way? Why or why not?

2. What areas of life does Epstein believe have been negatively affected by our immaturity? What are the consequences of youth culture's triumph over adulthood? What does Epstein's interpretation suggest about what he values?

3. Read John Taylor Gatto's "Against School" (page 682). What does he suggest are the benefits of treating adults like children? Who benefits? How does Gatto's argument about Americans' immaturity differ from Epstein's?

Kai Erikson

The Witches of Salem Village

Kai Erikson (b. 1931), son of renowned psychoanalyst Erik Erikson, is professor emeritus of sociology and American studies at Yale University. A noted scholar, Erikson has published several books and received numerous professional awards. His interests in communities and the effects of human disasters are reflected in Everything in Its Path: Destruction of Community in the Buffalo Creek Flood *(1976) and* A New Species of Trouble: Explorations in Disaster, Trauma, and Community *(1994). Erikson edited* Sociological Visions *(1997), a collection of writings on social problems. "The Witches of Salem Village" is from his study of Puritan New England,* Wayward Puritans: A Study in the Sociology of Deviance *(1966).*

No one really knows how the witchcraft hysteria began, but it originated in the home of the Reverend Samuel Parris, minister of the local church. In early 1692, several girls from the neighborhood began to spend their afternoons in the Parrises' kitchen with a slave named Tituba, and it was not long before a mysterious sorority of girls, aged between nine and twenty, became regular visitors to the parsonage. We can only speculate what was going on behind the kitchen door, but we know that Tituba had been brought to Massachusetts from Barbados and enjoyed a reputation in the neighborhood for her skills in the magic arts. As the girls grew closer together, a remarkable change seemed to come over them: perhaps it is not true, as someone later reported, that they went out into the forest to celebrate their own version of a black mass, but it is apparent that they began to live in a state of high tension and shared secrets with one another which were hardly becoming to quiet Puritan maidens.

Before the end of winter, the two youngest girls in the group succumbed to the shrill pitch of their amusements and began to exhibit a most unusual malady. They would scream unaccountably, fall into grotesque convulsions, and sometimes scamper along on their hands and knees making noises like the barking of a dog. No sooner had word gone around about this extraordinary affliction than it began to spread like a contagious disease. All over the community young girls were groveling on the ground in a panic of fear and excitement, and while some of the less credulous townspeople were tempted to reach for their belts in the hopes of strapping a little modesty into them, the rest could only stand by in helpless horror as the girls suffered their torments.

The town's one physician did what he could to stem the epidemic, but he soon exhausted his meagre store of remedies and was forced to conclude that the problem lay outside the province of medicine. The Devil had come to Salem Village, he announced; the girls were bewitched. At this disturbing news, ministers from many of the neighboring parishes came to consult with their colleague and offer what advice they might. Among the first to arrive was a thoughtful clergyman named Deodat Lawson, and he had been in town no more than a few hours when he happened upon a frightening exhibition of the devil's handiwork. "In the beginning of the evening," he later recounted of his first day in the village,

> I went to give Mr. Parris a visit. When I was there, his kinswoman, Abigail Williams, (about 12 years of age,) had a grievous fit; she was at first hurried with violence to and fro in the room, (though Mrs. Ingersoll endeavored to hold her,) sometimes making as if she would fly, stretching up her arms as high as she could, and crying "whish, whish, whish!" several times. . . . After that, she run to the fire, and began to throw fire brands about the house; and run against the back, as if she would run up the chimney, and, as they said, she had attempted to go into the fire in other fits.[1]

Faced by such clear-cut evidence, the ministers quickly agreed that Satan's new challenge would have to be met with vigorous action, and this meant that the afflicted girls would have to identify the witches who were harassing them.

It is hard to guess what the girls were experiencing during those early days of the commotion. They attracted attention everywhere they went and

---

[1]Deodat Lawson, "A Brief and True Narrative of Witchcraft at Salem Village," 1692, in *Narratives of the Witchcraft Cases, 1648–1706*, edited by George Lincoln Burr (New York: Scribner's, 1914), p. 154.

exercised a degree of power over the adult community which would have been exhilarating under the sanest of circumstances. But whatever else was going on in those young minds, the thought seems to have gradually occurred to the girls that they were indeed bewitched, and after they had been coaxed over and over again to name their tormentors, they finally singled out three women in the village and accused them of witchcraft.

Three better candidates could not have been found if all the gossips in New England had met to make the nominations. The first, understandably, was Tituba herself, a woman who had grown up among the rich colors and imaginative legends of Barbados and who was probably acquainted with some form of voodoo. The second, Sarah Good, was a proper hag of a witch if Salem Village had ever seen one. With a pipe clenched in her leathery face she wandered around the countryside neglecting her children and begging from others, and on more than one occasion the old crone had been overheard muttering threats against her neighbors when she was in an unusually sour humor. Sarah Osburne, the third suspect, had a higher social standing than either of her alleged accomplices, but she had been involved in a local scandal a year or two earlier when a man moved into her house some months before becoming her husband.

A preliminary hearing was set at once to decide whether the three accused women should be held for trial. The girls were ushered to the front row of the meeting house, where they took full advantage of the space afforded them by rolling around in apparent agony whenever some personal fancy (or the invisible agents of the devil) provoked them to it. It was a remarkable show. Strange creatures flew about the room pecking at the girls or taunting them from the rafters, and it was immediately obvious to everyone that the women on trial were responsible for all the disorder and suffering. When Sarah Good and Sarah Osburne were called to the stand and asked why they sent these spectres to torment the girls, they were too appalled to say much in their defense. But when Tituba took the stand she had a ready answer. A lifetime spent in bondage is poor training for standing up before a bench of magistrates, and anyway Tituba was an excitable woman who had breathed the warmer winds of the Caribbean and knew things about magic her crusty old judges would never learn. Whatever the reason, Tituba gave her audience one of the most exuberant confessions ever recorded in a New England courtroom. She spoke of the creatures who inhabit the invisible world, the dark rituals which bind them together in the service of Satan; and before she had ended her astonishing recital she had convinced everyone in Salem Village that the problem was far worse than they had dared imagine. For Tituba not only implicated Sarah Good and Sarah Osburne in her own confession but announced that many other people in the colony were engaged in the devil's conspiracy against the Bay.

So the hearing that was supposed to bring a speedy end to the affair only stirred up a hidden hornet's nest, and now the girls were urged to identify other suspects and locate new sources of trouble. Already the girls had become more than unfortunate victims: in the eyes of the community they were diviners, prophets, oracles, mediums, for only they could see the terrible spectres swarming over the countryside and tell what persons had sent them on their evil errands. As they became caught up in the enthusiasm of their new work, then, the girls began to reach into every corner of the community in a search for likely suspects. Martha Corey was an upstanding woman in the village whose main mistake was to snort incredulously at the girls' behavior. Dorcas Good, five years old, was a daughter of the accused Sarah. Rebecca Nurse was a saintly old woman who had been bedridden at the time of the earlier hearings. Mary Esty and Sarah Cloyce were Rebecca's younger sisters, themselves accused when they rose in energetic defense of the older woman. And so it went—John Proctor, Giles Corey, Abigail Hobbs, Bridgit Bishop, Sarah Wild, Susanna Martin, Dorcas Hoar, the Reverend George Burroughs: as winter turned into spring the list of suspects grew to enormous length and the Salem jail was choked with people awaiting trial. We know nothing about conditions of life in prison, but it is easy to imagine the tensions which must have echoed within those grey walls. Some of the prisoners had cried out against their relatives and friends in a desperate effort to divert attention from themselves, others were witless persons with scarcely a clue as to what had happened to them, and a few (very few, as it turned out) were accepting their lot with quiet dignity. If we imagine Sarah Good

The Trial of George Jacobs for Witchcraft in 1692. *Painting by Tompkins H. Matteson, 1855.*

sitting next to Rebecca Nurse and lighting her rancid pipe or Tituba sharing views on supernatural phenomena with the Reverend George Burroughs, we may have a rough picture of life in those crowded quarters.

By this time the hysteria had spread well beyond the confines of
Salem Village, and as it grew in scope so did the appetites of the young
girls. They now began to accuse persons they had never seen from places
they had never visited (in the course of which some absurd mistakes were
made),[2] yet their word was so little questioned that it was ordinarily war-
rant enough to put respected people in chains.

From as far away as Charlestown, Nathaniel Cary heard that his wife
had been accused of witchcraft and immediately traveled with her to
Salem "to see if the afflicted did know her." The two of them sat through
an entire day of hearings, after which Cary reported:

> I observed that the afflicted were two girls of about ten years old,
> and about two or three others, of about eighteen. . . . The prisoners were
> called in one by one, and as they came in were cried out of [at]. . . . The
> prisoner was placed about seven or eight feet from the Justices, and the
> accusers between the Justices and them; the prisoner was ordered to stand
> right before the Justices, with an officer appointed to hold each hand, lest
> they should therewith afflict them, and the prisoner's eyes must be con-
> stantly on the Justices; for if they looked on the afflicted, they would
> either fall into their fits, or cry out of being hurt by them. . . . Then the
> Justices said to the accusers, "which of you will go and touch the prisoner
> at the bar?" Then the most courageous would adventure, but before they
> had made three steps would ordinarily fall down as in a fit. The Justices
> ordered that they should be taken up and carried to the prisoner, that she
> might touch them; and as soon as they were touched by the accused, the
> Justices would say "they are well," before I could discern any alter-
> ation. . . . Thus far I was only as a spectator, my wife also was there part
> of the time, but no notice taken of her by the afflicted, except once or
> twice they came to her and asked her name.

After this sorry performance the Carys retired to the local inn for din-   10
ner, but no sooner had they taken seats than a group of afflicted girls
burst into the room and "began to tumble about like swine" at Mrs.
Cary's feet, accusing her of being the cause of their miseries. Remarkably,
the magistrates happened to be sitting in the adjoining room — "waiting
for this," Cary later decided — and an impromptu hearing took place on
the spot.

> Being brought before the Justices, her chief accusers were two girls.
> My wife declared to the Justices that she never had any knowledge of

---

[2]John Alden later reported in his account of the affair that the girls pointed their fingers at the wrong man when they first accused him of witchcraft and only realized their mistake when an obliging passerby corrected them. See Robert Calef, "More Wonders of the
Invisible World," Boston, 1701, in Burr, *Narratives*, p. 353.

In this 17th-century woodcut from Compendium Maleficarum *by Francisco Maria Guazzo, witches stand in line to show obedience to Satan by kissing his buttocks.*

them before that day; she was forced to stand with her arms stretched out. I did request that I might hold one of her hands, but it was denied me; then she desired me to wipe the tears from her eyes, and the sweat from her face, which I did; then she desired she might lean herself on me, saying she should faint. Justice Hathorne replied, she had strength enough to torment those persons, and she should have strength enough to stand. I speaking something against their cruel proceedings, they commanded me to be silent, or else I should be turned out of the room. An Indian . . . was also brought in to be one of her accusers: being come in, he now (when before the Justices) fell down and tumbled about like a hog, but said nothing. The Justices asked the girls, "who afflicted the Indian?", they answered "she" (meaning my wife). . . . The Justices ordered her to touch him, in order of his cure . . . but the Indian took hold of her in a barbarous manner; then his hand was taken off, and her hand put on his, and the cure was quickly wrought. . . . Then her mittimus was writ.[3]

For another example of how the hearings were going, we might listen for a moment to the examination of Mrs. John Proctor. This record was taken down by the Reverend Samuel Parris himself, and the notes in parentheses are his. Ann Putnam and Abigail Williams were two of the most energetic of the young accusers.

[3]Reproduced in Calef, "More Wonders," in Burr, *Narratives*, pp. 350–52.

Justice: Ann Putnam, doth this woman hurt you?

Putnam: Yes, sir, a good many times. (Then the accused looked upon them and they fell into fits.)

Justice: She does not bring the book to you, does she?[4]

Putnam: Yes, sir, often, and saith she hath made her maid set her hand to it.

Justice: Abigail Williams, does this woman hurt you?

Williams: Yes, sir, often.

Justice: Does she bring the book to you?

Williams: Yes.

Justice: What would she have you do with it?

Williams: To write in it and I shall be well.

Putnam to Mrs. Proctor: Did you not tell me that your maid had written?

Mrs. Proctor: Dear child, it is not so. There is another judgment, dear child. (Then Abigail and Ann had fits. By and by they cried out, "look you, there is Goody Proctor upon the beam." By and by both of them cried out of Goodman Proctor himself, and said he was a wizard. Immediately, many, if not all of the bewitched, had grievous fits.)

Justice: Ann Putnam, who hurt you?

Putnam: Goodman Proctor and his wife too. (Some of the afflicted cried, "there is Proctor going to take up Mrs. Pope's feet" — and her feet were immediately taken up.)

Justice: What do you say Goodman Proctor to these things?

Proctor: I know not. I am innocent.

Williams: There is Goodman Proctor going to Mrs. Pope (and immediately said Pope fell into a fit).

Justice: You see, the Devil will deceive you. The children could see what you was going to do before the woman was hurt. I would advise you to repentance, for the devil is bringing you out.[5]

This was the kind of evidence the magistrates were collecting in readiness for the trials; and it was none too soon, for the prisons were crowded with suspects. In June the newly arrived Governor of the Bay, Sir William Phips, appointed a special court of Oyer and Terminer to hear the growing number of witchcraft cases pending, and the new bench went immediately to work. Before the month was over, six women had been hanged from the gallows in Salem. And still the accused poured in.

As the court settled down to business, however, a note of uncertainty began to flicker across the minds of several thoughtful persons in the colony. To begin with, the net of accusation was beginning to spread out in wider arcs, reaching not only across the surface of the country but up the social ladder as well, so that a number of influential people were now among those in the overflowing prisons. Nathaniel Cary was an important citizen of Charlestown, and other men of equal rank (including the

---

[4]The "book" refers to the Devil's registry. The girls were presumably being tormented because they refused to sign the book and ally themselves with Satan.

[5]Hutchinson, *History*, II, pp. 27–28.

almost legendary Captain John Alden) were being caught up in the widening circle of panic and fear. Slowly but surely, a faint glimmer of skepticism was introduced into the situation; and while it was not to assert a modifying influence on the behavior of the court for some time to come, this new voice had become a part of the turbulent New England climate of 1692.

Meantime, the girls continued to exercise their extraordinary powers. Between sessions of the court, they were invited to visit the town of Andover and help the local inhabitants flush out whatever witches might still remain at large among them. Handicapped as they were by not knowing anyone in town, the girls nonetheless managed to identify more than fifty witches in the space of a few hours. Forty warrants were signed on the spot, and the arrest total only stopped at that number because the local Justice of the Peace simply laid down his pen and refused to go on with the frightening charade any longer—at which point, predictably, he became a suspect himself.

Yet the judges worked hard to keep pace with their young representatives in the field. In early August five persons went to the gallows in Salem. A month later fifteen more were tried and condemned, of which eight were hung promptly and the others spared because they were presumably ready to confess their sins and turn state's evidence. Nineteen people had been executed, seven more condemned, and one pressed to death under a pile of rocks for standing mute at his trial. At least two more persons had died in prison, bringing the number of deaths to twenty-two. And in all that time, not one suspect brought before the court had been acquitted.

At the end of this strenuous period of justice, the whole witchcraft mania began to fade. For one thing, the people of the Bay had been shocked into a mood of sober reflection by the deaths of so many persons. For another, the afflicted girls had obviously not learned very much from their experience in Andover and were beginning to display an ambition which far exceeded their credit. It was bad enough that they should accuse the likes of John Alden and Nathaniel Cary, but when they brought up the name of Samuel Willard, who doubled as pastor of Boston's First Church and President of Harvard College, the magistrates flatly told them they were mistaken. Not long afterwards, a brazen finger was pointed directly at the executive mansion in Boston, where Lady Phips awaited her husband's return from an expedition to Canada, and one tradition even has it that Cotton Mather's mother was eventually accused.[6]

This was enough to stretch even a Puritan's boundless credulity. One by one the leading men of the Bay began to reconsider the whole question and ask aloud whether the evidence accepted in witchcraft hearings was really suited to the emergency at hand. It was obvious that people were being condemned on the testimony of a few excited girls, and responsible minds in the community were troubled by the thought that the

15

[6]Burr, *Narratives*, p. 377.

girls' excitement may have been poorly diagnosed in the first place. Suppose the girls were directly possessed by the devil and not touched by intermediate witches? Suppose they were simply out of their wits altogether? Suppose, in fact, they were lying? In any of these events the rules of evidence used in court would have to be reviewed—and quickly.

Deciding what kinds of evidence were admissible in witchcraft cases was a thorny business at best. When the court of Oyer and Terminer had first met, a few ground rules had been established to govern the unusual situation which did not entirely conform to ordinary Puritan standards of trial procedure. In the first place, the scriptural rule that two eyewitnesses were necessary for conviction in capital cases was modified to read that any two witnesses were sufficient even if they were testifying about different events—on the interesting ground that witchcraft was a "habitual" crime. That is, if one witness testified that he had seen Susanna Martin bewitch a horse in 1660 and another testified that she had broken uninvited into his dreams twenty years later, then both were witnesses to the same general offense. More important, however, the court accepted as an operating principle the old idea that Satan could not assume the shape of an innocent person, which meant in effect that any spectres floating into view which resembled one of the defendants must be acting under his direct instruction. If an afflicted young girl "saw" John Proctor's image crouched on the window sill with a wicked expression on his face, for example, there could be no question that Proctor himself had placed it there, for the devil could not borrow that disguise without the permission of its owner. During an early hearing, one of the defendants had been asked: "How comes your appearance to hurt these [girls]?" "How do I know," she had answered testily, "He that appeared in the shape of Samuel, a glorified saint, may appear in anyone's shape."[7] Now this was no idle retort, for every man who read his Bible knew that the Witch of Endor had once caused the image of Samuel to appear before Saul, and this scriptural evidence that the devil might indeed be able to impersonate an innocent person proved a difficult matter for the court to handle. Had the defendant been able to win her point, the whole machinery of the court might have fallen in pieces at the magistrates' feet; for if the dreadful spectres haunting the girls were no more than free-lance apparitions sent out by the devil, then the court would have no prosecution case at all.

All in all, five separate kinds of evidence had been admitted by the court during its first round of hearings. First were trials by test, of which repeating the Lord's Prayer, a feat presumed impossible for witches to perform, and curing fits by touch were the most often used. Second was the testimony of persons who attributed their own misfortunes to the sorcery of a neighbor on trial. Third were physical marks like warts, moles, scars, or any other imperfection through which the devil might have

---

[7]Cotton Mather, "Wonders of the Invisible World," in Drake, *The Witchcraft Delusion*, p. 176.

sucked his gruesome quota of blood. Fourth was spectral evidence, of the sort just noted; and fifth were the confessions of the accused themselves.

Now it was completely obvious to the men who began to review the court's proceedings that the first three types of evidence were quite inconclusive. After all, anyone might make a mistake reciting the Lord's Prayer, particularly if the floor was covered with screaming, convulsive girls, and it did not make much sense to execute a person because he had spiteful neighbors or a mark upon his body. By those standards, half the people in Massachusetts might qualify for the gallows. This left spectral evidence and confessions. As for the latter, the court could hardly maintain that any real attention had been given to that form of evidence, since none of the executed witches had confessed and none of the many confessors had been executed. Far from establishing guilt, a well-phrased and tearfully delivered confession was clearly the best guarantee against hanging. So the case lay with spectral evidence, and legal opinion in the Bay was slowly leaning toward the theory that this form of evidence, too, was worthless. 20

In October, Governor Phips took note of the growing doubts by dismissing the special court of Oyer and Terminer and releasing several suspects from prison. The tide had begun to turn, but still there were 150 persons in custody and some 200 others who had been accused.

In December, finally, Phips appointed a new session of the Superior Court of Judicature to try the remaining suspects, and this time the magistrates were agreed that spectral evidence would be admitted only in marginal cases. Fifty-two persons were brought to trial during the next month, and of these, forty-nine were immediately acquitted. Three others were condemned ("two of which," a contemporary observer noted, "were the most senseless and ignorant creatures that could be found"),[8] and in addition death warrants were signed for five persons who had been condemned earlier. Governor Phips responded to these carefully reasoned judgments by signing reprieves for all eight of the defendants anyway, and at this, the court began to empty the jails as fast as it could hear cases. Finally Phips ended the costly procedure by discharging every prisoner in the colony and issuing a general pardon to all persons still under suspicion.

The witchcraft hysteria had been completely checked within a year of the day it first appeared in Salem Village.

The Reader's Presence

1. This essay appears in a larger work on social deviance. What is social deviance, in Erikson's perspective? How has it been perceived and controlled? Why might Erikson view the long-past historical events of Salem as relevant to questions of deviance today?

---

[8]Calef, "More Wonders," in Burr, *Narratives*, p. 382.

2. Erikson retells a familiar American story in a deceptively straight-forward manner. Does his tone endorse or undercut the surface meaning of his tale? In what way? What position toward the events does the essay appear to encourage in the reader? By what means?

3. Erikson's essay has a neat timeline: The essay begins with the onset of the witchcraft hysteria in 1692 and concludes at the end of that year by which point the "hysteria had been completely checked." Barbara Tuchman's historical account of the Black Death ("This Is the End of the World: The Black Death," page 548) covers a similarly brief period. Reread the essays together and note how each historian paces the telling of the historical narrative. When is primary evidence included? What comment does the writer offer, or withhold, and why? How is each essay's sense of momentum established? What makes you keep reading?

James Fallows

Throwing Like a Girl

Journalist James Fallows (b. 1949) has written extensively on government, war and defense, and the economy. He graduated with a BA degree in American history and literature from Harvard University, and received an MA degree in economics from Oxford University. Before becoming national correspondent for the Atlantic Monthly, *a position he has held for over 25 years, Fallows was an editor at the* Washington Monthly *and* U.S. News & World Report. *Fallows writes on a variety of national and international issues, most recently the war in Iraq. His latest book,* Blind into Baghdad: America's War in Iraq *(2006) is based on his many articles in the* Atlantic Monthly *since his 2002 cover story, "The Fifty-First State," won the National Magazine Award. His books include* National Defense *(1981), which won the National Book Award;* Looking at the Sun *(1995);* Breaking the News: How the Media Undermines American Democracy *(1996); and* Free Flight *(2001). His essay, "Throwing Like a Girl," first appeared in the* Atlantic Monthly *in August 1996.*

Most people remember the 1994 baseball season for the way it ended—with a strike rather than a World Series. I keep thinking about the way it began. On opening day, April 4, Bill Clinton went to Cleveland and, like many Presidents before him, threw out a ceremonial first pitch. That same day Hillary Rodham Clinton went to Chicago and, like no

First Lady before her, also threw out a first ball, at a Cubs game in Wrigley Field.

The next day photos of the Clintons in action appeared in newspapers around the country. Many papers, including the *New York Times* and the *Washington Post*, chose the same two photos to run. The one of Bill Clinton showed him wearing an Indians cap and warm-up jacket. The President, throwing lefty, had turned his shoulders sideways to the plate in preparation for delivery. He was bringing the ball forward from behind his head in a clean-looking throwing action as the photo was snapped. Hillary Clinton was pictured wearing a dark jacket, a scarf, and an oversized Cubs hat. In preparation for her throw she was standing directly facing the plate. A right-hander, she had the elbow of her throwing arm pointed out in front of her. Her forearm was tilted back, toward her shoulder. The ball rested on her upturned palm. As the picture was taken, she was in the middle of an action that can only be described as throwing like a girl.

The phrase "throwing like a girl" has become an embattled and offensive one. Feminists smart at its implication that to do something "like a girl" is to do it the wrong way. Recently, on the heels of the O. J. Simpson case, a book appeared in which the phrase was used to help explain why male athletes, especially football players, were involved in so many assaults against women. Having been trained (like most American boys) to dread the accusation of doing anything "like a girl," athletes were said to grow into the assumption that women were valueless, and natural prey.

I grant the justice of such complaints. I am attuned to the hurt caused by similar broad-brush stereotypes when they apply to groups I belong to—"dancing like a white man," for instance, or "speaking foreign languages like an American," or "thinking like a Washingtonian."

Still, whatever we want to call it, the difference between the two Clintons in what they were doing that day is real, and it is instantly recognizable. And since seeing those photos I have been wondering, Why, exactly, do so many women throw "like a girl"? If the motion were easy to change, presumably a woman as motivated and self-possessed as Hillary Clinton would have changed it. (According to her press secretary, Lisa Caputo, Mrs. Clinton spent the weekend before opening day tossing a ball in the Rose Garden with her husband, for practice.) Presumably, too, the answer to the question cannot be anything quite as simple as, because they *are* girls.

A surprising number of people think that there is a structural difference between male and female arms or shoulders—in the famous "rotator cuff," perhaps—that dictates different throwing motions. "It's in the shoulder joint," a well-educated woman told me recently. "They're hinged differently." Someday researchers may find evidence to support a biological theory of throwing actions. For now, what you'll hear if you ask an orthopedist, an anatomist, or (especially) the coach of a women's softball team is that there is no structural reason why men and women should throw in different ways. This point will be obvious to any male who grew up around girls who liked to play baseball and became good at it. It should be obvious on a larger scale this summer, in broadcasts of the Olympic Games. This year [1996], for the first time, women's fast-pitch softball teams will compete in the Olympics. Although the pitchers in these games will deliver the ball underhand, viewers will see female short-stops, center fielders, catchers, and so on pegging the ball to one another at speeds few male viewers could match.

Even women's tennis is a constant if indirect reminder that men's and women's shoulders are "hinged" the same way. The serving motion in tennis is like a throw—but more difficult, because it must be coordinated with the toss of the tennis ball. The men in professional tennis serve harder than the women, because they are bigger and stronger. But women pros serve harder than most male amateurs have ever done, and the service motion for good players is the same for men and women alike. There is no expectation in college or pro tennis that because of their anatomy female players must "serve like a girl." "I know many women who can throw a lot harder and better than the normal male," says Linda Wells, the coach of the highly successful women's softball team at Arizona State University. "It's not gender that makes the difference in how they throw."

So what is it, then? Since Hillary Clinton's ceremonial visit to Wrigley Field, I have asked men and women how they learned to throw, or didn't. Why did I care? My impetus was the knowledge that eventually my sons would be grown and gone. If my wife, in all other ways a talented athlete, could learn how to throw, I would still have someone to play catch with. My research left some women, including my wife, thinking that I am some kind of obsessed lout, but it has led me to the solution to the mystery. First let's be clear about what there is to be explained.

At a superficial level it's easy to tick off the traits of an awkward-looking throw. The fundamental mistake is the one Mrs. Clinton appeared to be making in the photo: trying to throw a ball with your body facing the target, rather than rotating your shoulders and hips ninety degrees away from the target and then swinging them around in order to accelerate the ball. A throw looks bad if your elbow is lower than your shoulder as your arm comes forward (unless you're throwing sidearm). A throw looks really bad if, as the ball leaves your hand, your wrist is "inside your elbow"—that is, your elbow joint is bent in such a way that your forearm angles back toward your body and your wrist is closer to your head than your elbow is. Slow-motion film of big-league pitchers shows that when they release the ball, the throwing arm is fully extended and straight from shoulder to wrist. The combination of these three elements—head-on stance, dropped elbow, and wrist inside the elbow—mechanically dictates a pushing rather than a hurling motion, creating the familiar pattern of "throwing like a girl."

It is surprisingly hard to find in the literature of baseball a deeper explanation of the mechanics of good and bad throws. Tom Seaver's pitching for the Mets and the White Sox got him into the Hall of Fame, but his

10

book *The Art of Pitching* is full of bromides that hardly clarify the process of throwing, even if they might mean something to accomplished pitchers. His chapter "The Absolutes of Pitching Mechanics," for instance, lays out these four unhelpful principles: "Keep the Front Leg Flexible!" "Rub Up the Baseball." "Hide the Baseball!" "Get it Out, Get it Up!" (The fourth refers to the need to get the ball out of the glove and into the throwing hand in a quick motion.)

A variety of other instructional documents, from *Little League's Official How-to-Play Baseball Book* to *Softball for Girls & Women*, mainly reveal the difficulty of finding words to describe a simple motor activity that everyone can recognize. The challenge, I suppose, is like that of writing a manual on how to ride a bike, or how to kiss. Indeed, the most useful description I've found of the mechanics of throwing comes from a man whose specialty is another sport: Vic Braden made his name as a tennis coach, but he has attempted to analyze the physics of a wide variety of sports so that they all will be easier to teach.

Braden says that an effective throw involves connecting a series of links in a "kinetic chain." The kinetic chain, which is Braden's tool for analyzing most sporting activity, operates on a principle like that of crack-the-whip. Momentum builds up in one part of the body. When that part is suddenly stopped, as the end of the "whip" is stopped in crack-the-whip, the momentum is transferred to and concentrated in the next link in the chain. A good throw uses six links of chain, Braden says. The first two links involve the lower body, from feet to waist. The first motion of a throw (after the body has been rotated away from the target) is to rotate the legs and hips back in the direction of the throw, building up momentum as large muscles move body mass. Then those links stop—a pitcher stops turning his hips once they face the plate—and the momentum is transferred to the next link. This is the torso, from waist to shoulders, and since its mass is less than that of the legs, momentum makes it rotate faster than the hips and legs did. The torso stops when it is facing the plate, and the momentum is transferred to the next link—the upper arm. As the upper arm comes past the head, it stops moving forward, and the momentum goes into the final links— the forearm and wrist, which snap forward at tremendous speed.

This may sound arcane and jerkily mechanical, but it makes perfect sense when one sees Braden's slow-mo movies of pitchers in action. And it explains why people do, or don't, learn how to throw. The implication of Braden's analysis is that throwing is a perfectly natural action (millions and millions of people can do it) but not at all innate. A successful throw involves an intricate series of actions coordinated among muscle groups, as each link of the chain is timed to interact with the next. Like bike riding or skating, it can be learned by anyone—male or female. No one starts out knowing how to ride a bike or throw a ball. Everyone has to learn.

Readers who are happy with their throwing skills can prove this to themselves in about two seconds. If you are right-handed, pick up a ball with your left hand and throw it. Unless you are ambidextrous or have some other odd advantage, you will throw it "like a girl." The problem is not that your left shoulder is hinged strangely or that you don't know what a good throw looks like. It is that you have not spent time training your leg, hip, shoulder, and arm muscles on that side to work together as required for a throw. The actor John Goodman, who played football seriously and baseball casually when he was in high school, is right-handed. When cast in the 1992 movie *The Babe*, he had to learn to bat and throw left-handed, for realism in the role of Babe Ruth. For weeks before the filming began, he would arrive an hour early at the set of his TV show, *Roseanne*, so that he could practice throwing a tennis ball against a wall left-handed. "I made damn sure no one could see me," Goodman told me recently. "I'm hard enough on myself without the derisive laughter of my so-called friends." When *The Babe* was released, Goodman told a newspaper interviewer, "I'll never say something like 'He throws like a girl' again. It's not easy to learn how to throw."

What Goodman discovered is what most men have forgotten: that if   15
they know how to throw now, it is because they spent time learning at some point long ago. (Goodman says that he can remember learning to ride a bicycle but not learning to throw with his right hand.) This brings us back to the roots of the "throwing like a girl" phenomenon. The crucial factor is not that males and females are put together differently but that they typically spend their early years in different ways. Little boys often learn how to throw without noticing that they are learning. Little girls are more rarely in environments that encourage them to learn in the same way. A boy who wonders why a girl throws the way she does is like a Frenchman who wonders why so many Americans speak French "with an accent."

"For young boys it is culturally acceptable and politically correct to develop these skills," says Linda Wells, of the Arizona State softball team. "They are mentored and networked. Usually girls are not coached at all, or are coached by Mom—or if it's by Dad, he may not be much of an athlete. Girls are often stuck with the bottom of the male talent pool as examples. I would argue that rather than learning to 'throw like a girl,' they learn to throw like poor male athletes. I say that a bad throw is 'throwing like an old man.' This is not gender, it's acculturation."

Almost any motor skill, from doing handstands to dribbling a basketball, is easier to learn if you start young, which is why John Goodman did not realize that learning to throw is difficult until he attempted it as an adult. Many girls reach adulthood having missed the chance to learn to throw when that would have been easiest to do. And as adults they have neither John Goodman's incentive to teach their muscles a new set of skills nor his confidence that the feat is possible. Five years ago, Joseph Russo, long a baseball coach at St. John's University, gave athletic-talent tests to actresses who were trying out for roles in *A League of Their*

Own, a movie about women's baseball. Most of them were "well coordinated in general, like for dancing," he says. But those who had not happened to play baseball or softball when they were young had a problem: "It sounds silly to say it, but they kept throwing like girls." (The best ball-field talents, by the way, were Madonna, Demi Moore, and the rock singer Joan Jett, who according to Russo "can really hit it hard." Careful viewers of *A League of Their Own* will note that only in a fleeting instant in one scene is the star, Geena Davis, shown actually throwing a ball.)

I'm not sure that I buy Linda Wells's theory that most boys are "mentored" or "networked" into developing ball skills. Those who make the baseball team, maybe. But for a far larger number the decisive ingredient seems to be the hundreds of idle hours spent throwing balls, sticks, rocks, and so on in the playground or the back yard. Children on the playground, I think, demonstrate the moment when the kinetic chain begins to work. It is when a little boy tries to throw a rock farther than his friend can or to throw a stick over a telephone wire thirty feet up. A toddler's first, instinctive throw is a push from the shoulder, showing the essential traits of "throwing like a girl." But when a child is really trying to put some oomph into the throw, his natural instinct is to wind up his body and let fly with the links of the chain. Little girls who do the same thing— compete with each other in distance throwing—learn the same way, but whereas many boys do this, few girls do. Tammy Richards, a woman who was raised on a farm in central California, says that she learned to throw by trying to heave dried cow chips farther than her brother could. It may have helped that her father, Bob Richards, was a former Olympic competitor in the decathlon (and two-time Olympic champion in the pole vault) and that he taught all his sons and daughters to throw not only the ball but also the discus, the shotput, and the javelin.

Is there a way to make up for lost time if you failed to invest those long hours on the playground years ago? Of course. Adults may not be able to learn to speak unaccented French, but they can learn to ride a bike, or skate, or throw. All that is required for developing any of these motor skills is time for practice—and spending that time requires overcoming the sense of embarrassment and futility that adults often have when attempting something new. Here are two tips that may help.

One is a surprisingly valuable drill suggested by the Little League's *How-to-Play* handbook. Play catch with a partner who is ten or fifteen feet away—but do so while squatting with the knee of your throwing side touching the ground. When you start out this low, you have to keep the throw high to get the ball to your partner without bouncing it. This encourages a throw with the elbow held well above the shoulder, where it belongs.

The other is to play catch with a person who can throw like an athlete but is using his or her off hand. The typical adult woman hates to play catch with the typical adult man. She is well aware that she's not

20

looking graceful and reacts murderously to the condescending tone in his voice ("That's more like it, honey!"). Forcing a right-handed man to throw left-handed is the great equalizer. He suddenly concentrates his attention on what it takes to get hips, shoulder, and elbow working together. He is suddenly aware of the strength of character needed to ignore the snickers of onlookers while learning new motor skills. He can no longer be condescending. He may even be nervous, wondering what he'll do if his partner makes the breakthrough first and he's the one still throwing like a girl.

The Reader's Presence

1. Fallows acknowledges the objections of feminists to the phrase "throwing like a girl." What other activities are linked to one gender or the other? Which gender gathers more negative associations? Why might feminists challenge the phrase? In your opinion, does Fallows satisfactorily answer such objections?

2. As a reporter, Fallows has covered many serious issues. Where does his use of language indicate that this essay is a lighter piece? Where does Fallows use an exaggerated or self-mocking tone? How does his use of humor affect the reader's reception of his message?

3. Reread the essay, focusing your attention on Fallows's descriptions of physical movement, especially paragraphs 9 through 14. Is it possible to understand his idea of the "kinetic chain" (paragraph 12) just by reading a description of it or must the reader also enact it with her or his body? Compare Fallows's anatomically detailed account to George Orwell's description of the dying elephant in "Shooting an Elephant" (page 203). How does each writer integrate such "close focus" descriptions into his larger argument? Do these passages slow down the essays? If not, why not?

Ian Frazier

All-Consuming Patriotism

The journalist and essayist Ian Frazier (b. 1951) started his career on the staff of the New Yorker, *writing "Talk of the Town" pieces as well as signed essays. Many of these essays can be found in his first two books:* Dating Your Mom *(1986) and* Nobody Better, Better than Nobody *(1987). In the mid-1980s Frazier left his job in New York and embarked on a journey across the North American prairies to Montana. The book that emerged after several years spent exploring this region,* Great Plains *(1989), was a huge success with both critics and readers. In* Family *(1994), Frazier turns to a subject closer to home and tells the story of twelve generations of his family. His books also include* Coyote v. Acme *(1996), a collection of comic essays;* On the Rez *(2000), the story of his experience on the Pine Ridge Indian Reservation;* The Fish's Eye: Essays about Angling and the Outdoors *(2002); and* Lamentations of the Father *(2008), based on his 1997 award-winning essay of the same name. Frazier coedited* The Best American Essays 1997 *and* The Best American Travel Writing 2003.

In all of his writing Frazier pays close attention to detail and location. "If you know something about a place it can save your sanity," he says, and a writer can find that knowledge through observation. "With a lot of writing, what you see is the top, the pinnacle, and the rest is invisible—all of these observations are ways of keeping yourself from flying off into space." In "All-Consuming Patriotism," which appeared in Mother Jones *in 2002, Frazier observes the expression of patriotism in the post–9/11 world.*

I think of myself as a good American. I follow current events, come to a complete stop at stop signs, show up for jury duty, vote. When the government tells me to shop, as it's been doing recently, I shop. Over the last few months, patriotically, I've bought all kinds of stuff I have no use for. Lack of money has been no obstacle; years ago I could never get a credit card, due to low income and lack of a regular job, and then one day for no reason credit cards began tumbling on me out of the mail. I now owe more to credit card companies than the average family of four earns in a year. So when buying something I don't want or need, I simply take out my credit card. That part's been easy; for me, it's the shopping itself that's hard. I happen to be a bad shopper—nervous, uninformed, prone to grab the first product I see on the shelf and pay any amount for it and run out the door. Frequently, trips I make to the supermarket end with my wife shouting in disbelief as she goes through the grocery bags and immediately transfers one wrongly purchased item after another directly into the garbage can.

It's been hard, as I say, but I've done my duty—I've shopped and then shopped some more. Certain sacrifices are called for. Out of concern

393

for the economy after the terror attacks, the president said that he wanted us to go about our business, and not stop shopping. On a TV commercial sponsored by the travel industry, he exhorted us to take the family for a vacation. The treasury secretary, financial commentators, leaders of industry — all told us not to be afraid to spend. So I've gone out of my comfort zone, even expanded my purchasing patterns. Not long ago I detected a look of respect in the eye of a young salesman with many piercings at the music store as he took in my heavy middle-aged girth and then the rap music CD featuring songs of murder and gangsterism that I had selflessly decided to buy. My life is usually devoid of great excitement or difficulty, knock wood and thank God, and I have nothing to cry about, but I've also noticed in the media recently a strong approval for uninhibited public crying. So now, along with the shopping, I've been crying a lot, too. Sometimes I cry and shop at the same time.

As I'm pushing my overfull shopping cart down the aisle, sobbing quietly, moving a bit more slowly because of the extra weight I've lately put on, a couple of troubling questions cross my mind. First, I start to worry about the real depth of my shopping capabilities. So far I have more or less been able to keep up with what the government expects of me. I'm at a level of shopping that I can stand. But what if, God forbid, events take a bad turn and the national crisis worsens, and more shopping is required? Can I shop with greater intensity than I am shopping now? I suppose I could eat even more than I've been eating, and order additional products in the mail, and go on costlier trips, and so on. But I'm not eager, frankly, to enter that "code red" shopping mode. I try to tell myself that I'd be equal to it, that in a real crisis I might be surprised by how much I could buy. But I don't know.

My other worry is a vague one, more in the area of atmospherics, intangibles. I feel kind of wrong even mentioning it in this time of trial. How can I admit that I am worried about my aura? I worry that my aura is not . . . well, that it's not what I had once hoped it would be. I can explain this only by comparison, obliquely. On the top shelf of my bookcase, among the works vital to me, is a book called *Trials and Triumphs: The Record of the Fifty-Fifth Ohio Volunteer Infantry*, by Captain Hartwell Osborn. I've read this book many times and studied it to the smallest detail, because I think the people in it are brave and cool and admirable in every way.

The Fifty-Fifth was a Union Army regiment, formed in the Ohio town of Norwalk, that fought throughout the Civil War. My great-great-grandfather served in the regiment, as did other relatives. The book lists every mile the regiment marched and every casualty it suffered. I like reading about the soldiering, but I can't really identify with it, having never been in the service myself. I identify more with the soldiers' wives and mothers and daughters, whose home-front struggles I can better imagine. *Trials and Triumphs* devotes a chapter to them, and to an organization they set up called the Soldiers' Aid Society.

5

The ladies of the Soldiers' Aid Society worked for the regiment almost constantly from the day it began. They sewed uniforms, made pillows, held ice-cream sociables to raise money, scraped lint for bandages, emptied their wedding chests of their best linen and donated it all. To provide the men with antiscorbutics while on campaign, they pickled everything that would pickle, from onions to potatoes to artichokes. Every other day they were shipping out a new order of home-made supplies. Some of the women spent so much time stooped over while packing goods in barrels that they believed they had permanently affected their postures. When the war ended the ladies of the Soldiers' Aid Society said that for the first time in their lives they understood what united womanhood could accomplish. The movements for prohibition and women's suffrage that grew powerful in the early 1900s got their start among those who'd worked in similar home-front organizations during the war.

I don't envy my forebears, or wish I'd lived back then. I prefer the greater speed and uncertainty and complicatedness of now. But I can't help thinking that in terms of aura, the Norwalk ladies have it all over me. I study the pages with their photographs, and admire the plainness of their dresses, the set of their jaws, the expression in their eyes. Next to them my credit card and I seem a sorry spectacle indeed. Their sense of purpose shames me. What the country needed from those ladies it asked for, and they provided, straightforwardly; what it wants from me it somehow can't come out and ask. I'm asked to shop more, which really means to spend more, which eventually must mean to work more than I was working before. In previous wars, harder work was a civilian sacrifice that the government didn't hesitate to ask. Nowadays it's apparently unwilling to ask for any sacrifice that might appear to be too painful, too real.

But I *want* it to be real. I think a lot of us do. I feel like an idiot with my tears and shopping cart. I want to participate, to do something—and shopping isn't it. Many of the donors who contributed more than half a billion dollars to a Red Cross fund for the families of terror attack victims became angry when they learned that much of the money would end up not where they had intended but in the Red Cross bureaucracy. People want to express themselves with action. In New York City so many have been showing up recently for jury duty that the courts have had to turn hundreds away; officials said a new surplus of civic consciousness was responsible for the upsurge. I'd be glad if I were asked to—I don't know—drive less or turn the thermostat down or send in seldom-used items of clothing or collect rubber bands or plant a victory garden or join a civilian patrol or use fewer disposable paper products at children's birthday parties. I'd be willing, if asked, just to sit still for a day and meditate on the situation, much in the way that Lincoln used to call for national days of prayer.

A great, shared desire to *do* something is lying around mostly untapped. The best we can manage, it seems, is to show our U.S.A. brand loyalty by putting American flags on our houses and cars. Some businesses across the country even display in their windows a poster on which the American flag appears as a shopping bag, with two handles at the top. Above the flag-bag are the words "America: Open for Business." Money and the economy have gotten so tangled up in our politics that we forget we're citizens of our government, not its consumers. And the leaders we elect, who got where they are by selling themselves to us with television ads, and who often are only on short loan from the corporate world anyway, think of us as customers who must be kept happy. There's a scarcity of ideas about how to direct all this patriotic feeling because usually the market, not the country, occupies our minds. I'm sure it's possible to transform oneself from salesman to leader, just as it is to go from consumer to citizen. But the shift of identity is awkward, without many precedents, not easily done. In between the two—between selling and leading, between consuming and being citizens—is where our leaders and the rest of us are now.

We see the world beyond our immediate surroundings mostly through   10
television, whose view is not much wider than that of a security peephole in a door. We hear over and over that our lives have forever changed, but the details right in front of us don't look very different, for all that. The forces fighting in Afghanistan are in more danger than we are back home, but perhaps not so much more; everybody knows that when catastrophe comes it could hit anywhere, most likely someplace it isn't expected. Strong patriotic feelings stir us, fill us, but have few means of expressing themselves. We want to be a country, but where do you go to do that? Surely not the mall. When Mayor Giuliani left office at the end of 2001, he said he was giving up the honorable title of mayor for the more honorable title of citizen. He got that right. Citizen is honorable; shopper is not.

The Reader's Presence

1. How does Frazier characterize shopping as an act of patriotism? What sacrifices does he make in the name of patriotic consumerism? What words and phrases exemplify the way he satirizes the call to shop?

2. Frazier discusses the sacrifices that patriotism asks of citizens. How is "sacrifice" defined in the first couple of paragraphs? Compare that definition to Frazier's discussion of sacrifice toward the end of the essay.

3. Frazier is well known as a humor writer. At what point did you recognize the humor in Frazier's writing? Where does his tone modulate and become more serious? Why? Compare Frazier's use of humor to Marjane Satrapi's "My Speech at West Point" (page 230). Compare the ways each author uses humor for political purposes.

Jon Gertner

The Futile Pursuit of Happiness

Journalist Jon Gertner writes about business and technology, and their links to society and culture. A graduate of Cornell University, Gertner is a contributing writer at the New York Times Magazine, *where he writes on a broad range of topics from global warming, to nuclear power, to economics. He has been senior editor at* Money *magazine and at* American Lawyer *magazine, and his articles have appeared in numerous business magazines, including* Fortune *and* Fast Company. *Gertner grew up in New Jersey, in the shadow of Bell Labs, the subject of his forthcoming book on the history of the company,* The Idea Factory: Bell Labs and the Invention of the Modern World.*

"The Futile Pursuit of Happiness" first appeared in the New York Times Magazine *in 2003, becoming the* Times's *most frequently e-mailed article of that year. The essay questions basic assumptions about human desire and our inability to really understand what we want in life and to "predict what will make us happy or unhappy."*

If Daniel Gilbert is right, then you are wrong. That is to say, if Daniel Gilbert is right, then you are wrong to believe that a new car will make you as happy as you imagine. You are wrong to believe that a new kitchen will make you happy for as long as you imagine. You are wrong to think that you will be more unhappy with a big single setback (a broken wrist, a broken heart) than with a lesser chronic one (a trick knee, a tense marriage). You are wrong to assume that job failure will be crushing. You are wrong to expect that a death in the family will leave you bereft for year upon year, forever and ever. You are even wrong to reckon that a cheeseburger you order in a restaurant—this week, next week, a year from now, it doesn't really matter when—will definitely hit the spot. That's because when it comes to predicting exactly how you will feel in the future, you are most likely wrong.

A professor in Harvard's department of psychology, Gilbert likes to tell people that he studies happiness. But it would be more precise to say that Gilbert—along with the psychologist Tim Wilson of the University of Virginia, the economist George Loewenstein of Carnegie Mellon, and the psychologist (and Nobel laureate in economics) Daniel Kahneman of Princeton—has taken the lead in studying a specific type of emotional and behavioral prediction. In the past few years, these four men have begun to question the decision-making process that shapes our sense of well-being: How do we predict what will make us happy or unhappy—and then how do we feel after the actual experience? For example, how do we suppose we'll feel if our favorite college football team wins or loses, and then how do we really feel a few days after the game? How do

397

we predict we'll feel about purchasing jewelry, having children, buying a big house, or being rich? And then how do we regard the outcomes? According to this small corps of academics, almost all actions—the decision to buy jewelry, have kids, buy a big house, or work exhaustively for a fatter paycheck—are based on our predictions of the emotional consequences of these events.

Until recently, this was uncharted territory. How we forecast our feelings, and whether those predictions match our future emotional states, had never been the stuff of laboratory research. But in scores of experiments, Gilbert, Wilson, Kahneman, and Loewenstein have made a slew of observations and conclusions that undermine a number of fundamental assumptions: namely, that we humans understand what we want and are adept at improving our well-being—that we are good at maximizing our utility, in the jargon of traditional economics. Further, their work on prediction raises some unsettling and somewhat more personal questions. To understand affective forecasting, as Gilbert has termed these studies, is to wonder if everything you have ever thought about life choices, and about happiness, has been at the least somewhat naïve and, at worst, greatly mistaken.

The problem, as Gilbert and company have come to discover, is that we falter when it comes to imagining how we will feel about something in the future. It isn't that we get the big things wrong. We know we will experience visits to Le Cirque and to the periodontist differently; we can accurately predict that we'd rather be stuck in Montauk[1] than in a Midtown elevator. What Gilbert has found, however, is that we overestimate the intensity and the duration of our emotional reactions—our "affect"—to future events. In other words, we might believe that a new BMW will make life perfect. But it will almost certainly be less exciting than we anticipated; nor will it excite us for as long as predicted. The vast majority of Gilbert's test participants through the years have consistently made just these sorts of errors both in the laboratory and in real-life situations. And whether Gilbert's subjects were trying to predict how they would feel in the future about a plate of spaghetti with meat sauce, the defeat of a preferred political candidate, or romantic rejection seemed not to matter. On average, bad events proved less intense and more transient than test participants predicted. Good events proved less intense and briefer as well.

Gilbert and his collaborator Tim Wilson call the gap between what we predict and what we ultimately experience the "impact bias"—"impact" meaning the errors we make in estimating both the intensity and duration of our emotions and "bias," our tendency to err. The phrase characterizes how we experience the dimming excitement over not just a BMW but also over any object or event that we presume will make us happy. Would a 20 percent raise or winning the lottery result in a contented life? You may predict it will, but almost surely it won't turn out that way. And a new plasma television? You may have high hopes, but

[5]

---

[1]*Montauk:* a small village on the easternmost point of Long Island, New York.—EDS.

the impact bias suggests that it will almost certainly be less cool, and in a shorter time, than you imagine. Worse, Gilbert has noted that these mistakes of expectation can lead directly to mistakes in choosing what we think will give us pleasure. He calls this "miswanting."

"The average person says, 'I know I'll be happier with a Porsche than a Chevy,'" Gilbert explains. "'Or with Linda rather than Rosalyn. Or as a doctor rather than as a plumber.' That seems very clear to people. The problem is, I can't get into medical school or afford the Porsche. So for the average person, the obstacle between them and happiness is actually getting the future that they desire. But what our research shows—not just ours, but Loewenstein's and Kahneman's—is that the real problem is figuring out which of those futures is going to have the high payoff and is really going to make you happy."

"You know, the Stones said, 'You can't always get what you want,'" Gilbert adds. "I don't think that's the problem. The problem is you can't always know what you want."

Gilbert's papers on affective forecasting began to appear in the late 1990s, but the idea to study happiness and emotional prediction actually came to him on a sunny afternoon in October 1992, just as he and his friend Jonathan Jay Koehler sat down for lunch outside the psychology building at the University of Texas at Austin, where both men were teaching at the time. Gilbert was uninspired about his studies and says he felt despair about his failing marriage. And as he launched into a discussion of his personal life, he swerved to ask why economists focus on the financial aspects of decision making rather than the emotional ones. Koehler recalls, "Gilbert said something like: 'It all seems so small. It isn't really about money; it's about happiness. Isn't that what everybody wants to know when we make a decision?'" For a moment, Gilbert forgot his troubles, and two more questions came to him. Do we even know what makes us happy? And if it's difficult to figure out what makes us happy in the moment, how can we predict what will make us happy in the future?

In the early 1990s, for an up-and-coming psychology professor like Gilbert to switch his field of inquiry from how we perceive one another to happiness, as he did that day, was just a hairsbreadth short of bizarre. But Gilbert has always liked questions that lead him somewhere new. Now forty-five, Gilbert dropped out of high school at fifteen, looking into what he calls "the tail end of the hippie movement" and hitchhiking aimlessly from town to town with his guitar. He met his wife on the road; she was hitching in the other direction. They married at seventeen, had a son at eighteen, and settled down in Denver. "I pulled weeds, I sold rebar, I sold carpet, I installed carpet, I spent a lot of time as a phone solicitor," he recalls. During this period he spent several years turning out science-fiction stories for magazines like *Amazing Stories*. Thus, in addition to being "one of the most gifted social psychologists of our age," as the psychology writer and professor David G. Myers describes him to me, Gilbert is the author of "The Essence of Grunk," a story about an encounter with a creature made of egg salad that jets around the galaxy in a rocket-powered refrigerator.

Psychology was a matter of happenstance. In the midst of his sci-fi   10
career, Gilbert tried to sign up for a writing course at the local community college, but the class was full; he figured that psych, still accepting registrants, would help him with character development in his fiction. It led instead to an undergraduate degree at the University of Colorado at Denver, then a Ph.D. at Princeton, then an appointment at the University of Texas, then the appointment at Harvard. "People ask why I study happiness," Gilbert says, "and I say, 'Why study anything else?' It's the holy grail. We're studying the thing that all human action is directed toward."

One experiment of Gilbert's had students in a photography class at Harvard choose two favorite pictures from among those they had just taken and then relinquish one to the teacher. Some students were told their choices were permanent; others were told they could exchange their prints after several days. As it turned out, those who had time to change their minds were less pleased with their decisions than those whose choices were irrevocable.

Much of Gilbert's research is in this vein. Another recent study asked whether transit riders in Boston who narrowly missed their trains experienced the self-blame that people tend to predict they'll feel in this situation. (They did not.) And a paper waiting to be published, "The Peculiar Longevity of Things Not So Bad," examines why we expect that bigger problems will always dwarf minor annoyances. "When really bad things happen to us, we defend against them," Gilbert explains. "People, of course, predict the exact opposite. If you ask, 'What would you rather have, a broken leg or a trick knee?' they'd probably say, 'Trick knee.' And yet, if your goal is to accumulate maximum happiness over your lifetime, you just made the wrong choice. A trick knee is a bad thing to have."

All of these studies establish the links between prediction, decision making, and well-being. The photography experiment challenges our common assumption that we would be happier with the option to change our minds when in fact we're happier with closure. The transit experiment demonstrates that we tend to err in estimating our regret over missed opportunities. The "things not so bad" work shows our failure to imagine how grievously irritations compromise our satisfaction. Our emotional defenses snap into action when it comes to a divorce or a disease but not for lesser problems. We fix the leaky roof on our house, but over the long haul, the broken screen door we never mend adds up to more frustration.

Gilbert does not believe all forecasting mistakes lead to similar results; a death in the family, a new gym membership, and a new husband are not the same, but in how they affect our well-being they are similar. "Our research simply says that whether it's the thing that matters or the thing that doesn't, both of them matter less than you think they will," he says. "Things that happen to you or that you buy or own—as much as you think they make a difference to your happiness, you're wrong by a certain amount. None of them makes the difference you think. And that's true of positive and negative events."

Much of the work of Kahneman, Loewenstein, Gilbert, and Wilson   15
takes its cue from the concept of adaptation, a term psychologists have used since at least the 1950s to refer to how we acclimate to changing circumstances. George Loewenstein sums up this human capacity as follows: "Happiness is a signal that our brains use to motivate us to do certain things. And in the same way that our eye adapts to different levels of illumination, we're designed to kind of go back to the happiness set point. Our brains are not trying to be happy. Our brains are trying to regulate us." In this respect, the tendency toward adaptation suggests why the impact bias is so pervasive. As Tim Wilson says: "We don't realize how quickly we will adapt to a pleasurable event and make it the backdrop of our lives. When any event occurs to us, we make it ordinary. And through becoming ordinary, we lose our pleasure."

It is easy to overlook something new and crucial in what Wilson is saying. Not that we invariably lose interest in bright and shiny things over time—this is a long-known trait—but that we're generally unable to recognize that we adapt to new circumstances and therefore fail to incorporate this fact into our decisions. So, yes, we will adapt to the BMW and the plasma TV, since we adapt to virtually everything. But Wilson and Gilbert and others have shown that we seem unable to predict that we will adapt. Thus, when we find the pleasure derived from a thing diminishing, we move on to the next thing or event and almost certainly make another error of prediction, and then another, ad infinitum.

As Gilbert points out, this glitch is also significant when it comes to negative events like losing a job or the death of someone we love, in response to which we project a permanently inconsolable future. "The thing I'm more interested in, that I've spent the most time studying, is our failure to recognize how powerful psychological defenses are once they're activated," Gilbert says. "We've used the metaphor of the 'psychological immune system'—it's just a metaphor, but not a bad one for that system of defenses that helps you feel better when bad things happen. Observers of the human condition since Aristotle have known that people have these defenses. Freud spent his life, and his daughter Anna spent her life, worrying about these defenses. What's surprising is that people don't seem to recognize that they have these defenses, and that these defenses will be triggered by negative events." During the course of my interviews with Gilbert, a close friend of his died. "I am like everyone in thinking, I'll never get over this and life will never be good again," he wrote to me in an e-mail message as he planned a trip to Texas for the funeral. "But because of my work, there is always a voice in the back of my head—a voice that wears a lab coat and has a lot of data tucked under its arm—that says, 'Yes, you will, and yes, it will.' And I know that voice is right."

Still, the argument that we imperfectly imagine what we want and how we will cope is nevertheless disorienting. On the one hand, it can cast a shadow of regret on some life decisions. Why did I decide that working one hundred hours a week to earn more would make me happy? Why did I think that retiring in Sun City, Arizona, would please me? On the other hand, it can be enlightening. No wonder this teak patio set hasn't made me as happy as I expected. Even if she dumps me, I'll be okay. Either way, predicting how things will feel to us over the long term is mystifying. A large body of research on well-being seems to suggest that wealth above middle-class comfort makes little difference to our happiness, for example, or that having children does nothing to improve well-being — even as it drives marital satisfaction dramatically down. We often yearn for a roomy, isolated home (a thing we easily adapt to), when, in fact, it will probably compromise our happiness by distancing us from neighbors. (Social interaction and friendships have been shown to give lasting pleasure.) The big isolated home is what Loewenstein, forty-eight, himself bought. "I fell into a trap I never should have fallen into," he told me.

Loewenstein's office is up a narrow stairway in a hidden corner of an enormous, worn brick building on the edge of the Carnegie Mellon campus in Pittsburgh. He and Gilbert make for an interesting contrast. Gilbert is garrulous, theatrical, dazzling in his speech and writing; he fills a room. Loewenstein is soft-spoken, given to abstraction, and lithe in the way of a hard-core athlete; he seems to float around a room. Both men profess tremendous admiration for the other, and their different disciplines — psychology and economics — have made their overlapping interests in affective forecasting more complementary than fraught. While Gilbert's most notable contribution to affective forecasting is the impact bias, Loewenstein's is something called the "empathy gap."

Here's how it expresses itself. In a recent experiment, Loewenstein 20 tried to find out how likely people might be to dance alone to Rick James's "Super Freak" in front of a large audience. Many agreed to do so for a certain amount of money a week in advance, only to renege when the day came to take the stage. This sounds like a goof, but it gets at the fundamental difference between how we behave in "hot" states (those of anxiety, courage, fear, drug craving, sexual excitation, and the like) and "cold" states of rational calm. This empathy gap in thought and behavior — we cannot seem to predict how we will behave in a hot state when we are in a cold state — affects happiness in an important but somewhat less consistent way than the impact bias. "So much of our lives involves making decisions that have consequences for the future," Loewenstein says. "And if our decision making is influenced by these transient emotional and psychological states, then we know we're not making decisions with an eye toward future consequences." This may be as simple as an unfortunate proclamation of love in a moment of lust, Loewenstein explains, or something darker, like an act of road rage or of suicide.

Among other things, this line of inquiry has led Loewenstein to collaborate with health experts looking into why people engage in unprotected sex when they would never agree to do so in moments of cool calculation. Data from tests in which volunteers are asked how they would behave in various "heat of the moment" situations—whether they would have sex with a minor, for instance, or act forcefully with a partner who asks them to stop—have consistently shown that different states of arousal can alter answers by astonishing margins. "These kinds of states have the ability to change us so profoundly that we're more different from ourselves in different states than we are from another person," Loewenstein says.

Part of Loewenstein's curiosity about hot and cold states comes from situations in which his emotions have been pitted against his intellect. When he's not teaching, he treks around the world, making sure to get to Alaska to hike or kayak at least once a year. A scholar of mountaineering literature, he once wrote a paper that examined why climbers have a poor memory for pain and usually ignore turn-back times at great peril. But he has done the same thing himself many times. He almost died in a white-water canoeing accident and vowed afterward that he never wanted to see his runaway canoe again. (A couple of hours later, he went looking for it.) The same goes for his climbing pursuits. "You establish your turn-back time, and then you find yourself still far from the peak," he says. "So you push on. You haven't brought enough food or clothes, and then as a result, you're stuck at thirteen thousand feet, and you have to just sit there and shiver all night without a sleeping bag or warm clothes. When the sun comes up, you're half-frozen, and you say, 'Never again.' Then you get back and immediately start craving getting out again." He pushes the point: "I have tried to train my emotions." But he admits he may make the same mistakes on his next trip.

Would a world without forecasting errors be a better world? Would a life lived without forecasting errors be a richer life? Among the academics who study affective forecasting, there seems little doubt that these sorts of questions will ultimately jump from the academy to the real world. "If people do not know what is going to make them better off or give them pleasure," Daniel Kahneman says, "then the idea that you can trust people to do what will give them pleasure becomes questionable." To Kahneman, who did some of the first experiments in the area in the early 1990s, affective forecasting could greatly influence retirement planning, for example, where mistakes in prediction (how much we save, how much we spend, how we choose a community we think we'll enjoy) can prove irreversible. He sees a role for affective forecasting in consumer spending, where a "cooling off" period might remedy buyer's remorse. Most important, he sees vital applications in health care, especially when it comes to informed consent. "We consider people capable of giving informed consent once they are told of the objective effects of a treatment," Kahneman says. "But can people anticipate how they and other people will react to a colostomy or to the removal of their vocal cords? The research on affective forecasting suggests that people may have little ability to anticipate their adaptation beyond the early stages." Loewenstein, along with his collaborator Dr. Peter Ubel, has done a great deal of work showing that nonpatients overestimate the displeasure of living with the loss of a limb, for instance, or paraplegia. To use affective forecasting to prove that people adapt to serious physical challenges far better and will be happier than they imagine, Loewenstein says, could prove invaluable.

There are downsides to making public policy in light of this research, too. While walking in Pittsburgh one afternoon, Loewenstein tells me that he doesn't see how anybody could study happiness and not find himself leaning left politically; the data make it all too clear that boosting the living standards of those already comfortable, such as through lower taxes, does little to improve their levels of well-being, whereas raising the living standards of the impoverished makes an enormous difference. Nevertheless, he and Gilbert (who once declared in an academic paper, "Windfalls are better than pratfalls, A's are better than C's, December 25 is better than April 15, and everything is better than a Republican administration") seem to lean libertarian in regard to pushing any kind of prescriptive agenda. "We're very, very nervous about overapplying the research," Loewenstein says. "Just because we figure out that X makes people happy and they're choosing Y, we don't want to impose X on them. I have a discomfort with paternalism and with using the results coming out of our field to impose decisions on people."

Still, Gilbert and Loewenstein can't contain the personal and philo-   25
sophical questions raised by their work. After talking with both men, I found it hard not to wonder about my own predictions at every turn. At times it seemed like knowing the secret to some parlor trick that was nonetheless very difficult to pull off—when I ogled a new car at the Honda dealership as I waited for a new muffler on my '92 Accord, for instance, or as my daughter's fever spiked one evening and I imagined something terrible, and then something more terrible thereafter. With some difficulty, I could observe my mind overshooting the mark, zooming past accuracy toward the sublime or the tragic. It was tempting to want to try to think about the future more moderately. But it seemed nearly impossible as well.

To Loewenstein, who is especially attendant to the friction between his emotional and deliberate processes, a life without forecasting errors would most likely be a better, happier life. "If you had a deep understanding of the impact bias and you acted on it, which is not always that easy to do, you would tend to invest your resources in the things that would make you happy," he says. This might mean taking more time with friends instead of more time for making money. He also adds that a better understanding of the empathy gap—those hot and cold states we all find ourselves in on frequent occasions—could save people from making regrettable decisions in moments of courage or craving.

Gilbert seems optimistic about using the work in terms of improving "institutional judgment"—how we spend health care dollars, for example — but less sanguine about using it to improve our personal judgment. He admits that he has taken some of his research to heart; for instance, his work on what he calls the psychological immune system has led him to believe that he would be able to adapt to even the worst turn of events. In addition, he says that he now takes more chances in life, a fact corroborated in at least one aspect by his research partner Tim Wilson, who says that driving with Gilbert in Boston is a terrifying, white-knuckle experience. "But I should have learned many more lessons from my research than I actually have," Gilbert admits. "I'm getting married in the spring because this woman is going to make me happy forever, and I know it." At this, Gilbert laughs, a sudden, booming laugh that fills his Cambridge office. He seems to find it funny not because it's untrue, but because nothing could be more true. This is how he feels. "I don't think I want to give up all these motivations," he says, "that belief that there's the good and there's the bad and that this is a contest to try to get one and avoid the other. I don't think I want to learn too much from my research in that sense."

Even so, Gilbert is currently working on a complex experiment in which he has made affective forecasting errors "go away." In this test, Gilbert's team asks members of Group A to estimate how they'll feel if they receive negative personality feedback. The impact bias kicks in, of course, and they mostly predict they'll feel terrible, when in fact they end up feeling okay. But if Gilbert shows Group B that others have gotten the same feedback and felt okay afterward, then its members predict they'll feel okay as well. The impact bias disappears, and the participants in Group B make accurate predictions.

This is exciting to Gilbert. But at the same time, it's not a technique he wants to shape into a self-help book, or one that he even imagines could be practically implemented. "Hope and fear are enduring features of the human experience," he says, "and it is because some psychologist told them they should." In fact, in his recent writings, he has wondered whether forecasting errors might somehow serve a larger functional purpose he doesn't yet understand. If he could wave a wand tomorrow and eliminate all affective-forecasting errors, I ask, would he? "The benefits of not making this error would seem to be that you get a little more happiness," he says. "When choosing between two jobs, you wouldn't sweat as much because you'd say: 'You know, I'll be happy in both. I'll adapt to either circumstance pretty well, so there's no use in killing myself for the next week.' But maybe our caricatures of the future — these overinflated assessments of how good or bad things will be — maybe it's these illusory assessments that keep us moving in one direction over the other. Maybe we don't want a society of people who shrug and say, 'It won't really make a difference.'

"Maybe it's important for there to be carrots and sticks in the world, even if they are illusions," he adds. "They keep us moving towards carrots and away from sticks."

30

The Reader's Presence:

1. Gertner leads his readers on an example-packed tour of the study of "affective forecasting." How, exactly, does Gertner define "affective forecasting" (paragraph 3)? What do the terms "impact bias" (paragraph 5), "empathy gap" (paragraph 19), a "'hot' state" (paragraph 20), and a "'cold' state" (paragraph 20) mean? Create a list of the examples Gertner uses to explain each of these terms. Which examples do you find most—and least—engaging? Explain why.

2. Summarize the areas of public and private life that seem to lend themselves to affective forecasting. Which does Gertner develop most effectively? Explain why. What examples can you point to in your own experience that reinforce the research of Daniel Gilbert and George Loewenstein? Please be as specific as possible. To what extent do you think this research on affective forecasting can be applied to issues of public policy? What concerns do Gilbert and Loewenstein express about the implications of their research?

3. How would you characterize Gertner's presence in this essay? Consider, for example, his opening paragraph. Comment on the effectiveness of Gertner's repetition of—and variations on—the phrase "you are wrong." What terms would you use to characterize his attitude toward "affective forecasting"? toward Gilbert and Loewenstein? toward the research they are conducting? toward the results—and implications—of that work? Comment on the effectiveness of Gertner's devoting time to applying the research findings of Gilbert and Loewenstein to the circumstances of his own life (paragraphs 25–26).

4. After you are reasonably confident that you understand the substance and spirit of the research Gilbert and Loewenstein are doing on affective forecasting, read Ian Frazier's essay, "All-Consuming Patriotism" (page 393). In what specific ways might Frazier's behavior—his willingness to buy "all kinds of stuff I have no use for" as an expression of his patriotism—be regarded as an example of affective forecasting?

Malcolm Gladwell
Big and Bad

Malcolm Gladwell was born in England in 1963 and grew up in Canada. He graduated with a degree in history from the University of Toronto in 1984. From 1987 to 1996, he was a reporter for the Washington Post, *first as a science writer and then as New York City bureau chief. Since 1996, he has been a staff writer for the* New Yorker. *He is known for writing clearly and engagingly on complex topics; he described his best-selling book,* The Tipping Point *(2001), as "an intellectual adventure story . . . it takes theories and ideas from the social sciences and shows how they can have real relevance to our lives." His most recent book is* Blink *(2004).*

"Big and Bad" first appeared in the New Yorker *in 2004.*

In the summer of 1996, the Ford Motor Company began building the Expedition, its new, full-sized S.U.V., at the Michigan Truck Plant, in the Detroit suburb of Wayne. The Expedition was essentially the F-150 pickup truck with an extra set of doors and two more rows of seats—and the fact that it was a truck was critical. Cars have to meet stringent fuel-efficiency regulations. Trucks don't. The handling and suspension and braking of cars have to be built to the demanding standards of drivers and passengers. Trucks only have to handle like, well, trucks. Cars are built with what is called unit-body construction. To be light enough to meet fuel standards and safe enough to meet safety standards, they have expensive and elaborately engineered steel skeletons, with built-in crumple zones to absorb the impact of a crash. Making a truck is a lot more rudimentary. You build a rectangular steel frame. The engine gets bolted to the front. The seats get bolted to the middle. The body gets lowered over the top. The result is heavy and rigid and not particularly safe. But it's an awfully inexpensive way to build an automobile. Ford had planned to sell the Expedition for thirty-six thousand dollars, and its best estimate was that it could build one for twenty-four thousand—which, in the automotive industry, is a terrifically high profit margin. Sales, the company predicted, weren't going to be huge. After all, how many Americans could reasonably be expected to pay a twelve-thousand-dollar premium for what was essentially a dressed-up truck? But Ford executives decided that the Expedition would be a highly profitable niche product. They were half right. The "highly profitable" part turned out to be true. Yet, almost from the moment Ford's big new S.U.V.s rolled off the assembly line in Wayne, there was nothing "niche" about the Expedition.

Ford had intended to split the assembly line at the Michigan Truck Plant between the Expedition and the Ford F-150 pickup. But, when the first flood of orders started coming in for the Expedition, the factory was entirely given over to S.U.V.s. The orders kept mounting. Assembly-line workers were put on sixty- and seventy-hour weeks. Another night shift was added. The plant was now running twenty-four hours a day, six days a week. Ford executives decided to build a luxury version of the Expedition, the Lincoln Navigator. They bolted a new grille on the Expedition, changed a few body panels, added some sound insulation, took a deep breath, and charged forty-five thousand dollars—and soon Navigators were flying out the door nearly as fast as Expeditions. Before long, the Michigan Truck Plant was the most profitable of Ford's fifty-three assembly plants. By the late nineteen-nineties, it had become the most profitable factory of any industry in the world. In 1998, the Michigan Truck Plant grossed eleven billion dollars, almost as much as McDonald's made that year. Profits were $3.7 billion. Some factory workers, with overtime, were making two hundred thousand dollars a year. The demand for Expeditions and Navigators was so insatiable that even when a blizzard hit the Detroit region in January of 1999—burying the city in snow, paralyzing the airport, and stranding hundreds of cars on the freeway—Ford officials got on their radios and commandeered parts bound for other factories so that the Michigan Truck Plant assembly line wouldn't slow for a moment. The factory that had begun as just another assembly plant had become the company's crown jewel.

In the history of the automotive industry, few things have been quite as unexpected as the rise of the S.U.V. Detroit is a town of engineers, and engineers like to believe that there is some connection between the success of a vehicle and its technical merits. But the S.U.V. boom was like Apple's bringing back the Macintosh, dressing it up in colorful plastic, and suddenly creating a new market. It made no sense to them. Consumers said they liked four-wheel drive. But the overwhelming majority of consumers don't need four-wheel drive. S.U.V. buyers said they liked the elevated driving position. But when, in focus groups, industry marketers probed further, they heard things that left them rolling their eyes. As Keith Bradsher writes in "High and Mighty"—perhaps the most important book about Detroit since Ralph Nader's "Unsafe at Any Speed"—what consumers said was "If the vehicle is up high, it's easier to see if something is hiding underneath or lurking behind it." Bradsher brilliantly captures the mixture of bafflement and contempt that many auto executives feel toward the customers who buy their S.U.V.s. Fred J. Schaafsma, a top engineer for General Motors, says, "Sport-utility owners tend to be more like 'I wonder how people view me,' and are more willing to trade off flexibility or functionality to get that." According to Bradsher, internal industry market research concluded that S.U.V.s tend to be bought by people who are insecure, vain, self-centered, and self-absorbed, who are frequently nervous about their marriages, and who lack confidence in their driving skills. Ford's S.U.V. designers took their cues from seeing "fashionably dressed women wearing hiking boots or even work boots while walking through expensive malls." Toyota's top marketing executive in the United States, Bradsher writes, loves to tell the story of how at a focus group in Los Angeles "an elegant woman in the group said that she needed her full-sized Lexus LX 470 to drive up over the curb and onto lawns to park at large parties in Beverly Hills." One of Ford's senior marketing executives was even blunter: "The only time those S.U.V.s are going to be off-road is when they miss the driveway at 3 a.m."

The truth, underneath all the rationalizations, seemed to be that S.U.V. buyers thought of big, heavy vehicles as safe: they found comfort in being surrounded by so much rubber and steel. To the engineers, of course, that didn't make any sense, either: if consumers really wanted something that was big and heavy and comforting, they ought to buy minivans, since minivans, with their unit-body construction, do much better in accidents than S.U.V.s. (In a thirty-five-m.p.h. crash test, for instance, the driver of a Cadillac Escalade—the G.M. counterpart to the Lincoln Navigator—has a sixteen-per-cent chance of a life-threatening head injury, a twenty-per-cent chance of a life-threatening chest injury, and a thirty-five-per-cent chance of a leg injury. The same numbers in a Ford Windstar minivan—a vehicle engineered from the ground up, as opposed to simply being bolted onto a pickup-truck frame—are, respectively, two per cent, four per cent, and one per cent.) But his desire for safety wasn't a rational calculation. It was a *feeling*. Over the past decade, a number of major automakers in America have relied on the services of a French-born cultural anthropologist, G. Clotaire Rapaille, whose speciality is getting beyond the rational—what he calls "cortex"—impressions of consumers and tapping into their deeper, "reptilian" responses. And what Rapaille concluded from countless, intensive sessions with car buyers was that when S.U.V. buyers thought about safety they were thinking about something that reached into their deepest unconscious. "The No. 1 feeling is that everything surrounding you should be round and soft, and should give," Rapaille told me. "There should be air bags everywhere. Then there's this notion that you need to be up high. That's a contradiction, because the people who buy these S.U.V.s know at the cortex level that if you are high there is more chance of a rollover. But at the reptilian level they think that if I am bigger and taller I'm safer. You feel secure because you are higher and dominate and look down. That you can look down is psychologically a very powerful notion. And what was the key element of safety when you were a child? It was that your mother fed you, and there was warm liquid. That's why cupholders are absolutely crucial for safety. If there is a car that has no cupholder, it is not safe. If I can put my coffee there, if I can have my food, if everything is round, if it's soft, and if I'm high, then I feel safe. It's amazing that intelligent, educated women will look at a car and the first thing they will look at is how many cupholders it has." During the design of Chrysler's PT Cruiser, one of the things Rapaille learned was that car buyers felt unsafe when they thought that an outsider could easily see inside their vehicles. So Chrysler made the back window of the PT Cruiser smaller. Of course, making windows smaller—and thereby reducing visibility—makes driving *more* dangerous, not less so. But that's the puzzle of what has happened to the automobile world: feeling safe has become more important than actually being safe.

One day this fall, I visited the automobile-testing center of Consumers Union, the organization that publishes *Consumer Reports*. It is tucked away in the woods, in south-central Connecticut, on the site of the old Connecticut Speedway. The facility has two skid pads to measure cornering, a long straightaway for braking tests, a meandering "handling" course that winds around the back side of the track, and an accident-avoidance obstacle course made out of a row of orange cones. It is headed by a trim, white-haired Englishman named David Champion, who previously worked as an engineer with Land Rover and with Nissan. On the day of my visit, Champion set aside two vehicles: a silver 2003 Chevrolet TrailBlazer—an enormous five-thousand-pound S.U.V.—and a shiny blue two-seater Porsche Boxster convertible.

We started with the TrailBlazer. Champion warmed up the Chevrolet with a few quick circuits of the track, and then drove it hard through the twists and turns of the handling course. He sat in the bucket seat with his back straight and his arms almost fully extended, and drove with practiced grace: every movement smooth and relaxed and unhurried. Champion, as an engineer, did not much like the TrailBlazer. "Cheap interior, cheap plastic," he said, batting the dashboard with his hand. "It's a little bit heavy, cumbersome. Quiet. Bit wallowy, side to side. Doesn't feel that secure. Accelerates heavily. Once it gets going, it's got decent power. Brakes feel a bit spongy." He turned onto the straightaway and stopped a few hundred yards from the obstacle course.

Measuring accident avoidance is a key part of the Consumers Union evaluation. It's a simple setup. The driver has to navigate his vehicle through two rows of cones eight feet wide and sixty feet long. Then he has to steer hard to the left, guiding the vehicle through a gate set off to the side, and immediately swerve hard back to the right, and enter a second sixty-foot corridor of cones that are parallel to the first set. The idea is to see how fast you can drive through the course without knocking over any cones. "It's like you're driving down a road in suburbia," Champion said. "Suddenly, a kid on a bicycle veers out in front of you. You have to do whatever it takes to avoid the kid. But there's a tractor-trailer coming toward you in the other lane, so you've got to swing back into your own lane as quickly as possible. That's the scenario."

Champion and I put on helmets. He accelerated toward the entrance to the obstacle course. "We do the test without brakes or throttle, so we can just look at handling," Champion said. "I actually take my foot right off the pedals." The car was now moving at forty m.p.h. At that speed, on the smooth tarmac of the raceway, the TrailBlazer was very quiet, and we were seated so high that the road seemed somehow remote. Champion

5

entered the first row of cones. His arms tensed. He jerked the car to the left. The TrailBlazer's tires squealed. I was thrown toward the passenger-side door as the truck's body rolled, then thrown toward Champion as he jerked the TrailBlazer back to the right. My tape recorder went skittering across the cabin. The whole maneuver had taken no more than a few seconds, but it felt as if we had been sailing into a squall. Champion brought the car to a stop. We both looked back: the TrailBlazer had hit the cone at the gate. The kid on the bicycle was probably dead. Champion shook his head. "It's very rubbery. It slides a lot. I'm not getting much communication back from the steering wheel. It feels really ponderous, clumsy. I felt a little bit of tail swing."

I drove the obstacle course next. I started at the conservative speed of thirty-five m.p.h. I got through cleanly. I tried again, this time at thirty-eight m.p.h., and that small increment of speed made a dramatic difference. I made the first left, avoiding the kid on the bicycle. But, when it came time to swerve back to avoid the hypothetical oncoming eighteen-wheeler, I found that I was wrestling with the car. The protests of the tires were jarring. I stopped, shaken. "It wasn't going where you wanted it to go, was it?" Champion said. "Did you feel the weight pulling you sideways? That's what the extra weight the S.U.V.s have tends to do. It pulls you in the wrong direction." Behind us was a string of toppled cones. Getting the TrailBlazer to travel in a straight line, after that sudden diversion, hadn't been easy. "I think you took out a few pedestrians," Champion said with a faint smile.

Next up was the Boxster. The top was down. The sun was warm on   10
my forehead. The car was low to the ground; I had the sense that if I dangled my arm out the window my knuckles would scrape on the tarmac. Standing still, the Boxster didn't feel safe: I could have been sitting in a go-cart. But when I ran it through the handling course I felt that I was in perfect control. On the straightaway, I steadied the Boxster at forty-five m.p.h., and ran it through the obstacle course. I could have balanced a teacup on my knee. At fifty m.p.h., I navigated the left and right turns with what seemed like a twitch of the steering wheel. The tires didn't squeal. The car stayed level. I pushed the Porsche up into the mid-fifties. Every cone was untouched. "Walk in the park!" Champion exclaimed as we pulled to a stop.

Most of us think that S.U.V.s are much safer than sports cars. If you asked the young parents of America whether they would rather strap their infant child in the back seat of the TrailBlazer or the passenger seat of the Boxster, they would choose the TrailBlazer. We feel that way because in the TrailBlazer our chances of surviving a collision with a hypothetical tractor-trailer in the other lane are greater than they are in the Porsche. What we forget, though, is that in the TrailBlazer you're also much more likely to hit the tractor-trailer because you can't get out of the way in time. In the parlance of the automobile world, the TrailBlazer is better at "passive safety." The Boxster is better when it comes to "active safety," which is every bit as important.

Consider the set of safety statistics compiled by Tom Wenzel, a scientist at Lawrence Berkeley National Laboratory, in California, and Marc Ross, a physicist at the University of Michigan. The numbers are expressed in fatalities per million cars, both for drivers of particular models and for the drivers of the cars they hit. (For example, in the first case, for every million Toyota Avalons on the road, forty Avalon drivers die in car accidents every year, and twenty people die in accidents involving Toyota Avalons.) The numbers below have been rounded:

Make/Model	Type	Driver Deaths	Other Deaths	Total
Toyota Avalon	large	40	20	60
Chrysler Town & Country	minivan	31	36	67
Toyota Camry	mid-size	41	29	70
Volkswagen Jetta	subcompact	47	23	70
Ford Windstar	minivan	37	35	72
Nissan Maxima	mid-size	53	26	79
Honda Accord	mid-size	54	27	82
Chevrolet Venture	minivan	51	34	85
Buick Century	mid-size	70	23	93
Subaru Legacy/ Outback	compact	74	24	98
Mazda 626	compact	70	29	99
Chevrolet Malibu	mid-size	71	34	105
Chevrolet Suburban	S.U.V.	46	59	105
Jeep Grand Cherokee	S.U.V.	61	44	106
Honda Civic	subcompact	84	25	109
Toyota Corolla	subcompact	81	29	110
Ford Expedition	S.U.V.	55	57	112
GMC Jimmy	S.U.V.	76	39	114
Ford Taurus	mid-size	78	39	117
Nissan Altima	compact	72	49	121
Mercury Marquis	large	80	43	123
Nissan Sentra	subcompact	95	34	129
Toyota 4Runner	S.U.V.	94	43	137
Chevrolet Tahoe	S.U.V.	68	74	141
Dodge Stratus	mid-size	103	40	143
Lincoln Town Car	large	100	47	147
Ford Explorer	S.U.V.	88	60	148
Pontiac Grand Am	compact	118	39	157
Toyota Tacoma	pickup	111	59	171
Chevrolet Cavalier	subcompact	146	41	186
Dodge Neon	subcompact	161	39	199
Pontiac Sunfire	subcompact	158	44	202
Ford F-Series	pickup	110	128	238

Are the best performers the biggest and heaviest vehicles on the road? Not at all. Among the safest cars are the midsize imports, like the Toyota Camry and the Honda Accord. Or consider the extraordinary performance of some subcompacts, like the Volkswagen Jetta. Drivers of the tiny Jetta die at a rate of just forty-seven per million, which is in the same range as drivers of the five-thousand-pound Chevrolet Suburban and almost half that of popular S.U.V. models like the Ford Explorer or the GMC Jimmy. In a head-on crash, an Explorer or a Suburban would crush a Jetta or a Camry. But, clearly, the drivers of Camrys and Jettas are finding a way to avoid head-on crashes with Explorers and Suburbans. The benefits of being nimble—of being in an automobile that's capable of staying out of trouble—are in many cases greater than the benefits of being big.

I had another lesson in active safety at the test track when I got in the TrailBlazer with another Consumers Union engineer, and we did three emergency-stopping tests, taking the Chevrolet up to sixty m.p.h. and then slamming on the brakes. It was not a pleasant exercise. Bringing five thousand pounds of rubber and steel to a sudden stop involves lots of lurching, screeching, and protesting. The first time, the TrailBlazer took 146.2 feet to come to a halt, the second time 151.6 feet, and the third time 153.4 feet. The Boxster can come to a complete stop from sixty m.p.h. in about 124 feet. That's a difference of about two car lengths, and it isn't hard to imagine any number of scenarios where two car lengths could mean the difference between life and death.

The S.U.V. boom represents, then, a shift in how we conceive of safety—from active to passive. It's what happens when a larger number of drivers conclude, consciously or otherwise, that the extra thirty feet that the TrailBlazer takes to come to a stop don't really matter, that the tractor-trailer will hit them anyway, and that they are better off treating accidents as inevitable rather than avoidable. "The metric that people use is size," says Stephen Popiel, a vice-president of Millward Brown Goldfarb, in Toronto, one of the leading automotive market-research firms. "The bigger something is, the safer it is. In the consumer's mind, the basic equation is, If I were to take this vehicle and drive it into this brick wall, the more metal there is in front of me the better off I'll be."

This is a new idea, and one largely confined to North America. In Europe and Japan, people think of a safe car as a nimble car. That's why they build cars like the Jetta and the Camry, which are designed to carry out the driver's wishes as directly and efficiently as possible. In the Jetta, the engine is clearly audible. The steering is light and precise. The brakes are crisp. The wheelbase is short enough that the car picks up the undulations of the road. The car is so small and close to the ground, and so dwarfed by other cars on the road, that an intelligent driver is constantly reminded of the necessity of driving safely and defensively. An S.U.V. embodies the opposite logic. The driver is seated as high and far from the road as possible. The vehicle is designed to overcome its environment, not to respond to it. Even four-wheel drive, seemingly the most beneficial feature of the S.U.V., serves to reinforce this isolation. Having the engine provide power to all four wheels, safety experts point out, does nothing to improve braking, although many S.U.V. owners erroneously believe this to be the case. Nor does the feature necessarily make it safer to turn across a slippery surface: that is largely a function of how much friction is generated by the vehicle's tires. All it really does is improve what engineers call tracking—that is, the ability to accelerate without slipping in perilous conditions or in deep snow or mud. Champion says that one of the occasions when he came closest to death was a snowy day, many years ago, just after he had bought a new Range Rover. "Everyone around me was slipping, and I was thinking, *Yeahhh*. And I came to a stop sign on a major road, and I was driving probably twice as fast as I should have been, because I could. I had traction. But also weighed probably twice as much as most cars. And I still had only four brakes and four tires on the road. I slid right across a four-lane road." Four-wheel drive robs the driver of feedback. "The car driver whose wheels spin once or twice while backing out of the driveway knows that the road is slippery," Bradsher writes. "The SUV driver who navigates the driveway and street without difficulty until she tries to brake may not find out that the road is slippery until it is too late." Jettas are safe because they make their drivers feel unsafe. S.U.V.s are unsafe because they make their drivers feel safe. That feeling of safety isn't the solution; it's the problem.

Perhaps the most troublesome aspect of S.U.V. culture is its attitude toward risk. "Safety, for most automotive consumers, has to do with the notion that they aren't in complete control," Popiel says. "There are unexpected events that at any moment in time can come out and impact them—an oil patch up ahead, an eighteen-wheeler turning over, something falling down. People feel that the elements of the world out of their control are the ones that are going to cause them distress."

Of course, those things really aren't outside a driver's control: an alert driver, in the right kind of vehicle, can navigate the oil patch, avoid the truck, and swerve around the thing that's falling down. Traffic-fatality rates vary strongly with driver behavior. Drunks are 7.6 times more likely to die in accidents than nondrinkers. People who wear their seat belts are almost half as likely to die as those who don't buckle up. Forty-year-olds are ten times less likely to get into accidents than sixteen-year-olds. Drivers of minivans, Wenzel and Ross's statistics tell us, die at a fraction of the rate of drivers of pickup trucks. That's clearly because minivans are family cars, and parents with children in the back seat are less likely to get into accidents. Frank McKenna, a safety expert at the University of Reading, in England, has done experiments where he shows drivers a series of videotaped scenarios—a child running out the front door of his house and onto the street, for example, or a car approaching an intersection at too great a speed to stop at the red light—and asks people to press a button the minute they become aware of the potential for an accident. Experienced drivers press the button between half a second and a second faster than new drivers, which, given that car accidents are events measured in milliseconds, is a significant difference. McKenna's work shows that, with experience, we all learn how to exert some degree of control over what might otherwise appear to be uncontrollable events. Any conception of safety that revolves entirely around the vehicle, then, is incomplete. Is the Boxster safer than the TrailBlazer? It depends on who's behind the wheel. In the hands of, say, my very respectable and prudent middle-aged mother, the Boxster is by far the safer car. In my hands, it probably isn't. On the open road, my reaction to the Porsche's extraordinary road manners and the sweet, irresistible wail of its engine would be to drive much faster than I should. (At the end of my day at Consumers Union, I parked the Boxster, and immediately got into my own car to drive home. In my mind, I was still at the wheel of the Boxster. Within twenty minutes, I had a two-hundred-and-seventy-one-dollar speeding ticket.) The trouble with the S.U.V. ascendancy is that it excludes the really critical component of safety: the driver.

In psychology, there is a concept called learned helplessness, which arose from a series of animal experiments in the nineteen-sixties at the University of Pennsylvania. Dogs were restrained by a harness, so that they couldn't move, and then repeatedly subjected to a series of electrical shocks. Then the same dogs were shocked again, only this time they could easily escape by jumping over a low hurdle. But most of them didn't; they just huddled in the corner, no longer believing that there was anything they could do to influence their own fate. Learned helplessness is now thought to play a role in such phenomena as depression and the failure of battered women to leave their husbands, but one could easily apply it more widely. We live in an age, after all, that is strangely fixated on the idea of helplessness: we're fascinated by hurricanes and terrorist acts and epidemics like SARS[1] — situations in which we feel powerless to affect our own destiny. In fact, the risks posed to life and limb by forces outside our control are dwarfed by the factors we can control. Our fixation with helplessness distorts our perceptions of risk. "When you feel safe, you can be passive," Rapaille says of the fundamental appeal of the S.U.V. "Safe means I can sleep. I can give up control. I can relax. I can take off my shoes. I can listen to music." For years, we've all made fun of the middle-aged man who suddenly trades in his sedate family sedan for a shiny red sports car. That's called a midlife crisis. But at least it involves some degree of engagement with the act of driving. The man who gives up his sedate family sedan for an S.U.V. is saying something far more troubling—that

---

[1] *SARS:* Severe acute respiratory syndrome is a respiratory disease in humans caused by the SARS coronavirus. The World Health Organization reported that between November 2002 and July 2003, there were 8,096 known infected cases and 774 deaths attributed to the SARS epidemic. — EDS.

he finds the demands of the road to be overwhelming. Is acting out really worse than giving up?

On August 9, 2000, the Bridgestone Firestone tire company announced one of the largest product recalls in American history. Because of mounting concerns about safety, the company said, it was replacing some fourteen million tires that had been used primarily on the Ford Explorer S.U.V. The cost of the recall—and of a follow-up replacement program initiated by Ford a year later—ran into billions of dollars. Millions more were spent by both companies on fighting and settling lawsuits from Explorer owners, who alleged that their tires had come apart and caused their S.U.V.s to roll over. In the fall of that year, senior executives from both companies were called to Capitol Hill, where they were publicly berated. It was the biggest scandal to hit the automobile industry in years. It was also one of the strangest. According to federal records, the number of fatalities resulting from the failure of a Firestone tire on a Ford Explorer S.U.V., as of September, 2001, was two hundred and seventy-one. That sounds like a lot, until you remember that the total number of tires supplied by Firestone to the Explorer from the moment the S.U.V. was introduced by Ford, in 1990, was fourteen million, and that the average life span of a tire is forty-five thousand miles. The allegation against Firestone amounts to the claim that its tires failed, with fatal results, two hundred and seventy-one times in the course of six hundred and thirty billion vehicle miles. Manufacturers usually win prizes for failure rates that low. It's also worth remembering that during that same ten-year span almost half a million Americans died in traffic accidents. In other words, during the nineteen-nineties hundreds of thousands of people were killed on the roads because they drove too fast or ran red lights or drank too much. And, of those, a fair proportion involved people in S.U.V.s who were lulled by their four-wheel drive into driving recklessly on slick roads, who drove aggressively because they felt invulnerable, who disproportionately killed those they hit because they chose to drive trucks with inflexible steel-frame architecture, and who crashed because they couldn't bring their five-thousand-pound vehicles to a halt in time. Yet, out of all those fatalities, regulators, the legal profession, Congress, and the media chose to highlight the .0005 percent that could be linked to an alleged defect in the vehicle.

But should that come as a surprise? In the age of the S.U.V., this is what people worry about when they worry about safety—not risks, however commonplace, involving their own behavior but risks, however rare, involving some unexpected event. The Explorer was big and imposing. It was high above the ground. You could look down on other drivers. You could see if someone was lurking behind or beneath it. You could drive it up on someone's lawn with impunity. Didn't it seem like the safest vehicle in the world?

20

The Reader's Presence

1. According to Gladwell, how do automobile companies regard consumer safety? What evidence does he provide to support his argument? Were you aware of any of the concerns Gladwell raises? Do you find his argument convincing? Why or why not?

2. Explain the terms "active safety" and "passive safety" (paragraph 11). What would be the priorities of a car buyer and driver interested in each? Do you agree with Gladwell that SUV drivers are giving up active safety for passive safety? What would be the consequences of such an exchange?

3. Gladwell points out that consumers' reasons for buying cars are frequently illogical. Read "Why McDonald's Fries Taste So Good" by Eric Schlosser (page 528). What basis do consumers have for choosing fast food over other options? Why do you think consumers sometimes make choices that are ultimately not in their best interest?

Stephen Jay Gould

Sex, Drugs, Disasters, and the Extinction of Dinosaurs

Stephen Jay Gould (1941–2002) was professor of geology and zoology at Harvard University and curator of invertebrate paleontology at Harvard's Museum of Comparative Zoology. He published widely on evolution and other topics and earned a reputation for making technical subjects readily comprehensible to lay readers without trivializing the material. His The Panda's Thumb *(1980) won the American Book Award, and* The Mismeasure of Man *(1981) won the National Book Critics Circle Award. Gould published more than one hundred articles in scientific journals, and he contributed to national magazines as well. "Sex, Drugs, Disasters, and the Extinction of Dinosaurs" appeared in* Discover *magazine in 1984. More recently, Gould wrote* Questioning the Millennium: A Rationalist's Guide to a Precisely Arbitrary Countdown *(1997),* Leonardo's Mountain of Clams and the Diet of Worms: Essays on Natural History *(1998),* Rocks of Ages: Science & Religion in the Fullness of Life *(1999),* The Lying Stones of Marrakesh *(2001), and* The Structure of Evolutionary Theory *(2001). Among many other honors and awards, he was a fellow of the National Science Foundation and the MacArthur Foundation. In 1999 Gould became president of the American Association for the Advancement of Science. John Updike comments that "Gould, in his scrupulous explication of [other scientists'] carefully wrought half-truths, abolishes the unnecessary distinction between the humanities and science, and honors the latter as a branch of humanistic thought, fallible and poetic."*

When asked if he found it difficult to write about complex scientific concepts in language that is accessible to general readers, Gould replied, "I don't see why it should be that difficult. . . . Every field has its jargon. I think scientists hide behind theirs perhaps more than people in other professions do—it's part of our mythology—but I don't think the concepts of science are intrinsically more difficult than the professional notions in any other field."

Science, in its most fundamental definition, is a fruitful mode of inquiry, not a list of enticing conclusions. The conclusions are the consequence, not the essence.

My greatest unhappiness with most popular presentations of science concerns their failure to separate fascinating claims from the methods that scientists use to establish the facts of nature. Journalists, and the public, thrive on controversial and stunning statements. But science is, basically, a way of knowing—in P. B. Medawar's[1] apt words, "the art of the soluble." If the growing corps of popular science writers would focus on *how* scientists develop and defend those fascinating claims, they would make their greatest possible contribution to public understanding.

Consider three ideas, proposed in perfect seriousness to explain that greatest of all titillating puzzles—the extinction of dinosaurs. Since these three notions invoke the primally fascinating themes of our culture—sex, drugs, and violence—they surely reside in the category of fascinating claims. I want to show why two of them rank as silly speculation, while the other represents science at its grandest and most useful.

Science works with the testable proposals. If, after much compilation and scrutiny of data, new information continues to affirm a hypothesis, we may accept it provisionally and gain confidence as further evidence mounts. We can never be completely sure that a hypothesis is right, though we may be able to show with confidence that it is wrong. The best scientific hypotheses are also generous and expansive: They suggest extensions and implications that enlighten related, and even far distant, subjects. Simply consider how the idea of evolution has influenced virtually every intellectual field.

Useless speculation, on the other hand, is restrictive. It generates no   5
testable hypothesis, and offers no way to obtain potentially refuting evidence. Please note that I am not speaking of truth or falsity. The speculation may well be true; still, if it provides, in principle, no material for

---

[1]*Sir Peter Brian Medawar:* (1915–1987) a Brazilian-born British scientist widely renowned for his research on how the immune system rejects or accepts tissue transplants. Co-winner of the 1960 Nobel Prize in Medicine.—Eds.

affirmation or rejection, we can make nothing of it. It must simply stand forever as an intriguing idea. Useless speculation turns in on itself and leads nowhere; good science, containing both seeds for its potential refutation and implications for more and different testable knowledge, reaches out. But, enough preaching. Let's move on to dinosaurs, and the three proposals for their extinction.

1. *Sex:* Testes function only in a narrow range of temperature (those of mammals hang externally in a scrotal sac because internal body temperatures are too high for their proper function). A worldwide rise in temperature at the close of the Cretaceous period caused the testes of dinosaurs to stop functioning and led to their extinction by sterilization of males.
2. *Drugs:* Angiosperms (flowering plants) first evolved toward the end of the dinosaurs' reign. Many of these plants contain psychoactive agents, avoided by mammals today as a result of their bitter taste. Dinosaurs had neither means to taste the bitterness nor livers effective enough to detoxify the substances. They died of massive overdoses.
3. *Disasters:* A large comet or asteroid struck the earth some 65 million years ago, lofting a cloud of dust into the sky and blocking sunlight, thereby suppressing photosynthesis and so drastically lowering world temperatures that dinosaurs and hosts of other creatures became extinct.

Before analyzing these three tantalizing statements, we must establish a basic ground rule often violated in proposals for the dinosaurs' demise. *There is no separate problem of the extinction of dinosaurs.* Too often we divorce specific events from their wider contexts and systems of cause and effect. The fundamental fact of dinosaur extinction is its synchrony with the demise of so many other groups across a wide range of habitats, from terrestrial to marine.

The history of life has been punctuated by brief episodes of mass extinction. A recent analysis by University of Chicago paleontologists Jack Sepkoski and Dave Raup, based on the best and most exhaustive tabulation of data ever assembled, shows clearly that five episodes of mass dying stand well above the "background" extinctions of normal times (when we consider all mass extinctions, large and small, they seem to fall in a regular 26-million-year cycle). The Cretaceous debacle, occurring 65 million years ago and separating the Mesozoic and Cenozoic eras of our geological time scale, ranks prominently among the five. Nearly all the marine plankton (single-celled floating creatures) died with geological suddenness; among marine invertebrates, nearly 15 percent of all families perished, including many previously dominant groups, especially the ammonites (relatives of squids in coiled shells). On land, the dinosaurs disappeared after more than 100 million years of unchallenged domination.

In this context, speculations limited to dinosaurs alone ignore the larger phenomenon. We need a coordinated explanation for a system of events that includes the extinction of dinosaurs as one component. Thus it makes little sense, though it may fuel our desire to view mammals as inevitable inheritors of the earth, to guess that dinosaurs died because small mammals ate their eggs (a perennial favorite among untestable speculations). It seems most unlikely that some disaster peculiar to dinosaurs befell these massive beasts—and that the debacle happened to strike just when one of history's five great dyings had enveloped the earth for completely different reasons.

The testicular theory, an old favorite from the 1940s, had its root in an interesting and thoroughly respectable study of temperature tolerances in the American alligator, published in the staid *Bulletin of the American Museum of Natural History* in 1946 by three experts on living and fossil reptiles—E. H. Colbert, my own first teacher in paleontology; R. B. Cowles; and C. M. Bogert.

The first sentence of their summary reveals a purpose beyond alliga-   10
tors: "This report describes an attempt to infer the reactions of extinct reptiles, especially the dinosaurs, to high temperatures as based upon reactions observed in the modern alligator." They studied, by rectal thermometry, the body temperatures of alligators under changing conditions of heating and cooling. (Well, let's face it, you wouldn't want to try sticking a thermometer under a 'gator's tongue.) The predictions under test go way back to an old theory first stated by Galileo in the 1630s—the unequal scaling of surfaces and volumes. As an animal, or an object, grows (provided its shape doesn't change), surface areas must increase more slowly than volumes—since surfaces get larger as length squared, while volumes increase much more rapidly, as length cubed. Therefore, small animals have high ratios of surface to volume, while large animals cover themselves with relatively little surface.

Among cold-blooded animals lacking any physiological mechanism for keeping their temperatures constant, small creatures have a hell of a time keeping warm—because they lose so much heat through their relatively large surfaces. On the other hand, large animals, with their relatively small surfaces, may lose heat so slowly that, once warm, they may maintain effectively constant temperatures against ordinary fluctuations of climate. (In fact, the resolution of the "hot-blooded dinosaur" controversy that burned so brightly a few years back may simply be that, while large dinosaurs possessed no physiological mechanism for constant temperature, and were not therefore warm-blooded in the technical sense, their large size and relatively small surface area kept them warm.)

Colbert, Cowles, and Bogert compared the warming rates of small and large alligators. As predicted, the small fellows heated up (and cooled down) more quickly. When exposed to a warm sun, a tiny 50-gram (1.76-ounce) alligator heated up one degree Celsius every minute and a half, while a large alligator, 260 times bigger at 13,000 grams (28.7 pounds), took seven and a half minutes to gain a degree. Extrapolating up to an adult 10-ton dinosaur, they concluded that a one-degree rise in body temperature would take eighty-six hours. If large animals absorb heat so slowly (through their relatively small surfaces), they will also be unable to shed any excess heat gained when temperatures rise above a favorable level.

The authors then guessed that large dinosaurs lived at or near their optimum temperatures; Cowles suggested that a rise in global temperatures just before the Cretaceous extinction caused the dinosaurs to heat up beyond their optimal tolerance—and, being so large, they couldn't shed the unwanted heat. (In a most unusual statement within a scientific paper, Colbert and Bogert then explicitly disavowed this speculative extension of their empirical work on alligators.) Cowles conceded that this excess heat probably wasn't enough to kill or even to enervate the great beasts, but since testes often function only within a narrow range of temperature, he proposed that this global rise might have sterilized all the males, causing extinction by natural contraception.

The overdose theory has recently been supported by UCLA psychiatrist Ronald K. Siegel. Siegel has gathered, he claims, more than 2,000 records of animals who, when given access, administer various drugs to themselves—from a mere swig of alcohol to massive doses of the big H. Elephants will swill the equivalent of twenty beers at a time, but do not like alcohol in concentrations greater than 7 percent. In a silly bit of anthropocentric speculation, Siegel states that "elephants drink, perhaps, to forget . . . the anxiety produced by shrinking rangeland and the competition for food."

Since fertile imaginations can apply almost any hot idea to the extinction of dinosaurs, Siegel found a way. Flowering plants did not evolve until late in the dinosaurs' reign. These plants also produced an array of aromatic, amino-acid-based alkaloids—the major group of psychoactive agents. Most mammals are "smart" enough to avoid these potential poisons. The alkaloids simply don't taste good (they are bitter); in any case, we mammals have livers happily supplied with the capacity to detoxify them. But, Siegel speculates, perhaps dinosaurs could neither taste the bitterness nor detoxify the substances once ingested. He recently told members of the American Psychological Association: "I'm not suggesting that all dinosaurs OD'd on plant drugs, but it certainly was a factor." He also argued that death by overdose may help explain why so many dinosaur fossils are found in contorted positions. (Do not go gentle into that good night.)[2]

Extraterrestrial catastrophes have long pedigrees in the popular literature of extinction, but the subject exploded again in 1979, after a long lull, when the father-son, physicist-geologist team of Luis and Walter Alvarez proposed that an asteroid, some 10 km in diameter, struck the earth 65 million years ago (comets, rather than asteroids, have since gained favor. Good science is self-corrective).

15

---

[2] "**Do not go gentle into that good night**": a poem composed in 1951 by the Welsh poet Dylan Thomas (1914–1953) and considered to be among the finest works.—EDS.

The force of such a collision would be immense, greater by far than the megatonnage of all the world's nuclear weapons. In trying to reconstruct a scenario that would explain the simultaneous dying of dinosaurs on land and so many creatures in the sea, the Alvarezes proposed that a gigantic dust cloud, generated by particles blown aloft in the impact, would so darken the earth that photosynthesis would cease and temperatures drop precipitously. (Rage, rage against the dying of the light.)[3] The single-celled photosynthetic oceanic plankton, with life cycles measured in weeks, would perish outright, but land plants might survive through the dormancy of their seeds (land plants were not much affected by the Cretaceous extinction, and any adequate theory must account for the curious pattern of differential survival). Dinosaurs would die by starvation and freezing; small, warm-blooded mammals, with more modest requirements for food and better regulation of body temperature, would squeak through. "Let the bastards freeze in the dark," as bumper stickers of our chauvinistic neighbors in sunbelt states proclaimed several years ago during the Northeast's winter oil crisis.

All three theories, testicular malfunction, psychoactive overdosing, and asteroidal zapping, grab our attention mightily. As pure phenomenology, they rank about equally high on any hit parade of primal fascination. Yet one represents expansive science, the others restrictive and untestable speculation. The proper criterion lies in evidence and methodology; we must probe behind the superficial fascination of particular claims.

How could we possibly decide whether the hypothesis of testicular frying is right or wrong? We would have to know things that the fossil record cannot provide. What temperatures were optimal for dinosaurs? Could they avoid the absorption of excess heat by staying in the shade, or in caves? At what temperatures did their testicles cease to function? Were late Cretaceous climates ever warm enough to drive the internal temperatures of dinosaurs close to this ceiling? Testicles simply don't fossilize, and how could we infer their temperature tolerances even if they did? In short, Cowles's hypothesis is only an intriguing speculation leading nowhere. The most damning statement against it appeared right in the conclusion of Colbert, Cowles, and Bogert's paper, when they admitted: "It is difficult to advance any definite arguments against the hypothesis." My statement may seem paradoxical—isn't a hypothesis really good if you can't devise any arguments against it? Quite the contrary. It is simply untestable and unusable.

Siegel's overdosing has even less going for it. At least Cowles extrapolated his conclusion from some good data on alligators. And he didn't completely violate the primary guideline of siting dinosaur extinction in the context of a general mass dying—for rise in temperature could be the root cause of a general catastrophe, zapping dinosaurs by testicular malfunction and different groups for other reasons. But Siegel's speculation cannot

20

---

[3] "*Rage, rage against the dying of the light.*": The final line of the poem "Do Not Go Gentle in That Good Night" by Dylan Thomas. —EDS.

touch the extinction of ammonites or oceanic plankton (diatoms make their own food with good sweet sunlight; they don't OD on the chemicals of terrestrial plants). It is simply a gratuitous, attention-grabbing guess. It cannot be tested, for how can we know what dinosaurs tasted and what their livers could do? Livers don't fossilize any better than testicles.

The hypothesis doesn't even make any sense in its own context. Angiosperms were in full flower ten million years before dinosaurs went the way of all flesh. Why did it take so long? As for the pains of a chemical death recorded in contortions of fossils, I regret to say (or rather I'm pleased to note for the dinosaurs' sake) that Siegel's knowledge of geology must be a bit deficient: muscles contract after death and geological strata rise and fall with motions of the earth's crust after burial—more than enough reason to distort a fossil's pristine appearance.

The impact story, on the other hand, has a sound basis in evidence. It can be tested, extended, refined, and, if wrong, disproved. The Alvarezes did not just construct an arresting guess for public consumption. They proposed their hypothesis after laborious geochemical studies with Frank Asaro and Helen Michael had revealed a massive increase of iridium in rocks deposited right at the time of extinction. Iridium, a rare metal of the platinum group, is virtually absent from indigenous rocks of the earth's crust; most of our iridium arrives on extraterrestrial objects that strike the earth.

The Alvarez hypothesis bore immediate fruit. Based originally on evidence from two European localities, it led geochemists throughout the world to examine other sediments of the same age. They found abnormally high amounts of iridium everywhere—from continental rocks of the western United States to deep sea cores from the South Atlantic.

Cowles proposed his testicular hypothesis in the mid-1940s. Where has it gone since then? Absolutely nowhere, because scientists can do nothing with it. The hypothesis must stand as a curious appendage to a solid study of alligators. Siegel's overdose scenario will also win a few press notices and fade into oblivion. The Alvarezes' asteroid falls into a different category altogether, and much of the popular commentary has missed this essential distinction by focusing on the impact and its attendant results, and forgetting what really matters to a scientist—the iridium. If you talk just about asteroids, dust, and darkness, you tell stories no better and no more entertaining than fried testicles or terminal trips. It is the iridium—the source of testable evidence—that counts and forges the crucial distinction between speculation and science.

The proof, to twist a phrase, lies in the doing. Cowles's hypothesis has generated nothing in thirty-five years. Since its proposal in 1979, the Alvarez hypothesis has spawned hundreds of studies, a major conference, and attendant publications. Geologists are fired up. They are looking for iridium at all other extinction boundaries. Every week exposes a new wrinkle in the scientific press. Further evidence that the Cretaceous iridium represents extraterrestrial impact and not indigenous volcanism continues to

25

accumulate. As I revise this essay in November 1984 (this paragraph will be out of date when the book is published),[4] new data include chemical "signatures" of other isotopes indicating unearthly provenance, glass spherules of a size and sort produced by impact and not by volcanic eruptions, and high-pressure varieties of silica formed (so far as we know) only under the tremendous shock of impact.

My point is simply this: Whatever the eventual outcome (I suspect it will be positive), the Alvarez hypothesis is exciting, fruitful science because it generates tests, provides us with things to do, and expands outward. We are having fun, battling back and forth, moving toward a resolution, and extending the hypothesis beyond its original scope.

As just one example of the unexpected, distant cross-fertilization that good science engenders, the Alvarez hypothesis made a major contribution to a theme that has riveted public attention in the past few months — so-called nuclear winter. In a speech delivered in April 1982, Luis Alvarez calculated the energy that a ten-kilometer asteroid would release on impact. He compared such an explosion with a full nuclear exchange and implied that all-out atomic war might unleash similar consequences.

This theme of impact leading to massive dust clouds and falling temperatures formed an important input to the decision of Carl Sagan[5] and a group of colleagues to model the climatic consequences of nuclear holocaust. Full nuclear exchange would probably generate the same kind of dust cloud and darkening that may have wiped out the dinosaurs. Temperatures would drop precipitously and agriculture might become impossible. Avoidance of nuclear war is fundamentally an ethical and political imperative, but we must know the factual consequences to make firm judgments. I am heartened by a final link across disciplines and deep concerns — another criterion, by the way, of science at its best.[6] A recognition of the very phenomenon that made our evolution possible by exterminating the previously dominant dinosaurs and clearing a way for the evolution of large mammals, including us, might actually help to save us from joining those magnificent beasts in contorted poses among the strata of the earth.

The Reader's Presence

1. Although the title of Gould's essay focuses on the extinction of dinosaurs, his overriding interest is in demonstrating the way science

---

[4]*The Flamingo's Smile* (1985), in which Gould included this essay. — EDS.

[5]*Carl Sagan:* (1934–1996) an American astronomer and astrochemist who did much to make the study of astronomy, astrophysics, and other natural sciences accessible to wide audiences. He also promoted the Search for Extra-Terrestrial Intelligence (SETI). — EDS.

[6]This quirky connection so tickles my fancy that I break my own strict rule about eliminating redundancies from [this essay]. . . . — GOULD'S NOTE.

works, and his purpose is to make that process fully accessible and understandable to the general public. Where does he lay out this central claim, and how does he demonstrate, clarify, and complicate it as his essay proceeds?

2. Reread Gould's essay with special attention to his use of tone, diction, syntax, and metaphor. How does he use these compositional strategies to make information accessible to his readers? Point to passages where Gould uses the diction and syntax of a serious scientist. When—and with what effects—does his prose sound more colloquial? Does his tone remain consistent throughout the essay? If not, when and how does it change? With what effects?

3. What distinctions does Gould draw among "testable proposals" (paragraph 4), "intriguing ideas" (paragraph 5), and "useless speculation" (paragaph 5)? What features of each does he identify? How does Gould encourage critical thinking in his reader? Compare his tactics to those of Malcolm Gladwell in "Big and Bad" (page 407). Where does each writer use humor to "translate" for the reader facts that might otherwise seem arcane?

Daniel Harris
Celebrity Bodies

Critic and essayist Daniel Harris (b. 1957) writes about a variety of social issues, with an emphasis on gay culture. In his seminal work, The Rise and Fall of Gay Culture *(1997), he argues that the once-vibrant gay world is being undermined by assimilation and rampant commercialization and that society at large is threatened with a loss of racial and cultural diversity. His other books include* Cute, Quaint, Hungry, and Romantic: The Aesthetics of Consumerism *(2000), A* Memoir of No One in Particular *(2002), and* Diary of a Drag Queen *(2005), his account of becoming a drag queen at age 46—all 6 foot 7 inches of him (in stilettos). An award-winning essayist, his work has appeared in* Harper's, Newsday, *the* New York Times Magazine, *the* Los Angeles Times, *and the* Nation, *among other publications. Harris was anthologized in* The Best American Essays 1993, *and he contributes to many literary journals, including the* Antioch Review *where his work was featured in their sixtieth anniversary issue. His work was awarded* Best Essay of 1993 *by* Southwest Review, *the literary quarterly in which his essay "Celebrity Bodies" appeared in 2008.*

Just months after the fatal heart attacks of two Uruguayan fashion models, one of whom collapsed within seconds after stepping off the runway, having eaten nothing but lettuce leaves in the months before her death, *Titanic* star Kate Winslet announced that she is suing *Grazia* magazine for slander. The British tabloid accused her of undergoing a crash diet at a fat farm in Santa Monica, a claim that the 5'8", 119–130-pound actress categorically denies, and with good reason, since she is by most estimates, despite her well-founded reputation of having one of the healthier appetites in Hollywood, already between fifteen and twenty pounds underweight. She is famous for banning fashion magazines from her house lest her seven-year-old daughter fall prey to their anorexic aesthetic, a sentiment with which her countryman, the 5'9", 120-pound Mischa Barton, herself anywhere from twenty to forty pounds underweight, heartily agrees, stating that "the unhealthy look should be abandoned" and "it's wrong to try to stifle womanly curves." The rail-thin actress has, however, done a remarkable job in quelling her own and is considered by some to look sickly and malnourished, a charge she dismisses, summing up her philosophy of dieting in the reassuring assertion that "I don't not eat anything."

Others are more candid. Kate Bosworth was recently spotted at an expensive Hollywood restaurant openly dining on cigarettes, bottled water, and—the main course—a wedge of iceberg lettuce, a repast as frugal as former model Cleo Glyde's green grape diet: three for breakfast, two for snacks, and six for binges. The typical American woman is 5'4", weighs 140 pounds, and wears a size 14; the typical fashion model is seven inches taller, twenty-three pounds lighter, and twelve to fourteen sizes smaller. In an MSN photo essay about the fluctuating weights of Hollywood actors, an alarming shot of "Men in Black" star Lara Flynn Boyle is captioned with the snide but accurate comment "the jewelry she was wearing weighed more than she did," while a sickly photo of Selma Blair shows the 'Legally Blonde' star looking "so slim she could seek cover behind the nearest swizzle stick." Teri Hatcher continues to flaunt the gams of a sub-Saharan famine victim while Calista Flockhart shocked the nation at the 1998 Emmys by wearing a backless gown that turned her spindly frame into a ghoulish anatomy lesson, an annotated diagram of frail scapulae and jutting vertebrae.

Few men are aroused by these stylishly accessorized carcasses, but their lack of sex appeal is what makes the new Hollywood aesthetic unique. It has been almost entirely detached from the biological function of beauty, that of attracting males. It is a man-made aesthetic, or, rather, a woman-made aesthetic, since the desire of men for voluptuous childbearing hips and pendulous breasts seems all but irrelevant to its look. Feminists have long complained that the so-called "beauty myth" consists entirely of male lust, of men looking at women as potential sex objects, subservient to their selfish demands. In fact, however, Hollywood is about women looking at women, not as sex objects, as a means for fulfilling the species's genetic mission, but as clothes hangers, as display mannequins for product lines. Men and their needs are entirely beside the point, which is why the aesthetic is so sterile, so sexless, because it has freed the female body from male desire, liberated it from its biological status as an organ of sex, which has given way to the commercial view of it as a wearer of commodities, a pretty face stuck on a stick. In many respects, the recent marriage of anorexia and glamour represents the final dehumanization of women who were once reduced to their bodies, objectified as tools for propagation, but have now been deprived of their corporeality altogether. A vision of the female body dictated by male desire would be far healthier and more attractive than one dictated by the imperatives of the closet, by manufacturers whose primary concern is showing off their goods to the best effect.

How much influence does this aesthetic have on the general public? Such well-known personalities as the withered Nicole Richie or the cadaverous Victoria "Posh" Beckham, a.k.a. "Skeletal Spice," are often cited as the chief culprits behind the endemic of eating disorders among the young but the fact remains that, while as many as one hundred thousand teenage girls suffer from excessive dieting, two out of three Americans are overweight and an estimated sixty million, or 20 percent of the population, are obese. Are Hollywood and the fashion world responsible for our ever-increasing girth or is the effect of our obsession with what many have dubbed "the rich and famished" as open to debate as the influence of television violence and the Xbox on actual crime statistics? Does Lindsay Lohan's waspish waistline make us skip meals and induce vomiting just as Mortal Kombat presumably makes us pick up assault rifles and open fire? How direct *is* the impact of Hollywood on our bodies, as direct as the *Daily Mirror* recently suggested when it ran a photograph of the emaciated Keira Knightley next to the headline "If Pictures Like This One of Keira Carried a Health Warning, My Darling Daughter Might Have Lived"? If many adolescents seek "thinspiration" from such desiccated waifs as Jessica Alba, who has admitted to being on a diet since age twelve, or Elisa Donovan, who dwindled to a mere 90 pounds after eating nothing but coffee, water, and toast for two years, the majority of Americans seem to be following the lead of reformed foodaholic Tom Arnold who, until he began taking the diet aid Xenical, regularly splurged on McDonald's and then hid his half-dozen Big Macs and Quarter Pounders from his equally gluttonous wife Roseanne, not out of shame, but because he didn't want to share.

What is dangerous about the influence of popular culture on our state 5
of physical health is not how slavishly we imitate the stars, attempting to acquire Hilary Swank's lats, Jennifer Lopez's glutes, and Beyoncé's quads, but how little they affect us at all, how they have turned us into quiescent spectators who worship an unattainable ideal so remote from our daily affairs that its exemplars seem to belong to another species. Celebrities are like athletes, a class of surrogates who live vigorous, aerobic lives while

we develop diabetes and arteriosclerosis on our sofas. Hollywood didn't create fat, anxious Americans; fat, anxious Americans created Hollywood, a vision of humanity that bears little resemblance to the typical dissipated physique, sagging from too many processed foods and sedentary hours watching lithe beauties cavort in haute couture. Fantasy worlds, like those inhabited by celebrities, are never fashioned in the image of the dreamer. The dreamer imagines an existence as unlike his own as possible and is content to admire this world from afar, not as a possible destination but as a wonderland all the more enticing the more unapproachable and exclusionary. Our fantasies engender a paralyzing awe that instills in us despair, a sense of hopelessness about maintaining our bodies, about achieving the buff perfections of stars spoon-fed by studio dieticians who force them to nibble on rice cakes and celery sticks and submit to grueling regimens of Pilates and kickboxing. In fact, we would almost certainly be healthier if we *did* imitate Hollywood, if we *did* work out and diet as compulsively as they do, if, like supermodel Dayle Haddon, we performed leg lifts while washing the dishes, side bends while standing in line at Starbucks, and thigh resistance exercises in the elevators of our four-star hotels.

We blame pop culture for turning us into diet-crazed bulimics, but how can celebrities be "role models," however derelict, when almost no one seems to imitate them, when we get fatter even as they get skinnier, exercise less even as they train like triathletes? Granted, we are preoccupied with celebrities, follow the evolution of their hair styles, take tours past the gates of their estates, make wild surmises about their sexual preferences, but obsession does not necessarily, or even usually, entail imitation. This does not keep us, however, from penalizing them with an unjust double standard, insisting that, in the name of public hygiene, they maintain scrupulously healthy diets, drink abstemiously, engage in unerringly faithful relations with their spouses, and indignantly turn down film roles in which they are asked to participate in such iniquitous activities as smoking. Never before have we demanded that popular culture be as virtuous as we have in the last forty years, that our stars, in the mistaken belief that they manufacture the moral templates of our lives, beat their breasts in remorse and enroll in rehab every time they fail a breathalyzer test, stumble on the red carpet, or light a cigarette in public. The anti-tobacco Web site Smokingsides.com provides exhaustive documentation of celebrated nicotine abusers; in its lengthy dossier on Nicole Kidman, for example, it cites no less than seventy-eight instances in which the actress was observed puffing away in full view of her fans, in particular at the infamous press conference at Cannes in 2003 in which, in an image broadcast around the world, she bummed a cigarette from a fellow actor, a faux pas that provoked such a vicious international backlash that an Australian senator threatened to slap parental advisories on films that depicted nicotine consumption favorably. We ourselves smoke like chimneys, drink like fish, swear like troopers, and copulate like rabbits, but those in Hollywood are expected to behave with unglamorous rectitude lest their misconduct deprave their malleable fans. We have moralized popular culture into one long tedious sermon, created a parallel universe far more chaste, more decorous, more modest and seemly than the one in which most of us live.

In the distant past, actors and artists occupied a seedy if alluring demimonde, a realm of license and nonconformity that flourished on the fringes of respectable society. Far from being role models, they were black sheep, bohemians high on cocaine and drunk on absinthe. Now, by contrast, we expect them to be the pillars of our society, moral leaders who scold us for the errors of our ways, elder statesmen who draft into the roles of goodwill ambassadors for the United Nations, environmentalists, and spokesmen for such causes as gingivitis, erectile dysfunction, and irritable bowel syndrome. A paucity of conventional heroes has led to the invention of an implausible new set of mentors — a NASCAR mom, like race car driver Shawna Robinson, who feels that, behind the wheel of her souped-up Chevrolet Monte Carlo, she is able "to reach a lot of people," or even a golfer, such as Tiger Woods, whom Rolemodel.net singles out as an inspirational figure, a champion who triumphed over racial prejudice on the links and transformed his sport from a senile pastime for retirees in madras pants into "a vehicle . . . to influence people." Celebrities are rapidly filling the roles that priests, politicians, and wealthy philanthropists once served, perhaps because, as the church is rocked by molestation scandals and the government seems less and less capable of addressing the difficulties of our times, we are transferring moral authority to the only public servants that remain: pop singers, Hollywood stars, and the casts of our favorite sitcoms.

We admire them and yet at the same time distrust them. We are always ill at ease with beautiful people who, through no special effort of their own, get better jobs, more friends, and sexier lovers, but it is seldom that we encounter them in groups as large as we do on the idyllic Wisteria Lane in "Desperate Housewives," a latter-day Peyton Place in which the entire cast — gardeners, pharmacists, plumbers, cable repairman — is gorgeous. Beautiful people in real life are scattered randomly throughout the population and it is statistically impossible that they should ever constitute more than a tiny, unthreatening minority. And yet with the international dissemination of American popular culture, they have triumphed over the statistical odds and done something they could never have done before the twentieth century: they have overcome their geographic dispersal, gravitated together, and emerged as a power elite, a physical aristocracy whose seat of government is one major U.S. city where they migrate at the invitation of directors, producers, talent scouts, and casting agents who scour the globe in search of the perfect photogenic face. For the first time in history, our daily lives are filled with images of a real live übermensch, a master race that flaunts the unfair privileges accorded to those whose talents are often little more than cheek bones and good genes. There have always been aristocracies, privileged classes whose social prestige derived from their material wealth or pedigree, but there has never been a Brahmin caste whose sole justification for power was its physical appeal. This unelected coalition of the sexually charismatic may not, like an actual government, regulate our daily affairs in any literal sense, but it does exercise autocratic authority over our imaginations, making us capitulate psychologically if not politically.

We seek to contain the influence of this new master race, to alleviate the sense of belittlement we experience from living in the shadow of its inconceivable affluence and glamour. Western culture affords us many ways of denigrating the beautiful, branding them stupid, egotistic, lonely, and unhappy, and our constant, self-abasing surveillance of their every move, our prurient eavesdropping on their private lives, from their sex tapes to the messages they leave on each other's answering machines, may itself be a method of diminishing their psychological power. Much as Louis XIV used Versailles as a glittering cage to imprison restive nobles, so we have surrounded our idols with an impregnable phalanx of flashbulbs, herding them together in Hollywood, forcing them to live in a kind of internment camp, albeit one with all the amenities of a spa. The paparazzi, in turn, have become our watch dogs who never let them out of our sight, staking out their gyms, grocery stores, and nightclubs where they are forced to submit to our mean-spirited and yet, at the same time, obsequious espionage. We think of fame as a form of homage, the adulation we lavish on the gifted, but it may contain a large measure of resentment and vengefulness as well. Living in the limelight, exposed to the scrutiny of anonymous multitudes, may be a method of punishment, a concerted campaign of ostracism, a discriminatory act that forces celebrities to live apart from us, immured in a gulag of tanning salons, acupuncture clinics, and trendy boutiques. Obviously, we are barred from entering their world, but so in many ways are they from ours.

Beauty is not democratic. It is unjust, distributed inequitably according   10
to the luck of the draw. Our obsession with Hollywood celebrates this injustice, the irrationality with which fortune bestows its gifts. People cannot simply crash the gates and appropriate the privileges of the genetically blessed, creating faces different from "the one [they] rode in on," as on blogger said of Nicole Kidman's suspiciously chiseled chin. When someone attempts to gain illegal entrance into the pantheon of the chosen few, manipulating Mother Nature through plastic surgery, we are both outraged and amused, angered that the inequalities we at once adore and fear are in fact phantasmal, and, at the same time, relieved that beauty is really just a con game, something we can control after all, an illusion fabricated through liposuction, collagen injections, and breast augmentations. Actors who submit to the knife are like athletes who inject steroids, fakes who should be disqualified from the race, interlopers who buy their way into the public's heart, who purchase their looks from any of the sixty-eight plastic surgeons in Beverly Hills, a number that translates into one surgeon for every 497 residents and compares astonishingly with the city's thirty-six pediatricians.

We are therefore thrilled when what Joan Rivers calls her "Simonizing," Dolly Parton her "fender work," and Demi Moore her "furniture" rearrangement goes hideously awry, as in the case of Tara Reid's left breast, which, mangled and misshapen, popped out of her dress at P-Diddy's thirty-fifth birthday party ("instead of a circle," Reid said of this scarred and lopsided protuberance, "it turned out to be a large square"); Sharon Osborne's tummy tuck, which chopped off so much loose skin as a result of her gastric bypass that they had to create a new belly button; or Stevie Nick's silicone implants, which caused such pain that, after their removal, she stored them in her freezer to remind herself of "the agony." "Scalpel slaves" — or "polysurgical patients," as they are known to industry insiders — are the butt of scathing Internet mockery: Mary Tyler Moore, whom doctors have now placed on "an unofficial plastic surgery blacklist" and whose mouth has been stretched like taffy into a perpetual grin; model Alicia Douvall who, after her silicone implants ruptured, installed valves to pump saline solution in and out so she can vary the size of her breasts as the occasion warrants; or, the poster child of sloppy work, Michael Jackson, who may have had as many as thirty to forty rhinoplasties, including one that grafted cartilage from his ear to keep his nose from sinking back into his nasal cavity, leaving a gaping chasm in the middle of his face. If we are to believe in the beauty elite, to worship its exclusivity, its insuperable remoteness, we must be convinced that our idols acquired their physical assets the old-fashioned way, from Mom and Dad, not from Robert Rey, M.D., a.k.a. "Dr. 90210," perhaps the most famous plastic surgeon in the world. Our admiration of celebrities is much like our belief in God, and when our faith is tested by clear evidence of inauthenticity, by imposters who achieve illegal access to the inner sanctum through procedures we are increasingly able to spot, having become, as one reporter called it, "surgically literate," we are furious and vindictive. We mutiny against such swindlers in our gossip columns and Internet bulletin boards where we laugh hysterically when Britney Spears checks into a hospital for knee surgery and emerges several days later, according to many reports, two cup sizes larger or when Hollywood is stricken with crippling shortages of Botox just before the Academy Awards, which one Beverly Hills surgeon refers to as "tax season."

Our relationship with celebrities is so pathological in part because they are an absent presence in our lives: while they are physically absent and rarely seen in person, we are nonetheless nearer to their bodies, through close-ups, nude scenes, and simulated sex, than we are to anyone outside of our immediate families. We rarely examine even our lovers as meticulously as the Web site TMZ.com did in a recent exposé entitled "Heinous Extremities," an unsparing collection of photographs of celebrities' gnarly hands and stunted feet, appalling shots of Iman's twisted toes spilling painfully out of her stilettos and Jenna Jameson's arthritic claws clutching a soft drink can. In "Basic Instinct," Sharon Stone uncrosses her legs during a notorious police interrogation scene and gives us a clear shot of her pantyless crotch, bringing us closer to her genitalia than many men venture to those of their wives and girlfriends. The psychological mechanism of our obsession with celebrities lies in this deceptive intimacy, in the paradox that they are both present and absent, within reach and hidden behind wrought-iron gates, flashing their crotches at us in our living rooms and cowering behind ballistic-grade steel doors and closed-circuit surveillance systems. The camera is a tease, simulating an intimacy we do not have, a familiarity that incites us to narrow the physical distance that divides us from the stars, to eliminate the mediation of the lens, and press ourselves against them, flesh to flesh. Those who stalk celebrities, like the woman who left cookies in David Letterman's foyer and camped out on his tennis courts, or the man who slashes his wrists outside of the ABC studios where Andrea Evans was filming an episode of "One Life to Live," are really just our ambassadors, envoys we send to do our investigative work for us, berserk enthusiasts whose actions are psychotic manifestations of a very normal impulse to ascertain the physical reality of bodies we know almost as well as our own, if only secondhand.

Not only do celebrities occupy a different space than their fans, they occupy a different, nonconsecutive time. They do not change as we do, gradually, imperceptibly. They exist only in photographs and films, outside of the passage of time, the chronology of their bodies scrambled by random encounters with images from various periods in their lives, one from the zenith of their careers, proudly cradling their Oscars, another decades later, unemployed has-beens, as in the notorious pair of photographs that many newspapers published side by side when Greta Garbo died in 1990—on the left, the young starlet in her twenties, untouchably beautiful; on the right, an aged crone with straggly white hair hobbling out of a health clinic just weeks before her death at the age of eighty-four. The descent of celebrities into infirmity, obesity, or even the terminal stages of an illness is telescoped by the very medium that at once celebrates their youth and beauty and, over time, renders them grotesque. Unlike the bodies of our friends and family, whom we see every day and who therefore do not age in any measurable way, stars seem to change in fits and starts. One minute, 5'4", 120-pound Janet Jackson has a six-pack and buns of steel, and the next she's 180 pounds wearing sweatpants and a baseball cap, a wardrobe malfunction far more troubling than that which occurred during so-called "Titgate" at the 2004 Super Bowl. Similarly, a famous photograph of her brother shows him when he is ten years old, sporting a huge Afro and an infectious smile, while his mug shot, taken some thirty-five years later after his arrest for child molestation, features the unforgettable image of a bleached mask, a macabre caricature of Caucasian features, a heartbreaking disavowal of his own blackness. Reruns and DVDs fast-forward the careers of the stars, allowing us to see them starting out fresh, exhilarated by their success, and then, with one flick of the remote control, sinking into the decrepitude of old age.

We are shocked by the essay film and photography inadvertently write on physical dissolution, by the way they document the remorseless changes, the ebbing vitality, that celebrities take such unavailing pains to arrest. Art is long, life short, but in the case of Hollywood celebrities, art—their careers, their beauty—is short and life long—for most, too long.

The Reader's Presence:

1. Harris offers a harrowing accounting of the causes and effects of what he calls "the new Hollywood aesthetic" (paragraph 3), of the ways in which "Celebrities are rapidly filling the roles that priests, politicians, and wealthy philanthropists once served" (paragraph 7). As you reread Harris's essay, create a list of each of the specific features of this new aesthetic. What makes it "unique" (paragraph 3)? What does Harris say about the origins of this new aesthetic? What role do men play in formulating it or promoting it or both? What examples does Harris use to illustrate his assertions about the damage done to individuals and to society as a result of the "influence of popular culture on our state of physical health" (paragraph 5)?

2. What do you notice about the number—and nature—of the paragraphs Harris uses to develop his analysis? To what extent does each of these paragraphs depend on Harris's formulating a topic sentence? Choose one of his paragraphs and analyze the strengths of its structure. What pattern does he establish for developing his paragraphs? Show how he reinforces these effects by his choices in diction and figurative language. What role does Harris's use of metaphor, simile, and analogy play in building his case against the general public's obsession with Hollywood celebrities? Which of his uses of figurative language are most effective? Which do you think might be strengthened or omitted? Explain how and why.

3. Comment on the effects of Harris's use of popular idioms—such as we "smoke like chimneys, drink like fish, swear like troopers, and copulate like rabbits" (paragraph 6). Characterize Harris's tone (his attitude) toward celebrities and the damage that they inflict on their bodies. What does he mean when he claims: "Our relationship with celebrities is so pathological" (paragraph 12)? Harris devotes the final few paragraphs to a painful irony: "The descent of celebrities into infirmity, obesity, or even the terminal stages of an illness is telescoped by the very medium that at once celebrates their youth and beauty and, over time, renders them grotesque" (paragraph 13). His examples include Greta Garbo as well as Janet and Michael Jackson. What other celebrities can you

identify who would exemplify Harris's bittersweet sentence: "Art is long, life short, but in the case of Hollywood celebrities, art—their careers, their beauty—is short and life long—for most too long" (paragraph 13)?

4. Harris observes, "What is dangerous about the influence of popular culture on our state of physical health is not how slavishly we imitate the stars . . . but how little they affect us at all, how they have turned us into quiescent spectators who worship an unattainable ideal so remote from our daily affairs that its exemplars seem to belong to another species" (paragraph 5). Compare and contrast Harris's analysis of our fascination with this "new Hollywood aesthetic" to Marie Winn's analysis of America's "addiction" to television in her essay "TV Addiction" (page 590). To what extent is Winn's definition of addiction applicable to the conditions Harris recounts in "Celebrity Bodies"? Please be as specific as possible in developing your response.

Siri Hustvedt

Eight Days in a Corset

Writer, essayist, and poet Siri Hustvedt (b. 1955) was born and raised in Northfield, Minnesota, where she attended St. Olaf's College before earning her PhD in English literature from Columbia University in New York City. She lives in Brooklyn, New York, with her husband, writer Paul Auster, and their daughter.

Hustvedt has authored numerous books of fiction and nonfiction, including four novels: The Blindfold *(1992),* The Enchantment of Lily Dahl *(1996),* What I Loved *(2003), and her most recent,* The Sorrows of an American *(2008). Her first book of essays,* Yonder, *was published in 1998, followed by* Mysteries of the Rectangle *(2005), a collection of personal essays on the paintings that "tell us something about what it means to be human." Her essay, "Eight Days in a Corset," is taken from* A Plea for Eros *(2006), a collection of personal and critical essays about writing and writers. Her work has appeared in a number of anthologies, journals, and magazines, including the* Paris Review Anthology *and* Best American Short Stories, Fiction *magazine, the* Observer, *and* Modern Painters. *A self-described "migraineur," she contributes to the* New York Times *blog, "Migraine: Perspectives on a Headache."*

In an interview with Powell's Books "Ink Q & A," Hustvedt was asked the inevitable question: Why do you write? "Writing isn't a job so much as a compul-

sion. I've been writing since I was very young because, for some strange reason, I must write, and also because when I write I feel more alive and closer to the world than when I'm not writing."

Last summer, I worked as an extra in the film version of Henry James's novel *Washington Square*. I am not an actress. Agnieszka Holland, the director, is a friend of my husband's and mine, and the person she was really interested in was our daughter, Sophie, who was cast as one of Mrs. Almond's children. Under a blasting June sun, Sophie and I arrived in Baltimore for a fitting. Sophie was dressed first, and she looked as pretty as a young heroine in any book. One of the two wardrobe women handed me a corset, a hoopskirt, and a petticoat, which I put on, and then she tightened my stays. They searched for a dress long enough to fit me, and I climbed into it in front of a long, wide mirror in the changing room.

Within a few minutes, I felt faint. I began to suffer from the feeling I always have when I am faint—acute embarrassment. This time there was the added burden of fear: that I would crash to the floor in front of my eight-year-old daughter: I began to sway, dropped, but did not black out. I wish I could say that they cried, "Loosen her stays!" hurried out for smelling salts, and waved my ashen face with a fan. But they didn't. They kindly brought me water and grapes as I recovered. I joked about filling the role too well, about becoming in a matter of minutes the classic image of a swooning nineteenth-century lady, and yet I don't believe it was the corset. I had almost fainted in front of a mirror once before—in a yoga class. That time I was wearing dance tights and a sweatshirt. My teacher was correcting my posture, and without warning I collapsed and found myself breathing deeply with my head between my knees.

Mirrors are where I check myself—for parsley stuck in my teeth, for blemishes and dirty hair—where I ponder which shoes go with which dress. But every once in a while, they become something more than that—the site of a body I know will eventually give up the ghost. As in fairy tales and folklore, the mirror displays for an instant my ghost double, and I don't like seeing her. It is a moment when I am a stranger to myself. But a foreign reflection in a mirror is not always a shock. There is something appealing about transformations, and clothes are the fastest route to leaping out of your own life and into someone else's. The whalebone corset I wore for eight days catapulted me into another time and another aesthetic, and I liked it.

The corset is a vilified article of clothing. It was and is blamed for a host of feminine miseries, both physical and spiritual, for ruining women's bodies and for closing their minds. It is interesting to note, however, that while women wore them, it was male doctors who led the campaign against the corset. Most women were for it. In the twentieth century, feminists joined physicians and attacked the garment as crippling. No doubt there were women who, in the heat of summer or in front of a parlor fire in winter, lost consciousness in corsets too tightly laced for their own good. But wearing mine day in and day out, I fell prey to its charms. Wearing a corset is a little like finding oneself in a permanent embrace, a hug around the middle that goes on and on. This is pleasant and vaguely erotic—a squeeze that lasts.

But the feeling of a corset is only part of its effect. Like all clothing,   5
more than anything else, it is an idea. In this case it promotes an idea of a woman's body as radically different from a man's. In the summer of 1986, I traveled in Asia with my three sisters and we visited both a Buddhist monastery and a Buddhist nunnery in the mountains of Taiwan. Those monks and nuns looked *exactly* alike—small, trim, hairless bodies with shaved heads. The monks had orange robes, the nuns white. Had they all stripped naked and stood together, the difference between them would have been ridiculously small, would have been no more nor less than what the difference truly is—genital variation and a few secondary sexual characteristics in the chest and hips. The truth about clothes, hairdos, and makeup had never hit me so hard. The cultural trappings of sex are overwhelming. We make them and live them and are them.

The corset takes the difference between men and women and runs wild with it. The inward slope of a woman's waist becomes extreme, and the tension of lacing the waist pushes the breasts upward. Suddenly, I had new breasts. I did not know how much my body had changed until I saw a photograph of myself in costume and marveled at this addition to my anatomy. The corset leaves most of the breasts free and does not cover the genitals. By lodging itself securely between upper and lower body parts, its effect is to articulate them more sharply and define them as separate erotic zones. The corset helped to create a notion of femininity, and the lines it produced have gone in and out of fashion ever since. If I had never seen a corset before or had never imagined myself in one, it probably wouldn't have had much power; but I grew up on nineteenth-century novels and studied the illustrations of Dickens and Thackeray very closely. Snug in my corset, with a body I had never seen before, I became an illustration to myself of a world I had only read about.

The corset did not live alone, however: In the 1860s, the time during which James set his novel, it was joined by other garments essential to the American bourgeois woman: the hoopskirt and the petticoat padded at the hips. The padding exaggerates the tiny waist created by the corset, and the hoop turns a woman into a kind of walking bell. The hoop's threat is real. You sit, and if you are not careful, it flies up over your head. No one can scrub floors in a hoop. If you're wearing one, it's a sign that during the day you are *never* on your knees. It is possible to arrange flowers in a hoop, life a teacup, read a book, and point out tasks to your servants. The hoop was a sign of class; its restriction meant luxury. Like the Chinese aristocrat with fingernails a yard long, it tells a story: "I do not work for money." And I did notice among some of the extras a touch of envy among those who were cast as maids in sad, gray dresses for those of us who swished along in our private balloons. Our movements might have been hampered, but we took up a lot of space, and that space, I realized, was a matter of pride.

And then, alas, they did my hair. I liked the corset. I was amused by my petticoats and laughed at the hoop, except when I had to back slowly into a bathroom stall wearing the crazy thing. (Women of the period did not back into stalls. Their underwear was open, and they could pee standing up. Yes, like a man.) The hairdo was another matter. I am six feet tall. I was forty-one years old. When they had finished with me, I looked like a giraffe in ringlets. The only people in the world who come by ringlets naturally are babies. During that period every woman who could afford to be curled was — young, old, and in between. It was baby fashion, and to my mind it made every woman over twenty look ridiculous. Like the hourglass figure, the longing for infancy through garments or hairdos comes and goes. The short shifts of the sixties were a movement back to childhood, as were the big eyes and ringlets of the same period. Only a few years ago I read about the fashion among teenagers and young club-goers to drape pacifiers around their necks after they had squeezed themselves into baby clothes. Female Peter Pans.

In other words, the idea is what matters. Clothes gives us insight into culture and its wishes, and into individuals and their desires. More than who you are, clothes articulate what you want to be. Ringlets were hard for me, because I like to think of myself as a grown-up, because I strive for a certain dignity in my apparel, but that dignity is no more than a message I want to communicate, and who knows if it is successful? I love clothes and have often pined for them — the beautiful dress or coat in the window. My desire is for a transformation I imagine will take place, a kind of enchantment of my own body.

Children are closer to fantastic transformations than adults, closer to the spell of costume and the change that comes from illusion, but we all are prone to it, and hiding behind the silk nightgown or the stockings or the pin-striped suit is a story we have heard and repeated to ourselves. These stories are often clichés, worn narratives we hold close to our hearts. I am changing into the silk nightgown, have brushed my hair and pinched my cheeks. I walk into the bedroom and there he is — the hero, Clark Gable or William Powell, depending on my mood. He turns, gasps, "You look . . ." Fill in the blank. Whatever the words are, it is never: "You look like yourself."

Any meaningful piece of clothing is a part of a broader cultural story. Years ago I went to a Halloween party as a man. In a borrowed suit, my face wiped clean of all makeup, and my hair hidden under a hat, I looked at myself in the mirror and was unprepared for the change. Women flirt with men's clothing all the time, but when you go all the way, the result is striking. I felt manly. My stride lengthened. My manner changed. It was easy to play at being a man, as easy as playing at being a woman. The suit unleashed a fantasy of maleness I heartily enjoyed. Another time, I was walking down a dark street in New York on my way to a large party. I was in

10

my early twenties then and experimented occasionally with wild attire. In a red jumpsuit and heels, which added several inches to my already towering frame, I passed a man who began spewing insults at me. I kept walking. It took several seconds for me to digest what was happening. The man had mistaken me for a transvestite. The experience, both comic and sad, gave me a sudden insight into the venom that appearances can produce, not to speak of the often hazy line between femininity and its parodic double.

Every once in a while, a piece of clothing jumps out of one culture and into another. I spent three months in Thailand in 1975 as a student, and I vividly remember seeing a gang of motorcycle toughs roaring through the streets of Chiang Mai in the rain, wearing shower caps. Several of those caps were decorated with flowers and other beacons of feminine adornment. I was amazed, but nobody else was. My cultural associations didn't apply. The shower cap had been born again somewhere else with a totally different signification.

While it is true that certain individuals are fixed on an idea that rigidly determines them—whether it be "I do not care about clothes at all" or "I am a sex goddess"—most of us have or have had over time many different dreams. I own a black dress that reminds me of Audrey Hepburn. I do not suffer from the delusion that I look like Audrey Hepburn in that dress, but her exquisite form wrapped in Givenchy has bewitched it nevertheless, and her magic is part of my pleasure in wearing it. Movies and books are strong drugs to clothes lovers. Katharine Hepburn striding along in trousers, Lana Turner in a towel, Claudette Colbert in a man's pajama top, Marilyn Monroe in anything. Tolstoy lavished his attention on the details of women's clothes and bodies, on Natasha at her first ball and Ellen's white shoulders above her low-cut gown. Jane Eyre's plain dress is a tonic against the frippery of the silly females who visit Rochester. And all these images are taken from moments in larger stories that captivate us, stories about people who are living out their lives and their romantic entanglements, both comic and tragic.

My daughter dresses up. She is a rich woman, then a poor one, starving in the streets. She is an old peasant woman selling apples. She is on the phone saying, "Let's have lunch," in an English accent. She sashays down the stairs snapping her gum and practicing her Brooklyn voice. She is wearing my shoes and singing "Adelaide's Lament." She is always somebody else. My husband says I have two personas at least, the stooped four-eyed scholar and the elegant lady. One lives at home. The other goes out. Thinking collapses my body, and I forget what I look like anyway. In a good dress, I stand up straight and never slump. I live up to the dress I know I am wearing even though I do not see myself wearing it. Others see me more often than I see myself. My family knows what I look like better than I do. I offer the mirror a placid face like an inanimate statue, and from time to time the frozen image may frighten me. But I also laugh a lot and smile. I wrinkle my face in concern, and I wave my hands when I talk, and this I never see.

In the end, wearing clothes is an act of the imagination, an invention   15
of self, a fiction. Several years ago, I was sitting in the Carlyle Hotel with
my husband having a drink. I was wearing a beautiful dress. I remember
that he looked across the table at me with pleasure and said, "When you
were a little girl growing up in the sticks of Minnesota, did you ever
imagine you would be sitting in this elegant hotel wearing that extraordinary dress?"

And I said, "Yes." Because of course, I did.

The Reader's Presence

1. Hustvedt builds her essay on her experience working as an extra—
   and wearing a corset for eight days—during the filming of Henry
   James's *Washington Square*. In paragraph 15, she observes: "In
   the end, wearing clothes is an act of imagination, an invention of
   self, a fiction." Throughout her essay, Hustvedt unfolds examples
   of the "transformations" that wearing different kinds of clothing
   afford her—and women more generally. Create a list of these
   transformations. Which do you find Hustvedt to have unpacked
   most engagingly? Explain why.

2. Summarize—and comment on—the literal and figurative importance of the mirror in her essay. What does she mean when she
   talks about her "ghost double" (paragraph 3)? Summarize—and
   then comment on—her attitudes toward the corset. In what specific ways does she illustrate and validate her assertion that the
   corset is responsible for "ruining women's bodies and for closing
   their minds" (paragraph 4)? In what specific ways—and why—
   does she fall "prey to its charms" (paragraph 4)? In addition to
   femininity and sexuality, what larger issues does Hustvedt address
   in her essay? How successfully?

3. In paragraph 10, she observes: "Children are closer to fantastic
   transformations than adults, closer to the spell of costume and the
   change that comes from illusion, but we are all prone to it . . . a
   story we have heard and repeated to ourselves. These stories are
   often clichés, worn narratives we hold close to our hearts." How
   does Hustvedt use specific word choices (especially verbs and adjectives) and phrasing to resist the lure of clichés in telling her
   story? Comment on the effectiveness of her use of simile and
   metaphor.

4. In paragraph 11, Hustvedt observes: "Any meaningful piece of
   clothing is part of a broader cultural story." She proceeds to recount the story of dressing as a man for a Halloween party and
   the effects of doing so on both her and on those who saw her. She
   concludes that the experience of dressing in a red jumpsuit and

being mistaken for a man was "both comic and sad, [and] gave me sudden insight into the venom that appearances can produce" (paragraph 11). Compare and contrast Hustvedt's conclusion about the relationship between clothing and social expectations, and between clothing and gender with that of Thomas Beller in "The Problem with T-Shirts" (page 53). Which writer makes the more convincing case for the relationship between clothing and social expectations and gender identity? Explain why.

Stephen King

Everything You Need to Know about Writing Successfully — in Ten Minutes

Stephen King was born in 1947 in Portland, Maine. He began writing stories early in his life, but it was his discovery of a box of horror and science fiction novels in the attic of his aunt's house that made him decide to pursue a career as a writer. He published his first short stories in pulp horror magazines while in high school. After graduating from the University of Maine at Orono in 1970, King, while working at a low-paying job in a laundry, began writing his first novel, Carrie *(1974).* Carrie *was followed by some forty more novels, including a series written under the pen name Richard Bachman, as well as numerous novellas, short story collections, and screenplays. His latest novel is* Duma Key *(2008). His critically acclaimed work of nonfiction,* On Writing *(2000), the source of the following essay, was completed while he was recovering painfully from a much-publicized accident.*

Stephen King has commented that, as a creative writer, he always hopes for "that element of inspiration which lifts you past the point where the characters are just you, where you do achieve something transcendental and the people are really people in the story."

I. THE FIRST INTRODUCTION

That's right. I know it sounds like an ad for some sleazy writers' school, but I really am going to tell you everything you need to pursue a successful and financially rewarding career writing fiction, and I really am going to do it in ten minutes, which is exactly how long it took me to learn.

It will actually take you twenty minutes or so to read this article, however, because I have to tell you a story, and then I have to write a second introduction. But these, I argue, should not count in the ten minutes.

II. THE STORY, OR, HOW STEPHEN KING LEARNED TO WRITE

When I was a sophomore in high school, I did a sophomoric thing which got me in a pot of fairly hot water, as sophomoric didoes often do. I wrote and published a small satiric newspaper called *The Village Vomit*. In this little paper I lampooned a number of teachers at Lisbon (Maine) High School, where I was under instruction. These were not very gentle lampoons; they ranged from the scatological to the downright cruel.

Eventually, a copy of this paper found its way into the hands of a faculty member, and since I had been unwise enough to put my name on it (a fault, some critics would argue, of which I have still not been entirely cured), I was brought into the office. The sophisticated satirist had by that time reverted to what he really was: a fourteen-year-old kid who was shaking in his boots and wondering if he was going to get a suspension . . . what we called a "three-day vacation" in those dim days of 1964.

I wasn't suspended. I was forced to make a number of apologies—they were warranted, but they tasted like dog-dirt in my mouth—and spent a week in detention hall. And the guidance counselor arranged what he no doubt thought of as a more constructive channel for my talents. This was a job—contingent upon the editor's approval—writing sports for the Lisbon Enterprise, a twelve-page weekly of the sort with which any small-town resident will be familiar. This editor was the man who taught me everything I know about writing in ten minutes. His name was John Gould—not the famed New England humorist or the novelist who wrote *The Greenleaf Fires*, but a relative of both, I believe.

He told me he needed a sports writer, and we could "try each other out," if I wanted.   5

I told him I knew more about advanced algebra than I did sports.

Gould nodded and said, "You'll learn."

I said I would at least try to learn. Gould gave me a huge roll of yellow paper and promised me a wage of 1/2 [cts.] per word. The first two pieces I wrote had to do with a high school basketball game in which a member of my school team broke the Lisbon High scoring record. One of these pieces was a straight piece of reportage. The second was a feature article.

I brought them to Gould the day after the game, so he'd have them for the paper, which came out Fridays. He read the straight piece, made two minor corrections, and spiked it. Then he started in on the feature piece with a large black pen and taught me all I ever needed to know about my craft. I wish I still had the piece,—it deserves to be framed, editorial corrections and all—but I can remember pretty well how it went and how it looked when he had finished with it. Here's an example:

Last night, in the ~~well-loved~~ gymnasium of Lisbon
High School, partisans and Jay Hills fans alike were
stunned by an athletic performance unequalled in
school history: Bob Ransom~~, known as Bullet Bob~~
~~for both his size and accuracy,~~ scored thirty-seven
points. Yes, you heard me right. ~~Plus~~ he did it with
grace, and speed...and with an odd courtesy as
well, committing only two personal fouls in his
~~knight-like~~ quest for a record which has eluded Lisbon ~~thinclads~~ since ~~the years of Korea~~...
       players   1953

When Gould finished marking up my copy in the manner I   10
have indicated above, he looked up and must have seen something
on my face. I think he must have thought it was horror, but it was
not: It was revelation.

"I only took out the bad parts, you know," he said. "Most of
it's pretty good."

"I know," I said, meaning both things; yes, most of it was
good, and yes, he had only taken out the bad parts. "I won't do it
again."

"If that's true," he said, "you'll never have to work again.
You can do this for a living."

Then he threw back his head and laughed.

And he was right: I am doing this for a living, and as long as I   15
can keep on, I don't expect ever to have to work again.

III. THE SECOND INTRODUCTION

All of what follows has been said before. If you are interested
enough in writing to be a purchaser of this magazine [*Writer*], you
will have either heard or read all (or almost all) of it before. Thousands of writing courses are taught across the United States each
year; seminars are convened; guest lecturers talk, then answer
questions, and it all boils down to what follows.

I am going to tell you these things again because often people
will only listen—really listen—to someone who makes a lot of
money doing the thing he's talking about. This is sad but true. And
I told you the story above not to make myself sound like a character out of a Horatio Alger novel but to make a point: I saw, I listened, and I learned. Until that day in John Gould's little office, I
had been writing first drafts of stories that might run 2,500 words.
The second drafts were apt to run 3,300 words. Following that
day, my 2,500-word first drafts became 2,200-word second drafts.
And two years after that, I sold the first one.

So here it is, with all the bark stripped off. It'll take ten minutes to read, and you can apply it right away . . . if you listen.

IV. EVERYTHING YOU NEED TO KNOW ABOUT WRITING SUCCESSFULLY

1. Be talented

This, of course, is the killer. What is talent? I can hear someone shouting, and here we are, ready to get into a discussion right up there with "What is the meaning of life?" for weighty pronouncements and total uselessness. For the purposes of the beginning writer, talent may as well be defined as eventual success — publication and money. If you wrote something for which someone sent you a check, if you cashed the check and it didn't bounce, and if you then paid the light bill with the money, I consider you talented.

Now some of you are really hollering. Some of you are calling me one   20
crass money-fixated creep. Nonsense. Worse than nonsense, off the subject. We're not talking about good or bad here. I'm interested in telling you how to get your stuff published, not in critical judgments of who's good or bad. As a rule, the critical judgments come after the check's been spent, anyway. I have my own opinions, but most times I keep them to myself. People who are published steadily and are paid for what they are writing may be either saints or trollops, but they are clearly reaching a great many someones who want what they have. Ergo, they are communicating. Ergo, they are talented. The biggest part of writing successfully is being talented, and in the context of marketing, the only bad writer is one who doesn't get paid. If you're not talented, you won't succeed. And if you're not succeeding, you should know when to quit.

When is that? I don't know. It's different for each writer. Not after six rejection slips, certainly, nor after sixty. But after six hundred? Maybe. After six thousand? My friend, after six thousand pinks, it's time you tried painting or computer programming.

Further, almost every aspiring writer knows when he is getting warmer — you start getting little jotted notes on your rejection slips, or personal letters . . . maybe a commiserating phone call. It's lonely out there in the cold, but there are encouraging voices . . . unless there is nothing in your words that warrants encouragement. I think you owe it to yourself to skip as much of the self-illusion as possible. If your eyes are open, you'll know which way to go . . . or when to turn back.

2. Be neat

Type. Double-space. Use a nice heavy white paper. If you've marked your manuscript a lot, do another draft.

3. Be self-critical

If you haven't marked up your manuscript a lot, you did a lazy job. Only God gets things right the first time. Don't be a slob.

4. Remove every extraneous word

You want to get up on a soapbox and preach? Fine. Get one, and try   25
your local park. You want to write for money? Get to the point. And if you remove the excess garbage and discover you can't find the point, tear up what you wrote and start all over again . . . or try something new.

5. Never look at a reference book while doing a first draft

You want to write a story? Fine. Put away your dictionary, your encyclopedias, your *World Almanac,* and your thesaurus. Better yet, throw your thesaurus into the wastebasket. The only things creepier than a thesaurus are those little paperbacks college students too lazy to read the assigned novels buy around exam time. Any word you have to hunt for in a thesaurus is the wrong word. There are no exceptions to this rule. You think you might have misspelled a word? O.K., so here is your choice: Either look it up in the dictionary, thereby making sure you have it right—and breaking your train of thought and the writer's trance in the bargain—or just spell it phonetically and correct it later. Why not? Did you think it was going to go somewhere? And if you need to know the largest city in Brazil and you find you don't have it in your head, why not write in Miami, or Cleveland? You can check it . . . but later. When you sit down to write, write. Don't do anything else except go to the bathroom, and only do that if it absolutely cannot be put off.

6. Know the markets

Only a dimwit would send a story about giant vampire bats surrounding a high school to *McCall's.* Only a dimwit would send a tender story about a mother and daughter making up their differences on Christmas Eve to *Playboy* . . . but people do it all the time. I'm not exaggerating; I have seen such stories in the slush piles of the actual magazines. If you write a good story, why send it out in an ignorant fashion? Would you send your kid out in a snowstorm dressed in Bermuda shorts and a tank top? If you like science fiction, read science fiction novels and magazines. If you want to write mysteries, read the magazines. And so on. It isn't just a matter of knowing what's right for the present story; you can begin to catch on, after a while, to overall rhythms, editorial likes and dislikes, a magazine's slant. Sometimes your reading can influence the next story, and create a sale.

7. Write to entertain

Does this mean you can't write "serious fiction"? It does not. Somewhere along the line pernicious critics have invested the American reading and writing public with the idea that entertaining fiction and serious ideas do not overlap. This would have surprised Charles Dickens, not to mention Jane Austen, John Steinbeck, William Faulkner, Bernard Malamud, and hundreds of others. But your serious ideas must always serve your story, not the other way around. I repeat: If you want to preach, get a soapbox.

8. Ask yourself frequently, "Am I having fun?"

The answer needn't always be yes. But if it's always no, it's time for a new project or a new career.

9. How to evaluate criticism

Show your piece to a number of people—ten, let us say. Listen carefully to what they tell you. Smile and nod a lot. Then review what was said very carefully. If your critics are all telling you the same thing about some facet of your story—a plot twist that doesn't work, a character who rings false, stilted narrative, or half a dozen other possibles—change it. It doesn't matter if you really like that twist or that character; if a lot of people are telling you something is wrong with your piece, it is. If seven or eight of them are hitting on that same thing, I'd still suggest changing it. But if everyone—or even most everyone—is criticizing something different, you can safely disregard what all of them say.

10. Observe all rules for proper submission

Return postage, self-addressed envelope, etc.

11. An agent? Forget it. For now.

Agents get 10 percent to 15 percent of monies earned by their clients. Fifteen percent of nothing is nothing. Agents also have to pay the rent. Beginning writers do not contribute to that or any other necessity of life. Flog your stories around yourself. If you've done a novel, send around query letters to publishers, one by one, and follow up with sample chapters and/or the complete manuscript. And remember Stephen King's First Rule of Writers and Agent, learned by bitter personal experience: You don't need one until you're making enough for someone to steal . . . and if you're making that much, you'll be able to take your pick of good agents.

12. If it's bad, kill it

When it comes to people, mercy killing is against the law. When it comes to fiction, it is the law.

That's everything you need to know. And if you listened, you can write everything and anything you want. Now I believe I will wish you a pleasant day and sign off.

My ten minutes are up.   35

The Reader's Presence

1. Why does King include sections I–III, even though they are not part of the "ten minutes"? What does the first introduction actually introduce? the second? How effectively does section II work with section IV? For example, how many rules did King learn when John Gould edited his story? Which rules does he break in his own essay? Why do you think he breaks them?

2. King is best known for writing horror novels, stories that scare people. What fears does he play on throughout this essay? How does he go about setting up suspenseful situations? What does he do to frighten people in this essay? If the rules are monsters, which ones do you think are the most frightening? Why?

3. By King's definition, a talented author is one who has been paid for his or her writing. Pick an author in this collection whom you consider talented and evaluate him or her according to King's rules. How successful should this writer be according to King? What other rules of success does the writer's essay suggest should be added to King's list?

4. King's essay represents an approach to an ongoing debate between money and art. Signalled by terms like *practicality* and *popularity*, the money side holds that you should write to make money. Signalled by phrases like *art for art's sake* or *selling out*, the art side holds that you should write to please yourself. George Orwell represents another approach to this debate when he lists "four great motives for writing" (page 521). Read Orwell's essay and determine

how well each of the motives would lead to the kind of successful writing that King imagines. For example, how well—or how poorly—does Orwell's desire to "share an experience which one feels is valuable" (page 521) lead to King's "eventual success— publication and money" (paragraph 19)?

Maxine Hong Kingston

No Name Woman

Maxine Hong Kingston (b. 1940) won the National Book Critics Circle Award for nonfiction with her first book, The Woman Warrior: Memoirs of a Girlhood among Ghosts *(1976). "No Name Woman" is the opening chapter of this book, which* Time *magazine named one of the top ten nonfiction works of the 1970s. Her other works include* China Men *(1980), which won the American Book Award;* Trip Master Monkey: His Fake Book *(1988), a picaresque novel; and* To Be a Poet *(2002), a collection of her lectures and verse. A manuscript entitled* The Fourth Book of Peace *was destroyed, along with her home and all of her possessions, in a 1991 Oakland–Berkeley fire, but Kingston started over and published* The Fifth Book of Peace *in 2003. Kingston's writing often blurs the distinction between fiction and nonfiction. She edited* Veterans of War, Veterans of Peace *(2006), a collection of writing by survivors of war compiled from her healing workshops. Her narratives blend autobiography, history, myth, and legend, drawing on the stories she remembers from her childhood in the Chinese American community of Stockton, California. Kingston's essays, stories, and poems also appear in numerous magazines, and she received the 1997 National Medal for the Humanities. In 2004, she retired as a senior lecturer for creative writing at the University of California, Berkeley.*

Kingston has said that before writing The Woman Warrior, *"My life as a writer had been a long struggle with pronouns. For 30 years I wrote in the first person singular. At a certain point I was thinking that I was self-centered and egotistical, solipsistic, and not very developed as a human being, nor as an artist, because I could only see from this one point of view." She began to write in the third person because "I thought I had to overcome this self-centeredness." As she wrote her third novel, Kingston experienced the disappearance of her authorial voice. "I feel that this is an artistic as well as psychological improvement on my part. Because I am now a much less selfish person."*

"You must not tell anyone," my mother said, "what I am about to tell you. In China your father had a sister who killed herself. She jumped into the family well. We say that your father has all brothers because it is as if she had never been born.

"In 1924 just a few days after our village celebrated seventeen hurry-up weddings—to make sure that every young man who went 'out on the road' would responsibly come home—your father and his brothers and your grandfather and his brothers and your aunt's new husband sailed for America, the Gold Mountain. It was your grandfather's last trip. Those lucky enough to get contracts waved good-bye from the decks. They fed and guarded the stowaways and helped them off in Cuba, New York, Bali, Hawaii. 'We'll meet in California next year,' they said. All of them sent money home.

"I remember looking at your aunt one day when she and I were dressing; I had not noticed before that she had such a protruding melon of a stomach. But I did not think, 'She's pregnant,' until she began to look like other pregnant women, her shirt pulling and the white tops of her black pants showing. She could not have been pregnant, you see, because her husband had been gone for years. No one said anything. We did not discuss it. In early summer she was ready to have the child, long after the time when it could have been possible.

"The village had also been counting. On the night the baby was to be born the villagers raided our house. Some were crying. Like a great saw, teeth strung with lights, files of people walked zigzag across our land, tearing the rice. Their lanterns doubled in the disturbed black water, which drained away through the broken bunds.[1] As the villagers closed in, we could see that some of them, probably men and women we knew well, wore white masks. The people with long hair hung it over their faces. Women with short hair made it stand up on end. Some had tied white bands around their foreheads, arms, and legs.

"At first they threw mud and rocks at the house. Then they threw eggs   5
and began slaughtering our stock. We could hear the animals scream their deaths—the roosters, the pigs, a last great roar from the ox. Familiar wild heads flared in our night windows; the villagers encircled us. Some of the faces stopped to peer at us, their eyes rushing like searchlights. The hands flattened against the panes, framed heads, and left red prints.

"The villagers broke in the front and the back doors at the same time, even though we had not locked the doors against them. Their knives dripped with the blood of our animals. They smeared blood on the doors and walls. One woman swung a chicken, whose throat she had slit, splattering blood in red arcs about her. We stood together in the middle of our house, in the family hall with the pictures and tables of the ancestors around us, and looked straight ahead.

[1]*Bunds:* an embankment around rice fields to help prevent flooding. —EDS.

"At that time the house had only two wings. When the men came back we would build two more to enclose our courtyard and a third one to begin a second courtyard. The villagers pushed through both wings, even your grandparents' rooms, to find your aunt's, which was also mine until the men returned. From this room a new wing for one of the younger families would grow. They ripped up her clothes and shoes and broke her combs, grinding them underfoot. They tore her work from the loom. They scattered the cooking fire and rolled the new weaving in it. We could hear them in the kitchen breaking our bowls and banging the pots. They over-turned the great waist-high earthenware jugs; duck eggs, pickled fruits, vegetables burst out and mixed in acrid torrents. The old woman from the next field swept a broom through the air and loosed the spirits-of-the-broom over our heads. 'Pig.' 'Ghost.' 'Pig,' they sobbed and scolded while they ruined our house.

"When they left, they took sugar and oranges to bless themselves. They cut pieces from the dead animals. Some of them took bowls that were not broken and clothes that were not torn. Afterward we swept up the rice and sewed it back up into sacks. But the smells from the spilled preserves lasted. Your aunt gave birth in the pigsty that night. The next morning when I went up for the water, I found her and the baby plugging up the family well.

"Don't let your father know that I told you. He denies her. Now that you have started to menstruate, what happened to her could happen to you. Don't humiliate us. You wouldn't like to be forgotten as if you had never been born. The villagers are watchful."

Whenever she had to warn us about life, my mother told stories that ran like this one, a story to grow up on. She tested our strength to establish realities. Those in the emigrant generations who could not reassert brute survival died young and far from home. Those of us in the first American generations have had to figure out how the invisible world the emigrants built around our childhoods fit in solid America.

The emigrants confused the gods by diverting their curses, misleading them with crooked streets and false names. They must try to confuse their offspring as well, who, I suppose, threaten them in similar ways — always trying to get things straight, always trying to name the unspeakable. The Chinese I know hide their names; sojourners take new names when their lives change and guard their real names with silence.

Chinese-Americans, when you try to understand what things in you are Chinese, how do you separate what is peculiar to childhood, to poverty, in-sanities, one family, your mother who marked your growing with stories, from what is Chinese? What is Chinese tradition and what is the movies?

If I want to learn what clothes my aunt wore, whether flashy or ordi-nary, I would have to begin, "Remember Father's drowned-in-the-well sister?" I cannot ask that. My mother has told me once and for all the use-ful parts. She will add nothing unless powered by Necessity, a riverbank that guides her life. She plants vegetable gardens rather than lawns; she carries the odd-shaped tomatoes home from the fields and eats food left for the gods.

Whenever we did frivolous things, we used up energy; we flew high kites. We children came up off the ground over the melting cones our parents brought home from work and the American movie on New Year's Day—*Oh, You Beautiful Doll* with Betty Grable one year, and *She Wore a Yellow Ribbon* with John Wayne another year. After the one carnival ride each, we paid in guilt; our tired father counted his change on the dark walk home.

Adultery is extravagance. Could people who hatch their own chicks   15
and eat the embryos and the heads for delicacies and boil the feet in vinegar for party food, leaving only the gravel, eating even the gizzard lining —could such people engender a prodigal aunt? To be a woman, to have a daughter in starvation time was a waste enough. My aunt could not have been the lone romantic who gave up everything for sex. Women in the old China did not choose. Some man had commanded her to lie with him and be his secret evil. I wonder whether he masked himself when he joined the raid on her family.

Perhaps she encountered him in the fields or on the mountain where the daughters-in-law collected fuel. Or perhaps he first noticed her in the marketplace. He was not a stranger because the village housed no strangers. She had to have dealings with him other than sex. Perhaps he worked an adjoining field, or he sold her the cloth for the dress she sewed and wore. His demand must have surprised, then terrified her. She obeyed him; she always did as she was told.

When the family found a young man in the next village to be her husband, she stood tractably beside the best rooster, his proxy, and promised before they met that she would be his forever. She was lucky that he was her age and she would be the first wife, an advantage secure now. The night she first saw him, he had sex with her. Then he left for America. She had almost forgotten what he looked like. When she tried to envision him, she only saw the black and white face in the group photograph the men had had taken before leaving.

The other man was not, after all, much different from her husband. They both gave orders: she followed. "If you tell your family, I'll beat you. I'll kill you. Be here again next week." No one talked sex, ever. And she might have separated the rapes from the rest of living if only she did not have to buy her oil from him or gather wood in the same forest. I want her fear to have lasted just as long as rape lasted so that the fear could have been contained. No drawn-out fear. But women at sex hazarded birth and hence lifetimes. The fear did not stop but permeated everywhere. She told the man, "I think I'm pregnant." He organized the raid against her.

On nights when my mother and father talked about their life back home, sometimes they mentioned an "outcast table" whose business they still seemed to be settling, their voices tight. In a commensal tradition, where food is precious, the powerful older people made wrongdoers eat alone. Instead of letting them start separate new lives like the Japanese, who could become samurais and geishas, the Chinese family, faces averted but eyes glowering sideways, hung on to the offenders and fed them left-overs. My aunt must have lived in the same house as my parents and eaten at an outcast table. My mother spoke about the raid as if she had seen it, when she and my aunt, a daughter-in-law to a different household, should not have been living together at all. Daughters-in-law lived with their husbands' parents, not their own; a synonym for marriage in Chinese is "taking a daughter-in-law." Her husband's parents could have sold her, mortgaged her, stoned her. But they had sent her back to her own mother and father, a mysterious act hinting at disgraces not told me. Perhaps they had thrown her out to deflect the avengers.

She was the only daughter; her four brothers went with her father, hus-   20
band, and uncles "out on the road" and for some years became western men. When the goods were divided among the family, three of the brothers took land, and the youngest, my father, chose an education. After my grandparents gave their daughter away to her husband's family, they had dispensed all the adventure and all the property. They expected her alone to keep the traditional ways, which her brothers, now among the barbarians, could fumble without detection. The heavy, deep-rooted women were to maintain the past against the flood, safe for returning. But the rare urge west had fixed upon our family, and so my aunt crossed boundaries not de-lineated in space.

The work of preservation demands that the feelings playing about in one's guts not be turned into action. Just watch their passing like cherry blossoms. But perhaps my aunt, my forerunner, caught in a slow life, let dreams grow and fade and after some months or years went toward what persisted. Fear at the enormities of the forbidden kept her desires delicate, wire and bone. She looked at a man because she liked the way the hair was tucked behind his ears, or she liked the question-mark line of a long torso curving at the shoulder and straight at the hip. For warm eyes or a soft voice or a slow walk—that's all—a few hairs, a line, a brightness, a sound, a pace, she gave up family. She offered us up for a charm that vanished with tiredness, a pigtail that didn't toss when the wind died. Why, the wrong lighting could erase the dearest thing about him.

It could very well have been, however, that my aunt did not take sub-tle enjoyment of her friend, but, a wild woman, kept rollicking company. Imagining her free with sex doesn't fit, though. I don't know any women like that, or men either. Unless I see her life branching into mine, she gives me no ancestral help.

To sustain her being in love, she often worked at herself in the mir-ror, guessing at the colors and shapes that would interest him, changing them frequently in order to hit on the right combination. She wanted to look back.

On a farm near the sea, a woman who tended her appearance reaped a reputation for eccentricity. All the married women blunt-cut their hair in flaps about their ears or pulled it back in tight buns. No nonsense. Neither style blew easily into heart-catching tangles. And at their weddings they displayed themselves in their long hair for the last time. "It brushed the back of my knees," my mother tells me. "It was braided, and even so, it brushed the backs of my knees."

At the mirror my aunt combed individuality into her bob. A bun could   25
have been contrived to escape into black streamers blowing in the wind or in quiet wisps about her face, but only the older women in our picture album wear buns. She brushed her hair back from her forehead, tucking the flaps behind her ears. She looped a piece of thread, knotted into a circle between her index fingers and thumbs, and ran the double strand across her forehead. When she closed her fingers as if she were making a pair of shadow geese bite, the string twisted together catching the little hairs. Then she pulled the thread away from her skin, ripping the hairs out neatly, her eyes watering from the needles of pain. Opening her fingers, she cleaned the thread, then rolled it along her hairline and the tops of the eyebrows. My mother did the same to me and my sisters and herself. I used to believe that the expression "caught by the short hairs" meant a captive held with a depilatory string. It especially hurt at the temples, but my mother said we were lucky we didn't have to have our feet bound when we were seven. Sisters used to sit on their beds and cry together, she said, as their mothers or their slave removed the bandages for a few minutes each night and let the blood gush back into their veins. I hope that the man my aunt loved appreciated a smooth brow, that he wasn't just a tits-and-ass man.

Once my aunt found a freckle on her chin, at a spot that the almanac said predestined her for unhappiness. She dug it out with a hot needle and washed the wound with peroxide.

More attention to her looks than these pullings of hairs and pickings at spots would have caused gossip among the villagers. They owned work clothes and good clothes, and they wore good clothes for feasting the new seasons. But since a woman combing her hair hexes beginnings, my aunt rarely found an occasion to look her best. Women looked like great sea snails—the corded wood, babies, and laundry they carried were the whorls on their backs. The Chinese did not admire a bent back; goddesses and warriors stood straight. Still there must have been a marvelous freeing of beauty when a worker laid down her burden and stretched and arched.

Such commonplace loveliness, however, was not enough for my aunt. She dreamed of a lover for the fifteen days of New Year's, the time for families to exchange visits, money, and food. She plied her secret comb. And sure enough she cursed the year, the family, the village, and herself.

Even as her hair lured her imminent lover, many other men looked at her. Uncles, cousins, nephews, brothers would have looked, too, had they been home between journeys. Perhaps they had already been restraining their curiosity, and they left, fearful that their glances, like a field of nesting birds, might be startled and caught. Poverty hurt, and that was their first reason for leaving. But another, final reason for leaving the crowded house was the never-said.

She may have been unusually beloved, the precious only daughter, 30 spoiled and mirror-gazing because of the affection the family lavished on her. When her husband left, they welcomed the chance to take her back from the in-laws; she could live like the little daughter for just a while longer. There are stories that my grandfather was different from other people, "crazy ever since the little Jap bayoneted him in the head." He used to put his naked penis on the dinner table, laughing. And one day he brought home a baby girl, wrapped up inside his brown western-style greatcoat. He had traded one of his sons, probably my father, the youngest, for her. My grandmother made him trade back. When he finally got a daughter of his own, he doted on her. They must have all loved her, except perhaps my father, the only brother who never went back to China, having once been traded for a girl.

Brothers and sisters, newly men and women, had to efface their sexual color and present plain miens. Disturbing hair and eyes, a smile like no other, threatened the ideal of five generations living under one roof. To focus blurs, people shouted face to face and yelled from room to room. The immigrants I know have loud voices, unmodulated to American tones even after years away from the village where they called their friendships out across the fields. I have not been able to stop my mother's screams in public libraries or over telephones. Walking erect (knees straight, toes pointed forward, not pigeon-toed, which is Chinese-feminine) and speaking in an inaudible voice, I have tried to turn myself American-feminine. Chinese communication was loud, public. Only sick people had to whisper. But at the dinner table, where the family members came nearest one another, no one could talk, not the outcasts nor any eaters. Every word that falls from the mouth is a coin lost. Silently they gave and accepted food with both hands. A preoccupied child who took his bowl with one hand got a sideways glare. A complete moment of total attention is due everyone alike. Children and lovers have no singularity here, but my aunt used a secret voice, a separate attentiveness.

She kept the man's name to herself throughout her labor and dying; she did not accuse him that he be punished with her. To save her inseminator's name she gave silent birth.

He may have been somebody in her own household, but intercourse with a man outside the family would have been no less abhorrent. All the village were kinsmen, and the titles shouted in loud country voices never let kinship be forgotten. Any man within visiting distance would have been neutralized as a lover — "brother," "younger brother," "older brother" — 115 relationship titles. Parents researched birth charts probably not so much to assure good fortune as to circumvent incest in a population that has but one hundred surnames. Everybody has eight million relatives. How useless then sexual mannerisms, how dangerous.

As if it came from an atavism deeper than fear, I used to add "brother" silently to boys' names. It hexed the boys, who would or would not ask me to dance, and made them less scary and as familiar and deserving of benevolence as girls.

But, of course, I hexed myself also — no dates. I should have stood up,   35 both arms waving, and shouted out across libraries, "Hey, you! Love me back." I had no idea, though, how to make attraction selective, how to control its direction and magnitude. If I made myself American-pretty so that the five or six Chinese boys in the class fell in love with me, everyone else — the Caucasian, Negro, and Japanese boys — would too. Sisterliness, dignified and honorable, made much more sense.

Attraction eludes control so stubbornly that whole societies designed to organize relationships among people cannot keep order, not even when they bind people to one another from childhood and raise them together. Among the very poor and the wealthy, brothers married their adopted sisters, like doves. Our family allowed some romance, paying adult brides' prices and providing dowries so that their sons and daughters could marry strangers. Marriage promises to turn strangers into friendly relatives — a nation of siblings.

In the village structure, spirits shimmered among the live creatures, balanced and held in equilibrium by time and land. But one human being flaring up into violence could open up a black hole, a maelstrom that pulled in the sky. The frightened villagers, who depended on one another to maintain the real, went to my aunt to show her a personal, physical representation of the break she made in the "roundness." Misallying couples snapped off the future, which was to be embodied in true offspring. The villagers punished her for acting as if she could have a private life, secret and apart from them.

If my aunt had betrayed the family at a time of large grain yields and peace, when many boys were born, and wings were being built on many houses, perhaps she might have escaped such severe punishment. But the men — hungry, greedy, tired of planting in dry soil, cuckolded — had been forced to leave the village in order to send food-money home. There were ghost plagues, bandit plagues, wars with the Japanese, floods. My Chinese brother and sister had died of an unknown sickness. Adultery, perhaps only a mistake during good times, became a crime when the village needed food.

The round moon cakes and round doorways, the round tables of graduated size that fit one roundness inside another, round windows and rice bowls — these talismans had lost their power to warn this family of the law: A family must be whole, faithfully keeping the descent line by having sons to feed the old and the dead who in turn look after the family. The villagers came to show my aunt and lover-in-hiding a broken house. The villagers were speeding up the circling of events because she was too shortsighted to see that her infidelity had already harmed the village, that waves of consequences would return unpredictably, sometimes in disguise, as now, to hurt her. This roundness had to be made coin-sized so that she would see its circumference: Punish her at the birth of her baby. Awaken her to the inexorable. People who refused fatalism because they could invent small resources insisted on culpability. Deny accidents and wrest fault from the stars.

After the villagers left, their lanterns now scattering in various directions toward home, the family broke their silence and cursed her. "Aiaa, we're going to die. Death is coming. Death is coming. Look what you've done. You've killed us. Ghost! Dead Ghost! Ghost! You've never been born." She ran out into the fields, far enough from the house so that she could no longer hear their voices, and pressed herself against the earth, her own land no more. When she felt the birth coming, she thought that she had been hurt. Her body seized together. "They've hurt me too much," she thought. "This is gall, and it will kill me." With forehead and knees against the earth, her body convulsed and then relaxed. She turned on her back, lay on the ground. The black well of sky and stars went out and out forever; her body and her complexity seemed to disappear. She was one of the stars, a bright dot in blackness, without home, without a companion, in eternal cold and silence. An agoraphobia rose in her, speeding higher and higher, bigger and bigger; she would not be able to contain it; there would be no end to fear.

Flayed, unprotected against space, she felt pain return, focusing her body. This pain chilled her—a cold, steady kind of surface pain. Inside, spasmodically, the other pain, the pain of the child, heated her. For hours she lay on the ground, alternately body and space. Sometimes a vision of normal comfort obliterated reality: She saw the family in the evening gambling at the dinner table, the young people massaging their elders' backs. She saw them congratulating one another, high joy on the mornings the rice shoots came up. When these pictures burst, the stars drew yet further apart. Black space opened.

She got to her feet to fight better and remembered that old-fashioned women gave birth in their pigsties to fool the jealous, pain-dealing gods, who do not snatch piglets. Before the next spasms could stop her, she ran to the pigsty, each step a rushing out into emptiness. She climbed over the fence and knelt in the dirt. It was good to have a fence enclosing her, a tribal person alone.

Laboring, this woman who had carried her child as a foreign growth that sickened her every day, expelled it at last. She reached down to touch the hot, wet, moving mass, surely smaller than anything human, and could feel that it was human after all—fingers, toes, nails, nose. She pulled it up on to her belly, and it lay curled there, butt in the air, feet precisely tucked one under the other. She opened her loose shirt and buttoned the child inside. After resting, it squirmed and thrashed and she pushed it up to her breast. It turned its head this way and that until it found her nipple. There,

40

it made little snuffling noises. She clenched her teeth at its preciousness, lovely as a young calf, a piglet, a little dog.

She may have gone to the pigsty as a last act of responsibility: She would protect this child as she had protected its father. It would look after her soul, leaving supplies on her grave. But how would this tiny child without family find her grave when there would be no marker for her anywhere, neither in the earth nor the family hall? No one would give her a family hall name. She had taken the child with her into the wastes. At its birth the two of them had felt the same raw pain of separation, a wound that only the family pressing tight could close. A child with no descent line would not soften her life but only trail after her, ghostlike, begging her to give it purpose. At dawn the villagers on their way to the fields would stand around the fence and look.

Full of milk, the little ghost slept. When it awoke, she hardened her   45 breasts against the milk that crying loosens. Toward morning she picked up the baby and walked to the well.

Carrying the baby to the well shows loving. Otherwise abandon it. Turn its face into the mud. Mothers who love their children take them along. It was probably a girl; there is some hope of forgiveness for boys.

"Don't tell anyone you had an aunt. Your father does not want to hear her name. She has never been born." I have believed that sex was unspeakable and words so strong and fathers so frail that "aunt" would do my father mysterious harm. I have thought that my family, having settled among immigrants who had also been their neighbors in the ancestral land, needed to clean their name, and a wrong word would incite the kinspeople even here. But there is more to this silence: They want me to participate in her punishment. And I have.

In the twenty years since I heard this story I have not asked for details nor said my aunt's name; I do not know it. People who comfort the dead can also chase after them to hurt them further—a reverse ancestor worship. The real punishment was not the raid swiftly inflicted by the villagers, but the family's deliberately forgetting her. Her betrayal so maddened them, they saw to it that she would suffer forever, even after death. Always hungry, always needing, she would have to beg food from other ghosts, snatch and steal it from those whose living descendants give them gifts. She would have to fight the ghosts massed at crossroads for the buns a few thoughtful citizens leave to decoy her away from village and home so that the ancestral spirits could feast unharassed. At peace, they could act like gods, not ghosts, their descent lines providing them with paper suits and dresses, spirit money, paper houses, paper automobiles, chicken, meat, and rice into eternity—essences delivered up in smoke and flames, steam and incense rising from each rice bowl. In an attempt to make the Chinese care for people outside the family, Chairman Mao encourages us now to give our paper replicas to the spirits of outstanding soldiers and workers, no matter whose ancestors they may be. My aunt remains forever hungry. Goods are not distributed evenly among the dead.

My aunt haunts me—her ghost drawn to me because now, after fifty years of neglect, I alone devote pages of paper to her, though not origamied into houses and clothes. I do not think she always means me well. I am telling on her, and she was a spite suicide, drowning herself in the drinking water. The Chinese are always very frightened of the drowned one, whose weeping ghost, wet hair hanging and skin bloated, waits silently by the water to pull down a substitute.

The Reader's Presence

1. Kingston's account of her aunt's life and death is a remarkable blend of fact and speculation. Consider the overall structure of "No Name Woman." How many versions of the aunt's story do we hear? Where, for example, does the mother's story end? Where does the narrator's begin? Which version do you find more compelling? Why? What does the narrator mean when she says that her mother's stories "tested our strength to establish realities" (paragraph 10)?

2. The narrator's version of her aunt's story is replete with such words and phrases as *perhaps* and *It could very well have been.* The narrator seems far more speculative about her aunt's life than her mother is. At what point does the narrator raise doubts about the veracity of her mother's version of the aunt's story? What purpose does the mother espouse in telling the aunt's story? Is it meant primarily to express family lore? to issue a warning? Point to specific passages to verify your response. What is the proposed moral of the story? Is that moral the same for the mother as for the narrator? Explain.

3. What line does Kingston draw between the two cultures represented in the story: between the mother, a superstitious, cautious Chinese woman, and the narrator, an American-born child trying to "straighten out" her mother's confusing story? How does the narrator resolve the issue by thinking of herself as neither Chinese nor American, but as Chinese American? How does she imagine her relationship to her distant aunt? Compare Kingston's depiction of relationships across generations and cultures to those in N. Scott Momaday's "The Way to Rainy Mountain" (page 487) and to those in Richard Rodriguez's "Aria: A Memoir of a Bilingual Childhood" (page 210). How does language feature in each writer's family? How do problems of comprehension become occasions for creative play in each essay?

THE WRITER AT WORK

Maxine Hong Kingston on Writing for Oneself

In the fire that raged through the Oakland, California, hills in 1991, Maxine Hong Kingston lost, along with her entire house, all her copies of a work in progress. In the following interview conducted by Diane Simmons at Kingston's new home in 1997, the writer discusses how the fire and the loss of her work have transformed her attitude toward her own writing. Confronted with a similar loss (whether the work was on paper or hard drive), most authors would try to recapture as best they could what they had originally written. Why do you think Kingston wants to avoid that sort of recovery? The following exchange is from the opening of that long interview, which appeared in a literary periodical, the Crab Orchard Review *(Spring/Summer 1998). Simmons is the author of* Maxine Hong Kingston *(New York: Twayne Publishers, 1999).*

I began by asking Ms. Kingston to talk about the book that was lost, and where she was going with her recent work.

Kingston: In the book that I lost in the fire, I was working on an idea of finding the book of peace again. There was a myth that there were three lost books of peace and so I was going to find the book of peace for our time. I imagine that it has to do with how to wage peace on earth and that there would be tactics on how to wage peace and how to stop war. I see that the books of war are popular; they are taught in the military academies; they're translated into all different languages. They [are used to] help corporate executives succeed in business. And people don't even think about the books of peace; people don't even know about them. I'm the only one that knows about it.

And so I was writing this and that was what was burned in the fire. What I'm working on now I'm calling *The Fifth Book of Peace.* I'm not recalling and remembering what I had written. To me it's the pleasure of writing to be constantly discovering, going into the new. To recall word by word what I had written before sounds like torture and agony for me. I know I can do it, I'm sure I can do it if I want to. One of my former students volunteered to hypnotize me so I could recall, but that seemed so wrong to me.

Simmons: How much was lost?

Kingston: About 200 written, rewritten pages, so it was very good.   5
But I had wanted to rewrite it again and I think to recall word by word would freeze me into a version and I didn't want to do that.

Simmons: Is the book you are working on now the same project, the same version?

Kingston: Yes, but it is not the same words. It's not the same story. It's the same idea that I want to work on peace. At one point I called it the global novel. But since then I've been thinking of it as a book of peace. And the one big difference is the Book of Peace was a work of fiction. I was imagining fictional characters. But after the fire I wanted to use writing for my personal self. I wanted to write directly what I was thinking and feeling, not imagining fictional other people. I wanted to write myself. I wanted to write in the way I wrote when I was a child which is to say my deepest feelings and thoughts as they could come out in a personal way and not for public consumption. It's not even for other people to read but for myself, to express myself, and it doesn't matter whether this would be published. I don't even want to think about publication or readers, but this is for my own expression of my own suffering or agony.

Simmons: You've said that that's how you wrote in the beginning.

Kingston: I always begin like that. I always have to begin like that. Getting back to the roots of language in myself. It's almost like diary writing which is not for others.

Simmons: You don't mean that you don't want other people to read it necessarily.

Kingston: That's not a consideration. I don't want to think about any of that. I think of this as going back to a primitive state of what writing is for me, which is that I am finding my own voice again.

Simmons: Was it lost?

Kingston: Well, I started not to think about it anymore. After a while I had such an effective public voice, from childhood to now, I had found it and I had created it.

Simmons: Where do we see that public voice?

Kingston: The public voice is the voice that's in all my books.

Simmons: Even *Woman Warrior*?

Kingston: Yes. All my works. That is a public voice. What I mean by the private, personal voice is what I write when I'm trying to figure out things, what I write that's just for me. I get to be the reader and nobody else gets to read this. For years now I have not written in that way. I usually don't write diaries as an adult and so after the fire I needed to get to that again. I had forgotten about it.

Simmons: You are going back to before *Woman Warrior*, to before being a writer.

Kingston: Yes. Before being a writer who publishes.

Simmons: Why do you think the fire caused you to turn away from fiction?

Kingston: At the same time my father died; he died a few weeks before the fire. At that time I felt I'd lost a lot. So I wanted to say what I felt about all that, about all my losses. And I don't see that as writing for publication. I see that as writing for myself, to put into words my losses. And so I started there, and wrote and wrote and wrote. But as I was writing, it became some of the things I was thinking in the book that burned; those would come into the writing, and then of course I go back to that very *id*[1] basic place. I'm old enough and civilized enough now so that the

---

[1] *id:* Latin for *it*; in Freudian psychonalysis it stands for primitive impulses that derive from the unconscious part of the human psyche.

sentences and the words that come out are very elegant, very good, very crafted. I don't return to a place that's not crafted anymore. So all this stuff that I wrote down is going to be part of *The Fifth Book of Peace.*

Abraham Lincoln
Gettysburg Address

Abraham Lincoln (1809–1865), the sixteenth president of the United States, led the country through a bloody civil war in which one side "would make war rather than let the nation survive; and the other would accept war rather than let it perish." During his presidency, Lincoln, who is still widely admired as both a political figure and a writer, wrote notable documents such as the Emancipation Proclamation and several poignant and moving speeches, including the Gettysburg Address.

Four months after the Battle of Gettysburg, Lincoln joined in a dedication of a national cemetery on the battlefield. The "Gettysburg Address," delivered on November 19, 1863, would become one of the most famous—and shortest— speeches given by a U.S. president. The text that follows has been widely accepted as the "final" version of the "Gettysburg Address." It comes from the "Bliss copy" of the speech—the fifth and final version of the text that Lincoln copied out by hand, probably sometime in early 1864.

Four score and seven years ago our fathers brought forth on this continent, a new nation, conceived in Liberty, and dedicated to the proposition that all men are created equal.

Now we are engaged in a great civil war, testing whether that nation, or any nation so conceived and so dedicated, can long endure. We are met on a great battle-field of that war. We have come to dedicate a portion of that field, as a final resting place for those who here gave their lives that that nation might live. It is altogether fitting and proper that we should do this.

But, in a larger sense, we can not dedicate—we can not consecrate— we can not hallow—this ground. The brave men, living and dead, who struggled here, have consecrated it, far above our poor power to add or detract. The world will little note, nor long remember what we say here, but it can never forget what they did here. It is for us the living, rather, to be dedicated here to the unfinished work which they who fought here have thus far so nobly advanced. It is rather for us to be here dedicated to the great task remaining before us—that from these honored dead we take increased devotion to that cause for which they gave the last full measure of devotion—that we here highly resolve that these dead shall not have died in vain—that this nation, under God, shall have a new birth of freedom—and that government of the people, by the people, for the people, shall not perish from the earth.

The Reader's Presence

1. What historical event does Lincoln refer to at the beginning and end of the "Gettysburg Address"? Why do you think he chose to place this information in a position of such prominence? Why is this event relevant to the dedication of a cemetery?

2. Consider Lincoln's strategy of repetition. What phrases and sentence structures does he repeat? What is the effect of the repetition? Read the speech aloud. Do you find the repetition more or less effective when the words are spoken? Why?

3. Compare and contrast the "Gettysburg Address" to Richard Ford's elegy to New Orleans after Hurricane Katrina, "A City Beyond the Reach of Empathy" (page 110). In what ways are Lincoln's words and sentiments echoed by Ford? How are the occasions similar? How are they different? Using the voice of Abraham Lincoln, write a "New Orleans Address." How does it differ from Lincoln's "Gettysburg Address"?

THE WRITER AT WORK

Abraham Lincoln's Hay Draft of the "Gettysburg Address"

Two of the five surviving versions of the "Gettysburg Address" in Lincoln's own handwriting were written down just before or just after he gave the speech on November 19, 1863. Scholars disagree about whether one of these two drafts—known as the "Nicolay Draft" and the "Hay Draft"—might have been the pages Lincoln read from on the field at Gettysburg; both drafts differ somewhat from contemporary accounts of the speech that the president delivered that day. Both also differ from the final "Bliss copy" that has become the standard version of the "Gettysburg Address" (see previous page).

The images on the following pages show the pages of the Hay Draft of the "Gettysburg Address," the second version that Lincoln wrote. Note the additions and changes Lincoln has made to this draft of his speech. Compare this version, written very close to the time of the speech's delivery, with the final version made several months later. As the fame of the "Gettysburg Address" continued to grow, Lincoln kept revising the words for an increasingly wide audience that had not been present to hear him speak. What do Lincoln's continuing revisions suggest about his hopes for this text? Which version do you find more compelling?

Four score and seven years ago our fathers brought forth, upon this continent, a new nation, conceived in Liberty, and dedicated to the proposition that all men are created equal.

Now we are engaged in a great civil war, testing whether that nation, or any nation, so conceived, and so dedicated, can long endure. We are met here on a great battle-field of that war. We have come to dedicate a portion of it, as a final resting place for those who here gave their lives that that nation might live. It is altogether fitting and proper that we should do this.

But in a larger sense we can not dedicate— we can not consecrate— we can not hallow this ground. The brave men, living and dead, who struggled here, have consecrated it far above our poor power to add or detract. The world will little note, nor long remember, what we say here, but can never forget what they did here. It is for us, the living, rather to be dedicated here to the unfinished work, which they have, thus far, so nobly carried on. It is rather *for us to be here dedicated to the great task remaining before us—that from these honored dead we take increased devotion to the cause for which they here gave the last full measure of devotion—that we here highly resolve that these dead shall not have died in vain; that this nation shall have a new birth of freedom, and that this government of the people, by the people, for the people, shall not perish from the earth.*

James McBride

Hip-Hop Planet

Writer, journalist, and musician James McBride (b. 1957) grew up in Harlem in New York City, the son of a black father and a white, Jewish mother, and the eighth of twelve siblings. The title of his best-selling memoir, The Color of Water: A Black Man's Tribute to His White Mother (1996), refers to the answer his mother gave him when he asked about the color of God's skin. McBride's first novel, Miracle of St. Anna (2002) has been made into a film by Spike Lee, scheduled for release in the fall of 2008. His latest novel is Song Yet Sung, published in 2008. McBride began his dual career as journalist and musician early, studying composition at the Oberlin Conservatory of Music in Ohio and receiving his masters in journalism from Columbia University in New York at age 22. He has been a staff writer for the Washington Post, People magazine, and the Boston Globe, and he has written articles for the New York Times, Essence, Rolling Stone, and

*National Geographic, where his essay "Hip-Hop Planet" appeared in April 2007.
McBride is a composer, lyricist, producer, and performer, playing tenor saxophone. He has written for such music luminaries as Anita Baker, Grover Washington Jr., and Gary Burton, and he has recorded and performed with numerous
jazz and pop artists. His collaboration with Ed Shockly on the musical Bobos
won the Stephen Sondheim Award and the Richard Rodgers Foundation Horizon
Award. He holds several honorary doctorates and was appointed a Distinguished
Writer in Residence at New York University in 2005. He is married with three
children and lives in Pennsylvania and New York.*

*McBride often talks about writing in the context of music, likening writing
fiction to playing jazz and, in an interview with Powell's Books, rap music to
storytelling: "The nice thing about rap music, and I know people give rap a bad
rap, good rap that's straight ahead and deals with truth really gets to the point and
takes you places, just like a good book will. And it's all valid. It's no more or less
valid than Def Leppard or Henri Salvador, the French singer. It's all storytelling."*

This is my nightmare: My daughter comes home with a guy and says,
"Dad, we're getting married." And he's a rapper, with a mouthful of gold
teeth, a do-rag on his head, muscles popping out of his arms, and a thug
attitude. And then the nightmare gets deeper, because before you know it,
I'm hearing the pitter-patter of little feet, their offspring, cascading
through my living room, cascading through my life, drowning me with
the sound of my own hypocrisy, because when I was young, I was a
knucklehead, too, hearing my own music, my own sounds. And so I curse
the day I saw his face, which is a reflection of my own, and I rue the day I
heard his name, because I realize to my horror that rap—music seemingly without melody, sensibility, instruments, verse, or harmony, music
with no beginning, end, or middle, music that doesn't even seem to be
music—rules the world. It is no longer my world. It is his world. And I
live in it. I live on a hip-hop planet.

HIGH-STEPPING

I remember when I first heard rap. I was standing in the kitchen at a
party in Harlem. It was 1980. A friend of mine named Bill had just gone
on the blink. He slapped a guy, a total stranger, in the face right in front
of me. I can't remember why. Bill was a fellow student. He was short-
circuiting. Problem was, the guy he slapped was a big guy, dude wearing
a do-rag who'd crashed the party with three friends, and, judging by the
fury on their faces, there would be no Martin Luther King moments in
our immediate future.

There were no white people in the room, though I confess I wished
there had been, if only to hide the paleness of my own frightened face. We
were black and Latino students about to graduate from Columbia University's journalism school, having learned the whos, whats, wheres, and whys
of American reporting. But the real storytellers of the American experience

came from the world of the guy that Bill had just slapped. They lived less than a mile from us in the South Bronx. They had no journalism degrees. No money. No credibility. What they did have, however, was talent.

Earlier that night, somebody tossed a record on the turntable, which sent my fellow students stumbling onto the dance floor, howling with delight, and made me, a jazz lover, cringe. It sounded like a broken record. It was a version of an old hit record called "Good Times," the same four bars looped over and over. And on top of this loop, a kid spouted a rhyme about how he was the best disc jockey in the world. It was called "Rapper's Delight." I thought it was the most ridiculous thing I'd ever heard. More ridiculous than Bill slapping that stranger.

Bill survived that evening, but in many ways, I did not. For the next 26 years, I high-stepped past that music the way you step over a crack in the sidewalk. I heard it pounding out of cars and alleyways from Paris to Abidjan, yet I never listened. It came rumbling out of boomboxes from Johannesburg to Osaka, yet I pretended not to hear. I must have strolled past the corner of St. James Place and Fulton Street in my native Brooklyn where a fat kid named Christopher Wallace, aka Biggie Smalls, stood amusing friends with rhyme, a hundred times, yet I barely noticed. I high-stepped away from that music for 26 years because it was everything I thought it was, and more than I ever dreamed it would be, but mostly, because it held everything I wanted to leave behind.

In doing so, I missed the most important cultural event of my lifetime.

Not since the advent of swing jazz in the 1930s has an American music exploded across the world with such overwhelming force. Not since the Beatles invaded America and Elvis packed up his blue suede shoes has a music crashed against the world with such outrage. This defiant culture of song, graffiti, and dance, collectively known as hip-hop, has ripped popular music from its moorings in every society it has permeated. In Brazil, rap rivals samba in popularity. In China, teens spray-paint graffiti on the Great Wall. In France it has been blamed, unfairly, for the worst civil unrest that country has seen in decades.

Its structure is unique, complex, and at times bewildering. Whatever music it eats becomes part of its vocabulary, and as the commercial world falls into place behind it to gobble up the powerful slop in its wake, it metamorphoses into the Next Big Thing. It is a music that defies definition, yet defines our collective societies in immeasurable ways. To many of my generation, despite all attempts to exploit it, belittle it, numb it, classify it, and analyze it, hip-hop remains an enigma, a clarion call, a cry of "I am" from the youth of the world. We'd be wise, I suppose, to start paying attention.

BURNING MAN

Imagine a burning man. He is on fire. He runs into the room. You put out the flames. Then another burning man arrives. You put him out and go about your business. Then two, three, four, five, ten appear. You extinguish them all, send them to the hospital. Then imagine no one bothers to examine why the men caught fire in the first place. That is the story of hip-hop.

It is a music dipped in the boiling cauldron of race and class, and for   10
that reason it is clouded with mystics, snake oil salesmen, two-bit scholars, race-baiters, and sneaker salesmen, all professing to know the facts, to be "real," when the reality of race is like shifting sand, dependent on time, place, circumstance, and who's telling the history. Here's the real story: In the mid-1970s, New York City was nearly broke. The public school system cut funding for the arts drastically. Gone were the days when you could wander into the band room, rent a clarinet for a minimal fee, and march it home to squeal on it and drive your parents nuts.

The kids of the South Bronx and Harlem came up with something else. In the summer of 1973, at 1595 East 174th Street in the Bronx River Houses, a black teenager named Afrika Bambaataa stuck a speaker in his mother's first-floor living room window, ran a wire to the turntable in his bedroom, and set the housing project of 3,000 people alight with party music. At the same time, a Jamaican teenager named Kool DJ Herc was starting up the scene in the East Bronx, while a technical whiz named Grandmaster Flash was rising to prominence a couple of miles south. The Bronx became a music magnet for Puerto Ricans, Jamaicans, Dominicans, and black Americans from the surrounding areas. Fab 5 Freddy, Kurtis Blow, and Melle Mel were only a few of the pioneers. Grand Wizard Theodore, Kool DJ AJ, the Cold Crush Brothers, Spoony Gee, and the Rock Steady Crew of B-boys showed up to "battle"—dance, trade quips and rhymes, check out each other's records and equipment—not knowing as they strolled through the doors of the community center near Bambaataa's mother's apartment that they were writing musical history. Among them was an MC named Lovebug Starski, who was said to utter the phrase "hip-hop" between breaks to keep time.

This is how it worked: One guy, the DJ, played records on two turntables. One guy—or girl—served as master of ceremonies, or MC. The DJs learned to move the record back and forth under the needle to create a "scratch," or to drop the needle on the record when the beat was the hottest, playing "the break" over and over to keep the folks dancing. The MCs "rapped" over the music to keep the party going. One MC sought to outchat the other. Dance styles were created—"locking" and "popping" and "breaking." Graffiti artists spread the word of the "I" because the music was all about identity: I am the best. I spread the most love in the Bronx, in Harlem, in Queens. The focus initially was not on the MCs, but on the dancers, or B-boys. Commercial radio ignored it. DJs sold mix tapes out of the back of station wagons. "Rapper's Delight" by the Sugarhill Gang—the song I first heard at that face-slapping party in Harlem— broke the music onto radio in 1979.

That is the short history.

The long history is that spoken-word music made its way here on slave ships from West Africa centuries ago: Ethnomusicologists trace hip-hop's roots to the dance, drum, and song of West African griots, or story-tellers, its pairing of word and music the manifestation of the painful journey of slaves who survived the middle passage. The ring shouts, field hollers, and spirituals[1] of early slaves drew on common elements of African music, such as call and response and improvisation. "Speech-song has been part of black culture for a long, long time," says Samuel A. Floyd, director of the Center for Black Music Research at Columbia College in Chicago. The "dozens," "toasts," and "signifying" of black Americans—verbal dueling, rhyming, self-deprecating tales, and stories of blacks outsmarting whites—were defensive, empowering strategies.

You can point to jazz musicians such as Oscar Brown Jr., Edgar "Eddie" Jefferson, and Louis Armstrong, and blues greats such as John Lee Hooker, and easily find the foreshadowing of rap music in the verbal play of their work. Black performers such as poet Nikki Giovanni and Gil Scott-Heron, a pianist and vocalist who put spoken political lyrics to music (most famously in "The Revolution Will Not Be Televised"), elevated spoken word to a new level.

But the artist whose work arguably laid the groundwork for rap as we know it was Amiri Baraka, a beat poet out of Allen Ginsberg's Greenwich Village scene. In the 1950s and '60s, Baraka performed with shrieks, howls, cries, stomps, verse floating ahead of or behind the rhythm, sometimes in staccato syncopation. It was performance art, delivered in a dashiki and Afro, in step with the anger of a bold and sometimes frightening nationalistic black movement, and it inspired what might be considered the first rap group, the Last Poets.

I was 13 when I first heard the Last Poets in 1970. They scared me. To black America, they were like the relatives you hoped wouldn't show up at your barbecue because the boss was there—the old Aunt Clementine who would arrive, get drunk, and pull out her dentures. My parents refused to allow us to play their music in our house—so my siblings waited until my parents went to work and played it anyway. They were the first musical group I heard to use the N-word on a record, with songs like "N——— Are Scared of Revolution." In a world where blacks were evolving from "Negroes" to "blacks," and the assassinations of civil rights leaders Malcolm X and Martin Luther King, Jr., still reverberated in the air like a shotgun blast, the Last Poets embodied black power. Their records consisted of percussion and spoken-word rhyme. They were wildly popular in my neighborhood. Their debut recording sold 400,000

15

[1]*ring shouts, field hollers, and spirituals:* Various types of music and circle dances that drew from African sources but were adapted by slave communities as they developed new forms of expression in the pre–Civil War American South.—EDS.

records in three months, says Last Poet member Umar Bin Hassan. "No videos, no radio play, strictly word of mouth." The group's demise coincided with hip-hop's birth in the 1970s.

It's unlikely that the Last Poets ever dreamed the revolution they sang of would take the form it has. "We were about the movement," Abiodun Oyewoke, a founder of the group, says. "A lot of today's rappers have talent. But a lot of them are driving the car in the wrong direction."

THE CROSSOVER

Highways wrap around the city of Dayton, Ohio, like a ribbon bow-tied on a box of chocolates from the local Esther Price candy factory. They have six ladies at the plant who do just that: Tie ribbons around boxes all day. Henry Rosenkranz can tell you about it. "I love candy," says Henry, a slim white teenager in glasses and a hairnet, as he strolls the factory, bucket in hand. His full-time after-school job is mopping the floors.

Henry is a model American teenager—and the prototypical con-   20
sumer at which the hip-hop industry is squarely aimed, which has his parents sitting up in their seats. The music that was once the purview of black America has gone white and gone commercial all at once. A sea of white faces now rises up to greet rap groups as they perform, many of them teenagers like Henry, a NASCAR fanatic and self-described redneck. "I live in Old North Dayton," he says. "It's a white, redneck area. But hip-hop is so prominent with country people . . . if you put them behind a curtain and hear them talk, you won't know if they're black or white. There's a guy I work with, when Kanye West sings about a gold digger, he can relate because he's paying alimony and child support."

Obviously, it's not just working-class whites, but also affluent, suburban kids who identify with this music with African-American roots. A white 16-year-old hollering rap lyrics at the top of his lungs from the driver's seat of his dad's late-model Lexus may not have the same rationale to howl at the moon as a working-class kid whose parents can't pay for college, yet his own anguish is as real to him as it gets. What attracts white kids to this music is the same thing that prompted outraged congressmen to decry jazz during the 1920s and Tipper Gore[2] to campaign decades later against violent and sexually explicit lyrics: life on the other side of the tracks; its "cool" or illicit factor, which black Americans, like it or not, are always perceived to possess.

Hip-hop has continually changed form, evolving from party music to social commentary with the 1982 release of Grandmaster Flash and the

---

[2]***Tipper Gore:*** Mary Elizabeth ("Tipper") Gore is the wife of former U.S. vice president Al Gore. In 1985 she founded an organization that advocated putting warning labels on albums with explicit lyrics. — EDS.

Furious Five's "The Message." Today, alternative hip-hop artists continue to produce socially conscious songs, but most commercial rappers spout violent lyrics that debase women and gays. Beginning with the so-called gangsta rap of the '90s, popularized by the still unsolved murders of rappers Biggie Smalls and Tupac Shakur, the genre has become dominated by rappers who brag about their lives of crime. 50 Cent, the hip-hop star of the moment, trumpets his sexual exploits and boasts that he has been shot nine times.

"People call hip-hop the MTV music now," scoffs Chuck D., of Public Enemy, known for its overtly political rap. "It's Big Brother controlling you. To slip something in there that's indigenous to the roots, that pays homage to the music that came before us, it's the Mount Everest of battles."

Most rap songs unabashedly function as walking advertisements for luxury cars, designer clothes, and liquor. Agenda Inc., a "pop culture brand strategy agency" listed Mercedes-Benz as the number one brand mentioned in *Billboard*'s top 20 singles in 2005. Hip-hop sells so much Hennessy cognac, listed at number six, that the French makers, deader than yesterday's beer a decade ago, are now rolling in suds. The company even sponsored a contest to win a visit to its plant in France with a famous rapper.

In many ways, the music represents an old dream. It's the pot of gold 25 to millions of kids like Henry, who quietly agonizes over how his father slaves 14 hours a day at two tool-and-die machine jobs to make ends meet. Like teenagers across the world, he fantasizes about working in the hip-hop business and making millions himself.

"My parents hate hip-hop," Henry says, motoring his 1994 Dodge Shadow through traffic on the way home from work on a hot October afternoon. "But I can listen to Snoop Dogg and hear him call women whores, and I know he has a wife and children at home. It's just a fantasy. Everyone has the urge deep down to be a bad guy or a bad girl. Everyone likes to talk the talk, but not everyone will walk the walk."

FULL CIRCLE

You breathe in and breathe out a few times and you are there. Eight hours and a wake-up shake on the flight from New York, and you are on the tarmac in Dakar, Senegal. Welcome to Africa. The assignment: Find the roots of hip-hop. The music goes full circle. The music comes home to Africa. That whole bit. Instead it was the old reporter's joke: You go out to cover a story and the story covers you. The stench of poverty in my nostrils was so strong it pulled me to earth like a hundred-pound ring in my nose. Dakar's Sandaga market is full of "local color"—unless you live there. It was packed and filthy, stalls full of new merchandise surrounded by shattered pieces of life everywhere, broken pipes, bicycle handlebars, fruit flies, soda bottles, beggars, dogs, cell phones. A teenager beggar, his body malformed by polio, crawled by on hands and feet, like a spider. He said, "Hey brother, help me." When I looked into his eyes, they were a bottomless ocean.

The Hotel Teranga is a fortress, packed behind a concrete wall where beggars gather at the front gate. The French tourists march past them, the women in high heels and stonewashed jeans. They sidle through downtown Dakar like royalty, haggling in the market, swimming in the hotel pool with their children, a scene that resembles Birmingham, Alabama in the 1950s—the blacks serving, the whites partying. Five hundred yards away, Africans eat off the sidewalk and sell peanuts for a pittance. There is a restlessness, a deep sense of something gone wrong in the air.

The French can't smell it, even though they've had a mouthful back home. A good amount of the torching of Paris suburbs in October 2005 was courtesy of the children of immigrants from former French African colonies, exhausted from being bottled up in housing projects for generations with no job prospects. They telegraphed the punch in their music— France is the second largest hip-hop market in the world—but the message was ignored. Around the globe, rap music has become a universal expression of outrage, its macho pose borrowed from commercial hip-hop in the U.S.

In Dakar, where every kid is a microphone and turntable away from   30
squalor, and American rapper Tupac Shakur's picture hangs in market stalls of folks who don't understand English, rap is king. There are hundreds of rap groups in Senegal today. French television crews troop in and out of Dakar's nightclubs filming the kora harp lute[3] and *tama*[4] talking drum with regularity. But beneath the drumming and the dance lessons and the jingling sound of tourist change, there is a quiet rage, a desperate fury among the Senegalese, some of whom seem to bear an intense dislike of their former colonial rulers.

"We know all about French history," says Abdou Ba, a Senegalese producer and musician. "We know about their kings, their castles, their art, their music. We know everything about them. But they don't know much about us."

Assane N'Diaye, 19, loves hip-hop music. Before he left his Senegalese village to work as a DJ in Dakar, he was a fisherman, just like his father, like his father's father before him. Tall, lean, with a muscular build and a handsome chocolate face, Assane became a popular DJ, but the equipment he used was borrowed, and when his friend took it back, success eluded him. He has returned home to Toubab Dialaw, about 25

---

[3]*kora harp lute:* In West Africa, a popular 21-string instrument played with both hands and used by storytellers and bards.—EDS.

[4]*tama:* A flexible West African drum, known as a "talking drum," popular in Senegal; it is placed under the shoulder and can be manipulated to produce a wide range of tones and sounds.—EDS.

miles south of Dakar, a village marked by a huge boulder, perhaps 40 feet high, facing the Atlantic Ocean.

About a century and a half ago, a local ruler led a group of people fleeing slave traders to this place. He was told by a white trader to come here, to Toubab Dialaw. When he arrived, the slavers followed. A battle ensued. The ruler fought bravely but was killed. The villagers buried him by the sea and marked his grave with a small stone, and over the years it is said to have sprouted like a tree planted by God. It became a huge, arching boulder that stares out to sea, protecting the village behind it. When the fishermen went deep out to sea, the boulder was like a lighthouse that marked the way home. The Great Rock of Toubab Dialaw is said to hold a magic spirit, a spirit that Assane N'Diaye believes in.

In the shadow of the Great Rock, Assane has built a small restaurant, Chez Las, decorated with hundreds of seashells. It is where he lives his hip-hop dream. At night, he and his brother and cousin stand by the Great Rock and face the sea. They meditate. They pray. Then they write rap lyrics that are worlds away from the bling-bling culture of today's commercial hip-hoppers. They write about their lives as village fishermen, the scarcity of catch forcing them to fish in deeper and deeper waters, the hardship of fishing for 8, 10, 14 days at a time in an open pirogue in rainy season, the high fee they pay to rent the boat, and the paltry price their catches fetch on the market. They write about the humiliation of poverty, watching their town sprout up around them with rich Dakarians and richer French. And they write about the relatives who leave in the morning and never return, surrendered to the sea, sharks, and God.

The dream, of course, is to make a record. They have their own demo, their own logo, and their own name, Salam T. D. (for Toubab Dialaw). But rap music represents a deeper dream: a better life. "We want money to help our parents," Assane says over dinner. "We watch our mothers boil water to cook and have nothing to put in the pot." 35

He fingers his food lightly. "Rap doesn't belong to American culture," he says. "It belongs here. It has always existed here, because of our pain and our hardships and our suffering."

On this cool evening in a restaurant above their village, these young men, clad in baseball caps and T-shirts, appear no different from their African-American counterparts, with one exception. After a dinner of chicken and rice, Assane says something in Wolof[5] to the others. Silently and without ceremony, they take every bit of the leftover dinner—the half-eaten bread, rice, pieces of chicken, the chicken bones—and dump them into a plastic bag to give to the children in the village. They silently rise from the table and proceed outside. The last I see of them, their regal figures are outlined in the dim light of the doorway, heading out to the darkened village, holding on to that bag as though it held money.

---

[5]**Wolof:** The most widely used language in Senegal; "banana" is a Wolof word.—Eds.

THE CITY OF GODS

Some call the Bronx River Houses the City of Gods, though if God has been by lately, he must've slipped out for a chicken sandwich. The 10 drab, red-brick buildings spread out across 14 acres, coming into view as you drive east across the East 174th Street Bridge. The Bronx is the hallowed holy ground of hip-hop, the place where it all began. Visitors take tours through this neighborhood now, care of a handful of fortyish "old-timers," who point out the high and low spots of hip-hop's birthplace.

It is a telling metaphor for the state of America's racial landscape that you need a permit to hold a party in the same parks and playgrounds that produced the music that changed the world. The rap artists come and go, but the conditions that produced them linger. Forty percent of New York City's black males are jobless. One in three black males born in 2001 will end up in prison. The life expectancy of black men in the U.S. ranks below that of men in Sri Lanka and Colombia. It took a massive hurricane in New Orleans for the United States to wake up to its racial realities.

That is why, after 26 years, I have come to embrace this music I tried   40
so hard to ignore. Hip-hop culture is not mine. Yet I own it. Much of it I hate. Yet I love it, the good of it. To confess a love for a music that, at least in part, embraces violence is no easy matter, but then again our national anthem talks about bombs bursting in air, and I love that song, too. At its best, hip-hop lays bare the empty moral cupboard that is our generation's legacy. This music that once made visible the inner culture of America's greatest social problem, its legacy of slavery, has taken the dream deferred to a global scale. Today, 2 percent of the Earth's adult population owns more than 50 percent of its household wealth, and indigenous cultures are swallowed with the rapidity of a teenager gobbling a bag of potato chips. The music is calling. Over the years, the instruments change, but the message is the same. The drums are pounding out a warning. They are telling us something. Our children can hear it.

They question is: Can we?

The Reader's Presence

1. "Hip-Hop Planet" features a popular topic covered by an experienced journalist. What characteristics of the selection seem to belong to the personal essay? What characteristics seem to belong to a journalistic article? How are these two components of the selection brought together? Would you prefer if the selection used only a single method—for example, interviews and information told in the third person without a personal response? Explain why or why not.

2. Discuss McBride's attitude toward hip-hop. Why did he dislike it at first? What did he come to admire about it? What does McBride

still not like about the music? What does he think about today's commercial rap artists? In what ways do they differ from the groups McBride enjoys most? How would you describe the differences? Do those differences matter to you?

3. Compare McBride's evaluation of hip-hop culture to Will Wright's discussion of video games in "Dream Machines" (page 605). Clearly, both hip-hop and video games — as each author claims — are tremendously popular among youth. After considering both selections, make a list of what you think both forms of popular entertainment, as different as they seem at first, have in common.

Charles McGrath

The Pleasures of the Text

Writer and editor Charles McGrath (b. 1947) is writer-at-large for the New York Times *and former editor of the* New York Times Book Review. *McGrath's career as a literary critic and journalist began after graduation from Yale University, when he joined the* New Yorker *as deputy editor, a position he held from 1974 to 1997. His articles appear regularly in the* New York Times Magazine *where the essay, "The Pleasures of the Text," was first published in January 2006.*

There used to be an ad on subway cars, next to the ones for bail bondsmen and hemorrhoid creams, that said: "if u cn rd ths u cn gt a gd job & mo pay." The ad was promoting a kind of stenography training that is now extinct, presumably. Who uses stenographers anymore? But the notion that there might be value in easily understood shorthand has proved to be prescient. If u cn rd these days, and just as important, if your thumbs are nimble enough so that u cn als snd, you can conduct your entire emotional life just by transmitting and receiving messages on the screen of your cellphone. You can flirt there, arrange a date, break up and — in Malaysia at least — even get a divorce.

Shorthand contractions, along with letter-number homophones ("gr8" and "2moro," for example), emoticons (like the tiresome colon-and-parenthesis smiley face) and acronyms (like the ubiquitous "lol," for "laughing out loud"), constitute the language of text-messaging — or txt msg, to use the term that txt msgrs prefer. Text-messaging is a refinement of computer instant-messaging, which came into vogue five or six years

ago. But because the typical cell phone screen can accommodate no more
than 160 characters, and because the phone touchpad is far less versatile
than the computer keyboard, text-messaging puts an even greater premium on concision. Here, for example, is a text-message version of "Paradise Lost" disseminated by some scholars in England: "Devl kikd outa
hevn coz jelus of jesus&strts war. pd'off wiv god so corupts man (md by
god) wiv apel, devl stays serpnt 4hole life&man ruind. Woe un2mnkind."

As such messages go, that one is fairly straightforward and un-
adorned. There is also an entire code book of acronyms and abbreviations, ranging from CWOT (complete waste of time) to DLTBBB (don't
let the bedbugs bite). And emoticonography has progressed way beyond
the smiley-face stage, and now includes hieroglyphics to indicate drool-
ing, for example (:-) . . .), as well as secrecy (:X), Hitler (/.#( ) and the rose
(@};—). Keep these in mind; we'll need them later.

As with any language, efficiency isn't everything. There's also the
issue of style. Among inventive users, and the younger ones especially,
text-messaging has taken on many of the characteristics of hip-hop, with
so much of which it conveniently overlaps — in the substitution of "z"
for "s," for example, "a," for "er," and "d" for "th." Like hip-hop,
text-messaging is what the scholars call "performative"; it's writing that
aspires to the condition of speech. And sometimes when it makes abun-
dant use of emoticons, it strives not for clarity so much as a kind of
rebus-like cleverness, in which showing off is part of the point. A text-
message version of "Paradise Lost" — or of the prologue, anyway — that
tries for little more than shnizzle might go like this: "Sing hvnly mewz dat
on d :X mtntp inspyrd dat shephrd hu 1st tot d chozn seed in d begnin hw
d hvn n erth @};— outa chaos."[1]

Not that there is much call for Miltonic messaging these days. To use   5
the scholarly jargon again, text-messaging is "lateral" rather than "pene-
trative," and the medium encourages blandness and even mindlessness.
On the Internet there are several Web sites that function as virtual Hallmark stores and offer ready-made text messages of breathtaking banality.
There are even ready-made Dear John letters, enabling you to dump
someone without actually speaking to him or her. Far from being considered rude, in Britain this has proved to be a particularly popular way of
ending a relationship — a little more thoughtful than leaving an e-mail
message but not nearly as messy as breaking up in person — and it's also
catching on over here.

Compared with the rest of the world, Americans are actually laggards
when it comes to text-messaging. This is partly for technical reasons. Because we don't have a single, national phone company, there are several
competing and incompatible wireless technologies in use, and at the same

---

[1]*"Sing hvnly . . . outa chaos":* From the prologue of John Milton's epic, *Paradise Lost*
(1667). "Sing Heav'nly Muse, that on the secret top / Of Oreb, or of Sinai, didst inspire /
That Shepherd, who first taught the chosen Seed, / In the beginning how the Heav'ns and
Earth / Rose out of Chaos." —EDS.

time actual voice calls are far cheaper here than in most places, so there is less incentive for texting. But in many developing countries, mobile-phone technology has so far outstripped land-line availability that cell-phones are the preferred, and sometimes the only, means of communication, and text messages are cheaper than voice ones. The most avid text-messagers are clustered in Southeast Asia, particularly in Singapore and the Philippines.

There are also cultural reasons for the spread of text-messaging elsewhere. The Chinese language is particularly well-suited to the telephone keypad, because in Mandarin the names of the numbers are also close to the sounds of certain words; to say "I love you," for example, all you have to do is press 520. (For "drop dead," it's 748.) In China, moreover, many people believe that to leave voice mail is rude, and it's a loss of face to make a call to someone important and have it answered by an underling. Text messages preserve everyone's dignity by eliminating the human voice.

This may be a universal attraction of text-messaging, in fact: it's a kind of avoidance mechanism that preserves the feeling of communication—the immediacy—without, for the most part, the burden of actual intimacy or substance. The great majority of text messages are of the "Hey, how are you, whassup?" variety, and they're sent sometimes when messenger and recipient are within speaking distance of each other—across classrooms, say, or from one row of a stadium to another. They're little electronic waves and nods, aren't meant to do much more than establish a connection—or disconnection, as the case may be—without getting into specifics.

"We're all wired together" is the collective message, and we'll signal again in a couple of minutes, not to say anything, probably, but just to make sure the lines are still working. The most depressing thing about the communications revolution is that when at last we have succeeded in making it possible for anyone to reach anyone else anywhere and at any time, it turns out that we really don't have much we want to say.

The Reader's Presence

1. In 1854, Henry David Thoreau wrote in his classic memoir, *Walden*: "Our inventions are wont to be pretty toys which distract our attention from serious things. . . . We are in great haste to construct a magnetic telegraph from Maine to Texas; but Maine and Texas, it may be, have nothing important to communicate." In what ways does Thoreau's remark anticipate the point McGrath makes in his essay? What does it say about advances in technology?

2. What does McGrath find missing in text-messaging? What do you think he means when he calls it an "avoidance mechanism" (paragraph 8)? What is being avoided? Do you agree with McGrath?

Why or why not? Can you offer counterarguments that would suggest the advantages text-messaging offers human communication?

3. In paragraph 4, McGrath says that "text-messaging has taken on many of the characteristics of hip-hop." What similarities does McGrath suggest? After reading McBride's essay "Hip-Hop Planet" (page 463), discuss the ways these two methods of communication are similar. Does McBride write anything about hip-hop that supports McGrath's comparison?

Louis Menand

Name That Tone

Pulitzer Prize–winning author, critic, and educator Louis Menand (b. 1952) has written and taught extensively on nineteenth- and twentieth-century cultural history and literature. He is the editor of numerous books on these subjects, including Pragmatism: A Reader *(1996),* The Future of Academic Freedom *(1997), and* The Cambridge History of Literary Criticism, Volume 7: Modernism and the New Criticism *(2000), and author of* Discovering Modernism: T. S. Eliot and His Context *(1987),* American Studies *(2002), and* The Metaphysical Club: A Story of Ideas *(2002), for which he won the 2002 Pulitzer Prize for History. Menand's essay, "Name That Tone," appeared in June 2006 in the "Talk of the Town" section of the* New Yorker, *where he is a staff writer. Prior to joining the* New Yorker *in 1991, Menand was an associate editor at the* New Republic, *and a contributing editor at the* New York Review of Books. *He is currently a professor of English and American literature and language at Harvard University, and he has taught at the Graduate Center of the City University of New York, Princeton University, Columbia University, and the University of Virginia School of Law.*

In an interview for Publisher's Weekly, *Menand wrote about his dual career as writer and academician: "I don't think of there being any division between my academic career and my career in journalism. To me, I'm just a writer. . . . And it happens that some of my interests are relatively scholarly and some are not."*

There is a new cell-phone ring tone that can't be heard by most people over the age of twenty, according to an NPR report. The tone is derived from something called the Mosquito, a device invented by a Welsh security firm for the noble purpose of driving hooligans, yobs, scamps, ne'er-do-wells, scapegraces, ruffians, tosspots, and bravos away from places where grownups are attempting to ply an honest trade. The device emits a seventeen-kilohertz buzz, a pitch that is too high for older ears to register but, as we learn from additional reporting by the *Times*, is "ear-splitting" for younger people. A person or persons unknown have produced a copy of the Mosquito buzz for use as a cell-phone ring tone, evidently with the idea that it will enable students to receive notification of text messages while sitting in class, without the knowledge of the teacher.

The *Times*, in a welcome but highly uncharacteristic embrace of anarchy, celebrated this development as an ingenious guerrilla tactic in youth's eternal war against adult authority—"a bit of technojujitsu," as the paper put it. But it's not entirely clear which side is the winner here. When you hear the tone, it apparently sets your teeth on edge, which means that, if the entire class suddenly grimaces, it's a good bet that one of the students just got a text message. (Which probably says "sup." Youth, as George Bernard Shaw[1] correctly observed, is wasted on the young.) Anyway, what was wrong with "vibrate only"?

The real interest of the story, of course, lies elsewhere. The news is not that students are fooling their teachers, which was never news, even in ancient Greece, or that technology is rapidly unraveling the fabric of trust and respect on which civil society depends which everyone already knows. It is that one more way for middle-aged people to feel that they're losing it has been discovered. The public concern over natural hearing loss—the *Times* explains that the medical term is "presbycusis"—is part of a trend that started when Bob Dole[2] told the nation that he had trouble getting an erection. Now television commercials inform us that thirty million American men may have trouble getting an erection. Wow. And these are big, friendly, touch-football-playing guys, with George Clooney smiles and luscious, adoring, patient wives. Decay is everywhere discussed, though it is always, weirdly, disguised. Young women with luminous skin explain the importance of fighting premature wrinkling. Thirty is the new forty. We know that this is just anxiety manufactured to sell products, but it does have an impact. People worry about being old before they get old. Americans are living longer but, somehow, aging sooner.

People tend to regard the gradual yet irreversible atrophying of their faculties as a bad thing. Is it, though? Sure, it's tied up with stuff that you don't want to think too much about. One day, you learn that you can't hear a sound that is perfectly audible to teen-agers and dogs. (Any significance in that symmetry, by the way? Do we feel diminished as a species because dogs can hear a noise that we can't?) Soon after that, you realize that you have forgotten how to calculate the area of a triangle, and how many pints there are in a quart. From there, it's not too long until you find that you are unable to stop talking about real estate, which is the

---

[1]*Shaw:* A world-renowned Irish playwright, Shaw (1856–1950) was applauded for his wit and memorable quotations.—EDS.

[2]*Dole:* The former U.S. Senator from Kansas was born in 1923; he ran for president on the Republican ticket in 1996, losing to Bill Clinton.—EDS.

first step down an increasingly rocky and overgrown path that leads, almost always—all right, always—to death. What is there to like about any
of this?

Well, first of all, who *wants* to hear someone else's cell phone? The   5
Mosquito tone is like the squirrel's heartbeat that George Eliot[3] refers to
in "Middlemarch": "If we had a keen vision and feeling of all ordinary
human life, it would be like hearing the grass grow and the squirrel's
heart beat, and we should die of that roar which lies on the other side of
silence. As it is, the quickest of us walk about well wadded with stupidity." The Mosquito tone is one of those things you're better off not
knowing. The world is probably full of such things (though how would
you know?). Maybe the area of a triangle isn't that important, either.
Maybe, in the end, it *is* all about real estate.

The point is that mental and physical development never stops, no
matter how old you are, and development is one of the things that make
it interesting to be a being. We imagine that we change our opinions or
our personalities or our taste in music as we ripen, often feeling that we
are betraying our younger selves. Really, though, our bodies just change,
and that is what changes our views, our temperament, and our tolerance
for Billy Joel. We can't help it. The chemistry has altered.

This means that some things that were once present to us become invisible, go off the screen; the compensation is that new things swim into
view. Ramps[4] are an example. Try getting a teen-ager to appreciate a grilled
ramp. Try getting a teen-ager to appreciate another person, for that matter. We may lose hormones, but we gain empathy. The deficits, in other
words, are not all at one end of the continuum. Readers who are over
twenty may not hear the new ring tone; if they had it on their phones, it
might as well be silent. But most readers who are under the age of twenty
will not be able to "hear" this Comment. Yes, they will see the words,
and they will imagine that they are reading something, and that it makes
sense; but they can never truly "get it." The Comment is simply beyond
the range of their faculties. For all intents and purposes, if you're under
twenty, this page might as well be blank.

The Reader's Presence

1. What does Menand claim is the "real interest" (paragraph 3) of
the news story about cell-phone ring tones that adults cannot
hear? How does his essay go about examining that "real interest"?

---

[3]*George Eliot:* The pen name of the esteemed British novelist, Mary Ann Evans
(1819–1880). Her major novel *Middlemarch* was published in 1872.—EDS.

[4]*ramps:* A plant native to America that is a member of the leek and onion family and
has become fashionable on restaurant menus.—EDS.

What aspects of his examination do you find humorous? What serious issues does he introduce?

2. How do you interpret the last four sentences of Menand's essay? Are they meant to be funny? Do you agree with his conclusion? Explain why or why not. Has he offered any evidence to support it? How would you summarize his overall assessment of teenagers?

3. Compare Menand's essay to Charles McGrath's essay "The Pleasures of the Text" (page 473). What do these short essays have in common? How would you describe the authors' attitudes toward technology? Provide specific quotations from each essay that you think best demonstrate each author's position. In your opinion, what attitudes toward young people characterize the essays?

Hanna Miller

American Pie

Foodie and food writer Hanna Miller Raskin was born in Ann Arbor, Michigan, in 1976. She received a degree in American history from Oberlin College in 1998 and a master's degree from the Cooperstown Graduate Program in American History Museum Studies in 2002. Her master's thesis "Identity Takeout: How American Jews Made Chinese Food Their Ethnic Cuisine" was published in the Journal of Popular Culture. *Using the name Hanna Rachel Raskin, she now lives in Asheville, North Carolina, where she is restaurant critic and food editor of the alternative weekly,* Mountain Xpress. *She also founded and directs American Culinary Tours, which escorts food-loving clients on "gastronomic adventures." Miller has explored the culinary heritage ("and good eating spots") of a variety of regions from Kentucky's Bourbon Trail to the Memphis barbeque scene. She continues to write about twentieth-century ethnic American food for such publications as* Repast *and* American Heritage, *where her essay, "American Pie," first appeared in 2006.*

Almost every American food—from egg foo young to empanadas—is covered in the phone book under the generic heading "Restaurants." Only pizza stands alone. Pizza, a Johnny-come-lately compared with such long-standing national favorites as the hamburger and hot dog, has secured a special place on the American table. Everybody likes pizza. Even those who claim to be immune to its charms must deign to have the occasional slice; a staggering 93 percent of Americans eat pizza at least once a month. According to one study, each man, woman, and child consumes an average of 23 pounds of pie every year.

But pizza wasn't always so popular. Food writers in the 1940s who were worldly enough to take note of the traditional Italian treat struggled to explain the dish to their readers, who persisted in imagining oversized apple-pie crusts stuffed with tomatoes and coated with cheese. "The pizza could be as popular a snack as the hamburger if Americans only knew about it," the *New York Times* lamented in 1947, illustrating its plaint with a photograph of a pie subdivided into dozens of canapé-sized slices.

That writer's wistful tone was supplanted in a very few years by a weary one, as culinary chroniclers became jaded by the nation's voracious appetite for pizza and the pie's never-ending parade of variations. "The highly seasoned pizza with its tough crust and tomato topping is such a gastronomical craze that the open pie threatens the preeminence of the hot dog and hamburger," the *Times* reported in a 1953 story about "what is perhaps inevitable — a packaged pizza mix."

Pizza had wedged its way into the nation's hearts and stomachs almost overnight, a phenomenon befitting a food that become synonymous with quick and easy. Americans seeking fun in the years after World War II found a good measure of it in pizza, a food that when eaten correctly (a matter of some debate among 1950s advice columnists) forced the diner's lips into a broad smile. Pizza, like teenagedom and rock 'n' roll, is a lasting relic of America's mid-century embrace of good times.

Modern pizza originated in Italy, although the style favored by Americans is more a friend than a relative of the traditional Neapolitan pie. Residents of Naples took the idea of using bread as a blank slate for relishes from the Greeks, whose bakers had been dressing their wares with oils, herbs, and cheese since the time of Plato. The Romans refined the recipe, developing a delicacy known as *placenta*, a sheet of fine flour topped with cheese and honey and flavored with bay leaves. Neapolitans earned the right to claim pizza as their own by inserting a tomato into the equation. Europeans had long shied away from the New World fruit, fearing it was plump with poison. But the intrepid citizens of Naples discovered the tomato was not only harmless but delicious, particularly when paired with pizza.

Cheese, the crowning ingredient, was not added until 1889, when the Royal Palace commissioned the Neapolitan *pizzaiolo* Raffaele Esposito to create a pizza in honor of the visiting Queen Margherita. Of the three contenders he created, the Queen strongly preferred a pie swathed in the colors of the Italian flag: red (tomato), green (basil), and white (mozzarella).

Thus ends the story of pizza, according to most histories of the pie. It's not a bad story, but it's only the beginning; Esposito's adventures in patriotic baking have little to do with why American pizza makers are taxed to exhaustion every Super Bowl Sunday.

·LOMBARDI'S in 1905·

Pizza crossed the Atlantic with the four million Italians who by the 1920s had sought a better life on American shores. Most Italians weren't familiar with the many regional variations their fragmented homeland had produced, but a longing for pan-Italian unity inspired a widespread embrace of a simplified pizza as their "national" dish. Fraternal "pizza and sausage" clubs, formed to foster Italian pride, sprouted in cities across the Northeast. Women got in on it too, participating in communal pizza exchanges in which entrants competed with unique pies, some molded into unusual shapes, some with the family name baked into the dough.

Although non-Italians could partake of pizza as early as 1905, when the venerable Lombardi's—the nation's first licensed pizzeria—opened its doors in Lower Manhattan, most middle-class Americans stuck to boiled fish and toast. The pungent combination of garlic and oregano signaled pizza as "foreign food," sure to upset native digestions. If pizza hoped to gain an American following beyond New York City and New Haven, it would have to become less like pizza. By the 1940s a few entrepreneurs had initiated the transformation, starting a craze that forever changed the American culinary landscape.

The modern pizza industry was born in the Midwest, not coincidentally a place of sparse Italian settlement. Although pizza had pushed into the suburbs as second-generation Italians relocated, most of the heartland was pizza-free. Its inhabitants had neither allegiance nor aversion to the traditional pie. The region also boasted an enviable supply of cheese.

10

Despite such advantages, Ike Sewell still wasn't thinking pies when he partnered with Ric Riccardo to open a Chicago restaurant. Sewell, a native of Texas, planned on offering a menu of Mexican specialties. Riccardo willingly agreed, having never tried Mexican food. His first meal changed his mind so completely that, he liked to say later, he fled to Italy to recover from it. While there, he sampled classic Neapolitan pizza and found it much better than Sewell's Mexican offerings. Sewell eventually agreed to forgo enchiladas for pizza, but not until he'd inflated the thin-crusted Neapolitan recipe to make it more palatable to Americans. "Ike tasted it and said nobody would eat it, it's not enough," Evelyne Slomon, author of *The Pizza Book*, said. "So he put gobs and gobs of stuff on it."

Sewell's lightly seasoned deep-dish pie, introduced in 1943, the signature item at Pizzeria Uno, was the first true American pizza. The pie was a uniquely Chicago institution, like a perennially losing major-league baseball team, that other cities showed no interest in adopting. Until Uno's opened its first location outside Chicago in 1979, people had to go to East Ohio Street to sample anything like Sewell's idea of a pie. But its success liberated pizzeria owners nationwide to tinker with their product, ultimately paving the way for the megafranchises.

Sewell was followed in the next two decades by scores of independent operators who deleted the traditional herbs and went easy on the garlic in hopes of gaining a bigger clientele. Pizza was no longer the province of first- and second-generation Italians. Americans of every ancestry wanted a slice of this pie. "I make any kinda pizza you want," the New York pizzeria owner Patsy D'Amore told the *Saturday Evening Post* in 1957. "One day a man order a lox pizza with cream cheese. It turn my stomach, but I make it for him." Professional pizza chefs like the unnamed Japanese-American woman who stumped the panel of the TV show "What's My Line?" in 1956, and the Mexican-Americans who helped make pizza the second-best seller at the 1952 Texas State Fair (edged out only by the irresistible corn dog), and fledgling franchises like Pizza Hut, gradually shed all Italian imagery from their advertising campaigns.

But despite the best entrepreneurial efforts, most Americans remained unfamiliar with pizza well into the 1940s. "We had to give it away at first," Eugenia DiCarlo told a McNeese State University interviewer of her husband's attempt to establish a pizzeria in Lake Charles, Louisiana, in 1947. "They had never, never heard of it down here. And, boy, every time they'd take a piece of it, they liked it. And more and more liked it, told other people, and then we got to the place where that was the biggest part of our business."

The urge to tell other people that pizza was apparently a universal   15
impulse that seized knowing literati like Ora Dodd—who in 1949 penned a two-page paean for the *Atlantic Monthly*: "It is piping hot; the brown crust holds a bubbling cheese-and-tomato filling. There is a wonderful savor of fresh bread, melted cheese and herbs. This is a *pizza*"—and World War II servicemen retiring from Italy. Veterans ranging from the lowliest private to Dwight D. Eisenhower talked up pizza.

Led by the servicemen's newfound cravings, Americans timidly sampled their first pies. Most weren't crisp, bathed in olive oil, or sprinkled with mozzarella; if cooks followed the advice offered by *Good Housekeeping* in 1951, their pizzas were biscuit rounds or English muffins topped with processed Cheddar cheese, chili sauce, salt, pepper, and salad oil. Cooks could also opt to add deviled ham, stuffed olives, or canned tuna to the "cheese treatment."

Americans who ate at any one of the country's rapidly proliferating pizzerias (the number of parlors in the United States skyrocketed from 500 in 1934 to 20,000 in 1956) enjoyed a pie that cut a neat compromise between the traditional Italian pizza and *Good Housekeeping*'s "Yankee" variety. Pizzas at the Pennsylvania parlor where Andy Zangrilli got his first job were massive rectangles speckled with slithery pepperoni disks. "It was a hit," said Zangrilli, who today owns a chain of pizzerias. "If you didn't like the pepperoni, you'd take it off. It was the Model T of food."

Unlike other ethnically derived foods that enjoyed faddish popularity in modern America, pizza never masqueraded as exotic. Its consumers didn't aspire to be cosmopolitan or courageous. They were simply drawn in by the bewitching interplay of tomatoes, bread, and cheese—drawn in so strongly that by 1958 the novelty singer Lou Monte could issue an album called *Songs for Pizza Lovers*.

But it wasn't just the taste that Americans liked. The social aspect of the pie appealed to a nation riding the postwar boom economy. It seemed uniquely suited to the fun that defined the 1950s, easy for "the gang" to share and informal enough to figure in slumber parties and sock hops. While the early New York pizzerias has been forced to sell by the slice to draw lunchtime business, most pies outside the five boroughs were sold whole, making it nearly impossible to eat pizza alone (although Jackie Gleason attributed his girth to having accomplished the feat many times, sometimes within the span of a single meal).

"I call it happy food," Slomon said. "It's a communal thing. You can have two people enjoying a pizza or you can have a group." Sophia Loren in 1959 told the *Los Angeles Times* that having been raised in Italy to consider pizza the food of poverty, she pitied Americans when she saw how many pizza joints they had. "So I think America not so rich after all. Then I find eating pizza here is like eating hot dog—for fun." 20

Eliminating cutlery made pizza eating seem raffish to more staid diners. Although Dear Abby[1] urged her readers to respect the pizza as a pie and reach for a fork, the etiquette authority Amy Vanderbilt condoned eating slices "out of hand," adding that "pizza tastes best as a finger food." *Look* magazine in 1954 published an illustrated step-by-step guide, instructing readers to hold pizza from "the arc edge," rather than the measly

---

[1]**Dear Abby:** Abigail Van Buren, the pseudonym for Pauline Esther Friedman Phillips (b. 1918), who began writing the "Dear Abby" syndicated personal advice column in 1956.—EDS.

tip, and "roll it in a log." Bob Hope still had reservations when his buddy Jerry Colonna prepared a pie. "It's a tough baby to cut," Hope complained. "I never cut it," Colonna responded. "It's hand food. Chew it down and have fun."

Pizzeria owners accelerated the fun by hiring dough-tossing showmen to divert patrons by spinning pies skyward, sometimes sending the dough 12 feet into the air (and creating an overly dry pizza in the process). Tossers such as Aldo Formica, who demonstrated his talent on Tennessee Ernie Ford's television show, became second-rung celebrities. "Then it started coming out that maybe the guy with the hairy arms in the dough wasn't turning people on, and maybe he was turning people off," the pizza consultant John Correll said of the tosser's ultimate disappearance from the scene. "But pizza has stayed locked in to the image of fun and frolic."

The image was polished in 1953 when Dean Martin swung his way through "That's Amore!," an Italian-flavored love song that famously compared the moon to "a big pizza pie" (a phrase that irritated exacting food writers, who insisted it was redundant).

By the mid-1950s pizza was everywhere. Although it would be another decade before baseball stadiums and zoos offered the snack, political parties, fundraising groups, and synagogue sisterhoods were plying their members with pizza. Fun and flavor aside, the price was right: Zangrilli sold two slices at his Pennsylvania State College parlor for a quarter. "Pizza fits students' needs perfectly," Zangrilli said. Sometimes too perfectly, as a 1950s Atlanta restaurateur discovered when he added pizza to his menu and immediately attracted hordes of Georgia Tech students who would congregate around a single pie and linger for hours. He dropped the pies.

An anonymous pizza baker in 1957 blamed James Dean for inducting teens into the pizza fraternity. "Jimmy loved pizza," he complained to the *Saturday Evening Post*. "His fans knew that, so they loved it too." Pizza was pitched as the ideal snack for hard-to-please high schoolers by companies such as General Mills, whose Betty Crocker character appeared in a 1960 comic strip to solve the "Problem of the Puzzled Parent," who is perplexed by what to serve her daughters' friends after a roller-skating outing. What do "most teenagers" like? she wonders. Refrigerated pizza dough, Betty Crocker assures her. Betty is proved right, as always. "Gee, Mrs. Steward, you sure know what's good," one handsome teen raves (although he disconcertingly appears to be eyeing her twin daughters rather than her pie). By 1963 pizza was a staple of the school lunch menu. The American School Foodservice Association that year announced it was bested only by hamburgers and hot dogs in the cafeteria popularity contest.

Adults weren't ready to cede pizza to children, though. People of every age and income bracket went for it, as Lucille Ball,[2] who met her

25

---

[2]***Ball:*** Lucille Ball (1911–1989) was one of America's most popular comediennes; a film, television, stage, and radio actress; and star of such iconic sitcoms as *I Love Lucy, The Lucy–Desi Comedy Hour, The Lucy Show,* and *Here's Lucy.* — EDS.

second husband, Gary Morton, on a blind date in a pizza parlor, could attest. George Liberace[3] was so enamored with pizza that in 1959 he contemplated abandoning the brothers Liberace to open a parlor, reconsidering only when brother Lee, the pianist of the duo, teased him ruthlessly.

Pizza's mid-century journey from unknown to unparalleled was captured in a raucous 1956 skit aired on "Caesar's Hour," the show's second gag that year grounded in pizza adoration. Pizza was to Sid Caesar's[4] writing team what domestic tranquility was to the creative staff over at "The Adventures of Ozzie and Harriet": a source of endless inspiration. In "The Commuters," three couples are absorbed in a competitive Scrabble game. The word *pizza* is played, but nobody's sure how to spell the name of their new favorite food (the word routinely shows up on first-grade spelling lists today). So the couples consult a dictionary, taking care not to drool on the definition. The men, now rapturous at the thought of a pie, flee for the nearest pizzeria, promising to return with pizza for everyone. This being comedy, they hit a snag on the way home: Their car breaks down, and the pizzas are in danger of getting wet. One of the men decides to shield the pizzas beneath the hood, a bit of chivalry that manages to jump-start the engine. Powered by pizza, the men arrive home to find their wives asleep, to be awoken only by having fragrant slices of pizza dragged beneath their noses. Pizza was a dream come true.

The premise of Caesar's skit quickly became dated as Tom Monaghan institutionalized the innovation that transformed America's infatuation with pizza into a lasting relationship: home delivery. In 1960 Monaghan and his brother James bought an Ypsilanti, Michigan, pizza joint called Dominick's (James traded his share to Tom one year later in exchange for a Volkswagen Beetle). According to Correll, Monaghan was forced to rechristen the store as Domino's when Dominick complained he was "besmirching his name" with a lousy product. But Monaghan wasn't fixated on quality: He decided to best the competition by offering free delivery, a service that every major chain later added to its repertoire. Pizza purveyors tested lots of new concepts in the 1970s and '80s: There were restaurants that explicitly wedded pizza to entertainment, such as Chuck E. Cheese's, where a life-sized rat boogied through the arcade, and restaurants that emphasized fresh and novel ingredients, such as California Pizza Kitchen, home to the caramelized pear and gorgonzola pie. Nothing, however, has yet supplanted the large pepperoni pie delivered hot within the hour as the quintessential American pizza experience.

Pizza's firm hold on the American appetite is unlikely to slip anytime soon. With very little nudging from pizza marketers, Americans have

---

[3]*George Liberace:* Wladziu Valentino Liberace (1919–1987), a popular entertainer and pianist.—EDS.

[4]*Caesar:* Isaac Sidney Caesar (b. 1922), an American comic actor and writer celebrated for the 1950s television series *Your Show of Shows* and *Caesar's Hour;* more recently as Coach Calhoun in *Grease* and *Grease 2.*—EDS.

made pizza the traditional food of the emerging national holiday Super Bowl Sunday; almost 70 percent of viewers eat pizza while watching the game. Both spontaneous and economical, ordering pizza remains a signifier of carefree camaraderie; pizza seems to automatically make any event a little more fun. "We will have PIZZA(!)," the Carleton College history department announced last year in a memo meant to lure students to a meeting. It's hard to imagine fried chicken or tofu having the same drawing power. "Pizza is more popular than ever," Slomon said. Not bad for a food that most Americans had to have explained to them just 50 years ago.

The Reader's Presence

1. Miller presents a brief but fact-filled history of how pizza "wedged its way" into American hearts and stomachs. What factors made pizza so appetizing to the American public across nationalities? How does Miller set up the history she recounts? She equates pizza with "teenagedom and rock 'n' roll" as "a lasting relic of America's mid-century embrace of good times" (paragraph 4). Comment on Miller's use of the word "relic" here. What associations does the word evoke? What other choices in diction and imagery (metaphor and simile, for example) does she make that reinforce the historical points she emphasizes? Point to specific words and phrases. Andy Zangrilli, the owner of "a chain of pizzerias," observes that pizza "was the Model T of food" (paragraph 17). What is the implication of this metaphor? What other metaphors can you summon to describe the role of pizza in the American diet?

2. Miller writes a delightful history of the origins — and presence — of pizza as a culinary staple in American life. How does she establish a presence for herself in the first paragraph of this essay? What do you notice about the choices she makes as a writer here? Consider, for example, her use of surprising information, her deft handling of irony and tone, as well as the verbs and nouns she places strategically in her opening sentences. After you have analyzed her compositional choices in the opening paragraph, reread the remainder of the essay. Which of these features does Miller continue to draw on as she recounts the history of a food that is consumed "at least once a month" by a "staggering 93 percent of Americans" (paragraph 1)? For example, how effectively does Miller incorporate such statistics into her essay? Point to specific instances and comment on what they contribute to her essay.

3. Consider the social dimensions of food. In what ways does pizza reflect class issues? In what ways does it transcend such issues? Near the end of her essay, Miller turns to examples of the ways in

which pizza has been integrated into American popular culture. Comment on the effectiveness of the examples Miller presents from such early television shows as those of Lucille Ball, Ozzie and Harriet, and Sid Caesar. Explain how Miller uses these references to transition into another facet of the history of pizza.

4. Pizza is one of the foods Lars Eighner discusses in his essay "On Dumpster Diving" (page 355). Eighner, much like Miller, is interested in the history of particular food products but for vastly different reasons. Consider the relationship Eighner and Miller establish both with food and with their audiences. To what extent do these writers consider themselves similar to—or different from— their readers in matters of taste and in their respective sensitivity to matters of history and the culinary arts?

N. Scott Momaday

The Way to Rainy Mountain

N. Scott Momaday (b. 1934) was born on a Kiowa Indian reservation in Oklahoma and grew up surrounded by the cultural traditions of his people. He has taught at the University of California, Berkeley; Stanford University; Columbia University, Princeton University, and the University of Arizona. His first novel, House Made of Dawn *(1968), won a Pulitzer Prize. The author of poetry and autobiography, Momaday has edited a collection of Kiowa oral literature. His books include* Ancestral Voice: Conversations with N. Scott Momaday *(1989),* The Ancient Child *(1989),* In the Presence of the Sun: Stories and Poems *(1991),* Circle of Wonder: A Native American Christmas Story *(1994),* The Man Made of Words: Essays, Stories, Passages *(1997), and* In the Bear's House *(1999). "The Way to Rainy Mountain" appears as the introduction to the book of that name, published in 1969. Among his more recent books is a collection of Momaday's plays,* Three Plays: The Indolent Boy, Children of the Sun, and the Moon in Two Windows *(2007) and* Four Arrows and Magpie *(2006), a book for young children, which he also illustrated. In 2007, Momaday was awarded the National Medal of Arts, "for his writings and his work that celebrate and preserve Native American art and oral tradition."*

Momaday thinks of himself as a storyteller. When asked to compare his written voice with his speaking voice, he replied, "My physical voice is something that bears on my writing in an important way. I listen to what I write. I work with it until it is what I want it to be in my hearing. I think that the voice of my writing

is very much like the voice of my speaking. And I think in both cases it's distinc-
tive. At least, I mean for it to be. I think that most good writers have individual
voices, and that the best writers are those whose voices are most distinctive—
most recognizably individual."

A single knoll rises out of the plain in Oklahoma, north and west of
the Wichita Range. For my people, the Kiowas, it is an old landmark, and
they gave it the name Rainy Mountain. The hardest winter in the world
is there. Winter brings blizzards, hot tornadic winds arise in the spring,
and in summer the prairie is an anvil's edge. The grass turns brittle and
brown, and it cracks beneath your feet. There are green belts along the
rivers and creeks, linear groves of hickory and pecan, willow and witch
hazel. At a distance in July or August, the steaming foliage seems almost
to writhe in fire. Great green and yellow grasshoppers are everywhere in
the tall grass, popping up like corn to sting the flesh, and tortoises crawl
about on the red earth, going nowhere in plenty of time. Loneliness is an
aspect of the land. All things in the plain are isolate; there is no confusion
of objects in the eye, but *one* hill or *one* tree or *one* man. To look upon
that landscape in the early morning, with the sun at your back, is to lose
the sense of proportion. Your imagination comes to life, and this, you
think, is where Creation was begun.

I returned to Rainy Mountain in July. My grandmother had died in
the spring, and I wanted to be at her grave. She had lived to be very old
and at last infirm. Her only living daughter was with her when she died,
and I was told that in death her face was that of a child.

I like to think of her as a child. When she was born, the Kiowas were
living the last great moment of their history. For more than a hundred
years they had controlled the open range from the Smoky Hill River to the
Red, from the headwaters of the Canadian to the fork of the Arkansas and
Cimarron. In alliance with the Comanches, they had ruled the whole of
the southern Plains. War was their sacred business, and they were among
the finest horsemen the world has ever known. But warfare for the Kiowas
was pre-eminently a matter of disposition rather than of survival, and they
never understood the grim, unrelenting advance of the U.S. Cavalry. When
at last, divided and ill-provisioned, they were driven onto the Staked Plains
in the cold rains of autumn, they fell into panic. In Palo Duro Canyon they
abandoned their crucial stores to pillage and had nothing then but their
lives. In order to save themselves, they surrendered to the soldiers of Fort
Sill and were imprisoned in the old stone corral that now stands as a military museum. My grandmother was spared the humiliation of those high
gray walls by eight or ten years, but she must have known from birth the
affliction of defeat, the dark brooding of old warriors.

Her name was Aho, and she belonged to the last culture to evolve in
North America. Her forebears came down from the high country in western Montana nearly three centuries ago. They were a mountain people, a
mysterious tribe of hunters whose language has never been positively clas-

sified in any major group. In the late seventeenth century they began a long migration to the south and east. It was a journey toward the dawn, and it led to a golden age. Along the way the Kiowas were befriended by the Crows, who gave them the culture and religion of the Plains. They acquired horses, and their ancient nomadic spirit was suddenly free of the ground. They acquired Tai-me, the sacred Sun Dance doll, from that moment the object and symbol of their worship, and so shared in the divinity of the sun. Not least, they acquired the sense of destiny, therefore courage and pride. When they entered upon the southern Plains they had been transformed. No longer were they slaves to the simple necessity of survival; they were a lordly and dangerous society of fighters and thieves, hunters and priests of the sun. According to their origin myth, they entered the world through a hollow log. From one point of view, their migration was the fruit of an old prophecy, for indeed they emerged from a sunless world.

Although my grandmother lived out her long life in the shadow of Rainy Mountain, the immense landscape of the continental interior lay like memory in her blood. She could tell of the Crows, whom she had never seen, and of the Black Hills, where she had never been. I wanted to see in reality what she had seen more perfectly in the mind's eye, and traveled fifteen hundred miles to begin my pilgrimage.

Yellowstone, it seemed to me, was the top of the world, a region of deep lakes and dark timber, canyons and waterfalls. But, beautiful as it is, one might have the sense of confinement there. The skyline in all directions is close at hand, the high wall of the woods and deep cleavages of shade. There is a perfect freedom in the mountains, but it belongs to the eagle and the elk, the badger and the bear. The Kiowas reckoned their stature by the distance they could see, and they were bent and blind in the wilderness.

Descending eastward, the highland meadows are a stairway to the plain. In July the inland slope of the Rockies is luxuriant with flax and buckwheat, stonecrop and larkspur. The earth unfolds and the limit of the land recedes. Clusters of trees, and animals grazing far in the distance, cause the vision to reach away and wonder to build upon the mind. The sun follows a longer course in the day, and the sky is immense beyond all comparison. The great billowing clouds that sail upon it are shadows that move upon the grain like water, dividing light. Farther down, in the land of the Crows and Blackfeet, the plain is yellow. Sweet clover takes hold of the hills and bends upon itself to cover and seal the soil. There the Kiowas paused on their way; they had come to the place where they must change their lives. The sun is at home on the plains. Precisely there does it have the certain character of a god. When the Kiowas came to the land of the Crows, they could see the dark lees of the hills at dawn across the Bighorn River, the profusion of light on the grain shelves, the oldest deity ranging after the solstices. Not yet would they veer southward to the caldron of the land that lay below; they must wean their blood from the

northern winter and hold the mountains a while longer in their view. They
bore Tai-me in procession to the east.

A dark mist lay over the Black Hills, and the land was like iron. At
the top of the ridge I caught sight of Devil's Tower upthrust against the
gray sky as if in the birth of time the core of the earth had broken
through its crust and the motion of the world was begun. There are
things in nature that engender an awful quiet in the heart of man; Devil's
Tower is one of them. Two centuries ago, because they could not do otherwise, the Kiowas made a legend at the base of the rock. My grandmother said:

> Eight children were there at play, seven sisters and their brother.
> Suddenly the boy was struck dumb; he trembled and began to run upon
> his hands and feet. His fingers became claws, and his body was covered
> with fur. Directly there was a bear where the boy had been. The sisters
> were terrified; they ran, and the bear ran after them. They came to the
> stump of a great tree, and the tree spoke to them. It bade them climb
> upon it, and as they did so it began to rise into the air. The bear came to
> kill them, but they were just beyond its reach. It reared against the tree
> and scored the bark all around with its claws. The seven sisters were
> borne into the sky, and they became the stars of the Big Dipper.

From that moment, and so long as the legend lives, the Kiowas have
kinsmen in the night sky. Whatever they were in the mountains, they
could be no more. However tenuous their well-being, however much
they had suffered and would suffer again, they had found a way out of the
wilderness.

My grandmother had a reverence for the sun, a holy regard that now
is all but gone out of mankind. There was a wariness in her, and an ancient awe. She was a Christian in her later years, but she had come a long
way about, and she never forgot her birthright. As a child she had been
to the Sun Dances; she had taken part in those annual rites, and by them
she had learned the restoration of her people in the presence of Tai-me.
She was about seven when the last Kiowa Sun Dance was held in 1887
in the Washita River above Rainy Mountain Creek. The buffalo were
gone. In order to consummate the ancient sacrifice — to impale the head
of a buffalo bull upon the medicine tree — a delegation of old men jour-
neyed into Texas, there to beg and barter for an animal from the Good-
night herd. She was ten when the Kiowas came together for the last time
as a living Sun Dance culture. They could find no buffalo; they had to
hang an old hide from the sacred tree. Before the dance could begin, a
company of soldiers rode out from Fort Sill under orders to disperse the
tribe. Forbidden without cause the essential act of their faith, having seen
the wild herds slaughtered and left to rot upon the ground, the Kiowas
backed away forever from the medicine tree. That was July 20, 1890, at
the great bend of the Washita. My grandmother was there. Without bitterness, and for as long as she lived, she bore a vision of deicide.

Now that I can have her only in memory, I see my grandmother in the several postures that were peculiar to her: standing at the wood stove on a winter morning and turning meat in a great iron skillet; sitting at the south window, bent above her beadwork, and afterwards, when her vision failed, looking down for a long time into the fold of her hands; going out upon a cane, very slowly as she did when the weight of age came upon her; praying. I remember her most often at prayer. She made long, rambling prayers out of suffering and hope, having seen many things. I was never sure that I had the right to hear, so exclusive were they of all mere custom and company. The last time I saw her she prayed standing by the side of her bed at night, naked to the waist, the light of a kerosene lamp moving upon her dark skin. Her long, black hair, always drawn and braided in the day, lay upon her shoulders and against her breasts like a shawl. I do not speak Kiowa, and I never understood her prayers, but there was something inherently sad in the sound, some merest hesitation upon the syllables of sorrow. She began in a high and descending pitch, exhausting her breath to silence; then again and again — and always the same intensity of effort, of something that is, and is not, like urgency in the human voice. Transported so in the dancing light among the shadows of her room, she seemed beyond the reach of time. But that was illusion; I think I knew then that I should not see her again.

Houses are like sentinels in the plain, old keepers of the weather watch. There, in a very little while, wood takes on the appearance of great age. All colors wear soon away in the wind and rain, and then the wood is burned gray and the grain appears and the nails turn red with rust. The windowpanes are black and opaque; you imagine there is nothing within, and indeed there are many ghosts, bones given up to the land. They stand here and there against the sky, and you approach them for a longer time than you expect. They belong in the distance; it is their domain.

Once there was a lot of sound in my grandmother's house, a lot of coming and going, feasting and talk. The summers there were full of excitement and reunion. The Kiowas are a summer people; they abide the cold and keep to themselves, but when the season turns and the land becomes warm and vital they cannot hold still; an old love of going returns upon them. The aged visitors who came to my grandmother's house when I was a child were made of lean and leather, and they bore themselves upright. They wore great black hats and bright ample shirts that shook in the wind. They rubbed fat upon their hair and wound their braids with strips of colored cloth. Some of them painted their faces and carried the scars of old and cherished enmities. They were an old council of warlords, come to remind and be reminded of who they were. Their wives and daughters served them well. The women might indulge themselves; gossip was at once the mark and compensation of their servitude. They made loud and elaborate talk among themselves, full of jest and gesture, fright and false alarm. They went abroad in fringed and flowered shawls, bright beadwork and German silver. They were at home in the kitchen, and they prepared meals that were banquets.

There were frequent prayer meetings, and great nocturnal feasts. When I was a child I played with my cousins outside, where the lamplight fell upon the ground and the singing of the old people rose up around us and carried away into the darkness. There were a lot of good things to eat, a lot of laughter and surprise. And afterwards, when the quiet returned, I lay down with my grandmother and could hear the frogs away by the river and feel the motion of the air.

Now there is a funereal silence in the rooms, the endless wake of some final word. The walls have closed in upon my grandmother's house. When I returned to it in mourning, I saw for the first time in my life how small it was. It was late at night, and there was a white moon, nearly full. I sat for a long time on the stone steps by the kitchen door. From there I could see out across the land; I could see the long row of trees by the creek, the low light upon the rolling plains, and the stars of the big dipper. Once I looked at the moon and caught sight of a strange thing. A cricket had perched upon the handrail, only a few inches away from me. My line of vision was such that the creature filled the moon like a fossil. It had gone there, I thought, to live and die, for there, of all places, was its small definition made whole and eternal. A warm wind rose up and purled like the longing within me.

The next morning I awoke at dawn and went out on the dirt road to   15
Rainy Mountain. It was already hot, and the grasshoppers began to fill the air. Still, it was early in the morning, and the birds sang out of the shadows. The long yellow grass on the mountain shone in the bright light, and a scissortail hied above the land. There, where it ought to be, at the end of a long and legendary way, was my grandmother's grave. Here and there on the dark stones were ancestral names. Looking back once, I saw the mountain and came away.

The Reader's Presence

1. Momaday tells several stories in this selection, including the history of the Kiowa people, the story of his grandmother's life and death, the story of his homecoming, and the legend of Devil's Tower. How does each story overlap and intertwine with the others? What forces compel the telling or creation of each story? What needs do the stories satisfy? Look, for example, at the legend related in paragraph 8. The Kiowas made this legend "because they could not do otherwise." Why could they have not done otherwise? How does this embedded legend enhance and complicate the other stories Momaday tells here?

2. From the beginning of this essay, Momaday sets his remarks very firmly in space and then in time. Discuss the importance of physical space in this essay. Why does Momaday take the journey to Rainy Mountain—a fifteen-hundred-mile "pilgrimage" (paragraph 5)? Why does he say that his grandmother's vision of this landscape is more perfect than his, even though she has never actually seen the landscape he travels? Consider the many remarks about perspective, and change of perspective, that Momaday includes, as well as his remarks on proportion. What significance does he attach to these remarks? More generally, consider the temporal journeys that run parallel to the spatial journeys: the Kiowas' "journey toward the dawn [that] led to a golden age" (paragraph 4) and Momaday's own journeys that he relates in the essay. How would you characterize the sense of space and time and the relation between the two that are conveyed in this essay?

3. In the interview quoted in the introductory note to this selection, Momaday talks about capturing his speaking voice in his writing. What are some of the phrases and passages that make you hear his distinctive voice as you read? Point to—and analyze—specific words and phrases to discuss how Momaday creates the effect he is aiming for. Compare Momaday's voice to Calvin Trillin's in "A Traditional Family" (page 545). What common techniques do these writers use to make their prose appealing to the reader's ear?

Azar Nafisi

From *Reading* Lolita *in Tehran*

Azar Nafisi (b. 1950) was raised in Tehran, Iran, and educated in England and the United States. Having returned to Iran in the 1970s to teach English literature, she experienced firsthand the revolution and its aftermath, when strict Islamic religious codes were imposed; the harshest restrictions were placed on women. Nafisi has said that "before the revolution I had an image of myself as a woman, as a writer, as an academician, as a person with a set of values." Afterward, even the smallest public gestures were forbidden, from kissing her husband in public to shaking hands with a colleague. Fearing she would "become someone who was a stranger to herself," Nafisi resigned her university position in 1995 and for two

years took a group of her best students "underground" for weekly discussions of
Western authors, including Vladimir Nabokov, the author of Lolita *and the sub-*
ject of Nafisi's scholarly work.

"Unfortunately you have to be deprived of something in order to understand
its worth," Nafisi told an interviewer. "I think if a civilization or a culture does
not take its own works of literature seriously it goes downhill. You need imagina-
tion in order to imagine a future that doesn't exist."

Nafisi left Iran with her family in 1997. She is currently a Visiting Fellow at
the Foreign Policy Institute of the Johns Hopkins University School of Advanced
International Studies and the director of the Dialogue Project, an education and
policy initiative for the development of democracy and human rights in the Mus-
lim world. This essay, adapted from Nafisi's memoir Reading Lolita *in* Tehran
(2003), first appeared in the Chronicle of Higher Education.

In the fall of 1995, after resigning from my last academic post, I decided to indulge myself and fulfill a dream. I chose seven of my best and
most committed students and invited them to come to my home every
Thursday morning to discuss literature. They were all women—to teach a
mixed class in the privacy of my home was too risky, even if we were discussing harmless works of fiction.

For nearly two years, almost every Thursday morning, rain or shine,
they came to my house, and almost every time, I could not get over the
shock of seeing them shed their mandatory veils and robes and burst into
color. When my students came into that room, they took off more than
their scarves and robes. Gradually, each one gained an outline and a
shape, becoming her own inimitable self. Our world in that living room
with its window framing my beloved Elburz Mountains became our sanc-
tuary, our self-contained universe, mocking the reality of black-scarved,
timid faces in the city that sprawled below.

The theme of the class was the relationship between fiction and reality. We would read Persian classical literature, such as the tales of our own
lady of fiction, Scheherazade, from *A Thousand and One Nights*, along
with Western classics—*Pride and Prejudice, Madame Bovary, Daisy
Miller, The Dean's December*, and *Lolita*, the work of fiction that perhaps
most resonated with our lives in the Islamic Republic of Iran. For the first
time in many years, I felt a sense of anticipation that was not marred by
tension: I would not need to go through the tortuous rituals that had
marked my days when I taught at the university—rituals governing what I
was forced to wear, how I was expected to act, the gestures I had to remember to control.

Life in the Islamic Republic was as capricious as the month of April,
when short periods of sunshine would suddenly give way to showers and
storms. It was unpredictable: The regime would go through cycles of
some tolerance, followed by a crackdown. Now, in the mid-1990s, after a
period of relative calm and so-called liberalization, we had again entered
a time of hardships. Universities had once more become the targets of attack by the cultural purists, who were busy imposing stricter sets of laws,

going so far as to segregate men and women in classes and punishing disobedient professors.

The University of Allameh Tabatabai, where I had been teaching   5
since 1987, had been singled out as the most liberal university in Iran. It
was rumored that someone in the Ministry of Higher Education had asked,
rhetorically, if the faculty at Allameh thought they lived in Switzerland.
Switzerland had somehow become a byword for Western laxity. Any program or action that was deemed un-Islamic was reproached with a mocking reminder that Iran was by no means Switzerland.

The pressure was hardest on the students. I felt helpless as I listened
to their endless tales of woe. Female students were being penalized for
running up the stairs when they were late for classes, for laughing in the
hallways, for talking to members of the opposite sex. One day Sanaz had
barged into class near the end of the session, crying. In between bursts
of tears, she explained that she was late because the female guards at
the door, finding a blush in her bag, had tried to send her home with a
reprimand.

Why did I stop teaching so suddenly? I had asked myself this question
many times. Was it the declining quality of the university? The ever-increasing indifference among the remaining faculty members and students?
The daily struggle against arbitrary rules and restrictions?

I often went over in my mind the reaction of the university officials
to my letter of resignation. They had harassed and limited me in all manner of ways, monitoring my visitors, controlling my actions, refusing
my long-overdue tenure; and when I resigned, they infuriated me by suddenly commiserating and by refusing to accept my resignation. The students had threatened to boycott classes, and it was of some satisfaction
to me to find out later that despite threats of reprisals, they in fact did
boycott my replacement. Everyone thought I would break down and
eventually return. It took two more years before they finally accepted my
resignation.

Teaching in the Islamic Republic, like any other vocation, was subservient to politics and subject to arbitrary rules. Always, the joy of teaching was marred by diversions and considerations forced on us by the
regime — how well could one teach when the main concern of university
officials was not the quality of one's work but the color of one's lips, the
subversive potential of a single strand of hair? Could one really concentrate on one's job when what preoccupied the faculty was how to
excise the word "wine" from a Hemingway story, when they decided not
to teach Brontë because she appeared to condone adultery?

In selecting students for study in my home, I did not take into consid-   10
eration their ideological or religious backgrounds. Later, I would count it
as the class's great achievement that such a mixed group, with different
and at times conflicting backgrounds, personal as well as religious and social, remained so loyal to its goals and ideals. One reason for my choice

of these particular girls was the peculiar mixture of fragility and courage I sensed in them. They were what you would call loners, who did not belong to any particular group or sect. I admired their ability to survive not despite but in some ways because of their solitary lives.

One of the first books we read was Nabokov's *Invitation to a Beheading*. Nabokov creates for us in this novel not the actual physical pain and torture of a totalitarian regime but the nightmarish quality of living in an atmosphere of perpetual dread. Cincinnatus C. is frail, he is passive, he is a hero without knowing or acknowledging it: He fights with his instincts, and his acts of writing are his means of escape. He is a hero because he refuses to become like all the rest.

We formed a special bond with Nabokov despite the difficulty of his prose. This went deeper than our identification with his themes. His novels are shaped around invisible trapdoors, sudden gaps that constantly pull the carpet from under the reader's feet. They are filled with mistrust of what we call everyday reality, an acute sense of that reality's fickleness and frailty. There was something, both in his fiction and in his life, that we instinctively related to and grasped, the possibility of a boundless freedom when all options are taken away.

Nabokov used the term "fragile unreality" to explain his own state of exile; it also describes our existence in the Islamic Republic of Iran. We lived in a culture that denied any merit to literary works, considering them important only when they were handmaidens to something seemingly more urgent—namely, ideology. This was a country where all gestures, even the most private, were interpreted in political terms. The colors of my head scarf or my father's tie were symbols of Western decadence and imperialist tendencies. Not wearing a beard, shaking hands with members of the opposite sex, clapping or whistling in public meetings, were likewise considered Western and therefore decadent, part of the plot by imperialists to bring down our culture.

Our class was shaped within this context. There, in that living room, we rediscovered that we were also living, breathing human beings; and no matter how repressive the state became, no matter how intimidated and frightened we were, like Lolita we tried to escape and to create our own little pockets of freedom. And, like Lolita, we took every opportunity to flaunt our insubordination: by showing a little hair from under our scarves, insinuating a little color into the drab uniformity of our appearances, growing our nails, falling in love, and listening to forbidden music.

How can I create this other world outside the room? I have no choice 15
but to appeal to your imagination. Let's imagine one of the girls, say Sanaz, leaving my house, and let us follow her from there to her final destination. She says her goodbyes and puts on her black robe and scarf over her orange shirt and jeans, coiling her scarf around her neck to cover her huge gold earrings. She directs wayward strands of hair under the scarf, puts her notes into her large bag, straps it on over her shoulder, and

walks out into the hall. She pauses for a moment on top of the stairs to put on thin, lacy, black gloves to hide her nail polish.

We follow Sanaz down the stairs, out the door, and into the street. You might notice that her gait and her gestures have changed. It is in her best interest not to be seen, not to be heard or noticed. She doesn't walk upright, but bends her head toward the ground and doesn't look at passers-by. She walks quickly and with a sense of determination. The streets of Tehran and other Iranian cities are patrolled by militia, who ride in white Toyota patrols—four gun-carrying men and women, sometimes followed by a minibus. They are called the Blood of God. They patrol the streets to make sure that women like Sanaz wear their veils properly, do not wear makeup, do not walk in public with men who are not their fathers, brothers, or husbands. If she gets on a bus, the seating is segregated. She must enter through the rear door and sit in the back seats, allocated to women.

You might well ask, What is Sanaz thinking as she walks the streets of Tehran? How much does this experience affect her? Most probably, she tries to distance her mind as much as possible from her surroundings. Perhaps she is thinking of her distant boyfriend and the time when she will meet him in Turkey. Does she compare her own situation with her mother's when she was the same age? Is she angry that women of her mother's generation could walk the streets freely, enjoy the company of the opposite sex, join the police force, become pilots, live under laws that were among the most progressive in the world regarding women? Does she feel humiliated by the new laws, by the fact that after the revolution, the age of marriage was lowered from eighteen to nine, that stoning became once more the punishment for adultery and prostitution?

In the course of nearly two decades, the streets have been turned into a war zone, where young women who disobey the rules are hurled into patrol cars, taken to jail, flogged, fined, forced to wash the toilets and humiliated—and, as soon as they leave, they go back and do the same thing. Is she aware, Sanaz, of her own power? Does she realize how dangerous she can be when her every stray gesture is a disturbance to public safety? Does she think how vulnerable are the Revolutionary Guards, who for over eighteen years have patrolled the streets of Tehran and have had to endure young women like herself, and those of other generations, walking, talking, showing a strand of hair just to remind them that they have not converted?

These girls had both a real history and a fabricated one. Although they came from very different backgrounds, the regime that ruled them had tried to make their personal identities and histories irrelevant. They were never free of the regime's definition of them as Muslim women.

Take the youngest in our class, Yassi. There she is, in a photograph I have of the students, with a wistful look on her face. She is bending her head to one side, unsure of what expression to choose. She is wearing a thin white-and-gray scarf, loosely tied at the throat—a perfunctory homage to her family's strict religious background. Yassi was a freshman who audited   20 my graduate courses in my last year of teaching. She felt intimidated by the older students, who, she thought, by virtue of their seniority, were blessed not only with greater knowledge and a better command of English but also with more wisdom. Although she understood the most difficult texts better than many of the graduate students, and although she read the texts more dutifully and with more pleasure than most, she felt secure only in her terrible sense of insecurity.

About a month after I had decided privately to leave Allameh Tabatabai, Yassi and I were standing in front of the green gate at the entrance of the university. What I remember most distinctly about the university now is that green gate. I owe my memory of that gate to Yassi: She mentioned it in one of her poems. The poem is called "How Small Are the Things That I Like." In it, she describes her favorite objects—an orange backpack, a colorful coat, a bicycle just like her cousin's—and she also describes how much she likes to enter the university through the green gate. The gate appears in this poem, and in some of her other writings, as a magical entrance into the forbidden world of all the ordinary things she had been denied in life.

Yet that green gate was closed to her, and to all my girls. Next to the gate there was a small opening with a curtain hanging from it. Through this opening all the female students went into a small, dark room to be inspected. Yassi would describe later what was done to her in this room: "I would first be checked to see if I have the right clothes: the color of my coat, the length of my uniform, the thickness of my scarf, the form of my shoes, the objects in my bag, the visible traces of even the mildest makeup, the size of my rings and their level of attractiveness, all would be checked before I could enter the campus of the university, the same university in which men also study. And to them the main door, with its immense portals and emblems and flags, is generously open."

In the sunny intimacy of our encounter that day, I asked Yassi to have an ice cream with me. We went to a small shop, where, sitting opposite each other with two tall *cafés glacés* between us, our mood changed. We became, if not somber, quite serious. Yassi came from an enlightened religious family that had been badly hurt by the revolution. They felt the Islamic Republic was a betrayal of Islam rather than its assertion. At the start of the revolution, Yassi's mother and older aunt joined a progressive Muslim women's group that, when the new government started to crack down on its former supporters, was forced to go underground. Yassi's mother and aunt went into hiding for a long time. This aunt had four daughters, all older than Yassi, all of whom in one way or another supported an opposition group that was popular with young religious Iranians. They were all but one arrested, tortured, and jailed. When they were released, every one of them married within a year. They married almost haphazardly, as if to negate their former rebellious selves. Yassi felt that they had survived the jail but could not escape the bonds of traditional marriage.

To me, Yassi was the real rebel. She did not join any political group or organization. As a teenager she had defied family traditions and, in the face of strong opposition, had taken up music. Listening to any form of nonreligious music, even on the radio, was forbidden in her family, but Yassi forced her will. Her rebellion did not stop there: She did not marry the right suitor at the right time and instead insisted on leaving her hometown, Shiraz, to go to college in Tehran. Now she lived partly with her older sister and husband and partly in the home of an uncle with fanatical religious leanings. The university, with its low academic standards, its shabby morality, and its ideological limitations, had been a disappointment to her.

What could she do? She did not believe in politics and did not want   25
to marry, but she was curious about love. That day, she explained why all the normal acts of life had become small acts of rebellion and political insubordination to her and to other young people like her. All her life she was shielded. She was never let out of sight; she never had a private corner in which to think, to feel, to dream, to write. She was not allowed to meet any young men on her own. Her family not only instructed her on how to behave around men, but seemed to think they could tell her how she should feel about them as well. What seems natural to someone like you, she said, is so strange and unfamiliar to me.

Again she repeated that she would never get married. She said that for her a man always existed in books, that she would spend the rest of her life with Mr. Darcy[1]—even in the books, there were few men for her. What was wrong with that? She wanted to go to America, like her uncles, like me. Her mother and her aunts had not been allowed to go, but her uncles were given the chance. Could she ever overcome all the obstacles and go to America? Should she go to America? She wanted me to advise her; they all wanted that. But what could I offer her, she who wanted so much more from life than she had been given?

There was nothing in reality that I could give her, so I told her instead about Nabokov's "other world." I asked her if she had noticed how in most of Nabokov's novels, there was always the shadow of another world, one that was attainable only through fiction. It is this world that prevents his heroes and heroines from utter despair, that becomes their refuge in a life that is consistently brutal.

Take *Lolita*. This was the story of a twelve-year-old girl who had nowhere to go. Humbert had tried to turn her into his fantasy, into his dead love, and he had destroyed her. The desperate truth of Lolita's story is not the rape of a twelve-year-old by a dirty old man but the confiscation of one individual's life by another. We don't know what Lolita would have become if Humbert had not engulfed her. Yet the novel, the finished work, is hopeful, beautiful even, a defense not just of beauty but

---

[1]*Mr. Darcy:* The leading male character in Jane Austen's classic novel *Pride and Prejudice* (1813).—Eds.

of life, ordinary everyday life, all the normal pleasures that Lolita, like Yassi, was deprived of.

Warming up and suddenly inspired, I added that, in fact, Nabokov had taken revenge against our own solipsizers; he had taken revenge on the Ayatollah Khomeini and those like him. They had tried to shape others according to their own dreams and desires, but Nabokov, through his portrayal of Humbert, had exposed all solipsists who take over other people's lives. She, Yassi, had much potential; she could be whatever she wanted to be—a good wife or a teacher and poet. What mattered was for her to know what she wanted.

I want to emphasize that we were not Lolita, the Ayatollah was not   30
Humbert, and this republic was not what Humbert called his princedom by the sea. *Lolita* was not a critique of the Islamic Republic, but it went against the grain of all totalitarian perspectives.

At some point, the truth of Iran's past became as immaterial to those who had appropriated it as the truth of Lolita's is to Humbert. It became immaterial in the same way that Lolita's truth, her desires and life, must lose color before Humbert's one obsession, his desire to turn a twelve-year-old unruly child into his mistress.

This is how I read *Lolita*. Again and again as we discussed *Lolita* in that class, our discussions were colored by my students' hidden personal sorrows and joys. Like tear stains on a letter, these forays into the hidden and the personal shaded all our discussions of Nabokov.

Humbert never possesses his victim; she always eludes him, just as objects of fantasy are always simultaneously within reach and inaccessible. No matter how they may be broken, the victims will not be forced into submission.

This was on my mind one Thursday evening after class, as I was looking at the diaries my girls had left behind, with their new essays and poems. At the start of our class, I had asked them to describe their image of themselves. They were not ready then to face that question, but every once in a while I returned to it and asked them again. Now, as I sat curled up on the love seat, I looked at dozens of pages of their recent responses.

I have one of these responses in front of me. It belongs to Sanaz, who   35
handed it in shortly after a recent experience in jail, on trumped-up morality charges. It is a simple drawing in black and white, of a naked girl, the white of her body caught in a black bubble. She is crouched in an almost fetal position, hugging one bent knee. Her other leg is stretched out behind her. Her long, straight hair follows the same curved line as the contour of her back, but her face is hidden. The bubble is lifted in the air by a giant bird with long black talons. What interests me is a small detail: the girl's hand reaches out of the bubble and holds on to the talon. Her subservient nakedness is dependent on that talon, and she reaches out to it.

The drawing immediately brought to my mind Nabokov's statement in his famous afterword to *Lolita*, about how the "first little throb of

Lolita" went through him in 1939 or early 1940, when he was ill with a severe attack of intercostal neuralgia. He recalls that "the initial shiver of inspiration was somehow prompted by a newspaper story about an ape in the Jardin des Plantes, who, after months of coaxing by a scientist, produced the first drawing ever charcoaled by an animal: this sketch showed the bars of the poor creature's cage."

The two images, one from the novel and the other from reality, reveal a terrible truth. Its terribleness goes beyond the fact that in each case an act of violence has been committed. It goes beyond the bars, revealing the victim's proximity and intimacy with its jailer. Our focus in each is on the delicate spot where the prisoner touches the bar, on the invisible contact between flesh and cold metal.

Most of the other students expressed themselves in words. Manna saw herself as fog, moving over concrete objects, taking on their form but never becoming concrete herself. Yassi described herself as a figment. Nassrin, in one response, gave me the *Oxford English Dictionary*'s definition of the word "paradox." Implicit in almost all of their descriptions was the way they saw themselves in the context of an outside reality that prevented them from defining themselves clearly and separately.

Manna had once written about a pair of pink socks for which she was reprimanded by the Muslim Students' Association. When she complained to a favorite professor, he started teasing her about how she had already ensnared and trapped her man, Nima, and did not need the pink socks to entrap him further.

These students, like the rest of their generation, were different from   40
my generation in one fundamental aspect. My generation complained of a loss, the void in our lives that was created when our past was stolen from us, making us exiles in our own country. Yet we had a past to compare with the present; we had memories and images of what had been taken away. But my girls spoke constantly of stolen kisses, films they had never seen, and the wind they had never felt on their skin. This generation had no past. Their memory was of a half-articulated desire, something they never had. It was this lack, their sense of longing for the ordinary, taken-for-granted aspects of life, that gave their words a certain luminous quality akin to poetry.

I had asked my students if they remembered the dance scene in *Invitation to a Beheading*: The jailer invites Cincinnatus to a dance. They begin a waltz and move out into the hall. In a corner they run into a guard: "They described a circle near him and glided back into the cell, and now Cincinnatus regretted that the swoon's friendly embrace had been so brief." This movement in circles is the main movement of the novel. As long as he accepts the sham world the jailers impose upon him, Cincinnatus will remain their prisoner and will move within the circles of their creation. The worst crime committed by totalitarian mind-sets is that they force their citizens, including their victims, to become complicit in their crimes. Dancing with your jailer, participating in your own execution, that is an act of utmost brutality. My students witnessed it in show trials on television and enacted it every time they went out into the streets dressed as they were told to dress. They had not become part of the crowd who watched the executions, but they did not have the power to protest them, either.

The only way to leave the circle, to stop dancing with the jailer, is to find a way to preserve one's individuality, that unique quality which evades description but differentiates one human being from the other. That is why, in their world, rituals—empty rituals—become so central.

There was not much difference between our jailers and Cincinnatus's executioners. They invaded all private spaces and tried to shape every gesture, to force us to become one of them, and that in itself is another form of execution.

In the end, when Cincinnatus is led to the scaffold, and as he lays his head on the block, in preparation for his execution, he repeats the magic mantra: "by myself." This constant reminder of his uniqueness, and his attempts to write, to articulate and create a language different from the one imposed upon him by his jailers, saves him at the last moment, when he takes his head in his hands and walks away toward voices that beckon him from that other world, while the scaffold and all the sham world around him, along with his executioner, disintegrate.

The Reader's Presence

1. What does literature represent to Nafisi's students? How do the young women's experiences in Iran shape their interpretations and understandings of Nabokov?

2. Why is Cincinnatus's execution a metaphor Nafisi's students can relate to? What is the meaning of Cincinnatus's mantra "by myself" (paragraph 44)? How does Cincinnatus "save" himself in the end? Is this ending hopeful for Nafisi's students? Why or why not?

3. The strict moral regulations imposed by the Islamic regime are, Nafisi suggests, motivated by fear. When picturing her student Sanaz on the street, Nafisi asks, "Does she realize how dangerous she can be when her every stray gesture is a disturbance to public safety?" (paragraph 18). How is the education of women a potential threat to public safety in Iran? Read Sherman Alexie's "The Joy of Reading and Writing: Superman and Me" (page 13). How does Alexie characterize his education as subversive? Who is threatened by his learning?

Danielle Ofri

SAT

Danielle Ofri (b. 1965) demonstrates that it is possible to be a productive writer while pursuing a busy life or career. The possessor of both an MD and a PhD, she is an attending physician at Bellevue Hospital and assistant professor of medicine at New York University School of Medicine. She is also editor-in-chief and co-founder of the Bellevue Literary Review *and the associate chief editor of the award-winning medical textbook* The Bellevue Guide to Outpatient Medicine. *Her essays have appeared in the* New York Times, *the* Los Angeles Times, Best American Essays, Best American Science Writing, *the* New England Journal of Medicine, *the* Missouri Review, Tikkun, *the* Journal of the American Medical Association, *and the* Lancet. *Her Web site, danielleofri.com, explores the relationship between literature and medicine. A frequent guest on National Public Radio, Ofri lives in New York City with her husband and three children.*

Her first collection, Singular Intimacies: Becoming a Doctor at Bellevue *(2003), was described by physician/author Perri Klass as "a beautiful book about souls and bodies, sadness and healing at a legendary hospital." Ofri co-edited with her colleagues the* Best of Bellevue Literary Review *(2008), a collection of writings from that journal. Her essay, "SAT," is taken from her 2005 book,* Incidental Findings: Lessons from My Patients in the Art of Medicine. *A* New York Times *profile reports, "To Dr. Ofri every patient's history is a mystery story, a narrative that unfolds full of surprises, exposing the vulnerability at the human core."*

"Nemesio Rios?" I called out to the crowded waiting room of our medical clinic. I'd just finished a long stint attending on the wards and I was glad to be back to the relatively sane life of the clinic. "Nemesio Rios?" I called out again.

"Yuh," came a grunt, as a teenaged boy in baggy jeans with a ski hat pulled low over his brow hoisted himself up. He sauntered into my office and slumped into the plastic chair next to my desk.

"What brings you to the clinic today?"

He shrugged. "Feel all right, but they told me to come today," he said, slouching lower into the chair, his oversize sweatshirt reaching nearly to his knees. The chart said he'd been in the ER two weeks ago for a cough.

"How about a regular checkup?" He shrugged again. His eyes were deep brown, tucked deep beneath his brow.

Past medical history? None. Past surgical history? None. Meds? None. Allergies? None. Family history? None.

"Where were you born?" I asked, wanting to know his nationality.

"Here."

"Here in New York?"

"Yeah, in this hospital."   10

"A Bellevue baby!" I said with a grin, noticing that his medical record number had only six digits (current numbers had nine digits). "A genuine Bellevue baby."

There was a small smile, but I could see him working hard to suppress it. "My mom's from Mexico."

"Have you ever been there?" I asked, curious.

"You sound like my mom." He rolled his eyes. "She's always trying to get me to go. She's over there right now visiting her sisters."

"You don't want to go visit?"   15

"Mexico? Just a bunch of corrupt politicians." Nemesio shifted his unlaced sneakers back and forth on the linoleum floor, causing a dull screech each time.

I asked about his family. In a distracted voice, as though he'd been through this a million times before, he told me that he was the youngest of eight, but now that his sister got married, it was only he and his mother left in the house. I asked about his father.

"He lives in Brooklyn." Nemesio poked his hand in and out of the pocket of his sweatshirt. "He's all right, I guess, but he drinks a lot," he said, his voice trailing off. "Doesn't do anything stupid, but he drinks."

"Are you in school now?"

"Me?" he said, his voice perking up for the first time from his base-   20
line mumble. "I'm twenty. I'm done! Graduated last year."

"What are you doing now?"

"Working in a kitchen. It's all right, I guess."

"Any thoughts about college?"

"You sound like my cousin in Connecticut. He's in some college there and he's always bugging me about going to college. But I'm lazy. No one to kick my lazy butt."

"What do you want to do when you grow up?"   25

"What I *really* want to do? I want to play basketball." He gave a small laugh. "But they don't take five-foot-seven guys in the NBA."

"Anything else besides basketball?"

He thought for a minute. "Comics. I like to draw comics. I guess I could be an artist that draws comics." His eye caught the tiny Monet poster I'd taped above the examining table. "That's pretty cool, that painting."

"There are a lot of great art schools here in New York." My comment floated off into empty space. We were silent for a few minutes. I made a few notes in the chart.

"That stuff about peer pressure is a bunch of crap," he said abruptly,   30
forcefully, sitting up in his chair, speaking directly toward the poster in front of him.

I leaned closer toward Nemesio, trying to figure out what this sudden outburst was related to. But he continued, staring straight forward, lecturing at the empty room, as if I weren't there.

"Anyone who tells you they do something because of peer pressure is full of crap." He was even more animated now, even angry. "People always asking me to do stuff, but I can make my own mind up." His hands came out of his sweatshirt pocket and began gesticulating in the air. "My brother and his friends, they're always drinking beer. But I don't like the taste of it. I don't believe in peer pressure."

Speech ended, Nemesio settled back into his chair, resumed his slouched posture, and repositioned his hands into his pockets. Then he glanced up at the ceiling and added quietly, almost wistfully, "But if beer tasted like apple juice, I might be drinking it every day."

He was quiet for a few minutes. One hand slid out of his pocket and started fiddling with the zipper on his sweatshirt.

Without warning he swiveled in his chair to face me directly, his 35 whole body leaning into my desk. "You ever face peer pressure, Doc?"

His eyes were right on mine, and I was caught off guard by this sudden shift in his voice and body language. I felt unexpectedly on the spot. Who does he see? I wondered. Do I represent the older generation or the medical profession or women or non-Hispanic whites? Or all of the above?

Nemesio refused to let my gaze wander off his. He demanded an answer to his question, and our doctor–patient encounter had obviously taken an abrupt turn. I could tell that a lot was riding on my answer, though I wasn't sure what exactly was at stake. Did he need me to provide a reassuring societal answer about how bad drugs are? Or did he need me to identify with him, to say that I've been where he's been, even if that was not exactly the truth?

"Yes," I said, after debating in my head for a moment, trying to think of something sufficiently potent to satisfy the question but not so sordid as to embarrass myself. "I have."

He stared at me, waiting for me to continue. His eyes looked younger and younger.

"In my first year of college," I said. "In the very first week. Everyone 40 was sitting in the stairwell and they were passing a joint around. Everyone took a drag. When it came to me I hesitated. I wasn't really interested in smoking, but everyone else was doing it."

"So what did you do?"

"I didn't want anyone to think I was a little kid, so I took a drag too."

"Did you like it?"

"No, I just hacked and coughed. I didn't even *want* the stupid joint to begin with, and I couldn't believe I was doing it just because everyone else was."

"That peer pressure is crap." Nemesio stated it as a fact and then 45 sank back into his seat.

"You're right. It is. It took me a little while to figure that out."

He pushed the ski hat back from his brow a few inches. "In my high school there was this teacher that was always on my case. She was always bugging me to study and take the tests. What a pain in the butt she was."

He pulled the hat all the way off. "But now there's no one around to kick my lazy butt. I could get to college easy, but I'm just lazy."

My mind wandered back to a crisp autumn day in my second month of medical school. Still overwhelmed by the pentose-phosphate shunt and other minutiae of biochemistry, our Clinical Correlation group—led by two fourth-year students—promised us first-year students a taste of clinical medicine.

The CC student leaders had obtained permission for a tour of the New York City medical examiner's office. All suspicious death—murders, suicides, and the like—were investigated here.

The autumn sun dazzled against the bright turquoise bricks of the ME   50
building, which stood out in sharp contrast to the gray concrete buildings lining First Avenue. We congregated on the steps, endeavoring to look nonchalant.

The security guard checked our ID cards as well as our letter of entry. We followed him through the metal detector, down the whitewashed concrete hallway, into the unpainted service elevator with a hand-pulled metal grate.

We stared at our sneakers as the elevator lurched downward. It creaked past several floors and landed with a jolt. Out we spilled, gingerly, onto the raw concrete floor. Our first stop was the morgue. The cavernous walk-in refrigerator was icy and silent. There was a Freon smell, the kind I recalled from the frozen food departments in grocery stores. As a child, when I went shopping with my mother I used to lean into the bins of ice cream and frozen waffles and inhale that curiously appealing, vaguely sweet, chemical fragrance. But here the odor was intensified—magnified by the rigid chill and bleak soundlessness of the room.

Nine naked corpses lay on shelves, their wizened bodies covered with skin that glowed a ghastly green from the low-wattage fluorescent lights. These were the unclaimed bodies, mostly elderly men found on the streets. The ones that were never identified, never claimed by relatives. The ones that were sent next door to the medical school. These were the subjects of our first-year anatomy course.

From there we were herded into the autopsy room. Loosely swinging doors delivered us into a shock of cacophonous noise and harsh bright lights. We stumbled into each other, a discombobulated mass at the entranceway, blinking to adjust from the stark silence of the morgue. The autopsy room was long and rectangular. The high ceilings and brisk yellow walls lent an odd air of cheeriness. Seven metal tables lay parallel in the center. Six of them were surrounded by groups of pathology residents performing autopsies. The residents wore long rubber gloves and industrial-strength aprons. The sound of their voices and their clanking instruments echoed in the room.

The only body I had ever opened was my cadaver in anatomy lab,   55
which was preserved in formaldehyde and completely dried out. I'd never

actually seen blood. In the autopsy room there was blood everywhere. Residents were handling organs—weighing hearts, measuring kidneys, taking samples from livers—then replacing them in the open corpses. Their aprons were spotted with scarlet streaks. Blood streamed down the troughs that surrounded each table.

It was disgusting, but I wasn't nauseated. These bodies didn't look like people anymore. It was more like a cattle slaughterhouse: cows and pigs lined up to be transformed into sterile packages of cellophane-wrapped chopped meat. The slaughterhouse that compelled you to vow lifetime vegetarianism, a resolve that lasted only until the next barbecue with succulent, browned burgers that looked nothing like the disemboweled carcasses you'd seen earlier.

Then I spied the last table, the only one without a sea of activity around it. Lying on the metal table was a young boy who didn't look older than twelve. He was wearing new Nikes and one leg of his jeans was rolled up to the knee. His bright red basketball jersey was pushed up, revealing a smooth brown chest. He looked as if he were sleeping.

I tiptoed closer. Could he really be dead? There was not a mark on his body. Every part was in its place. His clothes were crisp and clean. There was no blood, no dirt, no sign of struggle. He wasn't anything like the gutted carcasses on the other tables. His expression was serene, his face without blemish. His skin was plump. He was just a beautiful boy sleeping.

I wanted to rouse him, to tell him to get out of this house of death, quick, before the rubber-aproned doctors got to him. There is still time, I wanted to say. Get out while you can!

I leaned over his slender, exposed, adolescent chest. I peered closer.   60
There, just over his left nipple, was a barely perceptible hole. Smaller than the tip of my little finger. A tiny bullet hole.

I stared at that hole. That ignominious hole. That hole that stole this boy's life. I wanted to rewind the tape, to give him a chance to dodge six inches to the right. That's all he'd need—just six inches. Who would balk over six inches?

Somebody pulled on my arm. Time to go.

For months after my visit to the medical examiner's office, I had nightmares. But they weren't about bloody autopsies or refrigerated corpses. I dreamt only about the boy, that beautiful, untouched, intact boy. The one who'd had the misfortune to fall asleep in the autopsy room.

At night, he would creep into my bed. On the street, I could feel his breath on the back of my neck. In the library, while I battled the Krebs cycle and the branches of the trigeminal nerve, he would slip silently into the pages of my book. His body was so perfect, so untouched.

Except for that barely perceptible hole.   65

Now I looked at Nemesio Rios sitting before me; his beautiful body adrift in the uncertainty of adolescence, made all the rockier by the unfair burdens of urban poverty. Research has shown that health status and life expectancy are directly correlated with socioeconomic status and earning power. Whether this is related to having health insurance, or simply to having more knowledge to make healthier lifestyle choices, there is no doubt that being poor is bad for your health.

As I scribbled in his chart, an odd thought dawned on me: the best thing that I, as a physician, could recommend for Nemesio's long-term health would be to take the SAT and get into college. Too bad I couldn't just write a prescription for that.

"Have you taken the SAT yet?" I asked Nemesio.

"Nah. I can't stand U.S. history. What's the point of knowing U.S. history?"

I twisted my stethoscope around my finger. "Ever hear of McCarthy?"   70
He shrugged. "Yeah, maybe."

"McCarthy tried to intimidate people to turn in their friends and coworkers. Anyone who might believe differently from him. I'd hate to see that part of U.S. history repeated."

He nodded slowly. "Yeah, I guess. I wouldn't want nobody to tell me what to think. That peer pressure is crap."

"Besides," I added, "there's no U.S. history on the SAT."

Nemesio turned toward me, his eyes opened wide. "Yeah? No U.S.   75
history?" His cheeks were practically glowing.

"No history. Just math and English."

"Wow," he said. "No U.S. history. That's pretty cool." His tone of voice changed abruptly as his gaze plummeted to the floor. "But damn, I can't remember those fractions and stuff."

"Sure you can," I said. "It's all the same from high school. If you review it, it'll all come back to you."

In medical school, I had taught an SAT prep course on the weekends to help pay my living expenses. For kids in more affluent neighborhoods, these courses were standard. But it didn't seem fair, because for Nemesio, his health depended on it.

"Listen," I said. "I'll make you a deal. You go out and buy one of   80
those SAT review books and bring it to our next appointment. I bet we can brush you up on those fractions."

He shifted in his seat and I could just detect a hint of a swagger in his torso. "Okay, Doc. I'll take you on."

Nemesio stood up to go and then turned quickly back to me. "College ain't so bad, but what I really want is to play basketball."

Now it was my turn to nod. "There's nothing like a good ballgame. I played point guard in college."

"You? You even shorter than me."

"That's why I had to find another career."   85

He grinned. "You and me both." Nemesio put his ski hat on and pulled it carefully down over his forehead. Then he slouched out the door.

Nemesio and I met three times over the next two months. While my stethoscope and blood pressure cuff sat idle, we reviewed algebra, analogies, geometry, and reading comprehension. With only a little prodding, Nemesio was able to recall what he had learned in high school. And he thought it was "really cool" when I showed him the tricks and shortcuts that I recalled from the SAT prep course.

I lost touch with Nemesio after that. Many days I thought about him, wondering how things turned out. If this were a movie, he'd score a perfect 1600 and be off to Princeton on full scholarship. But Harlem isn't Hollywood, and the challenges in real life are infinitely more complex. I don't know if Nemesio ever got into college — any college — or if he even took the SAT exam. But he did learn a bit more about fractions, and I learned a bit more about the meaning of preventative medicine. At the end of each visit, I would face the clinic billing sheet. The top fifty diagnoses were listed — the most common and important medical issues, according to Medicaid, that faced our patients. I scrutinized them each time, because I was required to check one off, to check off Nemesio Rios's most salient medical diagnosis and treatment, to identify the most pressing issues for his health, to categorize the medical interventions deemed necessary for this patient's well-being, otherwise the clinic wouldn't get reimbursed.

SAT prep was not among them.   90

The Reader's Presence

1. Ofri uses dialogue extensively throughout the essay. What are the effects of this choice? How would the essay be different if she had not used her patient's own words?

2. Why does Ofri juxtapose the material about Nemesio Rios with the material about her experiences in the morgue? Is the fact that Ofri does not reveal the outcome of Nemesio's story disturbing? Does this uncertainty make the essay more or less believable? Why?

3. Ofri argues that continuing his education is the best step her patient can take to safeguard his health. Do you agree? Read John Taylor Gatto's "Against School" (page 682). Does Gatto's argument apply to a case like that of Ofri's young patient? Why or why not?

George Orwell

Politics and the English Language

During his lifetime, George Orwell was well known for the political positions he laid out in his essays. The events that inspired Orwell to write his essays have long since passed, but his writing continues to be read and enjoyed. Orwell demonstrates that political writing need not be narrowly topical — it can speak to enduring issues and concerns. He suggested as much in 1946 when he wrote, "What I have most wanted to do throughout the past ten years is to make political writing into an art. My starting point is always a feeling of partisanship, a feeling of injustice. . . . But I could not do the work of writing a book, or even a long magazine article, if it were not also an aesthetic experience." "Politics and the English Language" appears in Shooting an Elephant and Other Essays *(1950).*

For more information about Orwell, see page 203.

Most people who bother with the matter at all would admit that the English language is in a bad way, but it is generally assumed that we cannot by conscious action do anything about it. Our civilization is decadent and our language — so that argument runs — must inevitably share in the general collapse. It follows that any struggle against the abuse of language is a sentimental archaism, like preferring candles to electric light or hansom cabs to airplanes. Underneath this lies the half-conscious belief that language is a natural growth and not an instrument which we shape for our own purposes.

Now, it is clear that the decline of a language must ultimately have political and economic causes: It is not due simply to the bad influence of this or that individual writer. But an effect can become a cause, reinforcing the original cause and producing the same effect in an intensified form, and so on indefinitely. A man may take to drink because he feels himself to be a failure, and then fail all the more completely because he drinks. It is rather the same thing that is happening to the English language. It becomes ugly and inaccurate because our thoughts are foolish, but the slovenliness of our language makes it easier for us to have foolish thoughts. The point is that the process is reversible. Modern English, especially written English, is full of bad habits which spread by imitation and which can be avoided if one is willing to take the necessary trouble. If one gets rid of these habits one can think more clearly, and to think clearly is a necessary first step towards political regeneration: so that the fight against bad English is not frivolous and is not the exclusive concern of professional writers. I will come back to this presently, and I hope that by that time the meaning of what I have said here will have become clearer.

Meanwhile, here are five specimens of the English language as it is now habitually written.

These five passages have not been picked out because they are especially bad—I could have quoted far worse if I had chosen—but because they illustrate various of the mental vices from which we now suffer. They are a little below the average, but are fairly representative samples. I number them so that I can refer back to them when necessary:

(1) I am not, indeed, sure whether it is true to say that the Milton who once seemed not unlike a seventeenth-century Shelley had not become, out of an experience ever more bitter in each year, more alien [*sic*] to the founder of that Jesuit sect which nothing could induce him to tolerate.

Professor Harold Laski (*Essay in Freedom of Expression*).

(2) Above all, we cannot play ducks and drakes with a native battery of idioms which prescribes such egregious collections of vocals as the Basic *put up with* for *tolerate* or *put at a loss* for *bewilder*.

Professor Lancelot Hogben (*Interglossa*).

(3) On the one side we have the free personality: By definition it is not neurotic, for it has neither conflict nor dream. Its desires, such as they are, are transparent, for they are just what institutional approval keeps in the forefront of consciousness; another institutional pattern would alter their number and intensity; there is little in them that is natural, irreducible, or culturally dangerous. But *on the other side*, the social bond itself is nothing but the mutual reflection of these self-secure integrities. Recall the definition of love. Is not this the very picture of a small academic? Where is there a place in this hall of mirrors for either personality or fraternity?

Essay on psychology in *Politics* (New York).

(4) All the "best people" from the gentlemen's clubs, and all the frantic fascist captains, united in common hatred of Socialism and bestial horror of the rising tide of the mass revolutionary movement, have turned to acts of provocation, to foul incendiarism, to medieval legends of poisoned wells, to legalize their own destruction of proletarian organizations, and rouse the agitated petty-bourgeoisie to chauvinistic fervor on behalf of the fight against the revolutionary way out of the crisis.

Communist pamphlet.

(5) If a new spirit *is* to be infused into this old country, there is one thorny and contentious reform which must be tackled, and that is the humanization and galvanization of the B.B.C. Timidity here will bespeak cancer and atrophy of the soul. The heart of Britain may be sound and of strong beat, for instance, but the British lion's roar at present is like that of Bottom in Shakespeare's *Midsummer Night's Dream*—as gentle as any sucking dove. A virile new Britain cannot continue indefinitely to be traduced in the eyes or rather ears, of the world by the effete languors of Langham Place, brazenly masquerading as "standard English." When the *Voice of Britain* is heard at nine o'clock, better far and infinitely less

ludicrous to hear aitches honestly dropped than the present priggish, inflated, inhibited, school-ma'amish arch braying of blameless bashful mewing maidens!

Letter in *Tribune*.

Each of these passages has faults of its own, but, quite apart from avoidable ugliness, two qualities are common to all of them. The first is staleness of imagery: The other is lack of precision. The writer either has a meaning and cannot express it, or he inadvertently says something else, or he is almost indifferent as to whether his words mean anything or not. This mixture of vagueness and sheer incompetence is the most marked characteristic of modern English prose, and especially of any kind of political writing. As soon as certain topics are raised, the concrete melts into the abstract and no one seems able to think of turns of speech that are not hackneyed: Prose consists less and less of *words* chosen for the sake of their meaning, and more and more of *phrases* tacked together like the sections of a prefabricated hen-house. I list below, with notes and examples, various of the tricks by means of which the work of prose-construction is habitually dodged:

Dying Metaphors. A newly invented metaphor assists thought by   5
evoking a visual image, while on the other hand a metaphor which is technically "dead" (e.g., *iron resolution*) has in effect reverted to being an ordinary word and can generally be used without loss of vividness. But in between these two classes there is a huge dump of worn-out metaphors which have lost all evocative power and are merely used because they save people the trouble of inventing phrases for themselves. Examples are: *Ring the changes on, take up the cudgels for, toe the line, ride roughshod over, stand shoulder to shoulder with, play into the hands of, no axe to grind, grist to the mill, fishing in troubled waters, rift within the lute, on the order of the day, Achilles' heel, swan song, hotbed.* Many of these are used without knowledge of their meaning (what is a "rift," for instance?), and incompatible metaphors are frequently mixed, a sure sign that the writer is not interested in what he is saying. Some metaphors now current have been twisted out of their original meaning without those who use them even being aware of the fact. For example, *toe the line* is sometimes written *tow the line*. Another example is *the hammer and the anvil*, now always used with the implication that the anvil gets the worst of it. In real life it is always the anvil that breaks the hammer, never the other way about: A writer who stopped to think what he was saying would be aware of this, and would avoid perverting the original phrase.

Operators or Verbal False Limbs. These save the trouble of picking out appropriate verbs and nouns, and at the same time pad each sentence with extra syllables which give it an appearance of symmetry. Characteristic phrases are *render inoperative, militate against, make contact with, be subjected to, give rise to, give grounds for, have the effect of, play a lead-*

ing part (role) in, make itself felt, take effect, exhibit a tendency to, serve the purpose of, etc., etc. The keynote is the elimination of simple verbs. Instead of being a single word, such as *break, stop, spoil, mend, kill,* a verb becomes a *phrase,* made up of a noun or adjective tacked on to some general-purpose verb such as *prove, serve, form, play, render.* In addition, the passive voice is wherever possible used in preference to the active, and noun constructions are used instead of gerunds (*by examination of* instead of *by examining*). The range of verbs is further cut down by means of the *-ize* and *de-* formation, and the banal statements are given an appearance of profundity by means of the *not un-* formation. Simple conjunctions and prepositions are replaced by such phrases as *with respect to, having regard to, the fact that, by dint of, in view of, in the interests of, on the hypothesis that*; and the ends of sentences are saved from anticlimax by such resounding commonplaces as *greatly to be desired, cannot be left out of account, a development to be expected in the near future, deserving of serious consideration, brought to a satisfactory conclusion,* and so on and so forth.

Pretentious Diction. Words like *phenomenon, element, individual* (as noun), *objective, categorical, effective, virtual, basic, primary, promote, constitute, exhibit, exploit, utilize, eliminate, liquidate,* are used to dress up simple statements and give an air of scientific impartiality to biased judgments. Adjectives like *epoch-making, epic, historic, unforgettable, triumphant, age-old, inevitable, inexorable, veritable,* are used to dignify the sordid processes of international politics, while writing that aims at glorifying war usually takes on an archaic color, its characteristic words being: *realm, throne, chariot, mailed fist, trident, sword, shield, buckler, banner, jackboot, clarion.* Foreign words and expressions such as *cul de sac, ancien régime, deus ex machina, mutatis mutandis, status quo, gleichschaltung, weltanschauung,* are used to give an air of culture and elegance. Except for the useful abbreviations *i.e., e.g.,* and *etc.,* there is no real need for any of the hundreds of foreign phrases now current in English. Bad writers, and especially scientific, political, and sociological writers, are nearly always haunted by the notion that Latin or Greek words are grander than Saxon ones, and unnecessary words like *expedite, ameliorate, predict, extraneous, deracinated, clandestine, subaqueous,* and hundreds of others constantly gain ground from their Anglo-Saxon opposite numbers.[1] The jargon peculiar to Marxist writing (*hyena, hangman, cannibal, petty bourgeois, these gentry, lackey, flunkey, mad dog, White Guard, etc.*) consists largely of words and phrases translated from Russian, German, or French; but the normal way of coining a new word is to use a Latin or Greek root with the

---

[1]An interesting illustration of this is the way in which the English flower names which were in use till very recently are being ousted by Greek ones, *snapdragon* becoming *antirrhinum, forget-me-not* becoming *myosotis,* etc. It is hard to see any practical reason for this change of fashion: It is probably due to an instinctive turning away from the more homely word and a vague feeling that the Greek word is scientific.

appropriate affix and, where necessary, the *-ize* formation. It is often easier
to make up words of this kind (*deregionalize, impermissible, extramarital,
nonfragmentary*, and so forth) than to think up the English words that will
cover one's meaning. The result, in general, is an increase in slovenliness
and vagueness.

   Meaningless Words. In certain kinds of writing, particularly in art criticism and literary criticism, it is normal to come across long passages which
are almost completely lacking in meaning.[2] Words like *romantic, plastic, values, human, dead, sentimental, natural, vitality*, as used in art criticism, are
strictly meaningless, in the sense that they not only do not point to any dis-
coverable object, but are hardly ever expected to do so by the reader. When
one critic writes, "The outstanding feature of Mr. X's work is its living quality," while another writes, "The immediately striking thing about Mr. X's
work is its peculiar deadness," the reader accepts this as a simple difference
of opinion. If words like *black* and *white* were involved, instead of the jargon words *dead* and *living*, he would see at once that language was being
used in an improper way. Many political words are similarly abused. The
word *Fascism* has now no meaning except in so far as it signifies "something
not desirable." The words *democracy, socialism, freedom, patriotic, realistic, justice*, have each of them several different meanings which cannot be
reconciled with one another. In the case of a word like *democracy*, not only
is there no agreed definition, but the attempt to make one is resisted from all
sides. It is almost universally felt that when we call a country democratic we
are praising it: Consequently the defenders of every kind of regime claim
that it is a democracy, and fear that they might have to stop using the word
if it were tied down to any one meaning. Words of this kind are often used
in a consciously dishonest way. That is, the person who uses them has his
own private definition, but allows his hearer to think he means something
quite different. Statements like *Marshal Pétain[3] was a true patriot, The Soviet Press is the freest in the world, The Catholic Church is opposed to persecution*, are almost always made with intent to deceive. Other words used in
variable meanings, in most cases more or less dishonestly, are: *class, totalitarian, science, progressive, reactionary, bourgeois, equality.*

---

   [2]Example: "Comfort's catholicity of perception and image, strangely Whitmanesque in
range, almost the exact opposite in aesthetic compulsion, continues to evoke that trembling
atmospheric accumulative hinting at a cruel, an inexorably serene timelessness. . . . Wrey
Gardiner scores by aiming at simple bull's-eyes with precision. Only they are not so simple,
and through this contented sadness runs more than the surface bitter-sweet of resignation."
(*Poetry Quarterly*.)
   [3]*Pétain:* Henri Philippe Pétain was a World War I French military hero who served as
chief of state in France from 1940 to 1945, after France surrendered to Germany. A controversial figure, Pétain was regarded by some to be a patriot who had sacrificed himself for his
country, while others considered him to be a traitor. He was sentenced to life imprisonment
in 1945, the year before Orwell wrote his essay. — EDS.

Now that I have made this catalogue of swindles and perversions, let me give another example of the kind of writing that they lead to. This time it must of its nature be an imaginary one. I am going to translate a passage of good English into modern English of the worst sort. Here is a well-known verse from *Ecclesiastes*:

> I returned and saw under the sun, that the race is not to the swift, nor the battle to the strong, neither yet bread to the wise, nor yet riches to men of understanding, nor yet favor to men of skill; but time and chance happeneth to them all.

Here it is in modern English:

> Objective consideration of contemporary phenomena compels the conclusion that success or failure in competitive activities exhibits no tendency to be commensurate with innate capacity, but that a considerable element of the unpredictable must invariably be taken into account.

This is a parody, but not a very gross one. Exhibit (3), above, for instance, contains several patches of the same kind of English. It will be seen that I have not made a full translation. The beginning and ending of the sentence follow the original meaning fairly closely, but in the middle the concrete illustrations—race, battle, bread—dissolve into the vague phrase "success or failure in competitive activities." This had to be so, because no modern writer of the kind I am discussing—no one capable of using phrases like "objective consideration of contemporary phenomena"— would ever tabulate his thoughts in that precise and detailed way. The whole tendency of modern prose is away from concreteness. Now analyze these two sentences a little more closely. The first contains forty-nine words but only sixty syllables, and all its words are those of everyday life. The second contains thirty-eight words of ninety syllables: Eighteen of its words are from Latin roots, and one from Greek. The first sentence contains six vivid images, and only one phrase ("time and chance") that could be called vague. The second contains not a single fresh, arresting phrase, and in spite of its ninety syllables it gives only a shortened version of the meaning contained in the first. Yet without a doubt it is the second kind of sentence that is gaining ground in modern English. I do not want to exaggerate. This kind of writing is not yet universal, and outcrops of simplicity will occur here and there in the worst-written page. Still, if you or I were told to write a few lines on the uncertainty of human fortunes, we should probably come much nearer to my imaginary sentences than to the one from *Ecclesiastes*.

As I have tried to show, modern writing at its worst does not consist in picking out words for the sake of their meaning and inventing images in order to make the meaning clearer. It consists in gumming together long strips of words which have already been set in order by someone else, and making the results presentable by sheer humbug. The attraction of this way of writing is that it is easy. It is easier—even quicker once you have the

10

habit—to say *In my opinion it is a not unjustifiable assumption that* than to say *I think*. If you use ready-made phrases, you not only don't have to hunt about for words; you also don't have to bother with the rhythms of your sentences, since these phrases are generally so arranged as to be more or less euphonious. When you are composing in a hurry—when you are dictating to a stenographer, for instance, or making a public speech—it is natural to fall into a pretentious, Latinized style. Tags like *a consideration which we should do well to bear in mind* or *a conclusion to which all of us would readily assent* will save many a sentence from coming down with a bump. By using stale metaphors, similes, and idioms, you save much mental effort, at the cost of leaving your meaning vague, not only for your reader but for yourself. This is the significance of mixed metaphors. The sole aim of a metaphor is to call up a visual image. When these images clash—as in *The Fascist octopus has sung its swan song, the jackboot is thrown into the melting pot*—it can be taken as certain that the writer is not seeing a mental image of the objects he is naming; in other words he is not really thinking. Look again at the examples I gave at the beginning of this essay. Professor Laski (1) uses five negatives in fifty-three words. One of these is superfluous, making nonsense of the whole passage, and in addition there is the slip—*alien* for akin—making further nonsense, and several avoidable pieces of clumsiness which increase the general vagueness. Professor Hogben (2) plays ducks and drakes with a battery which is able to write prescriptions, and, while disapproving of the everyday phrase *put up with*, is unwilling to look *egregious* up in the dictionary and see what it means; (3), if one takes an uncharitable attitude towards it, is simply meaningless: Probably one could work out its intended meaning by reading the whole of the article in which it occurs. In (4), the writer knows more or less what he wants to say, but an accumulation of stale phrases chokes him like tea leaves blocking a sink. In (5), words and meaning have almost parted company. People who write in this manner usually have a general emotional meaning—they dislike one thing and want to express solidarity with another—but they are not interested in the detail of what they are saying. A scrupulous writer, in every sentence that he writes, will ask himself at least four questions, thus: What am I trying to say? What words will express it? What image or idiom will make it clearer? Is this image fresh enough to have an effect? And he will probably ask himself two more: Could I put it more shortly? Have I said anything that is avoidably ugly? But you are not obliged to go to all this trouble. You can shirk it by simply throwing your mind open and letting the ready-made phrases come crowding in. They will construct your sentences for you—even think your thoughts for you, to a certain extent—and at need they will perform the important service of partially concealing your meaning even from yourself. It is at this point that the special connection between politics and the debasement of language becomes clear.

In our time it is broadly true that political writing is bad writing. Where it is not true, it will generally be found that the writer is some kind of rebel, expressing his private opinions and not a "party line." Orthodoxy, of whatever color, seems to demand a lifeless, imitative style. The political dialects to be found in pamphlets, leading articles, manifestos, White Papers, and the speeches of under-secretaries do, of course, vary from party to party, but they are all alike in that one almost never finds in them a fresh, vivid, home-made turn of speech. When one watches some tired hack on the platform mechanically repeating the familiar phrases—*bestial atrocities, iron heel, bloodstained tyranny, free peoples of the world, stand shoulder to shoulder*—one often has a curious feeling that one is not watching a live human being but some kind of dummy: a feeling which suddenly becomes stronger at moments when the light catches the speaker's spectacles and turns them into blank discs which seem to have no eyes behind them. And this is not altogether fanciful. A speaker who uses that kind of phraseology has gone some distance towards turning himself into a machine. The appropriate noises are coming out of his larynx, but his brain is not involved as it would be if he were choosing his words for himself. If the speech he is making is one that he is accustomed to make over and over again, he may be almost unconscious of what he is saying, as one is when one utters the responses in church. And this reduced state of consciousness, if not indispensable, is at any rate favorable to political conformity.

In our time, political speech and writing are largely the defense of the indefensible. Things like the continuance of British rule in India, the Russian purges and deportations, the dropping of the atom bombs on Japan, can indeed be defended, but only by arguments which are too brutal for most people to face, and which do not square with the professed aims of political parties. Thus political language has to consist largely of euphemism, question-begging, and sheer cloudy vagueness. Defenseless villages are bombarded from the air, the inhabitants driven out into the countryside, the cattle machine-gunned, the huts set on fire with incendiary bullets: This is called *pacification*. Millions of peasants are robbed of their farms and sent trudging along the roads with no more than they can carry: This is called *transfer of population* or *rectification of frontiers*. People are imprisoned for years without trial, or shot in the back of the neck or sent to die of scurvy in Arctic lumber camps:[4] This is called *elimination of unreliable elements*. Such phraseology is needed if one wants to name things without calling up mental pictures of them. Consider for instance some comfortable English professor defending Russian totalitarianism. He cannot say outright, "I believe in killing off your opponents when you get good results by doing so." Probably, therefore, he will say something like this:

"While freely conceding that the Soviet régime exhibits certain features which the humanitarian may be inclined to deplore, we must, I think, agree that a certain curtailment of the right to political opposition is an unavoidable concomitant of transitional periods, and that the rigors

---

[4]*People . . . camps:* Though Orwell is decrying all totalitarian abuse of language, his examples are mainly pointed at the Soviet purges under Joseph Stalin. —EDS.

which the Russian people have been called upon to undergo have been amply justified in the sphere of concrete achievement."

The inflated style is itself a kind of euphemism. A mass of Latin words falls upon the facts like soft snow, blurring the outlines and covering up all the details. The great enemy of clear language is insincerity. When there is a gap between one's real and one's declared aims, one turns as it were instinctively to long words and exhausted idioms, like a cuttlefish squirting out ink. In our age there is no such thing as "keeping out of politics." All issues are political issues, and politics itself is a mass of lies, evasions, folly, hatred, and schizophrenia. When the general atmosphere is bad, language must suffer. I should expect to find—this is a guess which I have not sufficient knowledge to verify—that the German, Russian, and Italian languages have all deteriorated in the last ten or fifteen years, as a result of dictatorship.

But if thought corrupts language, language can also corrupt thought. A bad usage can spread by tradition and imitation, even among people who should and do know better. The debased language that I have been discussing is in some ways very convenient. Phrases like *a not unjustifiable assumption, leaves much to be desired, would serve no good purpose, a consideration which we should do well to bear in mind,* are a continuous temptation, a packet of aspirins always at one's elbow. Look back through this essay, and for certain you will find that I have again and again committed the very faults I am protesting against. By this morning's post I have received a pamphlet dealing with conditions in Germany. The author tells me that he "felt impelled" to write it. I open it at random, and here is almost the first sentence that I see: "(The Allies) have an opportunity not only of achieving a radical transformation of Germany's social and political structure in such a way as to avoid a nationalistic reaction in Germany itself, but at the same time of laying the foundations of a co-operative and unified Europe." You see, he "feels impelled" to write—feels, presumably, that he has something new to say—and yet his words, like cavalry horses answering the bugle, group themselves automatically into the familiar dreary pattern. The invasion of one's mind by ready-made phrases (*lay the foundations, achieve a radical transformation*) can only be prevented if one is constantly on guard against them, and every such phrase anaesthetizes a portion of one's brain.

I said earlier that the decadence of our language is probably curable. Those who deny this would argue, if they produced an argument at all, that language merely reflects existing social conditions, and that we cannot influence its development by any direct tinkering with words and constructions. So far as the general tone or spirit of a language goes, this may be true, but it is not true in detail. Silly words and expressions have often disappeared, not through any evolutionary process but owing to the conscious action of a minority. Two recent examples were *explore every avenue* and *leave no stone unturned,* which were killed by the jeers of a few journalists. There is a long list of flyblown metaphors which could similarly be got rid of if enough people would interest themselves in the jobs; and it should also be possible to laugh the *not un-* formation out of existence,[5] to reduce the amount of Latin and Greek in the average sentence, to drive out foreign phrases and strayed scientific words, and, in general, to make pretentiousness unfashionable. But all these are minor points. The defense of the English language implies more than this, and perhaps it is best to start by saying what it does *not* imply.

To begin with it has nothing to do with archaism, with the salvaging of obsolete words and turns of speech, or with the setting up of a "standard English" which must never be departed from. On the contrary, it is especially concerned with the scrapping of every word or idiom which has outworn its usefulness. It has nothing to do with correct grammar and syntax, which are of no importance so long as one makes one's meaning clear, or with the avoidance of Americanisms, or with having what is called a "good prose style." On the other hand it is not concerned with fake simplicity and the attempt to make written English colloquial. Nor does it even imply in every case preferring the Saxon word to the Latin one, though it does imply using the fewest and shortest words that will cover one's meaning. What is above all needed is to let the meaning choose the word, and not the other way about. In prose, the worst thing one can do with words is to surrender to them. When you think of a concrete object, you think wordlessly, and then, if you want to describe the thing you have been visualizing you probably hunt about till you find the exact words that seem to fit. When you think of something abstract you are more inclined to use words from the start, and unless you make a conscious effort to prevent it, the existing dialect will come rushing in and do the job for you, at the expense of blurring or even changing your meaning. Probably it is better to put off using words as long as possible and get one's meaning as clear as one can through pictures or sensations. Afterwards one can choose—not simply *accept*—the phrases that will best cover the meaning, and then switch round and decide what impression one's words are likely to make on another person. This last effort of the mind cuts out all stale or mixed images, all prefabricated phrases, needless repetitions, and humbug and vagueness generally. But one can often be in doubt about the effect of a word or a phrase, and one needs rules that one can rely on when instinct fails. I think the following rules will cover most cases:

(i) Never use a metaphor, simile, or other figure of speech which you are used to seeing in print.

(ii) Never use a long word where a short one will do.

(iii) If it is possible to cut a word out, always cut it out.

(iv) Never use the passive where you can use the active.

[5]One can cure oneself of the *not un-* formation by memorizing this sentence: *A not un-black dog was chasing a not unsmall rabbit across a not ungreen field.*

(v) Never use a foreign phrase, a scientific word, or a jargon word if you can think of an everyday English equivalent.

(vi) Break any of these rules sooner than say anything outright barbarous.

These rules sound elementary, and so they are, but they demand a deep change in attitude in anyone who has grown used to writing in the style now fashionable. One could keep all of them and still write bad English, but one could not write the kind of stuff that I quoted in those five specimens at the beginning of this article.

I have not here been considering the literary use of language, but merely language as an instrument for expressing and not for concealing or preventing thought. Stuart Chase and others have come near to claiming that all abstract words are meaningless, and have used this as a pretext for advocating a kind of political quietism. Since you don't know what Fascism is, how can you struggle against Fascism? One need not swallow such absurdities as these, but one ought to recognize that the present political chaos is connected with the decay of language, and the one can probably bring about some improvement by starting at the verbal end. If you simplify your English, you are freed from the worst follies of orthodoxy. You cannot speak any of the necessary dialects, and when you make a stupid remark its stupidity will be obvious, even to yourself. Political language — and with variations this is true of all political parties, from Conservatives to Anarchists — is designed to make lies sound truthful and murder respectable, and to give an appearance of solidity to pure wind. One cannot change this all in a moment, but one can at least change one's own habits, and from time to time one can even, if one jeers loudly enough, send some worn-out and useless phrase — some *jackboot, Achilles' heel, hotbed, melting pot, acid test, veritable inferno*, or other lump of verbal refuse — into the dustbin where it belongs.

The Reader's Presence

1. What characteristics of Orwell's own writing demonstrate his six rules for writing good prose? (See pages 521–522.) Can you identify five examples in which Orwell practices what he preaches? Can you identify any moments when he seems to slip?

2. Note that Orwell does not provide *positive* examples of political expression. Why do you think this is so? Is Orwell implying that all political language — regardless of party or position — is corrupt? From this essay can you infer his political philosophy? Explain your answer.

3. Look carefully at Orwell's five examples of bad prose. Would you have identified this writing as "bad" if you had come across it in

your college reading? Compare Orwell's list of rules for writing (paragraph 18), and the ideas expressed in paragraph 16, to Langston Hughes's "How to Be a Bad Writer (in Ten Easy Lessons)" (page 145). How does each writer use humor to persuade the reader of the serious effects of writing badly? What does each writer seem to think is at stake in how one writes?

THE WRITER AT WORK

George Orwell on the Four Reasons for Writing

As the preceding essay shows, George Orwell spent much time considering the art of writing. He believed it was of the utmost political importance to write clearly and accurately. In the following passage from another essay, "Why I Write," Orwell considers a more fundamental aspect of writing: the reasons behind why people write at all. You may observe that he doesn't list the reason most college students write — to respond to an assignment. Why do you think he omitted assigned writing? Can you think of other motives he doesn't take into account?

Putting aside the need to earn a living, I think there are four great motives for writing, at any rate for writing prose. They exist in different degrees in every writer, and in any one writer the proportions will vary from time to time, according to the atmosphere in which he is living. They are:

1. Sheer egoism. Desire to seem clever, to be talked about, to be remembered after death, to get your own back on grown-ups who snubbed you in childhood, etc., etc. It is humbug to pretend that this is not a motive, and a strong one. Writers share this characteristic with scientists, artists, politicians, lawyers, soldiers, successful businessmen — in short, with the whole top crust of humanity. The great mass of human beings are not acutely selfish. After the age of thirty they abandon individual ambition — in many cases, indeed, they almost abandon the sense of being individuals at all — and live chiefly for others, or are simply smothered under drudgery. But there is also the minority of gifted, willful people who are determined to live their own lives to the end, and writers belong in this class. Serious writers, I should say, are on the whole more vain and self-centered than journalists, though less interested in money.

2. Aesthetic enthusiasm. Perception of beauty in the external world, or, on the other hand, in words and their right arrangement. Pleasure in the impact of one sound on another, in the firmness of good prose or the rhythm of a good story. Desire to share an experience which one feels is valuable and ought not to be missed. The aesthetic motive is very feeble in a lot of writers, but even a pamphleteer or a writer of textbooks will have pet words and phrases which appeal to him for non-utilitarian reasons; or he may feel strongly about typography, width of margins, etc. Above the level of a railway guide, no book is quite free from aesthetic considerations.

3. Historical impulse. Desire to see things as they are, to find out true facts and store them up for the use of posterity.

4. Political purpose—using the word "political" in the widest possible sense. Desire to push the world in a certain direction, to alter other people's idea of the kind of society that they should strive after. Once again, no book is genuinely free from political bias. The opinion that art should have nothing to do with politics is itself a political attitude.

5

Katha Pollitt
Why Boys Don't Play with Dolls

Katha Pollitt was born in 1949 in New York City and is considered one of the leading poets of her generation. Her 1982 collection of poetry, Antarctic Traveller, *won a National Book Critics Circle Award. Her poetry has received many other honors and has appeared in the* Atlantic *and the* New Yorker. *Pollitt also writes essays, and she has gained a reputation for incisive analysis and persuasive argument. She contributes reviews, essays, and social commentary to numerous national publications, many of which are collected in* Reasonable Creatures *(1994). Her collections of essays,* Subject to Debate: Sense and Dissents on Women, Politics, and Culture *(2001) and* Virginity or Death! And Other Social and Political Issues of Our Time *(2006), draw on her twice-monthly column in the* Nation, *where she has been a writer, an associate editor, and a columnist for more than twenty-seven years. Her latest collection of personal essays is* Learning to Drive: and Other Life Stories *(2008). "Why Boys Don't Play with Dolls" appeared in the* New York Times Magazine *in 1995.*

Pollitt thinks of writing poems and political essays as two distinct endeavors. "What I want in a poem—one that I read or one that I write—is not an argument, it's not a statement, it has to do with language. . . . There isn't that much political poetry that I find I even want to read once, and almost none that I would want to read again."

It's twenty-eight years since the founding of NOW,[1] and boys still like trucks and girls still like dolls. Increasingly, we are told that the source of these robust preferences must lie outside society—in prenatal hormonal influences, brain chemistry, genes—and that feminism has reached its natural limits. What else could possibly explain the love of preschool girls

---

[1]*NOW:* The National Organization for Women was founded in 1966.—EDS.

for party dresses or the desire of toddler boys to own more guns than Mark from Michigan?[2]

True, recent studies claim to show small cognitive differences between the sexes: he gets around by orienting himself in space, she does it by remembering landmarks. Time will tell if any deserve the hoopla with which each is invariably greeted, over the protests of the researchers themselves. But even if the results hold up (and the history of such research is not encouraging), we don't need studies of sex-differentiated brain activity in reading, say, to understand why boys and girls still seem so unalike.

The feminist movement has done much for some women, and something for every woman, but it has hardly turned America into a playground free of sex roles. It hasn't even got women to stop dieting or men to stop interrupting them.

Instead of looking at kids to "prove" that differences in behavior by sex are innate, we can look at the ways we raise kids as an index to how unfinished the feminist revolution really is, and how tentatively it is embraced even by adults who fully expect their daughters to enter previously male-dominated professions and their sons to change diapers.

I'm at a children's birthday party. "I'm sorry," one mom silently 5 mouths to the mother of the birthday girl, who has just torn open her present — Tropical Splash Barbie. Now, you can love Barbie or you can hate Barbie, and there are feminists in both camps. But *apologize* for Barbie? Inflict Barbie, against your own convictions, on the child of a friend you know will be none too pleased?

Every mother in that room had spent years becoming a person who had to be taken seriously, not least by herself. Even the most attractive, I'm willing to bet, had suffered over her body's failure to fit the impossible American ideal. Given all that, it seems crazy to transmit Barbie to the next generation. Yet to reject her is to say that what Barbie represents — being sexy, thin, stylish — is unimportant, which is obviously not true, and children know it's not true.

Women's looks matter terribly in this society, and so Barbie, however ambivalently, must be passed along. After all, there are worse toys. The Cut and Style Barbie styling head, for example, a grotesque object intended to encourage "hair play." The grown-ups who give that probably apologize, too.

How happy would most parents be to have a child who flouted sex conventions? I know a lot of women, feminists, who complain in a comical, eyeball-rolling way about their sons' passion for sports: the ruined weekends, obnoxious coaches, macho values. But they would not think of discouraging their sons from participating in this activity they find so foolish. Or do they? Their husbands are sports fans, too, and they like their husbands a lot.

---

[2]*Mark from Michigan:* Mark Koernke, a former right-wing talk-show host who supports the militia movement's resistance to federal government. — EDS.

Could it be that even sports-resistant moms see athletics as part of manliness? That if their sons wanted to spend the weekend writing up their diaries, or reading, or baking, they'd find it disturbing? Too antisocial? Too lonely? Too gay?

Theories of innate differences in behavior are appealing. They let parents off the hook—no small recommendation in a culture that holds moms, and sometimes even dads, responsible for their children's every misstep on the road to bliss and success.

They allow grown-ups to take the path of least resistance to the dominant culture, which always requires less psychic effort, even if it means more actual work: just ask the working mother who comes home exhausted and nonetheless finds it easier to pick up her son's socks than make him do it himself. They let families buy for their children, without *too* much guilt, the unbelievably sexist junk that the kids, who have been watching commercials since birth, understandably crave.

But the thing that theories do most of all is tell adults that the *adult* world—in which moms and dads still play by many of the old rules even as they question and fidget and chafe against them—is the way it's supposed to be. A girl with a doll and a boy with a truck "explain" why men are from Mars and women are from Venus, why wives do housework and husbands just don't understand.

The paradox is that the world of rigid and hierarchical sex roles evoked by determinist theories is already passing away. Three-year-olds may indeed insist that doctors are male and nurses female, even if their own mother is a physician. Six-year-olds know better. These days, something like half of all medical students are female, and male applications to nursing school are inching upward. When tomorrow's three-year-olds play doctor, who's to say how they'll assign the roles?

With sex roles, as in every area of life, people aspire to what is possible, and conform to what is necessary. But these are not fixed, especially today. Biological determinism may reassure some adults about their present, but it is feminism, the ideology of flexible and converging sex roles, that fits our children's future. And the kids, somehow, know this.

That's why, if you look carefully, you'll find that for every kid who fits a stereotype, there's another who's breaking one down. Sometimes it's the same kid—the boy who skateboards *and* takes cooking in his afterschool program; the girl who collects stuffed animals *and* A-pluses in science.

Feminists are often accused of imposing their "agenda" on children. Isn't that what adults always do, consciously and unconsciously? Kids aren't born religious, or polite, or kind, or able to remember where they put their sneakers. Inculcating these behaviors, and the values behind them, is a tremendous amount of work, involving many adults. We don't have a choice, really, about *whether* we should give our children messages about what it means to be male and female—they're bombarded with them from morning till night.

The question, as always, is what do we want those messages to be?

The Reader's Presence

1. Pollitt notes in her opening paragraph that "it's twenty-eight years since the founding of NOW, and boys still like trucks and girls still like dolls." What does Pollitt identify as the competing theories to explain these differences between boys and girls? Which theory does Pollitt prefer, and how does she express her support of it?

2. As you reread the essay, consider carefully the role of the media in upholding the status quo with regard to differentiated roles for girls and boys. As you develop a response to this question, examine carefully both the media directed principally to children and the media targeted at adults. In the latter category, for instance, Pollitt refers to the media version of scientific research studies into gender differences (paragraph 2) and alludes to popular books that discuss the differences between men and women, such as *Men Are from Mars, Women Are from Venus,* and *You Just Don't Understand* (paragraph 12). Drawing on Pollitt's essay and on your own experience, identify — and discuss — the specific social responsibilities you would like to see America's mass media take more seriously.

3. How would you characterize Pollitt's stance toward today's parents? What are some of the reasons she gives to explain parents' choices and actions? Consider Pollitt's argument in the light of Bernard Cooper's essay "A Clack of Tiny Sparks: Remembrances of a Gay Boyhood" (page 75). How does Cooper's account of his parents' attitudes compare with Pollitt's portrait of parents? What general points about childrearing can you draw from the contrasts and commonalities between the essays? How does parenting figure in the transmission of beliefs and practices in America, according to these authors?

William Safire

Changing Warming

William Safire was born in New York City in 1929. A Pulitzer Prize–winning journalist, author, and self-described "libertarian conservative," Safire continues to write political and social commentary, as well as lessons on language. He wrote a regular political column for the New York Times *from 1973 to 2005 and continues contributing to the "On Language" feature of the* New York Times Magazine, *from which his 2005 essay "Changing Warming" is taken. Safire began his career as a reporter for the* New York Herald Tribune *and, before joining the* Times, *he was a senior White House speechwriter for President Richard Nixon. His interest in language and politics is reflected in his many books, including* Safire's Political Dictionary *(1978),* William Safire on Language *(1980),* What's the Good Word *(1982),* Coming to Terms *(1991),* Watching My Language: Adventures in the Word Trade *(1997), and* The Right Word in the Right Place at the Right Time *(2004). His novels, too, have a political tinge; they include* Full Disclosure *(1977),* Sleeper Spy *(1995), and* Scandalmonger *(2000). A dropout from Syracuse University, Safire returned a generation later to deliver the commencement address and is now a trustee.*

Safire is often the subject of criticism for his "opinionated reporting," a genre he claims to have invented. In a 2002 column, he wrote: "A columnist should play a hunch now and then, taking readers beyond the published news, using logic and experience to figure out what may be happening now or to predict what will happen soon. Win some, lose some."

The contentious phrase *global warming*, first used by United Press International in 1969, seems to be undergoing a certain cooling; contrariwise, the more temperate phrase *climate change* is getting hot.

Many think the terms are synonymous. "I think *climate change* and *global warming* are used interchangeably," says Jay Gulledge of the Pew Center on Global Climate Change (a name that, in squeezing the two terms together, notably drops *warming*). "When people talk about the general phenomenon of climate change, they assume the process of global warming." But he knows that scientists draw a distinction: "Since global warming has been well established, scientists have begun to focus more and more on other aspects of climate, necessitating the use of the more inclusive phrase *climate change*."

Over at the Brookings Institution, its environmental boss detects a whiff of terminological politics. "Polling data suggest that much of the public considers the term *climate change* less threatening than *global warming*," says David Sandalow. "As a result, politicians eager to downplay risks tend to use the term *climate change*."

At Greenpeace, an active environmentalist lobby, they don't like the change to *climate change*. "*Change* sounds mellow and gentle," notes Kert Davies, its research director. "Communications specialists during the Clinton administration determined that the term *climate change* was too benign, that it didn't evoke any urgency. Vice President Gore used *global warming* in his book *Earth in the Balance*. But now that the 90s label switch has switched back, Davies of Greenpeace argues that the verb change is not only weak but also misleading: "It's really 'disruption,' and it isn't benign at all."

The opposing view is heard from James Mahoney, the Bush adminis-   5
tration's director of the — you guessed it — Climate Change Science Program. "*Climate change* is a more encompassing and technically accurate term to describe the changes in earth systems," Mahoney says, adding that "*global warming* is an oversimplification, and by definition does not allow for the occurrence of warming in one region and simultaneous cooling or stability in others."

NASA's glossary tries valiantly to be apolitical, defining G.W. as "warming predicted to occur as a result of increased emissions of greenhouse gases," partly man-made, while C.C. is used by scientists "in a wider sense to also include natural changes in climate." United Nations usage differs, treating C.C. as change attributable directly or indirectly to human activity.

In the nomenclature struggle, who names an issue usually carries the day. Lexicographers and usagists take no sides, but in common parlance as reflected by the search engines, the neutral climate change has put a chill into the scarier global warming.

The Reader's Presence

1. Note the number of quotations used by Safire in this very short essay. If you add up the direct quotations from interviews and publications plus the paraphrases or summaries of other sources, how many of Safire's own words do you find in the selection? Why do you think he uses so many quotes? How does this technique affect your response to his main point about terminology? Do you think it supports it or detracts from it?

2. Safire claims that "lexicographers and usagists" (like himself) "take no sides" (paragraph 7). Do you agree? Why or why not? Where does he seem to stand on the issue? How do you interpret his final sentence? Can you find other instances in the essay where Safire seems to use a term for political effect?

3. Read Safire's essay in conjunction with Michiko Kakutani's essay "The Word Police" (page 710). In what sense do both authors

discuss a similar issue? After reading "The Word Police," discuss whether the terms "global warming" or "climate change" can be considered "politically correct." In your opinion, which term would be considered the more "politically correct," and why?

Eric Schlosser

Why McDonald's Fries Taste So Good

Investigative reporter and author Eric Schlosser was born in New York City in 1960. A correspondent for the Atlantic, *and contributor to* Rolling Stone *and the* New Yorker, *he has won numerous journalistic honors and awards. His two-part* Atlantic Monthly *series, "Reefer Madness" and "Marijuana and the Law," won the National Magazine Award in 1994 and became the basis for his best-selling collection of essays,* Reefer Madness: Sex, Drugs, and Cheap Labor in the American Black Market *(2003), an exposé of America's underground economy.* Fast Food Nation: The Dark Side of the All-American Meal *(2001), Schlosser's controversial and influential first book, prompted a reexamination of practices in the meat-processing industry. A best-seller, the book was adapted and released as a motion picture in 2006, followed by a companion book for young people,* Chew on This: Everything You Don't Want to Know About Fast Food *(2006).*

Of writing Fast Food Nation, *Schlosser said, "I care about the literary aspects of the book. I tried to make it as clear as possible, and make it an interesting thing to read, but I sacrificed some of that, ultimately, in order to get this out to people and let them know what's going on."*

The french fry was "almost sacrosanct for me," Ray Kroc, one of the founders of McDonald's, wrote in his autobiography, "its preparation a ritual to be followed religiously." During the chain's early years french fries were made from scratch every day. Russet Burbank potatoes were peeled, cut into shoestrings, and fried in McDonald's kitchens. As the chain expanded nationwide, in the mid-1960s, it sought to cut labor costs, reduce the number of suppliers, and ensure that its fries tasted the same at every restaurant. McDonald's began switching to frozen french fries in 1966 — and few customers noticed the difference. Nevertheless, the change had a profound effect on the nation's agriculture and diet. A familiar food had been transformed into a highly processed industrial commodity. McDonald's fries now come from huge manufacturing plants that can peel, slice, cook, and freeze two million pounds of potatoes a day. The rapid expansion of McDonald's and the popularity of its low-cost, mass-produced fries changed the way Americans eat. In 1960 Americans consumed an average of about eighty-one pounds of fresh potatoes and four pounds of frozen french fries. In 2000 they consumed an average of about fifty pounds of fresh potatoes and thirty pounds of frozen fries. Today McDonald's is the largest buyer of potatoes in the United States.

The taste of McDonald's french fries played a crucial role in the chain's success—fries are much more profitable than hamburgers—and was long praised by customers, competitors, and even food critics. James Beard loved McDonald's fries. Their distinctive taste does not stem from the kind of potatoes that McDonald's buys, the technology that processes them, or the restaurant equipment that fries them: other chains use Russet Burbanks, buy their french fries from the same large processing companies, and have similar fryers in their restaurant kitchens. The taste of a french fry is largely determined by the cooking oil. For decades McDonald's cooked its french fries in a mixture of about seven percent cottonseed oil and 93 percent beef tallow. The mixture gave the fries their unique flavor—and more saturated beef fat per ounce than a McDonald's hamburger.

In 1990, amid a barrage of criticism over the amount of cholesterol in its fries, McDonald's switched to pure vegetable oil. This presented the company with a challenge: how to make fries that subtly taste like beef without cooking them in beef tallow. A look at the ingredients in McDonald's french fries suggests how the problem was solved. Toward the end of the list is a seemingly innocuous yet oddly mysterious phrase: "natural flavor." That ingredient helps to explain not only why the fries taste so good but also why most fast food—indeed, most of the food Americans eat today—tastes the way it does.

Open your refrigerator, your freezer, your kitchen cupboards, and look at the labels on your food. You'll find "natural flavor" or "artificial flavor" in just about every list of ingredients. The similarities between these two broad categories are far more significant than the differences. Both are man-made additives that give most processed food most of its taste. People usually buy a food item the first time because of its packaging or appearance. Taste usually determines whether they buy it again. About 90 percent of the money that Americans now spend on food goes to buy processed food. The canning, freezing, and dehydrating techniques used in processing destroy most of food's flavor—and so a vast industry has arisen in the United States to make processed food palatable. Without this flavor industry today's fast food would not exist. The names of the leading American fast-food chains and their best-selling menu items have become embedded in our popular culture and famous worldwide. But few people can name the companies that manufacture fast food's taste.

The flavor industry is highly secretive. Its leading companies will not divulge the precise formulas of flavor compounds or the identities of clients. 5

The secrecy is deemed essential for protecting the reputations of beloved brands. The fast-food chains, understandably, would like the public to believe that the flavors of the food they sell somehow originate in their restaurant kitchens, not in distant factories run by other firms. A McDonald's french fry is one of countless foods whose flavor is just a component in a complex manufacturing process. The look and the taste of what we eat now are frequently deceiving — by design.

THE FLAVOR CORRIDOR

The New Jersey Turnpike runs through the heart of the flavor industry, an industrial corridor dotted with refineries and chemical plants. International Flavors & Fragrances (IFF), the world's largest flavor company, has a manufacturing facility off Exit 8A in Dayton, New Jersey; Givaudan, the world's second-largest flavor company, has a plant in East Hanover. Haarmann & Reimer, the largest German flavor company, has a plant in Teterboro, as does Takasago, the largest Japanese flavor company. Flavor Dynamics has a plant in South Plainfield; Frutarom is in North Bergen; Elan Chemical is in Newark. Dozens of companies manufacture flavors in the corridor between Teaneck and South Brunswick. Altogether the area produces about two-thirds of the flavor additives sold in the United States.

The IFF plant in Dayton is a huge pale-blue building with a modern office complex attached to the front. It sits in an industrial park, not far from a BASF plastics factory, a Jolly French Toast factory, and a plant that manufactures Liz Claiborne cosmetics. Dozens of tractor-trailers were parked at the IFF loading dock the afternoon I visited, and a thin cloud of steam floated from a roof vent. Before entering the plant, I signed a nondisclosure form, promising not to reveal the brand names of foods that contain IFF flavors. The place reminded me of Willy Wonka's chocolate factory. Wonderful smells drifted through the hallways, men and women in neat white lab coats cheerfully went about their work, and hundreds of little glass bottles sat on laboratory tables and shelves. The bottles contained powerful but fragile flavor chemicals, shielded from light by brown glass and round white caps shut tight. The long chemical names on the little white labels were as mystifying to me as medieval Latin. These odd-sounding things would be mixed and poured and turned into new substances, like magic potions.

I was not invited into the manufacturing areas of the IFF plant, where, it was thought, I might discover trade secrets. Instead I toured various laboratories and pilot kitchens, where the flavors of well-established brands are tested or adjusted, and where whole new flavors are created. IFF's snack-and-savory lab is responsible for the flavors of potato chips, corn chips, breads, crackers, breakfast cereals, and pet food. The confectionary lab devises flavors for ice cream, cookies, candies, toothpastes, mouthwashes, and antacids. Everywhere I looked, I saw famous, widely advertised products sitting on laboratory desks and tables. The beverage lab was full of brightly colored liquids in clear bottles. It comes up with flavors for popular soft drinks, sports drinks, bottled teas, and wine coolers, for all-natural juice drinks, organic soy drinks, beers, and malt liquors. In one pilot kitchen I saw a dapper food technologist, a middle-aged man with an elegant tie beneath his crisp lab coat, carefully preparing a batch of cookies with white frosting and pink-and-white sprinkles. In another pilot kitchen I saw a pizza oven, a grill, a milk-shake machine, and a french fryer identical to those I'd seen at innumerable fast-food restaurants.

In addition to being the world's largest flavor company, IFF manufactures the smells of six of the ten best-selling fine perfumes in the United States, including Estée Lauder's Beautiful, Clinique's Happy, Lancôme's Trésor, and Calvin Klein's Eternity. It also makes the smells of household products such as deodorant, dishwashing detergent, bath soap, shampoo, furniture polish, and floor wax. All these aromas are made through essentially the same process: the manipulation of volatile chemicals. The basic science behind the scent of your shaving cream is the same as that governing the flavor of your TV dinner.

"NATURAL" AND "ARTIFICIAL"

Scientists now believe that human beings acquired the sense of taste as   10
a way to avoid being poisoned. Edible plants generally taste sweet, harmful ones bitter. The taste buds on our tongues can detect the presence of half a dozen or so basic tastes, including sweet, sour, bitter, salty, astringent, and umami, a taste discovered by Japanese researchers—a rich and full sense of deliciousness triggered by amino acids in foods such as meat, shellfish, mushrooms, potatoes, and seaweed. Taste buds offer a limited means of detection, however, compared with the human olfactory system, which can perceive thousands of different chemical aromas. Indeed, "flavor" is primarily the smell of gases being released by the chemicals you've just put in your mouth. The aroma of a food can be responsible for as much as 90 percent of its taste.

The act of drinking, sucking, or chewing a substance releases its volatile gases. They flow out of your mouth and up your nostrils, or up the passageway in the back of your mouth, to a thin layer of nerve cells called the olfactory epithelium, located at the base of your nose, right between your eyes. Your brain combines the complex smell signals from your olfactory epithelium with the simple taste signals from your tongue, assigns a flavor to what's in your mouth, and decides if it's something you want to eat.

A person's food preferences, like his or her personality, are formed during the first few years of life, through a process of socialization. Babies innately prefer sweet tastes and reject bitter ones; toddlers can learn to enjoy hot and spicy food, bland health food, or fast food, depending on what the people around them eat. The human sense of smell is still not fully understood. It is greatly affected by psychological factors and expectations. The mind focuses intently on some of the aromas that surround us and filters out the overwhelming majority. People can grow accustomed to bad smells or good smells; they stop noticing what once seemed overpowering. Aroma and memory are somehow inextricably linked. A smell can suddenly evoke a long-forgotten moment. The flavors of childhood foods seem to leave an indelible mark, and adults often return to them, without always knowing why. These "comfort foods" become a source of pleasure and reassurance—a fact that fast-food chains use to their advantage. Childhood memories of Happy Meals, which come with french fries, can translate into frequent adult visits to McDonald's. On average, Americans now eat about four servings of french fries every week.

The human craving for flavor has been a largely unacknowledged and unexamined force in history. For millennia royal empires have been built, unexplored lands traversed, and great religions and philosophies forever changed by the spice trade. In 1492 Christopher Columbus set sail to find seasoning. Today the influence of flavor in the world marketplace is no less decisive. The rise and fall of corporate empires—of soft-drink companies, snack-food companies, and fast-food chains—is often determined by how their products taste.

The flavor industry emerged in the mid-nineteenth century, as processed foods began to be manufactured on a large scale. Recognizing the need for flavor additives, early food processors turned to perfume companies that had long experience working with essential oils and volatile aromas. The great perfume houses of England, France, and the Netherlands produced many of the first flavor compounds. In the early part of the twentieth century Germany took the technological lead in flavor production, owing to its powerful chemical industry. Legend has it that a German scientist discovered methyl anthranilate, one of the first artificial flavors, by accident while mixing chemicals in his laboratory. Suddenly the lab was filled with the sweet smell of grapes. Methyl anthranilate later became the chief flavor compound in grape Kool-Aid. After World War II much of the perfume industry shifted from Europe to the United States, settling in New York City near the garment district and the fashion houses. The flavor industry came with it, later moving to New Jersey for greater plant capacity. Man-made flavor additives were used mostly in baked goods, candies, and sodas until the 1950s, when sales of processed food began to soar. The invention of gas chromatographs and mass spectrometers—machines capable of detecting volatile gases at low levels—vastly increased the number of flavors that could be synthesized. By the mid-1960s flavor companies were churning out compounds to supply the taste of Pop Tarts, Bac-Os, Tab, Tang, Filet-O-Fish sandwiches, and literally thousands of other new foods.

The American flavor industry now has annual revenues of about $1.4   15
billion. Approximately 10,000 new processed-food products are introduced

every year in the United States. Almost all of them require flavor additives. And about nine out of ten of these products fail. The latest flavor innovations and corporate realignments are heralded in publications such as *Chemical Market Reporter*, *Food Chemical News*, *Food Engineering*, and *Food Product Design*. The progress of IFF has mirrored that of the flavor industry as a whole. IFF was formed in 1958, through the merger of two small companies. Its annual revenues have grown almost fifteenfold since the early 1970s, and it currently has manufacturing facilities in twenty countries.

Today's sophisticated spectrometers, gas chromatographs, and headspace-vapor analyzers provide a detailed map of a food's flavor components, detecting chemical aromas present in amounts as low as one part per billion. The human nose, however, is even more sensitive. A nose can detect aromas present in quantities of a few parts per trillion—an amount equivalent to about 0.000000000003 percent. Complex aromas, such as those of coffee and roasted meat, are composed of volatile gases from nearly a thousand different chemicals. The smell of a strawberry arises from the interaction of about 350 chemicals that are present in minute amounts. The quality that people seek most of all in a food—flavor—is usually present in a quantity too infinitesimal to be measured in traditional culinary terms such as ounces or teaspoons. The chemical that provides the dominant flavor of bell pepper can be tasted in amounts as low as 0.02 parts per billion; one drop is sufficient to add flavor to five average-size swimming pools. The flavor additive usually comes next to last in a processed food's list of ingredients and often costs less than its packaging. Soft drinks contain a larger proportion of flavor additives than most products. The flavor in a twelve-ounce can of Coke costs about half a cent.

The color additives in processed foods are usually present in even smaller amounts than the flavor compounds. Many of New Jersey's flavor companies also manufacture these color additives, which are used to make processed foods look fresh and appealing. Food coloring serves many of the same decorative purposes as lipstick, eye shadow, mascara—and is often made from the same pigments. Titanium dioxide, for example, has proved to be an especially versatile mineral. It gives many processed candies, frostings, and icings their bright white color; it is a common ingredient in women's cosmetics; and it is the pigment used in many white oil paints and house paints. At Burger King, Wendy's, and McDonald's coloring agents have been added to many of the soft drinks, salad dressings, cookies, condiments, chicken dishes, and sandwich buns.

Studies have found that the color of a food can greatly affect how its taste is perceived. Brightly colored foods frequently seem to taste better than bland-looking foods, even when the flavor compounds are identical. Foods that somehow look off-color often seem to have off tastes. For thousands of years human beings have relied on visual cues to help determine what is edible. The color of fruit suggests whether it is ripe, the color of meat whether it is rancid. Flavor researchers sometimes use colored lights to modify the influence of visual cues during taste tests. During one experiment in the early 1970s people were served an oddly tinted meal of steak and french fries that appeared normal beneath colored lights. Everyone thought the meal tasted fine until the lighting was changed. Once it became apparent that the steak was actually blue and the fries were green, some people became ill.

The federal Food and Drug Administration does not require companies to disclose the ingredients of their color or flavor additives so long as all the chemicals in them are considered by the agency to be GRAS ("generally recognized as safe"). This enables companies to maintain the secrecy of their formulas. It also hides the fact that flavor compounds often contain more ingredients than the foods to which they give taste. The phrase "artificial strawberry flavor" gives little hint of the chemical wizardry and manufacturing skill that can make a highly processed food taste like strawberries.

A typical artificial strawberry flavor, like the kind found in a Burger   20
King strawberry milk shake, contains the following ingredients: amyl acetate, amyl butyrate, amyl valerate, anethol, anisyl formate, benzyl acetate, benzyl isobutyrate, butyric acid, cinnamyl isobutyrate, cinnamyl valerate, cognac essential oil, diacetyl, dipropyl ketone, ethyl acetate, ethyl amyl ketone, ethyl butyrate, ethyl cinnamate, ethyl heptanoate, ethyl heptylate, ethyl lactate, ethyl methylphenylglycidate, ethyl nitrate, ethyl propionate, ethyl valerate, heliotropin, hydroxyphenyl-2-butanone (10 percent solution in alcohol), α-ionone, isobutyl anthranilate, isobutyl butyrate, lemon essential oil, maltol, 4-methylacetophenone, methyl anthranilate, methyl benzoate, methyl cinnamate, methyl heptine carbonate, methyl naphthyl ketone, methyl salicylate, mint essential oil, neroli essential oil, nerolin, neryl isobutyrate, orris butter, phenethyl alcohol, rose, rum ether, γ-undecalactone, vanillin, and solvent.

Although flavors usually arise from a mixture of many different volatile chemicals, often a single compound supplies the dominant aroma. Smelled alone, that chemical provides an unmistakable sense of the food. Ethyl-2-methyl butyrate, for example, smells just like an apple. Many of today's highly processed foods offer a blank palette: whatever chemicals are added to them will give them specific tastes. Adding methyl-2-pyridyl ketone makes something taste like popcorn. Adding ethyl-3-hydroxy butanoate makes it taste like marshmallow. The possibilities are now almost limitless. Without affecting appearance or nutritional value, processed foods could be made with aroma chemicals such as hexanal (the smell of freshly cut grass) or 3-methyl butanoic acid (the smell of body odor).

The 1960s were the heyday of artificial flavors in the United States. The synthetic versions of flavor compounds were not subtle, but they did not have to be, given the nature of most processed food. For the past twenty years food processors have tried hard to use only "natural flavors" in their products. According to the FDA, these must be derived entirely from natural sources — from herbs, spices, fruits, vegetables, beef, chicken, yeast, bark, roots, and so forth. Consumers prefer to see natural flavors on a label, out of a belief that they are more healthful. Distinctions between artificial and natural flavors can be arbitrary and somewhat absurd, based more on how the flavor has been made than on what it actually contains.

"A natural flavor," says Terry Acree, a professor of food science at Cornell University, "is a flavor that's been derived with an out-of-date technology." Natural flavors and artificial flavors sometimes contain exactly the same chemicals, produced through different methods. Amyl acetate, for example, provides the dominant note of banana flavor. When it is distilled from bananas with a solvent, amyl acetate is a natural flavor. When it is produced by mixing vinegar with amyl alcohol and adding sulfuric acid as a catalyst, amyl acetate is an artificial flavor. Either way it smells and tastes the same. "Natural flavor" is now listed among the ingredients of everything from Health Valley Blueberry Granola Bars to Taco Bell Hot Taco Sauce.

A natural flavor is not necessarily more healthful or purer than an artificial one. When almond flavor — benzaldehyde — is derived from natural sources, such as peach and apricot pits, it contains traces of hydrogen cyanide, a deadly poison. Benzaldehyde derived by mixing oil of clove and amyl acetate does not contain any cyanide. Nevertheless, it is legally considered an artificial flavor and sells at a much lower price. Natural and artificial flavors are now manufactured at the same chemical plants, places that few people would associate with Mother Nature.

A TRAINED NOSE AND A POETIC SENSIBILITY

The small and elite group of scientists who create most of the flavor in most of the food now consumed in the United States are called "flavorists." They draw on a number of disciplines in their work: biology, psychology, physiology, and organic chemistry. A flavorist is a chemist with a trained nose and a poetic sensibility. Flavors are created by blending scores of different chemicals in tiny amounts — a process governed by scientific principles but demanding a fair amount of art. In an age when delicate aromas and microwave ovens do not easily co-exist, the job of the flavorist is to conjure illusions about processed food and, in the words of one flavor company's literature, to ensure "consumer likeability." The flavorists with whom I spoke were discreet, in keeping with the dictates of their trade. They were also charming, cosmopolitan, and ironic. They not only enjoyed fine wine but could identify the chemicals that give each grape its unique aroma. One flavorist compared his work to composing music. A well-made flavor compound will have a "top note" that is often followed by a "dry-down" and a "leveling-off," with different chemicals responsible for each stage. The taste of a food can be radically altered by

25

minute changes in the flavoring combination. "A little odor goes a long way," one flavorist told me.

In order to give a processed food a taste that consumers will find appealing, a flavorist must always consider the food's "mouthfeel" — the unique combination of textures and chemical interactions that affect how the flavor is perceived. Mouthfeel can be adjusted through the use of various fats, gums, starches, emulsifiers, and stabilizers. The aroma chemicals in a food can be precisely analyzed, but the elements that make up mouthfeel are much harder to measure. How does one quantify a pretzel's hardness, a french fry's crispness? Food technologists are now conducting basic research in rheology, the branch of physics that examines the flow and deformation of materials. A number of companies sell sophisticated devices that attempt to measure mouthfeel. The TA.XT2i Texture Analyzer, produced by the Texture Technologies Corporation, of Scarsdale, New York, performs calculations based on data derived from as many as 250 separate probes. It is essentially a mechanical mouth. It gauges the most-important rheological properties of a food — bounce, creep, breaking point, density, crunchiness, chewiness, gumminess, lumpiness, rubberiness, springiness, slipperiness, smoothness, softness, wetness, juiciness, spreadability, springback, and tackiness.

Some of the most important advances in flavor manufacturing are now occurring in the field of biotechnology. Complex flavors are being made using enzyme reactions, fermentation, and fungal and tissue cultures. All the flavors created by these methods — including the ones being synthesized by fungi — are considered natural flavors by the FDA. The new enzyme-based processes are responsible for extremely true-to-life dairy flavors. One company now offers not just butter flavor but also fresh creamy butter, cheesy butter, milky butter, savory melted butter, and super-concentrated butter flavor, in liquid or powder form. The development of new fermentation techniques, along with new techniques for heating mixtures of sugar and amino acids, have led to the creation of much more realistic meat flavors.

The McDonald's Corporation most likely drew on these advances when it eliminated beef tallow from its french fries. The company will not reveal the exact origin of the natural flavor added to its fries. In response to inquiries from *Vegetarian Journal*, however, McDonald's did acknowledge that its fries derive some of their characteristic flavor from "an animal source." Beef is the probable source, although other meats cannot be ruled out. In France, for example, fries are sometimes cooked in duck fat or horse tallow.

Other popular fast foods derive their flavor from unexpected ingredients. McDonald's Chicken McNuggets contain beef extracts, as does Wendy's Grilled Chicken Sandwich. Burger King's BK Broiler Chicken Breast Patty contains "natural smoke flavor." A firm called Red Arrow Products specializes in smoke flavor, which is added to barbecue sauces, snack foods, and processed meats. Red Arrow manufactures natural smoke flavor by charring sawdust and capturing the aroma chemicals released into the air. The smoke is captured in water and then bottled, so that other companies can sell food that seems to have been cooked over a fire.

The Vegetarian Legal Action Network recently petitioned the FDA to   30
issue new labeling requirements for foods that contain natural flavors. The group wants food processors to list the basic origins of their flavors on their labels. At the moment vegetarians often have no way of knowing whether a flavor additive contains beef, pork, poultry, or shellfish. One of the most widely used color additives — whose presence is often hidden by the phrase "color added" — violates a number of religious dietary restrictions, may cause allergic reactions in susceptible people, and comes from an unusual source. Cochineal extract (also known as carmine or carminic acid) is made from the desiccated bodies of female *Dactylopius coccus Costa*, a small insect harvested mainly in Peru and the Canary Islands. The bug feeds on red cactus berries, and color from the berries accumulates in the females and their unhatched larvae. The insects are collected, dried, and ground into a pigment. It takes about 70,000 of them to produce a pound of carmine, which is used to make processed foods look pink, red, or purple. Dannon strawberry yogurt gets its color from carmine, and so do many frozen fruit bars, candies, and fruit fillings, and Ocean Spray pink-grapefruit juice drink.

In a meeting room at IFF, Brian Grainger let me sample some of the company's flavors. It was an unusual taste test — there was no food to taste. Grainger is a senior flavorist at IFF, a soft-spoken chemist with graying hair, an English accent, and a fondness for understatement. He could easily be mistaken for a British diplomat or the owner of a West End brasserie with two Michelin stars. Like many in the flavor industry, he has an Old World, old-fashioned sensibility. When I suggested that IFF's policy of secrecy and discretion was out of step with our mass-marketing, brand-conscious, self-promoting age, and that the company should put its own logo on the countless products that bear its flavors, instead of allowing other companies to enjoy the consumer loyalty and affection inspired by those flavors, Grainger politely disagreed, assuring me that such a thing would never be done. In the absence of public credit or acclaim, the small and secretive fraternity of flavor chemists praise one another's work. By analyzing the flavor formula of a product, Grainger can often tell which of his counterparts at a rival firm devised it. Whenever he walks down a supermarket aisle, he takes a quiet pleasure in seeing the well-known foods that contain his flavors.

Grainger had brought a dozen small glass bottles from the lab. After he opened each bottle, I dipped a fragrance-testing filter into it — a long white strip of paper designed to absorb aroma chemicals without producing off notes. Before placing each strip of paper in front of my nose, I closed my eyes. Then I inhaled deeply, and one food after another was conjured from the glass bottles. I smelled fresh cherries, black olives, sautéed onions, and shrimp. Grainger's most remarkable creation took me by surprise. After closing my eyes, I suddenly smelled a grilled hamburger. The aroma was uncanny, almost miraculous—as if someone in the room were flipping burgers on a hot grill. But when I opened my eyes, I saw just a narrow strip of white paper and a flavorist with a grin.

The Reader's Presence

1. What do McDonald's french fries have to do with Schlosser's primary aim in this selection? Why does he feature them in the title and use them in the opening to the essay? Why, in your opinion, didn't he use a different example?

2. Describe Schlosser's attitude toward "natural" and "artificial" flavoring. Does he think one is superior to the other? Why or why not? How critical does he appear toward food additives in general? Do you read his essay as a condemnation of fast food? How does his account of his laboratory visit color your response? Overall, were his laboratory experiences positive or negative? Explain what in his account makes you feel one way or the other.

3. Compare and contrast Schlosser's investigative techniques with those of James Fallows in "Throwing Like a Girl" (page 386), Amy Cunningham in "Why Women Smile" (page 324), or Malcolm Gladwell in "Big and Bad" (page 407). How does each writer establish a question to investigate, provoke your interest in the issue, gather information, and conduct the investigation? How important are sources and interviews? What information about sources and interviews is omitted from the essays?

Charles Simic

The Life of Images

Charles Simic (b. 1938) grew up in Belgrade, Yugoslavia (now Serbia), during World War II. He immigrated to the United States with his family when he was sixteen years old and became a naturalized citizen in 1971. "Being one of the millions of displaced persons made an impression on me. In addition to my own little story of bad luck, I heard plenty of others. I'm still amazed by all the vileness and stupidity I witnessed in my life," he says. Since his first volume of poetry, What the Grass Says *(1967), Simic has published more than sixty books and has won numerous awards, including the Pulitzer Prize in Poetry for* The World Doesn't End *(1989) and a MacArthur Foundation "genius grant." His book* Walking the Black Cat *(1996) was a finalist for the National Book Award for poetry;* The Voice at 3:00 A.M. *was nominated for the National Book Award and the* Los Angeles Times *Book Award in 2003. In 2008, he published two books of poetry,* Sixty Poems, *poems collected to celebrate his appointment as the U.S. Poet Laureate in 2007, and* On That Little Something *(2008), Simic's eighteenth collection of new poems. Simic is a noted translator of French, Serbian, Croatian, Macedonian, and Slovenian poetry, and his own work has also been translated into many languages. Professor emeritus at the University of New Hampshire in Durham, Simic also contributes frequently to magazines and journals, including the* Harvard Review, *in which his essay "The Life of Images" was published in 2003.*

When asked what he found hardest to write about, Simic replied, "Everything is hard to write about. Many of my shortest and seemingly simple poems took years to get right. I tinker with most of my poems even after publication. I expect to be revising in my coffin as it is being lowered into the ground."

In one of Berenice Abbott's[1] photographs of the Lower East Side, I recall a store sign advertising *Silk Underwear*. Underneath, there was the additional information about "reasonable prices for peddlers." How interesting, I thought. Did someone carry a suitcase full of ladies' underwear and try to peddle them on some street corner farther uptown? Or did he ring doorbells in apartment buildings and offer them to housewives? I imagine the underwear came in many different sizes, so he may have had to carry two suitcases. The peddler was most likely an immigrant and had difficulty making himself understood. What he wanted was for the lady of the house to feel how soft the silk was but she either did not understand him or she had other reasons for hesitating. She wore a house robe, her hair was loose as if she just got out of bed, so she was

---

[1]*Abbott:* Berenice Abbott (1898–1991), a photographer who is noted for her concentration on New York City. Combining artistry with documentary brilliance, her work ranks her among major American photographers. She wrote many articles on photography, and her best-known book is the one Simic refers to, *Changing New York* (1939).—EDS.

embarrassed to touch the undies draped over his extended hand. Then she finally did touch them.

The reason photographs live in my memory is that the city I continue to roam is rich with such visual delights. Everyone who does this is taking imaginary snapshots. For all I know my face, briefly glimpsed in a crowd, may live on in someone else's memory. The attentive eye makes the world mysterious. Some men or a woman going about their business seventy years ago either caught sight of a camera pointed at them or they passed by oblivious. It was like hide and seek. They thought they had concealed themselves in plain view and the camera found them out. It showed something even they did not know they were hiding. Often people had the puzzled look of someone who had volunteered to assist a hypnotist on a stage and awakened to the sound of the audience's applause.

I'm looking at the long-torn-down Second Avenue "El" at the intersection of Division Street and Bowery in another Abbott photograph. The date is April 24, 1936. It seems like a nice day, for the sunlight streams through the tracks and iron scaffold of the elevated train, making patterns of shadow and light on the sidewalk below. As far as I can make out, the street on both sides is lined with stores selling cheap furs. The entire area was for years a bargain hunter's paradise. My father knew a fellow in his office, an elderly, impeccably dressed man, who claimed that he did all his shopping on Orchard and Hester Streets, where he never paid more than five dollars for a suit. What interests me the most in this photograph is the shadowy couple under the El with their backs turned to us. She's willowy and taller than he is, as if she were a model or a salesgirl in one of these shops. They have drawn close together as if talking over something very important, or why would they otherwise stop like that in the middle of the street? The way this woman in a long skirt carries herself gives me the impression that she is young. Not so the man. With one hand casually resting on a post and his other stuck in his pocket, he appears confident, even brash. It's the way they stand together that suggests to me that they are not casual acquaintances. Most likely they work in the same neighborhood, but there is something else going on between them too. She seems very interested in what he is saying now. No one else in view pays them any attention. The fellow standing on the sidewalk in front of the Beauty Fur Shop looks off into the distance where a portly young man with glasses wearing an open overcoat over a three-piece suit is coming into view. He has just had lunch and is glancing idly at the shop windows as he strolls lazily back to the office. He is too young to be the boss, so he must be the son or the son-in-law of one of the store owners. Except for the couple who elude identification, there is nothing unusual here. A photograph such as this one, where time has stopped on an ordinary scene full of innuendoes, partakes of the infinite.

I cannot look long at any old photograph of the city without hearing some music in the background. The moment that happens, I'm transported into the past so vividly no one can convince me that I did not live in that

moment. I have heard just about every recording of popular music and jazz made between 1920 and 1950. This is probably the most esoteric knowledge I possess. It's easier to talk to people about Tibetan Buddhism, Arab poetry in Medieval Spain, or Russian icons, than about Helen Kane, Annette Hanshaw, and Ethel Waters. Or how about some Boswell Sisters or Joe Venuti and his Blue Four, Red McKenzie and his Mound City Blue Blowers, Ted Lewis and his Orchestra playing "Egyptian Ella"? It scares me how much of that music is in my head. I have friends who cannot believe that I can enjoy both Mahler's symphonies and Coleman Hawkins. Young Ella Fitzgerald singing "If That's What You're Thinking, You're Wrong" with Chick Webb's band would be just right for Abbott's shadowy couple.

Can one experience nostalgia for a time and place one did not know? I   5
believe so. You could put me in solitary with Abbott's photograph of "Blossom Restaurant"[2] and I wouldn't notice the months pass away as I studied the menu chalked on the blackboard at its entrance. The prices, of course, are incredibly low, but that's secondary. The dishes enumerated

[2]*"Blossom Restaurant":* Abbott's photograph of the restaurant, at 103 Bowery, was taken on October 3, 1935. —Eds.

here are what fascinates me. No one eats that kind of food today. Rare
Mongolian, Patagonian, and Afghan specialties are procurable in New
York, but not lamb oxtail stew, boiled beef, or even stuffed peppers. The
ethnic makeup of the city has changed in the last thirty years. Most of the
luncheonettes in the 1950s and 1960s served samplings of German, Hungarian, and Jewish cuisine. Pea and bean soup, stuffed cabbage, corned
beef and boiled potatoes, and veal cutlets were to be found regularly on
the menu, together with the usual assortment of sandwiches. On every
table, and all along the counter, there were containers stocked with dill
pickles and slices of raw onion. The portions were enormous. A cheap dish
like franks and kraut would stuff you for the rest of the day. I subsisted for
years on soups and chowders cooked by a Greek in a greasy spoon on East
8th Street. They gave you two thick slices of rye bread and butter with the
soup and all the pickles you could eat. After that, I could hardly keep my
eyes open for the rest of the day.

Abbott's photograph of the Blossom restaurant front also includes
the barbershop next door with its own price list. Does a tonsorial establishment anywhere in this country still offer electric massage? The gadget,
which resembled contraptions from a horror film, was a mesh of spring
coils and electric wires. Once the juice was turned on, the machine squirmed
and shook for a minute or two over the customer's scalp, supposedly
providing a stimulating, healthful, up-to-date treatment, while he sat
back in the chair pretending to be absorbed in some article in the *Police*

Gazette.[3] That ordeal was followed by a few sprinkles of strong-smelling cologne from a large bottle and a dusting of talcum powder on the freshly shaved neck.

The worst haircut I ever had in my life was at a barber college at the Union Square subway station. "Learn Barbering and make Money," the sign said. It was the cheapest haircut in town. But, before I realized what was happening, the apprentice barber had cut off all my hair with clippers except for a tuft right up in front. The kid was clearly a hair fashion visionary decades ahead of his time, but back then I was in total panic. I rushed immediately across the street into Klein's department store and found a beret, which I wore pulled down over my ears for the next six weeks. The problem was that it was summer, hot and humid as it usually is in New York. I also wore dark glasses to give the impression that I was simply affecting the appearance of a jazz musician. I saw both Dizzy Gillespie and Thelonius Monk similarly decked out, but they tended to make their appearance only after dark, while I had to go to work in the morning in the storeroom of a publishing company where everyone who saw me burst out laughing. Lunch was a hassle too. The customers at adjoining tables snickered and the waitress who knew me well gave me a puzzled look as she brought me my sandwich. I always held unpopular opinions and was not afraid to voice them, but to have people stare at me because I had a funny haircut or wore a necktie of some outrageous hue was something I had no stomach for.

"My place is no bigger than a closet," a woman said to her companion on the street the other day as they rushed past me, and I saw it instantly with its clutter of furniture and its piles of clothes on the bed and the floor. Dickinson's "Madonna dim" came to mind and I did not even take a good look at her before she was lost in the crowd. No sooner has one seen an interesting face in the street than one gives it a biography. Through a small window in her room, the evening casts its first shadow on a blank wall where the outline of a picture that once hung there is still visible. She is not home yet, but there is a small bird in the cage waiting for her and so am I.

Mr. Nobody is what I call the man in the subway. I catch sight of him from time to time. He has labored all his life to make himself inconspicuous in dress and manner and has nearly succeeded. He sits in the far corner in his gray hat, gray moustache, pale collapsing cheeks, and empty, watery eyes, staring off into space while the subway train grinds along and the overhead lights go out briefly and return to find us puzzled, looking up from newspapers at each other sitting there. Even more odd than these searching looks we give strangers are the times when we catch someone doing the same to us. They see me as I truly am, one imagines, wanting both to run away from them and to ask what it is they see.

---

[3]***Police Gazette:*** A century-old men's periodical that featured sensational news items and risqué photographs. It was especially popular in barbershops. —EDS.

Today dozens of people are sunning themselves on park benches, sit-   10
ting close together with eyes shut as if making a collective wish. An old
mutt who has done a lot of thinking and sighing in his life lies at their
feet, eyeing a rusty pigeon take wing as I pass by. The enigma of the
ordinary—that's what makes old photographs so poignant. An ancient
streetcar in sepia color. A few men holding on to their hats on a windy
day. They hurry with their faces averted except for one befuddled old fellow who has stopped and is looking over his shoulder at what we cannot
see, but where, we suspect, we ourselves will be coming into view someday, as hurried and ephemeral as any one of them.

The Reader's Presence

1. Consider the process Simic goes through when looking at a photograph. How does he make sense of the image? What does he
   add to it? What conclusions does he come to about the value of
   photography?

2. How does Simic move between interpreting the historic photographs by Berenice Abbott and interpreting scenes from his daily
   life in New York City? What does one have to do with the other?
   Does Simic read faces on the street or scenes in the city in the same
   way that he reads Abbott's photographs? Why or why not?

3. Consider Simic's essay compared to Nora Ephron's "The Boston
   Photographs" (page 676). How would you describe the different
   artistic perspectives of each writer? How are their perspectives
   shaped by the kind of photographs each writer is examining? In
   other words, how would you compare the photography of Berenice
   Abbott with that of Stanley Forman? After reading each selection
   carefully, discuss how you think Simic would have responded to
   Forman's photos. How would Ephron have responded to Abbott's?

Calvin Trillin

A Traditional Family

The journalist, critic, novelist, and humorist Calvin Trillin (b. 1935) was born in Kansas City but has lived in New York City for many years. He works as a staff writer at the New Yorker *and contributes to many other magazines, including the* Atlantic Monthly, Harper's, Life, *and the* Nation. *Trillin is especially well known for his nonfiction. His magazine columns are collected in* Uncivil Liberties *(1982),* With All Disrespect: More Uncivil Liberties *(1985),* If You Can't Say Something Nice *(1987), and* Enough's Enough *(1990); Trillin has also published a series of very popular books dealing with food and eating. In* American Fried *(1974) he paints a revealing portrait of American life through his discussion of regional and national eating habits. His love of traveling and eating in the company of his wife Alice also led him to write* Alice, Let's Eat *(1978),* Third Helpings *(1983), and* Travels with Alice *(1989). His latest book is* About Alice *(2006), a loving portrait of his wife five years after her death.*

Forswearing the temptation to "eat for a living," his later books take on subjects other than food (almost), with an emphasis on memoir and politics, and include Deadline Poet: My Life as a Doggerelist *(1994),* Messages from My Father *(1996),* Family Man *(1998),* Feeding a Yen: Savoring Local Specialties from Kansas City to Cuzco *(2003), and two books that take on the Bush administration "in rhyme,"* Obliviously on He Sails *(2004) and* Heck of a Job *(2006). "A Traditional Family" is excerpted from his book* Too Soon to Tell *(1995).*

When asked to describe the process he goes through when writing factual as opposed to imaginative columns, Trillin replied, "In a nonfiction piece . . . you really have to carry around a lot of baggage. You have what happened, your understanding of what happened, what you want to get across about what happened, all kinds of burdens of being fair to whatever sides there are. The facts are terribly restricting." Trillin typically writes at least four drafts of nonfiction articles, but finds that imaginative writing is less predictable. When writing his humor columns, for example, "it's a much less rigid system than that of writing nonfiction. Sometimes it only takes two drafts; sometimes it takes five."

I just found out that our family is no longer what the Census Bureau calls a traditional American family, and I want everyone to know that this is not our fault.

We now find ourselves included in the statistics that are used constantly to show the lamentable decline of the typical American household from something like Ozzie and Harriet and the kids to something like a bunch of kooks and hippies.

I want everyone to know right at the start that we are not kooks. Oh sure, we have our peculiarities, but we are not kooks. Also, we are not hippies. We have no children named Goodness. I am the first one to admit that reasonable people may differ on how to characterize a couple of my veteran sportcoats, and there may have been a remark or two passed in the neighborhood from time to time about the state of our front lawn. But no one has ever seriously suggested that we are hippies.

In fact, most people find us rather traditional. My wife and I have a marriage certificate, although I can't say I know exactly where to put my hands on it right at the moment. We have two children. We have a big meal on Christmas. We put on costumes at Halloween. (What about the fact that I always wear an ax murderer's mask on Halloween? That happens to be one of the peculiarities.) We make family decisions in the traditional American family way, which is to say the father is manipulated by the wife and the children. We lose a lot of socks in the wash. At our house, the dishes are done and the garbage is taken out regularly — after the glass and cans and other recyclable materials have been separated out. We're not talking about a commune here.

So why has the Census Bureau begun listing us with households   5
that consist of, say, the ex-stepchild of someone's former marriage living with someone who is under the mistaken impression that she is the aunt of somebody or other? Because the official definition of a traditional American family is two parents and one or more children under age eighteen. Our younger daughter just turned nineteen. Is that our fault?

As it happens, I did everything in my power to keep her from turning nineteen. When our daughters were about two and five, I decided that they were the perfect age, and I looked around for some sort of freezing process that might keep them there. I discovered that there was no such freezing process on the market. Assuming, in the traditional American way, that the technology would come along by and by, I renewed my investigation several times during their childhoods — they always seemed to be at the perfect age — but the freezing process never surfaced. Meanwhile, they kept getting older at what seemed to me a constantly accelerating rate. Before you could say "Zip up your jacket," the baby turned nineteen. What's a parent to do?

Ask for an easement. That's what a parent's to do. When I learned about the Census Bureau's definition of a traditional family — it was mentioned in an Associated Press story about how the latest census shows the traditional family declining at a more moderate pace than "the rapid and destabilizing rate" at which it declined between 1970 and 1980 — it occurred to me that we could simply explain the situation to the Census Bureau and ask that an exception be made in our case.

I realize that the Census Bureau would probably want to send out an inspector. I would acknowledge to him that our daughters are more or less away from home, but remind him that we have been assured by more experienced parents that we can absolutely count on their return. I would take the position, in other words, that we are just as traditional as any American family, just slightly undermanned at the moment — like a hockey team that has a couple of guys in the penalty box but is still a presence on the ice. We could show the official our Christmas tree decorations and our

Halloween costumes and a lot of single socks. We might, in the traditional American way, offer him a cup of coffee and a small bribe.

I haven't decided for sure to approach the Census Bureau. For one thing, someone might whisper in the inspector's ear that I have been heard to refer to my older daughter's room—the room where we now keep the exercise bike—as "the gym," and that might take some explaining. Also, I haven't discussed the matter with my wife. I would, of course, abide by her wishes. It's traditional.

The Reader's Presence

1. According to Trillin, how does the Census Bureau define "a traditional American family"? How does Trillin discover that his family would no longer be included in the Census Bureau's statistical compilations about "traditional" American families? Why does his family no longer satisfy the Census Bureau's criteria? What does Trillin try to do about this "problem"?

2. What characteristics of his family's behavior does Trillin identify as "traditional"? Examine the effect(s) of Trillin's verb choices. What patterns do you notice? What other patterns do you notice that he has woven into his word choices? When—and how—does Trillin poke fun at himself and the members of his family? To what extent does his humor depend on irony? on wit? Point to specific words and phrases to support your response.

3. When—and how—does Trillin use gender and familial stereotypes to reinforce the points he makes? Compare his light piece to the far more serious essay by David Mamet about his "new, cobbled-together family" who live in a new suburban development ("The Rake: A Few Scenes from My Childhood," page 183). How do both writers play with the reader's sense of the normative or the ideal? Can you imagine a comic version of Mamet's essay, and a serious version of Trillin's? If so, what might they look like?

Barbara Tuchman

"This Is the End of the World":
The Black Death

Barbara Tuchman (1912–1989) was an acclaimed historian who was noted for writing historical accounts in a literary style. Believing that most historians alienate their readers by including minute details and by ignoring the elements of well-written prose, Tuchman hoped to engage a broad audience with a well-told narrative. As she explained during a speech at the National Portrait Gallery in 1978, "I want the reader to turn the page and keep on turning to the end. . . . This is accomplished only when the narrative moves steadily ahead, not when it comes to a weary standstill, overloaded with every item uncovered in the re-search." Tuchman, a 1933 Radcliffe College graduate, never received formal training as a historian but developed an ability to document history early in her career while working as a research assistant for the Institute of Pacific Relations, a writer for the Nation, *a foreign correspondent during the Spanish Civil War, and an editor for the Office of War Information during World War II. Tuchman earned critical attention when her third book,* The Zimmermann Telegram, *be-came a best-seller in 1958. She received a Pulitzer Prize for* The Guns of August *(1962), a description of the early days of World War I, and for* Stilwell and the American Experience in China, 1911–1945 *(1970), a biographical account of Joseph Warren Stilwell, an American military officer during China's shift from feudalism to communism. Tuchman's other books include* The Proud Tower: A Portrait of the World before the War, 1890–1914 *(1966);* A Distant Mirror: The Calamitous Fourteenth Century *(1978), from which* "'This Is the End of the World': The Black Death" *is taken; and* The March of Folly: From Troy to Viet-nam *(1984).*

In October 1347, two months after the fall of Calais,[1] Genoese trading ships put into the harbor of Messina in Sicily with dead and dying men at the oars. The ships had come from the Black Sea port of Caffa (now Feo-dosiya) in the Crimea, where the Genoese maintained a trading post. The diseased sailors showed strange black swellings about the size of an egg or an apple in the armpits and groin. The swellings oozed blood and pus and were followed by spreading boils and black blotches on the skin from inter-nal bleeding. The sick suffered severe pain and died quickly within five days of the first symptoms. As the disease spread, other symptoms of continuous fever and spitting of blood appeared instead of the swellings or buboes. These victims coughed and sweated heavily and died even more quickly, within three days or less, sometimes in 24 hours. In both types everything

---

[1]*fall of Calais:* After a year-long siege, Calais, a town in France, surrendered to Ed-ward III, king of England and self-declared king of France. —EDS.

that issued from the body—breath, sweat, blood from the buboes and lungs, bloody urine, and blood-blackened excrement—smelled foul. Depression and despair accompanied the physical symptoms, and before the end "death is seen seated on the face."[2]

The disease was bubonic plague, present in two forms: one that infected the bloodstream, causing the buboes and internal bleeding, and was spread by contact; and a second, more virulent pneumonic type that infected the lungs and was spread by respiratory infection. The presence of both at once cause the high mortality and speed of contagion. So lethal was the disease that cases were known of persons going to bed well and dying before they woke, of doctors catching the illness at a bedside and dying before the patient. So rapidly did it spread from one to another that to a French physician, Simon de Covino, it seemed as if one sick person "could infect the whole world."[3] The malignity of the pestilence appeared more terrible because its victims knew no prevention and no remedy.

The physical suffering of the disease and its aspect of evil mystery were expressed in a strange Welsh lament[4] which saw "death coming into our midst like black smoke, a plague which cuts off the young, a rootless phantom which has no mercy for fair countenance. Woe is me of the shilling in the armpit! It is seething, terrible . . . a head that gives pain and causes a loud cry . . . a painful angry knob . . . Great is its seething like a burning cinder . . . a grievous thing of ashy color." Its eruption is ugly like the "seeds of black peas, broken fragments of brittle sea-coal . . . the early ornaments of black death, cinders of the peelings of the cockle weed, a mixed multitude, a black plague like halfpence, like berries. . . ."

Rumors of a terrible plague supposedly arising in China and spreading through Tartary (Central Asia) to India and Persia, Mesopotamia, Syria, Egypt, and all of Asia Minor had reached Europe in 1346. They told of a death toll so devastating that all of India was said to be depopulated, whole territories covered by dead bodies, other areas with no one left alive. As added up by Pope Clement VI at Avignon, the total of reported dead reached 23,840,000. In the absence of a concept of contagion, no serious alarm was felt in Europe until the trading ships brought their black burden of pestilence into Messina while other infected ships from the Levant carried it to Genoa and Venice.

By January 1348 it penetrated France via Marseille, and North Africa via Tunis. Shipborne along coasts and navigable rivers, it spread westward from Marseille through the ports of Languedoc to Spain and northward up the Rhône to Avignon, where it arrived in March. It reached Narbonne, Montpellier, Carcassonne, and Toulouse between February and May, and at the same time in Italy spread to Rome and Florence and their hinterlands. Between June and August it reached Bordeaux, Lyon, and

5

[2]"Death Is Seen Seated": Simon de Covino, q. Campbell, 80.
[3]"Could Infect the World": q. Gasquet, 41.
[4]Welsh Lament: q. Ziegler, 190.

Paris, spread to Burgundy and Normandy, and crossed the Channel from Normandy into southern England. From Italy during the same summer it crossed the Alps into Switzerland and reached eastward to Hungary.

In a given area the plague accomplished its kill within four to six months and then faded, except in the larger cities, where, rooting into the close-quartered population, it abated during the winter, only to reappear in the spring and rage for another six months.

In 1349 it resumed in Paris, spread to Picardy, Flanders, and the Low Countries, and from England to Scotland and Ireland as well as to Norway, where a ghost ship with a cargo of wool and a dead crew drifted offshore until it ran aground near Bergen. From there the plague passed into Sweden, Denmark, Prussia, Iceland, and as far as Greenland. Leaving a strange pocket of immunity in Bohemia, and Russia unattacked until 1351, it had passed from most of Europe by mid-1350. Although the mortality rate was erratic, ranging from one-fifth in some places to nine-tenths or almost total elimination in others, the overall estimate of modern demographers has settled — for the area extending from India to Iceland — around the same figure expressed in Froissart's casual words: "a third of the world died." His estimate, the common one at the time, was not an inspired guess but a borrowing of St. John's figure for mortality from plague in Revelation, the favorite guide to human affairs of the Middle Ages.

A third of Europe would have meant about 20 million deaths. No one knows in truth how many died. Contemporary reports were an awed impression, not an accurate count. In crowded Avignon, it was said, 400 died daily; 7,000 houses emptied by death were shut up; a single graveyard received 11,000 corpses in six weeks; half the city's inhabitants reportedly died, including 9 cardinals or one third of the total, and 70 lesser prelates. Watching the endlessly passing death carts, chroniclers let normal exaggeration take wings and put the Avignon death toll at 62,000 and even at 120,000 although the city's total population was probably less than 50,000.

When graveyards filled up, bodies at Avignon were thrown into the Rhône until mass burial pits were dug for dumping the corpses. In London in such pits corpses piled up in layers until they overflowed. Everywhere reports speak of the sick dying too fast for the living to bury. Corpses were dragged out of homes and left in front of doorways. Morning light revealed new piles of bodies. In Florence the dead were gathered up by the Compagnia della Misericordia — founded in 1244 to care for the sick — whose members wore red robes and hoods masking the face except for the eyes. When their efforts failed, the dead lay putrid in the streets for days at a time. When no coffins were to be had, the bodies were laid on boards, two or three at once, to be carried to graveyards or common pits. Families dumped their own relatives into the pits, or buried them so hastily and thinly "that dogs dragged them forth and devoured their bodies."[5]

---

[5]"Dogs Dragged Them Forth": Agnolo di Tura, q. Ziegler, 58.

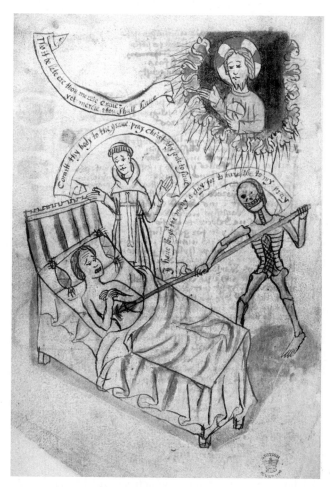

Plague victim receiving last rites, from a fifteenth-century collection of English religious texts

Amid accumulating death and fear of contagion, people died without   10
last rites and were buried without prayers, a prospect that terrified the
last hours of the stricken. A bishop in England gave permission to laymen
to make confession to each other as was done by the Apostles, "or if no
man is present then even to a woman,"[6] and if no priest could be found
to administer extreme unction, "then faith must suffice." Clement VI
found it necessary to grant remissions of sin to all who died of the plague
because so many were unattended by priests. "And no bells tolled,"[7]

[6]"Or if No Man Is Present": Bishop of Bath and Wells, q. Ziegler, 125.
[7]"No Bells Tolled": Agnolo di Tura, q. Schevill, *Siena*, 211. The same observation was
made by Gabriel de Muisis, notary of Piacenza, q. Crawford, 113.

wrote a chronicler of Siena, "and nobody wept no matter what his loss because almost everyone expected death. . . . And people said and believed, 'This is the end of the world.'"

In Paris, where the plague lasted through 1349, the reported death rate was 800 a day, in Pisa 500, in Vienna 500 to 600. The total dead in Paris numbered 50,000 or half the population. Florence, weakened by the famine of 1347, lost three- to four-fifths of its citizens, Venice two-thirds, Hamburg and Bremen, though smaller in size, about the same proportion. Cities, as centers of transportation, were more likely to be affected than villages, although once a village was infected, its death rate was equally high. At Givry, a prosperous village in Burgundy of 1,200 to 1,500 people, the parish register records 615 deaths in the space of fourteen weeks, compared to an average of thirty deaths a year in the previous decade.[8] In three villages of Cambridgeshire, manorial records show a death rate of 47 percent, 57 percent, and in one case 70 percent.[9] When the last survivors, too few to carry on, moved away, a deserted village sank back into the wilderness and disappeared from the map altogether, leaving only a grass-covered ghostly outline to show where mortals once had lived.

In enclosed places such as monasteries and prisons, the infection of one person usually meant that of all, as happened in the Franciscan convents of Carcassonne and Marseille, where every inmate without exception died. Of the 140 Dominicans at Montpellier only seven survived. Petrarch's brother Gherardo, member of a Carthusian monastery, buried the prior and 34 fellow monks one by one, sometimes three a day, until he was left alone with his dog and fled to look for a place that would take him in.[10] Watching every comrade die, men in such places could not but wonder whether the strange peril that filled the air had not been sent to exterminate the human race. In Kilkenny, Ireland, Brother John Clyn of the Friars Minor, another monk left alone among dead men, kept a record of what had happened lest "things which should be remembered perish with time and vanish from the memory of those who come after us."[11] Sensing "the whole world, as it were, placed within the grasp of the Evil One," and waiting for death to visit him too, he wrote, "I leave parchment to continue this work, if perchance any man survive and any of the race of Adam escape this pestilence and carry on the work which I have begun." Brother John, as noted by another hand, died of the pestilence, but he foiled oblivion.

The largest cities of Europe, with populations of about 100,000, were Paris and Florence, Venice and Genoa. At the next level, with more than 50,000, were Ghent and Bruges in Flanders, Milan, Bologna, Rome, Naples, and Palermo, and Cologne. London hovered below 50,000, the

---

[8]Givry Parish Register: Renouard, 111.
[9]Three Villages of Cambridgeshire: Saltmarsh.
[10]Petrarch's Brother: Bishop, 273.
[11]Brother John Clyn: q. Ziegler, 195.

only city in England except York with more than 10,000. At the level of 20,000 to 50,000 were Bordeaux, Toulouse, Montpellier, Marseille, and Lyon in France, Barcelona, Seville, and Toledo in Spain, Siena, Pisa, and other secondary cities in Italy, and the Hanseatic trading cities of the Empire. The plague raged through them all, killing anywhere from one-third to two-thirds of their inhabitants. Italy, with a total population of 10 to 11 million, probably suffered the heaviest toll. Following the Florentine bankruptcies, the crop failures and workers' riots of 1346–47, the revolt of Cola di Rienzi that plunged Rome into anarchy, the plague came as the peak of successive calamities. As if the world were indeed in the grasp of the Evil One, its first appearance on the European mainland in January 1348 coincided with a fearsome earthquake that carved a path of wreckage from Naples up to Venice. Houses collapsed, church towers toppled, villages were crushed, and the destruction reached as far as Germany and Greece. Emotional response, dulled by horrors, underwent a kind of atrophy epitomized by the chronicler who wrote, "And in these days was burying without sorrowe and wedding without friendschippe."[12]

In Siena, where more than half the inhabitants died of the plague, work was abandoned on the great cathedral, planned to be the largest in the world, and never resumed, owing to loss of workers and master masons and "the melancholy and grief" of the survivors. The cathedral's truncated transept still stands in permanent witness to the sweep of death's scythe. Agnolo di Tura, a chronicler of Siena, recorded the fear of contagion that froze every other instinct. "Father abandoned child, wife husband, one brother another," he wrote, "for this plague seemed to strike through the breath and sight.[13] And so they died. And no one could be found to bury the dead for money or friendship. . . . And I, Agnolo di Tura, called the Fat, buried my five children with my own hands, and so did many others likewise."

There were many to echo his account of inhumanity and few to balance it, for the plague was not the kind of calamity that inspired mutual help. Its loathsomeness and deadliness did not herd people together in mutual distress, but only prompted their desire to escape each other. "Magistrates and notaries refused to come and make the wills of the dying," reported a Franciscan friar of Piazza in Sicily;[14] what was worse, "even the priests did not come to hear their confessions." A clerk of the Archbishop of Canterbury reported the same of English priests who "turned away from the care of their benefices from fear of death."[15] Cases of parents deserting children and children their parents were reported across Europe from Scotland to Russia.[16] The calamity chilled the hearts of men, wrote

15

---

[12]Apathy; "And in These Days": q. Deaux, 143, citing only "an old northern chronicle."
[13]Agnolo di Tura, "Father Abandoned Child": q. Ziegler, 58.
[14]"Magistrates and Notaries": q. Deaux, 49.
[15]English Priests Turned Away: Ziegler, 261.
[16]Parents Deserting Children: Hecker, 30.

Boccaccio[17] in his famous account of the plague in Florence that serves as introduction to the *Decameron*. "One man shunned another . . . kinsfolk held aloof, brother was forsaken by brother, oftentimes husband by wife; nay, what is more, and scarcely to be believed, fathers and mothers were found to abandon their own children to their fate, untended, unvisited as if they had been strangers." Exaggeration and literary pessimism were common in the fourteenth century, but the Pope's physician, Guy de Chauliac, was a sober, careful observer who reported the same phenomenon: "A father did not visit his son, nor the son his father. Charity was dead."[18]

Yet not entirely. In Paris, according to the chronicler Jean de Venette, the nuns of the Hôtel Dieu or municipal hospital, "having no fear of death, tended the sick with all sweetness and humility."[19] New nuns repeatedly took the places of those who died, until the majority "many times renewed by death now rest in peace with Christ as we may piously believe."

When the plague entered northern France in July 1348, it settled first in Normandy and, checked by winter, gave Picardy a deceptive interim until the next summer. Either in mourning or warning, black flags were flown from church towers of the worst-stricken villages of Normandy. "And in that time," wrote a monk of the abbey of Fourcarment, "the mortality was so great among the people of Normandy that those of Picardy mocked them."[20] The same unneighborly reaction was reported of the Scots, separated by a winter's immunity from the English. Delighted to hear of the disease that was scourging the "southrons," they gathered forces for an invasion, "laughing at their enemies." Before they could move, the savage mortality fell upon them too, scattering some in death and the rest in panic to spread the infection as they fled.

In Picardy in the summer of 1349 the pestilence penetrated the castle of Coucy to kill Enguerrand's[21] mother, Catherine, and her new husband.[22] Whether her nine-year-old son escaped by chance or was perhaps living elsewhere with one of his guardians is unrecorded. In nearby Amiens, tannery workers, responding quickly to losses in the labor force, combined to bargain for higher wages.[23] In another place villagers were seen dancing to drums and trumpets, and on being asked the reason, answered that, seeing their neighbors die day by day while their village remained immune, they believed they could keep the plague from entering "by the jollity that is in us. That is why we dance."[24] Further north in Tournai on

[17]*Boccaccio:* Giovanni Boccaccio (1313–1375) was an Italian writer best known for his collection of stories about the Black Death, the *Decameron*.—EDS.

[18]Guy de Chauliac, "A Father": q. Gasquet, 50–51.

[19]Nuns of the Hôtel Dieu: *Chron. Jean de Venette*, 49.

[20]Picards and Scots Mock Mortality of Neighbors: Gasquet, 53, and Ziegler, 198.

[21]*Castle . . . Enguerrand:* Enguerrand de Coucy is the historical figure on whom Tuchman focuses in her account of the fourteenth century.—EDS.

[22]Catherine de Coucy: *L'Art de verifier*, 237.

[23]Amiens Tanners: Gasquet, 57.

[24]"By the Jollity That Is in Us": *Grandes Chrons.*, VI, 486–87.

the border of Flanders, Gilles li Muisis, Abbot of St. Martin's, kept one of the epidemic's most vivid accounts. The passing bells rang all day and all night, he recorded, because sextons were anxious to obtain their fees while they could. Filled with the sound of mourning, the city became oppressed by fear, so that the authorities forbade the tolling of bells and the wearing of black and restricted funeral services to two mourners. The silencing of funeral bells and of criers' announcements of deaths was ordained by most cities. Siena imposed a fine on the wearing of mourning clothes by all except widows.

Flight was the chief recourse of those who could afford it or arrange it. The rich fled to their country places like Boccaccio's young patricians of Florence, who settled in a pastoral palace "removed on every side from the roads" with "wells of cool water and vaults of rare wines." The urban poor died in their burrows, "and only the stench of their bodies informed neighbors of their death." That the poor were more heavily afflicted than the rich was clearly remarked at the time, in the north as in the south. A Scottish chronicler, John of Fordun, stated flatly that the pest "attacked especially the meaner sort and common people—seldom the magnates."[25] Simon de Covino of Montpellier made the same observation.[26] He ascribed it to the misery and want and hard lives that made the poor more susceptible, which was half the truth. Close contact and lack of sanitation was the unrecognized other half. It was noticed too that the young died in greater proportion than the old; Simon de Covino compared the disappearance of youth to the withering of flowers in the fields.[27]

In the countryside peasants dropped dead on the roads, in the fields, in their houses. Survivors in growing helplessness fell into apathy, leaving ripe wheat uncut and livestock untended. Oxen and asses, sheep and goats, pigs and chickens ran wild and they too, according to local reports, succumbed to the pest. English sheep, bearers of the precious wool, died throughout the country. The chronicler Henry Knighton, canon of Leicester Abbey, reported 5,000 dead in one field alone, "their bodies so corrupted by the plague that neither beast nor bird would touch them," and spreading an appalling stench.[28] In the Austrian Alps wolves came down to prey upon sheep and then, "as if alarmed by some invisible warning, turned and fled back into the wilderness."[29] In remote Dalmatia bolder wolves descended upon a plague-stricken city and attacked human survivors. For want of herdsmen, cattle strayed from place to place and died in hedgerows and ditches. Dogs and cats fell like the rest.[30]

20

[25]John of Fordun: q. Ziegler, 199.
[26]Simon de Covino on the Poor: Gasquet, 42.
[27]On Youth: Cazelles, *Peste*.
[28]Knighton on Sheep: q. Ziegler, 175.
[29]Wolves of Austria and Dalmatia: ibid., 84, 111.
[30]Dogs and Cats: Muisis, q. Gasquet, 44, 61.

The dearth of labor held a fearful prospect because the fourteenth century lived close to the annual harvest both for food and for next year's seed. "So few servants and laborers were left," wrote Knighton, "that no one knew where to turn for help." The sense of a vanishing future created a kind of dementia of despair. A Bavarian chronicler of Neuberg on the Danube recorded that "Men and women . . . wandered around as if mad" and let their cattle stray "because no one had any inclination to concern themselves about the future."[31] Fields went uncultivated, spring seed unsown. Second growth with nature's awful energy crept back over cleared land, dikes crumbled, salt water reinvaded and soured the lowlands. With so few hands remaining to restore the work of centuries, people felt, in Walsingham's words, that "the world could never again regain its former prosperity."[32]

Though the death rate was higher among the anonymous poor, the known and the great died too. King Alfonso XI of Castile was the only reigning monarch killed by the pest, but his neighbor King Pedro of Aragon lost his wife, Queen Leonora, his daughter Marie, and a niece in the space of six months. John Cantacuzene, Emperor of Byzantium, lost his son. In France the lame Queen Jeanne and her daughter-in-law Bonne de Luxemburg, wife of the Dauphin,[33] both died in 1349 in the same phase that took the life of Enguerrand's mother. Jeanne, Queen of Navarre, daughter of Louis X, was another victim. Edward III's second daughter, Joanna, who was on her way to marry Pedro, the heir of Castile, died in Bordeaux. Women appear to have been more vulnerable than men, perhaps because, being more housebound, they were more exposed to fleas. Boccaccio's mistress Fiammetta, illegitimate daughter of the King of Naples, died, as did Laura, the beloved—whether real or fictional—of Petrarch. Reaching out to us in the future, Petrarch cried, "Oh happy posterity who will not experience such abysmal woe and will look upon our testimony as a fable."[34]

In Florence Giovanni Villani, the great historian of his time, died at 68 in the midst of an unfinished sentence: "... *e dure questo pistolenza fino a* ... (in the midst of this pestilence there came to an end . . .)."[35] Siena's master painters, the brothers Ambrogio and Pietro Lorenzetti, whose names never appear after 1348, presumably perished in the plague, as did Andrea Pisano, architect and sculptor of Florence. William of Ockham and the English mystic Richard Rolle of Hampole both disappear from mention after 1349. Francisco Datini, merchant of Prato, lost both his parents and two siblings. Curious sweeps of mortality afflicted certain bodies of merchants in London. All eight wardens of the Company of Cutters, all six wardens of the Hatters, and four wardens of the Gold-

[31]Bavarian Chronicler of Neuberg: q. Ziegler, 84.
[32]Walsingham, "The World Could Never": Denifle, 273.
[33]*Dauphin:* The eldest son of a French king and presumably heir to the throne.—EDS.
[34]"Oh Happy Posterity": q. Ziegler, 45.
[35]Giovanni Villani, "*e dure questo*": q. Snell, 334.

smiths died before July 1350. Sir John Pulteney, master draper and four times Mayor of London, was a victim, likewise Sir John Montgomery, Governor of Calais.

Among the clergy and doctors the mortality was naturally high because of the nature of their professions. Out of 24 physicians in Venice, 20 were said to have lost their lives in the plague, although, according to another account, some were believed to have fled or to have shut themselves up in their houses.[36] At Montpellier, site of the leading medieval medical school, the physician Simon de Covino reported that, despite the great number of doctors, "hardly one of them escaped."[37] In Avignon, Guy de Chauliac confessed that he performed his medical visits only because he dared not stay away for fear of infamy, but "I was in continual fear."[38] He claimed to have contracted the disease but to have cured himself by his own treatment; if so, he was one of the few who recovered.

Clerical mortality varied with rank. Although the one-third toll of cardinals reflects the same proportion as the whole, this was probably due to their concentration in Avignon. In England, in strange and almost sinister procession, the Archbishop of Canterbury, John Stratford, died in August 1348, his appointed successor died in May 1349, and the next appointee three months later, all three within a year. Despite such weird vagaries, prelates in general managed to sustain a higher survival rate than the lesser clergy. Among bishops the deaths have been estimated at about one in twenty. The loss of priests, even if many avoided their fearful duty of attending the dying, was about the same as among the population as a whole.

Government officials, whose loss contributed to the general chaos, found, on the whole, no special shelter. In Siena four of the nine members of the governing oligarchy died, in France one third of the royal notaries, in Bristol 15 out of the 52 members of the Town Council or almost one third. Tax-collecting obviously suffered, with the result that Philip VI was unable to collect more than a fraction of the subsidy granted him by the Estates in the winter of 1347–48.

Lawlessness and debauchery accompanied the plague as they had during the great plague of Athens of 430 B.C., when according to Thucydides, men grew bold in the indulgence of pleasure: "For seeing how the rich died in a moment and those who had nothing immediately inherited their property, they reflected that life and riches were alike transitory and they resolved to enjoy themselves while they could."[39] Human behavior is timeless. When St. John had his vision of plague in Revelation, he knew from some experience or race memory that those who survived "repented not of the work of their hands. . . . Neither repented they of their murders, nor of their sorceries, nor of their fornication, nor of their thefts."

[36]Physicians of Venice: Campbell, 98.
[37]Simon de Covino: ibid., 31.
[38]Guy de Chauliac, "I Was in Fear": q. Thompson, *Ec. and Soc.*, 379.
[39]Thucydides: q. Crawfurd, 30–31.

Ignorance of the cause augmented the sense of horror. Of the real carriers, rats and fleas, the fourteenth century had no suspicion, perhaps because they were so familiar. Fleas, though a common household nuisance, are not once mentioned in contemporary plague writings, and rats only incidentally, although folklore commonly associated them with pestilence. The legend of the Pied Piper arose from an outbreak of 1284. The actual plague bacillus, *Pasturella pestis*, remained undiscovered for another 500 years. Living alternately in the stomach of the flea and the bloodstream of the rat who was the flea's host, the bacillus in its bubonic form was transferred to humans and animals by the bite of either rat or flea. It traveled by virtue of *Rattus rattus*, the small medieval black rat that lived on ships, as well as by the heavier brown or sewer rat. What precipitated the turn of the bacillus from innocuous to virulent form is unknown, but the occurrence is now believed to have taken place not in China but somewhere in central Asia and to have spread along the caravan routes. Chinese origin was a mistaken notion of the fourteenth century based on real but belated reports of huge death tolls in China from drought, famine, and pestilence which have since been traced to the 1330s, too soon to be responsible for the plague that appeared in India in 1346.[40]

The phantom enemy had no name. Called the Black Death only in later recurrences, it was known during the first epidemic simply as the Pestilence or Great Mortality. Reports from the East, swollen by fearful imaginings, told of strange tempests and "sheets of fire" mingled with huge hailstones that "slew almost all," or a "vast rain of fire" that burned up men, beasts, stones, trees, villages, and cities.[41] In another version, "foul blasts of wind" from the fires carried the infection to Europe "and now as some suspect it cometh round the seacoast." Accurate observation in this case could not make the mental jump to ships and rats because no idea of animal- or insect-borne contagion existed.

The earthquake was blamed for releasing sulfurous and foul fumes   30
from the earth's interior, or as evidence of a titanic struggle of planets and oceans causing waters to rise and vaporize until fish died in masses and corrupted the air. All these explanations had in common a factor of poisoned air, of miasmas and thick, stinking mists traced to every kind of natural or imagined agency from stagnant lakes to malign conjunction of the planets, from the hand of the Evil One to the wrath of God. Medical thinking, trapped in the theory of astral influences, stressed air as the communicator of disease, ignoring sanitation or visible carriers. The existence

---

[40]Chinese Origin: Although the idea of Chinese origin is still being repeated (e.g., by William H. McNeill, *Plagues and People*, New York, 1976, 161–63), it is disputed by L. Carrington Goodrich of the Association for Asian Studies, Columbia Univ., in letters to the author of 18 and 26 October 1973. Citing contemporary Chinese and other sources, he also quotes Dr. George A. Perera of the College of Physicians and Surgeons, an authority on communicable diseases, who "agrees with me that the spaces between epidemics in China (1334), Semirechyé (1338–9) and the Mediterranean basin (1347–9) seem too long for the first to be responsible for the last."

[41]Reports from the East: Barnes, 432; Coulton, *Black Death*, 9–11.

of two carriers confused the trail, the more so because the flea could live and travel independently of the rat for as long as a month and, if infected by the particularly virulent septicemic form of the bacillus, could infect humans without reinfecting itself from the rat. The simultaneous presence of the pneumonic form of the disease, which was indeed communicated through the air, blurred the problem further.

The mystery of the contagion was "the most terrible of all the terrors," as an anonymous Flemish cleric in Avignon wrote to a correspondent in Bruges. Plagues had been known before, from the plague of Athens (believed to have been typhus) to the prolonged epidemic of the sixth century A.D., to the recurrence of sporadic outbreaks in the twelfth and thirteenth centuries, but they had left no accumulated store of understanding.[42] That the infection came from contact with the sick or with their houses, clothes, or corpses was quickly observed but not comprehended. Gentile da Foligno, renowned physician of Perugia and doctor of medicine at the universities of Bologna and Padua, came close to respiratory infection when he surmised that poisonous material was "communicated by means of air breathed out and in."[43] Having no idea of microscopic carriers, he had to assume that the air was corrupted by planetary influences. Planets, however, could not explain the ongoing contagion. The agonized search for an answer gave rise to such theories as transference by sight. People fell ill, wrote Guy de Chauliac, not only by remaining with the sick but "even by looking at them." Three hundred years later Joshua Barnes, the seventeenth century biographer of Edward III, could write that the power of infection had entered into beams of light and "darted death from the eyes."

Doctors struggling with the evidence could not break away from the terms of astrology, to which they believed all human physiology was subject. Medicine was the one aspect of medieval life, perhaps because of its links with the Arabs, not shaped by Christian doctrine. Clerics detested astrology, but could not dislodge its influence. Guy de Chauliac, physician to three popes in succession, practiced in obedience to the zodiac. While his *Cirurgia* was the major treatise on surgery of its time, while he understood the use of anesthesia made from the juice of opium, mandrake, or hemlock, he nevertheless prescribed bleeding and purgatives by the planets and divided chronic from acute diseases on the basis of one being under the rule of the sun and the other of the moon.

In October 1348 Philip VI asked the medical faculty of the University of Paris for a report on the affliction that seemed to threaten human survival.[44] With careful thesis, antithesis, and proofs, the doctors ascribed it to a triple conjunction of Saturn, Jupiter, and Mars in the fortieth degree of

[42]Anonymous Flemish Cleric, "Most Terrible": His correspondence was edited in the form of a chronicle by De Smet, in *Recueil des chroniques de Flandres*, III, q. Ziegler, 22.

[43]Gentile da Foligno, "Communicated by air": Campbell, 38.

[44]Report of the University of Paris: Hecker, 51–53; Campbell, 15.

The Triumph of Death, from a fifteenth-century Catalan fresco

Aquarius said to have occurred on March 20, 1345. They acknowledged, however, effects "whose cause is hidden from even the most highly trained intellects." The verdict of the masters of Paris became the official version. Borrowed, copied by scribes, carried abroad, translated from Latin into various vernaculars, it was everywhere accepted, even by the Arab physicians of Cordova and Granada, as the scientific if not the popular answer. Because of the terrible interest of the subject, the translations of the plague tracts stimulated use of national languages. In that one respect, life came from death.

To the people at large there could be but one explanation—the wrath of God. Planets might satisfy the learned doctors, but God was closer to the average man. A scourge so sweeping and unsparing without any visible cause could only be seen as Divine punishment upon mankind for its sins. It might even be God's terminal disappointment in his creature. Matteo Villani compared the plague to the Flood in ultimate purpose and believed he was recording "the extermination of mankind."[45] Efforts to appease Divine

---

[45]M. Villani, "Extermination of Mankind": q. Meiss, *Painting . . . After the Black Death*, 66.

wrath took many forms, as when the city of Rouen ordered that everything that could anger God, such as gambling, cursing, and drinking, must be stopped.[46] More general were the penitent processions authorized at first by the Pope, some lasting as long as three days, some attended by as many as 2,000, which everywhere accompanied the plague and helped to spread it.

Barefoot in sackcloth, sprinkled with ashes, weeping, praying, tearing   35
their hair, carrying candles and relics, sometimes with ropes around their necks or beating themselves with whips, the penitents wound through the streets, imploring the mercy of the Virgin and saints at their shrines. In a vivid illustration for the *Très Riches Heures* of the Duc de Berry, the Pope is shown in a penitent procession attended by four cardinals in scarlet from hat to hem. He raises both arms in supplication to the angel on top of the Castel Sant'Angelo, while white-robed priests bearing banners and relics in golden cases turn to look as one of their number, stricken by the plague, falls to the ground, his face contorted with anxiety. In the rear, a gray-clad monk falls beside another victim already on the ground as the townspeople gaze in horror. (Nominally the illustration represents a sixth century plague in the time of Pope Gregory the Great, but as medieval artists made no distinction between past and present, the scene is shown as the artist would have seen it in the fourteenth century.) When it became evident that these processions were sources of infection, Clement VI had to prohibit them.

In Messina, where the plague first appeared, the people begged the Archbishop of neighboring Catania to lend them the relics of St. Agatha. When the Catanians refused to let the relics go, the Archbishop dipped them in holy water and took the water himself to Messina, where he carried it in a procession with prayers and litanies through the streets. The demonic, which shared the medieval cosmos with God, appeared as "demons in the shape of dogs" to terrify the people.[47] "A black dog with a drawn sword in his paws appeared among them, gnashing his teeth and rushing upon them and breaking all the silver vessels and lamps and candlesticks on the altars and casting them hither and thither. . . . So the people of Messina, terrified by this prodigious vision, were all strangely overcome by fear."

The apparent absence of earthly cause gave the plague a supernatural and sinister quality. Scandinavians believed that a Pest Maiden emerged from the mouth of the dead in the form of a blue flame and flew through the air to infect the next house.[48] In Lithuania the Maiden was said to wave a red scarf through the door or window to let in the pest. One brave man, according to legend, deliberately waited at his open window with drawn sword and, at the fluttering of the scarf, chopped off the hand. He died of his deed, but his village was spared and the scarf long preserved as a relic in the local church.

[46]Rouen Prohibits Gambling: Nohl, 74.
[47]At Messina, Demons Like Dogs: Coulton, *Black Death*, 22–27.
[48]Pest Maiden: Ziegler, 85.

Beyond demons and superstition the final hand was God's. The Pope acknowledged it in a Bull[49] of September 1348, speaking of the "pestilence with which God is afflicting the Christian people." To the Emperor John Cantacuzene it was manifest that a malady of such horrors, stenches, and agonies, and especially one bringing the dismal despair that settled upon its victims before they died, was not a plague "natural" to mankind but "a chastisement from Heaven."[50] To Piers Plowman "these pestilences were for pure sin."[51]

The general acceptance of this view created an expanded sense of guilt, for if the plague were punishment there had to be terrible sin to have occasioned it. What sins were on the fourteenth century conscience? Primarily greed, the sin of avarice, followed by usury, worldliness, adultery, blasphemy, falsehood, luxury, irreligion. Giovanni Villani, attempting to account for the cascade of calamity that had fallen upon Florence, concluded that it was retribution for the sins of avarice and usury that oppressed the poor. Pity and anger about the condition of the poor, especially victimization of the peasantry in war, was often expressed by writers of the time and was certainly on the conscience of the century. Beneath it all was the daily condition of medieval life, in which hardly an act or thought, sexual, mercantile, or military, did not contravene the dictates of the Church. Mere failure to fast or attend mass was sin. The result was an underground lake of guilt in the soul that the plague now tapped.

That the mortality was accepted as God's punishment may explain in part the vacuum of comment that followed the Black Death. An investigator has noticed that in the archives of Périgord references to the war are innumerable, to the plague few. Froissart mentions the great death but once, Chaucer gives it barely a glance. Divine anger so great that it contemplated the extermination of man did not bear close examination.

40

BIBLIOGRAPHY

L'Art de verifier les dates des faits historiques, par un Religieux de la Congregation de St. Maur, vol. XII. Paris, 1818.
Barnes, Joshua, The History of Edward III. Cambridge, 1688.
Campbell, Anna M., The Black Death and Men of Learning. Columbia University Press, 1931.
Chronicle of Jean de Venette. Trans. Jean Birdsall. Ed. Richard A. Newhall. Columbia University Press, 1853.
Crawfurd, Raymond, Plague and Pestilence in Literature and Art. Oxford, 1914.
Coulton, G. G., The Black Death. London, 1929.
Deaux, George, The Black Death, 1347. London, 1969.
Denifle, Henri, La Désolation des églises, monastères et hôpitaux en France pendant la guerre de cent ans, vol. I. Paris, 1899.
Gasquet, Francis Aidan, Abbot, The Black Death of 1348 and 1349, 2nd ed. London, 1908.

[49]*Bull:* A formal papal document. — EDS.
[50]Cantacuzene: Barnes, 435.
[51]Piers Plowman, "Pure Sin": B text, V, 13.

Grandes Chroniques de France, vol. VI (to 1380). Ed. Paulin Paris. Paris, 1838.

Hecker, J. F. C., *The Epidemics of the Middle Ages*. London, 1844.

Meiss, Millard, *Painting in Florence and Siena After the Black Death*. Princeton, 1951.

Nohl, Johannes, *The Black Death: A Chronicle of the Plague Compiled from Contemporary Sources*. Trans. C. H. Clarke. London, 1971.

Saltmarsh, John, "Plague and Economic Decline in England in the Latter Middle Ages," *Cambridge Historical Journal*, vol. VII, no. 1, 1941.

Schevill, Ferdinand, *History of Florence*. New York, 1961.

Snell, Frederick, *The Fourteenth Century*. Edinburgh, 1899.

Thompson, James Westfall, *Economic and Social History of Europe in the Later Middle Ages*. New York, 1931.

Ziegler, Philip, *The Black Death*. New York, 1969. (The best modern study.)

The Reader's Presence

1. History is a form of story. Which elements of Tuchman's account seem to pertain to pure fact and which to storytelling? Events are related in an objective tone. Is the writer's approval or disapproval ever evident? If so, where and in what ways?

2. This piece is drawn from a book titled *A Distant Mirror: The Calamitous Fourteenth Century*. In what ways does Tuchman's account suggest that fourteenth-century behaviors reflect our behaviors today?

3. At times Tuchman recounts history in the aggregate; at times she traces history through a specific figure. Find a few instances of this latter technique. Why might she have chosen to augment the general with the particular and vice versa? What is the effect of this technique on the reader?

4. "Ignorance of the cause augmented the sense of horror," Tuchman writes of the fourteenth-century plague (paragraph 28), but her statement can be taken as universally true. Use Tuchman's insight to sharpen your perception of the emotions expressed in Michihiko Hachiya's journal (from *Hiroshima Diary*, page 131) and in Don DeLillo's essay ("In the Ruins of the Future," page 332). How does each of these writers respond to problems of unspeakable horror? How do their approaches to narrating disaster compare?

Sherry Turkle

How Computers Change the Way We Think

Sherry Turkle (b. 1948) is Abby Rockefeller Mauzé Professor of the Social Studies of Science and Technology at the Massachusetts Institute of Technology. She is also the founder and current director of the MIT Initiative on Technology and Self, a research and education center concerned with the "subjective side of technology" and focused on the way technological change—particularly computers and the Internet—affects humans. A clinical psychologist, she has published a number of books, including The Second Self: Computers and the Human Spirit *(1984),* Psychoanalytic Politics: Jacques Lacan and Freud's French Revolution *(1992), and* Life on the Screen: Identity in the Age of the Internet *(1995). Turkle has edited several books of essays, including* Evocative Objects: Things We Think With *(2007), which describes the power of objects—a cello, a computer, an apple—to evoke emotion and thought, and her latest,* Falling for Science: Objects in Mind *(2008).*

Turkle sees computer-mediated reality as having the potential "to create a kind of crisis about the simulated and the real. The notion of what it is to live in a culture of simulation—how much of that counts as real experience and how much of that is discounted—is going to become more and more in the forefront of what people think and talk about, because so much experience is going to be about not being there." Her piece "How Computers Change the Way We Think" appeared in the Chronicle of Higher Education *in 2004.*

The tools we use to think change the ways in which we think. The invention of written language brought about a radical shift in how we process, organize, store, and transmit representations of the world. Although writing remains our primary information technology, today when we think about the impact of technology on our habits of mind, we think primarily of the computer.

My first encounters with how computers change the way we think came soon after I joined the faculty at the Massachusetts Institute of Technology in the late 1970s, at the end of the era of the slide rule and the beginning of the era of the personal computer. At a lunch for new faculty members, several senior professors in engineering complained that the transition from slide rules to calculators had affected their students' ability to deal with issues of scale. When students used slide rules, they had to insert decimal points themselves. The professors insisted that that required students to maintain a mental sense of scale, whereas those who relied on calculators made frequent errors in orders of magnitude. Additionally, the students with calculators had lost their ability to do "back of the envelope" calculations, and with that, an intuitive feel for the material.

That same semester, I taught a course in the history of psychology. There, I experienced the impact of computational objects on students' ideas about their emotional lives. My class had read Freud's essay on slips of the tongue, with its famous first example: The chairman of a parliamentary session opens a meeting by declaring it closed. The students discussed how Freud interpreted such errors as revealing a person's mixed emotions. A computer-science major disagreed with Freud's approach. The mind, she argued, is a computer. And in a computational dictionary—like we have in the human mind—"closed" and "open" are designated by the same symbol, separated by a sign for opposition. "Closed" equals "minus open." To substitute "closed" for "open" does not require the notion of ambivalence or conflict.

"When the chairman made that substitution," she declared, "a bit was dropped; a minus sign was lost. There was a power surge. No problem."

The young woman turned a Freudian slip into an information-processing error. An explanation in terms of meaning had become an explanation in terms of mechanism.   5

Such encounters turned me to the study of both the instrumental and the subjective sides of the nascent computer culture. As an ethnographer and psychologist, I began to study not only what the computer was doing *for* us, but what it was doing *to* us, including how it was changing the way we see ourselves, our sense of human identity.

In the 1980s, I surveyed the psychological effects of computational objects in everyday life—largely the unintended side effects of people's tendency to project thoughts and feelings onto their machines. In the 20 years since, computational objects have become more explicitly designed to have emotional and cognitive effects. And those "effects by design" will become even stronger in the decade to come. Machines are being designed to serve explicitly as companions, pets, and tutors. And they are introduced in school settings for the youngest children.

Today, starting in elementary school, students use e-mail, word processing, computer simulations, virtual communities, and PowerPoint software. In the process, they are absorbing more than the content of what appears on their screens. They are learning new ways to think about what it means to know and understand.

What follows is a short and certainly not comprehensive list of areas where I see information technology encouraging changes in thinking. There can be no simple way of cataloging whether any particular change is good or bad. That is contested terrain. At every step we have to ask, as educators and citizens, whether current technology is leading us in directions that serve our human purposes. Such questions are not technical; they are social, moral, and political. For me, addressing that subjective side of computation is one of the more significant challenges for the next decade of information technology in higher education. Technology does not determine change, but it encourages us to take certain directions. If we make those directions clear, we can more easily exert human choice.

Thinking about Privacy. Today's college students are habituated to a   10
world of online blogging, instant messaging, and Web browsing that leaves electronic traces. Yet they have had little experience with the right to privacy. Unlike past generations of Americans, who grew up with the notion that the privacy of their mail was sacrosanct, our children are accustomed to electronic surveillance as part of their daily lives.

I have colleagues who feel that the increased incursions on privacy have put the topic more in the news, and that this is a positive change. But middle-school and high-school students tend to be willing to provide personal information online with no safeguards, and college students seem uninterested in violations of privacy and in increased governmental and commercial surveillance. Professors find that students do not understand that in a democracy, privacy is a right, not merely a privilege. In ten years, ideas about the relationship of privacy and government will require even more active pedagogy. (One might also hope that increased education about the kinds of silent surveillance that technology makes possible may inspire more active political engagement with the issue.)

Avatars or a Self? Chat rooms, role-playing games, and other technological venues offer us many different contexts for presenting ourselves online. Those possibilities are particularly important for adolescents because they offer what Erik Erikson described as a moratorium, a time out or safe space for the personal experimentation that is so crucial for adolescent development. Our dangerous world—with crime, terrorism, drugs, and AIDS—offers little in the way of safe spaces. Online worlds can provide valuable spaces for identity play.

But some people who gain fluency in expressing multiple aspects of self may find it harder to develop authentic selves. Some children who write narratives for their screen avatars may grow up with too little experience of how to share their real feelings with other people. For those who are lonely yet afraid of intimacy, information technology has made it possible to have the illusion of companionship without the demands of friendship.

From Powerful Ideas to PowerPoint. In the 1970s and early 1980s, some educators wanted to make programming part of the regular curriculum for K–12 education. They argued that because information technology carries ideas, it might as well carry the most powerful ideas that computer science has to offer. It is ironic that in most elementary schools today, the ideas being carried by information technology are not ideas from computer science like procedural thinking, but more likely to be those embedded in productivity tools like PowerPoint presentation software.

PowerPoint does more than provide a way of transmitting content. It   15
carries its own way of thinking, its own aesthetic—which not surprisingly

shows up in the aesthetic of college freshmen. In that aesthetic, presentation becomes its own powerful idea.

To be sure, the software cannot be blamed for lower intellectual standards. Misuse of the former is as much a symptom as a cause of the latter. Indeed, the culture in which our children are raised is increasingly a culture of presentation, a corporate culture in which appearance is often more important than reality. In contemporary political discourse, the bar has also been lowered. Use of rhetorical devices at the expense of cogent argument regularly goes without notice. But it is precisely because standards of intellectual rigor outside the educational sphere have fallen that educators must attend to how we use, and when we introduce, software that has been designed to simplify the organization and processing of information.

In "The Cognitive Style of PowerPoint" (Graphics Press, 2003), Edward R. Tufte suggests that PowerPoint equates bulleting with clear thinking. It does not teach students to begin a discussion or construct a narrative. It encourages presentation, not conversation. Of course, in the hands of a master teacher, a PowerPoint presentation with few words and powerful images can serve as the jumping-off point for a brilliant lecture. But in the hands of elementary-school students, often introduced to Power-Point in the third grade, and often infatuated with its swooshing sounds, animated icons, and flashing text, a slide show is more likely to close down debate than open it up.

Developed to serve the needs of the corporate boardroom, the software is designed to convey absolute authority. Teachers used to tell students that clear exposition depended on clear outlining, but presentation software has fetishized the outline at the expense of the content.

Narrative, the exposition of content, takes time. PowerPoint, like so much in the computer culture, speeds up the pace.

Word Processing vs. Thinking. The catalog for the Vermont Country Store advertises a manual typewriter, which the advertising copy says "moves at a pace that allows time to compose your thoughts." As many of us know, it is possible to manipulate text on a computer screen and see how it looks faster than we can think about what the words mean. 20

Word processing has its own complex psychology. From a pedagogical point of view, it can make dedicated students into better writers because it allows them to revise text, rearrange paragraphs, and experiment with the tone and shape of an essay. Few professional writers would part with their computers; some claim that they simply cannot think without their hands on the keyboard. Yet the ability to quickly fill the page, to see it before you can think it, can make bad writers even worse.

A seventh grader once told me that the typewriter she found in her mother's attic is "cool because you have to type each letter by itself. You have to know what you are doing in advance or it comes out a mess." The idea of thinking ahead has become exotic.

Taking Things at Interface Value. We expect software to be easy to use, and we assume that we don't have to know how a computer works.

In the early 1980s, most computer users who spoke of transparency meant that, as with any other machine, you could "open the hood" and poke around. But only a few years later, Macintosh users began to use the term when they talked about seeing their documents and programs represented by attractive and easy-to-interpret icons. They were referring to an ability to make things work without needing to go below the screen surface. Paradoxically, it was the screen's opacity that permitted that kind of transparency. Today, when people say that something is transparent, they mean that they can see how to make it work, not that they know how it works. In other words, transparency means epistemic opacity.

The people who built or bought the first generation of personal computers understood them down to the bits and bytes. The next generation of operating systems were more complex, but they still invited that old-time reductive understanding. Contemporary information technology encourages different habits of mind. Today's college students are already used to taking things at (inter)face value; their successors in 2014 will be even less accustomed to probing below the surface.

Simulation and Its Discontents. Some thinkers argue that the new   25
opacity is empowering, enabling anyone to use the most sophisticated technological tools and to experiment with simulation in complex and creative ways. But it is also true that our tools carry the message that they are beyond our understanding. It is possible that in daily life, epistemic opacity can lead to passivity.

I first became aware of that possibility in the early 1990s, when the first generation of complex simulation games were introduced and immediately became popular for home as well as school use. SimLife teaches the principles of evolution by getting children involved in the development of complex ecosystems; in that sense it is an extraordinary learning tool. During one session in which I played SimLife with Tim, a 13-year-old, the screen before us flashed a message: "Your orgot is being eaten up." "What's an orgot?" I asked. Tim didn't know. "I just ignore that," he said confidently. "You don't need to know that kind of stuff to play."

For me, that story serves as a cautionary tale. Computer simulations enable their users to think about complex phenomena as dynamic, evolving systems. But they also accustom us to manipulating systems whose core assumptions we may not understand and that may not be true.

We live in a culture of simulation. Our games, our economic and political systems, and the ways architects design buildings, chemists envisage molecules, and surgeons perform operations all use simulation technology. In ten years the degree to which simulations are embedded in every area of life will have increased exponentially. We need to develop a new form of media literacy: readership skills for the culture of simulation.

We come to written text with habits of readership based on centuries of civilization. At the very least, we have learned to begin with the journalist's traditional questions: who, what, when, where, why, and how. Who wrote these words, what is their message, why were they written, and how are they situated in time and place, politically and socially? A central project for higher education during the next ten years should be creating programs in information-technology literacy, with the goal of teaching students to interrogate simulations in much the same spirit, challenging their built-in assumptions.

Despite the ever-increasing complexity of software, most computer environments put users in worlds based on constrained choices. In other words, immersion in programmed worlds puts us in reassuring environments where the rules are clear. For example, when you play a video game, you often go through a series of frightening situations that you escape by mastering the rules — you experience life as a reassuring dichotomy of scary and safe. Children grow up in a culture of video games, action films, fantasy epics, and computer programs that all rely on that familiar scenario of almost losing but then regaining total mastery: There is danger. It is mastered. A still-more-powerful monster appears. It is subdued. Scary. Safe.

Yet in the real world, we have never had a greater need to work our way out of binary assumptions. In the decade ahead, we need to rebuild the culture around information technology. In that new sociotechnical culture, assumptions about the nature of mastery would be less absolute. The new culture would make it easier, not more difficult, to consider life in shades of gray, to see moral dilemmas in terms other than a battle between Good and Evil. For never has our world been more complex, hybridized, and global. Never have we so needed to have many contradictory thoughts and feelings at the same time. Our tools must help us accomplish that, not fight against us.

Information technology is identity technology. Embedding it in a culture that supports democracy, freedom of expression, tolerance, diversity, and complexity of opinion is one of the next decade's greatest challenges. We cannot afford to fail.

When I first began studying the computer culture, a small breed of highly trained technologists thought of themselves as "computer people." That is no longer the case. If we take the computer as a carrier of a way of knowing, a way of seeing the world and our place in it, we are all computer people now.

The Reader's Presence

1. Reread the example that Turkle uses to open her essay. Does the young woman's reinterpretation of a Freudian slip show that computers can change the way we think? Does it show a change in the way we think of ourselves? Why or why not?

2. Turkle advocates critical dialogue about the consequences of technology, emphasizing that these "questions are not technical; they

are social, moral, and political" (paragraph 9). What are the so-
cial, moral, and political consequences that Turkle speaks of?
Which concern her most and why? Do you share her concerns?
Why or why not?

3. What is Turkle's opinion of the changes she outlines? Does she
present them uncritically or does she place value on certain ways
of thinking and being? Compare Turkle's essay to Ellen Ullman's
"Dining with Robots" (below). How do the two writers differ in
their responses to the changes that technology engenders? What
examples from Turkle's essay support Ullman's argument? Do
you think the two writers view technology in different or similar
ways? Why or why not?

Ellen Ullman

Dining with Robots

Ellen Ullman (b. 1950), writer, computer programmer, and technology con-
sultant, entered "computerdom" in the 1970s, just when business computing was
breaking wide open. "I've always written," she told an interviewer. "I'm from an
older generation of programmers. For the most part, we did not come out of engi-
neering (which was a much later development)." Ullman's experiences have shaped
her unique perspective on the upsides and downsides of technology and its effect
on human interaction. Close to the Machine: Technophilia and Its Discontents
(1997) *is Ullman's account of her life in "cyberculture" as a programmer running*
her own business out of a live-in office loft in San Francisco. Ullman turned that
experience into fiction in her first novel, The Bug *(2003). Ullman is a frequent*
guest commentator on National Public Radio and contributes to such publications
as Harper's, Wired, *and* Salon. *She is a contributing editor to the journal* American
Scholar, *in which "Dining with Robots" appeared in 2005. The essay was selected*
both for The Best American Essays *and* The Best American Science and Nature
Writing 2005.

In a 2002 interview, Ullman was asked if she thought that computers could
save the world, to which she emphatically replied: no. "Probably everything I've
written about technology is to get across the idea that computers can't save us. I
don't know where anyone ever got the idea that technology, in and of itself, was a
savior. Like all human-created 'progress,' computers are problematic, giving and
taking away."

On the first day of the first programming course I ever took, the instructor compared computer programming to creating a recipe. I remember he used the example of baking a cake. First you list the ingredients you'll need—flour, eggs, sugar, butter, yeast—and these, he said, are like the machine resources the program will need in order to run. Then you describe, in sequence, in clear declarative language, the steps you have to perform to turn those ingredients into a cake. Step one: preheat the oven. Two: sift together dry ingredients. Three: beat the eggs. Along the way were decisions he likened to the if/then/else branches of a program: if using a countertop mixer, then beat three minutes; else, if using a hand electric mixer, then beat four; else beat five. And there was a reference he described as a sort of subroutine: go to page 117 for details about varieties of yeast (with "return here" implied). He even drew a flow chart that took the recipe all the way through to the end: let cool, slice, serve.

I remember nothing, however, about the particulars of the cake itself. Was it angel food? Chocolate? Layered? Frosted? At the time, 1979 or 1980, I had been working as a programmer for more than a year, self-taught, and had yet to cook anything more complicated than poached eggs. So I knew a great deal more about coding than about cakes. It didn't occur to me to question the usefulness of comparing something humans absolutely must do to something machines never do: that is, eat.

In fact, I didn't think seriously about the analogy for another twenty-five years, not until a blustery fall day in San Francisco, when I was confronted with a certain filet of beef. By then I had learned to cook. (It was that or a life of programmer food: pizza, takeout, whatever's stocked in the vending machines.) And the person responsible for the beef encounter was a man named Joe, of Potter Family Farms, who was selling "home-raised and butchered" meat out of a stall in the newly renovated Ferry Building food hall.

The hall, with its soaring, arched windows, is a veritable church of food. The sellers are small, local producers; everything is organic, natural, free-range; the "baby lettuces" are so young one should perhaps call them "fetal"—it's that sort of place. Before shopping, it helps to have a glass of wine, as I had, to prepare yourself for the gasping shock of the prices. Sitting at the counter overlooking the bay, watching ships and ferries ply the choppy waters, I'd sipped down a nice Pinot Grigio, which had left me with lowered sales resistance by the time I wandered over to the Potter Farms meat stall. There Joe greeted me and held out for inspection a large filet—"a beauty," he said. He was not at all moved by my remonstrations that I eat meat but rarely cook it. He stood there as a man who had—personally—fed, slaughtered, and butchered this cow, and all for me, it seemed. I took home the beef.

I don't know what to do with red meat. There is something appalling about meat's sheer corporeality—meat meals are called *fleishidich* in Yiddish, a word that doesn't let you forget that what you are eating is *flesh*. So for help I turned to *The Art of French Cooking*, Volume I, the cookbook Julia Child[1] wrote with Louisette Bertholie and Simone Beck. I had bought this book when I first decided I would learn to cook. But I hadn't been ready for it then. I was scared off by the drawings of steer sides lanced for sirloins, porterhouses, and T-bones. And then there was all that talk of blanching, deglazing, and making a roux. But I had stayed with it, spurred on by my childhood memories of coming across Julia on her TV cooking show, when I'd be zooming around the dial early on weekend mornings and be stopped short at the sight of this big woman taking whacks at red lumps of meat. It was the physicality of her cooking that caught me, something animal and finger-painting-gleeful in her engagement with food.

And now, as rain hatched the windows, I came upon a recipe that Julia and her coauthors introduced as follows:

SAUTÉ DE BOEUF À LA PARISIENNE
[Beef Sauté with Cream and Mushroom Sauce]

> This sauté of beef is good to know about if you have to entertain important guests in a hurry. It consists of small pieces of filet sautéed quickly to a nice brown outside and a rosy center, and served in a sauce. In the variations at the end of the recipe, all the sauce ingredients may be prepared in advance. If the whole dish is cooked ahead of time, be very careful indeed in its reheating that the beef does not overcook. The cream and mushroom sauce here is a French version of beef Stroganoff, but less tricky as it uses fresh rather than sour cream, so you will not run into the problem of curdled sauce.
>
> Serve the beef in a casserole, or on a platter surrounded with steamed rice, risotto, or potato balls sautéed in butter. Buttered green peas or beans could accompany it, and a good red Bordeaux wine.

And it was right then, just after reading the words "a good red Bordeaux wine," that the programming class came back to me: the instructor at the board with his flow chart, his orderly procedural steps, the if/then decision branches, the subroutines, all leading to the final "let cool, slice, serve." And I knew in that moment that my long-ago instructor, like my young self, had been laughably clueless about the whole subject of cooking food.

If you have to entertain important guests.
A nice brown outside.
Rosy center.
Stroganoff.
Curdled.
Risotto.
Potato balls in butter
A good red Bordeaux.

---

[1]*Julia Child:* One of America's most popular cooks, Child (1912–2004) was one of the earliest TV chefs and the author of many best-selling cookbooks, including *Mastering the Art of French Cooking* (1961). —EDS.

I tried to imagine the program one might write for this recipe. And immediately each of these phrases exploded in my mind. How to tell a computer what "important guests" are? And how would you explain what it means to "have to" serve them dinner (never mind the yawning depths of "entertain")? A "nice brown," a "rosy center": you'd have to have a mouth and eyes to know what these mean, no matter how well you might translate them into temperatures. And what to do about "Stroganoff," which is not just a sauce but a noble family, a name that opens a chain of association that catapults the human mind across seven centuries of Russian history? I forced myself to abandon that line of thought and stay in the smaller realm of sauces made with cream, but this inadvertently opened up the entire subject of the chemistry of lactic proteins, and why milk curdles. Then I wondered how to explain "risotto": the special short-grained rice, the select regions on earth where it grows, opening up endlessly into questions of agriculture, its arrival among humans, the way it changed the earth. Next came the story of potatoes, that Inca food, the brutalities through which it arrives on a particular plate before a particular woman in Europe, before our eponymous Parisienne: how it is converted into a little round ball, and then, of course, buttered. (Then, lord help me, this brought up the whole subject of the French and butter, and how can they possibly get away with eating so much of it?)

But all of this was nothing compared to the cataclysm created by "a good red Bordeaux."

The program of this recipe expanded infinitely. Subroutine opened from subroutine, association led to exploding association. It seemed absurd even to think of describing all this to a machine. The filet, a beauty, was waiting for me.

Right around the time my programming teacher was comparing coding to cake making, computer scientists were finding themselves stymied in their quest to create intelligent machines. Almost from the moment computers came into existence, researchers believed that the machines could be made to think. And for the next thirty or so years, their work proceeded with great hope and enthusiasm. In 1967 the influential MIT computer scientist Marvin Minsky declared, "Within a generation the problem of creating 'artificial intelligence' will be substantially solved." But by 1982 he was less sanguine about the prospects, saying, "The AI problem is one of the hardest science has ever undertaken."

Computer scientists had been trying to teach the computer what human beings know about themselves and the world. They wanted to create inside the machine a sort of mirror of our existence, but in a form a computer could manipulate: abstract, symbolic, organized according to one theory or another of how human knowledge is structured in the brain. Variously called "micro worlds," "problem spaces," "knowledge representations," "classes," and "frames," these abstract universes contained systematized arrangements of facts, along with rules for operating

10

upon those — theoretically all that a machine would need to become intelligent. Although it wasn't characterized as such at the time, this quest for a symbolic representation of reality was oddly Platonic in motive, a computer scientist's idea of the pure, unchanging forms that lie behind the jumble of the physical world.

But researchers eventually found themselves in a position like mine when trying to imagine the computer program for my *boeuf à la Parisienne*: the network of associations between one thing and the next simply exploded. The world, the actual world we inhabit, showed itself to be too marvelously varied, too ragged, too linked and interconnected, to be sorted into any set of frames or classes or problem spaces. What we hold in our minds is not abstract, it turned out, not an ideal reflection of existence, but something inseparable from our embodied experience of moving about in a complicated world.

Hubert L. Dreyfus, a philosopher and early critic of artificial intelligence research, explained the problem with the example of a simple object like a chair. He pointed out the futility of trying to create a symbolic representation of a chair to a computer, which had neither a body to sit in it nor a social context in which to use it. "Chairs would not be equipment for sitting if our knees bent backwards like those of flamingoes, or if we had no tables, as in traditional Japan or the Australian bush," he wrote in his 1979 book *What Computers Can't Do*. Letting flow the myriad associations that radiate from the word *chair*, Dreyfus went on:

> Anyone in our culture understands such things as how to sit on kitchen chairs, swivel chairs, folding chairs; and in arm chairs, rocking chairs, deck chairs, barber's chairs, sedan chairs, dentist's chairs, basket chairs, reclining chairs . . . since there seems to be an indefinitely large variety of chairs and of successful (graceful, comfortable, secure, poised, etc.) ways to sit in them. Moreover, understanding chairs also includes social skills such as being able to sit appropriately (sedately, demurely, naturally, casually, sloppily, provocatively, etc.) at dinners, interviews, desk jobs, lectures, auditions, concerts . . .

At dinners where one has to entertain important guests . . . at the last minute . . . serving them beef in a French version of Stroganoff . . . with buttered potatoes . . . and a good red Bordeaux.

Several weeks after making Julia's *boeuf*, I was assembling twelve   15
chairs (dining chairs, folding chairs, deck chairs) around the dining table, and I was thinking not of Dreyfus but of my mother. In her younger days, my mother had given lavish dinner parties, and it was she who had insisted, indeed commanded, that I have all the necessary equipment for the sort of sit-down dinner I was giving that night. I surveyed the fancy wedding-gift stainless she had persuaded me to register for ("or else you'll get a lot of junk," she said), the Riedel wine glasses, also gifts, and finally the set of china she had given me after my father's death, when she sold their

small summer house—"the country dishes" is how I think of them, each one hand-painted in a simple design, blue cornflowers on white.

It wasn't until I started setting the table, beginning with the forks, that I thought of Dreyfus. Salad forks, fish forks, crab forks, entrée forks, dessert forks—at that moment it occurred to me that the paradigm for an intelligent machine had changed, but what remained was the knotty problem of teaching a computer what it needed to know to achieve sentience. In the years since Dreyfus wrote his book, computer scientists had given up on the idea of intelligence as a purely abstract proposition—a knowledge base and a set of rules to operate upon it—and were now building what are called social robots, machines with faces and facial expressions, who are designed to learn about the world the way human beings do: by interacting with other human beings. Instead of being born with a universe already inscribed inside them, these social machines will start life with only basic knowledge and skills. Armed with cute faces and adorable expressions, like babies, they must inspire humans to teach them about the world. And in the spirit of Dreyfus, I asked myself: if such a robot were coming to dinner, how could I, as a good human hostess and teacher, explain everything I would be placing before it tonight?

Besides the multiple forks, there will be an armory of knives: salad knife, fish knife, bread knife, dessert knife. We'll have soup spoons and little caviar spoons made of bone, tea spoons, tiny demitasse spoons, and finally the shovel-shaped ice cream spoons you can get only in Germany—why is it that only Germans recognize the need for this special ice cream implement? My robot guest could learn in an instant the name and shape and purpose of every piece of silverware, I thought; it would instantly understand the need for bone with caviar because metal reacts chemically with roe. But its mouth isn't functional; the mouthpart is there only to make us humans feel more at ease; my robot guest doesn't eat. So how will it understand the complicated interplay of implement, food, and mouth—how each tool is designed to hold, present, complement the intended fish or vegetable, liquid or grain? And the way each forkful or spoonful finds its perfectly dimensioned way into the moist readiness of the mouth, where the experience evanesces (one hopes) into the delight of taste?

And then there will be the wine glasses: the flutes for champagne, the shorter ones for white wine, the pregnant Burgundy glasses, the large ones for Cabernet blends. How could I tell a machine about the reasons for these different glasses, the way they cup the wine, shape the smell, and deliver it to the human nose? And how to explain wine at all? You could spend the rest of your life tasting wine and still not exhaust its variations, each bottle a little ecosystem of grapes and soils and weather, yeast and bacteria, barrels of wood from trees with their own soil and weather, the variables cross-multiplying until each glassful approaches a singularity, a moment in time on earth. Can a creature that does not drink or taste understand this pleasure? A good red Bordeaux!

I went to the hutch to get out the china. I had to move aside some of the pieces I never use: the pedestaled cigarette holders, the little ashtrays, the relish tray for the carrots, celery, and olives it was once de rigueur to put on the table. Then I came to the coffeepot, whose original purpose was not to brew coffee—that would have been done in a percolator—but to serve it. I remembered my mother presiding over the many dinners she had given, the moment when the table was scraped clean of crumbs and set for dessert, the coffee cups and saucers stacked beside her as she poured out each cup and passed it down the line. Women used to serve coffee at table, I thought. But my own guests would walk over and retrieve theirs from the automatic drip pot. My mother is now ninety-one; between her time as a hostess and mine, an enormous change had occurred in the lives of women. And, just then, it seemed to me that all that upheaval was contained in the silly fact of how one served coffee to dinner guests. I knew I would never want to go back to mother's time, but all the same I suddenly missed the world of her dinner parties, the guests waving their cigarettes as they chatted, my mother so dressed up, queenly by the coffee pot, her service a kind of benign rule over the table. I put the pot in the corner of the hutch and thought: it's no good trying to explain all this to my robot guest. The chain of associations from just this one piece of china has led me to regret and nostalgia, feelings I can't even explain to myself.

The real problem with having a robot to dinner is pleasure. What   20
would please my digital guest? Human beings need food to survive, but what drives us to choose one food over another is what I think of as the deliciousness factor. Evolution, that good mother, has seen fit to guide us to the apple instead of the poison berry by our attraction to the happy sweetness of the apple, its fresh crispness, and, in just the right balance, enough tartness to make it complicated in the mouth. There are good and rational reasons why natural selection has made us into creatures with fine taste discernment—we can learn what's good for us and what's not. But this very sensible survival imperative, like the need to have sex to reproduce, works itself out through the not very sensible, wilder part of our nature: desire for pleasure.

Can a robot desire? Can it have pleasure? When trying to decide if we should confer sentience upon another creature, we usually cite the question first posed by the philosopher Jeremy Bentham: can it suffer? We are willing to ascribe a kind of consciousness to a being whose suffering we can intuit. But now I wanted to look at the opposite end of what drives us, not at pain but at rapture: can it feel pleasure? Will we be able to look into the face of a robot and understand that some deep, inherent need has driven it to seek a particular delight?

According to Cynthia Breazeal, who teaches at MIT and is perhaps the best known of the new social-robot researchers, future digital creatures will have drives that are analogous to human desires but that will have nothing to do with the biological imperatives of food and sex. Robots will want the sort of things that machines need: to stay in good running order, to maintain physical homeostasis, to get the attention of human beings, upon whom they must rely, at least until they learn to take care of themselves. They will be intelligent and happy the way dolphins are: in their own form, in their own way.

Breazeal is very smart and articulate, and her defense of the eventual beingness of robotic creatures is a deep challenge to the human idea of sentience. She insists that robots will eventually become so lifelike that we will one day have to face the question of their inherent rights and dignity. "We have personhood because it's granted to us by society," she told me. "It's a status granted to one another. It's not innately tied to being a carbon-based life-form."

So challenged, I spent a long time thinking about the interior life of a robot. I tried to imagine it: the delicious swallowing of electric current, the connoisseurship of voltages, exquisite sensibilities sensing tiny spikes on the line, the pleasure of a clean, steady flow. Perhaps the current might taste of wires and transistors, capacitors and rheostats, some components better than others, the way soil and water make up the *terroir*[2] of wine, the difference between a good Bordeaux and a middling one. I think robots will delight in discerning patterns, finding mathematical regularities, seeing a world that is not mysterious but beautifully self-organized. What pleasure they will take in being fast and efficient — to run without cease! — humming along by their picosecond clocks, their algorithms compact, elegant, error-free. They will want the interfaces between one part of themselves and another to be defined, standardized, and modular, so that an old part can be unplugged, upgraded, and plugged back in their bodies forever renewed. Fast, efficient, untiring, correct, standardized, organized: the virtues we humans strive for but forever fail to achieve, the reasons we invented our helpmate, the machine.

The dinner party, which of course proceeded without a single robot guest, turned out to be a fine, raucous affair, everyone talking and laughing, eating and drinking to just the right degree of excess. And when each guest rose to pour his or her own cup of coffee, I knew it was one of those nights that had to be topped off with a good brandy. By the time the last friend had left, it was nearly two a.m., the tablecloth was covered with stains, dirty dishes were everywhere, the empty crab shells were beginning to stink, and the kitchen was a mess. Perfect.

Two days later I was wheeling a cart through the aisles at Safeway — food shopping can't always be about fetal lettuces — and I was thinking how neat and regular the food looked. All the packaged, prepared dinners

25

---

[2]*terroir:* French term that literally means terrain but that is often used today by experts to refer to the way a region's particular climate, soil, and other geographical features are expressed in its foods, wines, coffees, and such. — EDS.

lined up in boxes on the shelves. The meat in plastic-wrapped trays, in standard cuts, arranged in orderly rows. Even the vegetables looked cloned, identical bunches of spinach and broccoli, perfectly green, without an apparent speck of dirt. Despite the influence of Julia Child and California-cuisine guru Alice Waters, despite the movement toward organic, local produce, here it all still was: manufactured, efficient, standardized food.

But of course it was still here, I thought. Not everyone can afford the precious offerings of the food hall. And even if you could, who really has the time to stroll through the market and cook a meal based on what looks fresh that day? I have friends who would love to spend rainy afternoons turning a nice filet into *boeuf à la Parisienne*. But even they find their schedules too pressed these days; it's easier just to pick something up, grab a sauce out of a jar. Working long hours, our work life invading home life through e-mail and mobile phones, we all need our food-gathering trips to be brief and organized, our time in the kitchen efficiently spent, our meals downed in a hurry.

As I picked out six limes, not a bruise or blemish on them, it occurred to me that I was not really worried about robots becoming sentient, human, indistinguishable from us. That long-standing fear—robots who fool us into taking them for humans—suddenly seemed a comic-book peril, born of another age, as obsolete as a twenty-five-year-old computer.

What scared me now were the perfect limes, the five varieties of apples that seemed to have disappeared from the shelves, the dinner I'd make and eat that night in thirty minutes, the increasing rarity of those feasts that turn the dining room into a wreck of sated desire. The lines at the check-out stands were long; neat packages rode along on the conveyor belts; the air was filled with the beep of scanners as the food, labeled and bar-coded, identified itself to the machines. Life is pressuring us to live by the robots' pleasures, I thought. Our appetites have given way to theirs. Robots aren't becoming us, I feared; we are becoming them.

—in memory of Julia Child

The Reader's Presence

1. One of the techniques of the classic essay, dating from the sixteenth century, was for the writer to follow a "chain of associations" that would continually link up throughout the essay. In what ways does Ullman's essay resemble this classic form? Select a few images and references from the essay—recipes, wine, dinnerware, chairs, and so on—and try to map out their appearance and reappearances. What effect does this method have on the reader? In what ways does this method reinforce the essay's message about artificial intelligence?

2. Describe what you consider to be Ullman's central point about robots. How seriously should we take the prospects of robots becoming like human beings? According to Ullman, what will prevent that from happening? Does her argument persuade you? How does she deal with counterarguments in the essay? Do some of those counterarguments make sense to you? Explain. Discuss the essay's last sentence: How has Ullman prepared the reader for this viewpoint? Do you think she is correct? Explain why or why not.

3. Read Ullman's essay in conjunction with Michael J. Sandel's "The Case Against Perfection" (page 811). Compare the way each author considers the nature of human beings, their abilities and limitations. Could Sandel's perspective on perfection be applied to social robots? Do you believe humans are already as nearly perfect as they can be? Would improvements in human beings bring them closer to social robots or further away? Explain your answers based on a comparison of the two essays.

William Speed Weed

106 Science Claims and a Truckful of Baloney

William Speed Weed (b. 1971) graduated from Yale University in 1993. A science writer, essayist, and pop-culture critic, he has been a frequent contributor and columnist for GQ, Salon, Discover, *the* Washington Monthly, Current Science, Mother Jones, *and* Reader's Digest, *among others. Two of his essays were selected for the anthology* Best American Science and Nature Writing *for the years 2003 and 2005: "The Very Best Telescope," originally published in* Discover, *and "106 Science Claims and a Truckful of Baloney," which was published in* Popular Science *in 2005. Described in the* Washington Monthly *as "a science writer with a sly wit," Weed often questions conventional wisdom and blind cultural assumptions. For this essay, he recorded the many scientific claims he came across on product labels in stores, in print ads, in the media, and on the Internet. He then enlisted a number of experts to help him evaluate the "truckful of baloney" that he had collected.*

6:00 A.M.

I'm not up five minutes, and it looks like I'll get my RDA[1] of science claims at breakfast. Cheerios "can reduce your cholesterol."[1] My milk derives from a dairy whose cows "graze freely on lush natural pastures as nature intended."[2] My Concord Foods soy shake is "fat-free" and a "good source of fresh fruit."[3]

Then it's off to the e-mail inbox for some fresh scientific-sounding morning spam: A miracle pill guarantees I will "gain 3+ full inches in length."[4] A second promises me "huge breasts overnight."[5] A third will make me "look 20 years younger."[6] I wonder what I'd look like if I took all three.

In my first waking minutes of October 15, I wrote down thirteen scientific claims. Only one, for Cheerios, had any reasonable science behind it. According to the National Science Board's 2002 study *Science and Engineering Indicators*, only one-third of Americans can "adequately explain what it means to study something scientifically." Which presumably leaves those who would exploit scientific claims with two suckers born every three minutes. As a nation, we are easy prey to the pseudoscientific, and the National Science Board survey blames education and the media for this.

But how much "science" is the average American fed in a day, and how nutritious is it? I did not actively search through scientific journals, because the average American probably doesn't do that. Rather, I simply noted every claim to scientific veracity thrust upon me through radio, television, the Internet, product packaging, billboards, and a light read of the daily paper. By bedtime I had encountered more than one hundred (not all of which are detailed here, you'll be relieved to know; I've included a representative assortment). That's one science claim every ten minutes, on average.

The majority of the claims came from advertisers. Advertisers probably feed more science to Americans than anyone else, which is not surprising since they are in the business of making claims, and the same NSB study cited above noted that Americans are all ears about science: 90 percent of respondents were moderately or very interested in new scientific discoveries. Companies have a legal obligation to tell the truth (not always obeyed, of course; promising "3+ full inches" would seem to be a heartbreaking lie), but they have a marketing imperative to put the best possible spin on it. The marketing imperative is, of course, antithetical to the scientific method. Science proceeds slowly, painfully, and with considerable uncertainty: the cholesterol–heart disease connection has been researched for more than fifty years, and it's still not completely under-

5

---

[1]*RDA:* the Recommended Dietary Allowance is the daily dietary intake level of a nutrient considered to be sufficient to meet the requirements of nearly all healthy individuals in each life-stage. — EDS.

stood. In simplest terms, science is gray. Science in advertising wears makeup—it sometimes looks twenty years younger and has huge breasts and a, well, you get the picture. Very few of the one hundred claims I encountered proved completely true. A good number were patently false.

7:15 A.M.

The *New York Times* features a story on the Chinese astronaut's launch aboard the *Shenzhou 5* (which means "Divine Vessel") and a report that centenarians "have larger than average cholesterol-carrying molecules," which keep their arteries clear and healthy.[7]

On the radio, an ad for DuPont celebrates that "the fundamental understanding of life is something that didn't exist 15 years ago."[8] I Web surf, starting with MSN, where a banner ad tells me Pletal is my "claudication solution"[9]—whatever that means. Just a click away, WebMD reports "recommendations for breast cancer screening" from a panel of experts at the Cleveland Clinic: all women should have an annual mammogram starting at age forty.[10]

Just as I'm about to turn off the radio, Don Imus shoots a skeptical arrow at the Chinese astronaut: "How do we know those lying bastards got the guy up in the air?"

The breast cancer screening advice I clicked through to is a good example of how media—even careful media—simplify complex issues in order to give advice. Wait! I'm not allowed to call it *advice* because the site's legal disclaimer states that WebMD "does not provide medical advice." Whether or not "recommendations" and "advice" are synonyms is a moot point: in this case, the gray was rendered in black and white. Concerning whether women should have annual mammograms starting at age forty or (as some experts believe) at age fifty, the WebMD site acknowledges that "not all medical institutions and advocacy groups agree," but then comes down firmly on the age-forty standard. Further clicking does not easily reveal the full degree to which this recommendation remains controversial.

Oddly, the Imus joke about the Chinese astronaut embodied the sort   10
of attitude Americans could profit from in a world of promiscuous science claims. His "How do we know?" is a demand for fundamental evidence. (To answer the question: the Chinese launch and return were well documented, although some of the video was delayed by the Chinese government until it knew the taikonaut was safe on the ground.)

9:30 A.M.

Before I log off, I note an Atkins banner on my MSN homepage asking me to fill in my height and weight. I lie, typing in that I'm a 5-foot-10,

135-pound, 25-year-old female. When I punch "enter," the Web site tells me I'm perfectly healthy but pushes me to buy anyway. "Your low-carb meal plan will enable you to enjoy a lifetime of weight management."[11]

I throw some clothes on my 6-foot, 185-pound body and head for the grocery store. This place is a feast for a science-claim junkie. There's some Atkins low-carb bread, designed to contain as little as possible of the thing bread is famous for. There's a sign over the bread aisle: "Go for the grains! Bread and other grain foods are the foundation of healthy eating."[12] Meanwhile, the Wegmans brand bread claims to be "bromate-free."[13] Further along, a Perdue chicken assures me it's "all natural!"[14] and a bag of Diamond walnuts has a little flag saying "omega-3!"[15] A package of yeast brags that it's "gluten-free."[16] Puzzlingly, a nearby display suggests that gunky, white coconut oil may be a diet aid: a 2003 weekly magazine article conveniently posted over the bottles announces, "University of Colorado research has found coconut oil can increase your calorie-burning-power by up to 50%."[17]

"People in a grocery store assume the government is scrutinizing the claims products make, so if they're on the label, they must be accurate and important," notes William Hallman, a psychologist at the Food Policy Institute at Rutgers University. Of course, it's more complicated than that. The assumption of accuracy is correct, but the assumption of importance is not. Both Federal Trade Commission and FDA regulations require truthfulness on packages. Yes, the chicken is chicken. But, Hallman continues, "while the claim may be factually correct, the actual health benefits may lack practical significance."

Why make claims that "lack practical significance"? Because, says Hallman, "we jump to the conclusion that the benefits are substantial." Scientific language cues the consumer to take an insignificant claim and provide a significant health benefit *on the company's behalf.* "The beauty of this is that the manufacturer doesn't have to make the claim of benefits explicit." Doesn't have to, and, for the most part, couldn't. We do this because we generally believe science is good for us. The National Science Board survey found that although 90 percent of Americans consider themselves "interested" in science, only 15 percent consider themselves well informed. Ninety percent interested, 15 percent informed: That's a gap any marketing MBA could drive a truck of baloney through.

12:45 P.M.

Over lunch at the deli, my friend Charles mourns that neither of us orders a beer: "They're finding out alcohol is good for you,"[18] he says. On the car ride home, I hear a radio ad for eHarmony, the dating service that promises to find me a scientifically matched wife.[19] Near my exit, there's a billboard ad: "Is breast cancer's most avoidable risk factor elective abortion?"[20]

15

When I get home, I turn on the radio and hear the angry voice of Roger Hedgecock, the man sitting in for Rush Limbaugh, who is in rehab for drug addiction. "No U.S. animal species are falling extinct,"[21] he says.

Soon I'm off to the gym. I stop by the blood pressure reader and notice a warning label: "Only a physician is qualified to interpret the significance of blood pressure measurements." I am not a physician, so presumably I should note the measurements but not interpret them.

I'm offered a blood pressure machine but warned not to use the information. Science for the science-ignorant is talismanic. Roger Hedgecock hurls out claims so believers will believe. The billboard binds abortion to breast cancer with the scientific-sounding term "risk factor," giving an ethical argument—concerning the right to life—the halo of science.

This is the nub of the power of science claims in advertising and in slipshod media: science claims give permission to believe, even if the science itself, when examined, provides no such encouragement.

3:45 P.M.

CNN is on over the stationary bike at the gym. An FDA panel recommends lifting the ban on silicone breast implants.[22] In the shower afterward, I note that my conditioner "contains essential nucleic acids for pH 5.5 balance."[23] I brew in my travel mug some AllGoode-brand DigestibiliTea, containing fennel, which "promotes relaxation of the smooth muscles of the digestive tract." At the bottom of the package, there's a little disclaimer that reads: "The Food and Drug Administration has not evaluated these statements. This product is not intended to diagnose, treat, cure, or prevent any disease."[24]

At the GNC store, I spot that disclaimer on almost every product. It's even on a yellow shelf placard, underneath a pronouncement that "amino acids are the building blocks of proteins." Hmmm. Why the disclaimer? Amino acids *are* the building blocks of proteins, the same way letters are the building blocks of words. The FDA certainly knows this.

Curious about a radio ad that I hear on the drive home, I call up a company called CortiSlim, whose product, it claims, reduces levels of the stress hormone cortisol and thereby helps you lose weight.

Me: "So how does CortiSlim work to reduce cortisol?" Seller: "It decreases the level of cortisol in your body, just cancels it all out."[25] Me: "OK, but *how* does it do that?" Seller: "CortiSlim evaporates it and absorbs it and decreases it and cuts it down. So I want to tell you about a 'buy two get one free' special we're running this week."

Eager to establish its scientific credentials, CortiSlim's Web site features MRI images of fat deposits along with a bold motto: "The new science in weight loss." In the site's nether regions, however, you'll find the FDA disclaimer. Let's be clear: Wherever you see this disclaimer, it signals that you have no reason to believe that there will be "practical significance"

20

to using a product. The people wearing lab coats in the promo pics? They can be actors. Reported data from scientific studies? Could have been invented by someone who failed high school biology. Claims of health benefits? Well, you get the idea.

A 1994 federal law took the teeth out of the FDA's dietary supplement   25
regulations, which cover products that are neither foods nor drugs, such as CortiSlim and AllGoode teas. The FDA can yank a product off the shelves if it proves to be harmful (as it did to ephedra) and it can prohibit companies from claiming to cure specific diseases. AllGoode, therefore, can't be promoted as a cure to inflammatory bowel disease. But it can be sold to promote digestion, stimulate the digestive tract, maintain immune system balance—any medical-sounding thing that stimulates sales. Sellers of so-called "herbal Viagra alternatives" can imply the same benefits provided by heavily researched and FDA-approved pharmaceuticals—indeed, can imply the extra natural goodness of herbal drug alternatives—without reference to scientific research. Companies with names like Medicures can hawk "100% All Natural Doctor-Approved" pills, with names like Virility-Rx, which are neither medical nor, by their own disclaimered admission, cures.

6:30 P.M.

I drop by to visit my friends Mike and Jolynn, and they serve BLTs in front of the evening news. Tom Brokaw introduces the case of Terri Schiavo, a woman in a coma in Florida whose husband wants to pull the plug on her. "A medical dilemma wrapped in a family battle," he calls it.[26] A drug ad tells me that Lipitor reduces cholesterol[27] (just like Cheerios), although a disclaimer (not found on the Cheerios box) flashes on the screen: "Lipitor has not been shown to prevent heart disease or heart attacks." On a home shopping channel, a lady peddling skin cream tells me, "You know the benefits of vitamin A. Don't you want to use it on your skin?"[28] Actually, I don't know the benefits, and she never tells me.

Later, just before saying my good nights and heading home, I see a promo for *George of the Jungle 2*: George slams into a tree and Ape, his trusty gorilla butler, shakes his head: "And they say humans are more evolved."[29]

So the 106th and last item in my day of scientific-claim collecting turns out to be a joke. Fitting, perhaps, that it came from an actor dressed in a gorilla suit.

Psychologist William Hallman says that people really do learn their science from science claims, which is rather like learning the fundamentals of automobile engineering from a used-car salesman. "If you ask people, 'When you clean your kitchen, how clean do you need to get it to be safe?'" he says, "they respond: 'I need to clean 99.9 percent of germs on contact'—repeating the claims of antibacterial cleansers."

Or, you might say, aping them.   30

6:00 A.M.

1. CHEERIOS: **Fair enough. Good for sales.** In 1999 the FDA[2] allowed marketers to make unprecedented claims about the power of whole-grain foods to cut heart disease, based on its review of scientific research. General Mills, meanwhile, has funded Cheerios-specific research, and most recently published a 2003 study showing that if women eat two bowls a day, they can reduce their total cholesterol by 4 percent. A press release (not the study itself) concludes that Cheerios could save 24,000 lives per year, "if everybody in America ate Cheerios as recommended." Interesting extrapolation: 280 million Americans times 2 bowls times 365 days equals 204 billion bowls of Cheerios per year. Healthy indeed.

2. COWS: **Specious.** I'm happy for the cows—nature did evolve cows that wandered around and ate grass instead of the more efficient corn-based gruel some commercial dairies use. But "natural" is one of the most slippery words in marketing. Nature never "intended" humans to drink cow milk or to place cattle on pasture land in upstate New York. Cows descend from the wild aurochs, a now extinct native of Persia, and were bred and imported by humans who made pastures by clear-cutting the thick forests that had blanketed this land for eons.

3. SOY SHAKE: **Misleading.** The packaged powder contains no fresh fruit. The fruit is a banana you buy separately. Bananas contain fat, though not a lot. Only the powder is fat-free, and only the prepared shake has fresh fruit.

4. 3+ FULL INCHES: **Bogus.** Drugs can't extend penis length (except, of course, temporarily).

5. BREASTS: **Equally bogus.** No pill can enlarge breasts overnight.   35

6. YOUNGER: **Even more bogus.** No pill can make someone look twenty years younger. This pill further claims to increase emotional stability by 67 percent. Such pseudoscientific precision increases the absurdity of the claim by at least 68 percent.

7:15 A.M.

7. CENTENARIANS: **Well reported.** The science behind this story was published in the *Journal of the American Medical Association*, which, of course, doesn't guarantee its truth but does mean it has been peer-reviewed: vetted. The *Times* covered the study's method (comparing centenarians and their children to a control group of sixty- and seventy-year-olds); pointed out the unknowns, such as genetic links and the effect

[2]*FDA:* The U.S. Food and Drug Administration, an agency of the U.S. Department of Health and Human Services and responsible for regulating most types of food, dietary supplements, drugs, vaccines, biological medical products, blood products, medical devices, radiation-emitting devices, veterinary products, and cosmetics.—EDS.

on "good cholesterol"; and cautioned against overemphasizing the significance of the findings.

8. FUNDAMENTAL UNDERSTANDING OF LIFE: **Puffed up.** This corporate-identity ad, promoting DuPont and the New York Stock Exchange, vaguely suggests that genetics has profoundly deepened our understanding of life. Which of course it has. But the ring of finality here is meaningless. The life process is far from decoded.

9. CLAUDICATION: **Oversold.** The prescription drug Pletal can alleviate the limping (in other words, claudication) and pain old people get from arterial disease. However, Pletal does not work for everyone, and, as a potential patient learns on the company's Web site, it can kill patients with congestive heart failure. "Your claudication solution" is what happens when complex therapies are reduced to slogans; it implies the drug will help everyone who needs it. No drug works for everyone.

10. MAMMOGRAM: **Incomplete and potentially dangerous.** Hypothetically, if all women got annual mammograms starting at age twenty, we would catch even more breast cancers early. Doctors don't recommend doing so because we'd get too many false positives—resulting in a rash of unnecessary biopsies and worry, even lumpectomies. The critical public health question is: When does the risk of cancer outweigh the harm of false positives? While many doctors agree with the age-forty recommendation, others think forty is still too young and that fifty is the right *average* age. The most important guidelines, they say, are a woman's family medical history and her personal tolerance for risk.

40

9:30 A.M.

11. LOW-CARB PLAN: **Blanket pitch.** A healthy, right-weight twenty-five-year-old woman needs a lifetime plan?

12. GO FOR THE GRAINS: **Reasonable.** Despite the renewed controversy about low-carb diets, the evidence is not definitive. Balanced diet, calorie control, and exercise are still regarded as the best way to combat obesity. The FDA is reviewing the Food Pyramid, but it's unlikely to replace it with a Meat and Fat Pyramid. University of Colorado physician and nutritionist Holly Wyatt says, "All these diets mess up the message, saying, "It's carbs!' 'It's protein!' It's neither. Calories are what count."

13. BROMATE-FREE: **Voodoo use of chemical name.** Wegmans bread is indeed bromate-free, but it doesn't much matter. Some studies have shown that bromate, a dough enhancer, is a carcinogen if consumed in large amounts, though these findings are controversial. Bromate has never been found in baked breads at harmful levels. Most brands have stopped using bromate altogether.

14. ALL NATURAL: **Invokes a magic word.** "Natural" conjures up images of happy chickens prancing about a sunny barnyard under a wind-

mill. All this claim really means, though — insofar as FDA regulators are concerned — is that the chicken is not made of plastic. Chickens labeled "all natural" may have been crammed by the thousands into tight pens, their claws and beaks clipped, and stuffed full of antibiotics they'd never find in that "natural" barnyard.

15. OMEGA-3: **Cryptic.** Omega-3 fatty acids are a form of fat under-   45
represented in our diets, according to many nutritionists. All walnuts contain omega-3's, so the claim is accurate. But the message is reduced to code. Greek letter plus number equals "science-based," ergo good.

16. GLUTEN-FREE YEAST: **Duh.** Yeast is a fungus. Gluten is a product of plant protein. In evolutionary terms, yeast and gluten are as unrelated as a cow and an orange.

17. COCONUT OIL: **Fad.** Two public information officers at the University of Colorado canvassed their scientific faculty, trying to find anyone who had done this research. No luck. The notion that a saturated fat boosts "calorie-burning power" — rather than increasing the number of calories to be burned — is problematic. Well-known studies have shown that saturated fats *increase* the risk of heart disease. Still, the rumor of coconut oil's "power" created a run on the stuff in 2003.

12:45 P.M.

18. ALCOHOL IS GOOD FOR YOU: **Yes, and it's bad for you.** A landmark study that followed the drinking habits of nearly 90,000 male physicians showed that those who had one drink per day had significantly lower morbidity and mortality from diabetes, stroke, and heart disease. But people who drink excessively — and the definition of that is still debated — die at high rates from liver diseases, esophageal cancer, and car accidents.

19. eHARMONY: **Incomplete.** In the hot and heavy world of Web matchmaking, eHarmony distinguishes itself as, first, a service for the traditional alta-bound and, second, scientific in its approach, taking data points on clients' levels of obstreperousness, submissiveness, and other characteristics. The company now says it has conducted an internal scientific study of its matchmaking results using a standard methodology that gives "clear indication that the eHarmony matching algorithm works." Reviewing eHarmony's Web site, Arthur Aron, a professor of social psychology at the State University of New York at Stony Brook, notes that "it's true compatibility can be measured, but what they're measuring accounts for only a small portion of what makes a successful marriage."

20. ABORTION: **False.** The National Cancer Institute reviewed many   50
studies and concluded abortions do not increase risk of breast cancer.

21. EXTINCT: **Hogwash.** Tell that to one of the three remaining Hawaiian po'ouli birds; the po'ouli is just one of several Hawaiian birds at serious risk of extinction. Plenty of U.S. animals are endangered.

3:45 P.M.

22. BREAST IMPLANTS: **True.** The FDA panel did recommend lifting the ban, though the agency has since decided not to follow that recommendation.

23. CONDITIONER: *Sounds* **scientific!** Dermatologist Jerome Litt of Case Western Reserve University doesn't know what "essential nucleic acids for pH 5.5 balance" is supposed to mean in this phrase. "Any conditioner you like will work. They are all essentially the same."

24. FENNEL: **Unproven.** Fennel is a folk cure for indigestion (some folk cures, of course, have been scientifically proven to work). AllGoode did not respond to repeated requests for the science behind this claim. We searched PubMed and found one study on the subject that showed that fennel *stimulated* contractions of smooth muscle in guinea pigs and another that showed that fennel *relieved* smooth-muscle spasms in rats.

25. CANCELS OUT ALL THE CORTISOL: **Bogus.** Cortisol *is* a stress hormone — among other things, it regulates our fight-or-flight impulse — and has been weakly linked to one form of obesity. But "canceling out all cortisol would be disastrous," notes the University of Virginia endocrinologist Mary Vance. Perusing the ingredients listed on the company's Web site, she says: "You might as well eat tree bark." The Corti-Slim salesperson had apparently not read the Web site, which says the product helps "control cortisol levels within a healthy range." The site recommends the product for "millions of Americans . . . Anybody who leads a stressful lifestyle and wants to lose weight." Its homepage features a strong warning to consumers — against buying bogus CortiSlim.

6:30 P.M.

26. SCHIAVO COMA: **Incomplete.** The report never gives us the details of the medical dilemma behind this big story. Without more science, the dispute is difficult to understand.

27. LIPITOR: **True.** Lipitor lowers cholesterol, and cholesterol reduction is associated with lowering the risk of heart disease. But it's so difficult to prove a direct connection between a cholesterol-lowering medication and the long-term incidence of heart disease that Lipitor still runs this disclaimer, seven years after it hit the market. In contrast to the FDA's toothlessness with dietary supplements, the agency has the authority to ensure that all statements about prescription drugs are scientifically true. A Lipitor researcher predicted at press time that the disclaimer will be off the drug within a year because of new studies showing that its active ingredient does lower the risk of heart-disease mortality.

28. VITAMIN A: **Bogus.** Retinoic acid is the form of vitamin A used in prescription medications to rejuvenate skin. But according to the

Mount Sinai dermatology professor Susan Bershad, the form of vitamin A used in creams "sold over the counter won't have the same effect."

29. EVOLVED: **Misguided.** This joke only works because of the common misconception that evolution is progressive and that humans are the "most evolved." Indiana University biologist Rudolph Raff cautions, "Evolution is not a ladder of progress." All species alive today are, each in its own way, equally evolved. Humans have evolved higher intelligence. Apes are better adapted for eating leaves and, in some species, swinging from trees.

The Reader's Presence

1. In a series of footnotes, Weed evaluates each of the "scientific claims" that compete for his attention. What are the advantages — and disadvantages — of his decision to present his evaluations in footnote form? What would be the impact on his essay if he had chosen to weave many, most, or all of these evaluations into the heart of his essay?

2. How would you characterize Weed's tone in recounting each of the "scientific" claims presented to him during the course of a single day? Does his tone remain consistent throughout his essay? If it changes, point to where and how it shifts. In what specific ways is the tone of his footnotes consistent with — or different from — that in the main body of his essay? Point to specific passages to validate your reading.

3. What explanation does Weed offer for the benefits to companies who use scientific language and claims in promoting their products? Pay particular attention to paragraphs 13 through 19. Which of these explanations do you find most convincing? Explain why. Choose an example drawn from Weed's essay and compare and contrast it to one drawn from the items you purchase for either breakfast or lunch. What similarities and differences do you notice? Comment on the metaphors Weed uses. Which do you think are most effective? Explain why. From what aspect(s) of daily experience does Weed draw the majority of his metaphors and analogies? How does he resist what he calls the "marketing imperative" (paragraph 5) in his own choices of figurative language and diction? What does he mean when he says: "Science for the science-ignorant is talismanic" (paragraph 18)?

4. Weed's essay debunks most of the scientific language used in advertising. Compare and contrast the way Weed uses investigative techniques to those of such writers as Eric Schlosser in "Why

McDonald's Fries Taste So Good" (page 528), James Fallows in
"Throwing Like a Girl" (page 386), and Amy Cunningham in
"Why Women Smile" (page 324). How does each writer engage
an audience's attention, and how does each sustain that interest?
Which writer does the most credible work of investigative report-
ing? Explain why.

Marie Winn

TV Addiction

*Born in 1936 in Prague, Czechoslovakia, Marie Winn came to the United
States with her family in 1939. After receiving her education at Radcliffe College
and Columbia University, Winn became a freelance writer specializing in children's literature. In addition to having written more than a dozen books for children or for parents and teachers of children, she has contributed to the* New York
Times, *the* New York Times Book Review, *and the* Wall Street Journal. *Her publications include* Children without Childhood *(1983),* Unplugging the Plug-In
Drug *(1987),* Redtails in Love: A Wildlife Drama in Central Park *(1998), and*
Central Park in the Dark *(2008). "TV Addiction" is from* The Plug-In Drug: Television, Children and the Family *(originally published in 1977). The twenty-fifth
anniversary edition,* The Plug-In Drug: Television, Computers and Family Life
*(2002), adds the latest technological "addictions": video games, toys, and baby-
accessible television.*

The word "addiction" is often used loosely and wryly in conversation. People will refer to themselves as "mystery-book addicts" or "cookie
addicts." E. B. White wrote of his annual surge of interest in gardening:
"We are hooked and are making an attempt to kick the habit." Yet nobody really believes that reading mysteries or ordering seeds by catalogue
is serious enough to be compared with addictions to heroin or alcohol. In
these cases the word "addiction" is used jokingly to denote a tendency to
overindulge in some pleasurable activity.

People often refer to being "hooked on TV." Does this, too, fall into
the lighthearted category of cookie eating and other pleasures that people
pursue with unusual intensity? Or is there a kind of television viewing
that falls into the more serious category of destructive addiction?

Not unlike drugs or alcohol, the television experience allows the participant to blot out the real world and enter into a pleasurable and passive

mental state. To be sure, other experiences, notably reading, also provide a temporary respite from reality. But it's much easier to stop reading and return to reality than to stop watching television. The entry into another world offered by reading includes an easily accessible return ticket. The entry via television does not. In this way television viewing, for those vulnerable to addiction, is more like drinking or taking drugs—once you start it's hard to stop.

Just as alcoholics are only vaguely aware of their addiction, feeling that they control their drinking more than they really do ("I can cut it out any time I want—I just like to have three or four drinks before dinner"), many people overestimate their control over television watching. Even as they put off other activities to spend hour after hour watching television, they feel they could easily resume living in a different, less passive style. But somehow or other while the television set is present in their homes, it just stays on. With television's easy gratifications available, those other activities seem to take too much effort.

A heavy viewer (a college English instructor) observes: 5

> I find television almost irresistible. When the set is on, I cannot ignore it. I can't turn it off. I feel sapped, will-less, enervated. As I reach out to turn off the set, the strength goes out of my arms. So I sit there for hours and hours.

Self-confessed television addicts often feel they "ought" to do other things—but the fact that they don't read and don't plant their garden or sew or crochet or play games or have conversations means that those activities are no longer as desirable as television viewing. In a way, the lives of heavy viewers are as unbalanced by their television "habit" as drug addicts' or alcoholics' lives. They are living in a holding pattern, as it were, passing up the activities that lead to growth or development or a sense of accomplishment. This is one reason people talk about their television viewing so ruefully, so apologetically. They are aware that it is an unproductive experience, that by any human measure almost any other endeavor is more worthwhile.

It is the adverse effect of television viewing on the lives of so many people that makes it feel like a serious addiction. The television habit distorts the sense of time. It renders other experiences vague and curiously unreal while taking on a greater reality for itself. It weakens relationships by reducing and sometimes eliminating normal opportunities for talking, for communicating.

And yet television does not satisfy, else why would the viewer continue to watch hour after hour, day after day? "The measure of health," wrote the psychiatrist Lawrence Kubie, "is flexibility . . . and especially the freedom to cease when sated." But heavy television viewers can never be sated with their television experiences. These do not provide the true nourishment that satiation requires, and thus they find that they cannot stop watching.

The Reader's Presence

1. How does Winn characterize addiction? How does she apply that characterization to television watching? Do you think watching television is a genuine addiction, similar to addiction to drugs, alcohol, or tobacco? Why or why not?

2. Does Winn rely more heavily on evidence or opinion for her argument? Is her methodology convincing? What evidence do you find most persuasive?

3. Winn describes the feeling of powerlessness over television that some viewers experience. Compare Winn's description of television's effects to Sherry Turkle's assertion in "How Computers Change the Way We Think" (page 564) that "our tools carry the message that they are beyond our understanding" and that this "opacity can lead to passivity" (paragraph 25). What does Turkle say computer users take at face value? Is this effect significantly different from the powerlessness Winn describes, or are the effects of computers and television similar, in your view? Is either effect dangerous? Why or why not?

Tom Wolfe

Hooking Up

Tom Wolfe (b. 1931) grew up in Richmond, Virginia, and graduated from Washington and Lee University. He received his doctorate in American Studies from Yale University and began a career as a reporter, eventually writing for such papers as the New York Herald Tribune *and the* Washington Post. *His writing has also appeared in* New York *magazine,* Harper's, *and* Esquire, *where he has been a contributing editor since 1977. Writer, journalist, and social and cultural critic, Wolfe continues to be an arbiter (and satirist) of American cultural trends. His books* The Kandy-Kolored Tangerine-Flake Streamline Baby *(1965),* The Electric Kool-aid Acid Test *(1968),* The Pump House Gang *(1969), and* Radical Chic and Mau Mauing the Flak Catchers *(1970) were models of a flamboyant style known as "New Journalism." Wolfe's best-selling work of "extended" journalism,* The Right Stuff *(1979), won the American Book Award and National Book Critics Circle Award. His three novels,* The Bonfire of the Vanities *(1982),* A Man in Full *(1998), and* I Am Charlotte Simmons *(2004), contain the same blend of well-researched documentary journalism, entertainment, and realistic detail as his nonfiction work. Wolfe received the 2003* Chicago Tribune *Literary Prize for lifetime achievement.*

Wolfe has argued, "A novel of psychological depth without social depth isn't worth an awful lot because we are all individuals caught in an enormous web that consists of other people. It is in the social setting that the psychological battles take place." "Hooking Up" is from Wolfe's 2000 book Hooking Up: What Life Was Like at the Turn of the Second Millennium: An American's World, *a combination of fiction, memoir, and cultural and social observation.*

By the year 2000, the term "working class" had fallen into disuse in the United States, and "proletariat" was so obsolete it was known only to a few bitter old Marxist academics with wire hair sprouting out of their ears. The average electrician, air-conditioning mechanic, or burglar-alarm repairman lived a life that would have made the Sun King[1] blink. He spent his vacations in Puerto Vallarta, Barbados, or St. Kitts. Before dinner he would be out on the terrace of some resort hotel with his third wife, wearing his Ricky Martin cane-cutter shirt open down to the sternum, the better to allow his gold chains to twinkle in his chest hairs. The two of them would have just ordered a round of Quibel sparkling water, from the state of West Virginia, because by 2000 the once-favored European sparkling waters Perrier and San Pellegrino seemed so tacky.

European labels no longer held even the slightest snob appeal except among people known as "intellectuals," whom we will visit in a moment. Our typical mechanic or tradesman took it for granted that things European were second-rate. Aside from three German luxury automobiles — the Mercedes-Benz, the BMW, and the Audi — he regarded European-manufactured goods as mediocre to shoddy. On his trips abroad, our electrician, like any American businessman, would go to superhuman lengths to avoid being treated in European hospitals, which struck him as little better than those in the Third World. He considered European hygiene so primitive that to receive an injection in a European clinic voluntarily was sheer madness.

Indirectly, subconsciously, his views perhaps had to do with the fact that his own country, the United States, was now the mightiest power on earth, as omnipotent as Macedon under Alexander the Great, Rome under Julius Caesar, Mongolia under Genghis Khan, Turkey under Mohammed II, or Britain under Queen Victoria. His country was so powerful, it had begun to invade or rain missiles upon small nations in Europe, Africa, Asia, and the Caribbean for no other reason than that their leaders were lording it over their subjects at home.

Our air-conditioning mechanic had probably never heard of Saint-Simon,[2] but he was fulfilling Saint-Simon's and the other nineteenth-century

---

[1]*the Sun King:* Louis XIV, king of France (1638–1715), known for his absolutism and ostentation. — EDS.

[2]*Saint-Simon:* A French aristocrat, Henri de Saint-Simon (1760–1825) founded one of the most influential socialist programs of the nineteenth century. — EDS.

utopian socialists' dreams of a day when the ordinary workingman would have the political and personal freedom, the free time and the wherewithal to express himself in any way he saw fit and to unleash his full potential. Not only that, any ethnic or racial group—*any*, even recent refugees from a Latin country—could take over the government of any American city, if they had the votes and a modicum of organization. Americans could boast of a freedom as well as a power unparalleled in the history of the world.

Our typical burglar-alarm repairman didn't display one erg of chau-   5
vinistic swagger, however. He had been numbed by the aforementioned "intellectuals," who had spent the preceding eighty years being indignant over what a "puritanical," "repressive," "bigoted," "capitalistic," and "fascist" nation America was beneath its democratic façade. It made his head hurt. Besides, he was too busy coping with what was known as the "sexual revolution." If anything, "sexual revolution" was rather a prim term for the lurid carnival actually taking place in the mightiest country on earth in the year 2000. Every magazine stand was a riot of bare flesh, rouged areolae, moistened crevices, and stiffened giblets: boys with girls, girls with girls, boys with boys, bare-breasted female bodybuilders, so-called boys with breasts, riding backseat behind steroid-gorged body-building bikers, naked except for *cache-sexes* and Panzer helmets, on huge chromed Honda or Harley-Davidson motorcycles.

But the magazines were nothing compared with what was offered on an invention of the 1990s, the Internet. By 2000, an estimated 50 percent of all hits, or "log-ons," were at Web sites purveying what was known as "adult material." The word "pornography" had disappeared down the memory hole along with "proletariat." Instances of marriages breaking up because of Web-sex addiction were rising in number. The husband, some fifty-two-year-old MRI technician or systems analyst, would sit in front of the computer for twenty-four or more hours at a stretch. Nothing that the wife could offer him in the way of sexual delights or food could compare with the one-handing he was doing day and night as he sat be-fore the PC and logged on to such images as a girl with bare breasts and a black leather corset standing with one foot on the small of a naked boy's back, brandishing a whip.

In 1999, the year before, this particular sexual kink—sadomasochism —had achieved not merely respectability but high chic, and the word "perversion" had become as obsolete as "pornography" and "prole-tariat." Fashion pages presented the black leather and rubber parapher-nalia as style's cutting edge. An actress named Rene Russo blithely re-counted in the Living section of one of America's biggest newspapers how she had consulted a former dominatrix named Eva Norvind, who main-tained a dungeon replete with whips and chains and assorted baffling leather masks, chokers, and cuffs, in order to prepare for a part as an ag-gressive, self-obsessed agent provocateur in *The Thomas Crown Affair*, Miss Russo's latest movie.

"Sexy" was beginning to replace "chic" as the adjective indicating what was smart and up-to-the-minute. In the year 2000, it was standard practice for the successful chief executive officer of a corporation to shuck his wife of two to three decades' standing for the simple reason that her subcutaneous packing was deteriorating, her shoulders and upper back were thickening like a shot-putter's—in short, she was no longer sexy. Once he set up the old wife in a needlepoint shop where she could sell yarn to her friends, he was free to take on a new wife, a "trophy wife," preferably a woman in her twenties, and preferably blond, as in an expression from that time, a "lemon tart." What was the downside? Was the new couple considered radioactive socially? Did people talk *sotto voce*, behind the hand, when the tainted pair came by? Not for a moment. All that happened was that everybody got on the cell phone or the Internet and rang up or e-mailed one another to find out the spelling of the new wife's first name, because it was always some name like Serena and nobody was sure how to spell it. Once that was written down in the little red Scully & Scully address book that was so popular among people of means, the lemon tart and her big CEO catch were invited to all the parties, as though nothing had happened.

Meanwhile, sexual stimuli bombarded the young so incessantly and intensely they were inflamed with a randy itch long before reaching puberty. At puberty the dams, if any were left, burst. In the nineteenth century, entire shelves used to be filled with novels whose stories turned on the need for women, such as Anna Karenina or Madame Bovary, to remain chaste or to maintain a façade of chastity. In the year 2000, a Tolstoy or a Flaubert[3] wouldn't have stood a chance in the United States. From age thirteen, American girls were under pressure to maintain a façade of sexual experience and sophistication. Among girls, "virgin" was a term of contempt. The old term "dating"—referring to a practice in which a boy asked a girl out for the evening and took her to the movies or dinner—was now deader than "proletariat" or "pornography" or "perversion." In junior high school, high school, and college, girls headed out in packs in the evening, and boys headed out in packs, hoping to meet each other fortuitously. If they met and some girl liked the looks of some boy, she would give him the nod, or he would give her the nod, and the two of them would retire to a halfway-private room and "hook up."

"Hooking up" was a term known in the year 2000 to almost every American child over the age of nine, but to only a relatively small percentage of their parents, who, even if they heard it, thought it was being used in the old sense of "meeting" someone. Among the children, hooking up was always a sexual experience, but the nature and extent of what they did

10

---

[3] *a Tolstoy or a Flaubert:* The Russian novelist Leo Tolstoy published *Anna Karenina* in serial installment between 1875 and 1877; the French novelist Gustave Flaubert published *Madame Bovary* in 1865.—Eds.

could vary widely. Back in the twentieth century, American girls had used baseball terminology. "First base" referred to embracing and kissing; "second base" referred to groping and fondling and deep, or "French," kissing, commonly known as "heavy petting"; "third base" referred to fellatio, usually known in polite conversation by the ambiguous term "oral sex"; and "home plate" meant conception-mode intercourse, known familiarly as "going all the way." In the year 2000, in the era of hooking up, "first base" meant deep kissing ("tonsil hockey"), groping, and fondling; "second base" meant oral sex; "third base" meant going all the way; and "home plate" meant learning each other's names.

Getting to home plate was relatively rare, however. The typical Filofax entry in the year 2000 by a girl who had hooked up the night before would be: "Boy with black Wu-Tang T-shirt and cargo pants: O, A, 6." Or "Stupid cock diesel"—slang for a boy who was muscular from lifting weights—"who kept saying, 'This is a cool deal': TTC, 3." The letters referred to the sexual acts performed (e.g., TTC for "that thing with the cup"), and the Arabic number indicated the degree of satisfaction on a scale of 1 to 10.

In the year 2000, girls used "score" as an active verb indicating sexual conquest, as in: "The whole thing was like very sketchy, but I scored that diesel who said he was gonna go home and caff up [drink coffee in order to stay awake and study] for the psych test." In the twentieth century, only boys had used "score" in that fashion, as in: "I finally scored with Susan last night." That girls were using such a locution points up one of the ironies of the relations between the sexes in the year 2000.

The continuing vogue of feminism had made sexual life easier, even insouciant, for men. Women had been persuaded that they should be just as active as men when it came to sexual advances. Men were only too happy to accede to the new order, since it absolved them of all sense of responsibility, let alone chivalry. Men began to adopt formerly feminine attitudes when the subject of marriage came up, pleading weakness and indecisiveness, as in: "I don't know; I'm just not ready yet" or "Of course I love you, but like, you know, I start weirding out when I try to focus on it."

With the onset of puberty, males were able to get sexual enjoyment so easily, so casually, that junior high schools as far apart geographically and socially as the slums of the South Bronx and Washington's posh suburbs of Arlington and Talbot County, Virginia, began reporting a new discipline problem. Thirteen- and fourteen-year-old girls were getting down on their knees and fellating boys in corridors and stairwells during the two-minute break between classes. One thirteen-year-old in New York, asked by a teacher how she could do such a thing, replied: "It's nasty, but I need to satisfy my man." Nasty was an aesthetic rather than a moral or hygienic judgment. In the year 2000, boys and girls did not consider fellatio to be a truely sexual act, any more than tonsil hockey. It was just "fooling around." The President of the United States at the time used to have a twenty-two-year-old girl, an unpaid volunteer in the presidential palace, the White House, come around to his office for fellatio. He later testified under oath that he had never "had sex" with her. Older Americans tended to be shocked, but junior-high-school, high-school, and college students understood completely what he was saying and wondered what on earth all the fuss was about. The two of them had merely been on second base, hooking up.

Teenage girls spoke about their sex lives to total strangers without the least embarrassment or guile. One New York City newspaper sent out a man-on-the-street interviewer with the question: "How did you lose your virginity?" Girls as well as boys responded without hesitation, posed for photographs, and divulged their name, age, and the neighborhood where they lived.

Stains and stigmas of every kind were disappearing where sex was concerned. Early in the twentieth century the term "cohabitation" had referred to the forbidden practice of a man and woman living together before marriage. In the year 2000, nobody under forty had ever heard of the word, since cohabitation was now the standard form of American courtship. For parents over forty, one of the thornier matters of etiquette concerned domestic bed assignments. When your son or daughter came home for the weekend with the live-in consort, did you put the two of them in the same bedroom, which would indicate implicit approval of the discomforting fait accompli? Or did you put them in different bedrooms and lie awake, rigid with insomnia, fearful of hearing muffled footfalls in the hallway in the middle of the night?

Putting them in different rooms was a decidedly old-fashioned thing to do; and in the year 2000, thanks to the feverish emphasis on sex and sexiness, nobody wanted to appear old, let alone old-fashioned. From the city of Baltimore came reports of grandmothers having their eyebrows, tongues, and lips pierced with gold rings in order to appear younger, since body-piercing was a popular fashion among boys and girls in their teens and early twenties. Expectant mothers were having their belly buttons pierced with gold rings so that the shapelessness of pregnancy would not make them feel old. An old man who had been a prominent United States senator and a presidential candidate, emerged from what he confessed to have been a state of incapacity to go on television to urge other old men to take a drug called Viagra to free them from what he said was one of the scourges of modern times, the disease that dared not speak its name: impotence. He dared not speak it, either. He called it "E.D.," for erectile dysfunction. Insurance companies were under pressure to classify impotence in old men as a disease and to pay for treatment.

In the late nineteenth and early twentieth centuries, old people in America had prayed, "Please, God, don't let me look poor." In the year 2000, they prayed, "Please, God, don't let me look old." Sexiness was equated with youth, and youth ruled. The most widespread age-related disease was not senility but juvenility. The social ideal was to look twenty-three and dress thirteen. All over the country, old men and women were

dressing casually at every opportunity, wearing jeans, luridly striped
sneakers, shorts, T-shirts, polo shirts, jackets, and sweaters, heedless of
how such clothes revealed every sad twist, bow, hump, and webbed-up
vein clump of their superannuated bodies. For that matter, in the year
2000, people throughout American society were inverting norms of dress
that had persisted for centuries, if not millennia. Was the majesty of
America's global omnipotence reflected in the raiments of the rich and
prominent? Quite the opposite. In the year 2000, most American billionaires—and the press no longer took notice of men worth a mere $500
million or $750 million—lived in San Jose and Santa Clara Counties,
California, an area known nationally, with mythic awe, as the Silicon
Valley, the red-hot center of the computer and Internet industries. In
1999, the Internet industry alone had produced fourteen new billionaires.
The Valley's mythology was full of the sagas of young men who had gone
into business for themselves, created their own companies straight out of
college, or, better still, had dropped out of college to launch their "start-
ups," as these new digital-age enterprises were known. Such were the new
"Masters of the Universe," a term coined in the eighties to describe the
(mere) megamillionaires spawned by Wall Street during a boom in the
bond business. By comparison with the Valley's boy billionaires, the Wall
Streeters, even though they were enjoying a boom in the stock market in
the year 2000, seemed slow and dreary. Typically, they graduated from
college, worked for three years as number-crunching donkeys in some
large investment-banking firm, went off to business school for two years
to be certified as Masters of Business Administration, then returned to
some investment-banking firm and hoped to start making some real money
by the age of thirty. The stodginess of such a career was symbolized by
the stodginess of their dress. Even the youngest of them dressed like old
men: the dark blah suit, the light blah shirt, the hopelessly "interesting"
Hermès tie . . . Many of them even wore silk braces.

The new Masters of the Universe turned all that upside down. At Il
Fornaio restaurant in Palo Alto, California, where they gathered to tell
war stories and hand out business cards at breakfast, the billionaire
founders of the new wonder corporations walked in the door looking like
well-pressed, well-barbered beachcombers, but beachcombers all the
same. They wore khakis, boating moccasins (without socks), and ordinary cotton shirts with the cuffs rolled up and the front unbuttoned to the
navel, and that was it. You could tell at a glance that a Silicon Valley billionaire carried no cell phone, Palm Pilot, HP-19B calculator, or RIM
pager—he had people who did that for him. Having breakfast with him
at Il Fornaio would be a vice president whose net worth was $100 or
$200 million. He would be dressed just like the founder, except that he
would also be wearing a sport jacket. Why? So that he could carry . . . the
cell phone, the Palm Pilot, the HP-19B calculator, and the RIM pager,
which received e-mail and felt big as a brick. But why not an attaché
case? Because that was what old-fashioned businessmen Back East car-

ried. Nobody would be caught dead at Il Fornaio carrying an attaché case. The Back East attaché case was known scornfully as "the leather lunch pail."

When somebody walked into Il Fornaio wearing a suit and tie, he   20
was likely to be mistaken for a maître d'. In the year 2000, as in prior ages, service personnel, such as doormen, chauffeurs, waiters, and maître d's, were expected to wear the anachronistic finery of bygone eras. In Silicon Valley, wearing a tie was a mark of shame that indicated you were everything a Master of the Universe was not. Gradually, it would dawn on you. The poor devil in the suit and tie held one of those lowly but necessary executive positions, in public or investor relations, in which one couldn't avoid dealing with Pliocene old parties from . . . Back East.

Meanwhile, back East, the sons of the old rich were deeply involved in inverted fashions themselves. One of the more remarkable sights in New York City in the year 2000 was that of some teenage scion of an investment-banking family emerging from one of the forty-two Good Buildings, as they were known. These forty-two buildings on Manhattan's East Side contained the biggest, grandest, stateliest apartments ever constructed in the United States, most of them on Park and Fifth Avenues. A doorman dressed like an Austrian Army colonel from the year 1870 holds open the door, and out comes a wan white boy wearing a baseball cap sideways; an outsized T-shirt, whose short sleeves fall below his elbows and whose tail hangs down over his hips; baggy cargo pants with flapped pockets running down the legs and a crotch hanging below his knees, and yards of material pooling about his ankles, all but obscuring the Lugz sneakers. This fashion was deliberately copied from the "homeys" — black youths on the streets of six New York slums, Harlem, the South Bronx, Bedford-Stuyvesant, Fort Greene, South Ozone Park, and East New York. After passing the doorman, who tipped his visored officer's hat and said "Good day," the boy walked twenty feet to a waiting sedan, where a driver with a visored officer's hat held open a rear door.

What was one to conclude from such a scene? The costumes said it all. In the year 2000, the sons of the rich, the very ones in line to inherit the bounties of the all-powerful United States, were consumed by a fear of being envied. A German sociologist of the period, Helmut Schoeck, said that "fear of being envied" was the definition of guilt. But if so, guilt about what? So many riches, so much power, such a dazzling array of advantages? American superiority in all matters of science, economics, industry, politics, business, medicine, engineering, social life, social justice, and, of course, the military was total and indisputable. Even Europeans suffering the pangs of wounded chauvinism looked on with awe at the brilliant example the United States had set for the world as the third millennium began. And yet there was a cloud on the millennial horizon.

America had shown the world the way in every area save one. In matters intellectual and artistic, she remained an obedient colony of Europe. American architecture had never recovered from the deadening influence of the German Bauhaus[4] movement of the twenties. American painting and sculpture had never recovered from the deadening influence of various theory-driven French movements, beginning with Cubism early in the twentieth century. In music, the early-twentieth-century innovations of George Gershwin, Aaron Copland, Duke Ellington, and Ferde Grofé had been swept away by the abstract, mathematical formulas of the Austrian composer Arnold Schoenberg. Schoenberg's influence had faded in the 1990s, but the damage had been done. The American theater had never recovered from the Absurdism of Samuel Beckett, Bertolt Brecht, and Luigi Pirandello.

But, above all, there was the curious case of American philosophy—which no longer existed. It was as if Emerson, Charles Peirce, William James, and John Dewey had never lived. The reigning doctrine was deconstruction, whose hierophants were two Frenchmen, Michel Foucault and Jacques Derrida. They began with a hyperdilation of a pronouncement of Nietzsche's to the effect that there can be no absolute truth, merely many "truths," which are the tools of various groups, classes, or forces. From this, the deconstructionists proceeded to the doctrine that language is the most insidious tool of all. The philosopher's duty was to deconstruct the language, expose its hidden agendas, and help save the victims of the American "Establishment": women, the poor, nonwhites, homosexuals, and hardwood trees.

Oddly, when deconstructionists required appendectomies or bypass surgery or even a root-canal job, they never deconstructed medical or dental "truth," but went along with whatever their board-certified, profit-oriented surgeons proclaimed was the last word.   25

Confused and bored, our electrician, our air-conditioning mechanic, and our burglar-alarm repairman sat down in the evening and watched his favorite TV show (*The Simpsons*), played his favorite computer game (*Tony Hawk's Pro Skater*) with the children, logged on to the Internet, stayed up until 2 A.M. planning a trip to this fabulous-sounding resort just outside Bangkok, then "crashed" (went to bed exhausted), and fell asleep faster than it takes to tell it, secure in the knowledge that the sun would once more shine blessedly upon him in the morning. It was the year 2000.

The Reader's Presence

1. Wolfe makes frequent reference to how language has changed, pointing out defunct terms or newly coined phrases. What words does Wolfe say have been redefined or replaced? What are the connotations of the defunct term, and what is lost or gained with a new word?

[4]*Bauhaus:* A school of industrial design and architecture that developed in Germany during the early twentieth century.—EDS.

2. Examine Wolfe's tone throughout the essay. How does he approach his subject? Where does he uses humor, and for what purpose? Where does he use hyperbole (overstatement) and why?

3. Compare the way Wolfe covers current cultural trends to how Lauren Slater examines them in "The Trouble with Self-Esteem" (page 857). Which author strikes you as more objective and why? How does each writer establish credibility for his and her observations? What similarities can you see between both selections? Do you think Wolfe's comments on contemporary culture support Slater's and vice versa? Why or why not?

Virginia Woolf

The Death of the Moth

One of the most important writers of the twentieth century, Virginia Woolf (1882–1941) explored innovations in indirect narration and the impressionistic use of language that are now considered hallmarks of the modern novel and continue to influence novelists on both sides of the Atlantic. Together with her husband, Leonard Woolf, she founded the Hogarth Press, which published many experimental works that have now become classics, including her own. A central figure in the Bloomsbury group of writers, Woolf established her reputation with the novels Mrs. Dalloway *(1925),* To the Lighthouse *(1927), and* The Waves *(1931). The feminist movement has helped to focus attention on her work, and Woolf's nonfiction has provided the basis for several important lines of argument in contemporary feminist theory.* A Room of One's Own *(1929),* Three Guineas *(1938), and* The Common Reader *(1938) are the major works of nonfiction published in Woolf's lifetime; posthumously, her essays have been gathered together in* The Death of the Moth *(1942) (where the essay reprinted here appears) and in the four-volume* Collected Essays *(1967).*

Reflecting on her own writing life, Woolf wrote, "The novelist—it is his distinction and his danger—is terribly exposed to life. . . . He can no more cease to receive impressions than a fish in mid-ocean can cease to let the water rush through his gills." To turn those impressions into writing, Woolf maintained, requires solitude and the time for thoughtful selection. Given tranquility, a writer can, with effort, discover art in experience. "There emerges from the mist something stark, formidable and enduring, the bone and substance upon which our rush of indiscriminating emotion was founded."

Moths that fly by day are not properly to be called moths; they do not excite that pleasant sense of dark autumn nights and ivy-blossom which the commonest yellow-underwing asleep in the shadow of the curtain never fails to rouse in us. They are hybrid creatures, neither gay like butterflies nor somber like their own species. Nevertheless the present specimen, with his narrow hay-colored wings, fringed with a tassel of the same color, seemed to be content with life. It was a pleasant morning, mid-September, mild, benignant, yet with a keener breath than that of the summer months. The plough was already scoring the field opposite the window, and where the share had been, the earth was pressed flat and gleamed with moisture. Such vigor came rolling in from the fields and the down beyond that it was difficult to keep the eyes strictly turned upon the book. The rooks too were keeping one of their annual festivities; soaring round the tree tops until it looked as if a vast net with thousands of black knots in it had been cast up into the air; which, after a few moments sank slowly down upon the trees until every twig seemed to have a knot at the end of it. Then, suddenly, the net would be thrown into the air again in a wider circle this time, with the utmost clamor and vociferation, as though to be thrown into the air and settle slowly down upon the tree tops were a tremendously exciting experience.

The same energy which inspired the rooks, the ploughmen, the horses, and even, it seemed, the lean bare-backed downs, sent the moth fluttering from side to side of his square of the windowpane. One could not help watching him. One, was, indeed, conscious of a queer feeling of pity for him. The possibilities of pleasure seemed that morning so enormous and so various that to have only a moth's part in life, and a day moth's at that, appeared a hard fate, and his zest in enjoying his meager opportunities to the full, pathetic. He flew vigorously to one corner of his compartment, and after waiting there a second, flew across to the other. What remained for him but to fly to a third corner and then to a fourth? That was all he could do, in spite of the size of the downs, the width of the sky, the far-off smoke of houses, and the romantic voice, now and then, of a steamer out at sea. What he could do he did. Watching him, it seemed as if a fiber, very thin but pure, of the enormous energy of the world had been thrust into his frail and diminutive body. As often as he crossed the pane, I could fancy that a thread of vital light became visible. He was little or nothing but life.

Yet, because he was so small, and so simple a form of the energy that was rolling in at the open window and driving its way through so many narrow and intricate corridors in my own brain and in those of other human beings, there was something marvelous as well as pathetic about him. It was as if someone had taken a tiny bead of pure life and decking it as lightly as possible with down and feathers, had set it dancing and zigzagging to show us the true nature of life. Thus displayed one could not get over the strangeness of it. One is apt to forget all about life, seeing it humped and bossed and garnished and cumbered so that it has to move with the greatest circumspection and dignity. Again, the thought of all that life might have been had he been born in any other shape caused one to view his simple activities with a kind of pity.

After a time, tired by his dancing apparently, he settled on the window ledge in the sun, and, the queer spectacle being at an end, I forgot about him. Then, looking up, my eye was caught by him. He was trying to resume his dancing, but seemed either so stiff or so awkward that he could only flutter to the bottom of the windowpane; and when he tried to fly across it he failed. Being intent on other matters I watched these futile attempts for a time without thinking, unconsciously waiting for him to resume his flight, as one waits for a machine, that has stopped momentarily, to start again without considering the reason of its failure. After perhaps a seventh attempt he slipped from the wooden ledge and fell, fluttering his wings, on to his back on the windowsill. The helplessness of his attitude roused me. It flashed upon me that he was in difficulties; he could no longer raise himself; his legs struggled vainly. But, as I stretched out a pencil, meaning to help him to right himself, it came over me that the failure and awkwardness were the approach of death. I laid the pencil down again.

The legs agitated themselves once more. I looked as if for the enemy 5 against which he struggled. I looked out of doors. What had happened there? Presumably it was midday, and work in the fields had stopped. Stillness and quiet had replaced the previous animation. The birds had taken themselves off to feed in the brooks. The horses stood still. Yet the power was there all the same, massed outside, indifferent, impersonal, not attending to anything in particular. Somehow it was opposed to the little hay-colored moth. It was useless to try to do anything. One could only watch the extraordinary efforts made by those tiny legs against an oncoming doom which could, had it chosen, have submerged an entire city, not merely a city, but masses of human beings; nothing, I knew had any chance against death. Nevertheless after a pause of exhaustion the legs fluttered again. It was superb this last protest, and so frantic that he succeeded at last in righting himself. One's sympathies, of course, were all on the side of life. Also, when there was nobody to care or to know, this gigantic effort on the part of an insignificant little moth, against a power of such magnitude, to retain what no one else valued or desired to keep, moved one strangely. Again, somehow, one saw life, a pure bead. I lifted the pencil again, useless though I knew it to be. But even as I did so, the unmistakable tokens of death showed themselves. The body relaxed, and instantly grew stiff. The struggle was over. The insignificant little creature now knew death. As I looked at the dead moth, this minute wayside triumph of so great a force over so mean an antagonist filled me with wonder. Just as life had been strange a few minutes before, so death was now as strange. The moth having righted himself now lay most decently and uncomplainingly composed. O yes, he seemed to say, death is stronger than I am.

The Reader's Presence

1. Woolf calls her essay "The Death of *the* Moth" rather than "The Death of *a* Moth." Describe what difference this makes. What quality does the definite article add to the essay?

2. Reread the essay, paying special attention not to the moth but to the writer. What presence does Woolf establish for herself in the essay? How does the act of writing itself get introduced? Of what significance is the pencil? Can you discover any connection between the essay's subject and its composition?

3. Reread Woolf's concluding paragraph and paragraph 11 of George Orwell's "Shooting an Elephant" (page 203). How do the passages compare on the level of physical detail? How vivid is the death of each creature? Reread the paragraphs again, paying special attention to point of view. How do the writers implicate themselves in the deaths they witness? How do they appeal to the reader? Is the reader made into an "innocent bystander" or is he or she more intimately involved? If the latter, how does this intimacy come about?

THE WRITER AT WORK

Virginia Woolf on the Practice of Freewriting

At the time of her death (1941), Virginia Woolf, one of modern literature's outstanding creative voices, left twenty-six volumes of a handwritten diary that she had started in 1915. Her diary records her daily activities, social life, reading, and, most important, her thoughts about the writing process. In 1953, her husband, Leonard Woolf, extracted her remarks about writing and published them in a separate volume called A Writer's Diary. *Here, just having completed a newspaper article on the novelist Daniel Defoe, Woolf decides to take a break and think about the different ways she composes when she writes in her diary as opposed to when she writes more formally for publication.*

THIS LOOSE, DRIFTING MATERIAL OF LIFE
Easter Sunday, April 20, 1919

In the idleness which succeeds any long article, and Defoe is the second leader this month, I got out this diary and read, as one always does read one's own writing, with a kind of guilty intensity. I confess that the rough and random style of it, often so ungrammatical, and crying for a word altered, afflicted me somewhat. I am trying to tell whichever self it is that reads this hereafter that I can write very much better; and take no time over this; and forbid her to let the eye of man behold it. And now I may add my little compliment to the effect that it has a slapdash and vigor and sometimes hits an unexpected bull's eye. But what is more to the point is my belief that the habit of writing thus for my own eye only is good practice. It loosens the ligaments. Never mind the misses and the stumbles. Going at such a pace as I do I must make the most direct and instant shots at my object, and thus have to lay hands on words, choose them and shoot them with no more pause than is needed to put my pen in the ink. I believe that during the past year I can trace some increase of ease in my professional writing which I attribute to my casual half hours after tea. Moreover there looms ahead of me the shadow of some kind of form which a diary might attain to. I might in the course of time learn what it is that one can make of this loose, drifting material of life; finding another use for it than the use I put it to, so much more consciously and scrupulously, in fiction. What sort of diary should I like mine to be? Something loose knit and yet not slovenly, so elastic that it will embrace anything, solemn, slight, or beautiful that comes into my mind. I should like it to resemble some deep old desk, or capacious hold-all, in which one flings a mass of odds and ends without looking them through. I should like to come back, after a year or two, and find that the collection had sorted itself and refined itself and coalesced, as such deposits so mysteriously do, into a mould, transparent enough to reflect the light of our life, and yet steady, tranquil compounds with the aloofness of a work of art. The main requisite, I think on re-reading my old volumes, is not to play the part of censor, but to write as the mood comes or of anything whatever; since I was curious to find how I went for things put in haphazard, and found the significance to lie where I never saw it at the time. But looseness quickly becomes slovenly. A little effort is needed to face a character or an incident which needs to be recorded.

Will Wright

Dream Machines

Game designer Will Wright was born in Atlanta, Georgia, in 1960, and, at age 16, started college. Before dropping out, he studied architecture, mechanical engineering, computers, and robots—pursuits (or obsessions, as he calls them) that coalesced in his ultimate success as a genius inventor/designer of video games. "It usually starts with the research," he said in a Popular Science *interview. "I'll find some subject that I'm reading that fascinates me. It will pique my interest and I'll slowly become obsessed with it," By age 24, Wright had invented his first Nintendo video game,* Raid on Bungling Bay. *Next came* SimCity, *in which gamers build a city, followed by a family of simulation games, including* SimEarth, Sim-Farm, *and* The Sims, *in which entire virtual societies are built. Among the many awards Wright's work has received is* PC Magazine's Lifetime Achievement Award *and induction into the Academy of Arts and Sciences Hall of Fame. "Before Wright, computer simulation was the domain of the military, scientific research, and academics," the editors wrote. "He brought it to everyone." Wright wrote "Dream Machines" in 2006 as a guest editor at* Wired. *Always a different kind of designer, with games that create not destroy, that engage and educate, Wright told an interviewer that he wants to use gaming to get people more connected to the real world: "I think we all live in our own little bubbles, we have our own little lives and there's this whole world out there of things happening that we're kind of dimly aware of . . . if you could just get everybody to be a little bit more aware of the world around them, and how it works, and have that feedback in to the course the world is taking, gaming could be an incredibly powerful mechanism for steering the system."*

The human imagination is an amazing thing. As children, we spend much of our time in imaginary worlds, substituting toys and make-believe for the real surroundings that we are just beginning to explore and understand. As we play, we learn. And as we grow, our play gets more complicated. We add rules and goals. The result is something we call games.

Now an entire generation has grown up with a different set of games than any before it—and it plays these games in different ways. Just watch kids with a new videogame. The last thing they do is read the manual. Instead, they pick-up the controller and start mashing buttons to see what happens. This isn't a random process; it's the essence of the scientific method. Through trial and error, players build a model of the underlying game based on empirical evidence collected through play. As the players refine this model, they begin to master the game world. It's a rapid cycle of hypothesis, experiment, and analysis. And it's a fundamentally different take on problem-solving than the linear, read-the-manual-first approach of their parents.

In an era of structured education and standardized testing, this generational difference might not yet be evident. But the gamers' mindset—the fact that they are learning in a totally new way—means they'll treat the world as a place for creation, not consumption. This is the true impact videogames will have on our culture.

Society, however, notices only the negative. Most people on the far side of the generational divide—elders—look at games and see a list of ills (they're violent, addictive, childish, worthless). Some of these labels may be deserved. But the positive aspects of gaming—creativity, community, self-esteem, problem-solving—are somehow less visible to nongamers.

I think part of this stems from the fact that watching someone play a   5
game is a different experience than actually holding the controller and playing it yourself. Vastly different. Imagine that all you knew about movies was gleaned through observing the audience in a theater—but that you had never watched a film. You would conclude that movies induce

lethargy and junk-food binges. That may be true, but you're missing the big picture.

So it's time to reconsider games, to recognize what's different about them and how they benefit — not denigrate — culture. Consider, for instance, their "possibility space": Games usually start as a well-defined state (the setup in chess, for instance) and end when a specific state is reached (the king is checkmated). Players navigate this possibility space by their choices and actions; every player's path is unique.

Games cultivate — and exploit — possibility space better than any other medium. In linear storytelling, we can only imagine the possibility space that surrounds the narrative: What if Luke had joined the Dark Side? What if Neo isn't the One? In interactive media, we can explore it.

Like the toys of our youth, modern videogames rely on the player's active involvement. We're invited to create and interact with elaborately simulated worlds, characters, and story lines. Games aren't just fantasy worlds to explore; they actually amplify our powers of imagination.

Think of it this way: Most technologies can be seen as an enhancement of some part of our bodies (car/legs, house/skin, TV/senses). From the start, computers have been understood as an extension of the human brain; the first computers were referred to as mechanical brains and analytical engines. We saw their primary value as automated number crunchers that far exceeded our own meager abilities.

But the Internet has morphed what we used to think of as a fancy calculator into a fancy telephone with email, chat groups, IM, and blogs. It turns out that we don't use computers to enhance our math skills — we use them to expand our people skills.   10

The same transformation is happening in games. Early computer games were little toy worlds with primitive graphics and simple problems. It was up to the player's imagination to turn the tiny blobs on the screen into, say, people or tanks. As computer graphics advanced, game designers showed some Hollywood envy: They added elaborate cutscenes, epic plots, and, of course, increasingly detailed graphics. They bought into the idea that world building and storytelling are best left to professionals, and they pushed out the player. But in their rapture over computer processing, games designers forgot that there's a second processor at work: the player's imagination.

Now, rather than go Hollywood, some game designers are deploying that second processor to break down the wall between producers and consumers. By moving away from the idea that media is something developed by the few (movie and TV studios, book publishers, game companies) and consumed in a one-size-fits-all form, we open up a world of possibilities. Instead of leaving player creativity at the door, we are inviting it back to help build, design, and populate our digital worlds.

More games now include features that let players invent some aspect of their virtual world, from characters to cars. And more games entice players to become creative partners in world building, letting them mod its overall look and feel. The online communities that form around these imaginative activities are some of the most vibrant on the Web. For these players, games are not just entertainment but a vehicle for self-expression.

Games have the potential to subsume almost all other forms of entertainment media. They can tell us stories, offer us music, give us challenges, allow us to communicate and interact with others, encourage us to make things, connect us to new communities, and let us play. Unlike most other forms of media, games are inherently malleable. Player mods are just the first step down this path.

Soon games will start to build simple models of us, the players. They   15
will learn what we like to do, what we're good at, what interests and challenges us. They will observe us. They will record the decisions we make, consider how we solve problems, and evaluate how skilled we are in various circumstances. Over time, these games will become able to modify themselves to better "fit" each individual. They will adjust their difficulty on the fly, bring in new content, and create story lines. Much of this original material will be created by other players, and the system will move it to those it determines will enjoy it most.

Games are evolving to entertain, educate, and engage us individually. These personalized games will reflect who we are and what we enjoy, much as our choice of books and music does now. They will allow us to express ourselves, meet others, and create things that we can only dimly imagine. They will enable us to share and combine these creations, to build vast playgrounds. And more than ever, games will be a visible, external amplification of the human imagination.

The Reader's Presence

1. Wright says that "it's time to reconsider games" (paragraph 6). How would you define the essential characteristics of a game? Are video games like chess? like poker? like baseball? In what ways are video games like other games and in what ways does Wright suggest they are very different?

2. What does Wright mean by "the wall between producers and consumers" (paragraph 12)? Who are producers and who are consumers? Why does a barrier exist between the two? Where does Wright stand in relation to these two groups? What does Wright predict will occur when the barrier is dissolved?

3. Contrast Wright's essay with Marie Winn's "TV Addiction" (page 590). Does Wright feel the same way about video games as Winn does about television? Many people today claim that video games are just as addictive, perhaps more so, than TV. How would Wright counter that complaint?

Part III

Argumentative Writing: Contending with Issues

Kwame Anthony Appiah

The Case for Contamination

Philosopher and scholar Kwame Anthony Appiah was born in London in 1954 to a British mother and a Ghanaian father. Appiah was raised in Ghana and educated at Clare College, Cambridge University in England, where he received his PhD in philosophy. He has taught in a number of universities — from the University of Ghana to Yale, Cornell, Harvard, and Princeton, where he is currently the Laurance S. Rockefeller University Professor of Philosophy at the University Center for Human Values. A leading intellectual, his interests include the ethics and philosophy of mind and language, African and African American intellectual history and literary studies, and political philosophy. He is published widely as author and editor of numerous books, including his early work on the philosophy of language, Assertion and Conditionals *(1985) and* For Truth in Semantics *(1986);* In My Father's House *(1992), which explores the role of African and African American intellectuals in shaping contemporary African cultural life;* Color Conscious: The Political Morality of Race *(1996), co-written with Amy Gutmann; and* Bu Me Bé: The Proverbs of the Akan *(2002), written with his mother, writer Peggy Appiah. His extensive collaborations with Henry Louis Gates Jr. include a series on prominent black authors,* The Dictionary of Global Culture *(1997), out of which grew* Africana: The Encyclopedia of the African and African-American Experience *(1999). His most recent works are* The Ethics of Identity *(2005);* Cosmopolitanism: Ethics in a World of Strangers *(2006), from the "Issues of Our Time" series edited by Henry Louis Gates Jr.; and* Experiments in Ethics *(2008). Appiah has written for many journals, magazines, and newspapers, including the* New York Times, *where his essay "The Case for Contamination" appeared on January 1, 2006.*

In a 2006 interview with Mother Jones, *Appiah discussed his definition of "cosmopolitanism," an approach to the world that accepts and likes the fact that people live and express themselves in different ways: "What's distinctive about the cosmopolitan attitude is that it comes with a recognition that encounters with other people aren't about making them like us. . . . You enter a conversation, and conversation is about listening as well as talking; it's about being open to being changed yourself, but it's not about expecting consensus or seeking agreement. You can seek understanding without seeking agreement."*

1.

*I'm seated, with my mother, on a palace veranda, cooled by a breeze from
the royal garden. Before us, on a dais, is an empty throne, its arms and legs embossed with polished brass, the back and seat covered in black-and-gold silk. In
front of the steps to the dais, there are two columns of people, mostly men, facing
one another, seated on carved wooden stools, the cloths they wear wrapped
around their chests, leaving their shoulders bare. There is a quiet buzz of conversation. Outside in the garden, peacocks screech. At last, the blowing of a ram's
horn announces the arrival of the king of Asante, its tones sounding his honorific,
kotokohene, "porcupine chief." (Each quill of the porcupine, according to custom, signifies a warrior ready to kill and to die for the kingdom.) Everyone stands
until the king has settled on the throne. Then, when we sit, a chorus sings songs in
praise of him, which are interspersed with the playing of a flute. It is a Wednesday festival day in Kumasi, the town in Ghana where I grew up.*

Unless you're one of a few million Ghanaians, this will probably seem
a relatively unfamiliar world, perhaps even an exotic one. You might suppose that this Wednesday festival belongs quaintly to an African past. But
before the king arrived, people were taking calls on cellphones, and among
those passing the time in quiet conversation were a dozen men in suits,
representatives of an insurance company. And the meetings in the office
next to the veranda are about contemporary issues: HIV/AIDS, the educational needs of 21st-century children, the teaching of science and technology at the local university. When my turn comes to be formally presented,
the king asks me about Princeton, where I teach. I ask him when he'll
next be in the States. In a few weeks, he says cheerfully. He's got a meeting with the head of the World Bank.

Anywhere you travel in the world—today as always—you can find
ceremonies like these, many of them rooted in centuries-old traditions.
But you will also find everywhere—and this is something new—many intimate connections with places far away: Washington, Moscow, Mexico
City, Beijing. Across the street from us, when we were growing up, there
was a large house occupied by a number of families, among them a vast
family of boys; one, about my age, was a good friend. He lives in London. His brother lives in Japan, where his wife is from. They have another brother who has been in Spain for a while and a couple more brothers who, last I heard, were in the United States. Some of them still live in
Kumasi, one or two in Accra, Ghana's capital. Eddie, who lives in Japan,
speaks his wife's language now. He has to. But he was never very comfortable in English, the language of our government and our schools.
When he phones me from time to time, he prefers to speak Asante-Twi.[1]

Over the years, the royal palace buildings in Kumasi have expanded.
When I was a child, we used to visit the previous king, my great-uncle by
marriage, in a small building that the British had allowed his predecessor

---

[1] *Asante-Twi:* A language spoken and understood throughout Ghana.—EDS.

to build when he returned from exile in the Seychelles to a restored but diminished Asante kingship. That building is now a museum, dwarfed by the enormous house next door—built by his successor, my uncle by marriage—where the current king lives. Next to it is the suite of offices abutting the veranda where we were sitting, recently finished by the present king, my uncle's successor. The British, my mother's people, conquered Asante at the turn of the 20th century; now, at the turn of the 21st, the palace feels as it must have felt in the 19th century: a center of power. The president of Ghana comes from this world, too. He was born across the street from the palace to a member of the royal Oyoko clan. But he belongs to other worlds as well: he went to Oxford University; he's a member of one of the Inns of Court in London;[2] he's a Catholic, with a picture of himself greeting the pope in his sitting room.

What are we to make of this? On Kumasi's Wednesday festival day,   5
I've seen visitors from England and the United States wince at what they regard as the intrusion of modernity on timeless, traditional rituals— more evidence, they think, of a pressure in the modern world toward uniformity. They react like the assistant on the film set who's supposed to check that the extras in a sword-and-sandals movie aren't wearing wristwatches. And such purists are not alone. In the past couple of years, Unesco's[3] members have spent a great deal of time trying to hammer out a convention on the "protection and promotion" of cultural diversity. (It was finally approved at the Unesco General Conference in October 2005.) The drafters worried that "the processes of globalization . . . represent a challenge for cultural diversity, namely in view of risks of imbalances between rich and poor countries." The fear is that the values and images of Western mass culture, like some invasive weed, are threatening to choke out the world's native flora.

The contradictions in this argument aren't hard to find. This same Unesco document is careful to affirm the importance of the free flow of ideas, the freedom of thought and expression and human rights—values that, we know, will become universal only if we make them so. What's really important, then, cultures or people? In a world where Kumasi and New York—and Cairo and Leeds and Istanbul—are being drawn ever closer together, an ethics of globalization has proved elusive.

The right approach, I think, starts by taking individuals—not nations, tribes or "peoples"—as the proper object of moral concern. It doesn't much matter what we call such a creed, but in homage to Diogenes, the

---

[2]*Inns of Court in London:* Professional associations, one of which every English barrister (lawyer) and judge who was formerly a barrister must belong to. The Inns also provide libraries, dining facilities, and a church or chapel. There are now four: Lincoln's Inn, Gray's Inn, Inner Temple, and Middle Temple.—EDS.

[3]*Unesco:* United Nations Educational, Scientific, and Cultural Organization (UNESCO), an agency of the United Nations whose purpose is to contribute to peace and security by promoting international collaboration through education, science, and culture in order to further universal respect for justice, the rule of law, and the human rights and fundamental freedoms proclaimed in the UN Charter.—EDS.

fourth-century Greek Cynic and the first philosopher to call himself a "citizen of the world," we could call it cosmopolitan. Cosmopolitans take cultural difference seriously, because they take the choices individual people make seriously. But because cultural difference is not the only thing that concerns them, they suspect that many of globalization's cultural critics are aiming at the wrong targets.

Yes, globalization can produce homogeneity. But globalization is also a threat to homogeneity. You can see this as clearly in Kumasi as anywhere. One thing Kumasi isn't — simply because it's a city — is homogeneous. English, German, Chinese, Syrian, Lebanese, Burkinabe, Ivorian, Nigerian, Indian: I can find you families of each description. I can find you Asante people, whose ancestors have lived in this town for centuries, but also Hausa households that have been around for centuries, too. There are people there from every region of the country as well, speaking scores of languages. But if you travel just a little way outside Kumasi — 20 miles, say, in the right direction — and if you drive off the main road down one of the many potholed side roads of red laterite, you won't have difficulty finding villages that are fairly monocultural. The people have mostly been in Kumasi and seen the big, polyglot, diverse world of the city. Where they live, though, there is one everyday language (aside from English in the government schools) and an agrarian way of life based on some old crops, like yams, and some newer ones, like cocoa, which arrived in the late 19th century as a product for export. They may or may not have electricity. (This close to Kumasi, they probably do.) When people talk of the homogeneity produced by globalization, what they are talking about is this: Even here, the villagers will have radios (though the language will be local); you will be able to get a discussion going about Ronaldo, Mike Tyson, or Tupac; and you will probably be able to find a bottle of Guinness or Coca-Cola (as well as of Star or Club, Ghana's own fine lagers). But has access to these things made the place more homogeneous or less? And what can you tell about people's souls from the fact that they drink Coca-Cola?

It's true that the enclaves of homogeneity you find these days — in Asante as in Pennsylvania — are less distinctive than they were a century ago, but mostly in good ways. More of them have access to effective medicines. More of them have access to clean drinking water, and more of them have schools. Where, as is still too common, they don't have these things, it's something not to celebrate but to deplore. And whatever loss of difference there has been, they are constantly inventing new forms of difference: new hairstyles, new slang, even, from time to time, new religions. No one could say that the world's villages are becoming anything like the same.

So why do people in these places sometimes feel that their identities   10
are threatened? Because the world, their world, is changing, and some of them don't like it. The pull of the global economy — witness those cocoa trees, whose chocolate is eaten all around the world — created some of the life they now live. If chocolate prices were to collapse again, as they did in the early 1990's, Asante farmers might have to find new crops or

new forms of livelihood. That prospect is unsettling for some people (just as it is exciting for others). Missionaries came awhile ago, so many of these villagers will be Christian, even if they have also kept some of the rites from earlier days. But new Pentecostal messengers are challenging the churches they know and condemning the old rites as idolatrous. Again, some like it; some don't.

Above all, relationships are changing. When my father was young, a man in a village would farm some land that a chief had granted him, and his maternal clan (including his younger brothers) would work it with him. When a new house needed building, he would organize it. He would also make sure his dependents were fed and clothed, the children educated, marriages and funerals arranged and paid for. He could expect to pass the farm and the responsibilities along to the next generation.

Nowadays, everything is different. Cocoa prices have not kept pace with the cost of living. Gas prices have made the transportation of the crop more expensive. And there are new possibilities for the young in the towns, in other parts of the country and in other parts of the world. Once, perhaps, you would have commanded the young ones to stay. Now they have the right to leave — perhaps to seek work at one of the new data-processing centers down south in the nation's capital — and, anyway, you may not make enough to feed and clothe and educate them all. So the time of the successful farming family is passing, and those who were settled in that way of life are as sad to see it go as American family farmers are whose lands are accumulated by giant agribusinesses. We can sympathize with them. But we cannot force their children to stay in the name of protecting their authentic culture, and we cannot afford to subsidize indefinitely thousands of distinct islands of homogeneity that no longer make economic sense.

Nor should we want to. Human variety matters, cosmopolitans think, because people are entitled to options. What John Stuart Mill[4] said more than a century ago in "On Liberty" about diversity within a society serves just as well as an argument for variety across the globe.

> If it were only that people have diversities of taste, that is reason enough for not attempting to shape them all after one model. But different persons also require different conditions for their spiritual development; and can no more exist healthily in the same moral, than all the variety of plants can exist in the same physical, atmosphere and climate. The same things which are helps to one person toward the cultivation of his higher nature, are hindrances to another. . . . Unless there is a corresponding diversity in their modes of life, they neither obtain their fair share of happiness, nor grow up to the mental, moral, and aesthetic stature of which their nature is capable.

[4]*Mill:* (1806–1873) British philosopher, political economist, civil servant, and member of parliament, as well as an influential liberal thinker and advocate of utilitarianism — an ethical theory developed by Jeremy Bentham, who espoused the belief that the moral worth of an action is determined by its contribution to increasing happiness or pleasure. — EDS.

If we want to preserve a wide range of human conditions because it allows free people the best chance to make their own lives, we can't enforce diversity by trapping people within differences they long to escape.

2.

Even if you grant that people shouldn't be compelled to sustain the older cultural practices, you might suppose that cosmopolitans should side with those who are busy around the world "preserving culture" and resisting "cultural imperialism." Yet behind these slogans you often find some curious assumptions. Take "preserving culture." It's one thing to help people sustain arts they want to sustain. I am all for festivals of Welsh bards in Llandudno financed by the Welsh arts council. Long live the Ghana National Cultural Center in Kumasi, where you can go and learn traditional Akan dancing and drumming, especially since its classes are spirited and overflowing. Restore the deteriorating film stock of early Hollywood movies; continue the preservation of Old Norse and early Chinese and Ethiopian manuscripts; record, transcribe and analyze the oral narratives of Malay and Masai and Maori. All these are undeniably valuable.

But preserving culture—in the sense of such cultural artifacts—is different from preserving cultures. And the cultural preservationists often pursue the latter, trying to ensure that the Huli of Papua New Guinea (or even Sikhs in Toronto) maintain their "authentic" ways. What makes a cultural expression authentic, though? Are we to stop the importation of baseball caps into Vietnam so that the Zao will continue to wear colorful red headdresses? Why not ask the Zao? Shouldn't the choice be theirs?

"They have no real choice," the cultural preservationists say. "We've dumped cheap Western clothes into their markets, and they can no longer afford the silk they used to wear. If they had what they really wanted, they'd still be dressed traditionally." But this is no longer an argument about authenticity. The claim is that they can't afford to do something that they'd really like to do, something that is expressive of an identity they care about and want to sustain. This is a genuine problem, one that afflicts people in many communities: they're too poor to live the life they want to lead. But if they do get richer, and they still run around in T-shirts, that's their choice. Talk of authenticity now just amounts to telling other people what they ought to value in their own traditions.

Not that this is likely to be a problem in the real world. People who can afford it mostly like to put on traditional garb—at least from time to time. I was best man once at a Scottish wedding at which the bridegroom wore a kilt and I wore kente cloth. Andrew Oransay, the islander who piped us up the aisle, whispered in my ear at one point, "Here we all are then, in our tribal gear." In Kumasi, people who can afford them love to put on their kente cloths, especially the most "traditional" ones, woven in colorful silk strips in the town of Bonwire, as they have been for a couple of centuries. (The prices are high in part because demand outside Asante

15

has risen. A fine kente for a man now costs more than the average Ghanaian earns in a year. Is that bad? Not for the people of Bonwire.)

Besides, trying to find some primordially authentic culture can be like peeling an onion. The textiles most people think of as traditional West African cloths are known as Java prints; they arrived in the 19th century with the Javanese batiks sold, and often milled, by the Dutch. The traditional garb of Herero[5] women in Namibia derives from the attire of 19th-century German missionaries, though it is still unmistakably Herero, not least because the fabrics used have a distinctly un-Lutheran range of colors. And so with our kente cloth: the silk was always imported, traded by Europeans, produced in Asia. This tradition was once an innovation. Should we reject it for that reason as untraditional? How far back must one go? Should we condemn the young men and women at the University of Science and Technology, a few miles outside Kumasi, who wear European-style gowns for graduation, lined with kente strips (as they do now at Howard and Morehouse, too)? Cultures are made of continuities and changes, and the identity of a society can survive through these changes. Societies without change aren't authentic; they're just dead.

3.

The preservationists often make their case by invoking the evil of "cultural imperialism." Their underlying picture, in broad strokes, is this: There is a world system of capitalism. It has a center and a periphery. At the center—in Europe and the United States—is a set of multinational corporations. Some of these are in the media business. The products they sell around the world promote the creation of desires that can be fulfilled only by the purchase and use of their products. They do this explicitly through advertising, but more insidiously, they also do so through the messages implicit in movies and in television drama. Herbert Schiller, a leading critic of "media-cultural imperialism," claimed that "it is the imagery and cultural perspectives of the ruling sector in the center that shape and structure consciousness throughout the system at large."

That's the theory, anyway. But the evidence doesn't bear it out. Researchers have actually gone out into the world and explored the responses to the hit television series "Dallas" in Holland and among Israeli Arabs, Moroccan Jewish immigrants, kibbutzniks, and new Russian immigrants to Israel. Thy have examined the actual context of the television media—whose penetration in everyday life far exceeds that of film—in Australia, Brazil, Canada, India and Mexico. They have looked at how American popular culture was taken up by the artists of Sophiatown, in South Africa. They have discussed "Days of Our Lives" and

20

---

[5]*Herero:* One of the principal ethnic groups in Namibia, the Herero fought for control of the country's sparse pastureland. Dominated by German colonial rule in the nineteenth century, many were drawn to Christianity, especially Lutheranism.—EDS.

"The Bold and the Beautiful" with Zulu college students from traditional backgrounds.

And one thing they've found is that how people respond to these cultural imports depends on their existing cultural context. When the media scholar Larry Strelitz spoke to students from KwaZulu-Natal, he found that they were anything but passive vessels. One of them, Sipho—a self-described "very, very strong Zulu man"—reported that he had drawn lessons from watching the American soap opera "Days of Our Lives," "especially relationship-wise." It fortified his view that "if a guy can tell a woman that he loves her, she should be able to do the same." What's more, after watching the show, Sipho "realized that I should be allowed to speak to my father. He should be my friend rather than just my father." It seems doubtful that that was the intended message of multinational capitalism's ruling sector.

But Sipho's response also confirmed that cultural consumers are not dupes. They can adapt products to suit their own needs, and they can decide for themselves what they do and do not approve of. Here's Sipho again:

> In terms of our culture, a girl is expected to enter into relationships when she is about 20. In the Western culture, a girl can be exposed to a relationship as early as 15 or 16. That one we shouldn't adopt in our culture. Another thing we shouldn't adopt from the Western culture has to do with the way they treat elderly people. I wouldn't like my family to be sent into an old-age home.

It shouldn't matter whether the "old-age homes" in American soap operas were safe places, full of kindly people. That wouldn't sell the idea to Sipho. Dutch viewers of "Dallas" saw not the pleasures of conspicuous consumption among the superrich—the message that theorists of "cultural imperalism" find in every episode—but a reminder that money and power don't protect you from tragedy. Israeli Arabs saw a program that confirmed that women abused by their husbands should return to their fathers. Mexican telenovelas remind Ghanaian women that, where sex is at issue, men are not to be trusted. If the telenovelas tried to tell them otherwise, they wouldn't believe it.

Talk of cultural imperialism "structuring the consciousness" of those in the periphery treats people like Sipho as blank slates on which global capitalism's moving finger writes its message, leaving behind another cultural automaton as it moves on. It is deeply condescending. And it isn't true.

In fact, one way that people sometimes respond to the onslaught of ideas from the West is to turn them against their originators. It's no accident that the West's fiercest adversaries among other societies tend to come from among the most Westernized of the group. Who in Ghana excoriated the British colonizers and built the movement for independence? Not the farmers and the peasants. Not the chiefs. It was the Western-educated bourgeoisie. And when Kwame Nkrumah—who went to college in Pennsylvania and lived in London—created a nationalist mass movement, at its core were soldiers who had returned from fighting a war in the British Army, urban market women who traded Dutch prints, unionists who worked in industries created by colonialism and the so-called veranda boys, who had been to colonial schools, learned English and studied history and geography in textbooks written in England. Who led the resistance to the British Raj?[6] An Indian-born South African lawyer, trained in the British courts, whose name was Gandhi; an Indian named Nehru, who wore Savile Row suits and sent his daughter to an English boarding school; and Muhammad Ali Jinnah, founder of Pakistan, who joined Lincoln's Inn in London and became a barrister at the age of 19. The independence movements of the postwar world that led to the end of Europe's African and Asian empires were driven by the rhetoric that had guided the Allies' own struggle against Germany and Japan: democracy, freedom, equality. This wasn't a conflict between values. It was a conflict of interests couched in terms of the same values.

4.

Sometimes, though, people react to the incursions of the modern world not   25
by appropriating the values espoused by the liberal democracies but by inverting
them. One recent result has been a new worldwide fraternity that presents cos-
mopolitanism with something of a sinister mirror image. Indeed, you could think
of its members as counter-cosmopolitans. They believe in human dignity across
the nations, and they live their creed. They share these ideals with people in many
countries, speaking many languages. As thoroughgoing globalists, they make
full use of the World Wide Web. They resist the crass consumerism of modern
Western society and deplore its influence in the rest of the world. But they also
resist the temptations of the narrow nationalisms of the countries where they
were born, along with the humble allegiances of kith and kin. They resist such
humdrum loyalties because they get in the way of the one thing that matters:
building a community of enlightened men and women across the world. That is
one reason they reject traditional religious authorities (though they disapprove,
too, of their obscurantism and temporizing). Sometimes they agonize in their dis-
cussions about whether they can reverse the world's evils or whether their strug-
gle is hopeless. But mostly they soldier on in their efforts to make the world a
better place.

These are not the heirs of Diogenes the Cynic. The community these comrades are building is not a polis; it's what they call the ummah, the global community of Muslims, and it is open to all who share their faith. They are young, global Muslim fundamentalists. The ummah's new globalists consider that they have returned to the fundamentals of Islam; much of what passes for Islam in the world, much of what has passed as Islam for centuries, they think a sham. As the French scholar Olivier Roy has

---

[6]***British Raj:*** The British Indian Empire. —EDS.

observed, these religionists—his term for them is "neofundamentalists"—wish to cleanse Islam's pristine and universal message from the contingencies of mere history, of local cultures. For them, Roy notes, "globalization is a good opportunity to dissociate Islam from any given culture and to provide a model that could work beyond any culture." They have taken a set of doctrines that once came with a form of life, in other words, and thrown away that form of life.

Now, the vast majority of these fundamentalists are not going to blow anybody up. So they should not be confused with those other Muslims—the "radical neofundamentalists," Roy calls them—who want to turn jihad, interpreted as literal warfare against the West, into the sixth pillar of Islam. Whether to endorse the use of violence is a political decision, even if it is to be justified in religious terms. Nonetheless, the neofundamentalists present a classic challenge to cosmopolitanism, because they, too, offer a moral and, in its way, inclusive universalism.

Unlike cosmopolitanism, of course, it is universalist without being tolerant, and such intolerant universalism has often led to murder. It underlay the French Wars of Religion that bloodied the four decades before the Edict of Nantes of 1598, in which Henri IV of France finally granted to the Protestants in his realm the right to practice their faith. In the Thirty Years' War, which ravaged central Europe until 1648 and the Peace of Westphalia, Protestant and Catholic princes from Austria to Sweden struggled with one another, and hundreds of thousands of Germans died in battle. Millions starved or died of disease as roaming armies pillaged the countryside. The period of religious conflict in the British Isles, from the first Bishops' War of 1639 to the end of the English Civil War in 1651, which pitted Protestant armies against the forces of a Catholic king, resulted in the deaths of perhaps 10 percent of the population. All these conflicts involved issues beyond sectarian doctrine, of course. Still, many Enlightenment liberals drew the conclusion that enforcing one vision of universal truth could only lead the world back to the blood baths.

Yet tolerance by itself is not what distinguishes the cosmopolitan from the neofundamentalist. There are plenty of things that the heroes of radical Islam are happy to tolerate. They don't care if you eat kebabs or meatballs or kung pao chicken, as long as the meat is halal; your hijab can be silk or linen or viscose. At the same time, there are plenty of things that cosmopolitans will not tolerate. We will sometimes want to intervene in other places because what is going on there violates our principles so deeply. We, too, can see moral error. And when it is serious enough—genocide is the least-controversial case—we will not stop with conversation. Toleration has its limits.

Nor can you tell us apart by saying that the neofundamentalists believe in universal truth. Cosmopolitans believe in universal truth, too, though we are less certain that we already have all of it. It is not skepticism about the very idea of truth that guides us; it is realism about how hard the truth is to find. One tenet we hold to, however, is that every human being has obligations to every other. Everybody matters: that is our central idea. And again, it sharply limits the scope of our tolerance.

To say what, in principle, distinguishes the cosmopolitan from competing universalisms, we plainly need to go beyond talk of truth and tolerance. One distinctively cosmopolitan commitment is to pluralism. Cosmopolitans think that there are many values worth living by and that you cannot live by all of them. So we hope and expect that different people and different societies will embody different values. Another aspect of cosmopolitanism is what philosophers call fallibilism—the sense that our knowledge is imperfect, provisional, subject to revision in the face of new evidence.

The neofundamentalist conception of a global ummah, by contrast, admits of local variations—but only in matters that don't matter. These counter-cosmopolitans, like many Christian fundamentalists, do think that there is one right way for all human beings to live; that all the differences must be in the details. If what concerns you is global homogeneity, then this utopia, not the world that capitalism is producing, is the one you should worry about. Still, the universalisms in the name of religion are hardly the only ones that invert the cosmopolitan creed. In the name of universal humanity, you can be the kind of Marxist, like Mao[7] or Pol Pot,[8] who wants to eradicate all religion, just as easily as you can be the Grand Inquisitor supervising an auto-da-fé. All of these men want everyone on their side, so we can share with them the vision in their mirror. "Indeed, I'm a trustworthy adviser to you," Osama bin Laden said in a 2002 "message to the American people." "I invite you to the happiness of this world and the hereafter and to escape your dry, miserable, materialistic life that is without soul. I invite you to Islam, that calls to follow of the path of Allah alone Who has no partners, the path which calls for justice and forbids oppression and crimes." Join us, the counter-cosmopolitans say, and we will all be sisters and brothers. But each of them plans to trample on our differences—to trample us to death, if necessary—if we will not join them. Their motto might as well be the sardonic German saying *Und willst du nicht mein Bruder sein, So schlag' ich Dir den Schädel ein.* (If you don't want to be my brother, then I'll smash your skull in.)

That liberal pluralists are hostile to certain authoritarian ways of life—that they're intolerant of radical intolerance—is sometimes seen as a kind of self-refutation. That's a mistake: you can care about individual

---

[7] ***Mao:*** Mao Zedong (1893–1976), a Chinese military and political leader, who led the Communist party of China to victory against the Kuomintang (KMT) in the Chinese Civil War and remained the leader of the People's Republic of China from its inception in 1949 until his death in 1976.—EDS.

[8] ***Pol Pot:*** Saloth Sar (1925–1998), also known as Pol Pot, the leader of the Khmer Rouge. Prime Minister of Cambodia from 1976 to 1979, Pol Pot relocated city dwellers to the countryside to work in collective farms and forced labor projects. The combination of slave labor, malnutrition, poor medical care, and executions led to an estimated death toll of 750,000 to 1.7 million people.—EDS.

freedom and still understand that the contours of that freedom will vary considerably from place to place. But we might as well admit that a concern for individual freedom isn't something that will appeal to every individual. In politics, including cultural politics, there are winners and losers—which is worth remembering when we think about international human rights treaties. When we seek to embody our concern for strangers in human rights law, and when we urge our government to enforce it, we are seeking to change the world of law in every nation on the planet. We have declared slavery a violation of international law. And, in so doing, we have committed ourselves, at a minimum, to the desirability of its eradication everywhere. This is no longer controversial in the capitals of the world. No one defends enslavement. But international treaties define slavery in ways that arguably include debt bondage, and debt bondage is a significant economic institution in parts of South Asia. I hold no brief for debt bondage. Still, we shouldn't be surprised if people whose incomes and style of life depend upon it are angry.

It's the same with the international movements to promote women's equality. We know that many Islamists are deeply disturbed by the way Western men and women behave. We permit women to swim almost naked with strange men, which is our business, but it is hard to keep the news of these acts of immodesty from Muslim women and children or to protect Muslim men from the temptations they inevitably create. As the Internet extends its reach, it will get even harder, and their children, especially their girls, will be tempted to ask for these freedoms, too. Worse, they say, we are now trying to force our conception of how women and men should behave upon them. We speak of women's rights. We make treaties enshrining these rights. And then we want their governments to enforce them.

Like many people in every nation, I support those treaties; I believe   35
that women, like men, should have the vote, should be entitled to work outside their homes, should be protected from the physical abuse of men, including their fathers, brothers and husbands. But I also know that the changes these freedoms would bring will change the balance of power between men and women in everyday life. How do I know this? Because I have lived most of my adult life in the West as it has gone through just such a transition, and I know that the process is not yet complete.

So liberty and diversity may well be at odds, and the tensions between them aren't always easily resolved. But the rhetoric of cultural preservation isn't any help. Again, the contradictions are near to hand. Take another look at the Unesco Convention. It affirms the "principle of equal dignity of and respect for all cultures." (What, all cultures—including those of the KKK and the Taliban?) It also affirms "the importance of culture for social cohesion in general, and in particular its potential for the enhancement of the status and role of women in society." (But doesn't "cohesion" argue for uniformity? And wouldn't enhancing the status and role of women involve changing, rather than preserving, cultures?) In Saudi Arabia, people can watch "Will and Grace" on satellite TV—officially proscribed, but available all the same—knowing that, under Saudi law, Will could be beheaded in a public square. In northern Nigeria, mullahs[9] inveigh against polio vaccination while sentencing adulteresses to death by stoning. In India, thousands of wives are burned to death each year for failing to make their dowry payments. Vive la différence? Please.

5.

Living cultures do not, in any case, evolve from purity into contamination; change is more a gradual transformation from one mixture to a new mixture, a process that usually takes place at some distance from rules and rulers, in the conversations that occur across cultural boundaries. Such conversations are not so much about arguments and values as about the exchange of perspectives. I don't say that we change minds, but the reasons we offer in our conversation will seldom do much to persuade others who do not share our fundamental evaluative judgments already. When we make judgments, after all, it's rarely because we have applied well-thought-out principles to a set of facts and deduced an answer. Our efforts to justify what we have done—or what we plan to do—are typically made up after the event, rationalizations of what we have decided intuitively to do. And a good deal of what we intuitively take to be right, we take to be right just because it is what we are used to. That does not mean, however, that we cannot become accustomed to doing things differently.

Consider the practice of foot-binding in China, which persisted for a thousand years—and was largely eradicated within a generation. The anti-foot-binding campaign, in the 1910s and 1920s, did circulate facts about the disadvantages of bound feet, but those couldn't have come as news to most people. Perhaps more effective was the campaign's emphasis that no other country went in for the practice; in the world at large, then, China was "losing face" because of it. (To China's cultural preservationists, of course, the fact that the practice was peculiar to the region was entirely a mark of its favor.) Natural-foot societies were formed, with members foreswearing the practice and further pledging that their sons would not marry women with bound feet. As the movement took hold, scorn was heaped on older women with bound feet, and they were forced to endure the agonies of unbinding. What had been beautiful became ugly; ornamentation became disfigurement. The appeal to reason can explain neither the custom nor its abolition.

So, too, with other social trends. Just a couple of generations ago, most people in most of the industrialized world thought that middle-class women would ideally be housewives and mothers. If they had time on their hands, they could engage in charitable work or entertain one another; a few of them might engage in the arts, writing novels, painting, performing in music, theater and dance. But there was little place for them in the

---

[9]**Mullahs:** The name given to Islamic clerics and mosque leaders.—EDS.

"learned professions" — as lawyers or doctors, priests or rabbis; and if they were to be academics, they would teach young women and probably remain unmarried. They were not likely to make their way in politics, except perhaps at the local level. And they were not made welcome in science.

How much of the shift away from these assumptions is a result of arguments? Isn't a significant part of it just the consequence of our getting used to new ways of doing things? The arguments that kept the old pattern in place were not — to put it mildly — terribly good. If the reasons for the old sexist way of doing things had been the problem, the women's movement could have been done in a couple of weeks.

Consider another example: In much of Europe and North America, in places where a generation ago homosexuals were social outcasts and homosexual acts were illegal, lesbian and gay couples are increasingly being recognized by their families, by society and by the law. This is true despite the continued opposition of major religious groups and a significant and persisting undercurrent of social disapproval. Both sides make arguments, some good, most bad. But if you ask the social scientists what has produced this change, they will rightly not start with a story about reasons. They will give you a historical account that concludes with a sort of perspectival shift. The increasing presence of "openly gay" people in social life and in the media has changed our habits. And over the last 30 years or so, instead of thinking about the private activity of gay sex, many Americans and Europeans started thinking about the public category of gay people.

One of the great savants of the postwar era, John von Neumann, liked to say, mischievously, that "in mathematics you don't understand things, you get used to them." As in mathematical arguments, so in moral ones. Now, I don't deny that all the time, at every stage, people were talking, giving one another reasons to do things: accept their children, stop treating homosexuality as a medical disorder, disagree with their churches, come out. Still, the short version of the story is basically this: People got used to lesbians and gay men. I am urging that we should learn about people in other places, take an interest in their civilizations, their arguments, their errors, their achievements, not because that will bring us to agreement but because it will help us get used to one another — something we have a powerful need to do in this globalized era. If that is the aim, then the fact that we have all these opportunities for disagreement about values need not put us off. Understanding one another may be hard; it can certainly be interesting. But it doesn't require that we come to agreement.

6.

The ideals of purity and preservation have licensed a great deal of mischief in the past century, but they have never had much to do with lived culture. Ours may be an era of mass migration, but the global spread and hybridization of culture — through travel, trade, or conquest — is hardly a recent development. Alexander's empire molded both the states and the sculpture of Egypt and North India; the Mongols and then the Mughals shaped great swaths of Asia; the Bantu migrations populated half the African continent. Islamic states stretch from Morocco to Indonesia; Christianity reached Africa, Europe and Asia within a few centuries of the death of Jesus of Nazareth; Buddhism long ago migrated from India into much of East and Southeast Asia. Jews and people whose ancestors came from many parts of China have long lived in vast diasporas. The traders of the Silk Road changed the style of elite dress in Italy; someone buried Chinese pottery in 15th-century Swahili graves. I have heard it said that the bagpipes started out in Egypt and came to Scotland with the Roman infantry. None of this is modern.

Our guide to what is going on here might as well be a former African slave named Publius Terentius Afer, whom we know as Terence. Terence, born in Carthage, was taken to Rome in the early second century B.C., and his plays—witty, elegant works that are, with Plautus's earlier, less-cultivated works, essentially all we have of Roman comedy—were widely admired among the city's literary elite. Terence's own mode of writing—which involved freely incorporating any number of earlier Greek plays into a single Latin one—was known to Roman littérateurs as "contamination."

It's an evocative term. When people speak for an ideal of cultural purity, sustaining the authentic culture of the Asante or the American family farm, I find myself drawn to contamination as the name for a counterideal. Terence had a notably firm grasp on the range of human variety: "So many men, so many opinions" was a line of his. And it's in his comedy "The Self-Tormentor" that you'll find what may be the golden rule of cosmopolitanism—*Homo sum: humani nil a me alienum puto*; "I am human; nothing human is alien to me." The context is illuminating. A busybody farmer named Chremes is told by his neighbor to mind his own affairs; the *homo sum* credo is Chremes's breezy rejoinder. It isn't meant to be an ordinance from on high; it's just the case for gossip. Then again, gossip—the fascination people have for the small doings of other people—has been a powerful force for conversation among cultures.

The ideal of contamination has few exponents more eloquent than Salman Rushdie, who has insisted that the novel that occasioned his fatwa "celebrates hybridity, impurity, intermingling, the transformation that comes of new and unexpected combinations of human beings, cultures, ideas, politics, movies, songs. It rejoices in mongrelisation and fears the absolutism of the Pure. Mélange, hotch-potch, a bit of this and a bit of that is how newness enters the world." No doubt there can be an easy and spurious utopianism of "mixture," as there is of "purity" or "authenticity." And yet the larger human truth is on the side of contamination—that endless process of imitation and revision.

A tenable global ethics has to temper a respect for difference with a respect for the freedom of actual human beings to make their own choices. That's why cosmopolitans don't insist that everyone become cosmopolitan. They know they don't have all the answers. They're humble enough to think that they might learn from strangers; not too humble to

45

think that strangers can't learn from them. Few remember what Chremes says after his "I am human" line, but it is equally suggestive: "If you're right, I'll do what you do. If you're wrong, I'll set you straight."

The Reader's Presence

1. In Kwame Anthony Appiah's essay, what is being contaminated? What is the nature and extent of the contaminant? How does contamination work as an antidote for intolerance? Think carefully about Appiah's claim that the cure for intolerance is that we all "get used to one another" (paragraph 42). What does it mean to "get used" someone? How does this work in a way similar to — or different from — the way a tool "gets used" to do something?

2. Discuss the specific effects of Appiah's decision to divide his essay into six sections. You can answer this question by examining what — and how — each section contributes to Appiah's argument. How does each section differ from what comes before and after? What role does each section play in making the case for contamination? You can also imagine dividing the essay in other ways. Explain how the essay would change if it were divided into four sections or five.

3. How does Appiah's idea of cosmopolitan relations (paragraph 7) between individuals work within individuals? Think, for example, of Amy Tan's essay, "Mother Tongue" (page 249), where she writes about the "different Englishes" she uses: formal English at work and "broken" English with her mother. Which English represents authority and universalism and which pluralism and tolerance? What strategy do you use to negotiate the different languages you encounter (at home, at work, in class, online, etc.)? Drawing on Appiah's terms, describe yourself as a neofundamentalist, a universalist, or a cosmopolitan in relation to your cultures. Which is Tan? Explain why.

Rick Bass

Double-Talk

Rick Bass (b. 1957) was born in Fort Worth, Texas, the son of a geologist whose love of the land and passion for geology inspired the son to follow in his father's footsteps. Bass graduated from Utah State University with a degree in geology and set to work as a gas and oil geologist. He has said that he started writing on his lunch break from prospecting for oil in Jackson, Mississippi. The rugged south Texas hill country that generations of his family hiked and hunted was the basis of his first book of essays, The Deer Pasture *(1985). Nature, the environment, and the animals that inhabit it have been at the core of his nonfiction and fiction ever since. His collections of essays include* Oil Notes *(1988),* The Lost Grizzlies *(1995),* The New Wolves *(1998), and several books about northwestern Montana's Yaak Valley, where he has lived for many years with his wife, artist and frequent illustrator of his books, Elizabeth Hughes, and their children. His first collection of short stories,* The Watch *(1989), set in Texas, won the PEN/Nelson Algren Award. Among his many award-winning collections of short fiction are* Platte River *(1994),* The Hermit's Story *(2002), and* The Lives of Rocks *(2006); many of his stories have been selected in the* Best American Short Stories, *among other anthologies. He has written two novels,* Where the Sea Used to Be *(1998) and* The Diezmo *(2005), a work of historical fiction; his memoir,* Why I Came West, *was published in 2008. A noted environmental activist, Bass has contributed articles to* Paris Review, Esquire, GQ, Orion, OnEarth, *and* Audubon, *where his essay "Double-Talk" appeared in 2001.*

In an article for Orion, *Bass reflects on his beloved Yaak Valley, calling it a "vital linchpin, the narrowest bottleneck in a chain of wildness": "These roadless areas in the Yaak are public lands: lands owned by you, by me, by these writers, and by all Americans. Lands that, against overwhelming odds, have managed to retain the grace of their initial creation; fourteen last gardens where all the various and intensely interconnected cycles of life are still free to play out at the original pace with which they were first designed by the Creator."*

Next to vision, I believe language is our strongest sense. Allow me, then, some time to lament the corporate manipulation of my craft. To one who loves both language and wild country, it's infuriating to see the two loves pitted against each other, language being used to suck out the last good and vital marrow of wild country.

It's a platitude that big business runs the country, and frankly, whenever writers do battle with the monied interests, we expect to lose more than we win. But we writers like to think that at least we can help shape the future, by creating a purer, more mythical world in which the right thing is done, the right decision is made, and dignity, beauty, and nobility abound.

We can't. If anything, we're losing these battles even more decisively than we're losing the money wars.

Just as the forests, the wild prairies, the ocean, and the deserts are being taken from us, so, too—like an echo, or perhaps a foreshadowing—the language of wild places is being taken from us, insidiously, slyly, steadily. We are being given instead the language of machines, the language of the sick and the diseased. Individual words, used daily in government agencies, cede vast amounts of wild territory every time they are uttered. These words obscure the true beauty of wilderness and the possibility that there might exist a few landscapes that can do just fine without the curse of all our help and knowledge.

Clearcuts, for instance, are no longer exclusively called clearcuts. The   5
straightforward old Anglo-Saxon word has been replaced in most cases with the sinuous, almost lisping *seed trees with reserves*, which sounds more like some sort of Individual Retirement Account than a forest. Clearcuts are surrounded by "shelterbelts"—little more than beauty strips designed to obscure the public's view from the carnage beyond.

Engineers speak of the road "prism" as they make plans to enter the last roadless cores in benign fashion—the word *prism* conjuring not only the stability of the Pyramids but also, more subtly, the friendly kaleidoscopes of one's childhood. Where are the slaughterous runoffs of spring beneath that word *prism*? Where are the slumpage and collapse of roads, the sedimentation of streams, the crushing fragmentation of habitat?

Prescribed treatment. This phrase is used to describe an activity proposed by the Forest Service or some other agency—and rest assured, it usually involves chainsaws. Implicit in this notion of a prescription is that nature is sick, and we are the physician. That is not to say that there are not places where natural processes ("historic vegetative patterns") have not become slightly, temporarily unbalanced as a result of our past mistakes and transgressions, nor do I think that there aren't places where we can "manipulate" the forest to bring it closer to what most of us might describe as "health." But we use the terms *prescription* and *treatment* for every timber sale in the national forests. If your goal is to help preserve the sanctity, mystery, awe, and power of wild places, the battle is already half lost every time you open your mouth.

What are the cumulative effects of such usage—this daily refashioning of the woods into a thing that not only can but should always be controlled and manipulated?

How much room remains in that kind of language for what we are running out of, which is wilderness?

As a longtime resident of a logging community, and as a weekly re-   10
spondent to one proposed logging project after another, I am every bit as guilty of using this language. Not only do I use it in my letters of entreaty and outrage, I find myself sometimes *thinking* in that other language as I walk through the woods. Instead of seeing a fallen, rotting nurse log that

feeds insects and nurtures plants and soil, I see diseased trees, pathogens, fiber "wasted," value that is not "captured" in timely fashion.

Instead of seeing the mysteries of mycelium, I see root rot and dwarf mistletoe, and my mind skips ahead to the obvious "application": Fell the fir, girdle the larch. Stop the progress of death and dying. Stop the creation of new soil.

When a lot of trees in the wilderness die for one reason or another, then fall down or blow over, why is it called "fuel loading," rather than, say, "a bounty of carbon"? How did we lose even this battle? Is it the forests that elicit from us this exceptional deviousness of language? At first I think it is, but grassland activist George Wuerthner tells me about similar abuses of language in the prairies and the desert. "When the Bureau of Land Management is spending taxpayer money to develop water sources on public wildlands to benefit cow owners," he says, "they call them 'range-improvement' funds. But the only thing being improved is the ability to raise cows."

Wuerthner continues, "They call grazing a 'tool,' as a way of justifying livestock use of the land. There is 'Wildlife Services,' which serves wildlife by killing it. There is the 'Conservation Fund,' which pays for the eradication of prairie dogs with federal dollars."

In the depths of the sea, the language of wild and natural ecosystems is also egregiously abused. Carl Safina, author of *Song for the Blue Ocean* (and an Audubon Society vice-president), points out, "Fisheries people talk incessantly of 'harvesting' fishes, and even of 'harvesting' whales— trying to impart an agricultural tone, as though firing a bomb into the body of the largest creature ever to live on earth is analogous to picking watermelons that have been planted and cultivated."

Wuerthner agrees: "We see it with regard to hunting, where hunters don't kill wildlife, they 'harvest' it. Well, I don't harvest deer or elk, I kill them, and I'm quite willing to accept the proper term instead of hiding in some farm terminology."   15

This damning notion that natural resources are endless, controllable, easily manipulated to our desires is aided and abetted by the inability of wildlife to stand still and be quantified. Safina laments the use of the word *stock*—as if fish are but shoes on a shelf—and the glib interchangeability of two words, *fish* and *fishery*, that should not be interchangeable at all.

"In a trout stream," he says, "the trout themselves are not the fishery. They are simply fish—a population of wild animals. The people standing in the water in rubber pants are the fishery. On the Grand Banks, the weary cod and halibut are the fish; the boats whose wakes crisscross overhead as they pull the nets are the fishery."

The list of language abuses seems endless. In the forest, cyclic peaks of insect activity—exerting a healthy, selective force upon the living grace of the forest, providing nurse logs and hollow snags, recycling nutrients— are now called "outbreaks." In reality the insects are more surgeons than

we will ever be, one of the forces that have shaped and carved the wild
landscapes into their mosaic of health, much as wolves have whittled, in
the words of the poet Robinson Jeffers, "the fleet limbs of the antelope."

Catastrophic fires? We use these terms freely in our dialogue with the
government agencies, but would we ever have the temerity to suggest that
post-industrial management of the public lands has been its own kind of
"catastrophic" event? Why is industry so comfortable using such terms
of extremity, even violence? Such is the continuing, daily diminishment of
wilderness in this country.

Who defines for us what language to use and not use, when we may   20
and may not speak? In a true democracy, in true freedom, would we be
making these choices for ourselves? Would·we recognize when language
comes from the heart, versus when it is just trying to sell a product?

I fear increasingly that even as the wild country around us is being
compromised, like beach sand crumbling at the touch of the waves, so,
too, is our language of wilderness crumbling beneath us, until one day
our country will have forgotten how even to talk about wilderness, or
grizzly bears, or any of the other vanishing things, and the shadows, the
stories they cast.

I have been pleading on behalf of the last roadless cores in Montana
and the Yaak Valley for so long now that I rarely use the word *tree* anymore. Instead I choose the more familiar *timber*, whether the trees are
still standing or not. Dead and dying trees are usually called "material."
Even the relatively benign phrase *woody debris* sounds like something
you might comb out of your dog's hair after a hard day hunting: an an-
noyance, a nuisance. Often when there are a lot of dead, mulchy, crumbling logs in a stand (delicate fairy slipper orchids growing out of that
soft duff and powder, a richness of mushrooms), the official agency language will speak of how the groves need "sanitation."

How funny. It's in these tangled, unsanitary places that I like to sit
and rest, mesmerized by the intricacy of deadfall and blowdown, secure
in the faith that in such a forest, even in what looks to me like unstruc-
tured chaos, there is a grace and order and design. I cannot name it or
prove it or even see it, but sitting there in its midst, I can feel it, all
around me.

"When sea turtles that have drowned in nets wash up on beaches,
they are often referred to as 'stranded,'" says Safina. "I have been in
meetings with fishery managers who did not understand that all the
'stranded' turtles the fishermen were dismissing as 'not a problem' were,
in fact, dead. These are washed-up turtle carcasses, not stranded turtles."

Regeneration harvest? The forest is whacked and stacked, exposed to   25
the brutal, drying heat of an unprotected moonscape; and then little drift-
ing-in seedlings are expected to "regenerate." You "harvest" by taking it
all. I think I'll just keep using the word *clearcut*.

What are the consequences of a language that does not properly respect its subject?

This is certainly nothing that scientists can analyze, and yet I believe it is as real and significant a cumulative stress upon the ultimate future of the wilderness, and its wild inhabitants, as exists. Let the last few wild places escape the curse of our language and retain their eloquence. Let's keep the last precious bit as it is, rotting and burning and regenerating at its own pace and rhythm: a place where bears can be most fully bears, and where poets can be most fully poets, and even, perhaps, where scientists can be most fully scientists. Our dwindling wilderness areas should remain the greatest living sanctuaries on earth for our long, long list of endangered and threatened and sensitive species. But they are also one of the greatest available textbooks on the true possibilities of language, story, character, and imagination—both in individuals and in communities. We need to protect and preserve the last dark forest gardens, the last few unprotected public wildlands. But please, let's not go in there and "ecosystem manage" them.

Sometimes it seems as if our language is becoming as fragmented and manipulated as the dwindling wild landscape itself. I want more, not less, of the kind of landscape that reminds us that the wonders of life can exceed even the finest reaches of our language. We have enough, more than enough, of the chained and roaded, paved-over and cut-over lands, so subservient to our short-term hungers. We can never re-create our last few wildlands after they are gone or altered. We can only protect them, and treasure them—or, if we fail, tell stories about them after they are gone, with the echo of language.

The Reader's Presence

1. Bass argues strenuously against permitting corporate interests to continue to appropriate language "to suck out the last good and vital marrow of wild country" (paragraph 1). He claims, "The list of language abuses seems endless" (paragraph 18). Which of his examples do you find most memorable and convincing? Explain why. As soon as you understand the substance of Bass's argument, take a few moments to outline the structure of that argument. Where does Bass state most succinctly and effectively the idea— the thesis—that governs his essay? Comment on the extent to which you find his argument to be convincing and compelling. Choose one or two examples to illustrate your point. Shift your focus to more specific subjects, such as his word choices and phrasing. Point to specific examples of Bass's diction that you find especially effective in conveying the overarching idea of the essay.

Analyze the extent to which two of these word choices reinforce the effectiveness of his argument.

2. How would you characterize the tone Bass uses at the outset of his essay? Is it, for example, primarily strident? pensive? neither? Please support your response with specific examples. To what extent does Bass's tone remain consistent throughout the essay? Comment on his use of irony and paradox, and point to specific examples of his effective use of each. Bass also uses metaphor and analogy to reinforce the case he makes against the continued corruption of language used to describe wildlife and the wilderness. Choose one of these metaphors or analogies and discuss what is particularly effective about the ways he unfolds it. Track the changes in his pronoun references throughout the essay. For example, at what points does he shift from "I" to "we," and what are the benefits and disadvantages of making this move? What does Bass envision as the solution to the problem of "corporate manipulation of [his] craft" (paragraph 1)?

3. Bass's essay appeared in *Audubon* magazine. To what extent would his diction, tone, and use of metaphors need to change if he were to publish this essay as an editorial or a column in, say, a weekly newsmagazine, such as *Time* or *Newsweek*? Consider the same question after reading Cormac Cullinan's essay "If Nature Had Rights" (page 641). Each writer builds an argument to preserve the pristine character of the natural world and the basic rights of its objects and inhabitants. On which specific points would Bass and Cullinan agree—and disagree? Explain why.

Lakshmi Chaudhry
Mirror, Mirror on the Web

Journalist Lakshmi Chaudhry (b. 1968) grew up hearing stories about her grandfather, a noted journalist in India during the 1940s when India was battling for independence from Great Britain. Though her grandfather was dead by the time Chaudhry was born, she was inspired both by his antiestablishment politics and his work as a journalist. Chaudhry graduated with a degree in journalism from Mt. Holyoke College in 1990 and, after a year in India, pursued a graduate degree in political studies at the Maxwell School of Public Affairs at Syracuse

University. Chaudhry's career as a progressive journalist began with an internship at Mother Jones, *and she has since been a senior editor for* Alternet.org *and* In These Times. *Her articles on culture and politics have appeared in such publications as the* Village Voice, Wired, Bitch, *and* Ms. *and online in blogs for the* Huffington Post *and* RHRealityCheck.org. *She is currently a contributing writer at the* Nation, *where her essay, "Mirror, Mirror on the Web" first appeared in January 2007. Chaudhry co-wrote, with Christopher and Robert Scheer,* The Five Biggest Lies Bush Told Us about Iraq *(2003), and edited, with Don Hazen,* Start Making Sense: Turning the Lessons of 2004 into Winning Progressive Politics *(2005), a collection of essays by noted* AlterNet *contributors.*

In an interview on Feministing.com, *she talked about her work as a not-so-mainstream, "alternative" journalist: "The kind of journalism that attracted me was journalism that had a very clear point of view. That came to the world from this position that social justice is important, human rights are important, equality is important, feminism is important. And so, I really think* Mother Jones *was a big part of why I decided that journalism was for me. And so I've been [in journalism] since."*

"Everyone, in the back of his mind, wants to be a star," says YouTube co-founder Chad Hurley, explaining the dizzying success of the online mecca of amateur video in *Wired* magazine. And thanks to MySpace, YouTube, Facebook, LiveJournal and other bastions of the retooled Web 2.0, every Jane, Joe or Jamila can indeed be a star, be it as wannabe comics, citizen journalists, lip-syncing geeks, military bloggers, aspiring porn stars or even rodent-eating freaks.

We now live in the era of micro-celebrity, which offers endless opportunities to celebrate that most special person in your life, i.e., you—who not coincidentally is also *Time* magazine's widely derided Person of the Year for 2006. An honor once reserved for world leaders, pop icons and high-profile CEOs now belongs to "you," the ordinary netizen with the time, energy and passion to "make a movie starring my pet iguana . . . mash up 50 Cent's vocals with Queen's instrumentals . . . blog about my state of mind or the state of the nation or the *steak-frites* at the new bistro down the street."

The editors at *Time* tout this "revolution" in the headiest prose: "It's a story about community and collaboration on a scale never seen before. It's about the cosmic compendium of knowledge Wikipedia and the million-channel people's network YouTube and the online metropolis MySpace. It's about the many wresting power from the few and helping one another for nothing and how that will not only change the world, but also change the way the world changes."

This is the stuff of progressive fantasy: change, community, collaboration. And it echoes our cherished hope that a medium by, of and for the people will create a more democratic world. So it's easy to miss the editorial sleight of hand that slips from the "I" to the "we," substitutes individual self-expression for collective action and conflates popular attention with social consciousness.

For all the talk about coming together, Web 2.0's greatest successes   5
have capitalized on our need to feel significant and admired and, above
all, to be seen. The latest iteration of digital democracy had indeed
brought with it a new democracy of fame, but in doing so it has left us
ever more in the thrall of celebrity, except now we have a better shot at
being worshiped ourselves. As MySpace luminary Christine Dolce told
the *New York Post*, "My favorite comment is when people say that I'm
their idol. That girls look up to me."

So we upload our wackiest videos to YouTube, blog every sordid detail of our personal lives so as to insure at least fifty inbound links, add
200 new "friends" a day to our MySpace page with the help of friendflood
.com, all the time hoping that one day all our efforts at self-promotion
will merit—at the very least—our very own Wikipedia entry.

In *The Frenzy of Renown*, written in 1986, Leo Braudy documented
the long and intimate relationship between mass media and fame. The more
plentiful, accessible and immediate the ways of gathering and distributing
information have become, he wrote, the more ways there are to be known:
"In the past that medium was usually literature, theater, or public monu-
ments. With the Renaissance came painting and engraved portraits, and the
modern age added photography, radio, movies, and television. As each new
medium of fame appears, the human image it conveys is intensified and the
number of individuals celebrated expands." It's not surprise that the Internet, which offers vastly greater immediacy and accessibility than its top-
down predecessors, should further flatten the landscape of celebrity.

The democratization of fame, however, comes at a significant price.
"Through the technology of image reproduction and information reproduction, our relation to the increasing number of faces we see every day
becomes more and more transitory, and 'famous' seems as devalued a
term as 'tragic,'" Braudy wrote. And the easier it is to become known, the
less we have to do to earn that honor. In ancient Greece, when fame was
inextricably linked to posterity, an Alexander had to make his mark on
history to insure that his praises would be sung by generations to come.
The invention of the camera in the nineteenth century introduced the
modern notion of fame linked inextricably to a new type of professional:
the journalist. Aspiring celebrities turned increasingly to achievements
that would bring them immediate acclaim, preferably in the next day's
newspaper, and with the rise of television, on the evening news.

The broadcast media's voracious appetite for spectacle insured that
notoriety and fame soon became subsumed by an all-encompassing notion of celebrity, where simply being on TV became the ultimate stamp of
recognition. At the same time, advertisers sought to redefine fame in
terms of buying rather than doing, fusing the American Dream of material success with the public's hunger for stars in programs such as *Lifestyles of the Rich and Famous*.

But the advent of cyber-fame is remarkable in that it is divorced from 10
any significant achievement—farting to the tune of "Jingle Bells," for example, can get you on VH1. While a number of online celebrities are
rightly known for doing something (a blogger like Markos Moulitsas,
say), and still others have leveraged their virtual success to build lucrative
careers (as with the punk-rock group Fall Out Boy), it is no longer necessary to do either in order to be "famous."

Fame is now reduced to its most basic ingredient: public attention.
And the attention doesn't have to be positive either, as in the case of the
man in Belfast who bit the head off a mouse for a YouTube video. "In our
own time merely being looked at carries all the necessary ennoblement,"
Braudy wrote twenty years ago, words that ring truer than ever today.

Celebrity has become a commodity in itself, detached from and more
valuable than wealth or achievement. Even rich New York socialites feel
the need for their own blog, socialiterank.com, to get in on the action.
The advice for aspiring celebutantes may be tongue-in-cheek—"To become a relevant socialite, you are virtually required to have your name in
the press"—but no less true in this age of Paris Hilton wannabes.

Fame is no longer a perk of success but a necessary ingredient,
whether as a socialite, chef, scholar or skateboarder. "For a great many
people it is no longer enough to be very good at what you do. One also
has to be a public figure, noticed and celebrated, and preferably televised," writes Hal Niedzviecki in his book *Hello, I'm Special*. When it is
more important to be seen than to be talented, it is hardly surprising that
the less gifted among us are willing to fart our way into the spotlight.

The fantasy of fame is not new, but what is unprecedented is the pri-
macy of the desire, especially among young people. "I wanna be famous
because I would love it more than anything. . . . Sometimes I'll cry at
night wishing and praying for a better life to be famous. . . . To be like
the others someday too! Because i know that I can do it!" declares Britney Jo, writing on iWannaBeFamous.com.

She is hardly unusual. A 2000 Interprise poll revealed that 50 percent 15
of kids under 12 believed that becoming famous is part of the American
Dream. It's a dream increasingly shared by the rest of the world, as revealed in a recent survey of British children between 5 and 10, who most
frequently picked being famous as the "very best thing in the world." The
views of these young children are no different from American college
freshmen, who, according to a 2004 survey, most want to be an "actor or
entertainer."

Our preoccupation with fame is at least partly explained by our immersion in a media-saturated world that constantly tells us, as Braudy described it, "we should [be famous] if we possibly can, because it is the
best, perhaps the only, way to be." Less obvious, however, is how our
celebrity culture has fueled, and been fueled by, a significant generational
shift in levels of narcissism in the United States.

In the 1950s, only 12 percent of teenagers between 12 and 14 agreed with the statement, "I am an important person." By the late 1980s, the number had reached an astounding 80 percent, an upward trajectory that shows no sign of reversing. Preliminary findings from a joint study conducted by Jean Twenge, Keith Campbell and three other researchers revealed that an average college student in 2006 scored higher than 65 percent of the students in 1987 on the standard Narcissism Personality Inventory test, which includes statements such as "I am a special person," "I find it easy to manipulate people" and "If I were on the *Titanic*, I would deserve to be on the *first* lifeboat." In her recent book *Generation Me*, Twenge applies that overarching label to everyone born between 1970 and 2000.

According to Twenge and her colleagues, the spike in narcissism is linked to an overall increase in individualism, which has been fostered by a number of factors, including greater geographical mobility, breakdown of traditional communities and, more important, "the self-focus that blossomed in the 1970s [and] became mundane and commonplace over the next two decades." In schools, at home and in popular culture, children over the past thirty-odd years have been inculcated with the same set of messages: You're special; love yourself; follow your dreams; you can be anything you want to be.

These mantras, in turn, have been woven into an all-pervasive commercial narrative used to hawk everything from movie tickets to sneakers. Just do it, baby, but make sure you buy that pair of Nikes first. The idea that every self is important has been redefined to suit the needs of a cultural marketplace that devalues genuine community and selfhood in favor of "success." In this context, "feeling good about myself" becomes the best possible reason to staple one's stomach, buy that shiny new car, or strip for a Girls Gone Wild video. The corollary of individualism becomes narcissism, an inflated evaluation of self-worth devoid of any real sense of "self" or "worth."

Since a key component of narcissism is the need to be admired and   20
to be the center of attention, Generation Me's attraction to fame is inevitable. "You teach kids they're special. And when they watch TV, the impression they get is that everyone should be rich and famous. Then they hear, 'You can be anything you want.' So they're like, 'Well, I want to be rich and famous,'" says Twenge. Or if not rich and famous, at least to be "seen"—something the rest of us plebeians can now aspire to in the brave new media world. "To be noticed, to be wanted, to be loved, to walk into a place and have others care about what you're doing, even what you had for lunch that day: that's what people want, in my opinion," *Big Brother* contestant Kaysar Ridha told the *New York Times*, thus affirming a recent finding by Drew Pinsky and Mark Young that reality TV stars are far more narcissistic than actors, comedians, or musicians—perhaps because they reflect more closely the reason the rest of us are obsessed more than ever with "making it."

Not only do Americans increasingly want to be famous, but they also believe they *will* be famous, more so than any previous generation. A Harris poll conducted in 2000 found that 44 percent of those between the ages of 18 or 24 believed it was at least somewhat likely that they would be famous for a short period. Those in their late twenties were even more optimistic: Six in ten expected that they would be well-known, if only briefly, sometime in their lives. The rosy predictions of our destiny, however, contain within them the darker conviction that a life led outside of the spotlight would be without value. "People want the kind of attention that celebrities receive more than anything else," says Niedzviecki. "People want the recognition, the validation, the sense of having a place in the culture [because] we no longer know where we belong, what we're about or what we should be about."

Without any meaningful standard by which to measure our worth, we turn to the public eye for affirmation. "It's really the sense that Hey, I exist in this world, and that is important. That I matter," Niedzviecki says. Our "normal" lives therefore seem impoverished and less significant compared with the media world, which increasingly represents all that is grand and worthwhile, and therefore more "real."

No wonder that 16-year-old Rachel, Britney Jo's fellow aspirant to fame on iWannaBeFamous.com, rambles in desperation, "I figured out that I am tired of just dreaming about doing something, I am sick of looking for a 'regular' job . . . I feel life slipping by, and that 'something is missing' feeling begins to dominate me all day and night, I can't even watch the Academy Awards ceremony without crying . . . that is how I know . . . that is me. . . . I have to be . . . in the movies!!!"

The evolution of the Internet has both mirrored and shaped the intense focus on self that is the hallmark of the post-boomer generation. "If you aren't posting, you don't exist. People say, 'I post, therefore I am,'" Rishad Tobaccowala, CEO of Denuo, a new media consultancy, told *Wired*, inadvertently capturing the essence of Web 2.0, which is driven by our hunger for self-expression. Blogs, amateur videos, personal profiles, even interactive features such as Amazon.com's reviews offer ways to satisfy our need to be in the public eye.

But the virtual persona we project online is a carefully edited version 25
of ourselves, as "authentic" as a character on reality TV. People on reality TV "are ultra-self-aware versions of the ordinary, über-facsimiles of themselves in the same way that online personals are *recreations* of self constantly tweaked for maximum response and effect," writes Niedzviecki in his book.

Self-expression glides effortlessly into self-promotion as we shape our online selves—be it on a MySpace profile, LiveJournal blog or a YouTube video—to insure the greatest attention. Nothing beats good old-fashioned publicity even in the brave new world of digital media. So it should come as no shock that the oh-so-authentic LonelyGirl15 should turn out to be a

PR stunt or that the most popular person on MySpace is the mostly naked Tila Tequila, the proud purveyor of "skank-pop" who can boast of 1,626,097 friends, a clothing line, a record deal and making the cover of *Maxim UK* and *Stuff* magazines. YouTube has become the virtual equivalent of Los Angeles, the destination de rigueur for millions of celebrity aspirants, all hoping they will be the next Amanda Congdon, the video-blogger now with a gig on ABCNews.com, or the Spiridellis brothers, who landed venture capital funding because of their wildly popular video "This Land."

Beginning with the dot-com boom in the 1990s through to its present iteration as Web 2.0, the cultural power of the Internet has been fueled by the modern-day Cinderella fantasy of "making it." With their obsessive focus on A-list bloggers, upstart twentysomething CEOs and an assortment of weirdos and creeps, the media continually reframe the Internet as yet another shot at the glittering prize of celebrity. "We see the same slow channeling of the idea that your main goal in life is to reach as many people as possible all over the world with your product. And your product is you," says Niedzviecki. "As long as that's true, it's very hard to see how the Internet is going to change that." As long as more democratic media merely signify a greater democracy of fame—e.g., look how that indie musician landed a contract with that major label—we will remain enslaved to the same narrative of success that sustains corporate America.

In our eagerness to embrace the web as a panacea for various political ills, progressives often forget that the Internet is merely a medium like any other, and the social impact of its various features—interactivity, real-time publishing, easy access, cheap mass distribution—will be determined by the people who use them. There is no doubt that these technologies have facilitated greater activism, and new forms of it, both on- and offline. But we confuse the web's promise of increased visibility with real change. Political actions often enter the ether of the media world only to be incorporated into narratives of individual achievement. And the more successful among us end up as bold-faced names, leached dry of the ideas and values they represent—yet another face in the cluttered landscape of celebrity, with fortunes that follow the usual trajectory of media attention: First you're hot, and then you're not.

"It's all about you. Me. And all the various forms of the First Person Singular," writes cranky media veteran Brian Williams in his contribution to *Time*'s year-end package. "Americans have decided the most important person in their lives is . . . them, and our culture is now built upon that idea." So, have we turned into a nation of egoists, uninterested in anything that falls outside our narrow frame of self-reference?

As Jean Twenge points out, individualism doesn't necessarily preclude a social conscience or desire to do good. "But [Generation Me] articulates it as 'I want to make a difference,'" she says. "The outcome is still good, but it does put the self in the center." Stephen Duncombe, on

30

the other hand, author of the new book *Dream: Re-imagining Progressive Politics in an Age of Fantasy*, argues that rather than dismiss our yearning for individual recognition, progressives need to create real-world alternatives that offer such validation. For example, in place of vast anonymous rallies that aim to declare strength in numbers, he suggests that liberal activism should be built around small groups. "The size of these groups is critical. They are intimate affairs, small enough for each participant to have an active role in shaping the group's direction and voice," he writes. "In these 'affinity groups,' as they are called, every person is recognized: in short, they exist."

Such efforts, however, would have to contend with GenMe's aversion to collective action. "The baby boomers were self-focused in a different way. Whether it was self-examination like EST or social protest, they did everything in groups. This new generation is allergic to groups," Twenge says. And as Duncombe admits, activism is a tough sell for a nation weaned on the I-driven fantasy of celebrity that serves as "an escape from democracy with its attendant demands for responsibility and participation."

There is a happier alternative. If these corporate technologies of self-promotion work as well as promised, they may finally render fame meaningless. If everyone is onstage, there will be no one left in the audience. And maybe then we rock stars can finally turn our attention to life down here on earth. Or it may be life on earth that finally jolts us out of our admiring reverie in the mirrored hall of fame. We forget that this growing self-involvement is a luxury afforded to a generation that has not experienced a wide-scale war or economic depression. If and when the good times come to an end, so may our obsession with fame. "There are a lot of things on the horizon that could shake us out of the way we are now. And some of them are pretty ugly," Niedzviecki says. "We won't be able to say that my MySpace page is more important than my real life. . . . When you're a corpse, it doesn't matter how many virtual friends you have." Think global war, widespread unemployment, climate change. But then again, how cool would it be to vlog your life in the new Ice Age — kind of like starring in your very own *Day After Tomorrow*. LOL.

The Reader's Presence

1. Chaudhry argues that the digital democratization of fame has created a cultural environment on a global scale in which the pressure to establish oneself as a public figure, a celebrity of some notice, is intensifying, and rapidly so. Identify — and analyze — the factors that Chaudhry believes are essential features of contemporary definitions and illustrations of fame. In what specific ways are these characteristics different from — and similar to — definitions of "fame" and "celebrity" operative in earlier decades? How does

Chaudhry define "fantasy of fame" (paragraph 14)? Chaudhry plays with such terms as "netizen" and "celebutantes." Which does she use more effectively? Explain your answer. In what specific ways does Chaudhry support her assertion that "Celebrity has become a commodity in itself, detached from and more valuable than wealth or achievement" (paragraph 12)? What alternative(s) does she offer to a generation preoccupied with trying to devise ways to have self-expression glide "effortlessly into self-promotion" (paragraph 26)?

2. Comment on the ways Chaudhry uses diction, tone, and syntax to create a presence for herself in this essay. Consider, for example, the opening paragraph. What, specifically, are its strengths? What compositional strategies does Chaudhry use here to establish the purpose, tone, and direction for her essay? More generally, comment on the extent to which she succeeds in integrating secondary sources into her argument. What role does history play in the structure—and impact—of her essay? What does Chaudhry mean when she says, "Fame is no longer a perk of success but a necessary ingredient, whether as a socialite, chef, scholar, or skateboarder" (paragraph 13)? How would you characterize Chaudhry's attitude toward her subject? Give specific examples to support your response.

3. Lauren Slater, in her essay "The Trouble with Self-Esteem" (page 857), observes: "More than 2,000 books offering the attainment of self-esteem have been published; educational programs in schools designed to cultivate self-esteem continue to proliferate, as do rehabilitation programs for substance abusers that focus on cognitive realignment with self-affirming statements like, 'Today I will accept myself for who I am, not what I wish I were.'" Based on your reading of Slater's argument, in what ways would she agree—or disagree—with Chaudhry's analysis of the consequences of democratizing fame? Explain your answer. Be as specific as possible.

Cormac Cullinan

If Nature Had Rights

Cormac Cullinan (b. 1962) is an environmental lawyer and international consultant on the law and policy in the fields of environment and natural-resource management. Cullinan's broad-based law career has taken him from part-time law lecturer to shipping lawyer in Durban, South Africa, to an international commercial and tax practice in Luxembourg and London. A partner and director of the environmental law firm Winstanley and Cullinan Inc., he is also the founder of EnAct International, an environmental law and policy consultancy headquartered in Cape Town, South Africa. Cullinan is credited with creating a new approach to environmental law and policy, which he terms "Earth Jurisprudence," based on the belief that human societies should regulate themselves as members of a global community. Using his expertise in drafting legislation and international treaties, Cullinan works to develop new legal systems that foster a human connection to nature and encourage personal and social commitment to the sustainability of the planet. He has lectured and written widely on issues related to human interactions with the environment and is the author of Wild Law *(2002) as well as of several works commissioned and published by the Food and Agriculture Organization of the United Nations. This essay first appeared in the January–February 2008 issue of* Orion.*

It was the sudden rush of the goat's bodies against the side of the *boma*[1] that woke him. Picking up a spear and stick, the Kenyan farmer slipped out into the warm night and crept toward the pen. All he could see was the spotted, sloping hindquarters of the animal trying to force itself between the poles to get at the goats — but it was enough. He drove his spear deep into the hyena.

The elders who gathered under the meeting tree to deliberate on the matter were clearly unhappy with the farmer's explanation. A man appointed by the traditional court to represent the interests of the hyena had testified that his careful examination of the body had revealed that the deceased was a female who was still suckling pups. He argued that given the prevailing drought and the hyena's need to nourish her young, her behavior in attempting to scavenge food from human settlements was reasonable and that it was wrong to have killed her. The elders then cross-examined the farmer carefully. Did he appreciate, they asked, that such killings were contrary to customary law? Had he considered the hyena's situation and whether or not she had caused harm? Could he not have simply driven her away? Eventually the elders ordered the man's clan to pay compensation for the harm done by driving more than one hundred of their goats

---

[1] **Boma:** A traditional enclosure for livestock, also known as a corral or kraal. —EDS.

(a fortune in that community) into the bush, where they could be eaten by the hyenas and other wild carnivores.

The story, told to me by a Kenyan friend, illustrates African customary law's concern with restorative justice rather than retribution. Wrongdoing is seen as a symptom of a breakdown in relationships within the wider community, and the elders seek to restore the damaged relationship rather than focusing on identifying and punishing the wrongdoer.

The verdict of a traditional African court regarding hyenacide may seem of mere anthropological interest to contemporary Americans. In most of today's legal systems, decisions that harm ecological communities have to be challenged primarily on the basis of whether or not the correct procedures have been followed. Yet consider how much greater the prospects of survival would be for most of life on Earth if mechanisms existed for imposing collective responsibility and liability on human communities and for restoring damaged relations with the larger natural community. Imagine if we had elders with a deep understanding of the lore of the wild who spoke for the Earth as well as for humans. If we did, how might they order us to compensate for, say, the anticipated destruction of the entire Arctic ecosystem because of global climate change, to restore relations with the polar bears and other people and creatures who depend on that ecosystem? How many polluting power plants and vehicles would it be fair to sacrifice to make amends?

"So what would a radically different law-driven consciousness look   5
like?" The question was posed over three decades ago by a University of Southern California law professor as his lecture drew to a close. "One in which Nature had rights," he continued. "Yes, rivers, lakes, trees. . . . How could such a posture *in law* affect a community's view of *itself*?" Professor Christopher Stone may as well have announced that he was an alien life form. Rivers and trees are objects, not subjects, in the eyes of the law and are by definition incapable of holding rights. His speculations created an uproar.

Stone stepped away from that lecture a little dazed by the response from the class but determined to back up his argument. He realize that for nature to have rights the law would have to be changed so that, first, a suit could be brought in the name of an aspect of nature, such as a river; second, a polluter could be held liable for harming a river; and third, judgments could be made that would benefit a river. Stone quickly identified a pending appeal to the United States Supreme Court against a decision of the Ninth Circuit that raised these issues. The Ninth Circuit Court of Appeals had found that the Sierra Club Legal Defense Fund was not "aggrieved" or "adversely affected" by the proposed development of the Mineral King Valley in the Sierra Nevada by Walt Disney Enterprises, Inc. This decision meant that the Sierra Club did not have "standing" so the court didn't need to consider the merits of the matter. Clearly, if the Mineral King Valley itself had been recognized as having rights, it would have been an adversely affected party and would have had the necessary standing.

Fortuitously, Supreme Court Justice William O. Douglas was writing a preface to the next edition of the *Southern California Law Review*. Stone's seminal "Should Trees Have Standing? Toward Legal Rights for Natural Objects" ("Trees") was hurriedly squeezed into the journal and read by Justice Douglas before the Court issued its judgment. In "Trees," Stone argued that courts should grant legal standing to guardians to represent the rights of nature, in much the same way as guardians are appointed to represent the rights of infants. In order to do so, the law would have to recognize that nature was not just a conglomeration of objects that could be owned, but was a subject that itself had legal rights and the standing to be represented in the courts to enforce those rights. The article eventually formed the basis for a famous dissenting judgment by Justice Douglas in the 1972 case of *Sierra Club v. Morton* in which he expressed the opinion that "contemporary public concern for protecting nature's ecological equilibrium should lead to the conferral of standing upon environmental objects to sue for their own preservation."

Perhaps one of the most important things about "Trees" is that it ventured beyond the accepted boundaries of law as we know it and argued that the conceptual framework for law in the United States (and by analogy, elsewhere) required further evolution and expansion. Stone began by addressing the initial reaction that such ideas are outlandish. Throughout legal history, as he pointed out, each extension of legal rights had previously been unthinkable. The emancipation of slaves and the extension of civil rights to African Americans, women, and children were once rejected as absurd or dangerous by authorities. The Founding Fathers, after all, were hardly conscious of the hypocrisy inherent in proclaiming the inalienable rights of all men while simultaneously denying basic rights to children, women, and to African and Native Americans.

"Trees" has since become a classic for students of environmental law, but after three decades its impact on law in the United States has been limited. After it was written, the courts made it somewhat easier for citizens to litigate on behalf of other species and the environment by expanding the powers and responsibilities of authorities to act as trustees of areas used by the public (e.g., navigable waters, beaches, and parks). Unfortunately, these gains have been followed in more recent years by judicial attempts to restrict the legal standing of environmental groups. Damages for harm to the environment are now recoverable in some cases and are sometimes applied for the benefit of the environment. However, these changes fall far short of what Stone advocated for in "Trees." The courts still have not recognized that nature has directly enforceable rights.

Communities have always used laws to express the ideals to which   10
they aspire and to regulate how power is exercised. Law is also a social tool that is usually shaped and wielded most effectively by the powerful.

Consequently, law tends to entrench a society's fundamental idea of itself and of how the world works. So, for example, even when American society began to regard slavery as morally abhorrent, it was not able to peaceably end the practice because the fundamental concept that slaves were property had been hard-wired into the legal system. The abolition of slavery required not only that the enfranchised recognize that slaves were entitled to the same rights as other humans, but also a political effort to change the laws that denied those rights. It took both the Civil War and the Thirteenth Amendment to outlaw slavery. The Thirteenth Amendment, in turn, played a role in changing American society's idea of what was acceptable, thereby providing the bedrock for the subsequent civil rights movement.

In the eyes of American law today, most of the community of life on Earth remains mere property, natural "resources" to be exploited, bought, and sold just as slaves were. This means that environmentalists are seldom seen as activists fighting to uphold fundamental rights, but rather as criminals who infringe upon the property rights of others. It also means that actions that damage the ecosystems and the natural processes on which life depends, such as Earth's climate, are poorly regulated. Climate change is an obvious and dramatic symptom of the failure of human government to regulate human behavior in a manner that takes account of the fact that human welfare is directly dependent on the health of our planet and cannot be achieved at its expense.

In the scientific world there has been more progress. It's been almost forty years since James Lovelock first proposed the "Gaia hypothesis": a theory that Earth regulates itself in a manner that keeps the composition of the atmosphere and average temperatures within a range conducive to life. Derided or dismissed by most people at the time, the Gaia hypothesis is now accepted by many as scientific theory. In 2001, more than a thousand scientists signed a declaration that begins "The Earth is a self-regulating system made up from all life, including humans, and from the oceans, the atmosphere and the surface rocks," a statement that would have been unthinkable for most scientists when "Trees" was written.

The acceptance of Lovelock's hypothesis can be understood as part of a drift in the scientific world away from a mechanistic understanding of the universe toward the realization that no aspect of nature can be understood without looking at it within the context of the systems of which it forms a part. Unfortunately, this insight has been slow to penetrate the world of law and politics.

But what if we were to imagine a society in which our purpose was to act as good citizens of the Earth as a whole? What might a governance system look like if it were established to protect the rights of all members of a particular biological community, instead of only humans? Cicero pointed out that each of our rights and freedoms must be limited in order that others may be free. It is far past time that we should consider limiting the rights of humans so they cannot unjustifiably prevent nonhuman members of a community from playing their part. Any legal system designed to give effect to modern scientific understandings (or, indeed, to many cultures' ancient understandings) of how the universe functions would have to prohibit humans from driving other species to extinction or deliberately destroying the functioning of major ecosystems. In the absence of such regulatory mechanisms, an oppressive and self-destructive regime will inevitably emerge. As indeed it has.

In particular, we should examine the fact that, in the eyes of the law, corporations are considered people and entitled to civil rights. We often forget that corporations are only a few centuries old and have been continually evolving since their inception. Imagine what could be done if we changed the fiduciary responsibilities of directors to include obligations not only to profitability but also to the whole natural world, and if we imposed collective personal liability on corporate managers and stockholders to restore any damage that they cause to natural communities. Imagine if landowners who abused and degraded land lost the right to use it. In an Earth-centered community, all institutions through which humans act collectively would be designed to require behavior that is socially responsible from the perspective of the whole community. 15

A society whose concern is to maintain the integrity of wholeness of the Earth must also refine its ideas about what is "right" and "wrong." We may find it more useful to condone or disapprove of human conduct by considering the extent to which an action increases or decreases the health of the whole community and the quality or intimacy of the relationships between its members. As Aldo Leopold's famous land ethic states, "a thing is right when it tends to preserve the integrity, stability, and beauty of the biotic community. It is wrong when it tends otherwise." From this perspective, individual and collective human rights must be contextualized within, and balanced against, the rights of the other members and communities of Earth.

On September 19, 2006, the Tamaqua Borough of Schuylkill County, Pennsylvania, passed a sewage sludge ordinance that recognized natural communities and ecosystems within the borough as legal persons for the purposes of enforcing civil rights. It also strips corporations that engage in the land application of sludge of their rights to be treated as "persons" and consequently of their civil rights. One of its effects is that the borough or any of its residents may file a lawsuit on behalf of an ecosystem to recover compensatory and punitive damage for any harm done by the land application of sewage sludge. Damages recovered in this way must be paid to the borough and used to restore those ecosystems and natural communities.

According to Thomas Linzey, the lawyer from the Community Environmental Legal Defense Fund who assisted Tamaqua Borough, this ordinance marks the first time in the history of municipalities in the United States that something like this has happened. Coming after more than

150 years of judicially sanctioned expansion of the legal powers of corporations in the U.S., this ordinance is more than extraordinary—it is revolutionary. In a world where the corporation is king and all forms of life other than humans are objects in the eyes of the law, this is a small community's Boston tea party.

In Africa, nongovernmental organizations in eleven countries are also asserting local community rights in order to promote the conservation of biodiversity and sustainable development. Members of the African Biodiversity Network (ABN) have coined the term "cultural biodiversity" to emphasize that knowledge and practices that support biodiversity are embedded in cultural tradition. The ABN works with rural communities and schools to recover and spread traditional knowledge and practices. This is part of a wider effort to build local communities, protect the environment by encouraging those communities to value, retain, and build on traditional African cosmologies, and to govern themselves as part of a wider Earth community.

These small examples, emerging shoots of what might be termed   20
"Earth democracy," are pressing upward despite the odds. It may well be that Earth-centered legal systems will have to grow organically out of human-scale communities, and communities of communities, that understand that they must function as integrated parts of wider natural communities. In the face of climate change and other enormous environmental challenges, our future as a species depends on those people who are creating the legal and political spaces within which our connection to the rest of our community here on Earth is recognized. The day will come when the failure of our laws to recognize the right of a river to flow, to prohibit acts that destabilize Earth's climate, or to impose a duty to respect the intrinsic value and right to exist of all life will be as reprehensible as allowing people to be bought and sold. We will only flourish by changing these systems and claiming our identity, as well as assuming our responsibilities, as members of the Earth community.

The Reader's Presence

1. In paragraph 14, Cullinan invites his readers to "imagine a society in which our purpose was to act as good citizens of the Earth as a whole. What might a governance system look like if it were established to protect the rights of all members of a particular biological community, instead of only humans?" Following Cullinan's suggestion, imagine the following scenario: a court case in which a diamond sues the jeweler who cut and ground it into a heart shape before imprisoning the stone in a wedding ring. What points would the diamond use from Cullinan's essay to support its argument? What would the jeweler say in defense? Who would the

two parties bring in as witnesses and what would they say? For example, what would the bride who was supposed to wear the ring offer as testimony? What would the earth that was mined to procure the diamond contribute to the case? If you were the judge, what decision would you make and what punishments would you distribute? to whom? Why?

2. Cullinan's challenge in this essay is to argue about a subject not many readers have thought about or, if they have, have not taken seriously. What compositional strategies does Cullinan use in order to maintain a serious sense of purpose and tone to talk about the legal rights of nonhumans? To what extent does he cultivate his readers' generosity when, for example, he asks us to entertain the idea of rivers or trees being harmed? In effect, what specific strategies does Cullinan use to encourage us to take his argument seriously? Please examine carefully the story of Professor Stone (paragraphs 5–6). Explain how this story functions as an analogy for the relationship between Cullinan and his readers. In the story, what larger question is Professor Stone addressing? What was his students' reaction? How does Stone's response exemplify what Cullinan wants us to do? Analyze the opening story of the hyena in similar terms (paragraphs 1 and 2).

3. In the "Gettysburg Address" (page 460), Abraham Lincoln explains why the soldiers who gave their lives there did not "die in vain." Using the address as a model, how would you explain to Cullinan that the harm done to rivers, trees, and other members of Earth's community is not "in vain"? For example, what "birth of freedom" comes from damming up a river? How does drilling into oil reserves help ensure that the U.S. government "shall not perish"? Why would Cullinan not be convinced by your argument?

Jared Diamond

The Ends of the World as We Know Them

Pulitzer Prize–winning author Jared Diamond (b. 1937) is a physiologist, ecologist, and science writer known for his ability to make serious science accessible to a general audience. Diamond received his PhD from Cambridge University and has been on the UCLA faculty since 1966, currently serving as professor of geography. A recipient of many prestigious awards, he won the 1999 National Medal of Science for his work in the fields of evolutionary biology and conservation biology. He has done extensive fieldwork in South America, Africa, Indonesia, Australia, and New Guinea and written more than five hundred scholarly papers on evolutionary physiology, ecology, and ornithology.

Diamond's books include Why Is Sex Fun? *(1975);* The Third Chimpanzee *(1991), for which he was awarded the* Los Angeles Times *Book Prize and the* Science Book Prize; Guns, Germs, and Steel *(1997), for which he won the 1997 Pulitzer Prize for nonfiction; and his latest book,* Collapse *(2004), a historical analysis of the fates of societies faced with environmental or political catastrophe. He is a frequent contributor to such magazines as* Discover, Natural History, *and* Nature; *his essays are also found in such publications as the* Atlantic *and the* New York Times, *which published "The Ends of the World as We Know Them" on January 1, 2005.*

New Year's weekend traditionally is a time for us to reflect, and to make resolutions based on our reflections. In this fresh year, with the United States seemingly at the height of its power and at the start of a new presidential term, Americans are increasingly concerned and divided about where we are going. How long can America remain ascendant? Where will we stand ten years from now, or even next year?

Such questions seem especially appropriate this year. History warns us that when once-powerful societies collapse, they tend to do so quickly and unexpectedly. That shouldn't come as much of a surprise: peak power usually means peak population, peak needs, and hence peak vulnerability. What can be learned from history that could help us avoid joining the ranks of those who declined swiftly? We must expect the answers to be complex, because historical reality is complex: while some societies did indeed collapse spectacularly, others have managed to thrive for thousands of years without major reversal.

When it comes to historical collapses, five groups of interacting factors have been especially important: the damage that people have inflicted on their environment; climate change; enemies; changes in friendly trading partners; and the society's political, economic and social responses to these shifts. That's not to say that all five causes play a role in every case. Instead, think of this as a useful checklist of factors that should be examined, but whose relative importance varies from case to case.

For instance, in the collapse of the Polynesian society on Easter Island[1] three centuries ago, environmental problems were dominant, and climate change, enemies and trade were insignificant; however, the latter three factors played big roles in the disappearance of the medieval Norse colonies on Greenland. Let's consider two examples of declines stemming from different mixes of causes: the falls of classic Maya civilization and of Polynesian settlements on the Pitcairn Islands.

Maya Native Americans of the Yucatan Peninsula and adjacent parts   5
of Central America developed the New World's most advanced civilization before Columbus. They were innovators in writing, astronomy, architecture and art. From local origins around 2,500 years ago, Maya societies rose especially after the year A.D. 250, reaching peaks of population and sophistication in the late eighth century.

Thereafter, societies in the most densely populated areas of the southern Yucatan underwent a steep political and cultural collapse: between 760 and 910, kings were overthrown, large areas were abandoned, and at least 90 percent of the population disappeared, leaving cities to become overgrown by jungle. The last known date recorded on a Maya monument by their so-called Long Count calendar corresponds to the year 909. What happened?

A major factor was environmental degradation by people: deforestation, soil erosion and water management problems, all of which resulted in less food. Those problems were exacerbated by droughts, which may have been partly caused by humans themselves through deforestation. Chronic warfare made matters worse, as more and more people fought over less and less land and resources.

Why weren't these problems obvious to the Maya kings, who could surely see their forests vanishing and their hills becoming eroded? Part of the reason was that the kings were able to insulate themselves from problems afflicting the rest of society. By extracting wealth from commoners, they could remain well fed while everyone else was slowly starving.

What's more, the kings were preoccupied with their own power struggles. They had to concentrate on fighting one another and keeping up their images through ostentatious displays of wealth. By insulating themselves in the short run from the problems of society, the elite merely bought themselves the privilege of being among the last to starve.

Whereas Maya societies were undone by problems of their own mak-   10
ing, Polynesian societies on Pitcairn and Henderson Islands in the tropical Pacific Ocean were undone largely by other people's mistakes. Pitcairn,

---

[1]***Easter Island:*** Remote South Pacific island known for giant Moai statues, which were toppled during a period of decline for the Rapa Nui people there. —EDS.

the uninhabited island settled in 1790 by the *H.M.S. Bounty* mutineers, had actually been populated by Polynesians 800 years earlier. That society, which left behind temple platforms, stone and shell tools and huge garbage piles of fish and bird and turtle bones as evidence of its existence, survived for several centuries and then vanished. Why?

In many respects, Pitcairn and Henderson are tropical paradises, rich in some food sources and essential raw materials. Pitcairn is home to Southeast Polynesia's largest quarry of stone suited for making adzes, while Henderson has the region's largest breeding seabird colony and its only nesting beach for sea turtles. Yet the islanders depended on imports from Mangareva Island, hundreds of miles away, for canoes, crops, livestock and oyster shells for making tools.

Unfortunately for the inhabitants of Pitcairn and Henderson, their Mangarevan trading partner collapsed for reasons similar to those underlying the Maya decline: deforestation, erosion and warfare. Deprived of essential imports in a Polynesian equivalent of the 1973 oil crisis, the Pitcairn and Henderson societies declined until everybody had died or fled.

The Maya and the Henderson and Pitcairn Islanders are not alone, of course. Over the centuries, many other societies have declined, collapsed or died out. Famous victims include the Anasazi in the American Southwest, who abandoned their cities in the twelfth century because of environmental problems and climate change, and the Greenland Norse, who disappeared in the fifteenth century because of all five interacting factors on the checklist. There were also the ancient Fertile Crescent societies, the Khmer at Angkor Wat, the Moche society of Peru—the list goes on.

But before we let ourselves get depressed, we should also remember that there is another long list of cultures that have managed to prosper for lengthy periods of time. Societies in Japan, Tonga, Tikopia, the New Guinea Highlands and Central and Northwest Europe, for example, have all found ways to sustain themselves. What separates the lost cultures from those that survived? Why did the Maya fail and the shogun succeed?

Half of the answer involves environmental differences: geography deals worse cards to some societies than to others. Many of the societies that collapsed had the misfortune to occupy dry, cold or otherwise fragile environments, while many of the long-term survivors enjoyed more robust and fertile surroundings. But it's not the case that a congenial environment guarantees success: some societies (like the Maya) managed to ruin lush environments, while other societies—like the Incas, the Inuit, Icelanders and desert Australian Aborigines—have managed to carry on in some of the earth's most daunting environments.

The other half of the answer involves differences in a society's responses to problems. Ninth-century New Guinea Highland villagers, sixteenth-century German landowners, and the Tokugawa shoguns of seventeenth-century Japan all recognized the deforestation spreading around them and solved the problem, either by developing scientific reforestation (Japan and Germany) or by transplanting tree seedlings (New Guinea).

15

Conversely, the Maya, Mangarevans and Easter Islanders failed to address their forestry problems and so collapsed.

Consider Japan. In the 1600s, the country faced its own crisis of deforestation, paradoxically brought on by the peace and prosperity following the Tokugawa shoguns' military triumph that ended 150 years of civil war. The subsequent explosion of Japan's population and economy set off rampant logging for construction of palaces and cities, and for fuel and fertilizer.

The shoguns responded with both negative and positive measures. They reduced wood consumption by turning to light-timbered construction, to fuel-efficient stoves and heaters, and to coal as a source of energy. At the same time, they increased wood production by developing and carefully managing plantation forests. Both the shoguns and the Japanese peasants took a long-term view: the former expected to pass on their power to their children, and the latter expected to pass on their land. In addition, Japan's isolation at the time made it obvious that the country would have to depend on its own resources and couldn't meet its needs by pillaging other countries. Today, despite having the highest human population density of any large developed country, Japan is more than seventy percent forested.

There is a similar story from Iceland. When the island was first settled by the Norse around 870, its light volcanic soils presented colonists with unfamiliar challenges. They proceeded to cut down trees and stock sheep as if they were still in Norway, with its robust soils. Significant erosion ensued, carrying half of Iceland's topsoil into the ocean within a century or two. Icelanders became the poorest people in Europe. But they gradually learned from their mistakes, over time instituting stocking limits on sheep and other strict controls, and establishing an entire government department charged with landscape management. Today, Iceland boasts the sixth-highest per-capita income in the world.

What lessons can we draw from history? The most straightforward: 20
take environmental problems seriously. They destroyed societies in the past, and they are even more likely to do so now. If 6,000 Polynesians with stone tools were able to destroy Mangareva Island, consider what six billion people with metal tools and bulldozers are doing today. Moreover, while the Maya collapse affected just a few neighboring societies in Central America, globalization now means that any society's problems have the potential to affect anyone else. Just think how crises in Somalia, Afghanistan and Iraq have shaped the United States today.

Other lessons involve failures of group decision-making. There are many reasons why past societies made bad decisions, and thereby failed to solve or even to perceive the problems that would eventually destroy them. One reason involves conflicts of interest, whereby one group within a society (for instance, the pig farmers who caused the worst erosion in medieval Greenland and Iceland) can profit by engaging in practices that damage the rest of society. Another is the pursuit of short-term gains at the expense of long-term survival, as when fishermen overfish the stocks on which their livelihoods ultimately depend.

History also teaches us two deeper lessons about what separates successful societies from those heading toward failure. A society contains a built-in blueprint for failure if the elite insulates itself from the consequences of its actions. That's why Maya kings, Norse Greenlanders and Easter Island chiefs made choices that eventually undermined their societies. They themselves did not begin to feel deprived until they had irreversibly destroyed their landscape.

Could this happen in the United States? It's a thought that often occurs to me here in Los Angeles, when I drive by gated communities, guarded by private security patrols, and filled with people who drink bottled water, depend on private pensions, and send their children to private schools. By doing these things, they lose the motivation to support the police force, the municipal water supply, Social Security and public schools. If conditions deteriorate too much for poorer people, gates will not keep the rioters out. Rioters eventually burned the palaces of Maya kings and tore down the statues of Easter Island chiefs; they have also already threatened wealthy districts in Los Angeles twice in recent decades.

In contrast, the elite in seventeenth-century Japan, as in modern Scandinavia and the Netherlands, could not ignore or insulate themselves from broad societal problems. For instance, the Dutch upper class for hundreds of years has been unable to insulate itself from the Netherlands' water management problems for a simple reason: the rich live in the same drained lands below sea level as the poor. If the dikes and pumps keeping out the sea fail, the well-off Dutch know that they will drown along with everybody else, which is precisely what happened during the floods of 1953.

The other deep lesson involves a willingness to re-examine long-held   25
core values, when conditions change and those values no longer make sense. The medieval Greenland Norse lacked such a willingness: they continued to view themselves as transplanted Norwegian pastoralists, and to despise the Inuit as pagan hunters, even after Norway stopped sending trading ships and the climate had grown too cold for a pastoral existence. They died off as a result, leaving Greenland to the Inuit. On the other hand, the British in the 1950s faced up to the need for a painful reappraisal of their former status as rulers of a world empire set apart from Europe. They are now finding a different avenue to wealth and power, as part of a united Europe.

In this New Year, we Americans have our own painful reappraisals to face. Historically, we viewed the United States as a land of unlimited plenty, and so we practiced unrestrained consumerism, but that's no longer viable in a world of finite resources. We can't continue to deplete our own resources as well as those of much of the rest of the world.

Historically, oceans protected us from external threats; we stepped back from our isolationism only temporarily during the crises of two world wars. Now, technology and global interconnectedness have robbed us of our protection. In recent years, we have responded to foreign threats largely by seeking short-term military solutions at the last minute.

But how long can we keep this up? Though we are the richest nation on earth, there's simply no way we can afford (or muster the troops) to intervene in the dozens of countries where emerging threats lurk—particularly when each intervention these days can cost more than $100 billion and require more than 100,000 troops.

A genuine reappraisal would require us to recognize that it will be far less expensive and far more effective to address the underlying problems of public health, population and environment that ultimately cause threats to us to emerge in poor countries. In the past, we have regarded foreign aid as either charity or as buying support; now, it's an act of self-interest to preserve our own economy and protect American lives.

Do we have cause for hope? Many of my friends are pessimistic when   30
they contemplate the world's growing population and human demands colliding with shrinking resources. But I draw hope from the knowledge that humanity's biggest problems today are ones entirely of our own making. Asteroids hurtling at us beyond our control don't figure high on our list of imminent dangers. To save ourselves, we don't need new technology: we just need the political will to face up to our problems of population and the environment.

I also draw hope from a unique advantage that we enjoy. Unlike any previous society in history, our global society today is the first with the opportunity to learn from the mistakes of societies remote from us in space and in time. When the Maya and Mangarevans were cutting down their trees, there were no historians or archaeologists, no newspapers or television, to warn them of the consequences of their actions. We, on the other hand, have a detailed chronicle of human successes and failures at our disposal. Will we choose to use it?

The Reader's Presence

1. What societies does Diamond use as examples? How does he suggest that the fates of historical societies relate to the survival of modern societies like our own? Do you agree with his views about the factors that will be important for our society's survival? Why or why not?

2. What connections does Diamond make between choices made in modern American society and in defunct cultures of the past? What does he suggest is going wrong in American culture that could adversely affect our society's future? Does he leave out anything that you consider an important factor in the survival of the United States as a society? If so, what is that factor and why is it important?

3. Read "Worried? Us?" by Bill McKibben (page 761). How does McKibben's argument about the importance of concern for the environment compare with Diamond's? Which essay do you find more compelling? Why?

THE ACADEMIC VOICE

Jared Diamond on the "Ecological Collapses of Past Civilizations"

What happens when writers address an academic audience, rather than a general audience? What adjustments do they make in their vocabulary, tone of voice, organization, or argument? How do these adjustments take into account the level of knowledge and information they can expect an academic audience to possess? Here you will find the concluding section of Diamond's academic paper "Ecological Collapses of Past Civilizations," published in the Proceedings of the American Philosophical Society. *Compare this academic selection with the lessons from history (paragraphs 20–31) in the conclusion of Diamond's essay for a general audience, "The Ends of the World as We Know Them" (page 648).*

LESSONS FOR OUR TIMES

We have reviewed examples of ancient civilizations that collapsed, and whose collapses were caused by (or received contributions from) self-inflicted ecological damage. Yet there are other collapses for which such factors are not suspected. In still other areas, such as Japan, Java, and northwest Europe, complex societies have developed for thousands of years without evidence of interruption by a major collapse. Why are some societies apparently more vulnerable ecologically than are others?

By now, it may be apparent to readers that past ecological collapses occurred in environments or climates of types that we recognize today as ecologically vulnerable. Many of the collapses—such as those of Easter Island, Kahoolawe, the Anasazi, the Fertile Crescent, Greece, and northwest Africa—occurred in areas with dry climates. Since growth of vegetation is approximately proportional to rainfall, dry areas take much more time to recover from habitat destruction than do wet areas. If regrowth is too slow, erosion may remove topsoil and make recovery impossible, as happened on Kahoolawe. Many other collapses—such as those of New Zealand South Island and of Henderson Island—occurred after humans first colonized a land formerly uninhabited by humans. Animals with no evolutionary history of exposure to human predators are behaviorally naïve and easily exterminated by hunters (Olson and James 1982 et al. 1987, Steadman 1989, Steadman and Kirch 1990, Steadman 1991).

Thus, the pattern of ecological collapses of past civilizations is a familiar, almost banal, one. Of course, societies in more fragile environments are at a greater risk of collapse from undermining their own resource base! Today, many human societies in fragile environments are assaulting those environments with far greater human numbers and far more destructive technology than sufficed to degrade such environments in the past. Much of the U.S. West, the Himalayas, and Africa consists of such environments.

However, that reasoning should not be reversed to conclude that modern societies in ecologically more robust environments are secure. Unlike Easter Island society, which was totally self-sufficient for 1,500 years, all countries today depend economically on other countries for some essential resources, including food and energy. All countries today are interconnected through living together in the same increasingly polluted atmosphere and oceans. In the next century we risk more than just societies of fragile environments collapsing one by one. We also risk a collapse of world society, an outcome for which there are already warning signs.

Surprisingly, many educated people who should know better deny the seriousness of the risks ahead of us. History has important lessons to teach such people. Collapse has already befallen many societies that were at less risk than our societies are today.   5

REFERENCES

James, H. F., D. W. Stafford, D. W. Steadman, et al. 1987 Radiocarbon dates on bones of extinct birds from Hawaii. *Proc. Nat. Acad. Sci. USA* 84:2350–2354.

Olson, S. L., and H. F. James. 1982. Fossil birds from the Hawaiian Islands: evidence for wholesale extinction by man before Western contact. *Science* 217:633–635.

Steadman, D. W. 1989. Extinction of birds in eastern Polynesia: a review of the record, and comparisons with other Pacific island groups. *J. Archaeol. Sci.* 16:177–205.

———. 1991. Extinct and extirpated birds from Aitutaki and Atiu, southern Cook Islands. *Pacific Sci.* 45:325–347.

Steadman, D. W., and P. V. Kirch. 1990. Prehistoric extinction of birds on Mangaia, Cook Islands, Polynesia. *Proc. Nat. Acad. Sci. USA* 87:9605–9609.

Debra Dickerson

Who Shot Johnny?

Author, journalist, and "professional iconoclast" Debra Dickerson was born in 1959 in St. Louis, Missouri. "Having no clue what I was doing there," Dickerson dropped out of college and, in 1980, joined the United States Air Force, a move that got her an education: a degree in government and politics from the University of Maryland; a master's from St. Mary's University; and a career in the military as an intelligence officer, ultimately becoming the Chief of Intelligence in Ankara, Turkey, just as the Persian Gulf War was beginning in 1990–1991. After her discharge from the service, Dickerson went on to receive a law degree from Harvard Law School. In 1996, the New Republic published her essay, "Who Shot Johnny?" and her career as a journalist/writer/commentator on issues of race, gender, and culture was launched. She has won many awards for her work, including the New York Association of Black Journalists' award for personal commentary. Dickerson has written two books, An American Story (2000), a memoir; and The End of Blackness: Returning the Souls of Black Folk to their Rightful Owners (2004). Dickerson has been national correspondent for Salon, a Beliefnet columnist, and a senior editor at U.S. News & World Report, as well as a lawyer for the National Association for the Advancement of Colored People (NAACP) and a senior fellow at the New America Foundation. Her articles appear frequently in such publications as the Washington Post, the New York Times Magazine, the Village Voice, the Nation, and Mother Jones, where she is a contributing writer and blogger.

Given my level of political awareness, it was inevitable that I would come to view the everyday events of my life through the prism of politics and the national discourse. I read *The Washington Post, The New Republic, The New Yorker, Harper's, The Atlantic Monthly, The Nation, National Review, Black Enterprise,* and *Essence* and wrote a weekly column for the Harvard Law School *Record* during my three years just ended there. I do this because I know that those of us who are not well-fed white guys in suits must not yield the debate to them, however well-intentioned or well-informed they may be. Accordingly, I am unrepentant and vocal about having gained admittance to Harvard through affirmative action; I am a feminist, stoic about my marriage chances as a well-educated, thirty-six-year-old black woman who won't pretend to need help taking care of herself. My strength flags, though, in the face of the latest role assigned to my family in the national drama. On July 27, 1995, my sixteen-year-old nephew was shot and paralyzed.

Talking with friends in front of his house, Johnny saw a car he thought he recognized. He waved boisterously—his trademark—throwing both arms in the air in a full-bodied, hip-hop Y. When he got no response, he and his friends sauntered down the walk to join a group loitering in front of an apartment building. The car followed. The driver got out, brandished a revolver, and fired into the air. Everyone scattered. Then he took aim and shot my running nephew in the back.

Johnny never lost consciousness. He lay in the road, trying to understand what had happened to him, why he couldn't get up. Emotionlessly, he told the story again and again on demand, remaining apologetically firm against all demands to divulge the missing details that would make sense of the shooting but obviously cast him in a bad light. Being black, male, and shot, he must apparently be involved with gangs or drugs. Probably both. Witnesses corroborate his version of events.

Nearly six months have passed since that phone call in the night and my nightmarish headlong drive from Boston to Charlotte. After twenty hours behind the wheel, I arrived haggard enough to reduce my mother to fresh tears and to find my nephew reassuring well-wishers with an eerie sang-froid.

I take the day shift in his hospital room; his mother and grandmother, a clerk and cafeteria worker, respectively, alternate nights there on a cot. They don their uniforms the next day, gaunt after hours spent listening to Johnny moan in his sleep. How often must his subconscious replay those events and curse its host for saying hello without permission, for being carefree and young while a would-be murderer hefted the weight of his uselessness and failure like Jacob Marley's[1] chains? How often must he watch himself lying stubbornly immobile on the pavement of his nightmares while the sound of running feet syncopate his attacker's taunts?

I spend these days beating him at gin rummy and Scrabble, holding a basin while he coughs up phlegm and crying in the corridor while he catheterizes himself. There are children here much worse off than he. I should be grateful. The doctors can't, or won't, say whether he'll walk again.

I am at once repulsed and fascinated by the bullet, which remains lodged in his spine (having done all the damage it can do, the doctors say). The wound is undramatic — small, neat, and perfectly centered — an impossibly pink pit surrounded by an otherwise undisturbed expanse of mahogany. Johnny has asked me several times to describe it but politely declines to look in the mirror I hold for him.

Here on the pediatric rehab ward, Johnny speaks little, never cries, never complains, works diligently to become independent. He does whatever he is told; if two hours remain until the next pain pill, he waits quietly. Eyes bloodshot, hands gripping the bed rails. During the week of his intravenous feeding, when he was tormented by the primal need to masticate, he never asked for food. He just listened while we counted down the days for him and planned his favorite meals. Now required to dress himself back and forth unassisted, he does so without demur, rolling himself

5

---

[1]*Jacob Marley:* One of the ghosts in Charles Dickens's *A Christmas Carol.* —EDS.

back and forth valiantly on the bed and shivering afterward, exhausted. He "ma'am"s and "sir"s everyone politely. Before his "accident," a simple request to take out the trash could provoke a firestorm of teenage attitude. We, the women who have raised him, have changed as well; we've finally come to appreciate those boxer-baring, oversized pants we used to hate— it would be much more difficult to fit properly sized pants over his diaper.

He spends a lot of time tethered to rap music still loud enough to break my concentration as I read my many magazines. I hear him try to soundlessly mouth the obligatory "mothafuckers" overlaying the funereal dirge of the music tracks. I do not normally tolerate disrespectful music in my or my mother's presence, but if it distracts him now . . .

"Johnny," I ask later, "do you still like gangster rap?" During the   10
long pause I hear him think loudly, I'm paralyzed Auntie, not stupid. "I mostly just listen to hip-hop," he says evasively into his *Sports Illustrated*.

Miserable though it is, time passes quickly here. We always seem to be jerking awake in our chairs just in time for the next pill, his every-other-night bowel program, the doctor's rounds. Harvard feels a galaxy away—the world revolves around Family Members Living with Spinal Cord Injury class, Johnny's urine output, and strategizing with my sister to find affordable, accessible housing. There is always another long-distance uncle in need of an update, another church member wanting to pray with us, or Johnny's little brother in need of some attention.

We Dickerson women are so constant a presence the ward nurses and cleaning staff call us by name and join us for cafeteria meals and cigarette breaks. At Johnny's birthday pizza party, they crack jokes and make fun of each other's husbands (there are no men here). I pass slices around and try not to think, Seventeen with a bullet.

Oddly, we feel little curiosity or specific anger toward the man who shot him. We have to remind ourselves to check in with the police. Even so, it feels pro forma, like sending in those $2 rebate forms that come with new pantyhose: you know your request will fall into a deep, dark hole some-where, but still, it's your duty to try. We push for an arrest because we owe it to Johnny and to ourselves as citizens. We don't think about it other-wise—our low expectations are too ingrained. A Harvard aunt notwith-standing, for people like Johnny, Marvin Gaye was right that only three things are sure: taxes, death, and trouble. At least it wasn't the second.

We rarely wonder about or discuss the brother who shot him because we already know everything about him. When the call came, my first thought was the same one I'd had when I'd heard about Rosa Parks's beating: a brother did it. A non-job-having, middle-of-the-day malt-liquor-drinking, crotch-clutching, loud-talking brother with many neglected chil-dren born of many forgotten women. He lives in his mother's basement with furniture rented at an astronomical interest rate, the exact amount of which he does not know. He has a car phone, an $80 monthly cable bill, and every possible phone feature but no savings. He steals Social

Security numbers from unsuspecting relatives and assumes their identities to acquire large TV sets for which he will never pay. On the slim chance that he is brought to justice, he will have a colorful criminal history and no coherent explanation to offer his act. His family will raucously defend him and cry cover-up. Some liberal lawyer just like me will help him plea-bargain his way to yet another short stay in a prison pesthouse that will serve only to add another layer to the brother's sociopathology and form-less, mindless nihilism. We know him. We've known and feared him all our lives.

As a teenager, he called, "Hey, baby, gimme somma that boodie!" at us from car windows. Indignant at our lack of response, he followed up with, "Fuck you, then, 'ho!" He called me a "white-boy-lovin' nigger bitch oreo" for being in the gifted program and loving it. At twenty-seven, he got my seventeen-year-old sister pregnant with Johnny and lost interest without ever informing her that he was married. He snatched my wid-owed mother's purse as she waited in predawn darkness for the bus to work and then broke into our house while she soldered on an assembly line. He chased all the small entrepreneurs from our neighborhood with his violent thievery and put bars on our windows. He kept us from sitting on our own front porch after dark and laid the foundation for our peri-odic bouts of self-hating anger and racial embarrassment. He made our neighborhood a ghetto. He is the poster fool behind the maddening com-munity knowledge that there are still some black mothers who raise their daughters but merely love their sons. He and his cancerous carbon copies eclipse the vast majority of us who are not sociopaths and render us invis-ible. He is the Siamese twin who has died but cannot be separated from his living, vibrant sibling; which of us must attract more notice? We de-spise and disown this anomalous loser, but for many he *is* black America. We know him, we know that he is outside the fold, and we know that he will only get worse. What we didn't know is that, because of him, my lit-tle sister would one day be the latest hysterical black mother wailing over a fallen child on TV.

Alone, lying in the road bleeding and paralyzed but hideously con-scious, Johnny had lain helpless as he watched his would-be murderer come to stand over him and offer this prophecy: "Betch'ou won't be doin' nomo' wavin', mothafucker."

Fuck you, asshole. He's fine from the waist up. You just can't do any-thing right, can you?

The Reader's Presence

1. What information does Dickerson want us to know about her at the start of the essay? For example, why do you think she offers the reader a long list of the magazines she reads? What do these periodicals have in common? How does this personal information

prepare us for reading what follows in the essay? In what ways does it help establish Dickerson's credibility?

2. Note that the title of the essay is a question. How does Dickerson proceed to answer the question? Does she have an individual culprit in mind? Do you find any relevance to the fact that Dickerson (in paragraph 15) identifies the shooter as someone responsible for her sister's pregnancy with Johnny? What implication does this suggestion contain?

3. You might read "Who Shot Johnny?" in conjunction with two other personal essays on race and violence in America, Brent Staples's "Just Walk on By: A Black Man Ponders His Power to Alter Public Space" (page 240) and Jerald Walker's "Scattered Inconveniences" (page 265). In what ways are the authors of each essay similar? How does each one confront the fear of violence? To what extent do stereotypes figure in the essays? In your opinion, which author relies least on stereotypes? which most?

Annie Dillard

Living Like Weasels

Annie Dillard (b. 1945) was awarded the Pulitzer Prize for general nonfiction in 1974 for Pilgrim at Tinker Creek, *which she describes (borrowing from Henry David Thoreau) as "a meteorological journal of the mind." She graduated from Hollins College in 1967; Tinker Creek is nearby. She has also published poetry in* Tickets for a Prayer Wheel *(1975) and* Mornings Like This: Found Poems *(1995), literary theory in* Living by Fiction *(1982), essays in* Teaching a Stone to Talk *(1982) and* For the Time Being *(1999), and an autobiography in* An American Childhood *(1987). Dillard's first novel was* The Living *(1992), and her most recent is* The Maytrees *(2007); the* Annie Dillard Reader *was published in 1994. She was contributing editor to* Harper's *magazine for almost a decade, and she taught creative writing at Wesleyan University where she is now professor emeritus. "Living Like Weasels" appears in her book* Teaching a Stone to Talk.

In her 1997 essay "Advice to Young Writers," Dillard argues, "Don't use any extra words. A sentence is a machine; it has a job to do. An extra word in a sentence is like a sock in a machine."

A weasel is wild. Who knows what he thinks? He sleeps in his underground den, his tail draped over his nose. Sometimes he lives in his den for two days without leaving. Outside, he stalks rabbits, mice, muskrats, and birds, killing more bodies than he can eat warm, and often dragging the carcasses home. Obedient to instinct, he bites his prey at the neck, either splitting the jugular vein at the throat or crunching the brain at the base of the skull, and he does not let go. One naturalist refused to kill a weasel who was socketed into his hand deeply as a rattlesnake. The man could in no way pry the tiny weasel off, and he had to walk half a mile to water, the weasel dangling from his palm, and soak him off like a stubborn label.

And once, says Ernest Thompson Seton[1] — once, a man shot an eagle out of the sky. He examined the eagle and found the dry skull of a weasel fixed by the jaws to his throat. The supposition is that the eagle had pounced on the weasel and the weasel swiveled and bit as instinct taught him, tooth to neck, and nearly won. I would like to have seen that eagle from the air a few weeks or months before he was shot. Was the whole weasel still attached to his feathered throat, a fur pendant? Or did the eagle eat what he could reach, gutting the living weasel with his talons before his breast, bending his beak, cleaning the beautiful airborne bones?

I have been reading about weasels because I saw one last week. I startled a weasel who startled me, and we exchanged a long glance.

Near my house in Virginia is a pond — Hollins Pond. It covers two acres of bottomland near Tinker Creek with six inches of water and six thousand lily pads. There is a fifty-five mph highway at one end of the pond, and a nesting pair of wood ducks at the other. Under every bush is a muskrat hole or a beer can. The far end is an alternating series of fields and woods, fields and woods, threaded everywhere with motorcycle tracks — in whose bare clay wild turtles lay eggs.

One evening last week at sunset, I walked to the pond and sat on a downed log near the shore. I was watching the lily pads at my feet tremble and part over the thrusting path of a carp. A yellow warbler appeared to my right and flew behind me. It caught my eye; I swiveled around — and the next instant, inexplicably, I was looking down at a weasel, who was looking up at me. 5

Weasel! I'd never seen one wild before. He was ten inches long, thin as a curve, a muscled ribbon, brown as fruitwood, soft-furred, alert. His face was fierce, small and pointed as a lizard's; he would have made a good arrowhead. There was just a dot of chin, maybe two brown hairs' worth, and then the pure white fur began that spread down his underside. He had two black eyes I didn't see, any more than you see a window.

The weasel was stunned into stillness as he was emerging from beneath an enormous shaggy wild rose bush four feet away. I was stunned

---

[1]*Setton:* Ernest Thompson Seton (1860–1946), American author and naturalist who founded the wildlife organization upon which the Boy Scout movement was later patterned. — EDS.

into stillness twisted backward on the tree trunk. Our eyes locked, and someone threw away the key.

Our look was as if two lovers, or deadly enemies, met unexpectedly on an overgrown path when each had been thinking of something else: a clearing blow to the gut. It was also a bright blow to the brain, or a sudden beating of brains, with all the charge and intimate grate of rubbed balloons. It emptied our lungs. It felled the forest, moved the fields, and drained the pond; the world dismantled and tumbled into that black hole of eyes. If you and I looked at each other that way, our skulls would split and drop to our shoulders. But we don't. We keep our skulls.

He disappeared. This was only last week, and already I don't remember what shattered the enchantment. I think I blinked, I think I retrieved my brain from the weasel's brain, and tried to memorize what I was seeing, and the weasel felt the yank of separation, the careening splashdown into real life and the urgent current of instinct. He vanished under the wild rose. I waited motionless, my mind suddenly full of data and my spirit with pleadings, but he didn't return.

Please do not tell me about "approach-avoidance conflicts." I tell you   10
I've been in that weasel's brain for sixty seconds, and he was in mine. Brains are private places, muttering through unique and secret tapes—but the weasel and I both plugged into another tape simultaneously, for a sweet and shocking time. Can I help it if it was a blank?

What goes on in his brain the rest of the time? What does a weasel think about? He won't say. His journal is tracks in clay, a spray of feathers, mouse blood and bone: uncollected, unconnected, loose-leaf, and blown.

I would like to learn, or remember, how to live. I come to Hollins Pond not so much to learn how to live as, frankly, to forget about it. That is, I don't think I can learn from a wild animal how to live in particular— shall I suck warm blood, hold my tail high, walk with my footprints precisely over the prints of my hands?—but I might learn something of mindlessness, something of purity of living in the physical senses and the dignity of living without bias or motive. The weasel lives in necessity and we live in choice, hating necessity and dying at the last ignobly in its talons. I would like to live as I should, as the weasel lives as he should. And I suspect that for me the way is like the weasel's: open to time and death painlessly, noticing everything, remembering nothing, choosing the given with a fierce and pointed will.

I missed my chance. I should have gone for the throat. I should have lunged for that streak of white under the weasel's chin and held on, held on through mud and into the wild rose, held on for a dearer life. We could live under the wild rose wild as weasels, mute and uncomprehending. I could very calmly go wild. I could live two days in the den, curled, leaning on mouse fur, sniffing bird bones, blinking, licking, breathing musk, my hair tangled in the roots of grasses. Down is a good place to go, where the mind is single. Down is out, out of your ever-loving mind and back to your careless senses. I remember muteness as a prolonged and giddy fast, where every moment is a feast of utterance received. Time and events are merely poured, unremarked, and ingested directly, like blood pulsed into my gut through a jugular vein. Could two live that way? Could two live under the wild rose, and explore by the pond, so that the smooth mind of each is as everywhere present to the other, and as received and as unchallenged, as falling snow?

We could, you know. We can live any way we want. People take vows of poverty, chastity, and obedience—even of silence—by choice. The thing is to stalk your calling in a certain skilled and supple way, to locate the most tender and live spot and plug into that pulse. This is yielding, not fighting. A weasel doesn't "attack" anything; a weasel lives as he's meant to, yielding at every moment to the perfect freedom of single necessity.

I think it would be well, and proper, and obedient, and pure, to grasp your one necessity and not let it go, to dangle from it limp wherever it takes you. Then even death, where you're going no matter how you live, cannot you part. Seize it and let it seize you up aloft even, till your eyes burn out and drop; let your musky flesh fall off in shreds, and let your very bones unhinge and scatter, loosened over fields, over fields and woods, lightly, thoughtless, from any height at all, from as high as eagles. 15

The Reader's Presence

1. Dillard begins her essay with two documented accounts of weasels, presumably drawn from her reading. What do these accounts have in common? How do they establish the dominant characteristic of weasels and the theme of the essay?

2. "Our eyes locked," Dillard says in describing her encounter with the weasel. Why is this an appropriate image? How does the idea of "locking" run through the essay? She also uses the word *wild*. How does she characterize the wild? Could the wild be thought of differently, and in what ways?

3. Dillard's understanding of wild animals suggests a high degree of empathy on her part. Does she create the impression that her wish to live like a weasel is sincere? If not, what is the significance of this hypothetical argument? How does Dillard's sense of what she can learn from animals (in paragraph 14, especially) compare to Vicki Hearne's in "What's Wrong with Animal Rights" (page 697) or to Virginia Woolf's in "The Death of the Moth" (page 601)? Might Hearne or Woolf agree with Dillard's distinction between animals (who live "in necessity") and humans (who live "in choice")? What might each writer think her writing can do for the reader?

THE WRITER AT WORK

Annie Dillard on the Writing Life

One of the nation's outstanding nonfiction writers—who prefers to think of herself as an "all-purpose writer" rather than an essayist—Annie Dillard is also a professor emeritus of creative writing at Wesleyan University. Dillard once said that a commitment to writing is "like living any dedicated life." How is this idea reflected in the following excerpt from her book The Writing Life *(1989)? What does Dillard believe drives the creative artist and writer? Does her tough-minded advice apply only to artistic expression? In what other areas of human activity or expression might it also apply?*

Push it. Examine all things intensely and relentlessly. Probe and search each object in a piece of art. Do not leave it, do not course over it, as if it were understood, but instead follow it down until you see it in the mystery of its own specificity and strength. Giacometti's[1] drawings and paintings show his bewilderment and persistence. If he had not acknowledged his bewilderment, he would not have persisted. A twentieth-century master of drawing, Rico Lebrun, taught that "the draftsman must aggress; only by persistent assault will the live image capitulate and give up its secret to an unrelenting line." Who but an artist fierce to know—not fierce to seem to know—would suppose that a live image possessed a secret? The artist is willing to give all his or her strength and life to probing with blunt instruments those same secrets no one can describe in any way but with those instruments' faint tracks.

Admire the world for never ending on you—as you would admire an opponent, without taking your eyes from him, or walking away.

One of the few things I know about writing is this: spend it all, shoot it, play it, lose it, all, right away, every time. Do not hoard what seems good for a later place in the book, or for another book; give it, give it all, give it now. The impulse to save something good for a better place later is the signal to spend it now. Something more will arise for later, something better. These things fill from behind, from beneath, like well water. Similarly, the impulse to keep to yourself what you have learned is not only shameful, it is destructive. Anything you do not give freely and abundantly becomes lost to you. You open your safe and find ashes.

After Michelangelo died, someone found in his studio a piece of paper on which he had written a note to his apprentice, in the handwriting of his old age: "Draw, Antonio, draw, Antonio, draw and do not waste time."

---

[1]*Alberto Giacometti:* (1901–1966) A renowned Swiss sculptor, painter, draftsman, and printmaker.—EDS.

Gregg Easterbrook

The Myth of Fingerprints

Gregg Easterbrook (b. 1953) was educated at Colorado College and North-western University, earning an MA in journalism in 1977 and quickly gaining a national reputation for his investigative reporting. Easterbrook is a contributing editor of the New Republic; *he has served as editor and writer for a number of publications and venues, including the* Atlantic Monthly *and* Slate's *"Tuesday Morning Quarterback" sports column (from which assorted essays and haiku are collected in his 2001 book of the same name); and he is a frequent contributor to the* New York Times, *the* Washington Post, *the* Los Angeles Times, *and the* New Yorker. *He is a visiting fellow at the Brookings Institution and the author of many books, including* A Moment on the Earth: The Coming Age of Environmental Optimism *(1996),* Beside Still Waters: Searching for Meaning in an Age of Doubt *(1998),* Tuesday Morning Quarterback *(2001), and* The Progress Paradox: How Life Gets Better While People Feel Worse *(2003). He is also the author of two novels,* This Magic Moment *(1987) and* The Here and Now *(2002). "The Myth of Fingerprints" first appeared in the July 2000 issue of the* New Republic.

False convictions have been an important story this year [2000]. The reason? Genetic testing. So far, DNA tests have shown that at least sixty-eight people imprisoned by state and federal courts—including some sent to death row (though none executed)—were innocent. As a result, criminal defense lawyers Barry Scheck and Peter Neufeld are spearheading a national drive to make the tests available to thousands of inmates. They have dubbed their campaign the Innocence Project—creating the impression that DNA tests will serve mainly to exonerate.

In fact, genetic evidence will serve mainly to lock people up. In England, where DNA fingerprinting was invented and has been in widespread use for a decade, law enforcement agencies have already used genetic evidence to solve some 70,000 cases. In the fairly near future, a standard item in the trunks of American police cruisers—perhaps even on each officer's belt—may be a DNA analyzer. As a suspect is arrested, police will quickly swipe the inside of his cheek with a cotton swab and pop the results into the scanner. Within minutes the machine will produce a stream of data describing the suspect's unique genetic structure. The data will be uploaded to state or national DNA databases to determine whether the suspect's DNA matches that of blood, sweat, semen, or similar bodily fluids found at the scene of unsolved crimes around the nation. Such a procedure will be good for public safety and make our legal system more just, but in the long run it will be exactly the opposite of an "innocence project"—it will result in a steady stream of inmates about whose guilt we can be almost entirely certain.

665

The most striking effect of genetic fingerprinting may be on capital punishment, with some opponents suggesting that DNA exonerations could shift the debate in their favor. They're probably mistaken. Of the four people on Texas's death row who have been granted extra DNA testing, three have been executed anyway when genetic evidence either failed to clear them or confirmed their guilt. The fourth, Ricky McGinn, last month received a stay of execution from Governor George W. Bush so he too could be extended the tests—and they reportedly help support his conviction as well. The two big laboratories that process DNA tests, Cellmark Diagnostics and Forensic Science Associates, have exonerated an estimated 40 percent of the inmates whose "post-conviction" genetic evidence they have reviewed, but the other 60 percent have had their guilt confirmed—and what's being reviewed here is the genetic evidence from those with the strongest claims of mistaken conviction.

During the next few years, post-conviction DNA testing will analyze the evidence of death-row inmates convicted before genetic fingerprinting became practical, and some innocent people will surely be freed. But over time—as the system works through the backlog of those tried before genetic analysis was common—the test's main effect will be to increase society's confidence that the man or woman being strapped to the death gurney really did commit the crime. There are two basic arguments against capital punishment: that it is inherently wrong and that it might be used against the wrong person. Death-penalty opponents have been placing more and more emphasis in recent months on the second—precisely the one genetic fingerprinting will undermine.

DNA testing is not the first anti-crime device touted as infallible. Similar claims were made for fingerprinting, also developed in England, when it was introduced at the end of the nineteenth century. But criminals learned to wear gloves or to wipe the crime scene clean. What's more, because fingerprints don't readily convert into the kind of digital data that can be rapidly accessed and shared by police—searching files for a print match is laborious and expensive—regular fingerprints may solve one particular crime but are not usually much help in matching a suspect to others.

Genetic fingerprinting, however, may really allow close-to-infallible identification. In the early '80s, English geneticist Alec Jeffreys realized that the "markers" on human chromosomes—short, structural areas of the genome—are unique from person to person, except for identical twins. Jeffreys developed a test that converts gene markers into a readout similar to a bar code, which can be easily loaded into computers. Not only has the Jeffreys test proved extremely reliable in identifying individuals, but, because it generates a digital result, computers can cross-reference one genetic fingerprint with thousands or millions of others, quickly and cheaply linking suspects to past crimes.

In recent years, DNA-fingerprinting technology has advanced to the point that, rather than requiring a good sample of blood or semen—

5

which often meant securing warrants to jab suspects with needles—a speck of sweat or a swab from the inside of the mouth will do the trick. A test of mitochondrial DNA—which, while not unique to each individual, tells whether the DNA comes from a particular family's maternal line— can even be conducted on a strand of hair or "degraded" blood and bodily fluid samples that have been kept in storage. The cost of DNA fingerprinting has also dropped dramatically, from about $5,000 when the tests were first developed to about $100 for the newest versions, and is still falling.

Though very reliable, DNA fingerprinting won't solve every crime. It is useful mainly for what might be called intimate violent crimes, in which the perpetrator struggles with the victim and leaves behind blood, semen, or something else testable. (In the recent controversy over Bush's execution of Gary Graham,[1] for instance, genetic evidence was moot—the victim was shot from a distance, leaving nothing of the killer's to test.) At other times, DNA in itself may neither exculpate nor damn. A hair from the murderer of Ricky McGinn's twelve-year-old stepdaughter was found on her corpse, for instance, and a DNA test is believed to show that this hair came from either McGinn or a close maternal relative of his. So, although a prosecutor could not convict McGinn on the DNA evidence alone, it could be a critical component of a larger case.

While there is currently no way to beat a DNA test, that could change, especially if criminals grow more careful with bodily fluids—say, abandoning knives for guns shot from afar. And people won't be researching biotech just to cure diseases—perhaps some enterprising chemist will invent a pill that scrambles the genetic markers in sweat and semen. But for now, at least, genetic fingerprinting is just shy of foolproof.

For that reason, it is vital that DNA testing be used to exonerate the   10
innocent. There are two main questions about genetic evidence: whether people convicted before such tests were available can reopen their cases for post-conviction DNA reviews and whether genetic fingerprinting should become a standard element of new arrests, as it already is in England.

Today only a few states, among them New York and Illinois, unambiguously grant those already imprisoned access to additional DNA testing. Courts have traditionally put strict deadlines on how long after conviction someone can introduce new evidence, in part because experience teaches that the longer ago something happened, the easier it is to find someone willing to commit perjury about it. Prosecutors traditionally fight requests for post-conviction testing, too—which is shortsighted, since a

---

[1]*Gary Graham:* also known as Shaka Sankofa, was executed on June 22, 2000, after 19 years on death row. Graham, who was 17 at the time of his arrest, was accused of killing grocery clerk Bobby Lambert in 1981, during a robbery attempt. George W. Bush, then Governor of Texas, and the Texas Board of Pardons and Paroles rejected appeals to commute his death sentence.

false conviction not only imprisons an innocent person but lets the real perpetrator go free. The Justice Department recommends that post-conviction testing be allowed when it could prove "actual" innocence but not permitted in cases built on claims of technicalities or reversible error. This would be a substantial improvement, and a bill offered by Senator Patrick Leahy of Vermont would basically make it law.

Many states have compiled DNA databases and are scanning them to see if evidence from tested suspects matches evidence from unsolved cases. Virginia, which has enacted a law requiring convicted felons to submit to DNA analysis, now has about 120,000 DNA samples on record. It has already found 177 matches between suspects and genetic material at the scenes of past crimes. This June, Virginia detectives took the gene markers of a man convicted of robbing a local gas station and ran them through the state database; they matched the DNA fingerprint to blood found and stored after a horribly gruesome — and until then unsolved — 1992 murder. The gas-station robber was promptly arrested for the murder as well.

Yet, for routine police work, many states actually forbid DNA finger-printing or, nonsensically, allow it only after crimes of extreme violence — as though violent criminals should be caught but not mere thieves or carjackers. Leahy's bill, or something like it, would make genetic evidence more standard and also establish a national databank: had the accused murderer in the 1992 Virginia case robbed a gas station in another state and given his DNA sample there instead, Virginia detectives might never have found him. Fighting efforts to more effectively use genetic evidence is the American Civil Liberties Union [ACLU], which is lobbying against testing laws on the grounds that chromosome material deserves privacy protection because it might reveal such things as sexual orientation.

Why a murderer has a right to sexual privacy (or any kind of privacy) isn't clear, but in any case the ACLU claim evinces confusion about what Jeffreys-style DNA tests can show. The "markers" analyzed in police tests constitute only a small, structural part of the genome. Just as a traditional fingerprint doesn't tell you anything about the suspect's personality — it just tells you about the shape of his or her finger ridges — genetic markers don't reveal anything about IQ or disease disposition or sexual orientation. Analyzing such complex traits, assuming it can be done at all, would require far more sophisticated tests, along the lines of the years-long human genome initiative. Perhaps someday there will be a quick, cheap test that gives police personal information derived from genes; that may be a reason to enact legal safeguards. . . . For now, the main reason the ACLU seems to fear DNA fingerprinting is that it works.

And that should give death-penalty opponents pause as well. Ex-   15
panded use of DNA evidence will free a few death-row innocents, which would be a blessing. But the new technology will also make society much more confident that those receiving their last meals really are guilty of a mortal sin. Suspicions that the innocent are being executed will not grow

stronger as DNA testing spreads—they will grow weaker. And so opponents of capital punishment will lose the offensive they have claimed in recent months. They will be forced back to their real argument, the one that technology can't undermine: the inherent wickedness of execution itself.

The Reader's Presence

1. Who does Easterbrook think should be subject to mandatory DNA testing? According to him, why should these people be tested? Do you agree or disagree that mandatory genetic testing can "exonerate the innocent" (paragraph 10)? Why or why not?

2. What is Easterbrook's position on the death penalty? In what ways does his position on this issue influence his position on mandatory DNA testing? How does he relate the two issues? Who do you think would be more likely to support Easterbrook's ideas about DNA testing: an innocent person falsely accused of a crime or a guilty person who was rightly accused of a crime? Explain why.

3. Like Easterbrook, William Speed Weed ("106 Science Claims and a Truckful of Baloney," page 579) takes on an issue of science and tries to convince the reader to share his point of view. Compare the arguments made by these two essayists. What strategies do the authors use to convince their readers? What evidence do they introduce and how do they present it? How do they deal with possible objections? What would you say were "fair" argumentative strategies in these essays? What are unfair strategies? What, in particular, do you think makes one argument more convincing than the other?

Barbara Ehrenreich

Family Values

Barbara Ehrenreich (b. 1941) wrote some of her first articles and books on the inefficiency and inhumanity of the American health care system. In Complaints and Disorders: The Sexual Politics of Sickness *(coauthored with Deirdre English, 1973) she critiques the unjust and unequal treatment women receive in the medical system. She has written more than a dozen books, among them*

The Hearts of Men: American Dreams and the Flight from Commitment *(1983)*; The Worst Years of Our Lives: Irreverent Notes from a Decade of Greed *(1990), from which "Family Values" is taken; and* Kipper's Game *(1993). Ehrenreich is a contributing editor at the* Progressive *and the* Nation, *and her essays also appear regularly in magazines as varied as* Radical America, Time, Vogue, *and the* New York Times Magazine. *Her most recent books are* Nickel and Dimed: On (Not) Getting By in America *(2001),* Dancing in the Streets *(2007), and* This Land Is Their Land: Reports from a Divided Nation *(2008).*

Asked whether she writes in different voices for the alternative and the mainstream press, Ehrenreich replied, "I don't think it's really a different voice.... Obviously I assume more political sympathy for my views if I'm writing for Z or the Guardian *in England or the* Nation *than* Time, *but it might be the exact basic argument." She added, "An essay is like a little story, a short story, and I will obsess about what is the real point, what are the real connections, a long time before I ever put finger to keyboard."*

Sometime in the eighties, Americans had a new set of "traditional values" installed. It was part of what may someday be known as the "Reagan renovation," that finely balanced mix of cosmetic refinement and moral coarseness which brought $200,000 china to the White House dinner table and mayhem to the beleaguered peasantry of Central America. All of the new traditions had venerable sources. In economics, we borrowed from the Bourbons; in foreign policy, we drew on themes fashioned by the nomad warriors of the Eurasian steppes. In spiritual matters, we emulated the braying intolerance of our archenemies and esteemed customers, the Shi'ite fundamentalists.

A case could be made, of course, for the genuine American provenance of all these new "traditions." We've had our own robber barons, military adventures, and certainly more than our share of enterprising evangelists promoting ignorance and parochialism as a state of grace. From the vantage point of the continent's original residents, or, for example, the captive African laborers who made America a great agricultural power, our "traditional values" have always been bigotry, greed, and belligerence, buttressed by wanton appeals to a God of love.

The kindest—though from some angles most perverse—of the era's new values was "family." I could have lived with "flag" and "faith" as neotraditional values—not happily, but I could have managed—until "family" was press-ganged into joining them. Throughout the eighties, the winning political faction has been aggressively "profamily." They have invoked "the family" when they trample on the rights of those who hold actual families together, that is, women. They have used it to justify racial segregation and the formation of white-only, "Christian" schools. And they have brought it out, along with flag and faith, to silence any voices they found obscene, offensive, disturbing, or merely different.

Now, I come from a family—was raised in one, in fact—and one salubrious effect of right-wing righteousness has been to make me hew ever more firmly to the traditional values of my own progenitors. These were not people who could be accused of questionable politics or ethnicity. Nor were they members of the "liberal elite" so hated by our current conservative elite. They were blue-eyed, Scotch-Irish Democrats. They were small farmers, railroad workers, miners, shopkeepers, and migrant farm workers. In short, they fit the stereotype of "real" Americans; and their values, no matter how unpopular among today's opinion-shapers, are part of America's tradition, too. To my mind, of course, the finest part.

But let me introduce some of my family, beginning with my father, who was, along with my mother, the ultimate source of much of my radicalism, feminism, and, by the standards of the eighties, all-around bad attitude.

One of the first questions in a test of mental competency is "Who is the president of the United States?" Even deep into the indignities of Alzheimer's disease, my father always did well on that one. His blue eyes would widen incredulously, surprised at the neurologist's ignorance, then he would snort in majestic indignation, "Reagan, that dumb son of a bitch." It seemed to me a good deal—two people tested for the price of one.

Like so many of the Alzheimer's patients he came to know, my father enjoyed watching the president on television. Most programming left him impassive, but when the old codger came on, his little eyes twinkling piggishly above the disciplined sincerity of his lower face, my father would lean forward and commence a wickedly delighted cackle. I think he was prepared, more than the rest of us, to get the joke.

But the funniest thing was Ollie North. For an ailing man, my father did a fine parody. He would slap his hand over his heart, stare rigidly at attention, and pronounce, in his deepest bass rumble, "God Bless Am-ar-ica!" I'm sure he couldn't follow North's testimony—who can honestly say that they did?—but the main themes were clear enough in pantomime: the watery-eyed patriotism, the extravagant self-pity, the touching servility toward higher-ranking males. When I told my father that many people considered North a hero, a representative of the finest American traditions, he scowled and swatted at the air. Ollie North was the kind of man my father had warned me about, many years ago, when my father was the smartest man on earth.

My father had started out as a copper miner in Butte, Montana, a tiny mountain city famed for its bars, its brawls, and its distinctly unservile work force. In his view, which remained eagle-sharp even after a stint of higher education, there were only a few major categories of human beings. There were "phonies" and "decent" people, the latter group having hardly any well-known representative outside of Franklin Delano Roosevelt and John L. Lewis, the militant and brilliantly eloquent leader of the miners' union. "Phonies," however, were rampant, and, for reasons I would not understand until later in life, could be found clustered especially thick in the vicinity of money or power.

Well before he taught me other useful things, like how to distinguish fool's gold, or iron pyrite, from the real thing, he gave me some tips on the detection of phonies. For one thing, they broadened the *e* in "America" to

5

10

a reverent *ahh*. They were the first to leap from their seats at the playing of "The Star Spangled Banner," the most visibly moved participants in any prayer. They espoused clean living and admired war. They preached hard work and paid for it with nickels and dimes. They loved their country above all, but despised the low-paid and usually invisible men and women who built it, fed it, and kept it running.

Two other important categories figured in my father's scheme of things. There were dumb people and smart ones: a distinction which had nothing to do with class or formal education, the dumb being simply all those who were taken in by the phonies. In his view, dumbness was rampant, and seemed to increase in proportion to the distance from Butte, where at least a certain hard-bodied irreverence leavened the atmosphere. The best prophylactic was to study and learn all you could, however you could, and, as he adjured me over and over: always ask *why*.

Finally, there were the rich and the poor. While poverty was not seen as an automatic virtue—my parents struggled mightily to escape it—wealth always carried a presumption of malfeasance. I was instructed that, in the presence of the rich, it was wise to keep one's hand on one's wallet. "Well," my father fairly growled, "how do you think they got their money in the first place?"

It was my mother who translated these lessons into practical politics. A miner's daughter herself, she offered two overarching rules for comportment: never vote Republican and never cross a union picket line. The pinnacle of her activist career came in 1964, when she attended the Democratic Convention as an alternate delegate and joined the sit-in staged by civil rights leaders and the Mississippi Freedom Democratic Party. This was not the action of a "guilt-ridden" white liberal. She classified racial prejudice along with superstition and other manifestations of backward thinking, like organized religion and overcooked vegetables. The worst thing she could find to say about a certain in-law was that he was a Republican and a churchgoer, though when I investigated these charges later in life, I was relieved to find them baseless.

My mother and father, it should be explained, were hardly rebels. The values they imparted to me had been "traditional" for at least a generation before my parents came along. According to my father, the first great steps out of mental passivity had been taken by his maternal grandparents, John Howes and Mamie O'Laughlin Howes, sometime late in the last century [1800s]. You might think their rebellions small stuff, but they provided our family with its "myth of origins" and a certain standard to uphold.

I knew little about Mamie O'Laughlin except that she was raised as a   15
Catholic and ended up in western Montana sometime in the 1880s. Her father, very likely, was one of those itinerant breadwinners who went west to prospect and settled for mining. At any rate, the story begins when her father lay dying, and Mamie dutifully sent to the next town for a priest. The message came back that the priest would come only if

twenty-five dollars was sent in advance. This being the West at its wildest, he may have been justified in avoiding house calls. But not in the price, which was probably more cash than my great-grandmother had ever had at one time. It was on account of its greed that the church lost the souls of Mamie O'Laughlin and all of her descendents, right down to the present time. Futhermore, whether out of filial deference or natural intelligence, most of us have continued to avoid organized religion, secret societies, astrology, and New Age adventures in spiritualism.

As the story continues, Mamie O'Laughlin herself lay dying a few years later. She was only thirty-one, the mother of three small children, one of them an infant whose birth, apparently, led to a mortal attack of pneumonia. This time, a priest appeared unsummoned. Because she was too weak to hold the crucifix, he placed it on her chest and proceeded to administer the last rites. But Mamie was not dead yet. She pulled herself together at the last moment, flung the crucifix across the room, fell back, and died.

This was my great-grandmother. Her husband, John Howes, is a figure of folkloric proportions in my memory, well known in Butte many decades ago as a powerful miner and a lethal fighter. There are many stories about John Howes, all of which point to a profound inability to accept authority in any of its manifestations, earthly or divine. As a young miner, for example, he caught the eye of the mine owner for his skill at handling horses. The boss promoted him to an aboveground driving job, which was a great career leap for the time. Then the boss committed a foolish and arrogant error. He asked John to break in a team of horses for his wife's carriage. Most people would probably be flattered by such a request, but not in Butte, and certainly not John Howes. He declared that he was no man's servant, and quit on the spot.

Like his own wife, John Howes was an atheist or, as they more likely put it at the time, a freethinker. He, too, had been raised as a Catholic—on a farm in Ontario—and he, too, had had a dramatic, though somehow less glorious, falling out with the local clergy. According to legend, he once abused his position as an altar boy by urinating, covertly of course, in the holy water. This so enhanced his enjoyment of the Easter communion service that he could not resist letting a few friends in on the secret. Soon the priest found out and young John was defrocked as an altar boy and condemned to eternal damnation.

The full weight of this transgression hit a few years later, when he became engaged to a local woman. The priest refused to marry them and forbade the young woman to marry John anywhere, on pain of excommunication. There was nothing to do but head west for the Rockies, but not before settling his score with the church. According to legend, John's last act in Ontario was to drag the priest down from his pulpit and slug him, with his brother, presumably, holding the scandalized congregation at bay.

I have often wondered whether my great-grandfather was caught up 20 in the radicalism of Butte in its heyday: whether he was an admirer of Joe

Ehrenreich / *Family Values*

Hill, Big Bill Haywood, or Mary "Mother" Jones,[1] all of whom passed through Butte to agitate, and generally left with the Pinkertons[2] on their tails. But the record is silent on this point. All I know is one last story about him, which was told often enough to have the ring of another "traditional value."

According to my father, John Howes worked on and off in the mines after his children were grown, eventually saving enough to buy a small plot of land and retire to farming. This was his dream, anyway, and a powerful one it must have been for a man who had spent so much of his life underground in the dark. So he loaded up a horse-drawn cart with all his money and belongings and headed downhill, toward Montana's eastern plains. But along the way he came to an Indian woman walking with a baby in her arms. He offered her a lift and ascertained, pretty easily, that she was destitute. So he gave her his money, all of it, turned the horse around, and went back to the mines.

Far be it from me to interpret this gesture for my great-grandfather, whom I knew only as a whiskery, sweat-smelling, but straight-backed old man in his eighties. Perhaps he was enacting his own uncompromising version of Christian virtue, even atoning a little for his youthful offenses to the faithful. But at another level I like to think that this was one more gesture of defiance of the mine owners who doled out their own dollars so grudgingly—a way of saying, perhaps, that whatever they had to offer, he didn't really need all that much.

So these were the values, sanctified by tradition and family loyalty, that I brought with me to adulthood. Through much of my growing-up, I thought of them as some mutant strain of Americanism, an idiosyncracy which seemed to grow rarer as we clambered into the middle class. Only in the sixties did I begin to learn that my family's militant skepticism and odd-ball rebelliousness were part of a much larger stream of American dissent. I discovered feminism, the antiwar movement, the civil rights movement. I learned that millions of Americans, before me and around me, were "smart" enough, in my father's terms, to have asked "Why?"—and, beyond that, the far more radical question, "Why not?"

These are also the values I brought into the Reagan-Bush era, when all the dangers I had been alerted to as a child were suddenly realized. The "phonies" came to power on the strength, aptly enough, of a professional actor's finest performance. The "dumb" were being led and abetted by

---

[1]*Joe Hill . . . Jones:* Joe Hill (1879–1915), a writer of popular protest songs, was executed for murder in 1915 after a trial that many, including President Woodrow Wilson, believed suspicious; Big Bill Haywood (1869–1928) was president of the Western Federation of Miners during Colorado's bloody labor wars; Mary "Mother" Jones (1830–1930), the "Miner's Angel," was for decades a legendary union organizer as well as a lecturer for the Socialist Party of America and contributor to the founding of the International Workers of the World.—Eds.

[2]*Pinkertons:* Employees of the Pinkerton National Detective Agency, founded in 1850, were frequently hired to thwart strikes, sometimes violently.—Eds.

low-life preachers and intellectuals with expensively squandered educations. And the rich, as my father predicted, used the occasion to dip deep into the wallets of the desperate and the distracted.

It's been hard times for a traditionalist of my persuasion. Long-standing moral values—usually claimed as "Judeo-Christian" but actually of much broader lineage—were summarily tossed, along with most familiar forms of logic. We were told, at one time or another, by the president or his henchpersons, that trees cause pollution, that welfare causes poverty, and that a bomber designed for mass destruction may be aptly named the *Peacemaker*. "Terrorism" replaced missing children to become our national bugaboo and—simultaneously—one of our most potent instruments of foreign policy. At home, the poor and the middle class were shaken down, and their loose change funneled blithely upwards to the already overfed.

Greed, the ancient lubricant of commerce, was declared a wholesome stimulant. Nancy Reagan observed the deep recession of '82 and '83 by redecorating the White House, and continued with this Marie Antoinette theme while advising the underprivileged, the alienated, and the addicted to "say no." Young people, mindful of their elders' Wall Street capers, abandoned the study of useful things for finance banking and other occupations derived, ultimately, from three-card monte. While the poor donned plastic outerware and cardboard coverings, the affluent ran nearly naked through the streets, working off power meals of goat cheese, walnut oil, and crème fraîche.

Religion, which even I had hoped would provide a calming influence and reminder of mortal folly, decided to join the fun. In an upsurge of piety, millions of Americans threw their souls and their savings into evangelical empires designed on the principle of pyramid scams. Even the sleazy downfall of our telemessiahs—caught masturbating in the company of ten-dollar prostitutes or fornicating in their Christian theme parks—did not discourage the faithful. The unhappily pregnant were mobbed as "baby-killers"; sexual nonconformists—gay and lesbian—were denounced as "child molesters"; atheists found themselves lumped with "Satanists," Communists, and consumers of human flesh.

Yet somehow, despite it all, a trickle of dissent continued. There were homeless people who refused to be shelved in mental hospitals for the crime of poverty, strikers who refused to join the celebration of unions in faraway countries and scabs at home, women who insisted that their lives be valued above those of accidental embryos, parents who packed up their babies and marched for peace, students who protested the ongoing inversion of normal, nursery-school-level values in the name of a more habitable world.

I am proud to add my voice to all these. For dissent is also a "traditional value," and in a republic founded by revolution, a more deeply native one than smug-faced conservatism can ever be. Feminism was practically invented here, and ought to be regarded as one of our proudest exports to the world. Likewise, it tickles my sense of patriotism that Third World insurgents have often borrowed the ideas of our own

African-American movement. And in what ought to be a source of shame to some and pride to others, our history of labor struggle is one of the hardest-fought and bloodiest in the world.

No matter that patriotism is too often the refuge of scoundrels. Dissent, rebellion, and all-around hell-raising remain the true duty of patriots.   30

The Reader's Presence

1. Do you believe, with Ehrenreich, that different periods in American history have carried different social values? Why or why not? What is your impression of the 1980s, and what sources have you derived this impression from? How does Ehrenreich characterize the 1980s? What elements of 1980s culture does she recall in supporting her claims?

2. One catch phrase frequently heard during Ehrenreich's radical college years was "the personal is political." In what ways were Ehrenreich's father's personal principles political, in her view? How does Ehrenreich's use of her father as a model make the personal political and the political personal? Does this intermingling of the personal and the political undermine or enhance her larger argument? Why?

3. Ehrenreich uses her own impressions and experience as evidence in her argument. How might the essay read if it were argued in more objective terms (historical facts, statistics, etc.)? What sorts of examples does she use to make her point? What examples can you think of that are contrary to hers (counterexamples)? Contrast the type of evidence used by Ehrenreich with that used by Calvin Trillin in "A Traditional Family" (page 545).

Nora Ephron

The Boston Photographs

Nora Ephron (b. 1941) started her writing career as a reporter for the New York Post, *and since then has written for numerous magazines, including* New York Magazine, McCall's, *and* Cosmopolitan. *Ephron's collections of essays on popular culture include* Wall Flower at the Orgy *(1970),* Crazy Salad *(1975), and* Scribble, Scribble: Notes on the Media *(1978). The essay "The Boston Photographs" appeared originally in* Esquire *in 1975. She also wrote the screenplays for* Silkwood *(with Alice Arlen),* When Harry Met Sally, *and* Sleepless in Seattle. *In 1992 she directed her first movie,* This Is My Life, *written with her sister Delia Ephron; since then she has directed the films* Michael *(1996),* You've Got Mail *(1998), and* Lucky Numbers *(2000). Her most recent collection of essays and ruminations on aging is* I Feel Bad About My Neck: And Other Thoughts About Being a Woman *(2009).*

When Nora Ephron spoke at the Wellesley College commencement in 1979, she told the largely female audience, "We were sent off into a college environment that expected us to grow up to be soothing women. . . . We were to spend our lives making nice." Ephron believes that the world needs more troublemakers. In "The Boston Photographs," she makes a bold argument for publishing disturbing and controversial photographs.

"I made all kinds of pictures because I thought it would be a good rescue shot over the ladder . . . never dreamed it would be anything else. . . . I kept having to move around because of the light set. The sky was bright and they were in deep shadow. I was making pictures with a motor drive and he, the fire fighter, was reaching up and, I don't know, everything started falling. I followed the girl down taking pictures . . . I made three or four frames. I realized what was going on and I completely turned around, because I didn't want to see her hit."

You probably saw the photographs. In most newspapers, there were three of them. The first showed some people on a fire escape — a fireman, a woman and a child. The fireman had a nice strong jaw and looked very brave. The woman was holding the child. Smoke was pouring from the building behind them. A rescue ladder was approaching, just a few feet away, and the fireman had one arm around the woman and one arm reaching out toward the ladder. The second picture showed the fire escape slipping off the building. The child had fallen on the escape and seemed about to slide off the edge. The woman was grasping desperately at the legs of the fireman, who had managed to grab the ladder. The third picture showed the woman and child in midair, falling to the ground. Their arms and legs were outstretched, horribly distended. A potted plant was falling too. The caption said that the woman, Diana Bryant, nineteen, died in the fall. The child landed on the woman's body and lived.

The pictures were taken by Stanley Forman, thirty, of the *Boston Herald American*. He used a motor-driven Nikon F set at 1/250, f5.6-S. Because of the motor, the camera can click off three frames a second. More than four hundred newspapers in the United States alone carried the photographs; the tear sheets from overseas are still coming in. The *New York Times* ran them on the first page of its second section; a paper in south Georgia gave them nineteen columns; the *Chicago Tribune*, the *Washington Post* and the *Washington Star* filled almost half their front pages, the *Star* under a somewhat redundant headline that read: SENSATIONAL PHOTOS OF RESCUE ATTEMPT THAT FAILED.

The photographs are indeed sensational. They are pictures of death in action, of that split second when luck runs out, and it is impossible to look at them without feeling their extraordinary impact and remembering, in an almost subconscious way, the morbid fantasy of falling, falling off a building, falling to one's death. Beyond that, the pictures are classics, old-fashioned but perfect examples of photojournalism at its most spectacular. They're throwbacks, really, fire pictures, 1930s tabloid shots; at the same time they're technically superb and thoroughly modern — the sequence could not have been taken at all until the development of the motor-driven camera some sixteen years ago.

Most newspaper editors anticipate some reader reaction to photographs like Forman's; even so, the response around the country was enormous, and almost all of it was negative. I have read hundreds of the letters that were printed in letters-to-the-editor sections, and they repeat the same points. "Invading the privacy of death." "Cheap sensationalism." "I thought I was reading the *National Enquirer*." "Assigning the agony of a human being in terror of imminent death to the status of a side-show act." "A tawdry way to sell newspapers." The *Seattle Times* received sixty letters and calls; its managing editor even got a couple of them at home. A reader wrote the *Philadelphia Inquirer*: "*Jaws* and *Towering Inferno* are playing downtown; don't take business away from people who pay good money to advertise in your own paper." Another reader wrote the

Chicago Sun-Times: "I shall try to hide my disappointment that Miss Bryant wasn't wearing a skirt when she fell to her death. You could have had some award-winning photographs of her underpants as her skirt billowed over her head, you voyeurs." Several newspaper editors wrote columns defending the pictures: Thomas Keevil of the *Costa Mesa* (California) *Daily Pilot* printed a ballot for readers to vote on whether they would have printed the pictures; Marshall L. Stone of Maine's *Bangor Daily News*, which refused to print the famous assassination picture of the Vietcong prisoner in Saigon,[1] claimed that the Boston pictures showed the dangers of fire escapes and raised questions about slumlords. (The burning building was a five-story brick apartment house on Marlborough Street in the Back Bay section of Boston.)

For the last five years, the *Washington Post* has employed various journalists as ombudsmen, whose job is to monitor the paper on behalf of the public. The *Post*'s current ombudsman is Charles Seib, former managing editor of the *Washington Star*; the day the Boston photographs appeared, the paper received over seventy calls in protest. As Seib later wrote in a column about the pictures, it was "the largest reaction to a published item that I have experienced in eight months as the *Post*'s ombudsman. . . .

"In the *Post*'s newsroom, on the other hand, I found no doubts, no second thoughts . . . the question was not whether they should be printed but how they should be displayed. When I talked to editors . . . they used words like 'interesting' and 'riveting' and 'gripping' to describe them. The pictures told of something about life in the ghetto, they said (although the neighborhood where the tragedy occurred is not a ghetto, I am told). They dramatized the need to check on the safety of fire escapes. They dramatically conveyed something that had happened, and that is the business we're in. They were news. . . .

"Was publication of that [third] picture a bow to the same taste for the morbidly sensational that makes gold mines of disaster movies? Most papers will not print the picture of a dead body except in the most unusual circumstances. Does the fact that the final picture was taken a millisecond before the young woman died make a difference? Most papers will not print a picture of a bare female breast. Is that a more inappropriate subject for display than the picture of a human being's last agonized instant of life?" Seib offered no answers to the questions he raised, but he went on to say that although as an editor he would probably have run the pictures, as a reader he was revolted by them.

In conclusion, Seib wrote: "Any editor who decided to print those pictures without giving at least a moment's thought to what purpose they served and what their effect was likely to be on the reader should ask another question: Have I become so preoccupied with manufacturing a

---

[1]*famous assassination picture . . . in Saigon:* A 1968 photograph by Eddie Adams of the Associated Press showed Saigon's chief of police executing a prisoner with a pistol; the photograph helped turn American opinion against the war. — EDS.

product according to professional traditions and standards that I have forgotten about the consumer, the reader?"

It should be clear that the phone calls and letters and Seib's own 10 reaction were occasioned by one factor alone: the death of the woman. Obviously, had she survived the fall, no one would have protested; the pictures would have had a completely different impact. Equally obviously, had the child died as well—or instead—Seib would undoubtedly have received ten times the phone calls he did. In each case, the pictures would have been exactly the same—only the captions, and thus the responses, would have been different.

But the questions Seib raises are worth discussing—though not exactly for the reasons he mentions. For it may be that the real lesson of the Boston photographs is not the danger that editors will be forgetful of reader reaction, but that they will continue to censor pictures of death precisely because of that reaction. The protests Seib fielded were really a variation on an old theme—and we saw plenty of it during the Nixon-Agnew years—the "Why doesn't the press print the good news?" argument. In this case, of course, the objections were all dressed up and cleverly disguised as righteous indignation about the privacy of death. This is a form of puritanism that is often justifiable; just as often it is merely puritanical.

Seib takes it for granted that the widespread though fairly recent newspaper policy against printing pictures of dead bodies is a sound one; I don't know that it makes any sense at all. I recognize that printing pictures of corpses raises all sorts of problems about taste and titillation and sensationalism; the fact is, however, that people die. Death happens to be one of life's main events. And it is irresponsible—and more than that, inaccurate—for newspapers to fail to show it, or to show it only when an astonishing set of photos comes in over the Associated Press wire. Most papers covering fatal automobile accidents will print pictures of mangled cars. But the significance of fatal automobile accidents is not that a great deal of steel is twisted but that people die. Why not show it? That's what accidents are about. Throughout the Vietnam War, editors were reluctant to print atrocity pictures. Why *not* print them? That's what that war was about. Murder victims are almost never photographed; they are granted their privacy. But their relatives are relentlessly pictured on their way in and out of hospitals and morgues and funerals.

I'm not advocating that newspapers print these things in order to teach their readers a lesson. The *Post* editors justified their printing of the Boston pictures with several arguments in that direction; every one of them is irrelevant. The pictures don't show anything about slum life; the incident could have happened anywhere, and it did. It is extremely unlikely that anyone who saw them rushed out and had his fire escape strengthened. And the pictures were not news—at least they were not national news. It is not news in Washington, or New York, or Los Angeles that a woman was killed in a Boston fire. The only newsworthy thing about the pictures is that they were taken. They deserve to be printed because they are great pictures, breathtaking pictures of something that happened. That they disturb readers is exactly as it should be: that's why photojournalism is often more powerful than written journalism.

The Reader's Presence

1. At what point does Ephron's argument begin to emerge? How does she present information about the photographs? Why do you think she chooses to structure her argument as she does?

2. How does Ephron refute newspapers' justifications for printing the photographs? What might she argue should be the purpose of photojournalism? Do you agree with this purpose? Why or why not?

3. "Death happens to be one of life's main events," Ephron writes in paragraph 12, arguing that the photographs are important although they are "not news." How does knowing that the woman died in the fall affect the viewer's feelings about the photographs? Read Errol Morris's essay "Liar, Liar, Pants on Fire" (page 775), which focuses on "truth and photography." "It is also interesting," Morris observes, "how a photograph quickly changes when we learn more about what it depicts, when we provide a context, when we become familiar with an underlying story. And when we make claims about the photograph using language. For truth, properly considered, is about the relationship between language and the world, not about photographs and the world" (paragraph 18). Given your understanding of Ephron's points about photography, what would you anticipate would be her reaction to Morris's point here? Be as specific in your response as possible.

John Taylor Gatto

Against School

"I've taught public school for twenty-six years but I just can't do it anymore," began an impassioned op-ed piece published in the Wall Street Journal *in 1991. Its author, John Taylor Gatto (b. 1935), continued, "I've come slowly to understand what it is I really teach: A curriculum of confusion, class position, arbitrary justice, vulgarity, rudeness, disrespect for privacy, indifference to quality,*

*and utter dependency. I teach how to fit into a world I don't want to live in."
With the headline "I May Be a Teacher but I'm Not an Educator," the essay set
off a fierce debate among parents, teachers, and politicians about the system of
public education in the United States. It also launched Gatto's career as a speaker,
consultant, and writer.*

*After graduating from Columbia University, Gatto worked as a scriptwriter,
a songwriter, and an ad writer; drove a cab; sold hot dogs; and, finally, began a
distinguished career as a schoolteacher. He was recognized as New York City
Teacher of the Year for three years running. In 1991, the year he resigned in
protest from his position as a seventh-grade teacher at the Booker T. Washington
School in New York City, he was named New York State Teacher of the Year. He
has edited and written many books on education, including* Dumbing Us Down
(1992), The Exhausted School *(1993),* A Different Kind of Teacher *(2000), and*
Underground History of American Education *(2001). His essay "Against School"
first appeared in* Harper's *magazine in 2001.*

I taught for thirty years in some of the worst schools in Manhattan,
and in some of the best, and during that time I became an expert in boredom. Boredom was everywhere in my world, and if you asked the kids, as
I often did, *why* they felt so bored, they always gave the same answers:
They said the work was stupid, that it made no sense, that they already
knew it. They said they wanted to be doing something real, not just sitting around. They said teachers didn't seem to know much about their
subjects and clearly weren't interested in learning more. And the kids
were right: their teachers were every bit as bored as they were.

Boredom is the common condition of schoolteachers, and anyone
who has spent time in a teachers' lounge can vouch for the low energy,
the whining, the dispirited attitudes, to be found there. When asked why
they feel bored, the teachers tend to blame the kids, as you might expect.
Who wouldn't get bored teaching students who are rude and interested
only in grades? If even that. Of course, teachers are themselves products
of the same twelve-year compulsory school programs that so thoroughly
bore their students, and as school personnel they are trapped inside structures even more rigid than those imposed upon the children. Who, then,
is to blame?

We all are. My grandfather taught me that. One afternoon when I
was seven I complained to him of boredom, and he batted me hard on the
head. He told me that I was never to use that term in his presence again,
that if I was bored it was my fault and no one else's. The obligation to
amuse and instruct myself was entirely my own, and people who didn't
know that were childish people, to be avoided if possible. Certainly not to
be trusted. That episode cured me of boredom forever, and here and there
over the years I was able to pass on the lesson to some remarkable student. For the most part, however, I found it futile to challenge the official
notion that boredom and childishness were the natural state of affairs in
the classroom. Often I had to defy custom, and even bend the law, to help
kids break out of this trap.

The empire struck back, of course; childish adults regularly conflate opposition with disloyalty. I once returned from a medical leave to discover that all evidence of my having been granted the leave had been purposely destroyed, that my job had been terminated, and that I no longer possessed even a teaching license. After nine months of tormented effort I was able to retrieve the license when a school secretary testified to witnessing the plot unfold. In the meantime my family suffered more than I care to remember. By the time I finally retired in 1991, I had more than enough reason to think of our schools — with their long-term, cell-block–style, forced confinement of both students and teachers — as virtual factories of childishness. Yet I honestly could not see *why* they had to be that way. My own experience had revealed to me what many other teachers must learn along the way, too, yet keep to themselves for fear of reprisal: if we wanted to we could easily and inexpensively jettison the old, stupid structures and help kids *take* an education rather than merely *receive* a schooling. We could encourage the best qualities of youthfulness — curiosity, adventure, resilience, the capacity for surprising insight — simply by being more flexible about time, texts, and tests, by introducing kids to truly competent adults, and by giving each student what autonomy he or she needs in order to take a risk every now and then.

But we don't do that. And the more I asked why not, and persisted   5
in thinking about the "problem" of schooling as an engineer might, the more I missed the point: What if there is no "problem" with our schools? What if they are the way they are, so expensively flying in the face of common sense and long experience in how children learn things, not because they are doing something wrong but because they are doing something right? Is it possible that George W. Bush accidentally spoke the truth when he said we would "leave no child behind"? Could it be that our schools are designed to make sure not one of them ever really grows up?

Do we really need school? I don't mean education, just forced schooling: six classes a day, five days a week, nine months a year, for twelve years. Is this deadly routine really necessary? And if so, for what? Don't hide behind reading, writing, and arithmetic as a rationale, because two million happy homeschoolers have surely put that banal justification to rest. Even if they hadn't, a considerable number of well-known Americans never went through the twelve-year wringer our kids currently go through, and they turned out all right. George Washington, Benjamin Franklin, Thomas Jefferson, Abraham Lincoln? Someone taught them, to be sure, but they were not products of a school *system*, and not one of them was ever "graduated" from a secondary school. Throughout most of American history, kids generally didn't go to high school, yet the unschooled rose to be admirals, like Farragut; inventors, like Edison; captains of industry, like Carnegie and Rockefeller; writers, like Melville and

Twain and Conrad; and even scholars, like Margaret Mead.[1] In fact, until pretty recently people who reached the age of thirteen weren't looked upon as children at all. Ariel Durant, who co-wrote an enormous, and very good, multivolume history of the world with her husband, Will, was happily married at fifteen, and who could reasonably claim that Ariel Durant was an uneducated person? Unschooled, perhaps, but not uneducated.

We have been taught (that is, schooled) in this country to think of "success" as synonymous with, or at least dependent upon, "schooling," but historically that isn't true in either an intellectual or a financial sense. And plenty of people throughout the world today find a way to educate themselves without resorting to a system of compulsory secondary schools that all too often resemble prisons. Why, then, do Americans confuse education with just such a system? What exactly is the purpose of our public schools?

Mass schooling of a compulsory nature really got its teeth into the United States between 1905 and 1915, though it was conceived of much earlier and pushed for throughout most of the nineteenth century. The reason given for this enormous upheaval of family life and cultural traditions was, roughly speaking, threefold:

1. To make good people.
2. To make good citizens.
3. To make each person his or her personal best.

These goals are still trotted out today on a regular basis, and most of us accept them in one form or another as a decent definition of public education's mission, however short schools actually fall in achieving them. But we are dead wrong. Compounding our error is the fact that the national literature holds numerous and surprisingly consistent statements of compulsory schooling's true purpose. We have, for example, the great H. L. Mencken,[2] who wrote in *The American Mercury* for April 1924 that the aim of public education is not

> to fill the young of the species with knowledge and awaken their intelligence. . . . Nothing could be further from the truth. The aim . . . is simply to reduce as many individuals as possible to the same safe level, to breed and train a standardized citizenry, to put down dissent and originality. That is its aim in the United States . . . and that is its aim everywhere else.

Because of Mencken's reputation as a satirist, we might be tempted to dismiss this passage as a bit of hyperbolic sarcasm. His article, however, goes on to trace the template for our own educational system back to the

---

[1]*Mead:* Margaret Mead (1901–1978) became the most famous anthropologist in the world, best known for *Coming of Age in Samoa* (1928), a book that analyzed cultural influence on adolescence. — EDS.

[2]*H(enry) L(ouis) "H. L." Mencken:* (1880–1956) An influential journalist, essayist, magazine editor, satirist, and critic of American life and culture. — EDS.

now vanished, though never to be forgotten, military state of Prussia. And although he was certainly aware of the irony that we had recently been at war with Germany, the heir to Prussian thought and culture, Mencken was being perfectly serious here. Our educational system really is Prussian in origin, and that really is cause for concern.

The odd fact of a Prussian provenance for our schools pops up again and again once you know to look for it. William James[3] alluded to it many times at the turn of the century. Orestes Brownson, the hero of Christopher Lasch's 1991 book, *The True and Only Heaven*, was publicly denouncing the Prussianization of American schools back in the 1840s. Horace Mann's[4] "Seventh Annual Report" to the Massachusetts State Board of Education in 1843 is essentially a paean to the land of Frederick the Great and a call for its schooling to be brought here. That Prussian culture loomed large in America is hardly surprising, given our early association with that utopian state. A Prussian served as Washington's aide during the Revolutionary War, and so many German-speaking people had settled here by 1795 that Congress considered publishing a German-language edition of the federal laws. But what shocks is that we should so eagerly have adopted one of the very worst aspects of Prussian culture: an educational system deliberately designed to produce mediocre intellects, to hamstring the inner life, to deny students appreciable leadership skills, and to ensure docile and incomplete citizens—all in order to render the populace "manageable."

It was from James Bryant Conant—president of Harvard for twenty years, WWI poison-gas specialist, WWII executive on the atomic-bomb project, high commissioner of the American zone in Germany after WWII, and truly one of the most influential figures of the twentieth century—that I first got wind of the real purposes of American schooling. Without Conant, we would probably not have the same style and degree of standardized testing that we enjoy today, nor would we be blessed with gargantuan high schools that warehouse 2,000 to 4,000 students at a time, like the famous Columbine High in Littleton, Colorado. Shortly after I retired from teaching I picked up Conant's 1959 book-length essay, *The Child, the Parent and the State*, and was more than a little intrigued to see him mention in passing that the modern schools we attend were the result of a "revolution" engineered between 1905 and 1930. A revolution? He declines to elaborate, but he does direct the curious and the uninformed to Alexander Inglis's 1918 book, *Principles of Secondary Education*, in which "one saw this revolution through the eyes of a revolutionary."

10

---

[3]*William James:* (1842–1910) One of America's most important psychologists and philosophers. Trained as a medical doctor, he wrote important books on psychology, and particularly on education and religious experience, as well as on the philosophy of pragmatism. The brother of novelist Henry James and of diarist Alice James. — EDS.

[4]*Horace Mann:* (1796–1859) A celebrated American education reformer and also a member of the U.S. House of Representatives (Massachusetts) from 1848 to 1853. — EDS.

Inglis, for whom a lecture in education at Harvard is named, makes it perfectly clear that compulsory schooling on this continent was intended to be just what it had been for Prussia in the 1820s: a fifth column into the burgeoning democratic movement that threatened to give the peasants and the proletarians a voice at the bargaining table. Modern, industrialized, compulsory schooling was to make a sort of surgical incision into the prospective unity of these underclasses. Divide children by subject, by age-grading, by constant rankings on tests, and by many other more subtle means, and it was unlikely that the ignorant mass of mankind, separated in childhood, would ever re-integrate into a dangerous whole.

Inglis breaks down the purpose — the *actual* purpose — of modern schooling into six basic functions, any one of which is enough to curl the hair of those innocent enough to believe the three traditional goals listed earlier:

1. The *adjustive* or *adaptive* function. Schools are to establish fixed habits of reaction to authority. This, of course, precludes critical judgment completely. It also pretty much destroys the idea that useful or interesting material should be taught, because you can't test for *reflexive* obedience until you know whether you can make kids learn, and do, foolish and boring things.

2. The *integrating* function. This might well be called "the conformity function," because its intention is to make children as alike as possible. People who conform are predictable, and this is of great use to those who wish to harness and manipulate a large labor force.

3. The *diagnostic and directive* function. School is meant to determine each student's proper social role. This is done by logging evidence mathematically and anecdotally on cumulative records. As in "your permanent record." Yes, you do have one.

4. The *differentiating* function. Once their social role has been "diagnosed," children are to be sorted by role and trained only so far as their destination in the social machine merits — and not one step further. So much for making kids their personal best.

5. The *selective* function. This refers not to human choice at all but to Darwin's theory of natural selection as applied to what he called "the favored races." In short, the idea is to help things along by consciously attempting to improve the breeding stock. Schools are meant to tag the unfit — with poor grades, remedial placement, and other punishments — clearly enough that their peers will accept them as inferior and effectively bar them from the reproductive sweepstakes. That's what all those little humiliations from first grade onward were intended to do: wash the dirt down the drain.

6. The *propaedeutic* function. The societal system implied by these rules will require an elite group of caretakers. To that end, a small

fraction of the kids will quietly be taught how to manage this continuing project, how to watch over and control a population deliberately dumbed down and declawed in order that government might proceed unchallenged and corporations might never want for obedient labor.

That, unfortunately, is the purpose of mandatory public education in this country. And lest you take Inglis for an isolated crank with a rather too cynical take on the educational enterprise, you should know that he was hardly alone in championing these ideas. Conant himself, building on the ideas of Horace Mann and others, campaigned tirelessly for an American school system designed along the same lines. Men like George Peabody, who funded the cause of mandatory schooling throughout the South, surely understood that the Prussian system was useful in creating not only a harmless electorate and a servile labor force but also a virtual herd of mindless consumers. In time a great number of industrial titans came to recognize the enormous profits to be had by cultivating and tending just such a herd via public education, among them Andrew Carnegie and John D. Rockefeller.

There you have it. Now you know. We don't need Karl Marx's[5] conception of a grand warfare between the classes to see that it is in the interest of complex management, economic or political, to dumb people down, to demoralize them, to divide them from one another, and to discard them if they don't conform. Class may frame the proposition, as when Woodrow Wilson, then president of Princeton University, said the following to the New York City School Teachers Association in 1909: "We want one class of persons to have a liberal education, and we want another class of persons, a very much larger class, of necessity, in every society, to forgo the privileges of a liberal education and fit themselves to perform specific difficult manual tasks." But the motives behind the disgusting decisions that bring about these ends need not be class-based at all. They can stem purely from fear, or from the by now familiar belief that "efficiency" is the paramount virtue, rather than love, liberty, laughter, or hope. Above all, they can stem from simple greed.

There were vast fortunes to be made, after all, in an economy based on mass production and organized to favor the large corporation rather than the small business or the family farm. But mass production required mass consumption, and at the turn of the twentieth century most Americans considered it both unnatural and unwise to buy things they didn't actually need. Mandatory schooling was a godsend on that count. School didn't have to train kids in any direct sense to think they should consume nonstop, because it did something even better: it encouraged them not to

15

---

[5]*Karl Marx:* (1818–1883) Often identified as the father of communism, Marx was a philosopher, political economist, sociologist, political theorist, and revolutionary. — EDS.

think at all. And that left them sitting ducks for another great invention of the modern era — marketing.

Now, you needn't have studied marketing to know that there are two groups of people who can always be convinced to consume more than they need to: addicts and children. School has done a pretty good job of turning our children into addicts, but it has done a spectacular job of turning our children into children. Again, this is no accident. Theorists from Plato to Rousseau to our own Dr. Inglis knew that if children could be cloistered with other children, stripped of responsibility and independence, encouraged to develop only the trivializing emotions of greed, envy, jealousy, and fear, they would grow older but never truly grow up. In the 1934 edition of his once well-known book *Public Education in the United States*, Ellwood P. Cubberley detailed and praised the way the strategy of successive school enlargements had extended childhood by two to six years, and forced schooling was at that point still quite new. This same Cubberley — who was dean of Stanford's School of Education, a textbook editor at Houghton Mifflin, and Conant's friend and correspondent at Harvard — had written the following in the 1922 edition of his book *Public School Administration*: "Our schools are . . . factories in which the raw products (children) are to be shaped and fashioned. . . . And it is the business of the school to build its pupils according to the specifications laid down."

It's perfectly obvious from our society today what those specifications were. Maturity has by now been banished from nearly every aspect of our lives. Easy divorce laws have removed the need to work at relationships; easy credit has removed the need for fiscal self-control; easy entertainment has removed the need to learn to entertain oneself; easy answers have removed the need to ask questions. We have become a nation of children, happy to surrender our judgments and our wills to political exhortations and commercial blandishments that would insult actual adults. We buy televisions, and then we buy the things we see on the television. We buy computers, and then we buy the things we see on the computer. We buy $150 sneakers whether we need them or not, and when they fall apart too soon we buy another pair. We drive SUVs and believe the lie that they constitute a kind of life insurance, even when we're upside-down in them. And, worst of all, we don't bat an eye when Ari Fleischer[6] tells us to "be careful what you say," even if we remember having been told somewhere back in school that America is the land of the free. We simply buy that one too. Our schooling, as intended, has seen to it.

Now for the good news. Once you understand the logic behind modern schooling, its tricks and traps are fairly easy to avoid. School trains children to be employees and consumers; teach your own to be leaders

---

[6]*Ari Fleischer:* White House Press Secretary under President George W. Bush from 2001 to 2003. — Eds.

and adventurers. School trains children to obey reflexively; teach your own to think critically and independently. Well-schooled kids have a low threshold for boredom; help your own to develop an inner life so that they'll never be bored. Urge them to take on the serious material, the *grown-up* material, in history, literature, philosophy, music, art, economics, theology—all the stuff schoolteachers know well enough to avoid. Challenge your kids with plenty of solitude so that they can learn to enjoy their own company, to conduct inner dialogues. Well-schooled people are conditioned to dread being alone, and they seek constant companionship through the TV, the computer, the cell phone, and through shallow friendships quickly acquired and quickly abandoned. Your children should have a more meaningful life, and they can.

First, though, we must wake up to what our schools really are: laboratories of experimentation on young minds, drill centers for the habits and attitudes that corporate society demands. Mandatory education serves children only incidentally; its real purpose is to turn them into servants. Don't let your own have their childhoods extended, not even for a day. If David Farragut could take command of a captured British warship as a preteen, if Thomas Edison could publish a broadsheet at the age of twelve, if Ben Franklin could apprentice himself to a printer at the same age (then put himself through a course of study that would choke a Yale senior today), there's no telling what your own kids could do. After a long life, and thirty years in the public school trenches, I've concluded that genius is as common as dirt. We suppress our genius only because we haven't yet figured out how to manage a population of educated men and women. The solution, I think, is simple and glorious. Let them manage themselves.

The Reader's Presence

1. Would you agree with Gatto that compulsory schooling has the effect of creating conformity and obedience to authority? Why or why not? To what extent does schooling attempt to form citizens? To what extent are students trained to be consumers?

2. Gatto makes a distinction between "education" and "schooling." What is significant about this distinction? What are the consequences of conflating the two?

3. Gatto argues that compulsory schooling can effectively prevent students from becoming independent thinkers. Read Joseph Epstein's "The Perpetual Adolescent" (page 366). Do you think Epstein would agree that schooling is at least partly responsible for resistance to adulthood? Do you agree? Why or why not?

William Gibson

The Net Is a Waste of Time

William Gibson was born in 1948 in Conway, South Carolina, and now lives with his wife and children in Vancouver, British Columbia. Since Gibson coined the term cyberspace *and used it in his 1984* Neuromancer—*a debut novel that won all three major science fiction awards (the Hugo, Nebula, and Philip K. Dick awards)—he has been the foremost practitioner of the "cyberpunk" genre. His recent, post–9/11 sci-fi thrillers are* Pattern Recognition *(2003) and* Spook Country *(2007). He has also written a screenplay,* Johnny Mnemonic *(1995), and an episode of the television show* The X-Files. *Gibson is known for writing slowly and for being somewhat reclusive. Although he believes "most social change is technology-driven," until recently he did not have an e-mail address. (Today, he has his own "procrastinator's dream" of a Web site and blog: williamgibsonbooks.com.)*

The essay "The Net Is a Waste of Time" first appeared in the New York Times Magazine *in 1996.*

I coined the word "cyberspace" in 1981 in one of my first science fiction stories and subsequently used it to describe something that people insist on seeing as a sort of literary forerunner of the Internet. This being so, some think it remarkable that I do not use E-mail. In all truth, I have avoided it because I am lazy and enjoy staring blankly into space (which is also the space where novels come from) and because unanswered mail, e- or otherwise, is a source of discomfort.

But I have recently become an avid browser of the World Wide Web. Some people find this odd. My wife finds it positively perverse. I, however, scent big changes afoot, possibilities that were never quite as manifest in earlier incarnations of the Net.

I was born in 1948. I can't recall a world before television, but I know I must have experienced one. I do, dimly, recall the arrival of a piece of brown wooden furniture with sturdy Bakelite knobs and a screen no larger than the screen on this Powerbook.

Initially there was nothing on it but "snow," and then the nightly advent of a targetlike device called "the test pattern," which people actually gathered to watch.

Today I think about the test pattern as I surf the Web. I imagine that the World Wide Web and its modest wonders are no more than the test pattern for whatever the twenty-first century will regard as its equivalent medium. Not that I can even remotely imagine what that medium might actually be. 5

In the age of wooden television in the South where I grew up, leisure involved sitting on screened porches, smoking cigarettes, drinking iced tea, engaging in conversation and staring into space. It might also involve fishing.

Sometimes the Web does remind me of fishing. It never reminds me of conversation, although it can feel a lot like staring into space. "Surfing the Web" (as dubious a metaphor as "the information highway") is, as a friend of mine has it, "like reading magazines with the pages stuck together." My wife shakes her head in dismay as I patiently await the downloading of some Japanese Beatles fan's personal catalogue of bootlegs. "But it's from Japan!" She isn't moved. She goes out to enjoy the flowers in her garden.

I stay in. Hooked. Is this leisure — this browsing, randomly linking my way through these small patches of virtual real-estate — or do I somehow imagine that I am performing some more dynamic function? The content of the Web aspires to absolute variety. One might find anything there. It is like rummaging in the forefront of the collective global mind. Somewhere, surely, there is a site that contains . . . everything we have lost?

The finest and most secret pleasure afforded new users of the Web rests in submitting to the search engine of Alta Vista the names of people we may not have spoken aloud in years. Will she be here? Has he survived unto this age? (She isn't there. Someone with his name has recently posted to a news group concerned with gossip about soap stars.) What is this casting of the nets of identity? Do we engage here in something of a tragic seriousness?

In the age of wooden television, media were there to entertain, to sell   10 an advertiser's product, perhaps to inform. Watching television, then, could indeed be considered a leisure activity. In our hypermediated age, we have come to suspect that watching television constitutes a species of work. Post-industrial creatures of an information economy, we increasingly sense that accessing media is what we do. We have become terminally self-conscious. There is no such thing as simple entertainment. We watch ourselves watching. We watch ourselves watching Beavis and Butthead, who are watching rock videos. Simply to watch, without the buffer of irony in place, might reveal a fatal naïveté.

But that is our response to aging media like film and television, survivors from the age of wood. The Web is new, and our response to it has not yet hardened. That is a large part of its appeal. It is something half-formed, growing. Larval. It is not what it was six months ago; in another six months it will be something else again. It was not planned; it simply happened, is happening. It is happening the way cities happened. It *is* a city.

Toward the end of the age of wooden televisions the futurists of the Sunday supplements announced the advent of the "leisure society." Technology would leave us less and less to do in the Marxian sense of yanking the levers of production. The challenge, then, would be to fill our days with meaningful, healthful, satisfying activity. As with most products of an earlier era's futurism, we find it difficult today to imagine the exact coordinates from which this vision came. In any case, our world does not offer us a surplus of leisure. The word itself has grown somehow suspect, as quaint and vaguely melancholy as the battered leather valise in a Ralph Lauren window display. Only the very old or the economically disadvantaged (provided they are not chained to the schedules of their environment's more demanding addictions) have a great deal of time on their hands. To be successful, apparently, is to be chronically busy. As new technologies search out and lace over every interstice in the net of global communication, we find ourselves with increasingly less excuse for . . . slack.

And that, I would argue, is what the World Wide Web, the test pattern for whatever will become the dominant global medium, offers us. Today, in its clumsy, larval, curiously innocent way, it offers us the opportunity to waste time, to wander aimlessly, to daydream about the countless other lives, the other people, on the far sides of however many monitors in that postgeographical meta-country we increasingly call home. It will probably evolve into something considerably less random, and less fun—we seem to have a knack for that—but in the meantime, in its gloriously unsorted Global Ham[1] Television Postcard Universes phase, surfing the Web is a procrastinator's dream. And people who see you doing it might even imagine you're working.

The Reader's Presence

1. Of what importance is the age of television to Gibson's point about the World Wide Web? Why is television an "aging" medium? In what ways does Gibson believe the Web differs from television?

2. How does Gibson reach his conclusion that the best thing about the Web is that it "offers us the opportunity to waste time" (paragraph 13)? Why is that an advantage of this new "global medium"? Reread the essay, then explain how Gibson establishes the grounds for his conclusion.

3. Read Gibson's essay in conjunction with Marie Winn's "TV Addiction" (see page 590). Explain any similarities or differences between the way these two writers describe television. Winn was writing before the Internet had become a household reality. Does her description of television support Gibson's argument? Would you say that people are no longer addicted to television but are addicted now to the Internet? Explain your answer.

---

[1]*Global Ham:* Ham radio is amateur radio with mostly local or personal applications, its operators licensed by the government but forbidden to broadcast to the general public.—Eds.

Adam Gopnik

Shootings

Adam Gopnik was born in Philadephia, Pennsylvania, in 1956 and grew up in Montreal, Canada. After graduating from McGill University, he went to New York City to do graduate work in art history at the New York University Institute of Fine Arts. He arrived, he has said, with "a satchel full of ambitions," most of which centered on writing for the New Yorker, *a goal he realized in 1986 when he joined the magazine. In the more than twenty years since, Gopnik has served as reporter, journalist, essayist, and art critic, writing fiction and humor pieces, book reviews, profiles, and hundreds of articles for the magazine. As Paris correspondent, he moved to Paris in 1995 and began writing the magazine's "Paris Journal" column. These personal essays about his five years in Paris, which included the birth of his son among other adventures, were collected in his bestselling book* Paris to the Moon *(2000). Gopnik's post-Paris life after his return to New York with his family is described in his book of essays,* Through the Children's Gate: A Home in New York *(2006). Gopnik is also the author of a novel,* The King in the Window *(2005) and the editor of the anthology* Americans in Paris *(2004). He is a three-time winner of National Magazine Awards for Essays and for Criticism, and winner of the George Polk Award for Magazine Reporting.*

In a 2001 interview with Identity/Theory, *Gopnik talked about his favorite writing form, the personal comic essay: "It's a treacherous form because the line between entertainment and egomania is particularly fine and difficult. Essayists generally—and certainly me particularly—tend to be more like performers than novelists. . . . You have to have a bit of the ham in you. You like to do the thing and feel that the people are reacting."*

The cell phones in the pockets of the dead students were still ringing when we were told that it was wrong to ask why. As the police cleared the bodies from the Virginia Tech engineering building, the cell phones rang, in the eccentric varieties of ring tones, as parents kept trying to see if their children were O.K. To imagine the feelings of the police as they carried the bodies and heard the ringing is heartrending; to imagine the feelings of the parents who were calling—dread, desperate hope for a sudden answer and the bliss of reassurance, dawning grief—is unbearable. But the parents, and the rest of us, were told that it was not the right moment to ask how the shooting had happened—specifically, why an obviously disturbed student, with a history of mental illness, was able to buy guns whose essential purpose is to kill people—and why it happens over and over again in America. At a press conference, Virginia's governor, Tim Kaine, said, "People who want to . . . make it their political hobby horse to ride, I've got nothing but loathing for them. . . . At this point, what it's about is comforting family members . . . and helping this community heal. And so to those who want to try to make this into some little crusade, I say take that elsewhere."

If the facts weren't so horrible, there might be something touching in the Governor's deeply American belief that "healing" can take place magically, without the intervening practice called "treating." The logic is unusual but striking: the aftermath of a terrorist attack is the wrong time to talk about security, the aftermath of a death from lung cancer is the wrong time to talk about smoking and the tobacco industry, and the aftermath of a car crash is the wrong time to talk about seat belts. People talked about the shooting, of course, but much of the conversation was devoted to musings on the treatment of mental illness in universities, the problem of "narcissism," violence in the media and in popular culture, copycat killings, the alienation of immigrant students, and the question of Evil.

Some people, however—especially people outside America—were eager to talk about it in another way, and even to embark on a little crusade. The whole world saw that the United States has more gun violence than other countries because we have more guns and are willing to sell them to madmen who want to kill people. Every nation has violent loners, and they tend to have remarkably similar profiles from one country and culture to the next. And every country has known the horror of having a lunatic get his hands on a gun and kill innocent people. But on a recent list of the fourteen worst mass shootings in Western democracies since the nineteen-sixties the United States claimed seven, and, just as important, no other country on the list has had a repeat performance as severe as the first.

In Dunblane, Scotland, in 1996, a gunman killed sixteen children and a teacher at their school. Afterward, the British gun laws, already restrictive, were tightened—it's now against the law for any private citizen in the United Kingdom to own the kinds of guns that Cho Seung-Hui used at Virginia Tech—and nothing like Dunblane has occurred there since. In Quebec, after a school shooting took the lives of fourteen women in 1989, the survivors helped begin a gun-control movement that resulted in legislation bringing stronger, though far from sufficient, gun laws to Canada. (There have been a couple of subsequent shooting sprees, but on a smaller scale, and with far fewer dead.) In the Paris suburb of Nanterre, in 2002, a man killed eight people at a municipal meeting. Gun control became a key issue in the Presidential election that year, and there has been no repeat incident.

So there is no American particularity about loners, disenfranchised immigrants, narcissism, alienated youth, complex moral agency, or Evil. There is an American particularity about guns. The arc is apparent. Forty years ago, a man killed fourteen people on a college campus in Austin, Texas; this year, a man killed thirty-two in Blacksburg, Virginia. Not enough was done between those two massacres to make weapons of mass killing harder to obtain. In fact, while campus killings continued—Columbine being the most notorious, the shooting in the one-room Amish schoolhouse among the most recent—weapons have gotten more lethal, and, in states like Virginia, where the NRA [National Rifle Association] is powerful, no harder to buy.

Reducing the number of guns available to crazy people will neither relieve them of their insanity nor stop them from killing. Making it more difficult to buy guns that kill people is, however, a rational way to reduce the number of people killed by guns. Nations with tight gun laws have, on the whole, less gun violence; countries with somewhat restrictive gun laws have some gun violence; countries with essentially no gun laws have a lot of gun violence. (If you work hard, you can find a statistical exception hiding in a corner, but exceptions are just that. Some people who smoke their whole lives don't get lung cancer, while some people who never smoke do; still, the best way not to get lung cancer is not to smoke.)

It's true that in renewing the expired ban on assault weapons we can't guarantee that someone won't shoot people with a semi-automatic pistol, and that by controlling semi-automatic pistols we can't reduce the chances of someone killing people with a rifle. But the point of lawmaking is not to act as precisely as possible, in order to punish the latest crime; it is to act as comprehensively as possible, in order to prevent the next one. Semi-automatic Glocks and Walthers, Cho's weapons, are for killing people. They are not made for hunting, and it's not easy to protect yourself with them. (If having a loaded semi-automatic on hand kept you safe, cops would not be shot as often as they are.)

Rural America is hunting country, and hunters need rifles and shotguns—with proper licensing, we'll live with risk. There is no reason that any private citizen in a democracy should own a handgun. At some point, that simple truth will register. Until it does, phones will ring for dead children, and parents will be told not to ask why.

The Reader's Presence

1. Note the way Gopnik opens his essay. Why do you think he decided to start with the ringing cell phones on the dead students? Why didn't he begin with the act of shooting? What effect does he achieve with the ring tones? How would you describe its effect on you as a reader?

2. In constructing effective arguments, writers often concede points to an opponent to demonstrate their reasonableness. How does Gopnik achieve this? Does he take an absolute position against gun control? Point to several passages in which he entertains arguments that might be made by those who oppose gun control. How does he respond to those arguments? Do you find his responses persuasive? Why or why not?

3. Although Gopnik brings up the National Rifle Association (NRA), he doesn't introduce issues revolving around the Second Amendment directly. How do you think Gopnik would respond to constitutional scholar Akhil Reed Amar's opinions in "Second Thoughts: What the Right to Bear Arms Really Means" (page 293)? Explain the extent to which Gopnik could cite Amar's essay in support of his own beliefs in "Shootings."

Vicki Hearne

What's Wrong with Animal Rights

Vicki Hearne (1946–2001) had a unique career as a poet, an author, and an animal trainer, and she taught creative writing at Yale University and at the University of California. She published three volumes of poetry, Nervous Horses *(1980),* In the Absence of Horses *(1983), and* The Parts of Light *(1994). Hearne was known for her ability to train aggressive dogs (particularly pit bull terriers), and she wrote an account of her experiences in* Bandit: Dossier of a Dangerous Dog *(1991). Her other books include* Adam's Task: Calling Animals by Name *(1987),* The White German Shepherd *(1988), and* Animal Happiness *(1994). "What's Wrong with Animal Rights" was originally published in* Harper's *in 1991 and was selected for* The Best American Essays 1992.

Not all happy animals are alike. A Doberman going over a hurdle after a small wooden dumbbell is sleek, all arcs of harmonious power. A basset hound cheerfully performing the same exercise exhibits harmonies of a more lugubrious nature. There are chimpanzees who love precision the way musicians or fanatical housekeepers or accomplished hypochondriacs do; others for whom happiness is a matter of invention and variation—chimp vaudevillians. There is a rhinoceros whose happiness, as near as I can make out, is in needing to be trained every morning, all over again, or else he "forgets" his circus routine, and in this you find a clue to the slow, deep, quiet chuckle of his happiness and to the glory of the beast. Happiness for Secretariat[1] is in his ebullient bound, that joyful length of stride.

---

[1]*Secretariat:* (1970–1989) A celebrated American thoroughbred racehorse and winner of the 1973 Triple Crown (the Kentucky Derby, the Preakness, and the Belmont Stakes). —EDS.

For the draft horse or the weight-pull dog, happiness is of a different shape, more awesome and less obviously intelligent. When the pulling horse is at its most intense, the animal goes into himself, allocating all of the educated power that organizes his desire to dwell in fierce and delicate intimacy with that power, leans into the harness, and MAKES THAT SUCKER MOVE.

If we are speaking of human beings and use the phrase "animal happiness," we tend to mean something like "creature comforts." The emblems of this are the golden retriever rolling in the grass, the horse with his nose deep in the oats, the kitty by the fire. Creature comforts are important to animals — "Grub first, then ethics" is a motto that would describe many a wise Labrador retriever, and I have a pit bull named Annie whose continual quest for the perfect pillow inspires her to awesome feats. But there is something more to animals, a capacity for satisfactions that come from work in the fullest sense — what is known in philosophy and in this country's Declaration of Independence as "happiness." This is a sense of personal achievement, like the satisfaction felt by a good wood-carver or a dancer or a poet or an accomplished dressage horse. It is a happiness that, like the artist's must come from something within the animal, something trainers call "talent." Hence, it cannot be imposed on the animal. But it is also something that does not come *ex nihilo*. If it had not been a fairly ordinary thing, in one part of the world, to teach young children to play the pianoforte, it is doubtful that Mozart's music would exist.

Happiness is often misunderstood as a synonym for pleasure or as an antonym for suffering. But Aristotle associated happiness with ethics — codes of behavior that urge us toward the sensation of getting it right, a kind of work that yields the "click" of satisfaction upon solving a problem or surmounting an obstacle. In his *Ethics*, Aristotle wrote, "If happiness is activity in accordance with excellence, it is reasonable that it should be in accordance with the highest excellence." Thomas Jefferson identified the capacity for happiness as one of the three fundamental rights on which all others are based: "life, liberty, and the pursuit of happiness."

I bring up this idea of happiness as a form of work because I am an animal trainer, and work is the foundation of the happiness a trainer and an animal discover together. I bring up these words also because they cannot be found in the lexicon of the animal-rights movement. This absence accounts for the uneasiness toward the movement of most people, who sense that rights advocates have a point but take it too far when they liberate snails or charge that goldfish at the county fair are suffering. But the problem with the animal-rights advocates is not that they take it too far; it's that they've got it all wrong.

Animal rights are built upon a misconceived premise that rights were created to prevent us from unnecessary suffering. You can't find an animal-rights book, video, pamphlet, or rock concert in which someone doesn't mention the Great Sentence, written by Jeremy Bentham in 1789. Arguing

5

in favor of such rights, Bentham wrote: "The question is not, Can they *reason*? nor, can they *talk*? but, can they *suffer*?"

The logic of the animal-rights movement places suffering at the icono-graphic center of a skewed value system. The thinking of its proponents—given eerie expression in a virtually sado-pornographic sculpture of a tortured monkey that won a prize for its compassionate vision—has collapsed into a perverse conundrum. Today the loudest voices calling for—demanding—the destruction of animals are the humane organiza-tions. This is an inevitable consequence of the apotheosis of the drive to relieve suffering: death is the ultimate release. To compensate for their contradictions, the humane movement has demonized, in this century and the last, those who made animal happiness their business: veterinarians, trainers, and the like. We think of Louis Pasteur as the man whose work saved you and me and your dog and cat from rabies, but antivivisection-ists of the time claimed that rabies increased in areas where there were Pasteur Institutes.

An anti-rabies public relations campaign mounted in England in the 1880s by the Royal Society for the Prevention of Cruelty to Animals and other organizations led to orders being issued to club any dog found not wearing a muzzle. England still has her cruel and unnecessary law that re-quires an animal to spend six months in quarantine before being allowed loose in the country. Most of the recent propaganda about pit bulls—the crazy claim that they "take hold with their front teeth while they chew away with their rear teeth" (which would imply, incorrectly, that they have double jaws)—can be traced to literature published by the Humane Society of the United States during the fall of 1987 and earlier. If your neighbors want your dog or horse impounded and destroyed because he is a nuisance—say the dog barks, or the horse attracts flies—it will be the local Humane Society to whom your neighbors turn for action.

In a way, everyone has the opportunity to know that the history of the humane movement is largely a history of miseries, arrests, prosecutions, and death. The Humane Society is the pound, the place with the decom-pression chamber or the lethal injections. You occasionally find worried letters about this in Ann Landers's column.

Animal-rights publications are illustrated largely with photographs of two kinds of animals—"Helpless Fluff" and "Agonized Fluff," the two conditions in which some people seem to prefer their animals, because any other version of an animal is too complicated for propaganda. In the intro-duction to his book *Animal Liberation*, Peter Singer[2] says somewhat smugly that he and his wife have no animals and, in fact, don't much care for them. This is offered as evidence of his objectivity and ethical probity. But it strikes me as an odd, perhaps, obscene underpinning for an ethical

[2]For more on Peter Singer, see page 849.—EDS.

project that encourages university and high school students to cherish their ignorance of, say, great bird dogs as proof of their devotion to animals.

I would like to leave these philosophers behind, for they are inept   10
connoisseurs of suffering who might revere my Airedale for his capacity to scream when subjected to a blowtorch but not for his wit and courage, not for his natural good manners that are a gentle rebuke to ours. I want to celebrate the moment not long ago when, at his first dog show, my Airedale, Drummer, learned that there can be a public place where his work is respected. I want to celebrate his meticulousness, his happiness upon realizing at the dog show that no one would swoop down upon him and swamp him with the goo-goo excesses known as the "teddy-bear complex" but that people actually got out of his way, gave him room to work. I want to say, "There can be a six-and-a-half-month-old puppy who can care about accuracy, who can be fastidious, and whose fastidiousness will be a foundation for courage later." I want to say, "Leave my puppy alone!"

I want to leave the philosophers behind, but I cannot, in part because the philosophical problems that plague academicians of the animal-rights movement are illuminating. They wonder, do animals have rights or do they have interests? Or, if these rightists lead particularly unexamined lives, they dismiss that question as obvious (yes, of course animals have rights, prima facie) and proceed to enumerate them, James Madison style. This leads to the issuance of bills of rights—the right to an environment, the right not to be used in medical experiments—and other forms of trivialization.

The calculus of suffering can be turned against the philosophers of festering flesh, even in the case of food animals, or exotic animals who perform in movies and circuses. It is true that it hurts to be slaughtered by man, but it doesn't hurt nearly as much as some of the cunningly cruel arrangements meted out by "Mother Nature." In Africa, 75 percent of the lions cubbed do not survive to the age of two. For those who make it to two, the average age at death is ten years. Asali, the movie and TV lioness, was still working at age twenty-one. There are fates worse than death, but twenty-one years of a close working relationship with Hubert Wells, Asali's trainer, is not one of them. Dorset sheep and polled Herefords would not exist at all were they not in a symbiotic relationship with human beings.

A human being living in the "wild"—somewhere, say, without the benefits of medicine and advanced social organization—would probably have a life expectancy of from thirty to thirty-five years. A human being living in "captivity"—in, say, a middle-class neighborhood of what the Centers for Disease Control [and Prevention] call a Metropolitan Statistical Area—has a life expectancy of seventy or more years. For orangutans in the wild in Borneo and Malaysia, the life expectancy is thirty-five years; in captivity, fifty years. The wild is not a suffering-free zone or all that frolicsome a location.

The questions asked by animal-rights activists are flawed, because they are built on the concept that the origin of rights is in the avoidance of suffering rather than in the pursuit of happiness. The question that needs to be asked—and that will put us in closer proximity to the truth—is not, do they have rights? or, what are those rights? but rather, what is a right?

Rights originate in committed relationships and can be found, both 15 intact and violated, wherever one finds such relationships—in social compacts, within families, between animals, and between people and nonhuman animals. This is as true when the nonhuman animals in question are lions or parakeets as when they are dogs. It is my Airedale whose excellencies have my attention at the moment, so it is with reference to him that I will consider the question, what is a right?

When I imagine situations in which it naturally arises that A defends or honors or respects B's rights, I imagine situations in which the relationship between A and B can be indicated with a possessive pronoun. I might say, "Leave her alone, she's my daughter" or "That's what she wants, and she is my daughter. I think I am bound to honor her wants." Similarly, "Leave her alone, she's my mother." I am more tender of the happiness of my mother, my father, my child, than I am of other people's family members; more tender of my friends' happinesses than your friends' happinesses, unless you and I have a mutual friend.

Possession of a being by another has come into more and more disrepute, so that the common understanding of one person possessing another is slavery. But the important detail about the kind of possessive pronoun that I have in mind is reciprocity: if I have a friend, she has a friend. If I have a daughter, she has a mother. The possessive does not bind one of us while freeing the other; it cannot do that. Moreover, should the mother reject the daughter, the word that applies is "disown." The form of disowning that most often appears in the news is domestic violence. Parents abuse children; husbands batter wives.

Some cases of reciprocal possessives have built-in limitations, such as "my patient / my doctor" or "my student / my teacher" or "my agent / my client." Other possessive relations are extremely limited but still remarkably binding: "my neighbor" and "my country" and "my president."

The responsibilities and the ties signaled by reciprocal possession typically are hard to dissolve. It can be as difficult to give up an enemy as to give up a friend, and often the one becomes the other, as though the logic of the possessive pronoun outlasts the forms it chanced to take at a given moment, as though we were stuck with one another. In these bindings, nearly inextricable, are found the origin of our rights. They imply a possessiveness but also recognize an acknowledgment by each side of the other's existence.

The idea of democracy is dependent on the citizens' having knowl- 20 edge of the government; that is, realizing that the government exists and knowing how to claim rights against it. I know this much because I get mail from the government and see its "representatives" running about in uniforms. Whether I actually have any rights in relationship to the government is less clear, but the idea that I do is symbolized by the right to vote. I obey the government, and, in theory, it obeys me, by counting my ballot, reading the *Miranda* warning to me, agreeing to be bound by the Constitution. My friend obeys me as I obey her; the government "obeys" me to some extent, and, to a different extent, I obey it.

What kind of thing can my Airedale, Drummer, have knowledge of? He can know that I exist and through that knowledge can claim his happinesses, with varying degrees of success, both with me and against me. Drummer can also know about larger human or dog communities than the one that consists only of him and me. There is my household—the other dogs, the cats, my husband. I have had enough dogs on campuses to know that he can learn that Yale exists as a neighborhood or village. My older dog, Annie, not only knows that Yale exists but can tell Yalies from townies, as I learned while teaching there during labor troubles.

Dogs can have elaborate conceptions of human social structures, and even of something like their rights and responsibilities within them, but these conceptions are never elaborate enough to construct a rights relationship between a dog and the state, or a dog and the Humane Society. Both of these are concepts that depend on writing and memoranda, officers in uniform, plaques and seals of authority. All of these are literary constructs, and all of them are beyond a dog's ken, which is why the mail carrier who doesn't also happen to be a dog's friend is forever an intruder—this is why dogs bark at mailmen.

It is clear enough that natural rights relations can arise between people and animals. Drummer, for example, can insist, "Hey, let's go outside and do something!" if I have been at my computer several days on end. He can both refuse to accept various of my suggestions and tell me when he fears for his life—such as the time when the huge, white flapping flag appeared out of nowhere, as it seemed to him, on the town green one evening when we were working. I can (and do) say to him either, "Oh, you don't have to worry about that" or, "Uh oh, you're right, Drum, that guy looks dangerous." Just as the government and I—two different species of organism— have developed improvised ways of communicating, such as the vote, so Drummer and I have worked out a number of ways to make our expressions known. Largely through obedience, I have taught him a fair amount about how to get responses from me. Obedience is reciprocal; you cannot get responses from a dog to whom you do not respond accurately. I have enfranchised him in a relationship to me by educating him, creating the conditions by which he can achieve a certain happiness specific to a dog, maybe even specific to an Airedale, inasmuch as this same relationship has allowed me to plumb the happiness of being a trainer and writing this article.

Instructions in this happiness are given terms that are alien to a culture in which liver treats, fluffy windup toys, and miniature sweaters are confused with respect and work. Jack Knox, a sheepdog trainer originally from Scotland, will shake his crook at a novice handler who makes a promiscuous move to praise a dog, and will call out in his Scottish accent, "Eh! Eh! Get back, get BACK! Ye'll no be abusin' the dogs like that in my clinic." America is a nation of abused animals. Knox says, because we are always swooping at them with praise, "no gi'ing them their freedom." I am reminded of Rainer Maria Rilke's[3] account in which the Prodigal Son leaves — has to leave — because everyone loves him, even the dogs love him, and he has no path to the delicate and fierce truth of himself. Unconditional praise and love, in Rilke's story, disenfranchise us, distract us from what truly excites our interest.

In the minds of some trainers and handlers, praise is dishonesty.   25 Paradoxically, it is a kind of contempt for animals that masquerades as a reverence for helplessness and suffering. The idea of freedom means that you do not, at least not while Jack Knox is nearby, helpfully guide your dog through the motions of, say, herding over and over — what one trainer calls "explainy-wainy." This is rote learning. It works tolerably well on some handlers, because people have vast unconscious minds and can store complex preprogrammed behaviors. Dogs, on the other hand, have almost no unconscious minds, so they can learn only by thinking. Many children are like this until educated out of it.

If I tell my Airedale to sit and stay on the town green, and someone comes up and burbles, "What a pretty thing you are," he may break his stay to go for a caress. I pull him back and correct him for breaking. Now he holds his stay because I have blocked his way to movement but not because I have punished him. (A correction blocks one path as it opens another for desire to work; punishment blocks desire and opens nothing.) He holds his stay now, and — because the stay opens this possibility of work, new to a heedless young dog — he watches. If the person goes on talking, and isn't going to gush with praise, I may heel Drummer out of his stay and give him an "Okay" to make friends. Sometimes something about the person makes Drummer feel that reserve is in order. He responds to an insincere approach by sitting still, going down into himself, and thinking, "This person has no business pawing me. I'll sit very still, and he will go away." If the person doesn't take the hint from Drummer, I'll give the pup a little backup by saying, "Please don't pet him, he's working," even though he was not under any command.

The pup reads this, and there is a flicker of a working trust now stirring in the dog. Is the pup grateful? When the stranger leaves, does he lick my hand, full of submissive blandishments? This one doesn't. This one says nothing at all, and I say nothing much to him. This is a working trust we are developing, not a mutual congratulation society. My backup is praise enough for him; the use he makes of my support is praise enough for me.

Listening to a dog is often praise enough. Suppose it is just after dark and we are outside. Suddenly there is a shout from the house. The pup and I both

---

[3]*Rilke:* (1875–1926) Widely acclaimed as one of the German language's most important poets. — EDS.

look toward the shout and then toward each other: "What do you think?" I don't so much as cock my head, because Drummer is growing up, and I want to know what he thinks. He takes a few steps toward the house, and I follow. He listens again and comprehends that it's just Holly, who at fourteen is much given to alarming cries and shouts. He shrugs at me and goes about his business. I say nothing. To praise him for this performance would make about as much sense as praising a human being for the same thing. Thus:

A. What's that?

B. I don't know. [Listens] Oh, it's just Holly.

A. What a goooooood human being!

B. Huh?

This is one small moment in a series of like moments that will culminate in an Airedale who on a Friday will have the discrimination and confidence required to take down a man who is attacking me with a knife and on Saturday clown and play with the children at the annual Orange Empire Dog Club Christmas party.

People who claim to speak for animal rights are increasingly devoted   30
to the idea that the very keeping of a dog or a horse or a gerbil or a lion is in and of itself an offense. The more loudly they speak, the less likely they are to be in a rights relation to any given animal, because they are spending so much time in airplanes or transmitting fax announcements of the latest Sylvester Stallone anti-fur rally. In a 1988 *Harper's* forum, for example, Ingrid Newkirk, the national director of People for the Ethical Treatment of Animals [PETA], urged that domestic pets be spayed and neutered and ultimately phased out. She prefers, it appears, wolves—and wolves someplace else—to Airedales and, by a logic whose interior structure is both emotionally and intellectually forever closed to Drummer, claims thereby to be speaking for "animal rights."

She is wrong. I am the only one who can own up to my Airedale's inalienable rights. Whether or not I do it perfectly at any given moment is no more refutation of this point than whether I am perfectly my husband's mate at any given moment refutes the fact of marriage. Only people who know Drummer, and whom he can know, are capable of this relationship. PETA and the Humane Society and the ASPCA[4] and the Congress and NOW[5]—as institutions—do have the power to affect my ability to grant rights to Drummer but are otherwise incapable of creating conditions or laws or rights that would increase his happiness. Only Drummer's owner has the power to obey him—to obey who he is and what he is capable of—deeply enough to grant him his rights and open up the possibility of happiness.

---

[4]*ASPCA:* American Society for the Prevention of Cruelty to Animals.—EDS.
[5]*NOW:* National Organization for Women.—EDS.

The Reader's Presence

1. Hearne writes from an "expert" perspective as an animal trainer. Suppose she were not an expert. How would that change your reading of her argument?

2. Hearne takes issue both with the common definition of "animal," protesting that not all animals are alike, and with the common notion of "happiness" as comfort (paragraphs 1 and 2). How do questions of these definitions form the basis of her argument? Is it possible to disagree with Hearne's definitions and still support her overall argument, or vice-versa? Why or why not?

3. Throughout her essay, Hearne attends to the political dimensions of her argument. In paragraph 20, for example, she introduces "the idea of democracy" and in the final paragraph she refers to her "Airedale's inalienable rights." Find other such examples. How does Hearne incorporate American political history into her essay? Do you find her allusion to slavery (paragraph 17) persuasive? necessary? Compare Hearne's ideas about dogs to Annie Dillard's understanding of wild animals in "Living Like Weasels" (page 660). Is Dillard's essay as philosophical as Hearne's? as political? as poetical? How does each essay address the reader? What are their respective goals?

Thomas Jefferson

The Declaration of Independence

Thomas Jefferson (1743–1826) was born and raised in Virginia and attended William and Mary College. After being admitted to the bar, he entered politics and served in the Virginia House of Burgesses and the Continental Congress of 1775. During the Revolutionary War he was elected governor of Virginia, and after independence he was appointed special minister to France and later secretary of state. As the nation's third president, he negotiated the Louisiana Purchase. Of all his accomplishments as an inventor, an architect, a diplomat, a scientist, and a politician, Jefferson counted his work in designing the University of Virginia among the most important, along with his efforts to establish separation of church and state and the composition of the Declaration of Independence.

In May and June 1776, the Continental Congress had been vigorously debating the dangerous idea of independence and felt the need to issue a document that clearly pointed out the colonial grievances against Great Britain. A committee was appointed to "prepare a declaration" that would summarize the specific reasons for colonial discontent. The committee of five included Thomas Jefferson, Benjamin Franklin, and John Adams. Jefferson, who was noted for his skills in composition and, as Adams put it, "peculiar felicity of expression," was chosen to write the first draft. The assignment took Jefferson about two weeks, and he submitted the draft first to the committee, which made a few verbal alterations, and then on June 28 to Congress, where, after further alterations mainly relating to slavery, it was finally approved on July 4, 1776.

Jefferson claims to have composed the document without research, working mainly from ideas he felt were commonly held at the time. As Jefferson recalled many years later, he drafted the document as "an appeal to the tribunal of the world" and hoped "to place before mankind the common sense of the subject, in terms so plain and firm as to command their assent." He claims that "neither aiming at originality of principle or sentiment . . . it was intended to be an expression of the American mind, and to give to that expression the proper tone and spirit called for by the occasion."

When in the Course of human events, it becomes necessary for one people to dissolve the political bands which have connected them with another, and to assume among the Powers of the earth, the separate and equal station to which the Laws of Nature and of Nature's God entitle them, a decent respect to the opinions of mankind requires that they should declare the causes which impel them to the separation.

We hold these truths to be self-evident, that all men are created equal, that they are endowed by their Creator with certain inalienable Rights, that among these are Life, Liberty and the pursuit of Happiness. That to secure these rights, Governments are instituted among Men, deriving their just powers from the consent of the governed. That whenever any Form of Government becomes destructive of these ends, it is the Right of the People to alter or to abolish it, and to institute new Government, laying its foundation on such principles and organizing its powers in such form, as to them shall seem most likely to effect their Safety and Happiness. Prudence, indeed, will dictate that Governments long established should not be changed for light and transient causes; and accordingly all experience hath shown, that mankind are more disposed to suffer, while evils are sufferable, than to right themselves by abolishing the forms to which they are accustomed. But when a long train of abuses and usurpations, pursuing invariably the same Object evinces a design to reduce them under absolute Despotism, it is their right, it is their duty, to throw off such Government, and to provide new Guards for their future security. — Such has been the patient sufferance of these Colonies; and such is now the necessity which constrains them to alter their former Systems of Government. The history of the present King of Great Britain is a history of repeated injuries and usurpations, all having in direct object the establishment of an absolute Tyranny over these States. To prove this, let Facts be submitted to a candid world.

He has refused his Assent to Laws, the most wholesome and necessary for the public good.

He has forbidden his Governors to pass Laws of immediate and pressing importance, unless suspended in their operation till his Assent should be obtained; and when so suspended, he has utterly neglected to attend to them.

He has refused to pass other laws for the accommodation of large 5 districts of people, unless those people would relinquish the right of Representation in the Legislature, a right inestimable to them and formidable to tyrants only.

He has called together legislative bodies at places unusual, uncomfortable, and distant from the depository of their Public Records, for the sole purpose of fatiguing them into compliance with his measures.

He has dissolved Representative Houses repeatedly, for opposing with manly firmness his invasions on the rights of the people.

He has refused for a long time, after such dissolutions, to cause others to be elected; whereby the Legislative Powers, incapable of Annihilation, have returned to the People at large for their exercise; the State remaining in the mean time exposed to all the dangers of invasion from without, and convulsions within.

He has endeavoured to prevent the population of these States;[1] for that purpose obstructing the Laws for Naturalization of Foreigners; refusing to pass others to encourage their migration hither, and raising the conditions of new Appropriations of Lands.

He has obstructed the Administration of Justice, by refusing his Assent to Laws for establishing Judiciary Powers.

He has made Judges dependent on his Will alone, for the tenure of their offices, and the amount and payment of their salaries.

He has erected a multitude of New Offices, and sent hither swarms of Officers to harass our People, and eat out their substance.

He has kept among us, in times of peace, Standing Armies without the Consent of our legislature.

He has affected to render the Military independent of and superior to the Civil Power.

He has combined with others to subject us to a jurisdiction foreign to 15 our constitution, and unacknowledged by our laws; giving his Assent to their acts of pretended Legislation:

For quartering large bodies of armed troops among us:

For protecting them, by a mock Trial, from Punishment for any Murders which they should commit on the Inhabitants of these States:

For cutting off our Trade with all parts of the world:

---

[1] *prevent the population of these States:* This meant limiting emigration to the Colonies, thus controlling their growth. —Eds.

For imposing taxes on us without our Consent:

For depriving us in many cases, of the benefits of Trial by Jury: 20

For transporting us beyond Seas to be tried for pretended offenses:

For abolishing the free System of English Laws in a neighboring Province, establishing therein an Arbitrary government, and enlarging its Boundaries so as to render it at once an example and fit instrument for introducing the same absolute rule into these Colonies:

For taking away our Charters, abolishing our most valuable Laws, and altering fundamentally the Forms of our Governments:

For suspending our own Legislatures, and declaring themselves invested with Power to legislate for us in all cases whatsoever.

He has abdicated Government here, by declaring us out of his Protec-   25
tion and waging War against us.

He has plundered our seas, ravaged our Coasts, burnt our towns, and destroyed the lives of our people.

He is at this time transporting large armies of foreign mercenaries to compleat the works of death, desolation and tyranny, already begun with circumstances of Cruelty & perfidy scarcely paralleled in the most barbarous ages, and totally unworthy of the Head of a civilized nation.

He has constrained our fellow Citizens taken Captive on the high Seas to bear Arms against their Country, to become the executioners of their friends and Brethren, or to fall themselves by their Hands.

He has excited domestic insurrections amongst us, and has endeavoured to bring on the inhabitants of our frontiers, the merciless Indian Savages, whose known rule of warfare, is an undistinguished destruction of all ages, sexes and conditions.

In every stage of these Oppressions We have Petitioned for Readdress   30
in the most humble terms: Our repeated Petitions have been answered only by repeated injury. A Prince, whose character is thus marked by every act which may define a Tyrant, is unfit to be the ruler of a free People.

Nor have We been wanting in attention to our British brethren. We have warned them from time to time of attempts by their legislature to extend an unwarrantable jurisdiction over us. We have reminded them of the circumstances of our emigration and settlement here. We have appealed to their native justice and magnanimity, and we have conjured them by the ties of our common kindred to disavow these usurpations, which would inevitably interrupt our connections and correspondence. They too have been deaf to the voice of justice and of consanguinity. We must, therefore, acquiesce in the necessity, which denounces our Separation, and hold them, as we hold the rest of mankind, Enemies in War, in Peace Friends.

We, therefore, the Representatives of the United States of America, in General Congress, Assembled, appealing to the Supreme Judge of the world for the rectitude of our intentions, do in the Name, and by Authority of the good People of these Colonies, solemnly publish and declare, That these United Colonies are, and of Right ought to be Free and Independent States, that they are Absolved from all Allegiance to the British Crown, and that all political connection between them and the State of Great Britain, is and ought to be totally dissolved; and that as Free and Independent States, they have full Power to levy War, conclude Peace, contract Alliances, establish Commerce, and to do all other Acts and Things which Independent States may of right do. And for the support of this Declaration, with a firm reliance on the Protection of Divine Providence, we mutually pledge to each other our Lives, our Fortunes and our sacred Honor.

The Reader's Presence

1. How does Jefferson seem to define *independence*? Whom does the definition include? Whom does it exclude? How does Jefferson's definition of independence differ from your own? It has been pointed out that Jefferson disregards "interdependence." Can you formulate an argument contrary to Jefferson's?

2. Examine the Declaration's first sentence. Who is the speaker here? What is the effect of the omniscient tone of the opening? Why does the first paragraph have no personal pronouns or references to specific events? What might Jefferson's argument stand to gain in generalizing the American situation?

3. As in classical epics and the Bible, Jefferson frequently relies on the rhetorical devices of repetition and lists. What is the effect of such devices? What else about the Declaration strikes you as representative of eighteenth-century ideas and language? Choose another essay in this collection that relies on similar strategies. What, more specifically, do these essays have in common? What sets them apart? As you respond, you might find it helpful to read Akhil Reed Amar's essay "Second Thoughts: What the Right to Bear Arms Really Means" (page 293). Amar argues that "we need to understand how all the words of the [second] amendment fit together, and how they in turn, mesh with other words in the Constitution. The amendment's syntax seems odd only because modern readers persistently misread the words 'militia' and 'people,' imposing twentieth-century assumptions on an eighteenth-century text" (paragraph 5). What about the Declaration strikes you as representative of eighteenth-century ideas and language? Do you share Amar's view about the continuing misreadings of the second amendment? Why or why not?

Michiko Kakutani

The Word Police

Michiko Kakutani (b. 1955) graduated from Yale University in 1976 and then worked as a reporter at the Washington Post *and as a staff writer for* Time. *In 1979 she joined the cultural news department of the New York Times and has been the paper's senior book critic since 1983. She received the 1998 Pulitzer Prize for her "passionate, intelligent writing on books and contemporary literature." Kakutani has also published a collection of interviews,* The Poet at the Piano *(1988). "The Word Police" appeared in the* New York Times *in January 1993.*

This month's inaugural festivities, with their celebration, in Maya Angelou's words, of "humankind" — "the Asian, the Hispanic, the Jew / The African, the Native American, the Sioux, / The Catholic, the Muslim, the French, the Greek / The Irish, the Rabbi, the Priest, the Sheik, / The Gay, the Straight, the Preacher, / The privileged, the homeless, the Teacher" — constituted a kind of official embrace of multiculturalism and a new politics of inclusion.

The mood of political correctness, however, has already made firm inroads into popular culture. Washington boasts a store called Politically Correct that sells pro-whale, anti-meat, ban-the-bomb T-shirts, bumper stickers, and buttons, as well as a local cable television show called "Politically Correct Cooking" that features interviews in the kitchen with representatives from groups like People for the Ethical Treatment of Animals.

The Coppertone suntan lotion people are planning to give their long-time cover girl, Little Miss (Ms.?) Coppertone, a male equivalent, Little Mr. Coppertone. And even Superman (Superperson?) is rumored to be returning this spring, reincarnated as four ethnically diverse clones: an African-American, an Asian, a Caucasian and a Latino.

Nowhere is this P.C. mood more striking than in the increasingly noisy debate over language that has moved from university campuses to the country at large—a development that both underscores Americans' puritanical zeal for reform and their unwavering faith in the talismanic power of words.

Certainly no decent person can quarrel with the underlying impulse behind political correctness: a vision of a more just, inclusive society in which racism, sexism, and prejudice of all sorts have been erased. But the methods and fervor of the self-appointed language police can lead to a rigid orthodoxy—and unintentional self-parody—opening the movement to the scorn of conservative opponents and the mockery of cartoonists and late-night television hosts.

5

It's hard to imagine women earning points for political correctness by saying "ovarimony" instead of "testimony"—as one participant at the recent Modern Language Association convention was overheard to suggest. It's equally hard to imagine people wanting to flaunt their lack of prejudice by giving up such words and phrases as "bull market," "kaiser roll," "Lazy Susan," and "charley horse."

Several books on bias-free language have already appeared, and the 1991 edition of the *Random House Webster's College Dictionary* boasts an appendix titled "Avoiding Sexist Language." The dictionary also includes such linguistic mutations as "womyn" (women, "used as an alternative spelling to avoid the suggestion of sexism perceived in the sequence m-e-n") and "waitron" (a gender-blind term for waiter or waitress).

Many of these dictionaries and guides not only warn the reader against offensive racial and sexual slurs, but also try to establish and enforce a whole new set of usage rules. Take, for instance, *The Bias-Free Word Finder, a Dictionary of Nondiscriminatory Language* by Rosalie Maggio (Beacon Press)—a volume often indistinguishable, in its meticulous solemnity, from the tongue-in-cheek *Official Politically Correct Dictionary and Handbook* put out last year [1992] by Henry Beard and Christopher Cerf (Villard Books). Ms. Maggio's book supplies the reader intent on using kinder, gentler language with writing guidelines as well as a detailed listing of more than 5,000 "biased words and phrases."

Whom are these guidelines for? Somehow one has a tough time picturing them replacing *Fowler's Modern English Usage* in the classroom, or being adopted by the average man (sorry, individual) in the street.

The "pseudogeneric 'he,'" we learn from Ms. Maggio, is to be avoided   10
like the plague, as is the use of the word "man" to refer to humanity. "Fellow," "king," "lord" and "master" are bad because they're "male-oriented words," and "king," "lord" and "master" are especially bad because they're also "hierarchical, dominator society terms." The politically correct lion becomes the "monarch of the jungle," new-age children play "someone on the top of the heap," and the "Mona Lisa" goes down in history as Leonardo's "acme of perfection."

As for the word "black," Ms. Maggio says it should be excised from terms with a negative spin: she recommends substituting words like "mouse" for "black eye," "ostracize" for "blackball," "payola" for "blackmail" and "outcast" for "black sheep." Clearly, some of these substitutions work better than others: somehow the "sinister humor" of Kurt Vonnegut or *Saturday Night Live* doesn't quite make it; nor does the "denouncing" of the Hollywood 10.

For the dedicated user of politically correct language, all these rules can make for some messy moral dilemmas. Whereas "battered wife" is a gender-biased term, the gender-free term "battered spouse," Ms. Maggio notes, incorrectly implies "that men and women are equally battered."

On one hand, say Francine Wattman Frank and Paula A. Treichler in their book *Language, Gender, and Professional Writing* (Modern Language

Association), "he or she" is an appropriate construction for talking about an individual (like a jockey, say) who belongs to a profession that's predominantly male—it's a way of emphasizing "that such occupations are not barred to women or that women's concerns need to be kept in mind." On the other hand, they add, using masculine pronouns rhetorically can underscore ongoing male dominance in those fields, implying the need for change.

And what about the speech codes adopted by some universities in recent years? Although they were designed to prohibit students from uttering sexist and racist slurs, they would extend, by logic, to blacks who want to use the word "nigger" to strip the term of its racist connotations, or homosexuals who want to use the word "queer" to reclaim it from bigots.

In her book, Ms. Maggio recommends applying bias-free usage retro-   15
actively: she suggests paraphrasing politically incorrect quotations, or replacing "the sexist words or phrases with ellipsis dots and/or bracketed substitutes," or using "*sic*" "to show that the sexist words come from the original quotation and to call attention to the fact that they are incorrect."

Which leads the skeptical reader of *The Bias-Free Word Finder* to wonder whether "All the King's Men" should be retitled "All the Ruler's People"; "Pet Sematary," "Animal Companion Graves"; "Birdman of Alcatraz," "Birdperson of Alcatraz"; and "The Iceman Cometh," "The Ice Route Driver Cometh"?

Will making such changes remove the prejudice in people's minds? Should we really spend time trying to come up with non-male-based alternatives to "Midas touch," "Achilles' heel," and "Montezuma's revenge"? Will tossing out Santa Claus—whom Ms. Maggio accuses of reinforcing "the cultural male-as-norm system"—in favor of Belfana, his Italian female alter ego, truly help banish sexism? Can the avoidance of "violent expressions and metaphors" like "kill two birds with one stone," "sock it to 'em" or "kick an idea around" actually promote a more harmonious world?

The point isn't that the excesses of the word police are comical. The point is that their intolerance (in the name of tolerance) has disturbing implications. In the first place, getting upset by phrases like "bullish on America" or "the City of Brotherly Love" tends to distract attention from the real problems of prejudice and injustice that exist in society at large, turning them into mere questions of semantics. Indeed, the emphasis currently put on politically correct usage has uncanny parallels with the academic movement of deconstruction—a method of textual analysis that focuses on language and linguistic pyrotechnics—which has become firmly established on university campuses.

In both cases, attention is focused on surfaces, on words and metaphors; in both cases, signs and symbols are accorded more importance than content. Hence, the attempt by some radical advocates to remove *The Adventures of Huckleberry Finn* from curriculums on the grounds that Twain's use of the word "nigger" makes the book a racist text—never mind the fact that this American classic (written in 1884) depicts the spiritual kinship achieved between a white boy and a runaway slave, never mind the fact that the "nigger" Jim emerges as the novel's most honorable, decent character.

Ironically enough, the P.C. movement's obsession with language is 20 accompanied by a strange Orwellian willingness to warp the meaning of words by placing them under a high-powered ideological lens. For instance, the *Dictionary of Cautionary Words and Phrases*—a pamphlet issued by the University of Missouri's Multicultural Management Program to help turn "today's journalists into tomorrow's multicultural newsroom managers"—warns that using the word "articulate" to describe members of a minority group can suggest the opposite, "that 'those people' are not considered well educated, articulate and the like."

The pamphlet patronizes minority groups, by cautioning the reader against using the words "lazy" and "burly" to describe any member of such groups; and it issues a similar warning against using words like "gorgeous" and "petite" to describe women.

As euphemism proliferates with the rise of political correctness, there is a spread of the sort of sloppy, abstract language that Orwell said is "designed to make lies sound truthful and murder respectable, and to give an appearance of solidity to pure wind." "Fat" becomes "big boned" or "differently sized"; "stupid" becomes "exceptional"; "stoned" becomes "chemically inconvenienced."

Wait a minute here! Aren't such phrases eerily reminiscent of the euphemisms coined by the government during Vietnam and Watergate? Remember how the military used to speak of "pacification," or how President Richard M. Nixon's press secretary, Ronald L. Ziegler, tried to get away with calling a lie an "inoperative statement"?

Calling the homeless "the underhoused" doesn't give them a place to live; calling the poor "the economically marginalized" doesn't help them pay the bills. Rather, by playing down their plight, such language might even make it easier to shrug off the seriousness of their situation.

Instead of allowing free discussion and debate to occur, many gung-ho 25 advocates of politically correct language seem to think that simple suppression of a word or concept will magically make the problem disappear. In the *Bias-Free Word Finder*, Ms. Maggio entreats the reader not to perpetuate the negative stereotype of Eve. "Be extremely cautious in referring to the biblical Eve," she writes; "this story has profoundly contributed to negative attitudes toward women throughout history, largely because of misogynistic and patriarchal interpretations that labeled her evil, inferior, and seductive."

The story of Bluebeard, the rake (whoops!—the libertine) who killed his seven wives, she says, is also to be avoided, as is the biblical story of Jezebel. Of Jesus Christ, Ms. Maggio writes: "There have been few individuals in history as completely androgynous as Christ, and it does his message a disservice to overinsist on his maleness." She doesn't give the reader any hints on how this might be accomplished; presumably, one is supposed to avoid describing him as the Son of God.

Of course the P.C. police aren't the only ones who want to proscribe what people should say or give them guidelines for how they may use an idea; Jesse Helms and his supporters are up to exactly the same thing when they propose to patrol the boundaries of the permissible in art. In each case, the would-be censor aspires to suppress what he or she finds distasteful—all, of course, in the name of the public good.

In the case of the politically correct, the prohibition of certain words, phrases and ideas is advanced in the cause of building a brave new world free of racism and hate, but this vision of harmony clashes with the very ideals of diversity and inclusion that the multicultural movement holds dear, and it's purchased at the cost of freedom of expression and freedom of speech.

In fact, the utopian world envisioned by the language police would be bought at the expense of the ideas of individualism and democracy articulated in "The Gettysburg Address": "Fourscore and seven years ago our fathers brought forth on this continent a new nation, conceived in liberty and dedicated to the proposition that all men are created equal."

Of course, the P.C. police have already found Lincoln's words hopelessly "phallocentric." No doubt they would rewrite the passage: "Fourscore and seven years ago our foremothers and forefathers brought forth on this continent a new nation, formulated with liberty, and dedicated to the proposition that all humankind is created equal."   30

The Reader's Presence

1. Kakutani begins by dissecting what she sees as a current state of affairs. What kinds of words does she use to describe this state of affairs? Is she merely stating the facts or beginning her argument? Kakutani uses the term *language police* (paragraph 5) to describe those who would alter the English language. What does this term imply? Is it justified?

2. The author humorously cites rather awkward word substitutions from *The Bias-Free Word Finder*. Is this example sufficient and fair as evidence? Does mockery strengthen or weaken Kakutani's case?

3. Consider Kakutani's essay in relation to one of the best-known essays on the same topic, George Orwell's "Politics and the English Language" (page 510). Note in her essay where Kakutani covers some of the same ground as Orwell: What is similar about their critiques? How does Orwell deal with political correctness? How would you assess the political philosophy of each writer? Which writer, in your opinion, reflects more seriously on the political issues raised by certain English expressions and usages? Explain how you arrived at your opinion.

Martin Luther King Jr.

I Have a Dream

Martin Luther King Jr. (1929–1968) was born in Atlanta, Georgia, and after training for the ministry became pastor of the Dexter Avenue Baptist Church in Montgomery, Alabama. In 1956 he was elected president of the Montgomery Improvement Association, the group that organized a transportation boycott in response to the arrest of Rosa Parks. King later became president of the Southern Christian Leadership Conference, and under his philosophy of nonviolent direct action he led marches and protests throughout the South, to Chicago, and to Washington, D.C. In 1963 King delivered his most famous speech, "I Have a Dream," before 200,000 people in front of the Lincoln Memorial in Washington, D.C., and in 1964 he was awarded the Nobel Peace Prize. King was assassinated on April 3, 1968, in Memphis, Tennessee.

King was a masterful orator and a powerful writer. Along with his many speeches, King wrote several books, including Why We Can't Wait *(1963),* Where Do We Go from Here: Chaos or Community? *(1967),* The Measure of a Man *(1968), and* Trumpet of Conscience *(1968).*

For more on Martin Luther King Jr., see page 730.

Five score years ago, a great American, in whose symbolic shadow we stand, signed the Emancipation Proclamation.[1] This momentous decree came as a great beacon light of hope to millions of Negro slaves who had been seared in the flames of withering injustice. It came as a joyous daybreak to end the long night of captivity.

But one hundred years later, we must face the tragic fact that the Negro is still not free. One hundred years later, the life of the Negro is still sadly crippled by the manacles of segregation and the chains of discrimination. One hundred years later, the Negro lives on a lonely island of poverty in the midst of a vast ocean of material prosperity. One hundred years later, the Negro is still languishing in the corners of American society and finds himself an exile in his own land. So we have come here today to dramatize an appalling condition.

In a sense we have come to our nation's Capitol to cash a check. When the architects of our republic wrote the magnificent words of the Constitution and the Declaration of Independence, they were signing a promissory note to which every American was to fall heir. This note was a promise that all men would be guaranteed the unalienable rights of life, liberty, and the pursuit of happiness.

---

[1]*Emancipation Proclamation:* Abraham Lincoln signed the Emancipation Proclamation that officially freed the slaves in 1863. —EDS.

It is obvious today that America has defaulted on this promissory note insofar as her citizens of color are concerned. Instead of honoring this sacred obligation, America has given the Negro people a bad check; a check which has come back marked "insufficient funds." But we refuse to believe that the bank of justice is bankrupt. We refuse to believe that there are insufficient funds in the great vaults of opportunity of this nation. So we have come to cash this check—a check that will give us upon demand the riches of freedom and the security of justice. We have also come to this hallowed spot to remind America of the fierce urgency of *now*. This is no time to engage in the luxury of cooling off or to take the tranquilizing drug of gradualism. *Now* is the time to make real the promises of Democracy. *Now* is the time to rise from the dark and desolate valley of segregation to the sunlit path of racial justice. *Now* is the time to open the doors of opportunity to all of God's children. *Now* is the time to lift our nation from the quicksands of racial injustice to the solid rock of brotherhood.

It would be fatal for the nation to overlook the urgency of the moment and to underestimate the determination of the Negro. This sweltering summer of the Negro's legitimate discontent will not pass until there is an invigorating autumn of freedom and equality. 1963 is not an end, but a beginning. Those who hope that the Negro needed to blow off steam and will now be content will have a rude awakening if the nation returns to business as usual. There will be neither rest nor tranquility in America until the Negro is granted his citizenship rights. The whirlwinds of revolt will continue to shake the foundations of our nation until the bright day of justice emerges.

But there is something I must say to my people who stand on the warm threshold which leads into the palace of justice. In the process of gaining our rightful place we must not be guilty of wrongful deeds. Let us not seek to satisfy our thirst for freedom by drinking from the cup of bitterness and hatred. We must forever conduct our struggle on the high plane of dignity and discipline. We must not allow our creative protest to degenerate into physical violence. Again and again we must rise to the majestic heights of meeting physical force with soul force. The marvelous new militancy which has engulfed the Negro community must not lead us to a distrust of all white people, for many of our white brothers, as evidenced by their presence here today, have come to realize that their destiny is tied up with our destiny and their freedom is inextricably bound to our freedom. We cannot walk alone.

And as we walk, we must make the pledge that we shall march ahead. We cannot turn back. There are those who are asking the devotees of civil rights, "When will you be satisfied?" We can never be satisfied as long as the Negro is the victim of the unspeakable horrors of police brutality. We can never be satisfied as long as our bodies, heavy with the fatigue of travel, cannot gain lodging in the motels of the highways and the hotels of the cities. We cannot be satisfied as long as the Negro's basic mobility is from a smaller ghetto to a larger one. We can never be satisfied as long as a Negro

5

in Mississippi cannot vote and a Negro in New York believes he has nothing for which to vote. No, no, we are not satisfied, and we will not be satisfied until justice rolls down like waters and righteousness like a mighty stream.

I am not unmindful that some of you have come here out of great trials and tribulations. Some of you have come fresh from narrow jail cells. Some of you have come from areas where your quest for freedom left you battered by the storms of persecution and staggered by the winds of police brutality. You have been the veterans of creative suffering. Continue to work with the faith that unearned suffering is redemptive.

Go back to Mississippi, go back to Alabama, go back to South Carolina, go back to Georgia, go back to Louisiana, go back to the slums and ghettoes of our northern cities, knowing that somehow this situation can and will be changed. Let us not wallow in the valley of despair.

I say to you today, my friends, that in spite of the difficulties and frustrations of the moment I still have a dream. It is a dream deeply rooted in the American dream. 10

I have a dream that one day this nation will rise up and live out the true meaning of its creed: "We hold these truths to be self-evident; that all men are created equal."[2]

I have a dream that one day on the red hills of Georgia the sons of former slaves and the sons of former slaveowners will be able to sit down together at the table of brotherhood.

I have a dream that the state of Mississippi, a desert state sweltering with the heat of injustice and oppression, will be transformed into an oasis of freedom and justice.

I have a dream that my four little children will one day live in a nation where they will not be judged by the color of their skin but by the content of their character.

I have a dream today. 15

I have a dream that the state of Alabama, whose governor's[3] lips are presently dripping with the words of interposition and nullification, will be transformed into a situation where little black boys and black girls will be able to join hands with little white boys and white girls and walk together as sisters and brothers.

I have a dream today.

I have a dream that one day every valley shall be exalted, every hill and mountain shall be made low, the rough places will be made plain, and the crooked places will be made straight, and the glory of the Lord shall be revealed, and all flesh shall see it together.

---

[2]From the Declaration of Independence by Thomas Jefferson (page 705).—EDS.

[3]*governor's:* The governor of Alabama in 1963 was segregationist George Wallace (1919–1998), who eventually came to support integration and equal rights for African Americans.—EDS.

This is our hope. This is the faith with which I return to the South. With this faith we will be able to hew out of the mountain of despair a stone of hope. With this faith we will be able to transform the jangling discords of our nation into a beautiful symphony of brotherhood. With this faith we will be able to work together, to pray together, to struggle together, to go to jail together, to stand up for freedom together, knowing that we will be free one day.

This will be the day when all of God's children will be able to sing   20
with new meaning.

> My country, 'tis of thee
> Sweet land of liberty,
>   Of thee I sing:
> Land where my fathers died,
> Land of the pilgrims' pride,
> From every mountainside
>   Let freedom ring.

And if America is to be a great nation this must become true. So let freedom ring from the prodigious hilltops of New Hampshire. Let freedom ring from the mighty mountains of New York. Let freedom ring from the heightening Alleghenies of Pennsylvania!

Let freedom ring from the snowcapped Rockies of Colorado!

Let freedom ring from the curvaceous peaks of California!

But not only that; let freedom ring from Stone Mountain of Georgia!

Let freedom ring from Lookout Mountain of Tennessee!   25

Let freedom ring from every hill and molehill of Mississippi. From every mountainside, let freedom ring.

When we let freedom ring, when we let it ring from every village and every hamlet, from every state and every city, we will be able to speed up that day when all of God's children, black men and white men, Jews and Gentiles, Protestants and Catholics, will be able to join hands and sing in the words of the old Negro spiritual, "Free at last! free at last! thank God almighty, we are free at last!"

The Reader's Presence

1. How does King use familiar concepts and phrases from American democracy to create his message? What are some examples? How does he use repetition? How does he use rhythm? What are the effects of his rhetoric?

2. Make a list of the metaphors King uses throughout the speech. What connotations do they bring? What reccurring themes does he draw on for his metaphors? How do metaphors help extend the meanings of the words he describes?

3. Read Ho Che Anderson's graphic representation of King's "I Have a Dream" speech, which follows this piece. How does Anderson represent King as a speaker and leader? How does the juxtaposition of images and words influence your perception of the event?

THE ARTIST AT WORK

Ho Che Anderson Reenvisions Martin Luther King Jr.'s *I Have a Dream*

Ho Che Anderson (b. 1970) was born in the United Kingdom and raised in Canada, where he lives today. He has authored a number of graphic "comix" including Young Hoods in Love *(1994),* I Want to Be Your Dog *(1996), and, in collaboration with Wilfred Santiago, the series* Pop Life *(1998). His biographical trilogy,* King *(Volumes I–III), illustrates the life of Martin Luther King Jr. from his birth to his assassination. Anderson's complex rendering of the 1963 civil rights march on Washington, D.C., during which Dr. King delivered his most famous speech, "I Have a Dream," is excerpted from* King, *Volume II (2002). The first volume,* King *(1992), won a 1995 Parent's Choice Award;* King, *Volume III, was published in 2003.*

Martin Luther King Jr.

Letter from Birmingham Jail

> *Martin Luther King Jr. (1929–1968), one of the nation's best-known civil rights activists, led protests across the South in the years before the passage of the Civil Rights Act of 1964. He was arrested in 1960 for sitting at a whites-only lunch counter in Greensboro, North Carolina, and in 1962 he was jailed in Albany, Georgia. On April 12, 1963, King was again arrested, this time in Birmingham, Alabama, for demonstrating without a permit. He served eleven days in jail. While there, he wrote "Letter from Birmingham Jail" in response to a letter from eight clergymen who argued against King's acts of civil disobedience. The letter was published in King's book* Why We Can't Wait *(1963).*
>
> *Many of King's writings, including the letter printed here and the famous "I Have a Dream" speech (see page 730), are designed to educate his audiences and inspire them to act. "Through education we seek to break down the spiritual barriers to integration," he said, and "through legislation and court orders we seek to break down the physical barriers to integration. One method is not a substitute for the other, but a meaningful and necessary supplement."*
>
> *For more on Martin Luther King Jr., see page 715.*

The following is the public statement by eight Alabama clergymen that occasioned King's letter.

We the undersigned clergymen are among those who, in January, issued "an appeal for law and order and common sense," in dealing with racial problems in Alabama. We expressed understanding that honest convictions in racial matters could properly be pursued in the courts, but urged that decisions of those courts should in the meantime be peacefully obeyed.

Since that time there had been some evidence of increased forbearance and a willingness to face facts. Responsible citizens have undertaken to work on various problems which cause racial friction and unrest. In Birmingham, recent public events have given indication that we all have opportunity for a new constructive and realistic approach to racial problems.

However, we are now confronted by a series of demonstrations by some of our Negro citizens, directed and led in part by outsiders. We recognize the natural impatience of people who feel that their hopes are slow in being realized. But we are convinced that these demonstrations are unwise and untimely.

We agree rather with certain local Negro leadership which has called for honest and open negotiation of racial issues in our area. And we believe this kind of facing of issues can best be accomplished by citizens of our own metropolitan area, white and Negro, meeting with their knowledge and experience of the local situation. All of us need to face that responsibility and find proper channels for its accomplishment.

Just as we formerly pointed out that "hatred and violence have no sanction in our religious and political traditions," we also point out that such actions as incite to hatred and violence, however technically peaceful those actions may be, have not contributed to the resolution of our local problems. We do not believe that these days of new hope are days when extreme measures are justified in Birmingham.

We commend the community as a whole, and the local news media and law enforcement officials in particular, on the calm manner in which these demonstrations have been handled. We urge the public to continue to show restraint should the demonstrations continue, and the law enforcement officials to remain calm and continue to protect our city from violence.

We further strongly urge our own Negro community to withdraw support from these demonstrations, and to unite locally in working peacefully for a better Birmingham. When rights are consistently denied, a cause should be pressed in the courts and in negotiations among local leaders, and not in the streets. We appeal to both our white and Negro citizenry to observe the principles of law and order and common sense.

BISHOP C. C. J. CARPENTER, D.D., LL.D., Episcopalian Bishop of Alabama

BISHOP JOSEPH A. DURICK, D.D., Auxiliary Bishop, Roman Catholic Diocese of Mobile, Birmingham

RABBI MILTON L. GRAFMAN, Temple Emanu-El, Birmingham, Alabama

BISHOP PAUL HARDIN, Methodist Bishop of the Alabama–West Florida Conference

BISHOP NOLAN B. HARMON, Bishop of the North Alabama Conference of the Methodist Church

REV. GEORGE M. MURRAY, D.D., LL.D., Bishop Coadjutor, Episcopal Diocese of Alabama

REV. EDWARD V. RAMAGE, Moderator, Synod of the Alabama Presbyterian Church in the United States

REV. EARL STALLINGS, Pastor, First Baptist Church, Birmingham, Alabama

April 12, 1963

MARTIN LUTHER KING JR.
Birmingham City Jail
April 16, 1963

Bishop C. C. J. CARPENTER   *Bishop* NOLAN B. HARMON
Bishop JOSEPH A. DURICK   *The Rev.* GEORGE M. MURRAY
Rabbi MILTON L. GRAFMAN   *The Rev.* EDWARD V. RAMAGE
Bishop PAUL HARDIN   *The Rev.* EARL STALLINGS

My dear Fellow Clergymen,

While confined here in the Birmingham City Jail, I came across your recent statement calling our present activities "unwise and untimely." Seldom, if ever, do I pause to answer criticism of my work and ideas. If I
sought to answer all of the criticisms that cross my desk, my secretaries
would be engaged in little else in the course of the day and I would have
no time for constructive work. But since I feel that you are men of genuine
good will and your criticisms are sincerely set forth, I would like to answer
your statement in what I hope will be patient and reasonable terms.

I think I should give the reason for my being in Birmingham, since
you have been influenced by the argument of "outsiders coming in." I have
the honor of serving as president of the Southern Christian Leadership
Conference, an organization operating in every Southern state with headquarters in Atlanta, Georgia. We have some eighty-five affiliate organizations all across the South—one being the Alabama Christian Movement
for Human Rights. Whenever necessary and possible we share staff, educational, and financial resources with our affiliates. Several months ago our
local affiliate here in Birmingham invited us to be on call to engage in
a nonviolent direct action program if such were deemed necessary. We
readily consented and when the hour came we lived up to our promises. So
I am here, along with several members of my staff, because we were invited
here. I am here because I have basic organizational ties here. Beyond this, I
am in Birmingham because injustice is here. Just as the eighth century
prophets left their little villages and carried their "thus saith the Lord" far
beyond the boundaries of their home town, and just as the Apostle Paul
left his little village of Tarsus and carried the gospel of Jesus Christ to practically every hamlet and city of the Graeco-Roman world, I too am compelled to carry the gospel of freedom beyond my particular home town.
Like Paul, I must constantly respond to the Macedonian call for aid.

Moreover, I am cognizant of the interrelatedness of all communities
and states. I cannot sit idly by in Atlanta and not be concerned about what
happens in Birmingham. Injustice anywhere is a threat to justice everywhere. We are caught in an inescapable network of mutuality tied in a
single garment of destiny. Whatever affects one directly affects all indirectly. Never again can we afford to live with the narrow, provincial

"outside agitator" idea. Anyone who lives inside the United States can never be considered an outsider anywhere in this country.

You deplore the demonstrations that are presently taking place in Birmingham. But I am sorry that your statement did not express a similar concern for the conditions that brought the demonstrations into being. I am sure that each of you would want to go beyond the superficial social analyst who looks merely at effects, and does not grapple with underlying causes. I would not hesitate to say that it is unfortunate that so-called demonstrations are taking place in Birmingham at this time, but I would say in more emphatic terms it is even more unfortunate that the white power structure of this city left the Negro community with no other alternative.

In any nonviolent campaign there are four basic steps: (1) collection of the facts to determine whether injustices are alive; (2) negotiation; (3) self-purification; and (4) direct action. We have gone through all of these steps in Birmingham. There can be no gainsaying of the fact that racial injustice engulfs this community. Birmingham is probably the most thoroughly segregated city in the United States. Its ugly record of police brutality is known in every section of this country. Its unjust treatment of Negroes in the courts is a notorious reality. There have been more unsolved bombings of Negro homes and churches in Birmingham than any city in this nation. These are the hard, brutal, and unbelievable facts. On the basis of these conditions Negro leaders sought to negotiate with the city fathers. But the political leaders consistently refused to engage in good faith negotiation.

Then came the opportunity last September to talk with some of the leaders of the economic community. In these negotiating sessions certain promises were made by the merchants — such as the promise to remove the humiliating racial signs from the stores. On the basis of these promises Rev. Shuttlesworth and the leaders of the Alabama Christian Movement for Human Rights agreed to call a moratorium on any type of demonstrations. As the weeks and months unfolded we realized that we were the victims of a broken promise. The signs remained. As in so many experiences of the past we were confronted with blasted hopes, and the dark shadow of a deep disappointment settled upon us. So we had no alternative except that of preparing for direct action, whereby we would present our very bodies as a means of laying our case before the conscience of the local and national community. We were not unmindful of the difficulties involved. So we decided to go through a process of self-purification. We started having workshops on nonviolence and repeatedly asked ourselves the questions, "Are you able to accept blows without retaliating?" "Are you able to endure the ordeals of jail?"

We decided to set our direct action program around the Easter season, realizing that with the exception of Christmas, this was the largest shopping period of the year. Knowing that a strong economic withdrawal program would be the by-product of direct action, we felt that this was the best time to bring pressure on the merchants for the needed changes. Then it occurred to us that the March election was ahead, and so we speedily decided to postpone action until after election day. When we discovered that Mr. Connor[1] was in the run-off, we decided again to postpone so that the demonstrations could not be used to cloud the issues. At this time we agreed to begin our nonviolent witness the day after the run-off.

This reveals that we did not move irresponsibly into direct action. We too wanted to see Mr. Connor defeated; so we went through postponement after postponement to aid in this community need. After this we felt that direct action could be delayed no longer.

You may well ask, "Why direct action? Why sit-ins, marches, etc.? Isn't negotiation a better path?" You are exactly right in your call for negotiation. Indeed, this is the purpose of direct action. Nonviolent direct action seeks to create such a crisis and establish such creative tension that a community that has constantly refused to negotiate is forced to confront the issue. It seeks so to dramatize the issue that it can no longer be ignored. I just referred to the creation of tension as a part of the work of the nonviolent resister. This may sound rather shocking. But I must confess that I am not afraid of the word tension. I have earnestly worked and preached against violent tension, but there is a type of constructive nonviolent tension that is necessary for growth. Just as Socrates felt that it was necessary to create a tension in the mind so that individuals could rise from the bondage of myths and half-truths to the unfettered realm of creative analysis and objective appraisal, we must see the need of having nonviolent gadflies to create the kind of tension in society that will help men rise from the dark depths of prejudice and racism to the majestic heights of understanding and brotherhood. So the purpose of the direct action is to create a situation so crisis-packed that it will inevitably open the door to negotiation. We, therefore, concur with you in your call for negotiation. Too long has our beloved Southland been bogged down in the tragic attempt to live in monologue rather than dialogue.

One of the basic points in your statement is that our acts are untimely. Some have asked, "Why didn't you give the new administration time to act?" The only answer that I can give to this inquiry is that the new administration must be prodded about as much as the outgoing one before it acts. We will be sadly mistaken if we feel that the election of Mr. Boutwell will bring the millennium to Birmingham. While Mr. Boutwell is much more articulate and gentle than Mr. Connor, they are both segregationists dedicated to the task of maintaining the status quo. The hope I see in Mr. Boutwell is that he will be reasonable enough to see the futility

10

---

[1]**Mr. Connor:** Eugene "Bull" Connor and Albert Boutwell ran for mayor of Birmingham, Alabama, in 1963. Although Boutwell, the more moderate candidate, was declared the winner, Connor, the city commissioner of public safety, refused to leave office, claiming that he had been elected to serve until 1965. While the issue was debated in the courts, Connor was on the street ordering the police to use force to suppress demonstrations against segregation. — EDS.

of massive resistance to desegregation. But he will not see this without pressure from the devotees of civil rights. My friends, I must say to you that we have not made a single gain in civil rights without determined legal and nonviolent pressure. History is the long and tragic story of the fact that privileged groups seldom give up their privileges voluntarily. Individuals may see the moral light and voluntarily give up their unjust posture; but as Reinhold Niebuhr[2] has reminded us, groups are more immoral than individuals.

We know through painful experience that freedom is never voluntarily given by the oppressor; it must be demanded by the oppressed. Frankly I have never yet engaged in a direct action movement that was "well timed," according to the timetable of those who have not suffered unduly from the disease of segregation. For years now I have heard the word "Wait!" It rings in the ear of every Negro with a piercing familiarity. This "wait" has almost always meant "never." It has been a tranquilizing thalidomide, relieving the emotional stress for a moment, only to give birth to an ill-formed infant of frustration. We must come to see with the distinguished jurist of yesterday that "justice too long delayed is justice denied." We have waited for more than three hundred and forty years for our constitutional and God-given rights. The nations of Asia and Africa are moving with jet-like speed toward the goal of political independence, and we still creep at horse and buggy pace toward the gaining of a cup of coffee at a lunch counter.

I guess it is easy for those who have never felt the stinging darts of segregation to say wait. But when you have seen vicious mobs lynch your mothers and fathers at will and drown your sisters and brothers at whim; when you have seen hate-filled policemen curse, kick, brutalize, and even kill your black brothers and sisters with impunity; when you see the vast majority of your twenty million Negro brothers smothering in an air-tight cage of poverty in the midst of an affluent society; when you suddenly find your tongue twisted and your speech stammering as you seek to explain to your six-year-old daughter why she can't go to the public amusement park that has just been advertised on television, and see tears welling up in her little eyes when she is told that Funtown is closed to colored children, and see the depressing clouds of inferiority begin to form in her little mental sky, and see her begin to distort her little personality by unconsciously developing a bitterness toward white people; when you have to concoct an answer for a five-year-old son asking in agonizing pathos: "Daddy, why do white people treat colored people so mean?"; when you take a cross country drive and find it necessary to sleep night after night in the uncomfortable corners of your automobile because no motel will accept you; when you are humiliated day in and day out by nagging signs reading "white" men and "colored"; when your first name

---

[2]***Niebuhr:*** Protestant theologian Reinhold Niebuhr (1892–1971) best known for attempts to relate Christianity to modern politics. — EDS.

becomes "nigger" and your middle name becomes "boy" (however old you are) and your last name becomes "John," and when your wife and mother are never given the respected title "Mrs."; when you are harried by day and haunted by night by the fact that you are a Negro, living constantly at tiptoe stance never quite knowing what to expect next, and plagued with inner fears and outer resentments; when you are forever fighting a degenerating sense of "nobodiness";—then you will understand why we find it difficult to wait. There comes a time when the cup of endurance runs over, and men are no longer willing to be plunged into an abyss of injustice where they experience the bleakness of corroding despair. I hope, sirs, you can understand our legitimate and unavoidable impatience.

You express a great deal of anxiety over our willingness to break laws. This is certainly a legitimate concern. Since we so diligently urge people to obey the Supreme Court's decision of 1954 outlawing segregation in the public schools, it is rather strange and paradoxical to find us consciously breaking laws. One may well ask, "How can you advocate breaking some laws and obeying others?" The answer is found in the fact that there are two types of laws. There are *just* laws and there are *unjust* laws. I would be the first to advocate obeying just laws. One has not only a legal but moral responsibility to obey just laws. Conversely, one has a moral responsibility to disobey unjust laws. I would agree with Saint Augustine that "An unjust law is no law at all."

Now what is the difference between the two? How does one determine when a law is just or unjust? A just law is a man-made code that squares with the moral law or the law of God. An unjust law is a code that is out of harmony with the moral law. To put it in the terms of Saint Thomas Aquinas, an unjust law is a human law that is not rooted in eternal and natural law. Any law that uplifts human personality is just. Any law that degrades human personality is unjust. All segregation statutes are unjust because segregation distorts the soul and damages the personality. It gives the segregator a false sense of superiority and the segregated a false sense of inferiority. To use the words of Martin Buber, the great Jewish philosopher, segregation substitutes an "I-it" relationship for the "I-thou" relationship, and ends up relegating persons to the status of things. So segregation is not only politically, economically, and sociologically unsound, but it is morally wrong and sinful. Paul Tillich[3] has said that sin is separation. Isn't segregation an existential expression of man's tragic separation, an expression of his awful estrangement, his terrible sinfulness? So I can urge men to obey the 1954 decision of the Supreme Court[4] because it is morally right, and I can urge them to disobey segregation ordinances because they are morally wrong.

[3]*Tillich:* Paul Tillich (1886–1965), theologian and philosopher. —Eds.
[4]*1954 decision of the Supreme Court: Brown v. Board of Education,* the case in which the Supreme Court ruled racial segregation in the nation's public schools unconstitutional.—Eds.

Let us turn to a more concrete example of just and unjust laws. An
unjust law is a code that a majority inflicts on a minority that is not binding on itself. This is *difference* made legal. On the other hand a just law is
a code that a majority compels a minority to follow that it is willing to
follow itself. This is *sameness* made legal.

Let me give another explanation. An unjust law is a code inflicted
upon a minority which that minority had no part in enacting or creating
because they did not have the unhampered right to vote. Who can say the
legislature of Alabama which set up the segregation laws was democratically elected? Throughout the state of Alabama all types of conniving
methods are used to prevent Negroes from becoming registered voters
and there are some counties without a single Negro registered to vote despite the fact that the Negro constitutes a majority of the population. Can
any law set up in such a state be considered democratically structured?

These are just a few examples of unjust and just laws. There are some
instances when a law is just on its face but unjust in its application. For
instance, I was arrested Friday on a charge of parading without a permit.
Now there is nothing wrong with an ordinance which requires a permit
for a parade, but when the ordinance is used to preserve segregation and
to deny citizens the First Amendment privilege of peaceful assembly and
peaceful protest, then it becomes unjust.

I hope you can see the distinction I am trying to point out. In no
sense do I advocate evading or defying the law as the rabid segregationist
would do. This would lead to anarchy. One who breaks an unjust law
must do it *openly*, *lovingly* (not hatefully as the white mothers did in
New Orleans when they were seen on television screaming "nigger, nigger, nigger") and with a willingness to accept the penalty. I submit that
an individual who breaks a law that conscience tells him is unjust, and
willingly accepts the penalty by staying in jail to arouse the conscience of
the community over its injustice, is in reality expressing the very highest
respect for law.

Of course there is nothing new about this kind of civil disobedience.
It was seen sublimely in the refusal of Shadrach, Meshach, and Abed-
nego to obey the laws of Nebuchadnezzar because a higher moral law
was involved. It was practiced superbly by the early Christians who were
willing to face hungry lions and the excruciating pain of chopping
blocks, before submitting to certain unjust laws of the Roman Empire.
To a degree academic freedom is a reality today because Socrates practiced civil disobedience.

We can never forget that everything Hitler did in Germany was "legal"
and everything the Hungarian freedom fighters[5] did in Hungary was "illegal." It was "illegal" to aid and comfort a Jew in Hitler's Germany. But

15

20

---

[5]***Hungarian freedom fighters:*** Those who fought in the unsuccessful 1956 revolt against
Soviet oppression. — EDS.

I am sure that, if I had lived in Germany during that time, I would have aided and comforted my Jewish brothers even though it was illegal. If I lived in a communist country today where certain principles dear to the Christian faith are suppressed, I believe I would openly advocate disobeying those antireligious laws.

I must make two honest confessions to you, my Christian and Jewish brothers. First I must confess that over the last few years I have been gravely disappointed with the white moderate. I have almost reached the regrettable conclusion that the Negroes' great stumbling block in the stride toward freedom is not the White Citizens' "Counciler" or the Ku Klux Klanner, but the white moderate who is more devoted to "order" than to justice; who prefers a negative peace which is the absence of tension to a positive peace which is the presence of justice; who constantly says "I agree with you in the goal you seek, but I can't agree with your methods of direct action"; who paternalistically feels that he can set the timetable for another man's freedom; who lives by the myth of time and who constantly advises the Negro to wait until a "more convenient season." Shallow understanding from people of good will is more frustrating than absolute misunderstanding from people of ill will. Lukewarm acceptance is much more bewildering than outright rejection.

I had hoped that the white moderate would understand that law and order exist for the purpose of establishing justice, and that when they fail to do this they become the dangerously structured dams that block the flow of social progress. I had hoped that the white moderate would understand that the present tension in the South is merely a necessary phase of the transition from an obnoxious negative peace, where the Negro passively accepted his unjust plight, to a substance-filled positive peace, where all men will respect the dignity and worth of human personality. Actually, we who engage in nonviolent direct action are not the creators of tension. We merely bring to the surface the hidden tension that is already alive. We bring it out in the open where it can be seen and dealt with. Like a boil that can never be cured as long as it is covered up but must be opened with all its pus-flowing ugliness to the natural medicines of air and light, injustice must likewise be exposed, with all of the tension its exposing creates, to the light of human conscience and the air of national opinion before it can be cured.

In your statement you asserted that our actions, even though peaceful, must be condemned because they precipitate violence. But can this assertion be logically made? Isn't this like condemning the robbed man because his possession of money precipitated the evil act of robbery? Isn't this like condemning Socrates because his unswerving commitment to truth and his philosophical delvings precipitated the misguided popular mind to make him drink the hemlock? Isn't this like condemning Jesus because His unique God consciousness and never-ceasing devotion to His will precipitated the evil act of crucifixion? We must come to see, as federal courts have consistently affirmed, that it is immoral to urge an individual to withdraw his efforts to gain his basic constitutional rights because the quest precipitates violence. Society must protect the robbed and punish the robber.

I had also hoped that the white moderate would reject the myth of time. I received a letter this morning from a white brother in Texas which said: "All Christians know that the colored people will receive equal rights eventually, but is it possible that you are in too great of a religious hurry? It has taken Christianity almost 2000 years to accomplish what it has. The teachings of Christ take time to come to earth." All that is said here grows out of a tragic misconception of time. It is the strangely irrational notion that there is something in the very flow of time that will inevitably cure all ills. Actually time is neutral. It can be used either destructively or constructively. I am coming to feel that the people of ill will have used time much more effectively than the people of good will. We will have to repent in this generation not merely for the vitriolic words and actions of the bad people, but for the appalling silence of the good people. We must come to see that human progress never rolls in on wheels of inevitability. It comes through the tireless efforts and persistent work of men willing to be co-workers with God, and without this hard work time itself becomes an ally of the forces of social stagnation.

We must use time creatively, and forever realize that the time is always   25
ripe to do right. Now is the time to make real the promise of democracy, and transform our pending national elegy into a creative psalm of brotherhood. Now is the time to lift our national policy from the quicksand of racial injustice to the solid rock of human dignity.

You spoke of our activity in Birmingham as extreme. At first I was rather disappointed that fellow clergymen would see my nonviolent efforts as those of the extremist. I started thinking about the fact that I stand in the middle of two opposing forces in the Negro community. One is a force of complacency made up of Negroes who, as a result of long years of oppression, have been so completely drained of self-respect and a sense of "somebodiness" that they have adjusted to segregation, and of a few Negroes in the middle class who, because of a degree of academic and economic security, and because at points they profit by segregation, have unconsciously become insensitive to the problems of the masses. The other force is one of bitterness and hatred and comes perilously close to advocating violence. It is expressed in the various black nationalist groups that are springing up over the nation, the largest and best known being Elijah Muhammad's Muslim movement.[6] This movement is nourished by the contemporary frustration over the continued existence of racial discrimination. It is made up of people who have lost faith in America, who have absolutely repudiated Christianity, and who have concluded that the white

[6]*Elijah Muhammad's Muslim movement:* Led by Elijah Muhammad, the Black Muslims opposed integration and promoted the creation of a black nation within the United States. —EDS.

man is an incurable "devil." I have tried to stand between these two forces saying that we need not follow the "do-nothing-ism" of the complacent or the hatred and despair of the black nationalist. There is the more excellent way of love and nonviolent protest. I'm grateful to God that, through the Negro church, the dimension of nonviolence entered our struggle. If this philosophy had not emerged I am convinced that by now many streets of the South would be flowing with floods of blood. And I am further convinced that if our white brothers dismiss us as "rabble rousers" and "outside agitators"—those of us who are working through the channels of nonviolent direct action—and refuse to support our nonviolent efforts, millions of Negroes, out of frustration and despair, will seek solace and security in black nationalist ideologies, a development that will lead inevitably to a frightening racial nightmare.

Oppressed people cannot remain oppressed forever. The urge for freedom will eventually come. This is what has happened to the American Negro. Something within has reminded him of his birthright of freedom; something without has reminded him that he can gain it. Consciously and unconsciously, he has been swept in by what the Germans call the *Zeitgeist*,[7] and with his black brothers of Africa, and his brown and yellow brothers of Asia, South America, and the Caribbean, he is moving with a sense of cosmic urgency toward the promised land of racial justice. Recognizing this vital urge that has engulfed the Negro community, one should readily understand public demonstrations. The Negro has many pent-up resentments and latent frustrations. He has to get them out. So let him march sometime; let him have his prayer pilgrimages to the city hall; understand why he must have sit-ins and freedom rides. If his repressed emotions do not come out in these nonviolent ways, they will come out in ominous expressions of violence. This is not a threat; it is a fact of history. So I have not said to my people, "Get rid of your discontent." But I have tried to say that this normal and healthy discontent can be channeled through the creative outlet of nonviolent direct action. Now this approach is being dismissed as extremist. I must admit that I was initially disappointed in being so categorized.

But as I continued to think about the matter I gradually gained a bit of satisfaction from being considered an extremist. Was not Jesus an extremist in love? "Love your enemies, bless them that curse you, pray for them that despitefully use you." Was not Amos[8] an extremist for justice—"Let justice roll down like waters and righteousness like a mighty stream." Was not Paul an extremist for the gospel of Jesus Christ—"I bear in my body the marks of the Lord Jesus." Was not Martin Luther an extremist—"Here I stand; I can do none other so help me God." Was not John Bunyan[9] an extremist—"I will stay in jail to the end of my days be-

---

[7]*Zeitgeist:* A German word meaning "spirit of the time."—EDS.
[8]*Amos:* Prophet who preached against false worship and immorality.—EDS.
[9]*John Bunyan:* Puritan author (1628–1688) of *Pilgrim's Progress.*—EDS.

fore I make a butchery of my conscience." Was not Abraham Lincoln an extremist— "This nation cannot survive half slave and half free." Was not Thomas Jefferson an extremist— "We hold these truths to be self-evident, that all men are created equal." So the question is not whether we will be extremist but what kind of extremist will we be. Will we be extremists for hate or will we be extremists for love? Will we be extremists for the preservation of injustice—or will we be extremists for the cause of justice? In that dramatic scene on Calvary's hill three men were crucified. We must never forget that all three were crucified for the same crime—the crime of extremism. Two were extremists for immorality, and thus fell below their environment. The other, Jesus Christ, was an extremist for love, truth, and goodness, and thereby rose above His environment. So, after all, maybe the South, the nation, and the world are in dire need of creative extremists.

I had hoped that the white moderate would see this. Maybe I was too optimistic. Maybe I expected too much. I guess I should have realized that few members of a race that has oppressed another race can understand or appreciate the deep groans and passionate yearnings of those that have been oppressed, and still fewer have the vision to see that injustice must be rooted out by strong, persistent, and determined action. I am thankful, however, that some of our white brothers have grasped the meaning of this social revolution and committed themselves to it. They are still all too small in quantity, but they are big in quality. Some like Ralph McGill, Lillian Smith, Harry Golden, and James Dabbs have written about our struggle in eloquent, prophetic, and understanding terms. Others have marched with us down nameless streets of the South. They have languished in filthy, roach-infested jails, suffering the abuse and brutality of angry policemen who see them as "dirty nigger lovers." They, unlike so many of their moderate brothers and sisters, have recognized the urgency of the moment and sensed the need for powerful "action" antidotes to combat the disease of segregation.

Let me rush on to mention my other disappointment. I have been so 30 greatly disappointed with the white Church and its leadership. Of course there are some notable exceptions. I am not unmindful of the fact that each of you has taken some significant stands on this issue. I commend you, Rev. Stallings, for your Christian stand on this past Sunday, in welcoming Negroes to your worship service on a nonsegregated basis. I commend the Catholic leaders of this state for integrating Springhill College several years ago.

But despite these notable exceptions I must honestly reiterate that I have been disappointed with the Church. I do not say that as one of those negative critics who can always find something wrong with the Church. I say it as a minister of the gospel, who loves the Church; who was nurtured in its bosom; who has been sustained by its spiritual blessings and who will remain true to it as long as the cord of life shall lengthen.

I had the strange feeling when I was suddenly catapulted into the leadership of the bus protest in Montgomery[10] several years ago that we would have the support of the white Church. I felt that the white ministers, priests, and rabbis of the South would be some of our strongest allies. Instead, some have been outright opponents, refusing to understand the freedom movement and misrepresenting its leaders; all too many others have been more cautious than courageous and have remained silent behind the anesthetizing security of stained glass windows.

In spite of my shattered dreams of the past, I came to Birmingham with the hope that the white religious leadership of the community would see the justice of our cause and, with deep moral concern, serve as the channel through which our just grievances could get to the power structure. I had hoped that each of you would understand. But again I have been disappointed.

I have heard numerous religious leaders of the South call upon their worshippers to comply with a desegregation decision because it is the law, but I have longed to hear white ministers say follow this decree because integration is morally right and the Negro is your brother. In the midst of blatant injustices inflicted upon the Negro, I have watched white churches stand on the sideline and merely mouth pious irrelevancies and sanctimonious trivialities. In the midst of a mighty struggle to rid our nation of racial and economic injustice, I have heard so many ministers say, "Those are social issues with which the Gospel has no real concern," and I have watched so many churches commit themselves to a completely other-worldly religion which made a strange distinction between body and soul, the sacred and the secular.

So here we are moving toward the exit of the twentieth century with   35
a religious community largely adjusted to the status quo, standing as a tail-light behind other community agencies rather than a headlight leading men to higher levels of justice.

I have travelled the length and breadth of Alabama, Mississippi, and all the other Southern states. On sweltering summer days and crisp autumn mornings I have looked at her beautiful churches with their spires pointing heavenward. I have beheld the impressive outlay of her massive religious education buildings. Over and over again I have found myself asking: "Who worships here? Who is their God? Where were their voices when the lips of Governor Barnett[11] dripped with words of interposition and nullification? Where were they when Governor Wallace[12] gave the clarion call

---

[10]*bus protest in Montgomery:* After Rosa Parks was arrested on December 1, 1955, in Montgomery, Alabama, for refusing to give her seat on a bus to a white male passenger, a bus boycott began, which lasted nearly one year and was supported by nearly all of the city's black residents.—EDS.

[11]*Governor Barnett:* Ross R. Barnett, governor of Mississippi from 1960 to 1964.—EDS.

[12]*Governor Wallace:* George C. Wallace served as governor of Alabama from 1963 to 1966, 1971 to 1979, and 1983 to 1987.—EDS.

for defiance and hatred? Where were their voices of support when tired, bruised, and weary Negro men and women decided to rise from the dark dungeons of complacency to the bright hills of creative protest?"

Yes, these questions are still in my mind. In deep disappointment, I have wept over the laxity of the Church. But be assured that my tears have been tears of love. There can be no deep disappointment where there is not deep love. Yes, I love the Church; I love her sacred walls. How could I do otherwise? I am in the rather unique position of being the son, the grandson, and the great grandson of preachers. Yes, I see the Church as the body of Christ. But, oh! How we have blemished and scarred that body through social neglect and fear of being nonconformists.

There was a time when the Church was very powerful. It was during that period when the early Christians rejoiced when they were deemed worthy to suffer for what they believed. In those days the Church was not merely a thermometer that recorded the ideas and principles of popular opinion; it was a thermostat that transformed the mores of society. Wherever the early Christians entered a town the power structure got disturbed and immediately sought to convict them for being "disturbers of the peace" and "outside agitators." But they went on with the conviction that they were a "colony of heaven" and had to obey God rather than man. They were small in number but big in commitment. They were too God-intoxicated to be "astronomically intimidated." They brought an end to such ancient evils as infanticide and gladiatorial contest.

Things are different now. The contemporary Church is so often a weak, ineffectual voice with an uncertain sound. It is so often the arch-supporter of the status quo. Far from being disturbed by the presence of the Church, the power structure of the average community is consoled by the Church's silent and often vocal sanction of things as they are.

But the judgment of God is upon the Church as never before. If   40
the Church of today does not recapture the sacrificial spirit of the early Church, it will lose its authentic ring, forfeit the loyalty of millions, and be dismissed as an irrelevant social club with no meaning for the twentieth century. I am meeting young people every day whose disappointment with the Church has risen to outright disgust.

Maybe again I have been too optimistic. Is organized religion too inextricably bound to the status quo to save our nation and the world? Maybe I must turn my faith to the inner spiritual Church, the church within the Church, as the true *ecclesia*[13] and the hope of the world. But again I am thankful to God that some noble souls from the ranks of organized religion have broken loose from the paralyzing chains of conformity and joined us as active partners in the struggle for freedom. They have left their secure congregations and walked the streets of Albany, Georgia, with us. They have gone through the highways of the South on

[13]*ecclesia:* The Latin word for church. — EDS.

torturous rides for freedom. Yes, they have gone to jail with us. Some have been kicked out of their churches and lost the support of their bishops and fellow ministers. But they have gone with the faith that right defeated is stronger than evil triumphant. These men have been the leaven in the lump of the race. Their witness has been the spiritual salt that has preserved the true meaning of the Gospel in these troubled times. They have carved a tunnel of hope through the dark mountain of disappointment.

I hope the Church as a whole will meet the challenge of this decisive hour. But even if the Church does not come to the aid of justice, I have no despair about the future. I have no fear about the outcome of our struggle in Birmingham, even if our motives are presently misunderstood. We will reach the goal of freedom in Birmingham and all over the nation, because the goal of America is freedom. Abused and scorned though we may be, our destiny is tied up with the destiny of America. Before the pilgrims landed at Plymouth, we were here. Before the pen of Jefferson etched across the pages of history the majestic words of the Declaration of Independence, we were here. For more than two centuries our foreparents labored in this country without wages; they made cotton "king"; and they built the homes of their masters in the midst of brutal injustice and shameful humiliation—and yet out of a bottomless vitality they continued to thrive and develop. If the inexpressible cruelties of slavery could not stop us, the opposition we now face will surely fail. We will win our freedom because the sacred heritage of our nation and the eternal will of God are embodied in our echoing demands.

I must close now. But before closing I am impelled to mention one other point in your statement that troubled me profoundly. You warmly commended the Birmingham police force for keeping "order" and "preventing violence." I don't believe you would have so warmly commended the police force if you had seen its angry violent dogs literally biting six unarmed, nonviolent Negroes. I don't believe you would so quickly commend the policemen if you would observe their ugly and inhuman treatment of Negroes here in the city jail; if you would watch them push and curse old Negro women and young Negro girls; if you would see them slap and kick old Negro men and young Negro boys; if you will observe them, as they did on two occasions, refuse to give us food because we wanted to sing our grace together. I'm sorry that I can't join you in your praise for the police department.

It is true that they have been rather disciplined in their public handling of the demonstrators. In this sense they have been rather publicly "nonviolent." But for what purpose? To preserve the evil system of segregation. Over the last few years I have consistently preached that nonviolence demands that the means we use must be as pure as the ends we seek. So I have tried to make it clear that it is wrong to use immoral means to attain moral ends. But now I must affirm that it is just as wrong, or even more so, to use moral means to preserve immoral ends. Maybe Mr. Connor and his policemen have been rather publicly nonviolent, as Chief Pritchett[14] was in Albany, Georgia, but they have used the moral means of nonviolence to maintain the immoral end of flagrant racial injustice. T. S. Eliot has said that there is no greater treason than to do the right deed for the wrong reason.

I wish you had commended the Negro sit-inners and demonstrators 45 of Birmingham for their sublime courage, their willingness to suffer, and their amazing discipline in the midst of the most inhuman provocation. One day the South will recognize its real heroes. They will be the James Merediths,[15] courageously and with a majestic sense of purpose, facing jeering and hostile mobs and the agonizing loneliness that characterizes the life of the pioneer. They will be old, oppressed, battered Negro women, symbolized in a seventy-two year old woman of Montgomery, Alabama, who rose up with a sense of dignity and with her people decided not to ride the segregated buses, and responded to one who inquired about her tiredness with ungrammatical profundity: "My feets is tired, but my soul is rested." They will be young high school and college students, young ministers of the gospel and a host of the elders, courageously and nonviolently sitting in at lunch counters and willingly going to jail for conscience's sake. One day the South will know that when these disinherited children of God sat down at lunch counters they were in reality standing up for the best in the American dream and the most sacred values in our Judeo-Christian heritage, and thus carrying our whole nation back to great wells of democracy which were dug deep by the founding fathers in the formulation of the Constitution and the Declaration of Independence.

Never before have I written a letter this long (or should I say a book?). I'm afraid that it is much too long to take your precious time. I can assure you that it would have been much shorter if I had been writing from a comfortable desk, but what else is there to do when you are alone for days in the dull monotony of a narrow jail cell other than write long letters, think strange thoughts, and pray long prayers?

If I have said anything in this letter that is an overstatement of the truth and is indicative of an unreasonable impatience, I beg you to forgive me. If I have said anything in this letter that is an understatement of the truth and is indicative of my having a patience that makes me patient with anything less than brotherhood, I beg God to forgive me.

I hope this letter finds you strong in the faith. I also hope that circumstances will soon make it possible for me to meet each of you, not as an integrationist or a civil rights leader, but as a fellow clergyman and a

---

[14]***Chief Pritchett:*** Pritchett served as police chief in Albany, Georgia, during nonviolent demonstrations in 1961 and 1962. Chief Pritchett responded to the nonviolent demonstrations with nonviolence, refusing to allow his officers to physically or verbally abuse the demonstrators. —EDS.

[15]***James Merediths:*** Under the protection of federal marshals and the National Guard in 1962, James Meredith was the first black man to enroll at the University of Mississippi. —EDS.

Christian brother. Let us all hope that the dark clouds of racial prejudice will soon pass away and the deep fog of misunderstanding will be lifted from our fear-drenched communities and in some not too distant tomorrow the radiant stars of love and brotherhood will shine over our great nation with all of their scintillating beauty.

> *Yours for the cause of*
> *Peace and Brotherhood*
> MARTIN LUTHER KING JR.

The Reader's Presence

1. What does King gain by characterizing his "Fellow Clergymen" as "men of genuine good will," whose criticisms are "sincerely set forth" (paragraph 1)? What evidence can you point to in King's letter to verify the claim that his audience extends far beyond the eight clergymen he explicitly addresses? Comment on the overall structure of King's letter. What principle of composition underpins the structure of his response?

2. King establishes the tone of his response to the criticisms of the clergymen at the end of the opening paragraph: "I would like to answer your statement in what I hope will be patient and reasonable terms." As you reread his letter, identify specific words and phrases—as well as argumentative strategies—that satisfy these criteria that King imposes on himself. In what specific sense does King use the word *hope* here? As you reread his letter, point to each subsequent reference to hope. How does King emphasize the different meanings and connotations of the word as he unfolds his argument?

3. This letter has the ring of the oratory for which King was widely known and justly praised. Read passages aloud and note the ways that King appeals to his reader's ear (for example, with the balanced clauses of many of his sentences). How do the cadences of King's prose help to make his point? Compare King's letter to the famous "I Have a Dream" speech (page 715) he made in the same year. Although one is composed as a letter and the other was delivered as a stirring public address, what elements of language do they share?

THE WRITER AT WORK

Martin Luther King Jr. on Self-Importance

In the following piece, the famous African American political leader expresses his profound mistrust of the individual voice that rises above those for whom that voice speaks. In this, as in so many respects, King joins a long tradition of wrestling with the question of how to reconcile one's own creativity with the larger—and vastly more important—word and mission of God. King's spiritual mission was, of course, a social vision as well: that of racial equality in America. In speaking for those who believed with him in the possibility of making this dream a reality, King drew upon his consummate skills as a preacher, an orator, and an organizer. Throughout his short public life (spanning only twelve years, ending with his assassination on April 4, 1968, in Memphis, Tennessee), King struggled with the competing claims of personal celebrity and of the community he so forcefully represented. How do King's ideas about representation (standing for and speaking on behalf of others) resonate with the ideas of other notable Americans included in this anthology, for example, Thomas Jefferson (page 708), Malcolm X (page 168), and Abraham Lincoln (page 460)?

Would you allow me to share a personal experience with you this morning? And I say it only because I think it has bearing on this message. One of the problems that I have to face and even fight every day is this problem of self-centeredness, this tendency that can so easily come to my life now that I'm something special, that I'm something important. Living over the past year, I can hardly go into any city or any town in this nation where I'm not lavished with hospitality by peoples of all races and of all creeds. I can hardly go anywhere to speak in this nation where hundreds and thousands of people are not turned away because of lack of space. And then after speaking, I often have to be rushed out to get away from the crowd rushing for autographs. I can hardly walk the street in any city of this nation where I'm not confronted with people running up on the street, "Isn't this Reverend King of Alabama?" Living under this it's easy, it's a dangerous tendency that I will come to feel that I'm something special, that I stand somewhere in this universe because of my ingenuity and that I'm important, that I can walk around life with a type of arrogance because of an importance that I have. And one of the prayers that I pray to God every day is: "O God, help me to see my self in my true perspective. Help me, O God, to see that I'm just a symbol of a movement. Help me to see that I'm the victim of what the Germans call a *Zeitgeist* and that something was getting ready to happen in history; history was ready for it. And that a boycott would have taken place in Montgomery, Alabama, if I had never come to Alabama. Help me to realize that I'm where I am because of the forces of history and because of the fifty thousand Negroes of Alabama who will never get their names in the papers and in the headline. O God, help me to see that where I

stand today, I stand because others helped me to stand there and because
the forces of history projected me there. And this movement would have
come in history even if M. L. King had never been born." And when we
come to see that, we stand with humility. This is the prayer I pray to
God every day, "Lord help me to see M. L. King as M. L. King in his
true perspective." Because if I don't see that, I will become the biggest
fool in America.

Laura Kipnis

Against Love

    *Laura Kipnis is a cultural theorist, an author, and a videographer whose
work blends academic theory, social criticism, and witty analysis, all "richly informed by her post-marxist, post-structuralist, post-feminist, post-everything
sense of humor," according to a recent biography. A professor in the school of
communications at Northwestern University in Evanston, Illinois, she is the author of several books, including* Ecstasy Unlimited *(1993),* Bound and Gagged:
Pornography and the Politics of Fantasy in America *(1996),* Against Love: A
Polemic *(2003), and* The Female Thing: Dirt, Sex, Envy, Vulnerability *(2006).
Kipnis's video essays—including* Ecstasy Unlimited: The Interpenetrations of Sex
and Capital *(1985),* A Man's Woman *(1988), and* Marx: The Video *(1990)—
have been screened in such venues as the Museum of Modern Art, the American
Film Institute, and the Whitney Museum. Kipnis has also written essays and re-
views for* Slate, *the* Village Voice, Harper's, Critical Inquiry, Wide Angle, *and the*
New York Times Magazine, *where "Against Love" appeared in 2001.*

    *Kipnis's work has evolved over time, shifting from what was once a strictly
academic tone to her more recent playful and casual style. In an interview with
the editor of the* Minnesota Review, *she admits that she has developed a growing
interest in "creativity" over "theory." She explains, "I trace it back to my art
school origins. I started as a painter, actually, and there's something about the
writing I've been doing lately which has gotten really intricate and worked over,
that reminds me of my origins as a painter. I've started to write in a painterly
way, dabbing at it, endlessly revising."*

    In a discussion of Against Love *in 2001, Kipnis pointed out that "the voice
isn't precisely 'me,' it's some far more vivacious and playful version of me. It's a
polemic, so there are certain questions I don't have to address, or complications I
don't have to go into. I can be completely irresponsible. I love it."*

Love is, as we know, a mysterious and controlling force. It has vast power over our thoughts and life decisions. It demands our loyalty, and we, in turn, freely comply. Saying no to love isn't simply heresy; it is tragedy—the failure to achieve what is most essentially human. So deeply internalized is our obedience to this most capricious despot that artists create passionate odes to its cruelty, and audiences seem never to tire of the most deeply unoriginal mass spectacles devoted to rehearsing the litany of its torments, fixating their very beings on the narrowest glimmer of its fleeting satisfactions.

Yet despite near total compliance, a buzz of social nervousness attends the subject. If a society's lexicon of romantic pathologies reveals its particular anxieties, high on our own list would be diagnoses like "inability to settle down" or "immaturity," leveled at those who stray from the norms of domestic coupledom either by refusing entry in the first place or, once installed, pursuing various escape routes: excess independence, ambivalence, "straying," divorce. For the modern lover, "maturity" isn't a depressing signal of impending decrepitude but a sterling achievement, the sine qua non of a lover's qualifications to love and be loved.

This injunction to achieve maturity—synonymous in contemporary usage with thirty-year mortgages, spreading waistlines, and monogamy—obviously finds its raison d'être in modern love's central anxiety, that structuring social contradiction the size of the San Andreas Fault: namely, the expectation that romance and sexual attraction can last a lifetime of coupled togetherness despite much hard evidence to the contrary.

Ever optimistic, heady with love's utopianism, most of us eventually pledge ourselves to unions that will, if successful, far outlast the desire that impelled them into being. The prevailing cultural wisdom is that even if sexual desire tends to be a short-lived phenomenon, "mature love" will kick in to save the day when desire flags. The issue that remains unaddressed is whether cutting off other possibilities of romance and sexual attraction for the more muted pleasures of mature love isn't similar to voluntarily amputating a healthy limb: a lot of anesthesia is required and the phantom pain never entirely abates. But if it behooves a society to convince its citizenry that wanting change means personal failure or wanting to start over is shameful or simply wanting more satisfaction than what you have is an illicit thing, clearly grisly acts of self-mutilation will be required.

There hasn't always been quite such optimism about love's longevity. For the Greeks, inventors of democracy and a people not amenable to being pushed around by despots, love was a disordering and thus preferably brief experience. During the reign of courtly love, love was illicit and usually fatal. Passion meant suffering: the happy ending didn't yet exist in the cultural imagination. As far as togetherness as an eternal ideal, the 12th-century advice manual "De Amore et Amoris Remedio" ("On Love and

5

the Remedies of Love") warned that too many opportunities to see or chat with the beloved would certainly decrease love.

The innovation of happy love didn't even enter the vocabulary of romance until the 17th century. Before the 18th century—when the family was primarily an economic unit of production rather than a hothouse of Oedipal tensions—marriages were business arrangements between families; participants had little to say on the matter. Some historians consider romantic love a learned behavior that really only took off in the late 18th century along with the new fashion for reading novels, though even then affection between a husband and wife was considered to be in questionable taste.

Historians disagree, of course. Some tell the story of love as an eternal and unchanging essence; others, as a progress narrative over stifling social conventions. (Sometimes both stories are told at once; consistency isn't required.) But has modern love really set us free? Fond as we are of projecting our own emotional quandaries back through history, construing vivid costume dramas featuring medieval peasants or biblical courtesans sharing their feelings with the post-Freudian savvy of lifelong analysands, our amatory predecessors clearly didn't share all our particular aspirations about their romantic lives.

We, by contrast, feel like failures when love dies. We believe it could be otherwise. Since the cultural expectation is that a state of coupled permanence is achievable, uncoupling is experienced as crisis and inadequacy—even though such failures are more the norm than the exception.

As love has increasingly become the center of all emotional expression in the popular imagination, anxiety about obtaining it in sufficient quantities—and for sufficient duration—suffuses the population. Everyone knows that as the demands and expectations on couples escalated, so did divorce rates. And given the current divorce statistics (roughly 50 percent of all marriages end in divorce), all indications are that whomever you love today—your beacon of hope, the center of all your optimism—has a good chance of becoming your worst nightmare tomorrow. (Of course, that 50 percent are those who actually leave their unhappy marriages and not a particularly good indication of the happiness level or nightmare potential of those who remain.) Lawrence Stone, a historian of marriage, suggests—rather jocularly, you can't help thinking—that today's rising divorce rates are just a modern technique for achieving what was once taken care of far more efficiently by early mortality.

Love may or may not be a universal emotion, but clearly the social   10
forms it takes are infinitely malleable. It is our culture alone that has dedicated itself to allying the turbulence of romance and the rationality of the long-term couple, convinced that both love and sex are obtainable from one person over the course of decades, that desire will manage to sustain itself for thirty or forty or fifty years and that the supposed fate of social stability is tied to sustaining a fleeting experience beyond its given life span.

Of course, the parties involved must "work" at keeping passion alive (and we all know how much fun that is), the presumption being that even after living in close proximity to someone for a historically unprecedented length of time, you will still muster the requisite desire to achieve sexual congress on a regular basis. (Should passion fizzle out, just give up sex. Lack of desire for a mate is never an adequate rationale for "looking elsewhere.") And it is true, many couples do manage to perform enough psychic retooling to reshape the anarchy of desire to the confines of the marriage bed, plugging away at the task year after year (once a week, same time, same position) like diligent assembly-line workers, aided by the occasional fantasy or two to help get the old motor to turn over, or keep running, or complete the trip. And so we have the erotic life of a nation of workaholics: if sex seems like work, clearly you're not working hard enough at it.

But passion must not be allowed to die! The fear—or knowledge—that it does shapes us into particularly conflicted psychological beings, perpetually in search of prescriptions and professional interventions, regardless of cost or consequence. Which does have its economic upside, at least. Whole new sectors of the economy have been spawned, with massive social investment in new technologies from Viagra to couples' porn: capitalism's Lourdes[1] for dying marriages.

There are assorted low-tech solutions to desire's dilemmas too. Take advice. In fact, take more and more advice. Between print, airwaves, and the therapy industry, if there were any way to quantify the G.N.P. in romantic counsel, it would be a staggering number. Desperate to be cured of love's temporality, a love-struck populace has molded itself into an advanced race of advice receptacles, like some new form of miracle sponge that can instantly absorb many times its own body weight in wetness.

Inexplicably, however, a rebellious breakaway faction keeps trying to leap over the wall and emancipate themselves, not from love itself—unthinkable!—but from love's domestic confinements. The escape routes are well trodden—love affairs, midlife crises—though strewn with the left-behind luggage of those who encountered unforeseen obstacles along the way (panic, guilt, self-engineered exposures) and beat self-abashed retreats to their domestic gulags, even after pledging body and soul to newfound loves in the balmy utopias of nondomesticated romances. Will all the adulterers in the audience please stand up? You know who you are. Don't be embarrassed! Adulterers aren't just "playing around." These are our home-grown closet social theorists, because adultery is not just a referendum on the sustainability of monogamy; it is a veiled philosophical discussion about the social contract itself. The question on the table is thus "How much renunciation of desire does society demand of us, versus the degree of gratification it provides?" Clearly, the adulterer's answer, following a long line of venerable social critics, would be, "Too much."

---

[1]*Lourdes:* Notre Dame de Lourdes in France has been a site of Catholic pilgrimage ever since a fourteen-year-old girl reportedly received a vision there in 1858.—Eds.

But what exactly is it about the actual lived experience of modern do-   15
mestic love that would make flight such a compelling option for so many?
Let us briefly examine those material daily life conditions.

Fundamentally, to achieve love and qualify for entry into that realm
of salvation and transcendence known as the couple (the secular equivalent of entering a state of divine grace), you must *be* a lovable person.
And what precisely does being lovable entail? According to the tenets of
modern love, it requires an advanced working knowledge of the intricacies of *mutuality*.

Mutuality means recognizing that your partner has needs and being
prepared to meet them. This presumes, of course, that the majority of
those needs can and should be met by one person. (Question this, and
you question the very foundations of the institution. So don't.) These
needs of ours run deep, a tangled underground morass of ancient, gnarled
roots, looking to ensnarl any hapless soul who might accidentally trod
upon their outer radices.

Still, meeting those needs is the most effective way to become the object
of another's desire, thus attaining intimacy, which is required to achieve the
state known as psychological maturity. (Despite how closely it reproduces
the affective conditions of our childhoods, since trading compliance for love
is the earliest social lesson learned; we learn it in our cribs.)

You, in return, will have your own needs met by your partner in matters large and small. In practice, many of these matters turn out to be
quite small. Frequently, it is the tensions and disagreements over the
minutiae of daily living that stand between couples and their requisite intimacy. Taking out the garbage, tone of voice, a forgotten errand—these
are the rocky shoals upon which intimacy so often founders.

Mutuality requires *communication*, since in order to be met, these   20
needs must be expressed. (No one's a mind reader, which is not to say that
many of us don't expect this quality in a mate. Who wants to keep having
to tell someone what you need?) What you need is for your mate to understand you—your desires, your contradictions, your unique sensitivities,
what irks you. (In practice, that means what about your mate irks you.)
You, in turn, must learn to understand the mate's needs. This means
being willing to hear what about yourself irks your mate. Hearing is not a
simple physiological act performed with the ears, as you will learn. You
may think you know how to *hear*, but that doesn't mean that you know
how to *listen*.

With two individuals required to coexist in enclosed spaces for
extended periods of time, domesticity requires substantial quantities of
compromise and adaptation simply to avoid mayhem. Yet with the post-
Romantic ideal of unconstrained individuality informing our most fundamental ideas of the self, this can prove a perilous process. Both parties
must be willing to jettison whatever aspects of individuality might prove
irritating while being simultaneously allowed to retain enough individual-

ity to feel their autonomy is not being sacrificed, even as it is being surgically excised.

Having mastered mutuality, you may now proceed to *advanced intimacy*. Advanced intimacy involves inviting your partner "in" to your most interior self. Whatever and wherever our "inside" is, the widespread—if somewhat metaphysical—belief in its existence (and the related belief that whatever is in there is dying to get out) has assumed a quasi-medical status. Leeches once served a similar purpose. Now we "express our feelings" in lieu of our fluids because everyone knows that those who don't are far more prone to cancer, ulcers or various dire ailments.

With love as our culture's patent medicine, prescribed for every ill (now even touted as a necessary precondition for that other great American obsession, longevity), we willingly subject ourselves to any number of arcane procedures in its quest. "Opening up" is required for relationship health, so lovers fashion themselves after doctors wielding long probes to penetrate the tender regions. Try to think of yourself as one big orifice: now stop clenching and relax. If the procedure proves uncomfortable, it just shows you're not open enough. Psychotherapy may be required before sufficient dilation can be achieved: the world's most expensive lubricant.

Needless to say, this opening-up can leave you feeling quite vulnerable, lying there psychically spread-eagled and shivering on the examining table of your relationship. (A favored suspicion is that your partner, knowing exactly where your vulnerabilities are, deliberately kicks you there—one reason this opening-up business may not always feel as pleasant as advertised.) And as anyone who has spent much time in—or just in earshot of—a typical couple knows, the "expression of needs" is often the Trojan horse of intimate warfare, since expressing needs means, by definition, that one's partner has thus far failed to meet them.

In any long-term couple, this lexicon of needs becomes codified over time into a highly evolved private language with its own rules. Let's call this couple grammar. Close observation reveals this as a language composed of one recurring unit of speech: the interdiction—highly nuanced, mutually imposed commands and strictures extending into the most minute areas of household affairs, social life, finances, speech, hygiene, allowable idiosyncrasies and so on. From bathroom to bedroom, car to kitchen, no aspect of coupled life is not subject to scrutiny, negotiation and codes of conduct.

A sample from an inexhaustible list, culled from interviews with numerous members of couples of various ages, races and sexual orientations: You can't leave the house without saying where you're going. You can't not say what time you'll return. You can't go out when the other person feels like staying at home. You can't be a slob. You can't do less than 50 percent of the work around the house, even if the other person wants to do 100 percent more cleaning than you find necessary or even reasonable. You can't leave the dishes for later, load them the way that seems best to you, drink straight from the carton or make crumbs. You can't leave the bathroom door open — it's offensive. You can't leave the bathroom door closed — your partner needs to get in. You can't not shave your underarms or legs. You can't gain weight. You can't watch soap operas. You can't watch infomercials or the pregame show or Martha Stewart. You can't eat what you want — goodbye Marshmallow Fluff; hello tofu meatballs. You can't spend too much time on the computer. And stay out of those chat rooms. You can't take risks, unless they are agreed-upon risks, which somewhat limits the concept of "risk." You can't make major purchases alone, or spend money on things the other person considers excesses. You can't blow money just because you're in a bad mood, and you can't be in a bad mood without being required to explain it. You can't begin a sentence with "You always. . . ." You can't begin a sentence with "I never. . . ." You can't be simplistic, even when things are simple. You can't say what you really think of that outfit or color combination or cowboy hat. You can't be cynical about things the other person is sincere about. You can't drink without the other person counting your drinks. You can't have the wrong laugh. You can't bum cigarettes when you're out because it embarrasses your mate, even though you've explained the unspoken fraternity between smokers. You can't tailgate, honk or listen to talk radio in the car. And so on. The specifics don't matter. What matters is that the operative word is "can't."

Thus is love obtained.

Certainly, domesticity offers innumerable rewards: companionship, child-rearing convenience, reassuring predictability and many other benefits too varied to list. But if love has power over us, domesticity is its enforcement wing: the iron dust mop in the velvet glove. The historian Michel Foucault[2] has argued that modern power made its mark on the world by inventing new types of enclosures and institutions, places like factories, schools, barracks, prisons and asylums, where individuals could be located, supervised, processed and subjected to inspection, order and the clock. What current social institution is more enclosed than modern intimacy? What offers greater regulation of movement and time, or more precise surveillance of body and thought, to a greater number of individuals?

Of course, it is your choice — as if any of us could really choose not   30
to desire love or not to feel like hopeless losers should we fail at it. We moderns are beings yearning to be filled, yearning to be overtaken by love's mysterious power. We prostrate ourselves at love's portals, like social strivers waiting at the rope line outside some exclusive club hoping to gain admission and thereby confirm our essential worth. A life without love lacks an organizing narrative. A life without love seems so barren,

---

[2]*Foucault:* (1926–1984) French philosopher and historian who questioned assumptions about the constitution of power and knowledge. — EDS.

and it might almost make you consider how empty the rest of the world is, as if love were vital plasma and everything else just tap water.

Exchanging obedience for love comes naturally — after all, we all were once children whose survival depended on the caprices of love. And there you have the template for future intimacies. If you love me, you'll do what I want — or need, or demand — and I'll love you in return. We all become household dictators, petty tyrants of the private sphere, who are, in our turn, dictated to.

And why has modern love developed in such a way as to maximize submission and minimize freedom, with so little argument about it? No doubt a citizenry schooled in renouncing desire instead of imagining there could be something more would be, in many respects, advantageous. After all, wanting more is the basis for utopian thinking, a path toward dangerous social demands, even toward imagining the possibilities for altogether different social arrangements. But if the most elegant forms of social control are those that came packaged in the guise of individual needs and satisfactions, so wedded to the individual psyche that any opposing impulse registers as the anxiety of unlovability, who needs a soldier on every corner? We are more than happy to police ourselves and those we love and call it living happily ever after. Perhaps a secular society needed another metaphysical entity to subjugate itself to after the death of God, and love was available for the job. But isn't it a little depressing to think we are somehow incapable of inventing forms of emotional life based on anything other than subjugation?

The Reader's Presence

1. How does Kipnis reevaluate the meaning of adultery and mid-life crises? What sort of evidence are these phenomena, in her opinion?

2. What elements of Kipnis's writing mark this essay as a scholarly argument? Do you agree that it is also a "polemic," as the subtitle of her book indicates? Is it more effective as a scholarly argument or as a polemic? Why?

3. Kipnis suggests that society benefits from convincing its populace to marry and that people have been brainwashed into believing that these long-term arrangements are natural. What benefits does society gain from long-term relationships? What, in Kipnis's opinion, do individuals give up? Read John Taylor Gatto's "Against School" (page 682). What, according to his argument, does the individual lose in submitting to compulsory schooling? Who, according to Gatto, benefits from it?

Steven D. Levitt and Stephen J. Dubner

Trading Up: Where Do Baby Names Come From?

Steven D. Levitt (b. 1967) and Stephen J. Dubner (b. 1963) teamed up to write the enormously popular and influential book Freakonomics. *Published in 2005, the book was on the* New York Times *best-seller list for over two years, selling more than 3 million copies worldwide. Their selection, "Trading Up: Where Do Baby Names Come From?" is excerpted from the book and appeared on* Slate *in 2005.*

Levitt graduated from Harvard University and received his PhD from the Massachusetts Institute of Technology. He has been a professor of economics at the University of Chicago since 1997 and is the director of the Becker Center on Chicago Price Theory, a research center administered by the Graduate School of Business that emphasizes the role of markets and incentives in understanding economics and human behavior—fundamental elements of the new study of "freakonomics." An award-winning economist, Levitt was named one of Time *magazine's "100 People Who Shape Our World" and, in 2004, received the John Bates Clark Medal, which recognizes the most influential economist in America under the age of 40.*

Author and journalist Stephen J. Dubner received his MFA from Columbia University in New York City. In addition to co-writing Freakonomics, *he is the author of two books of nonfiction/memoir,* Turbulent Souls: A Catholic Son's Return to His Jewish Family *(1998) and* Confessions of a Hero-Worshipper *(2003); and a book for young children,* The Boy with Two Belly Buttons *(2007). His work appears frequently in the* New Yorker *and the* New York Times, *and has been anthologized in* Best American Sports Writing *and* Best American Crime Writing, *among others. Both writers contribute to the* New York Times *blog, "Freakonomics."*

The California names data tell a lot of stories in addition to the one about the segregation of white and black first names. Broadly speaking, the data tell us how parents see themselves—and, more significantly, what kinds of expectations they have for their children.

The actual source of a name is usually obvious: There's the Bible, there's the huge cluster of traditional English and Germanic and Italian and French names, there are princess names and hippie names, nostalgic names and place names. Increasingly, there are brand names (Lexus, Armani, Bacardi, Timberland) and what might be called aspirational names. The California data show eight Harvards born during the 1990s (all of them black), 15 Yales (all white), and 18 Princetons (all black). There were no Doctors but three Lawyers (all black), nine Judges (eight of them white), three Senators (all white), and two Presidents (both black).

But how does a name migrate through the population, and why? Is it purely a matter of zeitgeist, or is there a more discernible pattern to these movements?

Consider the 10 most popular names given to white girls in California in 1980 and then in 2000. A single holdover: Sarah. So, where do these Emilys and Emmas and Laurens all come from? Where on earth did *Madison* come from? It's easy enough to see that new names become very popular very fast—but why?

Most Popular Overall White Girl Names

1980	2000
1. Jennifer	1. Emily
2. Sarah	2. Hannah
3. Melissa	3. Madison
4. Jessica	4. Sarah
5. Christina	5. Samantha
6. Amanda	6. Lauren
7. Nicole	7. Ashley
8. Michelle	8. Emma
9. Heather	9. Taylor
10. Amber	10. Megan

Let's take a look at the top five girls' names and top five boys' names ⁵ given during the 1990s among high-income white families and low-income white families, ranked in order of their relative rarity in the opposite category.

Most Popular High-End White Girl Names in the 1990s

1. Alexandra
2. Lauren
3. Katherine
4. Madison
5. Rachel

Most Popular Low-End White Girl Names in the 1990s

1. Amber
2. Heather
3. Kayla
4. Stephanie
5. Alyssa

Most Popular High-End White Boy Names

1. Benjamin
2. Samuel
3. Jonathan
4. Alexander
5. Andrew

Most Popular Low-End White Boy Names

1. Cody
2. Brandon
3. Anthony
4. Justin
5. Robert

Now compare the "high-end" and "low-end" girls' names with the most popular ones overall from 1980 and 2000. Lauren and Madison, two of the most popular high-end names from the 1990s, made the overall top-10 list in 2000. Amber and Heather, meanwhile, two of the overall most popular names from 1980, are now among the low-end names.

Most Popular Overall

1980	2000
1. Jennifer	1. Emily
2. Sarah	2. Hannah
3. Melissa	3. Madison
4. Jessica	4. Sarah
5. Christina	5. Samantha
6. Amanda	6. Lauren
7. Nicole	7. Ashley
8. Michelle	8. Emma
9. Heather	9. Taylor
10. Amber	10. Megan

Most Popular High-End	**Most Popular Low-End**
1990s	1990s
1. Alexandra	1. Amber
2. Lauren	2. Heather
3. Katherine	3. Kayla
4. Madison	4. Stephanie
5. Rachel	5. Alyssa

There is a pattern at play: Once a names catches on among high-income, highly educated parents, it starts working its way down the socioeconomic ladder. Amber, Heather, and Stephanie started out as high-end names. For every high-end baby given those names, however, another *five* lower-income girls received those names within 10 years.

Many people assume that naming trends are driven by celebrities. But how many Madonnas do you know? Or, considering all the Brittanys, Britneys, Brittanis, Brittanies, Brittneys, and Brittnis you encounter these days, you might think of Britney Spears; but she is in fact a symptom, not a cause, of the Brittany/Britney/Brittani/Brittanie/Brittney/Brittni explosion—and hers is a name that began on the high end and has since fallen to the low. Most families don't shop for baby names in Hollywood. They look to the family just a few blocks over, the one with the bigger house and newer car. The kind of families that were the first to call their daughters Amber or Heather, and are now calling them Alexandra or Katherine. The kind of families that used to name their sons Justin or Brandon and are now calling them Alexander or Benjamin. Parents are reluctant to poach a name from someone too near—family members or close friends—

but many parents, whether they realize it or not, like the sound of names that sound "successful."

Once a high-end name is adopted en masse, however, high-end parents begin to abandon it. Eventually, it will be considered so common that even lower-end parents may not want it, whereby it falls out of the rotation entirely. The lower-end parents, meanwhile, go looking for the next name that the upper-end parents have broken in.

So, the implication is clear: The parents of all those Alexandras and   10
Katherines, Madisons and Rachels should not expect the cachet to last much longer. Those names are just now peaking and are already on their way to overexposure. Where, then, will the new high-end names come from? Considering the traditionally strong correlation between income and education, it probably makes sense to look at the most popular current names among parents with the most years of education. Here, drawn from a pair of databases that provide the years of parental education, is a sampling of such names. Some of them, as unlikely as it seems, may well become tomorrow's mainstream names. Before you scoff, ask yourself this: Do Aviva or Clementine seem any more ridiculous than Madison might have seemed 10 years ago?

Most Popular Girls' Names of 2015?	Most Popular Boys' Names of 2015?
Annika	Aidan
Ansley	Aldo
Ava	Anderson
Avery	Ansel
Aviva	Asher
Clementine	Beckett
Eleanor	Bennett
Ella	Carter
Emma	Cooper
Fiona	Finnegan
Flannery	Harper
Grace	Jackson
Isabel	Johan
Kate	Keyon
Lara	Liam
Linden	Maximilian
Maeve	McGregor
Marie-Claire	Oliver
Maya	Reagan
Philippa	Sander
Phoebe	Sumner
Quinn	Will
Sophie	
Waverly	

Obviously, a variety of motives are at work when parents consider a name for their child. It would be an overstatement to suggest that all parents are looking—whether consciously or not—for a smart name or a high-end name. But they are all trying to signal *something* with a name, and an overwhelming number of parents are seemingly trying to signal their own expectations of how successful they hope their children will be. The name itself isn't likely to make a shred of difference. But the parents may feel better knowing that, from the very outset, they tried their best.

The Reader's Presence

1. Why would economists be interested in the names parents give their children? In what ways does naming seem appropriate or inappropriate to the field of economics? How do Levitt and Dubner use an economic approach to understand the subject? Do they persuade you that our names have a distinct economic significance? Why or why not?

2. Levitt and Dubner's research leads them to believe that popular names move over time down the class scale—that is, the "high-end" names of the 1980s become the "low-end" names of the 1990s. But where do the high-end names originate? In your opinion, if parents hope to signify success in giving their child a name that isn't on its way down the social scale, how do they select the new name that's on its way up? Can you explain that part of their theory?

3. Examine Levitt and Dubner's theory of names against Barry Schwartz's essay, "The Tyranny of Choice" (page 834). For new parents, the choice of names to give their baby is enormous; entire books exist listing hundreds of names. How might Schwartz's argument engage with Levitt and Dubner's theory? Can it help explain why a certain few names are used over and over in a population? Why or why not? Look at Levitt and Dubner's theory with respect to a personal essay, Maya Angelou's "What's Your Name, Girl?" (page 17). Explain whether you think an economic interpretation can be applied to the conflict dramatized in that essay.

Bill McKibben

Worried? Us?

Bill McKibben (b. 1960) advocates human behavior toward Earth that is "sound and elegant and civilized and respectful of community." Born in Palo Alto, California, and raised in Massachusetts, he now lives with his family in New York's Adirondack Mountains. After graduating from Harvard University in 1982, McKibben immediately went to work as a writer, and later as an editor, at the New Yorker, *where he wrote more than four hundred articles for the magazine's "Talk of the Town" column. His essays, reporting, and criticism appear regularly in publications such as the* Atlantic Monthly, Harper's, *the* New York Review of Books, *the* New York Times, Natural History, Orion, Rolling Stone, *and* Outside. *McKibben is currently scholar-in-residence in environmental studies at Middlebury College in Vermont.*

McKibben's 1989 book, The End of Nature, *sounded one of the earliest alarms about global warming and catalyzed an international debate on the issue that is still ongoing. His long list of books catalogs his concerns about the health of our global ecosystem, particularly the relationship between humanity and nature and the impact of our consumer society on both. His recent books include* Long Distance *(2000),* Enough: Staying Human in an Engineered Age *(2003),* Wandering Home *(2005),* Comforting Whirlwind: God, Job, and the Scale of Creation *(2005),* The Age of Missing Information *(2006),* Deep Economy: The Wealth of Communities and the Durable Future *(2007), and* Fight Global Warming *(2007). His collected essays,* The Bill McKibben Reader, *was published in 2008, as was* American Earth: Environmental Writing Since Thoreau, *which he edited.*

In a 1999 interview, McKibben discussed the competing visions of what is good for people and the planet on which we live: "The market forces pushing convenience, individualism, and comfort are still stronger than the attraction of community, fellowship, and connection with the natural world. . . . What we call the environmental crisis is really a crisis of desire. We're losing the battle to offer people an alternative set of things to desire."

McKibbens's essay "Worried? Us?" asks why, in the face of mainstream scientific evidence to the contrary, so many people continue to ignore the threat of global warming. It was first published in Granta *in 2003.*

For fifteen years now, some small percentage of the world's scientists and diplomats and activists has inhabited one of those strange dreams where the dreamer desperately needs to warn someone about something bad and imminent; but somehow, no matter how hard he shouts, the other person in the dream—standing smiling, perhaps, with his back to an oncoming train—can't hear him. This group, this small percentage, knows that the world is about to change more profoundly than at any time in the history of human civilization. And yet, so far, all they have achieved is to add another line to the long list of human problems—people

761

think about "global warming" in the way they think about "violence on televison" or "growing trade deficits," as a marginal concern to them, if a concern at all. Enlightened governments make smallish noises and negotiate smallish treaties; enlightened people look down on America for its blind piggishness. Hardly anyone, however, has fear in their guts.

Why? Because, I think, we are fatally confused about time and space. Though we know that our culture has placed our own lives on a demonic fast-forward, we imagine that the earth must work on some other timescale. The long slow accretion of epochs—the Jurassic, the Cretaceous, the Pleistocene—lulls us into imagining that the physical world offers us an essentially stable background against which we can run our race. Humbly, we believe that the world is big and that we are small. This humility is attractive, but also historic and no longer useful. In the world as we have made it, the opposite is true. Each of us is big enough, for example, to produce our own cloud of carbon dioxide. As a result, we—our cars and our industry—have managed to raise the atmospheric level of carbon dioxide, which had been stable at 275 parts per million throughout human civilization, to about 380 parts per million, a figure that is climbing by one and a half parts per million each year. This increase began with the Industrial Revolution in the eighteenth century, and it has been accelerating ever since. The consequence, if we take a median from several respectable scientific projections, is that the world's temperature will rise by five degrees Fahrenheit (roughly two and a half degrees Celsius) over the next hundred years, to make it hotter than it has been for 400 million years. At some level, these are the only facts worth knowing about our earth.

Fifteen years ago, it was a hypothesis. Those of us who were convinced that the earth was warming fast were a small minority. Science was skeptical, but set to work with rigor. Between 1988 and 1995, scientists drilled deep into glaciers, took core samples from lake bottoms, counted tree rings, and, most importantly, refined elaborate computer models of the atmosphere. By 1995, the almost impossibly contentious world of science had seen enough. The world's most distinguished atmospheric chemists, physicists and climatologists, who had organized themselves into a large collective called the Intergovernmental Panel on Climate Change, made their pronouncement: "The balance of evidence suggests that there is a discernible human influence on global climate." In the eight years since, science has continued to further confirm and deepen these fears, while the planet itself has decided, as it were, to peer-review their work with a succession of ominously hot years (1998 was the hottest ever, with 2002 trailing by only a few hundredths of a degree). So far humanity has raised the planet's temperature by about one degree Fahrenheit, with most of that increase happening after 1970—from about fifty-nine degrees Fahrenheit, where it had been stuck since the first cities rose and the first crops grew, to about sixty degrees. Five more degrees in the offing, as I have said, but already we understand, with an almost desperate clarity, how finely balanced our world has been. One degree turns out to be a lot. In the cryosphere—the frozen portions of the planet's surface—glaciers are everywhere in rapid retreat (spitting out Bronze Age hunter-gatherers). The snows of Kilimanjaro are set to become the rocks of Kilimanjaro by 2015. Montana's Glacier National Park is predicted to lose its last glaciers by 2030. We know how thick Arctic ice is—we know it because Cold War nuclear-powered submarines needed the information for their voyages under the ice cap. When the data was declassified in the waning days of the Clinton administration, it emerged that Arctic ice was forty per cent thinner than it had been forty years before. *Perma*frost is melting. Get it?

"Global warming" can be a misleading phrase—the temperature is only the signal that extra solar radiation is being trapped at the earth's surface. That extra energy drives many things: wind-speeds increase, a reflection of the increasing heat-driven gradients between low and high pressure; sea level starts to rise, less because of melting ice caps than because warm air holds more water vapor than cold; hence evaporation increases and with it drought, and then, when the overloaded clouds finally part, deluge and flood. Some of these effects are linear. A recent study has shown that rice fertility drops by ten per cent for each degree Celsius that the temperature rises above thirty degrees Celsius during the rice plant's flowering. At forty degrees Celsius, rice fertility drops to zero. But science has come to understand that some effects may not follow such a clear progression. To paraphrase Orwell, we may all be hot, but some will be hotter than others. If the Gulf Stream fails because of Arctic melting, some may, during some seasons, even be colder.

The success of the scientific method underlines the failure of the political method. It is clear what must happen—the rapid conversion of our energy system from fossil to renewable fuels. And it is clear that it could happen—much of the necessary technology is no longer quixotic, no longer the province of backyard tinkerers. And it is also clear that it isn't happening. Some parts of Europe have made material progress—Denmark has built great banks of windmills. Some parts of Europe have made promises—the United Kingdom thinks it can cut its carbon emissions by sixty per cent by 2050. But China and India are still building power plants and motorways, and the United States has made it utterly clear that nothing will change soon. When Bill Clinton was President he sat by while American civilians traded up from cars to troop-transport vehicles; George Bush has not only rejected the Kyoto treaty,[1] he has ordered the Environmental Protection Agency to replace "global warming" with the less ominous "climate change," and issued a national energy

[1]*Kyoto treaty:* A treaty drawn up in 1997 with the aim of reducing worldwide emissions of greenhouse gases. President George W. Bush withdrew it from U.S. consideration in 2001.—EDS.

policy that foresees ever more drilling, refining and burning. Under it, American carbon emissions will grow another forty per cent in the next generation.

As satisfying as it is to blame politicians, however, it will not do. Politicians will follow the path of least resistance. So far there has not been a movement loud or sustained enough to command political attention. Electorates demand economic prosperity—more of it—above all things. Gandhianism, the political philosophy that restricts material need, is now only a memory even in the country of its birth. And our awareness that the world will change in every aspect, should we be so aware, is muted by the future tense, even though that future isn't far away, so near in fact that preventing global warming is a lost cause—all we can do now is to try to keep it from getting utterly out of control.

This is a failure of imagination, and in this way a literary failure. Global warming has still to produce an Orwell or a Huxley, a Verne or a Wells, a *Nineteen Eighty-Four* or a *War of the Worlds*, or in film any equivalent of *On the Beach*[2] or *Doctor Strangelove*. It may never do so. It may be that because—fingers crossed—we have escaped our most recent fear, nuclear annihilation via the Cold War, we resist being scared all over again. Fear has its uses, but fear on this scale seems to be disabling, paralyzing. Anger has its uses too, but the rage of anti-globalization demonstrators has yet to do more than alienate majorities. Shame sends a few Americans shopping for small cars, but on the whole America, now the exemplar to the world, is very nearly unshameable.

My own dominant feeling has always been sadness. In 1989, I published *The End of Nature*, the first book for a lay audience about global warming. Half of it was devoted to explaining the science, the other half to my unease. It seemed, and still seems, to me that humanity has intruded into and altered every part of the earth (or very nearly) with our habits and economies. Thoreau once said that he could walk half an hour from his home in Concord, Massachusetts, and come to a place where no man stood from one year to the next, and "there consequently politics are not, for politics are but the cigar smoke of a man." Now that cigar smoke blows everywhere.

Paradoxically, the world also seems more lonely. Everything else exists at our sufferance. Biologists guess that the result of a rapid warming will be the greatest wave of extinction since the last asteroid crashed into the earth. Now we are the asteroid. The notion that we live in a God-haunted

---

[2]*Huxley . . . On the Beach:* Aldous Huxley (1894–1963), author of the dystopian novel *Brave New World* (1932); Jules Verne (1828–1905), French speculative and science fiction writer, author of *Journey to the Center of the Earth* (1864) and *20,000 Leagues under the Sea* (1870); H. G. Wells (1866–1946), British author of *Island of Dr. Moreau* (1896) and *War of the Worlds* (1898); *On the Beach*, a 1959 film based on a 1957 novel of the same name by Australian writer Nevil Shute, about a group waiting for inevitable death by radiation after a nuclear war. — EDS.

world is harder to conjure up. God rebuked Job: "Were you there when I wrapped the ocean in clouds . . . and set its boundaries, saying, 'Here you may come but no farther. Here shall your proud waves break . . . Who gathers up the stormclouds, slits them and pours them out?'" Job, and everyone else until our time, had the sweet privilege of shutting up in the face of that boast—it was clearly God or gravity or some force other than us. But as of about 1990 we can answer back, because we set the sea level now, and we run the storm systems. The excretion of our economy has become the most important influence on the planet we were born into. We're what counts.

Our ultimate sadness lies in the fact that we know that this is not a pre-ordained destiny; it isn't fate. New ways of behaving, of getting and spending, can still change the future: there is, as the religious evangelist would say, still time, though not much of it, and a miraculous conversion is called for—Americans in the year 2000 produced fifteen per cent more carbon dioxide than they had ten years before.

The contrast between two speeds is the key fact of our age: between the pace at which the physical world is changing and the pace at which human society is reacting to this change. In history, if it exists, we shall be praised or damned.

The Reader's Presence

1. How does McKibben use his opening metaphor to explain his attitude toward the conversation about global warming? What is his tone in the opening paragraph? How would you explain the tone of the title? By the end of the essay, how has his tone changed?

2. What does McKibben say in the essay to support his case that global warming is a major threat to our survival? How does he establish himself as a credible expert on the subject?

3. Compare McKibben's essay to Ian Frazier's "All-Consuming Patriotism" (page 393). Does Frazier's analysis of American culture explain the reluctance of Westerners to take global warming seriously? Why or why not? How might Frazier's theory on the relationship between government and its citizens explain the stance of the United States on environmental policies?

Walter Benn Michaels

The Trouble with Diversity

Walter Benn Michaels (b. 1948) entered a swirl of controversy — from both right and left — with his 2006 book, The Trouble with Diversity, *his polemic against identity politics and economic inequality on college campuses and in the greater society. In his book, he argues that the thorniest problem in American society is not racism or sexism or any of the other isms but the "increasing gap between the rich and the poor." Michaels received his PhD at the University of California, Santa Barbara, and taught English at the University of California, Berkeley, and at Johns Hopkins University before joining the faculty at the University of Illinois at Chicago, where he has taught American literature and literary theory since 2001. His books and monographs include* The Gold Standard and the Logic of Naturalism *(1987),* Our America: Nativism, Modernism and Pluralism *(1995),* The Shape of the Signifier: 1967 to the End of History *(2004), and* Promises of American Life: 1880–1920 *in volume three of the* Cambridge History of American Literature. *His essay, "The Trouble with Diversity," excerpted from his 2006 book, appeared in the* American Prospect *in 2006.*

In a 2004 essay in the New York Times Magazine, *Michaels argued that focusing on diversity keeps our eyes off the real problem. "As long as we think that our best universities are fair if they are appropriately diverse, we don't have to worry that most people can't go to them, while others get to do so because they've had the good luck to be born into relatively wealthy families. In other words, as long as the left continues to worry about diversity, the right won't have to worry about inequality."*

"The rich are different from you and me" is a famous remark supposedly made by F. Scott Fitzgerald to Ernest Hemingway, although what made it famous — or at least made Hemingway famously repeat it — was not the remark itself but Hemingway's reply: "Yes, they have more money." In other words, to Hemingway, the rich really aren't very different from you and me. Fitzgerald's mistake, he thought, was that he mythologized or sentimentalized the rich, treating them as if they were a different kind of person instead of the same kind of person with more money. It was as if, according to Fitzgerald, what made rich people different was not what they *had* — their money — but what they *were*, "a special glamorous race."

To Hemingway, this difference — between what people owned and what they were — seemed obvious. No one cares much about Robert Cohn's money in *The Sun Also Rises*, but everybody feels the force of the fact that he's a "race conscious . . . little kike." And whether or not it's true that Fitzgerald sentimentalized the rich, it's certainly true that he, like Hemingway, believed that the fundamental differences — the ones that really mattered—ran deeper than the question of how much money you had. That's why in *The Great Gatsby*, the fact that Gatsby has made a great deal of money isn't quite enough to win Daisy Buchanan back. Rich as he has become, he's still "Mr. Nobody from Nowhere," not Jay Gatsby but Jimmy Gatz. The change of name is what matters. One way to look at *The Great Gatsby* is as a story about a poor boy who makes good, which is to say, a poor boy who becomes rich—the so-called American Dream. But *Gatsby* is not really about someone who makes a lot of money; it is instead about someone who tries and fails to change who he is. Or, more precisely, it's about someone who pretends to be something he's not; it's about Jimmy Gatz pretending to by Jay Gatsby. If, in the end, Daisy Buchanan is very different from Jimmy Gatz, it's not because she's rich and he isn't but because Fitzgerald treats them as if they really belong to different races, as if poor boys who made a lot of money were only "passing" as rich. "We're all white here," someone says, interrupting one of Tom Buchanan's racist outbursts. Jimmy Gatz isn't quite white enough.

What's important about *The Great Gatsby*, then, is that it takes one kind of difference (the difference between the rich and the poor) and redescribes it as another kind of difference (the difference between the white and the not-so-white). To put the point more generally, books like *The Great Gatsby* (and there have been a great many of them) give us a vision of our society divided into races rather than into economic classes. And this vision has proven to be extraordinarily attractive. Indeed, it has survived even though what we used to think were the races have not. In the 1920s, racial science was in its heyday; now very few scientists believe that there are any such things as races. But many of those who are quick to remind us that there are no biological entities called races are even quicker to remind us that races have not disappeared; they should just be understood as social entities instead. And these social entities have turned out to be remarkably tenacious, both in ways we know are bad and in ways we have come to think of as good. The bad ways involve racism, the inability or refusal to accept people who are different from us. The good ways involve just the opposite: embracing difference, celebrating what we have come to call diversity.

Indeed, in the United States, the commitment to appreciating diversity emerged out of the struggle against racism, and the word diversity itself began to have the importance it does for us today in 1978 when, in *Bakke v. Board of Regents*, the Supreme Court ruled that taking into consideration the race of an applicant to the University of California (the medical school at UC Davis, in this case) was acceptable if it served "the interest of diversity." The Court's point here was significant. It was not asserting that preference in admissions could be given, say, to black people because they had previously been discriminated against. It was saying instead that universities had a legitimate interest in taking race into account in exactly the same way they had a legitimate interest in taking into account what part of the country an applicant came from or what his or her nonacademic interests were. They had, in other words, a legitimate interest in having a "diverse student body," and racial diversity, like geographic diversity, could thus be an acceptable goal for an admissions policy.

Two things happened there. First, even though the concept of diver- 5 sity was not originally connected with race (universities had long sought diverse student bodies without worrying about race at all), the two now came to be firmly associated. When universities publish their diversity statistics today, they're not talking about how many kids come from Oregon. My university—the University of Illinois at Chicago—is ranked as one of the most diverse in the country, but well over half the students in it come from Chicago. What the rankings measure is the number of African Americans and Asian Americans and Latinos we have, not the number of Chicagoans.

And, second, even though the concept of diversity was introduced as a kind of end run around the historical problem of racism (the whole point was that you could argue for the desirability of a diverse student body without appealing to the history of discrimination against blacks and so without getting accused by people like Alan Bakke of reverse discrimination against whites), the commitment to diversity became deeply associated with the struggle against racism. Indeed, the goal of overcoming racism—of creating a "color-blind" society—was now reconceived as the goal of creating a diverse, that is, a color-conscious, society. Instead of trying to treat people as if their race didn't matter, we would not only recognize but celebrate racial identity. Indeed, race has turned out to be a gateway drug for all kinds of identities, cultural, religious, sexual, even medical. To take what may seem like an extreme case, advocates for the disabled now urge us to stop thinking of disability as a condition to be "cured" or "eliminated" and to start thinking of it instead on the model of race: We don't think black people should want to stop being black; why do we assume the deaf want to hear?

Our commitment to diversity has thus redefined the opposition to discrimination as the appreciation (rather than the elimination) of difference. So with respect to race, the idea is not just that racism is a bad thing (which of course it is) but that race itself is a good thing.

And what makes it a good thing is that it's not class. We love race—we love identity—because we don't love class. We love thinking that the differences that divide us are not the differences between those of us who have money and those who don't but are instead the differences between those who are black and those who are white or Asian or Latino or whatever. A world where some of us don't have money is a world where the differences between us present a problem: the need to get rid of inequality or to justify it. A world where some of us are black and some of us are white—or bi-racial or Native American or transgendered—is a world where the differences between us present a solution: appreciating our diversity. So we like to talk about the differences we can appreciate, and we don't like to talk about the ones we can't. Indeed, we don't even like to acknowledge that they exist. As survey after survey has shown, Americans are very reluctant to identify themselves as belonging to the lower class and even more reluctant to identify themselves as belonging to the upper class. The class we like is the middle class.

But the fact that we all like to think of ourselves as belonging to the same class doesn't, of course, mean that we actually do belong to the same class. In reality, we obviously and increasingly don't. "The last few decades," as *The Economist* puts it, "have seen a huge increase in inequality in America." The rich *are* different from you and me, and one of the ways they're different is that they're getting richer and we're not. And while it's not surprising that most of the rich and their apologists on the intellectual right are unperturbed by this development, it is at least a little surprising that the intellectual left has managed to remain almost equally unperturbed. Giving priority to issues like affirmative action and committing itself to the celebration of difference, the intellectual left has responded to the increase in economic inequality by insisting on the importance of cultural identity. So for 30 years, while the gap between the rich and the poor has grown larger, we've been urged to respect people's identities—as if the problem of poverty would be solved if we just appreciated the poor. From the economic standpoint, however, what poor people want is not to contribute to diversity but to minimize their contribution to it—they want to stop being poor. Celebrating the diversity of American life has become the American left's way of accepting their poverty, of accepting inequality.

Our current notion of cultural diversity—trumpeted as the repudiation of racism and biological essentialism—in fact grew out of and perpetuates the very concepts it congratulates itself on having escaped. The American love affair with race—especially when you can dress race up as culture—has continued and even intensified. Almost everything we say about culture (that the significant differences between us are cultural, that such differences should be respected, that our cultural heritages should be perpetuated, that there's a value in making sure that different cultures survive) seems to me mistaken. We must shift our focus from cultural diversity to economic equality to help alter the political terrain of contemporary American intellectual life.

In the last year, it has sometimes seemed as if this terrain might in fact be starting to change, and there has been what at least looks like the beginning of a new interest in the problem of economic inequality. Various newspapers have run series noticing the growth of inequality and the decline of class mobility; it turns out, for example, that the Gatsby-style American Dream—poor boy makes good, buys beautiful, beautiful shirts—now has a better chance of coming true in Sweden than it does in America, and as good a chance of coming true in western Europe (which is to say, not very good) as it does here. People have begun to notice also that the intensity of interest in the race of students in our universities has coincided with more or less complete indifference to their wealth. We're getting to the point where there are more black people than poor people in elite universities (even though there are still precious few black people). And Hurricane Katrina—with its televised images of the people left to fend for themselves in drowning New Orleans—provided both a reminder that there still are poor people in America and a vision of what the consequences of that poverty can be.

At the same time, however, the understanding of these issues has proven to be more a symptom of the problem than a diagnosis. In the *Class Matters* series in the *New York Times*, for example, the differences that mattered most turned out to be the ones between the rich and the really rich and between the old rich and the new rich. Indeed, at one point, the *Times* started treating class not as an issue to be addressed in addition to race but as itself a version of race, as if the rich and poor really were different races and so as if the occasional marriage between them were a kind of interracial marriage.

But classes are not like races and cultures, and treating them as if they were—different but equal—is one of our strategies for managing inequality rather than minimizing or eliminating it. White is not better than black, but rich is definitely better than poor. Poor people are an endangered species in elite universities not because the universities put quotas on them (as they did with Jews in the old days) and not even because they can't afford to go to them (Harvard will lend you or even give you the money you need to go there) but because they can't get into them. Hence the irrelevance of most of the proposed solutions to the systematic exclusion of poor people from elite universities, which involve ideas like increased financial aid for students who can't afford the high tuition, support systems for the few poor students who manage to end up there anyway, and, in general, an effort to increase the "cultural capital" of the poor. Today, says David Brooks, "the rich don't exploit the poor, they just out-compete them." And if out-competing people means tying their ankles together and loading them down with extra weight while hiring yourself the most expensive coaches and the best practice facilities, he's right. The entire U.S. school system, from pre-K up, is structured from the very start to enable the rich to out-compete the poor, which is to say, the race is fixed. And the kinds of solutions that might actually make a difference—financing every school district equally, abolishing private schools, making high-quality child care available to every family—are treated as if they were positively un-American.

But it's the response to Katrina that is most illuminating for our purposes, especially the response from the left, not from the right. "Let's be honest," Cornel West told an audience at the Paul Robeson Student Center at Rutgers University, "we live in one of the bleakest moments in the history of black people in this nation." "Look at the Super Dome," he went on to say. "It's not a big move from the hull of the slave ship to the living hell of the Super Dome." This is what we might call the "George Bush doesn't care about black people" interpretation of the government's failed response to the catastrophe. But nobody doubts that George Bush cares about Condoleezza Rice, who is very much a black person and who is fond of pointing out that she's been black since birth. And there are, of course, lots of other black people—like Clarence Thomas[1] and Thomas Sowell[2] and Janice Rogers Brown[3] and, at least once upon a time, Colin Powell—for whom George Bush almost certainly has warm feelings. But what American liberals want is for our conservatives to be racists. We want the black people George Bush cares about to be "some of my best friends are black" tokens. We want a fictional George Bush who doesn't care about black people rather than the George Bush we've actually got, one who doesn't care about poor people.

Although that's not quite the right way to put it. First because, for all I know, George Bush does care about poor people; at least he cares as much about poor people as anyone else does. What he doesn't care about—and what Bill Clinton, judging by his eight years in office, didn't much care about, and what John Kerry, judging from his presidential campaign, doesn't much care about, and what we on the so-called left, judging by our own willingness to accept Kerry as the alternative to Bush, don't care about either—is taking any steps to get them to stop being poor. We would much rather get rid of racism than get rid of poverty. And we would much rather celebrate cultural diversity than seek to establish economic equality.

Indeed, diversity has become virtually a sacred concept in American life today. No one's really against it; people tend instead to differ only in their degrees of enthusiasm for it and their ingenuity in pursuing it. Microsoft, for example, is very ingenious indeed. Almost every company has the standard racial and sexual "employee relations groups," just as every college has the standard student groups: African American, Black and Latino Brotherhood, Alliance of South Asians, Chinese Adopted Sibs (this one's pretty cutting-edge), and the standard GLBTQ (the Q is for *Questioning*) support center. But (as reported in a 2003 article in *Workforce Management*) Microsoft also includes groups for "single parents, dads, Singaporean, Malaysian, Hellenic, and Brazilian employees, and one for those with attention deficit disorder." And the same article goes on to quote Patricia Pope, CEO of a diversity management firm in Cincinnati, describing companies that "tackle other differences" like "diversity of

15

---

[1]*Clarence Thomas:* (b. 1948) Associate Justice of the Supreme Court of the United States since 1991 and the second African American to serve on the Supreme Court, after Justice Thurgood Marshall.—EDS.

[2]*Thomas Sowell:* (b. 1930) An American economist, social commentator, author of numerous books, and a senior fellow of the Hoover Institution.—EDS.

[3]*Janice Rogers Brown:* (b. 1949) A federal judge on the United States Court of Appeals for the District of Columbia Circuit and previously an Associate Justice of the California Supreme Court.—EDS.

birth order" and, most impressive of all, "diversity of thought." If it's a little hard to imagine the diversity of birth order workshops (all the oldest siblings trying to take care of each other, all the youngest competing to be the baby), it's harder still to imagine how the diversity of thought workshops go. What if the diversity of thought is about your sales plan? Are you supposed to reach agreement (but that would eliminate diversity) or celebrate disagreement (but that would eliminate the sales plan)?

Among the most enthusiastic proponents of diversity, needless to say, are the thousands of companies providing "diversity products," from diversity training (a $10-billion-a-year industry) to diversity newsletters (I subscribe to *Diversity Inc.*, but there are dozens of them) to diversity rankings to diversity gifts and clothing—you can "show your support for multiculturalism" *and* "put an end to panty lines" with a "Diversity Rocks Classic Thong" ($9.99). The "Show Me the Money Diversity Venture Capital Conference" says what needs to be said here. But it's not all about the benjamins.[4] There's no money for the government in proclaiming Asian Pacific American Heritage Month (it used to be just a week, but the first President Bush upgraded it) or in Women's History Month or National Disability Employment Awareness Month or Black History Month or American Indian Heritage Month. And there's no money for the Asians, Indians, blacks, and women whose history gets honored.

In fact, the closest thing we have to a holiday that addresses economic inequality instead of identity is Labor Day, which is a product not of the multicultural cheerleading at the end of the 20th century but of the labor unrest at the end of the 19th. The union workers who took a day off to protest President Grover Cleveland's deployment of 12,000 troops to break the Pullman strike weren't campaigning to have their otherness respected. And when, in 1894, their day off was made official, the president of the American Federation of Labor, Samuel Gompers, looked forward not just to a "holiday" but to "the day for which the toilers in past centuries looked forward, when their rights and wrongs would be discussed." The idea was not that they'd celebrate their history but that they'd figure out how to build a stronger labor movement and make the dream of economic justice a reality.

Obviously, it didn't work out that way, either for labor (which is weaker than it's ever been) or for Labor Day (which mainly marks the end of summer). You get bigger crowds, a lot livelier party and a much stronger sense of solidarity for Gay Pride Day. But Gay Pride Day isn't about economic equality, and celebrating diversity shouldn't be an acceptable alternative to seeking economic equality.

In an ideal universe we wouldn't be celebrating diversity at all—we wouldn't even be encouraging it—because in an ideal universe the ques-   20

---

[4]*"benjamins":* 100 dollar bills; so called because the face of Benjamin Franklin is on the bill. — EDS.

tion of who you wanted to sleep with would be a matter of concern only to you and to your loved (or unloved) ones. As would your skin color; some people might like it, some people might not, but it would have no political significance whatsoever. Diversity of skin color is something we should happily take for granted, the way we do diversity of hair color. No issue of social justice hangs on appreciating hair color diversity; no issue of social justice hangs on appreciating racial or cultural diversity.

If you're worried about the growing economic inequality in American life, if you suspect that there may be something unjust as well as unpleasant in the spectacle of the rich getting richer and the poor getting poorer, no cause is less worth supporting, no battles are less worth fighting, than the ones we fight for diversity. While some cultural conservatives may wish that everyone should be assimilated to their fantasy of one truly American culture, and while the supposed radicals of the "tenured left" continue to struggle for what they hope will finally become a truly inclusive multiculturalism, the really radical idea of redistributing wealth becomes almost literally unthinkable. In the early 1930s, Senator Huey Long of Louisiana proposed a law making it illegal for anyone to earn more than $1 million a year and for anyone to inherit more than $5 million. Imagine the response if—even suitably adjusted for inflation—any senator were to propose such a law today, cutting off incomes at, say, $15 million a year and inheritances at $75 million. It's not just the numbers that wouldn't fly; it's the whole concept. Long's proposal never became law, but it was popular and debated with some seriousness. Today, such a restriction would seem as outrageous and unnatural as interracial—not to mention gay—marriage would have seemed then. But we don't need to purchase our progress in civil rights at the expense of a commitment to economic justice. More fundamentally still, we should not allow—or we should not continue to allow—the phantasm of respect for difference to take the place of that commitment to economic justice. Commitment to diversity is at best a distraction and at worst an essentially reactionary position that prevents us from putting equality at the center of the national agenda.

Our identity is the least important thing about us. And yet, it is the thing we have become most committed to talking about. From the standpoint of a left politics, this is a profound mistake since what it means is that the political left—increasingly invested in the celebration of diversity and the redress of historical grievance—has converted itself into the accomplice rather than the opponent of the right. Diversity has become the left's way of doing neoliberalism, and antiracism has become the left's contribution to enhancing market efficiency. The old Socialist leader Eugene Debs used to be criticized for being unwilling to interest himself in any social reform that didn't involve attacking economic inequality. The situation now is almost exactly the opposite; the left obsessively interests itself in issues that have nothing to do with economic inequality.

And, not content with pretending that our real problem is cultural difference rather than economic difference, we have also started to treat economic difference as if it were cultural difference. So now we're urged to be more respectful of poor people and to stop thinking of them as victims, since to treat them as victims is condescending—it denies them their "agency." And if we can stop thinking of the poor as people who have too little money and start thinking of them instead as people who have too little respect, then it's our attitude toward the poor, not their poverty, that becomes the problem to be solved, and we can focus our efforts of reform not on getting rid of classes but on getting rid of what we like to call classism. The trick, in other words, is to stop thinking of poverty as a disadvantage, and once you stop thinking of it as a disadvantage then, of course, you no longer need to worry about getting rid of it. More generally, the trick is to think of inequality as a consequence of our prejudices rather than as a consequence of our social system and thus to turn the project of creating a more egalitarian society into the project of getting people (ourselves and, especially, others) to stop being racist, sexist, classist homophobes. The starting point for a progressive politics should be to attack that trick.

The Reader's Presence

1. According to Michaels, why does celebrating diversity distract us from minimizing inequality? Specifically, how does Michaels establish connections between race and class? What would happen if we followed his advice and focused only on economic inequalities? For example, describe how colleges would be affected if they did not take the diversity of their student body into account during the admissions process. Michaels is not specific about how eliminating race as a political category will eliminate class as a social misery. Applying Michaels's logic to his Hurricane Katrina example (paragraph 14), how would ignoring race have led to a better response for the hurricane's victims?

2. Michaels skillfully uses wit and humor at strategic moments in his essay. Consider, for example, such lines as "what poor people want is not to contribute to diversity but to minimize their contribution to it" (paragraph 9). What are the effects of using wit and humor to write about such a serious subject? What risks does Michaels take in doing so? How effectively would his essay read if such wit and humor were omitted? In formulating your response, identify a few humorous or witty moments and rewrite them with a serious tone. How did changing the tone affect the argument? Do you think a reader would be more—or less—convinced by an argument that was formulated without wit and humor? Explain why.

3. Stephen Jay Gould's "Sex, Drugs, Disasters, and the Extinction of Dinosaurs" (page 417) demonstrates how to distinguish ideas that are "silly speculation" from solid hypotheses. Use Gould's methods to evaluate the specific claims Michaels makes in his essay. For example, what would Gould make of Michaels's notion that "no issue of social justice hangs on appreciating racial or cultural diversity" (paragraph 20)? Is it fair to use scientific standards for argument to evaluate cultural claims about race and class? Why or why not?

Errol Morris

Liar, Liar, Pants on Fire

Writer and documentary filmmaker Errol Morris was born in Hewlett, New York, in 1948. After graduating from the University of Wisconsin, Morris studied philosophy at the University of California, Berkeley, until his "obsession" with film ended his graduate-school career. His first film was Gates of Heaven, *released in 1978. Financed by family, friends, and the kindness of strangers, the film met with critical acclaim and launched a career that would result in seven more feature-length documentaries, a Guggenheim Fellowship, a MacArthur Fellowship "genius award," a retrospective at the Museum of Modern Art, a tribute at Sundance film festival, and an Oscar. His films include* Vernon, Florida *(1980);* The Thin Blue Line *(1988);* Fast, Cheap, and Out of Control *(1997);* A Brief History of Time *(1992);* Mr. Death *(2000); and* The Fog of War: Eleven Lessons from the Life of Robert S. McNamara, *which won the Academy Award for best documentary feature in 2004. Between films, Morris created the Bravo television series "First Person" and became a sought-after, and highly successful, director of commercials. Morris's latest film,* Standard Operating Procedure, *is slated for a 2008 release. The film explores the incidents at Abu Ghraib prison in Iraq through the infamous photos taken there. "It all starts with the photographs," he said in an interview. "*Standard Operating Procedure *is my attempt to tell the stories behind these photographs, to examine the context in which they were taken." Morris's essay, "Liar, Liar, Pants on Fire," part of a series written for the* New York Times *blog "Zoom," explores the same themes. "You look at a photograph, you think you know what it means, but more often than not, you could be wrong. Photographs provide evidence, but usually, it takes some investigative effort to uncover evidence of what?"*

Pictures are supposed to be worth a thousand words. But a picture unaccompanied by words may not mean anything at all. Do pictures provide evidence? And if so, evidence of what? And, of course, the underlying question: do they tell the truth?

I have beliefs about the photographs I see. Often—when they appear in books or newspapers—there are captions below them, or they are embedded in explanatory text. And even where there are no explicit captions on the page, there are captions in my mind. What I think I'm looking at. What I think the photograph is about.

I have often wondered: would it be possible to look at a photograph shorn of all its context, captionless, unconnected to current thought and ideas? It would be like stumbling on a collection of photographs in a curiosity shop—pictures of people and places that we do not recognize and know nothing about. I might imagine things about the people and places in the photographs but know nothing about them. Nothing.

This collection could even involve my own past. I recently was handed a collection of photographs taken by my father—dead now for over fifty years. I looked at it, somewhat confused. I suppose saddened by the passage of time. Even though I am in the photographs, the people in them are mysterious, inherently foreign. Maybe because photographs tamper with the glue that holds life and memory together.

Who are these people? Do they have anything to do with me? Do I   5
really know them?

As disconnected from the present as these photographs might be, they do not seem devoid of context. I know too much about them—even if I know very little. They are pictures of my own family. It's too easy for me to concoct some story about them. To find a picture shorn of context, it would be important to pick a photograph that's sufficiently removed for me in time and context—a photograph preternaturally unfamiliar. Perhaps a war photograph, but a war photograph from an unfamiliar war. It should be a war six or seven wars ago. Passions, presumably, have been diminished. No one in the photographs will still be alive.

I want to ask a relatively simple question. Are these photographs true or false? Do they tell the truth?

Look at the photograph below. Is it true or false?

I find the question ridiculous: "True or false in regard to what?"

Without a caption, without a context, without some idea about what   10
the picture is a picture of, I can't answer. I simply cannot talk about the photograph as being true or false independently of beliefs about the picture. A captionless photograph, stripped of all context, is virtually meaningless. I need to know more.

And yet, this idea that photographs can be true or false independent of context is so ingrained in our thinking that we are reluctant to part with it.

Let's add a caption to the photograph.

The Lusitania

Only now can we ask questions that have true or false answers. The caption asserts that this is a photograph of the *Lusitania*, a British ship launched in 1907. I found the photograph on a website entitle "Maritime Quest." I made no effort to check it; I simply took their word for it. That could be a mistake on my part. With no malice intended, the wrong caption could have inadvertently been placed under the photograph. The photograph could actually be a photograph of the *Titanic*. Or malice could have been involved. Someone could have maliciously switched the captions of pictures of the *Lusitania* and the *Titanic*.

But one thing is clear. When I look at these pictures—whether it is a picture of the *Lusitania* or the *Titanic*—I imagine that someone stood on a dry dock, or some vantage point, looked through the viewfinder of the camera, and took a photograph of something that was floating out there in the water. If it was the *Lusitania*, then he took a photograph of the *Lusitania*. If it was the *Titanic*, then he took a picture of the *Titanic*. This may seem hopelessly obvious, but I have this saying—and I believe there's something to it—that there is nothing so obvious that it's obvious.

But we need language, and we need context, in order to know which   15
ship it is, and a host of other sundry facts.

In discussing truth and photograph, we are asking whether a caption or a belief—whether a statement about a photograph—is true or false about (the things depicted in) the photograph. A caption is like a statement. It trumpets the claim, "This is the *Lusitania*." And when we wonder "Is this a photograph of the *Lusitania*?" we are wondering whether the claim is true or false. The issue of the truth or falsity of a photograph is only meaningful with respect to statements about the photograph. Truth or falsity "adheres" not to the photograph itself but to the statements we make about a photograph. Depending on the statements, our answers change. All alone—shorn of context, without captions—a photograph is neither true nor false.

But why this photograph? It's so terribly bland. I wanted to begin this series of essays on photography with an image chosen particularly for its blandness. Removed in time, far from our core knowledge, it is unfamiliar. We know little about it. We most likely do not recognize it as the *Lusitania*. We might think it's an early-20th-century ocean liner, and perhaps even imagine it may be the *Titanic*—at which point we have placed a kind of mental caption under the photograph, and we begin to see the photograph in terms of our associations and beliefs, about what it seems to say about reality.

It is also interesting how a photograph quickly changes when we learn more about what it depicts, when we provide a context, when we become familiar with an underlying story. And when we make claims about the photograph using language. For truth, properly considered, is about the relationship between language and the world, not about photographs and the world.

So here's a story.

On the evening of May 7th, 1915, the RMS *Lusitania* was off the   20
coast of Ireland en route to Liverpool from New York when it was torpe-
doed by a German U-Boat and sank. About 1,200 of the nearly 2,000
passengers and crew aboard drowned, including more than 100 Americans. The loss of life provoked America out of a hereunto neutrality in
the ongoing war in Europe. With cries of "Remember the *Lusitania*" the
U.S. entered into WWI within two years.

To modern viewers, this image of the *Lusitania* is emotionally un-
charged, if not devoid of interest. But to a viewer in the summer of 1915,
it was charged with meaning. It was surrounded by many, many other
photographs, images and accounts of the sinking of the *Lusitania*, a cause
célèbre.

Let's look at some of these other images.

"ENLIST" was a WWI Recruitment poster designed by Fred Spears.
Spears's design was inspired by a news report from Cork, Ireland, that
described, among the recovered bodies from the *Lusitania*, "a mother

with a three-month-old child clasped tightly in her arms. Her face wears a half smile. Her baby's head rests against her breast. No one has tried to separate them."

And here is a photograph from the same period with the following caption.

"SOME OF THE SIXTY-SIX COFFINS BURIED IN ONE OF THE   25
HUGE GRAVES IN THE QUEENSTOWN CHURCHYARD"

The caption is from a two-page pictorial spread in the May 30, 1915, *New York Times*: "BURYING THE LUSITANIA'S DEAD AND SUC-CORING HER SURVIVORS"

One more photograph and an accompanying article from the *Toronto Star*.

Watch's Fixed Hands Record Lusitania's Last 30 Minutes

At 2.30 p.m. today it will be exactly 27 years since a small pocket watch owned by Percy Rogers, Toronto, was stopped by the action of a German submarine.

It was 2 o'clock on the afternoon of May 7, 1915. The giant Cunard liner, Lusitania, with 1,906 aboard, was eight miles off the south coast of Ireland, and New York bound. In the domed dining saloon, Percy Rogers, then secretary of the C.N.E., had just finished lunch.

Mr. Rogers got up from the table, glanced at his watch and walked to his stateroom. At the very moment he was reaching to pick up a letter, he heard a "tremendous thud." He rushed on deck.

"People were running around like a flock of sheep with no one to direct them," he recalls. "Some of them clambered into lifeboats. The ship took a heavy list." His watch ticked off the fateful minutes. It was 2.15.

"I helped women and children near me into a boat. Then, as there were no more there, I got in. We had barely pulled a little way off before the ship turned on its side and sank." Five minutes had ticked by. It was 2.20.

"There was very little suction from the ship's sinking. But our boat upset. I struck out. Women and children were floating, mothers seeking to hold babies up. . . ." The watch ticked on, minute after minute. More than 1,000 lives were being snuffed out, and as the cold salt water seeped through Percy Rogers' clothes and finally into the delicate mechanism, his watch stopped. The minute hand, which had ticked off 30 of the most terrible minutes in history, was turned

downward in defeat. It was exactly 2.30.

Mr. Rogers floated with the help of a cupboard for an hour and a half. He was then picked up by a trawler and taken to Queenstown. When he looks at his watch today, one thing sticks in his mind. It is the official German statement at the time of the torpedoing: "Every German heart is filled with joy, pride and gratification." Mr. Rogers has never had the watch repaired. The hands have remained where they stopped as a reminder of the Lusitania.

The photograph is of a pocket watch. We learn from the accompanying article that the watch belonged to Percy Rogers and that the watch stopped at exactly 2:30 after "ticking off 30 of the most terrible minutes in history." Mr. Rogers was in a stateroom when the torpedo struck the *Lusitania*. He spent his last minutes on board helping women and children climb into lifeboats. Then he climbed into a lifeboat as well. And then the ship sank. The last paragraph of the article is memorable. It quotes "the official German statement" following the sinking of the *Lusitania*: "Every German heart is filled with joy, pride and gratification."

Now look at the photograph of the ship one more time.

The image remains the same, but clearly we look at it in a different   30
way.

Is that really a photograph of the *Lusitania*? When was it taken?
Could it have been taken on May 7, 1915? If it was, what was the exact
time that it was taken? Two o'clock? Two fifteen? Just seconds before the
German torpedo hit? Ah, can we see the torpedo in the water? Is that the
mother and her child (depicted in the poster) standing on the deck looking out over the water? Is that Percy Rogers with his pocket watch, helping that same woman and child climb into a lifeboat?

The idea that photographs hand us an objective piece of reality, that
they by themselves provide us with the truth, is an idea that has been with
us since the beginning of photography. But photographs are neither true
nor false in and of themselves. They are only true or false with respect to
statements that we make about them or the questions that we might ask
of them.

The photograph doesn't give me answers. A lot of additional investigation could provide those answers, but who has time for that?

Pictures may be worth a thousand words, but there are two words
that you can never apply to them: "true" and "false."

The Reader's Presence

1. In the opening of his essay, Morris mentions receiving a collection
   of family photographs taken by his father a long time ago. Of
   what relevance are these photos to the point Morris is making
   about truth and photography? Why don't these photographs
   allow him to establish his point?

2. Morris writes: "A captionless photograph, stripped of all context,
   is virtually meaningless" (paragraph 10). Yet in many museums

and galleries across the nation photographs by leading photographers are exhibited and many are deliberately without captions.
Are these works "virtually meaningless"? Do such exhibits dis-
prove Morris's point? How might Morris respond to such uncap-
tioned photographs?

3. How does Morris's assessment of photography compare with
   Charles Simic's in "The Life of Images" (page 539)? What similarities and differences do you find between these two approaches
   to photographs? How does each writer "make sense" of photographic images?

Martha Nussbaum

Can Patriotism Be Compassionate?

*Martha Nussbaum (b. 1947) received her BA from New York University and
her PhD from Harvard University, and has taught at Harvard, Brown, and Oxford
universities. She has published many books, including* The Fragility of Goodness:
Luck and Ethics in Greek Tragedy and Philosophy *(1986/2001),* Love's Knowledge:
Essays on Philosophy and Literature *(1990),* Upheavals of Thought: The Intelli-
gence of Emotions *(2001),* Hiding from Humanity: Disgust, Shame, and the Law
(2004), and, with co-editor Cass R. Sunstein, Animal Rights: Current Debates and
New Directions *(2004). Her most recent books are* The Clash Within: Democracy,
Religious Violence, and India's Future *(2007);* Frontiers of Justice: Disability, Na-
tionality, Species Membership *(2007); and* Liberty of Conscience: In Defense of
America's Tradition of Religious Equality *(2008). The essay "Can Patriotism Be
Compassionate?" first appeared in the* Nation *in December 2001.*

*The Ernst Freund Distinguished Professor at the University of Chicago,
Nussbaum teaches in the law school, the philosophy department, the divinity
school, and the classics department. She has said that, in order to act ethically on
the global stage, it is necessary to cultivate "the ability to imagine what it might
be like to be in the shoes of someone who's different from yourself."*

In the aftermath of September 11, we have all experienced strong
emotions for our country: fear, outrage, grief, astonishment. Our media
portray the disaster as a tragedy that has happened to our nation, and
that is how we very naturally see it. So too the ensuing war: It is called
"America's New War," and most news reports focus on the meaning of

events for us and our nation. We think these events are important because they concern us—not just human lives, but American lives. In one way, the crisis has expanded our imaginations. We find ourselves feeling sympathy for many people who did not even cross our minds before: New York firefighters, that gay rugby player who helped bring down the fourth plane, bereaved families of so many national and ethnic origins. We even sometimes notice with a new attention the lives of Arab-Americans among us, or feel sympathy for a Sikh taxi driver who complains about customers who tell him to go home to "his country," even though he came to the United States as a political refugee from Punjab. Sometimes our compassion even crosses that biggest line of all, the national boundary. Events have led many Americans to sympathize with the women and girls of Afghanistan, for example, in a way that many feminists had been trying to get people to do for a long time, without success.

All too often, however, our imaginations remain oriented to the local; indeed, this orientation is implicit in the unusual level of our alarm. The world has come to a stop in a way that it never has for Americans when disaster has befallen human beings in other places. Floods, earthquakes, cyclones—and the daily deaths of thousands from preventable malnutrition and disease—none of these typically make the American world come to a standstill, none elicit a tremendous outpouring of grief and compassion. The plight of innocent civilians in the current war evokes a similarly uneven and flickering response.

And worse: Our sense that the "us" is all that matters can easily flip over into a demonizing of an imagined "them," a group of outsiders who are imagined as enemies of the invulnerability and the pride of the all-important "us." Just as parents' compassion for their own children can all too easily slide into an attitude that promotes the defeat of other people's children, so too with patriotism: Compassion for our fellow Americans can all too easily slide over into an attitude that wants America to come out on top, defeating or subordinating other peoples or nations. Anger at the terrorists themselves is perfectly appropriate; so is the attempt to bring them to justice. But "us versus them" thinking doesn't always stay focused on the original issue; it too easily becomes a general call for American supremacy, the humiliation of "the other."

One vivid example of this slide took place at a baseball game I went to at Chicago's Comiskey Park, the first game played there after September 11—and a game against the Yankees, so there was a heightened awareness of the situation of New York and its people. Things began well, with a moving ceremony commemorating the firefighters who had lost their lives and honoring local firefighters who had gone to New York afterward to help out. There was even a lot of cheering when the Yankees took the field, a highly unusual transcendence of local attachments. But as the game went on and the beer flowed, one heard, increasingly, "U-S-A, U-S-A," echoing the chant from the 1980 Olympic hockey match in which the United States defeated Russia. This chant seemed to express a wish for

America to defeat, abase, humiliate its enemies. Indeed, it soon became a general way of expressing the desire to crush one's enemies, whoever they were. When the umpire made a bad call that went against the Sox, the same group in the stands turned to him, chanting "U-S-A." In other words, anyone who crosses us is evil, and should be crushed. It's not surprising that Stoic philosopher and Roman emperor Marcus Aurelius, trying to educate himself to have an equal respect for all human beings, reported that his first lesson was "not to be a fan of the Greens or Blues at the races, or the light-armed or heavy-armed gladiators at the Circus."

Compassion is an emotion rooted, probably, in our biological heritage. (Although biologists once portrayed animal behavior as egoistic, primatologists by now recognize the existence of altruistic emotion in apes, and it may exist in other species as well.) But this history does not mean that compassion is devoid of thought. In fact, as Aristotle argued long ago, human compassion standardly requires three thoughts: that a serious bad thing has happened to someone else; that this bad event was not (or not entirely) the person's own fault; and that we ourselves are vulnerable in similar ways. Thus compassion forms a psychological link between our own self-interest and the reality of another person's good or ill. For that reason it is a morally valuable emotion — when it gets things right. Often, however, the thoughts involved in the emotion, and therefore the emotion itself, go astray, failing to link people at a distance to ones' own current possibilities and vulnerabilities. (Rousseau said that kings don't feel compassion for their subjects because they count on never being human, subject to the vicissitudes of life.) Sometimes, too, compassion goes wrong by getting the seriousness of the bad event wrong: Sometimes, for example, we just don't take very seriously the hunger and illness of people who are distant from us. These errors are likely to be built into the nature of compassion as it develops in childhood and then adulthood: We form intense attachments to the local first, and only gradually learn to have compassion for people who are outside our own immediate circle. For many Americans, that expansion of moral concern stops at the national boundary.

Most of us are brought up to believe that all human beings have equal worth. At least the world's major religions and most secular philosophies tell us so. But our emotions don't believe it. We mourn for those we know, not for those we don't know. And most of us feel deep emotions about America, emotions we don't feel about India or Russia or Rwanda. In and of itself, this narrowness of our emotional lives is probably acceptable and maybe even good. We need to build outward from meanings we understand, or else our moral life would be empty of urgency. Aristotle long ago said, plausibly, that the citizens in Plato's ideal city, asked to care for all citizens equally, would actually care for none, since care is learned in small groups with their more intense attachments. Reading Marcus Aurelius bears this out: The project of weaning his imagination from its intense erotic attachments to the familial and the local gradually turns into the rather alarming project of weaning his heart from deep investment in the world. He finds that the only way to be utterly evenhanded is to cultivate a kind of death within life, seeing all people as distant and shadowlike, "vain images in a procession." If we want our life with others to contain strong passions—for justice in a world of injustice, for aid in a world where many go without what they need—we would do well to begin, at least, with our familiar strong emotions toward family, city and country. But concern should not stop with these local attachments.

Americans, unfortunately, are prone to such emotional narrowness. So are all people, but because of the power and geographical size of America, isolationism has particularly strong roots here. When at least some others were finding ways to rescue the Jews during the Holocaust, America's inactivity and general lack of concern were culpable, especially in proportion to American power. It took Pearl Harbor to get us even to come to the aid of our allies. When genocide was afoot in Rwanda, our own sense of self-sufficiency and invulnerability stopped us from imagining the Rwandans as people who might be us; we were therefore culpably inactive toward them. So too in the present situation. Sometimes we see a very laudable recognition of the interconnectedness of all peoples, and of the fact that we must join forces with people in all nations to defeat terrorists and bring them to justice. At other times, however, we see simplifying slogans ("America Fights Back") that portray the situation in terms of a good "us" crusading against an evil "them"—failing to acknowledge, for instance, that people in all nations have strong reasons to oppose terrorism, and that the fight has many active allies.

Such simplistic thinking is morally wrong, because it encourages us to ignore the impact of our actions on innocent civilians and to focus too little on the all-important project of humanitarian relief. It is also counterproductive. We now understand, or ought to, that if we had thought more about support for the educational and humanitarian infrastructure of Pakistan, for example, funding good local nongovernmental organizations there the way several European nations have done in India, young people in Pakistan might possibly have been educated in a climate of respect for religious pluralism, the equality of women and other values that we rightly prize instead of having fundamentalist *madrassahs*[1] as their only educational option. Our policy in South Asia has exhibited for many years a gross failure of imagination and sympathy; we basically thought in terms of cold war values, ignoring the real lives of people to whose prospects our actions could make a great difference. Such crude thinking is morally obtuse; it is also badly calculated to advance any good cause we wish to embrace, in a world where all human lives are increasingly interdependent.

---

[1]*madrassahs:* A group of buildings used for teaching Islamic theology and religious law, typically including a mosque.—EDS.

Compassion begins with the local. But if our moral natures and our emotional natures are to live in any sort of harmony, we must find devices through which to extend our strong emotions—and our ability to imagine the situation of others—to the world of human life as a whole. Since compassion contains thought, it can be educated. We can take this disaster as occasion for narrowing our focus, distrusting the rest of the world, and feeling solidarity with Americans alone. Or we can take it as an occasion for expansion of our ethical horizons. Seeing how vulnerable our great country is, we can learn something about the vulnerability that all human beings share, about what it is like for distant others to lose those they love to a disaster not of their own making, whether it is hunger or flood or war.

Because human beings find the meaning of life in attachments that are local, we should not ask of people that they renounce patriotism, any more than we now ask them to renounce the love of their parents and children. But we typically do ask parents not to try to humiliate or thwart other people's children, and we work (at least sometimes) for schools that develop the abilities of all children, that try to make it possible for everyone to support themselves and find rewarding work. So too with the world: We may love our own nation most, but we should also strive for a world in which the capacities of human beings will not be blighted by hunger or misogyny or lack of education—or by being in the vicinity of a war one has not caused. We should therefore demand an education that does what it can to encourage the understanding of human predicaments—and also to teach children to recognize the many obstacles to that pursuit, the many pitfalls of the self-centered imagination as it tries to be just. There are hopeful signs in the present situation, particularly in attempts to educate the American public about Islam, about the histories of Afghanistan and Pakistan, and about the situation and attitudes of Arab-Americans in this country. But we need to make sure these educational efforts are consistent and systematic, not just fear-motivated responses to an immediate crisis.

Our media and our systems of education have long given us far too little information about lives outside our borders, stunting our moral imaginations. The situation of America's women and its racial, ethnic, and sexual minorities has to some extent worked its way into curricula at various levels, and into our popular media. We have done less well with parts of the world that are unfamiliar. This is not surprising, because such teaching requires a lot of investment in new curricular initiatives, and such television programming requires a certain temporary inattention to the competition for ratings. But we now know that we live in a complex, interconnected world, and we know our own ignorance. As Socrates said, this is at least the beginning of progress. At this time of national crisis we can renew our commitment to the equal worth of humanity, demanding media, and schools, that nourish and expand our imaginations by presenting non-American lives as deep, rich, and compassion-worthy. "Thus from our weakness," said Rousseau of such an education, "our fragile happiness is born." Or, at least, it might be born.

10

The Reader's Presence

1. Evaluate the validity of Nussbaum's claim that becoming compassionate requires an "expansion of our ethical horizons" (paragraph 9) by looking at the instances where she sees a lack of compassion. For each instance, how would you expand people's horizons? According to Nussbaum, what conditions are necessary to make people feel compassionate? Which do you think would work? Which wouldn't? Why and why not?

2. Beginning with a twenty-first-century U.S. perspective, Nussbaum expands and contracts her temporal focus several times. For example, she talks about recent events (a baseball game) and then immediately switches to a discussion of Aristotle's argument about compassion. By writing this way, she broadens "this narrowness of our emotional lives" (paragraph 6), which she feels constricts America. In what other ways does she try to broaden our horizons? In how many other ways does she contract and expand her focus? Which ways create compassion most effectively? Why?

3. Compare Nussbaum's view of post–9/11 patriotism with that of Ian Frazier in "All–Consuming Patriotism" (page 393). How does each writer broadly define patriotism? How does each essay include a personal point of view? Which essay in your opinion is based more on personal experience? Why? How does each writer use historical comparisons to support his or her position? Although both authors rely on different perspectives, in what way do emotions figure in each essay?

THE ACADEMIC VOICE

Martha Nussbaum on "Cultivating Humanity in Legal Education"

What happens when writers address an academic audience, rather than a general audience? What adjustments do they make in their vocabulary, tone of voice, organization, or argument? How do these adjustments take into account the level of knowledge and information they can expect an academic audience to possess? Here you will find a section of Martha Nussbaum's academic paper "Cultivating Humanity in Legal Education," published in the University of Chicago Law Review. *Compare this academic selection with Nussbaum's comments on the effect of 9/11 on American education (paragraphs 10–11) in the conclusion of her essay for a general audience, "Can Patriotism Be Compassionate?" (page 783).*

ANCIENT PHILOSOPHY AND CONTEMPORARY COOPERATION

The theory of education developed in *Cultivating Humanity*[1] has two very different sources: study of the ancient Greek and Roman Stoics, and experience working with an international agency on issues of poverty in developing countries. For the Greek and Roman Stoics, all human beings are fundamentally members of one world order, no matter in what nation they dwell. The view is often referred to as "cosmopolitanism," from the fact that they say that each of us is a "citizen of the world" (in Greek, *kosmou politês*).[2] For thinkers such as Cicero,[3] Seneca, and Marcus Aurelius, the fact that we share a common humanity with people in distant parts of the world means that we have moral obligations to them that transcend the reach of current positive law. These thinkers' ideas became the basis for later development of international law, especially in the area of war and peace.[4]

Since the Stoics believed that people should cooperate across national borders, they had some radical ideas about education. Seneca, a Roman philosopher born in Spain and a regent of the Roman Empire during Nero's youth, was well placed to reflect on these issues, since he lived in a Rome already heterogeneous in ethnic makeup and complexly connected to many different parts of the world. Seneca's *Moral Epistle 88*, often called "letter on liberal education," is the founding text for our modern idea of liberal education.[5]

[1]Martha C. Nussbaum, *Cultivating Humanity: A Classical Defense of Reform in Liberal Education* 50–84 (Harvard 1997) (arguing for a conception of liberal education that will prepare students for global citizenship).

[2]See, for example, Martha C. Nussbaum, *For Love of Country?* (Beacon 2002) (discussing the negative effects of excessive patriotic pride on cosmopolitanism and its ideals); Martha C. Nussbaum, *Duties of Justice, Duties of Material Aid: Cicero's Problematic Legacy*, 8 J Polit Phil 170, 185 (1999) (describing Cicero's conception of the duties of justice as "fully cosmopolitan"); Martha C. Nussbaum, *Kant and Stoic Cosmopolitanism*, 5 J Polit Phil 4–12 (1997). My book in progress, *The Cosmopolitan Tradition*, is under contract with Yale University Press (unpublished manuscript on file with author).

For an overall account of Greek and Roman Stoicism, see Martha C. Nussbaum, *The Therapy of Desire: Theory and Practice in Hellenistic Ethics* (Princeton 1994). See also Malcolm Schofield, *The Stoic Idea of the City* (Chicago 2d ed 1999) (discussing Stoic political thought).

[3]Cicero is not a Stoic, and he has many objections to their ideas in some areas; in his political thought, however, he is quite close to orthodox Stoicism, and *De Officiis* (*On Duties*) is one of our fullest accounts of Stoic cosmopolitan ideas. For an English-language version of this account, see Cicero, *On Duties* (Cambridge 1991) (M.T. Griffin and E.M. Atkins, eds).

[4]See Nussbaum, 8 J Polit Phil at 185 (cited in note 2) (outlining "the material in Cicero that became the foundation of modern international law"). A more detailed discussion is in the Grotius chapter of Nussbaum, *The Cosmopolitan Tradition* (cited in note 2).

[5]The best Latin edition is Seneca, *Ad Lucilium Epistulae Morales* 312–23 (Oxford 1965) (L.D. Reynolds, ed). A complete but unsatisfactory English translation is available in Seneca, *Ad Lucilium Epistulae Morales* (G.P. Putnam's Sons 1917) (Richard M. Gummere, trans). The epistles were probably published around 64–65 A.D. Thus they are a bit later than *On Anger*, but quite consistent in thought.

Seneca begins his letter by describing the traditional style of education, noting that it is called "liberal" (*liberalis*, "connected to freedom"), because it is understood to be an education for well-brought-up young gentlemen, who were called the *liberales*, the "free-born." He then announces that he will use the term "liberal" in a very different way. In his view, an education is truly "liberal" only if it is one that "liberates" the student's mind, encouraging him or her to take charge of his or her own thinking, leading the Socratic-examined life, and becoming a reflective critic of traditional practices.[6] Seneca goes on to argue that only this sort of education will develop each person's capacity to be fully human, by which he means self-aware, self-governing, and capable of recognizing and respecting the humanity of all our fellow human beings, no matter where they are born, no matter what social class they inhabit, no matter what their gender or ethnic origin. "Soon we shall breathe our last," he concludes in his related treatise *On Anger*. "Meanwhile, while we live, while we are among human beings, let us cultivate our humanity."[7]

These ideas, I believe, can help us see what is well and not well done in contemporary reforms of liberal education. Liberal education in the United States used to be like the old type of education Seneca describes, an education designed for well-brought-up young gentlemen, to acculturate them into the traditional norms and values of the community. During the past twenty years or so, the idea of preparing many different kinds of students for citizenship in a complex world has been gradually taking hold. But there are many conflicting views of how this idea should be realized in practice, and many bitter controversies about new forms of study such as women's studies, the study of human sexuality, the study of non-Western cultures, and the study of race and ethnicity. It is important to develop some general principles to guide the assessment of new curricular initiatives, inspired by what was good in Stoic philosophical ideas and by the best in current educational practice.[8]

---

[6]I use "him or her" not just out of contemporary political correctness: Stoic philosophers of the first century A.D. wrote at length about the equal education of women, and defended the view that women as much as men should lead the examined life. See Martha C. Nussbaum, *The Incomplete Feminism of Musonius Rufus, Platonist, Stoic and Roman*, in Martha C. Nussbaum and Juha Sihvola, eds, *The Sleep of Reason: Erotic Experience and Sexual Ethics in Ancient Greece and Rome* 283, 286–98 (Chicago 2002).

[7]All translations from Seneca's Latin are my own. The best edition of the Latin text of *De Ira* (*On Anger*) is in Seneca, *Dialogorum Libri Duodecim* 39–128 (Oxford 1977) (L. D. Reynolds, ed). An English-language version may be found at Seneca, *On Anger*, in Seneca, *Moral and Political Essays* 17, 117 (Cambridge 1995) (John M. Cooper and J. F. Procopé, eds).

[8]Nussbaum, *Cultivating Humanity* (cited in note 1) focuses on a group of fifteen highly diverse colleges and universities, studying their curricula in especially close detail.

Camille Paglia

The Pitfalls of Plastic Surgery

Camille Paglia (b. 1947), academic, author, and Salon's "fave pop intellectual," earned her PhD at Yale University and taught at Bennington College, Wesleyan University, and Yale University; in 1984, she joined the faculty at the University of the Arts in Philadelphia, where she is professor of humanities and media studies. Her academic study, and first book, Sexual Personae: Art and Decadence from Nefertiti to Emily Dickinson *(1990) caused heated debate and launched her career as a noted feminist, cultural critic, and social commentator. By early 1991, she was featured on the cover of* New York Magazine, *under the headline: "Woman Warrior." In 1992, her second book was published,* Sex, Art and American Culture, *followed by* Vamps and Tramps *(1994). In 1998, she published a volume about Alfred Hitchcock's film* The Birds, *for the British Film Institute Films Classics series. Her latest book is* Break, Blow, Burn: Camille Paglia Reads Forty-Three of the World's Best Poems *(2005). Paglia is a contributing editor at* Interview *magazine; she is a founding contributor to* Salon; *and she writes about art, literature, culture, media, and politics for numerous publications throughout the world, including the* Advocate, *the* New York Times, *the* Independent *of London, the* American Enterprise, *and* Harper's Bazaar, *where "The Pitfalls of Plastic Surgery" appeared in 2005.*

Paglia describes her life after turning sixty and becoming a parent, with her partner, of a baby boy—and reveals the trials of writing her first book. "I'm deeply enjoying being a parent—which I certainly would not have been able to do while I was writing Sexual Personae *for 20 years," she told an interviewer. "That 700-page tome was a round-the-clock operation, requiring a fanaticism of attention and persistence that could not possibly have been combined with a responsible family life."*

Plastic surgery is living sculpture: a triumph of modern medicine. As a revision of nature, cosmetic surgery symbolizes the conquest of biology by human free will. With new faces and bodies, people have become their own works of art.

Once largely confined to the entertainment and fashion industries, plastic surgery has become routine in the corporate workplace in the U.S., even for men. A refreshed, youthful look is now considered essential for job retention and advancement in high-profile careers. As cosmetic surgery has become more widespread and affordable, it has virtually become a civil right, an equal-opportunity privilege once enjoyed primarily by a moneyed elite who could fly to Brazil for a discreet nip and tuck.

The questions raised about plastic surgery often have a moralistic hue. Is cosmetic surgery a wasteful frivolity, an exercise in narcissism? Does the pressure for alteration of face and body fall more heavily on women because of endemic sexism? And are coercive racist stereotypes at work in the trend among black women to thin their noses and among Asian women to "Westernize" their eyes?

All these ethical issues deserve serious attention. But nothing, I submit, will stop the drive of the human species toward beauty and the shimmering illusion of perfection. It is one of our deepest and finest instincts. From prehistory on, tribal peoples flattened their skulls, pierced their noses, elongated their necks, stretched their earlobes and scarred or tattooed their entire bodies to achieve the most admired look. Mutilation is in the eye of the beholder.

Though cosmetic surgery is undoubtedly an unstoppable movement,   5
we may still ask whether its current application can be improved. I have not had surgery and have no plans to do so, on the theory that women intellectuals, at least, should perhaps try to hold out. (On the other hand, one doesn't want to scare the horses!) Over the past 15 years, I have become increasingly uneasy about ruling styles of plastic surgery in the U.S. What norms are being imposed on adult or aging women?

I would suggest that the current models upon which many American surgeons are basing their reworking of the female face and body are far too parochial. The eye can be retrained over time, and so we have come to accept a diminished and even demeaning view of woman as ingenue, a perky figure of ingratiating girliness. Neither sex bomb nor dominatrix, she is a cutesy sex kitten without claws.

In the great era of the Hollywood studio system, from the 1920s to the early '60s, pioneering makeup techniques achieved what plastic surgery does now to remold the appearance of both male and female stars. For example, the mature Lana Turner[1] of *Imitation of Life* or *Peyton Place* was made to look like a superglamorous and ravishingly sensual version of a woman of Turner's own age. The problem today is that Hollywood expects middle-aged female actors to look 20 or even 30 years younger than they are. The ideal has become the bouncy Barbie doll or simpering nymphet, not a sophisticated woman of the world. Women's faces are erased, blanked out as in a cartoon. In Europe, in contrast, older women are still considered sexy: Women are granted the dignity of accumulated experience. The European woman has a reserve or mystique because of her assumed mastery of the esoteric arts of love.

Why this cultural discrepancy? Many of the founders of Hollywood, from studio moguls to directors, screenwriters, makeup artists, and composers, were European émigrés whose social background ranged from peasant to professional. European models of beauty are based on classical precedents: on luminous Greek sculpture, with its mathematical symmetry and proportion, or on Old Master oil paintings, with their magnificent

---

[1]*Lana Turner:* One of Hollywood's most glamorous stars in the 1940s and 1950s, Lana Turner (1921–1995) appeared in countless films, including *Peyton Place* (1957) and *Imitation of Life* (1959).

portraiture of elegant aristocrats and hypnotic femme fatales. As an upstart popular form with trashy roots in nickelodeons and penny arcades, Hollywood movies strove to elevate their prestige by invoking a noble past. The studios presented their stable of stars as a Greek pantheon of resurrected divinities, sex symbols with an unattainable grandeur.

But Hollywood's grounding in great art has vanished. In this blockbuster era of computerized special effects and slam-bang action-adventure films, few producers and directors root their genre in the ancestry of the fine arts. On the contrary, they are more likely to be inspired by snarky television sitcoms or holographic video games, with their fantasy cast of overmuscled heroes and pneumatic vixens. The profound influence of video games can be seen in the redefining of today's ultimate female body type, inspired by Amazonian superheroines like Lara Croft: large breasts with a flat midriff and lean hips, a hormonally anomalous profile that few women can attain without surgical intervention and liposuction.

Maximizing one's attractiveness and desirability is a justifiable aim 10 in any society, except for the most puritanical. But it is worrisome that the American standard of female sexual allure may be regressing. In the post-1960s culture of easy divorce on demand, middle-aged women have found themselves competing with nubile women in their 20s, who are being scooped up as trophy second wives by ambitious men having a midlife crisis. Cosmetic surgery seems to level the playing field. But at what cost?

Good surgery discovers and reveals personality; bad surgery obscures or distorts it. The facial mask should not be frozen or robotic. We still don't know what neurological risks there might be in long term use of nonsurgical Botox, a toxin injected subcutaneously to paralyze facial muscles and smooth out furrows and wrinkles. What is clear, however, is that unskilled practitioners are sometimes administering Botox in excessive amounts, so that even major celebrities in their late 30s and 40s can be seen at public events with frighteningly waxen, mummified foreheads. Actors who overuse Botox are forfeiting the mobile expressiveness necessary to portray character. We will probably never again see "great faces" among accomplished older women—the kind of severe, imperious, craggy look of formidable visionaries like Diana Vreeland or Lillian Hellman.[2]

The urgent problem is that today's cosmetic surgeons are drawing from too limited a repertoire of images. Plastic surgery is an art form: Therefore, surgeons need training in art as well as medicine. Without a broader visual vocabulary, too many surgeons will continue to homogenize women, divesting them of authority and reducing them to a generic cookie-cutter sameness. And without a gift for psychology, surgeons cannot intuit and reinforce a woman's unique personality.

---

[1]*Diana Vreeland or Lillian Hellman:* Vreeland (1903–1989), the celebrated fashion editor of *Vogue* magazine, and Hellman (1905–1984), the well-known American playwright, were known for their strikingly craggy facial features.

For cosmetic surgery to maintain or regain subtlety and nuance, surgeons should meditate on great painting and sculpture. And women themselves must draw the line against seeking and perpetuating an artificial juvenility that obliterates their own cultural value.

The Reader's Presence

1. How would you describe Paglia's attitude toward cosmetic surgery? What ethical issues does it raise for her? In what ways does cosmetic surgery affect Paglia's artistic sensibility? What distinction does she make between good surgery and bad surgery?

2. How does Paglia connect the popularity of cosmetic surgery today to the history of the American film industry? How did changes in the movie industry alter American notions of what is beautiful? According to Paglia, what are the sources of today's standards of attractiveness and how are they affecting cosmetic surgery? Do you find her analysis persuasive? Why or why not?

3. Consider Paglia's short essay in conjunction with Daniel Akst's "What Meets the Eye" (page 281) and Daniel Harris's "Celebrity Bodies" (page 425). In what ways do these other selections help reinforce Paglia's point? Which author, in your opinion, provides the most interesting explanation of what Americans find physically attractive? Give specific reasons for why you find one analysis more interesting than the others.

Steven Pinker

Sex Ed: The Science of Difference

Cognitive scientist, psychologist, linguist, and scholar Steven Pinker (b. 1954) has been variously described as the "bad boy" of language, "agent provocateur" of science, "wunderkind," and "evolutionary pop star," labels earned as much from his best-selling books and articles in the mainstream press as from his many, and masterful, scholarly works. His books include The Language Instinct *(1994), which argues that language is a biological adaptation; followed by* How the Mind Works *(1997), which includes the rest of the mind in his synthesis— "from vision and reasoning to the emotions, humor, and art"; and* The Blank

Slate: The Modern Denial of Human Nature *(2002), which explores the political, moral, and emotional aspects of human nature. His latest book is* The Stuff of Thought: Language as a Window into Human Nature *(2007). Pinker is a professor in the department of psychology at Harvard University and, until 2003, was director of the Center for Cognitive Neuroscience at the Massachusetts Institute of Technology (MIT), where he specialized in psycholinguistics, particularly language development in children. Born in Montreal, Canada, he earned a degree in experimental psychology at McGill University, then immigrated to the United States in 1976 to do his graduate work at Harvard, followed by a postdoctoral fellowship at MIT. He became a naturalized U.S. citizen in 1980. Pinker's essay, "Sex Ed: The Science of Difference," appeared in the* New Republic *in 2005. A defense of Harvard president Lawrence Summers's remarks about the gender gap in mathematics and science, the essay caused a firestorm of criticism from within the academic community and from the general public.*

When I was an undergraduate in the early 1970s, I was assigned a classic paper published in *Scientific American* that began: "There is an experiment in psychology that you can perform easily in your home. . . . Buy two presents for your wife, choosing things . . . she will find equally attractive." Just ten years after those words were written, the author's blithe assumption that his readers were male struck me as comically archaic. By the early '70s, women in science were no longer an oddity or a joke but a given. Today, in my own field, the study of language development in children, a majority of the scientists are women. Even in scientific fields with a higher proportion of men, the contributions of women are so indispensable that any talk of turning back the clock would be morally heinous and scientifically ruinous.

Yet to hear the reaction to Harvard President Lawrence Summers's[1] remarks at a conference on gender imbalances in science, in which he raised the possibility of innate sex differences, one might guess that he had proposed exactly that. Nancy Hopkins, the eminent MIT biologist and advocate for women in science, stormed out of the room to avoid, she said, passing out from shock. An engineering dean called his remarks "an intellectual tsunami," and, with equal tastelessness, a *Boston Globe* columnist compared him to people who utter racial epithets or wear swastikas. Alumnae threatened to withhold donations, and the National Organization for Women called for his resignation. Summers was raked in a letter signed by more than 100 Harvard faculty members and shamed into issuing serial apologies.

Summers did not, of course, say that women are "natively inferior," that "they just can't cut it," that they suffer "an inherent cognitive deficit in the sciences," or that men have "a monopoly on basic math ability," as many academics and journalists assumed. Only a madman could believe

[1]***Summers:*** Summers (b. 1954), a leading economist, served as Secretary of the Treasury toward the close of Bill Clinton's presidency and was president of Harvard University from 2001 to 2006. Summers resigned as a result of the controversy Pinker discusses. —EDS.

such things. Summers's analysis of why there might be fewer women in mathematics and science is commonplace among economists who study gender disparities in employment, though it is rarely mentioned in the press or in academia when it comes to discussions of the gender gap in science and engineering. The fact that women make up only 20 percent of the workforce in science, engineering, and technology development has at least three possible (and not mutually exclusive) explanations. One is the persistence of discrimination, discouragement, and other barriers. In popular discussions of gender imbalances in the workforce, this is the explanation most mentioned. Although no one can deny that women in science still face these injustices, there are reasons to doubt they are the only explanation. A second possibility is that gender disparities can arise in the absence of discrimination as long as men and women differ, on average, in their mixture of talents, temperaments, and interests—whether this difference is the result of biology, socialization, or an interaction of the two. A third explanation is that child-rearing, still disproportionately shouldered by women, does not easily coexist with professions that demand Herculean commitments of time. These considerations speak against the reflex of attributing every gender disparity to gender discrimination and call for research aimed at evaluating the explanations.

The analysis should have been unexceptionable. Anyone who has fled a cluster of men at a party debating the fine points of flat-screen televisions can appreciate that fewer women than men might choose engineering, even in the absence of arbitrary barriers. (As one female social scientist noted in *Science Magazine*, "Reinventing the curriculum will not make me more interested in learning how my dishwasher works.") To what degree these and other differences originate in biology must be determined by research, not fatwa.[2] History tells us that how much we want to believe a proposition is not a reliable guide as to whether it is true.

Nor is a better understanding of the causes of gender disparities in-   5
consequential. Overestimating the extent of sex discrimination is not without costs. Unprejudiced people of both sexes who are responsible for hiring and promotion decisions may be falsely charged with sexism. Young women may be pressured into choosing lines of work they don't enjoy. Some proposed cures may do more harm than good; for example, gender quotas for grants could put deserving grantees under a cloud of suspicion, and forcing women onto all university committees would drag them from their labs into endless meetings. An exclusive focus on overt discrimination also diverts attention from policies that penalize women inadvertently because of the fact that, as the legal theorist Susan Estrich has put it, "Waiting for the connection between gender and parenting to be broken is waiting for Godot."[3] A tenure clock that conflicts with

---

[2]*fatwa:* An Arabic word that refers to a binding religious edict or ruling. —EDS.
[3]*waiting for Godot:* A reference to Samuel Beckett's play *Waiting for Godot*, used here to imply a sense of endless or fruitless waiting. —EDS.

women's biological clocks, and family-unfriendly demands like evening seminars and weekend retreats, are obvious examples. The regrettably low proportion of women who have received tenured job offers from Harvard during Summers's presidency may be an unintended consequence of his policy of granting tenure to scholars early in their careers, when women are more likely to be bearing the full burdens of parenthood.

Conservative columnists have had a field day pointing to the Harvard hullabaloo as a sign of runaway political correctness at elite universities. Indeed, the quality of discussion among the nation's leading scholars and pundits is not a pretty sight. Summers's critics have repeatedly mangled his suggestion that innate differences might be one cause of gender disparities (a suggestion that he drew partly from a literature review in my book, *The Blank Slate*) into the claim that they must be the only cause. And they have converted his suggestion that the statistical distributions of men's and women's abilities are not identical to the claim that all men are talented and all women are not—as if someone heard that women typically live longer than men and concluded that every woman lives longer than every man. Just as depressing is an apparent unfamiliarity with the rationale behind political equality, as when Hopkins sarcastically remarked that, if Summers were right, Harvard should amend its admissions policy, presumably to accept fewer women. This is a classic confusion between the factual claim that men and women are not indistinguishable and the moral claim that we ought to judge people by their individual merits rather than the statistics of their group.

Many of Summers's critics believe that talk of innate gender differences is a relic of Victorian pseudoscience, such as the old theory that cogitation harms women by diverting blood from their ovaries to their brains. In fact, much of the scientific literature has reported numerous statistical differences between men and women. As I noted in *The Blank Slate*, for instance, men are, on average, better at mental rotation and mathematical word problems; women are better at remembering locations and at mathematical calculation. Women match shapes more quickly, are better at reading faces, are better spellers, retrieve words more fluently, and have a better memory for verbal material. Men take greater risks and place a higher premium on status; women are more solicitous to their children.

Of course, just because men and women are different does not mean that the differences are triggered by genes. People develop their talents and personalities in response to their social milieu, which can change rapidly. So some of today's sex differences in cognition could be as culturally determined as sex differences in hair and clothing. But the belief, still popular among some academics (particularly outside the biological sciences), that children are born unisex and are molded into male and female roles by their parents and society is becoming less credible. Many sex differences are universal across cultures (the twentieth-century belief in sex-reversed tribes is as specious as the nineteenth-century belief in blood-deprived ovaries), and some are found in other primates. Men's and women's brains vary in numerous ways, including the receptors for sex hormones. Variations in these hormones, especially before birth, can exaggerate or minimize the typical male and female patterns in cognition and personality. Boys with defective genitals who are surgically feminized and raised as girls have been known to report feeling like they are trapped in the wrong body and to show characteristically male attitudes and interests. And a meta-analysis of 172 studies by psychologists Hugh Lytton and David Romney in 1991 found virtually no consistent difference in the way contemporary Americans socialize their sons and daughters. Regardless of whether it explains the gender disparity in science, the idea that some sex differences have biological roots cannot be dismissed as Neanderthal ignorance.

Since most sex differences are small and many favor women, they don't necessarily give an advantage to men in school or on the job. But Summers invoked yet another difference that may be more consequential. In many traits, men show greater variance than women, and are disproportionately found at both the low and high ends of the distribution. Boys are more likely to be learning disabled or retarded but also more likely to reach the top percentiles in assessments of mathematical ability, even though boys and girls are similar in the bulk of the bell curve. The pattern is readily explained by evolutionary biology. Since a male can have more offspring than a female—but also has a greater chance of being childless (the victims of other males who impregnate the available females)—natural selection[4] favors a slightly more conservative and reliable baby-building process for females and a slightly more ambitious and error-prone process for males. That is because the advantages of an exceptional daughter (who still can have only as many children as a female can bear and nurse in a lifetime) would be canceled out by her unexceptional sisters, whereas an exceptional son who might sire several dozen grandchildren can more than make up for his dull childless brothers. One doesn't have to accept the evolutionary explanation to appreciate how greater male variability could explain, in part, why more men end up with extreme levels of achievement.

What are we to make of the breakdown of standards of intellectual discourse in this affair—the statistical innumeracy, the confusion of fairness with sameness, the refusal to glance at the scientific literature? It is not a disease of tenure radicals; comparable lapses can be found among the political right (just look at its treatment of evolution). Instead, we must be seeing the operation of a fascinating bit of human psychology.

The psychologist Philip Tetlock has argued that the mentality of taboo—the belief that certain ideas are so dangerous that it is sinful even to think them—is not a quirk of Polynesian culture or religious supersti-

10

---

[4]***natural selection:*** A biological term associated with evolution and the concept that stronger species survive and flourish while weaker species fade out. —EDS.

tion but is ingrained into our moral sense. In 2000, he reported asking university students their opinions of unpopular but defensible proposals, such as allowing people to buy and sell organs or auctioning adoption licenses to the highest-bidding parents. He found that most of his respondents did not even try to refute the proposals but expressed shock and outrage at having been asked to entertain them. They refused to consider positive arguments for the proposals and sought to cleanse themselves by volunteering for campaigns to oppose them. Sound familiar?

The psychology of taboo is not completely irrational. In maintaining our most precious relationships, it is not enough to say and do the right thing. We have to show that our heart is in the right place and that we don't weigh the costs and benefits of selling out those who trust us. If someone offers to buy your child or your spouse or your vote, the appropriate response is not to think it over or to ask how much. The appropriate response is to refuse even to consider the possibility. Anything less emphatic would betray the awful truth that you don't understand what it means to be a genuine parent or spouse or citizen. (The logic of taboo underlies the horrific fascination of plots whose protagonists are agonized by unthinkable thoughts, such as *Indecent Proposal* and *Sophie's Choice*.)[5]

Sacred and tabooed beliefs also work as membership badges in coalitions. To believe something with a perfect faith, to be incapable of apostasy, is a sign of fidelity to the group and loyalty to the cause. Unfortunately, the psychology of taboo is incompatible with the ideal of scholarship, which is that any idea is worth thinking about, if only to determine whether it is wrong.

At some point in the history of the modern women's movement, the belief that men and women are psychologically indistinguishable became sacred. The reasons are understandable: Women really had been held back by bogus claims of essential differences. Now anyone who so much as raises the question of innate sex differences is seen as "not getting it" when it comes to equality between the sexes. The tragedy is that this mentality of taboo needlessly puts a laudable cause on a collision course with the findings of science and the spirit of free inquiry.

The Reader's Presence

1. Where would you say Pinker stands on the issue of differences between the sexes? Does he believe that men and women are innately the same or that they are innately different? Point to the evidence he uses to support his position. How do you evaluate his evidence? How does that evidence affect Pinker's response to the comments by Harvard's former president?

---

[5]**Indecent Proposal** *and* **Sophie's Choice***:* A reference to two films in which the main characters are confronted with difficult moral choices. —EDS.

2. In paragraph 10, Pinker's essay takes a turn. How would you describe that turn? How does his topic change? Discuss why you think he introduces a new topic. What is the relationship of this topic to the issue he began with—the response to remarks made by Lawrence Summers? What is Pinker's larger point in his essay? Do you think it is a fair point to make or relevant to the specific issue he began with? Explain why or why not.

3. Consider Pinker's essay along with two other essays on sex and gender: James Fallows's "Throwing Like a Girl" (page 386) and Katha Pollitt's "Why Boys Don't Play with Dolls" (page 522). How do gender stereotypes enter into all three of these selections? How would you distinguish among the three approaches to sex differences? Which author do you think makes the most compelling argument, and why? You might also want to consider Pinker's point about taboo subjects as a larger issue that applies to a number of essays in this collection. Select an essay in this book that you think takes an approach to a topic that most people would prefer not to discuss and evaluate it according to Pinker's notion of the "psychology of taboo."

Michael Pollan

What's Eating America

Journalist, author, and educator Michael Pollan (b. 1955), has become a leading voice for change in our industrialized food system—what we grow and what we eat. The theme of his latest book, In Defense of Food: An Eater's Manifesto *(2008), comes down to seven words: Eat Food. Not Too Much. Mostly Plants. His previous books include* The Botany of Desire: A Plant's-Eye View of the World *(2001), in which he argues that domesticated plants have shaped humans as much as humans have shaped them, and* The Omnivore's Dilemma: A Natural History of Four Meals *(2006), which focuses on the impact of corn on the American diet and the environment. Pollan was born and raised on Long Island, New York, and educated at Bennington College, Mansfield College, Oxford, and Columbia University, where he received his MA in English. Since then, he has written books and articles, lectured, and taught about food, agriculture, nature, and the environment. He is currently the Knight Professor of Journalism and director of the Knight Program in Science and Environmental Journalism at the University of California, Berkeley. An award-winning journalist, Pollan is a regular contributor to the* New York Times Magazine. *"What's Eating America" appeared in July 2006.*

Descendants of the Maya living in Mexico still sometimes refer to themselves as "the corn people." The phrase is not intended as metaphor. Rather, it's meant to acknowledge their abiding dependence on this miraculous grass, the staple of their diet for almost 9,000 years.

For an American like me, growing up linked to a very different food chain, yet one that is also rooted in corn, not to think of himself as a corn person suggests either a failure of imagination or a triumph of capitalism.

Or perhaps a little of both. For the great edifice of variety and choice that is an American supermarket rests on a remarkably narrow biological foundation: corn. It's not merely the feed that the steers and the chickens and the pigs and the turkeys ate; it's not just the source of the flour and the oil and the leavenings, the glycerides and the coloring in the processed foods; it's not just sweetening the soft drinks or lending a shine to the magazine cover over by the checkout. The supermarket itself—the wall-board and joint compound, the linoleum and fiberglass and adhesives out of which the building itself has been built—is in no small measure a manifestation of corn.

There are some 45,000 items in the average American supermarket, and more than a quarter of them contain corn. At the same time, the food industry has done a good job of persuading us that the 45,000 different items or SKUs (stock keeping units) represent genuine variety rather than the clever rearrangements of molecules extracted from the same plant.

How this peculiar grass, native to Central America and unknown to 5 the Old World before 1492, came to colonize so much of our land and bodies is one of the plant world's greatest success stories. I say the plant world's success story because it is no longer clear that corn's triumph is such a boon to the rest of the world.

At its most basic, the story of life on earth is the competition among species to capture and store as much energy as possible—either directly from the sun, or, in the case of animals, by eating plants and plant eaters. The energy is stored in the form of carbon molecules and measured in calories: the calories we eat, whether in an ear of corn or a steak, represent packets of energy once captured by a plant. Few plants can manufacture quite as much organic matter (and calories) from the same quantities of sunlight and water and basic elements as corn.

The great turning point in the modern history of corn, which in turn marks a key turning point in the industrialization of our food, can be dated with some precision to the day in 1947 when the huge munitions plant at Muscle Shoals, Alabama, switched over from making explosives to making chemical fertilizer. After World War II, the government had found itself with a tremendous supply of ammonium nitrate, the principal ingredient in the making of explosives. Ammonium nitrate also happens to be an excellent source of nitrogen for plants. Serious thought was given to spraying America's forests with the surplus chemical, to help the timber industry. But agronomists in the Department of Agriculture had a better idea: spread the ammonium nitrate on farmland as fertilizer. The chemical fertilizer industry (along with that of pesticides, which are based on the poison gases developed for war) is the product of the government's effort to convert its war machine to peacetime purposes. As the Indian farmer activist Vandana Shiva says in her speeches, "We're still eating the leftovers of World War II."

F1 hybrid corn is the greediest of plants, consuming more fertilizer than any other crop. Though F1 hybrids were introduced in the 1930s, it wasn't until they made the acquaintance of chemical fertilizers in the 1950s that corn yields exploded. The discovery of synthetic nitrogen changed everything — not just for the corn plant and the farm, not just for the food system, but also for the way life on earth is conducted.

All life depends on nitrogen; it is the building block from which nature assembles amino acids, proteins and nucleic acid; the genetic information that orders and perpetuates life is written in nitrogen ink. But the supply of usable nitrogen on earth is limited. Although earth's atmosphere is about 80 percent nitrogen, all those atoms are tightly paired, nonreactive and therefore useless; the 19th-century chemist Justus von Liebig spoke of atmospheric nitrogen's "indifference to all other substances." To be of any value to plants and animals, these self-involved nitrogen atoms must be split and then joined to atoms of hydrogen.

Chemists call this process of taking atoms from the atmosphere and   10
combining them into molecules useful to living things "fixing" that element. Until a German Jewish chemist named Fritz Haber figured out how to turn this trick in 1909, all the usable nitrogen on earth had at one time been fixed by soil bacteria living on the roots of leguminous plants (such as peas or alfalfa or locust trees) or, less commonly, by the shock of electrical lightning, which can break nitrogen bonds in the air, releasing a light rain of fertility.

In his book *Enriching the Earth: Fritz Haber, Carl Bosch and the Transformation of World Food Production*, Vaclav Smil pointed out that "there is no way to grow crops and human bodies without nitrogen." Before Haber's invention, the sheer amount of life earth could support — the size of crops and therefore the number of human bodies — was limited by the amount of nitrogen that bacteria and lightning could fix. By 1900, European scientists had recognized that unless a way was found to augment this naturally occurring nitrogen, the growth of the human population would soon grind to a very painful halt. The same recognition by Chinese scientists a few decades later is probably what compelled China's opening to the West: after Nixon's 1972 trip, the first major order the Chinese government placed was for 13 massive fertilizer factories. Without them, China would have starved.

This is why it may not be hyperbole to claim, as Smil does, that the Haber-Bosch process for fixing nitrogen (Bosch gets the credit for commercializing Haber's idea) is the most important invention of the 20th century. He estimates that two of every five humans on earth today would not be alive if not for Fritz Haber's invention. We can easily imagine a world without computers or electricity, Smil points out, but without synthetic fertilizer billions of people would never have been born. Though, as these numbers suggest, humans may have struck a Faustian bargain[1] with nature when Fritz Haber gave us the power to fix nitrogen.

Fritz Haber? No, I'd never heard of him either, even though he was awarded the Nobel Prize in 1918 for "improving the standards of agriculture and the well-being of mankind." But the reason for his obscurity has less to do with the importance of his work than an ugly twist of his biography, which recalls the dubious links between modern warfare and industrial agriculture: during World War I, Haber threw himself into the German war effort, and his chemistry kept alive Germany's hopes for victory, by allowing it to make bombs from synthetic nitrate. Later, Haber put his genius for chemistry to work developing poisonous gases—ammonia, then chlorine. (He subsequently developed Zyklon B, the gas used in Hitler's concentration camps.) His wife, a chemist sickened by his contributions to the war effort, used his army pistol to kill herself; Haber died, broken and in flight from Nazi Germany, in a Basel hotel room in 1934.

His story has been all but written out of the 20th century. But it embodies the paradoxes of science, the double edge to our manipulations of nature, the good and evil that can flow not only from the same man but from the same knowledge. Even Haber's agricultural benefaction has proved to be a decidedly mixed blessing.

When humankind acquired the power to fix nitrogen, the basis of soil   15
fertility shifted from a total reliance on the energy of the sun to a new reliance on fossil fuel. That's because the Haber-Bosch process works by combining nitrogen and hydrogen gases under immense heat and pressure in the presence of a catalyst. The heat and pressure are supplied by prodigious amounts of electricity, and the hydrogen is supplied by oil, coal or, most commonly today, natural gas. True, these fossil fuels were created by the sun, billions of years ago, but they are not renewable in the same way that the fertility created by a legume nourished by sunlight is. (That nitrogen is fixed by a bacterium living on the roots of the legume, which trades a tiny drip of sugar for the nitrogen the plant needs.)

Liberated from the old biological constraints, the farm could now be managed on industrial principles, as a factory transforming inputs of raw material—chemical fertilizer—into outputs of corn. And corn adapted brilliantly to the new industrial regime, consuming prodigious quantities

---

[1]*"Faustian bargain":* In the legend, Faust traded his soul to the devil in exchange for knowledge. To "strike a Faustian bargain" is to be willing to give up anything for knowledge or power.—EDS.

of fossil fuel energy and turning out ever more prodigious quantities of food energy. Growing corn, which from a biological perspective had always been a process of capturing sunlight to turn it into food, has in no small measure become a process of converting fossil fuels into food. More than half of all the synthetic nitrogen made today is applied to corn.

From the standpoint of industrial efficiency, it's too bad we can't simply drink petroleum directly, because there's a lot less energy in a bushel of corn (measured in calories) than there is in the half-gallon of oil required to produce it. Ecologically, this is a fabulously expensive way to produce food — but "ecologically" is no longer the operative standard. In the factory, time is money, and yield is everything.

One problem with factories, as opposed to biological systems, is that they tend to pollute. Hungry for fossil fuels as hybrid corn is, farmers still feed it far more than it can possibly eat, wasting most of the fertilizer they buy. And what happens to that synthetic nitrogen the plants don't take up? Some of it evaporates into the air, where it acidifies the rain and contributes to global warming. Some seeps down to the water table, whence it may come out of the tap. The nitrates in water bind to hemoglobin, compromising the blood's ability to carry oxygen to the brain. (I guess I was wrong to suggest we don't sip fossil fuels directly; sometimes we do.)

It has been less than a century since Fritz Haber's invention, yet already it has changed earth's ecology. More than half of the world's supply of usable nitrogen is now man-made. (Unless you grew up on organic food, most of the kilo or so of nitrogen in your body was fixed by the Haber-Bosch process.) "We have perturbed the global nitrogen cycle," Smil wrote, "more than any other, even carbon." The effects may be harder to predict than the effects of the global warming caused by our disturbance of the carbon cycle, but they are no less momentous.

The flood of synthetic nitrogen has fertilized not just the farm fields but   20
the forests and oceans, too, to the benefit of some species (corn and algae being two of the biggest beneficiaries) and to the detriment of countless others. The ultimate fate of the nitrates spread in Iowa or Indiana is to flow down the Mississippi into the Gulf of Mexico, where their deadly fertility poisons the marine ecosystem. The nitrogen tide stimulates the wild growth of algae, and the algae smother the fish, creating a "hypoxic," or dead, zone as big as New Jersey — and still growing. By fertilizing the world, we alter the planet's composition of species and shrink its biodiversity.

And yet, as organic farmers (who don't use synthetic fertilizer) prove every day, the sun still shines, plants and their bacterial associates still fix nitrogen, and farm animals still produce vast quantities of nitrogen in their "waste," so-called. It may take more work, but it's entirely possible to nourish the soil, and ourselves, without dumping so much nitrogen into the environment. The key to reducing our dependence on synthetic nitrogen is to build a more diversified agriculture — rotating crops and using animals to recycle nutrients on farms — and give up our vast, nitrogen-guzzling monocultures of corn. Especially as the price of fossil fuels climbs, even the world's most industrialized farmers will need to take a second look at how nature, and those who imitate her, go about creating fertility without diminishing our world.

The Reader's Presence

1. In paragraph 4, Pollan announces,

   > There are some 45,000 items in the average American supermarket, and more than a quarter of them contain corn. At the same time, the food industry has done a good job of persuading us that the 45,000 different items or SKUs (stock keeping units) represent genuine variety rather than the clever rearrangements of molecules extracted from the same plant.

   Comment on Pollan's use of statistics throughout his essay. In which instances does he use them most effectively to reinforce his argument? Consider field-testing his assertion. Visit your local supermarket and check out the label of ingredients on 50 items—to assess how accurate Pollan's claim that a quarter of the items there rely on corn either directly (corn syrup) or indirectly (corn feed). In what specific products were you surprised to find corn? Pollan suggests that our ignorance about the large role corn-based products play in our lives is not an accident. Based on Pollan's description of agri-business, why would companies not announce that their products are grounded in corn? Summarize the flow of nitrogen during corn production and explain why Pollan thinks this has dangerous consequences for the environment.

2. Pollan published his essay in *Smithsonian* magazine, which characterizes itself as "World renowned for its unparalleled coverage of nature, history, science and the arts." *Smithsonian* "explores lifestyles, cultures, people, technology, music and Americana for an inquisitive and educated readership." What would you identify as some of the expectations about writing that this "inquisitive and educated readership" would have of authors publishing in this magazine? To what extent does Pollan take liberty with some of these expectations? Point to specific examples and analyze the effectiveness of each. For example, re-read Pollan's essay carefully; how often does he use incomplete sentences (fragments)? With what effect(s)? Or, consider the nature and length of his paragraphs. Many young writers are instructed that a paragraph must have at least three sentences. How many of Pollan's paragraphs have fewer? With what effect(s)? Pollan, of course, is aware of his readers' expectations about sentence and paragraph structure. What tradition(s) does he draw on in constructing his essay? What effects are the nature of his sentence and paragraph structure likely have on his readers?

3. Compare Eric Schlosser's explanation of the chemistry of French fries (see "Why McDonald's Fries Taste So Good," page 528) to Pollan's chemistry of corn. Both authors try to make technical subjects easily understandable for nontechnical readers. To what extent does each writer use similar methods? Describe as specifically as possible what they share, or how they differ. What purpose does each establish for his essay? Overall, which author was more successful in achieving his purpose? Which process did you understand more easily? Explain why. Choose a complex food subject, such as the chemistry that makes soda fizz, and prepare a nontechnical but accurate description using the strategies that make Pollan's and Schlosser's explanations successful.

Virginia Postrel

In Praise of Chain Stores

Born in 1960 in Asheville, North Carolina, and educated at Princeton University, Virginia Postrel is a journalist, an author, a speaker, and a self-styled libertarian. She is especially interested in what she calls the "aesthetic imperative," a concept based on her conviction that aesthetics, "the look and feel of people, places, and things," are an increasingly important source of economic and cultural value. She is the author of The Future and Its Enemies: The Growing Conflict over Creativity, Enterprise and Progress *(1998) and* The Substance of Style: How the Rise of Aesthetic Value Is Remaking Commerce, Culture, and Consciousness *(2003), as well as co-editor of* Free Minds and Free Markets: Twenty-Five Years of Reason *(1993), a collection of work from* Reason *magazine, where she was an editor for more than ten years. Postrel writes the "Culture & Commerce" column for* The Atlantic, *where her essay, "In Praise of Chain Stores," appeared in December 2006. Over the course of her career as a journalist, she has been a columnist for the business section of the* New York Times, *a regular contributor to* Forbes, *and a staff writer for* Inc. *magazine.*

Every well-traveled cosmopolite knows that America is mind-numbingly monotonous—"the most boring country to tour, because everywhere looks like everywhere else," as the columnist Thomas Friedman once told Charlie Rose. Boston has the same stores as Denver, which has the same stores as Charlotte or Seattle or Chicago. We live in a "Stepford world,"[1] says Rachel Dresbeck, the author of *Insiders' Guide to Portland, Oregon*. Even Boston's historic Faneuil Hall,[2] she complains, is "dominated by the Gap, Anthropologie, Starbucks, and all the other usual suspects. Why go anywhere? Every place looks the same." This complaint is more than the old worry, dating back to the 1920s, that the big guys are putting Mom and Pop out of business. Today's critics focus less on what isn't there—Mom and Pop—than on what is. Faneuil Hall actually has plenty of locally owned businesses, from the Geoclassics store selling minerals and jewelry, to Pizzeria Regina ("since 1926"). But you do find the same chains everywhere.

The suburbs are the worst. Take Chandler, Arizona, just south of Phoenix. At Chandler Fashion Center, the area's big shopping mall, you'll find P. F. Chang's, California Pizza Kitchen, Chipotle Mexican Grill, and the Cheesecake Factory. Drive along Chandler's straight, flat boulevards, and you'll see Bed Bath & Beyond and Linens-n-Things; Barnes & Noble and Borders; PetSmart and Petco; Circuit City and Best Buy; Lowe's and Home Depot; CVS and Walgreens. Chandler has the Apple Store and Pottery Barn, the Gap and Ann Taylor, Banana Republic and DSW, and, of course, Target and Wal-Mart, Starbucks and McDonald's. For people allergic to brands, Chandler must be hell—even without the 110-degree days.

One of the fastest-growing cities in the country, Chandler is definitely the kind of place urbanists have in mind as they intone, "When every place looks the same, there is no such thing as place anymore." Like so many towns in America, it has lost much of its historic character as a farming community. The annual Ostrich Festival still honors one traditional product, but these days Chandler raises more subdivisions and strip malls than ostrich plumes or cotton, another former staple. Yet it still refuses the common assertion that national chains are a blight on the landscape, that they've turned American towns into an indistinguishable "geography of nowhere."

The first thing you notice in Chandler is that, as a broad empirical claim, the cliché that "everywhere looks like everywhere else" is obvious nonsense. Chandler's land and air and foliage are peculiar to the desert Southwest. The people dress differently. Even the cookie-cutter housing developments with their xeriscaping and washed-out desert palette, remind you where you are. Forget New England clapboard, Carolina columns, or yellow Texas brick. In the intense sun of Chandler, the red-tile roofs common in California turn a pale, pale pink.

Stores don't give places their character. Terrain and weather and culture do. Familiar retailers may take some of the discovery out of travel—to the consternation of journalists looking for obvious local color—but by holding some of the commercial background constant, chains make it

       5

---

[1]*"Stepford world":* An allusion to *The Stepford Wives*, a 1972 novel by Ira Levin, which focuses on the lives of suburban women in Connecticut. —EDS.

[2]*Faneuil Hall:* Since 1742, a marketplace and meeting hall in downtown Boston near the current Government Center. —EDS.

easier to discern the real differences that define a place: the way, for instance, that people in Chandler come out to enjoy the summer twilight, when the sky glows purple and the dry air cools.

Besides, the idea that America was once filled with wildly varied business establishments is largely a myth. Big cities could, and still can, support more retail niches than small towns. And in a less competitive national market, there was certainly more variation in business efficiency — in prices, service, and merchandise quality. But the range of retailing *ideas* in any given town was rarely that great. One deli or diner or lunch counter or cafeteria was pretty much like every other one. A hardware store was a hardware store, a pharmacy a pharmacy. Before it became a ubiquitous part of urban life, Starbucks was, in most American cities, a radically new idea.

Chains do more than bargain down prices from suppliers or divide fixed costs across a lot of units. They rapidly spread economic discovery — the scarce and costly knowledge of what retail concepts and operational innovations actually work. That knowledge can be gained only through the expensive and time-consuming process of trial and error. Expecting each town to independently invent every new business is a prescription for real monotony, at least for the locals. Chains make a large range of choices available in more places. They increase local variety, even as they reduce the differences from place to place. People who mostly stay put get to have experiences once available only to frequent travelers, and this loss of exclusivity is one reason why foreign travelers are the ones who complain. When Borders was a unique Ann Arbor institution, people in places like Chandler — or, for that matter, Philadelphia and Los Angeles — didn't have much in the way of bookstores. Back in 1986, when California Pizza Kitchen [CPK] was an innovative local restaurant about to open its second location, food writers at the L.A. *Daily News* declared it "the kind of place every neighborhood should have." So what's wrong if the country has 158 neighborhood CPKs instead of one or two?

The process of multiplication is particularly important for fast-growing towns like Chandler, where rollouts of established stores allow retail variety to expand as fast as the growing population can support new businesses. I heard the same refrain in Chandler that I've heard in similar boomburgs elsewhere, and for similar reasons. "It's got all the advantages of a small town, in terms of being friendly, but it's got all the things of a big town," says Scott Stephens, who moved from Manhattan Beach, California, in 1998 to work for Motorola. Chains let people in a city of 250,000 enjoy retail amenities once available only in a huge metropolitan center. At the same time, familiar establishments make it easier for people to make a home in a new place. When Nissan recently moves its headquarters from Southern California to Tennessee, an unusually high percentage of its Los Angeles–area employees accepted the transfer: "The fact that Starbucks are everywhere helps make moving a lot easier these days," a rueful Greg Whitney, vice president of business development for the Los Angeles County Economic Development Corporation, told the *Los Angeles Times* reporter John O'Dell. Orth Hedrick, a Nissan product manager, decided he could stay with the job he loved when he turned off the interstate near Nashville and realized, "You could really be Anywhere, U.S.A. There's a great big regional shopping mall, and most of the stores and restaurants are the same ones we see in California. Yet a few miles away you're in downtown, and there's lots of local color, too."

Contrary to the rhetoric of bored cosmopolites, most cities don't exist primarily to please tourists. The children toddling through the Chandler mall hugging their soft Build-A-Bear animals are no less delighted because kids can also build a bear in Memphis or St. Louis. For them, this isn't tourism; it's life—the experiences that create the memories from which the meaning of a place arises over time. Among Chandler's most charming sites are the business-casual dads joining their wives and kids for lunch in the mall food court. The food isn't the point, let alone whether it's from Subway or Dairy Queen. The restaurants merely provide the props and setting for the family time. When those kids grow up, they'll remember the food court as happily as an older generation recalls the diners and motels of Route 66—not because of the businesses' innate appeal but because of the memories they evoke.

The contempt for chains represents a brand-obsessed view of place, as if store names were all that mattered to a city's character. For many critics, the name of the store really *is* all that matters. The planning consultant Robert Gibbs works with cities that want to revive their downtowns, and he also helps developers find space for retailers. To his frustration, he finds that many cities actually turn away national chains, preferring a moribund downtown that seems authentically local. But, he says, the same local activists who oppose chains "want specialty retail that sells exactly what the chains sell—the same price, the same fit, the same brands, even." You can show people pictures of a Pottery Barn with nothing but the name changed, he says, and they'll love the store. So downtown stores stay empty, or sell low-value tourist items like candles and kites, while the chains open on the edge of town. In the name of urbanism, officials and activists in cities like Ann Arbor and Fort Collins, Colorado, are driving business to the suburbs. "If people like shopping at the Banana Republic or the Gap, it that's your market—or Payless Shoes—why not?" says an exasperated Gibbs. "Why not sell the goods and services people want?"

10

The Reader's Presence

1. Postrel sets out to dismantle the traditional arguments and popular misconceptions that inform what she calls the "contempt for chains" (paragraph 10) that marks the reaction of many local

officials to chain stores and retail malls. Postrel opens with a quotation from Thomas Friedman, a columnist from the *New York Times* and the author of the best-selling study of globalization, *The World Is Flat*. The United States, Friedman observes, is "the most boring country to tour, because everywhere looks like everywhere else." Summarize—and analyze—each of the moves Postrel makes as she refutes Friedman's contention. When and how does she broaden her argument into an essay praising chain stores and suburban malls? What advantages does she associate with these places and products? Which points in her argument do you find most—and least—convincing? Explain why. Based on your analysis, discuss the extent to which you agree or disagree with Postrel's conclusion that chain stores do not destroy the local flavor but rather add variety, convenience, and comfort to a community. What role does resistance to brand names play in the argument opposing chain stores and retail malls?

2. Consider the extent to which Postrel anticipates the arguments of those who would charge that chain stores and retail malls contribute little more to the American landscape than duplicating the same scenes and the same merchandise. For example, how successfully does Postrel counter the claim that "national chains are a blight on the landscape, that they've turned American towns into an indistinguishable 'geography of nowhere'" (paragraph 3)? How does she counter each of the arguments against these places and products?

3. With the exception of Boston's Faneuil Hall, Postrel draws her examples of the positive impact of chain stores and retail malls from communities in the western United States. Comment on the extent to which you would agree with her critics' claim that her argument is weakened as a result. What myths does she debunk about the local flavor of big cities and small towns? Explain why you agree—or disagree—with her claim that "Stores don't give places their character. Terrain and weather and culture do" (paragraph 5). What clichés does Postrel deflate in the process?

4. In "The Trouble with Diversity" (page 766), Walter Benn Michaels argues against the belief that what he calls "two great liberal preoccupations—the celebration of cultural difference and the fight against inequality" go hand in hand. Based on your reading of the case Postrel makes in favor of chain stores and retail malls, comment on the ways issues of class and race are implicit in her argument.

Michael J. Sandel

The Case Against Perfection

Michael J. Sandel (b. 1953) is a recognized scholar of public philosophy, ethics, and civic life, and a well-known intellectual opponent of liberal thought. His seminal work, Liberalism and the Limits of Justice *(1982; 2nd edition, 1997), critiques the very basis of liberalism as a public philosophy. His other books include* Democracy's Discontent: America in Search of a Public Philosophy *(1996),* Public Philosophy: Essays on Morality in Politics *(2005), and* The Case Against Perfection: Ethics in the Age of Genetic Engineering *(2007), which grew out of his 2004 essay in the* Atlantic Monthly. *His articles have also appeared in numerous academic publications and journals, and in the* New Republic *and the* New York Times, *among others. Sandel is Anne T. and Robert M. Bass Professor of Government at Harvard University, where he teaches graduate and undergraduate courses in contemporary political philosophy. Sandel has received fellowships from the Carnegie Corporation, the National Endowment for the Humanities, the Ford Foundation, and the American Council of Learned Societies, and from 2002 to 2005 he served on the President's Council on Bioethics, a national council appointed by the president to examine the ethical implications of new biomedical technologies. He is a graduate of Brandeis University and received his PhD in 1981 from Oxford University, where he was a Rhodes Scholar.*

Sandel writes frequently about what he finds most morally troubling about the genetic engineering of "designer" children: "To appreciate children as gifts is to accept them as they come, not as objects of our design or products of our will or instruments of our ambition."

Breakthroughs in genetics present us with a promise and a predicament. The promise is that we may soon be able to treat and prevent a host of debilitating diseases. The predicament is that our newfound genetic knowledge may also enable us to manipulate our own nature—to enhance our muscles, memories, and moods; to choose the sex, height, and other genetic traits of our children; to make ourselves "better than well." When science moves faster than moral understanding, as it does today, men and women struggle to articulate their unease. In liberal societies they reach first for the language of autonomy, fairness, and individual rights. But this part of our moral vocabulary is ill equipped to address the hardest questions posed by genetic engineering. The genomic revolution has induced a kind of moral vertigo.

Consider cloning. The birth of Dolly the cloned sheep, in 1997, brought a torrent of concern about the prospect of cloned human beings. There are good medical reasons to worry. Most scientists agree that cloning is unsafe, likely to produce offspring with serious abnormalities. (Dolly recently died a premature death.) But suppose technology improved

811

to the point where clones were at no greater risk than naturally conceived offspring. Would human cloning still be objectionable? Should our hesitation be moral as well as medical? What, exactly, is wrong with creating a child who is a genetic twin of one parent, or of an older sibling who has tragically died—or, for that matter, of an admired scientist, sports star, or celebrity?

Some say cloning is wrong because it violates the right to autonomy: by choosing a child's genetic makeup in advance, parents deny the child's right to an open future. A similar objection can be raised against any form of bioengineering that allows parents to select or reject genetic characteristics. According to this argument, genetic enhancements for musical talent, say, or athletic prowess, would point children toward particular choices, and so designer children would never be fully free.

At first glance the autonomy argument seems to capture what is troubling about human cloning and other forms of genetic engineering. It is not persuasive, for two reasons. First, it wrongly implies that absent a designing parent, children are free to choose their characteristics for themselves. But none of us chooses his genetic inheritance. The alternative to a cloned or genetically enhanced child is not one whose future is unbound by particular talents but one at the mercy of the genetic lottery.

Second, even if a concern for autonomy explains some of our worries   5
about made-to-order children, it cannot explain our moral hesitation about people who seek genetic remedies or enhancements for themselves. Gene therapy on somatic (that is, nonreproductive) cells, such as muscle cells and brain cells, repairs or replaces defective genes. The moral quandary arises when people use such therapy not to cure a disease but to reach beyond health, to enhance their physical or cognitive capacities, to lift themselves above the norm.

Like cosmetic surgery, genetic enhancement employs medical means for nonmedical ends—ends unrelated to curing or preventing disease or repairing injury. But unlike cosmetic surgery, genetic enhancement is more than skin-deep. If we are ambivalent about surgery or Botox injections for sagging chins and furrowed brows, we are all the more troubled by genetic engineering for stronger bodies, sharper memories, greater intelligence, and happier moods. The question is whether we are right to be troubled, and if so, on what grounds.

In order to grapple with the ethics of enhancement, we need to confront questions largely lost from view—questions about the moral status of nature, and about the proper stance of human beings toward the given world. Since these questions verge on theology, modern philosophers and political theorists tend to shrink from them. But our new powers of biotechnology make them unavoidable. To see why this is so, consider four examples already on the horizon: muscle enhancement, memory enhancement, growth-hormone treatment, and reproductive technologies that enable parents to choose the sex and some genetic traits of their children. In each case what began as an attempt to treat a disease or prevent a genetic disorder now beckons as an instrument of improvement and consumer choice.

MUSCLES

Everyone would welcome a gene therapy to alleviate muscular dystrophy and to reverse the debilitating muscle loss that comes with old age. But what if the same therapy were used to improve athletic performance? Researchers have developed a synthetic gene that, when injected into the muscle cells of mice, prevents and even reverses natural muscle deterioration. The gene not only repairs wasted or injured muscles but also strengthens healthy ones. This success bodes well for human applications. H. Lee Sweeney, of the University of Pennsylvania, who leads the research, hopes his discovery will cure the immobility that afflicts the elderly. But Sweeney's bulked-up mice have already attracted the attention of athletes seeking a competitive edge. Although the therapy is not yet approved for human use, the prospect of genetically enhanced weight lifters, home-run sluggers, linebackers, and sprinters is easy to imagine. The widespread use of steroids and other performance-improving drugs in professional sports suggests that many athletes will be eager to avail themselves of genetic enhancement.

Suppose for the sake of argument that muscle-enhancing gene therapy, unlike steroids, turned out to be safe—or at least no riskier than a rigorous weight-training regimen. Would there be a reason to ban its use in sports? There is something unsettling about the image of genetically altered athletes lifting SUVs or hitting 650-foot home runs or running a three-minute mile. But what, exactly, is troubling about it? Is it simply that we find such superhuman spectacles too bizarre to contemplate? Or does our unease point to something of ethical significance?

It might be argued that a genetically enhanced athlete, like a drug-enhanced athlete, would have an unfair advantage over his unenhanced competitors. But the fairness argument against enhancement has a fatal flaw: it has always been the case that some athletes are better endowed genetically than others, and yet we do not consider this to undermine the fairness of competitive sports. From the standpoint of fairness, enhanced genetic differences would be no worse than natural ones, assuming they were safe and made available to all. If genetic enhancement in sports is morally objectionable, it must be for reasons other than fairness.

10

MEMORY

Genetic enhancement is possible for brains as well as brawn. In the mid-1990s scientists managed to manipulate a memory-linked gene in fruit flies, creating flies with photographic memories. More recently researchers have produced smart mice by inserting extra copies of a memory-related gene into mouse embryos. The altered mice learn more quickly and remember things longer than normal mice. The extra copies were programmed to remain active even in old age, and the improvement was passed on to offspring.

Human memory is more complicated, but biotech companies, including Memory Pharmaceuticals, are in hot pursuit of memory-enhancing drugs, or "cognition enhancers," for human beings. The obvious market for such drugs consists of those who suffer from Alzheimer's and other serious memory disorders. The companies also have their sights on a bigger market: the 81 million Americans over fifty, who are beginning to encounter the memory loss that comes naturally with age. A drug that reversed age-related memory loss would be a bonanza for the pharmaceutical industry: a Viagra for the brain. Such use would straddle the line between remedy and enhancement. Unlike a treatment for Alzheimer's, it would cure no disease; but insofar as it restored capacities a person once possessed, it would have a remedial aspect. It could also have purely nonmedical uses: for example, by a lawyer cramming to memorize facts for an upcoming trial, or by a business executive eager to learn Mandarin on the eve of his departure for Shanghai.

Some who worry about the ethics of cognitive enhancement point to the danger of creating two classes of human beings: those with access to enhancement technologies, and those who must make do with their natural capacities. And if the enhancements could be passed down the generations, the two classes might eventually become subspecies—the enhanced and the merely natural. But worry about access ignores the moral status of enhancement itself. Is the scenario troubling because the unenhanced poor would be denied the benefits of bioengineering, or because the enhanced affluent would somehow be dehumanized? As with muscles, so with memory: the fundamental question is not how to ensure equal access to enhancement but whether we should aspire to it in the first place.

HEIGHT

Pediatricians already struggle with the ethics of enhancement when confronted by parents who want to make their children taller. Since the 1980s human growth hormone has been approved for children with a hormone deficiency that makes them much shorter than average. But the treatment also increases the height of healthy children. Some parents of healthy children who are unhappy with their stature (typically boys) ask why it should make a difference whether a child is short because of a hormone deficiency or because his parents happen to be short. Whatever the cause, the social consequences are the same.

In the face of this argument some doctors began prescribing hormone 15 treatments for children whose short stature was unrelated to any medical problem. By 1996 such "off-label" use accounted for 40 percent of human-growth-hormone prescriptions. Although it is legal to prescribe drugs for purposes not approved by the Food and Drug Administration [FDA], pharmaceutical companies cannot promote such use. Seeking to expand its market, Eli Lilly & Co. recently persuaded the FDA to approve its human growth hormone for healthy children whose projected adult height is in the bottom one percentile—under five feet three inches for boys and four feet eleven inches for girls. This concession raises a large question about the ethics of enhancement: If hormone treatments need not be limited to those with hormone deficiencies, why should they be available only to very short children? Why shouldn't all shorter-than-average children be able to seek treatment? And what about a child of average height who wants to be taller so that he can make the basketball team?

Some oppose height enhancement on the grounds that it is collectively self-defeating; as some become taller, others become shorter relative to the norm. Except in Lake Wobegon,[1] not every child can be above average. As the unenhanced began to feel shorter, they, too, might seek treatment, leading to a hormonal arms race that left everyone worse off, especially those who couldn't afford to buy their way up from shortness.

But the arms-race objection is not decisive on its own. Like the fairness objection to bioengineered muscles and memory, it leaves unexamined the attitudes and dispositions that prompt the drive for enhancement. If we were bothered only by the injustice of adding shortness to the problems of the poor, we could remedy that unfairness by publicly subsidizing height enhancements. As for the relative height deprivation suffered by innocent bystanders, we could compensate them by taxing those who buy their way to greater height. The real question is whether we want to live in a society where parents feel compelled to spend a fortune to make perfectly healthy kids a few inches taller.

SEX SELECTION

Perhaps the most inevitable nonmedical use of bioengineering is sex selection. For centuries parents have been trying to choose the sex of their children. Today biotech succeeds where folk remedies failed.

One technique for sex selection arose with prenatal tests using amniocentesis and ultrasound. These medical technologies were developed to detect genetic abnormalities such as spina bifida and Down syndrome. But they can also reveal the sex of the fetus—allowing for the abortion of

[1]*Lake Wobegon:* A fictional town (in Minnesota) and the childhood home of Garrison Keillor (b. 1942), an American author, storyteller, humorist, musician, satirist, and host of the Minnesota Public Radio show "A Prairie Home Companion." —EDS.

a fetus of an undesired sex. Even among those who favor abortion rights, few advocate abortion simply because the parents do not want a girl. Nevertheless, in traditional societies with a powerful cultural preference for boys, this practice has become widespread.

Sex selection need not involve abortion, however. For couples under-   20
going *in vitro* fertilization (IVF), it is possible to choose the sex of the child before the fertilized egg is implanted in the womb. One method makes use of pre-implantation genetic diagnosis (PGD), a procedure developed to screen for genetic diseases. Several eggs are fertilized in a petri dish and grown to the eight-cell stage (about three days). At that point the embryos are tested to determine their sex. Those of the desired sex are implanted; the others are typically discarded. Although few couples are likely to undergo the difficulty and expense of IVF simply to choose the sex of their child, embryo screening is a highly reliable means of sex selection. And as our genetic knowledge increases, it may be possible to use PGD to cull embryos carrying undesired genes, such as those associated with obesity, height, and skin color. The science-fiction movie *Gattaca* depicts a future in which parents routinely screen embryos for sex, height, immunity to disease, and even IQ. There is something troubling about the *Gattaca* scenario, but it is not easy to identify what exactly is wrong with screening embryos to choose the sex of our children.

One line of objection draws on arguments familiar from the abortion debate. Those who believe that an embryo is a person reject embryo screening for the same reasons they reject abortion. If an eight-cell embryo growing in a petri dish is morally equivalent to a fully developed human being, then discarding it is no better than aborting a fetus, and both practices are equivalent to infanticide. Whatever its merits, however, this "pro-life" objection is not an argument against sex selection as such.

The latest technology poses the question of sex selection unclouded by the matter of an embryo's moral status. The Genetics & IVF Institute, a for-profit infertility clinic in Fairfax, Virginia, now offers a sperm-sorting technique that makes it possible to choose the sex of one's child before it is conceived. X-bearing sperm, which produce girls, carry more DNA than Y-bearing sperm, which produce boys; a device called a flow cytometer can separate them. The process, called MicroSort, has a high rate of success.

If sex selection by sperm sorting is objectionable, it must be for reasons that go beyond the debate about the moral status of the embryo. One such reason is that sex selection is an instrument of sex discrimination—typically against girls, as illustrated by the chilling sex ratios in India and China. Some speculate that societies with substantially more men than women will be less stable, more violent, and more prone to crime or war. These are legitimate worries—but the sperm-sorting company has a clever way of addressing them. It offers MicroSort only to couples who want to choose the sex of a child for purposes of "family balancing." Those with more sons than daughters may choose a girl, and vice versa. But customers may not use the technology to stock up on children of the same sex, or even to choose the sex of their firstborn child. (So far the majority of MicroSort clients have chosen girls.) Under restrictions of this kind, do any ethical issues remain that should give us pause?

The case of MicroSort helps us isolate the moral objections that would persist if muscle-enhancement, memory-enhancement, and height-enhancement technologies were safe and available to all.

It is commonly said that genetic enhancements undermine our humanity by threatening our capacity to act freely, to succeed by our own efforts, and to consider ourselves responsible—worthy of praise or blame—for the things we do and for the way we are. It is one thing to hit seventy home runs as the result of disciplined training and effort, and something else, something less, to hit them with the help of steroids or genetically enhanced muscles. Of course, the roles of effort and enhancement will be a matter of degree. But as the role of enhancement increases, our admiration for the achievement fades—or, rather, our admiration for the achievement shifts from the player to his pharmacist. This suggests that our moral response to enhancement is a response to the diminished agency of the person whose achievement is enhanced.

Though there is much to be said for this argument, I do not think the main problem with enhancement and genetic engineering is that they undermine effort and erode human agency. The deeper danger is that they represent a kind of hyperagency—a Promethean[2] aspiration to remake nature, including human nature, to serve our purposes and satisfy our desires. The problem is not the drift to mechanism but the drive to mastery. And what the drive to mastery misses and may even destroy is an appreciation of the gifted character of human powers and achievements.

To acknowledge the giftedness of life is to recognize that our talents and powers are not wholly our own doing, despite the effort we expend to develop and to exercise them. It is also to recognize that not everything in the world is open to whatever use we may desire or devise. Appreciating the gifted quality of life constrains the Promethean project and conduces to a certain humility. It is in part a religious sensibility. But its resonance reaches beyond religion.

It is difficult to account for what we admire about human activity and achievement without drawing upon some version of this idea. Consider two types of athletic achievement. We appreciate players like Pete Rose, who are not blessed with great natural gifts but who manage, through striving, grit, and determination, to excel in their sport. But we also admire players like Joe DiMaggio, who display natural gifts with grace and effortlessness. Now, suppose we learned that both players took

25

---

[2]**Promethean:** Prometheus is a character in Greek mythology, punished by the gods for stealing fire from the heavens to give to humans. A "Promethean aspiration" is regarded as inventive or innovative, groundbreaking, or opening new fields of inquiry or abilities.—EDS.

performance-enhancing drugs. Whose turn to drugs would we find more deeply disillusioning? Which aspect of the athletic ideal—effort or gift— would be more deeply offended?

Some might say effort: the problem with drugs is that they provide a shortcut, a way to win without striving. But striving is not the point of sports; excellence is. And excellence consists at least partly in the display of natural talents and gifts that are no doing of the athlete who possesses them. This is an uncomfortable fact for democratic societies. We want to believe that success, in sports and in life, is something we earn, not something we inherit. Natural gifts, and the admiration they inspire, embarrass the meritocratic faith;[3] they cast doubt on the conviction that praise and rewards flow from effort alone. In the face of this embarrassment we inflate the moral significance of striving, and depreciate giftedness. This distortion can be seen, for example, in network-television coverage of the Olympics, which focuses less on the feats the athletes perform than on heartrending stories of the hardships they have overcome and the struggles they have waged to triumph over an injury or a difficult upbringing or political turmoil in their native land.

But effort isn't everything. No one believes that a mediocre basketball   30
player who works and trains even harder than Michael Jordan deserves greater acclaim or a bigger contract. The real problem with genetically altered athletes is that they corrupt athletic competition as a human activity that honors the cultivation and display of natural talents. From this standpoint, enhancement can be seen as the ultimate expression of the ethic of effort and willfulness—a kind of high-tech striving. The ethic of willfulness and the biotechnological powers it now enlists are arrayed against the claims of giftedness.

The ethic of giftedness, under siege in sports, persists in the practice of parenting. But here, too, bioengineering and genetic enhancement threaten to dislodge it. To appreciate children as gifts is to accept them as they come, not as objects of our design or products of our will or instruments of our ambition. Parental love is not contingent on the talents and attributes a child happens to have. We choose our friends and spouses at least partly on the basis of qualities we find attractive. But we do not choose our children. Their qualities are unpredictable, and even the most conscientious parents cannot be held wholly responsible for the kind of children they have. That is why parenthood, more than other human relationships, teaches what the theologian William F. May calls an "openness to the unbidden."

May's resonant phrase helps us see that the deepest moral objection to enhancement lies less in the perfection it seeks than in the human dis-

---

[3]*meritocratic faith:* Those who believe in meritocracy, a system in which appointments and advancement depend on demonstrated ability (merit) and not talent or wealth (plutocracy), family connections (nepotism), class privilege, or popularity, as in democracy.—EDS.

position it expresses and promotes. The problem is not that parents usurp the autonomy of a child they design. The problem lies in the hubris of the designing parents, in their drive to master the mystery of birth. Even if this disposition did not make parents tyrants to their children, it would disfigure the relation between parent and child, and deprive the parent of the humility and enlarged human sympathies that an openness to the unbidden can cultivate.

To appreciate children as gifts or blessings is not, of course, to be passive in the face of illness or disease. Medical intervention to cure or prevent illness or restore the injured to health does not desecrate nature but honors it. Healing sickness or injury does not override a child's natural capacities but permits them to flourish.

Nor does the sense of life as a gift mean that parents must shrink from shaping and directing the development of their child. Just as athletes and artists have an obligation to cultivate their talents, so parents have an obligation to cultivate their children, to help them discover and develop their talents and gifts. As May points out, parents give their children two kinds of love: accepting love and transforming love. Accepting love affirms the being of the child, whereas transforming love seeks the well-being of the child. Each aspect corrects the excesses of the other, he writes: "Attachment becomes too quietistic if it slackens into mere acceptance of the child as he is." Parents have a duty to promote their children's excellence.

These days, however, overly ambitious parents are prone to get carried away with transforming love—promoting and demanding all manner of accomplishments from their children, seeking perfection. "Parents find it difficult to maintain an equilibrium between the two sides of love," May observes. "Accepting love, without transforming love, slides into indulgence and finally neglect. Transforming love, without accepting love, badgers and finally rejects." May finds in these competing impulses a parallel with modern science: it, too, engages us in beholding the given world, studying and savoring it, and also in molding the world, transforming and perfecting it.   35

The mandate to mold our children, to cultivate and improve them, complicates the case against enhancement. We usually admire parents who seek the best for their children, who spare no effort to help them achieve happiness and success. Some parents confer advantages on their children by enrolling them in expensive schools, hiring private tutors, sending them to tennis camp, providing them with piano lessons, ballet lessons, swimming lessons, SAT-prep courses, and so on. If it is permissible and even admirable for parents to help their children in these ways, why isn't it equally admirable for parents to use whatever genetic technologies may emerge (provided they are safe) to enhance their children's intelligence, musical ability, or athletic prowess?

The defenders of enhancement are right to this extent: improving children through genetic engineering is similar in spirit to the heavily managed, high-pressure child-rearing that is now common. But this similarity does not vindicate genetic enhancement. On the contrary, it highlights a problem with the trend toward hyperparenting. One conspicuous example of this trend is sports-crazed parents bent on making champions of their children. Another is the frenzied drive of overbearing parents to mold and manage their children's academic careers.

As the pressure for performance increases, so does the need to help distractible children concentrate on the task at hand. This may be why diagnoses of attention deficit and hyperactivity disorder [ADHD] have increased so sharply. Lawrence Diller, a pediatrician and the author of *Running on Ritalin*, estimates that five to six percent of American children under eighteen (a total of four to five million kids) are currently prescribed Ritalin, Adderall, and other stimulants, the treatment of choice for ADHD. (Stimulants counteract hyperactivity by making it easier to focus and sustain attention.) The number of Ritalin prescriptions for children and adolescents has tripled over the past decade, but not all users suffer from attention disorders or hyperactivity. High school and college students have learned that prescription stimulants improve concentration for those with normal attention spans, and some buy or borrow their classmates' drugs to enhance their performance on the SAT or other exams. Since stimulants work for both medical and nonmedical purposes, they raise the same moral questions posed by other technologies of enhancement.

However those questions are resolved, the debate reveals the cultural distance we have traveled since the debate over marijuana, LSD, and other drugs a generation ago. Unlike the drugs of the 1960s and 1970s, Ritalin and Adderall are not for checking out but for buckling down, not for beholding the world and taking it in but for molding the world and fitting in. We used to speak of nonmedical drug use as "recreational." That term no longer applies. The steroids and stimulants that figure in the enhancement debate are not a source of recreation but a bid for compliance—a way of answering a competitive society's demand to improve our performance and perfect our nature. This demand for performance and perfection animates the impulse to rail against the given. It is the deepest source of the moral trouble with enhancement.

Some see a clear line between genetic enhancement and other ways   40
that people seek improvement in their children and themselves. Genetic manipulation seems somehow worse—more intrusive, more sinister—than other ways of enhancing performance and seeking success. But morally speaking, the difference is less significant than it seems. Bioengineering gives us reason to question the low-tech, high-pressure child-rearing practices we commonly accept. The hyperparenting familiar in our time represents an anxious excess of mastery and dominion that misses the sense of life as a gift. This draws it disturbingly close to eugenics.[4]

---

[4]*eugenics:* A social philosophy advocating improving human hereditary traits through various forms of intervention.—EDS.

The shadow of eugenics hangs over today's debates about genetic engineering and enhancement. Critics of genetic engineering argue that human cloning, enhancement, and the quest for designer children are nothing more than "privatized" or "free-market" eugenics. Defenders of enhancement reply that genetic choices freely made are not really eugenic—at least not in the pejorative sense. To remove the coercion, they argue, is to remove the very thing that makes eugenic policies repugnant.

Sorting out the lesson of eugenics is another way of wrestling with the ethics of enhancement. The Nazis gave eugenics a bad name. But what, precisely, was wrong with it? Was the old eugenics objectionable only insofar as it was coercive? Or is there something inherently wrong with the resolve to deliberately design our progeny's traits?

James Watson, the biologist who, with Francis Crick, discovered the structure of DNA, sees nothing wrong with genetic engineering and enhancement, provided they are freely chosen rather than state-imposed. And yet Watson's language contains more than a whiff of the old eugenic sensibility. "If you really are stupid, I would call that a disease," he recently told *The Times* of London. "The lower 10 percent who really have difficulty, even in elementary school, what's the cause of it? A lot of people would like to say, 'Well, poverty, things like that.' It probably isn't. So I'd like to get rid of that, to help the lower 10 percent." A few years ago Watson stirred controversy by saying that if a gene for homosexuality were discovered, a woman should be free to abort a fetus that carried it. When his remark provoked an uproar, he replied that he was not singling out gays but asserting a principle: women should be free to abort fetuses for any reason of genetic preference—for example, if the child would be dyslexic, or lacking musical talent, or too short to play basketball.

Watson's scenarios are clearly objectionable to those for whom all abortion is an unspeakable crime. But for those who do not subscribe to the pro-life position, these scenarios raise a hard question: If it is morally troubling to contemplate abortion to avoid a gay child or a dyslexic one, doesn't this suggest that something is wrong with acting on any eugenic preference, even when no state coercion is involved?

Consider the market in eggs and sperm. The advent of artificial insemination allows prospective parents to shop for gametes with the genetic traits they desire in their offspring. It is a less predictable way to design children than cloning or pre-implantation genetic screening, but it offers a good example of a procreative practice in which the old eugenics meets the new consumerism. A few years ago some Ivy League newspapers ran an ad seeking an egg from a woman who was at least five feet ten inches tall and athletic, had no major family medical problems, and had a combined SAT score of 1400 or above. The ad offered $50,000 for an egg from a donor with these traits. More recently a Web site was launched claiming to auction eggs from fashion models whose photos appeared on the site, at starting bids of $15,000 to $150,000.

45

On what grounds, if any, is the egg market morally objectionable? Since no one is forced to buy or sell, it cannot be wrong for reasons of coercion. Some might worry that hefty prices would exploit poor women by presenting them with an offer they couldn't refuse. But the designer eggs that fetch the highest prices are likely to be sought from the privileged, not the poor. If the market for premium eggs gives us moral qualms, this, too, shows that concerns about eugenics are not put to rest by freedom of choice.

A tale of two sperm banks helps explain why. The Repository for Germinal Choice, one of America's first sperm banks, was not a commercial enterprise. It was opened in 1980 by Robert Graham, a philanthropist dedicated to improving the world's "germ plasm" and counteracting the rise of "retrograde humans." His plan was to collect the sperm of Nobel Prize–winning scientists and make it available to women of high intelligence, in hopes of breeding supersmart babies. But Graham had trouble persuading Nobel laureates to donate their sperm for his bizarre scheme, and so settled for sperm from young scientists of high promise. His sperm bank closed in 1999.

In contrast, California Cryobank, one of the world's leading sperm banks, is a for-profit company with no overt eugenic mission. Cappy Rothman, M.D., a co-founder of the firm, has nothing but disdain for Graham's eugenics, although the standards Cryobank imposes on the sperm it recruits are exacting. Cryobank has offices in Cambridge, Massachusetts, between Harvard and MIT, and in Palo Alto, California, near Stanford. It advertises for donors in campus newspapers (compensation up to $900 a month), and accepts less than five percent of the men who apply. Cryobank's marketing materials play up the prestigious source of its sperm. Its catalogue provides detailed information about the physical characteristics of each donor, along with his ethnic origin and college major. For an extra fee prospective customers can buy the results of a test that assesses the donor's temperament and character type. Rothman reports that Cryobank's ideal sperm donor is six feet tall, with brown eyes, blond hair, and dimples, and has a college degree—not because the company wants to propagate those traits, but because those are the traits his customers want: "If our customers wanted high school dropouts, we would give them high school dropouts."

Not everyone objects to marketing sperm. But anyone who is troubled by the eugenic aspect of the Nobel Prize sperm bank should be equally troubled by Cryobank, consumer-driven though it be. What, after all, is the moral difference between designing children according to an explicit eugenic purpose and designing children according to the dictates of the market? Whether the aim is to improve humanity's "germ plasm" or to cater to consumer preferences, both practices are eugenic insofar as both make children into products of deliberate design.

A number of political philosophers call for a new "liberal eugenics."   50
They argue that a moral distinction can be drawn between the old eugenic

policies and genetic enhancements that do not restrict the autonomy of the child. "While old-fashioned authoritarian eugenicists sought to produce citizens out of a single centrally designed mould," writes Nicholas Agar, "the distinguishing mark of the new liberal eugenics is state neutrality." Government may not tell parents what sort of children to design, and parents may engineer in their children only those traits that improve their capacities without biasing their choice of life plans. A recent text on genetics and justice, written by the bioethicists Allen Buchanan, Dan W. Brock, Norman Daniels, and Daniel Wikler, offers a similar view. The "bad reputation of eugenics," they write, is due to practices that "might be avoidable in a future eugenic program." The problem with the old eugenics was that its burdens fell disproportionately on the weak and the poor, who were unjustly sterilized and segregated. But provided that the benefits and burdens of genetic improvement are fairly distributed, these bioethicists argue, eugenic measures are unobjectionable and may even be morally required.

The libertarian philosopher Robert Nozick proposed a "genetic supermarket" that would enable parents to order children by design without imposing a single design on the society as a whole: "This supermarket system has the great virtue that it involves no centralized decision fixing the future human type(s)."

Even the leading philosopher of American liberalism, John Rawls, in his classic *A Theory of Justice* (1971), offered a brief endorsement of non-coercive eugenics. Even in a society that agrees to share the benefits and burdens of the genetic lottery, it is "in the interest of each to have greater natural assets," Rawls wrote. "This enables him to pursue a preferred plan of life." The parties to the social contract "want to insure for their descendants the best genetic endowment (assuming their own to be fixed)." Eugenic policies are therefore not only permissible but required as a matter of justice. "Thus over time a society is to take steps at least to preserve the general level of natural abilities and to prevent the diffusion of serious defects."

But removing the coercion does not vindicate eugenics. The problem with eugenics and genetic engineering is that they represent the one-sided triumph of willfulness over giftedness, of dominion over reverence, of molding over beholding. Why, we may wonder, should we worry about this triumph? Why not shake off our unease about genetic enhancement as so much superstition? What would be lost if biotechnology dissolved our sense of giftedness?

From a religious standpoint the answer is clear: To believe that our talents and powers are wholly our own doing is to misunderstand our place in creation, to confuse our role with God's. Religion is not the only source of reasons to care about giftedness, however. The moral stakes can also be described in secular terms. If bioengineering made the myth of the "self-made man" come true, it would be difficult to view our talents as gifts for which we are indebted, rather than as achievements for which we are responsible. This would transform three key features of our moral landscape: humility, responsibility, and solidarity.

In a social world that prizes mastery and control, parenthood is a   55
school for humility. That we care deeply about our children and yet cannot choose the kind we want teaches parents to be open to the unbidden. Such openness is a disposition worth affirming, not only within families but in the wider world as well. It invites us to abide the unexpected, to live with dissonance, to rein in the impulse to control. A *Gattaca*-like world in which parents became accustomed to specifying the sex and genetic traits of their children would be a world inhospitable to the unbidden, a gated community writ large. The awareness that our talents and abilities are not wholly our own doing restrains our tendency toward hubris.

Though some maintain that genetic enhancement erodes human agency by overriding effort, the real problem is the explosion, not the erosion, of responsibility. As humility gives way, responsibility expands to daunting proportions. We attribute less to chance and more to choice. Parents become responsible for choosing, or failing to choose, the right traits for their children. Athletes become responsible for acquiring, or failing to acquire, the talents that will help their teams win.

One of the blessings of seeing ourselves as creatures of nature, God, or fortune is that we are not wholly responsible for the way we are. The more we become masters of our genetic endowments, the greater the burden we bear for the talents we have and the way we perform. Today when a basketball player misses a rebound, his coach can blame him for being out of position. Tomorrow the coach may blame him for being too short. Even now the use of performance-enhancing drugs in professional sports is subtly transforming the expectations players have for one another; on some teams players who take the field free from amphetamines or other stimulants are criticized for "playing naked."

The more alive we are to the chanced nature of our lot, the more reason we have to share our fate with others. Consider insurance. Since people do not know whether or when various ills will befall them, they pool their risk by buying health insurance and life insurance. As life plays itself out, the healthy wind up subsidizing the unhealthy, and those who live to a ripe old age wind up subsidizing the families of those who die before their time. Even without a sense of mutual obligation, people pool their risks and resources and share one another's fate.

But insurance markets mimic solidarity only insofar as people do not know or control their own risk factors. Suppose genetic testing advanced to the point where it could reliably predict each person's medical future and life expectancy. Those confident of good health and long life would opt out of the pool, causing other people's premiums to skyrocket. The solidarity of insurance would disappear as those with good genes fled the actuarial company of those with bad ones.

The fear that insurance companies would use genetic data to assess 60
risks and set premiums recently led the Senate to vote to prohibit genetic
discrimination in health insurance. But the bigger danger, admittedly more
speculative, is that genetic enhancement, if routinely practiced, would make
it harder to foster the moral sentiments that social solidarity requires.

Why, after all, do the successful owe anything to the least-advantaged
members of society? The best answer to this question leans heavily on the
notion of giftedness. The natural talents that enable the successful to flourish are not their own doing but, rather, their good fortune—a result of the
genetic lottery. If our genetic endowments are gifts, rather than achievements for which we can claim credit, it is a mistake and a conceit to assume that we are entitled to the full measure of the bounty they reap in a
market economy. We therefore have an obligation to share this bounty
with those who, through no fault of their own, lack comparable gifts.

A lively sense of the contingency of our gifts—a consciousness that
none of us is wholly responsible for his or her success—saves a meritocratic society from sliding into the smug assumption that the rich are rich
because they are more deserving than the poor. Without this, the successful would become even more likely than they are now to view themselves
as self-made and self-sufficient, and hence wholly responsible for their
success. Those at the bottom of society would be viewed not as disadvantaged, and thus worthy of a measure of compensation, but as simply
unfit, and thus worthy of eugenic repair. The meritocracy, less chastened
by chance, would become harder, less forgiving. As perfect genetic knowledge would end the simulacrum of solidarity in insurance markets, so perfect genetic control would erode the actual solidarity that arises when
men and women reflect on the contingency of their talents and fortunes.

Thirty-five years ago Robert L. Sinsheimer, a molecular biologist at
the California Institute of Technology, glimpsed the shape of things to
come. In an article titled "The Prospect of Designed Genetic Change" he
argued that freedom of choice would vindicate the new genetics, and set it
apart from the discredited eugenics of old.

> To implement the older eugenics . . . would have required a massive so-
> cial programme carried out over many generations. Such a programme
> could not have been initiated without the consent and co-operation of a
> major fraction of the population, and would have been continuously
> subject to social control. In contrast, the new eugenics could, at least in
> principle, be implemented on a quite individual basis, in one generation,
> and subject to no existing restrictions.

According to Sinsheimer, the new eugenics would be voluntary rather
than coerced, and also more humane. Rather than segregating and eliminating the unfit, it would improve them. "The old eugenics would have
required a continual selection for breeding of the fit, and a culling of the

unfit," he wrote. "The new eugenics would permit in principle the conversion of all the unfit to the highest genetic level."

Sinsheimer's paean to genetic engineering caught the heady, Promethean self-image of the age. He wrote hopefully of rescuing "the losers in that chromosomal lottery that so firmly channels our human destinies," including not only those born with genetic defects but also "the 50,000,000 'normal' Americans with an IQ of less than 90." But he also saw that something bigger than improving on nature's "mindless, age-old throw of dice" was at stake. Implicit in technologies of genetic intervention was a more exalted place for human beings in the cosmos. "As we enlarge man's freedom, we diminish his constraints and that which he must accept as given," he wrote. Copernicus and Darwin had "demoted man from his bright glory at the focal point of the universe," but the new biology would restore his central role. In the mirror of our genetic knowledge we would see ourselves as more than a link in the chain of evolution: "We can be the agent of transition to a whole new pitch of evolution. This is a cosmic event."

There is something appealing, even intoxicating, about a vision of human freedom unfettered by the given. It may even be the case that the allure of that vision played a part in summoning the genomic age into being. It is often assumed that the powers of enhancement we now possess arose as an inadvertent by-product of biomedical progress — the genetic revolution came, so to speak, to cure disease, and stayed to tempt us with the prospect of enhancing our performance, designing our children, and perfecting our nature. That may have the story backwards. It is more plausible to view genetic engineering as the ultimate expression of our resolve to see ourselves astride the world, the masters of our nature. But that promise of mastery is flawed. It threatens to banish our appreciation of life as a gift, and to leave us with nothing to affirm or behold outside our own will.

The Reader's Presence

1. Sandel frames his essay as a series of questions, each designed to explore the implications of his opening sentence: "Breakthroughs in genetics present us with a promise and a predicament." List each of the questions Sandel poses, and summarize the main points of his argument in response to each. Which questions — and which responses — do you find most convincing and compelling? Explain why. To what extent does Sandel anticipate — and then respond effectively to — the arguments and points of view of those advocating for what he calls "genetic enhancements" (paragraph 3)?

2. At the end of the first paragraph, Sandel observes, "The genomic revolution has induced a kind of moral vertigo." At the beginning of paragraph 7, he notes, "In order to grapple with the ethics of enhancement, we need to confront questions largely lost from view—questions about the moral status of nature, and about the proper stance of human beings toward the given world." Summarize the nature of Sandel's arguments about this "mortal vertigo" and "the ethics of enhancement." What differences does Sandel draw between moral and ethical questions?

3. Sandel focuses his argument about the "new powers of biotechnology" (paragraph 7) on the scientific horizon: "muscle enhancement, memory enhancement, growth-hormone treatment, and reproductive technologies." Which of these examples does he address most convincingly? most compellingly? Explain why. Consider Sandel's use of analogy and metaphor in making his case against perfection. Choose two examples of moments when his use of analogy, metaphor, and other forms of figurative language are most effectively employed, and explain why. What, in Sandel's view, are the consequences of "the trend toward hyperparenting" (paragraph 37)? What prominence does Sandel give to religious arguments in his case against perfection? Comment on the effectiveness of the conclusion he builds for his argument.

4. In addressing issues about the ethics and morality of biotechnology, Sandel writes from the point of view of a political philosopher. How would you read—and respond to—this essay differently if a scientist, reasoning through inside knowledge of the subject, wrote it? Like Sandel, Gregg Easterbrook tackles an increasingly prominent issue within—and beyond—science (see "The Myth of Fingerprints," page 665) and tries to convince his readers of the validity of his point of view. Compare and contrast how each nonscientist uses scientific evidence to support his argument. Which writer stakes a claim that he defends more successfully? Explain why.

Scott Russell Sanders

The Men We Carry in Our Minds

Scott Russell Sanders (b. 1945) writes in a variety of genres: science fiction, realistic fiction, folktales, children's stories, essays, and historical novels. In all his work, however, he is concerned with the ways in which people live in communities. His books include The Paradise of Bombs *(1987), from which "The Men We Carry in Our Minds" is taken;* Staying Put: Making a Home in a Restless World *(1993);* Here Comes the Mystery Man *(1993);* Writing from the Center *(1995);* Hunting for Hope: A Father's Journey *(1998);* The Country of Language *(1999);* Bad Man Ballad *(2004); and a memoir,* A Private History of Awe *(2006). Sanders contributes to both literary and popular magazines. He is a professor of English at Indiana University.*

Sanders has said, "I believe that a writer should be a servant of language, community, and nature. Language is the creation and sustenance of community. . . . My writing is driven by a deep regard for particular places and voices, persons and tools, plants and animals, for human skills and stories. . . . If my writing does not help my neighbors to live more alertly, pleasurably, or wisely, then it is worth little."

"This must be a hard time for women," I say to my friend Anneke. "They have so many paths to choose from, and so many voices calling them."

"I think it's a lot harder for men," she replies.

"How do you figure that?"

"The women I know feel excited, innocent, like crusaders in a just cause. The men I know are eaten up with guilt."

We are sitting at the kitchen table drinking sassafras tea, our hands wrapped around the mugs because this April morning is cool and drizzly. "Like a Dutch morning," Anneke told me earlier. She is Dutch herself, a writer and midwife and peacemaker, with the round face and sad eyes of a woman in a Vermeer painting who might be waiting for the rain to stop, for a door to open. She leans over to sniff a sprig of lilac, pale lavender, that rises from a vase of cobalt blue.

"Women feel such pressure to be everything, do everything," I say. "Career, kids, art, politics. Have their babies and get back to the office a week later. It's as if they're trying to overcome a million years' worth of evolution in one lifetime."

"But we help one another. We don't try to lumber on alone, like so many wounded grizzly bears, the way men do." Anneke sips her tea. I gave her the mug with the owls on it, for wisdom. "And we have this deep-down sense that we're in the *right*—we've been held back, passed

828

over, used—while men feel they're in the wrong. Men are the ones who've been discredited, who have to search their souls."

I search my soul. I discover guilty feelings aplenty—toward the poor, the Vietnamese, Native Americans, the whales, an endless list of debts—a guilt in each case that is as bright and unambiguous as a neon sign. But toward women I feel something more confused, a snarl of shame, envy, wary tenderness, and amazement. This muddle troubles me. To hide my unease I say, "You're right, it's tough being a man these days."

"Don't laugh." Anneke frowns at me, mournful-eyed, through the sassafras steam. "I wouldn't be a man for anything. It's much easier being the victim. All the victim has to do is break free. The persecutor has to live with his past."

How deep is that past? I find myself wondering after Anneke has left. 10 How much of an inheritance do I have to throw off? Is it just the beliefs I breathed in as a child? Do I have to scour memory back through father and grandfather? Through St. Paul? Beyond Stonehenge and into the twilit caves? I'm convinced the past we must contend with is deeper even than speech. When I think back on my childhood, on how I learned to see men and women, I have a sense of ancient, dizzying depths. The back roads of Tennessee and Ohio where I grew up were probably closer, in their sexual patterns, to the campsites of Stone Age hunters than to the genderless cities of the future into which we are rushing.

The first men, besides my father, I remember seeing were black convicts and white guards, in the cottonfield across the road from our farm on the outskirts of Memphis. I must have been three or four. The prisoners wore dingy gray-and-black zebra suits, heavy as canvas, sodden with sweat. Hatless, stooped, they chopped weeds in the fierce heat, row after row, breathing the acrid dust of boll-weevil poison. The overseers wore dazzling white shirts and broad shadowy hats. The oiled barrels of their shotguns flashed in the sunlight. Their faces in memory are utterly blank. Of course those men, white and black, have become for me an emblem of racial hatred. But they have also come to stand for the twin poles of my early vision of manhood—the brute toiling animal and the boss.

When I was a boy, the men I knew labored with their bodies. They were marginal farmers, just scraping by, or welders, steelworkers, carpenters; they swept floors, dug ditches, mined coal, or drove trucks, their forearms ropy with muscle; they trained horses, stoked furnaces, built tires, stood on assembly lines wrestling parts onto cars and refrigerators. They got up before light, worked all day long whatever the weather, and when they came home at night they looked as though somebody had been whipping them. In the evenings and on weekends they worked on their own places, tilling gardens that were lumpy with clay, fixing broken-down cars, hammering on houses that were always too drafty, too leaky, too small.

The bodies of the men I knew were twisted and maimed in ways visible and invisible. The nails of their hands were black and split, the hands tattooed with scars. Some had lost fingers. Heavy lifting had given many of them finicky backs and guts weak from hernias. Racing against conveyor belts had given them ulcers. Their ankles and knees ached from years of standing on concrete. Anyone who had worked for long around machines was hard of hearing. They squinted, and the skin of their faces was creased like the leather of old work gloves. There were times, studying them, when I dreaded growing up. Most of them coughed, from dust or cigarettes, and most of them drank cheap wine or whiskey, so their eyes looked bloodshot and bruised. The fathers of my friends always seemed older than the mothers. Men wore out sooner. Only women lived into old age.

As a boy I also knew another sort of men, who did not sweat and break down like mules. They were soldiers, and so far as I could tell they scarcely worked at all. During my early school years we lived on a military base, an arsenal in Ohio, and every day I saw GIs in the guardshacks, on the stoops of barracks, at the wheels of olive drab Chevrolets. The chief fact of their lives was boredom. Long after I left the Arsenal I came to recognize the sour smell the soldiers gave off as that of souls in limbo. They were all waiting—for wars, for transfers, for leaves, for promotions, for the end of their hitch—like so many braves waiting for the hunt to begin. Unlike the warriors of older tribes, however, they would have no say about when the battle would start or how it would be waged. Their waiting was broken only when they practiced for war. They fired guns at targets, drove tanks across the churned-up fields of the military reservation, set off bombs in the wrecks of old fighter planes. I knew this was all play. But I also felt certain that when the hour for killing arrived, they would kill. When the real shooting started, many of them would die. This was what soldiers were *for*, just as a hammer was for driving nails.

Warriors and toilers: those seemed, in my boyhood vision, to be the   15
chief destinies for men. They weren't the only destinies, as I learned from having a few male teachers, from reading books, and from watching television. But the men on television—the politicians, the astronauts, the generals, the savvy lawyers, the philosophical doctors, the bosses who gave orders to both soldiers and laborers—seemed as remote and unreal to me as the figures in tapestries. I could no more imagine growing up to become one of these cool, potent creatures than I could imagine becoming a prince.

A nearer and more hopeful example was that of my father, who had escaped from a red-dirt farm to a tire factory, and from the assembly line to the front office. Eventually he dressed in a white shirt and tie. He carried himself as if he had been born to work with his mind. But his body, remembering the earlier years of slogging work, began to give out on him in his fifties, and it quit on him entirely before he turned sixty-five. Even such a partial escape from man's fate as he had accomplished did not seem possible for most of the boys I knew. They joined the army, stood in line for jobs in the smoky plants, helped build highways. They were bound to work as their fathers had worked, killing themselves or preparing to kill others.

A scholarship enabled me not only to attend college, a rare enough feat in my circle, but even to study in a university meant for the children of the rich. Here I met for the first time young men who had assumed from birth that they would lead lives of comfort and power. And for the first time I met women who told me that men were guilty of having kept all the joys and privileges of the earth for themselves. I was baffled. What privileges? What joys? I thought about the maimed, dismal lives of most of the men back home. What had they stolen from their wives and daughters? The right to go five days a week, twelve months a year, for thirty or forty years to a steel mill or a coal mine? The right to drop bombs and die in war? The right to feel every leak in the roof, every gap in the fence, every cough in the engine, as a wound they must mend? The right to feel, when the lay-off comes or the plant shuts down, not only afraid but ashamed?

I was slow to understand the deep grievances of women. This was because, as a boy, I had envied them. Before college, the only people I had ever known who were interested in art or music or literature, the only ones who read books, the only ones who ever seemed to enjoy a sense of ease and grace were the mothers and daughters. Like the menfolk, they fretted about money, they scrimped and made-do. But, when the pay stopped coming in, they were not the ones who had failed. Nor did they have to go to war, and that seemed to me a blessed fact. By comparison with the narrow, ironclad days of fathers, there was an expansiveness, I thought, in the days of mothers. They went to see neighbors, to shop in town, to run errands at school, at the library, at church. No doubt, had I looked harder at their lives, I would have envied them less. It was not my fate to become a woman, so it was easier for me to see the graces. Few of them held jobs outside the home, and those who did filled thankless roles as clerks and waitresses. I didn't see, then, what a prison a house could be, since houses seemed to me brighter, handsomer places than any factory. I did not realize—because such things were never spoken of—how often women suffered from men's bullying. I did learn about the wretchedness of abandoned wives, single mothers, widows; but I also learned about the wretchedness of lone men. Even then I could see how exhausting it was for a mother to cater all day to the needs of young children. But if I had been asked, as a boy, to choose between tending a baby and tending a machine, I think I would have chosen the baby. (Having now tended both, I know I would choose the baby.)

So I was baffled when the women at college accused me and my sex of having cornered the world's pleasures. I think something like my bafflement has been felt by other boys (and by girls as well) who grew up in dirt-poor farm country, in mining country, in black ghettos, in Hispanic barrios, in the shadows of factories, in Third World nations—any place where the fate of men is as grim and bleak as the fate of women. Toilers and warriors. I realize now how ancient these identities are, how deep the tug they exert on men, the undertow of a thousand generations. The miseries I saw, as a

boy, in the lives of nearly all men I continue to see in the lives of many—
the body-breaking toil, the tedium, the call to be tough, the humiliating
powerlessness, the battle for a living and for territory.

When the women I met at college thought about the joys and privi-   20
leges of men, they did not carry in their minds the sort of men I had
known in my childhood. They thought of their fathers, who were bankers,
physicians, architects, stockbrokers, the big wheels of the big cities. These
fathers rode the train to work or drove cars that cost more than any of
my childhood houses. They were attended from morning to night by female helpers, wives, and nurses and secretaries. They were never laid off,
never short of cash at month's end, never lined up for welfare. These fathers made decisions that mattered. They ran the world.

The daughters of such men wanted to share in this power, this glory.
So did I. They yearned for a say over their future, for jobs worthy of their
abilities, for the right to live at peace, unmolested, whole. Yes, I thought,
yes yes. The difference between me and these daughters was that they saw
me, because of my sex, as destined from birth to become like their fathers,
and therefore as an enemy to their desires. But I knew better. I wasn't an
enemy, in fact or in feeling. I was an ally. If I had known, then, how to
tell them so, would they have believed me? Would they now?

The Reader's Presence

1. Sanders begins the essay by jumping directly into a conversation
   (paragraphs 1–9). What initial effect does this conversation have
   on the reader? What does Sanders want you to think of him as
   you read the dialogue? How does he move from the conversation
   to the body of the essay (paragraphs 10 and following)? How
   might you describe the transition? Does Sanders's voice change at
   paragraph 10? Does Sanders return to Anneke's distinction between the victim and the persecutor (end of paragraph 9)? If so,
   how? Finally, how do you understand the opening dialogue by the
   end of the essay, having encountered the full passion of Sanders's
   beliefs about his legacy of masculinity?

2. Consider the title of the essay. Why does Sanders use the word
   carry? What image does the word convey? How is that image reinforced throughout the essay?

3. Read Sanders's essay in connection with Katha Pollitt's "Why
   Boys Don't Play with Dolls" (page 522). In what ways does Pollitt's view of sex roles reinforce or contradict Sanders's opinions
   about gender and class? After a careful reading of both essays, do
   you think Sanders would agree with Pollitt, in whole or in part?
   Why or why not? To what extent does Sanders endorse or deny
   conventional sex roles and expectations?

THE WRITER AT WORK

Scott Russell Sanders on Writing Essays

The well-known American essayist Scott Russell Sanders is also a professor of English at Indiana University and the author of several novels, short story collections, and books of criticism. In the following passage from "The Singular First Person," which was originally delivered as a keynote talk at an academic conference on the essay at Seton Hall University in 1988, Sanders argues for the relevance of essay writing in a society that increasingly relies on abstract and formulaic language. If you compare this passage with the style of argument Sanders makes in the preceding essay, you will see that he is a writer who practices what he preaches. He also raises an interesting question about the difference between essays and fiction that you might consider when reading the stories in Part IV: Do essayists put more of themselves at risk than novelists and short story writers?

The essay is a haven for the private, idiosyncratic voice in an era of anonymous babble. Like the bland burgers served in their millions along our highways, most language served up in public these days is textureless, tasteless mush. On television, over the phone, in the newspaper, wherever humans bandy words about, we encounter more and more abstractions, more empty formulas. Think of the pablum ladled out by politicians. Think of the fluffy white bread of advertising. Think, Lord help us, of committee reports. In contrast, the essay remains stubbornly concrete and particular: it confronts you with an oil-smeared toilet at the Sunoco station, a red vinyl purse shaped like a valentine heart, a bow-legged dentist hunting deer with an elephant gun. As Orwell forcefully argued,[1] and as dictators seem to agree, such a bypassing of abstractions, such an insistence on the concrete, is a politically subversive act. Clinging to this door, that child, this grief, following the zigzag motions of an inquisitive mind, the essay renews language and clears trash from the springs of thought. A century and a half ago, Emerson called on a new generation of writers to cast off the hand-me-down rhetoric of the day, to "pierce this rotten diction and fasten words again to visible things." The essayist aspires to do just that.

As if all these virtues were not enough to account for a renaissance of this protean genre, the essay has also taken over some of the territory abdicated by contemporary fiction. Pared down to the brittle bones of plot, camouflaged with irony, muttering in brief sentences and grade-school vocabulary, today's fashionable fiction avoids disclosing where the author stands on anything. Most of the trends in the novel and short story over the past twenty years have led away from candor—toward satire, artsy jokes, close-lipped coyness, metafictional hocus-pocus, anything but a direct statement of what the author thinks and feels. If you hide behind

---

[1] See "Politics and the English Language," page 510.—EDS.

enough screens, no one will ever hold you to an opinion or demand from you a coherent vision or take you for a charlatan.

The essay is not fenced round by these literary inhibitions. You may speak without disguise of what moves and worries and excites you. In fact, you had better speak from a region pretty close to the heart, or the reader will detect the wind of phoniness whistling through your hollow phrases. In the essay you may be caught with your pants down, your ignorance and sentimentality showing, while you trot recklessly about on one of your hobbyhorses. You cannot stand back from the action, as Joyce instructed us to do, and pare your fingernails. You cannot palm off your cockamamie notions on some hapless character. If the words you put down are foolish, everyone knows precisely who the fool is.

To our list of the essay's contemporary attractions we should add the perennial ones of verbal play, mental adventure, and sheer anarchic high spirits. The writing of an essay is like finding one's way through a forest without being quite sure what game you are chasing, what landmark you are seeking. You sniff down one path until some heady smell tugs you in a new direction, and then off you go, dodging and circling, lured on by the songs of unfamiliar birds, puzzled by the tracks of strange beasts, leaping from stone to stone across rivers, barking up one tree after another. Much of the pleasure in writing an essay—and, when the writing is any good, the pleasure in reading it—comes from this dodging and leaping, this movement of the mind. It must not be idle movement, however, if the essay is to hold up; it must be driven by deep concerns. The surface of a river is alive with lights and reflections, the breaking of foam over rocks, but beneath that dazzle it is going somewhere. We should expect as much from an essay: the shimmer and play of mind on the surface and in the depths a strong current.

Barry Schwartz

The Tyranny of Choice

Author and professor Barry Schwartz (b. 1946) has taught psychology and economics at Swarthmore College in Pennsylvania since receiving his PhD from the University of Pennsylvania in 1971. He is currently the Dorwin Cartwright Professor of Social Theory and Social Action, and his classes and seminars focus on thinking and decision-making, the interaction of morality and self-interest, work satisfaction, and the intersection of psychology and economics—all subjects found in his many writings and books. In addition to co-writing a number of text-books on the psychology of learning, memory, and behaviorism, he has written The Battle for Human Nature: Science, Morality and Modern Life *(1987)*, The Costs of Living: How Market Freedom Erodes the Best Things in Life *(2000)*, *and* The Paradox of Choice: Why More Is Less *(2003)*, *in which he explores how choice overload in the marketplace can lead to anxiety and the inability to choose anything at all. Schwartz has written articles for numerous professional journals and mainstream periodicals, including the* New York Times Magazine, USA Today, Scientific American, *and the* Chronicle of Higher Education, *where his essay, "The Tyranny of Choice," appeared in January 2004.*

The modern university has become a kind of intellectual shopping mall. Universities offer a wide array of different "goods" and allow, even encourage, students—the "customers"—to shop around until they find what they like. Individual customers are free to "purchase" whatever bundles of knowledge they want, and the university provides whatever its customers demand. In some rather prestigious institutions, this shopping-mall view has been carried to an extreme. In the first few weeks of classes, students sample the merchandise. They go to a class, stay 10 minutes to see what the professor is like, then walk out, often in the middle of the professor's sentence, to try another class. Students come and go in and out of classes just as browsers go in and out of stores in a mall.

This explosion of choice in the university is a reflection of a pervasive social trend. Americans are awash in choice, not only in the courses they take, but also in the products they buy (300 kinds of cereal, 50 different cellphones, thousands of mutual funds) and in virtually all aspects of life. Increasingly, people are free to choose when and how they will work, how they will worship, where they will live, and what they will look like (thanks to liposuction, Botox, and cosmetic surgery of every description), and what kind of romantic relationships they will have. Further, freedom of choice is greatly enhanced by increased affluence. In the last 40 years, the inflation-adjusted, per capita income of Americans has more than doubled. The proportion of homes with dishwashers has increased from 9 to 50 percent, with clothes dryers from 20 to 70 percent, and with air-conditioning from 15 to 73 percent. And of course, no one had cable TV, home computers, or the Internet in 1964. This increased affluence con-tributes to freedom of choice by giving people the means to act on their various goals and desires, whatever they may be.

Does increased affluence and increased choice mean we have more happy people? Not at all. Three recently published books—by the psy-chologist David Myers, the political scientist Robert E. Lane, and the journalist Gregg Easterbrook—point out how the growth of material affluence has not brought with it an increase in subjective well-being. In-deed, they argue that we are actually experiencing a *decrease* in well-being. In the last 30 years, the number of Americans describing themselves as "very happy" declined by 5 percent, which means that about 14 million fewer people report being very happy today than in 1974. And, as a recent study published in the *Journal of the American Medical Association* indicates, the rate of serious clinical depression has more than tripled over the last two generations, and increased by perhaps a factor of 10 from 1900 to 2000. Suicide rates are also up, not only in the United States, but in almost every developed country. And both serious depression and suicide are occurring among people younger than ever before. Deans at virtually every college and university in the United States can testify to this malaise, as they witness a demand for psychological services that they are unable to meet.

Why are people increasingly unhappy even as they experience greater material abundance and freedom of choice? Recent psychological research suggests that increased choice may itself be part of the problem.

It may seem implausible that there can be too much choice. As a matter of logic, it would appear that adding options will make no one worse off and is bound to make someone better off. If you're content choosing among three different kinds of breakfast cereal, or six television stations, you can simply ignore the dozens or hundreds that get added to your supermarket shelves or cable provider's menu. Meanwhile, one of those new cereals or TV stations may be just what some other person was hoping for. Given the indisputable fact that choice is good for human well-being, it seems only logical that if some choice is good, more choice is better.

Logically true, yes. Psychologically true, no. My colleagues and I, along with other researchers, have begun amassing evidence—both in the laboratory and in the field—that increased choice can lead to *decreased* well-being. This is especially true for people we have termed "maximizers," people whose goal is to get the best possible result when they make decisions. Choice overload is also a problem for people we call "satisficers," people who seek only "good enough" results from their choices, but the problem is greatly magnified for maximizers. Much of the relevant research is summarized in my book, *The Paradox of Choice: Why More Is Less.* Here are some examples:

- Shoppers who confront a display of 30 jams or varieties of gourmet chocolate are less likely to purchase *any* than when they encounter a display of six.

- Students given 30 topics from which to choose to write an extra-credit essay are less likely to write one than those given six. And if they do write one, it tends to be of lower quality.

- The majority of medical patients do not want the decision authority that the canons of medical ethics have thrust upon them. Responsibility for medical decisions looks better to people in prospect than in actuality: Sixty-five percent of respondents say that if they were to get cancer, they would want to be in charge of treatment decisions, but among those who actually have cancer, only 12 percent want that control and responsibility.

- The more funds employers offer their employees in 401(k) retirement plans, the less likely the employees are to invest in *any*, even though in many cases, failing to do so costs them employer-matching funds of up to several thousand dollars a year.

- When maximizers, as opposed to satisficers, go shopping for big items or small ones, they spend more time looking, have a harder time deciding, look around more at what others are buying, and are less satisfied with their purchases.

- Maximizing college seniors send out more résumés, investigate more different fields, go on more job interviews, and get better, higher-paying jobs than satisficers. But they are less satisfied with their jobs, and are much more stressed, anxious, frustrated, and unhappy in the process.

These examples paint a common picture: Increasing options does not increase well-being, especially for maximizers, even when it enables choosers to do better by some objective standard. We have identified several processes that help explain why increased choice decreases satisfaction. Greater choice:

- Increases the burden of gathering information to make a wise decision.

- Increases the likelihood that people will regret the decisions they make.

- Increases the likelihood that people will *anticipate* regretting the decision they make, with the result that they can't make a decision at all.

- Increases the feeling of missed opportunities, as people encounter the attractive features of one option after another that they are rejecting.

- Increases expectations about how good the chosen option should be. Since assessments of the quality of a choice are almost always made relative to one's expectations, as expectations rise, actual choices have a rising standard to meet if they are to produce satisfaction.

- Increases the chances that people will blame themselves when their choices fail to live up to expectations. After all, with so many options out there, there is really no excuse for a disappointing choice.

To illustrate these last two points, I recall buying a bottle of wine to accompany dinner when I was vacationing with my family in a seaside cottage in a small town in Oregon. The tiny general store had about five options from which to choose. The wine I chose wasn't very good, but I didn't expect it to be, and I knew that I couldn't really have done much better. Contrast that with how it would feel to bring home a disappointing bottle of wine from a store that offered thousands of bottles from which to choose.

What are the implications of an abundance of choice for higher education today? College students don't have to worry about choosing 401(k) plans, and most of them don't have major health issues to make decisions about. Nonetheless, the world of the modern college student is so laden with choice, much of it extremely consequential, that for many, it has become overwhelming, perhaps contributing to the rush of students to university counseling services.

When I went to college, 35 years ago, there were almost two years' worth of general-education requirements that all students had to complete. We had *some* choices among courses that met those requirements, but they were rather narrow. Almost every department had a single, introductory course that prepared the student for more advanced work in the field. You could be fairly certain, if you ran into a fellow student you didn't know, that the two of you would have at least a year's worth of courses in common to discuss. In the shopping mall that is the modern university, the chances that any two students have significant intellectual experiences in common are much reduced.

About 30 years ago, somewhat dismayed that their students no longer shared enough common intellectual experiences, the Harvard faculty revised its general-education requirements to form a "core curriculum." With this new curriculum (which is currently undergoing another revision), students take at least one course in each of 11 different broad areas of inquiry. But among those areas, there are dozens and dozens of courses from which to choose. What are the odds that two random students will have courses in common to discuss?

At the advanced end of the curriculum, Harvard offers about 40 majors. For students with interdisciplinary interests, these can be combined into an almost endless array of joint majors. If that doesn't do the trick, students can create their own degree plan. And within majors, at least many of them, internal structure has largely disappeared. Students can begin almost anywhere in the curriculum and end almost anywhere.

Harvard is not unusual. Princeton offers its students a choice of several hundred courses from which to satisfy its general-education requirements. Stanford, which has a larger student body, offers even more. Even at my small college, Swarthmore, with only 1,350 students, we offer about 120 courses to meet our version of the general-education requirement, from which students must select nine. And don't think that this range of choices is peculiar to elite, private institutions. At Pennsylvania State University, for example, liberal-arts students can choose from more than 40 majors and from hundreds of courses intended to meet basic requirements.

Within classes, the digital revolution has made access to information unbelievably easy. The Internet and the "digital library" can be a term-paper writer's blessing. But they can also be a curse. With so much information so readily available, when do you stop looking? There is no excuse for failing to examine all of it.

10

And outside the classroom, the range of recreational and extracurric-   15
ular activities afforded to students has become mind-boggling. As elite
universities compete with one another for elite students (an example of
social waste that I think rivals the SUV), the institutions engage in an
arms race of amenity provision—fitness centers, indoor rock-climbing
walls, hot tubs that accommodate dozens of people at once, espresso
bars—in their effort to attract every student they want. The result is a set
of choices of things to do outside of class that makes one's head spin.

There are many benefits to expanded educational opportunities. The
traditional bodies of knowledge transmitted from teachers to students in
the past were constraining and often myopic. The tastes and interests of the
idiosyncratic students often were stifled and frustrated. In the modern university, each individual student is free to pursue almost any interest, without having to be harnessed to what his intellectual ancestors thought was
worth knowing. Moreover, the advent of the digital age has opened up the
intellectual world to all students, even those at resource-poor institutions.

But this freedom comes at a price. Now, students are required to make
many choices about education that will affect them for the rest of their
lives, and they are forced to make them at a point in their intellectual development when many students lack the wisdom to choose intelligently. In
my own experience I see this manifested in several ways. Advisees ask me
to approve course selections that have no rhyme or reason behind them
and that the advisees themselves can't justify. Students are eager to have
double and triple majors, partly, I know, to pad their résumés, but also because they can't figure out which discipline they really want to commit to.
And I learned some time ago that "What are you doing when you graduate?" is not a friendly question to ask many college seniors.

In addition, students are faced with all this curricular choice while also
trying to figure out what kinds of people they are going to be. Matters of
ethnic, religious, and sexual identity are up for grabs. So are issues of romantic intimacy (to marry or not to marry; to have kids or not to have kids;
to have kids early or to wait until careers are established). Students can live
and work anywhere after they graduate, and in a wired world, they can
work at any time, from any place. Of course it is true that students have
always had to make these kinds of life decisions. College is an unsettled,
and often unsettling, time. But in the past, in virtually each of these areas of
life, there was a "default" option that was so powerful that many decisions
didn't *feel* like decisions, because alternatives to the default weren't seriously considered. Nowadays, almost nothing is decided by default.

The result is a generation of students who use university counseling
services and antidepressants in record numbers, and who provide places
like Starbucks with the most highly educated minimum-wage work force
in the world, as they bide their time hoping that the answer to the "what
should I be when I grow up" question will eventually emerge. Choice
overload is certainly not the only reason for the anxiety and uncertainty

experienced by modern college students, but I believe it is an important one. I believe that by offering our students this much freedom of choice, we are doing them no favor. Indeed, I think that this obsession with choice constitutes an abdication of responsibility by university faculty members and administrators to provide college students with the guidance they badly need.

In an important respect, the "liberation" of the university experience   20
mirrors the embrace of choice in American society at large. The dominant political trend in the last 25 years, influenced by the principles and assumptions of neoclassical economics, has been to stop trying to have the government provide services that serve the welfare of citizens and instead offer citizens choices so that each of us can pursue our own welfare. The push to privatize Social Security, to offer senior citizens choice among prescription-drug plans, and to offer parents choice in the public education their children receive — these are all instances of the view that choice cannot help but make people better off. And so it is with the modern university. What I have tried to indicate is that though all this choice no doubt makes *some* people better off, it makes *many* people worse off, even when their choices work out well.

If enhanced freedom of choice and increased affluence don't enhance well-being, what does? The most important factor seems to be close social relations. People who are married, who have good friends, and who are close to their families are happier than those who are not. People who participate in religious communities are happier than those who do not. Being connected to others seems to be more important to well-being than being rich or "keeping your options open."

In the context of this discussion of choice, it is important to note that, in many ways, social ties actually *decrease* freedom of choice. Marriage, for example, is a commitment to a particular other person that curtails freedom of choice of sexual or emotional partners. Serious friendship also entails weighty responsibilities and obligations that at times may limit one's own freedom. The same is true, obviously, of family. And most religious institutions call on their members to live their lives in a certain way, and to take responsibility for the well-being of their fellow congregants. So, counterintuitive as it may appear, what seems to contribute most to happiness binds us rather than liberates us.

Yet more than a quarter of Americans report being lonely, and loneliness seems to come not from being alone, but from lack of intimacy. We spend less time visiting with neighbors. We spend less time visiting with our parents, and much less time visiting with other relatives. Partly this is because we *have* less time, since we are busy trying to determine what choices to make in other areas of life. But partly this is because close social relations have themselves become matters of choice. As Robert Lane writes: "What was once given by neighborhood and work now must be achieved; people have had to make their own friends . . . and actively cultivate their own family connections." In other words, our social fabric is no longer a birthright but has become a series of deliberate and demanding choices.

Universities should acknowledge the role they have played in creating a world of choice overload and move from being part of the problem to being a part of the solution. The "culture wars" over the canon that rocked college campuses for years have subsided, and most of us were not sorry to see them go. It is deeply troubling to face up to the fact that you and your colleagues can't agree on something as basic as what a college curriculum should consist of. There were no winners in these wars; they subsided, I think, because people got tired of fighting them. And they subsided because giving students choice seemed like a benign resolution of what were sometimes virulent conflicts. Some choice is good, we thought, so more choice is better. Let students choose and we never have to figure out what to choose for them.

But offering more choice is *not* benign. It is a major source of stress,   25
uncertainty, anxiety—even misery. It is not serving our students well. They would be better served by a faculty and an institution that offered choice within limits, freedom within constraints. The poet and essayist Katha Pollitt observed some years ago that the real reason why battles over the curriculum were so intense—the reason that the stakes seemed so high—is that faculty members knew that for the vast majority of students, the last serious book they would *ever* read would be the last book they read in their college careers. I think we are less likely to turn our students off to the life of the mind if we offer them curricular options that are well structured and coherent than if we simply let them choose whatever they want on their own.

There is a *New Yorker* cartoon that depicts a parent goldfish and an offspring in a small goldfish bowl. "You can be anything you want to be—no limits," says the myopic parent, not realizing how limited an existence the fishbowl allows. I'd like to suggest that perhaps the parent is not so myopic. Freedom without limits, choice within constraints, is indeed liberating. But if the fishbowl gets shattered—if the constraints disappear—freedom of choice can turn into a tyranny of choice.

The Reader's Presence

1. Schwartz, a professor of psychology at Swarthmore College, begins his essay with the provocative assertion: "The modern university has become a kind of intellectual shopping mall." Explore the nature of this metaphor. What aspects of it do you find most— and least—convincing? Explain why. If "increased choice" leads to a "*decrease* in well-being," as Schwartz argues (paragraph 3), then to what extent should we decrease curriculum choice to increase our educational well-being? Which parts of Schwartz's essay support eliminating our opportunity to choose college courses?

Would Schwartz endorse the recommendation that all students should take the same classes through their undergraduate years? Explain why or why not. Develop a counterargument that defends increased choice, taking care to reply to each of Schwartz's points. In your judgment, what are some reasons to keep a university as "a kind of intellectual shopping mall"?

2. Identify—and comment on the effectiveness of—the different kinds of evidence Schwartz draws on to make his points (for example, statistics, stories, logic). In what circumstances—and why—does he use one kind of proof rather than another? For example, why do the statistics that begin the essay disappear toward the end? Which kinds of proof are the most convincing to support his points? Reread Schwartz's account of choosing a bottle of wine. These are personal facts, but this is the only personal story he tells. Why does he choose to tell it here? How is it more or less persuasive than citing another statistic or research study?

3. What might Schwartz say about people who have no choices? For example, read Lars Eighner's "On Dumpster Diving" (page 355), which partly tells about what happens when we can no longer exercise choice about where we get our food and what we eat. As Schwartz predicts, Eighner comes to "a healthy state of mind" by losing his material choices (food, cable channels, etc.). But explain the extent to which Eighner's mental well-being increases because he has lost his choices.

Leslie Marmon Silko

In the Combat Zone

Poet, novelist, screenwriter, and storyteller Leslie Marmon Silko (b. 1948) is of mixed heritage, part Pueblo Indian, part Mexican, and part white. She was raised on the Laguna Pueblo and educated at the University of New Mexico, where she taught English for many years. Her published work includes Storyteller *(1981), a montage of stories, legends, poems, and photographs;* Sacred Water: Narratives and Pictures *(1993), an illustrated autobiography;* Yellow Woman and a Beauty of the Spirit *(1996), a collection of essays;* Love Poem and Slim Man Canyon *(1999); and the novels* Almanac of the Dead *(1991) and* Garden in the Dunes *(1999). A collection of rare interviews with Silko,* Conversations with

Leslie Marmon Silko, *edited by Ellen L. Arnold, was published in 2000. "In the Combat Zone" appeared in* Hungry Mind Review *in 1995. In 1981, Silko was awarded a MacArthur Fellowship prize for her writing. She has taught in New Mexico, Alaska, and Arizona and holds academic appointments at both the universities of New Mexico and Arizona.*

When asked by an interviewer why she writes, she replied, "I don't know what I know until it comes out in narrative." Speaking specifically of the process of composing her novel Almanac of the Dead, *she said, "It's like a do-it-yourself psychoanalysis. It's sort of dangerous to be a novelist . . . you're working with language and all kinds of things can escape with the words of a narrative."*

Women seldom discuss our wariness or the precautions we take after dark each time we leave the apartment, car, or office to go on the most brief errand. We take for granted that we are targeted as easy prey by muggers, rapists, and serial killers. This is our lot as women in the United States. We try to avoid going anywhere alone after dark, although economic necessity sends women out night after night. We do what must be done, but always we are alert, on guard, and ready. We have to be aware of persons walking on the sidewalk behind us; we have to pay attention to others who board an elevator we're on. We try to avoid all staircases and deserted parking garages when we are alone. Constant vigilance requires considerable energy and concentration seldom required of men.

I used to assume that most men were aware of this fact of women's lives, but I was wrong. They may notice our reluctance to drive at night to the convenience store alone, but they don't know or don't want to know the experience of a woman out alone at night. Men who have been in combat know the feeling of being a predator's target, but it is difficult for men to admit that we women live our entire lives in a combat zone. Men have the power to end violence against women in the home, but they feel helpless to protect women from violent strangers. Because men feel guilt and anger at their inability to shoulder responsibility for the safety of their wives, sisters, and daughters, we don't often discuss random acts of violence against women.

When we were children, my sisters and I used to go to Albuquerque with my father. Sometimes strangers would tell my father it was too bad that he had three girls and no sons. My father, who has always preferred the company of women, used to reply that he was glad to have girls and not boys, because he might not get along as well with boys. Furthermore, he'd say, "My girls can do anything your boys can do, and my girls can do it better." He had in mind, of course, shooting and hunting.

When I was six years old, my father took me along as he hunted deer; he showed me how to walk quietly, to move along, and then to stop and listen carefully before taking another step. A year later, he traded a pistol for a little single shot .22 rifle just my size.

He took me and my younger sisters down to the dump by the river   5
and taught us how to shoot. We rummaged through the trash for bottles

and glass jars; it was great fun to take aim at a pickle jar and watch it shatter. If the Río San Jose had water running in it, we threw bottles for moving targets in the muddy current. My father told us that a .22 bullet can travel a mile, so we had to be careful where we aimed. The river was a good place because it was below the villages and away from the houses; the high clay riverbanks wouldn't let any bullets stray. Gun safety was drilled into us. We were cautioned about other children whose parents might not teach them properly; if we ever saw another child with a gun, we knew to get away. Guns were not toys. My father did not approve of BB guns because they were classified as toys. I had a .22 rifle when I was seven years old. If I felt like shooting, all I had to do was tell my parents where I was going, take my rifle and a box of .22 shells and go. I was never tempted to shoot at birds or animals because whatever was killed had to be eaten. Now, I realize how odd this must seem; a seven-year-old with a little .22 rifle and a box of ammunition, target shooting alone at the river. But that was how people lived at Laguna when I was growing up; children were given responsibilities from an early age.

Laguna Pueblo people hunted deer for winter meat. When I was thirteen, I carried George Pearl's saddle carbine, a .30–30, and hunted deer for the first time. When I was fourteen, I killed my first male deer buck with one shot through the heart.

Guns were for target shooting and guns were for hunting, but also I knew that Grandma Lily carried a little purse gun with her whenever she drove alone to Albuquerque or Los Lunas. One night my mother and my grandmother were driving the fifty miles from Albuquerque to Laguna down Route 66 when three men in a car tried to force my grandmother's car off the highway. Route 66 was not so heavily traveled as Interstate 40 is now, and there were many long stretches of highway where no other car passed for minutes on end. Payrolls at the Jackpile Uranium Mine were large in the 1950s, and my mother or my grandmother had to bring home thousands from the bank in Albuquerque to cash the miners' checks on paydays.

After that night, my father bought my mother a pink nickel-plated snub-nose .22 revolver with a white bone grip. Grandma Lily carried a tiny Beretta as black as her prayer book. As my sisters and I got older, my father taught us to handle and shoot handguns, revolvers mostly, because back then, semiautomatic pistols were not as reliable—they frequently jammed. I will never forget the day my father told us three girls that we never had to let a man hit us or terrorize us because no matter how big and strong the man was, a gun in our hand equalized all differences of size and strength.

Much has been written about violence in the home and spousal abuse. I wish to focus instead on violence from strangers toward women because this form of violence terrifies women more, despite the fact that most women are murdered by a spouse, relative, fellow employee, or next-door neighbor, not a stranger. Domestic violence kills many more women and children than strangers kill, but domestic violence also follows more predictable patterns and is more familiar: He comes home drunk and she knows what comes next. A good deal of the terror of a stranger's attack comes from its suddenness and unexpectedness. Attacks by strangers occur with enough frequency that battered women and children often cite their fears of such attacks as reasons for remaining in abusive domestic situations. They fear the violence they imagine strangers will inflict on them more than they fear the abusive home. More than one feminist has pointed out that rapists and serial killers help keep the patriarchy securely in place.

An individual woman may be terrorized by her spouse, but women are not sufficiently terrorized that we avoid marriage. Yet many women I know, including myself, try to avoid going outside of their homes alone after dark. Big deal, you say; well, yes, it is a big deal since most lectures, performances, and films are presented at night; so are dinners and other social events. Women out alone at night who are assaulted by strangers are put on trial by public opinion: Any woman out alone after dark is asking for trouble. Presently, for millions of women of all socio-economic backgrounds, sundown is lockdown. We are prisoners of violent strangers.

Daylight doesn't necessarily make the streets safe for women. In the early 1980s, a rapist operated in Tucson in the afternoon near the University of Arizona campus. He often accosted two women at once, forced them into residential alleys, then raped each one with a knife to her throat and forced the other to watch. Afterward the women said that part of the horror of their attack was that all around them, everything appeared normal. They could see people inside their houses and cars going down the street—all around them life was going on as usual while their lives were being changed forever.

The afternoon rapist was not the only rapist in Tucson at that time; there were the prime-time rapist, the potbellied rapist, and the apologetic rapist all operating in Tucson in the 1980s. The prime-time rapist was actually two men who invaded comfortable foothills homes during television prime time when residents were preoccupied with television and eating dinner. The prime-time rapists terrorized entire families; they raped the women and sometimes they raped the men. Family members were forced to go to automatic bank machines to bring back cash to end the ordeal. Potbelly rapist and apologetic rapist need little comment, except to note that the apologetic rapist was good looking, well educated, and smart enough to break out of jail for one last rape followed by profuse apologies and his capture in the University of Arizona library. Local papers recounted details about Tucson's last notorious rapist, the red bandanna rapist. In the late 1970s, this rapist attacked more than twenty women over a three-year period, and Tucson police were powerless to stop him. Then one night, the rapist broke into a midtown home where the lone resident, a woman, shot him four times in the chest with a .38 caliber revolver.

In midtown Tucson, on a weekday afternoon, I was driving down Campbell Avenue to the pet store. Suddenly the vehicle behind me began to weave into my lane, so I beeped the horn politely. The vehicle swerved back to its lane, but then in my rearview mirror I saw the small late-model truck change lanes and begin to follow my car very closely. I drove a few blocks without looking in the rearview mirror, but in my sideview mirror I saw the compact truck was right behind me. OK. Some motorists stay upset for two or three blocks, some require ten blocks or more to recover their senses. Stoplight after stoplight, when I glanced into the rearview mirror I saw the man—in his early thirties, tall, white, brown hair, and dark glasses. This guy must not have a job if he has the time to follow me for miles—oh, ohhh! No beast more dangerous in the U.S.A. than an unemployed white man.

At this point I had to make a decision: Do I forget about the trip to the pet store and head for the police station downtown, four miles away? Why should I have to let this stranger dictate my schedule for the afternoon? The man might dare to follow me to the police station, but by the time I reach the front door of the station, he'd be gone. No crime was committed; no Arizona law forbids tailgating someone for miles or for turning into a parking lot behind them. What could the police do? I had no license plate number to report because Arizona requires only one license plate, on the rear bumper of the vehicle. Anyway, I was within a block of the pet store where I knew I could get help from the pet store owners. I would feel better about this incident if it was not allowed to ruin my trip to the pet store.

The guy was right on my rear bumper; if I'd had to stop suddenly for   15
any reason, there'd have been a collision. I decide I will not stop even if he does ram into the rear of my car. I study this guy's face in my rearview mirror; six feet two inches tall, 175 pounds, medium complexion, short hair, trimmed moustache. He thinks he can intimidate me because I am a woman, five feet five inches tall, 140 pounds. But I am not afraid, I am furious. I refuse to be intimidated. I won't play his game. I can tell by the face I see in the mirror this guy has done this before, he enjoys using his truck to menace lone women.

I keep thinking he will quit, or he will figure that he's scared me enough, but he seems to sense that I am not afraid. It's true. I am not afraid because years ago my father taught my sisters and me that we did not have to be afraid. He'll give up when I turn into the parking lot outside the pet store, I think. But I watch in my rearview mirror; he's right on my rear bumper. As his truck turns into the parking lot behind my car, I reach over and open the glove compartment. I take out the holster with my .38 special and lay it on the car seat beside me.

I turned my car into a parking spot so quickly that I was facing my stalker who had momentarily stopped his truck and was watching me. I slid the .38 out of its holster onto my lap. I watched the stranger's face, trying to determine whether he would jump out of his truck with a baseball bat or gun and come after me. I felt calm. No pounding heart or rapid breathing. My early experience deer hunting had prepared me well. I did not panic because I felt I could stop him if he tried to harm me. I was in no hurry. I sat in the car and waited to see what choice my stalker would make. I looked directly at him without fear because I had my .38 and I was ready to use it. The expression on my face must have been unfamiliar to him; he was used to seeing terror in the eyes of the women he followed. The expression on my face communicated a warning: If he approached the car window, I'd kill him.

He took a last look at me then sped away. I stayed in my car until his truck disappeared in the traffic of Campbell Avenue.

I walked into the pet store shaken. I had felt able to protect myself throughout the incident, but it left me emotionally drained and exhausted. The stranger had only pursued me — how much worse to be battered or raped.

Years before, I was unarmed the afternoon that two drunken deer hunters threatened to shoot me off my horse with razor-edged hunting arrows from fiberglass crossbows. I was riding a colt on a national park trail near my home in the Tucson Mountains. These young white men in their late twenties were complete strangers who might have shot me if the colt had not galloped away erratically bucking and leaping — a moving target too difficult for the drunken bow hunters to aim at. The colt brought me to my ranch house where I called the county sheriff's office and the park ranger. I live in a sparsely populated area where my nearest neighbor is a quarter-mile away. I was afraid the men might have followed me back to my house so I took the .44 magnum out from under my pillow and strapped it around my waist until the sheriff or park ranger arrived. Forty-five minutes later, the park ranger arrived; the deputy sheriff arrived fifteen minutes after him. The drunken bow hunters were apprehended in the national park and arrested for illegally hunting; their bows and arrows were seized as evidence for the duration of bow hunting season. In southern Arizona that is enough punishment; I didn't want to take a chance of stirring up additional animosity with these men because I lived alone then; I chose not to make a complaint about their threatening words and gestures. I did not feel that I backed away by not pressing charges; I feared that if I pressed assault charges against these men, they would feel that I was challenging them to all-out war. I did not want to have to kill either of them if they came after me, as I thought they might. With my marksmanship and my .243 caliber hunting rifle from the old days, I am confident that I could stop idiots like these. But to have to take the life of another person is a terrible experience I will always try to avoid.

It isn't height or weight or strength that make women easy targets; from infancy women are taught to be self-sacrificing, passive victims. I was taught differently. Women have the right to protect themselves from death or bodily harm. By becoming strong and potentially lethal individuals, women destroy the fantasy that we are sitting ducks for predatory strangers.

In a great many cultures, women are taught to depend on others, not themselves, for protection from bodily harm. Women are not taught to defend themselves from strangers because fathers and husbands fear the consequences themselves. In the United States, women depend on the courts and the police, but as many women have learned the hard way, the police cannot be outside your house twenty-four hours a day. I don't want more police. More police on the streets will not protect women. A few policemen are rapists and killers of women themselves; their uniforms and squad cars give them an advantage. No, I will be responsible for my own safety, thank you.

Women need to decide who has the primary responsibility for the health and safety of their bodies. We don't trust the State to manage our reproductive organs, yet most of us blindly trust that the State will protect us (and our reproductive organs) from predatory strangers. One look at the rape and murder statistics for women (excluding domestic incidents) and it is clear that the government FAILS to protect women from the violence of strangers. Some may cry out for a "stronger" State, more police, mandatory sentences, and swifter executions. Over the years we have seen the U.S. prison population become the largest in the world, executions take place every week now, inner-city communities are occupied by the National Guard, and people of color are harassed by police, but guess what? A woman out alone, night or day, is confronted with more danger of random violence from strangers than ever before. As the U.S. economy continues "to downsize," and the good jobs disappear forever, our urban and rural landscapes will include more desperate, angry men with nothing to lose.

Only women can put a stop to the "open season" on women by strangers. Women are TAUGHT to be easy targets by their mothers, aunts, and grandmothers, who themselves were taught that "a woman doesn't kill" or "a woman doesn't learn how to use a weapon." Women must learn how to take aggressive action individually, apart from the police and the courts.

Presently, twenty-one states issue permits to carry concealed weapons; 25 most states require lengthy gun safety courses and a police security check before issuing a permit. Inexpensive but excellent gun safety and self-defense courses designed for women are also available from every quality gun dealer who hopes to sell you a handgun at the end of the course. Those who object to firearms need trained companion dogs or collectives of six or more women to escort one another day and night. We must destroy the myth that women are born to be easy targets.

The Reader's Presence

1. What does Silko mean by a "combat zone" (paragraph 3)? What is the origin of the term? How does she apply it to women's experiences? Do you think the term is applicable? What behavior does the term legitimize? Why do you think she concentrates on violence from strangers instead of domestic violence?

2. Why do you think Silko introduces stories about hunting experiences? In what ways do those experiences shape her background? Do you think they have shaped her present attitude? How do the experiences help reinforce her point about gun ownership? In what ways do they make her more qualified to speak on the issue?

3. In her opening two paragraphs, Silko describes the precautions women take in public every day, of which men are often ignorant. Read Brent Staples's "Just Walk on By" (page 240), which details his experiences of being stereotyped as a threat. How do you think Staples and Silko might discuss this idea of safety? Does Staples show himself to be aware of women's safety concerns? If so, in what ways? What might Silko say in response to Staples's feelings about "being perceived as dangerous"?

Peter Singer

The Singer Solution to World Poverty

Peter Singer, born in Melbourne, Australia, in 1946, has had a long career as the dean of the animal rights movement and is one of today's most controversial contemporary philosophers. He has taught at the University of Colorado at Boulder and the University of California at Irvine and is now the DeCamp Professor of Bioethics at Princeton University's Center for Human Values. His book Animal Liberation, *first published in 1975 and reprinted many times since, has become a basic sourcebook for animal rights activists. His* Practical Ethics (1979) *is one of the most widely recognized works of applied ethics. He has also written* Rethinking Life and Death, *which received an award from the National Book Council in 1995. In 2000, Singer published* Writings on an Ethical Life *and* A Darwinian Left: Politics, Evolution, and Cooperation, *which argues that the left should replace Marx with Darwin. Singer's other books include* One World: The

Ethics of Globalization *(2002),* Pushing Time Away: My Grandfather and the Tragedy of Jewish Vienna *(2003), and* President of Good and Evil: The Ethics of George W. Bush *(2004). He co-wrote with Jim Mason* The Ethics of What We Eat: Why Our Food Choices Matter *(2006) and co-edited the* Cambridge Textbook of Bioethics, *published in 2008. "The Singer Solution to World Poverty" was first published in the* New York Times *in September 1999.*

A reviewer of Writings on an Ethical Life *commented: "Singer argues that value judgments should be matters of rational scrutiny and not matters of taste about which argument is futile. . . . For Singer, living ethically is living a meaningful life. It is a life that makes a difference in the world. It is a life that reduces the sum total of suffering."*

In the Brazilian film *Central Station,* Dora is a retired schoolteacher who makes ends meet by sitting at the station writing letters for illiterate people. Suddenly she has an opportunity to pocket $1,000. All she has to do is persuade a homeless nine-year-old boy to follow her to an address she has been given. (She is told he will be adopted by wealthy foreigners.) She delivers the boy, gets the money, spends some of it on a television set, and settles down to enjoy her new acquisition. Her neighbor spoils the fun, however, by telling her that the boy was too old to be adopted—he will be killed and his organs sold for transplantation. Perhaps Dora knew this all along, but after her neighbor's plain speaking, she spends a troubled night. In the morning Dora resolves to take the boy back.

Suppose Dora had told her neighbor that it is a tough world, other people have nice new TVs too, and if selling the kid is the only way she can get one, well, he was only a street kid. She would then have become, in the eyes of the audience, a monster. She redeems herself only by being prepared to bear considerable risks to save the boy.

At the end of the movie, in cinemas in the affluent nations of the world, people who would have been quick to condemn Dora if she had not rescued the boy go home to places far more comfortable than her apartment. In fact, the average family in the United States spends almost one-third of its income on things that are no more necessary to them than Dora's new TV was to her. Going out to nice restaurants, buying new clothes because the old ones are no longer stylish, vacationing at beach resorts—so much of our income is spent on things not essential to the preservation of our lives and health. Donated to one of a number of charitable agencies, that money could mean the difference between life and death for children in need.

All of which raises a question: In the end, what is the ethical distinction between a Brazilian who sells a homeless child to organ peddlers and an American who already has a TV and upgrades to a better one—knowing that the money could be donated to an organization that would use it to save the lives of kids in need?

Of course, there are several differences between the two situations   5
that could support different moral judgments about them. For one thing,

to be able to consign a child to death when he is standing right in front of you takes a chilling kind of heartlessness; it is much easier to ignore an appeal for money to help children you will never meet. Yet for a utilitarian philosopher like myself—that is, one who judges whether acts are right or wrong by their consequences—if the upshot of the American's failure to donate the money is that one more kid dies on the streets of a Brazilian city, then it is, in some sense, just as bad as selling the kid to the organ peddlers. But one doesn't need to embrace my utilitarian ethic to see that, at the very least, there is a troubling incongruity in being so quick to condemn Dora for taking the child to the organ peddlers while, at the same time, not regarding the American consumer's behavior as raising a serious moral issue.

In his 1996 book, *Living High and Letting Die*, the New York University philosopher Peter Unger presented an ingenious series of imaginary examples designed to probe our intuitions about whether it is wrong to live well without giving substantial amounts of money to help people who are hungry, malnourished, or dying from easily treatable illnesses like diarrhea. Here's my paraphrase of one of these examples:

Bob is close to retirement. He has invested most of his savings in a very rare and valuable old car, a Bugatti, which he has not been able to insure. The Bugatti is his pride and joy. In addition to the pleasure he gets from driving and caring for his car, Bob knows that its rising market value means that he will always be able to sell it and live comfortably after retirement. One day when Bob is out for a drive, he parks the Bugatti near the end of a railway siding and goes for a walk up the track. As he does so, he sees that a runaway train, with no one aboard, is running down the railway track. Looking farther down the track, he sees the small figure of a child very likely to be killed by the runaway train. He can't stop the train and the child is too far away to warn of the danger, but he can throw a switch that will divert the train down the siding where his Bugatti is parked. Then nobody will be killed—but the train will destroy his Bugatti. Thinking of his joy in owning the car and the financial security it represents, Bob decides not to throw the switch. The child is killed. For many years to come, Bob enjoys owning his Bugatti and the financial security it represents.

Bob's conduct, most of us will immediately respond, was gravely wrong. Unger agrees. But then he reminds us that we, too, have opportunities to save the lives of children. We can give to organizations like Unicef or Oxfam America. How much would we have to give one of these organizations to have a high probability of saving the life of a child threatened by easily preventable diseases? (I do not believe that children are more worth saving than adults, but since no one can argue that children have brought their poverty on themselves, focusing on them simplifies the issues.) Unger called up some experts and used the information they provided to offer some plausible estimates that include the cost of raising money, administrative expenses, and the cost of delivering aid where it is most needed. By

his calculation, $200 in donations would help a sickly two-year-old trans-
form into a healthy six-year-old—offering safe passage through childhood's most dangerous years. To show how practical philosophical argument can be, Unger even tells his readers that they can easily donate funds
by using their credit card and calling one of these toll-free numbers: (800)
367-5437 for Unicef; (800) 693-2687 for Oxfam America.

Now you, too, have the information you need to save a child's life.
How should you judge yourself if you don't do it? Think again about Bob
and his Bugatti. Unlike Dora, Bob did not have to look into the eyes of the
child he was sacrificing for his own material comfort. The child was a complete stranger to him and too far away to relate to in an intimate, personal
way. Unlike Dora, too, he did not mislead the child or initiate the chain
of events imperiling him. In all these respects, Bob's situation resembles
that of people able but unwilling to donate to overseas aid and differs
from Dora's situation.

If you still think that it was very wrong of Bob not to throw the switch   10
that would have diverted the train and saved the child's life, then it is hard
to see how you could deny that it is also very wrong not to send money to
one of the organizations listed above. Unless, that is, there is some morally
important difference between the two situations that I have overlooked.

Is it the practical uncertainties about whether aid will really reach the
people who need it? Nobody who knows the world of overseas aid can
doubt that such uncertainties exist. But Unger's figure of $200 to save a
child's life was reached after he had made conservative assumptions about
the proportion of the money donated that will actually reach its target.

One genuine difference between Bob and those who can afford to donate to overseas aid organizations but don't is that only Bob can save the
child on the tracks, whereas there are hundreds of millions of people who
can give $200 to overseas aid organizations. The problem is that most of
them aren't doing it. Does this mean that it is all right for you not to do it?

Suppose that there were more owners of priceless vintage cars—
Carol, Dave, Emma, Fred, and so on, down to Ziggy—all in exactly the
same situation as Bob, with their own siding and their own switch, all sacrificing the child in order to preserve their own cherished car. Would that
make it all right for Bob to do the same? To answer this question affirma-
tively is to endorse follow-the-crowd ethics—the kind of ethics that led
many Germans to look away when the Nazi atrocities were being committed. We do not excuse them because others were behaving no better.

We seem to lack a sound basis for drawing a clear moral line between
Bob's situation and that of any reader of this article with $200 to spare
who does not donate it to an overseas aid agency. These readers seem to
be acting at least as badly as Bob was acting when he chose to let the runaway train hurtle toward the unsuspecting child. In the light of this conclusion, I trust that many readers will reach for the phone and donate
that $200. Perhaps you should do it before reading further.

Now that you have distinguished yourself morally from people who   15
put their vintage cars ahead of a child's life, how about treating yourself
and your partner to dinner at your favorite restaurant? But wait. The
money you will spend at the restaurant could also help save the lives of
children overseas! True, you weren't planning to blow $200 tonight, but
if you were to give up dining out just for one month, you would easily
save that amount. And what is one month's dining out, compared to a
child's life? There's the rub. Since there are a lot of desperately needy children in the world, there will always be another child whose life you could
save for another $200. Are you therefore obliged to keep giving until you
have nothing left? At what point can you stop?

Hypothetical examples can easily become farcical. Consider Bob.
How far past losing the Bugatti should he go? Imagine that Bob had got
his foot stuck in the track of the siding, and if he diverted the train, then
before it rammed the car it would also amputate his big toe. Should he
still throw the switch? What if it would amputate his foot? His entire leg?

As absurd as the Bugatti scenario gets when pushed to extremes, the
point it raises is a serious one: Only when the sacrifices become very
significant indeed would most people be prepared to say that Bob does
nothing wrong when he decides not to throw the switch. Of course, most
people could be wrong; we can't decide moral issues by taking opinion
polls. But consider for yourself the level of sacrifice that you would demand of Bob, and then think about how much money you would have to
give away in order to make a sacrifice that is roughly equal to that. It's almost certainly much, much more than $200. For most middle-class Amer-
icans, it could easily be more like $200,000.

Isn't it counterproductive to ask people to do so much? Don't we run
the risk that many will shrug their shoulders and say that morality, so
conceived, is fine for saints but not for them? I accept that we are unlikely
to see, in the near or even medium-term future, a world in which it is normal for wealthy Americans to give the bulk of their wealth to strangers.
When it comes to praising or blaming people for what they do, we tend
to use a standard that is relative to some conception of normal behavior.
Comfortably off Americans who give, say, 10 percent of their income to
overseas aid organizations are so far ahead of most of their equally comfortable fellow citizens that I wouldn't go out of my way to chastise them
for not doing more. Nevertheless, they should be doing much more, and
they are in no position to criticize Bob for failing to make the much
greater sacrifice of his Bugatti.

At this point various objections may crop up. Someone may say: "If
every citizen living in the affluent nations contributed his or her share I
wouldn't have to make such a drastic sacrifice, because long before such
levels were reached, the resources would have been there to save the lives
of all those children dying from lack of food or medical care. So why
should I give more than my fair share?" Another, related objection is that

the government ought to increase its overseas aid allocations, since that would spread the burden more equitably across all taxpayers.

Yet the question of how much we ought to give is a matter to be de-   20
cided in the real world—and that, sadly, is a world in which we know that most people do not, and in the immediate future will not, give substantial amounts to overseas aid agencies. We know, too, that at least in the next year, the United States government is not going to meet even the very modest United Nations–recommended target of 0.7 percent of gross national product; at the moment it lags far below that, at 0.09 percent, not even half of Japan's 0.22 percent or a tenth of Denmark's 0.97 percent. Thus, we know that the money we can give beyond that theoretical "fair share" is still going to save lives that would otherwise be lost. While the idea that no one need do more than his or her fair share is a powerful one, should it prevail if we know that others are not doing their fair share and that children will die preventable deaths unless we do more than our fair share? That would be taking fairness too far.

Thus, this ground for limiting how much we ought to give also fails. In the world as it is now, I can see no escape from the conclusion that each one of us with wealth surplus to his or her essential needs should be giving most of it to help people suffering from poverty so dire as to be life-threatening. That's right: I'm saying that you shouldn't buy that new car, take that cruise, redecorate the house, or get that pricey new suit. After all, a $1,000 suit could save five children's lives.

So how does my philosophy break down in dollars and cents? An American household with an income of $50,000 spends around $30,000 annually on necessities, according to the Conference Board, a nonprofit economic research organization. Therefore, for a household bringing in $50,000 a year, donations to help the world's poor should be as close as possible to $20,000. The $30,000 required for necessities holds for higher incomes as well. So a household making $100,000 could cut a yearly check for $70,000. Again, the formula is simple: Whatever money you're spending on luxuries, not necessities, should be given away.

Now, evolutionary psychologists tell us that human nature just isn't sufficiently altruistic to make it plausible that many people will sacrifice so much for strangers. On the facts of human nature, they might be right, but they would be wrong to draw a moral conclusion from those facts. If it is the case that we ought to do things that, predictably, most of us won't do, then let's face that fact head-on. Then, if we value the life of a child more than going to fancy restaurants, the next time we dine out we will know that we could have done something better with our money. If that makes living a morally decent life extremely arduous, well, then that is the way things are. If we don't do it, then we should at least know that we are failing to live a morally decent life—not because it is good to wallow in guilt but because knowing where we should be going is the first step toward heading in that direction.

When Bob first grasped the dilemma that faced him as he stood by that railway switch, he must have thought how extraordinarily unlucky he was to be placed in a situation in which he must choose between the life of an innocent child and the sacrifice of most of his savings. But he was not unlucky at all. We are all in that situation.

The Reader's Presence

1. How convincing do you find Singer's hypothetical examples, such as Bob and his uninsured Bugatti? Do you think the examples support his basic argument or weaken it? Explain your response.

2. Singer defines a utilitarian philosopher as one who "judges whether acts are right or wrong by their consequences" (paragraph 5). Can you think of utilitarian solutions other than Singer's to the problems of world poverty? For example, would population-control methods that drastically reduced the number of impoverished children born into the world also be a utilitarian solution? Would donations to organizations that fund population control be more effective than charitable donations that directly assist children? If Singer's solution were adopted and more and more children were assisted, would that eventually encourage higher birth rates and thus worsen the very problem Singer wants to solve?

3. Consider Singer's essay in conjunction with Jonathan Swift's classic satirical essay on poverty, "A Modest Proposal" (page 866). In what ways does Swift's essay also take a utilitarian position? How do you think Swift would react to Singer's solution to world poverty?

THE ACADEMIC VOICE

Peter Singer on "Utility and the Survival Lottery"

What happens when writers address an academic audience, rather than a general audience? What adjustments do they make in their vocabulary, tone of voice, organization, or argument? How do these adjustments take into account the level of knowledge and information they can expect an academic audience to possess? Here you will find the beginning of Peter Singer's academic paper "Utility and the Survival Lottery," published in the journal Philosophy. *Compare this academic selection with Singer's imaginary example of Bob and his Bugatti (paragraphs 7–14) in his essay for a general audience, "The Singer Solution to World Poverty" (page 849).*

In an ingenious article John Harris has proposed a "survival lottery," which would minimize the total number of deaths in a community by sacrificing randomly chosen individuals so that their organs could be transplanted to other people, each of whom needs to have an organ replaced. Since, assuming the perfection of transplant technology, the parts of one "donor" (if that is the right word) could save the lives of four or five others, the proposal appears to be a rational one. If we had the option of joining such a scheme it seems, at first glance anyway, that we would be imprudent to refuse to join. More lives will be saved by the transplants than will be lost by the sacrifices required; hence our prospects of living to a ripe old age are better if we join.[1]

Rational as Harris's idea seems, it will no doubt evoke numerous objections based on the idea of the sanctity of human life and the wrongness of killing an innocent human being.[2] It is not my present purpose to discuss such objections, although my inclinations are to side with Harris against them, on the ground that if human life is valuable, a scheme that saves human lives must be desirable. To say that one violates the sanctity of human life by killing one person to save four, while one does not violate it if one allows four to die because one refuses to kill one, invokes a very dubious notion of moral responsibility. Moral responsibility, as Harris and others have argued, must apply to what we deliberately allow to occur as well as to what we directly bring about.[3]

Similarly, the charge that it is arbitrary or unfair to be called upon to die just because one's number has been drawn in a lottery can be met by pointing out that it is arbitrary and unfair to die just because one has contracted a kidney disease; and if the only way to prevent four arbitrary and unfair deaths is to inflict one arbitrary and unfair death, that procedure is itself neither arbitrary nor unfair.

In any case, the charge of unfairness, or of infringing on individual rights, can be overcome by the stipulation that the scheme be a voluntary one. Instead of simply giving everyone a lottery number, as Harris suggests, we could invite applications for membership in a kind of mutual benefit society, benefits and risks being restricted to members only. Provided people consent to the arrangement, in full knowledge of what it is to which they are consenting, it seems difficult to hold it unfair or an infringement of their rights if they are later selected to be sacrificed.

The major drawback to the survival lottery seems to be, then, not that it infringes some justifiable moral prohibition against killing; rather, I shall suggest, it is a problem of a utilitarian kind. This is surprising, for the scheme looks like an example of utilitarian planning carried to a new   5

---

[1]John Harris, "The Survival Lottery," *Philosophy* 50 (1975), 81.

[2]Alan Ryan has suggested (though not necessarily endorsed) some of these objections in "Two Kinds of Morality," *The Hastings Center Report* 5, no. 5 (1975), 5.

[3]See, for instance, Jonathan Bennett, "Whatever the Consequences," *Analysis* 26 (1966); Michael Tooley, "Abortion and Infanticide," *Philosophy and Public Affairs* 2, no. 1 (1972); and Jonathan Glover's book, *Causing Death and Saving Lives* (1990).

extreme. Harris himself says that utilitarians ought to favor it, and devotes most of his article to meeting absolutist objections. But the survival lottery faces a problem that is faced—though in a milder form—by a wide range of social welfare schemes: by transferring the consequences of imprudent action from the imprudent individual to society at large, the scheme removes the natural disincentive to imprudent action. Thus if I like rich food, and am a member of the survival lottery, I can eat what I like without worrying about growing obese or straining my heart; when it fails, I can always get a new one from a healthier person. My obesity does not increase my chances of being selected by the lottery, and so does not decrease my expected life-span; nor does another person's sensible diet and regular exercise increase his expected life-span. There may even be a tendency toward the reverse, since unhealthy people whose organs have already deteriorated to some extent will be of little use as donors and so presumably would be eliminated from the draw, leaving the healthy to bear the burden of providing organs when required.

Lauren Slater

The Trouble with Self-Esteem

Lauren Slater (b. 1962) began her writing career after earning a doctorate in clinical psychology from Boston University. Her first book, Welcome to My Country: A Therapist's Memoir of Madness *(1996), tells the stories of some of the patients she treated over the course of her eleven-year career. She is perhaps best known, however, for her accounts of her own mental illness and recovery,* Prozac Diary *(1998) and* Lying: A Metaphorical Memoir *(2000). Discussing the difference between writing about her patients and about herself, Slater explains, "I think I found it easier to write about other people, about patients, because I could portray the enormity and dignity of their suffering without risking self-absorption, or blatant narcissism. In writing about myself, I feel much more constricted. I worry about solipsism, shortsightedness, self-aggrandizement, self-denigration, and all the other treacherous territories that come with the fascinating pursuit of autobiography."*

Slater has also published numerous books combining scientific research, a professional's perspective, and personal experience, including Love Works Like This *(2002),* Opening Skinner's Box: Great Psychological Experiments of the Twentieth Century *(2004), and* Blue Beyond Blue *(2005), a collection of stories told as fairy tales. She has contributed pieces to the* New York Times, Harper's,

Elle, *and* Nerve, *and her essays are found in numerous anthologies, including* Best American Essays *of 1994 and 1997,* Best American Science Writing 2002, *and* Best American Magazine Writing 2002. *Her essay "The Trouble with Self-Esteem" appeared in the* New York Times Magazine *in 2002.*

Take this test:

1. On the whole I am satisfied with myself.
2. At times I think that I am no good at all.
3. I feel that I have a number of good qualities.
4. I am able to do things as well as most other people.
5. I feel I do not have much to be proud of.
6. I certainly feel useless at times.
7. I feel that I am a person of worth, at least the equal of others.
8. I wish I could have more respect for myself.
9. All in all, I am inclined to feel that I am a failure.
10. I take a positive attitude toward myself.

Devised by the sociologist Morris Rosenberg, this questionnaire is one of the most widely used self-esteem assessment scales in the United States. If your answers demonstrate solid self-regard, the wisdom of the social sciences predicts that you are well adjusted, clean and sober, basically lucid, without criminal record and with some kind of college cum laude under your high-end belt. If your answers, on the other hand, reveal some inner shame, then it is obvious: you were, or are, a teenage mother; you are prone to social deviance; and if you don't drink, it is because the illicit drugs are bountiful and robust.

It has not been much disputed, until recently, that high self-esteem — defined quite simply as liking yourself a lot, holding a positive opinion of your actions and capacities — is essential to well-being and that its opposite is responsible for crime and substance abuse and prostitution and murder and rape and even terrorism. Thousands of papers in psychiatric and social-science literature suggest this, papers with names like "Characteristics of Abusive Parents: A Look at Self-Esteem" and "Low Adolescent Self-Esteem Leads to Multiple Interpersonal Problems." In 1990, David Long published "The Anatomy of Terrorism," in which he found that hijackers and suicide bombers suffer from feelings of worthlessness and that their violent, fluorescent acts are desperate attempts to bring some inner flair to a flat mindscape.

This all makes so much sense that we have not thought to question it. The less confidence you have, the worse you do; the more confidence you have, the better you do; and so the luminous loop goes round. Based on our beliefs, we have created self-esteem programs in schools in which the main objective is, as Jennifer Coon-Wallman, a psychotherapist based in

Boston, says, "to dole out huge heapings of praise, regardless of actual accomplishment." We have a National Association for Self-Esteem with about a thousand members, and in 1986, the State Legislature of California founded the "California Task Force to Promote Self-Esteem and Personal and Social Responsibility." It was galvanized by Assemblyman John Vasconcellos, who fervently believed that by raising his citizens' self-concepts, he could divert drug abuse and all sorts of other social ills.

It didn't work.

In fact, crime rates and substance abuse rates are formidable, right   5
along with our self-assessment scores on paper-and-pencil tests. (Whether these tests are valid and reliable indicators of self-esteem is a subject worthy of inquiry itself, but in the parlance of social-science writing, it goes "beyond the scope of this paper.") In part, the discrepancy between high self-esteem scores and poor social skills and academic acumen led researchers like Nicholas Emler of the London School of Economics and Roy Baumeister of Case Western Reserve University to consider the unexpected notion that self-esteem is overrated and to suggest that it may even be a culprit, not a cure.

"There is absolutely no evidence that low self-esteem is particularly harmful," Emler says. "It's not at all a cause of poor academic performance; people with low self-esteem seem to do just as well in life as people with high self-esteem. In fact, they may do better, because they often try harder." Baumeister takes Emler's findings a bit further, claiming not only that low self-esteem is in most cases a socially benign if not beneficent condition but also that its opposite, high self-regard, can maim and even kill. Baumeister conducted a study that found that some people with favorable views of themselves were more likely to administer loud blasts of ear-piercing noise to a subject than those more tepid, timid folks who held back the horn. An earlier experiment found that men with high self-esteem were more willing to put down victims to whom they had administered electric shocks than were their low-level counterparts.

Last year alone there were three withering studies of self-esteem released in the United States, all of which had the same central message: people with high self-esteem pose a greater threat to those around them than people with low self-esteem and feeling bad about yourself is not the cause of our country's biggest, most expensive social problems. The research is original and compelling and lays the groundwork for a new, important kind of narrative about what makes life worth living—if we choose to listen, which might be hard. One of this country's most central tenets, after all, is the pursuit of happiness, which has been strangely joined to the pursuit of self-worth. Shifting a paradigm is never easy. More than 2,000 books offering the attainment of self-esteem have been published; educational programs in schools designed to cultivate self-esteem continue to proliferate, as do rehabilitation programs for substance abusers that focus on cognitive realignment with self-affirming

statements like, "Today I will accept myself for who I am, not who I wish
I were." I have seen therapists tell their sociopathic patients to say "I
adore myself" every day or to post reminder notes on their kitchen cabi-
nets and above their toilet-paper dispensers, self-affirmations set side by
side with waste.

Will we give these challenges to our notions about self-esteem their
due or will the research go the way of the waste? "Research like that is
seriously flawed," says Stephen Keane, a therapist who practices in New-
buryport, Mass. "First, it's defining self-esteem according to very conventional and problematic masculine ideas. Second, it's clear to me that
many violent men, in particular, have this inner shame; they find out
early in life they're not going to measure up, and they compensate for it
with fists. We need, as men, to get to the place where we can really honor
and expand our natural human grace."

Keane's comment is rooted in a history that goes back hundreds of
years, and it is this history that in part prevents us from really tussling
with the insights of scientists like Baumeister and Emler. We have long
held in this country the Byronic[1] belief that human nature is essentially
good or graceful, that behind the sheath of skin is a little globe of glow to
be harnessed for creative uses. Benjamin Franklin, we believe, got that
glow, as did Joseph Pulitzer and scads of other, lesser, folks who eagerly
caught on to what was called, in the 19th century, "mind cure."

Mind cure augurs New Age healing, so that when we lift and look at   10
the roots, New Age is not new at all. In the 19th century, people fervently
believed that you were what you thought. Sound familiar? Post it above
your toilet paper. You are what you think. What you think. What you
think. In the 1920's, a French psychologist, Émile Coué, became all the
rage in this country; he proposed the technique of autosuggestion and before long had many citizens repeating, "Day by day in every way I am
getting better and better."

But as John Hewitt says in his book criticizing self-esteem, it was
maybe Ralph Waldo Emerson more than anyone else who gave the modern self-esteem movement its most eloquent words and suasive philosophy. Emerson died more than a century ago, but you can visit his house
in Concord, Mass., and see his bedroom slippers cordoned off behind
plush velvet ropes and his eyeglasses, surprisingly frail, the frames of thin
gold, the ovals of shine, perched on a beautiful desk. It was in this house
that Emerson wrote his famous transcendentalist essays like "On Self-
Reliance," which posits that the individual has something fresh and authentic within and that it is up to him to discover it and nurture it apart
from the corrupting pressures of social influence. Emerson never mentions "self-esteem" in his essay, but his every word echoes with the self-

---

[1] *Byronic:* After the English poet George Gordon, Lord Byron (1788–1824). —Eds.

esteem movement of today, with its romantic, sometimes silly and clearly humane belief that we are special, from head to toe.

Self-esteem, as a construct, as a quasi-religion, is woven into a tradition that both defines and confines us as Americans. If we were to deconstruct self-esteem, to question its value, we would be, in a sense, questioning who we are, nationally and individually. We would be threatening our self-esteem. This is probably why we cannot really assimilate research like Baumeister's or Emler's; it goes too close to the bone and then threatens to break it. Imagine if you heard your child's teacher say, "Don't think so much of yourself." Imagine your spouse saying to you, "You know, you're really not so good at what you do." We have developed a discourse of affirmation, and to deviate from that would be to enter another arena, linguistically and grammatically, so that what came out of our mouths would be impolite at best, unintelligible at worst.

Is there a way to talk about the self without measuring its worth? Why, as a culture, have we so conflated the two quite separate notions — (a) self and (b) worth? This may have as much to do with our entrepreneurial history as Americans, in which everything exists to be improved, as it does, again, with the power of language to shape beliefs. How would we story the self if not triumphantly, redemptively, enhanced from the inside out? A quick glance at amazon.com titles containing the word "self" shows that a hefty percentage also have -improvement or -enhancement tucked into them, oftentimes with numbers — something like 101 ways to improve your self-esteem or 503 ways to better your outlook in 60 days or 604 ways to overcome negative self-talk. You could say that these titles are a product of a culture, or you could say that these titles and the contents they sheathe shape the culture. It is the old argument: do we make language or does language make us? In the case of self-esteem, it is probably something in between, a synergistic loop-the-loop.

On the subject of language, one could, of course, fault Baumeister and Emler for using "self-esteem" far too unidimensionally, so that it blurs and blends with simple smugness. Baumeister, in an attempt at nuance, has tried to shade the issue by referring to two previously defined types: high *unstable* self-esteem and high *well-grounded* self-esteem. As a psychologist, I remember once treating a murderer, who said, "The problem with me, Lauren, is that I'm the biggest piece of [expletive] the world revolves around." He would have scored high on a self-esteem inventory, but does he really "feel good" about himself? And if he doesn't really feel good about himself, then does it not follow that his hidden low, not his high, self-esteem leads to violence? And yet as Baumeister points out, research has shown that people with overt low self-esteem aren't violent, so why would low self-esteem cause violence only when it is hidden? If you follow his train of thinking, you could come up with the sort of silly conclusion that covert low self-esteem causes aggression, but overt low self-esteem does not, which means concealment, not cockiness, is the real culprit. That makes little sense.

"The fact is," Emler says, "we've put antisocial men through every self-   15
esteem test we have, and there's *no* evidence for the old psychodynamic
concept that they secretly feel bad about themselves. These men are racist
or violent because they don't feel bad *enough* about themselves." Baumeister and his colleagues write: "People who believe themselves to be
among the top 10 percent on any dimension may be insulted and threatened whenever anyone asserts that they are in the 80th or 50th or 25th
percentile. In contrast, someone with lower self-esteem who regards himself or herself as being merely in the top 60 percent would only be threatened by the feedback that puts him or her at the 25th percentile. . . . In
short, the more favorable one's view of oneself, the greater the range of
external feedback that will be perceived as unacceptably low."

Perhaps, as these researchers are saying, pride really is dangerous,
and too few of us know how to be humble. But that is most likely not the
entire reason why we are ignoring flares that say, "Look, sometimes self-
esteem can be bad for your health." There are, as always, market forces,
and they are formidable. The psychotherapy industry, for instance, would
take a huge hit were self-esteem to be re-examined. After all, psychology
and psychiatry are predicated upon the notion of the self, and its enhancement is the primary purpose of treatment. I am by no means saying
mental health professionals have any conscious desire to perpetuate a perhaps simplistic view of self-esteem, but they are, we are (for I am one of
them, I confess), the "cultural retailers" of the self-esteem concept, and
were the concept to falter, so would our pocketbooks.

Really, who would come to treatment to be taken down a notch?
How would we get our clients to pay to be, if not insulted, at least uncomfortably challenged? There is a profound tension here between psychotherapy as a business that needs to retain its customers and psychotherapy as a
practice that has the health of its patients at heart. Mental health is not
necessarily a comfortable thing. Because we want to protect our patients
and our pocketbooks, we don't always say this. The drug companies that
underwrite us never say this. Pills take you up or level you out, but I have
yet to see an advertisement for a drug of deflation.

If you look at psychotherapy in other cultures, you get a glimpse into
the obsessions of our own. You also see what a marketing fiasco we
would have on our hands were we to dial down our self-esteem beliefs. In
Japan, there is a popular form of psychotherapy that does not focus on
the self and its worth. This psychotherapeutic treatment, called Morita,
holds as its central premise that neurotic suffering comes, quite literally,
from extreme self-awareness. "The most miserable people I know have
been self-focused," says David Reynolds, a Morita practitioner in Oregon. Reynolds writes, "Cure is not defined by the alleviation of discomfort or the attainment of some ideal state (which is impossible) but by
taking constructive action in one's life which helps one to live a full and
meaningful existence and not be ruled by one's emotional state."

Morita therapy, which emphasizes action over reflection, might have some trouble catching on here, especially in the middle-class West, where folks would be hard pressed to garden away the 50-minute hour. That's what Morita patients do; they plant petunias and practice patience as they wait for them to bloom.

Like any belief system, Morita has its limitations. To detach from   20
feelings carries with it the risk of detaching from their significant signals, which carry important information about how to act: reach out, recoil. But the current research on self-esteem does suggest that we might benefit, if not fiscally then at least spiritually, from a few petunias on the Blue Cross bill. And the fact that we continue, in the vernacular, to use the word "shrink" to refer to treatment means that perhaps unconsciously we know we sometimes need to be taken down a peg.

Down to . . . what? Maybe self-control should replace self-esteem as a primary peg to reach for. I don't mean to sound puritanical, but there is something to be said for discipline, which comes from the word "disciple," which actually means to comprehend. Ultimately, self-control need not be seen as a constriction; restored to its original meaning, it might be experienced as the kind of practiced prowess an athlete or an artist demonstrates, muscles not tamed but trained, so that the leaps are powerful, the spine supple and the energy harnessed and shaped.

There are therapy programs that teach something like self-control, but predictably they are not great moneymakers and they certainly do not attract the bulk of therapy consumers, the upper middle class. One such program, called Emerge, is run by a psychologist named David Adams in a low-budget building in Cambridge, Mass. Emerge's clients are mostly abusive men, 75 percent of them mandated by the courts. "I once did an intake on a batterer who had been in psychotherapy for three years, and his violence wasn't getting any better," Adams told me. "I said to him, 'Why do you think you hit your wife?' He said to me, 'My therapist told me it's because I don't feel good about myself inside.'" Adams sighs, then laughs. "We believe it has *nothing* to do with how good a man feels about himself. At Emerge, we teach men to evaluate their behaviors honestly and to interact with others using empathy and respect." In order to accomplish these goals, men write their entire abuse histories on 12-by-12 sheets of paper, hang the papers on the wall and read them. "Some of the histories are so long, they go all around the room," Adams says. "But it's a powerful exercise. It gets a guy to really concretely *see*." Other exercises involve having the men act out the abuse with the counselor as the victim. Unlike traditional "suburban" therapies, Emerge is under no pressure to keep its customers; the courts do that for them. In return, they are free to pursue a path that has to do with "balanced confrontation," at the heart of which is critical reappraisal and self- — no, not esteem — responsibility.

While Emerge is for a specific subgroup of people, it might provide us with a model for how to reconfigure treatment — and maybe even life — if we do decide the self is not about how good it feels but how well it does, in work and love. Work and love. That's a phrase fashioned by Freud himself, who once said the successful individual is one who has achieved meaningful work and meaningful love. Note how separate this sentence is from the notion of self. We blame Freud for a lot of things, but we can't blame that cigar-smoking Victorian for this particular cultural obsession. It was Freud, after all, who said that the job of psychotherapy was to turn neurotic suffering into ordinary suffering. Freud never claimed we should be happy, and he never claimed confidence was the key to a life well lived.

I remember the shock I had when I finally read this old analyst in his native tongue. English translations of Freud make him sound maniacal, if not egomaniacal, with his bloated words like id, ego and superego. But in the original German, id means under-I, ego translates into I and superego is not super-duper but, quite simply, over-I. Freud was staking a claim for a part of the mind that watches the mind, that takes the global view in an effort at honesty. Over-I. I can see. And in the seeing, assess, edit, praise and prune. This is self-appraisal, which precedes self-control, for we must first know both where we flail and stumble, and where we are truly strong, before we can make disciplined alterations. Self-appraisal. It has a certain sort of rhythm to it, does it not? Self-appraisal may be what Baumeister and Emler are actually advocating. If our lives are stories in the making, then we must be able to edit as well as advertise the text. Self-appraisal. If we say self-appraisal again and again, 101 times, 503 times, 612 times, maybe we can create it. And learn its complex arts.

The Reader's Presence

1. How does Slater establish her credibility? Identify techniques, words, phrases, and evidence that enhance your view of her as an expert. What makes establishing credibility especially important in this essay?

2. In Slater's opinion, how is self-esteem tied to American identity? What have Americans invested in the idea of self-esteem? What might be lost if self-esteem were no longer seen as valuable?

3. In refuting the idea that self-esteem is highly valuable, Slater honestly addresses what would be threatened by such a change in perspective. How does Slater address each of these threats? Compare Slater's technique of arguing against a widely accepted ideal to Laura Kipnis's argument in "Against Love" (page 748) and John Taylor Gatto's in "Against School" (page 682). Which argument(s) do you find most convincing? Why?

THE WRITER AT WORK

Lauren Slater on Writing Groups

Many professional writers find it stimulating and inspiring to share their work with friends and colleagues. They prefer to do this while the writing is in progress so that they can discover problems they haven't anticipated, take note of alternate directions they might pursue, or simply obtain a "gut reaction" from a supportive audience. For Slater, a key advantage of working with a writing group is the impetus provided by a dialogue: "You feel like you're really involved in a dialogue as opposed to a monologue. I do better in engaging in dialogues" (paragraph 2). These comments on writing groups are part of an interview Slater did with Alys Culhane that appeared in the creative nonfiction journal Fourth Genre *in spring 2005.*

Culhane: I recently read that your writing group is integral to your writing process. Is this so? And if so, what's its history?

Slater: It's been quite critical. I was 24 when I started working with this group and I've just turned 40. My writing group has shortened or abolished the state between writer and reader. It can be weeks on end that you are writing, and when you send something out, weeks on end before you hear anything back. But you can bring something to group, and people will hear it right away. This provides a real impetus. You feel like you're really involved in a dialogue as opposed to a monologue. I do better in engaging in dialogues.

Culhane: Why do you think this is?

Slater: Probably everything I write is kind of a co-construction of what I think and what other people think and I just don't see myself as being someone who's pulling ideas out of her own head. I dialogue with people, with books, with pictures, with everything—the world is always giving me things and I'm always taking them and turning them over. I often feel like a quilt maker—and the members of my writing group have, in a way, provided me with ways of thinking about a design and given me some of the squares. So have other friends, other writers, other books. I'm a very derivative writer and I rely heavily on other texts.

Culhane: Can you provide a specific instance where a reliance upon other texts appears in your work?

5

Slater: Yes. I just finished a book of fairy tales, *Blue Beyond Blue*. In this book I take established fairy tales and established fairy-tale characters and tell the story of Snow White through the eyes of the stepmother, Hansel and Gretel through the eyes of the witch.

Culhane: How has the structure of your writing group changed over time?

Slater: It's always been very loose. There's been considerable discussion about life issues that have changed over the years, from getting a boyfriend, to having breast cancer, to having kids or not having kids; the issues have changed as we've changed. In terms of structure, we have always followed the same set of "rules." We convene around 8:30 P.M. every Thursday night. We eat. We talk. At around about 11 P.M. we start to read our work. We stay for as long as it takes for everyone who has work to read it. After a person is finished reading, we go around the room and give our own comments on the piece. When this is done, we plunge into a discussion. We're all very tired on Fridays.

Culhane: Now after many years of sharing your writing with the same people do you find that you anticipate their response when you're writing?

Slater: Yes. For example, to some degree I know that one person is   10 going to feel that a particular, say, meditative or internal beginning is slow because her writing style favors very action-oriented scenes. Others are more partial to memoir, or to fiction. Some of us adhere to the "Show, Don't Tell" rule whereas others are more likely to analyze and interpret.

Culhane: Do you anticipate their specific responses?

Slater: Yes. As a writer, what I'm really looking for is a very visceral kind of response; I take visceral reactions much more to heart than studious ones. I ask myself, did they connect with this piece, does it resonate? What I should do with this paragraph or that paragraph isn't an issue to me.

Jonathan Swift

A Modest Proposal

For Preventing the Children of Poor People in Ireland from Being a Burden to Their Parents or Country, and for Making Them Beneficial to the Public

Jonathan Swift (1667–1745) was born and raised in Ireland, the son of English parents. He was ordained an Anglican priest and, although as a young man he lived a literary life in London, he was appointed against his wishes to be dean of St. Patrick's Cathedral in Dublin. Swift wrote excellent poetry but is remembered principally for his essays and political pamphlets, most of which were published under pseudonyms. Swift received payment for only one work in his entire life, Gulliver's Travels *(1726), for which he earned £200. Swift's political pamphlets were very influential in his day; among other issues, he spoke out against English exploitation of the Irish. Some of Swift's more important publications include* A Tale of a Tub *(1704),* The Importance of the Guardian Considered *(1713),* The Public Spirit of the Whigs *(1714), and* A Modest Proposal *(1729).*

Writing to his friend Alexander Pope, Swift commented that "the chief end I propose to myself in all my labors is to vex the world rather than divert it, and if I could compass that design without hurting my own person or Fortune I would be the most Indefatigable writer you have ever seen."

It is a melancholy object to those who walk through this great town[1] or travel in the country, when they see the streets, the roads, and cabin doors, crowded with beggars of the female sex, followed by three, four, or six children, all in rags and importuning every passenger for an alms. These mothers instead of being able to work for their honest livelihood, are forced to employ all their time in strolling to beg sustenance for their helpless infants: who as they grow up either turn thieves for want of work, or leave their dear native country to fight for the pretender in Spain,[2] or sell themselves to the Barbadoes.[3]

I think it is agreed by all parties that this prodigious number of children in the arms, or on the backs, or at the heels of their mothers, and frequently of their fathers, is in the present deplorable state of the kingdom a very great additional grievance; and, therefore, whoever could find out a fair, cheap, and easy method of making these children sound, useful members of the commonwealth, would deserve so well of the public as to have his statute set up for a preserver of the nation.

But my intention is very far from being confined to provide only for the children of professed beggars; it is of a much greater extent, and shall take in the whole number of infants at a certain age who are born of parents in effect as little able to support them as those who demand our charity in the streets.

As to my own part, having turned my thoughts for many years upon this important subject, and maturely weighed the several schemes of our projectors,[4] I have always found them grossly mistaken in their computation. It is true, a child just dropped from its dam may be supported by her milk for a solar year, with little other nourishment; at most not above the

---

[1]*this great town:* Dublin. —EDS.

[2]*pretender in Spain:* James Stuart (1688–1766); exiled in Spain, he laid claim to the English crown and had the support of many Irishmen who had joined an army hoping to restore him to the throne. —EDS.

[3]*the Barbadoes:* Inhabitants of the British colony in the Caribbean where Irishmen emigrated to work as indentured servants in exchange for their passage. —EDS.

[4]*projectors:* Planners. —EDS.

value of 2s.,[5] which the mother may certainly get, or the value in scraps, by her lawful occupation of begging; and it is exactly at one year old that I propose to provide for them in such a manner as instead of being a charge upon their parents or the parish, or wanting food and raiment for the rest of their lives, they shall on the contrary contribute to the feeding, and partly to the clothing, of many thousands.

There is likewise another great advantage in my scheme, that it will prevent those voluntary abortions, and that horrid practice of women murdering their bastard children, alas! too frequent among us! sacrificing the poor innocent babes I doubt more to avoid the expense than the shame, which would move tears and pity in the most savage and inhuman breast.

The number of souls in this kingdom being usually reckoned one million and a half, of these I calculate there may be about 200,000 couple whose wives are breeders; from which number I subtract 30,000 couple who are able to maintain their own children (although I apprehend there cannot be so many, under the present distress of the kingdom); but this being granted, there will remain 170,000 breeders. I again subtract 50,000 for those women who miscarry, or whose children die by accident or disease within the year. There only remain 120,000 children of poor parents annually born. The question therefore is, how this number shall be reared and provided for? which, as I have already said, under the present situation of affairs, is utterly impossible by all the methods hitherto proposed. For we can neither employ them in handicraft or agriculture; we neither build houses (I mean in the country) nor cultivate land; they can very seldom pick up a livelihood by stealing, till they arrive at six years old, except where they are of towardly parts,[6] although I confess they learn the rudiments much earlier; during which time they can, however, be properly looked upon only as probationers; as I have been informed by a principal gentleman in the county of Cavan, who protested to me that he never knew above one or two instances under the age of six, even in a part of the kingdom so renowned for the quickest proficiency in that art.

I am assured by our merchants, that a boy or a girl before twelve years old is no salable commodity; and even when they come to this age they will not yield above 3£. or 3£. 2s. 6d. at most on the exchange; which cannot turn to account either to the parents or kingdom, the charge of nutriment and rags having been at least four times that value.

I shall now therefore humbly propose my own thoughts, which I hope will not be liable to the least objection.

5

---

[5]*2s.:* Two shillings; in Swift's time one shilling was worth less than twenty-five cents. Other monetary references in the essay are to pounds sterling ("£"), pence ("d."), a crown, and a groat. A pound consisted of twenty shillings; a shilling of twelve pence; a crown was five shillings; a groat was worth a few cents.—Eds.

[6]*towardly parts:* Natural abilities.—Eds.

I have been assured by a very knowing American of my acquaintance in London, that a young healthy child well nursed is at a year old a most delicious, nourishing, and wholesome food, whether stewed, roasted, baked, or broiled; and I make no doubt that it will equally serve in a fricassee or a ragout.[7]

I do therefore humbly offer it to public consideration that of the 120,000 children already computed, 20,000 may be reserved for breed, whereof only one-fourth part to be males; which is more than we allow to sheep, black cattle, or swine; and my reason is, that these children are seldom the fruits of marriage, a circumstance not much regarded by our savages; therefore one male will be sufficient to serve four females. That the remaining 100,000 may, at a year old, be offered in sale to the persons of quality and fortune through the kingdom; always advising the mother to let them suck plentifully in the last month, so as to render them plump and fat for a good table. A child will make two dishes at an entertainment for friends; and when the family dines alone, the fore and hind quarter will make a reasonable dish, and seasoned with a little pepper or salt will be very good boiled on the fourth day, especially in winter.

I have reckoned upon a medium that a child just born will weigh 12 pounds, and in a solar year, if tolerably nursed, will increase to 28 pounds.

I grant this food will be somewhat dear, and therefore very proper for landlords, who, as they have already devoured most of the parents, seem to have the best title to the children.

Infants' flesh will be in season throughout the year, but more plentiful in March, and a little before and after: for we are told by a grave author, an eminent French physician,[8] that fish being a prolific diet, there are more children born in Roman Catholic countries about nine months after Lent than at any other season; therefore, reckoning a year after Lent, the markets will be more glutted than usual, because the number of popish infants is at least three to one in this kingdom: and therefore it will have one other collateral advantage, by lessening the number of papists among us.

I have already computed the charge of nursing a beggar's child (in which list I reckon all cottagers, laborers, and four-fifths of the farmers) to be about 2s. per annum, rags included; and I believe no gentleman would repine to give 10s. for the carcass of a good fat child, which, as I have said, will make four dishes of excellent nutritive meat, when he has only some particular friend or his own family to dine with him. Thus the squire will learn to be a good landlord, and grow popular among the tenants; the mother will have 8s. net profit, and be fit for work till she produces another child.

---

[7]*ragout:* A stew. —Eds.

[8]*French physician:* François Rabelais (c. 1494–1553), the great Renaissance humanist and author of the comic masterpiece *Gargantua and Pantagruel*. Swift is being ironic in calling Rabelais "grave." —Eds.

Those who are more thrifty (as I must confess the times require)   15
may flay the carcass; the skin of which artificially[9] dressed will make
admirable gloves for ladies, and summer boots for fine gentlemen.

As to our city of Dublin, shambles[10] may be appointed for this
purpose in the most convenient parts of it, and butchers we may be assured will not be wanting: although I rather recommend buying the children alive, and dressing them hot from the knife as we do roasting pigs.

A very worthy person, a true lover of his country, and whose virtues I
highly esteem, was lately pleased in discoursing on this matter to offer a
refinement upon my scheme. He said that many gentlemen of this kingdom, having of late destroyed their deer, he conceived that the want of
venison might be well supplied by the bodies of young lads and maidens,
not exceeding fourteen years of age nor under twelve; so great a number
of both sexes in every country being now ready to starve for want of
work and service; and these to be disposed of by their parents, if alive, or
otherwise by their nearest relations. But with due deference to so excellent a friend and so deserving a patriot, I cannot be altogether in his sentiments; for as to the males, my American acquaintance assured me from
frequent experience that their flesh was generally tough and lean, like that
of our schoolboys by continual exercise, and their taste disagreeable; and
to fatten them would not answer the charge. Then as to the females, it
would, I think, with humble submission be a loss to the public, because
they soon would become breeders themselves: and besides, it is not improbable that some scrupulous people might be apt to censure such a
practice (although indeed very unjustly), as a little bordering upon cruelty; which, I confess, has always been with me the strongest objection
against any project, how well soever intended.

But in order to justify my friend, he confessed that this expedient was
put into his head by the famous Psalmanazar[11] a native of the island Formosa, who came from thence to London about twenty years ago: and in
conversation told my friend, that in his country when any young person
happened to be put to death, the executioner sold the carcass to persons
of quality as a prime dainty; and that in his time the body of a plump girl
of fifteen, who was crucified for an attempt to poison the emperor, was
sold to his imperial majesty's prime minister of state, and other great
mandarins of the court, in joints from the gibbet, at 400 crowns. Neither
indeed can I deny, that if the same use were made of several plump young
girls in this town, who without one single groat to their fortunes cannot
stir abroad without a chair,[12] and appear at the playhouse and assemblies
in foreign fineries which they never will pay for, the kingdom would not
be the worse.

---

[9]*artificially:* Artfully.—EDS.

[10]*shambles:* Slaughterhouses.—EDS.

[11]*Psalmanazar:* George Psalmanazar (c. 1679–1763) was a Frenchman who tricked
London society into believing he was a native of Formosa (now Taiwan).—EDS.

[12]*a chair:* A sedan chair in which one is carried about.—EDS.

Some persons of a desponding spirit are in great concern about the vast number of poor people, who are aged, diseased, or maimed, and I have been desired to employ my thoughts what course may be taken to ease the nation of so grievous an encumbrance. But I am not in the least pain upon that matter, because it is very well known that they are every day dying and rotting by cold and famine, and filth and vermin, as fast as can be reasonably expected. And as to the young laborers, they are now in as hopeful condition: They cannot get work, and consequently pine away for want of nourishment, to a degree that if at any time they are accidentally hired to common labor, they have not strength to perform it; and thus the country and themselves are happily delivered from the evils to come.

I have too long digressed, and therefore shall return to my subject. I think the advantages by the proposal which I have made are obvious and many, as well as of the highest importance.   20

For first, as I have already observed, it would greatly lessen the number of papists, with whom we are yearly overrun, being the principal breeders of the nation as well as our most dangerous enemies; and who stay at home on purpose to deliver the kingdom to the Pretender, hoping to take their advantage by the absence of so many good Protestants, who have chosen rather to leave their country than stay at home and pay tithes against their conscience to an Episcopal curate.

Secondly, The poor tenants will have something valuable of their own, which by law may be made liable to distress[13] and help to pay their landlord's rent, their corn and cattle being already seized, and money a thing unknown.

Thirdly, Whereas the maintenance of 100,000 children from two years old and upward, cannot be computed at less that 10s. a-piece per annum, the nation's stock will be thereby increased £50,000 per annum, beside the profit of a new dish introduced to the tables of all gentlemen of fortune in the kingdom who have any refinement in taste. And the money will circulate among ourselves, the goods being entirely of our own growth and manufacture.

Fourthly, The constant breeders beside the gain of 8s. sterling per annum by the sale of their children, will be rid of the charge of maintaining them after the first year.

Fifthly, This food would likewise bring great custom to taverns,   25
where the vintners will certainly be so prudent as to procure the best receipts[14] for dressing it to perfection, and consequently have their houses frequented by all the fine gentlemen, who justly value themselves upon their knowledge in good eating; and a skillful cook who understands how to oblige his guests, will contrive to make it as expensive as they please.

---

[13]*distress:* Seizure for payment of debt. — EDS.
[14]*receipts:* Recipes. — EDS.

Sixthly, This would be a great inducement to marriage, which all wise nations have either encouraged by rewards or enforced by laws and penalties. It would increase the care and tenderness of mothers toward their children, when they were sure of a settlement for life to the poor babes, provided in some sort by the public, to their annual profit instead of expense. We should see an honest emulation among the married women, which of them would bring the fattest child to the market. Men would become as fond of their wives during the time of their pregnancy as they are now of their mares in foal, their cows in calf, their sows when they are ready to farrow; nor offer to beat or kick them (as is too frequent a practice) for fear of a miscarriage.

Many other advantages might be enumerated. For instance, the addition of some thousand carcasses in our exportation of barreled beef, the propagation of swine's flesh, and improvement in the art of making good bacon, so much wanted among us by the great destruction of pigs, too frequent at our table; which are no way comparable in taste or magnificence to a well-grown, fat, yearling child, which roasted whole will make a considerable figure at a lord mayor's feast or any other public entertainment. But this and many others I omit, being studious of brevity.

Supposing that 1,000 families in this city would be constant customers for infants' flesh, besides others who might have it at merry-meetings, particularly at weddings and christenings, I compute that Dublin would take off annually about 20,000 carcasses; and the rest of the kingdom (where probably they will be sold somewhat cheaper) the remaining 80,000.

I can think of no one objection that will possibly be raised against this proposal unless it should be urged that the number of people will be thereby much lessened in the kingdom. This I freely own, and it was indeed one principal design in offering it to the world. I desire the reader will observe, that I calculate my remedy for this one individual kingdom of Ireland and for no other that ever was, is, or I think ever can be upon earth. Therefore let no man talk to me of other expedients: of taxing our absentees at 5s. a pound: of using neither clothes nor household furniture except what is of our own growth and manufacture: of utterly rejecting the materials and instruments that promote foreign luxury: of curing the expensiveness of pride, vanity, idleness, and gaming in our women: of introducing a vein of parsimony, prudence, and temperance: of learning to love our country, in the want of which we differ even from Laplanders and the inhabitants of Topinamboo:[15] of quitting our animosities and factions, nor acting any longer like the Jews, who were murdering one another at the very moment their city was taken:[16] of being a little cautious not to sell our country and conscience for nothing: of teaching landlords

---

[15]*Laplanders and the inhabitants of Topinamboo:* Lapland is the area of Scandinavia above the Arctic Circle; Topinamboo, in Brazil, was known in Swift's time for the savagery of its tribes.—EDS.

[16]*was taken:* A reference to the Roman seizure of Jerusalem (70 CE).—EDS.

to have at least one degree of mercy toward their tenants: lastly, of putting a spirit of honesty, industry, and skill into our shopkeepers; who, if a resolution could now be taken to buy only our native goods, would immediately unite to cheat and exact upon us in the price the measure, and the goodness, nor could ever yet be brought to make one fair proposal of just dealing, though often and earnestly invited to it.

Therefore I repeat, let no man talk to me of these and the like expedients, till he has at least some glimpse of hope that there will be ever some hearty and sincere attempt to put them in practice.

But as to myself, having been wearied out for many years with offering vain, idle, visionary thoughts, and at length utterly despairing of success, I fortunately fell upon this proposal; which, as it is wholly new, so it has something solid and real, of no expense and little trouble, full in our own power, and whereby we can incur no danger in disobliging England. For this kind of commodity will not bear exportation, the flesh being of too tender a consistence to admit a long continuance in salt, although perhaps I could name a country which would be glad to eat up our whole nation without it.

After all, I am not so violently bent upon my own opinion as to reject any offer proposed by wise men, which shall be found equally innocent, cheap, easy, and effectual. But before something of that kind shall be advanced in contradiction to my scheme, and offering a better, I desire the author or authors will be pleased maturely to consider two points. First, as things now stand, how they will be able to find food and raiment for 100,000 useless mouths and backs. And secondly, there being a round million of creatures in human figure throughout this kingdom, whose subsistence put into a common stock would leave them in debt 2,000,000£. sterling, adding those who are beggars by profession to the bulk of farmers, cottagers, and laborers, with the wives and children who are beggars in effect; I desire those politicians who dislike my overture, and may perhaps be so bold as to attempt an answer, that they will first ask the parents of these mortals, whether they would not at this day think it a great happiness to have been sold for food at a year old in the manner I prescribe, and thereby have avoided such a perpetual scene of misfortunes as they have since gone through by the oppression of landlords, the impossibility of paying rent without money or trade, the want of common sustenance, with neither house nor clothes to cover them from the inclemencies of the weather, and the most inevitable prospect of entailing the like or greater miseries upon their breed for ever.

I profess, in the sincerity of my heart, that I have not the least personal interest in endeavoring to promote this necessary work, having no other motive than the public good of my country, by advancing our trade, providing for infants, relieving the poor, and giving some pleasure to the rich. I have no children by which I can propose to get a single penny; the youngest being nine years old, and my wife past childbearing.

The Reader's Presence

1. Consider Swift's title. In what sense is the proposal "modest"? What is modest about it? What synonyms would you use for *modest* that appear in the essay? In what sense is the essay a "proposal"? Does it follow any format that resembles a proposal? If so, what type of format? What aspects of its language seem to resemble proposal writing?

2. For this essay Swift invents a speaker, an unnamed, fictional individual who "humbly" proposes a plan to relieve poverty in Ireland. What attitudes and beliefs in the essay do you attribute to the speaker? Which do you attribute to Swift, the author? Having considered two authors (the speaker of the proposal and Swift), now consider two readers—the reader the speaker imagines and the reader Swift imagines. How do these two readers differ? Reread the final paragraph of the essay from the perspective of each of these readers. How do you think each reader is expected to respond?

3. In the introductory comment, Swift is quoted as wanting "to vex the world rather than divert it" with his writing. Where in the essay do you find Swift most vexing? How does he attempt to provoke the reader's outrage? Where does the first, most visceral indication of the speaker's plan appear? Does he heighten the essay's effect after this point? If so, where and how? How does Swift mount a serious political argument in the midst of such hyperbole? Read "Against Love" by Laura Kipnis (page 748). How does Kipnis use hyperbole or satire in the presentation of her argument? Does she make a serious point? Why or why not?

Sojourner Truth

And Ain't I a Woman?

Sojourner Truth was born Isabella Baumfree in New York, circa 1797. After being liberated from slavery by the New York State Emancipation Act of 1827, she lived briefly in New York, working as a domestic servant. She took the name Sojourner Truth as a sign of her religious vocation and soon became famous as a wandering preacher, spellbinding crowds wherever she spoke. Eventually she joined the abolitionist movement and lectured on her experiences as a slave before

white audiences throughout the North. She became friendly with the major aboli-
tionists of the era, including Harriet Beecher Stowe, who called her "the Libyan
sibyl." She lived for many years in Florence, Massachusetts, and in the 1850s relo-
cated to Battle Creek, Michigan, where she spent the rest of her life. During the
Civil War she helped to raise relief funds for escaped slaves and to gather supplies
for black volunteer regiments. In 1864, she was received warmly at the White
House by President Abraham Lincoln. Sojourner Truth's autobiography, The
Narrative of Sojourner Truth *(narrated to Olive Gilbert), was published in 1850.*
She died in 1883. "And Ain't I a Woman?" is a speech she gave at the Women's
Rights Convention in 1851.

The leaders of the movement trembled on seeing a tall, gaunt black woman in a gray dress and white turban, surmounted with an uncouth sun-bonnet, march deliberately into the church, walk with the air of a queen up the aisle, and take her seat upon the pulpit steps. A buzz of disapprobation was heard all over the house, and there fell on the listening ear, "An aboli-tion affair!" "Woman's rights and niggers!" "I told you so!" . . .

I chanced on that occasion to wear my first laurels in public life as president of the meeting. At my request order was restored, and the busi-ness of the Convention went on. Morning, afternoon, and evening exer-cises came and went. Through all these sessions old Sojourner, quiet and reticent as the "Lybian Statue," sat crouched against the wall on the cor-ner of the pulpit stairs, her sun-bonnet shading her eyes, her elbows on her knees, her chin resting upon her broad, hard palms. At intermission she was busy selling the "Life of Sojourner Truth," a narrative of her own strange and adventurous life. Again and again, timorous and trembling ones came to me and said, with earnestness, "Don't let her speak, Mrs. Gage, it will ruin us. Every newspaper in the land will have our cause mixed up with abolition and niggers, and we shall be utterly denounced." My only answer was, "We shall see when the time comes."

The second day the work waxed warm. Methodist, Baptist, Episcopal, Presbyterian, and Universalist ministers came in to hear and discuss the resolutions presented. One claimed superior rights and privileges for man, on the ground of "superior intellect"; another, because of the "manhood of Christ; if God had desired the equality of woman, He would have given some token of His will through the birth, life, and death of the Saviour." Another gave us a theological view of the "sin of our first mother."

There were very few women in those days who dared to "speak in meeting"; and the august teachers of the people were seemingly getting the better of us, while the boys in the galleries, and the sneerers among the pews, were hugely enjoying the discomfiture, as they supposed, of the "strong-minded." Some of the tender-skinned friends were on the point of losing dignity, and the atmosphere betokened a storm. When, slowly from her seat in the corner rose Sojourner Truth, who, till now, had scarcely lifted her head. "Don't let her speak!" gasped half a dozen in my ear. She moved slowly and solemnly to the front, laid her old bonnet at her feet, and

turned her great speaking eyes to me. There was a hissing sound of disapprobation above and below. I rose and announced "Sojourner Truth," and
begged the audience to keep silence for a few moments.

The tumult subsided at once, and every eye was fixed on this almost   5
Amazon form, which stood nearly six feet high, head erect, and eyes
piercing the upper air like one in a dream. At her first word there was a
profound hush. She spoke in deep tones, which, though not loud, reached
every ear in the house, and away through the throng at the doors and
windows.

"Wall, chilern, whar dar is so much racket dar must be somethin' out
o' kilter. I tink dat 'twixt de niggers of de Souf and de womin at de Norf,
all talkin' 'bout rights, de white men will be in a fix pretty soon. But
what's all dis here talkin' 'bout?

"Dat man ober dar say dat womin needs to be helped into carriages,
and lifted ober ditches, and to hab de best place everywhar. Nobody eber
helps me into carriages, or ober mud-puddles, or gibs me any best place!"
And raising herself to her full height, and her voice to a pitch like rolling
thunder, she asked, "And a'n't I a woman? Look at me! Look at my arm!
(and she bared her right arm to the shoulder, showing her tremendous
muscular power). I have ploughed, and planted, and gathered into barns,
and no man could head me! And a'n't I a woman? I could work as much
and eat as much as a man—when I could get it—and bear de lash as
well! And a'n't I a woman? I have borne thirteen chilern, and seen 'em
mos' all sold off to slavery, and when I cried out with my mother's grief,
none but Jesus heard me! And a'n't I a woman?

"Den dey talks 'bout dis ting in de head; what dis dey call it?" ("Intellect," whispered some one near.) "Dat's it, honey. What's dat got to do
wid womin's rights or nigger's rights? If my cup won't hold but a pint,
and yourn holds a quart, wouldn't ye be mean not to let me have my little
half-measure full?" And she pointed her significant finger, and sent a
keen glance at the minister who had made the argument. The cheering
was long and loud.

"Den dat little man in black dar, he say women can't have as much
rights as men, 'cause Christ wan't a woman! Whar did your Christ come
from?" Rolling thunder couldn't have stilled that crowd, as did those
deep, wonderful tones, as she stood there with outstretched arms and eyes
of fire. Raising her voice still louder, she repeated, "Whar did your Christ
come from? From God and a woman! Man had nothin' to do wid Him."
Oh, what a rebuke that was to that little man.

Turning again to another objector, she took up the defense of Mother   10
Eve. I can not follow her through it all. It was pointed, and witty, and
solemn; eliciting at almost every sentence deafening applause; and she
ended by asserting: "If de fust woman God ever made was strong enough
to turn de world upside down all alone, dese women togedder (and she
glanced her eye over the platform) ought to be able to turn it back, and
get it right side up again! And now dey is asking to do it, de men better

let 'em." Long-continued cheering greeted this. " 'Bleeged to ye for hearin' on me, and now ole Sojourner han't got nothin' more to say."

Amid roars of applause, she returned to her corner, leaving more than one of us with streaming eyes, and hearts beating with gratitude. She had taken us up in her strong arms and carried us safely over the slough of difficulty turning the whole tide in our favor. I have never in my life seen anything like the magical influence that subdued the mobbish spirit of the day, and turned the sneers and jeers of an excited crowd into notes of respect and admiration. Hundreds rushed up to shake hands with her, and congratulate the glorious old mother, and bid her God-speed on her mission of "testifyin' agin concerning the wickedness of this 'ere people."

The Reader's Presence

1. Imagine yourself as the two men whom Truth directly addresses: "[that] man [over there]" and "[that] little man in black" (paragraphs 7 and 9). Continue the conversation. What might each one have said in reply to her points? How would she have responded? In developing your dialogue, focus on maintaining Truth's style and rhythm as much as possible. How convincing was your version of the dialogue? What was the most difficult challenge you faced in making her voice sound "right"? What was the easiest aspect of recreating her voice?

2. Truth was illiterate when she spoke at the Women's Rights Convention in 1851. Recollecting the speech in 1863—twelve years later—the convention's president, Frances Gage, wrote what has become the official version of Truth's words. Reread the speech carefully. What indications do you find that the speech has been changed from spoken language to written word? How do these changes affect the overall meaning of the speech? In answering this question, think about what has been left out of the written version (for example, facial expressions, gestures, tone). What has been added (for example, punctuation, asides)? Do you think the changes make the speech more powerful and successful, or less powerful? How?

3. Why has Truth's speech continued to be popular for over 150 years? Examine another selection that is dated from at least 20 years ago, such as Martin Luther King Jr.'s "Letter from Birmingham Jail" (page 730) or Thomas Jefferson's "The Declaration of Independence" (page 705). What characteristics do the selections share? How do the pieces continue to be relevant to a world very different from the world in which they were written? What indications do you find that the essays are past their time? How long do you think the essays will continue to be important? Why?

Mark Twain

Corn-pone Opinions

Mark Twain, the pseudonym of Samuel Clemens (1835–1910), was a master satirist, journalist, novelist, orator, and steamboat pilot. He grew up in Hannibal, Missouri, a frontier setting that appears in different forms in several of his novels, most notably in his masterpiece Adventures of Huckleberry Finn *(1869). His satirical eye spared very few American political or social institutions, including slavery, and for this reason, as well as because it violated conventional standards of taste,* Huckleberry Finn *created a minor scandal when it was published. Nonetheless, with such books as* The Innocents Abroad *(1869),* Roughing It *(1872),* The Adventures of Tom Sawyer *(1876), and* The Prince and the Pauper *(1882), Twain secured himself a position as one of the most popular authors in American history. Twain built his career on his experiences in the western states and his travels in Europe and the Middle East, but he eventually settled in Hartford, Connecticut. His last years were spent as one of the most celebrated public speakers and social figures in the United States.*

Reflecting on the experience of writing, Twain once wrote in his notebook, "The time to begin writing an article is when you have finished it to your satisfaction. By that time you begin to clearly and logically perceive what it is that you really want to say."

"Corn-pone Opinions" was found in Mark Twain's papers after his death and first published in 1923 in Europe and Elsewhere, *edited by Albert Bigelow Paine.*

Fifty years ago, when I was a boy of fifteen and helping to inhabit a Missourian village on the banks of the Mississippi, I had a friend whose society was very dear to me because I was forbidden by my mother to partake of it. He was a gay and impudent and satirical and delightful young black man—a slave—who daily preached sermons from the top of his master's woodpile, with me for sole audience. He imitated the pulpit style of the several clergymen of the village, and did it well, and with fine passion and energy. To me he was a wonder. I believed he was the greatest orator in the United States and would some day be heard from. But it did not happen; in the distribution of rewards he was overlooked. It is the way, in this world.

He interrupted his preaching, now and then, to saw a stick of wood; but the sawing was a pretense—he did it with his mouth; exactly imitating the sound the bucksaw makes in shrieking its way through the wood. But it served its purpose; it kept his master from coming out to see how the work was getting along. I listened to the sermons from the open window of a lumber room at the back of the house. One of his texts was this:

"You tell me whar a man gits his corn pone,[1] en I'll tell you what his 'pinions is."

I can never forget it. It was deeply impressed upon me. By my mother. Not upon my memory, but elsewhere. She had slipped in upon me while I was absorbed and not watching. The black philosopher's idea was that a man is not independent, and cannot afford views which might interfere with his bread and butter. If he would prosper, he must train with the majority; in matters of large moment, like politics and religion, he must think and feel with the bulk of his neighbors, or suffer damage in his social standing and in his business prosperities. He must restrict himself to corn-pone opinions—at least on the surface. He must get his opinions from other people; he must reason out none for himself; he must have no first-hand views.

I think Jerry was right, in the main, but I think he did not go far enough.   5

1. It was his idea that a man conforms to the majority view of his locality by calculation and intention.

This happens, but I think it is not the rule.

2. It was his idea that there is such a thing as a first-hand opinion; an original opinion; an opinion which is coldly reasoned out in a man's head, by a searching analysis of the facts involved, with the heart unconsulted, and the jury room closed against outside influences. It may be that such an opinion has been born somewhere, at some time or other, but I suppose it got away before they could catch it and stuff it and put it in the museum.

I am persuaded that a coldly-thought-out and independent verdict upon a fashion in clothes, or manners, or literature, or politics, or religion, or any other matter that is projected into the field of our notice and interest, is a most rare thing—if it has indeed ever existed.

A new thing in costume appears—the flaring hoopskirt, for example—and the passers-by are shocked, and the irreverent laugh. Six months later everybody is reconciled; the fashion has established itself; it is admired, now, and no one laughs. Public opinion resented it before, public opinion accepts it now, and is happy in it. Why? Was the resentment reasoned out? Was the acceptance reasoned out? No. The instinct that moves to conformity did the work. It is our nature to conform; it is a force which not many can successfully resist. What is its seat? The inborn requirement of self-approval. We all have to bow to that; there are no exceptions. Even the woman who refuses from first to last to wear the hoopskirt comes under that law and is its slave; she could not wear the skirt and have her own approval; and that she *must* have, she cannot help herself.   10

[1]*Corn pone:* Southern expression that dates from the mid-nineteenth century for a simple corn bread or muffin; *pone* comes from a Native American word for something baked.—Eds.

But as a rule our self-approval has its source in but one place and not elsewhere—the approval of other people. A person of vast consequences can introduce any kind of novelty in dress and the general world will presently adopt it—moved to do it, in the first place, by the natural instinct to passively yield to that vague something recognized as authority, and in the second place by the human instinct to train with the multitude and have its approval. An empress introduced the hoopskirt, and we know the result. A nobody introduced the bloomer, and we know the result. If Eve should come again, in her ripe renown, and reintroduce her quaint styles—well, we know what would happen. And we should be cruelly embarrassed, along at first.

The hoopskirt runs its course and disappears. Nobody reasons about it. One woman abandons the fashion; her neighbor notices this and follows her lead; this influences the next woman; and so on and so on, and presently the skirt has vanished out of the world, no one knows how nor why, nor cares, for that matter. It will come again, by and by and in due course will go again.

Twenty-five years ago, in England, six or eight wine glasses stood grouped by each person's plate at a dinner party, and they were used, not left idle and empty; to-day there are but three or four in the group, and the average guest sparingly uses about two of them. We have not adopted this new fashion yet, but we shall do it presently. We shall not think it out; we shall merely conform, and let it go at that. We get our notions and habits and opinions from outside influences; we do not have to study them out.

Our table manners, and company manners, and street manners change from time to time, but the changes are not reasoned out; we merely notice and conform. We are creatures of outside influences; as a rule we do not think, we only imitate. We cannot invent standards that will stick; what we mistake for standards are only fashions, and perishable. We may continue to admire them, but we drop the use of them. We notice this in literature. Shakespeare is a standard, and fifty years ago we used to write tragedies which we couldn't tell from—from somebody else's; but we don't do it any more, now. Our prose standard, three quarters of a century ago, was ornate and diffuse; some authority or other changed it in the direction of compactness and simplicity, and conformity followed, without argument. The historical novel starts up suddenly, and sweeps the land. Everybody writes one, and the nation is glad. We had historical novels before; but nobody read them, and the rest of us conformed—without reasoning it out. We are conforming in the other way, now, because it is another case of everybody.

The outside influences are always pouring in upon us, and we are always obeying their orders and accepting their verdicts. The Smiths like the new play; the Joneses go to see it, and they copy the Smith verdict. Morals, religions, politics, get their following from surrounding influences and atmospheres, almost entirely; not from study, not from thinking. A man must and will have his own approval first of all, in each and every moment and circumstance of his life—even if he must repent of a self-approved act the moment after its commission, in order to get his self-approval *again*: but, speaking in general terms, a man's self-approval in the large concerns of life has its source in the approval of the peoples about him, and not in a searching personal examination of the matter. Mohammedans are Mohammedans because they are born and reared among that sect, not because they have thought it out and can furnish sound reasons for being Mohammedans; we know why Catholics are Catholics; why Presbyterians are Presbyterians; why Baptists are Baptists; why Mormons are Mormons; why thieves are thieves; why monarchists are monarchists; why Republicans are Republicans and Democrats, Democrats. We know it is a matter of association and sympathy, not reasoning and examination; that hardly a man in the world has an opinion upon morals, politics, or religion which he got otherwise than through his associations and sympathies. Broadly speaking, there are none but corn-pone opinions. And broadly speaking, corn-pone stands for self-approval. Self-approval is acquired mainly from the approval of other people. The result is conformity. Sometimes conformity has a sordid business interest—the bread-and-butter interest—but not in most cases, I think. I think that in the majority of cases it is unconscious and not calculated; that it is born of the human being's natural yearning to stand well with his fellows and have their inspiring approval and praise—a yearning which is commonly so strong and so insistent that it cannot be effectually resisted, and must have its way.

A political emergency brings out the corn-pone opinion in fine force   15
in its two chief varieties—the pocketbook variety, which has its origin in self-interest, and the bigger variety, the sentimental variety—the one which can't bear to be outside the pale; can't bear to be in disfavor; can't endure the averted face and the cold shoulder; wants to stand well with his friends, wants to be smiled upon, wants to be welcome, wants to hear the precious words, "*He's* on the right track!" Uttered, perhaps by an ass, but still an ass of high degree, an ass whose approval is gold and diamonds to a smaller ass, and confers glory and honor and happiness, and membership in the herd. For these gauds many a man will dump his lifelong principles into the street, and his conscience along with them. We have seen it happen. In some millions of instances.

Men think they think upon great political questions, and they do; but they think with their party, not independently; they read its literature, but not that of the other side; they arrive at convictions, but they are drawn from a partial view of the matter in hand and are of no particular value. They swarm with their party, they feel with their party, they are happy in their party's approval; and where the party leads they will follow, whether for right and honor, or through blood and dirt and a mush of mutilated morals.

In our late canvass half of the nation passionately believed that in silver lay salvation, the other half as passionately believed that that way lay destruction. Do you believe that a tenth part of the people, on either side, had any rational excuse for having an opinion about the matter at all? I studied that mighty question to the bottom—came out empty. Half of our people passionately believe in high tariff, the other half believe otherwise. Does this mean study and examination, or only feeling? The latter, I think. I have deeply studied that question, too—and didn't arrive. We all do no end of feeling, and we mistake it for thinking. And out of it we get an aggregation which we consider a boon. Its name is Public Opinion. It is held in reverence. It settles everything. Some think it the Voice of God.

The Reader's Presence

1. "Corn pone" was a dish eaten, in Twain's time, by poor Southerners. How might this image of a lowly, common foodstuff be tied to the opinions of Twain's commonsense slave "philosopher"? What is Twain's position on Jerry's everyday wisdom? What sort of audience does Twain appear to be writing for? How does Twain "translate" Jerry's statement?

2. Twain agrees with Jerry's statement but feels he "did not go far enough." How do Twain's opinions differ from Jerry's? How does Twain use Jerry's opinions, starting in paragraph 9, to launch his own? Twain does not return to Jerry in the essay. How does the dramatic technique of ending the essay with topics far from those with which it was begun affect your reading of it?

3. About ten years after Samuel Clemens was born in Missouri, the New England philosopher Ralph Waldo Emerson wrote an essay called "Self-Reliance" in which he sharply criticized *his* fellow Americans' tendency toward conformism. "If I know your sect," he wrote, "I anticipate your argument." How does Twain invoke the ideal of self-reliance? Twain calls Jerry's mode of oratory a kind of "pulpit style"; Emerson, too, was a preacher whose essays loosely resemble sermons. What does Twain's essay have in common with the structure of a traditional sermon? Compare the essay to that of another preacher, Martin Luther King Jr.'s "Letter from Birmingham Jail" (page 730). Why might Twain, a deeply irreverent writer, participate in the American sermon tradition? What is the effect of this "sermon" on you as reader? Is Twain's essay as sharp a piece of oratory as King's? Why or why not? How does it appeal to the reader's ear?

Gore Vidal

Drugs

Gore Vidal (b. 1925), author, playwright, screenwriter, essayist, and reviewer, is known for his satirical observations, acerbic wit, and eloquence. He is a prolific author of more than twenty books, including The City and the Pillar *(1948),* Myra Breckinridge *(1968),* Myron *(1974),* Palimpsest: A Memoir *(1995), and* The Smithsonian Institution *(1998). Among Vidal's irreverent historical novels are* Julian *(1964),* Burr *(1973),* 1876 *(1976),* Lincoln *(1984), and* The Golden Age *(2000). His best-known dramatic work is* Visit to a Small Planet *(1957), which was made into a movie. Vidal has published collections of his writings in* The Essential Gore Vidal *(1999),* Gore Vidal, Sexually Speaking *(1999), and* The Last Empire *(2001). His more recent work includes* Imperial America: Reflections on the United States of Amnesia *(2004);* Clouds and Eclipses *(2006), his collected short stories; and* Point to Point Navigation *(2006), a memoir, and sequel to* Palimpsest, *covering the years 1964–2006.* Conversations with Gore Vidal, *a series of interviews, was published in 2005, and, in 2008,* The Selected Essays of Gore Vidal, *edited by Jay Parini. The essay "Drugs" originally appeared in 1970 as an editorial in the* New York Times *and was later included in his book* Homage to Daniel Shays: Collected Essays 1952–1972 *(1972).*

It is possible to stop most drug addiction in the United States within a very short time. Simply make all drugs available and sell them at cost. Label each drug with a precise description of what effect—good and bad—the drug will have on the taker. This will require heroic honesty. Don't say that marijuana is addictive or dangerous when it is neither, as millions of people know—unlike "speed," which kills most unpleasantly, or heroin, which is addictive and difficult to kick.

For the record, I have tried—once—almost every drug and liked none, disproving the popular Fu Manchu theory that a single whiff of opium will enslave the mind. Nevertheless many drugs are bad for certain people to take and they should be told why in a sensible way.

Along with exhortation and warning, it might be good for our citizens to recall (or learn for the first time) that the United States was the creation of men who believed that each man has the right to do what he wants with his own life as long as he does not interfere with his neighbor's pursuit of happiness. (That his neighbor's idea of happiness is persecuting others does confuse matters a bit.)

This is a startling notion to the current generation of Americans. They reflect a system of public education which has made the Bill of Rights, literally, unacceptable to a majority of high school graduates (see the annual Purdue reports) who now form the "silent majority"—a phrase which that underestimated wit Richard Nixon took from Homer, who used it to describe the dead.

Now one can hear the warning rumble begin: If everyone is allowed to take drugs everyone will and the GNP will decrease, the Commies will stop us from making everyone free, and we shall end up a race of zombies, passively murmuring "groovy" to one another. Alarming thought. Yet it seems most unlikely that any reasonably sane person will become a drug addict if he knows in advance what addiction is going to be like.

Is everyone reasonably sane? No. Some people will always become drug addicts just as some people will always become alcoholics, and it is just too bad. Every man, however, has the power (and should have the legal right) to kill himself if he chooses. But since most men don't, they won't be mainliners either. Nevertheless, forbidding young people things they like or think they might enjoy only makes them want those things all the more. This psychological insight is, for some mysterious reason, perennially denied our governors.

It is a lucky thing for the American moralist that our country has always existed in a kind of time-vacuum: We have no public memory of anything that happened before last Tuesday. No one in Washington today recalls what happened during the years alcohol was forbidden to the people by a Congress that thought it had a divine mission to stamp out Demon Rum— launching, in the process, the greatest crime wave in the country's history, causing thousands of deaths from bad alcohol, and creating a general (and persisting) contempt among the citizenry for the laws of the United States.

The same thing is happening today. But the government has learned nothing from past attempts at prohibition, not to mention repression.

Last year when the supply of Mexican marijuana was slightly curtailed by the Feds, the pushers got the kids hooked on heroin and deaths increased dramatically, particularly in New York. Whose fault? Evil men like the Mafiosi? Permissive Dr. Spock? Wild-eyed Dr. Leary?[1] No.

The government of the United States was responsible for those deaths. The bureaucratic machine has a vested interest in playing cops and robbers. Both the Bureau of Narcotics and the Mafia want strong laws against the sale and use of drugs because if drugs are sold at cost there would be no money in it for anyone.

If there was no money in it for the Mafia, there would be no friendly playground pushers, and addicts would not commit crimes to pay for the next fix. Finally, if there was no money in it, the Bureau of Narcotics would wither away, something they are not about to do without a struggle.

Will anything sensible be done? Of course not. The American people are as devoted to the idea of sin and its punishment as they are to making

---

[1]**Dr. Leary:** Timothy Leary (1926–1996) was a lecturer in psychology at Harvard and a noted proponent of psychedelic drugs who urged young Americans in the late 1960s to "tune in, turn on, drop out." —EDS.

money—and fighting drugs is nearly as big a business as pushing them. Since the combination of sin and money is irresistible (particularly to the professional politician), the situation will only grow worse.

The Reader's Presence

1. Writing in 1970, Vidal admits to having tried "almost every drug" (paragraph 1). What might the impact of such an admission by a public figure have been at that time? Would the impact be the same today? What sort of audience might Vidal's piece be directed to? Does his admission seem casual or calculated? Does it strengthen or weaken his argument? Why?

2. In paragraph 5, Vidal constructs a hypothetical scenario of what would happen if drugs were not illegal. Does he endorse or mock this scenario? Whose opinion does he seem to be representing? What sorts of words does he use to describe a drug-addicted world? Does his use of humor enhance or undermine his argument?

3. Vidal asserts that the U.S. government profits from drug sales and prosecution, and he links the government to organized crime. He argues, finally, that drugs will continue to be a problem in this society as long as Americans are "devoted" to making money: For all their dangers, drugs are big business. How does Vidal support these claims? What is his view of the American people? How does it compare to Martha Nussbaum's portrait of American compassion in "Can Patriotism Be Compassionate?" (page 783)? Cite specific examples from each text.

John Edgar Wideman

The Night I Was Nobody

John Edgar Wideman was born in 1941 in Washington, D.C., and grew up in Homewood, a Pittsburgh ghetto. Much of his fiction is set in Homewood or neighborhoods like it, and it explores issues facing the black urban poor in America. He has published more than a dozen books, including Brothers and Keepers *(1984), a memoir that focuses on his brother Robby; the novel* Philadelphia Fire *(1990);* The Stories of John Edgar Wideman *(1992);* Fatheralong: A Meditation on Fathers and Sons, Race and Society *(1994); and* Hoop Roots *(2001), a memoir about his obsession with basketball. Wideman's most recent work includes* The Island: Martinique *(2003);* God's Gym *(2005), a collection of short stories; and his first novel in over a decade,* Fanon *(2008). Wideman has been honored with numerous awards and prizes, including the Lannan Literary Fellowship for Fiction (1991) and a MacArthur Fellowship (1993–1998). Wideman was a Rhodes scholar at Oxford University (1963) and a Kent fellow at the University of Iowa Writing Workshop (1966). Wideman has taught at the University of Pennsylvania and at the University of Massachusetts at Amherst; he is currently a professor of Africana Studies and Creative Writing at Brown University. He lectures widely in colleges across the United States. He is also an athlete and a member of the Philadelphia Big Five Basketball Hall of Fame. "The Night I Was Nobody" appeared in* Speak My Name: Black Men on Masculinity and the American Dream *(1995).*

When Wideman lived in Cheyenne and taught at the University of Wyoming (1975–1986), an interviewer inquired whether he felt a distance between his life and his fiction. "My particular imagination has always worked well in a kind of exile," he responded. "It fits the insider-outsider view I've always had. It helps to write away from the center of action."

On July 4th, the fireworks day, the day for picnics and patriotic speeches, I was in Clovis, New Mexico, to watch my daughter, Jamila, and her team, the Central Massachusetts Cougars, compete in the Junior Olympics Basketball national tourney. During our ten-day visit to Clovis the weather had been bizarre. Hailstones as large as golf balls. Torrents of rain flooding streets hubcap deep. Running through the pelting rain from their van to a gym, Jamila and several teammates cramming through a doorway had looked back just in time to see a funnel cloud touch down a few blocks away. Continuous sheet lightning had shattered the horizon, crackling for hours night and day. Spectacular, off-the-charts weather flexing its muscles, reminding people what little control they had over their lives.

Hail rat-tat-tatting against our windshield our first day in town wasn't exactly a warm welcome, but things got better fast. Clovis people were glad to see us and the mini-spike we triggered in the local economy. Hospitable, generous, our hosts lavished upon us the same hands-on affection and attention to detail that had transformed an unpromising place in the middle of nowhere into a very livable community.

On top of all that, the Cougars were kicking butt, so the night of July 3rd I wanted to celebrate with a frozen margarita. I couldn't pry anybody else away from "Bubba's," the movable feast of beer, chips, and chatter the adults traveling with the Cougars improvised nightly in the King's Inn Motel parking lot, so I drove off alone to find one perfect margarita.

Inside the door of Kelley's Bar and Lounge I was flagged by a guy collecting a cover charge and told I couldn't enter wearing my Malcolm X hat. I asked why; the guy hesitated, conferred for a moment with his partner, then declared that Malcolm X hats were against the dress code. For a split second I thought it might be that *no* caps were allowed in Kelley's. But the door crew and two or three others hanging around the entranceway all wore the billed caps ubiquitous in New Mexico, duplicates of mine, except theirs sported the logos of feed stores and truck stops instead of a silver X.

What careened through my mind in the next couple of minutes is essentially unsayable but included scenes from my own half-century of life as a black man, clips from five hundred years of black/white meetings on slave ships, auction blocks, plantations, basketball courts, in the Supreme Court's marble halls, in beds, back alleys and back rooms, kisses and lynch ropes and contracts for millions of dollars so a black face will grace a cereal box. To tease away my anger I tried joking with folks in other places. Hey, Spike Lee. That hat you gave me on the set of the Malcolm movie in Cairo ain't legal in Clovis.

But nothing about these white guys barring my way was really funny. Part of me wanted to get down and dirty. Curse the suckers. Were they prepared to do battle to keep me and my cap out? Another voice said, Be cool. Don't sully your hands. Walk away and call the cops or a lawyer. Forget these chumps. Sue the owner. Or should I win hearts and minds? Look, fellas, I understand why the X on my cap might offend or scare you. You probably don't know much about Malcolm. The incredible metamorphoses of his thinking, his soul. By the time he was assassinated he wasn't a racist, didn't advocate violence. He was trying to make sense of America's impossible history, free himself, free us from the crippling legacy of race hate and oppression.

While all the above occupied my mind, my body, on its own, had assumed a gunfighter's vigilance, hands ready at sides, head cocked, weight poised, eyes tight and hard on the doorkeeper yet alert to anything stirring on the periphery. Many other eyes, all in white faces, were checking out the entranceway, recognizing the ingredients of a racial incident. Hadn't they witnessed Los Angeles going berserk on their TV screens just a couple months ago? That truck driver beaten nearly to death in the street, those packs of black hoodlums burning and looting? Invisible lines were being drawn in the air, in the sand, invisible chips bristled on shoulders.

The weather again. Our American racial weather, turbulent, unchanging in its changeability, its power to rock us and stun us and smack

5

us from our routines and tear us apart as if none of our cities, our pieties, our promises, our dreams, ever stood a chance of holding on. The racial weather. Outside us, then suddenly, unforgettably, unforgivingly inside, reminding us of what we've only pretended to have forgotten. Our limits, our flaws. The lies and compromises we practice to avoid dealing honestly with the contradictions of race. How dependent we are on luck to survive—*when* we survive—the racial weather.

One minute you're a person, the next moment somebody starts treating you as if you're not. Often it happens just that way, just that suddenly. Particularly if you are a black man in America. Race and racism are a force larger than individuals, more powerful than law or education or government or the church, a force able to wipe these institutions away in the charged moments, minuscule or mountainous, when black and white come face to face. In Watts in 1965,[1] or a few less-than-glorious minutes in Clovis, New Mexico, on the eve of the day that commemorates our country's freedom, our inalienable right as a nation, as citizens, to life, liberty, equality, the pursuit of happiness, those precepts and principles that still look good on paper but are often as worthless as a sheet of newspaper to protect you in a storm if you're a black man at the wrong time in the wrong place.

None of this is news, is it? Not July 3rd in Clovis, when a tiny misfire   10
occurred, or yesterday in your town or tomorrow in mine? But haven't we made progress? Aren't things much better than they used to be? Hasn't enough been done?

We ask the wrong questions when we look around and see a handful of fabulously wealthy black people, a few others entering the middle classes. Far more striking than the positive changes are the abiding patterns and assumptions that have not changed. Not all black people are mired in social pathology, but the bottom rung of the ladder of opportunity (and the space *beneath* the bottom rung) is still defined by the color of the people trapped there—and many *are* still trapped there, no doubt about it, because their status was inherited, determined generation after generation by blood, by color. Once, all black people were legally excluded from full participation in the mainstream. Then fewer. Now only some. But the mechanisms of disenfranchisement that originally separated African Americans from other Americans persist, if not legally, then in the apartheid mind-set, convictions and practices of the majority. The seeds sleep but don't die. Ten who suffer from exclusion today can become ten thousand tomorrow. Racial weather can change that quickly.

How would the bouncer have responded if I'd calmly declared, "This is a free country, I can wear any hat I choose"? Would he thank me for standing up for our shared birthright? Or would he have to admit, if pushed, that American rights belong only to *some* Americans, white Americans?

---

[1]*Watts in 1965:* In August of 1965, a police traffic stop provoked six days of rioting in which thirty-four people died in the Watts neighborhood of Los Angeles.—EDS.

We didn't get that far in our conversation. We usually don't. The girls' faces pulled me from the edge—girls of all colors, sizes, shapes, gritty kids bonding through hard clean competition. Weren't these guys who didn't like my X cap kids too? Who did they think I was? What did they think they were protecting? I backed out, backed down, climbed in my car and drove away from Kelley's. After all, I didn't want Kelley's. I wanted a frozen margarita and a mellow celebration. So I bought plenty of ice and the ingredients for a margarita and rejoined the festivities at Bubba's. Everybody volunteered to go back with me to Kelley's, but I didn't want to spoil the victory party, taint our daughters' accomplishments, erase the high marks Clovis had earned hosting us.

But I haven't forgotten what happened in Kelley's. I write about it now because this is my country, the country where my sons and daughter are growing up, and your daughters and sons, and the crisis, the affliction, the same ole, same ole waste of life continues across the land, the nightmarish weather of racism, starbursts of misery in the dark.

The statistics of inequality don't demonstrate a "black crisis"—that   15
perspective confuses cause and victim, solutions and responsibility. When the rain falls, it falls on us all. The bad news about black men—that they die sooner and more violently than white men, are more ravaged by unemployment and lack of opportunity, are more exposed to drugs, disease, broken families, and police brutality, more likely to go to jail than college, more cheated by the inertia and callousness of a government that represents and protects the most needy the least—this is not a "black problem," but a *national* shame affecting us all. Wrenching ourselves free from the long nightmare of racism will require collective determination, countless individual acts of will, gutsy, informed, unselfish. To imagine the terrible cost of not healing ourselves, we must first imagine how good it would feel to be healed.

The Reader's Presence

1. The incident Wideman recounts in this essay takes place on the eve of the Fourth of July, "the fireworks day, the day for picnics and patriotic speeches" (paragraph 1). Look closely at the modifiers he chooses to describe the Fourth of July. Given the events that took place in Clovis that night, comment on the significance of each phrase. How else might Wideman have described this holiday, and why might he have intentionally discarded those descriptions? Identify—and comment on the effectiveness of—other moments in the essay when Wideman refers to the Fourth of July in related themes.

2. An extended metaphor of weather runs through this essay. Trace the analogy through the comparisons and contrasts Wideman makes or implies. In what specific ways, for instance, are the townsfolk described in paragraph 2 like or unlike the weather? How does this

change as the essay progresses? How does racism resemble and differ from the weather? Given this guiding metaphor, does Wideman leave his reader with much hope for an end to racism? Explain your answer.

3. Wideman's Malcolm X hat is the object that sparks the inciting incident of the essay. The hat, Wideman tells his reader, was a gift from director Spike Lee during the making of the film *Malcolm X* in 1992. Wideman's allusion to the famous African American leader, Malcolm X, is not trivial. What does Malcolm X's "presence" in the essay do for Wideman's argument? Compare Wideman's essay to the excerpt from Malcolm X's autobiography included in this anthology ("Homeboy," page 168). How do these authors express their emotions about racism? How does each writer use vernacular language (everyday speech), and to what effects? How does each of them justify the recording of their experiences for others to read? Compare how the two discuss ideas of rage, violence, shame, and hope.

Terry Tempest Williams

The Clan of One-Breasted Women

The environmentalist and writer Terry Tempest Williams (b. 1953) lives in Utah, where she is active in the movement to expand federally protected wilderness areas. She is currently the Annie Clark Tanner Scholar in Environmental Humanities at the University of Utah, where she has taught English for many years, and naturalist-in-residence at the Utah Museum of Natural History. In 2006, the Wilderness Society awarded her the Robert Marshall Award, their highest honor given to an American citizen. In Refuge: An Unnatural History of Family and Place *(1991), she documents the epidemic of cancer caused by nuclear weapons testing in Utah during the 1950s and meditates on the meaning of this tragedy for her family. "The Clan of One-Breasted Women" appears in* Refuge. *Her first book,* Pieces of a White Shell: A Journey to Navajoland *(1984), received a Southwest Book Award. Other books include* Coyote's Canyon *(1989), An* Unspoken Hunger: Stories from the Field *(1994),* Desert Quartet *(1995),* Leap *(2000), and* Red: Passion and Patience in the Desert *(2001). She also co-edited* Testimony: Writers of the West Speak on Behalf of Utah Wilderness *(1996),* New Genesis: Mormons Writing on the Environment *(1999), and* The Open Space of Democracy *(2004). Her latest book is* Mosaic: Finding Beauty in a Broken World *(2008).*

Reflecting on her motivation for writing about her personal experience with cancer, Williams notes, "Perhaps I am telling this story in an attempt to heal myself, to confront what I do not know, to create a path for myself with the idea that 'memory is the only way home.'"

I belong to a Clan of One-Breasted Women. My mother, my grandmothers, and six aunts have all had mastectomies. Seven are dead. The two who survive have just completed rounds of chemotherapy and radiation.

I've had my own problems: two biopsies for breast cancer and a small tumor between my ribs diagnosed as a "borderline malignancy."

This is my family history.

Most statistics tell us that breast cancer is genetic, hereditary, with rising percentages attached to fatty diets, childlessness, or becoming pregnant after thirty. What they don't say is that living in Utah may be the greatest hazard of all.

We are a Mormon family with roots in Utah since 1847. The "word   5
of wisdom" in my family aligned us with good foods—no coffee, no tea, tobacco, or alcohol. For the most part, our women were finished having their babies by the time they were thirty. And only one faced breast cancer prior to 1960. Traditionally, as a group of people, Mormons have a low rate of cancer.

Is our family a cultural anomaly? The truth is, we didn't think about it. Those who did, usually the men, simply said, "bad genes." The women's attitude was stoic. Cancer was part of life. On February 16, 1971, the eve of my mother's surgery, I accidentally picked up the telephone and overheard her ask my grandmother what she could expect.

"Diane, it is one of the most spiritual experiences you will ever encounter."

I quietly put down the receiver.

Two days later, my father took my brothers and me to the hospital to visit her. She met us in the lobby in a wheelchair. No bandages were visible. I'll never forget her radiance, the way she held herself in a purple velvet robe, and how she gathered us around her.

"Children, I am fine. I want you to know I felt the arms of God   10
around me."

We believed her. My father cried. Our mother, his wife, was thirty-eight years old.

A little over a year after Mother's death, Dad and I were having dinner together. He had just returned from St. George, where the Tempest Company was completing the gas lines that would service southern Utah. He spoke of his love for the country, the sandstoned landscape, bare-boned and beautiful. He had just finished hiking the Kolob trail in Zion National Park. We got caught up in reminiscing, recalling with fondness our walk up Angel's Landing on his fiftieth birthday and the years our family had vacationed there.

Over dessert, I shared a recurring dream of mine. I told my father that for years, as long as I could remember, I saw this flash of light in the night in the desert—that this image had so permeated my being that I could not venture south without seeing it again, on the horizon, illuminating buttes and mesas.

"You did see it," he said.

"Saw what?"   15

"The bomb. The cloud. We were driving home from Riverside, California. You were sitting on Diane's lap. She was pregnant. In fact, I remember the day, September 7, 1957. We had just gotten out of the Service. We were driving north, past Las Vegas. It was an hour or so before dawn, when this explosion went off. We not only heard it, but felt it. I thought the oil tanker in front of us had blown up. We pulled over and suddenly, rising from the desert floor, we saw it, clearly, this golden-stemmed cloud, the mushroom. The sky seemed to vibrate with an eerie pink glow. Within a few minutes, a light ash was raining on the car."

I stared at my father.

"I thought you knew that," he said. "It was a common occurrence in the fifties."

It was at this moment that I realized the deceit I had been living under. Children growing up in the American Southwest, drinking contaminated milk from contaminated cows, even from the contaminated breasts of their mothers, my mother—members, years later, of the Clan of One-Breasted Women.

It is a well-known story in the Desert West, "The Day We Bombed   20
Utah,"[1] or more accurately, the years we bombed Utah: aboveground atomic testing in Nevada took place from January 27, 1951, through July 11, 1962. Not only were the winds blowing north covering "low-use segments of the population" with fallout and leaving sheep dead in their tracks but the climate was right. The United States of the 1950s was red, white, and blue. The Korean War was raging. McCarthyism[2] was rampant. Ike[3] was it, and the cold war was hot. If you were against nuclear testing, you were for a communist regime.

Much has been written about this "American nuclear tragedy." Public health was secondary to national security. The Atomic Energy Commissioner, Thomas Murray, said, "Gentlemen, we must not let anything interfere with this series of tests, nothing."[4]

Again and again, the American public was told by its government, in spite of burns, blisters, and nausea, "It has been found that the tests may

[1]John G. Fuller., *The Day We Bombed Utah* (New York: New American Library, 1984).

[2]*McCarthyism:* The practice of publicizing accusations of political disloyalty or subversion without sufficient regard to evidence. Associated with Senator Joseph McCarthy (1908–1957).—EDS.

[3]*Ike:* President Dwight D. Eisenhower (1890–1969) was known as "Ike."—EDS.

[4]Ferenc M. Szasz, "Downward from the Bomb," *Nevada Historical Society Quarterly* 30, no. 3 (Fall 1987): 185.

be conducted with adequate assurance of safety under conditions prevailing at the bombing reservations."[5] Assuaging public fears was simply a matter of public relations. "Your best action," an Atomic Energy Commission booklet read, "is not to be worried about fallout." A news release typical of the times stated, "We find no basis for concluding that harm to any individual has resulted from radioactive fallout."[6]

On August 30, 1979, during Jimmy Carter's presidency, a suit was filed, *Irene Allen v. The United States of America*. Mrs. Allen's case was the first on an alphabetical list of twenty-four test cases, representative of nearly twelve hundred plaintiffs seeking compensation from the United States government for cancers caused by nuclear testing in Nevada.

Irene Allen lived in Hurricane, Utah. She was the mother of five children and had been widowed twice. Her first husband, with their two oldest boys, had watched the tests from the roof of the local high school. He died of leukemia in 1956. Her second husband died of pancreatic cancer in 1978.

In a town meeting conducted by Utah Senator Orrin Hatch, shortly before the suit was filed, Mrs. Allen said, "I am not blaming the government, I want you to know that, Senator Hatch. But I thought if my testimony could help in any way so this wouldn't happen again to any of the generations coming up after us . . . I am happy to be here this day to bear testimony of this."[7]   25

God-fearing people. This is just one story in an anthology of thousands.

On May 10, 1984, Judge Bruce S. Jenkins handed down his opinion. Ten of the plaintiffs were awarded damages. It was the first time a federal court had determined that nuclear tests had been the cause of cancers. For the remaining fourteen test cases, the proof of causation was not sufficient. In spite of the split decision, it was considered a landmark ruling.[8] It was not to remain so for long.

In April 1987, the Tenth Circuit Court of Appeals overturned Judge Jenkins's ruling on the ground that the United States was protected from suit by the legal doctrine of sovereign immunity, a centuries-old idea from England in the days of absolute monarchs.[9]

In January 1988, the Supreme Court refused to review the Appeals Court decision. To our court system it does not matter whether the United States government was irresponsible, whether it lied to its citizens, or even that citizens died from the fallout of nuclear testing. What matters is that our government is immune: "The King can do no wrong."

---

[5]Philip L. Fradkin, *Fallout* (Tucson: University of Arizona Press, 1989), 98.
[6]Ibid., 109.
[7]Town meeting held by Senator Orrin Hatch in St. George, Utah, April 17, 1979, transcript, 26–28.
[8]Fradkin, *Fallout*, 228.
[9]*U.S. v. Allen*, 816 Federal Reporter, 2d/1417 (10th Circuit Court 1987), cert. denied, 108 St. Ct. 694 (1988).

In Mormon culture, authority is respected, obedience is revered, and   30
independent thinking is not. I was taught as a young girl not to "make
waves" or "rock the boat."

"Just let it go," Mother would say. "You know how you feel, that's
what counts."

For many years, I have done just that—listened, observed, and quietly formed my own opinions, in a culture that rarely asks questions because it has all the answers. But one by one, I have watched the women in
my family die common, heroic deaths. We sat in waiting rooms hoping
for good news, but always receiving the bad. I cared for them, bathed
their scarred bodies, and kept their secrets. I watched beautiful women
become bald as Cytoxan, cisplatin, and Adriamycin were injected into
their veins. I held their foreheads as they vomited green-black bile, and I
shot them with morphine when the pain became inhuman. In the end, I
witnessed their last peaceful breaths, becoming a midwife to the rebirth of
their souls.

The price of obedience has become too high.

The fear and inability to question authority that ultimately killed
rural communities in Utah during atmospheric testing of atomic weapons
is the same fear I saw in my mother's body. Sheep. Dead sheep. The evidence is buried.

I cannot prove that my mother, Diane Dixon Tempest, or my grand-   35
mothers, Lettie Romney Dixon and Kathryn Blackett Tempest, along
with my aunts developed cancer from nuclear fallout in Utah. But I can't
prove they didn't.

My father's memory was correct. The September blast we drove
through in 1957 was part of Operation Plumbbob, one of the most intensive series of bomb tests to be initiated. The flash of light in the night in
the desert, which I had always thought was a dream, developed into a
family nightmare. It took fourteen years, from 1957 to 1971, for cancer
to manifest in my mother—the same time, Howard L. Andrews, an authority in radioactive fallout at the National Institutes of Health, says radiation cancer requires to become evident.[10] The more I learn about what
it means to be a "downwinder," the more questions I drown in.

What I do know, however, is that as a Mormon woman of the fifth
generation of Latter-day Saints, I must question everything, even if it
means losing my faith, even if it means becoming a member of a border
tribe among my own people. Tolerating blind obedience in the name of
patriotism or religion ultimately takes our lives.

When the Atomic Energy Commission described the country north of
the Nevada Test Site as "virtually uninhabited desert terrain," my family
and the birds at Great Salt Lake were some of the "virtual uninhabitants."

[10]Fradkin, *Fallout*, 116.

One night, I dreamed women from all over the world circled a blazing fire in the desert. They spoke of change, how they hold the moon in their bellies and wax and wane with its phases. They mocked the presumption of even-tempered beings and made promises that they would never fear the witch inside themselves. The women danced wildly as sparks broke away from the flames and entered the night sky as stars.

And they sang a song given to them by Shoshone grandmothers: 40

Ah ne nah, nah	Consider the rabbits
nin nah nah —	How gently they walk on the earth —
ah ne nah, nah	Consider the rabbits
nin nah nah —	How gently they walk on the earth —
Nyaga mutzi	We remember them
oh ne nay —	We can walk gently also —
Nyaga mutzi	We remember them
oh ne nay[11]	We can walk gently also

The women danced and drummed and sang for weeks, preparing themselves for what was to come. They would reclaim the desert for the sake of their children, for the sake of the land.

A few miles downwind from the fire circle, bombs were being tested. Rabbits felt the tremors. Their soft leather pads on paws and feet recognized the shaking sands, while the roots of mesquite and sage were smoldering. Rocks were hot from the inside out and dust devils hummed unnaturally. And each time there was another nuclear test, ravens watched the desert heave. Stretch marks appeared. The land was losing its muscle.

The women couldn't bear it any longer. They were mothers. They had suffered labor pains but always under the promise of birth. The red hot pains beneath the desert promised death only, as each bomb became a stillborn. A contract had been made and broken between human beings and the land. A new contract was being drawn by the women, who understood the fate of the earth as their own.

Under the cover of darkness, ten women slipped under a barbed-wire fence and entered the contaminated country. They were trespassing. They walked toward the town of Mercury, in moonlight, taking their cues from coyote, kit fox, antelope squirrel, and quail. They moved quietly and deliberately through the maze of Joshua trees. When a hint of daylight appeared they rested, drinking tea and sharing their rations of food. The women closed their eyes. The time had come to protest with the heart, that to deny one's genealogy with the earth was to commit treason against one's soul.

---

[11]This song was sung by the Western Shoshone women as they crossed the line at the Nevada Test Site on March 18, 1988, as part of their "Reclaim the Land" action.

At dawn, the women draped themselves in mylar, wrapping long streamers of silver plastic around their arms to blow in the breeze. They wore clear masks that became the faces of humanity. And when they arrived at the edge of Mercury, they carried all the butterflies of a summer day in their wombs. They paused to allow their courage to settle.

The town that forbids pregnant women and children to enter because   45
of radiation risks was asleep. The women moved through the streets as winged messengers, twirling around each other in slow motion, peeking inside homes and watching the easy sleep of men and women. They were astonished by such stillness and periodically would utter a shrill note or low cry just to verify life.

The residents finally awoke to these strange apparitions. Some simply stared. Others called authorities, and in time, the women were apprehended by wary soldiers dressed in desert fatigues. They were taken to a white, square building on the edge of Mercury. When asked who they were and why they were there, the women replied, "We are mothers and we have come to reclaim the desert for our children."

The soldiers arrested them. As the ten women were blindfolded and handcuffed, they began singing:

> *You can't forbid us everything*
> *You can't forbid us to think —*
> *You can't forbid our tears to flow*
> *And you can't stop the songs that we sing.*

The women continued to sing louder and louder, until they heard the voices of their sisters moving across the mesa:

> *Ah ne nah, nah*
> *nin nah nah —*
> *Ah ne nah, nah*
> *nin nah nah —*
> *Nyaga mutzi*
> *oh ne nay —*
> *Nyaga mutzi*
> *oh ne nay —*

"Call for reinforcements," one soldier said.

"We have," interrupted one woman, "we have—and you have no idea of our numbers."

I crossed the line at the Nevada Test Site and was arrested with nine other Utahns for trespassing on military lands. They are still conducting nuclear tests in the desert. Ours was an act of civil disobedience. But as I walked toward the town of Mercury, it was more than a gesture of peace. It was a gesture on behalf of the Clan of One-Breasted Women.

As one officer cinched the handcuffs around my wrists, another   50
frisked my body. She found a pen and a pad of paper tucked inside my left boot.

"And these?" she asked sternly.

"Weapons," I replied.

Our eyes met. I smiled. She pulled the leg of my trousers back over my boot.

"Step forward, please," she said as she took my arm.

We were booked under an afternoon sun and bused to Tonopah, Nevada. It was a two-hour ride. This was familiar country. The Joshua trees standing their ground had been named by my ancestors, who believed they looked like prophets pointing west to the Promised Land. These were the same trees that bloomed each spring, flowers appearing like white flames in the Mojave. And I recalled a full moon in May, when Mother and I had walked among them, flushing out mourning doves and owls.

The bus stopped short of town. We were released.

The officials thought it was a cruel joke to leave us stranded in the desert with no way to get home. What they didn't realize was that we were home, soul-centered and strong, women who recognized the sweet smell of sage as fuel for our spirits.

The Reader's Presence

1. Paragraph 3 reads, "This is my family history." Which parts of Williams's essay are particular to her family, and what do they add to the larger social history of her time and place? How does her family's religion, Mormonism, play into the family history? What does she gain by drawing on the earlier spiritual tradition of the Shoshones, which is rooted in the same geographical area? What other "families," besides her nuclear and extended family, might Williams belong to?

2. Examine carefully—and discuss in detail—the roles of dream and reality in this essay. Characterize the power of each. Consider also the relationship between dream and nightmare. How do you read the "dream" Williams recounts in paragraph 39 and following? Characterize the relationship between that dream and the "civil disobedience" she recounts in the following section (paragraph 49 and following).

3. Consider the role of language in Williams's essay. Do you see instances of what might be termed "Orwellian doublespeak"? If so, where? What effects is Williams trying to achieve? Does she successfully use pen and paper as "weapons," as she says is her intention? Why or why not? Read George Orwell's "Politics and the English Language" (page 510). Would you expect Orwell to approve or disapprove of the political purposes to which Williams puts language? Why?

Howard Zinn

Stories Hollywood Never Tells

Howard Zinn (b. 1922), professor emeritus of political science at Boston University, is known both for his active involvement in the civil rights and peace movements and for his scholarship. He has published scores of books that reflect the issues of their times yet remain in print, demonstrating their continuing relevance. A sampling includes The Southern Mystique *(1964);* Vietnam: The Logic of Withdrawal *(1967);* Disobedience and Democracy: Nine Fallacies on Law and Order *(1968);* The Politics of History *(1970);* A People's History of the United States: 1492 to the Present *(1980), which has sold more than a million copies;* Declarations of Independence *(1990);* The Zinn Reader: Writings on Disobedience and Democracy *(1997);* Howard Zinn on History *(2000);* Three Strikes: Stories of American Labor *(2001); and* Artists in Times of War *(2003). His most recent book,* Voices of a People's History of the United States *(2004), is a companion to* A People's History. *The essay "Stories Hollywood Never Tells," adapted from* Artists in Times of War, *was published in* The Sun *in 2004.*

Zinn has also written plays, a musical, and an autobiography, You Can't Be Neutral on a Moving Train *(1994). Zinn continues to write, travel, and lecture, and he is a frequent contributor to such magazines as the* Nation *and the* Progressive.

Zinn has argued that perseverance in the face of opposition is essential: "I am totally confident not that the world will get better, but that we should not give up the game before all the cards have been played. The metaphor is deliberate; life is a gamble. Not to play is to foreclose any chance of winning. To play, to act, is to create at least a possibility of changing the world."

However hateful they may be sometimes, I have always loved the movies. When I began reading and studying history, I kept coming across incidents and events that led me to think, *Wow, what a movie this would make.* I would look to see if a movie had been made about it, but I'd never find one. It took me a while to realize that Hollywood isn't going to make movies like the ones I imagined. Hollywood isn't going to make movies that are class-conscious, or antiwar, or conscious of the need for racial equality or gender equality.

I wondered about this. It seemed to me that the people in Hollywood didn't all get together in a room and decide, "We're going to do just this kind of film and not the other kind of film." Yet it's not just an oversight or an accident, either. Leon Trotsky once used an expression to describe events that are not accidents, and are not planned deliberately, but are something in between. He called this the "natural selection of accidents," in which, if there's a certain structure to a situation, then these "accidents" will inevitably happen, whether anyone plans them or not. It seems that the structure of Hollywood is such that it will not produce the kinds of films that I imagined. It's a structure where money and profit are absolutely the first consideration: before art, before aesthetics, before human values.

When you consider the films about war that have come out of Hollywood—and there have been hundreds and hundreds, maybe even thousands—they almost always glorify military heroism. We need to think about telling the story of war from a different perspective.

Let's take one of our most popular wars to begin with: the Revolutionary War. How can you speak against the Revolutionary War, right? But to tell the story of the American Revolution, not from the standpoint of the schoolbooks, but from the standpoint of war as a complex phenomenon intertwined with moral issues, we must acknowledge not just that Americans were oppressed by the English, but that some Americans were oppressed by other Americans. For instance, American Indians did not rush to celebrate the victory of the colonists over England, because for them it meant that the line that the British had drawn to limit westward expansion in the Proclamation of 1763 would now be obliterated. The colonists would be free to move west into Indian lands.

John Adams, one of the Founding Fathers and a revolutionary leader, estimated that one-third of the colonists supported the American Revolution, one-third were opposed, and one-third were neutral. It would be interesting to tell the story of the American Revolution from the viewpoint of an ordinary workingman who hears the Declaration of Independence read to him from a balcony in Boston, promising freedom and equality and so on, and immediately is told that rich men can get out of service by paying several hundred dollars. This man then joins the army, despite his misgivings, despite his own feelings of being oppressed—not just by the British, but by the leaders of the colonial world—because he is promised some land. But as the war progresses and he sees the mutilations and the killing, he becomes increasingly disaffected. There's no place in society where class divisions are more clear-cut than in the military, and he sees that the officers are living in splendor while the ordinary enlisted men don't have any clothes or shoes, aren't being paid, and are being fed slop. So he joins the mutineers.

In the Revolutionary War, there were two mutinies against Washington's army: the mutiny of the Pennsylvania Line, and the mutiny of the New Jersey Line. Let's say our workingman joins the Pennsylvania Line, and they march on the Continental Congress, but eventually are surrounded by Washington's army, and several of their former comrades are forced to shoot several of the mutineers. Then this soldier, embittered by what he's seen, gets out of the army and gets some land in western Massachusetts. After the war is over, he becomes part of Shays's Rebellion, in which a group of small farmers rebel against the rich men who control the legislature in Boston and who are imposing heavy taxes on them, taking away their land and farms. The farmers, many of them Revolutionary War veterans, surround the courthouses and refuse to let the auctioneer go in to auction off their farms. The militia is called out to suppress them, and the militia also goes over to their side. Finally an army is raised by the moneyed class in Boston to suppress Shays's Rebellion.

I have never seen Hollywood tell this kind of story. If you know of a film that has been made about it, I wish you'd tell me so that we could have a celebration of that rare event.

Wars are more complicated than the simple good-versus-evil scenario presented to us in our history books and our culture. Wars are not simply conflicts of one people against another; wars always involve class differences within each side, and victory is very often not shared by everybody, but only among a few. The people who fight the wars are not the people who benefit from the wars.

I think somebody should make a new movie about the Mexican War. I haven't seen one that tells how the Mexican War started, or how the president of the United States deceived the American people. I know it's surprising to hear that a president would willfully deceive the people of the United States, but this was one of those rare cases. President James Polk told Americans that Mexican troops had fired at our troops on U.S. soil. Really the fighting broke out on disputed soil that both Mexico and the U.S. had claimed. The war had been planned in advance by the Polk administration, because it coveted this beautiful territory of the Southwest.

It would be interesting to tell that story from the viewpoint of an or- 10
dinary soldier, who sees the mayhem and the bloodshed as the army moves into Mexico and destroys town after town. More and more U.S. soldiers grow disaffected from the war, and as they make their final march toward Mexico City, General Scott wakes up one morning to discover that half his army has deserted.

It would be interesting, too, to tell the story from the point of view of one of the Massachusetts volunteers who comes back at the end of the war and is invited to a victory celebration. When the commander of the Massachusetts volunteers gets up to speak, he is booed off the platform by the surviving half of his men, who resent what happened to their comrades in the war and who wonder what they were fighting for. I should tell you: this really happened.

The film could also include a scene after the war in which the U.S. Army is moving to suppress a rebellion in Santa Fe, because mostly Mexicans still live there. The army marches through the streets of Santa Fe, and all the townspeople go into their houses and close the shutters. The army is met by total silence, an expression of how the population feels about this great American victory.

Another little story about the Mexican War is the tale of the deserters. Many of those who volunteered to fight in the Mexican War did so for the same reason that people volunteer for the military today: they were desperately poor and hoped that their fortunes would improve as a result of enlisting. During the Mexican War, some of these volunteers were recent Irish immigrants. When these immigrant soldiers saw what was being done to the people of Mexico, a number of them deserted and went over to the Mexican side. They formed their own battalion, which they called St. Patrick's Battalion, or the San Patricio Battalion, and they fought for the Mexicans.

It's not easy to make the Spanish-American War look like a noble enterprise—though of course Hollywood can do anything. The war has gotten a certain amount of attention, because of the heroism of Theodore Roosevelt and his Rough Riders, but not a lot. In the history textbooks, the Spanish-American War is called "a splendid little war." It lasted three months. We fought it to free the Cubans, because we're always going to war to free somebody. We expelled the Spaniards from Cuba, but we didn't expel ourselves, and the United States in effect took over Cuba after the war. One grievance we have against Fidel Castro is that he ended U.S. control of Cuba. We're certainly not against him simply because he's a dictator. We've never had anything against dictators in general.

I remember learning in school that, as a result of the Spanish-American War, we somehow took over the Philippines, but I never knew the details. When you look into it, you'll find that the Spanish-American War lasted three months; the Philippine War lasted for years and was a brutal, bloody suppression of the Filipino movement for independence. In many ways, it was a precursor of the Vietnam War, in terms of the atrocities committed by the U.S. Army. Now, that's a story that has never been told. 15

Black American soldiers in the Philippines soon began to identify more with the Filipinos than with their fellow white Americans. While these black soldiers were fighting to suppress the Filipinos, they also were hearing from relatives about the lynchings and race riots in their hometowns. They were hearing about black people being killed in large numbers—and here they were, fighting against a nonwhite people on behalf of the United States government. A number of black soldiers deserted and went over to fight with the Filipinos.

In 1906, when the Philippine War was supposedly over—but really the U.S. Army was still suppressing pockets of rebellion—there was a massacre. That's the only way to describe it. The Moros are inhabitants of a southern island in the Philippines. The army swooped down and annihilated a Moro village of six hundred men, women, and children—all of whom were unarmed. Every last one of them was killed. Mark Twain wrote angrily about this. He was especially angry about the fact that President Theodore Roosevelt sent a letter of congratulations to the military commander who had ordered this atrocity, saying it was a great military victory. Have you ever seen a movie in which Theodore Roosevelt was presented as a racist? As an imperialist? As a supporter of massacres? And there he is, up on Mount Rushmore. I've had the thought: *A hammer, a chisel.* But no, it wouldn't do.

War needs to be presented on film in such a way as to encourage the population simply to say no to war. We need a film about those heroic Americans who protested World War I. When you look at them, you see socialists, pacifists, and just ordinary people who saw the stupidity of entering a war that was taking the lives of ten million people in Europe. You see Emma Goldman, the feminist and anarchist, who went to prison for opposing the draft and the war. You see Helen Keller. Every film about Helen Keller concentrates on the fact that she was disabled. I've never seen a film in which Helen Keller is presented as what she was: a radical, a socialist, an antiwar agitator. You also see Kate Richards O'Hare, a socialist who was put in jail for opposing World War I. There is a story from her time in prison that would make a great scene in a movie: The prisoners are stifling for lack of air, and O'Hare takes a book that she's been reading, reaches through the bars, and hurls the book through a skylight to let the air in. All the prisoners applaud and cheer.

I have to acknowledge that there have been a few antiwar films made about World War I. *All Quiet on the Western Front* is an extraordinary film. I recently wrote an article comparing it to *Saving Private Ryan*. Despite the mayhem, *Saving Private Ryan* was essentially a glorification of war, whereas *All Quiet on the Western Front* expresses a diamond-clear antiwar sentiment.

What about the many films devoted to World War II, the "good war"?   20
When Studs Terkel did his oral history of World War II, he called it *The "Good War,"* with quotation marks around *Good War*. In that war, we fought against a terrible evil—fascism—but our own atrocities multiplied as the war went on, culminating in the bombings of Hiroshima and Nagasaki. I have not seen a Hollywood film about the bombing of Hiroshima. The closest we've come to a movie that deals with our bombing of civilian populations was the film version of Kurt Vonnegut's book *Slaughterhouse-Five*, about the bombing of Dresden, Germany, and that was a rarity.

Films about the Civil War tend to focus on the famous battles, like Gettysburg, Fredericksburg, and Bull Run. The Civil War is, again, one of our "good wars"—the slaves were freed because of it—but it is not that simple. There is the class element of who was and who was not drafted, who paid substitutes, who made huge amounts of money off the war. And then there is what happened to the Indians. In the midst of the Civil War, while the armies were fighting in the South, another part of the Union Army was out west, destroying Indian settlements and taking over Indian land. In 1864, not long after the Emancipation Proclamation, the U.S. Army was in Colorado attacking an Indian village, killing hundreds of men, women, and children at Sand Creek, in one of the worst Indian massacres in American history. This massacre occurred during the war to end slavery. In the years of the Civil War, more land was taken from the Indians than in any other comparable period in history.

There's a lot of historical work to be done, a lot of films that need to be made. There are so many class struggles in the U.S. that could be dealt with in movies. We've seen movies that deal with working-class people, but it's always some individual who rises up out of his or her situation and "makes it" in society. Stories of Americans who organize and get together to oppose the powers that hold them down have been very rare.

The American political system and the revered and celebrated Constitution of the United States do not grant any economic rights to the American people. We very often forget that the Constitution gives political rights but not economic rights. If you are not wealthy, then your political rights are limited, even though they are guaranteed on paper in the Constitution. The freedom of speech is granted there, but how much free speech you have depends on how much money and what access to resources you have. The Declaration of Independence talks about the right to life, liberty, and the pursuit of happiness. But how can you have life, liberty, and the pursuit of happiness if you don't have food, housing, and healthcare?

Working people throughout history have had to organize, struggle, go on strike, declare boycotts, and face the police and the army. They have had to do it themselves, against the opposition of government, in order to win the eight-hour workday and other slight improvements to their working conditions. A great film remains to be made about the Haymarket Affair of 1886, which was part of the struggle for the eight-hour work-day. The Haymarket Affair culminated in the execution of four anarchists who were charged with planting a bomb, though in the end nobody ever found out who really had planted it.

The great railroad strike of 1894 tied up the railway system of the United States, and all the power of the army and the courts had to be   25

Engraving depicting the 1886 Haymarket Riot

brought against the striking workers. Eugene Debs, who organized the railroad workers, has never been the central figure in a movie. He was sent to prison for opposing World War I, and he made such an impression on his fellow prisoners that, when he was released, the warden let all the inmates out into the yard, and they applauded as Debs was granted his freedom.

I've met someone who is actually writing a script about the Lawrence textile strike of 1912, a magnificent episode in American history, because the striking workers won. It was a multicultural strike. A working population that spoke twelve different languages got together and defied the textile companies and the police, who were sent to the railroad station to prevent the children of the workers from leaving town. Police literally attacked the women and children at the station, because the company wanted to starve out the strikers, and that would be less likely to happen

Immigrant women striking in Lawrence, Massachusetts, 1912

if their children were safe. But the strikers held out, and with the help of the Industrial Workers of the World, they finally won.

Then there's the Ludlow Massacre, which took place during the Colorado coal strike of 1913–1914, one of the most bitter, bloody, dramatic strikes in American history. The workers were up against the Rockefeller interests. (It's not easy to make an unflattering film about the Rockefellers.) One of the strike's leaders was Mother Jones, an eighty-three-year-old woman who had previously organized textile workers in West Virginia and Pennsylvania. That's another story that should be told. There were kids working in the textile mills at the age of eleven and twelve. Mother Jones led these children on a march from Pennsylvania to Oyster Bay, New York, where President Theodore Roosevelt was on summer vacation. They stood there outside the resort with signs that said, WE WANT TIME TO PLAY. Has there ever been a film made about that?

We've had films on Christopher Columbus, but I don't know of any film that shows Columbus as what he was: a man ruled by the capitalist ethic. Columbus and the Spaniards were killing people for gold. The Catholic priest Bartolomé de Las Casas was an eyewitness. He exposed what was going on, and a remarkable debate took place before the Royal Commission of Spain in 1650. The debate was between las Casas and Sepulveda, another priest, who argued that the Indians were not human and therefore you could do anything you wanted to them.

There's also the story of the Trail of Tears—the expulsion of the Cherokees from the Southeast. Andrew Jackson, one of our national heroes, signed the order to expel them. That was ethnic cleansing on a large scale: the march across the continent, the U.S. Army driving the Indians from their homeland to a little space in Oklahoma that was then called "Indian Territory." When oil was later discovered there, the Indian population was once again evicted. Of the sixteen thousand people who marched westward, four thousand died on the march, while the U.S. Army pushed them, and the U.S. president extolled what happened.

Of course someone should finally tell the story of black people in the United States from a black person's point of view. We've had a number of films about the civil-rights movement from white points of view. *The Long Walk Home* (1991) tells the story of the Montgomery bus boycott from Sissy Spacek's point of view. *Mississippi Burning* (1988) is about the murder of three civil-rights workers in Mississippi in 1964. The FBI agents are the heroes of the film, but every person who was in Mississippi in 1964—my wife and I were both there at the time—knew that the FBI was the enemy. The FBI was watching people being beaten and not doing anything about it. The FBI was silent and absent when people needed protection against murderers. In this Hollywood film, they become heroes. We need the story of the civil-rights movement told from the viewpoint of black people.

Of course, many good movies and wonderful documentaries have been made. Michael Moore's film *Roger and Me*, which has been seen by tens of millions of people, is a remarkable success story. So the possibilities do exist to practice a kind of guerrilla warfare and make films outside of the Hollywood establishment.

If such films are made — about war, about class conflict, about the history of governmental lies, about broken treaties and official violence — if those stories reach the public, we might produce a new generation. As a teacher, I'm not interested in just reproducing class after class of graduates who will get out, become successful, and take their obedient places in the slots that society has prepared for them. What we must do — whether we teach or write or make films — is educate a new generation to do this very modest thing: change the world.

The Reader's Presence

1. Explain what Zinn means by what Leon Trotsky called the "natural selection of accidents" (paragraph 2) preventing true depictions of war, class, and race from appearing in films. Do you agree that Hollywood's structure works against such depictions? Why or why not?

2. Reading the essay, who did you imagine Zinn's audience to be? How sympathetic to his argument would you expect them to be? What evidence can you find for your answers?

3. Zinn says, "Stories of Americans who organize and get together to oppose the powers that hold them down have been very rare" in Hollywood (paragraph 22), but he presents examples to indicate that such stories have appeared again and again throughout American history. In "Family Values" (page 669), Barbara Ehrenreich argues that too few Americans recognize the kind of progressive views espoused for generations in her family as "traditional American values." What "American values" would Zinn and Ehrenreich be likely to share? Do you see these values as traditional? as important? Why or why not?

Part IV

Voices of Modern Fiction: Six Short Stories

Sherman Alexie

This Is What It Means to Say Say Phoenix, Arizona

Sherman Alexie's short story "This Is What It Means to Say Phoenix, Arizona" appears in The Lone Ranger and Tonto Fistfight in Heaven *(1993). Alexie has said, "Most of my heroes are just decent people. Decency is rare and underrated. I think my writing is somehow just about decency." Victor and Thomas, two "decent people" in this story, are also characters in Alexie's first screenplay. The film,* Smoke Signals, *premiered at the 1998 Sundance Film Festival, where it won the Audience Award and the Filmmakers Trophy. Alexie describes the film as "a very basic story, a road trip/buddy movie about a lost father." The narrative structure, as he has pointed out, appears "in everything from the Bible to the* Iliad *and the* Odyssey.*"*

For additional information on Sherman Alexie, see page 13.

Just after Victor lost his job at the BIA,[1] he also found out that his father had died of a heart attack in Phoenix, Arizona. Victor hadn't seen his father in a few years, only talked to him on the telephone once or twice, but there still was a genetic pain, which was soon to be pain as real and immediate as a broken bone.

Victor didn't have any money. Who does have money on a reservation, except the cigarette and fireworks salespeople? His father had a savings account waiting to be claimed, but Victor needed to find a way to get to Phoenix. Victor's mother was just as poor as he was, and the rest of his family didn't have any use at all for him. So Victor called the Tribal Council.

"Listen," Victor said. "My father just died. I need some money to get to Phoenix to make arrangements."

---

[1]*BIA:* Bureau of Indian Affairs, an agency that has historically often been at odds with the tribes it was created to administer. — EDS.

"Now, Victor," the council said. "You know we're having a difficult time financially."

"But I thought the council had special funds set aside for stuff like this."   5

"Now, Victor, we do have some money available for the proper return of tribal members' bodies. But I don't think we have enough to bring your father all the way back from Phoenix."

"Well," Victor said. "It ain't going to cost all that much. He had to be cremated. Things were kind of ugly. He died of a heart attack in his trailer and nobody found him for a week. It was really hot, too. You get the picture."

"Now, Victor, we're sorry for your loss and the circumstances. But we can really only afford to give you one hundred dollars."

"That's not even enough for a plane ticket."

"Well, you might consider driving down to Phoenix."   10

"I don't have a car. Besides, I was going to drive my father's pickup back up here."

"Now, Victor," the council said. "We're sure there is somebody who could drive you to Phoenix. Or is there somebody who could lend you the rest of the money?"

"You know there ain't nobody around with that kind of money."

"Well, we're sorry, Victor, but that's the best we can do."

Victor accepted the Tribal Council's offer. What else could he do? So   15
he signed the proper papers, picked up his check, and walked over to the Trading Post to cash it.

While Victor stood in line, he watched Thomas Builds-the-Fire standing near the magazine rack, talking to himself. Like he always did. Thomas was a storyteller that nobody wanted to listen to. That's like being a dentist in a town where everybody has false teeth.

Victor and Thomas Builds-the-Fire were the same age, had grown up and played in the dirt together. Ever since Victor could remember, it was Thomas who always had something to say.

Once, when they were seven years old, when Victor's father still lived with the family, Thomas closed his eyes and told Victor this story: "Your father's heart is weak. He is afraid of his own family. He is afraid of you. Late at night he sits in the dark. Watches the television until there's nothing but that white noise. Sometimes he feels like he wants to buy a motorcycle and ride away. He wants to run and hide. He doesn't want to be found."

Thomas Builds-the-Fire had known that Victor's father was going to leave, knew it before anyone. Now Victor stood in the Trading Post with a one-hundred-dollar check in his hand, wondering if Thomas knew that Victor's father was dead, if he knew what was going to happen next.

Just then Thomas looked at Victor, smiled, and walked over to him.   20

"Victor, I'm sorry about your father," Thomas said.

"How did you know about it?" Victor asked.

"I heard it on the wind. I heard it from the birds. I felt it in the sunlight. Also, your mother was just in here crying."

"Oh," Victor said and looked around the Trading Post. All the other Indians stared, surprised that Victor was even talking to Thomas. Nobody talked to Thomas anymore because he told the same damn stories over and over again. Victor was embarrassed, but he thought that Thomas might be able to help him. Victor felt a sudden need for tradition.

"I can lend you the money you need," Thomas said suddenly. "But   25
you have to take me with you."

"I can't take your money," Victor said. "I mean, I haven't hardly talked to you in years. We're not really friends anymore."

"I didn't say we were friends. I said you had to take me with you."

"Let me think about it."

Victor went home with his one hundred dollars and sat at the kitchen table. He held his head in his hands and thought about Thomas Builds-the-Fire, remembered little details, tears and scars, the bicycle they shared for a summer, so many stories.

Thomas Builds-the-Fire sat on the bicycle, waited in Victor's yard. He   30
was ten years old and skinny. His hair was dirty because it was the Fourth of July.

"Victor," Thomas yelled. "Hurry up. We're going to miss the fireworks."

After a few minutes, Victor ran out of his house, jumped the porch railing, and landed gracefully on the sidewalk.

"And the judges award him a 9.95, the highest score of the summer," Thomas said, clapped, laughed.

"That was perfect, cousin," Victor said. "And it's my turn to ride the bike."

Thomas gave up the bike and they headed for the fairgrounds. It was   35
nearly dark and the fireworks were about to start.

"You know," Thomas said. "It's strange how us Indians celebrate the Fourth of July. It ain't like it was *our* independence everybody was fighting for."

"You think about things too much," Victor said. "It's just supposed to be fun. Maybe Junior will be there."

"Which Junior? Everybody on this reservation is named Junior."

And they both laughed.

The fireworks were small, hardly more than a few bottle rockets and   40
a fountain. But it was enough for two Indian boys. Years later, they would need much more.

Afterwards, sitting in the dark, fighting off mosquitoes, Victor turned to Thomas Builds-the-Fire.

"Hey," Victor said. "Tell me a story."

Thomas closed his eyes and told this story: "There were these two Indian boys who wanted to be warriors. But it was too late to be warriors in the old way. All the horses were gone. So the two Indian boys stole a car and drove to the city. They parked the stolen car in front of the police station and then hitchhiked back home to the reservation. When they got back, all their friends cheered and their parents' eyes shone with pride. *You were very brave*, everybody said to the two Indian boys. *Very brave.*"

"Ya-hey," Victor said. "That's a good one. I wish I could be a warrior."

"Me, too," Thomas said.   45

They went home together in the dark, Thomas on the bike now, Victor on foot. They walked through shadows and light from the streetlamps.

"We've come a long ways," Thomas said. "We have outdoor lighting."

"All I need is the stars," Victor said. "And besides, you still think about things too much."

They separated then, each headed for home, both laughing all the way.

Victor sat at his kitchen table. He counted his one hundred dollars   50
again and again. He knew he needed more to make it to Phoenix and back. He knew he needed Thomas Builds-the-Fire. So he put his money in his wallet and opened the front door to find Thomas on the porch.

"Ya-hey, Victor," Thomas said. "I knew you'd call me."   .

Thomas walked into the living room and sat down on Victor's favorite chair.

"I've got some money saved up," Thomas said. "It's enough to get us down there, but you have to get us back."

"I've got this hundred dollars," Victor said. "And my dad had a savings account I'm going to claim."

"How much in your dad's account?"   55

"Enough. A few hundred."

"Sounds good. When we leaving?"

When they were fifteen and had long since stopped being friends, Victor and Thomas got into a fistfight. That is, Victor was really drunk and beat Thomas up for no reason at all. All the other Indian boys stood around and watched it happen. Junior was there and so were Lester, Seymour, and a lot of others. The beating might have gone on until Thomas was dead if Norma Many Horses hadn't come along and stopped it.

"Hey, you boys," Norma yelled and jumped out of her car. "Leave him alone."

If it had been someone else, even another man, the Indian boys   60
would've just ignored the warnings. But Norma was a warrior. She was powerful. She could have picked up any two of the boys and smashed their skulls together. But worse than that, she would have dragged them all over to some tipi and made them listen to some elder tell a dusty old story.

The Indian boys scattered, and Norma walked over to Thomas and picked him up.

"Hey, little man, are you okay?" she asked.

Thomas gave her a thumbs up.

"Why they always picking on you?"

Thomas shook his head, closed his eyes, but no stories came to him,   65
no words or music. He just wanted to go home, to lie in his bed and let
his dreams tell his stories for him.

Thomas Builds-the-Fire and Victor sat next to each other in the air-
plane, coach section. A tiny white woman had the window seat. She was
busy twisting her body into pretzels. She was flexible.

"I have to ask," Thomas said, and Victor closed his eyes in
embarrassment.

"Don't," Victor said.

"Excuse me, miss," Thomas asked. "Are you a gymnast or something?"

"There's no something about it," she said. "I was first alternate on   70
the 1980 Olympic team."

"Really?" Thomas asked.

"Really."

"I mean, you used to be a world-class athlete?" Thomas asked.

"My husband still thinks I am."

Thomas Builds-the-Fire smiled. She was a mental gymnast, too. She   75
pulled her leg straight up against her body so that she could've kissed her
kneecap.

"I wish I could do that," Thomas said.

Victor was ready to jump out of the plane. Thomas, that crazy Indian
storyteller with ratty old braids and broken teeth, was flirting with a beautiful Olympic gymnast. Nobody back home on the reservation would ever
believe it.

"Well," the gymnast said. "It's easy. Try it."

Thomas grabbed at his leg and tried to pull it up into the same position as the gymnast. He couldn't even come close, which made Victor and
the gymnast laugh.

"Hey," she asked. "You two are Indian, right?"   80

"Full-blood," Victor said.

"Not me," Thomas said. "I'm half magician on my mother's side and
half clown on my father's."

They all laughed.

"What are your names?" she asked.

"Victor and Thomas."   85

"Mine is Cathy. Pleased to meet you all."

The three of them talked for the duration of the flight. Cathy the
gymnast complained about the government, how they screwed the 1980
Olympic team by boycotting.

"Sounds like you all got a lot in common with Indians," Thomas said.

Nobody laughed.

After the plane landed in Phoenix and they had all found their way to   90
the terminal, Cathy the gymnast smiled and waved good-bye.

"She was really nice," Thomas said.

"Yeah, but everybody talks to everybody on airplanes," Victor said. "It's too bad we can't always be that way."

"You always used to tell me I think too much," Thomas said. "Now it sounds like you do."

"Maybe I caught it from you."

"Yeah."   95

Thomas and Victor rode in a taxi to the trailer where Victor's father died.

"Listen," Victor said as they stopped in front of the trailer. "I never told you I was sorry for beating you up that time."

"Oh, it was nothing. We were just kids and you were drunk."

"Yeah, but I'm still sorry."

"That's all right."   100

Victor paid for the taxi and the two of them stood in the hot Phoenix summer. They could smell the trailer.

"This ain't going to be nice," Victor said. "You don't have to go in."

"You're going to need help."

Victor walked to the front door and opened it. The stink rolled out and made them both gag. Victor's father had lain in that trailer for a week in hundred-degree temperatures before anyone found him. And the only reason anyone found him was because of the smell. They needed dental records to identify him. That's exactly what the coroner said. They needed dental records.

"Oh, man," Victor said. "I don't know if I can do this."   105

"Well, then don't."

"But there might be something valuable in there."

"I thought his money was in the bank."

"It is. I was talking about pictures and letters and stuff like that."

"Oh," Thomas said as he held his breath and followed Victor into   110
the trailer.

When Victor was twelve, he stepped into an underground wasp nest. His foot was caught in the hole, and no matter how hard he struggled, Victor couldn't pull free. He might have died there, stung a thousand times, if Thomas Builds-the-Fire had not come by.

"Run," Thomas yelled and pulled Victor's foot from the hole. They ran then, hard as they ever had, faster than Billy Mills,[2] faster than Jim Thorpe,[3] faster than the wasps could fly.

---

[2]*Mills:* An Oglala Lakota (Sioux), Billy Mills (b. 1938) was the only American to win an Olympic gold medal in the 10,000-meter race—at the 1964 Tokyo Olympic Games.—EDS.

[3]*Thorpe:* A member of the Sac and Fox tribe and acclaimed to be the greatest athlete of the twentieth century, Jim Thorpe (1887–1953) won gold medals in the pentathlon and decathlon in the 1912 Olympic games and played both professional football and baseball. —EDS.

Victor and Thomas ran until they couldn't breathe, ran until it was cold and dark outside, ran until they were lost and it took hours to find their way home. All the way back, Victor counted his stings.

"Seven," Victor said. "My lucky number."

Victor didn't find much to keep in the trailer. Only a photo album and   115
a stereo. Everything else had that smell stuck in it or was useless anyway.

"I guess this is all," Victor said. "It ain't much."

"Better than nothing," Thomas said.

"Yeah, and I do have the pickup."

"Yeah," Thomas said, "it's in good shape."

"Dad was good about that stuff."   120

"Yeah, I remember your dad."

"Really?" Victor asked. "What do you remember?"

Thomas Builds-the-Fire closed his eyes and told this story: "I remember when I had this dream that told me to go to Spokane, to stand by the Falls in the middle of the city and wait for a sign. I knew I had to go there but I didn't have a car. Didn't have a license. I was only thirteen. So I walked all the way, took me all day, and I finally made it to the Falls. I stood there for an hour waiting. Then your dad came walking up. *What the hell are you doing here?* he asked me. I said, *Waiting for a vision.* Then your father said, *All you're going to get here is mugged.* So he drove me over to Denny's, bought me dinner, and then drove me home to the reservation. For a long time I was mad because I thought my dreams had lied to me. But they didn't. Your dad was my vision. *Take care of each other* is what my dreams were saying. *Take care of each other.*"

Victor was quiet for a long time. He searched his mind for memories of his father, found the good ones, found a few bad ones, added it all up, and smiled.

"My father never told me about finding you in Spokane," Victor said.   125

"He said he wouldn't tell anybody. Didn't want me to get in trouble. But he said I had to watch out for you as part of the deal."

"Really?"

"Really. Your father said you would need the help. He was right."

"That's why you came down here with me, isn't it?" Victor asked.

"I came because of your father."   130

Victor and Thomas climbed into the pickup, drove over to the bank, and claimed the three hundred dollars in the savings account.

Thomas Builds-the-Fire could fly.

Once, he jumped off the roof of the tribal school and flapped his arms like a crazy eagle. And he flew. For a second, he hovered, suspended above all the other Indian boys who were too smart or too scared to jump.

"He's flying," Junior yelled, and Seymour was busy looking for the trick wires or mirrors. But it was real. As real as the dirt when Thomas lost altitude and crashed to the ground.

He broke his arm in two places.   135

"He broke his wing," Victor chanted, and the other Indian boys joined in, made it a tribal song.

"He broke his wing, he broke his wing, he broke his wing," all the Indian boys chanted as they ran off, flapping their wings, wishing they could fly, too. They hated Thomas for his courage, his brief moment as a bird. Everybody has dreams about flying. Thomas flew.

One of his dreams came true for just a second, just enough to make it real.

Victor's father, his ashes, fit in one wooden box with enough left over to fill a cardboard box.

"He was always a big man," Thomas said.   140

Victor carried part of his father and Thomas carried the rest out to the pickup. They set him down carefully behind the seats, put a cowboy hat on the wooden box and a Dodgers cap on the cardboard box. That's the way it was supposed to be.

"Ready to head back home?" Victor asked.

"It's going to be a long drive."

"Yeah, take a couple days, maybe."

"We can take turns," Thomas said.   145

"Okay," Victor said, but they didn't take turns. Victor drove for six-teen hours straight north, made it halfway up Nevada toward home before he finally pulled over.

"Hey, Thomas," Victor said. "You got to drive for a while."

"Okay."

Thomas Builds-the-Fire slid behind the wheel and started off down the road. All through Nevada, Thomas and Victor had been amazed at the lack of animal life, at the absence of water, of movement.

"Where is everything?" Victor had asked more than once.   150

Now when Thomas was finally driving they saw the first animal, maybe the only animal in Nevada. It was a long-eared jackrabbit.

"Look," Victor yelled. "It's alive."

Thomas and Victor were busy congratulating themselves on their dis-covery when the jackrabbit darted out into the road and under the wheels of the pickup.

"Stop the goddamn car," Victor yelled, and Thomas did stop, backed the pickup to the dead jackrabbit.

"Oh, man, he's dead," Victor said as he looked at the squashed   155
animal.

"Really dead."

"The only thing alive in this whole state and we just killed it."

"I don't know," Thomas said, "I think it was suicide."

Victor looked around the desert, sniffed the air, felt the emptiness and loneliness, and nodded his head.

"Yeah," Victor said, "it had to be suicide."   160

"I can't believe this," Thomas said. "You drive for a thousand miles and there ain't even any bugs smashed on the windshield. I drive for ten seconds and kill the only living thing in Nevada."

"Yeah," Victor said. "Maybe I should drive."

"Maybe you should."

Thomas Builds-the-Fire walked through the corridors of the tribal school by himself. Nobody wanted to be anywhere near him because of all those stories. Story after story.

Thomas closed his eyes and this story came to him: "We are all given   165
one thing by which our lives are measured, one determination. Mine are the stories which can change or not change the world. It doesn't matter which as long as I continue to tell the stories. My father, he died on Okinawa in World War II, died fighting for this country, which had tried to kill him for years. My mother, she died giving birth to me, died while I was still inside her. She pushed me out into the world with her last breath. I have no brothers or sisters. I have only my stories which came to me before I even had the words to speak. I learned a thousand stories before I took my first thousand steps. They are all I have. It's all I can do."

Thomas Builds-the-Fire told his stories to all those who would stop and listen. He kept telling them long after people had stopped listening.

Victor and Thomas made it back to the reservation just as the sun was rising. It was the beginning of a new day on earth, but the same old shit on the reservation.

"Good morning," Thomas said.

"Good morning."

The tribe was waking up, ready for work, eating breakfast, reading   170
the newspaper, just like everybody else does. Willene LeBret was out in her garden wearing a bathrobe. She waved when Thomas and Victor drove by.

"Crazy Indians made it," she said to herself and went back to her roses.

Victor stopped the pickup in front of Thomas Builds-the-Fire's HUD[4] house. They both yawned, stretched a little, shook dust from their bodies.

"I'm tired," Victor said.

"Of everything," Thomas added.

They both searched for words to end the journey. Victor needed to   175
thank Thomas for his help, for the money, and make the promise to pay it all back.

---

[4]*HUD:* The U.S. Department of Housing and Urban Development. —EDS.

"Don't worry about the money," Thomas said. "It don't make any difference anyhow."

"Probably not, enit?"

"Nope."

Victor knew that Thomas would remain the crazy storyteller who talked to dogs and cars, who listened to the wind and pine trees. Victor knew that he couldn't really be friends with Thomas, even after all that had happened. It was cruel but it was real. As real as the ashes, as Victor's father, sitting behind the seats.

"I know how it is," Thomas said. "I know you ain't going to treat me   180
any better than you did before. I know your friends would give you too much shit about it."

Victor was ashamed of himself. Whatever happened to the tribal ties, the sense of community? The only real thing he shared with anybody was a bottle and broken dreams. He owed Thomas something, anything.

"Listen," Victor said and handed Thomas the cardboard box which contained half of his father. "I want you to have this."

Thomas took the ashes and smiled, closed his eyes, and told this story: "I'm going to travel to Spokane Falls one last time and toss these ashes into the water. And your father will rise like a salmon, leap over the bridge, over me, and find his way home. It will be beautiful. His teeth will shine like silver, like a rainbow. He will rise, Victor, he will rise."

Victor smiled.

"I was planning on doing the same thing with my half," Victor said.   185
"But I didn't imagine my father looking anything like a salmon. I thought it'd be like cleaning the attic or something. Like letting things go after they've stopped having any use."

"Nothing stops, cousin," Thomas said. "Nothing stops."

Thomas Builds-the-Fire got out of the pickup and walked up his driveway. Victor started the pickup and began the drive home.

"Wait," Thomas yelled suddenly from his porch. "I just got to ask one favor."

Victor stopped the pickup, leaned out the window, and shouted back. "What do you want?"

"Just one time when I'm telling a story somewhere, why don't you   190
stop and listen?" Thomas asked.

"Just once?"

"Just once."

Victor waved his arms to let Thomas know that the deal was good. It was a fair trade, and that was all Victor had ever wanted from his whole life. So Victor drove his father's pickup toward home while Thomas went into his house, closed the door behind him, and heard a new story come to him in the silence afterwards.

The Reader's Presence

1. Thomas is portrayed as an outcast in the community, "a story-teller that nobody wanted to listen to" (paragraph 16). What stories does Thomas tell? Why are they unpopular with listeners? What do Thomas's stories have to do with his role as an outcast?

2. Describe Victor's state of mind and place in life at the beginning of the story. What is he like? What has happened to him? Compare this Victor to the Victor who appears at the end of the story. Has he changed? Do you think that he will change in the future? Why or why not?

3. Compare the characters of Thomas and Victor to Alexie's description in "The Joy of Reading and Writing: Superman and Me" (page 13) of the children on the Spokane Indian Reservation of Alexie's youth. What characteristics does Thomas share with the children Alexie describes (including himself as a boy)? What characteristics does Victor share with them? How are Alexie's fictional reservation and the people who live there like — and unlike — the reservation and people he describes in his essay?

Raymond Carver

The Bath

Raymond Carver (1938–1988) is best known for his tightly crafted, spare, and often grim short stories. In fact, his mastery of dialogue and his fine eye for detail have made his collections of short stories best-sellers in the United States and abroad. These collections include Will You Please Be Quiet, Please? *(1976);* What We Talk about When We Talk about Love *(1981), in which "The Bath" can be found;* Cathedral *(1984); and* Where I'm Calling From *(1988). Carver worked and reworked his stories, even after they were published. Another version of "The Bath" was later published in* Cathedral; *this later story, called "A Small Good Thing," won the 1983 O. Henry Award. In 1993, Robert Altman made the critically acclaimed film* Short Cuts *based on a number of Carver's short stories.*

Describing the process of writing fiction, Carver says, "I never start with an idea. I always see something. I start with an image, a cigarette being put out in a jar of mustard, for instance, or the remains, the wreckage, of a dinner left on the table. Pop cans in the fireplace, that sort of thing. And a feeling goes with that. And that feeling seems to transport me back to that particular time and place, and the ambience of time. But it is the image, and the emotion that goes with that image—that's what's important."

For more information on Raymond Carver, see page 57.

Saturday afternoon the mother drove to the bakery in the shopping center. After looking through a loose-leaf binder with photographs of cakes taped onto the pages, she ordered chocolate, the child's favorite. The cake she chose was decorated with a spaceship and a launching pad under a sprinkling of white stars. The name SCOTTY would be iced on in green as if it were the name of the spaceship.

The baker listened thoughtfully when the mother told him Scotty would be eight years old. He was an older man, this baker, and he wore a curious apron, a heavy thing with loops that went under his arms and around his back and then crossed in front again where they were tied in a very thick knot. He kept wiping his hands on the front of the apron as he listened to the woman, his wet eyes examining her lips as she studied the samples and talked.

He let her take her time. He was in no hurry.

The mother decided on the spaceship cake, and then she gave the baker her name and her telephone number. The cake would be ready Monday morning, in plenty of time for the party Monday afternoon. This was all the baker was willing to say. No pleasantries, just this small exchange, the barest information, nothing that was not necessary.

Monday morning, the boy was walking to school. He was in the company of another boy, the two boys passing a bag of potato chips back and forth between them. The birthday boy was trying to trick the other boy into telling what he was going to give in the way of a present.   5

At an intersection, without looking, the birthday boy stepped off the curb, and was promptly knocked down by a car. He fell on his side, his head in the gutter, his legs in the road moving as if he were climbing a wall.

The other boy stood holding the potato chips. He was wondering if he should finish the rest or continue on to school.

The birthday boy did not cry. But neither did he wish to talk anymore. He would not answer when the other boy asked what it felt like to be hit by a car. The birthday boy got up and turned back for home, at which time the other boy waved good-bye and headed off for school.

The birthday boy told his mother what had happened. They sat together on the sofa. She held his hands in her lap. This is what she was doing when the boy pulled his hands away and lay down on his back.

Of course, the birthday party never happened. The birthday boy was in the hospital instead. The mother sat by the bed. She was waiting for   10 the boy to wake up. The father hurried over from his office. He sat next to the mother. So now the both of them waited for the boy to wake up. They waited for hours, and then the father went home to take a bath.

The man drove home from the hospital. He drove the streets faster than he should. It had been a good life till now. There had been work, fatherhood, family. The man had been lucky and happy. But fear made him want a bath.

He pulled into the driveway. He sat in the car trying to make his legs work. The child had been hit by a car and he was in the hospital, but he was going to be all right. The man got out of the car and went up to the door. The dog was barking and the telephone was ringing. It kept ringing while the man unlocked the door and felt the wall for the light switch.

He picked up the receiver. He said, "I just got in the door!"

"There's a cake that wasn't picked up."

This is what the voice on the other end said.   15

"What are you saying?" the father said.

"The cake," the voice said. "Sixteen dollars."

The husband held the receiver against his ear, trying to understand. He said, "I don't know anything about it."

"Don't hand me that," the voice said.

The husband hung up the telephone. He went into the kitchen and   20
poured himself some whiskey. He called the hospital.

The child's condition remained the same.

While the water ran into the tub, the man lathered his face and shaved. He was in the tub when he heard the telephone again. He got himself out and hurried through the house, saying, "Stupid, stupid," because he wouldn't be doing this if he'd stayed where he was in the hospital. He picked up the receiver and shouted, "Hello!"

The voice said, "It's ready."

The father got back to the hospital after midnight. The wife was sitting in the chair by the bed. She looked up at the husband and then she looked back at the child. From an apparatus over the bed hung a bottle with a tube running from the bottle to the child.

"What's this?" the father said.   25

"Glucose," the mother said.

The husband put his hand to the back of the woman's head.

"He's going to wake up," the man said.

"I know," the woman said.

In a little while the man said, "Go home and let me take over."   30

She shook her head. "No," she said.

"Really," he said. "Go home for a while. You don't have to worry. He's sleeping, is all."

A nurse pushed open the door. She nodded to them as she went to the bed. She took the left arm out from under the covers and put her fingers on the wrist. She put the arm back under the covers and wrote on the clipboard attached to the bed.

"How is he?" the mother said.

"Stable," the nurse said. Then she said, "Doctor will be in again   35
shortly."

"I was saying maybe she'd want to go home and get a little rest," the man said. "After the doctor comes."

"She could do that," the nurse said.

The woman said, "We'll see what the doctor says." She brought her hand up to her eyes and leaned her head forward.

The nurse said, "Of course."

The father gazed at his son, the small chest inflating and deflating   40
under the covers. He felt more fear now. He began shaking his head. He talked to himself like this. The child is fine. Instead of sleeping at home, he's doing it here. Sleep is the same wherever you do it.

The doctor came in. He shook hands with the man. The woman got up from the chair.

"Ann," the doctor said and nodded. The doctor said, "Let's just see how he's doing." He moved to the bed and touched the boy's wrist. He peeled back an eyelid and then the other. He turned back the covers and listened to the heart. He pressed his fingers here and there on the body. He went to the end of the bed and studied the chart. He noted the time, scribbled on the chart, and then he considered the mother and the father.

This doctor was a handsome man. His skin was moist and tan. He wore a three-piece suit, a vivid tie, and on his shirt were cufflinks.

The mother was talking to herself like this. He has just come from somewhere with an audience. They gave him a special medal.

The doctor said, "Nothing to shout about, but nothing to worry   45
about. He should wake up pretty soon." The doctor looked at the boy again. "We'll know more after the tests are in."

"Oh, no," the mother said.

The doctor said, "Sometimes you see this."

The father said, "You wouldn't call this a coma, then?"

The father waited and looked at the doctor.

"No, I don't want to call it that," the doctor said. "He's sleeping. It's   50
restorative. The body is doing what it has to do."

"It's a coma," the mother said. "A kind of coma."

The doctor said, "I wouldn't call it that."

He took the woman's hands and patted them. He shook hands with the husband.

The woman put her fingers on the child's forehead and kept them there for a while. "At least he doesn't have a fever," she said. Then she said, "I don't know. Feel his head."

The man put his fingers on the boy's forehead. The man said, "I 55 think he's supposed to feel this way."

The woman stood there awhile longer, working her lip with her teeth. Then she moved to her chair and sat down.

The husband sat in the chair beside her. He wanted to say something else. But there was no saying what it should be. He took her hand and put it in his lap. This made him feel better. It made him feel he was saying something. They sat like that for a while, watching the boy, not talking. From time to time he squeezed her hand until she took it away.

"I've been praying," she said.

"Me too," the father said. "I've been praying too."

A nurse came back in and checked the flow from the bottle. 60

A doctor came in and said what his name was. This doctor was wearing loafers.

"We're going to take him downstairs for more pictures," he said. "And we want to do a scan."

"A scan?" the mother said. She stood between this new doctor and the bed.

"It's nothing," he said.

"My God," she said. 65

Two orderlies came in. They wheeled a thing like a bed. They unhooked the boy from the tube and slid him over onto the thing with wheels.

It was after sunup when they brought the birthday boy back out. The mother and father followed the orderlies into the elevator and up to the room. Once more the parents took up their places next to the bed.

They waited all day. The boy did not wake up. The doctor came again and examined the boy again and left after saying the same things again. Nurses came in. Doctors came in. A technician came in and took blood.

"I don't understand this," the mother said to the technician.

"Doctor's orders," the technician said. 70

The mother went to the window and looked out at the parking lot. Cars with their lights on were driving in and out. She stood at the window with her hands on the sill. She was talking to herself like this. We're into something now, something hard.

She was afraid.

She saw a car stop and a woman in a long coat get into it. She made believe she was that woman. She made believe she was driving away from here to someplace else.

The doctor came in. He looked tanned and healthier than ever. He went to the bed and examined the boy. He said, "His signs are fine. Everything's good."

The mother said, "But he's sleeping."   75

"Yes," the doctor said.

The husband said, "She's tired. She's starved."

The doctor said, "She should rest. She should eat. Ann," the doctor said.

"Thank you," the husband said.

He shook hands with the doctor and the doctor patted their shoul-   80
ders and left.

"I suppose one of us should go home and check on things," the man said. "The dog needs to be fed."

"Call the neighbors," the wife said. "Someone will feed him if you ask them to."

She tried to think who. She closed her eyes and tried to think anything at all. After a time she said, "Maybe I'll do it. Maybe if I'm not here watching, he'll wake up. Maybe it's because I'm watching that he won't."

"That could be it," the husband said.

"I'll go home and take a bath and put on something clean," the   85
woman said.

"I think you should do that," the man said.

She picked up her purse. He helped her into her coat. She moved to the door, and looked back. She looked at the child, and then she looked at the father. The husband nodded and smiled.

She went past the nurses' station and down to the end of the corridor, where she turned and saw a little waiting room, a family in there, all sitting in wicker chairs, a man in a khaki shirt, a baseball cap pushed back on his head, a large woman wearing a housedress, slippers, a girl in jeans, hair in dozens of kinky braids, the table littered with flimsy wrappers and styrofoam and coffee sticks and packets of salt and pepper.

"Nelson," the woman said. "Is it about Nelson?"

The woman's eyes widened.   90

"Tell me now, lady," the woman said. "Is it about Nelson?"

The woman was trying to get up from her chair. But the man had his hand closed over her arm.

"Here, here," the man said.

"I'm sorry," the mother said. "I'm looking for the elevator. My son is in the hospital. I can't find the elevator."

"Elevator is down that way," the man said, and he aimed a finger in   95
the right direction.

"My son was hit by a car," the mother said. "But he's going to be all right. He's in shock now, but it might be some kind of coma too. That's what worries us, the coma part. I'm going out for a little while. Maybe I'll take a bath. But my husband is with him. He's watching. There's a chance everything will change when I'm gone. My name is Ann Weiss."

The man shifted in his chair. He shook his head.
He said, "Our Nelson."

She pulled into the driveway. The dog ran out from behind the house.
He ran in circles on the grass. She closed her eyes and leaned her head
against the wheel. She listened to the ticking of the engine.

She got out of the car and went to the door. She turned on lights and   100
put on water for tea. She opened a can and fed the dog. She sat down on
the sofa with her tea.
The telephone rang.
"Yes!" she said. "Hello!" she said.
"Mrs. Weiss," a man's voice said.
"Yes," she said. "This is Mrs. Weiss. Is it about Scotty?" she said.

"Scotty," the voice said. "It is about Scotty," the voice said. "It has   105
to do with Scotty, yes."

The Reader's Presence

1. What information does the omniscient point of view provide that
   would be unavailable if the story were told by the mother? by the
   father? How does the inclusion of this information affect the story?

2. In the hospital scenes, what clues does Carver give to the woman's
   feelings? How do her dialogue, her actions, and the things she notices indicate her emotional state?

3. What information does the story not provide that you might have
   expected it to? Why do you think Carver chose to tell this story
   about events affecting a family in such minimal detail? Read
   Carver's essay "My Father's Life" (page 57). What similarities
   does the nonfiction piece share with the short story? What details
   does Carver leave out of the essay? Why do you think he made
   these choices?

Jamaica Kincaid

Girl

Jamaica Kincaid was born in Antigua in 1949 and came to the United States at the age of seventeen to work for a New York family as an au pair. Her novel Lucy *(1990) is an imaginative account of her experience of coming into adulthood in a foreign country and continues the narrative of her personal history begun in the novel* Annie John *(1985). She has also published a collection of short stories,* At the Bottom of the River *(1983), a collection of essays,* A Small Place *(1988), and a third novel,* The Autobiography of My Mother *(1995). Her most recent publications include* My Brother *(1997), which was a National Book Award Finalist for Nonfiction,* My Favorite Plant: Writers and Gardeners on the Plants They Love *(1998),* My Garden *(2001),* Mr. Potter *(2002), and* Among Flowers: A Walk in the Himalaya *(2005). Her writing also appears in national magazines, especially the* New Yorker, *where she worked as a staff writer until 1995. "Girl" is the first piece of fiction Kincaid published; it appeared in the* New Yorker *in 1978.*

Wash the white clothes on Monday and put them on the stone heap; wash the color clothes on Tuesday and put them on the clothesline to dry; don't walk barehead in the hot sun; cook pumpkin fritters in very hot sweet oil; soak your little clothes right after you take them off; when buying cotton to make yourself a nice blouse, be sure that it doesn't have gum on it, because that way it won't hold up well after a wash; soak salt fish overnight before you cook it; is it true that you sing benna[1] in Sunday School?; always eat your food in such a way that it won't turn someone else's stomach; on Sundays try to walk like a lady and not like the slut you are so bent on becoming; don't sing benna in Sunday School; you mustn't speak to wharf-rat boys, not even to give directions; don't eat fruits on the street—flies will follow you; *but I don't sing benna on Sundays at all and never in Sunday School;* this is how to sew on a button; this is how to make a buttonhole for the button you have just sewed on; this is how to hem a dress when you see the hem coming down and so to prevent yourself from looking like the slut I know you are so bent on becoming; this is how you iron your father's khaki shirt so that it doesn't have a crease; this is how you iron your father's khaki pants so that they don't have a crease; this is how you grow okra—far from the house, because okra tree harbors red ants; when you are growing dasheen,[2] make sure it gets plenty of water or else it makes your throat itch when you are eating it; this is how you sweep a corner; this is how you sweep a whole

---

[1]*benna:* Popular calypso-like music.—EDS.
[2]*dasheen:* A starchy vegetable.—EDS.

house; this is how you sweep a yard; this is how you smile to someone you don't like too much; this is how you smile to someone you don't like at all; this is how you smile to someone you like completely; this is how you set a table for tea; this is how you set a table for dinner; this is how you set a table for dinner with an important guest; this is how you set a table for lunch; this is how you set a table for breakfast; this is how to behave in the presence of men who don't know you very well, and this way they won't recognize immediately the slut I have warned you against becoming; be sure to wash every day, even if it is with your own spit; don't squat down to play marbles—you are not a boy, you know; don't pick people's flowers—you might catch something; don't throw stones at blackbirds, because it might not be a blackbird at all; this is how to make a bread pudding; this is how to make doukona;[3] this is how to make pepper pot; this is how to make a good medicine for a cold; this is how to make a good medicine to throw away a child before it even becomes a child; this is how to catch a fish; this is how to throw back a fish you don't like, and that way something bad won't fall on you; this is how to bully a man; this is how a man bullies you; this is how to love a man, and if this doesn't work there are other ways, and if they don't work don't feel too bad about giving up; this is how to spit up in the air if you feel like it, and this is how to move quick so that it doesn't fall on you; this is how to make ends meet; always squeeze bread to make sure it's fresh; *but what if the baker won't let me feel the bread?*; you mean to say that after all you are really going to be the kind of woman who the baker won't let near the bread?

The Reader's Presence

1. Whose voice dominates this story? To whom is the monologue addressed? What effect(s) does the speaker seek to have on the listener? Where does the speaker appear to have acquired her values? Categorize the kinds of advice you find in the story. Identify sentences in which one category of advice merges into another. How are the different kinds of advice alike, and to what extent are they contradictory?

2. "Girl" speaks only two lines, both of which are italicized. In each case, what prompts her to speak? What is the result? Stories generally create the expectation that at least one main character will undergo a change. What differences, if any, do you notice between Girl's first and second lines of dialogue (and the replies she elicits), differences that might suggest that such a change has taken place? If you do notice any differences, in whom do you

[3]*doukona:* Cornmeal. — EDS.

notice them? Analyze the girl's character based not only on what she says but on what she hears (if one can assume that this monologue was not delivered all in one sitting, but is rather the distillation of years' worth of advice, as heard by the girl).

3. Consider the role of gender in this story. What gender stereotypes does the main speaker perpetuate? Look not only at the stereotypes that affect women but also at those that define the roles of men. What can you infer about the males who remain behind the scenes? Read Amy Cunningham's "Why Women Smile" (page 324). What gender stereotypes influence whether—and when—women smile? To what extent do gender roles and cultural expectations determine the patterns—and consequences—of when men and women smile?

THE WRITER AT WORK

Jamaica Kincaid on *Girl*

To many readers, "Girl" appears to be an odd and confusing short story. It's far shorter than most published stories and consists almost entirely of a monologue spoken by a mother to her daughter. Readers may wonder: "What makes this a story?" In the following passage from an interview with Jamaica Kincaid, Allan Varda asks the author some questions about this intriguing little story and discovers behind its composition a larger agenda that we might not perceive from a single reading. Do Kincaid's answers to Varda's questions help you better understand what's happening in the story? In what ways?

AV: There is a litany of items in "Girl" from a mother to her daughter about what to do and what *not* to do regarding the elements of being "a nice young lady." Is this the way it was for you and other girls in Antigua?

JK: In a word, yes.

AV: Was that good or bad?

JK: I don't think it's the way I would tell my daughter, but as a mother I would tell her what I think would be best for her to be like. This mother in "Girl" was really just giving the girl an idea about the things she would need to be a self-possessed woman in the world.

AV: But you didn't take your mother's advice?   5

JK: No, because I had other ideas on how to be a self-possessed woman in the world. I didn't know that at the time. I only remember these things. What the mother in the story sees as aids to living in the world, the girl might see as extraordinary oppression, which is one of the things I came to see.

AV: Almost like she's Mother England.

JK: I was just going to say that. I've come to see that I've worked through the relationship of the mother and the girl to a relationship between Europe and the place that I'm from, which is to say, a relationship between the powerful and the powerless. The girl is powerless and the mother is powerful. The mother shows her how to be in the world, but at the back of her mind she thinks she never will get it. She's deeply skeptical that this child could ever grow up to be a self-possessed woman and in the end she reveals her skepticism; yet even within the skepticism is, of course, dismissal and scorn. So it's not unlike the relationship between the conquered and the conqueror.

Joyce Carol Oates

Where Are You Going, Where Have You Been?

Joyce Carol Oates (b. 1938) has published more than a hundred works of fiction and nonfiction in every genre, including novels, short stories, essays, poetry, screenplays, and a libretto — frequently publishing several projects simultaneously while working and reworking the manuscript for the next. Describing herself as a "chronicler of the American experience," Oates often explores violent behavior "in a nation prone to violence" and its effect on the lives of ordinary people, particularly women and children. Among her long list of novels are A Garden of Earthly Delights *(1967) and* them *(1969), which won the National Book Award for fiction in 1970. Her most recent works of fiction include the novels* Missing Mom *(2005),* Black Girl / White Girl *(2006),* The Gravedigger's Daughter *(2007), and* My Sister, My Love: The Intimate Story of Skyler Rampike *(2008) and short story collections* The Museum of Dr. Moses: Tales of Mystery and Suspense *(2007) and* Wild Nights! *(2008). Oates's interests and versatility are also reflected in her nonfiction prose, which includes* The Profane Art *(1983),* On Boxing *(1987),* Where I've Been, and Where I'm Going *(1999), and, her latest,* Uncensored: Views and (Re)views *(2005).*

Oates's short story "Where Are You Going, Where Have You Been?" first appeared in 1966 and has been anthologized frequently since. She has said that the idea came from a magazine piece she saw — but never finished reading — about a "thrill killer" in Tucson, Arizona. "Where Are You Going, Where Have You Been?" was the basis for the film Smooth Talk *in 1985.*

For Bob Dylan

Her name was Connie. She was fifteen and she had a quick nervous giggling habit of craning her neck to glance into mirrors, or checking other people's faces to make sure her own was all right. Her mother, who noticed everything and knew everything and who hadn't much reason any longer to look at her own face, always scolded Connie about it. "Stop gawking at yourself, who are you? You think you're so pretty?" she would say. Connie would raise her eyebrows at these familiar complaints and look right through her mother, into a shadowy vision of herself as she was right at that moment: she knew she was pretty and that was everything. Her mother had been pretty once too, if you could believe those old snapshots in the album, but now her looks were gone and that was why she was always after Connie.

"Why don't you keep your room clean like your sister? How've you got your hair fixed—what the hell stinks? Hair spray? You don't see your sister using that junk."

Her sister June was twenty-four and still lived at home. She was a secretary in the high school Connie attended, and if that wasn't bad enough—with her in the same building—she was so plain and chunky and steady that Connie had to hear her praised all the time by her mother and her mother's sisters. June did this, June did that, she saved money and helped clean the house and cooked and Connie couldn't do a thing, her mind was all filled with trashy daydreams. Their father was away at work most of the time and when he came home he wanted supper and he read the newspaper at supper and after supper he went to bed. He didn't bother talking much to them, but around his bent head Connie's mother kept picking at her until Connie wished her mother was dead and she herself was dead and it was all over. "She makes me want to throw up sometimes," she complained to her friends. She had a high, breathless, amused voice which made everything she said a little forced, whether it was sincere or not.

There was one good thing: June went places with girl friends of hers, girls who were just as plain and steady as she, and so when Connie wanted to do that her mother had no objections. The father of Connie's best girl friend drove the girls the three miles to town and left them off at a shopping plaza, so that they could walk through the stores or go to a movie, and when he came to pick them up again at eleven he never bothered to ask what they had done.

They must have been familiar sights, walking around that shopping plaza in their shorts and flat ballerina slippers that always scuffed the sidewalk, with charm bracelets jingling on their thin wrists; they would lean together to whisper and laugh secretly if someone passed by who amused or interested them. Connie had long dark blond hair that drew anyone's eye to it, and she wore part of it pulled up on her head and puffed out and the rest of it she let fall down her back. She wore a pullover jersey blouse that looked one way when she was at home and another way when she was

5

away from home. Everything about her had two sides to it, one for home and one for anywhere that was not home: her walk that could be childlike and bobbing, or languid enough to make anyone think she was hearing music in her head, her mouth which was pale and smirking most of the time, but bright and pink on these evenings out, her laugh which was cynical and drawling at home—"Ha, ha, very funny"—but high-pitched and nervous anywhere else, like the jingling of the charms on her bracelet.

Sometimes they did go shopping or to a movie, but sometimes they went across the highway, ducking fast across the busy road, to a drive-in restaurant where older kids hung out. The restaurant was shaped like a big bottle, though squatter than a real bottle, and on its cap was a revolving figure of a grinning boy who held a hamburger aloft. One night in midsummer they ran across, breathless with daring, and right away someone leaned out a car window and invited them over, but it was just a boy from high school they didn't like. It made them feel good to be able to ignore him. They went up through the maze of parked and cruising cars to the bright-lit, fly-infested restaurant, their faces pleased and expectant as if they were entering a sacred building that loomed out of the night to give them what haven and what blessing they yearned for. They sat at the counter and crossed their legs at the ankles, their thin shoulders rigid with excitement and listened to the music that made everything so good: the music was always in the background like music at a church service, it was something to depend upon.

A boy named Eddie came in to talk with them. He sat backwards on his stool, turning himself jerkily around in semi-circles and then stopping and turning again, and after a while he asked Connie if she would like something to eat. She said she did and so she tapped her friend's arm on her way out—her friend pulled her face up into a brave droll look—and Connie said she would meet her at eleven, across the way. "I just hate to leave her like that," Connie said earnestly, but the boy said that she wouldn't be alone for long. So they went out to his car and on the way Connie couldn't help but let her eyes wander over the windshields and faces all around her, her face gleaming with the joy that had nothing to do with Eddie or even this place; it might have been the music. She drew her shoulders up and sucked in her breath with the pure pleasure of being alive, and just at that moment she happened to glance at a face just a few feet from hers. It was a boy with shaggy black hair, in a convertible jalopy painted gold. He stared at her and then his lips widened into a grin. Connie slit her eyes at him and turned away, but she couldn't help glancing back and there he was still watching her. He wagged a finger and laughed and said, "Gonna get you, baby," and Connie turned away again without Eddie noticing anything.

She spent three hours with him, at the restaurant where they ate hamburgers and drank Cokes in wax cups that were always sweating, and then down an alley a mile or so away, and when he left her off at five to eleven only the movie house was still open at the plaza. Her girl friend was there, talking with a boy. When Connie came up the two girls smiled at each other and Connie said, "How was the movie?" and the girl said, "*You* should know." They rode off with the girl's father, sleepy and pleased, and Connie couldn't help but look at the darkened shopping plaza with its big empty parking lot and its signs that were faded and ghostly now, and over at the drive-in restaurant where cars were still circling tirelessly. She couldn't hear the music at this distance.

Next morning June asked her how the movie was and Connie said, "So-so."

She and that girl and occasionally another girl went out several times a   10
week that way, and the rest of the time Connie spent around the house—it was summer vacation—getting in her mother's way and thinking, dreaming, about the boys she met. But all the boys fell back and dissolved into a single face that was not even a face, but an idea, a feeling, mixed up with the urgent insistent pounding of the music and the humid night air of July. Connie's mother kept dragging her back to the daylight by finding things for her to do or saying suddenly, "What's this about the Pettinger girl?"

And Connie would say nervously, "Oh, her. That dope." She always drew thick clear lines between herself and such girls, and her mother was simple and kindly enough to believe her. Her mother was so simple, Connie thought, that it was maybe cruel to fool her so much. Her mother went scuffling around the house in old bedroom slippers and complained over the telephone to one sister about the other, then the other called up and the two of them complained about the third one. If June's name was mentioned her mother's tone was approving, and if Connie's name was mentioned it was disapproving. This did not really mean she disliked Connie and actually Connie thought that her mother preferred her to June because she was prettier, but the two of them kept up a pretense of exasperation, a sense that they were tugging and struggling over something of little value to either of them. Sometimes, over coffee, they were almost friends, but something would come up—some vexation that was like a fly buzzing suddenly around their heads—and their faces went hard with contempt.

One Sunday Connie got up at eleven—none of them bothered with church—and washed her hair so that it could dry all day long, in the sun. Her parents and sister were going to a barbecue at an aunt's house and Connie said no, she wasn't interested, rolling her eyes, to let mother know just what she thought of it. "Stay home alone then," her mother said sharply. Connie sat out back in a lawn chair and watched them drive away, her father quiet and bald, hunched around so that he could back the car out, her mother with a look that was still angry and not at all softened through the windshield, and in the back seat poor old June all dressed up as if she didn't know what a barbecue was, with all the running yelling kids and the flies. Connie sat with her eyes closed in the sun, dreaming and dazed with the warmth about her as if this were a kind of love, the caresses of love, and her mind slipped over onto thoughts of the boy she had been with the night before and how nice he had been, how sweet it always was, not the way someone like June would suppose but sweet, gentle, the way it was in movies and promised in songs; and when she opened her eyes she hardly knew where she was, the back yard ran off into weeds and a fenceline of trees and behind it the sky was perfectly blue and still. The asbestos "ranch house" that was now three years old startled her—it looked small. She shook her head as if to get awake.

It was too hot. She went inside the house and turned on the radio to drown out the quiet. She sat on the edge of her bed, barefoot, and listened for an hour and a half to a program called XYZ Sunday Jamboree, record after record of hard, fast, shrieking songs she sang along with, interspersed by exclamations from "Bobby King": "An' look here you girls at Napoleon's—Son and Charley want you to pay real close attention to this song coming up!"

And Connie paid close attention herself, bathed in a glow of slow-pulsed joy that seemed to rise mysteriously out of the music itself and lay languidly about the airless little room, breathed in and breathed out with each gentle rise and fall of her chest.

After a while she heard a car coming up the drive. She sat up at once, startled, because it couldn't be her father so soon. The gravel kept crunching all the way in from the road—the driveway was long—and Connie ran to the window. It was a car she didn't know. It was an open jalopy, painted a bright gold that caught the sun opaquely. Her heart began to pound and her fingers snatched at her hair, checking it, and she whispered "Christ. Christ," wondering how bad she looked. The car came to a stop at the side door and the horn sounded four short taps as if this were a signal Connie knew. 15

She went into the kitchen and approached the door slowly, then hung out the screen door, her bare toes curling down off the step. There were two boys in the car and now she recognized the driver: he had shaggy, shabby black hair that looked crazy as a wig and he was grinning at her.

"I ain't late, am I?" he said.

"Who the hell do you think you are?" Connie said.

"Toldja I'd be out, didn't I?"

"I don't even know who you are." 20

She spoke sullenly, careful to show no interest or pleasure, and he spoke in a fast bright monotone. Connie looked past him to the other boy, taking her time. He had fair brown hair, with a lock that fell onto his forehead. His sideburns gave him a fierce, embarrassed look, but so far he hadn't even bothered to glance at her. Both boys wore sunglasses. The driver's glasses were metallic and mirrored everything in miniature.

"You wanta come for a ride?" he said.

Connie smirked and let her hair fall loose over one shoulder.

"Don'tcha like my car? New paint job," he said. "Hey."

"What?" 25

"You're cute."

She pretended to fidget, chasing flies away from the door.

"Don'tcha believe me, or what?" he said.

"Look, I don't even know who you are," Connie said in disgust.

"Hey, Ellie's got a radio, see. Mine's broke down." He lifted his   30
friend's arm and showed her the little transistor the boy was holding, and
now Connie began to hear the music. It was the same program that was
playing inside the house.

"Bobby King?" she said.

"I listen to him all the time. I think he's great."

"He's kind of great," Connie said reluctantly.

"Listen, that guy's *great*. He knows where the action is."

Connie blushed a little, because the glasses made it impossible for her   35
to see just what this boy was looking at. She couldn't decide if she liked
him or if he was just a jerk, and so she dawdled in the doorway and
wouldn't come down or go back inside. She said, "What's all that stuff
painted on your car?"

"Can'tcha read it?" He opened the door very carefully, as if he was
afraid it might fall off. He slid out just as carefully, planting his feet firmly
on the ground, the tiny metallic world in his glasses slowing down like
gelatin hardening and in the midst of it Connie's bright green blouse.
"This here is my name, to begin with," he said. ARNOLD FRIEND was written in tar-like black letters on the side, with a drawing of a round grinning
face that reminded Connie of a pumpkin, except it wore sunglasses. "I
wanta introduce myself, I'm Arnold Friend and that's my real name and
I'm gonna be your friend, honey, and inside the car's Ellie Oscar, he's
kinda shy." Ellie brought his transistor up to his shoulder and balanced it
there. "Now these numbers are a secret code, honey," Arnold Friend explained. He read off the numbers 33, 19, 17 and raised his eyebrows at her
to see what she thought of that, but she didn't think much of it. The left
rear fender had been smashed and around it was written, on the gleaming
gold background: DONE BY CRAZY WOMAN DRIVER. Connie had to laugh
at that. Arnold Friend was pleased at her laughter and looked up at her.
"Around the other side's a lot more—you wanta come and see them?"

"No."

"Why not?"

"Why should I?"

"Don'tcha wanta see what's on the car? Don'tcha wanta go for a   40
ride?"

"I don't know."

"Why not?"

"I got things to do."

"Like what?"

"Things."   45

He laughed as if she had said something funny. He slapped his thighs.
He was standing in a strange way, leaning back against the car as if he were

balancing himself. He wasn't tall, only an inch or so taller than she would be if she came down to him. Connie liked the way he was dressed, which was the way all of them dressed: tight faded jeans stuffed into black, scuffed boots, a belt that pulled his waist in and showed how lean he was, and a white pull-over shirt that was a little soiled and showed the hard small muscles of his arms and shoulders. He looked as if he probably did hard work, lifting and carrying things. Even his neck looked muscular. And his face was a familiar face, somehow: the jaw and chin and cheeks slightly darkened, because he hadn't shaved for a day or two, and the nose long and hawk-like, sniffing as if she were a treat he was going to gobble up and it was all a joke.

"Connie, you ain't telling the truth. This is your day set aside for a ride with me and you know it," he said, still laughing. The way he straightened and recovered from his fit of laughing showed that it had been all fake.

"How do you know what my name is?" she said suspiciously.

"It's Connie."

"Maybe and maybe not."   50

"I know my Connie," he said, wagging his finger. Now she remembered him even better, back at the restaurant, and her cheeks warmed at the thought of how she sucked in her breath just at the moment she passed him—how she must have looked to him. And he had remembered her. "Ellie and I come out here especially for you," he said. "Ellie can sit in back. How about it?"

"Where?"

"Where what?"

"Where're we going?"

He looked at her. He took off the sunglasses and she saw how pale   55
the skin around his eyes was, like holes that were not in shadow but instead in light. His eyes were like chips of broken glass that catch the light in an amiable way. He smiled. It was as if the idea of going for a ride somewhere, to some place, was a new idea to him.

"Just for a ride, Connie sweetheart."

"I never said my name was Connie," she said.

"But I know what it is. I know your name and all about you, lots of things," Arnold Friend said. He had not moved yet but stood still leaning back against the side of his jalopy. "I took a special interest in you, such a pretty girl, and found out all about you like I know your parents and sister are gone somewheres and I know where and how long they're going to be gone, and I know who you were with last night, and your best friend's name is Betty. Right?"

He spoke in a simple lilting voice, exactly as if he were reciting the words to a song. His smile assured her that everything was fine. In the car Ellie turned up the volume on his radio and did not bother to look around at them.

"Ellie can sit in the back seat," Arnold Friend said. He indicated his   60
friend with a casual jerk of his chin, as if Ellie did not count and she
could not bother with him.

"How'd you find out all that stuff?" Connie said.

"Listen: Betty Schultz and Tony Fitch and Jimmy Pettinger and Nancy
Pettinger," he said, in a chant. "Raymond Stanley and Bob Hutter—"

"Do you know all those kids?"

"I know everybody."

"Look, you're kidding. You're not from around here."   65

"Sure."

"But—how come we never saw you before?"

"Sure you saw me before," he said. He looked down at his boots, as
if he were a little offended. "You just don't remember."

"I guess I'd remember you," Connie said.

"Yeah?" He looked up at this, beaming. He was pleased. He began   70
to mark time with the music from Ellie's radio, tapping his fists lightly
together. Connie looked away from his smile to the car, which was
painted so bright it almost hurt her eyes to look at it. She looked at that
name, ARNOLD FRIEND. And up at the front fender was an expression
that was familiar—MAN THE FLYING SAUCERS. It was an expression kids
had used the year before, but didn't use this year. She looked at it for a
while as if the words meant something to her that she did not yet know.

"What're you thinking about? Huh?" Arnold Friend demanded.
"Not worried about your hair blowing around in the car, are you?"

"No."

"Think I maybe can't drive good?"

"How do I know?"

"You're a hard girl to handle. How come?" he said. "Don't you   75
know I'm your friend? Didn't you see me put my sign in the air when you
walked by?"

"What sign?"

"My sign." And he drew an X in the air, leaning out toward her.
They were maybe ten feet apart. After his hand fell back to his side the X
was still in the air, almost visible. Connie let the screen door close and
stood perfectly still inside it, listening to the music from her radio and the
boy's blend together. She stared at Arnold Friend. He stood there so
stiffly relaxed, pretending to be relaxed, with one hand idly on the door
handle as if he were keeping himself up that way and had no intention of
ever moving again. She recognized most things about him, the tight jeans
that showed his thighs and buttocks and the greasy leather boots and the
tight shirt, and even that slippery friendly smile of his, that sleepy dreamy
smile that all the boys used to get across ideas they didn't want to put
into words. She recognized all this and also the singsong way he talked,
slightly mocking, kidding, but serious and a little melancholy, and she
recognized the way he tapped one fist against the other in homage to the
perpetual music behind him. But all these things did not come together.

She said suddenly, "Hey, how old are you?"

His smile faded. She could see then that he wasn't a kid, he was much older—thirty, maybe more. At this knowledge her heart began to pound faster.

"That's a crazy thing to ask. Can'tcha see I'm your own age?"   80

"Like hell you are."

"Or maybe a coupla years older, I'm eighteen."

"Eighteen?" she said doubtfully.

He grinned to reassure her and lines appeared at the corners of his mouth. His teeth were big and white. He grinned so broadly his eyes became slits and she saw how thick the lashes were, thick and black as if painted with a black tar-like material. Then he seemed to become embarrassed, abruptly, and looked over his shoulder at Ellie. "*Him*, he's crazy," he said. "Ain't he a riot, he's a nut, a real character." Ellie was still listening to the music. His sunglasses told nothing about what he was thinking. He wore a bright orange shirt unbuttoned halfway to show his chest, which was a pale, bluish chest and not muscular like Arnold Friend's. His shirt collar was turned up all around and the very tips of the collar pointed out past his chin as if they were protecting him. He was pressing the transistor radio up against his ear and sat there in a kind of daze, right in the sun.

"He's kinda strange," Connie said.   85

"Hey, she says you're kinda strange! Kinda strange!" Arnold Friend cried. He pounded on the car to get Ellie's attention. Ellie turned for the first time and Connie saw with shock that he wasn't a kid either—he had a fair, hairless face, cheeks reddened slightly as if the veins grew too close to the surface of his skin, the face of a forty-year-old baby. Connie felt a wave of dizziness rise in her at this sight and she stared at him as if waiting for something to change the shock of the moment, make it all right again. Ellie's lips kept shaping words, mumbling along with the words blasting his ear.

"Maybe you two better go away," Connie said faintly.

"What? How come?" Arnold Friend cried. "We come out here to take you for a ride. It's Sunday." He had the voice of the man on the radio now. It was the same voice, Connie thought. "Don'tcha know it's Sunday all day and honey, no matter who you were with last night today you're with Arnold Friend and don't you forget it!—Maybe you better step out here," he said, and this last was in a different voice. It was a little flatter, as if the heat was finally getting to him.

"No. I got things to do."

"Hey."   90

"You two better leave."

"We ain't leaving until you come with us."

"Like hell I am—"

"Connie, don't fool around with me. I mean—I mean, don't fool *around*," he said, shaking his head. He laughed incredulously. He placed his sunglasses on top of his head, carefully, as if he were indeed wearing a wig, and brought the stems down behind his ears. Connie stared at him, another wave of dizziness and fear rising in her so that for a moment he wasn't even in focus but was just a blur, standing there against his gold car, and she had the idea that he had driven up the driveway all right but had come from nowhere before that and belonged nowhere and that everything about him and even the music that was so familiar to her was only half real.

"If my father comes and sees you—"   95

"He ain't coming. He's at a barbecue."

"How do you know that?"

"Aunt Tillie's. Right now they're—uh—they're drinking. Sitting around," he said vaguely, squinting as if he were staring all the way to town and over to Aunt Tillie's back yard. Then the vision seemed to clear and he nodded energetically. "Yeah. Sitting around. There's your sister in a blue dress, huh? And high heels, the poor sad bitch—nothing like you, sweetheart! And your mother's helping some fat woman with the corn, they're cleaning the corn—husking the corn—"

"What fat woman?" Connie cried.

"How do I know what fat woman. I don't know every goddamn fat   100
woman in the world!" Arnold Friend laughed.

"Oh, that's Mrs. Hornby. . . . Who invited her?" Connie said. She felt a little light-headed. Her breath was coming quickly.

"She's too fat. I don't like them fat. I like them the way you are, honey," he said, smiling sleepily at her. They stared at each other for a while, through the screen door. He said softly, "Now what you're going to do is this: you're going to come out that door. You're going to sit up front with me and Ellie's going to sit in the back, the hell with Ellie, right? This isn't Ellie's date. You're my date. I'm your lover, honey."

"What? You're crazy—"

"Yes, I'm your lover. You don't know what that is but you will," he said. "I know that too. I know all about you. But look: it's real nice and you couldn't ask for nobody better than me, or more polite. I always keep my word. I'll tell you how it is, I'm always nice at first, the first time. I'll hold you so tight you won't think you have to try to get away or pretend anything because you'll know you can't. And I'll come inside you where it's all secret and you'll give in to me and you'll love me—"

"Shut up! You're crazy!" Connie said. She backed away from the door.   105
She put her hands against her ears as if she'd heard something terrible, some-thing not meant for her. "People don't talk like that, you're crazy," she muttered. Her heart was almost too big now for her chest and its pumping made sweat break out all over her. She looked out to see Arnold Friend pause and then take a step toward the porch lurching. He almost fell. But, like a clever drunken man, he managed to catch his balance. He wobbled in his high boots and grabbed hold of one of the porch posts.

"Honey?" he said. "You still listening?"

"Get the hell out of here!"

"Be nice, honey. Listen."

"I'm going to call the police—"

He wobbled again and out of the side of his mouth came a fast spat   110
curse, an aside not meant for her to hear. But even this "Christ!" sounded
forced. Then he began to smile again. She watched this smile come, awkward as if he were smiling from inside a mask. His whole face was a mask,
she thought wildly, tanned down onto his throat but then running out as if
he had plastered make-up on his face but had forgotten about his throat.

"Honey—? Listen, here's how it is. I always tell the truth and I
promise you this: I ain't coming in that house after you."

"You better not! I'm going to call the police if you—if you don't—"

"Honey," he said, talking right through her voice, "honey, I'm not
coming in there but you are coming out here. You know why?"

She was panting. The kitchen looked like a place she had never seen
before, some room she had run inside but which wasn't good enough,
wasn't going to help her. The kitchen window had never had a curtain,
after three years, and there were dishes in the sink for her to do—probably—and if you ran your hand across the table you'd probably feel something sticky there.

"You listening, honey? Hey?"   115

" —going to call the police—"

"Soon as you touch the phone I don't need to keep my promise and
can come inside. You won't want that."

She rushed forward and tried to lock the door. Her fingers were shaking. "But why lock it," Arnold Friend said gently, talking right into her
face. "It's just a screen door. It's just nothing." One of his boots was at a
strange angle, as if his foot wasn't in it. It pointed out to the left, bent at
the ankle. "I mean, anybody can break through a screen door and glass
and wood and iron or anything else if he needs to, anybody at all and specially Arnold Friend. If the place got lit up with a fire, honey, you'd come
runnin' out into my arms, right into my arms an' safe at home—like you
knew I was your lover and'd stopped fooling around, I don't mind a nice
shy girl but I don't like no fooling around." Part of those words were spoken with a slight rhythmic lilt, and Connie somehow recognized them—
the echo of a song from last year, about a girl rushing into her boy
friend's arms and coming home again—

Connie stood barefoot on the linoleum floor, staring at him. "What
do you want?" she whispered.

"I want you," he said.   120

"What?"

"Seen you that night and thought, that's the one, yes sir. I never
needed to look any more."

"But my father's coming back. He's coming to get me. I had to wash
my hair first—" She spoke in a dry, rapid voice, hardly raising it for him
to hear.

"No, your daddy is not coming and yes, you had to wash your hair and you washed it for me. It's nice and shining and all for me. I thank you, sweetheart," he said, with a mock bow, but again he almost lost his balance. He had to bend and adjust his boots. Evidently his feet did not go all the way down; the boots must have been stuffed with something so that he would seem taller. Connie stared out at him and behind him at Ellie in the car, who seemed to be looking off toward Connie's right, into nothing. Then Ellie said, pulling the words out of the air one after another as if he were just discovering them, "You want me to pull out the phone?"

"Shut your mouth and keep it shut," Arnold Friend said, his face red 125 from bending over or maybe from embarrassment because Connie had seen his boots. "This ain't none of your business."

"What—what are you doing? What do you want?" Connie said. "If I call the police they'll get you, they'll arrest you—"

"Promise was not to come in unless you touch that phone, and I'll keep that promise," he said. He resumed his erect position and tried to force his shoulders back. He sounded like a hero in a movie, declaring something important. He spoke too loudly and it was as if he were speaking to someone behind Connie. "I ain't made plans for coming in that house where I don't belong but just for you to come out to me, the way you should. Don't you know who I am?"

"You're crazy," she whispered. She backed away from the door but did not want to go into another part of the house, as if this would give him permission to come through the door. "What do you . . . You're crazy, you. . . ."

"Huh? What're you saying, honey?"

Her eyes darted everywhere in the kitchen. She could not remember 130 what it was, this room.

"This is how it is, honey: you come out and we'll drive away, have a nice ride. But if you don't come out we're gonna wait till your people come home and then they're all going to get it."

"You want that telephone pulled out?" Ellie said. He held the radio away from his ear and grimaced, as if without the radio the air was too much for him.

"I toldja shut up, Ellie," Arnold Friend said, "you're deaf, get a hearing aid, right? Fix yourself up. This little girl's no trouble and's gonna be nice to me, so Ellie keep to yourself, this ain't your date—right? Don't hem in on me, don't hog, don't crush, don't bird dog, don't trail me," he said in a rapid, meaningless voice, as if he were running through all the expressions he'd learned but was no longer sure which one of them was in style, then rushing on to new ones, making them up with his eyes closed. "Don't crawl under my fence, don't squeeze in my chipmunk hole, don't sniff my glue, suck my pop-sicle, keep your own greasy fingers on yourself!" He shaded his eyes and peered in at Connie, who was backed against the kitchen table. "Don't mind him, honey, he's just a creep. He's a dope. Right? I'm the boy for you and like I said, you come out here nice like a lady and give me your hand, and nobody else gets hurt, I mean, your nice old bald-headed daddy and your mummy and your sister in her high heels. Because listen: why bring them in this?"

"Leave me alone," Connie whispered.

"Hey, you know that old woman down the road, the one with the 135 chickens and stuff—you know her?"

"She's dead!"

"Dead? What? You know her?" Arnold Friend said.

"She's dead—"

"Don't you like her?"

"She's dead—she's—she isn't here any more—" 140

"But don't you like her, I mean, you got something against her? Some grudge or something?" Then his voice dipped as if he were conscious of rudeness. He touched the sunglasses on top of his head as if to make sure they were still there. "Now you be a good girl."

"What are you going to do?"

"Just two things, or maybe three," Arnold Friend said. "But I promise it won't last long and you'll like me that way you get to like people you're close to. You will. It's all over for you here, so come on out. You don't want your people in any trouble, do you?"

She turned and bumped against a chair or something, hurting her leg, but she ran into the back room and picked up the telephone. Something roared in her ear, a tiny roaring, and she was so sick with fear that she could do nothing but listen to it—the telephone was clammy and very heavy and her fingers groped down to the dial but were too weak to touch it. She began to scream into the phone, into the roaring. She cried out, she cried for her mother, she felt her breath start jerking back and forth in her lungs as if it were something Arnold Friend was stabbing her with again and again with no tenderness. A noisy sorrowful wailing rose all about her and she was locked inside it the way she was locked inside this house.

After a while she could hear again. She was sitting on the floor, with 145 her wet back against the wall.

Arnold Friend was saying from the door, "That's a good girl. Put the phone back."

She kicked the phone away from her.

"No, honey. Pick it up. Put it back right."

She picked it up and put it back. The dial tone stopped.

"That's a good girl. Now you come outside." 150

She was hollow with what had been fear but what was now just an emptiness. All that screaming had blasted it out of her. She sat, one leg cramped under her, and deep inside her brain was something like a pinpoint of light that kept going and would not let her relax. She thought, I'm not going to see my mother again. She thought, I'm not going to sleep in my bed again. Her bright green blouse was all wet.

Arnold Friend said, in a gentle-loud voice that was like a stage voice, "The place where you came from ain't there any more, and where you had in mind to go is cancelled out. This place you are now — inside your daddy's house — is nothing but a cardboard box I can knock down any time. You know that and always did know it. You hear me?"

She thought, I have got to think. I have got to know what to do.

"We'll go out to a nice field, out in the country here where it smells so nice and it's sunny," Arnold Friend said. "I'll have my arms tight around you so you won't need to try to get away and I'll show you what love is like, what it does. The hell with this house! It looks solid all right," he said. He ran a fingernail down the screen and the noise did not make Connie shiver, as it would have the day before. "Now put your hand on your heart, honey. Feel that? That feels solid too but we know better. Be nice to me, be sweet like you can because what else is there for a girl like you but to be sweet and pretty and give in? — and get away before her people get back?"

She felt her pounding heart. Her hand seemed to enclose it. She   155
thought for the first time in her life that it was nothing that was hers, that belonged to her, but just a pounding, living thing inside this body that wasn't really hers either.

"You don't want them to get hurt," Arnold Friend went on. "Now get up, honey. Get up all by yourself."

She stood.

"Now turn this way. That's right. Come over to me — Ellie, put that away, didn't I tell you? You dope. You miserable creepy dope," Arnold Friend said. His words were not angry but only part of an incantation. The incantation was kindly. "Now come out through the kitchen to me honey and let's see a smile, try it, you're a brave sweet little girl and now they're eating corn and hotdogs cooked to bursting over an outdoor fire, and they don't know one thing about you and never did and honey you're better than them because not a one of them would have done this for you."

Connie felt the linoleum under her feet; it was cool. She brushed her hair back out of her eyes. Arnold Friend let go of the post tentatively and opened his arms for her, his elbows pointing in toward each other and his wrists limp, to show that this was an embarrassed embrace and a little mocking, he didn't want to make her self-conscious.

She put out her hand against the screen. She watched herself push the   160
door slowly open as if she were back safe somewhere in the other doorway, watching this body and this head of long hair moving out into the sunlight where Arnold Friend waited.

"My sweet little blue-eyed girl," he said in a half-sung sigh that had nothing to do with her brown eyes but was taken up just the same by the vast sunlit reaches of the land behind him and on all sides of him — so much land that Connie had never seen before and did not recognize except to know that she was going to it.

The Reader's Presence

1. Oates describes Connie as having "two sides . . . , one for home and one for anywhere that was not home" (paragraph 5). What are the differences between the two sides? In what ways does Arnold Friend also seem to have two sides? How are these characters alike? How are they different?

2. Compare the ending of this story to the conclusion of Raymond Carver's "The Bath" (page 919). What do you think happens after each story ends? Why do you think Carver and Oates made the decision to end the story without discussing how the characters' situations will resolve? Does the ending increase or decrease each story's emotional tension? Why?

3. Read Oates's essay that follows. In what specific ways does reading this essay help you to understand better—and appreciate more—Oates's achievements as a writer of fiction? What specific aspects of the essay help you to understand Connie and, especially, her relationship with adults? What does Oates admire about the film *Smooth Talk*? What reservations does she express about the film? Characterize Oates's response to the contrast between the end of the story and of the film. Which does she prefer? Explain why.

THE WRITER AT WORK

Joyce Carol Oates on Smooth Talk: *Short Story into Film*

Joyce Carol Oates's "Where Are You Going, Where Have You Been?" has been described as "a study in the peril that lurks beneath the surface of everyday life." In 1985, Joyce Chopra directed a film, Smooth Talk, with a screenplay by Tom Cole based on Oates's story. The film continues after the story ends, giving viewers an unexpectedly optimistic glimpse of Connie's fate. Smooth Talk won the Grand Jury Prize at the Sundance Film Festival in 1986. The following article appeared in the New York Times in 1986. Does Oates's original conception of the story fit with your expectations of what might happen to Connie? Does considering a happy ending—or at least an ending without tragedy—make a difference in your view of the story as a whole?

Some years ago in the American Southwest there surfaced a tabloid psychopath known as "The Pied Piper of Tucson." I have forgotten his name, but his specialty was the seduction and occasional murder of teenaged girls. He may or may not have had actual accomplices, but his bizarre activities were known among a circle of teenagers in the Tucson area; for some reason they kept his secret, deliberately did not inform parents or police. It was this fact, not the fact of the mass murderer him-self, that struck me at the time. And this was a pre-Manson time, early or mid-1960s.

The Pied Piper mimicked teenagers in their talk, dress, and behavior, but he was not a teenager—he was a man in his early thirties. Rather short, he stuffed rags in his leather boots to give himself height. (And sometimes walked unsteadily as a consequence: did none among his ad-miring constituency notice?) He charmed his victims as charismatic psy-chopaths have always charmed their victims, to the bewilderment of others who fancy themselves free of all lunatic attractions. The Pied Piper of Tuc-son: a trashy dream, a tabloid archetype, sheer artifice, comedy, cartoon—surrounded, however improbably, and finally tragically by real people. You think that, if you look twice, he won't be there. But there he is.

I don't remember any longer where I first read about this Pied Piper—very likely in *Life* Magazine. I do recall deliberately not reading the full article because I didn't want to be distracted by too much detail. It was not after all the mass murderer himself who intrigued me, but the disturb-ing fact that a number of teenagers—from "good" families—aided and abetted his crimes. This is the sort of thing authorities and responsible cit-izens invariably call "inexplicable" because they can't find explanations for it. *They* would not have fallen under this maniac's spell, after all.

An early draft of my short story "Where Are You Going, Where Have You Been?"—from which the film *Smooth Talk* was adapted by Joyce Chopra and Tom Cole—had the rather too explicit title "Death and the Maiden." It was cast in a mode of fiction to which I am still partial—in-deed, every third or fourth story of mine is probably in this mode—"real-istic allegory," it might be called. It is Hawthornean,[1] romantic, shading into parable. Like the medieval German engraving from which my title was taken, the story was minutely detailed yet clearly an allegory of the fatal attractions of death (or the devil). An innocent young girl is seduced by way of her own vanity; she mistakes death for erotic romance of a par-ticularly American/trashy sort.

In subsequent drafts the story changed its tone, its focus, its language, its title. It became "Where Are You Going, Where Have You Been?" Written at a time when the author was intrigued by the music of Bob Dylan, particularly the hauntingly elegiac song "It's All Over Now, Baby Blue," it was dedicated to Bob Dylan. The charismatic mass murderer drops into the background and his innocent victim, a fifteen-year-old, moves into the foreground. She becomes the true protagonist of the tale, courting and being courted by her fate, a self-styled 1950s pop figure, alternately ab-surd and winning. There is no suggestion in the published story that "Arnold Friend" has seduced and murdered other young girls, or even that he necessarily intends to murder Connie. Is his interest "merely" sex-

5

---

[1] *"Hawthornean":* Similar in style to that of Nathaniel Hawthorne (1804–1864), the acclaimed American novelist and short story writer.—EDS.

ual? (Nor is there anything about the complicity of other teenagers. I saved that yet more provocative note for a current story, "Testimony.") Connie is shallow, vain, silly, hopeful, doomed—but capable nonetheless of an unexpected gesture of heroism at the story's end. Her smooth-talking seducer, who cannot lie, promises her that her family will be unharmed if she gives herself to him; and so she does. The story ends abruptly at the point of her "crossing over." We don't know the nature of her sacrifice, only that she is generous enough to make it.

In adapting a narrative so spare and thematically foreshortened as "Where Are You Going, Where Have You Been?" film director Joyce Chopra and screenwriter Tom Cole were required to do a good deal of filling in, expanding, inventing. Connie's story becomes lavishly, and lovingly, textured; she is not an allegorical figure so much as a "typical" teen-aged girl (if Laura Dern, spectacularly good-looking, can be so defined). Joyce Chopra, who has done documentary films on contemporary teenage culture and, yet more authoritatively, has an adolescent daughter of her own, creates in *Smooth Talk* a vivid and absolutely believable world for Connie to inhabit. Or worlds: as in the original story there is Connie-at-home, and there is Connie-with-her-friends. Two fifteen-year-old girls, two finely honed styles, two voices, sometimes but not often overlapping. It is one of the marvelous visual features of the film that we *see* Connie and her friends transform themselves, once they are safely free of parental observation. The girls claim their true identities in the neighborhood shopping mall. What freedom, what joy!

Smooth Talk is, in a way, as much Connie's mother's story as it is Connie's; its center of gravity, its emotional nexus, is frequently with the mother—warmly and convincingly played by Mary Kay Place. (Though the mother's sexual jealousy of her daughter is slighted in the film.) Connie's ambiguous relationship with her affable, somewhat mysterious father (well played by Levon Helm) is an excellent touch: I had thought, subsequent to the story's publication, that I should have built up the father, suggesting, as subtly as I could, an attraction there paralleling the attraction Connie feels for her seducer, Arnold Friend. And Arnold Friend himself— "A. Friend" as he says—is played with appropriately overdone sexual swagger by Treat Williams, who is perfect for the part; and just the right age. We see that Arnold Friend isn't a teenager even as Connie, mesmerized by his presumed charm, does not seem to *see* him at all. What is so difficult to accomplish in prose—nudging the reader to look over the protagonist's shoulder, so to speak—is accomplished with enviable ease in film.

Treat Williams as Arnold Friend is supreme in his very awfulness, as, surely, the original Pied Piper of Tucson must have been. (Though no one involved in the film knew about the original source.) Mr. Williams flawlessly impersonates Arnold Friend as Arnold Friend impersonates—is it James Dean? James Dean regarding himself in mirrors, doing James Dean impersonations? That Connie's fate is so trashy is in fact her fate.

What is outstanding in Joyce Chopra's *Smooth Talk* is its visual freshness, its sense of motion and life; the attentive intelligence the director has brought to the semi-secret world of the American adolescent—shopping mall flirtations, drive-in restaurant romances, highway hitchhiking, the fascination of rock music played very, very loud. (James Taylor's music for the film is wonderfully appropriate. We hear it as Connie hears it; it is the music of her spiritual being.) Also outstanding, as I have indicated, and numerous critics have noted, are the acting performances. Laura Dern is so dazzlingly right as "my" Connie that I may come to think I modeled the fictitious girl on her, in the way that writers frequently delude themselves about motions of causality.

My difficulties with *Smooth Talk* have primarily to do with my chronic hesitation—about seeing/hearing work of mine abstracted from its contexture of language. All writers know that language is their subject; quirky word choices, patterns of rhythm, enigmatic pauses, punctuation marks. Where the quick scanner sees "quick" writing, the writer conceals nine tenths of the iceberg. Of course we all have "real" subjects, and we will fight to the death to defend those subjects, but beneath the tale-telling it is the tale-telling that grips us so very fiercely. The writer works in a single dimension, the director works in three. I assume they are professionals to their fingertips; authorities in their medium as I am an authority (if I am) in mine. I would fiercely defend the placement of a semicolon in one of my novels but I would probably have deferred in the end to Joyce Chopra's decision to reverse the story's conclusion, turn it upside down, in a sense, so that the film ends not with death, not with a sleepwalker's crossing over to her fate, but upon a scene of reconciliation, rejuvenation.

A girl's loss of virginity, bittersweet but not necessarily tragic. Not today. A girl's coming-of-age that involves her succumbing to, but then rejecting, the "trashy dreams" of her pop teenage culture. "Where Are You Going, Where Have You Been?" defines itself as allegorical in its conclusion: Death and Death's chariot (a funky souped-up convertible) have come for the Maiden. Awakening is, in the story's final lines, moving out into the sunlight where Arnold Friend waits:

> "My sweet little blue-eyed girl," he said in a half-sung sigh that had nothing to do with [Connie's] brown eyes but was taken up just the same by the vast sunlit reaches of the land behind him and on all sides of him—so much land that Connie had never seen before and did not recognize except to know that she was going to it.

—a conclusion impossible to transfigure into film.

Flannery O'Connor
A Good Man Is Hard to Find

Flannery O'Connor (1925–1964) was born in Savannah, Georgia, the only child of devout Catholic parents. At the age of thirteen, O'Connor moved with her parents to her mother's ancestral home in Milledgeville, Georgia, after her father became terminally ill with lupus. In 1945 she received a BA degree from Georgia State College for Women, where she contributed regularly to the school's literary magazine. While earning an MFA from the Writers' Workshop at the University of Iowa, O'Connor published her first short story, "The Geranium," in 1946. After graduation O'Connor was a resident at Yaddo, an artists' retreat in New York, and lived in New York City and in Connecticut until 1951, when she was diagnosed with lupus and returned to Georgia for treatment. She and her mother moved a short distance from Milledgeville to their family farm, Andalusia, where O'Connor lived until her death at the age of thirty-nine, raising peafowl, painting, and writing daily. During her short yet distinguished life, O'Connor published two novels, Wise Blood *(1952) and* The Violent Bear It Away *(1960), and a collection of short stories,* A Good Man Is Hard to Find *(1955), the title story of which appears here. A book of essays,* Mystery and Manners *(1969); two other short story collections,* Everything That Rises Must Converge *(1965) and* The Complete Stories of Flannery O'Connor *(1971), winner of a National Book Award; and a collection of letters,* The Habit of Being *(1979), were published posthumously.*

The grandmother didn't want to go to Florida. She wanted to visit some of her connections in east Tennessee and she was seizing at every chance to change Bailey's mind. Bailey was the son she lived with, her only boy. He was sitting on the edge of his chair at the table, bent over the orange sports section of the *Journal.* "Now look here, Bailey," she said, "see here, read this," and she stood with one hand on her thin hip and the other rattling the newspaper at his bald head. "Here this fellow that calls himself The Misfit is aloose from the Federal Pen and headed toward Florida and you read here what it says he did to these people. Just you read it. I wouldn't take my children in any direction with a criminal like that aloose in it. I couldn't answer to my conscience if I did."

Bailey didn't look up from his reading so she wheeled around then and faced the children's mother, a young woman in slacks, whose face was as broad and innocent as a cabbage and was tied around with a green head-kerchief that had two points on the top like a rabbit's ears. She was sitting on the sofa, feeding the baby his apricots out of a jar. "The children have been to Florida before," the old lady said. "You all ought to take them somewhere else for a change so they would see different parts of the world and be broad. They never have been to east Tennessee."

The children's mother didn't seem to hear her but the eight-year-old boy, John Wesley, a stocky child with glasses, said, "If you don't want to go to Florida, why dontcha stay at home?" He and the little girl, June Star, were reading the funny papers on the floor.

"She wouldn't stay at home to be queen for a day," June Star said without raising her yellow head.

"Yes and what would you do if this fellow, The Misfit, caught you?" the grandmother asked.   5

"I'd smack his face," John Wesley said.

"She wouldn't stay at home for a million bucks," June Star said. "Afraid she'd miss something. She has to go everywhere we go."

"All right, Miss," the grandmother said. "Just remember that the next time you want me to curl your hair."

June Star said her hair was naturally curly.

The next morning the grandmother was the first one in the car, ready   10
to go. She had her big black valise that looked like the head of a hippopotamus in one corner, and underneath it she was hiding a basket with Pitty Sing, the cat, in it. She didn't intend for the cat to be left alone in the house for three days because he would miss her too much and she was afraid he might brush against one of the gas burners and accidentally asphyxiate himself. Her son, Bailey, didn't like to arrive at a motel with a cat.

She sat in the middle of the back seat with John Wesley and June Star on either side of her. Bailey and the children's mother and the baby sat in front and they left Atlanta at eight forty-five with the mileage on the car at 55890. The grandmother wrote this down because she thought it would be interesting to say how many miles they had been when they got back. It took them twenty minutes to reach the outskirts of the city.

The old lady settled herself comfortably, removing her white cotton gloves and putting them up with her purse on the shelf in front of the back window. The children's mother still had on slacks and still had her head tied up in a green kerchief, but the grandmother had on a navy blue straw sailor hat with a bunch of white violets on the brim and a navy blue dress with a small white dot in the print. Her collars and cuffs were white organdy trimmed with lace and at her neckline she had pinned a purple spray of cloth violets containing a sachet. In case of an accident, anyone seeing her dead on the highway would know at once that she was a lady.

She said she thought it was going to be a good day for driving, neither too hot nor too cold, and she cautioned Bailey that the speed limit was fifty-five miles an hour and that the patrolmen hid themselves behind billboards and small clumps of trees and sped out after you before you had a chance to slow down. She pointed out interesting details of the scenery: Stone Mountain; the blue granite that in some places came up to both sides of the highway; the brilliant red clay banks slightly streaked with purple; and the various crops that made rows of green lace-work on the ground. The trees were full of silver-white sunlight and the meanest of them sparkled. The children were reading comic magazines and their mother had gone back to sleep.

"Let's go through Georgia fast so we won't have to look at it much," John Wesley said.

"If I were a little boy," said the grandmother, "I wouldn't talk about   15
my native state that way. Tennessee has the mountains and Georgia has the hills."

"Tennessee is just a hillbilly dumping ground," John Wesley said, "and Georgia is a lousy state too."

"You said it," June Star said.

"In my time," said the grandmother, folding her thin veined fingers, "children were more respectful of their native states and their parents and everything else. People did right then. Oh look at the cute little pickaninny!" she said and pointed to a Negro child standing in the door of a shack. "Wouldn't that make a picture, now?" she asked and they all turned and looked at the little Negro out of the back window. He waved.

"He didn't have any britches on," June Star said.

"He probably didn't have any," the grandmother explained. "Little   20
niggers in the country don't have things like we do. If I could paint, I'd paint that picture," she said.

The children exchanged comic books.

The grandmother offered to hold the baby and the children's mother passed him over the front seat to her. She set him on her knee and bounced him and told him about the things they were passing. She rolled her eyes and screwed up her mouth and stuck her leathery thin face into his smooth bland one. Occasionally he gave her a faraway smile. They passed a large cotton field with five or six graves fenced in the middle of it, like a small island. "Look at the graveyard!" the grandmother said, pointing it out. "That was the old family burying ground. That belonged to the plantation."

"Where's the plantation?" John Wesley asked.

"Gone With the Wind," said the grandmother. "Ha. Ha."

When the children finished all the comic books they had brought,   25
they opened the lunch and ate it. The grandmother ate a peanut butter sandwich and an olive and would not let the children throw the box and the paper napkins out the window. When there was nothing else to do they played a game by choosing a cloud and making the other two guess what shape it suggested. John Wesley took one the shape of a cow and June Star guessed a cow and John Wesley said, no, an automobile, and June Star said he didn't play fair, and they began to slap each other over the grandmother.

The grandmother said she would tell them a story if they would keep quiet. When she told a story, she rolled her eyes and waved her head and was very dramatic. She said once when she was a maiden lady she had been courted by a Mr. Edgar Atkins Teagarden from Jasper, Georgia. She said he was a very good-looking man and a gentleman and that he brought her a watermelon every Saturday afternoon with his initials cut in it, E. A. T. Well, one Saturday, she said, Mr. Teagarden brought the watermelon and there was nobody at home and he left it on the front porch and returned in his buggy to Jasper, but she never got the watermelon, she said, because a nigger boy ate it when he saw the initials, E. A. T.! This story tickled John Wesley's funny bone and he giggled and giggled but June Star didn't think it was any good. She said she wouldn't marry a man that just brought her a watermelon on Saturday. The grandmother said she would have done well to marry Mr. Teagarden because he was a gentleman and had bought Coca-Cola stock when it first came out and that he had died only a few years ago, a very wealthy man.

They stopped at The Tower for barbecued sandwiches. The Tower was a part stucco and part wood filling station and dance hall set in a clearing outside of Timothy. A fat man named Red Sammy Butts ran it and there were signs stuck here and there on the building and for miles up and down the highway saying, TRY RED SAMMY'S FAMOUS BARBECUE. NONE LIKE FAMOUS RED SAMMY'S! RED SAM! THE FAT BOY WITH THE HAPPY LAUGH! A VETERAN! RED SAMMY'S YOUR MAN!

Red Sammy was lying on the bare ground outside The Tower with his head under a truck while a gray monkey about a foot high, chained to a small chinaberry tree, chattered nearby. The monkey sprang back into the tree and got on the highest limb as soon as he saw the children jump out of the car and run toward him.

Inside, The Tower was a long dark room with a counter at one end and tables at the other and dancing space in the middle. They all sat down at a board table next to the nickelodeon and Red Sam's wife, a tall burnt-brown woman with hair and eyes lighter than her skin, came and took their order. The children's mother put a dime in the machine and played "The Tennessee Waltz," and the grandmother said that tune always made her want to dance. She asked Bailey if he would like to dance but he only glared at her. He didn't have a naturally sunny disposition like she did and trips made him nervous. The grandmother's brown eyes were very bright. She swayed her head from side to side and pretended she was dancing in her chair. June Star said play something she could tap to so the children's mother put in another dime and played a fast number and June Star stepped out onto the dance floor and did her tap routine.

"Ain't she cute?" Red Sam's wife said, leaning over the counter. 30 "Would you like to come be my little girl?"

"No I certainly wouldn't," June Star said. "I wouldn't live in a broken-down place like this for a million bucks!" and she ran back to the table.

"Ain't she cute?" the woman repeated, stretching her mouth politely.

"Aren't you ashamed?" hissed the grandmother.

Red Sam came in and told his wife to quit lounging on the counter and hurry up with these people's order. His khaki trousers reached just to his hip bones and his stomach hung over them like a sack of meal swaying under his shirt. He came over and sat down at a table nearby and let out a combination sigh and yodel. "You can't win," he said. "You can't win," and he wiped his sweating red face off with a gray handkerchief. "These days you don't know who to trust," he said. "Ain't that the truth?"

"People are certainly not nice like they used to be," said the grand-   35
mother.

"Two fellers come in here last week," Red Sammy said, "driving a Chrysler. It was an old beat-up car, but it was a good one and these boys looked all right to me. Said they worked at the mill and you know I let them fellers charge the gas they bought? Now why did I do that?"

"Because you're a good man!" the grandmother said at once.

"Yes'm, I suppose so," Red Sam said as if he were struck with this answer.

His wife brought the orders, carrying the five plates all at once without a tray, two in each hand and one balanced on her arm. "It isn't a soul in this green world of God's that you can trust," she said. "And I don't count nobody out of that, not nobody," she repeated, looking at Red Sammy.

"Did you read about that criminal, The Misfit, that's escaped?"   40
asked the grandmother.

"I wouldn't be a bit surprised if he didn't attact this place right here," said the woman. "If he hears about it being here, I wouldn't be none surprised to see him. If he hears it's two cent in the cash register, I wouldn't be at all surprised if he . . ."

"That'll do," Red Sam said. "Go bring these people their Co'-Colas," and the woman went off to get the rest of the order.

"A good man is hard to find," Red Sammy said. "Everything is getting terrible. I remember the day you could go off and leave your screen door unlatched. Not no more."

He and the grandmother discussed better times. The old lady said that in her opinion Europe was entirely to blame for the way things were now. She said the way Europe acted you would think we were made of money and Red Sam said it was no use talking about it, she was exactly right. The children ran outside into the white sunlight and looked at the monkey in the lacy chinaberry tree. He was busy catching fleas on himself and biting each one carefully between his teeth as if it were a delicacy.

They drove off again into the hot afternoon. The grandmother took   45
cat naps and woke up every few minutes with her own snoring. Outside of Toombsboro she woke up and recalled an old plantation that she had visited in this neighborhood once when she was a young lady. She said the house had six white columns across the front and that there was an avenue of oaks leading up to it and two little wooden trellis arbors on either side in front where you sat down with your suitor after a stroll in the garden. She recalled exactly which road to turn off to get to it. She knew that Bailey would not be willing to lose any time looking at an old house, but the more she talked about it, the more she wanted to see it once again and find out if the little twin arbors were still standing. "There was a

secret panel in this house," she said craftily, not telling the truth but wishing that she were, "and the story went that all the family silver was hidden in it when Sherman[1] came through but it was never found . . ."

"Hey!" John Wesley said. "Let's go see it! We'll find it! We'll poke all the woodwork and find it! Who lives there? Where do you turn off at? Hey Pop, can't we turn off there?"

"We never have seen a house with a secret panel!" June Star shrieked. "Let's go to the house with the secret panel! Hey Pop, can't we go see the house with the secret panel!"

"It's not far from here, I know," the grandmother said. "It wouldn't take over twenty minutes."

Bailey was looking straight ahead. His jaw was as rigid as a horseshoe. "No," he said.

The children began to yell and scream that they wanted to see the house with the secret panel. John Wesley kicked the back of the front seat and June Star hung over her mother's shoulder and whined desperately into her ear that they never had any fun even on their vacation, that they could never do what THEY wanted to do. The baby began to scream and John Wesley kicked the back of the seat so hard that his father could feel the blows in his kidney. 50

"All right!" he shouted and drew the car to a stop at the side of the road. "Will you all shut up? Will you all just shut up for one second? If you don't shut up, we won't go anywhere."

"It would be very educational for them," the grandmother murmured.

"All right," Bailey said, "but get this: this is the only time we're going to stop for anything like this. This is the one and only time."

"The dirt road that you have to turn down is about a mile back," the grandmother directed. "I marked it when we passed."

"A dirt road," Bailey groaned. 55

After they had turned around and were headed toward the dirt road, the grandmother recalled other points about the house, the beautiful glass over the front doorway and the candle-lamp in the hall. John Wesley said that the secret panel was probably in the fireplace.

"You can't go inside this house," Bailey said. "You don't know who lives there."

"While you all talk to the people in front, I'll run around behind and get in a window," John Wesley suggested.

"We'll all stay in the car," his mother said.

They turned onto the dirt road and the car raced roughly along in a swirl of pink dust. The grandmother recalled the times when there were no paved roads and thirty miles was a day's journey. The dirt road was hilly and there were sudden washes in it and sharp curves on dangerous 60

[1]*Sherman:* General William Tecumseh Sherman (1820–1891) was the Union general who captured Atlanta in 1864. —EDS.

embankments. All at once they would be on a hill, looking down over the blue tops of trees for miles around, then the next minute, they would be in a red depression with the dust-coated trees looking down on them.

"This place had better turn up in a minute," Bailey said, "or I'm going to turn around."

The road looked as if no one had traveled on it in months.

"It's not much farther," the grandmother said and just as she said it, a horrible thought came to her. The thought was so embarrassing that she turned red in the face and her eyes dilated and her feet jumped up, upsetting her valise in the corner. The instant the valise moved, the newspaper top she had over the basket under it rose with a snarl and Pitty Sing, the cat, sprang onto Bailey's shoulder.

The children were thrown to the floor and their mother, clutching the baby, was thrown out the door onto the ground; the old lady was thrown into the front seat. The car turned over once and landed right-side-up in a gulch off the side of the road. Bailey remained in the driver's seat with the cat—gray-striped with a broad white face and an orange nose—clinging to his neck like a caterpillar.

As soon as the children saw they could move their arms and legs, they scrambled out of the car, shouting, "We've had an ACCIDENT!" The grandmother was curled up under the dashboard, hoping she was injured so that Bailey's wrath would not come down on her all at once. The horrible thought she had had before the accident was that the house she had remembered so vividly was not in Georgia but in Tennessee.

Bailey removed the cat from his neck with both hands and flung it out the window against the side of a pine tree. Then he got out of the car and started looking for the children's mother. She was sitting against the side of the red gutted ditch, holding the screaming baby, but she only had a cut down her face and a broken shoulder. "We've had an ACCIDENT!" the children screamed in a frenzy of delight.

"But nobody's killed," June Star said with disappointment as the grandmother limped out of the car, her hat still pinned to her head but the broken front brim standing up at a jaunty angle and the violet spray hanging off the side. They all sat down in the ditch, except the children, to recover from the shock. They were all shaking.

"Maybe a car will come along," said the children's mother hoarsely.

"I believe I have injured an organ," said the grandmother, pressing her side, but no one answered her. Bailey's teeth were clattering. He had on a yellow sport shirt with bright blue parrots designed in it and his face was as yellow as the shirt. The grandmother decided that she would not mention that the house was in Tennessee.

The road was about ten feet above and they could see only the tops of the trees on the other side of it. Behind the ditch they were sitting in there were more woods, tall and dark and deep. In a few minutes they saw a car some distance away on top of a hill, coming slowly as if the occupants were watching them. The grandmother stood up and waved both

65

70

arms dramatically to attract their attention. The car continued to come on slowly, disappeared around a bend and appeared again, moving even slower, on top of the hill they had gone over. It was a big black battered hearselike automobile. There were three men in it.

It came to a stop just over them and for some minutes, the driver looked down with a steady expressionless gaze to where they were sitting, and didn't speak. Then he turned his head and muttered something to the other two and they got out. One was a fat boy in black trousers and a red sweat shirt with a silver stallion embossed on the front of it. He moved around on the right side of them and stood staring, his mouth partly open in a kind of loose grin. The other had on khaki pants and a blue striped coat and a gray hat pulled down very low, hiding most of his face. He came around slowly on the left side. Neither spoke.

The driver got out of the car and stood by the side of it, looking down at them. He was an older man than the other two. His hair was just beginning to gray and he wore silver-rimmed spectacles that gave him a scholarly look. He had a long creased face and didn't have on any shirt or undershirt. He had on blue jeans that were too tight for him and was holding a black hat and a gun. The two boys also had guns.

"We've had an ACCIDENT!" the children screamed.

The grandmother had the peculiar feeling that the bespectacled man was someone she knew. His face was as familiar to her as if she had known him all her life but she could not recall who he was. He moved away from the car and began to come down the embankment, placing his feet carefully so that he wouldn't slip. He had on tan and white shoes and no socks, and his ankles were red and thin. "Good afternoon," he said. "I see you all had you a little spill."

"We turned over twice!" said the grandmother.   75

"Oncet," he corrected. "We seen it happen. Try their car and see will it run, Hiram," he said quietly to the boy with the gray hat.

"What you got that gun for?" John Wesley asked. "Whatcha gonna do with that gun?"

"Lady," the man said to the children's mother, "would you mind calling them children to sit down by you? Children make me nervous. I want all you all to sit down right together there where you're at."

"What are you telling US what to do for?" June Star asked.

Behind them the line of woods gaped like a dark open mouth. "Come   80
here," said their mother.

"Look here now," Bailey began suddenly, "we're in a predicament! We're in . . ."

The grandmother shrieked. She scrambled to her feet and stood staring. "You're The Misfit!" she said. "I recognized you at once!"

"Yes'm," the man said, smiling slightly as if he were pleased in spite of himself to be known, "but it would have been better for all of you, lady, if you hadn't of reckernized me."

Bailey turned his head sharply and said something to his mother that shocked even the children. The old lady began to cry and The Misfit reddened.

"Lady," he said, "don't you get upset. Sometimes a man says things   85
he don't mean. I don't reckon he meant to talk to you thataway."

"You wouldn't shoot a lady, would you?" the grandmother said and removed a clean handkerchief from her cuff and began to slap at her eyes with it.

The Misfit pointed the toe of his shoe into the ground and made a little hole and then covered it up again. "I would hate to have to," he said.

"Listen," the grandmother almost screamed, "I know you're a good man. You don't look a bit like you have common blood. I know you must come from nice people!"

"Yes ma'am," he said, "finest people in the world." When he smiled he showed a row of strong white teeth. "God never made a finer woman than my mother and my daddy's heart was pure gold," he said. The boy with the red sweat shirt had come around behind them and was standing with his gun at his hip. The Misfit squatted down on the ground. "Watch them children, Bobby Lee," he said. "You know they make me nervous." He looked at the six of them huddled together in front of him and he seemed to be embarrassed as if he couldn't think of anything to say. "Ain't a cloud in the sky," he remarked, looking up at it. "Don't see no sun but don't see no cloud neither."

"Yes, it's a beautiful day," said the grandmother. "Listen," she said,   90
"you shouldn't call yourself The Misfit because I know you're a good man at heart. I can just look at you and tell."

"Hush!" Bailey yelled. "Hush! Everybody shut up and let me handle this!" He was squatting in the position of a runner about to sprint forward but he didn't move.

"I pre-chate that, lady," The Misfit said and drew a little circle in the ground with the butt of his gun.

"It'll take a half a hour to fix this here car," Hiram called, looking over the raised hood of it.

"Well, first you and Bobby Lee get him and that little boy to step over yonder with you," The Misfit said, pointing to Bailey and John Wesley. "The boys want to ask you something," he said to Bailey. "Would you mind stepping back in them woods there with them?"

"Listen," Bailey began, "we're in a terrible predicament! Nobody re-   95
alizes what this is," and his voice cracked. His eyes were as blue and intense as the parrots in his shirt and he remained perfectly still.

The grandmother reached up to adjust her hat brim as if she were going to the woods with him but it came off in her hand. She stood staring at it and after a second she let it fall on the ground. Hiram pulled Bailey up by the arm as if he were assisting an old man. John Wesley caught hold of his father's hand and Bobby Lee followed. They went off toward the woods and just as they reached the dark edge, Bailey turned and supporting himself against a gray naked pine trunk, he shouted, "I'll be back in a minute, Mamma, wait on me!"

"Come back this instant!" his mother shrilled but they all disappeared into the woods.

"Bailey Boy!" the grandmother called in a tragic voice but she found she was looking at The Misfit squatting on the ground in front of her. "I just know you're a good man," she said desperately. "You're not a bit common!"

"Nome, I ain't a good man," The Misfit said after a second as if he had considered her statement carefully, "but I ain't the worst in the world neither. My daddy said I was a different breed of dog from my brothers and sisters. 'You know,' Daddy said, 'it's some that can live their whole life out without asking about it and it's others has to know why it is, and this boy is one of the latters. He's going to be into everything!'" He put on his black hat and looked up suddenly and then away deep into the woods as if he were embarrassed again. "I'm sorry I don't have on a shirt before you ladies," he said, hunching his shoulders slightly. "We buried our clothes that we had on when we escaped and we're just making do until we can get better. We borrowed these from some folks we met," he explained.

"That's perfectly all right," the grandmother said. "Maybe Bailey has   100
an extra shirt in his suitcase."

"I'll look and see terrectly," The Misfit said.

"Where are they taking him?" the children's mother screamed.

"Daddy was a card himself," The Misfit said. "You couldn't put anything over on him. He never got in trouble with the Authorities though. Just had the knack of handling them."

"You could be honest too if you'd only try," said the grandmother. "Think how wonderful it would be to settle down and live a comfortable life and not have to think about somebody chasing you all the time."

The Misfit kept scratching in the ground with the butt of his gun as if   105
he were thinking about it. "Yes'm, somebody is always after you," he murmured.

The grandmother noticed how thin his shoulder blades were just behind his hat because she was standing up looking down on him. "Do you ever pray?" she asked.

He shook his head. All she saw was the black hat wiggle between his shoulder blades. "Nome," he said.

There was a pistol shot from the woods, followed closely by another. Then silence. The old lady's head jerked around. She could hear the wind move through the tree tops like a long satisfied insuck of breath. "Bailey Boy!" she called.

"I was a gospel singer for a while," The Misfit said. "I been most everything. Been in the arm service, both land and sea, at home and abroad, been twict married, been an undertaker, been with the railroads, plowed Mother Earth, been in a tornado, seen a man burnt alive oncet," and looked up at the children's mother and the little girl who were sitting close together, their faces white and their eyes glassy; "I even seen a woman flogged," he said.

"Pray, pray," the grandmother began, "pray, pray . . ."   110

"I never was a bad boy that I remember of," The Misfit said in an almost dreamy voice, "but somewheres along the line I done something wrong and got sent to the penitentiary. I was buried alive," and he looked up and held her attention to him by a steady stare.

"That's when you should have started to pray," she said. "What did you do to get sent to the penitentiary that first time?"

"Turn to the right, it was a wall," The Misfit said, looking up again at the cloudless sky. "Turn to the left, it was a wall. Look up it was a ceiling, look down it was a floor. I forget what I done, lady. I set there and set there, trying to remember what it was I done and I ain't recalled it to this day. Oncet in a while, I would think it was coming to me, but it never come."

"Maybe they put you in by mistake," the old lady said vaguely.

"Nome," he said. "It wasn't no mistake. They had the papers on me."   115

"You must have stolen something," she said.

The Misfit sneered slightly. "Nobody had nothing I wanted," he said. "It was a head-doctor at the penitentiary said what I had done was kill my daddy but I known that for a lie. My daddy died in nineteen ought nineteen of the epidemic flu and I never had a thing to do with it. He was buried in the Mount Hopewell Baptist churchyard and you can go there and see for yourself."

"If you would pray," the old lady said, "Jesus would help you."

"That's right," The Misfit said.

"Well then, why don't you pray?" she asked, trembling with delight   120
suddenly.

"I don't want no hep," he said. "I'm doing all right by myself."

Bobby Lee and Hiram came ambling back from the woods. Bobby Lee was dragging a yellow shirt with bright blue parrots in it.

"Throw me that shirt, Bobby Lee," The Misfit said. The shirt came flying at him and landed on his shoulder and he put it on. The grandmother couldn't name what the shirt reminded her of. "No, lady," The Misfit said while he was buttoning it up, "I found out the crime don't matter. You can do one thing or you can do another, kill a man or take a tire off his car, because sooner or later you're going to forget what it was you done and just be punished for it."

The children's mother had begun to make heaving noises as if she couldn't get her breath. "Lady," he asked, "would you and that little girl like to step off yonder with Bobby Lee and Hiram and join your husband?"

"Yes, thank you," the mother said faintly. Her left arm dangled help-   125
lessly and she was holding the baby, who had gone to sleep, in the other. "Hep that lady up, Hiram," The Misfit said as she struggled to climb out of the ditch, "and Bobby Lee, you hold onto that little girl's hand."

"I don't want to hold hands with him," June Star said. "He reminds me of a pig."

The fat boy blushed and laughed and caught her by the arm and pulled her off into the woods after Hiram and her mother.

Alone with The Misfit, the grandmother found that she had lost her voice. There was not a cloud in the sky nor any sun. There was nothing around her but woods. She wanted to tell him that he must pray. She opened and closed her mouth several times before anything came out. Finally she found herself saying, "Jesus, Jesus," meaning, Jesus will help you, but the way she was saying it, it sounded as if she might be cursing.

"Yes'm," the Misfit said as if he agreed. "Jesus thown everything off balance. It was the same case with Him as with me except He hadn't committed any crime and they could prove I had committed one because they had the papers on me. Of course," he said, "they never shown me my papers. That's why I sign myself now. I said long ago, you get you a signature and sign everything you do and keep a copy of it. Then you'll know what you done and you can hold up the crime to the punishment and see do they match and in the end you'll have something to prove you ain't been treated right. I call myself The Misfit," he said, "because I can't make what all I done wrong fit what all I gone through in punishment."

There was a piercing scream from the woods, followed closely by a   130
pistol report. "Does it seem right to you, lady, that one is punished a heap and another ain't punished at all?"

"Jesus!" the old lady cried. "You've got good blood! I know you wouldn't shoot a lady! I know you come from nice people! Pray! Jesus, you ought not to shoot a lady. I'll give you all the money I've got!"

"Lady," The Misfit said, looking beyond her far into the woods, "there never was a body that give the undertaker a tip."

There were two more pistol reports and the grandmother raised her head like a parched old turkey hen crying for water and called, "Bailey Boy, Bailey Boy!" as if her heart would break.

"Jesus was the only One that ever raised the dead." The Misfit continued, "and He shouldn't have done it. He thown everything off balance. If He did what He said, then it's nothing for you to do but thow away everything and follow Him, and if He didn't, then it's nothing for you to do but enjoy the few minutes you got left the best way you can—by killing somebody or burning down his house or doing some other meanness to him. No pleasure but meanness," he said and his voice had become almost a snarl.

"Maybe He didn't raise the dead," the old lady mumbled, not know-   135
ing what she was saying and feeling so dizzy that she sank down in the ditch with her legs twisted under her.

"I wasn't there so I can't say He didn't," The Misfit said. "I wisht I had of been there," he said, hitting the ground with his fist. "It ain't right I wasn't there because if I had of been there I would of known. Listen lady," he said in a high voice, "if I had of been there I would of known and I wouldn't be like I am now." His voice seemed about to crack and the grandmother's head cleared for an instant. She saw the man's face twisted close to her own as if he was going to cry and she murmured, "Why you're one of my babies. You're one of my own children!" She reached out and touched him on the shoulder. The Misfit sprang back as if a snake had bitten him and shot her three times through the chest. Then he put his gun down on the ground and took off his glasses and began to clean them.

Hiram and Bobby Lee returned from the woods and stood over the ditch, looking down at the grandmother who half sat and half lay in a puddle of blood with her legs crossed under her like a child's and her face smiling up at the cloudless sky.

Without his glasses, The Misfit's eyes were red-rimmed and pale and defenseless-looking. "Take her off and thow her where you thown the others," he said, picking up the cat that was rubbing itself against his leg.

"She was a talker, wasn't she?" Bobby Lee said, sliding down the ditch with a yodel.

"She would of been a good woman," The Misfit said, "if it had been somebody there to shoot her every minute of her life."   140

"Some fun!" Bobby Lee said.

"Shut up, Bobby Lee," The Misfit said. "It's no real pleasure in life."

The Reader's Presence

1. The grandmother is described only indirectly, through her words, actions, and interactions with others. Reread paragraphs 1–9. How does the grandmother appear to see herself? How do you see her? In what ways does the writer's "voice" influence your impression of the character?

2. What might the Misfit figure symbolize in relation to the grandmother and her family? Does his nickname have any significance? What sort of tone does O'Connor establish in the Misfit encounter? Is it eerie, comedic, or somewhere in between? Imagine the story as presented in a different tone; how would it differ? What does O'Connor's position on the characters and events appear to be? What clues in her approach lead you to your conclusion? (See also O'Connor's commentary on the story.)

3. In the "Writer at Work" that follows, O'Connor discusses the crucial action or gesture that makes a story work. "[I]t is probably some action, some gesture of a character that is unlike any other in the story, one which indicates where the real heart of the story lies. . . . It would be a gesture which somehow made contact with mystery" (paragraph 12). O'Connor locates this key moment in paragraph 136 of "A Good Man Is Hard to Find," when "the grandmother's head cleared for an instant." Locate the crucial

gesture or action in Raymond Carver's story "The Bath" (page 919) and in Sherman Alexie's story "This Is What It Means to Say Phoenix, Arizona" (page 909). Is O'Connor's description of such a gesture and its key role in "making a story hold up" applicable to stories by writers other than herself? Is "mystery" as important to Carver and to Alexie as it is to O'Connor?

THE WRITER AT WORK

Flannery O'Connor on Her Own Work

Flannery O'Connor's "A Good Man Is Hard to Find" ranks as one of American fiction's most durable short stories. It has been reprinted and analyzed in critical periodicals hundreds of times since it first appeared in 1953. Ten years after its first publication and shortly before her untimely death, O'Connor was invited to read the story at Hollins College (now Hollins University) in Virginia, where she made the following remarks. Her comments on the story were then included in a collection of nonfiction published by her editor in 1969 under the very appropriate title "Mystery and Manners." As you consider the story, you may want to focus on these terms: mystery and manners. How does each word describe an important aspect of the story? How are they interrelated? You should also consider the story from the perspective O'Connor herself provides in the following selection. Do you think her comments on her own story are critically persuasive? Did you come away from the story with a different sense of its significance? Do you think that what an author says about his or her own work must always be the final word?

Last fall I received a letter from a student who said she would be "graciously appreciative" if I would tell her "just what enlightenment" I expected her to get from each of my stories. I suspect she had a paper to write. I wrote her back to forget about the enlightenment and just try to enjoy them. I knew that was the most unsatisfactory answer I could have given because, of course, she didn't want to enjoy them, she just wanted to figure them out.

In most English classes the short story has become a kind of literary specimen to be dissected. Every time a story of mine appears in a Freshman anthology, I have a vision of it, with its little organs laid open, like a frog in a bottle.

I realize that a certain amount of this what-is-the-significance has to go on, but I think something has gone wrong in the process when, for so many students, the story becomes simply a problem to be solved, something which you evaporate to get Instant Enlightenment.

A story really isn't any good unless it successfully resists paraphrase, unless it hangs on and expands in the mind. Properly, you analyze to enjoy, but it's equally true that to analyze with any discrimination, you have to have enjoyed already, and I think that the best reason to hear a story read is that it should stimulate that primary enjoyment.

I don't have any pretensions to being an Aeschylus or Sophocles and providing you in this story with a cathartic experience out of your mythic background, though this story I'm going to read certainly calls up a good deal of the South's mythic background, and it should elicit from you a degree of pity and terror, even though its way of being serious is a comic one. I do think, though, that like the Greeks you should know what is going to happen in this story so that any element of suspense in it will be transferred from its surface to its interior.

I would be most happy if you had already read it, happier still if you knew it well, but since experience has taught me to keep my expectations along these lines modest, I'll tell you that this is the story of a family of six which, on its way driving to Florida, gets wiped out by an escaped convict who calls himself the Misfit. The family is made up of the Grandmother and her son, Bailey, and his children, John Wesley and June Star and the baby, and there is also the cat and the children's mother. The cat is named Pitty Sing, and the Grandmother is taking him with them, hidden in a basket.

Now I think it behooves me to try to establish with you the basis on which reason operates in this story. Much of my fiction takes its character from a reasonable use of the unreasonable, though the reasonableness of my use of it may not always be apparent. The assumptions that underlie this use of it, however, are those of the central Christian mysteries. These are assumptions to which a large part of the modern audience takes exception. About this I can only say that there are perhaps other ways than my own in which this story could be read, but none other by which it could have been written. Belief, in my own case anyway, is the engine that makes perception operate.

The heroine of this story, the Grandmother, is in the most significant position life offers the Christian. She is facing death. And to all appearances she, like the rest of us, is not too well prepared for it. She would like to see the event postponed. Indefinitely.

I've talked to a number of teachers who use this story in class and who tell their students that the Grandmother is evil, that in fact, she's a witch, even down to the cat. One of these teachers told me that his students, and particularly his Southern students, resisted this interpretation with a certain bemused vigor, and he didn't understand why. I had to tell him that they resisted it because they all had grandmothers or great-aunts just like her at home, and they knew, from personal experience, that the old lady lacked comprehension, but that she had a good heart. The Southerner is usually tolerant of those weaknesses that proceed from innocence, and he knows that a taste for self-preservation can be readily combined with the missionary spirit.

This same teacher was telling his students that morally the Misfit was several cuts above the Grandmother. He had a really sentimental attachment to the Misfit. But then a prophet gone wrong is almost always more interesting than your grandmother, and you have to let people take their pleasures where they find them.

It is true that the old lady is a hypocritical old soul; her wits are no match for the Misfit's, nor is her capacity for grace equal to his; yet I think the unprejudiced reader will feel that the Grandmother has a special kind of triumph in this story which instinctively we do not allow to someone altogether bad.

I often ask myself what makes a story work, and what makes it hold up as a story, and I have decided that it is probably some action, some gesture of a character that is unlike any other in the story, one which indicates where the real heart of the story lies. This would have to be an action or a gesture which was both totally right and totally unexpected; it would have to be one that was both in character and beyond character; it would have to suggest both the world and eternity. The action or gesture I'm talking about would have to be on the anagogical level, that is, the level which has to do with the Divine life and our participation in it. It would be a gesture that transcended any neat allegory that might have been intended or any pat moral categories a reader could make. It would be a gesture which somehow made contact with mystery.

There is a point in this story where such a gesture occurs. The Grandmother is at last alone, facing the Misfit. Her head clears for an instant and she realizes, even in her limited way, that she is responsible for the man before her and joined to him by ties of kinship which have their roots deep in the mystery she has been merely prattling about so far. And at this point, she does the right thing, she makes the right gesture.

I find that students are often puzzled by what she says and does here, but I think myself that if I took out this gesture and what she says with it, I would have no story. What was left would not be worth your attention. Our age not only does not have a very sharp eye for the almost imperceptible intrusions of grace, it no longer has much feeling for the nature of the violences which precede and follow them. The devil's greatest wile, Baudelaire has said, is to convince us that he does not exist.

I suppose the reasons for the use of so much violence in modern fic-   15
tion will differ with each writer who uses it, but in my own stories I have found that violence is strangely capable of returning my characters to reality and preparing them to accept their moment of grace. Their heads are so hard that almost nothing else will do the work. This idea, that reality is something to which we must be returned at considerable cost, is one which is seldom understood by the casual reader, but it is one which is implicit in the Christian view of the world.

I don't want to equate the Misfit with the devil. I prefer to think that, however unlikely this may seem, the old lady's gesture, like the mustard-seed, will grow to be a great crow-filled tree in the Misfit's heart, and will be enough of a pain to him there to turn him into the prophet he was meant to become. But that's another story.

This story has been called grotesque, but I prefer to call it literal. A good story is literal in the same sense that a child's drawing is literal. When a child draws, he doesn't intend to distort but to set down exactly what he sees, and as his gaze is direct, he sees the lines that create motion. Now the lines of motion that interest the writer are usually invisible. They are lines of spiritual motion. And in this story you should be on the lookout for such things as the action of grace in the Grandmother's soul, and not for the dead bodies.

We hear many complaints about the prevalence of violence in modern fiction, and it is always assumed that this violence is a bad thing and meant to be an end in itself. With the serious writer, violence is never an end in itself. It is the extreme situation that best reveals what we are essentially, and I believe these are times when writers are more interested in what we are essentially than in the tenor of our daily lives. Violence is a force which can be used for good or evil, and among other things taken by it is the kingdom of heaven. But regardless of what can be taken by it, the man in the violent situation reveals those qualities least dispensable in his personality, those qualities which are all he will have to take into eternity with him; and since the characters in this story are all on the verge of eternity, it is appropriate to think of what they take with them. In any case, I hope that if you consider these points in connection with the story, you will come to see it as something more than an account of a family murdered on the way to Florida.

THE CRITIC AT WORK

William Caverlee on "The Best Southern Short Story Ever?"

"A Good Man Is Hard to Find" has been considered one of the greatest American short stories for decades and it has been included in nearly every short fiction anthology since it first appeared in Partisan Review *in 1953. Given its enigmatic quality and its eerie combination of humor and horror, the story has been the subject of much serious criticism over the years. The following essay by William Caverlee, a contributing writer to the Southern magazine* Oxford American, *is one of the latest attempts to come to terms with the story's mystery. You might compare Caverlee's understanding of the story to O'Connor's in the preceding selection. How do you think O'Connor might respond to Caverlee's interpretation and assessment?*

Without ever leaving her hideout in Milledgeville, Georgia, Flannery O'Connor knew all there was to know about the two-lane, dirt and blacktop Southern roads of the 1950s—with their junkyards and tourist courts, gravel pits and pine trees that pressed at the edges of the road. She knew the slogans of the Burma Shave signs, knew the names of barbecue joints and the chicken baskets on their menus. She also knew a backwoods American cadence and vocabulary you'd think was limited to cops, truckers, runaway teens, and the patrons of the Teardrop Inn, where at midnight somebody could always be counted on to go out to a pickup truck and come back with a shotgun. She was a virtuoso mimic, and she assimilated whole populations of American sounds and voices, and then offered them back to us from time to time in her small fictional detonations, one of which she named, in 1953, "A Good Man Is Hard to Find."

The plot is sewn together through a devious coincidence: While planning a car trip to Florida, a Georgia family (grandmother, son, wife, and three children) learns that an escaped criminal named The Misfit is roaming about the region. The family embarks anyway, stops for lunch at a country restaurant, has a car accident, and is slaughtered by The Misfit and his two cohorts.

In a characteristic sleight of hand, O'Connor decided to give the story to the grandmother, a pint-sized heroine for this tale of mayhem and death. The grandmother (that's her name in the story) appears in every scene and speaks nearly all of the dialogue, rivaled only by the two menacing, boisterous older children and an unexpected visitor in the final scene. She takes control of things from the outset—wheedling, conniving, whining, and manipulating the entire family to go along with her plans. She's a self-pitying narcissist, a megalomaniacal, self-delighting tyrant of her middle-class family. She utters clichés day and night and considers herself, in the end, always a proper lady:

> I wouldn't take my children in any direction with a criminal like that aloose in it. I couldn't answer to my conscience if I did. [1]

> In my time, children were more respectful of their native states and their parents and everything else. [18]

> People are certainly not nice like they used to be. [25]

And naturally, it is the grandmother's hiding of her cat in the car's back seat (couldn't bear leaving Pitty Sing home alone) and her maneuvers to visit a roadside attraction that lead to the car accident and the family's destruction.

In the final scene, the grandmother meets her narcissistic match, who just so happens to be a sociopathic killer. The duet that plays between her and The Misfit is a pinnacle of American comic writing—a dizzying dialogue that takes place at the same time as the gunshot murders of two adults, two children, and an infant. Like a pair of theological vaudevillians, they speak of Christ, fate, good and evil, and the discovery of their respective salvation. For the first time in her life, the grandmother is nearly dumb with terror, reduced to stammering out pleas for her life. The middle-aged Misfit, scholarly in his spectacles, recounts his horrific past. He is at once ominous and detached, despairing and alert, a kind of proselytizing antiprophet utterly given over to impulse and violence, and who, in spite of (or perhaps because of) his complete solipsism, speaks one or two words of unwitting truth—truth that, improbably enough, sets the old woman free.

5

Along with the grandmother, everyone in the story speaks in banalities — the children, John Wesley and June Star, the garrulous restaurateur Red Sammy, The Misfit's two henchmen, Hiram and Bobby Lee — everyone including The Misfit (perhaps especially The Misfit), although his language also manages to be complex and self-aware. With The Misfit, the reader is jerked out of an impatient restlessness and distaste for these tiresome people. He's the only charismatic figure in these pages, and his compressed life story has the cadence and richness of a poem:

> I was a gospel singer for a while. I been most everything. Been in the arm service, both land and sea, at home and abroad, been twict married, been an undertaker, been with the railroads, plowed Mother Earth, been in a tornado. . . .

In one sense, The Misfit is a co-hero, as significant as the grandmother — a hypnotic, dazzling Iago, of sorts. But O'Connor is doing a number on us with the magnetic Misfit, has intentionally made him the most interesting character, so that we would be drawn to him for a time, so that we would be curious about him, half-believe him. Indeed, we're spellbound, laughing and wincing at his eerie language until the moment he reminds us of his horrific potential.

The Shakespeare critic A. C. Bradley once said that the first thing to keep in mind about Iago is that you can't believe a single word he says. You have to distrust everything. Certainly, the same holds for The Misfit, who, like his predecessor, is so penetrated with untruth that he lies before he thinks, lies as he breathes. He's in that great line of backwoods con men — quite capable of rewriting his charismatic life story on every ditch-bank in Georgia, the biblical language in which he is so fluent being another form of the con.

The story, which had begun as a cartoon, a comedy of '50s manners, takes, in a handful of pages, a remarkable turn. All the events have occurred in a single day, during this balmy summer car trip in rural Georgia. There is no chance that a reader should accept O'Connor's plot, with its blatantly placed clue in the first paragraph. Yet she makes it work. We laugh our way through a brief series of scenes, ride along in the crowded car, have lunch at Red Sammy's, get lost on the dirt road, laugh again when Pitty Sing (who, it must be said, had been suspiciously well behaved for most of the trip) jumps on the son's shoulder and causes the wreck; and then somehow, not quite knowing how it has happened, we find ourselves slumped in shock alongside the doomed family at the bottom of a ditch, looking up at a cloudless sky and three men looming above.

The grandmother's son is named Bailey, but we never learn his wife's name. She is simply "the children's mother," anonymous, almost selfless in the grandmother's characteristic worldview. O'Connor makes her the butt of an early joke on page one, giving her a face "as broad and innocent as a cabbage." During the accident, she is thrown from the car, still holding the infant, and breaks her shoulder. She sits there, stiffening in shock as her husband and young son are led away by The Misfit's henchmen to be slaughtered in the woods. Soon the murderers come for her, and The Misfit quietly asks her "to step off yonder with Bobby Lee and Hiram and join your husband."

Nearly mute in pain and horror, she can only say, "Yes, thank you." Then she takes the two remaining children and obediently walks off to her death. O'Connor, who had humiliated the young woman earlier, gives her back to us now in something close to tragedy, in a miraculous dignity; and her "Yes, thank you" becomes the most poignant moment of the story.

Only the grandmother remains. Grasping at straws, she mutters, "Jesus, Jesus," and The Misfit chimes right in. And then, in the midst of his philosophizing, he speaks the central line of the story: "Jesus thown everything off balance." We know that The Misfit is speaking out of his own insanity and violence, but O'Connor is stretching language so far here that, for a moment at least, the reality of these Georgia trees and skies starts to crack apart. We've been working our way through some of the strangest American prose ever written. Six people are dead. And The Misfit becomes the most memorable religious character in recent American fiction.

In the last moments of the story, the grandmother has reached the limits of despair. She alone is left alive. She has begged for her life, twisted and turned every way she knows, has reached some unspeakable point of horror and fear and catastrophe, and she cries out to The Misfit, "Why you're one of my babies. You're one of my own children!" Her entire atrocious, selfish, ignorant, useless life has led to this. And in its last moments, the improbable occurs: She breaks through, speaks words she doesn't even realize she is speaking. She reaches out to The Misfit and touches him on the shoulder—a common enough rural gesture. And at her touch, The Misfit, a fully realized nihilist, shoots her dead.

The story runs quickly to its close. One or two more sentences. The Misfit tells Bobby Lee, "She would of been a good woman, if it had been somebody there to shoot her every minute of her life." It has taken the extremity of death for the grandmother to escape the shell of her egoism—a transformation The Misfit, a shrewd psychologist, readily comprehends, even as he is the very agent of her destruction.

Thus, in the guise of a Deep South horror story, O'Connor gave   15
American letters something else altogether: a religiously audacious work of literature, a spiritual puzzle—a small miracle.

John Updike

A & P

Over the course of his career as a novelist, short story writer, poet, essayist, and dramatist, John Updike (b. 1932) has been awarded every major American literary award; in 1998 he was awarded the National Book Foundation Medal for Distinguished Contribution to American Letters. For one novel alone, Rabbit Is Rich *(1981), he won the Pulitzer Prize, the American Book Award, and the National Book Critics Circle Award. Among more than a dozen published novels, his recurring themes include religion, sexuality, and middle-class experience. In his essays, Updike's concerns range widely over literary and cultural issues. One volume of his collected essays,* Hugging the Shore: Essays and Criticism *(1983), was also awarded a National Book Critics Circle Award. His most recent publications include the novels* Terrorist *(2006) and* The Widows of Eastwick *(2008); and the nonfiction collections* Still Looking: Essays on American Art *(2005) and* Due Considerations: Essays and Criticism *(2007).*

"A&P" is one of nineteen stories from John Updike's 1962 collection titled Pigeon Feathers and Other Stories, *which appeared early in the writer's long and impressive career. In a 2001 interview, Updike commented on his goals as a writer and what he appreciates in other writing: "I've just tried to write in a way that would entertain and please me, if I were the reader . . . the kind of writer I'm attracted to is a writer who gives pleasure—the prose writer who does a little more than what is strictly called for to deliver the image or the facts. I'm not a very fast reader, so I like to open up a book and feel some whiff of poetry or of extra effort or of something inventive going on, so that even read backwards, a paragraph of prose will yield something to the sense." Updike has said humorously of his approach to reading: "My purpose in reading has ever secretly been not to come and judge but to come and steal."*

In walks these three girls in nothing but bathing suits. I'm in the third checkout slot, with my back to the door, so I don't see them until they're over by the bread. The one that caught my eye first was the one in the plaid green two-piece. She was a chunky kid, with a good tan and a sweet broad soft-looking can with those two crescents of white just under it, where the sun never seems to hit, at the top of the backs of her legs. I stood there with my hand on a box of HiHo crackers trying to remember if I rang it up or not. I ring it up again and the customer starts giving me hell. She's one of these cash-register-watchers, a witch about fifty with rouge on her cheekbones and no eyebrows, and I know it made her day to trip me up. She'd been watching cash registers for fifty years and probably never seen a mistake before.

By the time I got her feathers smoothed and her goodies into a bag—she gives me a little snort in passing, if she'd been born at the right time they would have burned her over in Salem—by the time I get her on her way the girls had circled around the bread and were coming back, without a pushcart, back my way along the counters, in the aisle between the checkouts and the Special bins. They didn't even have shoes on. There was this chunky one, with the two-piece — it was bright green and the seams on the bra were still sharp and her belly was still pretty pale so I guessed she just got it (the suit) — there was this one, with one of those chubby berry-faces, the lips all bunched together under her nose, this one, and a tall one, with black hair that hadn't quite frizzed right, and one of these sunburns right across under the eyes, and a chin that was too long — you know, the kind of girl other girls think is very "striking" and "attractive" but never quite makes it, as they very well know, which is why they like her so much — and then the third one, that wasn't quite so tall. She was the queen. She kind of led them, the other two peeking around and making their shoulders round. She didn't look around, not this queen, she just walked straight on slowly, on these long white prima-donna legs. She came down a little hard on her heels, as if she didn't walk in her bare feet that much, putting down her heels and then letting the weight move along to her toes as if she was testing the floor with every step, putting a little deliberate extra action into it. You never know for sure how girls' minds work (do you really think it's a mind in there or just a little buzz like a bee in a glass jar?) but you got the idea she had talked the other two into coming in here with her, and now she was showing them how to do it, walk slow and hold yourself straight.

She had on a kind of dirty-pink — beige maybe, I don't know — bathing suit with a little nubble all over it and, what got me, the straps were down. They were off her shoulders looped loose around the cool tops of her arms, and I guess as a result the suit had slipped a little on her, so all around the top of the cloth there was this shining rim. If it hadn't been there you wouldn't have known there could have been anything whiter than those shoulders. With the straps pushed off, there was nothing between the top of the suit and the top of her head except just *her*, this clean bare plane of the top of her chest down from the shoulder bones like a dented sheet of metal tilted in the light. I mean, it was more than pretty.

She had sort of oaky hair that the sun and salt had bleached, done up in a bun that was unraveling, and a kind of prim face. Walking into the A & P with your straps down, I suppose it's the only kind of face you *can* have. She held her head so high her neck, coming up out of those white shoulders, looked kind of stretched, but I didn't mind. The longer her neck was, the more of her there was.

She must have felt in the corner of her eye me and over my shoulder Stokesie in the second slot watching, but she didn't tip. Not this queen. She kept her eyes moving across the racks, and stopped, and turned so slow it made my stomach rub the inside of my apron, and buzzed to the other two, who kind of huddled against her for relief, and then they all three of them went up the cat-and-dog-food-breakfast-cereal-macaroni-rice-raisins-seasonings-spreads-spaghetti-soft-drinks-crackers-and-cookies aisle. From the third slot I look straight up this aisle to the meat counter,

5

and I watched them all the way. The fat one with the tan sort of fumbled with the cookies, but on second thought she put the package back. The sheep pushing their carts down the aisle — the girls were walking against the usual traffic (not that we have one-way signs or anything) — were pretty hilarious. You could see them, when Queenie's white shoulders dawned on them, kind of jerk, or hop, or hiccup, but their eyes snapped back to their own baskets and on they pushed. I bet you could set off dynamite in an A & P and the people would by and large keep reaching and checking oatmeal off their lists and muttering "Let me see, there was a third thing, began with A, asparagus, no, ah, yes, applesauce!" or whatever it is they do mutter. But there was no doubt, this jiggled them. A few houseslaves in pin curlers even looked around after pushing their carts past to make sure what they had seen was correct.

You know, it's one thing to have a girl in a bathing suit down on the beach, where what with the glare nobody can look at each other much anyway, and another thing in the cool of the A & P, under the fluorescent lights, against all those stacked packages, with her feet paddling along naked over our checkerboard green-and-cream rubber-tile floor.

"Oh Daddy," Stokesie said beside me. "I feel so faint."

"Darling," I said. "Hold me tight." Stokesie's married, with two babies chalked up on his fuselage already, but as far as I can tell that's the only difference. He's twenty-two, and I was nineteen this April.

"Is it done?" he asks, the responsible married man finding his voice. I forgot to say he thinks he's going to be manager some sunny day, maybe in 1990 when it's called the Great Alexandrov and Petrooshki Tea Company or something.

What he meant was, our town is five miles from a beach, with a big summer colony out on the Point, but we're right in the middle of town, and the women generally put on a shirt or shorts or something before they get out of the car into the street. And anyway these are usually women with six children and varicose veins mapping their legs and nobody, including them, could care less. As I say, we're right in the middle of town, and if you stand at our front doors you can see two banks and the Congregational church and the newspaper store and three real-estate offices and about twenty-seven old freeloaders tearing up Central Street because the sewer broke again. It's not as if we're on the Cape, we're north of Boston and there's people in this town haven't seen the ocean for twenty years.

10

The girls had reached the meat counter and were asking McMahon something. He pointed, they pointed, and they shuffled out of sight behind a pyramid of Diet Delight peaches. All that was left for us to see was old McMahon patting his mouth and looking after them sizing up their joints. Poor kids, I began to feel sorry for them, they couldn't help it.

Now here comes the sad part of the story, at least my family says it's sad, but I don't think it's so sad myself. The store's pretty empty, it being Thursday afternoon, so there was nothing much to do except lean on the register and wait for the girls to show up again. The whole store was like a pinball machine and I didn't know which tunnel they'd come out of.

After a while they come around out of the far aisle, around the light bulbs, records at discount of the Caribbean Six or Tony Martin Sings or some such gunk you wonder they waste the wax on, sixpacks of candy bars, and plastic toys done up in cellophane that fall apart when a kid looks at them anyway. Around they come, Queenie still leading the way, and holding a little gray jar in her hands. Slots Three through Seven are unmanned and I could see her wondering between Stokes and me, but Stokesie with his usual luck draws an old party in baggy gray pants who stumbles up with four giant cans of pineapple juice (what do these bums *do* with all that pineapple juice? I've often asked myself). So the girls come to me. Queenie puts down the jar and I take it into my fingers icy cold. Kingfish Fancy Herring Snacks in Pure Sour Cream: 49¢. Now her hands are empty, not a ring or a bracelet, bare as God made them, and I wonder where the money's coming from. Still with that prim look she lifts a folded dollar bill out of the hollow at the center of her nubbled pink top. The jar went heavy in my hand. Really, I thought that was so cute.

Then everybody's luck begins to run out. Lengel comes in from haggling with a truck full of cabbages on the lot and is about to scuttle into that door marked MANAGER behind which he hides all day when the girls touch his eye. Lengel's pretty dreary, teaches Sunday school and the rest, but he doesn't miss that much. He comes over and says, "Girls, this isn't the beach."

Queenie blushes, though maybe it's just a brush of sunburn I was noticing for the first time, now that she was so close. "My mother asked me to pick up a jar of herring snacks." Her voice kind of startled me, the way voices do when you see the people first, coming out so flat and dumb yet kind of tony, too, the way it ticked over "pick up" and "snacks." All of a sudden I slid right down her voice into the living room. Her father and the other men were standing around in ice-cream coats and bow ties and the women were in sandals picking up herring snacks on toothpicks off a big glass plate and they were all holding drinks the color of water with olives and sprigs of mint in them. When my parents have somebody over they get lemonade and if it's a real racy affair Schlitz in tall glasses with "They'll Do It Every Time" cartoons stenciled on.

"That's all right," Lengel said. "But this isn't the beach." His repeating this struck me as funny, as if it had just occurred to him, and he had been thinking all these years the A & P was a great big dune and he was the head lifeguard. He didn't like my smiling—as I say he doesn't miss much—but he concentrates on giving the girls that sad Sunday-school-superintendent stare.   15

Queenie's blush is no sunburn now, and the plump one in plaid, that I liked better from the back—a really sweet can—pipes up, "We weren't doing any shopping. We just came in for the one thing."

"That makes no difference," Lengel tells her, and I could see from the way his eyes went that he hadn't noticed she was wearing a two-piece before. "We want you decently dressed when you come in here."

"We *are* decent," Queenie says suddenly, her lower lip pushing, getting sore now that she remembers her place, a place from which the crowd that runs the A & P must look pretty crummy. Fancy Herring Snacks flashed in her very blue eyes.

"Girls, I don't want to argue with you. After this come in here with your shoulders covered. It's our policy." He turns his back. That's policy for you. Policy is what the kingpins want. What the others want is juvenile delinquency.

All this while, the customers had been showing up with their carts but, you know, sheep, seeing a scene, they had all bunched up on Stokesie, who shook open a paper bag as gently as peeling a peach, not wanting to miss a word. I could feel in the silence everybody getting nervous, most of all Lengel, who asks me, "Sammy, have you rung up their purchase?"

I thought and said "No" but it wasn't about that I was thinking. I go through the punches, 4, 9, GROC. TOT—it's more complicated than you think, and after you do it often enough, it begins to make a little song, that you hear words to, in my case "Hello (*bing*) there, you (*gung*) hap-py *pee*-pul (*splat*)!"—the *splat* being the drawer flying out. I uncrease the bill, tenderly as you may imagine, it just having come from between the two smoothest scoops of vanilla I had ever known were there, and pass a half and a penny into her narrow pink palm, and nestle the herrings in a bag and twist its neck and hand it over, all the time thinking.

The girls, and who'd blame them, are in a hurry to get out, so I say "I quit" to Lengel quick enough for them to hear, hoping they'll stop and watch me, their unsuspected hero. They keep right on going, into the electric eye; the door flies open and they flicker across the lot to their car, Queenie and Plaid and Big Tall Goony-Goony (not that as raw material she was so bad), leaving me with Lengel and a kink in his eyebrow.

"Did you say something, Sammy?"

"I said I quit."

"I thought you did."

"You didn't have to embarrass them."

"It was they who were embarrassing us."

I started to say something that came out "Fiddle-de-doo." It's a saying of my grandmother's, and I know she would have been pleased.

"I don't think you know what you're saying," Lengel said.

"I know you don't," I said. "But I do." I pull the bow at the back of my apron and start shrugging it off my shoulders. A couple customers that had been heading for my slot begin to knock against each other, like scared pigs in a chute.

Lengel sighs and begins to look very patient and old and gray. He's been a friend of my parents for years. "Sammy, you don't want to do this to your Mom and Dad," he tells me. It's true, I don't. But it seems to me that once you begin a gesture it's fatal not to go through with it. I fold the apron, "Sammy" stitched in red on the pocket, and put it on the counter, and drop the bow tie on top of it. The bow tie is theirs, if you've ever wondered. "You'll feel this for the rest of your life," Lengel says, and I know that's true, too, but remembering how he made the pretty girl blush makes me so scrunchy inside I punch the No Sale tab and the machine whirs "pee-pul" and the drawer splats out. One advantage to this scene taking place in summer, I can follow this up with a clean exit, there's no fumbling around getting your coat and galoshes, I just saunter into the electric eye in my white shirt that my mother ironed the night before, and the door heaves it-self open, and outside the sunshine is skating around on the asphalt.

I look around for my girls, but they're gone, of course. There wasn't anybody but some young married screaming with her children about some candy they didn't get by the door of a powder-blue Falcon station wagon. Looking back in the big windows, over the bags of peat moss and aluminum lawn furniture stacked on the pavement, I could see Lengel in my place in the slot, checking the sheep through. His face was dark gray and his back stiff, as if he'd just had an injection of iron, and my stomach kind of fell as I felt how hard the world was going to be to me hereafter.

The Reader's Presence

1. The story is written in colloquial language. Reread the first two paragraphs. What does the narrator's style of expression convey about him? What effect does the narrator's style of expression have upon your reading of the story? Are you more, or less, inclined to believe his words? Why? Suppose the same story were re-counted in more conventional English. Would its meaning differ? If so, in what ways? How do you think Updike wishes the reader to view the narrator? Does Updike seem to agree, partially agree, or disagree with the narrator's point of view? What clues in the narrative lead you to your conclusion?

2. A great deal of the story hinges on what the narrator doesn't know or say. Is the girls' attire the only issue in the confrontation? What other tensions are evident in the store and in the town? What im-pression of the situation do you glean "between the lines"? How does the writer convey information beyond the scope of what the narrator is able to articulate?

3. Updike's story presents a seemingly minor event at a supermarket as the catalyst for a major change in the narrator's life. "I felt how hard the world was going to be to me hereafter," Sammy says in the story's final sentence. How do the perceptions of the past, pre-sent, and future intersect in the story? How seriously do you take the narrator's grim view of his future? Read Judith Ortiz Cofer's essay "Silent Dancing" (page 64), which is also prompted by a seemingly insignificant occasion: watching a home movie. Com-pare and contrast the ways in which past, present, and future in-tersect in Cofer's essay and Updike's story. Which writer handles these intersections more effectively? Explain why.

Acknowledgments

Daniel Akst. "What Meets the Eye." First published in *Wilson Quarterly*, Summer 1997. Copyright © 2005 Daniel Akst. Reprinted by permission of the author.

Sherman Alexie. "Superman and Me." From *The Most Wonderful Books*, edited by Michael Dorris and Emilie Buchwald. Copyright © 1997 by Milkweed Editions. Reprinted with permission of the author. "This Is What It Means to Say Phoenix, Arizona." From *The Lone Ranger and Tonto Fistfight in Heaven*. Copyright © 1993 by Sherman Alexie. Used by permission of Grove/Atlantic, Inc.

Akhil Reed Amar. "Second Thoughts." First published in the July 12, 1999, issue of *The New Republic*. Copyright © 1999. All rights reserved by Akhil Amar c/o Writers Representatives LLC, New York, NY. Reprinted with permission of Writers Representatives LLC, New York, NY.

Ho Che Anderson. "Reenvisioning *I Have a Dream*." From *King*, Volume 2. Copyright © 2002 by Ho Che Anderson. Reprinted courtesy of Fantagraphic Books.

Maya Angelou. "What's Your Name, Girl?" From *I Know Why the Caged Bird Sings* by Maya Angelou. Copyright © 1969 and renewed 1997 by Maya Angelou. Used by permission of Random House, Inc.

Kwame Anthony Appiah. "The Case for Contamination." From *The New York Times*, Magazine Section, January 1, 2006, issue, page 30. Copyright © 2006 The New York Times. All rights reserved. Used by permission and protected by the Copyright Laws of the United States. The printing, copying, redistribution, or retransmission of the Material without express written permission is prohibited.

Marie Arana. "*Ghosts*/Pishtacos." From *American Chica: Two Worlds, One Childhood*. Copyright © 2001 by Marie Arana. Used by permission of The Dial Press/Dell Publishing, a Division of Random House, Inc.

James Baldwin. Excerpt from *Notes of a Native Son* by James Baldwin. Copyright © 1955 renewed 1983 by James Baldwin. Reprinted by permission of Beacon Press, Boston. "Black English." Originally titled, "If Black English Isn't a Language, Then Tell Me, What Is?" © 1979 was originally published in *The New York Times*, collected in *The Price of the Ticket*, published by St. Martin's. Used by arrangement with the James Baldwin Estate.

Rick Bass. "Double-Talk." Originally published in *Audubon*, November–December 2001. Copyright © 2001 Rick Bass. Used by permission of the author.

Thomas Beller. "The Problem with T-Shirts." From *How to Be a Man: Scenes from a Protracted Boyhood* by Thomas Beller. Copyright © 2005 by Thomas Beller. Used by permission of W. W. Norton & Company, Inc.

Michael Bérubé. "Analyze, Don't Summarize." Originally published in *The Chronicle of Higher Education*, October 1, 2004. Copyright © 2004 Michael Bérubé. Used by permission of the author.

David Brooks. "People Like Us." Originally published in *The Atlantic Monthly*, September 2003. Used by permission of the author.

Stephen Budiansky. "The Physics of Gridlock." Originally published in *The Atlantic Monthly*, December 9, 2003. Copyright © 2003 Stephen Budiansky. Used by permission of the author.

Stephen L. Carter. "The Insufficiency of Honesty." From *Integrity*. Copyright © 1996 by Stephen L. Carter. Used by permission of Basic Books, a member of Perseus Books, LLC.

Raymond Carver. "My Father's Life." First published in *Esquire* (1984). Copyright © 1983 by the estate of Raymond Carver. Reprinted with permission of The Wylie Agency. "The Bath." From *What We Talk About When We Talk About Love* by Raymond Carver. Copyright © 1981 by Raymond Carver. Used by permission of Alfred A. Knopf, a division of Random House.

William Caverlee. "The Best Southern Short Story Ever?" Originally published in *The Oxford American*, Spring 2006, pp. 134–136. Copyright © 2006 William Caverlee. Used by permission of the author.

Lakshmi Chaudhry. "Mirror, Mirror on the Web." From the January 29, 2007, issue of *The Nation*. Reprinted with permission. For subscription information, call 1-800-333-8536. Portions of each week's *Nation* magazine can be accessed at http://www.thenation.com.

Judith Ortiz Cofer. "Silent Dancing" and "On Memory and Personal Essays" (excerpted from "Preface"). From *Silent Dancing: A Partial Remembrance of a Puerto-Rican Childhood*. Copyright © 1990. Reprinted with permission from the publisher.

Bernard Cooper. "A Clack of Tiny Sparks: Remembrances of a Gay Boyhood." Copyright © 1990 by *Harper's Magazine*. All rights reserved. Reproduced from the January 2001 issue by special permission.

Henry Louis Gates Jr. "In the Kitchen" and "On the Writer's Voice," excerpt from "Introduction" from *Colored People* by Henry Louis Gates Jr. Copyright © 1994 by Henry Louis Gates Jr. Used by permission of Alfred A. Knopf, a division of Random House, Inc.

John Taylor Gatto. "Against School." Copyright © 2003 by *Harper's Magazine*. All rights reserved. Reproduced from the September issue by special permission.

Jon Gertner. "The Futile Pursuit of Happiness." From *The New York Times* Magazine Section, September 7, 2003, issue, page 44. Copyright © 2003 by The New York Times. All rights reserved. Used by permission and protected by the Copyright Laws of the United States. The printing, copying, redistribution, retransmission of the Material without express written permission is prohibited.

William Gibson. "The Net Is a Waste of Time (and That's Probably What's Right About It)." Originally appeared in *The New York Times Magazine*. Copyright © 1996 by William Gibson. Reprinted by permission of the Martha Millard Literary Agency.

Malcolm Gladwell. "Big and Bad." Originally published in *The New Yorker*, January 12, 2004. Copyright © 2004 Malcolm Gladwell. Reprinted with permission of the author.

Adam Gopnik. "Shootings." From *The New Yorker* (Talk of the Town), April 30, 2007, pp. 27–28. Copyright © 2007. Used by permission of the author.

Stephen Jay Gould. "Sex, Drugs, Disasters, and the Extinction of Dinosaurs." From *The Flamingo's Smile: Reflections in Natural History* by Stephen Jay Gould. Copyright © 1984 by Stephen Jay Gould. Used by permission of W. W. Norton & Company, Inc.

Michihiko Hachiya. "What Had Happened?" August 6, 1945, pages 1–4. "Pikadon," pages 36–38 from *Hiroshima Diary: The Journal of a Japanese Physician, August 6–September 30, 1945* by Michihiko Hachiya, translated and edited by Warner Wells, M.D. Copyright © 1955 by the University of North Carolina Press. Renewed 1983 by Warner Wells. Foreword by John W. Dower. © 1995 by the University of North Carolina Press. Used by permission of the publisher.

Daniel Harris. "Celebrity Bodies." First appeared in *Southwest Review*, Vol. 93, No. 1, 2008. Copyright © 2008 Daniel Harris. Used with permission of Malaga Baldi Agency on behalf of the author.

Vicki Hearne. "What's Wrong with Animal Rights." Copyright © 1991 by *Harper's Magazine*. All rights reserved. Reproduced from the September issue by special permission.

Edward Hoagland. "On Stuttering." Originally published as "The Football Game in My Head" in *U.S. News & World Report*, April 2, 2001. Copyright 2001 U.S. News & World Report, L.P. Reprinted with permission. "What an Essay Is." Excerpted from "To the Point: Truths Only Essays Can Tell." Copyright © 1993 by *Harper's Magazine*. All rights reserved. Reproduced from the March issue by special permission.

Langston Hughes. "Salvation." From *The Big Sea* by Langston Hughes. Copyright © 1940 by Langston Hughes. Copyright renewed 1968 by Arna Bontemps and George Houston Bass. Reprinted by permission of Hill and Wang, a division of Farrar, Straus and Giroux, LLC. "How to Be a Bad Writer (in Ten Easy Lessons)." From *The Langston Hughes Reader*. Reprinted by permission of Harold Ober Associates Incorporated. "That word *Black*" from *The Return of Simple*, edited by Akiba Sullivan Harper. Copyright © 1994 by Ramona Bass and Arnold Rampersad. Reprinted by permission of Hill and Wang, a division of Farrar, Straus & Giroux, LLC.

Siri Hustvedt. "Eight Days in a Corset." Copyright © 2006 by Siri Hustvedt. Reprinted by permission of International Creative Management, Inc.

"An Interview with Jamaica Kincaid" from *Face to Face: Interviews with Contemporary Novelists*, edited by Allan Vorda (Houston: Rice University Press, 1993). Reprinted by permission.

Michiko Kakutani. "The Word Police." From *The New York Times*, Style Section, January 31, 1993, issue, page 1. Copyright © 1993 The New York Times. All rights reserved. Used by permission and protected by the Copyright Laws of the United States. The printing, copying, redistribution, or retransmission of the Material without express written permission is prohibited.

Jamaica Kincaid. "Girl." From *At the Bottom of the River*. Copyright © 1993 by Jamaica Kincaid. Reprinted by permission of Farrar, Straus and Giroux, LLC. "Jamaica Kincaid On *Girl*."

Martin Luther King Jr. "Letter from Birmingham Jail" and "I Have a Dream." Copyright 1963 Dr. Martin Luther King Jr; copyright renewed 1991 Coretta Scott King. "On Self-Importance" excerpted from "Conquering Self-Centeredness." Copyright 1957 by Martin Luther King Jr. and renewed 1991 by Coretta Scott King. Reprinted by

The University of Chicago Law Review, Vol. 70, No. 1, Centennial Tribute Essays (Winter 2003), pp. 265–279. Reprinted with permission of the author.

Joyce Carol Oates. "Where Are You Going, Where Have You Been?" Originally published in 1970 by Vanguard Press. Copyright © 1970 Ontario Review. Reprinted by permission of John Hawkins & Associates, Inc. "District School #7, Niagara County, New York." Originally published in *The Faith of a Writer: Life, Craft, Art* by Joyce Carol Oates. Copyright © 2003 Ontario Review. Reprinted by permission of John Hawkins & Associates, Inc.

Barack Obama. "Origins." From *Dreams from My Father* by Barack Obama. Copyright © 1995, 2004 by Barack Obama. Used by permission of Three Rivers Press, a division of Random House, Inc. "On the Hazards of Autobiography," from the introduction to *Dreams from My Father*, by Barack Obama.

Flannery O'Connor. "A Good Man Is Hard to Find." From *A Good Man Is Hard to Find and Other Stories*. Copyright 1953 by Flannery O'Connor and renewed 1981 by Regina O'Connor. Reprinted by permission of Houghton Mifflin Harcourt Publishing Company. "A Reasonable Use of the Unreasonable" from "On Her Own Work" from *Mystery and Manners* by Flannery O'Connor. Copyright © 1969 by the Estate of Mary Flannery O'Connor. Reprinted by permission of Farrar, Straus and Giroux, LLC.

Danielle Ofri. "SAT." From *Incidental Findings* by Danielle Ofri. Copyright © 2005 by Danielle Ofri. Reprinted by permission of Beacon Press, Boston.

George Orwell. "Shooting an Elephant" and "Politics and the English Language." From *Shooting an Elephant and Other Essays*. Copyright © 1946 by Sonia Brownell Orwell and renewed 1974 by Sonia Orwell. Reprinted by permission of Houghton Mifflin Harcourt Publishing Company. "Four Reasons for Writing." From *Such, Such Were the Joys*. Copyright 1953 by Sonia Brownell Orwell and renewed 1981 by Mrs. George K. Perutz, Mrs. Miriam Gross, and Dr. Michael Dickson, Executors of the Estate of Sonia Brownell Orwell. Reprinted by permission of Houghton Mifflin Harcourt Publishing Company.

Camille Paglia. "The Pitfalls of Plastic Surgery." Reprinted by permission of the author.

Stephen Pinker. "Sex Ed: The Science of Difference." From *The New Republic*, February 14, 2005. Copyright © 2005 The New Republic, LLC. Reprinted by permission.

Michael Pollan. "What's Eating America." First published in *Smithsonian* magazine, July, 2006. Copyright © 2006 by Michael Pollan. Reprinted by permission of International Creative Management, Inc.

Katha Pollitt. "Why Boys Don't Play with Dolls." From *The New York Times*, October 8, 1995. Copyright © 1995 Katha Pollitt. Used by permission of the author.

Virginia Postrel. "In Praise of Chain Stores." First published in *The Atlantic Monthly*, December 2006. Copyright © 2006 Virginia Postrel. Used by permission of the author.

Richard Rodriguez. "Aria: A Memoir of a Bilingual Childhood." From *Aria: A Memoir of a Bilingual Childhood* by Richard Rodriguez. © 1980 by Richard Rodriguez. Originally appeared in *The American Scholar*. Reprinted by permission of Georges Borchardt, Inc., on behalf of the author. "On a Writer's Identity" excerpted from "Crossing Borders: An Interview with Richard Rodriguez" by Scott London. Originally published in *The Sun 260* (August 1997). Copyright © 1997 by Scott London. Used by permission of the author.

Robert Root. "Interview with Marjane Satrapi." From *Fourth Genre: Explorations in Nonfiction* V9, No. 2, Fall 2007, pp. 147–57. Copyright © 2007. Used by permission of the publisher.

William Safire. "Changing Warming." From *The New York Times*, magazine section, August 14, 2005. Copyright © 2005 William Safire. Used by permission of Wallin, Simon, Black & Co., on behalf of William Safire.

Michael J. Sandel. "The Case Against Perfection." First published in *The Atlantic Monthly*, April 2004. Copyright © 2004 Michael Sandel. Used by permission of the author.

Scott Russell Sanders. "The Men We Carry in Our Minds." First appeared in *Milkweed Chronicle*; from *The Paradise of Bombs*. Copyright © 1984 by Scott Russell Sanders. Reprinted by permission of the author and the author's agents, the Virginia Kidd Agency, Inc. "On Writing Essays," excerpted from "The Singular First Person." © 1988 Scott Russell Sanders. First appeared in *Sewanee Review*. Reprinted by permission of the author.

Eric Schlosser. "Why McDonald's Fries Taste So Good." From *Fast Food Nation: The Dark Side of the All-American Meal* by Eric Schlosser. First published in the *Atlantic*

E. B. White. "Once More to the Lake." From *One Man's Meat*. Text copyright © 1941 by E. B. White. Copyright renewed. Reprinted by permission of Tillbury House Publishers, Gardiner, Maine. "On the Essayist." From pp. vii–viii of E. B. White's Foreword from *Essays of E. B. White* by E. B. White. Copyright © 1977 by E. B. White. Reprinted by permission of HarperCollins Publishers.

John Edgar Wideman. "The Night I Was Nobody." Copyright © 1996 by John Edgar Wideman. Reprinted with the permission of The Wylie Agency.

Terry Tempest Williams. "The Clan of One-Breasted Women." From *Refuge: An Unnatural History of Family and Place* by Terry Tempest Williams. Copyright © 1991 by Terry Tempest Williams. Used by permission of Pantheon Books, a division of Random House, Inc.

Marie Winn. "TV Addiction." Excerpted from "Cookies or Heroin?" from *The Plug-In Drug, Revised and Updated 25th Anniversary Edition*. Copyright © 1977, 1985, 2002 by Marie Winn Miller. Used by permission of Viking Penguin, a division of Penguin Group (USA).

Tom Wolfe. Excerpt from *Hooking Up*. Copyright © 2000 by Tom Wolfe. Reprinted by permission of Farrar, Straus & Giroux, LLC.

Virginia Woolf. "The Death of the Moth." From *The Death of the Moth and Other Essays* by Virginia Woolf. Copyright 1942 by Houghton Mifflin Harcourt Publishing Company and renewed 1970 by Majorie T. Parsons, Executrix. Reprinted by permission of the publisher. "This Loose, Drifting Material of Life." From *A Writer's Diary* by Virginia Woolf. Copyright 1954 by Leonard Woolf. Renewed 1982 by Quentin Bell and Angelica Garnett. Reprinted by permission of Harcourt, Inc.

Will Wright. "Dream Machines." First published in *Wired*, April, 2006. Copyright © 2006 Will Wright. Reprinted with permission of the author.

Howard Zinn. "Stories Hollywood Never Tells." From *The Sun*, July 2004. Reprinted with permission of the author.

Art

102 Photo by Ray A. Dove. © by Rita Dove; **112** © Chris Jordan; **123** Michael Ochs Archives/© 2007 Getty Images; **124** © Bettmann/CORBIS; **128** © Bettmann/CORBIS; **135** Bernard Hoffman/© Time & Life Pictures/Getty Images; **144** Jacob Lawrence, *Eight Studies for the Book of Genesis, #3: And God said, "Let the Earth bring forth the grass, trees, fruits, and herbs."* 1989. Gouache on paper, 29¾" x 22". © 2008 The Jacob and Gwendolyn Lawrence Foundation, Seattle/Artists Rights Society (ARS), New York. The Jacob and Gwendolyn Lawrence Foundation/Art Resource, NY; **231** © Marjane Satrapi. Reprinted by permission; **256** DOONESBURY©2003 G. B. Trudeau. Reprinted with permission of UNIVERSAL PRESS SYNDICATE. All rights reserved; **291** Paramount/The Kobal Collection; **291** Philippe Halsman/Magnum Photos; **326** © Paul Ekman, Ph.D.; **328** Réunion des Musées Nationaux/Art Resource, NY; **379** Library of Congress; **462** Library of Congress; **481** Courtesy of Lombardi's. Reprinted by permission; **541** Photography Collection, Miriam and Ira D. Wallach Division of Art, Prints and Photographs, The New York Public Library, Astor, Lenox and Tilden Foundations; **542** Photography Collection, Miriam and Ira D. Wallach Division of Art, Prints and Photographs, The New York Public Library, Astor, Lenox and Tilden Foundations; **551** © British Library/HIP/Art Resource, NY. British Library, London, Great Britain; **560** Scala/Art Resource, NY. Galleria Nazionale della Sicilia, Palermo, Sicily, Italy; **678** © Stanley J. Forman, Pulitzer Prize 1976; **776** The Wylie Agency, Inc. Photo courtesy of Errol Morris. Reprinted by permission; **777** Courtesy of Mary Evans Picture Library; **779** © Topham/The Image Works; **780** Library of Congress, Serials and Government Publications Division, Washington, D.C. 20540; **781** Toronto Star archives. Reprinted by permission; **903** Library of Congress, Prints and Photographs Division, Washington, D.C. 20540; **904** Collection of Immigrant City Archives, Lawrence, Massachusetts.

Index of Authors and Titles _____